The Institutes

of

Biblical Law

by

ROUSAS JOHN RUSHDOONY

A Chalcedon Study
with three appendices by
GARY NORTH

THE PRESBYTERIAN AND REFORMED
PUBLISHING COMPANY

Library of Congress Catalog Card Number 72-79485
Printed in the United States of America

TABLE OF CONTENTS

PREFACE

The chapters of this study were delivered, over a period of three years, before a large number of groups—students, civil officials, businessmen, housewives, and a great variety of persons. All of this study was also delivered at a single place during the course of the three years, with discussion and comment: At the Chapel of the Palms, Westwood, Los Angeles, James and Clarence Pierce have made their facility available for a continuing Chalcedon study group, and their cooperation is gratefully acknowledged.

Various persons have contributed generously to the Chalcedon publication fund, and have made this study possible: Frederick Vreeland, Keith Harnish, Mrs. S. W. North, Jr., my associate Gary North, and many others. The faithful work of the Chalcedon Guild is undergirding the publication of this and other Chalcedon Studies.

The indexing is the work of Bernard Ladouceur. The typing and proofreading have been done by my beloved wife, Dorothy, whose thinking and questioning have greatly furthered this study.

Many of the ideas developed in this study were discussed at times with Burton S. Blumert, who in more ways than one has been a source of encouragement. David L. Thoburn supplied me with several books which were helpful. Many other friends have, by their encouragement and help, made my work possible, and, to one and all, I am deeply grateful.

ROUSAS JOHN RUSHDOONY

INTRODUCTION

The Importance of the Law

When Wyclif wrote of his English Bible that "This Bible is for the government of the people, by the people, and for the people," his statement attracted no attention insofar as his emphasis on the centrality of Biblical law was concerned. That law should be God's law was held by all; Wyclif's departure from accepted opinion was that the people themselves should not only read and know that law but also should in some sense govern as well as be governed by it. At this point, Heer is right in saying that "Wyclif and Hus were the first to demonstrate to Europe the possibility of an alliance between the university and the people's yearning for salvation. It was the freedom of Oxford that sustained Wyclif."[1] The concern was less with church or state than with government by the law word of God.

Brin has said, of the Hebrew social order, that it differed from all others in that it was believed to be grounded on and governed by the law of God, who gave it specifically for man's government.[2] No less than Israel of old, Christendom believed itself to be God's realm because it was governed by the law of God as set forth in Scripture. There were departures from that law, variations of it, and laxity in faithfulness to it, but Christendom saw itself as the new Israel of God and no less subject to His law.

When New England began its existence as a law-order, its adoption of Biblical law was both a return to Scripture and a return to Europe's past. It was a new beginning in terms of old foundations. It was not an easy beginning, in that the many servants who came with the Puritans later were in full scale revolt against any Biblical faith and order.[3] Nevertheless, it was a resolute return to the fundamentals of Christendom. Thus, the New Haven Colony records show that the law of God, without any sense of innovation, was made the law of the Colony:

> *March 2, 1641/2*: And according to the fundamental agreem(en)t, made and published by full and gen(e)r(a)ll consent, when the plantation began and government was settled, that the judiciall law

1. Friedrich Heer, *The Intellectual History of Europe* (Cleveland: The World Publishing Co., 1966), p. 184.
2. Joseph G. Brin, "The Social Order Under Hebrew Law," *The Law Society Journal,* vol. VII, no. 3 (August, 1936), pp. 383-387.
3. Henry Bamford Parkes, "Morals and Law Enforcement in Colonial England," *The New England Quarterly,* vol. 5 (July, 1932), pp. 431-452.

of God given by Moses and expounded in other parts of scripture, so far as itt is a hedg and a fence to the moral law, and neither ceremoniall nor typical nor had any reference to Canaan, hath an everlasting equity in itt, and should be the rule of their proceedings.[4]

April 3, 1644: Itt was ordered thatt the judiciall lawes of God, as they were delivered by Moses . . . be a rule to all the courts in this jurisdiction in their proceeding against offenders. . . .[5]

Thomas Shepard wrote, in 1649, "For all laws, whether ceremonial or judicial, may be referred to the decalogue, as appendices to it, or applications of it, and so to comprehend all other laws as their summary."[6]

It is an illusion to hold that such opinions were simply a Puritan aberration rather than a truly Biblical practice and an aspect of the persisting life of Christendom. It is a modern heresy that holds that the law of God has no meaning nor any binding force for man today. It is an aspect of the influence of humanistic and evolutionary thought on the church, and it posits an evolving, developing god. This "dispensational" god expressed himself in law in an earlier age, then later expressed himself by grace alone, and is now perhaps to express himself in still another way. But this is not the God of Scripture, whose grace and law remain the same in every age, because He, as the sovereign and absolute lord, changes not, nor does He need to change. The strength of man is the absoluteness of his God.

To attempt to study Scripture without studying its law is to deny it. To attempt to understand Western civilization apart from the impact of Biblical law within it and upon it is to seek a fictitious history and to reject twenty centuries and their progress.

The Institutes of Biblical Law has as its purpose a reversal of the present trend. It is called "Institutes" in the older meaning of that word, i.e., fundamental principles, here of law, because it is intended as a beginning, as an instituting consideration of that law which must govern society, and which shall govern society under God.

1. The Validity of Biblical Law

A central characteristic of the churches and of modern preaching and Biblical teaching is antinomianism, an anti-law position. The antinomian believes that faith frees the Christian from the law, so that

---

4. Charles Hoadly, ed., *Records of the Colony and Plantation of New Haven from 1638 to 1649* (Hartford: for the Editor, 1857), p. 69.

5. *Ibid.*, p. 130.

6. John A. Albro, ed., *The Works of Thomas Shepard*, III, *Theses Sabbatical* (1649) (Boston: Doctrinal Tract and Book Society, 1853; New York: AMS Press, 1967), p. 49.

he is not outside the law but is rather dead to the law. There is no warrant whatsoever in Scripture for antinomianism. The expression, "dead to the law," is indeed in Scripture (Gal. 2:9; Rom. 7:4), but it has reference to the believer in relationship to the atoning work of Christ as the believer's representative and substitute; the believer is dead to the law as an indictment, a legal sentence of death against him, Christ having died for him, but the believer is alive to the law as the righteousness of God. The purpose of Christ's atoning work was to restore man to a position of covenant-keeping instead of covenant-breaking, to enable man to keep the law by freeing man "from the law of sin and death" (Rom. 8:2), "that the righteousness of the law might be fulfilled in us" (Rom. 8:4). Man is restored to a position of law-keeping. The law thus has a position of centrality in man's indictment (as a sentence of death against man the sinner), in man's redemption (in that Christ died, Who although the perfect law-keeper as the new Adam, died as man's substitute), and in man's sanctification (in that man grows in grace as he grows in law-keeping, for the law is the way of sanctification).

Man as covenant-breaker is in "enmity against God" (Rom. 8:7) and is subject to "the law of sin and death" (Rom. 8:2), whereas the believer is under "the law of the Spirit of life in Christ" (Rom. 8:2). The law is one law, the law of God. To the man on death row in a prison, the law is death; to the godly man, the same law which places another on death row is life, in that it protects him and his property from criminals. Without law, society would collapse into anarchy and fall into the hands of hoodlums. The faithful and full execution of the law is death to the murderer but life to the godly. Similarly, the law in its judgment upon God's enemies is death; the law in its sustaining care and blessings is for the law-abiding a principle of life.

God, in creating man, ordered him to subdue the earth and to exercise dominion over the earth (Gen. 1:28). Man, in attempting to establish separate dominion and autonomous jurisdiction over the earth (Gen. 3:5), fell into sin and death. God, in order to re-establish the Kingdom of God, called Abraham, and then Israel, to be His people, to subdue the earth, and to exercise dominion under God. The law, as given through Moses, established the laws of godly society, of true development for man under God, and the prophets repeatedly recalled Israel to this purpose.

The purpose of Christ's coming was in terms of this same creation mandate. Christ as the new Adam (I Cor. 15:45) kept the law perfectly. As the sin-bearer of the elect, Christ died to make atonement for their sins, to restore them to their position of righteousness under God. The redeemed are recalled to the original purpose of man, to exercise dominion under God, to be covenant-keepers, and to fulfil "the righteousness of the law" (Rom. 8:4). The law remains central to God's purpose. Man has been re-established into God's original purpose and calling. Man's *justification* is by the *grace* of God in Jesus Christ; man's *sanctification* is by means of the *law* of God.

As the new chosen people of God, the Christians are commanded to do that which Adam in Eden, and Israel in Canaan, failed to do. One and the same covenant, under differing administrations, still prevails. Man is summoned to create the society God requires. The determination of man and of history is from God, but the reference of God's law is to this world. "To be spiritually minded is life and peace" (Rom. 8:6), and to be spiritually minded does not mean to be other-worldly but to apply the mandates of the written word under the guidance of the Spirit to this world.

Lawless Christianity is a contradiction in terms: it is anti-Christian. The purpose of grace is not to set aside the law but to fulfil the law and to enable man to keep the law. If the law was so serious in the sight of God that it would require the death of Jesus Christ, the only-begotten Son of God, to make atonement for man's sin, it seems strange for God then to proceed to abandon the law! The goal of the law is not lawlessness, nor the purpose of grace a lawless contempt of the giver of grace.

The increasing breakdown of law and order must first of all be attributed to the churches and their persistent antinomianism. If the churches are lax with respect to the law, will not the people follow suit? And civil law cannot be separated from Biblical law, for the Biblical doctrine of law includes all law, civil, ecclesiastical, societal, familial, and all other forms of law. The social order which despises God's law places itself on death row: it is marked for judgment.

2. The Law as Revelation and Treaty

Law is in every culture *religious in origin.* Because law governs man and society, because it establishes and declares the meaning of justice and righteousness, law is inescapably religious, in that it establishes in practical fashion the ultimate concerns of a culture. Accordingly, a fundamental and necessary premise in any and every study of law must be, *first,* a recognition of this religious nature of law.

Second, it must be recognized that in any culture *the source of law is the god of that society.* If law has its source in man's reason, then reason is the god of that society. If the source is an oligarchy, or in a court, senate, or ruler, then that source is the god of that system. Thus, in Greek culture law was essentially a religiously humanistic concept.

In contrast to every law derived from revelation, *nomos* for the Greeks originated in the mind (*nous*). So the genuine *nomos* is no mere obligatory law, but something in which an entity valid in itself is discovered and appropriated. . . . It is "the order which exists (from time immemorial), is valid and is put into operation."[1]

Because for the Greeks mind was one being with the ultimate order of things, man's mind was thus able to discover ultimate law (*nomos*) out of its own resources, by penetrating through the maze of accident and matter to the fundamental ideas of being. As a result, Greek culture became both humanistic, because man's mind was one with ultimacy, and also neoplatonic, ascetic, and hostile to the world of matter, because *mind*, to be truly itself, had to separate itself from non-mind.

Modern humanism, the religion of the state, locates law in the state and thus makes the state, or the people as they find expression in the state, the god of the system. As Mao Tse-Tung has said, "Our God is none other than the masses of the Chinese people."[2] In Western culture, law has steadily moved away from God to the people (or the state) as its source, although the historic power and vitality of the West has been in Biblical faith and law.

Third, in any society, any change of law is an explicit or implicit change of religion. Nothing more clearly reveals, in fact, the religious change in a society than a legal revolution. When the legal foundations shift from Biblical law to humanism, it means that the society now draws its vitality and power from humanism, not from Christian theism.

Fourth, no disestablishment of religion as such is possible in any society. A church can be disestablished, and a particular religion can be supplanted by another, but the change is simply to another religion. Since the foundations of law are inescapably religious, no society exists without a religious foundation or without a law-system which codifies the morality of its religion.

Fifth, there can be no tolerance in a law-system for another religion. Toleration is a device used to introduce a new law-system as a prelude to a new intolerance. Legal positivism, a humanistic faith, has been savage in its hostility to the Biblical law-system and has claimed to be an "open" system. But Cohen, by no means a Christian, has aptly described the logical positivists as "nihilists" and their faith as "nihilistic absolutism."[3] Every law-system must maintain its existence

---

1. Hermann Kleinknecht and W. Gutbrod, *Law* (London: Adam and Charles Black, 1962), p. 21.
2. Mao Tse-Tung, *The Foolish Old Man Who Removed Mountains* (Peking: Foreign Languages Press, 1966), p. 3.
3. Morris Raphael Cohen, *Reason and Law* (New York: Collier Books, 1961), p. 84 f.

by hostility to every other law-system and to alien religious foundations, or else it commits suicide.

In analyzing now the nature of Biblical law, it is important to note *first* that, for the Bible, law is revelation. The Hebrew word for law is *torah*, which means instruction, authoritative direction.[4] The Biblical concept of law is broader than the legal codes of the Mosaic formulation. It applies to the divine word and instruction in its totality:

> . . . the earlier prophets also use *torah* for the divine word proclaimed through them (Isa. viii. 16, cf. also v. 20; Isa. xxx. 9 f.; perhaps also Isa. i. 10). Besides this, certain passages in the earlier prophets use the word *torah* also for the commandment of Yahweh which was written down: thus Hos. viii. 12. Moreover there are clearly examples not only of ritual matters, but also of ethics.
>
> Hence it follows that at any rate in this period *torah* had the meaning of a divine instruction, whether it had been written down long ago as a law and was preserved and pronounced by a priest, or whether the priest was delivering it at that time (Lam. ii. 9; Ezek. vii. 26; Mal. ii. 4 ff.), or the prophet is commissioned by God to pronounce it for a definite situation (so perhaps Isa. xxx. 9).
>
> Thus what is objectively essential in *torah* is not the form but the divine authority.[5]

The law is the revelation of God and His righteousness. There is no ground in Scripture for despising the law. Neither can the *law* be relegated to the Old Testament and *grace* to the New:

> The time-honored distinction between the OT as a book of law and the NT as a book of divine grace is without grounds or justification. Divine grace and mercy are the presupposition of law in the OT; and the grace and love of God displayed in the NT events issue in the legal obligations of the New Covenant. Furthermore, the OT contains evidence of a long history of legal developments which must be assessed before the place of law is adequately understood. Paul's polemics against the law in Galatians and Romans are directed against an understanding of law which is by no means characteristic of the OT as a whole.[6]

There is no contradiction between law and grace. The question in James's Epistle is faith and works, not faith and law.[7] Judaism had made *law* the *mediator* between God and man, and between God and the world. It was this view of law, not the law itself, which Jesus attacked.

---

4. Ernest F. Kevan, *The Moral Law* (Jenkintown, Penna.: Sovereign Grace Publishers, 1963) p. 5 f. S. R. Driver, "Law (In Old Testament)," in James Hastings, ed., *A Dictionary of the Bible*, vol. III (New York: Charles Scribner's Sons, 1919), p. 64.
5. Kleinknecht and Gutbrod, *Law*, p. 44.
6. W. J. Harrelson, "Law in the OT," in *The Interpreter's Dictionary of the Bible*, (New York: Abingdon Press, 1962), III, 77.
7. Kleinknecht and Gutbrod, *Law*, p. 125.

As Himself the Mediator, Jesus rejected the law as mediator in order to re-establish the law in its God-appointed role as law, the way of holiness. He established the law by dispensing forgiveness as the law-giver in full support of the law as the convicting word which makes men sinners.[8] The law was rejected only as mediator and as the source of justification.[9] Jesus fully recognized the law, and obeyed the law. It was only the absurd interpretations of the law He rejected. Moreover,

> We are not entitled to gather from the teaching of Jesus in the Gospels that He made any formal distinction between the Law of Moses and the Law of God. His mission being not to destroy but to fulfil the Law and the Prophets (Mt. 5:17), so far from saying anything in disparagement of the Law of Moses or from encouraging His disciples to assume an attitude of independence with regard to it, He expressly recognized the authority of the Law of Moses as such, and of the Pharisees as its official interpreters (Mt. 23:1-3).[10]

With the completion of Christ's work, the role of the Pharisees as interpreters ended, but not the authority of the Law. In the New Testament era, only apostolically received revelation was ground for any alteration in the law. The authority of the law remained unchanged:

> St. Peter, e.g., required a special revelation before he would enter the house of the uncircumcised Cornelius and admit the first Gentile convert into the Church by baptism (Acts 10:1-48)—a step which did not fail to arouse opposition on the part of those who "were of the circumcision" (cf. 11:1-18).[11]

The *second* characteristic of Biblical law is that it is a *treaty* or *covenant*. Kline has shown that the form of the giving of the law, the language of the text, the historical prologue, the requirement of exclusive commitment to the suzerain, God, the pronouncement of imprecations and benedictions, and much more, all point to the fact that the law is a treaty established by God with His people. Indeed, "the revelation committed to the two tables was rather a suzerainty treaty or covenant than a legal code."[12] The full covenant summary, the Ten Commandments, was inscribed on each of the two tables of stone, one table or copy of the treaty for each party in the treaty, God and Israel.[13]

The two stone tables are not, therefore, to be likened to a stele

---

8. *Ibid.*, pp. 74, 81-91.
9. *Ibid.*, p. 95.
10. Hugh H. Currie, "Law of God," in James Hastings, ed., *A Dictionary of Christ and the Gospels* (New York: Charles Scribner's Sons, 1908), II, 15.
11. Olaf Moe, "Law," in James Hastings, ed., *Dictionary of the Apostolic Church* (New York: Charles Scribner's Sons, 1919), I, 685.
12. Meredith G. Kline, *Treaty of the Great King, The Covenant Structure of Deuteronomy: Studies and Commentary* (Grand Rapids: William B. Eerdmans, 1963), p. 16. See also J. A. Thompson: *The Ancient Near Eastern Treaties and the Old Testament* (London: The Tyndale Press, 1964).
13. Kline, *op. cit.*, p. 19.

containing one of the half-dozen or so known legal codes earlier
than or roughly contemporary with Moses as though God had
engraved on these tables a corpus of law. The revelation they contain is nothing less than an epitome of the covenant granted by
Yahweh, the sovereign Lord of heaven and earth, to his elect and
redeemed servant, Israel.

Not law, but covenant. That must be affirmed when we are seeking a category comprehensive enough to do justice to this revelation
in its totality. At the same time, the prominence of the stipulations,
reflected in the fact that "the ten words" are the element used as
pars pro toto, signalizes the centrality of law in this type of covenant.
There is probably no clearer direction afforded the biblical theologian
for defining with biblical emphasis the type of covenant God adopted
to formalize his relationship to his people than that given in the
covenant he gave Israel to perform, even "the ten commandments."
Such a covenant is a declaration of God's lordship, consecrating a
people to himself in a sovereignly dictated order of life.[14]

This latter phrase needs re-emphasis: the covenant is "a sovereignly
dictated order of life." God as the sovereign Lord and Creator gives His
law to man as an act of sovereign grace. It is an act of election, of
electing grace (Deut. 7:7 f.; 8:17; 9:4-6, etc.).

The God to whom the earth belongs will have Israel for His own
property, Ex. xix. 5. It is only on the ground of the gracious election
and guidance of God that the divine commands to the people are
given, and therefore the Decalogue, Ex. xx. 2, places at its forefront
the fact of election.[15]

In the law, *the total life of man* is ordered: "there is no primary distinction between *the inner and the outer life*; the holy calling of the people
must be realized in both."[16]

The *third* characteristic of the Biblical law or covenant is that it
constitutes a plan for *dominion under God*. God called Adam to
exercise dominion in terms of God's revelation, God's law (Gen. 1:26 ff.;
2:15-17). This same calling, after the fall, was required of the godly
line, and in Noah it was formally renewed (Gen. 9:1-17). It was again
renewed with Abraham, with Jacob, with Israel in the person of Moses,
with Joshua, David, Solomon (whose Proverbs echo the law), with
Hezekiah and Josiah, and finally with Jesus Christ. The sacrament of
the Lord's Supper is the renewal of the covenant: "this is my blood of
the new testament" (or covenant), so that *the sacrament itself re-estab-
lishes the law*, this time with a new elect group (Matt. 26:28; Mark
14:24; Luke 22:20; I Cor. 11:25). *The people of the law* are now the

14. *Ibid.*, p. 17.
15. Gustave Friedrich Oehler, *Theology of the Old Testament* (Grand Rapids:
Zondervan, 1883), p. 177.
16. *Ibid.*, p. 182.

people of Christ, the believers redeemed by His atoning blood and
called by His sovereign election. Kline, in analyzing Hebrews 9:16, 17,
in relation to the covenant administration, observes:

> . . . the picture suggested would be that of Christ's children (cf.
> 2:13) inheriting his universal dominion as their eternal portion
> (note 9:15b; cf. also 1:14; 2:5 ff.; 6:17; 11:7 ff.). And such is the
> wonder of the messianic Mediator-Testator that the royal inheritance
> of his sons, which becomes of force only through his death, is
> nevertheless one of co-regency with the living Testator! For (to
> follow the typological direction provided by Heb. 9:16, 17 according
> to the present interpretation) Jesus is both dying Moses and suc-
> ceeding Joshua. Not merely after a figure but in truth a royal
> Mediator *redivivus*, he secures the divine dynasty by succeeding
> himself in resurrection power and ascension glory.[17]

The purpose of God in requiring Adam to exercise dominion over the
earth remains His continuing covenant word: man, created in God's
image and commanded to subdue the earth and exercise dominion over
it in God's name, is *recalled to this task and privilege* by his redemption
and regeneration.

The law is therefore the law for Christian man and Christian society.
Nothing is more deadly or more derelict than the notion that the Christian is at liberty with respect to the kind of law he can have. Calvin,
whose classical humanism gained ascendancy at this point, said of the
laws of states, of civil governments:

> I will briefly remark, however, by the way, what laws it (the state)
> may piously use before God, and be rightly governed by among men.
> And even this I would have preferred passing over in silence, if I
> did not know that it is a point on which many persons run into
> dangerous errors. For some deny that a state is well constituted,
> which neglects the polity of Moses, and is governed by the common
> laws of nations. The dangerous and seditious nature of this opinion
> I leave to the examination of others; it will be sufficient for me to
> have evinced it to be false and foolish.[18]

Such ideas, common in Calvinist and Lutheran circles, and in virtually
all churches, are still heretical nonsense.[19] Calvin favored "the common
law of nations." But the common law of nations in his day was
Biblical law, although extensively denatured by Roman law. And this
"common law of nations" was increasingly evidencing a new religion,
humanism. Calvin wanted the establishment of the Christian religion;

---

17. Kline, *Treaty of the Great King*, p. 41.
18. John Calvin, *Institutes of the Christian Religion*, bk. IV, chap. XX, para.
xiv. In the John Allen translation (Philadelphia: Presbyterian Board of Christian
Education, 1936), II, 787 f.
19. See H. de Jongste and J. M. van Krimpen, *The Bible and the Life of the
Christian*, for similar opinions (Philadelphia: Presbyterian and Reformed Publishing Co., 1968), p. 66 ff.

he could not have it, nor could it last long in Geneva, without Biblical law.

Two Reformed scholars, in writing of the state, declare, "It is to be God's servant, for our welfare. It must exercise justice, and it has the power of the sword."[20] Yet these men follow Calvin in rejecting Biblical law for "the common law of nations." But can the state be God's servant and by-pass God's law? And if the state "must exercise justice," how is justice defined, by the nations, or by God? There are as many ideas of justice as there are religions.

The question then is, what law for the state? Shall it be *positive law, the law of nations, a relativistic law*? De Jongste and van Krimpen, after calling for "justice" in the state, declare, "A static legislation valid for all times is an impossibility."[21] Indeed! Then what about the commandment, Biblical legislation, if you please, "Thou shalt not kill," and "Thou shalt not steal"? Are they not intended to be valid for all time and in every civil order? By abandoning Biblical law, these Protestant theologians end up in moral and legal relativism.

Roman Catholic scholars offer *natural law*. The origins of this concept are in Roman law and religion. For the Bible, there is no law in nature, because nature is fallen and cannot be normative. Moreover, the source of law is not nature but God. There is no law *in* nature but a law *over* nature, God's law.[22]

Neither positive law nor natural law can reflect more than the sin and apostasy of man: *revealed law* is the need and privilege of Christian society. It is the *only* means whereby man can fulfil his creation mandate of exercising dominion under God. Apart from revealed law, man cannot claim to be under God but only in rebellion against God.

3. The Direction of the Law

In order to understand Biblical law, it is necessary to understand also certain basic characteristics of that law. *First*, certain broad premises or principles are declared. These are declarations of basic law. The Ten Commandments give us such declarations. The Ten Commandments are not therefore laws among laws, but are the basic laws, of which the various laws are specific examples. An example of such a basic law is Exodus 20:15 (Deut. 5:19), "Thou shalt not steal."

In analyzing this commandment, "Thou shalt not steal," it is important to note, *a*), that this is the establishment, positively, of private property, even as, negatively, it punishes offenses against property.

---

20. *Ibid.*, p. 73.
21. *Ibid.*, p. 75.
22. The very term "nature" is mythical. See R. J. Rushdoony, "The Myth of Nature," in *The Mythology of Science* (Nutley, N. J.: The Craig Press, 1967), pp. 96-98.

The commandments thus *establish and protect* a basic area of life. But, *b*), even more important, this establishment of property issues, not from the state or man but from the sovereign and omnipotent God. The commandments all have their origin in God, who, as the sovereign lord, issues the law to govern His realm. Further, it follows, *c*), since God issues the law, that any offense against the law is an offense against God. Whether the law has reference to property, person, family, labor, capital, church, state, or anything else, its first frame of reference is to God. In essence, law-breaking is entirely against God, since everything and every person is His creation. But, David declared, with reference to his acts of adultery and murder, "Against thee, thee only, have I sinned and done this evil in thy sight" (Ps. 51:4). This means then, *d*), that lawlessness is also sin, i.e., that any civil, familial, ecclesiastical, or other social act of disobedience is also a religious offense *unless* the disobedience is required by the prior obedience to God.

With this in mind, that the law, *first*, lays down broad and basic principles, let us examine a *second* characteristic of Biblical law, namely, that the major portion of the law is *case law*, i.e., the illustration of the basic principle in terms of specific cases. These specific cases are often illustrations of the extent of the application of the law; that is, by citing a minimal type of case, the necessary jurisdictions of the law are revealed. To prevent us from having any excuse for failing to understand and utilize this concept, the Bible gives us its own interpretation of such a law, and the illustration, being given by St. Paul, makes clear the New Testament's undergirding of the law. We cite therefore, first, the basic principle, second, the case law, and, third, the Pauline declaration of the application of the law:

1. Thou shalt not steal (Ex. 20:15). The basic law, declaration of principle.
2. Thou shalt not muzzle the ox when he treadeth out the corn (Deut. 25:4). Illustration of the basic law, a case law.
3. For it is written in the law of Moses, Thou shalt not muzzle the mouth of the ox that treadeth out the corn. Doth God take care for oxen? Or saith he it altogether for our sakes? For our sakes, no doubt, this is written: that he that ploweth should plow in hope; and that he that thresheth in hope should be partaker of his hope. . . . Even so hath the Lord ordained that they which preach the gospel should live of the gospel (I Cor. 9:9, 10, 14; the entire passage, 9:1-14, is an interpretation of the law).

   For the scripture saith, Thou shalt not muzzle the ox that treadeth out the corn. And, The labourer is worthy of his reward (I Tim. 5:18, cf. v. 17; the illustration is to buttress the requirement of "honour," or "double honour" for presbyters or elders, i.e., pastors of the church). These two passages illustrate the requirement, "Thou shalt not steal," in terms of a specific case law, revealing the extent of that case in its implications. In his epistle to Timothy, Paul refers also to the law which in effect declares, by case law, that "The labourer is worthy of his reward." The reference is to Leviticus 19:13, "Thou shalt not defraud thy neighbour, neither rob him: the wages of him that is hired shall not abide with thee all night until the morning," and Deut. 24:14, "Thou shalt not oppress an hired servant that is poor and needy, whether he be of thy brethren, or of thy strangers that are in thy land within thy gates (cf. v. 15). This is cited by Jesus, Luke 10:7, "The laborer is worthy of his hire."

If it is a sin to defraud an ox of his livelihood, then it is also a sin to defraud a man of his wages: it is *theft* in both cases. If theft is God's classification of an offense against an animal, how much more so an offense against God's apostle and minister? The implication then is, how much more deadly is stealing from God. Malachi makes this very clear:

> Will a man rob God? Yet ye have robbed me. But ye say, Wherein have we robbed thee? in tithes and offerings. Ye are cursed with a curse: for ye have robbed me, even this whole nation. Bring ye all the tithes into the storehouse, that there may be meat in mine house, and prove me now herewith, saith the LORD of hosts, if I will not open you the windows of heaven, and pour you out a blessing, that there shall not be room enough to receive it. And I will rebuke the devourer for your sakes, and he shall not destroy the fruits of your ground; neither shall your vine cast her fruit before the time in the field, saith the LORD of hosts. And all the nations shall call you blessed: for ye shall be a delightsome land, saith the LORD of hosts (Mal. 3:8-12).

This example of case law illustrates not only the *meaning* of case law in Scripture, but also its *necessity*. Without case law, God's law would soon be reduced to an extremely limited area of meaning. This, of course, is precisely what has happened. Those who deny the present validity of the law apart from the Ten Commandments have as a consequence a very limited definition of theft. Their definition usually follows the civil law of their country, is humanistic, and is not radically different from the definitions given by Moslems, Buddhists, and humanists. But, in analyzing later the case laws illustrative of the law, "Thou shalt not steal," we shall see how far-reaching its meaning is.

The law, then, *first* asserts principles, *second*, it cites cases to develop the implications of those principles, and, *third*, the law has as its purpose and direction *the restitution of God's order*.

This *third* aspect is basic to Biblical law, and it illustrates again the difference between Biblical law·and humanistic law. According to one scholar, "Justice in its true and proper sense is *a principle of co-ordination between subjective beings*."[1] Such a concept of justice is not only

---

1. Giorgio Del Vecchio, *Justice, An Historical and Philosophical Essay*, edited with additional notes by A. H. Campbell (Edinburgh: Edinburgh University Press, 1956 [1952, 1924 Italian edition]), p. 2.

humanistic but also subjective. Instead of a basic *objective order* of justice, there is instead merely an *emotional condition* called justice.

In a humanistic law-system, restitution is possible and often exists, but again it is not the restoration of God's fundamental order but of man's condition. Restitution then is entirely to man.[2] Biblical law requires restitution to the offended person, but even more basic to the law is the demand for the restoration of God's order. It is not merely the courts of law which are operative in terms of restitution. For Biblical law, restitution is indeed, *a*), to be required by courts of law of all offenders, but, even more, *b*), is the purpose and direction of the law in its entirety, the restoration of God's order, a glorious and good creation which serves and glorifies its Creator. Moreover, *c*), God's sovereign court and law operates in terms of restitution at all times, to curse disobedience and hamper thereby its challenge to and devastation of God's order, and to bless and prosper the obedient restoration of God's order. Malachi's declaration concerning tithes, to return to our illustration, implies this, and, indeed, states it explicitly: they are "cursed with a curse" for robbing God of His tithes. Therefore, their fields are not productive, since they work against God's restitutive purpose. Obedience to God's law of the tithe, honoring instead of robbing God, will deluge His people with blessings. The word "deluge" is appropriate: the expression "open . . . the windows of heaven" recalls the Flood (Gen. 7:11), which was a central example of a curse. But the purpose of curses is also restitution: the curse prevents the ungodly from overthrowing God's order. The men of Noah's generation were destroyed in their evil imaginations, as they conspired against God's order (Gen. 6:5), in order to institute the process of restoration through Noah.

But to return to our original illustration of Biblical law, "Thou shalt not steal." The New Testament illustrates restitution after extortion in the form of unjust taxation in the person of Zaccheus (Luke 19:2-9), who was pronounced a saved man after declaring his intention of making full restitution. Restitution is clearly in view in the Sermon on the Mount (Matt. 5:23-26). According to one scholar,

> In Eph. iv. 28, St. Paul shows how the principle of restitution was to be extended. He who had been a robber must not only cease from theft, but must labour with his hands that he might restore what he had wrongfully taken away, but in case those whom he had wronged could not be found, restitution should be made to the poor.[3]

This fact of restitution or restoration is spoken of, in its relationship

---

2. See, for a study of such a concept, Dr. Stephen Schafer, *Restitution to Victims of Crimes* (London: Stevens and Sons; Chicago: Quadrangle Books, 1960).
3. John Henry Blunt, ed., *Dictionary of Doctrinal and Historical Theology* (London: Longmans, Green, 1891), p. 645.

to God, in three ways. *First,* there is the restitution or restoration of God's sovereign law-word by proclamation. St. John the Baptist, by his preaching, restored the law-word to the life of God's people. Jesus so declared it: "Elias truly shall first come, and restore all things. But I say unto you, That Elias is come already, and they knew him not" (Matt. 17:11, 12). There is then, *second,* the restoration which comes by subjecting all things to Christ and establishing a godly order over the world (Matt. 28:18-20; II Cor. 10:5; Rev. 11:15, etc.). *Third,* with the second coming, there is the total, final restoration which comes with the second coming, and towards which history moves; the second coming is the total and culminating rather than sole act of "the times of restitution" (Acts 3:21).

God's covenant with Adam required him to exercise dominion over the earth and to subdue it (Gen. 1:26 ff) under God and according to God's law-word. This relationship of man to God was a covenant (Hosea 6:7; cp. marginal reading).

> But all of Scripture proceeds from the truth that man always stands in covenant relation to God. All God's dealings with Adam in paradise presuppose this relation: for God talked with Adam and revealed Himself to him, and Adam knew God in the wind of day. Besides, salvation is always presented as the establishment and realization of God's covenant. . . .
>
> . . . this covenant relation is not to be conceived as something incidental, as a means to an end, as a relation that was established by way of an agreement, but as a fundamental relationship in which Adam stood to God by virtue of his creation.[4]

The restoration of that covenant relationship was the work of Christ, His grace to His elect people. The fulfilment of that covenant is their great commission: to subdue all things and all nations to Christ and His law-word.

The creation mandate was precisely the requirement that man subdue the earth and exercise dominion over it. There is not one word of Scripture to indicate or imply that this mandate was ever revoked. There is every word of Scripture to declare that this mandate must and shall be fulfilled, and "scripture cannot be broken," according to Jesus (John 10:35). Those who attempt to break it shall themselves be broken.[5]

---

4. Herman Hoeksema, *Reformed Dogmatics* (Grand Rapids: Reformed Free Publishing Association, 1966), p. 221 f.
5. H. de Jongste and J. M. van Krimpen, *The Bible and the Life of the Christian,* p. 27, recognize this, "That mandate has never been revoked," and then proceed to revoke it by their amillennial presuppositions by foreseeing the revocation of the mandate by the triumph of the anti-Christ: "There is no room for optimism: towards the end, in the camps of the satanic and the anti-Christ, culture will sicken, and the Church will yearn to be delivered from its distress" (p. 85).

I

THE FIRST COMMANDMENT

1. The First Commandment and the Shema Israel

The prologue to the Ten Commandments introduces not only the law as a whole but leads directly to the first commandment.

> And God spake all these words, saying,
> I am the LORD thy God, which have brought thee out of the land of Egypt, out of the house of bondage.
> Thou shalt have no other gods before me (Ex. 20:1-3).

In this declaration, God identifies Himself, *first*, as the LORD, the self-existent and absolute One. *Second*, He reminds Israel that He is their Savior, and that their relationship to Him ("thy God") is therefore one of grace. God chose Israel, not Israel God. *Third*, the law is given to the people of grace. All men are already judged, fallen, and lost; all men are under the wrath of the law, a fact which the quaking mountain and the fact of death for unhallowed approach underscored (Ex. 19:16-25). The law is given to the people saved by grace as their way of grace, to set forth the privilege and blessing of the covenant. *Fourth*, it follows then that the first response of grace, as well as the first principle of the law, is this, "Thou shalt have no other gods before me."

In analyzing this commandment, we must examine the implications of it cited by Moses:

> Now these are the commandments, the statutes, and the judgments, which the LORD your God commanded to teach you, that ye might do them in the land whither ye go to possess it:
> That thou mightest fear the LORD thy God, to keep all his statutes and his commandments, which I command thee, thou, and thy son, and thy son's son, all the days of thy life; and that thy days may be prolonged.
> Hear therefore, O Israel and observe to do it: that it may be well with thee, and that ye may increase mightily, as the Lord God of thy fathers hath promised thee, in the land that floweth with milk and honey (Deut. 6:1-3).

But this is a mythical and unbiblical definition of antichrist, who, according to St. John, is simply anyone, present from the beginning, who denies the Father and the Son (I John 2:22; 4:3; II John 7). To ascribe such deniers the role of final dominion and power is without any Biblical warrant.

First, the reason for the giving of these commandments is to awaken the fear of God, and that fear might prompt obedience. Because God is God, the absolute lord and law-giver, fear of God is the essence of sanity and common sense. To depart from a fear of God is to lack any sense of reality. *Second,* "The maintenance of the fear of God would bring prosperity, and the increase of the nation promised to the fathers. . . . The increase of the nation had been promised to the patriarchs from the very first (Gen. xii. 1; . . . cf. Lev. xxvi. 9)."[1] It is therefore necessary to maintain this fear and obedience from generation to generation.

In Deuteronomy 6:4-9, we come to a central and basic declaration of the first principle of the law:

> Hear, O Israel: the LORD our God is one LORD.
> And thou shalt love the LORD thy God with all thine heart, and with all thy soul, and with all thy might.
> And these words, which I command thee this day, shall be in thine heart:
> And thou shalt teach them diligently unto thy children, and shall talk of them when thou sittest in thine house, and when thou walkest by the way, and when thou liest down and when thou risest up.
> And thou shalt bind them for a sign upon thine hand, and they shall be as frontlets between thine eyes.
> And thou shalt write them upon the posts of thy house, and on thy gates.

The first two verses (6:4, 5) are the *Shema Israel,* recited as the morning and evening prayer of Israel, and "considered by the Rabbis to contain the principles of the Decalogue."[2] The second portion of the *Shema,* v. 5, is echoed in Deuteronomy 10:12, 13:

> And now, Israel, what doth the LORD thy God require of thee, but to fear the LORD thy God, to walk in all His ways, and to love Him, and to serve the LORD thy God with all thy heart and with all thy soul; to keep for thy good the commandments of the LORD, and His statutes, which I command thee this day?[3]

Deuteronomy 6:5 is cited by Christ as "the first and great commandment" (Matt. 22:37; Mark 12:30; Luke 10:27), i.e., as the essential and basic principle of the law. The premise of this commandment is, however, Deuteronomy 6:4: "Hear, O Israel, the LORD our God is one LORD." The Christian affirmation of this is the declaration, "We worship one God in Trinity, and Trinity in Unity." It is the faith in the

---

1. C. F. Keil and Delitzsch, *Biblical Commentary on the Old Testament,* vol. III, *The Pentateuch* (Grand Rapids: Eerdmans, 1949), p. 322.
2. Rabbi Dr. I. Epstein, ed., *The Babylonian Talmud, Seder Nezikin,* vol. IV, *Aboth* (London: The Soncino Press, 1935), p. 22, n. 8.
3. *The Holy Scriptures According to the Masoretic Text* (Philadelphia: Jewish Publication Society of America, 1917, 1961).

unity of the Godhead as opposed to the belief in "gods many and lords many."[4]

The consequences for law of this fact are total: it means *one God, one law*. The premise of polytheism is that we live in a multiverse, not a universe, that a variety of law-orders and hence lords exist, and that man cannot therefore be under one law *except* by virtue of imperialism. Modern legal positivism denies the existence of any absolute; it is hostile, because of its relativism, to the concept of a universe and of a universe of law. Instead, societies of men exist, each with its order of positive law, and each order of law lacks any absolute or universal validity. The law of Buddhist states is seen as valid for Buddhist nations, the law of Islam for Moslem states, the laws of pragmatism for humanistic states, and the laws of Scripture for Christian states, but none, it is held, have the right to claim that their law represents truth in any absolute sense. This, of course, militates against the Biblical declaration that God's order is absolute and absolutely binding on men and nations.

Even more, because an absolute law is denied, it means that the only universal law possible is an *imperialistic law*, a law imposed by force and having no validity other than the coercive imposition. Any one world order on such a premise is of necessity imperialistic. Having denied absolute law, it cannot appeal to men to return to the true order from whence man has fallen. A relativistic, pragmatic law has no premise for missionary activity: the "truth" it proclaims is no more valid than the "truth" held by the people it seeks to unite to itself. If it holds, "we are better off one," it cannot justify this statement except by saying, "I hold it to be so," to which the resister can reply, "I hold that we are better off many." Under pragmatic law, it is held that every man is his own law-system, because there is no absolute over-arching law-order. But this means anarchy. Thus, while pragmatism or relativism (or existentialism, positivism, or any other form of this faith) holds to the absolute immunity of the individual implicitly or explicitly, in effect its only argument is the coercion of the individual, because it has no other bridge between man and man. It can speak of love, but there is no ground calling love more valid than hate. Indeed, the Marquis de Sade logically saw no crime in murder; on nominalistic, relativistic grounds, what could be wrong with murder?[5] If there is no absolute law, then every man is his own law. As the writer of Judges

4. C. H. Waller, "Deuteronomy," in Charles John Ellicott, ed., *Ellicott's Commentary on the Whole Bible* (Grand Rapids: Zondervan), II, 25.
5. Richard Seaver and Austryn Wainhouse, eds., *The Marquis de Sade: The Complete Justine, Philosophy in the Bedroom, and other writings* (New York: Grove Press, 1965), pp. 329-337.

declared, "In those days there was no king in Israel (i.e., the people had rejected God as King); every man did that which was right in his own eyes" (Judges 21:25; cf. 17:6; 18:1; 19:1). The law forbids man's self-law: "Ye shall not do after all the things that we do here this day, every man whatsoever is right in his own eyes" (Deut. 12:8), and this applies to worship as well as to moral order. The *first* principle of the *Shema Israel* is thus *one God, one law*. It is the declaration of an absolute moral order to which man must conform. If Israel cannot admit another god and another law-order, it cannot recognize any other religion or law-order as valid either for itself or for anyone else. *Because God is one, truth is one*. Other people will perish in their way, lest they turn and be converted (Ps. 2:12). The basic coercion is reserved to God.

Because God is one, and truth is one, the one law has an inner coherence. The unity of the Godhead appears in the unity and coherence of the law. Instead of being strata of diverse origins and utility, the law of God is essentially one word, a unified whole.

Modern political orders are polytheistic imperial states, but the churches are not much better. To hold, as the churches do, Roman Catholic, Greek Orthodox, Lutheran, Calvinist, and all others virtually, that the law was good for Israel, but that Christians and the church are under grace and without law, or under some higher, newer law, is implicit polytheism. The Joachimite heresy has deeply infected the church. According to this heresy, the first age of man was the age of the Father, the age of justice and the law. The second age was the age of the Son, of Christianity, of the church, and of grace. The third age is the age of the Spirit, when men become gods and their own law.

Dispensationalism is also either evolutionary or polytheistic or both. God changes or alters His ways with man, so that law is administered in one age, and not in another. One age sees salvation by works, another by grace, and so on. But Scripture gives us a contrary assertion: "I am the LORD, I change not" (Mal. 3:6). To attempt to pit law against grace is polytheistic or at least Manichaean: it assumes two ultimate ways and powers in contradiction to one another. But the word of God is one word, and the law of God is one law, because God is one. The word of God is a law-word, and it is a grace-word: the difference is in men, by virtue of God's election, not in God. The word blesses and it condemns in terms of our response to it. To pray for grace is also to pray for judgment, and it is to affirm the truth and the validity of the law and the justice of the law. The whole doctrine of Christ's atonement upholds the unity of law, judgment, and grace.

Every form of antinomianism has elements of polytheism in it. Of antinomians Fairbairn wrote:

Some so magnify grace in order to get their consciences at ease respecting the claims of holiness, and vindicate for themselves a liberty to sin that grace may abound—or, which is even worse, deny that anything they do can have the character of sin, because they are through grace released from the demands of law, and so cannot sin. These are Antinomians of the grosser kind, who have not particular texts merely of the Bible, but its whole tenor and spirit against them. Others, however, and these the only representatives of the idea who in present times can be regarded as having an outstanding existence, are advocates of holiness after the example and teaching of Christ. They are ready to say, "Conformity to the Divine will, and that as obedience to commandments, is alike the joy and the duty of the renewed mind. Some are afraid of the word obedience, as if it would weaken love and the idea of a new creation. Scripture is not. Obedience and keeping the commandments of one we love is the proof of that love, and the delight of the new creature. Did I do all right, and not do it in obedience, I should do nothing right, because my true relationship and heart-reference to God would be left out. This is love, that we keep His commandments" (Darby "On the Law," pp. 3, 4). So far excellent; but then these commandments are not found in the revelation of law, distinctively so called. The law, it is held, had a specific character and aim, from which it cannot be dissociated, and which makes it for all time the minister of evil. "It is a principle of dealing with men which necessarily destroys and condemns them. This is the way (the writer continues) the Spirit of God uses law in contrast with Christ, and never in Christian teaching puts men under it. Nor does Scripture ever think of saying, You are not under the law in one way, but you are in another; you are not for justification, but you are for a rule of life. It declares, You are not under law, but under grace; and if you are under law, you are condemned and under a curse. How is that obligatory which a man is not under—from which he is delivered?" (*Ibid.*, p. 4). Antinomianism of this description—distinguishing between the teaching or commandments of Christ and the commandments of the law, holding the one to be binding on the conscience of Christians and the other not—is plainly but partial Antinomianism; it does not, indeed, essentially differ from Neonomianism, since law only as connected with the earlier dispensation is repudiated, while it is received as embodying the principles of Christian morality, and associated with the life and power of the Spirit of Christ.[6]

One "evangelistic" association given to campus work has actually taught that "the law was given by Satan." (Reported by this writer's daughter, from a course taught on campus by a leader of this movement.) Such a position can only be described as blasphemy.

An example of this antinomianism from some unofficial Lutheran circles comes from a Sunday School manual. The Old Testament is

6. Patrick Fairbairn, *The Revelation of Law in Scripture* (Grand Rapids: Zondervan, 1957 [1869]), pp. 29-31.

treated, as is the New, as a book to be mined or searched out for "truths," so that studies of various books are prefaced with a few summary statements titled "Truths You Will Find in the Book of Habakkuk," or "Truths You Will Find in the Book of Matthew," and so on. Are we to assume the rest of each book is lies? In the "Introduction to the New Testament," we are told, "The New Testament is the presentation of life under grace as it differs from life under law."[7] But the Old Testament also presents life under grace, and both Old and New Testaments present life under grace as life under law, *never* as lawlessness. *The alternative to law is not grace; it is lawlessness.* Grace and election move in terms of law and under law; reprobation is anti-law and anti-grace. Is it the purpose of churchmen to make the churches schools of reprobation?

All this illustrates a *second* principle of the *Shema Israel*: one absolute, unchanging God means *one absolute, unchanging law.* Men's social applications and approximations of the righteousness of God may alter, vary, and waver, but the absolute law does not. To speak of the law as "for Israel" but not for Christians is not only to abandon the law but also to abandon the God of the law. Since there is only one true God, and His law is the expression of His unchanging nature and righteousness, then to abandon the Biblical law for another law-system is to change gods. The moral collapse of Christendom is a product of this current process of changing gods.

Barthianism, by asserting the "freedom" of God to change (implying the evolving of an imperfect god), is asserting polytheism. Polytheism asserts many gods and many ways of salvation. It is not surprising that Karl Barth is at least implicitly universalistic. For Barth, all men can be or will be saved, because there is no one absolute, unchanging law which judges all men. In his polytheistic world view, all men can find one of any number of roads to salvation, if, indeed, it is salvation they need. For Barth, salvation is more realistically to be seen as self-realization; it is the gnosis of election, the realization that all men are elect in Christ, i.e., free from an absolute God and an absolute decree and law.

A *third* principle of the *Shema Israel* is that one God, one law, requires *one total, unchanging, and unqualified obedience*: "thou shalt love the LORD thy God with all thine heart, and with all thy soul, and with all thy might" (Deut. 6:5). The Talmud translates "might" as "money."[8] The meaning is that man must obey God totally, in any and

---

7. Dr. J. A. Huffman and Knute Larson, *Through the Bible in Two Years,* Book 6, pp. 5, 32, 33. Second year, second quarter (Winona Lake, Ind.: Lambert Huffman, 1962).

8. Talmud: *Seder Mo'ed*, vol. I, p. 264, n. 9.

every condition, with all his being. Since man is totally the creature of God, and since there is not a fiber of his being which is not the handiwork of God and therefore subject to the total law of God, there is not an area of man's life and being which can be held in reservation from God and His law. Therefore, as Deuteronomy 6:6 declares, "And these words, which I command thee this day, shall be in thine heart." Luther's comment on this verse is of interest, in that it contained the seeds of antinomianism which later became so deeply rooted in Lutheranism:

> He (Moses) wants you to know that the First Commandment is the measure and yardstick of all others, to which they are to yield and give obedience. Therefore, if it is for the sake of faith and charity, you may kill, in violation of the Fifth Commandment, just as Abraham killed the kings (Gen. 14:15) and King Ahab sinned because he did not kill the King of Syria (I Kings 20:34 ff.). Similar is the case of theft, ambush, and trickery against the enemies of God; you may take spoils, goods, wives, daughters, sons, and servants of enemies. So you should hate father and mother that you may love the Lord (Luke 14:26). In short, where anything will be against faith and love, there you shall not know that anything else is commanded by either God or man. Where it is for faith and love, however, you shall know that everything is commanded in all cases and everywhere. For the statement stands: "These words shall be in your heart"; there they shall rule. Furthermore, unless they are also in the heart, certainly no one will understand or follow this *epieikeia*, or ever employ laws successfully, safely, or legally. Therefore Paul says also in I Tim. 1:9, that "the Law is not set up for the righteous," for the reason that the fulfilling of the Law is love from a good heart and from faith that is not feigned (I Tim. 1:5), which uses law lawfully when it has no laws and has all laws—no laws, because none bind unless they serve faith and love; all, because all bind when they serve faith and love.
>
> Therefore this is Moses' meaning there: If you desire to understand the First Commandment correctly and truly not to have other gods, act so that you believe and love one God, deny yourself, receive everything by grace, and do everything gratefully.[9]

The confusions of this statement could only beget confusion.

A *fourth* principle which follows from the *Shema Israel* is stated in Deuteronomy 6:7-9, 20-25: education in the law is basic to and inseparable both from obedience to the law and from worship. The law requires education in terms of the law. Anything other than a Biblically grounded schooling is thus an act of apostasy for a believer: it involves having another god and bowing down before him to learn from

---

9. Jaroslav Pelikan, Daniel Poellot, eds., *Luther's Works*, vol. 9, *Lectures on Deuteronomy* (St. Louis: Concordia, 1960), p. 70.

him. There can be no true worship without true education, because the law prescribes and is absolute, and no man can approach God in contempt of God's prescription.

From Deuteronomy 6:8 Israel derived the use of the Tephillin, the portions of the law bound upon the head or arm at prayer. Of 6:8, 9 it has been observed:

> As these words are figurative, and denote an undeviating observance of the divine commands, so also the commandment which follows, viz. to write the words upon the door-posts of the house, and also upon the gates, are to be understood spiritually; and the literal fulfilment of such a command could only be a praiseworthy custom or well-pleasing to God when resorted to as the means of keeping the commandments of God constantly before the eye. The precept itself, however, presupposes the existence of this custom, which is not only met with in the Mahometan countries of the East at the present day, but was also a common custom in ancient Egypt.[10]

What is required, certainly, is that mind and action, family and home, man's vision and man's work, be all viewed in the perspective of God's law-word.

But this is not all. The literal fulfilment of the command concerning the frontlets and the posts (Deut. 6:8, 9) is clearly required, as Numbers 15:37-41 (cf. Deut. 11:18-20) makes clear. The blue thread required cannot be spiritualized away. God requires that He be worshiped according to His own word. Calvin's comment here on Numbers 15:38 was to the point:

> And, first of all, by contrasting "the hearts and eyes" of men with His Law, He shews that He would have His people contented with that one rule which He prescribes, without the admixture of any of their own imaginations; and again, He denounces the vanity of whatever men invent for themselves, and however pleasing any human scheme may appear to them, He still repudiates and condemns it. And this is still more clearly expressed in the last word, when he says that men "go a whoring" whenever they are governed by their own counsels. This declaration is deserving of our especial observation, for whilst they have much self-satisfaction who worship God according to their own will, and whilst they account their zeal to be very good and very right, they do nothing else but pollute themselves by spiritual adultery. For what by the world is considered to be the holiest devotion, God with his own mouth pronounces to be fornication. By the word "eyes" he unquestionably means man's power of discernment.[11]

It is regrettable that Calvin mars this by calling it a "need of these coarse

---

10. Keil and Delitzsch, *op. cit.*, III, 324.
11. John Calvin, *Commentaries on the Four Last Books of Moses in the Form of a Harmony* (Grand Rapids: Eerdmans, 1950), I, 265.

rudiments."[12] Our Lord fulfilled this law, and a woman touched a fringe or hem of His garment to be healed (Matt. 9:20). Jesus criticized the Pharisees for making large their fringes (Matt. 23:5) to boast of their ostensibly larger loyalty to the law. The commandment is repeated in Deuteronomy 22:12, so as to make clear its importance.

Men dress in diverse and strange ways to conform to the world and its styles. What is so difficult or "coarse" about any conformity to God's law, or any mode God specifies? There is nothing difficult or strange about this law, nor any thing absurd or impossible.

It is *not* observed by Christians, because it was, like circumcision, the Sabbath, and other aspects of the Mosaic form of the covenant, superseded by new signs of the covenant as renewed by Christ. The law of the covenant remains; the covenant rites and signs have been changed. But the forms of covenant signs are no less honorable, profound, and beautiful in the Mosaic form than in the Christian form. The change does not represent an evolutionary advance or a higher or lower relationship. The covenant was fulfilled in Jesus Christ; but God did not treat Moses, David, Isaiah, Hezekiah, or any of His Old Testament covenant people as lesser in His sight or more childish in ability and hence in need of "coarse rudiments." In every age, the covenant is all-holy and wise; in every age, the people of the covenant stand in terms of grace, not because of a "higher" personal ability or maturity.

Worship in an unknown tongue (I Cor. 14) is a violation of this commandment, as is worship which lacks the faithful proclamation of God's word, or is without the education of the people of the covenant in terms of the covenant law-word.

A *fifth* principle which is also proclaimed in this same passage, in Deuteronomy 6:20-25, is that, in this required education, it must be stressed that *the response to grace is the keeping of the law.* Children are to be taught that the meaning of the law is that God redeemed Israel out of bondage, and, "that he might preserve us alive," "commanded us to do all these statutes, to fear the LORD our God, for our good always" (6:24). There is no warrant for setting this aside in either the Old or New Testament. Where the churches of the Old or New Testament have set up a false meaning to the law, that false meaning is attacked by prophets and apostles, but never the law of God itself. Because God is one, His grace and law are one in their purpose and direction. This passage makes pointedly clear the priority of God's electing grace in the call and redemption of His chosen people. The relationship of Israel was a relationship of grace, and the law was given in order to

---

12. *Ibid.*

provide God's people with the necessary and required response to grace, and manifestation of grace: the keeping of the law.

In Deuteronomy 6:10-15, another central point is made with respect to the implications of the *Shema Israel*:

> And it shall be, when the LORD thy God shall bring thee into the land which He swore unto thy fathers, to Abraham, to Isaac, and to Jacob, to give thee—great and goodly cities, which thou didst not build, and houses full of good things, which thou didst not fill, and cisterns hewn out, which thou didst not hew, vineyards and olive-trees, which thou didst not plant, and thou shalt eat and be satisfied—then beware lest thou forget the LORD, who brought thee forth out of the land of Egypt, out of the house of bondage. Thou shalt fear the LORD thy God; and Him shalt thou serve, and by His name shalt thou swear. Ye shall not go after other gods, of the gods of the peoples that are round about you; for a jealous God, even the LORD thy God, is in the midst of thee; lest the anger of the LORD thy God be kindled against thee, and He destroy thee from off the face of the earth.[13]

Thus, the *sixth* principle is *the jealousy of God*. This is a fact of cardinal importance. The chosen people are warned, as they occupy and possess a rich land which they did not develop, lest they forget God, who delivered and prospered them. Seeing the wealth which came from a culture hostile to God, God's covenant people will be tempted to see other means to success and prosperity than the Lord. The temptation will be to "go after other gods, . . . the gods of the people round about." This is to believe that there is another law-order than God's order; it is to forget that the success and the destruction of the Canaanites was alike the work of God. It is the provocation of God's wrath and jealousy. The fact that jealousy is associated repeatedly with the law, and invoked by God in the giving of the law, is of cardinal importance in understanding the law. The law of God is not a blind, impersonal, and mechanically operative force. It is neither *Karma* nor fate. The law of God is the law of the absolute and totally personal Creator whose law operates within the context of His love and hate, His grace towards His people and His wrath towards His enemies. A current of electricity is impersonal: it flows in its specified energy when the conditions for a flow or discharge of energy are met; otherwise, it does not flow. But the law of God is not so: it is personal; God restrains His wrath in patience and grace, or He destroys His enemies with an over-running flood of judgment (Nahum 1:8). From a humanistic and impersonalistic perspective, both the mercy of God to Assyria (Jonah 3:1–4:3) and the judgment of God on Assyria (Nahum 1:1–3:19)

---

13. Masoretic Text of the Jewish Publication Society of America, hereinafter referred to as MTV.

seem disproportionate, because an impersonal law is also an external law: it knows only actions, not the heart. Man, as he applies the law of God, must judge the actions of man, but God, being absolute, judges the total man with total judgment. The jealousy of God is therefore the certain assurance of the infallibility of God's court of law. The evil which so easily escapes the courts of state cannot escape the judgment of God, which, both in time as well as beyond time, moves in terms of the total requirements of His law. The jealousy of God is the guarantee of justice. An impersonal justice in a world of persons means that evil, being personal, can escape the net of the law and reign in laughing triumph. But the jealous God prevents the triumph either of Canaan or an apostate Israel or church. Without a jealous, personal God, no justice is possible. The doctrine of *Karma* only enthrones injustice: it leads to the most vicious and callous kind of externalism and impersonalism. The people of *Karma* spare their monkeys but destroy one another; *Karma* knows no grace, because *Karma* in essence knows no persons, only actions and consequences. The escape from *Karma* becomes *Nirvana*, the escape from life.

This same passage declares, "Thou shalt fear the LORD thy God; and Him shalt thou serve, and by His name shalt thou swear" (Deut. 6:13). Luther's comment here is excellent:

> Therefore you swear by the name of God if you relate that by which you swear to God and grasp it in the name of God; otherwise you would not swear if you knew it displeased Him. Similarly you serve God alone when you serve men in the name of God; otherwise you would not serve. By such swearing you safeguard your service to God alone and are not drawn toward a godless work or oath. Thus Christ also says in Matt. 23:16-22 that he who swears by the temple and altar and heaven swears by God; and in Matt. 5:35-36 He forbids to swear by Jerusalem, by one's head, by heaven, or by anything else, because in all these one swears by God. But to swear by God frivolously and emptily is to take the name of God in vain.
>
> When, therefore, He desires oaths to be made by the name of God and no other, the reason is not only this, that for the truth (which is God) the confirmation of no one should be introduced except that of God Himself, but also this, that man should remain in the service of God alone, learn to relate everything to Him, and to do, possess, use, and endure all in His name. Otherwise, if they employ another name, they would be diverted and become used to swearing as if it had nothing to do with God; and finally through bad usage they would begin to distinguish between the deeds by which God is served and those by which He is not served, when He wants to be served in all and wants all things to be done in fear, because He is present to see and judge.
>
> Therefore the oath is to be used in the same way as the sword and

sexual intercourse are used. It is forbidden to take the sword, as
Christ says (Matt. 26:52): "He who takes the sword shall perish
by the sword," because he takes it without a command and because
of his own lust. But it is a command and a divine service to bear
the sword if this is assigned by God or through man; for then it is
borne in the name of the Lord, for the good of the neighbor, as
Paul says: "He is the servant of God for your good" (Rom. 13:4).
Thus the fleshly use of sex is forbidden, because it is a disorderly
lust. Where, however, sex is associated with you by marriage, then
the flesh should be used, and you render to the divine Law, that is,
to love what is demanded. In the same way one should make use
of an oath: you should swear not for your own sake but for the sake
of God or your neighbor in the name of the Lord. Thus you will
always remain in the service of God alone.[14]

In the Temptation of Jesus, two of the three answers to Satan are
from Deuteronomy 6: "It is written again, Thou shalt not tempt the
Lord thy God" (Matt. 4:7; Deut. 6:16), and "Get thee hence, Satan:
for it is written, Thou shalt worship the Lord thy God, and him only
shalt thou serve" (Matt. 4:10; Deut. 6:13; 10:20). The third answer
is taken from a related passage, Deuteronomy 8:3: "But he answered
and said, It is written, Man shall not live by bread alone, but by every
word that proceedeth out of the mouth of God" (Matt. 4:4). All three
answers were responses to the temptation to test God, implicit to which
was not merely questioning but actually challenging God and His
law word.

A *seventh* principle which follows from the *Shema Israel* is declared
in Deuteronomy 6:16-19:

> Ye shall not try the LORD your God, as ye tried Him in Massah.
> Ye shall diligently keep the commandments of the LORD your God,
> and His testimonies, and His statutes, which He hath commanded
> thee. And thou shalt do that which is right and good in the sight of
> the LORD; that it may be well with thee and that thou mayest go
> in and possess the good land which the LORD swore unto thy
> fathers, to thrust out all thine enemies from before thee, as the
> LORD hath spoken (MTV).

It was this that Satan tried to tempt Jesus to do: to try God, to put
God to the test. Israel tempted God at Massah by raising the question,
"Is the LORD among us, or not?" (Ex. 17:7).

> The worship of Jehovah not only precludes all idolatry, which the
> Lord, as a jealous God, will not endure (see at Ex. xx.5), but will
> punish with destruction from the earth ("the face of the ground,"
> as in Ex. xxxii.12): but it also excludes tempting the Lord by an
> unbelieving murmuring against God, if He does not remove any kind

---

14. Luther, *Deuteronomy*, p. 73 f.

of distress immediately, as the people had already sinned at Massah, i.e., at Rephidim (Ex. xvii. 1-7).[15]

This *seventh* principle thus *forbids the unbelieving testing of God: God's law is the testing of man; therefore, man cannot presume to be god and put God and His law-word on trial.* Such a step is a supreme arrogance and blasphemy; it is the opposite of obedience, because it is the essence of disobedience to the law. Hence, it is contrasted to a diligent keeping of the law. This obedience is the condition of blessing: it is the ground of conquest and of possession, in terms of which the covenant people of God, His law-people, enter into their inheritance.

Tempting or trying God has other implications. According to Luther,

> The first way is not to use the necessary things that are at hand but to seek others, which are not at hand. . . . So he tempts God who snores and does not want to work, taking for granted that he must be sustained by God without work, although God has promised to provide for him through his work, as Prov: 10:4 says: "The hands of the busy prepare wealth, but the slack hand will hunger." This vulgar celibacy is like that too. . . .
>
> Secondly, God is tempted when nothing needed is at hand except the bare and lone Word of God. . . . For here the godless are not content with the Word; and unless God does what He promised at the time, in the place, and in the manner prescribed by themselves, they give up and do not believe. But to prescribe place, time, or manner to God is actually to tempt Him and to feel about, as it were, whether He is there. But this is nothing else than to want to put limits on God and subject Him to our will; in fact, to deprive Him of His divinity. He should be free, not subject to bounds and limitations, and be the one who prescribes places, means, and time to us. Therefore both temptations are against the First Commandment. . . .[16]

The neglect of the *Shema Israel* and Deuteronomy 6 has been part and parcel of the neglect of the law.

2. The Undivided Word

A number of prologues or prefatory declarations appear in the law, which are not generally regarded as a part of the law. Calvin called these passages "The Preface to the Law," which in an accurate sense they are, but they are equally a part of the law, the first commandment in particular, because they affirm the exclusive nature of the one true God and bar from the allegiance of Israel all other gods. These passages are Exodus 20:1, 2; 23:20-31; Leviticus 19:36, 37; 20:8; 22: 31-33; Deuteronomy 1:1–4:49; 5:1-6; 7:6-8; 8:1-18; 10:14-17; 11: 1-7; 13:18; 26:16-19; 27:9, 10.

---

15. Keil and Delitzsch, *op. cit.*, III, 325 f.
16. Luther, *op. cit.*, p. 74 f.

First, the premise of commandment is asserted, even as in the *Shema Israel*, that God is the LORD (Jehovah or Yahweh, He Who Is, the self-existent, absolute, and eternal One), and, *second*, that Israel stands before God because of His electing grace:

> And God spake all these words, saying,
> I am the LORD thy God, which have brought thee out of the land of Egypt, out of the house of bondage (Ex. 20:1, 2).

> And Moses called all Israel, and said unto them, Hear, O Israel, the statutes and judgments which I speak in your ears this day, that ye may learn them, and keep and do them.
> The LORD our God made a covenant with us in Horeb.
> The LORD made not this covenant with our fathers, but with us, even us, who are all of us here alive this day.
> The LORD talked with you face to face in the mount, out of the midst of the fire.
> (I stood between the LORD and you at that time, to shew you the word of the LORD; for ye were afraid by reason of the fire, and went not up into the mount,) saying,
> I am the LORD thy God, which brought thee out of the land of Egypt, from the house of bondage (Deut. 5:1-6).

> But the LORD hath taken you, and brought you forth out of the iron furnace, even out of Egypt, to be unto him a people of inheritance, as ye are this day (Deut. 4:20).

In these and many of the other passages cited above, the sovereignty of God, and His electing grace, are declared. In Deuteronomy 5:3, the "fathers" who perished in the wilderness, while outwardly of the covenant, are excluded from it by God's declaration: the covenant is "with us, even us, who are all of us here alive this day." Those who perished had been cut off from God by their unbelief. The "people of inheritance" (Deut. 4:20) are the believing Israelites.

The history of grace, and the fact of God's saving grace to Israel, is cited repeatedly, to deter the people from presumption and pride (Deut. 1–4; 7:6-8; 8:1-6, 11-18; 9:1-6; 10:14-17, 21-22; 11:1-8; 26:16-19; 27:9, 10; 29:2-9). The history of grace is also a promise of grace if man's response is one of grateful obedience to the law and an unswerving devotion to the only true God.

Third, the Angel of the LORD will go before His people, to keep them and to deliver them:

> Behold, I send an Angel before thee, to keep thee in the way, and to bring thee into the place which I have prepared.
> Beware of him, and obey his voice, provoke him not; for he will not pardon your transgressions: for my name is in him.
> But if thou shalt indeed obey his voice, and do all that I speak; then I will be an enemy unto thine enemies, and an adversary unto thine adversaries.

For mine Angel shall go before thee, and bring thee in unto the Amorites, and the Hittites, and the Perizzites, and the Canaanites, the Hivites, and the Jebusites: and I will cut them off.

Thou shalt not bow down to their gods, nor serve them, nor do after their works: but thou shalt utterly overthrow them, and quite break down their images.

And ye shall serve the LORD your God, and he shall bless thy bread, and thy water; and I will take sickness away from the midst of thee.

There shall nothing cast their young, nor be barren, in thy land: the number of thy days I will fulfil.

I will send my fear before thee, and will destroy all the people to whom thou shalt come, and I will make all thine enemies turn their backs unto thee.

And I will send hornets before thee, which shall drive out the Hivite, the Canaanite, and the Hittite, from before thee.

I will not drive them out from before thee in one year; lest the land become desolate, and the beast of the field multiply against thee.

By little and little I will drive them out before thee, until thou be increased, and inherit the land.

And I will set thy bounds from the Red sea even unto the sea of the Philistines, and from the desert unto the river: for I will deliver the inhabitants of the land into your hand; and thou shalt drive them out before thee.

Thou shalt make no covenant with them, nor with their gods.

They shall not dwell in thy land, lest they make thee sin against me: for if thou serve their gods, it will surely be a snare against thee (Ex. 23:20-33).

The Angel of the Lord (Gen. 16:10, 13; 18:2-4,13, 14, 33; 22:11, 12, 15, 16; 31:11, 13; 32:30; Ex. 3:2, 4; 20:20 ff.; 32:34; 33:14; Josh. 5: 13-15; 6:2; Isa. 63:9; Zech. 1:10-13; 3:1-2) identifies Himself with the Lord; those to whom He reveals Himself recognize Him as God; He is called the LORD by Biblical writers; the Scripture here implies a plurality of persons in the Godhead.[1] Moreover, the statement is clearly made by God that "my name is in him," which is the same as "I am in him" (Ex. 23:20).[2] The Angel of the Lord appears in the New Testament repeatedly, for example, in Acts 5:19; 12:7-11, 17, etc. St. Paul identified the Angel as Jesus Christ (I Cor. 10:9).

Fourth, they shall be preserved from plagues and epidemics (Ex. 23:25-27), so that obedience is followed by material blessings. These material blessings include driving out their enemies before them and giving them a great inheritance (Ex. 23:27-31). That all of this is tied to the first commandment appears from Exodus 23:32, 33; they must separate themselves from other gods: "no covenant" can be made

---

1. H. C. Leupold, *Exposition of Genesis* (Columbus, Ohio: The Wartburg Press, 1942), p. 500 f.
2. Oswald T. Allis, *God Spake By Moses* (Philadelphia: Presbyterian and Reformed Publishing Co., 1951), p. 62 f.

with unbelievers (by marriage, treaty, or community) or with their gods.

An important verse which comes at the conclusion of the law is still an exposition of the approach of man to the law. In Deuteronomy 29: 29, Moses, after warning them of the curse on disobedience, declared:

> The secret things belong unto the LORD our God: but those things which are revealed belong unto us and to our children for ever, that we may do all the words of this law.

An interpretation which is most relevant to the context of this statement comments:

> That which is revealed includes the law with its promises and threats: consequently that which is hidden can only refer to the mode in which God will carry out in the future His counsel and will, which He has revealed in the law, and complete His work of salvation notwithstanding the apostasy of the people.[3]

This means, *fifth*, that the law, God's revelation, has behind it God's secret will whereby His counsel shall stand and man's rebellion shall be confounded, to the triumph of His Kingdom in His own time and way. In brief, the law is revealed; the fulfilment of the law is assured because God is God; the mode and time is extensively hidden. The court is called by God, not by man.

Sixth, the law is one undivided word:

> Ye shall not add unto the word which I command you, neither shall ye diminish ought from it, that ye may keep the commandments of the LORD your God which I command you (Deut. 4:2).

The meaning clearly is that all Scripture, law, prophets, and gospel, is one word. Words can be added, until the close of revelation, when even the addition (or subtraction) of words is forbidden (Rev. 22:18, 19). There can be no arbitrary separation of the law from the gospel: *one God means one word.* To divide the word is to deny God.

3. God versus Moloch

Calvin, in his excellent classification of the law in his *Commentaries on the Four Last Books of Moses Arranged in the Form of a Harmony,* cites Deut. 18:9-22; 13:1-4; Lev. 18:21; 19:26, 31; and Deut. 12: 29-32, as basic to the first commandment. These passages relate to man's attempt to know and control the future. Since God is the LORD, the Maker of heaven and earth, and the determiner of all things, any attempt to know and control the future outside of God is to set up another god in contempt of the LORD.

---

3. Keil and Delitzsch, *op. cit.*, III, 451.

Every form of illicit probing of the future is cited by Moses:

> When thou art come into the land which the LORD thy God giveth thee, thou shalt not learn to do after the abominations of those nations.
> There shall not be found among you any one that maketh his son or his daughter to pass through the fire, or that useth divination, or an observer of times, or an enchanter, or a witch,
> Or a charmer, or a consulter with familiar spirits, or a wizard, or a necromancer.
> For all that do these things are an abomination unto the LORD: and because of these abominations the LORD thy God doth drive them out from before thee.
> Thou shalt be perfect (or, upright) with the LORD thy God.
> For these nations, which thou shalt possess, hearkened unto observers of times, and unto diviners; but as for thee, the LORD thy God hath not suffered thee so to do (Deut. 18:9-14).

> And thou shalt not let any of thy seed pass through the fire to Molech, neither shalt thou profane the name of thy God: I am the LORD (Lev. 18:21).

> Ye shall not eat any thing with the blood; neither shall ye use enchantment, nor observe times (Lev. 19:26).

> Regard not them that have familiar spirits, neither seek after wizards, to be defiled by them: I am the LORD your God (Lev. 19:31).

> When the LORD thy God shall cut off the nations from before thee, whither thou goest to possess them, and thou succeedest them, and dwellest in their land;
> Take heed to thyself that thou be not snared by following them, after that they be destroyed from before thee; and that thou enquire not after their gods, saying, How did these nations serve their gods? even so will I do likewise.
> Thou shalt not do so unto the LORD thy God: for every abomination to the LORD, which he hateth, have they done unto their gods; for even their sons and their daughters they have burnt in the fire to their gods.
> What thing soever I command you, observe to do it: thou shalt not add thereto, nor diminish from it (Deut. 12:29-32).

Calvin's comment on Deuteronomy 18:9-14 gets to the heart of the matter:

> Moses explains clearly in this passage what it is to have other gods, viz. to mix up the worship of God with things profane, since its purity is only thus maintained by banishing from it all uncongenial superstitions. The sum, therefore, is, that the people of God should abstain from all the inventions of men, whereby pure and simple religion is adulterated.[1]

---

1. John Calvin, *Commentaries on the Four Last Books of Moses*, vol. I, p. 424.

Equally to the point is the observation of another commentator:

> Moses groups together all the words which the language contained for the different modes of exploring the future and discovering the will of God, for the purpose of forbidding every description of soothsaying, and places the prohibition of Moloch-worship at the head, to show the inward connection between soothsaying and idolatry, possibly because februation, or passing children through the fire in the worship of Moloch, was more intimately connected with soothsaying and magic than any other description of idolatry.[2]

A wide variety of practices is cited. An "enchanter" is a whisperer or snake charmer; a witch, one who uses charms or spells; a wizard, one who claimed to know the secrets of the other world; a necromancer, one who enquires of the dead, and so on.[3] But the key evil is Moloch-worship. The word Moloch (or Melech, Melek, Malik), meaning *king*, is a misvocalization of the name of a pagan, the consonants of *king* being retained and the vowels of *shame* used. Human sacrifice was made to this god, who is identified as the god of Ammon in I Kings 11:7, 33. There are references to Moloch in Jeremiah 49:1, 3; Amos 1:15; Zephaniah 1:5; Leviticus 18:21; 20:2-5; II Kings 23:10; Jeremiah 32:35, etc., and the location of Moloch worship in Israel was the Valley of Hinnom (Jer. 32:35; II Kings 23:10). Moloch worship was not limited to Ammon.[4]

Moloch is "the king" or "kingship." The name of Moloch is also given as Milcom (I Kings 6:5, 33) and Malcam (Jer. 49:1, 3, RV; Zeph. 1:5). Moloch was an aspect of Baal (Jer. 32:35), *Baal* meaning *lord*. Under the name of Melcarth, king of Tyre, Baal was worshiped with human sacrifices at Tyre.[5]

While relatively little is known of Moloch, much more is known of the concept of divine kingship, the king as god, and the god as king, as the divine-human link between heaven and earth. The god-king represented man on a higher scale, man ascended, and the worship of such a god, i.e., of such a *Baal*, was the assertion of the *continuity* of heaven and earth. It was the belief that all being was one being, and the god therefore was an ascended man on that scale of being. The power manifested in the political order was thus a manifestation or apprehension and seizure of divine power. It represented the triumph of a man and of his people. Moloch worship was thus a political religion.

Since Moloch represented kingship and power, sacrifices to Moloch represented the purchase, at the very least, of immunity or insurance

---

2. Keil and Delitzsch, *The Pentateuch*, III, 393.
3. C. H. Waller, "Deuteronomy," in *Ellicott*, II, 54.
4. J. Gray, "Molech, Moloch," in *The Interpreter's Dictionary of the Bible,* K–Q, p. 422 f.
5. John D. Davis, *A Dictionary of the Bible* (Philadelphia: Westminster Press, 1924, 1936), p. 510.

and protection, and, at its highest claim, of power. The "higher" sacrifices in paganism, and especially Baal worship, were sacrifices of humanity, i.e., self-mutilations, notably castration, the sacrifice of children or of posterity, and the like. The priest became identified with the god to the degree that he "departed" from humanity by his castration, his separation from normal human relationships, and his abnormalities. The king became identified with the god to the degree that he manifested absolute power. The sacrifice of children was the supreme sacrifice to Moloch. Moloch worship entered Israel when Solomon built an altar for Moloch for his foreign wives, the Ammonites in particular. Apparently, Solomon limited the sacrificial scope of that altar, because many generations passed before the first human sacrifice, but Solomon's act (I Kings 11:7, 8) had introduced the cult into Israel.

Moloch worship was thus state worship. The state was the true and ultimate order, and religion was a department of state. The state claimed *total jurisdiction* over man; it was therefore entitled to *total sacrifice*. T. Robert Ingram, in his excellent study of law, virtually the only work of merit on the law in generations, rightly links the first commandment to the proscription of statism and totalitarianism. Speaking of "the government which would arrogate to itself all power and bow before no other," Ingram comments:

> The modern word for such a government is totalitarian: a government that arrogates to itself total power. The crowning goal of Satan is to have a totalitarian world government. We who have known something of God the Creator know that total power can reside *only* in Him. Clearly the maker of anything is greater than anything he might make. The very possibility of a Frankenstein monster, the creation of human hands that can destroy humans and not be destroyed by them, is a false image of distorted reason. It presupposes a supernatural evil genius which deceives men into thinking they have made something while really they have been but passive agents of an unknown power. The potter can do what he will with his clay.

> It is certain that the ultimate in supremacy, the greatest power there is, is the power to give existence to everything that is. God alone owes His own being to no other and has eternal existence in Himself. The mere possibility of total power residing anywhere forces us to recognize it in the Creator. Total power can be seated nowhere else. Any person who refuses to acknowledge that all things were made (and hence there is a Maker) simply rules out any consideration of the fact that total power exists anywhere. Thus we may say that for both Christians and non-Christians there is no reasonable way to establish total power anywhere but in the Creator of all things. Apart from Him, all power is divided and thereby limited.[6]

---

6. T. Robert Ingram, *The World Under God's Law* (Houston: St. Thomas Press, 1962), p. 24.

For a state to claim total jurisdiction, as the modern state does, is to claim to be as god, to be the total governor of man and the world. Instead of limited law and limited jurisdiction, the modern antichristian state claims jurisdiction from cradle to grave, from womb to tomb, over welfare, education, worship, the family, business and farming, capital and labor, and all things else. The modern state is a Moloch, demanding Moloch worship: it claims total jurisdiction over man and hence requires total sacrifice.

But, as Ingram observes, with respect to worship, "Only the power who is to be worshipped can ordain the manner in which he is to be worshipped."[7] Similarly, only the power who is ultimate has the right to be the source of law. God is the only true *source* of law; the state is an *agency* of law, one agency among many (church, school, family, etc.), and has a specified and limited area of law to administer under God. The Moloch state denies any such boundaries: it insists on taxing at will, expropriating at its pleasure by "eminent domain," and it claims the right to force the youth into warfare and death at the pleasure of the state.

The Moloch state is the product of apostasy. When a people reject God as their King, and make a man or the state their king (I Sam. 8:7-9), God declares the consequences:

> This will be the manner of the king that shall reign over you: he will take your sons, and appoint them unto him, for his chariots, and to be his horsemen; and they shall run before his chariots. And he will appoint them unto him for captains of thousands, and captains of fifties; and to plow his ground, and to reap his harvest, and to make his instruments of war, and the instruments of his chariots. And he will take your daughters to be perfumers, and to be cooks, and to be bakers. And he will take your fields, and your vineyards, and your oliveyards, even to the best of them, and give them to his servants. And he will take the tenth of your seed, and of your vineyards, and give to his officers, and to his servants. And he will take your men-servants, and your maid-servants, and your goodliest young men, and your asses, and put them to his work. He will take the tenth of your flocks; and ye shall be his servants. And ye shall cry out in that day because of your king whom ye shall have chosen you; and the LORD will not answer you in that day (I Sam. 8:11-18 MTV).

Several aspects of the state which rejects God are here cited: *First*, an anti-Biblical military conscription will be instituted and enforced. *Second*, there will be compulsory labor battalions conscripted for state service. *Third*, the conscription will be of young men and young women, and of animals as well. *Fourth*, the state will expropriate

---

7. *Ibid.*, p. 25.

property, both landed property and livestock. *Fifth*, because the state is now playing god-king, it will demand like God a tithe, a tenth of man's increase as its tax. *Sixth*, God will not hear a people who are complaining at paying the price for their sins.

All these conditions are met and surpassed by the modern Moloch state, which refuses to be content with a tithe but demands a tax equal to several tithes. In some countries, the local tax required is an incredible seizure. Thus, "The late Luigi Einaudi, Italy's foremost economist and ex-President of the Republic, calculated that, if every tax on the statute books was fully collected, the State would absorb 110% of the national income."[8]

The Moloch state simply represents the supreme effort of man to command the future, to predestine the world, and to be as God. Lesser efforts, divination, spirit-questing, magic, and witchcraft, are equally anathema to God. All represent efforts to have the future on other than God's terms, to have a future apart from and in defiance of God. They are assertions that the world is not of God but of brute factuality, and that man can somehow master the world and the future by going directly to the raw materials thereof. Thus King Saul outwardly conformed to God's law by abolishing all black arts, but, when faced with a crisis, he turned to the witch of Endor (I Sam. 28). Saul knew where he stood with God: in rebellion and unrepentant. Saul knew moreover the judgment of the law and of the prophet Samuel concerning him (I Sam. 15:10-35). Samuel alive had declared God's future to Saul. In going to the witch of Endor, Saul attempted to reach Samuel dead, in the faith and hope that Samuel dead was now in touch with and informed concerning a world of brute factuality outside of God which could offer Saul a God-free, law-free future. But the word from the grave only underscored God's law-word (I Sam. 28:15-19): it was the word of judgment.

Astrology is to be included in the ungodly probings which cannot put off or charm away judgment (Isa. 47:10-14).

In Leviticus 19:26, divination and soothsaying are forbidden in the same sentence as the eating of blood. Davis' definition of the meaning of blood in the Bible deserves quotation in full as a succinct statement of the matter:

> BLOOD. The vital fluid circulating through the body, and conveyed by a system of deep-seated arteries from the heart to the extremities, and by a system of superficial veins back again to the heart. . . . The life is in the blood (Lev. xvii. 11, 14): or the blood is the life (Deut. xii. 23), though not exclusively (Ps. civ. 30). The blood represented the life, and so sacred is life before God that the

8. Luigi Barzini, *The Italians* (New York: Bantam Books, 1965), p. 109.

blood of murdered Abel could be described as crying to God from the ground for vengeance (Gen. iv. 10); and immediately after the flood the eating of the blood of the lower animals was forbidden, although their slaughter for food was authorized (ix. 3, 4; Acts xv. 20, 29), and the law was laid down, "Whoso sheddeth man's blood, by man shall his blood be shed" (Gen. ix. 6). The loss of life is the penalty for sin, and its typical vicarious surrender was necessary for remission (Heb. ix. 22), and so, under the Mosaic law the blood of animals was used in all offerings for sin, and the blood of beasts killed on the hunt or slaughtered for food was poured out and covered with earth, because withheld by God from man's consumption and reserved for purposes of atonement (Lev. xvii. 10-14; Deut. xii. 15, 16). The "blood of Jesus," the "blood of Christ," the "blood of Jesus Christ," or "the blood of the Lamb," are figurative expressions for his atoning death (I Cor. x. 16; Eph. ii. 13; Heb. ix. 14; x. 19; I Pet. i. 2, 19; I John i:7; Rev. vii. 14; xii. 11).[9]

Since life is given by God and is to be lived on His terms alone, no life of man or beast can be taken except on God's terms, whether by the state, by man to eat, or by man in his self-defense. To attempt to govern or to take life apart from God's permission, and apart from His service, is like attempting to govern the world and the future apart from God. For this reason, Lev. 19:26 puts the eating of blood, divination, and soothsaying all on the same level as the same sin in essence.

Deuteronomy 18:13 commands, "Thou shalt be perfect (or, upright; "whole-hearted" MTV; "blameless," Berkeley Version) with the LORD thy God." This is part of the often repeated commandment, "Ye shall be holy: for I the LORD your God am holy" (Lev. 19:2; 11:44; Ex. 19:6; Lev. 20:7, 26; I Thess. 4:7; I Peter 1:15, 16, etc.). To be *holy* means literally to be separated, i.e., set apart from a common to a sacred use. The utensils and vessels of the sanctuary, the ministers, and certain days, were separated unto God's special service and hence holy (Ex. 20:8; 30:31; 31:10, 11; Num. 5:17; Zech. 14:21). The defilement from lack of separation could be ceremonial and physical (Ex. 22:31; Lev. 20:26), or it could be spiritual and moral (II Cor. 7:1; I Thess. 4:7; Lev. 20:6, 7; 21:6). The holiness of God is His separation from all created being as the uncreated and creating Being, infinite in wisdom, power, justice, goodness, truth, and glory. The true holiness of man is man's separation unto God in faith and in obedience to God's law. The law is thus the specified way of holiness.

Moloch worship seeks a non-theistic, a non-Biblical way to holiness. It seeks to set itself apart as the power and the glory by means of sacrifices designed to transcend humanity. St. Paul specified some of these ways of false holiness as "forbidding to marry, and commanding to

---

9. Davis, *Dictionary of the Bible*, p. 99.

abstain from meats, which God hath created to be received with thanksgiving: for it is sanctified (made holy) by the word of God and prayer" (I Tim. 4:4, 5).

Very often, societies have sacrificed men in order to dedicate and sanctify a building, to give it power. Writing in 1909, Lawson reported, in his study of lingering paganism in Greece: ". . . it was reported from Zacynthos only a generation ago that a strong feeling still existed there in favour of sacrificing a Mohammedan or a Jew at the foundation of important bridges and other buildings; and there is a legend of a black man having been actually immured in the bridge of an aqueduct near Lebadea in Boeotia."[10] Strack, in the course of disproving any special racial blood ritual among the Jews, did call attention to extensive evidences of superstitious human sacrifices and animal sacrifices in modern Europe.[11]

Man's attempts to control the world and to be the source of predestination lead also to false prophets. The law governing this declares:

> If there arise among you a prophet, or a dreamer of dreams, and giveth thee a sign or a wonder,
> And the sign or the wonder come to pass, whereof he spake unto thee, saying, Let us go after other gods, which thou has not known, and let us serve them;
> Thou shalt not hearken unto the words of that prophet, or that dreamer of dreams: for the LORD your God proveth you, to know whether ye love the LORD your God with all your heart and with all your soul.
> Ye shall walk after the LORD your God, and fear him, and keep his commandments, and obey his voice, and ye shall serve him, and cleave unto him (Deut. 13:1-4).

> The LORD thy God will raise up unto thee a Prophet from the midst of thee, of thy brethren, like unto me; unto him ye shall hearken;
> According to all that thou desirest of the LORD thy God in Horeb in the day of the assembly, saying, Let me not hear again the voice of the LORD my God, neither let me see this great fire any more, that I die not.
> And the LORD said unto me, They have well spoken that which they have spoken.
> I will raise them up a Prophet from among their brethren, like unto thee, and will put my words in his mouth; and he shall speak unto them all that I command him.
> And it shall come to pass, that whosoever will not hearken unto my words which he shall speak in my name, I will require it of him.
> But the prophet, which shall presume to speak a word in my name,

---

10. John Cuthbert Lawson, *Modern Greek Folklore and Ancient Greek Religion* (New Hyde Park, N. Y.: University Books [1909], 1964), p. 276 f.
11. Hermann L. Strack, *The Jew and Human Sacrifice* (London: Cope and Fenwick, 1909).

which I have not commanded him to speak, or that shall speak in
the name of other gods, even that prophet shall die.
And if thou say in thine heart, How shall we know the word which
the LORD hath spoken?
When a prophet speaketh in the name of the LORD, if the thing
follow not, nor come to pass, that is the thing which the LORD hath
not spoken, but the prophet hath spoken it presumptuously: thou
shall not be afraid of him (Deut. 18:15-22).

Deuteronomy 13 cites three cases of instigation to idolatry, *first*, in
vv. 1-5, by the false prophet; *second*, in vv. 6-11, by a private individual;
and, *third*, by a city, vv. 12-18.[12] The penalty in every case is death
without mercy. To the modern mind, this seems drastic. Why death
for idolatry? If idolatry is unimportant to a man, then a penalty for it
is outrageous. But modern man thinks nothing of death penalties for
crimes against the state, or against the "people," or against "the revolution," because these things are important to him. The death penalty
is *not* required here for private belief: it is for attempts to subvert others
and to subvert the social order by enticing others to idolatry. Because
for Biblical law the foundation is the one true God, the central offense
is therefore treason to that God by idolatry. Every law-order has its
concept of treason. No law-order can permit an attack on its foundations without committing suicide. Those states which claim to abolish
the death penalty still retain it on the whole for crimes against the state.
The foundations of a law-order must be protected.

Criminal offenses *always* exact a penalty. The critical question in
any society is this: who shall be penalized? Biblical law declares that
restitution must prevail: if a man steals $100, he must restore the $100
plus another $100; the criminal is penalized. In certain crimes, his
restitution is his own death. In modern humanistic society, the victim
is penalized. There is no restitution, and there is increasingly lighter
punishment of the criminal. Without restitution, crime becomes potentially profitable, and the victim is penalized by the state. The victim
is penalized by the crime, by the court costs, and the prison costs as
they appear in taxation.

But crime always exacts a penalty above and beyond the individuals
involved as victims and as criminals. The law-order is breached; the
peace and the health of society are broken. A society which tolerates
penalties against itself and against its law-abiding citizens is a dangerous
and a dying society.

Basic to the health of a society is the integrity of its foundation. To
allow tampering with its foundation is to allow its total subversion.
Biblical law can no more permit the propagation of idolatry than

---

12. Waller, in *Ellicott*, II, 42.

Marxism can permit counter-revolution, or monarchy a move to execute the king, or a republic an attempt to destroy the republic and create a dictatorship.

It should be noted that Deuteronomy 13:5-18 does not call for the death penalty for unbelief or for heresy. It condemns false prophets (vv. 1-5) who seek to lead the people, with signs and wonders, into idolatry. It does condemn individuals who secretly try to start a movement into idolatry (vv. 6-11). It does condemn cities which establish another religion and subvert the law-order of the nation (vv. 13-18), and this condemnation must be enforced by man to turn away the judgment of God (v. 17).

This condemnation does not apply to a missionary situation, where the land is anti-God to begin with: this is a situation for conversion. It does require a nation grounded in God's law-system to preserve that order by punishing the basic treason against it. No society is without testing, and God tests man by these challenges, to see whether man will stand in terms of God's order or not (v. 3).

Having dealt with false prophets, i.e., false mediators, the law turns to the one true Mediator:

> The LORD thy God will raise up unto thee a Prophet from the midst of thee, of thy brethren, like unto me; unto him ye shall hearken (Deut. 18:15).

This Prophet and His work is described in vv. 15-19. Men must either obey Him, or else God will require it of men (v. 19). Waller's comment concerning the Prophet is especially good:

> The connection between these verses and the preceding is well illustrated by Isaiah's question (chap. viii. 19): "And when they shall say unto you, Seek unto them that have familiar spirits, and unto wizards that peep, and that mutter: should not a people seek unto their God? for the living to the dead?" Or, as the angel turned the phrase on Easter morning: "Why seek ye Him that liveth among the dead?"[13]

According to Calvin, "the expression 'a Prophet,' is used by *enallage* for a number of prophets. . . . Not at all more correct is their opinion, who apply it to Christ alone."[14] Clearly, the passage does refer to prophets generally, and in vv. 20-22, the false prophet is identified and called presumptuous: "thou shalt not be afraid of him." The term, however, equally clearly and more obviously applies to the one great Prophet and Mediator, as against the many false mediators. All prophets are speakers for the one Prophet who speaks the word of the LORD. Since there is one true God, there is one word, and one speaker. All prophets

---

13. Waller, in *Ellicott*, II, 54.
14. Calvin, *op. cit.*, I, 434.

were speakers for the one Prophet, Jesus Christ, the second person of the Trinity.

The commandment is, "Thou shalt have no other gods before me." In our polytheistic world, the many other gods are the many peoples, every man his own god. Every man under humanism is his own law, and his own universe. Anarchism is the personal creed, and totalitarian statism the social creed, since only coercion can, in a polytheistic world, bring men together.

> During the recent occupation of the Sorbonne a student obliterated a large "No Smoking" sign near the entrance to the auditorium and wrote: "You Have the Right to Smoke." In due time another student added: "It is Forbidden to Forbid." This slogan has caught on and is now appearing in many places which have been taken over by the students. In foot-high letters in the grand hall of the Sorbonne, someone has written: "I take my desires for the truth because I believe in the truth of my desires."[15]

These lawless students, while affirming that none had the right to forbid them anything, to coerce them into any behaviour, were bent on coercing an entire nation. Total anarchy means total coercion. This is Moloch worship with a vengeance: all society must be sacrificed to satisfy these modern worshipers of destruction. The student revolution is a fitting climax to statist education. To surrender children to the state is to turn them over to the enemy. For the surrendered children, as the new Janizaries of the new Turks, to turn on the society which begat them and to destroy it is a judgment on the Moloch worship of their elders. To have other gods and other laws, other schools, and other hopes than the one true God is to invoke the whole weight of the law in judgment.

Our culture today resembles the legend of Empedocles, the Greek philosopher:

> Even in his life-time Empedocles was a charismatic figure. Diodorus describes him as laurel-wreathed, robed like a god in purple, sandalled in gold. He taught that the highest forms of human life, the closest to the divine, were the prophet and the physician. He was both. As a living myth, he attracted legend. Most spectacular of unsupported tales is the account of his death by suicidal leap into Aetna's crater: self-immolation in the expectation of becoming, or at least being worshipped as a god. The mountain, it is said, later gave back one golden sandal.[16]

Like the legendary Empedocles of old, our world today is seeking to make itself god by self-immolation.

---

15. *The Review of the News,* vol. IV, no. 22 (May 29, 1968), p. 16.
16. Helen Hill Miller, *Sicily and the Western Colonies of Greece* (New York: Charles Scribner's Sons, 1965), p. 146. For a reference to the sacrifice of a boy to Moloch by Himilco of Carthage, see. p. 165.

4. The Laws of Covenant Membership

Those who obey the first commandment, "Thou shalt not have other gods before me," are members of the covenant. The two basic rites of the covenant in the Old Testament were circumcision and the passover, and, in the New Testament, baptism and communion.

Genesis 17:9-14 gives us the institution of circumcision as the sign of the covenant. The requirement of the covenant is obedience to the moral law (Gen. 17:1; 18:17-19). "Further, the ethical character of O.T. religion is symbolized by circumcision."[1] Circumcision was widely prevalent in all cultures, and always religious. It is the act of cutting off the foreskin of the male genital organ.

> For the doctrinal understanding of circumcision two facts are significant; first, it was instituted before the birth of Isaac; secondly, in the accompanying revelation only the second promise, relating to numerous posterity is referred to. These two facts together show that circumcision has something to do with the process of propagation. Not in the sense that the act is in itself sinful, for there is no trace of this anywhere in the O.T. It is not the act but the product, that is, *human nature*, which is unclean, and stands in need of purification and qualification. Hence circumcision is not, as among pagans, applied to grown-up men, but to infants on the eighth day. Human nature is unclean and disqualified in its very source. Sin, consequently is a matter of the race and not of the individual only. The need of qualification had to be specially emphasized under the O.T. At that time the promises of God had proximate reference to temporal, natural things. Hereby the danger was created that natural descent might be understood as entitling to the grace of God. Circumcision teaches that physical descent from Abraham is not sufficient to make true Israelites. The uncleanness and disqualification of nature must be taken away. Dogmatically speaking, therefore, circumcision stands for justification and regeneration, plus sanctification (Rom. 4:9-12; Col. 2:11-13).[2]

Circumcision is required by the law in Leviticus 12:3, on the eight day. All who desired to partake of the passover, whether Hebrew or foreigner, had to be circumcised (Ex. 12:48-49). Both Jesus and John the Baptist were circumcised (Luke 1:59; 2:21), as was St. Paul (Phil. 3:5), who insisted on the circumcision of Timothy, who had a Jewish mother and a Greek father (Acts 16:3), but Paul did not require it of Titus (Gal. 2:3).

From the beginning, the meaning of circumcision and its spiritual consequences were understood:

1. Geerhardus Vos, *Biblical Theology, Old and New Testaments* (Grand Rapids: Eerdmans, 1948), p. 103.
2. *Ibid.*, p. 104 f.

Circumcise therefore the foreskin of your heart, and be no more
stiffnecked (Deut. 10:16).

And the LORD thy God will circumcise thine heart, and the heart
of thy seed, to love the LORD thy God with all thine heart, and with
all thy soul, that thou mayest live (Deut. 30:6).

Similar expressions are to be found in Leviticus 26:41; Jeremiah 4:4;
6:10; Romans 2:28-29; Colossians 2:11, etc.

Modern commentators see no great distinction between Hebrew and
pagan circumcisions.[3] The differences, of course, are very great. For
the Christian, the paramount difference is that the Biblical rite was
ordained by God as a part of His revelation. With respect to the meaning of the rite, it is in paganism a ritual of initiation into manhood, and
into the tribe or clan. Whereas other religions commonly recognize a
defect in human nature, they also hold that the defect can be remedied
by man: hence the connection of circumcision with the onset of manhood. The young man assumes his responsibilities in society, and also
his religious responsibility to conform to the religious standard by an act
of will. Paganism is Pelagian to the core. Circumcision on the eighth
day removes the power of the rite from man to God: the young child
is not capable of justifying, regenerating, or sanctifying himself: he is
entirely passive in the rite. The fact of divine grace is thus set forth.
Just as the covenant wholly represents God's initiative and grace, so
the sign of the covenant represents the same. The commandment therefore was clear: circumcision was to be on (or after) the eighth day,
when the child's blood would coagulate properly and permit the operation.

A ceremony related to circumcision is the purification of women after
childbirth (Lev. 12). The uncleanness of the woman has reference to
a religious and sacramental impurity. Micklem observed of Leviticus
12:2:

> The translation *unclean* is peculiarly infelicitous here, for it inevi-
> tably suggests disapprobation or disgust, and it anticipates a Mani-
> chaean view of evil inherent in the flesh. The passage might be
> paraphrased: "When a woman has borne a son, proper feeling re-
> quires that she remain in seclusion for a week; then the child is to
> be circumcised; even then she is to stay at home for a month, and
> her first journey abroad shall be to church."[4]

The point with respect to Manichaeanism is well taken, but more is
at stake than "proper feeling"! Neither the flesh nor the spirit of fallen
man is clean before God. There is no more hope in things spiritual

---

3. See, for example, Nathaniel Micklem, "Leviticus," in *The Interpreter's
Bible*, vol. II, p. 60 f., and J. P. Hyatt, "Circumcision," in *The Interpreter's Dictionary of the Bible*, A–D, pp. 629-631.

4. Micklem, *Interpreter's Bible*, II, 60.

than in things material. Circumcision witnesses to the fact that man's hope is not in generation but in regeneration, and the witness of the ceremony of the purification of women is the same.

The days of uncleanness for a man-child were seven: circumcision, by its witness to covenant grace, terminated that period. For a female child, the days of uncleanness were fourteen, during which time the woman touched no hallowed thing and was forbidden entrance to the sanctuary. These periods of time were followed by the days of purification, thirty-three after a male birth, and sixty-six days after a daughter's birth, after which the mother came to the sanctuary with an offering, a yearling lamb, or, in cases of poverty, as with Mary (Luke 2:21-24), two pigeons or doves. Circumcision served to shorten the time with respect to male births, and the ritual of purification was the witness to covenant membership for the daughters. It was a reminder that covenant righteousness was of the grace of God, to mother and child, and that grace, not race or blood, is the fountainhead of salvation.

The service continues in the church, and appears, for example, in *The Book of Common Prayer* as "The Thanksgiving of Woman after Child-birth" or "the Churching of Women." It begins with the pastoral declaration, "Forasmuch as it hath pleased Almighty God, of his goodness, to give you safe deliverance, and to preserve you in the great danger of child-birth: You shall give hearty thanks unto God," and it concluded with the presentation by the woman of a required gift.

The rite has reference, not to actual sin but original sin, and it is a recognition of the fall of man and of covenant grace. By birth the old rebellion of Adam is re-introduced into the covenant household in the form of a child whose nature is inherited from Adam. This hereditary corruption is acknowledged, and the covenant grace beseeched, in the ritual of the purification of women. There is no valid reason for the discontinuance of the rite. It has been reduced to a simple thanksgiving in *The Book of Common Prayer*, which is an atrophy of meaning, but this still far surpasses the practice of other churches.

Baptism is the sign of the renewed covenant, replacing circumcision. It was a sign of religious purification and consecration in the Old Testament (Ex. 29:4; 30:19, 20; 40:12; Lev. 15; 16:26, 28; 17:15; 22:4, 6; Num. 19:8). In Ezekiel 36:25, 26, we are given baptism ("sprinkling") as a sign of the regeneration of the covenant people after the captivity, and it is associated with a "new heart." Jeremiah 31:31-34 associates this "new heart" with the new covenant in Christ. In terms of these texts, proselytes into Israel were baptized prior to circumcision, indicating that the new covenant was in mind. John the Baptist, by summoning all Israel to baptism, created a sensation, in that it indicated that the age of the Messiah was at hand.

Baptism like circumcision is to be administered to children, unless it is to an adult newly converted, as the sign of covenant membership by grace. Not surprisingly, most opponents of infant baptism are logically also Pelagian or at the least Arminian. They insist on claiming the prerogative in salvation for man.

The other rite of covenant membership, the passover, was instituted in Egypt (Ex. 12; 13:3-10; Num. 9:1-14; Deut. 16:3-4; Ex. 23:18) to celebrate the culminating act of redemption by God in His judgment on Egypt. All the firstborn of Egypt were killed by God, who passed over those Israelite and other believers' houses where the blood of a lamb or a kid had been sprinkled above and on the sides of the door, and the members of the household stood, staff in hand, waiting to move in terms of God's promised deliverance. The lamb or kid was roasted whole and eaten with unleavened bread (to signify the incorruptibility of the sacrifice, Lev. 2:11; I Cor. 5:7, 8) and bitter herbs, to signify the bitterness of their slavery in Egypt.

Central to the passover is the blood. In the covenant with Abraham (Gen. 15:7-21), Abraham was required to pass between the divided pieces of slain animals, which set forth the death of the covenant maker, i.e., the death of the true sacrifice who was to come, Jesus Christ, and the judgment of death upon those who betrayed His covenant. Moses at Sinai took the blood and sprinkled it both upon the altar and on the people (Ex. 24:4-8) to indicate both that the covenant rested upon an atonement provided entirely by God, and that the penalty for apostasy from the covenant is death. Stibbs has ably summarized the main significance of "blood" in Scripture:

> Blood is a visible token of life violently ended; it is a sign of life either given or taken in death. Such giving or taking of life is in this world the extreme both of gift or price and of crime or penalty. Man knows no greater. So, first, the greatest offering or service one can render is to give one's blood or life. "Greater love hath no man than this, that a man lay down his life for his friends" (Jn. 15: 13). Second, the greatest earthly crime or evil is to take blood or life, that is, manslaughter or murder. Third, the great penalty or loss is to have one's blood shed or life taken. So, it says of the blood-shedder, "by man shall his blood be shed"; and so Paul says of the magistrate, ". . . He bareth not the sword in vain: for he is a minister of God, an avenger for wrath to him that doeth evil" (Rom. 13:4, R.V.). "The wages of sin is death" (Rom. 6:23). Fourth, the only possible or adequate expiation or atonement is life for life and blood for blood. This expiation man cannot give. (See Ps. 49:7, 8; Mk. 8:36, 37.) Not only is his own life already forfeit as a sinner. But also all life is God's. (See Ps. 50:9, 10.) So man has no "blood" that he can give. This necessary but otherwise unobtainable gift God has given. He has given the blood to make atonement (Lv. 17:11). Atonement is, therefore, only possible by

the gift of God. Or as P. T. Forsyth expressed it, "Sacrifice is the fruit and not the root of grace." What is more, when our Lord claimed to have come "to give his life a ransom for many" (Mk. 10:45), He was implying His Deity as well as His human sinlessness, and indicating the fulfilment of that which the shed blood of animal sacrifices merely typified. Here in Jesus, the incarnate Son, was God come in person to give as Man the blood which only can make atonement. The Church of God is, therefore, purchased with His own blood (Acts 20:28).

All these four significances of "blood" as shed meet in the Cross of Christ. There the Son of Man in our flesh and blood for us men and for our salvation made the greatest offering. He gave His life. (See Jn. 10:17, 18.) Second, He became the victim of mankind's greatest crime. He was vilely and unjustly put to death. Third, "He was reckoned with transgressors" (Lk. 22:37 R.V. from Is. 53:12), and endured the extreme penalty of the wrongdoer. The hand of the law and of the Roman magistrate put Him to death. By man was His blood shed. Fourth, He, as God made flesh, gave, as He alone could do, His human blood to make atonement. Repentance and remission of sins can, therefore, now be preached in His name. We are justified by His blood.[5]

The passover celebrated Israel's redemption, even as the sacrament of the Lord's Table celebrates the redemption of the true Church of God by the blood of Jesus Christ. The celebration of the sacrament means the reception by faith of the redemption and cleansing from sin, and the blessings of the covenant life, in Christ through His atoning sacrifice.

The passover was doubly a witness to blood required. Blood was required, *first*, of all Egypt for their unbelief. The firstborn represented in their person the whole household, and the sentence of death passed against them was a death sentence against all. *Second*, Israel no less than Egypt was under sentence of death. There was no merit in them to save them, nor could there be. But the death sentence passed against the covenant people was assumed by God the Son in the type of the blood of the lamb.

The same double witness to blood appears in the cross. *First*, Israel was sentenced to death (Matt. 24) and destined for destruction for its treason to the covenant. *Second*, the people of Christ were redeemed from sin by the blood of the covenant and were delivered from the judgment on Jerusalem and Judea.

The sacrament of the Lord's Table is the Christian passover, "for even Christ our passover is sacrificed for us: Therefore let us keep the feast, not with old leaven, neither with the leaven of malice and wickedness; but with the unleavened bread of sincerity and truth" (I Cor.

---

5. A. M. Stibbs, *The Meaning of the Word 'Blood' in Scripture* (London: The Tyndale Press, 1948, 1962), p. 30 f.

5:7, 8). The first celebration of the Lord's Supper, in the Upper Room, was at the conclusion, and in fulfilment, of the passover.

The same double witness is basic to the Lord's Table, and it cannot be truly celebrated if this aspect is denied or overlooked. *First*, the passover of Israel was celebrated in the expectation of victory. The Hebrews were to eat in haste: God would deliver them that very night from their oppressor and enemy by a mighty judgment against Egypt and a spoiling of the Egyptians (Ex. 12:11, 29-36). The Christian passover sets forth the believer's deliverance from sin and death *and* his deliverance from the enemy. It is both a spiritual and a material salvation. To celebrate the death of God's firstborn for our salvation is to celebrate the death of God's enemies, of their firstborn, their totality, under His judgment. It requires us to move in terms of victory (Ex. 12:11) if we are to receive it. To limit the sacrament to a spiritual victory is to act as a Manichaean rather than as a Christian; it is to see God as lord only of the spiritual and not of the material realm. Thus, *second*, as is clearly apparent, the Lord's Table is victory because it is judgment. St. Paul declared the sacrament to be judgment against believers who partook thereof "unworthily . . . not discerning the Lord's body" (I Cor. 11:27-30). If it is judgment against believers who transgress, how much more does the Lord's Supper proclaim damnation to a world in rebellion against God?

But, *third*, the children of the covenant, i.e., circumcised male children, and daughters of the covenant, partook of it. Indeed, the service was designed to declare the meaning of the sacrament to the youngest male child able to speak, to whom was assigned the ritual role of asking, "What mean ye by this service?" (Ex. 12:26). The father then declared its meaning to all. In the early church, children partook of the sacrament, according to all the records. The evidence of St. Paul indicates that entire families attended and participated: it was the evening meal (I Cor. 11). Joseph Bingham's *Antiquities of the Christian Church* cites the evidence of a long-standing practice of participation by children and infants. This practice was clearly a carry-over from the passover of Israel, and there is no Scriptural evidence for a departure from it. At the same time, it should be noted, the early church strictly excluded outsiders from the sacraments. Arguments against this inclusion of children are more rationalistic and Pelagian than Biblical.

The commandment, "Thou shalt have no other gods before me," requires, *first*, that a man know that his only hope of salvation is in the blood of God's sacrifice, the Lamb of God, and to live in grateful obedience. *Second*, man must recognize that *all* blood is governed by God and His law-word, and to do anything apart from God and His

law-word, is *sin*, "for whatsoever is not of faith is sin" (Rom. 14:23).
As Stibbs has written,

> Further, the conviction that underlies the Old Testament Scriptures
> is that physical life is God's creation. So it belongs to Him not to
> men. Also, particularly in the case of man made in God's image,
> this life is precious in God's sight. Therefore, not only has no man
> any independent right of freedom to shed blood and take life, but
> also if he does, he will be accountable to God for his action. God
> will require blood of any man that sheds it. The murderer brings
> blood upon himself not only in the eyes of men but first of all in
> the sight of God. And the penalty which was due to God, and
> which other men were made responsible to inflict, was that the mur-
> derer's own life must be taken. Such a man is not worthy to enjoy
> further the stewardship of the Divine gift of life. He must pay the
> extreme earthly penalty and lose his own life in the flesh. Further,
> the character of the punishment is also significantly described by the
> use of the word "blood." "Whoso sheddeth man's blood, by man
> shall his blood be shed" (Gen. 9:5, 6).[6]

To have none other gods, means to have no other law than God's law,
and no activity or thought apart from His law-word. Whether for food,
to uphold the civil law, in warfare, or in self-defense, blood can be shed
only in terms of God's word. Where God permits it, man cannot contradict God or propose a "better" or "higher" way without sin. Thus,
to regard vegetarianism, pacifism, or non-resistance in all cases, as a
"higher" way is to treat God's way as lower than man's.

Very closely related to the doctrine of the passover is the redemption
of the first-born and their sanctification.

> And the LORD spake unto Moses, saying,
> Sanctify unto me all the firstborn, whatsoever openeth the womb
> among the children of Israel, both of man and of beast: it is mine
> (Ex. 13:1, 2).

> And it shall be when the LORD shall bring thee into the land of
> the Canaanites, as he sware unto thee and to thy fathers, and shall
> give it thee,
> That thou shalt set apart unto the LORD all that openeth the matrix,
> and every firstling that cometh of a beast which thou hast; the males
> shall be the LORD'S.
> And every firstling of an ass thou shalt redeem with a lamb; and if
> thou wilt not redeem it, then thou shalt break his neck: and all the
> firstborn of man among thy children shalt thou redeem.
> And it shall be when thy son asketh thee in time to come, saying,
> What is this? that thou shalt say unto him, By strength of hand the
> LORD brought us out from Egypt, from the house of bondage:
> And it came to pass, when Pharaoh would hardly let us go, that the
> LORD slew all the firstborn in the land of Egypt, both the firstborn
> of man, and the firstborn of beast: therefore I sacrifice to the LORD

---

6. Stibbs, *op. cit.*, p. 11.

all that openeth the matrix, being males: but all the firstborn of my children I redeem.
And it shall be for a token upon thine hand, and for frontlets between thine eyes: for by strength of hand the LORD brought us forth out of Egypt (Ex. 13:11-16).

Thou shalt not delay to offer the first of thy ripe fruits, and of thy liquors: the firstborn of thy sons shalt thou give unto me.
Likewise shalt thou do with thine oxen, and with thy sheep; seven days it shall be with his dam: on the eighth day then shalt thou give it me (Ex. 22:29, 30).

All that openeth the matrix is mine; and every firstling among thy cattle, whether ox or sheep, that is male.
But the firstling of an ass thou shalt redeem with a lamb: and if thou redeem him not, then thou shalt break his neck. All the firstborn of thy sons thou shalt redeem. And none shall appear before me empty (Ex. 34:19, 20).

Only the firstling of the beasts, which should be the LORD'S firstling, no man shall sanctify it; whether it be ox, or sheep: it is the LORD'S (Lev. 27:26).

All the firstling males that come of thy herd and of thy flock thou shalt sanctify unto the LORD thy God: thou shalt do no work with the firstling of thy bullock, nor shear the firstling of thy sheep.
Thou shalt eat it before the LORD thy God year by year in the place which the LORD shall choose, thou and thy household (Deut. 15: 19, 20).

For if the firstfruit be holy, the lump is also holy: and if the root be holy, so are the branches (Rom. 11:16).

Redemption is here a very physical matter, because redemption is never to be separated from the world of the physical or the spiritual. Israel was physically enslaved to Egypt as well as in bondage to sin. The fall of man placed man, body and soul, into bondage, and redemption therefore is total, affecting man's total being, not merely an aspect thereof. To limit salvation to man's soul and not to his body, his society, and his every aspect and relationship, is to deny its Biblical meaning. Indeed, the whole creation is finally involved in redemption (Rom. 8:20-21).

The first-born referred to in the law is the first-born of a mother rather than of a father: it is "the first issue of every womb" (Ex. 13:2).[7] Fairbairn's analysis of the redemption of the first-born is particularly good:

We have a three-fold act of God—first, the infliction of death on the first-born of man and beast in Egypt; then exemption from this judgment on the part of Israel in consideration of the paschal sacri-

7. *The Torah, The Five Books of Moses*, A New Translation (Philadelphia: Jewish Publication Society, 1962).

fice; and finally, in commemoration of the exemption, the consecrating to the Lord of all the first-born in time to come. The fundamental element on which the whole proceeds, is evidently the representative character of the first-born; the first offspring of the producing parent stands for the entire fruit of the womb, being that in which the whole takes its beginning; so that the slaying of the first-born of Egypt was virtually the slaying of all—it implied that one and the same doom was suspended over all; and, consequently, that the saving of the first-born of Israel and their subsequent consecration to the Lord, was, in regard to divine intention and efficacious virtue, the saving and consecration of all. Hence Israel as a whole was designated God's first-born: "Thou shalt say unto Pharaoh, Thus saith the Lord, Israel is my son, my first-born; and I say unto thee, Let my son go, that he may serve me; and if thou refuse to let him go, behold I will slay thy son, thy first-born." Ex. iv. 22, 23.[8]

The act of redemption was thus the ritual of *confirmation* of covenant membership. All Israel, man and beast, was acknowledged to be God's possession, His "first-born" by grace and adoption. Israel deserved to die no less than Egypt: its redemption was an act of sovereign grace. This fact had been demonstrated by God to Abraham, in calling for the sacrifice of Isaac. The Bible does not condemn human sacrifice in principle. "All Biblical sacrifice rests on the idea that the gift of life to God, either in consecration or in expiation, is necessary to the action or the restoration of religion." On the other hand, "man in the abnormal relation of sin is disqualified for offering this gift of his life in his own person. Hence the principle of vicariousness is brought into play: one life takes the place of another life."[9] But even without sin, man can give nothing to God that man has not already received from God. The fact that the redemption of the first-born was normally linked with the eighth day, the time of circumcision, of entrance into the covenant, made it at the same time a confirmation of the covenant by the parents. The animals were often given directly to the priest. The tribe of Levi became a substitute priestly tribe, devoted to God, as the first-born (Num. 3:40, 41). The law took care to protect the parents from an exorbitant redemption fee (Lev. 27:1-8). Other laws with respect to the first-born, i.e., re-stating it, are Numbers 8:16, 17, which connects God's right to Israel's first-born with the slaying of Egypt's first-born; Numbers 8:18, which established the Levites as the substitute; and Numbers 3:11-13, 44-51, which gives specific details of this substitution. The first-born of flocks and herds are specified in Exodus 13:11-13 and Exodus 22:30, as well as in Exodus 34:19, 20; Leviticus 27:26, 27; and Numbers 18:

---

8. Patrick Fairbairn, "First-Born," in Fairbairn's *Imperial Standard Bible Encyclopedia* (Grand Rapids: Zondervan [1891], 1957), II, 297 f.
9. G. Vos, *Biblical Theology*, p. 107.

15, 17. In Numbers 18:15, 17, it is specified that the firstling of a cow, a sheep, or a goat cannot be redeemed but must, according to Deuteronomy 14:23; 15:19-22, together with the tithe of the corn, wine, and oil, be eaten before the Lord for the second tithe. Waller commented on Deuteronomy 14:22, 23, 28:

> (22) *Thou shalt truly tithe.*—The Talmud and Jewish interpreters in general are agreed in the view that the tithe mentioned in this passage, both here and in verse 28, and also the tithe described in chap. xxvi. 12-15, are all one thing—"the second tithe"; and entirely distinct from the ordinary tithe assigned to the Levites for their subsistence in Num. xviii. 21, and by them tithed again for the priest (Num. xviii. 26). . . .
> (23) *And thou shalt eat before the LORD thy God*—i.e., thou shalt eat the second tithe. This was to be done two years; but in the third and sixth years there was a different arrangement (see verse 28). In the seventh year, which was Sabbatical, there would probably be no tithe, for there was to be no harvest. The profit of the earth was for all, and every one was free to eat at pleasure. . . .
> (28) *At the end of three years thou shalt bring forth all the tithe.*— This is called by the Jews Ma'aser 'Ani. "the poor's tithe." They regard it as identical with the second tithe, which was ordinarily eaten by the owners at Jerusalem; but in every third and sixth year was bestowed upon the poor.[10]

It should be noted that this second tithe was not strictly a tenth, in that a second tenth was not set apart from the specified livestock, but "*the firstlings* take the place of a second tithe on animals."[11]

In addition to the redemption of the firstborn, a head tax was required of every male twenty years old and over (Ex. 30:11-16), which was used originally for the construction of the tabernacle (Ex. 38:25-28). It was paid by Levites and all others. It was a reminder that all were preserved alive only by the grace of God. It was used to maintain the civil order after the tabernacle (the throne room and palace of God's government) was built. Formal enrolment at maturity meant the payment of a half-shekel in acknowledgment of God's providential grace. All paid the same amount. "It was an acknowledgment of sin, equally binding upon all, and so made equal for all; and it saved from God's vengeance those who, if they had been too proud to make it, would have been punished by some 'plague' or another."[12] The poll tax was a reminder that they lived by God's grace, and that their lives and

---

10. Waller, in *Ellicott*, II, 44 f.
11. P. W. Thompson, *All the Tithes or Terumah* (London: The Covenant Publishing Co., 1946), p. 19.
12. Rev. George Rawlinson, in H. D. M. Spence and J. S. Exell, eds., *The Pulpit Commentary: Exodus*, vol. II (New York: Funk & Wagnalls), p. 305. See also J. C. Connell, "Exodus," F. Davidson, A. M. Stibbs, E. F. Kevan, eds., *The New Bible Commentary* (Grand Rapids: Eerdmans, 1953), p. 128; Keil and Delitzsch, *The Pentateuch*, III, 210-212.

substance were forfeited by treason against God. It was therefore a ceremony associated in meaning with the redemption of the firstborn, the passover, and the Day of Atonement, rather than the tithe.

Both the first-fruits of the flock, and of the field, were, with the exception noted, to be given to the Lord for Levitical maintenance, according to the Law of the Covenant.[13] The law of the first-fruits appears in Leviticus 23:10, 17 and Deuteronomy 26:1-11, also Numbers 15: 17-21; Exodus 22:29; 23:19. The New Testament refers to the first-fruits in Romans 8:13; 11:16; 16:5; I Corinthians 15:20-23; 16:15; James 1:18; Revelation 14:4. Jesus Christ is declared to be, when risen from the dead, "the first sheaf waved before the Lord on the second Paschal day, just as Christ actually burst the bonds of death at that very time."[14] St. Paul declared, "Ourselves also, which have the first-fruits of the Spirit, even we ourselves groan within ourselves, waiting for the adoption, to wit, the redemption of our body" (Rom. 8:23).

The offering of the first-born and of the firstfruits was closely connected with the *tithe*, and, with it, constituted a symbolic offering of the whole. The tithe, however, was in addition to the offering of the first-born and of the firstfruits.

The early church saw the offering of the first-born fulfilled in Jesus Christ, the offering given by God in fulfillment of the requirement for the household of faith. The offering of the firstfruits was, however, continued, although it too was in equal measure fulfilled by Christ. The collection of firstfruits took various forms, such as the payment of the first year's produce of benefices demanded by the pope of benefices in England which had been granted to foreigners. Henry VIII took over these collections, but Queen Anne restored them to the Church of England to augment small livings.[15]

With respect to the tithe, according to Bingham, "the ancients believed the law about tithes not to be merely a ceremonial or political command, but of moral and perpetual obligation."[16] For many centuries, the tithe was paid in produce, i.e., a literal tenth of the field rather than its monetary equivalent. Tithe-barns were built to house the tithes.[17] The tithe was commanded by the Council of Trent on pain of excom-

---

13. U. Z. Rule, *Old Testament Institutions Their Origin and Development* (London: S.P.C.K., 1910), p. 322.

14. A. Edersheim, *The Temple, Its Ministry and Services as they were at the time of Christ* (New York: Hodder and Stoughton, n.d.), p. 385.

15. John M'Clintock and James Strong, *Cyclopaedia of Biblical, Theological, and Ecclesiastical Literature* (New York: Harper, 1894), III, 574.

16. Joseph Bingham, *The Antiquities of the Christian Church* (London: Bohn, 1850), I, 189.

17. For pictures of tithe-barns of medieval England, see Sacheverell Sitwell, *Monks, Nuns and Monasteries* (New York: Holt, Rinehart, and Winston, 1965), illust. between pp. 42 and 43.

munication, but it was abolished in France in 1789 and has gradually fallen into neglect. It was required in Protestant circles at one time but here too it has fallen into neglect or become simply a tithe to the church.[18]

The tithe or tenth appears very early, long before Moses; when Abraham tithed (Gen. 14:20; Heb. 7:4, 6), it was apparently an established practice, so that its origin may go back to the original revelation to Adam. Jacob also spoke of the tithe (Gen. 28:20-22). A Lord's portion related to the tithe appears in the war against Midian, where God fixed the proportion of the spoils of war which were to be the Lord's as one out of fifty, and one out of five hundred, depending on the booty (Num. 31:25-54).

The law of the tithe appears in Leviticus 27:30-33; Numbers 18:21-26; Deuteronomy 14:22-27; 26:12, 15. The rabbis and many orthodox scholars distinguished three tithes; some orthodox scholars and virtually all modernists see only one tithe.[19] The existence of three tithes from early years is a matter of record, i.e., from the earliest period of Hebraic documents related to Scripture, i.e., from the Apocrypha. Tobit, dated 350 B.C., or from 250 to 200 B.C. by Davis,[20] and "toward the close of the 3d century B.C." by Gehman,[21] gives evidence of three tithes very plainly (Tobit 1:5-8). Similar evidence is to be found in Josephus' *Antiquities*, bk. IV, and in Jerome, at a later date.[22] The historical evidence reveals the practice; the Scripture refers to three kinds of tithing. The burden of proof is on those who insist on reducing it to one tithe.

In analyzing the tithe, therefore, it becomes apparent that, *first*, there are three kinds of tithes, a first tithe, the Lord's tithe (Num. 18:21-24), which went to the Levites, who rendered a tenth of this to the priests (Num. 18:26-28); a second tithe, a festival tithe to rejoice before the Lord (Deut. 12:6-7, 17-18); a third tithe, a poor tithe, every third year, to be shared locally with the local Levite, the stranger, the fatherless, and the widow (Deut. 14:27-29).[23]

Second, the Lord as Creator of all things, established the terms of man's life and the use of man's substance. Certain specified amounts are holy unto the Lord. The tithe was of substance, i.e., of the increase of the flock or herd, or the yield of the field. If redeemed, i.e., paid to the

18. George C. M. Douglas, "Tithe," in *Fairbairn's Bible Encyclopedia*, VI, 290.
19. For the tithe, see Oswald T. Allis, "Leviticus," in Davidson, Stibbs, and Kevan, *op. cit.*, p. 161; Davis, *op. cit.*, p. 783 f.; H. H. Guthrie, Jr., "Tithe," in *Interpreter's Dictionary of the Bible*, R–Z, p. 654, see the three tithes as the practice of later Judaism, i.e., prior to and including the N.T. era.
20. Davis, *op. cit.*, p. 44.
21. Henry Snyder Gehman revision of John D. Davis, *The Westminster Dictionary of the Bible* (Philadelphia: The Westminster Press, 1944), p. 34.
22. Henry Lansdell, *The Tithe in Scripture* (London: SPCK, 1908), p. 32 f.
23. See *ibid.*, pp. 23-36.

Lord in money, a fifth of the amount had to be added. In tithing, a man was not to choose the good or bad for the Lord, but to take every tenth animal for his tithe. If a man counted sixteen calves, he thus tithed one only, the tenth as he numbered them. By adding a fifth to the monetary tithe, he tended to equalize the tithe, but, on the whole, the requirement favored man (Lev. 27:30-33).

Third, the second tithe was to be used in rejoicing before the Lord at the three annual religious festivals. It could be taken to the sanctuary in the form of money, to be spent there on himself at the Passover, the Feast of Tabernacles, and the Feast of Weeks, over two weeks of religious "vacationing" (Deut. 12:6-7; 14:22-27; 16:3, 13,16). Except for the Levites, with whom a portion was shared, this tithe remained with the tither and was used for his pleasure. There was no second tithe on animals in the second tithe; the firstlings of the flock took their place in the second tithe (Deut. 12:17, 18).

Fourth, the third tithe was the poor tithe, to be used locally with the poor, widows, orphans, helpless foreigners, people unable to help themselves because of age, illness, or other special conditions. The Levites were also to be remembered (Deut. 14:27-29).

Fifth, the tithe, according to Thompson, amounted thus to a tenth for the Lord, a tenth for the poor, and a slight amount from the second tithe for the Levites. Thompson called it "one-sixth of a man's income," since the third or poor tithe came twice in each six-year period.[24] In terms of this, Thompson saw the total tithe as equal to one day's labor in six.[25] This may be a little high, but it is close. Without reckoning the second tithe as a cost (i.e., the Levite's portion), it comes to 13.33 percent annually, whereas Thompson's reckoning takes it to a higher percentage.

Sixth, there was no tithe of the produce of farming in the seventh or sabbath year (Lev. 25:1-7). In that year, there was to be no sowing, pruning, reaping, or gathering. The trees and vines were to drop their fruit, except for what the poor harvested for their use, or cattle and wild animals ate, or for table use by the owner (Ex. 23:11). Rawlinson commented:

> Under the system thus Divinely imposed upon the Israelites, three beneficent purposes were accomplished. 1. *The proprietor was benefited.* Not only was he prevented from exhausting his farm by overcropping, and so sinking into poverty, but he was forced to form habits of forethought and providence. He necessarily laid by something for the seventh year, and hence learnt to calculate his needs, to store his grain, and to keep something in hand against the future. In this way his reason and reflective powers were developed, and he

---

24. P. W. Thompson, *All the Tithes*, p. 30.
25. *Ibid.*, p. 22 f.

was advanced from a mere labouring hand to a thoughtful cultivator.
2. *The poor were benefited.* As whatever grew in the seventh year
grew spontaneously, without expense or trouble on the part of the
owner, it could not be rightfully considered to belong exclusively to
him. The Mosaic law placed it on a par with ordinary wild fruits,
and granted it to the first comer (Lev. xxv. 5, 6). By this arrangement the poor were enabled to profit, since it was they especially
who gathered the store that Nature's bounty provided. In the dry
climate of Palestine, where much grain is sure to be shed during the
gathering in of the harvest, the spontaneous growth would probably
be considerable, and would amply suffice for the sustenance of those
who had no other resource. 3. *The beasts were benefited.* God
"careth for cattle." He appoints the Sabbatical year, in part, that
"the beasts of the field" may have abundance to eat. When men dole
out their food, they have often a scanty allowance. God would have
them, for one year in seven at least, eat their fill.[26]

Rawlinson to the contrary at one point, the sabbath use of the field and
vineyard was unquestionably similar to gleaning, i.e., the owner governed the admission of the deserving poor. More will be said of the
agricultural sabbath later.

Seventh, tithing meant proportionate giving. The tenth of a poor man
is as pleasing to God as the tenth of the rich. The principle of the tithe
is stated clearly in the law: "Every man shall give as he is able" (Deut.
16:17). This same principle is restated by St. Paul in II Corinthians
8:12 as the essence of Christian giving. St. Paul wrote with respect
to the collection for the poor, and he cited the principle of the tithe to
collect the poor tithe from Christians. By means of proportionate giving,
no undue burden was placed on anyone: the rich were not expected to
do all the giving, nor was the burden left to the willing.

Eighth, by means of the tithe, a concrete and realistic relationship
with God existed. According to Malachi 3:7-12, God's curse goes out
against those who deny God's ordinance of tithing, for this is to turn
away from God's law (Mal. 3:7). Similarly, God's blessing is poured
out like a flood to those who obey the law of the tenth. As Samuel
Rutherford (1600-1661) wrote, "I am persuaded that Christ is re-
sponsal and law-abiding, to make recompense for anything that is haz-
arded or given out for Him; losses for Christ are but our goods given
out in bank in Christ's hand."[27] This is not pay from God, who owes
no man anything, but blessing. Primarily, Malachi promises a national
blessing, as we shall later see, but the personal aspect is not absent.
G. H. Pember wrote, in *Earth's Earliest Ages,*

We know generally that the grace of God follows every act of direct

26. Rawlinson in *Pulpit Commentary, Exodus,* II, 205.
27. P. W. Thompson, *All Thine Increase* (London: Marshall, Morgan & Scott,
1937, 3rd edition), p. 109.

obedience on our part. *If we search out even the most minute commands of His law, and do them: if we show that we would not have a word uttered by Him fall to the ground,* we testify both to ourselves and to others that we do in very deed, and not in word only recognize Him as our God and our King. . . . Nor will He on His part be slow in acknowledging us as His subjects, as those who have a claim upon His aid and protection.[28]

And, as the Rev. Samuel Chadwick (1860-1912) wrote "No man can rob God without starving his own soul."[29]

Ninth, the Lord's tithe, and the poor tithe, took care of the basic social functions which, under modern totalitarianism, have become the province of the state, namely, education and welfare. Education was one of the functions of the Levites (not of the sanctuary). The Levites assisted the priests in the religious duties related to the sanctuary (I Chron. 23:28-31; II Chron. 29:34; 35:11), and as officers, judges, and musicians (I Chron. 23:1-5). In a godly civil order, the group best instructed in the law of God will clearly have far-reaching social services to render. Since their support is undergirded by the tithe, the basic cost to society for civil government becomes slight. The tithe is an acknowledgement of God's kingship; in I Samuel 8:4-19, the consequences of a rejection of God's kingship are cited: they are totalitarianism, oppression, a loss of liberty, *and* an increased cost of civil government. Without the tithe, basic social functions fall into two kinds of pitfalls: on the one hand, the state assumes these functions, and, on the other, wealthy individuals and foundations exercise a preponderant power over society. Tithing releases society from this dependence on the state and on wealthy individuals and foundations. The tithe places the basic control of society with the tithing people of God. They are commanded to bring "the whole tithe into the storehouse" (Mal. 3:10, MTV). The storehouse Malachi spoke of was literally that: a physical storage-place which was the Lord's, i.e., belonged to that religious tradition of Levites who, instead of being apostate or syncretistic, were faithful to God and His law-word. The tither was not tithing if his tithe went to a faithless storehouse; it was his duty to judge then between godly and ungodly Levites. Similarly, the tither today is not tithing unless his tenth goes to truly godly work, to churches, missionary causes, and schools which teach the law-word faithfully. Again, the poor tithe is in the tither's hands: he cannot use it, or his sabbath-year produce, or the gleanings of his field to subsidize evil, sloth, or apostasy. The poor tithe has as its purpose the strengthening of godly society, not its destruction.

As we have seen, the tithe went to the Levites, who gave a tenth of

---

28. Cited in *ibid*, p. 140.
29. *Ibid.*, p. 216.

the tithe to the priests. Thus, only a small portion of the tithe went to the priests and for the maintenance of worship. In the wilderness period, the Levites had important duties in the care and transportation of the tabernacle, but these duties later disappeared. The Levites assumed the broader social functions, and no prophet ever criticized or challenged these broader functions, which means they were clearly within the declared calling of God. The Levites, as the tribe of the "firstborn" by choice of God, were thus the tribe with the basic functions of the first-born, which were governmental in the broad sense of the term. While the "scepter" was given to Judah (Gen. 49:10), in other respects Levi as the tribe of the firstborn (Num. 8:18) had the basic governmental duties. There was thus a *basic division of powers* between the state (Judah and the throne) and broad governmental functions (Levi). This division has been destroyed by the disappearance of the tithe as a governmental factor.

In medieval and Reformation Europe, broad governmental functions belonged to the world of the tithe. One reason for the frequent lack of distrust for the state was the usually limited role of the state. Schools, hospitals, lazar-houses for lepers, charity to orphans, widows, strangers, and the poor, all this and more was the province of the tithe. Granted that there was corruption in the medieval church, yet that corruption has been far overshadowed by the degenerate and profligate modern state.

It should be remembered too that the tithe went to the local church or diocese. The laws of Edmund issued at an assembly at London, 942-946, chap. 2, read: "We command every Christian on his Christianity to pay tithes, and church dues, and Peter's pence, and plough-alms. And if any one will not do this, let him be excommunicated." The laws of Ethelred, 1008, chap. 11, declared:

> And church-dues shall be paid promptly every year, namely, plough-alms a fortnight after Easter, the tithe of the increase of the flocks at Pentecost, and of the fruits of the earth at the mass of All Saints, and Peter's pence at Peter's mass, and the fees for lights three times in the year.[30]

The Bible provides, as the foundation law of a godly social order, the law of the tithe. To understand the full implication of the tithe, it is important to know that Biblical law has *no property tax*; the right to tax real property is implicitly denied to the state, because the state has no earth to tax. "The earth is the Lord's" (Ex. 9:29; Deut. 10:14; Ps. 24:1; I Cor. 10:26, etc.); therefore, only God can tax the earth. For the state to claim the right to tax the earth is for the state to make itself the

---

30. William E. Lunt, *Papal Revenues in the Middle Ages*, vol. II, Records of Civilization, Columbia University, n. XIX (New York: Columbia University Press, 1934), p. 56 f.

god and creator of the earth, whereas the state is instead God's ministry of justice (Rom. 13:1-8). For the state to enter into God's realm is to invite judgment.

The immunity of land from taxation by the state means liberty. A man then cannot be dispossessed of his land; every man has a basic security in his property. As Rand pointed out,

> It was impossible to dispossess men of their inheritance under the law of the Lord as no taxes were levied against land. Regardless of a man's personal commitments he could not disinherit his family by being dispossessed of his land forever.[31]

Because the land is not the property of the state, nor is land a part of the state's jurisdiction, the state therefore has no right under God to levy taxes against God's earth. Moreover, for the state to claim as much as God, i.e., a tenth of a man's income, is a sign of apostasy and tyranny, according to I Samuel 8:4-19. The modern state, of course, claims several tithes in taxes.

The tithe is *not* a gift to God; it is God's tax for the use of the earth, which is at all points under God's law and jurisdiction. Only when the payment to the Lord exceeds ten percent is it called a gift and a "free-will offering" (Deut. 16:10,11; Ex. 36:3-7; Lev. 22:21, etc.).

The tithe was for centuries legally collected, i.e., the state provided the legal requirement that tithes be paid to the church. When Virginia repealed its law which made payment of the tithe mandatory, George Washington expressed his disapproval in a letter to George Mason, October 3, 1785. He believed, he said, in "making people pay toward the support of that which they profess."[32] From the 4th century on, civil governments began to require the tithe, because it was believed that a country could only deny God His tax at its peril. From the end of the 18th century, and especially in recent years, such laws have disappeared under the impact of atheistic and revolutionary movements. Instead of freeing men from an "oppressive" tax, the abolition of the tithe has opened the way for truly oppressive taxation by the state in order to assume the social responsibilities once maintained by tithe money. Basic social functions must be paid for. If they are not paid by a responsible, tithing Christian people, they will be paid for by a tyrant state which will use welfare and education as stepping-stones to totalitarian power.

The matter was ably summed up by Lansdell:

> It seems clear, then, in the light of revelation, and from the practice of, perhaps, all ancient nations, that the man who denies God's

31. Howard B. Rand, *Digest of the Divine Law* (Merrimac, Mass.: Destiny Publishers, 1943, 1959), p. 111.
32. Jared Sparks, ed., *The Writings of George Washington* (Boston: Ferdinand Andrews, 1838), IX, 137.

claim to a portion of the wealth that comes to his hands, is much
akin to a spiritual anarchist; whilst he who so apportions less than
a tenth of his income or increase is condemned by Scripture as a
robber. Indeed, if in the days of Malachi not to pay the tithe was
counted robbery, can a Christian who with-holds the tenth be—now,
any more than then—counted honest towards God?

Right giving is a part of right living. The living is not right when the
giving is wrong. The giving is wrong when we steal God's portion to
spend it on ourselves.[33]

It is significant that in the Soviet Union, any charitable activity is
strictly forbidden to religious groups.[34] If a church group were to
collect funds or goods to administer relief to sick and needy members
of the congregation or community, it would immediately create a power
independent of the state as the remedy for social problems. It would
moreover create a power which would reach people more directly,
efficiently, and powerfully. The consequence would be a direct affront
to the preëminence of the state. For this reason, in the democracies
orphanages have been steadily the target of repressive legislation to
eliminate them, and charity has been preëmpted by the state increasingly
as a major step towards totalitarianism.

Lansdell was right. Those who do not tithe are spiritual anarchists:
they destroy both the freedom and order of society and unleash the
demons of statism.

5. The Law as Power and Discrimination

The fact of *power* is inseparable from law. Law is not law if it lacks
the power to bind, to compel, and to punish. While it is a fallacy to
define law simply as compulsion or coercion, it is a serious error to
define law without recognizing that coercion is basic to it. To empty
God of absolute power is to deny that He is God. To separate power
from law is to deny it the status of law. The fact that God repeatedly
identifies Himself in Scripture as "the Almighty" (Gen. 17:1, 35; Ex.
6:3, etc.) is a part of His assertion of total sovereignty and hence His
call to obedience.

Power is a religious concept, and the god or gods of any system of
thought have been the sources of power for that system. The monarch
or ruler has a religious significance precisely because of his power.
When the democratic state gains power, it too arrogates to itself religious claims and prerogatives. Because the Marxist state has more
power, and claims more power, than other contemporary states, its

---

33. Lansdell, *Tithe in Scripture*, p. 148.
34. St. Mary's School of Religion for Adults, *An Illustrated Digest of the
Church and State Under Communism* (Port Richmond, Staten Island, N. Y.,
1964), p. 15.

rejection of Christianity is all the more radical: it cannot tolerate ascription of absolute power to a god other than itself. Power is jealously guarded in the anti-Christian state, and any division of powers in the state, designed to limit its power and prevent its concentration, is bitterly contested.

The law is applied power, otherwise it ceases to be law. The law is more than power, but, apart from coercion, there is no law. Those who object to the coercive element in law are in fact objecting to law, whether knowingly or unknowingly. The purpose of the law is in part to be a "terror" to evil-doers (Rom. 13:4); the word "terror" is given a milder translation in modern versions, but the whole tenor of Scripture requires the element of fear as man faces God, and as sinful, lawless man faces the law. St. Paul makes it clear, however, that power is ordained of God, "for there is no power but of God: the powers that be are ordained of God" (Rom. 13:1). Since God is absolute power, all subordinate and created powers derive their office, power, and moral authority only from God, and they must exercise it only on His terms and under His jurisdiction or else face His judgment. Lord Acton's dictum, "All power corrupts, and absolute power corrupts absolutely," is a liberal half-truth and reflects liberal illusions. *First* of all, all power does not corrupt. The power of a godly husband and father to govern his family does not corrupt him; he exercises it under God and in terms of God's law-word. Instead of being corrupted by his power, the godly man is blessed by means of his power, and he makes it a blessing to his family and society. A godly ruler, who uses his power readily for legitimate and moral ends, prospers the society under his power. The two evils with respect to power and the exercise thereof are, on the one hand, the fear of using power, and, on the other, the immoral use of power. Both evils extensively prevail in any humanistic society. Men who are afraid to use power lawfully and morally corrupt their families and societies. The failure to exercise due power reduces a society to lawlessness and anarchy. The immoral use of power leads to the corruption of society and the suppression of freedom, but it is not the use of power which causes this decay but the immoral use thereof. Power does not corrupt when it is used properly under God: it blesses, prospers, orders, and governs society to its advantage and welfare.

Second, if "absolute power corrupts absolutely," then God must be called corrupt, because He alone has absolute power. But Acton is wrong: man cannot have absolute power. He may strive for it, and the striving is corrupt and it corrupts society, but man remains, in all his pretensions, totally under the absolute power of God.

Not only is all power derived from God and decreed by His absolute power, but it is also decreed and bound by His absolute righteousness.

Law therefore is, when it is true law, not only power but also righteousness. It is therefore a "terror" to evil-doers but the security and "praise" of the godly citizenry (Rom. 13:2-5). Because true law has its roots in the sovereign God, the very nature of all being works to uphold it. As Deborah sang, "They fought from heaven, The stars in their courses fought against Sisera" (Judges 5:20). The law is either righteous, or it is anti-law masquerading as law. Modern legal positivism, Marxism, and other legal philosophies are thus exponents of anti-law, in that they deny law as an approximation of ultimate order and truth and recognize only a humanistic doctrine of law. If law is severed from righteousness and truth, it leads on the one hand to the anarchy of a lawless and meaningless world, or, on the other, to the totalitarianism of an elite group which imposes its relative "truth" on other men by sheer and unprincipled coercion.

But law is required to be a ministry of justice under God, and the civil officer "a minister of God" (Rom. 13:5-6). This concept of the law as a ministry of justice is all but forgotten today, and, where remembered, it is derided. But it is all the same the only possible foundation for a just and prosperous social order. The law as a ministry lacks the arrogance of positivist legal theorists, who see no law or truth beyond themselves. Ministerial law is law under God: it is required to have a humility which positivist law cannot have. The champions of legal positivism are prone to accuse Christians of pride, but the world has never seen more ruthless arrogance and pride than that manifested by the relativists, whether of ancient Greece, the Renaissance, or of the twentieth century.

Another aspect of law is implicit in St. Paul's statement in Romans 13:1-6: the law is always discriminatory. It is impossible to escape or evade this aspect of law. If the law fulfils its function, to establish justice and to protect godly, law-abiding men, then the law must discriminate against law-breakers and rigorously seek their judgment. The law cannot favor equality without ceasing to be law: at all times, the law defines, in any and every society, those who constitute the legitimate and the illegitimate members of society. The fact of law introduces a fundamental and basic inequality in society. The abolition of law will not eliminate inequality, because then the very fact of sheer survival will create an elite and establish a fundamental inequality.

The law has often been used as an ostensible weapon to gain equality, but such attempts represent either self-deception or an attempt to deceive by the group in power.

The "civil rights" revolutionary groups are a case in point. Their goal is not equality but power. The background of Negro culture is African and magic, and the purposes of magic are control and power over God, man, nature, and society. Voodoo, or magic, was the religion and life of American Negroes. Voodoo songs underlie jazz, and old voodoo, with its power goal, has been merely replaced with revolutionary voodoo, a modernized power drive.[1]

The student revolution attacks the inequality between students and faculty, between students and the ruling powers, but it has consistently rejected favorable concessions in favor of broader claims to power. The goal from the beginning is power.

The list could be extended indefinitely. The goal of the equalitarians has always been power, and equality has been an argument to tickle the sick conscience of a faithless and shaky ruling element.

The law will always require inequality. The question is simply this: will it be an inequality in terms of fundamental justice, i.e., the rewarding of good and the punishing of evil, or will it be the inequalities of injustice and evil triumphant?

The commandment, "Thou shalt have no other gods before me," requires that we recognize no power as true and ultimately legitimate if it be not grounded in God and His law-word. It requires that we see true law as righteousness, the righteousness of God, and as a ministry of justice, and it requires us to recognize that the inequalities of just law faithfully applied are the basic ingredients of a free and healthy society. The body politic, no less than the physical body, cannot equate sickness with health without perishing.

The commandment, "Thou shalt have no other gods before me," means also "Thou shalt have no other powers before me," independent of me or having priority over me. The commandment can also read, "Thou shalt have no other law before me." The powers which today more than ever present themselves as the other gods are the antichristian states. The antichristian state makes itself god and therefore sees itself as the source of both law and power. Apart from a Biblical perspective, the state becomes another god, and, instead of law, legality prevails.

This devotion to legality has a long history in the modern world. Gohier, minister of justice in France during the years of the Reign of Terror, came to be known as "the casuist of the guillotine" because of his dedication to legality. Later, as a member of the Directory, when faced with the threat of Napoleon's seizure of power, he declared, "At the worst, how can there be any revolution in St. Cloud? As President, I have here in my possession the seal of the Republic."[2] Stalin operated his continuing terror under the umbrella of legality.

---

1. See, for the voodoo background of jazz, Robert Tallant, *Voodoo in New Orleans* (New York: Collier Books, 1946, 1965).
2. Donald J. Goodspeed, *Napoleon's Eighty Days* (Boston: Houghton Mifflin, 1965), pp. 53, 124 f.

But legality is not law. A state can by strict legality embark on a course of radical lawlessness. Legality has reference to the rules of the game as established by a state and its courts. Law has reference to fundamental, God-given order. The modern state champions legality as a tool in opposing law. The result is a legal destruction of law and order.

As a result, the state, instead of being a "terror" to evil-doers, is a terror progressively to the law-abiding citizenry, to the righteous and godly people. Hoodlums terrorize the country with riots and violence, and without fear. Moreover, even as Rome declared war on the Christians, so socialism and communism, and progressively the democracies, are at war against orthodox or Biblical faith. The consequence of such a desertion by the state of its calling as the ministry of justice can only be finally the fall of the state. The state which ceases to be a terror to evil-doers and becomes a terror to the godly is committing suicide.

II

THE SECOND COMMANDMENT

1. The Lawful Approach to God

Thou shalt not make unto thee any graven image, or any likeness of any thing that is in heaven above, or that is in the earth beneath, or that is in the water under the earth:
Thou shalt not bow down thyself to them, nor serve them: for I the LORD thy God am a jealous God, visiting the iniquity of the fathers upon the children unto the third and fourth generation of them that hate me;
And shewing mercy unto thousands of them that love me, and keep my commandments (Ex. 20:4-6, cf. Deut. 5:8-10).

The first commandment prohibits idolatry in the broad sense. There can be none other god than the Lord. These other gods are man-made substitutes for the true God. As Ingram noted, "the other gods about whom we must be concerned are, as they ever have been, to be found in the seats of temporal, or human, government."[1] The Biblical definition of idolatry is obviously a broad one; thus, St. Paul declares that "no covetous man, who is an idolater, hath any inheritance in the Kingdom of Christ and of God" (Eph. 5:5). Again, in Colossians 3:5, reference is made to "covetousness, which is idolatry." Lenski noted, "A Catholic priest states that during his long years of service all kinds of sins and crimes were confessed to him in the confessional but never the sin of covetousness."[2]

Thus, in analyzing the second commandment, we must say, *first,* that the literal use of idols and images in worship is strictly forbidden. Leviticus 26:1, 2 makes this very clear:

Ye shall make you no idols nor graven image, neither shall ye set up any image of stone in your land, to bow down unto it: for I am the LORD your God.
Ye shall keep my sabbaths, and reverence my sanctuary: I am the LORD.

Leviticus 19:4 also commands:

Turn ye not unto idols, nor make to yourselves molten gods: I am the LORD your God (cf. Ex. 34:17).

---

1. Ingram, *World Under God's Law*, p. 33.
2. R. C. H. Lenski, *The Interpretation of St. Paul's Epistles to the Colossians, to the Thessalonians, to Timothy, to Titus and to Philemon* (Columbus, Ohio: Wartburg Press, 1937, 1946), p. 158.

Other legislation reads:

> And the LORD said unto Moses, Thus thou shalt say unto the children of Israel, Ye have seen that I have talked with you from heaven.
> Ye shall not make with me gods of silver, neither shall ye make unto you gods of gold.
> An altar of earth thou shalt make unto me, and shalt sacrifice thereon thy burnt offerings, and thy peace offerings, thy sheep, and thine oxen: in all places where I record my name I will come unto thee, and I will bless thee.
> And if thou wilt make me an altar of stone, thou shalt not build it of hewn stone: for if thou lift up thy tool upon it, thou hast polluted it.
> Neither shalt thou go up by steps unto mine altar, that thy nakedness be not discovered thereon (Ex. 20:22-26).

> Take ye therefore good heed unto yourselves—for ye saw no manner of form on the day that the LORD spake unto you in Horeb out of the midst of the fire—lest ye deal corruptly, and make you a graven image, even the form of any figure, the likeness of male or female, the likeness of any beast that is on the earth, the likeness of any winged fowl that flieth in the heaven, the likeness of any thing that creepeth on the ground, the likeness of any fish that is in the water under the earth; and lest thou lift up thine eyes unto heaven, and when thou seest the sun and the moon and the stars, even all the host of heaven, thou be drawn away and worship them, and serve them, which the LORD thy God hath allotted unto all the peoples under the whole heaven. But you hath the LORD taken and brought forth out of the iron furnace, out of Egypt, to be unto Him a people of inheritance, as ye are this day. Now the LORD was angered with me for your sakes, and swore that I should not go over the Jordan, and that I should not go in unto that good land, which the LORD thy God giveth thee for an inheritance; but I must die in this land, I must not go over the Jordan, but ye are to go over, and possess that good land. Take heed unto yourselves, lest ye forget the covenant of the LORD your God, which He made with you, and make you a graven image, even the likeness of anything which the LORD thy God hath forbidden thee. For the LORD thy God is a devouring fire, a jealous God (Deut. 4:15-24, MTV).

> Take heed to yourselves, that your heart be not deceived, and ye turn aside, and serve other gods, and worship them;
> And then the LORD'S wrath be kindled against you, and he shut up the heaven, and there be no rain, and that the land yield not her fruit; and lest ye perish quickly from off the good land which the LORD giveth you (Deut. 11:16, 17).

> Cursed be the man that maketh any graven or molten image, an abomination unto the LORD, the work of the hands of the craftsman, and putteth it in a secret place. And all the people shall answer and say, Amen (Deut. 27:15).

This law does not forbid engraving, picturing, or art work in general.

The priest's garment, for example, pictured pomegranates (Ex. 28: 33-34; 39:24); the mercy seat had at either end two cherubim of gold (Ex. 25:18-22; 37:7), and the sanctuary as a whole was richly ornamented. It is not the religious use of such things which is forbidden, for the pomegranates and cherubim had a religious function, but it is the unauthorized use on the one hand, and their use as a mediation or a way to God that is strongly forbidden. They cannot be "helps" to worship; man needs no aid to worship other than God's provision.

Thus, idolatry is generally banned by the first commandment, whereas the second law-word prohibits it more specifically with reference to worship. Man can only approach God on God's terms; there can be no mediation between God and man except that which is ordered by God.

The rationale of idolatry is quite logical. As one writer has pointed out, with reference to Hindu idols, the purpose of the idols is to convey abstract concepts to the simple mind. The god depicted with many hands symbolizes thereby the omnipotence of the supreme being, and the many-eyed god sets forth omniscience, and so on. This is an intelligent and logical thesis, but it is also totally wrong. It is forbidden by God and therefore dishonors Him and thus receives no blessing. It has also been productive of social decadence and personal depravity. Wherever man begins by establishing his own approach to God, he ends up by establishing his own will, his own lusts, and finally himself as God. If the terms of man's approach to God are set by man, then the terms of man's life and prosperity are dictated also by man rather than by God. But the initiative belongs entirely to God, and therefore the only lawful approach to God is on His terms entirely and by His grace. This, then, is the *second* aspect of the second commandment: the lawful approach to God is entirely of God's ordination. Hence the altar had to be a natural one, not of man's making; hence too the priest could not reveal his nakedness: he was to be entirely covered by raiment setting forth the office of mediation, God's appointed mediator. Since the order of worship set forth the mediatorial work of Christ, the God-appointed approach to God, there could be no departure from that order without apostasy.

A *third* aspect of this law-word is this: even as a very literal idolatry is forbidden, so a very literal blessing and cursing are attached to the law. This is clearly stated in the declaration of the commandment. It appears sharply in Leviticus 26; vv. 1-3 forbid idolatry, order sabbath-keeping, and reverence for the sanctuary; and call as well for walking in the Lord's statutes and commandments generally. In vv. 4-46, the very literal material consequences to the nation are fully depicted. A very literal law has very literal and material consequences. Obedience and disobedience have central historical consequences and results.

In brief, religion, true religion, is not a matter of voluntary choice which is without repercussions. It is required by God, and failure to meet His requirements leads to His judgment. To assume that men are free to worship or not to worship without radical consequences for society is to negate the very meaning of Biblical faith. The life of a society is its religion, and if that religion be false, then the society is headed for death. Remarkable and signal material blessings are promised for obedience, but, "And if ye will not be reformed by me by these things, but will walk contrary unto me; Then will I also walk contrary unto you, and will punish you seven times for your sins" (Lev. 26:23, 24). Obedience is thus not a matter of taste: it is a question of life or death.

Fourth, social health requires the prohibition of idolatry, because its toleration means social suicide. Idolatry is thus not only punishable by law as socially detrimental, it is in fact a capital offense. It constitutes treason to the King or Sovereign, to Almighty God.

> If there be found among you, within any of thy gates which the LORD thy God giveth thee, man or woman, that hath wrought wickedness in the sight of the LORD thy God, in transgressing his covenant,
> And hath gone and served other gods, and worshipped them, either the sun, or moon, or any of the host of heaven, which I have not commanded;
> And it be told thee, and thou hast heard of it, and enquired diligently, and, behold, it be true, and the thing certain, that such abomination is wrought in Israel:
> Then shalt thou bring forth that man or that woman, which have committed that wicked thing, unto thy gates, even that man or that woman, and shalt stone them with stones, till they die.
> At the mouth of two witnesses, or three witnesses, shall he that is worthy of death be put to death; but at the mouth of one witness he shall not be put to death.
> The hands of the witnesses shall be first upon him to put him to death, and afterwards the hands of all the people. So thou shalt put the evil away from among you (Deut. 17:2-7).

To the modern mind, treason to the state is logically punishable by death, but not treason to God. But no law-order can survive if it does not defend its core faith by rigorous sanctions. The law-order of humanism leads only to anarchy. Lacking absolutes, a humanistic law-order tolerates everything which denies absolutes while warring against Biblical faith. The only law of humanism is ultimately this, that there is no law except self-assertion. It is "Do what thou wilt." The result is the arrogant contempt for law manifested in a 1968 broadside issued by the Riverside County (California) Cleaver for President Committee, promoting the candidacy of Eldridge Cleaver, Black Panther "Minister of

Information," and Peace and Freedom Party candidate for U. S. president. The statement describes Cleaver in part thus:

> Now consider Eldridge Cleaver. His "American history" can be told quickly. First he was invisible and irrelevant—a slum kid in Little Rock, a ghetto expendable in Watts. Then he was a local nuisance—in 1954, when he was busted for the first time, aged 18, for smoking pot. Then he became a Savage Menace—that was when he was jailed for the second time, in 1958, for disturbing the beauty sleep of some of suburban Los Angeles' white goddesses. Later, when in his own beautiful way and against incredible odds he achieved his own distinctive manhood, what was he then?—A political prisoner, in a nation that pretends not even to know the meaning of these words.[3]

The terms in which a record of rape is described indicate the utter contempt for Biblical law-order on the part of the committee. To tolerate an alien law-order is a very real subsidy of it: it is a warrant for life to that alien law-order, and a sentence of death against the established law-order.

Sir Patrick Devlin has pointed to the dilemma of the law today:

> I think it is clear that the criminal law as we know it is based upon moral principle. In a number of crimes its function is simply to enforce a moral principle and nothing else. The law, both criminal and civil, claims to be able to speak about morality and immorality generally. Where does it get its authority to do this and how does it settle the moral principles which it enforces? Undoubtedly, as a matter of history, it derives both from Christian teaching. But I think that the strict logician is right when he says that the law can no longer rely on doctrines in which citizens are entitled to disbelieve. It is necesary therefore to look for some other source.[4]

The legal crisis is due to the fact that the law of Western civilization has been Christian law, but its faith is increasingly humanism. The old law is therefore neither understood, nor obeyed, nor enforced. But the new "law" simply makes every man his own law and increasingly leads to anarchy and totalitarianism. The law, says Devlin, cannot function "in matters of morality about which the community as a whole is not deeply imbued with a sense of sin; the law sags under a weight which it is not constructed to bear and may become permanently warped." Moreover,

> A man who concedes that morality is necessary to society must support the use of those instruments without which morality cannot

---

3. Peace and Freedom Party, Riverside County Cleaver for President Committee, *Eldridge Cleaver for President* (Riverside, Calif., 1968). For more on Cleaver, see *Peace and Freedom News*, Special Issue (May 6, 1968), Berkeley, Calif.

4. Sir Patrick Devlin, *The Enforcement of Morals*, Maccabaean Lecture in Jurisprudence of the British Academy, 1959 (London: Oxford University Press, 1959, 1962), p. 9.

be maintained. The two instruments are those of teaching, which is doctrine, and of enforcement, which is the law. If morals could be taught simply on the basis that they are necessary to society, there would be no social need for religion; it could be left as a purely personal affair. But morality cannot be taught in that way. Loyalty is not taught in that way either. No society has yet solved the problem of how to teach morality without religion. So the law must base itself on Christian morals and to the limit of its ability enforce them, not simply because they are the morals of most of us, nor simply because they are the morals which are taught by the established Church—on these points the law recognizes the right to dissent—but for the compelling reason that without the help of Christian teaching the law will fail.[5]

In short, the laws of a society cannot raise a people above the level of the faith and morality of the people and of the society. A people cannot legislate itself above its level. If it holds to Christian faith in truth and in deed, it can establish and maintain godly law and order. If its faith be humanistic, the people will be traitors to any law-order which does not condone their self-assertion and their irresponsibility.

The question thus is a basic one: what constitutes treason in a culture? Idolatry, i.e., treason to God, or treason to the state? What is the fundamental principle of order, the necessary ground of man's existence and salvation, God or the state? Treason to the state is a concept which can be used to destroy the godly, and it is so done in Marxist countries. Treason can be defined, as the U. S. Constitution in Article III, Section 3, defined it, very narrowly and cautiously, but what if the enemy of the citizen turns out to be the state turned traitor to its own Constitution? For the Christian, it is idolatry which above all else constitutes treason to the social order.

Fifth, we have seen that, while idolatry is narrowly defined, it is also broadly defined, i.e., as covetousness. But idolatry involves any and every attempt by man to be guided by his own word rather than God's law-word. This is often devoutly and piously done. Many parents are sinfully patient or indulgent with their lawless children, or husbands with wives, and wives with husbands, in the fond hope that God will miraculously change the wayward one. "I am in continual prayer," they will assert, adding that all things are possible with God. But this is a fearful arrogance and sin. Indeed, all things are possible with God, but we cannot live in terms of what God might do but only in terms of what His law-word requires. To wait on conversion, or move in hope, is a sinful substitute, however much piously disguised, for obedience to God and the acceptance of reality under God. Such a course is to make our hope the law-word, and God's law-word of none effect. Sam-

5. *Ibid.,* p. 25.

uel made this clear to Saul, declaring, "For rebellion is as the sin of witchcraft, and stubbornness is as iniquity and idolatry" (I Sam. 15:23). We are not permitted to call our stubbornness and rebellion anything other than sin.

The only lawful approach to God is thus the way He provides, and that way is summed up in the person of Jesus Christ. Any other way is idolatry, even when presented in the name of the Lord.

2. The Throne of Law

In Exodus 25–31; 35:4–39:43, the law is given concerning the building of the tabernacle, i.e., the tent of meeting: "And let them make me a sanctuary: that I may dwell among them. According to all that I shew thee, after the pattern of the tabernacle, and the pattern of all the instruments thereof, even so shall ye make it" (Ex. 25:8, 9). This pattern had to be strictly followed, without variation. When the ideal or symbolic temple of the future, i.e., the Kingdom of Christ, is portrayed through Ezekiel, again adherence to the pattern is required (Ezek. 43:10). This emphasis on the absoluteness of the pattern is spoken of also in Hebrews 8:5; 9:23.

Thus, first, the pattern of the tabernacle is given by God and is entirely His work. J. Edgar Park sees it as man's work and "man's response to God." "As the Creator made the earth for man to dwell in, so man must make a dwelling for the Creator." Park does not see this as a historical account, nor as revelation.[1] This may be a pretty thought, but it is not true. The pattern and materials are required by God, and His subjects are expected to obey. When subjects build a palace for their monarch, it is not as a "response" to him, but in obedience to their king.

This, of course, points to the *second* aspect of the law of the sanctuary: the tabernacle is more than a tent of meeting: "It is the palace of the King in which the people render Him homage."[2] At this point a central fallacy of the ecclesiastical approach to the subject appears. Earnest Biblical scholars have, while affirming their faith in the fundamentals, still shared in the modern belief that religion is an ecclesiastical matter. In their analysis of the typology and symbolism of the tabernacle, they stress its relation to ecclesiastical worship.[3] But the reduction of religion to the church is a modern heresy; the domain of religion is the whole of life, and the concern of the sanctuary was the total life. The tabernacle was the palace of God the King, covenant Lord of Israel, from whence He ruled the nation absolutely. Israel presented

---

1. J. Edgar Park, "Exodus," in *The Interpreter's Bible*, I, 1021.
2. Vos, *Biblical Theology*, p. 168.
3. See W. G. Moorehead, *The Tabernacle* (Grand Rapids: Kregel, 1895, 1957).

itself at the palace, not only to worship but to be commanded in every respect and in every area.

Third, as a result, there could only be one sanctuary, because there is only one true God, one God, one throne, one realm to govern. Since there was one law governing God's realm, there was one source of law, the palace. Because of the ecclesiastical point of view, it is difficult for men to see the tabernacle as primarily and essentially God's palace or dwelling-place; for the church-oriented mind, it was primarily and essentially a place of worship. Even a moment's reflection will make this point clear. The law required all males to appear thrice annually at the palace:

> Three times thou shalt keep a feast unto me in the year (Ex. 23:14).
>
> Three times in the year all thy males shall appear before the Lord GOD (Ex. 23:17).
>
> Thrice in the year shall all your men children appear before the Lord GOD, the God of Israel (Ex. 34:23).

It will be objected by some that these three feasts are described as "holy" convocations (Lev. 23:4) and are thus clearly and essentially worship. But it is a serious error to associate holiness with worship; worship in itself is not holy and can be blasphemy; holiness does not refer to worship but to God in all His ways and in all His being. Thus, all godly activity, whether it be in the home, field, court, church, or school, is holy activity. The "medieval" perspective, although corrupted by neo-platonism, was still more Biblical than the modern concept of the state as a profane and secular agency, i.e., outside the palace of God and separate from Him. Because the monarch represented God's ministry of justice, and because he ruled as the vicegerent of Christ the King, the office of the monarch was thus seen as a holy office.

> The king was, indeed, a likeness of Christ. The coronation rite transformed him sacramentally into a *Christus Domini*, that is, not only into a person of episcopal rank, but into an image of Christ himself. By this rite, Professor Kantorowicz writes, "the new government was linked with the divine government and with that of Christ, the true governor of the world; and the images of King and Christ (were) brought together as nearly as possible." Such dramatic representations of the meaning of the monarchy were not confined to the king's coronation. On the great religious feasts of the year, "the king's day of exaltation was made to coincide with the . . . exaltation of the Lord" in order to make "terrestrial kingship all the more transparent against the background of the kingship of Christ." In Capetian France as elsewhere, such religious feasts often were made the occasion for the king's festive coronation; and, as the political assemblies of the realm were likewise held on these feasts, the interweaving of the two spheres was underscored by liturgical pageants that stressed the sacerdotal dignity of kingship.

What appears to us as no more than festive pageantry was, in point of fact, an act of sacramental as well as constitutional significance. It was precisely his anointment as *Christus Domini* that raised the king above even the most powerful dukes. In the political controversies of the early twelfth century this fact is adduced again and again.[4]

However, because of neo-platonism, the concept of continuity made for a oneness of being between God and the king which led to ruler worship and an antichristian order. In terms of the Biblical discontinuity of being between God and man, the typology of king as vicegerent must be maintained. The typology cannot be transformed into a continuity concept.[5]

Holiness has reference, thus, primarily and essentially to God, and, secondarily, to all things done in His name, according to His word, and to His glory. All things were created by God wholly good, and therefore holy, separated and dedicated to Him. Men, by their fall, have become profane. The goal of redemption is the restoration of the universe to holiness, its recreation, and the separation of the reprobate or Canaanite from "the house of the LORD of hosts" (Zech. 14:20, 21).

The tabernacle was God's palace; it was the sanctuary because it was God's palace or dwelling-place. In the wilderness, and in the early years, God made His palace as the people made their dwellings, in a tent. It was tardily, with David, that the people became mindful of the contrast between their houses and God's palace, still in a tent (II Sam. 7:2). The building of this temple, house, or palace of God, was deferred by God to the reign of Solomon (II Sam. 7:4-29).

The tabernacle, and the temple after it, remained primarily as palace, not house of worship. Worship was local, and its place was in the family. The sabbath was kept in the home, not in the sanctuary. To see the tabernacle and the temple as church structures is to misread the Bible. That there was worship at the sanctuary does not alter this fact. Man worshiped God everywhere: when he killed meat, game or domestic animals, the blood was shed in worship. Prayers and sacrifices were offered before battle, and the sin of Saul was that he did not wait for Samuel to come and perform the offering (I Sam. 13). But the normal place of worship was the home, where the sabbath was observed.

---

4. Otto von Simson, *The Gothic Cathedral, Origins of Gothic Architecture and the Medieval Concept of Order.* Bollingen Series XLVIII, revised edition (New York: Pantheon Books, 1962, 1965), p. 138.
5. See the writings of Ernst H. Kantorowicz, esp. *Laudes Regiae, A Study in Liturgical Acclamations and Mediaeval Ruler Worship* (University of California Press, 1946); *The King's Two Bodies, A Study in Mediaeval Political Theology* (Princeton: Princeton University Press, 1957); *Frederick the Second, 1194–1250* (New York: Frederick Ungar, 1931, 1957).

Fourth, the tabernacle thus has no counterpart in the church. When at the death of Christ, the veil of the temple was rent in twain (Matt. 27:51), the end of the temple as God's palace was openly set forth. The new temple is Jesus Christ, who was crucified for declaring Himself to be the true temple, built by His resurrection (Matt. 26:61; 27:40; John 2:19-21, etc.). By the indwelling Holy Spirit, believers are now in a sense temples of God (I Cor. 3:16,17), as is the church also, which is spoken of as "the house of God" (I Tim. 3:15; I Peter 4:17), but the "church" as so designated is not a visible habitation or structure but the entire visible congregation or church of Christ. The temple, or, more accurately, the tabernacle, has its fulfilment in Christ, and the true holy of holies is now opened to men of faith in that through "the blood of Jesus" God's covenant people have access to the throne (Heb. 10:19-22).

The tabernacle had three rooms. First, there was the court, open only to the covenant people and, while fenced off, was open to the sky. The second room was open only to priests and was veiled while still lighted. The third, the holy of holies, was veiled and dark, and only the high priest entered it, once a year. In heaven, God dwells as Ruler of the universe; in the tabernacle, God dwelled "in His condescending grace" as ruler of His covenant people.[6]

With the incarnation, the tabernacling presence gave way to the incarnate God-man, Jesus Christ. With the ascension, the Holy Spirit continues the work of government; the Holy Spirit thus cannot be separated from law and government in any sense. However, even more, a new stage appeared with Christ in the rule of God the King. The heavenly sanctuary, the throne of the world, became the throne of Christ, who reigns now to subjugate all His enemies (I Cor. 15:25), so that the triumphant prophecy be fulfilled, "The kingdoms of this world are become the kingdoms of our Lord, and of his Christ; and he shall reign for ever and ever" (Rev. 11:15). In terms of this purpose, the covenant men were told by Jesus Christ, "All power (all authority or dominion) is given unto me in heaven and in earth. Go ye therefore, and teach all nations . . ." (Matt. 28:18,19). The church is sent into the world as part of Christ's imperialism, to subjugate the world to His reign.

Fifth, in the holy of holies, the throne of God is the law. Fairbairn called attention to this clearly:

> The connection now indicated between the revelation of law in the stricter sense, and the structure and use of the sacred dwelling, comes out very strikingly in the description given of the tabernacle, which, after mentioning the different kinds of material to be provided, begins first with the ark of the covenant—the repository, as

6. Oehler, *Theology of the O.T.*, p. 254 f.

it might equally be called, of the Decalogue, since it was merely a chest for containing the tables of the law, and as such was taken for the very seat or throne from which Jehovah manifested His presence and glory (Ex. xxv. 2, 9, 40 etc.). It was, therefore, the most sacred piece of furniture belonging to the Tabernacle—the centre from which all relating to men's fellowship with God was to proceed, and to derive its essential character.[7]

The ark contained the treaty, the covenant law between God and man. The ark was thus the repository of the law and symbolized the law. The giving of the law was God's grace to His covenant people, and His throne is that same law. The law sets forth the justice and righteousness of God, and it is His government declared in its details and principles. The central meaning of the ark is to be seen in terms of the law. "There can be no doubt—that the proper contents of the ark were the two tables of the covenant, and that to be the repository of these was the special purpose for which it was made."[8] The ark was not a normal chair: it was more obviously a chest, and the emphasis was on the contents of the chest as the covenant between God and man, as the basis of God's rule, and the throne of His kingship. It does impossible violence to the kingship of Christ, therefore, to separate it from the law, or to see His work as the end of the law.

God did not make the altar His throne, because the altar, however important, set forth atonement, the beginning of new life for God's people. The goal of atonement, of redemption, is the rule of God over a kingdom wholly subject to the law of the covenant, and joyfully so. This joyful submission to law was fully manifested in Jesus Christ, who declared, "Lo, I come to do thy will, O God" (Heb. 10:5-9), and who, as King, reigns in terms of a law He gave and He fulfilled.

The tabernacle thus has a central significance to Biblical law: it declares God's throne to be His law, and it declares that the throne of law governs the world.

It is truncated and defective faith which stops at the altar. The altar signifies redemption. It sets forth thus the rebirth of the believer. But rebirth for what? Without the dimension of law, life is denied the meaning and purpose of rebirth. Not surprisingly, altar-centered faith is heaven-centered and rapture-centered rather than God-centered. It seeks an escape from the world rather than the fulfilment of God's calling and law-word in the world. It has no knowledge of the throne.

3. The Altar and Capital Punishment

Provision is made in the law for an altar. The first word concerning

---

7. Fairbairn, *The Revelation of Law in Scripture*, p. 136.
8. Fairbairn: "Ark of the Covenant," in *Fairbairn's Imperial Standard Bible Cyclopedia*, I, 194.

the altar appears in Exodus 20:22-26, an altar of natural materials for the pre-tabernacle period, for the interim until its construction. This altar was not to be of man's design or making, "for the altar was not to represent the creature, but to be the place to which God came to receive man into His fellowship there. For this reason the altar was to be made of the same material, which formed the earthly soil for the kingdom of God, either of earth or else of stones."[1]

God's pattern for the altar was subsequently given as a part of the law of the tabernacle (Ex. 27:1-8; 38:1-7).[2] It was built of acacia wood covered entirely with bronze, five by five by three cubits in size.[3]

The altar is, of course, of central significance religiously. Sacrifice sets forth the fact of atonement, that God provided a way for sinful man to gain salvation. This is clearly the *first* and central meaning of the altar. The animals offered on the altar typified Jesus Christ, "the Lamb of God, which taketh away the sin of the world" (John 1:29). In Revelation 1:5 Jesus Christ is described as the one who "loved us, and washed us from our sins in his own blood." Apart from acceptance of the atoning sacrifice of Jesus Christ, there can be neither salvation nor Christian faith. Sacrifice is basic to Biblical faith. A very large and fundamental aspect of all Scripture is the declaration of vicarious sacrifice and of a God-provided atonement. Chapter after chapter gives laws pertaining to sacrifice. Jesus Christ declared Himself to be the Son of man, come "to give his life a ransom for many" (Matt. 20:28; Mark 10:45). The apostolic declaration was this, "For there is one God, and one mediator between God and man, the man Christ Jesus: Who gave himself a ransom for all, to be testified in due time" (I Tim. 2:5, 6). The altar signified Jesus Christ and His atoning sacrifice.

Unfortunately, it is at this point that the ecclesiastical interpretation of the Bible begins and ends. The significance of the altar is ably discussed at great length, but almost always with respect to a transaction basic to the life of the church, whereas it is in reality basic to the life of man in church, state, and all of life.

Fairbairn called attention to this *second* aspect of the altar:

> And there can be no doubt, that the representations just noticed, and others of a like description, concerning the death of Christ, do in their natural sense carry a legal aspect; they bear respect to the demands of law, or the justice of which law is the expression. They declare that, to meet these demands in behalf of sinners, Christ bore a judicial death—a death which, while all-undeserved on the part of Him who suffered, must be regarded as the merited judgment of Heaven on human guilt. To be made a curse, that He might redeem

---

1. Keil and Delitzsch, *The Pentateuch*, II, 127.
2. See Fairbairn, "Altar," in *Fairbairn's Bible Encyclopedia*, I, 136-141.
3. J. C. Rylaarsdam, "Exodus," *Interpreter's Bible*, I, 1034.

men from the curse of the law, can have no other meaning than to endure the penalty, which as transgressors of the law they had incurred, in order that they might escape; nor can the exchange indicated in the words, "He was made sin for us, that we might be made the righteousness of God in Him," be justly understood to import less than that He, the righteous One, took the place of sinners in suffering, that they might take His place in favour and blessing. And the stern necessity for the transaction—a necessity which even the resources of infinite wisdom, at the earnest cry of Jesus, found it impossible to evade (Matt. 26:39)—on what could it rest but the bosom of law, whose violated claims called for satisfaction? Not that God delights in blood, but that the paramount interests of truth and righteousness must be upheld, even though blood unspeakably precious may have to be shed in their vindication.[4]

The altar thus sets forth, no less than the ark, *the law and the justice of the law.* So central is the law to God, that the demands of the law are fulfilled as the necessary condition of grace, and God fulfils the demands of the law on Jesus Christ. Jesus Christ, as the new Adam, head of the new humanity, kept the law perfectly, *to set forth the obedience of the new race or humanity,* and died on the cross as the sinless Lamb of God, *to fulfil the requirement of the law against sinners.* Grace does not set aside the law: it provides the necessary fulfilment of the law. Thus, the grace of God witnesses to the validity of the law and the full and absolute justice of the claims of the law.

Here again Fairbairn stated the case eloquently and clearly:

We must have a solid foundation for our feet to stand on, a sure and living ground for our confidence before God. And this we can find only in the old church view of the sufferings and death of Christ as a satisfaction to God's justice for the offense done by our sin to His violated law. *Satisfaction*, I say emphatically, *to God's justice*—which some, even evangelical writers, seem disposed to stumble at; they would say, satisfaction to God's honour, indeed, but by no means to God's justice. What, then, I would ask, is God's honour apart from God's justice? His honour can be nothing but the reflex action or display of His moral attributes; and in the exercise of these attributes, the fundamental and controlling element is justice. Every one of them is conditioned; love itself is conditioned by the demands of justice; and to provide scope for the operation of love in justifying the ungodly consistently with those demands, is the very ground and reason of the atonement—its ground and reason primarily in the mind of God, and because there, then also in its living image, the human conscience, which instinctively regards punishment as "the recoil of the eternal law of right against the transgressor," and cannot attain to solid peace but through a medium of valid expiation. So much so, indeed, that wherever the true expiation is unknown, or but partially understood, it ever goes about to provide expiations of its own.

---

4. Patrick Fairbairn, *The Revelation of Law in Scripture*, p. 247 f.

Thus has the law been established (Rom. iii. 31)—most signally established by that very feature of the Gospel, which specially distinguished it from the law—its display of the redeeming love of God in Christ.[5]

To deny this second aspect of the altar is to fall into antinomianism. Such a perspective sees the altar as a witness to God's unconditioned love rather than to a love "conditioned by the demands of justice," to use Fairbairn's phrase.

It must be recognized then that either the witness of the altar to, and the meaning of the altar as, law and justice are affirmed and upheld, or another religion, which is antichristian to the core has assumed the garb of the Christian faith. The blood of the altar was a grim and sustained declaration of the inflexible and abiding demand of the law that the justice of God be fulfilled.

Third, then, the altar was clearly also a witness to *capital punishment* as basic to the law. The doctrine of capital punishment is not normally associated with the altar or the second commandment but rather with the sixth, "Thou shalt not kill." This fallacy both limits the meaning of the sixth commandment and also deprives capital punishment of its profound theological foundation. If capital punishment is not basic to God's law, then Christ died in vain, for some easier way of satisfying God's justice could have been found. If capital punishment is not basic to the second commandment, then the altar was a bloody mistake, and God has been needlessly worshiped by wantonly shed blood. But to imagine that atonement is possible without death, or that the altar can be by-passed in man's approach to God, is to set up a graven image of man, and of man's capacity to save himself, in the stead of the triune God.

Not only is the death penalty required by the law, but it is specified that there can be no remission of the penalty: "Moreover ye shall take no satisfaction for the life of a murderer, which is guilty of death: but he shall be surely put to death" (Num. 35:31). Thus, when various Protestant and Roman Catholic church leaders, including Pope Paul VI, and civil authorities such as Queen Elizabeth II, tried to persuade the Rhodesian authorities to set aside the death penalty for some murderers on the claim that these were "freedom fighters," they were defying and despising the law of God. They were also expressing their contempt of the cross of Christ, which sets forth the necessity of the death penalty in the sight of God, and establishing *their* word above God's word.

The laws concerning the death penalty can be briefly summarized:

Numbers 35:31: Shall not be remitted.

---

5. *Ibid.*, pp. 250-252.

Genesis 9:5, 6; Numbers 35:16-21, 30-33; Deuteronomy 17:6; Leviticus 24:17: Inflicted for murder.

Leviticus 20:10; Deuteronomy 22:21-24: For adultery.

Leviticus 20:11, 12, 14: For incest.

Exodus 22:19; Leviticus 20:15, 16: For bestiality.

Leviticus 18:22; 20:13: For sodomy.

Deuteronomy 22:25: For rape of a betrothed virgin.

Deuteronomy 19:16-20: For false witness in a case involving a capital offense.

Exodus 21:16; Deuteronomy 24:7: Kidnapping.

Leviticus 21:9: For a priest's daughter who committed fornication.

Exodus 22:18: For witchcraft.

Leviticus 20:2-5: For offering human sacrifice.

Exodus 21:15, 17; Leviticus 20:9: For striking or cursing father or mother.

Deuteronomy 21:18-21: For incorrigible juvenile delinquents.

Leviticus 24:11-14, 16, 23: For blasphemy.

Exodus 35:2; Numbers 15:32-36: For sabbath desecration.

Deuteronomy 13:1-10: For prophesying falsely, or propagating false doctrines.

Exodus 22:20: For sacrificing to false gods.

Deuteronomy 17:12: For lawless refusal to abide by godly law and order, anti-law, anti-court attitudes and actions.

Deuteronomy 13:9; 17:7: Execution by the witnesses.

Numbers 15:35, 36; Deuteronomy 13:9: Execution by the congregation.

Numbers 35:30; Deuteronomy 17:6; 19:15: Not inflicted on testimony of less than two witnesses.

At a few points the penalties were altered in the New Testament, but the basic principle of the death penalty was undergirded and set forth by Christ's atoning death, which made clear that the penalty for man's treason to God and departure from God's law is death without remission.

The blood of the altar and the fact of the altar are thus a declaration of the necessity of capital punishment. To oppose capital punishment as prescribed by God's law is thus to oppose the cross of Christ and to deny the validity of the altar.

The altar therefore sets forth the principle of capital punishment. But, *fourth*, the altar is a *declaration of life* because it witnesses to death. It declares that our life rests in the death of the Lamb of God. It declares moreover that our life's safety is hedged in and walled about by the fact of capital punishment. If God's law in this respect is denied, then "the land is defiled; therefore I do visit the iniquity thereof upon it, and the land itself vomiteth out her inhabitants" (Lev. 18:25). But the godly exercise of capital punishment cleanses the land of evil and protects the righteous. In calling for the death of incorrigible juvenile delinquents, which means, therefore, in terms of case law, the death of incorrigible adult delinquents; the law declares, "so shalt thou put evil away from among you; and all Israel shall hear, and fear" (Deut. 21:21).

To deny the death penalty is to insist on life for the evil; it means that evil men are given the right to kill, kidnap, rape, and violate law and order, and their life is guaranteed against death in the process. The murderer is given the right to kill without losing his life, and the victim and potential victims are denied their right to live. Men may speak of unconditional love, and unconditional mercy, but every act of love and mercy is conditional, because, in granting it to one man, I am affirming the conditions of his life and denying others in the process. If I am loving and merciful to a murderer, I am unloving and merciless to his present and future victims. Moreover, I am then in open contempt of God and His law, which requires no mercy to a man guilty of death: "Moreover ye shall take no satisfaction for the life of a murderer, which is guilty of death: but he shall surely be put to death" (Num. 35:31). Moreover,

> So ye shall not pollute the land wherein ye are: for blood it defileth the land: and the land cannot be cleansed of the blood that is shed therein, but by the blood of him that shed it.
> Defile not therefore the land which ye shalt inhabit, wherein I dwell, for I the LORD dwell among the children of Israel (Num. 35:33, 34).

Leviticus 26 makes clear the curse which rests upon the land which despises God's law: if the people will not cleanse the land of evil, God will cleanse the land of its people. In terms of this, it is not surprising that history has been so continuously on a disaster course apart from God's law-word.

This, then, is the meaning of the altar: it is life to the righteous in Christ, who are redeemed by His atoning blood, because it represents inflexible and immutable death to evil. The altar is the supreme witness to the death penalty, and to the fact that it is never set aside. For us, by the grace of God, it is fulfilled on the person of Jesus Christ. We cannot trifle with the law of God without despising Christ and His sacrifice and thereby revealing our own reprobate nature, "For if we sin wilfully after that we have received the knowledge of the truth, there remaineth no more sacrifice for sins, But a certain fearful looking for of judgment and fiery indignation, which shall devour the adversaries" (Heb. 10:26, 27).

But for us who stand in terms of the altar, it is our life, and the guarantee of judgment against the enemies of God and His kingdom.

4. Sacrifice and Responsibility

Sacrifice is commonly treated as a relic of man's primitive past; attempts to direct attention to a divine origin in terms of Scripture are discounted, and we are told that "all monogenetic theories of the origin of sacrifice may be safely discountenanced from the start."[1] These cavalier dismissals rest on a faith in autonomous man and his anti-God world view.

Sacrifice is basic to the Biblical faith, and it is basic to Biblical law. Any consideration of Biblical law must of necessity recognize the centrality of sacrifice.

In analyzing the meaning of sacrifice to law (for our interest here is legal rather than soteriological), it is necessary, *first*, to recognize that *Biblical sacrifice requires a doctrine of human sacrifice while rejecting sinful man as the sacrifice*. As Vos observed in commenting on the sacrifice of Isaac (Gen. 22), "the sacrifice of a human being cannot be condemned on principle."[2] Moreover,

> All Biblical sacrifice rests on the idea that the gift of life to God, either in consecration or in expiation, is necessary to the action or the restoration of religion. What passes from man to God is not regarded as property but, even though it be property for a symbolic purpose, means always in the last analysis the gift of life. And this is, in the original conception, neither in expiation nor in conse-cration of the gift of alien life; it is the gift of the life of the offerer himself. The second principle underlying the idea is that man in the abnormal relation of sin is disqualified for offering this gift of his life in his own person. Hence the principle of vicariousness is brought into play: one life takes the place of another life. . . . Not sacrifice of human life as such, but the sacrifice of average sinful human life, is deprecated by the O.T. In the Mosaic law these things are taught by an elaborate symbolism.[3]

Notice that sacrifice serves both for *expiation* and for *consecration*. It is, as Vos pointed out, "the gift of the life of the offerer himself," and yet, be-cause of *the disqualification of sin*, "the principle of vicariousness," i.e., a God-provided substitute, is introduced. Oehler, in dealing with all forms of offerings and sacrifices, declared, "*The essential nature of an offering in general is the devotion of man to God, expressed in an out-ward act*."[4] This, then, is the essence of sacrifice, *man's total devotion to God*.

Second, this true and total devotion to God requires *obedience to the law of God* in love and faith. The Ten Commandments are followed by the summons to obey in total devotion: "And thou shalt love the LORD thy God with all thine heart, and with all thy soul, and with all thy might" (Deut. 6:5; cf. vv. 1-6). Before sacrifices were described

---

1. T. H. Gaster, "Sacrifice," in *Interpreter's Dictionary of the Bible*, vol. 4, R–Z, p. 147.
2. Vos, *Biblical Theology*, p. 106.
3. *Ibid.*, p. 107.
4. Oehler, *Theology of the Old Testament*, p. 261.

by the law, Moses at Sinai on the first day commanded obedience (Ex. 19:5, 6) and, on the third day, the law was given and sacrifices offered (Ex. 19:10–24:8). It is apparently to this primacy of obedience to the law that Jeremiah referred (Jer. 7:21-24). Sacrifices should be linked to obedience, according to Jeremiah 33:10, 11, and will be in the day of restoration. The prophets denounced a purely formal sacrifice: obedience was required to give the sacrifice meaning as man's full devotion to God.[5]

Third, the physical sacrifice of sinful man as an offering to God is a fearful offense against Him and invites judgment (Jer. 7:30-34). Since the essence of sacrifice is the devotion of man to God, human sacrifice represents an attempt to by-pass God's law and find a man-made way to God. Human sacrifice is thus humanistic to the core: it is atonement by man on his own terms.

Fourth, it is obvious that the sacrifices, as distinct from the offerings, typified Christ, the sinless and perfect man, who, in perfect devotion to God, kept the law fully. Christ, as the sinless man, was the acceptable sacrifice in atonement for the sins of His elect, who are redeemed by His atoning blood. Hence, to represent Christ, the offered animal had to be without blemish.

Fifth, the sacrifices were required of all believers as their bond of peace and unity with God. Those not covered by the sacrifice of Christ are under sentence of death. In the sacrificial system, the believer "put his hand upon the head of the burnt-offering" (Lev. 1:4), or, more literally, *leaned* his hand.[6] Certain portions of the sacrifice and of all meats were reserved portions, forbidden to man: the blood, the omentum or fat, the kidneys with the fat on them, and, in the case of sheep, the tail (also fat); these were the continually reserved portions, as distinct from portions reserved for the priest (Ex. 29:22; Lev. 3:9; 7:3, 4; 8:25; 9:19, 20). The animal sacrifices which were acceptable were cattle (bovine), sheep (ovine), and kids (caprine); of fowl, turtle-doves and young pigeons; all these were in the class of "clean" animals (Lev. 9:3; 14:10; 5:7; 12:8; Num. 28:3, 9, 11; 7:16, 17, 22, 23; etc.).

The shedding of blood was basic to the unity of the believer with God. Oehler noted:

> The mediator of the covenant first offers to God in the blood a *pure life,* which comes in between God and the people, covering and atoning for the latter. In this connection the sprinkling of the altar does not merely signify God's acceptance of the blood, but at the

---

5. See Vos, *Biblical Theology,* pp. 282-294.
6. Andrew Bonar, *Leviticus* (London: Banner of Truth Trust, 1846, 1966), p. 15.

same time serves to consecrate the place in which Jehovah enters into intercourse with his people. But when a portion of the blood accepted by God is further applied to the people by an act of sprinkling, this is meant to signify that the same life which is offered up in atonement for the people is also intended to consecrate the people themselves to covenant fellowship with God. The act of consecration thus becomes an act of renewal of life,—a translation of Israel into the kingdom of God, in which it is filled with divine vital energy, and is sanctified to be a kingdom of priests, a holy people.[7]

All must be under the blood or they are under judgment.

Sixth, the sacrificial system incorporated into law a basic principle: *the greater the responsibility, the greater the culpability, the greater the sin.* This is very clearly set forth in Leviticus 4, according to which there are four levels or grades of sin: 1) of the high priest, 4:3-12, whose sin-offering required a bullock, the largest and most expensive sacrifice. "This is the very same kind of offering as when the whole congregation sins."[8] Religious leaders, because they have a central responsibility with respect to the law of God, are all the more guilty, and all the more severely judged by God. 2) The sin of the whole congregation is next in consequence, 4:13-21; "the congregation" here had reference to the Hebrew nation. The sin of a people collectively is a real one; it can be a sin of ignorance, or of falling short in obeying the law, but it is still a sin. The required sacrifice was again a bullock. 3) The sin of a ruler, a civil magistrate or officer, is next in order of consequence. The sin-offering here was "a kid of the goats, a male without blemish" (4:22-26). The "ruler" clearly "includes all civil magistrates. His high responsibility is here shewn just as in Prov. xxiv. 12, 'If a ruler hearken to lies, all his servants will be wicked.'" Moreover, the text speaks of "The Lord his God" because "A ruler is specially bound to be a man of God."[9] 4) The sins of individuals, of any of the people of the land, are last in the order of sins (4:27-35). For the well-to-do, the prosperous, a female kid was required; if they were unable to bring the kid, a lamb could be offered. For sins of inadvertency, the poor could bring two turtle-doves or two young pigeons (Lev. 5:11); for other sacrifices also, this poor man's offering was possible. Thus, some individuals have a responsibility almost equal to that of rulers, in that they rule an estate or a segment of society. Psychologically, a female kid is lesser than a male kid; productively, its potential is greater. Some private individuals can often wield a power greater than civil authorities, and their sin is commensurate to their responsibility. Most telling in

---

7. Oehler, *Theology of the Old Testament*, p. 264.
8. Bonar, *Leviticus*, p. 67.
9. *Ibid.*, p. 80.

this list is the clear and great prominence given to the religious leaders, and the markedly lower place given to civil authorities. According to Proverbs 29:18, "Where there is no vision, the people perish: but he that keepeth the law, happy is he." The Berkeley Version notes that "vision" has reference to a "prophetic ministry," without which "the people run wild." Law and order are dependent on the faithful proclamation of God's prophetic law-word, and, without it, social anarchy ensues.

Seventh, ignorance of the law is no excuse, nor are sins of inadvertency any the less sins. This is clear from Leviticus 4 and 5, which specify the sacrifices for such sins. Bonar called attention to the significance of this aspect of the law:

> Here, too, we learn that "sin is the *transgression of the law*" (I John iii. 4). It is not merely when we act contrary *to the dictates of conscience* that we sin; we may often be sinning when conscience never upbraids us.[10]

Modern autonomous man regards as sin, if he considers the subject at all, only that which offends his conscience. But Biblical law holds that sin and lawlessness can occur without knowledge and without conscience. Man, in fact, may sin with good conscience, but this does not alter the fact that he sins: the criterion of transgression is not man's conscience but the law of God. Cannibalism and human sacrifice have both been practiced as matters of conscience, and much else also. The conscience of fallen man is no law criterion.

The main offerings of the Mosaic law were burnt offerings, meal offerings, peace offerings, sin offerings, and trespass offerings. The burnt offerings, consisting of bullocks, goats, rams, lambs, turtle-doves, or young pigeons, were entirely burnt on the altar, except for the animal skins, the priest's portion (Lev. 1; 6:8-13; 7:8). The sin offerings and trespass offerings, as we have seen, were males or females of the herd, flock, or turtle-doves and young pigeons, and one-tenth ephah of flour. All of the sin offerings save God's reserved portions went to the priest (Lev. 6:24-30); the same was true of some of the trespass offerings (Lev. 7:1-7). The meal offering consisted of fine flour, green ears of grain, frankincense, oil, and salt; again, a portion went to the priests (Lev. 2; 6:14-23). The peace offerings were male and female of the herd and flock, of bullocks, lambs, and goats; there were also unleavened cakes and wafers mingled with oil. But leavened bread was also to be used (Lev. 3; 7:11-13). The priest's portion was the heave-shoulder and the wave-breast. The fact that offerings which were vicarious representatives of man's sin became acceptable food for the priests had a

10. Bonar, *Leviticus*, p. 88.

symbolic aspect; "The memorial of the mass of sin is consumed in the fire of wrath; but the priest takes his portion, in order to show that the sin is cleansed out from the mass."[11]

But, *eighth*, before this cleansing could occur the law required *restitution*. The goal of sacrifice as well as of law is the restoration of God's law order. The requirement of restitution is both man-ward and God-ward. Bonar commented, with reference to Leviticus 16,

> The trespasser is to be no gainer by defrauding God's house. He is to suffer, even in temporal things, as a punishment for his sin. He is to bring, in addition to the thing of which he had defrauded God, money to the extent of one-fifth of the value of the thing. This was given to the priest as the head of the people in things of God, and representative of God in holy duties. It was to be a *double tithe* because of the attempt to defraud God. (The tithe regularly paid was an acknowledgement that God had a right to the things tithed; and this double tithe was an acknowledgment that, in consequence of this attempt to defraud Him, His right must be *doubly* acknowledged.)[12]

Finally, *ninth*, a leavened offering was a part of the peace offering, an important fact (Lev. 7:13). Leaven is taken by some as a symbol or type of sin; it is rather a symbol of corruptibility. As a peace offering, this was acceptable. Other offerings had established man's atonement through the blood of the unblemished and innocent one. Man was now in communion with God, and man's works, however faulty, become thereby acceptable to God. All man's services to God have an element of corruptibility; his works, buildings, gifts, and efforts decay and pass away. They are none the less a fulfilment of God's law and an acceptable sacrifice. The acceptability of man's works rests not on their perfection, but on the perfection of God and on God's provision of atonement for His elect. Man's obedience to the law is a leavened offering, clearly corruptible, yet when faithful and obedient to God's authority and order, a "sacrifice" well-pleasing in His sight and assured of His reward.

5. Holiness and Law

The relationship of holiness to law is a very real and important one, however much neglected. Attention has been diverted, in recent years, to erroneous concepts by the influential work of Rudolf Otto: *The Idea of the Holy* (1923). Holiness cannot be defined in and of itself. It is a "transcendental attribute" of God and must be defined first of all in relation to Him.

Thus, *first*, holiness must be defined, in terms of Scripture, as *separa-*

---

11. *Ibid.*, p. 97.
12. *Ibid.*, p. 102 f.

tion, non-trespassable, with the implication of *devotion*. It has reference to the "unapproachableness" of God. As Vos pointed out, it has an ethical significance: it refers to God's majesty and omnipotence.[1] In reference to man, "the meaning is never simply that of moral goodness, considered in itself, but always ethical goodness seen in relation to God."[2] Israel became holy because God in His electing grace made His covenant people His son by adoption (Deut. 14:1-2).[3]

Now the fact that *holiness* involves *separation*, or, very literally, *a cutting*, makes apparent immediately its basic and essential relation to *law*. The law simply states *the principle of the cutting or separation*. Wherever there is law, there is inescapably a line of separation. Conversely, wherever there is no law, there is no line of separation. Antinomian sects may speak earnestly of holiness, but, because of their denial of law, they have denied the principle of holiness.

It follows, therefore, that we can say, *second*, that *every Biblical law is concerned with holiness*. Every law, by setting a line of division between the people of the law as against the outlaws, the people outside the law, is concerned with establishing a principle of separation in terms of God. Some laws set forth also the principle of separation in a symbolic as well as a literal form. For example, in Numbers 19:11-22, separation from death is required, and ritual purification after contact with the dead (see also Lev. 5:2, 3; 11:8; Num. 31:19, 20; 9:10; Lev. 21:1-4; 22:4, 6). Israel had been called to be a holy people (Ex. 19:6; 22:31; 23:24; Lev. 19:2; Deut. 7:6; 14:2, 21; 26:18, 19). Since "God is not the God of the dead, but of the living (Matt. 22:32), to be God's covenant man means separation from death itself ultimately. This separation is set forth in these laws. Their destiny being *life*, the covenant people of God are to regard death as something from which they are being separated by God. It is clear that the Mosaic law affirmed the principle of quarantine against communicable diseases in full recognition of their contagious nature, but, even more basically, the law of separation was operative in such legislation to affirm the holiness of God's people (Deut. 24:8; Lev. 13). God's people are destined for health as well as life, and hence they are "cut off" from diseases symbolically as well as in protection from contagion.

Not only death and disease were to be separated from the people of life, but also eunuchs and bastards (Deut. 23:1-2). Various forms of self-mutilation (Deut. 14:1, 2; Lev. 19:27) were forbidden, as was tatooing (Lev. 19:28). Sickness and age might mar the body; the people of God were forbidden to mar it. Some of these marks repre-

1. Vos, *Biblical Theology*, pp. 264-269.
2. *Ibid.*, p. 270.
3. Oehler, *Theology of the O.T.*, p. 178 f.

sented covenants with other gods, an added factor in separation from them.

With respect to the ban on eunuchs and bastards, i.e., their being barred from the congregation, it is to the tenth generation. According to one editorial footnote in the Talmud, entering in to the congregation of the Lord meant "eligible to intermarry with Israelites,"[4] and, according to another editorial note, the expression "to his tenth generation" meant "the stigma is perpetual."[5] The ban on intermarriage was probably a real factor; certainly the penalty would work to make intermarriage difficult. But this does not get to the root of the matter. The ban was not on faith; i.e., it is not stated that the bastards and eunuchs nor, in Deuteronomy 23:3, that Ammonites and Moabites, cannot be believers. There is, in fact, a particularly strong promise of blessing to believing eunuchs in Isaiah 56:4, 5, and their place as proselytes was real even in the era of hardened Phariseeism (Acts 8:27, 28). The Moabitess Ruth intermarried twice, first with a son of Naomi, then with Boaz, to become an ancestress of Jesus Christ (Ruth 1:4; 4:13, 18-21; Matt. 1:5). There is no reason to doubt that eunuchs, bastards, Ammonites, and Moabites regularly became believers and were faithful worshipers of God. *Congregation* has reference to the whole nation in its governmental function as God's covenant people. G. Ernest Wright defined it as "the whole organized commonwealth as it assembled officially for various purposes, particularly worship."[6] The *men* of the legitimate blood line constituted the heads of houses and of tribes. These *men* were the congregation of Israel, not the women and children nor excluded persons. All the integrity and honesty required by the law was due to every "stranger" (Lev. 19:33, 34), and it was certainly not denied to a man's illegitimate child, nor to a eunuch, an Ammonite, or a Moabite. The purpose of the commandment is here the protection of authority. Authority among God's people is *holy*; it does require a separateness. It does not belong to every man simply on the ground of his humanity.

The Berkeley Version reading of Deuteronomy 23:1-3 would allow for the admission of these excluded persons at the tenth generation. There is some ground for such an interpretation in terms of Deuteronomy 23:7, 8, where the Edomites are given entrance into "the assembly of the LORD" on the third generation.

The grounds for exclusion are significant. Edom met Israel with open, honest enmity (Num. 26:18, 20), and Egypt worked to destroy them (Ex. 1:22), but Ammon and Moab instead worked to pervert Israel

4. *Babylonian Talmud, Seder Nezekin*, vol. III, Sanhedrin 36b, p. 229n.
5. *Seder Nezekin*, vol. IV, *Makkoth* 13a, p. 90n.
6. G. Ernest Wright, "Deuteronomy," *The Interpreter's Bible*, II, 468.

(Num. 22:25; 31:16), after Israel showed them forebearance (Deut. 2:9,19, 29). A faint echo of this principle appeared in Napoleon's treatment of Surgeon-major Mouton, who had demeaned the Princess of Lichtenstein and the men of her household. Napoleon, summoning Mouton before his staff, declared, "Understand this, gentlemen, one kills men, but one never puts them to shame. Let him (Mouton) be shot!" Later, Mouton's life was spared and he understood the lesson.[7] Edom and Egypt sought to kill Israel; Ammon and Moab tried to pervert and degrade Israel, and their judgment was accordingly severe.

Other causes of ceremonial and physical uncleanness were cited: an issue of blood (Lev. 15:2-16, 19-26); childbirth (Lev. 12:1, 2, 4, 5); menstruation (Lev. 15:19-31; 18:19); sexual intercourse, as against the fertility cult belief that it involved communion with the gods (Lev. 15:16-18; 18:20); unclean persons (Num. 19:22); the spoils of war (Num. 31:21-24); and also the unauthorized touching or eating of holy things (Lev. 22:3, 14). The humanistic approach sees a daintiness with respect to things in these laws, or else a puritanical abhorrence of them. Nothing could be further from the truth. The point at issue is not man's response to things but his holiness in terms of separation to the living God. Many of the things cited constituted, in paganism, particular ways of holiness; here, the ground of holiness is separation unto God.

The subject of vows is closely linked to holiness. To vow is to devote something or one's self to God, to sanctify it to Him. The laws of vows, as well as the laws of redemption of things vowed, appear in Leviticus 22:21; 27:1-29; Numbers 6:3-21; 30:1-15; Deuteronomy 12:6, 26; 23:21-33. Vows were voluntary, but an important aspect of the vow brings us to a *third* aspect of the laws of holiness. A man was always bound by his vow. Man, created in the image of God, was called to walk under God's law and in obedience to the creation mandate. John Marsh has called attention to a telling aspect of man's image-responsibility:

> A man is always unconditionally bound by either kind of vow (i.e., vows of every kind, and . . . a vow of abstinence). It is interesting to note that for the Hebrew mind even a man's word should accomplish that which is imposed: God's word, of course, always did: it could not return to him void. A man might cherish intentions to do certain things and not be bound by them. But once his intention was expressed in words, then the obligation was laid upon him unconditionally.[8]

Such a vow could only be made by a free man. Once made, the vow had to be fulfilled. The vow of an unmarried woman could be over-

---

7. Jean Savant, *Napoleon in His Time* (New York: Thomas Nelson & Sons, 1958), p. 223.
8. John Marsh, "Numbers," in *Interpreter's Bible*, II, 281 f.

ruled by her father; being under authority, she was not free to do as she pleased. The same was true of a married woman (Num. 30:1-16). A divorced woman or a widow was free to vow, being independent. The implication was clear. A woman's holiness and devotion is subject first of all to the authority of her husband. God's law disallows all vows of service which a woman vows without her husband's or father's consent. A woman's holiness is not to be found in an evasion of her place.

A special kind of vow was that of the Nazirite (Num. 6:2-21). A Nazirite was a man or a woman who vowed a vow and for a season observed strict laws of separation in the course of the discharge of his vow. Abstinence from strong drink of any kind, and from grapes and raisins, no cutting of the hair, and separation from the dead marked the noticeable aspect of his vow. The usual period of the vow was brief. There was no separation from the routine of family life and work. The essence of the Nazirite's separation was not in the abstinence but in the separation "unto the Lord" in the discharge of a particular service or vow.

A fourth aspect of holiness appears in matters of food. No flesh torn by beasts of the field could be eaten (Ex. 22:31), i.e., meat not properly butchered (Lev. 7:22-27). The first-fruits were given to the Lord (Ex. 23:19; 34:26), indicating thereby the holiness of the entirety. The eating of fat and blood was forbidden (Lev. 7:22-27; 19:26). Clean and unclean animals for eating are listed (Lev. 11); while dead animals and other unclean animals are forbidden to the covenant people, if foreigners regard them as good food, there is no harm in selling them such items (Lev. 17:10-16). Fruit trees should be allowed five years growth before they are regarded as "circumcised" and edible (Lev. 19:23-26); the circumcision of the tree was its ceremonial picking in the fourth year in dedication to the Lord. Foods forbidden by God should be "abominable" to His people (Lev. 20:25; Deut. 14:13-21). There is no question but that these laws were and are basic to good health; there is also no question about the fact that they are laws of holiness. These laws of holiness are a "blessing" (Deut. 12:15) to the physical life of God's people, i.e., to their health. In this respect, they are another law of *separation from death. Health* is thus an aspect of holiness, and the fulness of health is in the resurrection.

A *fifth* aspect of holiness has reference to dress. Tranvestite dress is an "abomination" to the Lord (Deut. 22:5); it is a sterile and perverse hostility to God's created order. Similarly, wearing a garment of mingled materials, wool and linen together (Deut. 22:11; cf. Lev. 19:19) is forbidden. To bring diverse things together in an unnatural union is to despise the order of God's creation.

Sixth, the very land itself is holy and can be defiled even by leaving a hanged man up overnight (Deut. 21:22, 23). In brief, the land itself must be regarded as separated and devoted to God. We have here an instance of case law. If a body left out overnight *defiles* a land, how much more so man's abusive use of the soil, his contempt of God's creation, and his attempt to hybridize and mingle what God ordained to be separate?

Finally, *seventh,* it should be noted that, while evangelical Christians today are greatly concerned with *personal* holiness, the Bible is also concerned with *national* holiness. The summons to be a holy people, repeatedly declared, has reference to the nation, called to be "an holy Nation" (Ex. 19:6). The holiness of a nation rests in its law-structure. Where God's laws are enforced, and true faith protected, there a holy nation exists. The cutting edge of the law is the principle of national holiness. Without this foundation of law, no holiness can exist. By means of God's law, a nation devotes itself to life; without God's law, it is devoted to death, "cut off" from the only true principle of life.

At every point, thus, holiness brings us face to face with very material laws. Every Biblical law is concerned with holiness. All law creates a line of division, a separation between the law-abiding and the law-breaking peoples. Without law, there can be no separation. The modern antipathy to and open hatred of law is also a hatred of holiness. It is an attempt to destroy the line of separation between good and evil by abolition of law. But, because God is holy, law is written into the structure of all being; law cannot be abolished: it can only be enforced, if not by man, then surely by God.

6. Law as Warfare

The Biblical laws deal at length with the details of worship as it was ordained for Israel. With these details we are not concerned, except where they involve and set forth concepts and principles of law.

Turning to such instances, *first,* the ephod and the breastplate of the high priest is of significance. In Exodus 28:6-14, the ephod, a priestly garment, is described, and in Exodus 28:15-30, the breastplate. Both articles had a common characteristic: the ephod had two stones on the shoulder on which the names of the tribes of Israel were engraved, to be borne before the Lord by the high priest (Ex. 28:12), and the breastplate had twelve stones, one for each tribe (Ex. 28:21, 29). Both religiously and legally, these stones are important. As the high priest approached the altar and the throne, he represented the covenant people before God. His prayers thus were basically for the people of God. Legally, the stones, representing the covenant people, indicated that God's government is essentially for God's purposes, which plainly includes God's covenant people. At God's orders, the high priest's primary function, God-ward, is to intercede for the covenant people. He does not pray promiscuously: his essential calling is to pray for God's own. The throne functions to protect the people of the throne. The priority of God's people, as set forth in the ephod and breastplate, is of God's ordering.

There is thus both a partiality and an impartiality to God's law. In a general sense, God's law functions impartially to cause the sun to shine on the good and evil alike, and the rain to fall on the just and the unjust (Matt. 5:45). Moreover, with respect to the nation, the equal protection and government of the law applied to all, to the "home-born" and the "stranger" or alien (Ex. 12:49; Lev. 24:22; Num. 9:14; 15:15, 16, 29). The principle of "one law" for all is basic to Biblical law.

On the other hand, there is a definite *partiality* to the Biblical law. In instances too numerous to cite, God "intervenes" in history to over-throw the enemies of His covenant people; the weather is used; plague is used, and a variety of means, from the plagues against Egypt on. Moreover, the law as given to Israel is partial in that it protects an order, God's law-order, and the people of that order. Idolatry is forbidden; violations of the law-order are punished, and, at every point, God's law is the protection of God's order and the people of God's law-order. The modern concept of total toleration is not a valid legal principle but an advocacy of anarchism. Shall all religions be tolerated? But, as we have seen, every religion is a concept of law-order. Total toleration means total permissiveness for every kind of practice: idolatry, adultery, cannibalism, human sacrifice, perversion, and all things else. Such total toleration is neither possible nor desirable. The stones of the ephod and breastplate set forth the principle of partiality. For men, by prayer and by law, to move in terms of this partiality is neither evil nor selfish, but simply godly. To pray for others is certainly godly, but to be un-mindful of all of our household and our own needs is not godly; it makes a man worse than an unbeliever or infidel (I Tim. 5:8). And for a law-order to forsake its self-protection is both wicked and suicidal. *To tolerate subversion is itself a subversive activity.*

A *second* principle appears in another case law, Deuteronomy 23:18, "Thou shalt not bring the hire of a whore, or the price of a dog, into the house of the LORD thy God for any vow: for even both these are abomi-nation unto the LORD thy God"; the previous verse, 23:17, states, "There shall be no whore of the daughters of Israel, nor sodomite of the sons of Israel" (cf. Lev. 19:29). The word "whore" in Deuter-onomy 23:17 is given in the marginal reading as "sodomitess"; the prohibition of prostitution was previously made in Leviticus 19:29. The reference here is to Lesbians, apparently. The law against homosexuality appears in Leviticus 18:22 and 20:13. The reference in Deuteronomy 23:17, 18 is to sacred prostitution as a part of fertility cult worship. This practice appeared later in the nation (I Kings 14:24; 15:12; II Kings 23:7; Amos 2:7; it is used to describe Israel's apostasy in Jer. 3:2, 6; 8:9, 13). It is of note that the Bible uses a term of contempt, "dog," for the male homosexual. The point, however, of the law is this: the very religious impulse of the whore and the homosexual are especially contemptible in the sight of God; their wages can never be an acceptable gift to God. It is not sinners who are barred from giving, but rather it is the profits of sin which cannot be accepted. The point is a significant one. We are accustomed to thinking ecclesiastically of such gifts. But the "vow" sets forth a case, a religious case law. The terms of a vow have an especial sanctity. But when the vow and its pledge represent an *alien* law order, then that pledge is not admissible and is an "abomination." The person making the vow has no place before the law, no standing before the throne. The whore and the sodomite who brought their pledges were not simply sinners before the law, but, more than that, outlaws, outside the law. There is a marked difference between a *sinner before the law and an enemy of the law*. *No* tax or offering from an enemy of the law was thus acceptable. The sinner was *commanded* to bring an offering; the outlaw was *forbidden* to offer it. Because there was "one law" for all, the outlaw was entitled to justice under that law, as witness the appeal to Solomon's court of the two harlots (I Kings 3:16-28). The outlaw received justice, but *not* citizenship. To tax crime is to give it legitimacy and a legal standing before the law as a financial supporter of the law: the next step then is equal rights to the protection of the law, which means immunity from prosecution. Under the Biblical influence, most countries have ruled that criminals lose their citizenship, and condemned men have no legal existence. The pressure today is against such legislation, and taxation is applied to all, with increasing representation for all. Deuteronomy 23:17, 18 is the legal foundation for an exclusive citizenship in terms of the law-order. It is significant that the common term for prostitute in Scripture is a "stranger" or "strange woman," that is, a foreigner. Not only was prostitution in essence a foreign practice to the covenant people, but an Israelite girl was "profane" (Lev. 19:19), i.e., outside the temple, outside the principle of citizenship, a foreigner, if she became a prostitute. The homosexual was also outside the law; at least the prostitute, while called a "strange woman" (Prov. 2:16; 5:3, 20; 6:24; 7:5; 23:27, 33; 27:13) was still included in mankind by the term, but the homosexual, as a "dog" (Deut. 23:18; Rev. 22:15), is regarded as outside the race of man; he is, as the Greek text of Romans 1:27 makes clear, the *burned out* end product of rebellion.

There are, broadly, three possible ways for the law to regard the out-law and the dissenter, and the difference between the two is a great one, although both are against the law. First, there is the attitude that can be summarized as that of the "medieval" church, that heretics have forfeited their rights before the law. Thus, John Hus was given safe conduct to the Council of Constance, and then the safe conduct was revoked on the ground that he was a heretic. Sigismund was pressured to break his pledge of safe conduct, on the grounds of his own safety, "for he who protected heretics was himself a heretic."[1] Such an attitude made difficult any protection from the established order by means of the law. The law supposedly guarded society against heresy, but in actuality the establishment, itself free to practice heresy, could destroy any critic simply by accusation. Suspicion destroyed rights; a person was guilty by implication before proven guilty.

A second possible way for the law to regard the outlaw and the dis-senter is to be found in the modern liberal state, as in the United States. Attempts have been made directly to strike at the law denying citizen-ship to guilty criminals. Indirectly, their rights have been more than restored. The U. S. Supreme Court has virtually destroyed laws with respect to libel and slander; the "criminal" thus is favored over his victims. Self-confessed rapists and murderers have been freed on imaginary technicalities, in clear partiality to the criminal as against the victim. Gardner has observed, of the courts and "law" today, "The rights of the individual are being protected, *provided the individual has committed a crime.*"[2] Although the laws of many states admit and in some cases *require* capital punishment for certain offenses, the U. S. Supreme Court declared that "The death sentence cannot be imposed by a jury from which persons with conscientious or religious scruples against capital punishment were automatically excluded."[3] In other words, the court demanded that people who *deny* the validity of the law be asked to "enforce" the law! This is, of course, a clear-cut attack on capital punishment and in effect an abolition of it. No question was raised by the court as to the possible innocence of the condemned man; his guilt was implicitly admitted. But the court again ruled in favor of the superior rights of the criminal and the dissenter as against the law and the law-abiding.

A third possible way for the law to regard the outlaw and the dissenter is the Biblical way: "One law shall be to him that is homeborn, and unto

1. Paul Roubicek and Joseph Kalmer, *Warrior of God, the Life and Death of John Hus* (London: Nicholson and Watson, 1947), p. 172.
2. Earle Stanley Gardner, "Crime in the Streets," *This Week Magazine* (August 18, 1968), p. 4.
3. "Top Court Hits at 'Stacking of Juries,'" in Los Angeles *Herald Examiner* (Monday, June 3, 1968), p. 1.

the stranger that sojourneth among you" (Ex. 12:49). The law must afford equal justice to all. A person is innocent until proven guilty, and two witnesses are required (Num. 35:30; Deut. 17:6). The two prostitutes in Solomon's day were able to appeal their case all the way to Solomon (I Kings 3:16-28). But their right of appeal did not make them citizens: whether the two women were of Israelite blood or of foreign extraction, they were by law foreigners, with no rights of citizenship. Their gifts were excluded from the temple. Since the Holy of Holies was the throne-room of God, the prohibition of any vow to the throne was a denial of citizenship; it was an exemption from taxation, since the person had no legal existence as a member of the state.

In analyzing Leviticus 4, we saw that levels or grades of sacrifice stressed the principle that, *the greater the responsibility, the greater the culpability, the greater the sin.* It is also apparent now that *criminal irresponsibility means a loss of rights.* A man who is not within the law is an outlaw; the rights conferred by the law-order belong to those who live within the law-order. The right have the rights. There is thus a signal difference between due process of law and the privileges of citizenship.

We have seen, thus far, *first*, with respect to the breastplate and ephod, the partiality as well as the impartiality of the law; *second*, we have seen, moreover, that criminal irresponsibility means a loss of rights. Now, *third*, we come to the crux of the issue, namely, that *law is a form of warfare, and, indeed, the major and continuing form of warfare.* The second commandment prohibits graven images in worship; it *requires* the destruction of all such forms of worship: "Thou shalt not bow down to their gods, nor serve them, nor do after their works: but thou shalt utterly overthrow them, and quite break down their images" (Ex. 23: 24). In Deuteronomy 12:1-14, the contrast is drawn clearly: obedience means on the one hand destroying all places of idolatrous worship, and, on the other hand, bringing offerings to God in the prescribed manner and to the prescribed place. The commandment to destroy idolatrous places and images is restated in Deuteronomy 7:5; 16:21, 22, Numbers 33:52; and Exodus 34:13, 14. But, in certain instances, the destruction of graven images required also the destruction of the people of the images (Deut. 7:1-5); not only are covenants with the Canaanites forbidden, but inter-marriage also. The Canaanites were "devoted" or set apart, "sanctified" unto death by God's order. This is an important point and needs careful attention. The law specifically forbad reprisals against Egyptians or any other foreigner; instead of vengeance, they should remember their oppression in Egypt as a means of greater dedication to justice for all under God's law (Lev. 19:33-37). Having suffered injustice at foreign hands, they should themselves be careful to avoid being like the Egyptians, themselves the instruments of injustice. Egypt sought to exterminate all Hebrews (Ex. 1:15-22), but Israel was required to render justice to all Egyptians in terms of their individual obedience or disobedience to the law. But all Canaanites were devoted to death. The criterion was not enmity to Israel but the law of God. Egypt was an enemy of God as was Canaan, but the iniquity of the Canaanites was "full" or total in God's sight (Gen. 15:16; Lev. 18: 24-28, etc.). Prostitution and homosexuality had become religious practices to the point where the people were entrenched in depravity and proud of it. Their iniquity was "full" or total. Accordingly, God sentenced them to death and made Israel the executioner. Now this fact has been repeatedly cited as "evidence" that the Bible represents an immoral God and an ugly morality; such a charge represents hatred, not intelligence. If individuals and nations have repeatedly disappeared abruptly from history, this clearly indicates some kind of "judgment" by history, or dialectical materialism, or evolution, or whatever other gods one holds to, on these persons and nations. Such judgments are repeatedly cited and concurred in by historians. The point of offense with respect to the Canaanite judgment is the *criterion* of judgment used by God. Had God declared the Canaanites to be cruel, capitalistic oppressors, and hence under judgment, His verdict would gain hearty praise from many intellectuals. But God is God, not the intellectuals, and, as a result, God's criterion prevails, not man's. The Canaanites as a whole were deserving of death; God's patience allowed them a few centuries from Abraham's day to Joshua's and then His judgment was ordered executed. The failure of Israel to execute it fully became finally their own judgment.

The sentence of death against Canaan is simply a realistic fact of warfare. Warfare is sometimes waged with limited objectives; at other times, war is unto death, because the nature of the struggle requires it. When, in earlier centuries, warfare did not involve deeply rooted principles but merely local issues, warfare was limited in scope and in deadliness. When revolution became a fact on the Western scene with the French Revolution, total warfare became a reality, war unto death in terms of mutually exclusive principles. Where warfare against heaven is waged, the consequences are death, not the death of God but the death of the contending peoples.

In brief, every law-order is a state of war against the enemies of that order, *and all law is a form of warfare.* Every law declares that certain offenders are enemies of the law-order and must be arrested. For limited offenses, there are limited penalties; for capital offences, capital punishment. *Law is a state of war*; it is the organization of the powers of civil government to bring the enemies of the law-order to justice.

The officers of the law are properly armed; in a godly state, they should
be armed by the justice of the law as well as weapons of warfare,
in order to defend society against its enemies.

Friends of the law will therefore seek at all times to improve,
strengthen, and confirm a godly law-order. Enemies of the law will
accordingly be in continuing warfare against the law. The enmity to the
law will be direct and indirect, it will resort to internal subversion
through the legislatures and the courts, and to external assault by disobedience, contempt, and intellectual attack. Every law-order will be
subject to attacks, because, short of heaven, every law-order will have
its enemies within. The critical question, therefore, is not, "Will the law
be attacked?" but rather, "Will the law-order resist attack?" Is there
health in the body politic to resist the disease? When Israel was commanded to destroy the Canaanites (Deut. 7:1-11), it was also told that
obedience would result in health: fertility for man and beast, and immunity from the evil diseases of Egypt (7:12-26). Note the juxtaposi-
tion of the promise and the command:

> Wherefore it shall come to pass, if ye hearken to these judgments,
> and keep, and do them, that the LORD thy God shall keep unto thee
> the covenant and the mercy which he sware unto thy fathers;
> And he will love thee, and bless thee, and multiply thee; he will also
> bless the fruit of thy womb, and the fruit of thy land, thy corn, and
> thy wine, and thine oil, the increase of thy kine, and the flocks of
> of thy sheep, in the land which he sware unto thy fathers to give thee.
> Thou shalt be blessed above all people; there shall not be male or
> female barren among you, or among your cattle.
> And the LORD will take away from thee all sickness, and will put
> none of the evil disease of Egypt, which thou knowest, upon thee;
> but will lay them upon all that hate thee.
> And thou shalt consume all the people which the LORD thy God
> shall deliver thee; thine eye shall have no pity upon them: neither
> shalt thou serve their gods; for that will be a snare unto thee
> (Deut. 7:12-16).

Clearly, a predicate and condition of social health is the destruction of
social evil.

Since law is a form of warfare, it follows that there is a required
continual barrier to peace with evil. Man cannot seek co-existence with
evil without thereby declaring war against God. The law declares,
speaking of Ammorites and Moabites, apparently in this case in their
continued life in terms of their law-culture, "Thou shalt not seek their
peace nor their prosperity all thy days forever" (Deut. 23:6, RV). *A
law-order cannot escape warfare:* if it makes peace in one area, it
thereby declares war against another. A law-system is a form of warfare.
The *fact* of warfare remains constant: the *object* of warfare can change.
Marxist states claim to be for "world peace," but this is only in terms of

total conquest *and* total warfare against God and against all men. *The more total the peace desired, the more total the warfare required.* The new creation of Jesus Christ is the end result of His total warfare against a fallen world; it requires the permanent suppression of evil in hell. The new creation demanded by the various forms of socialism requires the permanent suppression of the God of Scripture and of His covenant people. There can be peace *in* heaven, but *no* peace *between* heaven and hell. A law-order can have peace only by denying the possibility of peace with evil. The Irish Protestant jurist, John Philpot Curran (1750-1817), said, in 1790, in a speech on "The Right of Election," "It is the common fate of the indolent to see their rights become a prey to the active. The condition upon which God hath given liberty to man is eternal vigilance; which condition, if he break, servitude is at once the consequence of his crime and the punishment of his guilt."

Those who seek peace with evil are seeking not the peace they profess but slavery, and the surest peace of all is death and the tomb.

7.　Law and Equality

Death is the end of the conflict, and a society in search of a false peace is in search of death. An anthropologist has written:

> Conflict is useful. In fact, society is impossible without conflict. But society is worse than impossible without control of conflict. The analogy to sex is relevant again: society is impossible without *regulated* sexuality: the degree of regulation differs among societies. But total repression leads to extinction; total lack of repression also leads to extinction. Total repression of conflict leads to anarchy just as surely as does total conflict.

> We Westerners are afraid of conflict today because we no longer understand it. We see conflict in terms of divorce, rioting, war. And we reject them out of hand. And, when they happen, we have no "substitute institutions" to do the job that should have been done by the institution that failed. In the process—and to our cost—we do not allow ourselves to see that marriage, civil rights, and national states are all institutions built on conflict and its sensible, purposeful control.

> . . . There are basically two forms of conflict resolution: administered rules and fighting. Law and war. Too much of either destroys what it is meant to protect or aggrandize.[1]

Bohannan's position is humanistic and relativistic. As a result, the conflict in a society of his character will tend to anarchy. With every man a law unto himself, with no absolute other than man's will, total con-

---

1. Paul Bohannan, "Introduction" to Paul Bohannan, ed., *Law and Warfare, Studies in the Anthropology of Conflict* (Garden City, N. Y.: The Natural History Press, 1967), pp. xii-xiii.

flict and total anarchy will be the only alternative to a totalitarian regime.

The problem of conflict cannot be resolved in any just and orderly manner in a relativistic society. Since every perspective, religion, and philosophy is made legitimate, and all people are made citizens, in effect every possible kind of law, and every possible culture, is admitted to legality. Either a repressive and totalitarian state then suppresses all, or all prevail and anarchy reigns.

Individualism and collectivism are both products of liberalism. Ellul has observed:

> It is believed that an individualist society, in which the individual is thought to have a higher value than the group, tends to destroy groups that limit the individual's range of action, whereas a mass society negates the individual and reduces him to a cipher. But this contradiction is purely theoretical and a delusion. In actual fact, an individualist society *must* be a mass society, because the first move toward liberation of the individual is to break up the small groups that are an organic fact of the entire society. In this process the individual frees himself completely from family, village, parish, or brotherhood bonds—only to find himself directly vis-a-vis the entire society. When individuals are not held together by local structures, the only form in which they can live together is in an unstructured mass society. Similarly, a mass society can only be based on individuals—that is, on men in their isolation, whose identities are determined by their relationships with one another. Precisely because the individual claims to be equal to all other individuals, he becomes an abstraction and is in effect reduced to a cipher.
>
> As soon as local organic groupings are reformed, society tends to cease being individualistic, and thereby to lose its mass character as well. What then occurs is the formation of organic groups of *elite* in what remains a mass society, but which rests on the framework of strongly structured and centralized political parties, unions, and so on. These organizations reach only an active minority, and the members of this minority cease to be individualistic by being integrated into such organic associations. From this perspective, individualist society and mass society are two corollary aspects of the same reality. This corresponds to what we have said about the mass media: to perform a propagandistic function they must capture the individual and the mass at the same time.[2]

Liberalism dissolves the religious and familial ties of a society and leaves only the rootless individual and the humanistic state. Society then veers between collectivism and individualism.

A social order which denies that God is the source of law must of

---

2. Jacques Ellul, *Propaganda, The Formation of Men's Attitudes* (New York: Knopf, 1965), p. 90.

necessity seek its principle of law from within history or from man. The conflict of law then is no longer between God's law and man's sin, but it is now the law of some men's ordering, which now makes sinners of all other men who differ. The law also shows then an ambivalence between an aristocracy suppressing the people, and a democracy seeking to suppress the aristocracy. Gray's comment on the purpose of civil government shows the problem clearly:

> That order is usually regarded as the prime object of governments will not be denied. The means of enforcing order differ in different communities; and it is reasonably plain, *other things being equal,* that the best government for *enforcing* order is the government which is able, without check of any sort, to impose its restraints upon the individual—that is, a despotic government.
>
> Why then, if order is the first object, and a despotic government is the best means of enforcing order, are not all governments despotic?
>
> Because "all men are born equal," because every man born on the earth has the same right to use the earth, as every other man. Thus it is perceived that this order, which is the object of government, is not the ultimate end of government, but is merely a means whereby the equality to which men are born may be enjoyed. If this be true the ultimate principle upon which governments depend is equality, and the law of unity which regulates the operation and the organization of governments is the law of equality.[3]

Gray admitted that "Equality is a mathematical term,"[4] and one would expect that he would have seen the impossibility of applying a mathematical abstraction to man. On the contrary, he favored its application to taxation, the subject of his study. He admitted that the principle of equality was an American development of the past 50 years, i.e., which would be since the Civil War, since Gray published in 1906.[5] Gray's concept of equality was close to the Marxist principle of equality, since he felt that

> It is plain that equality does not necessarily consist in mere equality of contribution. For every man, rich or poor, to pay the same, would be the greatest inequality. Whether it consists in proportionate contribution according to property, is a question which has been much discussed. In the common forms of property taxation, this is the method in which the courts have usually found that sufficient equality inheres.
>
> A great economist has said that equality in taxation consists of *equality of sacrifice.*
>
> The courts have usually measured equality in taxation by reference

---

3. James M. Gray, *Limitations of the Taxing Power including Limitations Upon Public Indebtedness* (San Francisco: Bancroft-Whitney, 1906), para. 2, p. 2.
4. *Ibid.,* 5, p. 4.
5. *Ibid.,* 7, p. 5.

to the amount of benefits received, rather than by considering the sacrifice of the taxpayer.

The economists of the present day seem to prefer the idea of equality of sacrifice. A glance at the two chief economic theories of taxation shows the distinction between the equality based on proportionate contribution and equality of sacrifice.[6]

Gray denied the "benefits" theory of taxation; if those who benefited the most paid the most taxes, then the poor and weak would pay the most, and the rich and strong the least.[7] From Gray, it is clear why the income tax amendment came into being; it was "necessary" in terms of existing presuppositions.

But the consequence of Gray's theory is that the people are levelled, stripped of power, to create a state which is not "equal" to the people but far superior and able to crush them:

> The power of the state, acting through its governmental agencies, to tax its citizens, is absolute and unlimited as to persons and property. Every person within the jurisdiction of the state, whether citizen or not, is subject to this power, every form of property, tangible or intangible, stationary or transitory, every privilege, right, or income which exists within the jurisdiction, may be reached and taken for the support of the state.
>
> This doctrine is involved in the general theory of the state. The state exists for the purposes of law, order, and justice; the institution of property, the preservation and security of life, liberty, and property depend upon the existence of the state. Inasmuch as all private ownership of property is postulated on the existence of the state, the state may properly exhaust all the resources of private property in the support and preservation of that existence; inasmuch as all privileges and liberties derive their value from the protection of the state, the state may take any share of the value of those privileges and franchises for its support, even to the extent of the whole value.[8]

The state thus becomes the total institution, comprehending the life and property of man. The state can confiscate all things to insure its own existence, because the state has implicitly become the basic value.

In the United States, the property tax developed in New England in the 17th century, but it was limited at first in its extent. The South resisted it for a time. The transition to a humanistic concept of the state was both gradual and steady. In the 20th century, taxation began to serve as an instrument of social and economic change. Thus, taxation no longer serves simply to support civil government but also to reorganize society in terms of levelling and equalitarian concepts.

In this newer concept of taxation, the new established religion of the United States, humanism, came to focus. God being denied as the source

---

6. *Ibid.*, 20a, p. 11 f.
7. *Ibid.*, 21-23, p. 12 f.
8. *Ibid.*, 44, p. 29 f.

of law, law has moved steadily to enforce a totalitarian and equalitarian principle.

In Biblical law, neither equalitarianism nor an oligarchy have any standing. God as the source of law established the covenant as the principle of citizenship. Only those within the covenant are citizens. The covenant is restrictive in terms of God's law; it is also restrictive in terms of a bar against membership, which appears specifically, naming certain kinds and groups of persons. This aspect of the law is usually overlooked, because it is embarrassing to modern man. It needs therefore especial attention. In Deuteronomy 23:1-8, eunuchs are barred from citizenship; bastards are banned through the tenth generation. Ammonites and Moabites are either banned through the tenth generation, or they are totally excluded, depending on the reading of the text. Edomites and Egyptians were eligible for citizenship "in their third generation"; the implication is that they are eligible after three generations of faith, after demonstrating for three generations that they believed in the covenant God and abided by His law. The throne being the ark in the tabernacle, and the tabernacle being also the central place of atonement, membership in the nation-civil and in the nation-ecclesiastical were one and the same. Citizenship rested on faith. Apostasy was treason. The believing alien had some kind of access to the sanctuary (II Chron. 6:32-33), at least for prayer, but this act did not give him citizenship. The alien—Egyptian, Babylonian, Ethiopian, Philistine, Phoenician, and any others—could be citizens of the true or heavenly Zion, the city of God (Ps. 87), but the local Zion, Israel, was not to admit the banned groups except on God's terms. Entrance was possible by marriage to a male Israelite (Ruth 4:6), but not directly; a woman assumed the status of her husband. Now in all this one thing is certainly absolutely clear: there is *no* equalitarianism here. There is an obvious discrimination and distinction made which no straining can eliminate. At the same time, the one-law requirement of Exodus 12:49 made clear the absolute requirement of justice for all without respect of persons.

Thus, it would appear from the evidence of the law that, *first*, a restrictive membership or citizenship was a part of the practice of Israel by law. There is evidence of a like standard in the New Testament church: instead of being forced into rigid uniformity, Gentiles and Jews were free to establish their separate congregations and maintain their distinctive character.[9] Moreover, Acts 15, the Council of Jerusalem, makes clear that the differences in cultural heritage and stages of moral and spiritual growth made possible major conflicts in

---

9. See Adolf Schlatter, *The Church in the New Testament Period* (London: SPCK, 1961).

case of uniform membership. As a result, separate congregations were authorized. On the other hand, Jews were not barred from Gentile congregations, so that, while restrictive groups were valid, integrated groups were not invalid.

Second, the predominant fact in Israel was one-law for all, irrespective of faith or national origin, that is, the absolute requirement of justice for all without respect of persons. Similarly, in the church of the New Testament, there was "one Lord, one faith, one baptism" (Eph. 4:5) in the true church and the true Kingdom of God. The limited local membership was valid, but the universal sway of the kingdom and the common citizenship of all believers are the basic and governing fact. The reality of local distinctions cannot, however, be obliterated by the ultimate and essential unity which is not to be confused with uniformity. Equalitarianism is a modern politico-religious concept: it did not exist in the Biblical world, and it cannot with any honesty be forced onto Biblical law. Equalitarianism is a product of humanism, of the worship of a new idol, man, and a new image carved out of man's imagination. As a standard in religion, politics, and economics it is a product of the modern era; to read it into the Biblical faith is to do violence to Scripture and to be guilty of dishonesty.

The excluded persons of Deuteronomy 23:1-8 are of interest: bastards were excluded to the tenth generation, eunuchs were excluded, whether eunuchs by an accident or by act of man. Because eunuchs are without posterity, they have no interest or stake in the future, and hence no citizenship. Persons of a lower moral culture, such as Ammonites and Moabites, were also excluded. The purpose of exclusion was the preservation of the covenant in the hands of responsible leadership. The limitations on Edomite and Egyptian membership served the same function.

Eunuchs were commonly used in antiquity for civil office, and, in Byzantium, were the civil service; precisely because they had no stake in the future, eunuchs were entrusted with positions calling for an exclusively present loyalty. The eunuch, as a kind of existentialist mentality, was severed from past and future and bound to the present; hence he was preferred over family men.

In colonial New England, the covenantal concept of church and state was applied. Everyone went to church, but only a limited number had voting rights in the church and therefore in the state, because there was a coincidence of church membership and citizenship. The others were no less believers, but the belief was that *only the responsible must be given responsibility.* One faith, one law, and one standard of justice did not mean democracy. The heresy of democracy has since then worked havoc in church and state, and it has worked towards reducing society to anarchy.

III

THE THIRD COMMANDMENT

1. The Negativism of the Law

The third commandment declares, "Thou shalt not take the name of the LORD thy God in vain; for the LORD will not hold him guiltless that taketh his name in vain" (Ex. 20:7; Deut. 5:11).

Before beginning an analysis of this commandment, it is important to call attention to an aspect of the law which makes it especially offensive to the modern mind: its *negativism*. Of the ten commandments, eight are stated in negative terms. The other two, "Remember the sabbath day to keep it holy," and "Honor thy father and thy mother," are undergirded by a number of subordinate laws which are all negative in character. The sabbath commandment is negative: "thou shalt not do any work" (Ex. 20:10; Deut. 5:14), so that, in their full form, nine of the ten commandments are negative.

To the modern mind, laws of negation seem oppressive and tyrannical, and the longing is for positive officials of the law to replace the police. Thus the Black Panther leader, and Peace and Freedom presidential candidate, Eldridge Cleaver, declared in 1968, that, "if elected, he would do away with the poverty program, and substitute 'public safety officials' for police."[1] Public safety officials produced a reign of terror in the French Revolution, and not without reason, because a positive law can only lead to tyranny and totalitarianism.

The best statement of a positive concept of law was the Roman legal principle: the health of the people is the highest law. This principle has so thoroughly passed into the world's legal systems that to question it is to challenge a fundamental premise of the state. The Roman principle is basic to the American development, in that the courts have interpreted the "general welfare" clause of the U. S. Constitution in terms radically alien to the original intent in 1787.

A *negative* concept of law confers a double benefit: first, it is practical, in that a negative concept of law deals realistically with a particular evil. It states, "Thou shalt not steal," or, "Thou shalt not bear false witness." A negative statement thus deals with a particular evil directly and plainly: it prohibits it, makes it illegal. The law thus has a *modest* function; *the*

---

1. Van Nuys, California, *The News*, "Channel 28 to Interview Black Panther Leader"(Sunday, August 11, 1968), p. 10-A.

law is limited, and therefore the state is limited. The state, as the enforcing agency, is limited to dealing with evil, not controlling all men.

Second, and directly related to this first point, *a negative concept of law insures liberty*: except for the prohibited areas, all of man's life is beyond the law, and the law is of necessity indifferent to it. If the commandment says, "Thou shalt not steal," it means that the law can only govern theft: it cannot govern or control honestly acquired property. When the law prohibits blasphemy and false witness, it guarantees that all other forms of speech have their liberty. *The negativity of the law is the preservation of the positive life and freedom of man.*

But, if the law is positive in its function, and if the health of the people is the highest law, then the state has total jurisdiction to compel the total health of the people. The immediate consequence is a double penalty on the people. *First*, an omnicompetent state is posited, and a totalitarian state results. Everything becomes a part of the state's jurisdiction, because everything can potentially contribute to the health or the destruction of the people. *Because the law is unlimited, the state is unlimited. It becomes the business of the state, not to control evil, but to control all men.* Basic to every totalitarian regime is a positive concept of the function of law.

This means, *second*, that no area of liberty can exist for man; there is then no area of things indifferent, of actions, concerns, and thoughts which the state cannot govern in the name of public health. To credit the state with ability to minister to the general welfare, to govern for the general and total health of the people, is to assume an omnicompetent state, and to assume an all-competent state is to assume an incompetent people. The state then becomes a nursemaid to a citizenry whose basic character is childish and immature. The theory that law must have a positive function assumes thus that the people are essentially childish.

At this point some might comment that Biblical faith, with its doctrines of the fall and of total depravity, holds to a similar view of man. Nothing could be farther from the truth. Evolutionary faith, by positing long ages of development for man, holds on the one hand that man's being is still governed by ancient, primitive drives and impulses, and, on the other, that man today is still a child in relationship to future evolutionary growth.

Biblical faith, on the contrary, holds to the original creation of a mature and good man. The human problem is not a primitive nature, not childishness, but irresponsibility, a rebellion against maturity and responsibility. Man is a rebel, and his course is not childishness but sin, not ignorance but wilful folly.

Essentially, a fool cannot be protected, because a fool's problem is not other people but himself. The book of Proverbs gives considerable attention to the fool. As Kidner has summarized the teaching of Proverbs, it declares, concerning the fool, that

> The root of his trouble is spiritual, not mental. He *likes* his folly, going back to it "like a dog that returns to his vomit" (26:11); he has no reverence for truth, preferring comfortable illusions (see 14: 8, and note). At bottom, what he is rejecting is the fear of the Lord (1:29): it is this that constitutes him a fool, and this that makes his complacency tragic; for "the careless ease of fools shall destroy them" (1:32).
>
> *In society* the fool is, in a word, a menace. At best, he wastes your time: "you will not find a word of sense in him" (14:7, Moffatt); and he may be a more serious nuisance. If he has an idea in his head, nothing will stop him: "let a bear robbed of her whelps meet a man, rather than a fool in his folly" (17:12)—whether that folly is some prank that is beyond a joke (10:23), or some quarrel he must pick (18:6) and run to death (29:11). Give him a wide berth, for "the companion of fools shall smart for it" (13:20), and if you want to send him away, don't send him with a message (26:6).[2]

Numerous incidents could be cited to illustrate how prone a fool is to folly: rescue him from one plight, and he falls into another. A sick man, finally persuaded to leave a quack who was treating him, went then instead only to a worse one. And this should surprise no one; a fool is by nature folly prone.

To examine an area where the law has functioned positively, most people would believe with notable success, let us review the situation in medicine. The state control of the medical profession was largely promoted and advanced by Rockefeller funds. Medical schools were brought under state control, as well as the medical profession. Unapproved medical practices were outlawed, and, we are told, the result has been remarkable progress.

But has the progress been due to state control or the work of the medical profession? Has not the profession itself been responsible for its own progress? And, obviously, there are as many quacks now as then, and perhaps more. The federal government estimates that more than two billion dollars was spent in 1966 on what some authorities would term medical quackery, although the term, significantly, covers everything from fraud to unofficial or unapproved practices.[3] Moreover, the danger now is that any medical researcher whose work fails to gain

---

2. Derek Kidner, *Proverbs, An Introduction and Commentary* (Chicago: Inter-Varsity Press, 1964), p. 40.

3. See James Harvey Young, *The Medical Messiah, A Social History of Health Quackery in Twentieth-Century America* (Princeton, N. J.: Princeton University Press, 1967).

approval not only is classified a quack but can be in serious legal trouble. Even more, the standard, accepted medical profession, together with the drug companies, has been under very serious attack from Congress for serious malpractice. A variety of "wonder drugs" used experimentally and released with inadequate testing have had serious consequences.[4] Medical journals have also spoken of serious over-dosing in hospitals.[5]

Granted the responsibility of doctors in prescribing unwisely, the fact remains that many patients, well aware of the hazards in new drugs (and old drugs as well), demand to be dosed. And, given all possible legal safeguards, how can perfection be expected either of doctors or patients? Some doctors and some patients will always be fools.

But the real issue lies deeper. Even as the state controls over medicine have increased, so, at the same time, charges of medical malpractice have increased, and doctors today are in constant danger of lawsuits. American medical skill and surgery have never been better, nor the legal complaints greater. This points up a curious fact: the state has taken over the basic policing power from the medical profession, but the state, instead of assuming responsibility, has increased the culpability of the doctors. A federal agency approves a drug, but the doctor pays the penalty if there are bad reactions.

When the law of the state assumes a positive function in protecting the health and general welfare of its people, it then does not assume the liability. The people are absolved of responsibility, but the medical profession (or business firms, property owners, and the like) assume *total liability*. The steps towards total liability are gradual, but they are inevitable with a welfare economy.

Historians often praise the medical practice of pagan antiquity, and they commonly credit it with far more merit than it had. At the same time, they blame Christianity for corrupting and halting medical progress. But the decline in ancient medicine began by their own admission in the third century B.C.[6] Entralgo has pointed out that, in fact, Christianity rescued medicine from sterile presuppositions.[7]

But, in ancient Egypt, Babylon, and elsewhere, the doctor was subject to total liability. If the patient lost his life, the doctor lost his life. Even

4. See Morton Mintz, *By Prescription Only*. Second edition, revised (Boston: Houghton Mifflin, 1967).

5. See "Medical Care Can Be Dangerous," in *Prevention* (August, 1968), p. 80 ff.

6. J. Beaujeu, "Medicine," in Rene Taton, ed., *History of Science: Ancient and Medieval Science, from the Beginnings to 1450* (New York: Basic Books, 1957, 1963), p. 365.

7. Pedro L. Entralgo, *Mind and Body, Psychosomatic Pathology: A Short History of the Evolution of Medical Thought* (New York: P. J. Kenedy and Sons, n.d.).

though the fault was not his, the doctor was totally liable. But, even when the doctor was at fault, what made the doctor totally liable? The patient, after all, had come voluntarily, and the doctor was not a god. Or should he be? The European pagan background, as well as other pagan practices, associated medicine with the gods. Ascetic practices were required of the doctor, so that the doctor was gradually converted into a monk. This pagan influence, combining with neoplatonism in the early centuries of the Christian era, led to an ascetic as doctor. Pickman noted, of Gaul,

> Evidently asceticism's popular appeal in those days was less on account of its psychological effect on the ascetic himself, than of its physical effect on those to whom he ministered. It was the chosen weapon of the humanitarian. That is why before long a physician who did not become a monk lost his practice.[8]

Only gradually, with the Christianization of the West, was this pagan concept of medicine abandoned, and, with it, the concept of liability which required the doctor to be a god or else suffer.

State controls over the medical profession have steadily restored the old concept of liability, and the doctors find themselves especially prone to lawsuits. It has become dangerous for a doctor to administer emergency roadside care in an accident because of this proneness to liability. The day may not be too far distant, if the present trend continues, when doctors may be tried for murder if their patient dies. There were hints of this in the Soviet Union in Stalin's closing days.

If the law assumes a positive function, it is because it is believed that the people are a negative factor, i.e., incompetent and child-like. Then, in such a situation, *responsible men are penalized with total liability.* If a criminal, who is by his criminality an incompetent, enters a man's home, he is protected in his rights by law, but the responsible and law-abiding citizen can face a murder charge if he kills the invader when his own life is not clearly threatened, and every recourse to escape is not exhausted. A hoodlum can trespass on a man's property, climbing a fence or breaking down a gate to do so, but if he then breaks his leg in an uncovered post-hole or trench, the home owner is liable for damages.

When the law loses its negativity, when the law assumes a positive function, it protects the criminals and the fools, and it penalizes responsible men.

Responsibility and liability are inescapable facts: if denied in one area, they are not abolished but rather simply transferred to another area. If alcoholics and criminals are not responsible people but merely

---

8. Edward Motley Pickman, *The Mind of Latin Christendom* (New York: Oxford University Press, 1937), I, 457.

sick, then someone is guilty of making them sick. Thus, Dr. Richard R. Korn, professor at the University of California School of Criminology at Berkeley, has said that prostitutes should not be arrested and imprisoned, because they are "alienated poor children looking for a better way of life."[9] If these prostitutes are simply "alienated poor children looking for a better way of life," then someone is responsible for their plight other than themselves, because their intentions were good ones. More than a few are ready to name the responsible party: *society*. But the prostitutes, their pimps, and the criminal underworld are all a part of our society in the general sense, and it is obvious that they are not being blamed. It is clear also that by guilty society the responsible and successful people are meant. Under communism, this means the total liability of the Christians and capitalists as guilty of all of society's ills. As totally liable, they must be liquidated.

Responsibility and liability cannot be avoided: if a Biblical doctrine of responsibility be denied, a pagan doctrine takes over. And if the Biblical negativism of the law is replaced with a law having a positive function, a revolution against Christianity and freedom has taken place. A negative concept of law is not only a safeguard to liberty but to life as well.

2. Swearing and Revolution

The third commandment once had central attention in church and society; today, its significance has waned greatly for modern man. Even in such a work as Rand's *Digest of the Divine Law*, there is no mention of this commandment other than a listing of it in the table of ten, and a brief citation later.[1] On the other hand, the champions of swearing are increasingly in evidence, as witness the work of an anthropologist, Ashley Montagu, in defense of swearing.

Montagu's informative study gives us a frank statement of the meaning of swearing:

> Swearing serves clearly definable social as well as personal purposes. A social purpose? But has not swearing always been socially condemned and proscribed? It has. And that is precisely the point. Because the early forms of swearing were often of a nature regarded as subversive of social and religious institutions, as when the names of the gods were profanely invoked, their use in such a manner was strictly forbidden.[2]

An important point is made here: false swearing is somehow linked with subversion. We shall return to this later.

---

9. "New Approach to S.F. Vice," Oakland, Calif., *Tribune* (Friday, August 16, 1968), p. 10.
1. Rand, *Digest*, pp. 51, 56.
2. Ashley Montagu, *The Anatomy of Swearing* (New York: Macmillan, 1967), p. 1.

Swearing is "not a universal phenomenon." It is not found among American Indians, Japanese, Malayans, and most Polynesians. The examples Montagu gives of its existence among other peoples, as the aborigines of Australia, represent not theistic swearing but swearing as filthy speech, and there is a marked difference between the two.[3]

Montagu has an interesting classification of the various forms of "swearing":

Swearing is the act of verbally expressing the feeling of aggressiveness that follows upon frustration in words possessing strong emotional associations.

Cursing, often used as a synonym for swearing, is a form of swearing distinguished by the fact that it invokes or calls down some evil upon its object.

Profanity, often used as a synonym for swearing and cursing, is the form of swearing in which the names or attributes of the figures or objects of religion are uttered.

Blasphemy, often identified with cursing and profanity, is the act of vilifying or ridiculing the figures or objects of religious veneration. . . .

Obscenity, a form of swearing that makes use of indecent words and phrases.

Vulgarity, a form of swearing that makes use of crude words, such as *bloody*.

Euphemistic swearing, a form of swearing in which mild, vague, or corrupted expressions are substituted for the original strong ones.[4]

This classification is, of course, non-Biblical in orientation. There is, *first* of all, a prohibition only of false swearing or false cursing. It is taking the name of the Lord *in vain*, or "profanely" (Berkeley Version) that is forbidden. Clearly, not all swearing or cursing is forbidden. *Second*, from the Biblical perspective, all false swearing or cursing is *profane*, and thus profanity is not a separate category. The word *profane* comes from the Latin *pro*, before, *fanum*, temple, i.e., before or outside the temple; profanity is thus all speech, action, and living which is outside God. Profanity thus includes filthy speech, false swearing and cursing, and also polite and courteous speech and action which is outside God and which does not recognize His sovereignty. *Third*, only one kind of deserved cursing cannot be permitted. In cursing, a man invokes the judgment of God upon an evil-doer. But, however evil one's parents may be, and however deserving of judgment, no man may curse his father or mother. In fact, "he that curseth (or revileth) his father or his mother, shall surely be put to death" (Ex. 21:17). *Honor* to parents is so fundamental to godly society that not even in extreme cases can the son or daughter curse either parent. Children must *obey*

---

3. *Ibid.*, pp. 10-18, 55 f.
4. *Ibid.*, p. 105.

their parents. Adults are simply required to *honor* them; they may, and sometimes must, disagree with them, but to *curse* them is to violate a fundamental principle of order and authority.

Fourth, blasphemy is more than taking the name of God profanely. It is defamatory, wicked, and rebellious language directed against God (Ps. 74:10-18; Isa. 52:5; Rev. 16:9, 11, 21). It was punishable by death (Lev. 24:16). Naboth was falsely accused of blasphemy (I Kings 21:10-13), as was Stephen (Acts 6:11), and Jesus Christ (Matt. 9:3; 26:65, 66; John 10:36). "Blasphemy against the Holy Ghost consisted in attributing the miracles of Christ, which were wrought by the Spirit of God, to Satanic power (Mat. xii. 22-32; Mark iii. 22-30)."[5]

Montagu points out that, according to the law, "In England, and in every one of the United States, it is still a legal offense to swear."[6] Such laws are rarely enforced now. In recent years, women, once not normally associated with profanity, have become increasingly addicted to it. During World War II, in one aircraft factory where many women were employed, a notice read, "No swearing. There may be gentlemen about."[7] On the other hand, Montagu points out, while in the slums of English towns extreme profanity and obscenity can be heard among women, it is "seldom, if ever, encountered in a civilized English village in which the taboos upon 'bad language' of any kind still remain Victorian in their rigor."[8] It is interesting to note that there is some hostility of late to profanity in the U.S.S.R.[9] Profanity does have associations with social disorientation and deterioration.

To analyze now a few basic facts with respect to swearing, it must be noted, *first*, that forbidden swearing is essentially and necessarily linked to *religion*. It is *profanity*, outside God and against God. It represents, where the name of God is involved, an illicit and hostile use of God's name, or a dishonest use thereof. Much of the primitive and modern swearing cited by Montagu is obscenity rather than profanity. Primitive swearing as well as modern invokes sexual and excremental words and subjects.[10] This is a significant fact. In order to appreciate its significance, let us review a few of the central facts. Godly oath-taking is a solemn and important religious act. Man aligns himself under God and in conformity to His righteousness to abide by his word even as God abides by His word. Godly swearing is a form of vow-taking. But ungodly swearing is a deliberate profanation of the purpose of the oath or vow; it is light use of it, a contemptuous use of it, to express contempt for God. But ungodly swearing cannot remain merely negative or hostile: it denies God as the ultimate, but it must posit another ultimate in

---

5. Davis, *Dictionary of the Bible*, p. 98.
6. Montagu, *Anatomy of Swearing*, p. 2.
7. *Ibid.*, p. 87.
8. *Ibid.*, p. 134.
9. *Ibid.*, p. 333 f.
10. *Ibid.*, p. 10 f.

God's place. Godly oaths seek their confirmation and strength from above; ungodly swearing looks below for its power. Its concept of the "below" is Manichaean to the core: it is material. Hence, ungodly swearing finds its power, its "below," in sex and in excrement. The association is significant. Even while protesting the "Puritanism" of Biblical morality, the ungodly reveal that to them sex and excrement are linked together as powers of the "underworld" of the unconscious, the primitive, and the vital.

The direction of profanity is thus progressively downward. After the middle of the 20th century, a new profane word gained popularity, apparently "an American Negro invention," whose blunt fact was mother-incest. The term actually gained some "honorific" senses.[11] Since then, other profane words having reference to homosexuality have become more popularly used. The references to other perversions have also increased. In brief, the direction of profanity is progressively downward. When the religion of the triune God is denied, the religion of revolution, the cults of chaos, take over. Vitality, power, and force are seen as coming from below; profane language seeks to be forceful, and the forceful is that which is below.

Second, as is already apparent, there is a religious progression in profanity: it moves from a defiance of God to an invocation of excrement and sex, and then perverted forms of sex. This religious progression is social as well as verbal. The profane society invokes, not God, but the world of the illicit, the obscene, and the perverted. What it invokes in word it also invokes in act. The downward trend of society is a quest for renewed energy, the shock of new force and vitality, and it is a perpetual quest for new profanations. White men will go to a colored prostitute for "a change of luck," i.e., to renew their vitality and power to prosper for a time. By "going down," they are recharged in order to "go up." Verbal profanity is an oral witness to a social profanity. As the verbal profanity delves downward, so does society in its actions.

This means, therefore, that, *third,* profanity is a barometer. It is indicative of revolution in process. It is an index to social deterioration and degeneration. The psychological significance of profanity is not lost on a revolutionary age; profanity is championed with evangelical fervor. It should surprise no one that a dictionary of slang and profanity was widely promoted as an invaluable reference work for high school libraries in the early 1960s.[12] True education involves, for a

---

11. *Ibid.,* p. 313 f. It is interesting to note that Stalin's favorite Russian oath also referred to mother-incest; Francis B. Randall, *Stalin's Russia* (New York: The Free Press, 1965), p. 37.

12. Harold Wentworth and Stuart Berg Flexner, *Dictionary of American Slang* (New York: Crowell, 1960).

profane world, an integration downward into the void, to use Cornelius Van Til's apt phrase. Knowledge of God is barred from the schools, but knowledge of profanity is encouraged. Revolution is invited and encouraged in a society which seeks an integration downward, and profanity is an index, a barometer, of this revolutionary integration downward.

Fourth, we can now recognize why, in Montagu's words, "the early forms of swearing were often of a nature regarded as subversive of social and religious institutions."[13] They still are. All swearing is religious, and false swearing represents a subversive drive in society. We saw earlier that some societies, like the aborigines of Australia, have no theistic swearing but that their swearing is simply filthy language, excremental and sexual in content. In such a society, such swearing is not subversive, since the society is already by its total character regressive and on a low level. But when such swearing assumes major proportions and constitutes literary and artistic realism in Western society, it is subversive, and it is religious. Montagu's interesting study is also a religious work; he finds health in such profanity, and we must remember that *health* and *salvation* (Latin *salus, salve,* health) are the same words. The wit and scholarship of his study serve only to heighten his religious purpose: swearing is a healthy social expression. But when it comes to a knowledge of his motives in desiring this health, or why it constitutes health, he is silent.

An interesting point is made by Sir John Harington in his poem, "Against Swearing," in *Epigrams*, published in London "some three years after his death." Montagu cites this poem for documentation on the development of oaths:

> In elder times an ancient custom was,
> To sweare in weighty matters by the Masse.
> But when the Masse went downe (as old men note)
> They sware then by the crosse of this same grote.
> And when the Crosse was likewise held in scorne,
> Then by their faith, the common oath was sworne.
> Last, having swore away all faith and trothe,
> Only God damn them is their common oath.
> > Thus custome kept *decorum* by gradation,
> > That losing Masse, Crosse, Faith, they find damnation.[14]

Harington noted the religious progression. The major change has come since then.

The commandment declares: Thou shalt not take the name of the LORD thy God *in vain*. Positively, this means: Thou *shalt* take the

---

13. Montagu, *Anatomy of Swearing*, p. 1.
14. *Ibid.*, p. 287.

name of the LORD thy God in righteousness and truth. Negatively, it also means: Thou shalt *not* take the name of other gods or powers. In each case, the implications are far-reaching.

3. The Oath and Society

The third and ninth commandments are closely related. The third declares, "Thou shalt not take the name of the LORD thy God in vain: for the LORD will not hold him guiltless that taketh his name in vain" (Ex. 20:7). The ninth states, "Thou shalt not bear false witness against thy neighbour" (Ex. 20:16). Both commandments are concerned with speech: the one has reference to God, the other to man. Moreover, Ingram is right in seeing the legal reference of both. The third in particular is normally seen, as Ingram states, "as a sort of good mannered objection to coarse or vulgar language," whereas it is "a prohibition against perjury, heresy and lying."[1] We have already seen the implications of swearing as obscenity. The law covers this and more. But the heart of the third commandment is in its nature as the foundation of a legal system. Citing Ingram again, "the foundation for all legal procedure involving so-called civil disputes is clearly in the Third Commandment, and it would certainly carry over its importance into the realm of criminal law."[2] The oath of office, the trustworthiness of witnesses, the stability of a society in terms of a common regard for truth, the faithfulness of the clergy to their ordination vows, of wives and husbands to their marital vows, and much more all hinge on the holiness of the oath or vow. Where there is no regard for truth, when men can subscribe to oaths and vows with no intention of abiding by their terms, then social anarchy and degeneration ensue. Where there is no fear of God, then the sanctity of oaths and vows disappears, and men shift the foundations of society from the truth to a lie. It is significant that prosecutions for perjury are today almost unheard of, although perjury is a daily routine in the courts. But, as Ingram points out, God's law makes clear in the third commandment, "that, whatever man may do in this regard, God will not hold him guiltless that taketh His name in vain."[3]

The presidential oath of office, and every other oath of office in the United States, was in earlier years recognized precisely as coming under the third commandment, and, in fact, invoking it. By taking the oath, a man promised to abide by his word and his obligations even as God is faithful to His word. If he failed, by his oath of office, the public official invoked divine judgment and the curse of the law upon himself.

---

1. Ingram, *World Under God's Law*, p. 46.
2. *Ibid.*, p. 44.
3. *Ibid.*, p. 44.

Although, even in the face of this, corrupt office-holders were not lacking, it is also clear that a large measure of real political responsibility was in evidence. Godly men took oaths seriously. George Washington, whose belief in a compulsory tithe we previously noted, felt very strongly about the meaning of the oath. In his farewell address, he expressed his dismay over skepticism, agnosticism, Deism, and atheism creeping in from France and the French Revolution. Unbelief worked, he saw, great damage. Among other things, by destroying the faith behind the oath, unbelief undercut the security of society. He declared,

> Of all the dispositions and habits which lead to political prosperity, religion and morality are indispensable supports. In vain would that man claim the tribute of patriotism, who should labor to subvert these great pillars of human happiness, these firmest props of the duties of men and citizens. The mere politician, equally with the pious man, ought to respect and cherish them. A volume could not trace all their connexions with private and public felicity. Let it simply be asked, Where is the security for property, for reputation, for life, if the sense of religious obligation desert the oaths, which are the instruments of investigation in courts of justice? And let us with caution indulge the supposition, that morality can be maintained without religion. Whatever may be conceded to the influence of refined education on minds of peculiar structure, reason and experience both forbid us to expect, that national morality can prevail in exclusion of religious principle.

To despise, abuse, or profane the oath is therefore an offense which denies the validity of all law and order, of all courts and offices, and it is an act of anarchy and revolution. In terms of this, we can better understand Leviticus 24:10-16, the incident of blasphemy and the death sentence meted out. The offending party in this case was half Danite and half Egyptian. The Hebrew text assumes a knowledge which has since been largely forgotten. The ancient Chaldee version paraphrases as follows:

> And while the Israelites were dwelling in the wilderness, he sought to pitch his tent in the midst of the tribe of the children of Dan; but they would not let him, because, according to the order of Israel, every man, according to his order, dwelt with his family by the ensign of his father's house. And they strove together in the camp. Whereupon the son of the Israelitish woman and the man of Israel who was of the tribe of Dan went into the house of judgment.[4]

The judgment was against the half Danite, half Egyptian, and his reaction was that he "blasphemed the name of the LORD and cursed" (Lev. 24:11). He denied the entire structure of Israelite society and law, the very principle of order. As a result, the sentence of death was

---

4. C. D. Ginsburg, "Leviticus," in *Ellicott*, I, 451.

passed for blasphemy. His offense was in effect that he affirmed total revolution, absolute secession from any society which denied him his wishes. No society can long exist which permits such subversion. God's law in this case is of particular importance: "Whosoever curseth his God shall bear his sin. And he that blasphemeth the name of the LORD, he shall surely be put to death" (Lev. 24:15, 16). Any and all Gentiles who despised or violated the oath of their religion were subject to the laws of their religion, to whatever penalties their law imposed for such blasphemy, or cursing, for to despise the oath of one's faith is to curse his God. Ginsberg summarized the law here ably:

> If such a Gentile curses his own God in whom he still professes to believe, he shall bear his sin; he must suffer the punishment for his sin from the hands of his co-religionists, whose feelings he has outraged. The Israelites are not to interfere to save him from the consequences of his guilt; for a heathen who reviles the god in whom he believes is not to be trusted in other respects, and sets a bad example to others, who might be led to imitate his conduct.[5]

There is a point of very great significance in this legislation, one which requires particular attention. *First*, we must note that the modern mind sees "good" in all religions, supposedly, while denying them in favor of the autonomous mind of man. To deny Christianity and its exclusive truth, the modern mind professes to find truth in all religions. The Bible, however, has no such tolerance towards a lie. The psalmist summed up the matter: "For all the gods of the nation are idols: but the LORD made the heavens" (Ps. 96:5). Without any qualification, all other religions are condemned by the Bible. The modern mind, while fully religious, is not institutionally religious, and so it can offer contemptuous toleration to all religions. But the modern mind is politically religious; that is, it regards the political order as its ultimate and religious order, and this leads us to a *second* observation, namely, political intolerance is basic to the modern mind, and it denies the validity of every other order than its dream state, and of all law and order alien to its own whims and will, because it regards all these orders as fearful lies. The Bible, on the other hand, extends a limited tolerance to other social orders. The only true order is founded on Biblical law. All law is religious in nature, and every non-Biblical law-order represents an anti-Christian religion. But the key to remedying the situation is *not* revolution, nor any kind of resistance that works to subvert law and order. The New Testament abounds in warnings against disobedience and in summons to peace. The key is regeneration, propagation of the gospel, and the conversion of men and nations to God's law-word. Meanwhile, the existing law-order must be respected, and neighboring

5. *Ibid.*, I, 451 f.

law-orders must be respected as far as is possible without offense to one's own faith. The pagan law-order represents the faith and religion of the people; it is better than anarchy, and it does provide a God-given framework of existence under which God's work can be furthered. The modern perspective leads to revolutionary intolerance: either a one-world order in terms of a dream, or "perpetual warfare for perpetual peace."

So seriously was the abuse of the oath regarded, that for a person to witness such an oath, or an oath to do evil uttered anywhere, and to take no action, required a trespass offering of atonement (Lev. 5:1-7).

Proverbs 29:24, in the Berkeley Version, reads, "The partner of a thief hates himself; he heard the curse (i.e., pronounced on the thief), but says nothing." Delitzsch commented:

> The oath is, after Lev. v. 1, that of the judge who adjured the partner of the thief by God to tell the truth; but he conceals it, and burdens his soul with a crime worthy of death, for from a concealer he becomes in addition a perjured man.[6]

More serious than the act of stealing, or of murder even, is the false oath. Theft robs a single man, and murder takes the life of a single man, or perhaps a group of men, but *a false oath is an assault on the life of an entire society.* The fact that its seriousness is lightly viewed is a good barometer to social degeneration. The godly hatred of false swearing is clearly reflected in Psalm 109:17-19. The trifling use of the oath was forbidden by Christ in Matthew 5:33-37, whose words had a partial reference to Numbers 30:7. False swearing was already banned in the law; Christ made clear that the oath or vow was not to be used for private purposes except on such serious occasions as the lawful intended use allowed. The cheap recourse to vows to prop up one's word, however true, was forbidden.

The godly man's communication is "yea, yea," and "nay, nay"; it is honest and forthright (Matt. 5:37). The godly man swears or testifies honestly to his own hurt, and he does not change his witness to suit his interests (Ps. 15:7). Being under God, the godly man's word is in a sense always under oath. As Ingram has observed, "It is significant that under some European Christian systems, a wilful violation of a promissory oath is treated as perjury."[7]

Ingram has very rightly stressed the relationship of heresy to this commandment. Members and clergymen who deny their baptismal and ordination vows to affirm heresy are violating their oaths. More-

6. Franz Delitzsch, *Biblical Commentary on the Proverbs of Solomon* (Grand Rapids: Eerdmans, 1950), II, 257 f.
7. Ingram, *World Under God's Law*, p. 44.

over, the heretic, "in all the horror of raging pride . . . declares, 'It is right for me to be wrong.' "[8]

Today, in many countries and in some American states, the name of God is removed from oaths of office and from the swearing in of witnesses. This means that, when a man is sworn into office, he is not bound by God to fulfil the constitutional requirements of the office or the law; the man solemnly swears by himself; if it is agreeable to him to alter the law, if he regards his own ideas as superior, then he can move to circumvent the law. The major changes in the American constitution have occurred over a period of time when no fundamental changes have been made in the U. S. Constitution. The reason is that the letter and the spirit of the law now have very little meaning as against the political wills of men and parties.

If a witness is asked to swear to tell the whole truth and nothing but the truth without any reference to God, truth then can be and is commonly redefined in terms of himself. The oath in God's name is the "legal recognition of God"[9] as the source of all things and the only true ground of all being. It establishes the state under God and under His law. The removal of God from oaths, and the light and dishonest use of oaths, is a declaration of independence from Him, and it is warfare against God in the name of the new gods, apostate man and his totalitarian state.

The modern American oath, which omits all reference to God, is set in the context of a pragmatic philosophy, a faith taught in the schools and upheld by the state and federal governments. Truth in terms of pragmatism is *what works*. The consequence can only be revolutionary anarchy. It means not only warfare against God, but warfare by every man against his neighbor.

4. Swearing and Worship

Calvin in a very perceptive analysis of the third commandment, called attention to the relationship of swearing to worship. He observed that

> We shall soon see that to swear by God's name is a species or part of religious worship, and this is manifest too from the words of Isaiah (xlv. 23), for when he predicts that all nations shall devote themselves to pure religion, he thus speaks, "As I live, saith the Lord, every knee shall bow to me, and every tongue shall swear by me."[1]

The verse cited, Isaiah 45:23, reads in full: "I have sworn by myself, the word is gone out of my mouth in righteousness, and shall not return,

---

8. *Ibid.*, p. 45.
9. *Ibid.*, p. 46.
1. John Calvin, *Commentaries on the Four Last Books of Moses*, II, 408.

That unto me every knee shall bow, every tongue shall swear." God declares that history shall culminate in a universal worship of Him, and
the godly oath as the foundation of every society. Alexander's comment
brought out the meaning clearly:

> The kneeling and swearing in the last clause are acts of homage,
> fealty, or allegiance, which usually went together (I Kings xix. 18),
> and involved a solemn recognition of the sovereignty of him to whom
> they were tendered. . . . This text is twice applied by Paul to Christ
> (Rom. xiv. 11; Phil. ii. 10), in proof of his regal and judicial sov-
> ereignty. It does not necessarily predict that all shall be converted
> to him, since the terms are such as to include both a voluntary and
> a compulsory submission, and in one of these ways all, without ex-
> ception, shall yet recognize him as their rightful sovereign.[2]

Alexander's interpretation restores the basic perspective of the law:
God is the absolute, sovereign lord and king over all, man's only
creator, sustainer, and savior. To worship Him truly requires a
total submission to Him not only with respect to salvation but also
with respect to all things else. God alone is lord of the church, state,
school, home, and every sphere and area of all creation. Thus, as
Calvin noted, to swear by God's name is truly "a species or part of
religious worship."

Commenting further on the meaning of taking the *name* of the Lord
in vain, Calvin noted,

> It is silly and childish to restrict this to the name Jehovah, as if
> God's majesty were confined to letters or syllables; but, whereas
> His essence is invisible, His name is set before us as an image, in
> so far as God manifests Himself to us, and is distinctly made known
> to us by His own marks, just as men are each by his own name.
> On this ground Christ teaches that God's name is comprehended
> in the heavens, the earth, the temple, the altar (Matt. v. 34), because
> His glory is conspicuous in them. Consequently, God's name is
> profaned whenever any detraction is made from His supreme wis-
> dom, infinite power, justice, truth, clemency, and rectitude. If a
> shorter definition be preferred, let us say that His name is what
> Paul calls . . . "that which may be known" of Him (Rom. 1. 19).[3]

The Lord's name is thus taken in vain whenever and wherever man
treats lightly and profanely the fact that God's sovereignty undergirds
the whole of reality. Man dare not take lightly God's sovereignty nor
man's obligation to speak the truth at all times in every normal sphere
of life.

The close relationship of this commandment to the ninth is readily
apparent. Calvin observed,

---

2. Joseph Addison Alexander, *Commentary on the Prophecies of Isaiah* (Grand
Rapids: Zondervan), p. 188.
3. Calvin, *op. cit.*, II, 408 f.

God will again condemn perjury in the Fifth Commandment of the Second Table, viz., in so far as it offends against and violates charity by injuring our neighbours. The aim and object of this Commandment is different, i.e., that the honour due to God may be unsullied; that we should only speak of Him religiously; that becoming veneration of Him should be maintained among us.[4]

If swearing and worship are so closely related, and if trifling and false usage of the Lord's "name," His wisdom, power, justice, truth, mercy, and righteousness constitutes blasphemy, then we must count most preaching of our day to be thoroughly blasphemous. It is amusing to note that some clergymen regard the expression, originally English, "I don't care a dam," in America, usually "not worth a dam" as profanity, but they fail to see how profane much of their preaching is. This expression, "I don't care a dam," came from India through the Duke of Wellington. The *dam* is the Indian coin of least value; the expression is thus related to, "not worth a *sou*," i.e., the lowest of French coins, now long since gone.[5] Thus, "I don't care a dam" means "I couldn't care less."

Now it must be plainly stated that most preaching today is not worth a dam, nor worth a sou, nor worth anything. More than that, it is blasphemous, in that it either denies the faith on the one hand, or reduces it to trifling dimensions on the other. Much preaching *may* be pious in intention which is blasphemous in execution.

When man fell, when the curse was laid upon mankind, it was because man had submitted to the Satanic temptation to be his own god (Gen. 3:5). Man separated himself from God, and from the name of God, to define reality in terms of man and in the name of man. When men began again to call on the name of the Lord (Gen. 4:26), men looked to God as lord and creator as well as savior. They took the name of the Lord, not in vain, but in truth; they recognized God as their only savior, law-giver, and hope. To the degree that they truly called upon the name of the Lord, to the degree that they brought all of life under the dominion of God, to that degree they were out from under the curse and under blessing.

To take the name of the Lord *in truth* means thus to ground our lives and actions, our thoughts and possessions, and every law-sphere of life firmly and fully on God and His law-word.

To take the name of the Lord *in vain* is to deny in reality the only true God; it is empty profession of Him when our lives and actions, and often every thought, possession, and every law-sphere is alienated from God or blasphemously ascribed to ourselves.

---

4. *Ibid.*, II, 409.
5. See Montagu, *Anatomy of Swearing*, pp. 92 f., 296-298.

Thus, as Oehler observed, "Perjury does not concern the transgressor alone, but his whole race."[6] It moves man and his society from the world of blessing to the world of the curse.

True swearing is thus true worship: it ascribes to God the glory due to His name.

Only when we begin to understand the relationship of the oath to the foundations of society, to revolution, and to religion, can we begin to understand the ancient horror of blasphemy. The horror expressed by the high priest at the words of Jesus, as he accused Jesus of blasphemy (Matt. 26:65), may have been hypocritical, but it mirrored all the same, the shock men normally felt. Prior to World War II, this horror was still very much a reality in Japan; whenever any blasphemy was uttered with respect to Shintoism, it constituted a very serious civil offense. Quite rightly, the Japanese recognized it as treason, revolution, and anarchy.

Because the sense of blasphemy, and horror for it, are gone, there is now a changing concept of *treason*. It is of interest to examine the concept of treason. Rebecca West has given an able summary of the historic concept:

> According to tradition and logic, the state gives protection to all men within its confines, and in return exacts their obedience to its laws; and the process is reciprocal. When men within the confines of the state are obedient to its laws they have a right to claim its protection. It is a maxim of the law, quoted by Coke in the sixteenth century, that "protection draws allegiance, and allegiance draws protection" (*protectio trahit subjectionem, et subjectio protectionem*). It was laid down in 1608, by reference to the case of Sherley, a Frenchman who had come to England and joined in a conspiracy against the King and Queen, that such a man "owed to the King obedience, that is, so long as he was within the King's protection."[7]

But in an age when men deny God and His sovereignty, the world is torn then between two conflicting claimants to the authority of God: the totalitarian state on the one hand, and the totaliarian, anarchistic individual on the other hand. The totalitarian state permits no dissent, and the anarchistic individual admits no possible loyalty outside of himself. When all the world is black, no concept of black is possible, since no differentiation exists. Everything being black, there is no principle of definition and description left. When all the world is in blasphemy, no definition of blasphemy is possible: everything is the same. As the world moves towards total blasphemy, its ability to define

---

6. Oehler, *Theology of the Old Testament*, p. 250.
7. Rebecca West, *The New Meaning of Treason* (New York: The Viking Press, 1964), p. 12 f.

and to recognize anything diminishes. Hence the necessity and health of judgment, which, as a catharsis, restores perspective and definition to the world.

The basic premise of the law and of society today is relativism. Relativism reduces all things to a common color, to a common gray. As a result, there is no longer any definition for treason, or for crime. The criminal is protected by law, because the law knows no criminal, since modern law denies that absoluteness of justice which defines good and evil. What cannot be defined cannot be delimited or protected. A definition is a fencing and a protection around an object: it separates it from all things else and protects its identity. An absolute law set forth by the absolute God separates good and evil and protects good. When that law is denied, and relativism sets in, there no longer exists any valid principle of differentiation and identification. What needs protecting from whom, when all the world is equal and the same? When all the world is water, there is no shore line to be guarded. When all reality is death, there is no life to be protected. Because the courts of law are increasingly unable to define anything due to their relativism, they are increasingly unable to protect the righteous and the law-abiding in a world where crime cannot be properly defined. For Emile Durkheim, the criminal may be and often is an evolutionary pioneer, charting the next direction of society.[8] In terms of Durkheim's relativistic sociology, the criminal may be a more valuable man than the law-abiding citizen, whose interests will be conservative or reactionary.

The relativistic society is indeed then an "open society," open to all evil and to no good. Since the relativistic society is beyond good and evil by definition, it cannot offer its citizens any protection from evil. Instead, a relativistic society will seek to protect its people from those who seek to restore a definition of good and evil in terms of Scripture.

When Chief Justice Frederick Moore Vinson of the U. S. asserted after World War II, "Nothing is more certain in modern society than the principle that there are no absolutes," he made it clear that, before the law, the one clear-cut evil is to stand in terms of God's absolute law. "The principle that there are no absolutes," enthroned as law, means warfare against the Biblical absolutes. It means that the banner of the law is the standard of the Enlightenment, Ecrasez L'infame, 'The shame and infamy of Christianity,' must be wiped out. In terms of this Voltaire welcomed the affectionate salutation of Diderot describing him as his "sublime, honorable, and dear Anti-Christ." Had not Voltaire made

---

8. Emile Durkheim, "On the Normality of Crime," in his *The Rules of Sociological Method*, in Talcott Parsons, Edward Shils, Kaspar D. Nargele, Jesse R. Pitts, eds., *Theories of Society* (New York: Free Press of Glencoe, 1961), II, 872-875.

it his principle that "Every sensible man, every honorable man, must hold the Christian sect in horror."[9] Voltaire only talked; the modern court acts on this faith. The conclusion of such a course can only be the reign of terror magnified. We can only say with the Hebrew observer of old, "They that fear the Lord will prepare their hearts and humble their souls in his sight, saying, We will fall into the hands of the Lord, and not into the hands of men: for as his majesty is, so is his mercy" (Ecclus. 2:17, 18).

5. The Oath and Authority

A case law which has already been cited deserves particular attention, Exodus 21:17: "And he that curseth his father, or his mother, shall surely be put to death." This statement is one of three in Exodus 21: 15-17 which follow the requirement in Exodus 21:12-14 of death for murder. They are thus linked in a sense with murder. *First*, "And he that smiteth his father, or his mother, shall be surely put to death" (Ex. 21:15). *Second*, "And he that stealeth a man and selleth him, or if he be found in his hand, he shall surely be put to death" (Ex. 21:16). Kidnapping and enforced slavery are punishable by death. The Biblical law recognizes voluntary slavery, because there are men who prefer security to freedom, but it strictly forbids involuntary servitude except as a punishment. *Third*, the law against cursing parents, already cited, is also cited as comparable to murder. Rawlinson's commentary is to the point:

> With homicide are conjoined some other offences, regarded as of a heinous character, and made punishable by death: viz. (1) striking a parent; (2) kidnapping; and (3) cursing a parent. The immediate sequence of these crimes upon murder, and their punishment by the same penalty, marks strongly God's abhorrence of them. The parent is viewed as God's representative, and to smite him is to offer God an insult in his person. To curse him implies, if possible, a greater want of reverence; and, since curses can only be effectual as appeals to God, it is an attempt to enlist God on our side against His representative. Kidnapping is a crime against the person only a very little short of murder, since it is to deprive a man of that which gives life its chief value—liberty.[1]

Related laws appear in other ancient cultures. Thus, ancient Babylonian law declared, "If a son has struck his father, they shall cut off his hand."[2] The authority of the entire society was endangered in any

---

9. Peter Gay, *The Enlightenment, An Interpretation. The Rise of Modern Paganism* (New York: Knopf, 1967), 391.
1. George Rawlinson, "Exodus," in *Ellicott*, I, 267.
2. H. W. F. Saggs, *Everyday Life in Babylonia and Assyria* (New York: G. P. Putnam's Sons, 1965), p. 143. See also James B. Pritchard, ed., *Ancient Near Eastern Texts* (Princeton, N. J.: Princeton University Press, 1955), p. 175.

assault on parental authority or any other authority. Exodus 21:15, 17 was enacted very early into Massachusetts' law; there is no record of any death penalty, but several cases prior to 1650 record severe whippings inflicted by the courts on rebellious sons, and on sons who struck a parent.[3]

Both the oath, or curse, and physical resistance are important matters. The oath or curse is an appeal to God to stand with us for righteousness and against evil. Similarly, physical resistance, whether in the form of warfare or personal resistance to murderous attack, or the attempts by evil men to overwhelm us, is a godly stand and by no means wrong. In an evil world, such resistance is often necessary; it is an unpleasant and ugly necessity, but not an evil. David could thank God for teaching him to war successfully (II Sam. 22:35; Ps. 18:34; 144:1). In an evil world, God requires men to stand in terms of His word and law.

At this point, many will cite Matthew 5:39, "resist not evil." The point made by Christ in this passage (Matt. 5:38-42) has reference to resistance to an alien power which governs the land, can "compel" man by a forced draft to serve the Roman imperial forces for a mile or more, seize property, enforce loans, and generally conscript property, money, and labor for its needs. In such a case, resistance is futile and wrong, and cooperation, going the second mile, is more productive of good. Ellicott's comment on Matthew 5:41 was to the point:

> The Greek word implies the special compulsion of forced service as courier or messenger under Government, and was imported from the Persian postal system, organised on the plan of employing men thus impressed to convey Government dispatches from stage to stage (Herod. viii. 98). The use of the illustration here would seem to imply the adoption of the same system by the Roman Government under the empire. Roman soldiers and their horses were billeted on Jewish householders. Others were impressed for service of longer or shorter duration.[4]

Christ's words were thus a warning against revolutionary resistance. His warning was repeated by St. Paul in Romans 13:1, 2, with the warning that resistance to duly constituted authority is resistance to the ordinance of God. At the same time, we must note that "Peter and the other apostles," when forbidden to preach by the authorities, declared, "We ought to obey God rather than men" (Acts 5:29).

There is no discrepancy between these positions. Respect for duly constituted authorities is required both as a religious duty and a practical policy. The world is not bettered by disobedience and anarchy;

---

3. George Lee Haskins, *Law and Authority in Early Massachusetts* (New York: Macmillan, 1960), p. 81.
4. *Ellicott*, VI, 30.

evil men cannot produce a good society. The key to social renewal is individual regeneration. All authorities are to be obeyed, parents, husbands, masters, rulers, pastors, always subject to the prior obedience to God. All obedience is under God, because required by His word. Therefore, *first*, the covenant people cannot violate any due authority without taking the name of the Lord in vain. Disobedience at any level constitutes disobedience to God. *Second*, to strike a parent, or to assault a police officer, or any due authority, is thus to strike at God's authority also and to use the right of self-defense for an aggression against authority. *Third*, to curse one's parents is to attempt to place God on the side of rebellion against God's central authority, the parent, and God's central institution, the family. In murder, a man assaults and takes the life of an individual, or several individuals. In every anarchistic assault on authority, the assailant attacks the life of an entire society and the very authority of God.

The excuse for such assault is *conscience*. The autonomous and absolute authority of conscience has been progressively asserted since the Enlightenment, and especially with the rise of Romanticism. In the United States, the name of Thoreau comes most readily to mind as an example of Romantic Anarchism. *Conscience* means responsibility with reference to right and wrong; conscience implies creaturehood and subjection. Conscience must be under authority, or it ceases to be conscience and becomes a god. The humanistic desire to live beyond good and evil is actually a desire to live beyond responsibility and beyond conscience. Under the facade of conscience, an assault is launched against conscience and authority.

The appeal of anarchistic revolutionists to conscience is clearly a lie and a fraud. Conscience in the modern philosophy and mood is simply a term for our own desires, enthroned as law. Thus, James Joyce, in *A Portrait of the Artist as a Young Man*, has Stephen Dedalus say, "Welcome, O life! I go to encounter for the millionth time the reality of experience and to forge in the smithy of my soul the uncreated conscience of my race." For those under the influence of Freud, the conscience, or super-ego, is simply the external authorities, parents, religion, state, and school, internalized. The super-ego is the successor and representative of the parents and other authorities; for Freud, the super-ego is the enemy of the *id*, the pleasure principle and will to live, and it is therefore to be broken. The *id* and the *ego* cannot be escaped, but the *super-ego*, as an immediate social product, can be broken in its power over man. Despite variations, Freud's view of the conscience is the view of modern man. The conscience has no standing in modern thought, and is actually in disrepute, *except* when it is useful as an appeal against the law. The conscience of autonomous man is a studied rebellion against conscience and authorities as symbols of oppression and tyranny.

True conscience is under authority, godly authority. True conscience is governed by Scripture; it does not set itself up as an arbiter over God and His word, or as the voice of God and itself a special revelation. True conscience subjects itself to God's authority: it is at all times *under God*, never itself a god and lord. In 1788, the Presbyterian Synod of New York and Philadelphia declared, in its "Preliminary Principles" to "The Form of Government," that "God alone is the Lord of the conscience; and hath left it free from the doctrine and commandments of men, which are in any thing contrary to his word, or beside it in matters of faith or worship." The declaration then defended the right of private judgment. The purpose was to free man from arbitrary demands of the state and men in terms of the absolute authority of God over the conscience. The humanistic concept of conscience, by denying the lordship of God, makes inescapable the tyranny of men. Every man's conscience is made by humanism an absolute lord; the student rioters of the 1960s and 1970s, the anarchistic revolutionists, the "civil rights" protestors, all claim the right by "conscience" to destroy law and order and overthrow society.

The death penalty of Exodus 21:15, 17 makes clear that no evil can become an excuse for more evil. The family, as God's central law-order, even when parents are most evil, cannot be attacked by a child. The child is not asked to obey its parents by doing evil; the child is not asked to call evil good. But honor must be given to whom honor is due (Rom. 13:7), and honor is due to parents.

This means that, while man must work to further righteousness, *there is a limit to the extent of his right to war against evil*. The Scripture is emphatic that vengeance belongs to God (Deut. 32:35; Ps. 94:1; Heb. 10:30; Rom. 12:19). St. Paul states plainly: "Do not revenge yourselves, dear friends, but leave room for divine retribution, for it is written, 'It is Mine to punish; I will pay them back,' the LORD says" (Rom. 12:19, Berkeley Version).

Two legitimate forms of godly vengeance exist: *First*, the absolute and perfect justice of God finally and totally administers perfect justice. History culminates in Christ's triumph, and eternity settles all scores. *Second*, the authorities ordained by God, parents, pastors, civil authorities, and others, have a duty to exercise the justice and vengeance of God. As themselves sinners, they can never do this perfectly, but imperfect justice can be justice still. A cloudy day cannot be called midnight; imperfect justice is not injustice.

A godly man does not expect perfect justice and vindication, and, at times, recognizes he cannot expect it at all of men. The Bible gives us instances of vengeance, of righting of ancient wrongs, but no such thing occurred for Joseph in relationship to Potiphar. Joseph had gone to prison for attempted rape; he was summoned out of prison to great power. His past was immaterial to the pharaoh. No doubt, to Joseph's dying day vicious critics whispered behind his back that Joseph was an ex-convict, guilty of attempted rape, but Joseph's exercise of power was godly. Where it mattered, as with his brethren, he exacted a vengeance designed to test their character. To punish Potiphar or Potiphar's wife would have accomplished nothing; and no punishment could have been more frightening for that couple than to know that their ex-slave was now the greatest power in Egypt next to pharaoh. God was Joseph's vindication.

For a man to dream of effecting perfect justice, gaining vindication in all things, and righting the record at all points, is to assume the role of vengeance which properly belongs only to God. It means joining the very forces of evil. While such a presumption is cloaked in the name of the Lord, it involves blasphemy. "And he that curseth his father, or his mother, shall surely be put to death" (Ex. 21:17).

6. The Name of God

In July, 1968, a man was convicted in Westminster, Maryland, on charges that he "did unlawfully use profanity by taking the Lord's name in vain in a public place." The man in question was arrested for fighting on Main Street and for resisting arrest. The reason for the conviction was a revealing one. The steady erosion of the law under Supreme Court interpretations made conviction on the usual charges more difficult. Magistrate Charles J. Simpson used the old law of 1723, because "sometimes an obscure law like this is the only way we have to solve some of these problems."[1]

The judge's dilemma is not surprising. Under the influence of the new doctrine of equality, crime has steadily been equalized with good, and even given an edge. Walt Whitman, regarded by many as America's greatest poet, asserted this equalitarian principle bluntly: "What is called good is perfect and what is called bad is just as perfect."[2] When good and evil are equalized, then the erosion of the law is inescapable and inevitable.

But it is not enough to deny equality. Law premised on equality will simply assert the tyrannical supremacy of an elite group of men. True law must rest on the absolute and only true God. God as absolute

---

1. "In Jail for Blasphemy; But Lucky?," Los Angeles *Herald Examiner* (Thursday, July 18, 1968), p. A-14.
2. Quoted by William James, in F. O. Matthiesen, *The James Family, A Group Biography* (New York: Knopf [1947], 1961), p. 496.

Lord and Judge is the ultimate arbiter of all things, and, as the determiner of men's destinies, His word and fear are compelling in the lives of believers. Hence, the sworn statement by a true believer has always been basic to all rules of evidence. A principle canon law, which has been influential in civil courts, is this:

> An oath, taken in the sense of a means of judicial proof, while preserving its own individual character as an invocation of the Divine Name in testimony or guarantee of the truth of a particular assertion, is the most powerful and effective means of obtaining proof and of arriving at the truth of the facts of a case and is necessary before a judge may give sentence.[3]

This same authority defines blasphemy in these terms:

> This crime may take the form of heretical blasphemy, i.e., that by which the existence of God or His attributes are impugned or denied; or of simple blasphemy or imprecation, i.e., reviling or profaning the name of God or of the saints.[4]

Both aspects of this definition have been previously considered. It is important now to deal more specifically with the *name* of God: "Thou shalt not take the *name* of the Lord thy God in vain; for the LORD will not hold him guiltless that taketh his name in vain."

Names in Scripture are revelatory of the character and nature of the person named. A man's name changed as his character changed. As Meredith wrote,

> The *third commandment* deals with God's *name*, His *office*, His *position* as the great sovereign RULER of the universe. . . .
>
> In the Bible, personal names have a *meaning*.
>
> Every name or title of God reveals some attribute of the Divine *character*. In studying God's Word, we learn new facts about God's *nature* and *character* with each new name by which He reveals Himself. In other words, God *names* Himself *what He is!*
>
> If men use the *name* of God in a way which denies the true *meaning* and *character* of God, they are BREAKING the third commandment.[5]

Not only the Old but the New Testament meaning of *name* bears out Meredith's point. Thus, in the Greek New Testament,

> By a usage chiefly Hebraistic the *name* is used for everything which the name covers, everything the thought or feeling of which is roused in the mind by mentioning, hearing, remembering, the name,

---

3. Fernando Della Rocca, *Manual of Canon Law*, trans. by the Rev. Anselm Thatcher, O.S.B. (Milwaukee: Bruce, 1969), p. 396 f.
4. *Ibid.*, p. 586.
5. Roderick C. Meredith, *The Ten Commandments* (Pasadena, Calif.: Ambassador College, 1960), p. 19.

i.e., for *one's rank, authority, interests, pleasure, command, excellences, deeds, etc.*[6]

Moreover, as Meredith noted,

> The Hebrew word here rendered "guiltless" may be better translated "clean"—"the Lord will not hold him to be *clean* that taketh his name in vain." *The test of spiritual cleanliness is the attitude of a man to the NAME of God!* A man is clean or unclean according as he uses the name of God *in truth*—or for *vanity*.[7]

This definition of the third commandment was clearly brought out by the Puritan divine, Thomas Watson, in *The Ten Commandments*, a continuation of his study, *A Body of Divinity*. The Larger Catechism of the Westminster Assembly also brought this out plainly:

> Q. 112. What is required in the third commandment?
> A. The third commandment requires, That the name of God, his titles, attributes, ordinances, the word, sacraments, prayer, oaths, vows, lots, his works, and whatsoever else there is whereby he makes himself known, be holily and reverently used in thought, meditation, word, and writing; by an holy profession, and answerable conversation, to the glory of God, and the good of ourselves, and others.
>
> Q. 113. What are the sins forbidden in the third commandment?
> A. The sins forbidden in the third commandment are, the not using of God's name as is required, and the abuse of it in ignorant, vain, irreverent, profane, superstitious, or wicked mentioning or otherwise using his titles, attributes, ordinances, or works, by blasphemy, perjury; all sinful cursings, oaths, vows and lots; violating of our oaths and vows, if lawful; and fulfilling them, if of things unlawful; murmuring and quarrelling at, curious prying into, and misapplying of God's decrees and providences; misinterpreting, misapplying, or any way perverting the word, or any part of it, to profane jests, curious or unprofitable questions, vain janglings, or the maintaining of false doctrines; abusing it, the creatures, or any thing contained under the name of God, to charms, or sinful lusts and practices; the maligning, scorning, reviling, or any wise opposing of God's truth, grace, and ways; making profession of religion in hypocrisy, or for sinister ends; being ashamed of it, or a shame to it, by unconformable, unwise, unfruitful, and offensive walking, or backsliding from it.

It is apparent thus that blasphemy is today more common than the true use of God's name. Dr. Willis Elliott of the United Church of Christ has said, "I consider adherence to the infallibility of Scripture demonic."[8] B. D. Olsen, who claims to adhere to the infallibility of Scripture, lays

---

6. Joseph Henry Thayer, *A Greek-English Lexicon of the New Testament* (New York: Harper & Brothers, 1889), p. 447.
7. Meredith, *op. cit.*, p. 19 f.
8. "COCU 'Unifying,'" in *The Presbyterian Journal*, vol. XXVI, no. 9 (June 28, 1967), p. 9.

claim to "vision."⁹ Both assertions are alike blasphemy. To cite Meredith again,

> God declares through Isaiah: "Hear ye this, O house of Jacob, which are called by the name of Israel, and are come forth out of the waters of Judah, which swear by the name of the Lord, and make mention of the God of Israel, but not in truth, nor in righteousness" (Isaiah 48:1). People to whom this prophecy applies use the *name* of God, but fail to obey the *revelation of God* contained in His name.¹⁰

Many *titles* for God appear in Scripture; these are revelatory of aspects of His nature. His name, however, is given as Jehovah or Yahweh (the true vowel construction is unknown), and it means He Who Is, the self-existent One, I am that I am. This is the revelation of God contained in His name.

God is thus the principle of definition, of law, and of all things. He is the premise of all thinking, and the necessary presupposition for every sphere of thought. It is blasphemy therefore to attempt to "prove" God; God is the necessary presupposition of all proof. To ground any sphere of thought, life, or action, or any sphere of being, on anything other than the triune God is thus blasphemy. Education without God as its premise, law which does not presuppose God and rest on His law, a civil order which does not derive all authority from God, or a family whose foundation is not God's word, is blasphemous.

---

9. B. D. Olsen, *Divers Seeds and the Kingdom* (Richmond, Calif.: The Triumph of God Publishing Co, c. 1967).
10. Meredith, *op. cit.*, p. 19.

IV

THE FOURTH COMMANDMENT

1. The Sign of Freedom

The fourth commandment, the sabbath law, is important in terms of its prophetic significance, as well as its legal status. Kline, in discussing the Deuteronomic formulation of the law, states:

> Most significant of the variations from the form of the Decalogue as presented in Exodus 20:2-17 is the new formulation of the fourth word. The sabbatic cycle of covenant life symbolizes the consummation principle characteristic of divine action. God works, accomplishes his purpose and, rejoicing, rests. Exodus 20:11 refers to the exhibition of the consummation pattern in creation for the original model of the Sabbath; Deuteronomy 5:15 refers to its manifestation in redemption, where the divine triumph is such as to bring God's elect to their rest also. Most appropriately, therefore, was the Sabbath appointed as a sign of God's covenant with the people he redeemed from the bondage of Egypt to inherit the rest of Canaan (cf. Ex. 31:13-17). In keeping with the Deuteronomic interpretation of the Sabbath in terms of the progress of God's redemptive purpose is the New Testament's orientation of the Sabbath to the Saviour's resurrection triumph by which his redeemed people attain with him unto eternal rest.[1]

The pattern of the sabbath is God's creation rest; the goal of the sabbath is man's redemption rest.

There is no record or evidence for the sabbath prior to Exodus. The word "remember" in the commandment harks back to the creation and does not recall a past observance but commands the people to remember the sabbath thereafter. A weekly day of rest is unknown to other cultures. Only where Biblical faith and culture have brought it about does it exist to this day. In some cultures of the ancient world, an occasional day of rest marked the celebration of the divine-human king's birthday. But the Biblical concept of a redemption rest as the goal of history, i.e., a perfect order in which work is totally blessed, and the order is entirely of God's making, is unknown outside of Biblical faith. God, speaking through Isaiah, declared, "But the wicked are like the troubled sea, when it cannot rest, whose waters cast up mire and dirt. There is no peace, saith my God, to the wicked" (Isa. 57:20, 21).

---

1. Kline, *Treaty of the Great King*, p. 63 f.

The world of the unregenerate is in perpetual search of the sabbath, of the glorious rest of creation, but its self-defeating quest leads only to greater disturbances: it casts up "mire and dirt."

The sabbath is not an infringement of man's liberty but rather the liberation of man.[2]

The sabbath asserts the principle of freedom under God, of liberty under law, God's law. It summons man to obedience to the ordinance of rest in order to free man from himself and from this work. The essence of humanism is its belief in the plenary ability of man. Man is able, it is held, to save himself, to guide his own evolution and that of society, to control himself, his world, the weather, and all things else. When man controls and re-orders all things, then man will have re-created the world into a paradise. Whether Marxist, Fabian, or democratic, this is the dream of humanism.

It is also the assurance of *the proletarianization of man.* As Pieper has noted, "the proletarian is the man who is fettered to the process of work."[3] The leaders of the proletarian revolution dream of freeing man from work. For them, this means freeing man from God also. According to Stalin,

> If God exists, He must have ordained slavery, feudalism, and capitalism. He must want humanity to suffer, as the monks were always telling me. Then there would be no hope for the toiling masses to free themselves from their oppressors. But when I learned that there is no God, I knew that humanity could fight its way to freedom.[4]

If there is no God, Stalin held, then there is no divine Providence, and man must work to become his own providence. The total government of God would have to be replaced by the total government of man. This means tremendous work and sacrifice. The end result would be the liberated and ideal man.

> Each man, Stalin predicted, would be developed under socialism to a point at which he and all his fellows would surpass the giants of the pre-socialist past, such as Michelangelo, or Goethe. Yet nothing sounds less like Michelangelo or Goethe than these hints of Stalin's about the ideal future condition of man. The men of the future were in fact intended by Stalin to resemble the New Soviet Men of his day—hard-working, utterly devoted, utterly self-effacing, utterly submissive Stakhanovite workers and other heroes. The world was to be transformed into what the Communist ideology of

---

2. For a study of "The Sabbath, Satanism, and the Proletarian Revolution," see R. J. Rushdoony, *The Politics of Guilt and Pity, Studies in Political Justification* (Nutley, N. J.: The Craig Press, 1970), sec. I, chap. 7.

3. Josef Pieper, *Leisure, The Basis of Culture* (New York: Mentor-Omega, [1952] 1963), p. 50.

4. Stalin, in *Finskii Vestnik* (December 17, 1928), p. 11; cited by Francis B. Randall, *Stalin's Russia* (New York: The Free Press, 1965), p. 65.

Stalin's day said it ought to be. And that was essentially Stalin's Russia, writ large, spread over the whole world, made prosperous at last, and rid of all save those who obeyed voluntarily and perfectly the perfect laws of Communism.[5]

Stalin, in the course of this quest for the true sabbath, man's true rest, did two things: *First*, he enslaved more men than any other tyrant in all history, and, *second*, he had more men killed than any other man in all history. Man's attempt to enter heaven on his own terms places him instead in hell.

Now to examine the sabbath laws more specifically, it is at once apparent that, while the principle of the sabbath remains basic to Biblical law, the specific form of sabbath observance changed radically in terms of the new covenant in Christ.

First, the sabbath in the Old Testament law was not primarily a day of *worship* but a day of rest. The pattern of weekly worship did not exist in the Old Testament law. The synagogue introduced it in the inter-testamental period, and the New Testament clearly practiced it and urged it (Heb. 10:25). In the Old Testament, worship was family-centered, and woven into the fabric of daily life. It should still be so embedded in the common life of man, but there is now also the duty of corporate worship. This corporate *worship* cannot, however, be confused or equated with *rest,* although the two are closely associated. *Rest* has reference here to the soteriological reality, to the fact of redemption, liberation, and wholeness of life. *Rest* here means confidence in God's work, so that we cease from our own labors in symbolic representation of our total confidence in God's accomplishment. The manna in the wilderness set forth God's rest, and the order to observe the sabbath with confidence in the sufficiency of manna reinforced this fact of God's provision. When such a God works, man can and must rest (Ex. 16:14-36).

Second, severe laws enforced the sabbath *rest*. It was not *worship* which the laws demanded, but *rest*. The general law was that no work should be done on the sabbath (Ex. 34:21; Deut. 5:12-15; Ex. 20:8-11; Lev. 23:3; Jer. 17:22). "The gates should be shut" (Neh. 13:19). "Abide ye every man in his place, let no man go out of his place on the seventh day" (Ex. 16:29). Asses should not be laden (Neh. 13:15), nor burdens borne (Jer. 17:21, 22), nor fires kindled (Ex. 35:3), nor sheaves brought in (Neh. 13:15), nor sticks gathered (Num. 15:32-35), nor victuals or wares bought (Neh. 10:31) or sold (Neh. 13:15), nor wine treaded in the presses (Neh. 13:15). Life, however, could be saved on the sabbath (Mark 3:4; Luke 6:9), since redemption is the

5. Randall, p. 94. For Stalin on the future man, *Finskii Vestnik* (December 17, 1928), p. 41. Marx and Trotsky held to the same opinion.

essence of the Sabbath. This can mean healing the sick (Matt. 12:10-
13; Mark 3:1-5; Luke 14:3, 4; 6:8-10; 13:14-16; John 7:23), or res-
cuing an animal that has fallen into a pit (Matt. 12:11; Luke 14:5).
Since hunger alleviated is a part of redemption, it is proper for one
who is hungry to "pluck and eat corn" on the Sabbath (Matt. 12:1-8;
Mark 2:23-28; Luke 6:1-5), and the same is true of thirst, so that a
thirsty animal can be taken to water in fulfilment of the sabbath (Luke
13:15). Since redemption means defeating God's enemies, the Maccabees finally came to the logical conclusion that it was in conformity
with the sabbath to resist attacks by the enemy (I Mac. 2:41).[6] These
laws make clear that the essence of the sabbath is the victory of
redemption rest. Mary's Magnificat, because it celebrates the redemption through the Messiah, is a sabbath song in essence, and it properly
forms a part of sabbath worship:

My soul doth magnify the Lord,
And my spirit hath rejoiced in God my Saviour.
For he hath regarded the low estate of his handmaiden: for, behold,
from henceforth all generations shall called me blessed.
For he that is mighty hath done to me great things; and holy is his
name.
And his mercy is on them that fear him from generation to genera-
tion.
He hath shewed strength with his arm; he hath scattered the proud
in the imagination of their hearts.
He hath put down the mighty from their seats, and exalted them of
low degree.
He hath filled the hungry with good things; and the rich he hath
sent empty away.
He hath holpen his servant Israel, in remembrance of his mercy;
As he spake to our fathers, to Abraham, and to his seed for ever
(Luke 1:46-55).

Third, there is not a trace of the maintenance of the sabbath penalties in the church after the resurrection. Because the early disciples
and members were Jews, they continued for a time to observe the Old
Testament sabbath (Acts 13:14-26; 16:11-13; 17:2, 3; 18:1, 11). But
the Christian day of worship was the first day of the week, the day of
resurrection as well as of Pentecost (Matt. 28:1; Mark 16:1, 2, 9; Luke
24:1; John 20:1-19; Acts 20:6-8; I Cor. 16:1, 2). Many Reformed
churchmen seem to assume that the one law of Scripture is sabbath
observance. Clearly, this is not derived from Calvin, who held, in his
"Catechism of the Churches of Geneva," that

M. Does he order us to labour on six days, that we may rest on the
seventh?

6. Clark, *Biblical Law*, p. 210 f.

S. Not absolutely; but allowing man six days for labour, he excepts the seventh, that it may be devoted to rest.

M. Does he interdict us from all kinds of labour?

S. This commandment has a separate and peculiar reason. As the observance of rest is part of the old ceremonies, it was abolished by the advent of Christ.

M. Do you mean that this commandment properly refers to the Jews, and was therefore merely temporary?

S. I do, in as far as it is ceremonial.

M. What then? Is there any thing under it beyond ceremony?

S. It was given for three reasons.

M. State them to me.

S. To figure spiritual rest; for the preservation of ecclesiastical polity; and for the relief of slaves.

M. What do you mean by spiritual rest?

S. When we keep holiday from our own works, that God may perform his own work in us.

M. What, moreover, is the method of thus keeping holiday?

S. By crucifying our flesh,—that is, renouncing our own inclination, that we may be governed by the Spirit of God.

M. Is it sufficient to do so on the seventh day?

S. Nay, continually. After we have once begun, we must continue during the whole course of life.

M. Why then, is a certain day appointed to figure it?

S. There is no necessity that the reality should agree with the figure in every respect, provided it be suitable in so far as is required for the purpose of figuring.

M. But why is the seventh day prescribed rather than any other day?

S. In Scripture the number seven implies perfection. It is, therefore, apt for denoting perpetuity. It, at the same time, indicates that this spiritual rest is only begun in this life, and will not be perfect until we depart from this world.

M. But what is meant when the Lord exhorts us to rest by his own example?

S. Having finished the creation of the world in six days, he dedicated the seventh to the contemplation of his works. The more strongly to stimulate us to this, he set before us his own example. For nothing is more desirable than to be formed after his image.

M. But ought meditation on the works of God to be continual, or is it sufficient that one day out of seven be devoted to it?

S. It becomes us to be daily exercised in it, but because of our weakness, one day is specially appointed. And this is the polity which I mentioned.

M. What order, then, is to be observed on that day?

S. That the people meet to hear the doctrine of Christ, to engage in public prayer, and make profession of their faith.

M. Now explain what you meant by saying that the Lord intended by this commandment to provide also for the relief of slaves.

S. That some relaxation might be given to those under the power of others. Nay, this, too, tends to maintain a common polity. For when one day is devoted to rest, every one accustoms himself to labour during the other days.

M. Let us now see how far this command has reference to us.

S. In regard to the ceremony, I hold that it was abolished, as the reality existed in Christ (Col. ii. 17).

M. How?

S. Because, by virtue of his death, our old man is crucified, and we are raised up to a newness of life (Rom. vi. 6).

M. What of the commandment then remains for us?

S. Not to neglect the holy ordinances which contribute to the spiritual polity of the Church; especially to frequent sacred assemblies, to hear the word of God, to celebrate the sacraments, and engage in the regular prayers, as enjoined.

M. But does the figure give us nothing more?

S. Yes, indeed. We must give heed to the thing meant by it; namely, that being engrafted into the body of Christ, and made his members, we cease from our own works, and so resign ourselves to the government of God.[7]

St. Paul was emphatic in stating that the sabbath regulations no longer had their old binding force: "Let no man therefore judge you in meat, or in drink, or in respect of an holy day, or of the new moon, or of the sabbath days: Which are a shadow of things to come: but the body is of Christ" (Col. 2:16, 17). None will argue that the old death penalty for violations of the sabbath is still binding, or ever has been since Christ. The whole of the New Testament forbids such an interpretation. But, equally clearly, any law which at one time brought forth a death penalty for violation must involve a principle so basic to man and nature that obviously a hard central core remains in some sense binding in every age. (In another chapter, this will be considered.)

Fourth, not only is the legal status of the sabbath altered, but the day of rest has been changed from the Hebrew sabbath to the Christian day of resurrection. The Deuteronomic law (Deut. 5:12-15) made clear that the Hebrew sabbath celebrated the deliverance from Egypt: "And remember that thou wast a servant in the land of Egypt, and that the LORD thy God brought thee out thence, through a mighty hand, and by a stretched out arm; therefore the LORD thy God commanded thee to keep the sabbath day" (Deut. 5:16). The Hebrew redemption was thus celebrated in the sabbath; the Christian sabbath commemorates Christ's triumph over sin and death, and hence it is celebrated on the day of resurrection, the first day of the week. To reject this day is to reject Christ's redemption and to seek salvation by another and inadmissible way.

---

7. John Calvin, *Tracts and Treatises* (Grand Rapids: Eerdmans, 1958), II, 61-63.

Fifth, the Hebrew sabbath and the modern Saturday cannot be equated. As Curtis Clair Ewing has clearly shown, the calendar of Israel does not permit such an identification. The calendar of Israel at Sinai was a solar calendar, and it is not to be confused with the modern Jewish solar-lunar calendar of A.D. 359. Ewing has called attention to the unfortunate translation at times of "moon" for "month," thus creating some confusion. There are three sabbaths spoken of in Scripture: the creation sabbath; the Hebrew sabbath, which commemorated the deliverance from Egypt; and the Christian sabbath, which is "kept in commemoration of Christ's finished resurrection and is the only sabbath that remains."[8] As Ewing points out, the fourth commandment orders remembrance, because it recalls the creation sabbath, God's rest, as the pattern of the covenant rest:

> Remember the sabbath day, to keep it holy.
> Six days shalt thou labour, and do all thy work:
> But the seventh day is the sabbath of the LORD thy God: in it thou shalt not do any work, thou, nor thy son, nor thy daughter, thy manservant, nor thy maidservant, nor thy cattle, nor thy stranger that is within thy gates;
> For in six days the LORD made heaven and earth, the sea, and all that in them is, and rested the seventh day: wherefore the LORD blessed the sabbath day and hallowed it (Ex. 20:8-11).

In Deuteronomy, they are not commanded to *remember,* since it is not the pattern of the creation sabbath in view, but they are commanded to *keep* the sabbath, in commemoration of the deliverance of Israel from Egypt:

> Keep the sabbath day to sanctify it, as the LORD thy God hath commanded thee.
> Six days thou shalt labour, and do all thy work:
> But the seventh day is the sabbath of the LORD thy God: in it thou shalt not do any work, thou, nor thy son, nor thy daughter, nor thy manservant, nor thy maidservant, nor thine ox, nor thine ass, nor any of thy cattle, nor thy stranger that is within thy gates; that thy manservant and thy maidservant may rest as well as thou.
> And remember that thou wast a servant in the land of Egypt, and that the LORD thy God brought thee out thence through a mighty hand and by a stretched out arm: therefore the LORD thy God commanded thee to keep the sabbath day (Deut. 5:12-15).

Because of the deliverance from Egypt, Israel is "therefore" to keep the sabbath. The extent of the required rest is more specifically spelled out in Deuteronomy.

The Hebrew calendar began its dating from the deliverance from Egypt. As Ewing points out, the Hebrews retained the Egyptian cal-

---

8. Curtis Clair Ewing, *Israel's Calendar and the True Sabbath* (Los Angeles: The National Message Ministry, n.d.), p. 9.

endar of 12 months of 30 days, but, instead of adding the five supplementary days at the end of the year, they added three at the end of the sixth month, and two at the end of the twelfth month. The 15th day of Abib, the first month, had to be a sabbath every year, which meant that the first and eighth of Abib were fixed sabbaths, as were the seven sabbaths following the 15th of Abib (Lev. 23:6, 7, 11, 15-16). The 50th day would then be Pentecost:

> Now the Sabbath of Abib 15th being fixed by date, it follows that these seven successive Sabbaths must also have been on fixed dates and would fall as follows: Abib 22, 29; Iyar 6, 13, 20, 27; and Sivan 4. By no possibility can there be seven Sabbaths complete from Abib 15 to Sivan 4th unless those Sabbaths came on fixed dates of the month every year.[9]

Since the *date of the month* was constant, the *day of the week* was variable. "This means that once in seven years each of them would fall on every single day of the week, just as your birthday comes on a different day of the week every year."[10] To cite Ewing further,

> But this is not all. According to Exodus 12:3, 5, 6, 24 and Leviticus 23:15, the 10th, 14th and 16th of Abib could never be Sabbaths because they were work days of specific command: real work like cleaning house, butchering cattle, and reaping fields. We know these dates would fall on Saturday once every seven years and if Saturday were the Sabbath there would be a conflict of commands. There would be three dates in which Israel is commanded to work falling every seventh year on days in which Israel was commanded not to work. We know that never happened, because God is not the author of confusion.

> We have now shown by Scripture, and the calendar disclosed therein, that Israel's Sabbaths were fixed to fall on the same dates of the month every year. With these fifteen regular Sabbaths coming on the same dates every year and the three commanded work days coming on the same dates every year, *it is impossible for Saturday to have been the Sabbath.*

> If the year had 365 days in it and we divide 365 by 7 we get 52 weeks and one day left over. The question then is, where did the extra day go? That was absorbed by a 48-hour Sabbath on the 4th and 5th of Sivan as shown by Leviticus 23:15, 16, and 21. This changed the day of the week on which the Sabbath was celebrated each year, but also maintained the fixed Sabbaths on the same day of the month and the 7-day cycle. . . .

> There is nothing in the Bible to determine the length of a Sabbath. The Scriptures use the same word to describe: (1) A rest one day long (Ex. 20:8-11; Deut. 5:12-15), (2) A rest two days long (Lev. 23:15, 16, 21), (3) A rest one year long (Lev. 25:4, 8),

---

9. *Ibid.,* p. 14.
10. *Ibid.,* p. 15.

(4) A rest two years long (Lev. 25:8-12), (5) A rest seventy years long (II Chron. 36:21).

The meaning of the word "Sabbath" is *cessation* or *rest*. One cannot rest twice unless he has worked between those rests. This 48-hour Sabbath was not two rests or Sabbaths but a lengthening out of the one rest or Sabbath through two days. As an illustration, note that the rest of the land during the whole of every 49th and 50th year was not two rests to the land, but one rest to the land during the two whole years, hence a Sabbath two years long once in fifty years. Just so, when God required "the seventh Sabbath" and the "morrow after the seventh Sabbath" both to be a Sabbath, it was one Sabbath 48 hours long because no work came between them.

In like manner, by *a law of necessity*, we know that 3 days of the additional 5 days at the end of the year were added at the end of the month Elul, because we have shown that the 1st of Tisri had to be a Sabbath every year. The last Sabbath of Elul was the 27th of the month, thus leaving only 3 more days in the month; but, in order to have 6 days labor before another Sabbath, 3 days have to be added here. After the same manner we know that the 2 remaining days of the 5 supplementary days were added at the end of Adar. We have shown that the 1st of Abib in every year was a Sabbath; but the last Sabbath of Adar was on the 26th, leaving 4 days of the 30. So, in order to have 6 days labor before the next Sabbath, we must insert the 2 extra days of labor here.[11]

Ewing's carefully documented study, quoted here in its barest outline, clearly establishes that attempts to treat Saturdays as the true sabbath, apart from being non-Christian, are also non-Biblical in their radical variance from the sabbath of Israel.

Sixth, the sabbath, as we have seen, is the day of rest, redemption, and liberation. The great proclamation of the jubilee sabbath is "proclaim liberty throughout all the land unto all the inhabitants thereof" (Lev. 25:10). But the security and "rest" of slavery could constitute a pseudo-rest.

Slavery could be involuntary as a punishment. A thief who did not make restitution was sold as a slave (Ex. 22:3). A man could also be sold for debt (Deut. 15:12). As Clark noted, "The servitude ceased when labor had been performed equivalent to the amount which would have been required to make restitution, and it is thought to have been limited to six years."[12]

A man could renounce his liberty and make himself a slave. He was then set free on the sabbath year. If he chose the security of slavery, his ear was pierced, to indicate that he was now like a woman, permanently in subjection, and he remained a slave (Ex. 21:5-7). Since

11. *Ibid.*, p. 15 f.
12. Clark, *Biblical Law*, p. 268.

unbelievers are by nature slaves, they could be held as life-long slaves without this formality (Lev. 25:44-45). The slave could be flogged by the master (Ex. 21:20; Deut. 23:15), but if maimed by abusive treatment, the slave, domestic or foreign, went free (Ex. 21:26-27; Lev. 24:17). They were to be circumcised (Ex. 12:44; Gen. 17:12), and could eat holy things (Lev. 22:10 ff.; Ex. 12:44). The slave had some rights and position in a home (Gen. 24:2): he could share in the inheritance (Prov. 17:2). He was entitled to rest on the sabbath, as the fourth commandment makes clear.

Since the slave was, except where debt and theft were concerned, a slave by nature and by choice, a fugitive slave went free, and the return of such fugitives was forbidden (Deut. 23:15, 16).

Christians cannot become slaves voluntarily; they are not to become the slaves of men (I Cor. 7:23), nor "entangled again with the yoke of bondage" (Gal. 5:1). The road of pseudo-security, of pseudo-liberation in slavery, socialism, and welfarism, is forbidden to the Christian. The Christian sabbath is not the slavery of socialism.

2. The Sabbath and Life

The death penalties attached to the violation of the sabbath in the Old Testament era convey two very obvious assumptions. *First*, the sabbath law involves a principle so important and basic that violation thereof is a capital offense. *Second*, the law conveys also the fact that violation of the sabbath laws involves a kind of death in and of itself, i.e., that violation brings on death. The prophets clearly made this assumption. Obedience, by implication, means life.

Our familiarity with a matter sometimes makes for ignorance, in that we fail to examine it. We are accustomed also to fitting facts into a framework familiar to us. Thus, generations of teachers have cited, as an example of humility, the statement to a Roman general in a triumphal march, "Remember that you are a man." But the reality was quite different:

> The triumphator was something rather different even from the highest official of the state. In the triumph the Roman general was endowed with the highest insignia that ancient Rome possessed, the attributes of the chief god of the state, Jupiter. It is true that the slave who held the golden wreath over the triumphant general's head as he drove along in a chariot drawn by four white horses had to repeat to him, "Remember that you are a man," but that only meant that in the moment of his triumph the general was regarded as equivalent to the chief god of the state.[1]

---

1. Heinz Kahler, *The Art of Rome and Her Empire* (New York: Crown Publishers, 1963), p. 65.

To us, these words mean, Remember, you are human, mortal; to the Romans, they meant, Remember, you are a god. Thus, to understand anything, it is important to know the context.

Jesus said, "The sabbath was made for man, and not man for the sabbath: Therefore the Son of man is Lord also of the sabbath" (Mark 2:27-28). The sabbath was made for the true and perfect Man, Jesus Christ, who is therefore Lord of the sabbath; it was therefore also made for the redeemed of Christ, for covenant man, and as a principle of life and regeneration to him.

To understand the meaning of this, it is perhaps necessary to do two things, *first*, to remember that the principle purpose of the sabbath is not worship but rest. Only as worship qualifies as rest and refreshing to the man, as true worship does, is it a necessary aspect of the sabbath rest. But the essence of the sabbath is rest. *Second*, we view the sabbath in terms of man *exclusively* rather than man *centrally*, and as a result, we miss its meaning. By approaching the sabbath from the standpoint of the earth, we can better understand its meaning.

The commandment makes clear that the sabbath day of rest is for man and beast alike. But the details of the law spell out the fact that a sabbatical *year* is required for the land itself. The comments on this sabbatical year are of interest. Thus, according to Galer, "The custom of letting the land lie fallow is common throughout the East, made necessary no doubt by the lack of fertilizers and knowledge of proper methods of rotating crops."[2] There is no evidence that they lacked in ancient times a knowledge of either fertilizers or crop rotation; such knowledge is ancient, although men have disregarded their knowledge of it in many eras. Rylaarsdam holds that "The original function of the custom is probably religious, to appease the spiritual powers controlling the land or to give them opportunity to restore its fertility."[3] Such "interpretations" are not exegesis at all, but indications of a lordly sense of superiority over our forebears who were lower on the evolutionary ladder of history.

The law reads:

> And six years thou shalt sow thy land, and shall gather in the fruits thereof:
> But the seventh year thou shalt let it rest and lie still; that the poor of thy people may eat: and what they leave the beasts of the field shall eat. In like manner thou shalt deal with thy vineyard and with thy oliveyard (Ex. 23:10, 11).

And the LORD spake unto Moses in mount Sinai, saying,

---

2. Roger Sherman Galer, *Old Testament Law For Bible Students* (New York: Macmillan, 1922), p. 105.
3. J. C. Rylaarsdam, "Exodus," in *Interpreter's Bible*, I, 1012.

Speak unto the children of Israel, and say unto them, When ye come into the land which I give you, then shall the land keep a sabbath unto the LORD.
Six years thou shalt sow thy field, and six years thou shalt prune thy vineyard, and gather in the fruit thereof:
But in the seventh year shall be a sabbath of rest unto the land, a sabbath for the LORD: thou shalt neither sow thy field, nor prune the vineyard.
That which groweth of its own accord of thy harvest thou shalt not reap, neither gather the grapes of thy vine undressed: for it is a year of rest unto the land.
And the sabbath of the land shall be meat for you; for thee, and for thy servant and for thy maid, and for thy hired servant, and for thy stranger that sojourneth with thee.
And for thy cattle, and for the beast that are in thy land, shall all the increase thereof be meat (Lev. 25:1-7).

And if ye shall say, What shall we eat the seventh year? behold we shall not sow, nor gather in our increase:
Then I will command my blessing upon you in the sixth year, and it shall bring forth fruit for three years.
And ye shall sow the eighth year, and eat yet of old fruit unto the ninth year: until her fruits come in ye shall eat of the old store (Lev. 25:20-22).

These laws, it should be noted, were not too well observed in much of Israel's history. Between the Exodus and the Babylonian captivity, it was neglected 70 times, and hence 70 years of captivity were imposed to give the land rest (II Chron. 36:21). This means that more than half the time, the law was not observed. After the captivity, this law was observed (but others broken), and Tacitus (*Hist.* v. 4) commented on it. Julius Caesar remitted Jewish taxes in the seventh year in recognition of their custom (Josephus, *Ant. Jud.* XIV. 10, 6). However, according to Oehler, the jubilee was not observed, only the sabbatical years.[4]

There was to be no pruning or planting in the sabbath year, nor any attempt to kill the insects, or otherwise interfere with natural processes in the field. The fruit had to remain in the field, except for what passersby, servants, or owners plucked to eat; no real harvesting was permitted, only eating. This prohibition of any real harvesting or storing of produce in the sabbatical year is clearly stated in Leviticus 25:20.[5]

But the law has still more to say about the sabbath of the land: the jubilee year. Every 50th year was a jubilee year, inaugurated by blowing the trumpet on the Day of Atonement. Since the 49th year was a sabbath year, the jubilee marked two sabbath years in a row:

4. Oehler, *Theology of the O.T.*, p. 344.
5. C. D. Ginsburg, "Leviticus," in Ellicott, *op. cit.*, I, 453.

And thou shalt number seven sabbaths of years unto thee, seven
times seven years; and the space of the seven sabbaths of years
shall be unto thee forty and nine years.
Then shalt thou cause the trumpet of the jubile to sound on the
tenth day of the seventh month, in the day of atonement shall ye
make the trumpet sound throughout all your land.
And ye shall hallow the fiftieth year, and proclaim liberty throughout
all the land unto all the inhabitants thereof: it shall be a jubile unto
you; and ye shall return every man unto his possession, and ye
shall return every man unto his family.
A jubile shall that fiftieth year be unto you: ye shall not sow,
neither reap that which groweth of itself in it, nor gather the grapes
in it of thy vine undressed.
For it is the jubile; it shall be holy unto you: ye shall eat the increase thereof out of the field (Lev. 25:8-12).

Micklem regarded it as "very" curious that the jubilee, which he is
not sure existed, began on the Day of Atonement.[6] The answer appears
in the laws which immediately follow:

In the year of this jubile ye shall return every man unto his possession.
And if thou sell ought unto thy neighbour, or buyest ought of thy
neighbour's hand, ye shall not oppress one another:
According to the number of years after the jubile thou shalt buy of
thy neighbour, and according unto the number of years of the
fruits he shall sell unto thee:
According to the multitude of years thou shalt increase the price
thereof, and according to the fewness of years thou shalt diminish
the price of it: for according to the number of the years of the fruits
doth he sell unto thee.
Ye shall not therefore oppress one another; but thou shalt fear thy
God: for I am the LORD your God (Lev. 25:13-17).

To analyze this legislation, it is apparent, *first* that the purpose is
not, as many hold, "humanitarian." Certainly, "the poor of thy people"
ate of the field in the sabbath year, but they could glean the fields every
year, so that no special sabbatical year was necessary to provide for
the poor. To attempt to justify the sabbath day or year for reasons
other than the sabbath itself is to deny that this is a separate commandment, embodying in and of itself a particular aspect of God's
righteousness and law. The purpose of the sabbath is the sabbath,
i.e., the rest and release of redemption and regeneration.

Second, in the supreme expression in the Mosaic legislation of the
sabbath principle, the jubilee year, the jubilee is begun by the sounding
of the trumpet or ram's horn, on the Day of Atonement. Micklem found
this strange, but Ginsburg's comment stated its meaning very clearly, in
his comment on Leviticus 25:9.

---

6. Nathaniel Micklem, "Leviticus," in *Interpreter's Bible*, II, 121.

On the close of the great Day of Atonement, when the Hebrews realised that they had peace of mind, that their heavenly Father had annulled their sins, and that they had become re-united to Him through His forgiving mercy, every Israelite was called upon to proclaim throughout the land, by nine blasts of the cornet, that he too had given the soil rest, that he had freed every encumbered family estate, and that he had given liberty to every slave, who was now to rejoin his kindred. Inasmuch as God has forgiven his debts, he also is to forgive his debtors.[7]

The sabbath recalled the creation sabbath. The institution of the Israelite sabbath recalled Israel's redemption and regeneration. The goal of the sabbath, as Hebrews 3 makes clear, is the promised land, the new creation in Jesus Christ. The sabbath therefore sets forth the restoration and restitution of all things in Christ. In the jubilee year, as in each sabbatical year, debts ran out. The modern statute of limitations on the collection of debts is an adaptation of this Biblical law. In the jubilee year also, the rural land holdings reverted to their original owners; slaves were freed, as on each sabbatical year. The jubilee marked a two-year holiday in which covenant man celebrated the foretaste of the great sabbath of the new creation. Because the jubilee began on the evening of the Day of Atonement, it made clear the foundation of the new creation, atonement through the blood of the Lamb of the Covenant. Creation and recreation were thus basic to the sabbath: man *rests* in God's finished work of redemption proclaimed before the time. By faith, man, anticipating the final victory and rejoicing in the present deliverance, lives by faith in the sufficiency of God.

Third, the great work of restoration, of undoing the work of the Fall, includes the soil also. By this rest, the soil also is restored and revitalized. By allowing the field to go to weeds, the weeds of the field are given the opportunity to bring to the topsoil minerals from below and to revitalize the soil. The vines and trees are given free growth, unpruned, and again renew their vitality. The fruit which falls and rots again contributes to the soil. The value of the sabbath in regenerating the soil is very great. But man, lacking faith, prefers his own work to God's work, and his proposed rest to God's sabbath. God's method is called crude, and modern sprays, manufactured fertilizers, and other devices are used, and the soil is steadily mined and abused. The soil is treated as something science can make and re-make, and even do without. Very few scientists treat the soil with any respect. Notable exceptions are Sir Albert Howard: *An Agricultural Testament;* Friend Sykes: *Modern Humus Farming*; William A. Albrecht: *Soil Fertility and Animal Health*; Joseph A. Cocannouer: *Weeds, Guardians of the*

---

7. C. D. Ginsburg, "Leviticus," in Ellicott, I, 454.

Soil, and *Water and the Cycle of Life.* These and other writers make clear the extensive abuse of the soil, the function of microorganisms in the soil, the value of compost and of trees in regenerating the soil, and much more. The value of wild animals and birds in the life cycles of the earth has scarcely been touched. The earth clearly is renewed by rest, or it is exploited ruthlessly and finally turned into a desert. Many once populous areas are today desert, as witness Babylon and the Sahara. When God ordained that Israel and Judah go into captivity, it was not only to punish the people but to restore the land. We are plainly told that Judah went into captivity "To fulfil the word of the Lord by the mouth of Jeremiah, until the land had enjoyed her sabbaths: for as long as she lay desolate she kept sabbath, to fulfil threescore and ten years" (II Chron. 36:21). The prophecy of Jeremiah referred to is Jeremiah 25:9-12; it is recalled in Daniel 9:2. The captivity was in fulfilment of the prophecy of the law concerning violations of the sabbaths:

> Then shall the land enjoy her sabbaths, as long as it lieth desolate, and ye be in your enemies' land; even then shall the land rest and enjoy her sabbath (Lev. 26:34).

> The land shall be left of them, and shall enjoy her sabbaths, while she lieth desolate without them: and they shall accept of the punishment of their iniquity: because, even they despised my judgments, and because their soul abhorred my statutes (Lev. 26:43).

This seventy-year-long sabbath was God's mercy on the land and on Israel. After the crucifixion of Christ, no such mercy was extended to the land, and its history has been one of the steady erosion of soil and men. The land and the people show the effects of the curse. Although Israel between the captivity and the crucifixion observed the sabbaths of the earth, at other points they despised God, and they crucified His Son, so that the curse fell upon them, and the earth for their sake.

Clearly, the renewal of the earth is a basic aspect of the sabbath. The renewal of all things is basic to the sabbath, and the earth is central to this renewal. Men can ignore the sabbath requirements of the earth only at the peril of judgment and death. Clearly, the death penalty is operative in history, and nations which mine the earth and use its resources abusively are doomed to die. The logical assumption then is this: if contempt of the sabbath is so serious with respect to the earth, is it not equally serious with respect to man and beast?

We do know that modern poultry methods, with the round the clock lighting of the cages, chemically "fortified" foods to step up growth, and various methods used to increase egg-laying, result in hens which are no longer profitable for retention after they begin moulting. Dairy cows similarly have a limited life span now. Not surprisingly, the produce from such animals no longer has the nutritional value it once did.

With regard to men, continued stress leads to death, we are told. Man's inability to rest, his lack of a true sabbath, his lack of faith, lead to a stress-filled life which ends in death. The study of stress, from a non-Christian perspective, has been extensively made in recent years by Dr. Selye.[8]

Man needs *rest*; he requires the sabbath truly to live; but, without faith, he cannot have true rest, nor can he give rest to others, to the soil, or to the animal creation. Very often pagan societies, on a limited scale, have practiced excellent soil policies from a pragmatic perspective. But the practice, being purely pragmatic, has not been joined with a similarly wise policy with respect to animals. More often than not, pagan cultures have been prevented from large-scale destruction only by their small-scale abilities.

When man destroys the soil, pollutes food, and poisons the air and the water, he does pass a death sentence against himself. The extent of the pollution is very great, and it is aggravated by man's confidence that "science" can somehow cope with it by some new artificial device.[9]

The essence of the sabbath is the work of restoration, God's new creation; the goal of the sabbath is the second creation rest of God. Man is required to rest and to allow earth and animals to rest, that God's restoration may work, and creation be revitalized. Every sabbath rest points to the new creation, the regeneration and restoration of all things. God's work of restoration is from the ground up, and His sabbath must therefore apply to the soil also.

But, *fourth*, the sabbath cannot be reduced to soil conservation any more than it can be reduced to humanitarianism. It is "a sabbath unto the LORD." It is a *covenant sign* according to God's own declaration:

> Wherefore I caused them to go forth out of the land of Egypt, and brought them into the wilderness.
> And I gave them my statutes, and shewed them my judgments, which if a man do, he shall even live in them.
> Moreover also I gave them my sabbaths, to be a sign between me and them, that they might know that I am the LORD that sanctify them.
> But the house of Israel rebelled against me in the wilderness: they walked not in my statutes, and they despised my judgments, which if a man do he shall even live in them; and my sabbaths they greatly polluted: then I said, I would pour out my fury upon them in the wilderness, to consume them (Ezek. 20:10-13).

---

8. Hans Selye, M.D., *The Stress of Life* (New York: McGraw-Hill, 1956).
9. For an account of the pollution, see J. I. Rodale and Staff, *Our Poisoned Earth and Sky* (Emmaus, Penna.: Rodale Books, 1964).

144   *The Institutes of Biblical Law*

The sabbath derives its essential meaning thus from the fact that it witnesses to an essential and life-giving covenant between God and man. The *source* of that life is God, *not* the law or the sabbath in and of itself. Israel, after the captivity, kept the sabbath rigidly, applying it to man, earth, and animals, but the *form* gave no life. They denied the sabbath by trusting in their works, and their blood (their descent from Abraham), and they died in their blindness. Observance of the sabbath did not save them who denied and crucified the Lord of the sabbath.

Churchmen who limit the meaning of the sabbath, or who feel it is obeyed in worship and inactivity, have no knowledge of its meaning. Certain Pharisees debated over the inadvisability of eating eggs, because the hen may have labored over them on the sabbath, but they did not trust in God for their salvation. Their emphasis on "no work" was in itself a work of man, a proud boast in their ability to fulfil a law, and this same Phariseeism is apparent in some churches today. The sabbath is life to the man who looks to the Lord for life, and allows God to work throughout all creation as the great re-creator. It is more than an outward observance, and it cannot be joined with any humanistic confidence in man's works, or the state's works, as man's source of rest and salvation.

Fifth, forgiveness is a basic aspect of the sabbath. The grace of God unto the remission of sins is the covenant of man's sabbath. It means rest, release from the burden of sin and guilt. The Lord's Prayer, which looks forward to the great sabbath ("Thy kingdom come"), has as a central petition the jubilee release: "And forgive us our debts, as we forgive our debtors" (Matt. 6:12). Lenski translated this, "And dismiss for us our debts as we, too, did dismiss our debtors."[10] The translation "trespasses" is good, in that it points more clearly to our sins; but the word "debts" has a broader connotation often, as it definitely does here. As Lenski observed, "So great are our debts to God that we can never hope to pay them, and our only help is that God will remit them gratis, by way of gift, for Christ's sake."[11]

The sabbath means rest, forgiveness, the cancellation of debt and weariness. It means fresh life. Since the unbeliever is by nature a slave, he is not released from debts:

> At the end of every seven years there must be a canceling of debts, and this shall be the way of canceling: Every creditor shall cancel the loan he made to his neighbor or to his brother: he shall make no demand for repayment, because the LORD'S release has been proclaimed. A foreigner you may press for payment, but whatever

10. R. C. H. Lenski, *The Interpretation of St. Matthew's Gospel* (Columbus, Ohio: The Wartburg Press, 1943), p. 269.
11. *Ibid.*, p. 269.

of yours was due from a brother you shall cancel. However, there should be no poor among you, for the LORD your God will abundantly bless you in the land He will give to possess as an heritage, if you listen to the LORD your God and rightly observe all these commandments which today I am enjoining upon you. When the LORD your God blesses you as He promised you, then you shall lend to many nations, but not borrow; you shall rule many nations, but they shall not rule over you (Deut. 15:1-6, Berkeley Version).

God's goal is a debt-free society which is also poverty-free, and this is only possible in terms of His law.

The effect of the sabbath law here is marked in Christendom. As Clark noted:

Modern statutes of limitation and bankruptcy acts fulfill the purpose of the ancient law of sabbatical release—the former by forbidding the bringing of an action upon a debt after a certain number of years and the latter enabling a debtor to turn over his property in satisfaction of his debts.[12]

The modern statutes are thoroughly secular and profane in intention, however, and, while derived from the Biblical sabbath law of release, are alien in spirit from it. The sabbath release confers life, but, to those alien to God, neither the sabbath nor its release can have their true meaning.

3. The Sabbath and Work

In his analysis of "The Idea of the Sabbath," Gustave Oehler observed, concerning it, that, *first*, "Man, like God is to work and to rest; thus human life is to be a copy of Divine life." The work of God's people is to be instrumental in the restoration of the divine order to the earth. *Second*,

Divine labor terminates in happy rest; not till the Creator rests satisfied in the contemplation of His works is His creation itself complete. So, too, human labor is not to run on in resultless circles, but to terminate in a happy harmony of existence.

The jubilee in part brings out this aspect of the sabbath. Moreover, because "the whole course of human history is not to run on in dreary endlessness," because its goal is a glorious victory, we too "are to find a completion in an harmonious and God-given order" which "is guaranteed by the Sabbath of creation, and prefigured by the sabbatical seasons." The sabbath of creation, unlike the previous six days, is not ended with an evening. "The Divine rest of the seventh day of creation, which has no evening, hovers over the world's progress, that it may at last absorb it into itself."

---

12. Clark, *Biblical Law*, p. 179.

Work and goal, effort and result, these are the two concepts which are basic to the idea of the sabbath, according to Oehler. The sabbath gives purpose to man's life, in that it makes labor meaningful and purposive: it links it to a joyful consummation. The sabbath, Oehler noted, looks *backward* to the creation rest for its pattern and faith; it looks *upward* to God in the assurance of His grace and victory; it looks *forward* to the great sabbath consummation.

> The full purport, however, of the idea of the Sabbath is not attained until that dominion of *sin* and *death*, which have entered into the development of mankind, is taken into account. It was after the curse of God was imposed upon the earth, and man condemned to labor in the sweat of his brow in the service of his perishable existence, that the desire for the rest of God took the form of a longing for *redemption* (Gen. v. 29). Israel, too, learned, by suffering under Egyptian oppression without any refreshing intermission, to sigh for rest. When their God bestowed upon them their regularly recurring period of rest, by leading them out of bondage, this ordinance became at the same time *a thankful solemnity in remembrance of the deliverance they had experienced.* Hence it is said, in the second version of the Decalogue (Deut. v. 15): "Remember that thou wast a bondman in the land of Egypt, and the Lord thy God brought thee out thence, with a mighty hand and a stretched-out arm; therefore the Lord thy God commanded thee to keep the Sabbath-day." This passage does not, as it has often been understood, merely urge a motive for the special duty of not hindering servants from resting on the seventh day: nor, on the other hand, does it contain, as has also been asserted, the proper objective reason for the sanctification of the sabbath, which is, on the contrary, expressed, as already said, in the first version of the Decalogue, Ex. xx. 11; but it applies to the keeping of the Sabbath, in particular, that consideration which is the deepest subjective incitement to the fulfilling of the whole law. How closely the remembrance of the deliverance from Egyptian bondage was bound up with this very institution of the Sabbath, is evident from what, according to the testimony of Roman authors given above (Tacitus, *Hist.* v. 4; Justin, *Hist.* 36. 2), was known to the heathen concerning the reason for the celebration of the Sabbath.[1]

Attention has been called to the fact that *restoration* is basic to the concept of the sabbath. But restoration clearly involves *work.* As Oehler pointed out, "one point, important in an ethical aspect, remains to be noticed. The Sabbath has its significance only as the seventh day, preceded by six days of labor. . . . Thus it is only upon the *foundation of preceding labor in our vocation* that the rest of the Sabbath is to be reared."[2]

The sabbath is God's covenant sign with man, declaring God's grace

---

1. Oehler, *Theology of the O.T.*, p. 332 f.
2. *Ibid.*, p. 333.

and God's efficacious work unto salvation, so that man can rest, "forasmuch as ye know that your labour is not in vain in the Lord" (I Cor. 15:58).

It must be remembered that an important aspect of the fourth law-word is this, "Six days thou shalt labour," i.e., six days are set aside for work. There is a positive command, therefore, to work. The creation mandate declared to man, "Be fruitful, multiply; fill the earth and subdue it; bear rule over the fish of the sea; over the birds of the air and over every living, moving creature on earth" (Gen. 1:28, Berkeley Version). This mandate was declared before the fall. The duties of fertility, work, and dominion were established thus before the fall; they continued after the fall, but with a serious impediment. Without regenerating grace, man cannot keep God's law and discharge his duties. The redeemed man's work is not an attempt to *create* a paradise on earth, but to *fulfill* God's requirements within the kingdom. The redeemed man is a citizen of the Kingdom of God, and he abides by the laws thereof: this is his work, his duty, and his path to dominion. The fact of the sabbath presupposes the fact of work.

The relationship between the sabbath and work is one that brings all things into relationship to God and in dedication to Him. Nothing can be, nor can be deemed to be, outside of God. Not only covenant man but all his work must be circumcised in a sense, or baptized, into the kingdom. The custom of the first-fruits was an aspect of this. But another law bears even more plainly on this matter:

> And when ye shall come into the land, and shall have planted all manner of trees for food, then ye shall count the fruit thereof as uncircumcised; three years shall it be as uncircumcised unto you: it shall not be eaten of. But in the fourth year all the fruit thereof shall be holy to praise the Lord withal. And in the fifth year shall ye eat of the fruit thereof, that it may yield unto you the increase thereof: I am the LORD your God (Lev. 19:23-25).

This law clearly is linked with laws previously discussed which bear on soil conservation, the fertility of the trees, and respect for the life of all creation. Ginsburg's comments bring out this aspect excellently:

> Trees which bore fruit unfit for human food, which grew up by themselves, or which were planted for hedges or timber, did not come under this law.
>
> Then ye shall count the fruit thereof as uncircumcised.—Literally, *then shall ye circumcise the uncircumcision, its fruit*, that is, cut off or pinch off its uncircumcision, which the text itself explains as "its fruit." The metaphorical use of circumcision is thus explained by the text itself: it denotes the fruit as disqualified or unfit. In chap. xxvi. 41 the same metaphor is used for the heart which is stubborn or not ripe to listen to the Divine admonitions. And in

other passages of Scripture it is used with reference to lips (Ex. vi. 12, 30) and ears (Jer. vi. 10) which do not perform their proper functions.[3]

For the first three years the fruit must be pinched off and allowed to rot on the ground. In the fourth year, it could be eaten if redeemed from the lord by paying its value plus a fifth part: it belonged to God. In the fifth year, the fruit could be harvested, and for five years thereafter, or, until the next sabbath year.

This law is concerned with the preservation of life by due respect for the conditions of life, but more is involved, because the word *uncircumcised* is deliberately and emphatically used. It means that the ground is indeed cursed for man's sake, because of his sin, and all man's work is futile and uncirmumcised apart from God.

Concerning the uncircumcised fruit, Peake's comment is an illustration of the absurdity of unbelief:

> The point is perhaps that during the first three years it is taboo and must be left alone; it may originally have been left for the field-spirits. Notice that animal firstlings were also not used till they were three years old. The Arabs propitiate the jinn with blood when a piece of land is ploughed for the first time.[4]

This masterpiece of irrelevance is so treasured by the modernist mind that Nathaniel Micklem perpetuated it a generation later by quoting Peake in his own commentary on Leviticus 19:23-25.[5] Bonar, whom neither Peake nor Micklem would recognize as a commentator, since he took God's law seriously, observed:

> Was this precept not a memorial of the *Forbidden Tree of Paradise?* Every fruit-tree was to stand unused for three years, as a test of their obedience. Every stranger saw, in Israel's orchards and vineyards, proofs of their obedience to their supreme Lord—a witness for Him.[6]

The conservation of the soil and the preservation of the fertility of the tree are important: they underlie this fact of uncircumcision. The earth is the Lord's, and it is to be used on His terms and under His law. The sabbath is not kept merely by inactivity, nor can any man commend himself to God by abstaining from eggs over which a hen labored on the sabbath. *The sabbath presupposes work, work fulfilling God's creation mandate and performed under God's law, and the sabbath is the joyful rest from the exercise of this godly dominion.* On the sabbath, a man rejoices that the earth is the Lord's, and all the fulness

3. Ginsburg, "Leviticus," in Ellicott, I, 426.
4. Arthur S. Peake, *A Commentary on the Bible* (London: T. C. & E. C. Jack, 1920), p. 208.
5. Micklem, "Leviticus," *Interpreter's Bible*, II, 98.
6. Bonar, *Leviticus*, p. 351.

thereof (Ps. 24:1). In that confidence man rests, and in that joy he surveys the work of his hands, knowing that his "labour is not in vain in the Lord" (I Cor. 15:58). On that day, and in the sabbatical season, he abstains from the fruit and the tree, now like a forbidden tree to him, because the Lord, who commands work in order that man may exercise dominion, also sets the boundaries on that dominion.

Man knows that his "labour is not in vain in the Lord" (I Cor. 15:58) because the sovereign God makes *all* things work together for good unto them that love Him, who are the called according to His purpose (Rom. 8:28). Covenant man recognizes, or is called to recognize, that to break the law at one point is to break the whole law (James 2:10), for to disregard the law at any point is to place ourselves in the position of gods at that point. The fact that Adam and Eve obeyed at all other points but disobeyed with respect to *one* tree did not give them a favorable balance with God. At that point they revealed a new operating principle: to be as gods, knowing or determining good and evil for themselves (Gen. 3:5). Both work and rest must be unto the Lord, and their presupposition must be the sovereignty of the triune God.

4. The Sabbath and Authority

There is a description of marriage in Scripture which often brings a snort of dissent from women. Naomi, in planning marriage for Ruth, declared, "My daughter shall I not seek rest for thee, that it may be well with thee?" (Ruth 3:1). The word *rest* here used in Hebrew is *manaoch*, place of rest, or, rest, whereas the *rest* which refers to cessation or sabbath is in Hebrew *shabbathon*. Nonetheless, while there is a distinction of importance between the two words, and the sabbath rest has a fulness lacking in the other, there is also a relationship.

It will not do to say that marriage was a *rest* to Ruth because, prior to that, she was working as a gleaner. The *rest* for Ruth was that she would in marriage be under the care and authority of a man, even as a man's *rest* is to be under Christ, "for the head of every man is Christ; and the head of the woman is the man" (I Cor. 11:3). True rest exists in that marriage where, despite the extensive work which may be the lot of husband and wife, each is under authority and walks in the confidence of that authority. The woman's long hair and covered head is a sign of submission to authority, and that authority is "power on her head." It signifies both her submission to authority and the power and protection that authority affords her. Historically and psychologically, the unprotected woman is open game.

The references to *rest, shabbathon* (Ex. 16:23; 31:15; 35:2; Lev.

16:31; 23:3, 32; 25:4, 5), speak of it as a "holy" rest, or a "rest to the Lord," or "holy to the Lord," or the like. Because it is a covenant sign, the sabbath is a sign of subjection to God, of an acceptance of God's authority on God's terms. "I gave them my sabbaths, to be a sign between me and them, that they might know that I am the LORD that sanctify them" (Ezek. 20:12).

The sabbaths were as follows:

1. *The Weekly Sabbaths*

2. *The New Moon Sabbaths,* Numbers 28:11-15, when labor was not forbidden but sacrifices were required. Later, according to Amos 8:5, a cessation of work became customary, but the original law did not require it. Earlier, it was a day of family observances (I Sam. 20:5 ff.). Also the Feast of Trumpets, or the New Year, was a sabbath.

3. *The Sabbatical Year and the Year of Jubilee* (Ex. 23:10 ff.; Lev. 25:1-7; 25:8-10; Deut. 15:1-11; 31:10-13, etc.). Debts could only be contracted for a six year period; the seventh year was a sabbath and a year of release (Deut. 15:1-11).

4. *The Passover* (Ex. 12:1-28, 43-49; 13:3-9; 23:15; Lev. 23:5 ff.; Num. 28:16-25; Deut. 16:1 ff.).

5. *Feast of Unleavened Bread* (seven days) (Ex. 13:17).

6. *The Feast of Weeks* (Pentecost) celebrated seven weeks after the Passover (Lev. 23:15 ff.). This was a harvest thanksgiving, on the 16th Nisan.

7. *The Feast of Tabernacles,* kept seven days, by dwelling in booths made of boughs, recalled the exodus journey (Lev. 23:36, 42). It ended the agricultural year with rejoicing and feasting.

There is thus a wide difference between the sabbaths. On the weekly sabbath, not even a fire could be built, food had to be cooked on the previous day. On the other hand, the new moon sabbaths originally did not call for a cessation of work, so that *rest* is not the essence of every sabbath; rejoicing and faith are. The other sabbaths were largely seasons of feasting and celebration. *All* the sabbaths were to be a *delight* to the covenant people.

To return to the relationship of the sabbath to authority, Ezekiel cited it as closely related to godly living, in speaking of the priests: "And in controversy they shall stand in judgment; and they shall judge it according to my judgments: and they shall keep my laws and my statutes in all mine assemblies; and they shall hallow my sabbaths" (Ezek. 44:24). The merely external rest of the sabbath was important, but an even deeper and more basic rest was the rest in the authority and work of God, and man's delight in it. The commandment does not merely require a cessation of work but "Remember . . . to keep it holy" (Ex. 20:8). Both work and rest were under authority and set apart or sanctified unto the Lord. Holiness in itself implies authority: it is separation and dedication in terms of God.

From the foregoing, three things are apparent. *First*, the *rest* of the sabbath comes from the fact that covenant man is *under authority*. *Second*, the sabbath is kept as a "sabbath to Jehovah thy God" (Ex. 20:10), as Bush rendered it,[1] as a *sign of the covenant*. *Third*, the sabbath is *holy* unto the Lord. All three things show clearly the basic fact of the sovereignty and authority of God, so that the sabbath must set forth God's authority and sovereignty, or else it is not truly a sabbath.

At this point, the development of synagogue and church worship appears as a logical development of the sabbath. Although it had no part in the original sabbath, it was still a necessary and logical development. To be under authority and to acknowledge sovereignty requires *knowledge*. The Levites very early became expositors of the law, and the schools of prophets were training centers for a teaching ministry. The synagogue was the result, so the Council of Jerusalem could observe, "For Moses of old time hath in every city them that preach him, being read in the synagogues every sabbath day" (Acts 15:21).

Growth in knowledge of God and His law-word is thus important to the celebration of the sabbath, and the evidence of the New Testament is eloquent to this fact. The Christian sabbath is thus geared to *knowledge* as an important aspect of the sabbath rest. Thus, a *first* and central aspect of the Christian sabbath is that it is a day for the proclamation of the word of God, a day when its meaning is studied and the knowledge of its application furthered. The joy and the song associated with the sabbath is associated with this knowledge. The knowledge of salvation, and the confidence in the divine law-word, give to the covenant people a delight and a certainty expressed in song and praise.

Second, while the Christian sabbath is inescapably and closely linked to the sabbath of Israel, there is still a very important difference. St. Paul's words in Colossians 2:16, 17 make clear that the old ordinance has undergone a radical change. Calvin commented on the Colossians passage:

> To *judge* means here to hold one to be guilty of a crime, or to impose a scruple of conscience, so that we are no longer free. He says, therefore, that it is not in the power of men to make us subject to the observance of rites which Christ has by his death abolished, and exempts us from their yoke, that we may not allow ourselves to be fettered by the laws which they have imposed. He tacitly, however, places Christ in contrast with all mankind, lest any one

---

1. George Bush, *Notes, Critical and Practical, on the Book of Exodus* (Boston: Henry A. Young, 1870), I, 270.

should extol himself so daringly as to attempt to take away what he has given him.

. . . The reason why he frees Christians from the observance of them is, that they were *shadows* at a time when Christ was still, in a manner, absent. For he contrasts shadows with revelation, and absence with manifestation. Those, therefore, who still adhere to these *shadows*, act like one who should judge of a man's appearance from his shadow, while in the mean time he had himself personally before his eyes. For Christ is now manifested to us, and hence we enjoy him as being present. *The body*, says he, is *of Christ*, that is, IN *Christ*.[2]

Luther cited the old sabbath "among the ceremonies that were necessary for the people of Moses but free for us."[3] Calvin's commentary on the law brought to focus the importance of the old as well as the change to the new:

And first of all, that this was a ceremonial precept, Paul clearly teaches, calling it a shadow of these things, the body of which is only Christ (Col. ii. 17). But if the outward rest was nothing but a ceremony, the substance of which must be sought in Christ, it now remains to be considered how Christ actually exhibited what was then prefigured; and this the same Apostle declares, when he states that "our old man is crucified with Christ," and that we are buried with Him, that His resurrection may be to us newness of life (Rom. vi. 4). It is to be gathered without doubt from many passages, that the keeping of the sabbath was a serious matter, since God inculcates no other commandment more frequently, nor more strictly requires obedience to any; and again when He complains that He is despised, and that the Jews have fallen into extreme ungodliness, He simply says that His "Sabbaths are polluted," as if religion principally consisted in their observance (Jer. xvii. 24; Ez. xx. 21; xxii. 8; xxiii. 38). Moreover, if there had not been some peculiar excellency in the Sabbath, it might have appeared to be an act of atrocious injustice to command a man to be put to death for cutting wood upon it (Numb. xv. 32). Wherefore it must be concluded that the substance of the Sabbath, which Paul declares to be in Christ, must have been no ordinary good thing.[4]

These words of Calvin are in marked contrast to the savage persecution ascribed to Calvin by antichristian writers. The "savage severity" of Calvin is a myth.[5] The Sunday laws and other moral legislations were medieval laws which were in force in Geneva when Calvin was not

---

2. John Calvin, *Commentaries on the Epistles of Paul to the Philippians, Colossians, and Thessalonians* (Grand Rapids: Eerdmans, 1957), p. 191 f.
3. Luther, *Lectures on Deuteronomy*, p. 81.
4. Calvin, *Commentaries on the Four Last Books of Moses in the Form of a Harmony*, II, 435.
5. See G. Rattray Taylor, *Sex in History* (New York: The Vanguard Press, 1954), p. 162.

there, and were enforced by persons who were often strongly opposing Calvin.[6]

To return to Calvin's point, a law which once called for death involved something very important and unusually good. Christ is that great good, and our rest in Him. As Calvin noted, "the Sabbath is violated even by good works, so long as we regard them as our own."[7] The essence of the sabbath is our rest in Christ, and our growth in the knowledge of that salvation by His grace.

The point of difference between Israel's sabbath and the Christian sabbath is not only in the day but in the end of the old restrictions. The first day of the week was a work-day in Palestine and also throughout the Roman Empire. The church normally met on the evening of the first day, because the members worked during the day. On one occasion, a sleepy member fell out the window and was killed (Acts 20:7-12). Obviously, if work on the Lord's day was still illegal, the New Testament would have had much to say concerning it. The old law was clearly altered here. The duty now, as stated by St. Paul, was "not forsaking the assembling of ourselves together, as the manner of some is" (Heb. 10:25).

Some, however, would call the work of the early Christians "works of necessity." In an alien culture, their work was comparable in a sense to enforced labor, slave labor. There is a good case for this. When Christian states were established, some forms of mandatory sabbath observance followed. When the sabbath laws began to break down, the reaction was an anguished one, as witness Robert Murray McCheyne, in a famous sermon of December 18, 1841:

> Dear fellow countrymen, as a servant of God in this dark and cloudy day, I feel constrained to lift up my voice in behalf of the Lord's Day. The daring attack that is now made by some of the directors of the Edinburgh and Glasgow Railway on the law of God and the peace of our Scottish Sabbath, the blasphemous motion which they mean to propose to the shareholders next February, and the wicked pamphlets which are now being circulated in thousands, full of all manner of lies and impieties, call loudly for the calm, deliberate testimony of all faithful ministers and private Christians in behalf of God's holy day. In the name of all God's people in this town and in this land, I commend for your consideration the following reasons for loving the Lord's Day.[8]

McCheyne then eloquently gave reasons for, let it be noted, "loving" the

---

6. See Phillip E. Hughes, "Introduction," in Hughes, *The Register of the Company of Pastors of Geneva in the Time of Calvin* (Grand Rapids: Eerdmans, 1966), pp. 3-31.
7. Calvin, *Commentaries on the Four Last Books of Moses*, II, 436.
8. Andrew A. Bonar, ed., *Memoirs of McCheyne, Including His Letters and Messages* (Chicago: Moody Press, 1947), p. 393.

Lord's day. While he opposed Sunday trains, and called it sabbath-breaking, he could not place it fully on the Old Testament level. The world, with increasingly round-the-clock operation of power plants, food transports, and the like, was rendering McCheyne's concept of the sabbath untenable. But the modern concept of the no-sabbath is equally untenable and destructive of man's peace. The sabbath of Israel is gone, and its laws, but the Christian sabbath does require Christian order, and an aspect of that order is the Christian sabbath.

But the sabbath is a sign of the *covenant*; it is not a law for a humanistic state, and has no meaning for it, nor can it be required of it. In a Christian state, it cannot be made anything resembling the sabbath of Israel. It must be a day of rest, and of peace and quiet, but the basic emphasis is on the authority of God, knowledge of Him, and rest in His government and salvation. The shifting of emphasis from the meaning of the sabbath to quibbling about regulations for the sabbath is certainly no honor to the sabbath. The words of St. Paul in Colossians 2:16, 17 remain true: if no man is to judge us with respect to the sabbaths, we then are similarly to judge none.

But, *third*, those who are members of the covenant, instead of being judges and law-makers over others with respect to the sabbath, are instead happy keepers of the day. It is for them truly a day of rest, because they alone are truly capable of resting. It is for them a day when God works in them by His word and His Spirit, so that they grow in grace and in wisdom, and in favor with God in the sight of men.

Psalm 1 states the relationship of man to the law very plainly:

> Blessed is the man that walketh not in the counsel of the lawless, nor standeth in the way of the unlawful, nor sitteth in the seat of the scornful. But his delight is in the law of YAHWEH; and in His Law doth he meditate day and night. And he shall be like a tree planted by the rivers of water, that bringeth forth his fruit in his season; his leaf also shall not wither; and whatsoever he doeth shall flourish.
>
> The lawless are not so: but are like the chaff which the wind driveth away. Therefore the lawless shall not stand in The Judgment, nor the unlawful in the Congregation of the Righteous. For YAHWEH knoweth the way of the righteous; but the way of the lawless shall perish.[9]

It is the vitality of faith which rejoices in the sabbath, and which flourishes because of the sabbath rest. To rest in the Lord is to accept His authority and to trust in Him.

---

9. Trans. by Theodore M. Jackman, *Psalms for Today* (Taylors, S. C.; 1968), p. 7.

5. The Sabbath and Law

St. Augustine spoke of the goal of history as "the great Sabbath which has no evening."[1] He concluded his *Confessions* with a statement on the meaning of the sabbath as the goal of history:

> (XXXV.) 50. *O Lord God, give peace unto us*: (for Thou hast given us all things;) the peace of rest, the peace of the Sabbath which hath no evening. For all this most goodly array of things *very good,* having finished their courses, is to pass away, for in them there was *morning and evening.*

> (XXXVI.) 51. But the seventh day hath no evening, nor hath it setting; because Thou hast sanctified it to an everlasting continuance; that that which Thou didst *after Thy works* which were *very good, resting on the seventh day,* although Thou madest them in unbroken rest, that may the voice of Thy Book announce beforehand unto us, that we also after our works (therefore *very good,* because Thou hast given them us,) shall *rest* in Thee also in the Sabbath of eternal life.

> (XXXVII.) 52. For then shalt Thou so rest in us, as now Thou workest in us; and so shall that be Thy rest through us, as these are Thy works through us. But Thou, Lord, ever workest, and art ever at rest. Nor dost Thou see in time, nor art moved in time, nor restest in a time; and yet Thou makest things seen in time, yea the times themselves, and the rest which results from time.

> (XXXVIII.) 53. We therefore see these things which Thou madest, because they are: but they are, because Thou seest them. And we see without, that they are, and within, that they are good, but Thou sawest them there, when made, where Thou sawest them, yet to be made. And we were at a later time moved to do well, after our hearts had conceived of Thy Spirit; but in the former time we were moved to do evil, forsaking Thee; but Thou, the One, the Good God, didst never cease doing good. And we also have some *good works,* of Thy gift, but not eternal; *after them* we trust *to rest* in Thy great *hallowing.* But Thou, being the Good which needeth no good, art ever at rest, because Thy rest is Thou Thyself. And what man can teach man to understand this? or what Angel, an Angel? or what Angel, a man? Let it be *asked* of Thee, *sought* in Thee, *knocked* for at Thee; so, shall it be *received,* so shall it be found, so shall it be *opened.* Amen.[2]

Westcott spoke of the sabbath rest of Hebrews 4:9 as "a rest which closes the manifold forms of earthly preparation and work (the Hexaemeron of human toil): not an isolated sabbath but a sabbath-life. . . . The Sabbath rest answers to the Creation as its proper consummation." Westcott, citing St. Augustine, then called attention to rabbinical commentaries:

---

1. St. Augustine, *The City of God,* bk. XXII, chap. xxx.
2. St. Augustine, *Confessions* (London: J. M. Dent, 107, Everyman's Library), bk. XIII, p. 347 f.

The Jewish teachers dwelt much upon the symbolic meaning of the Sabbath as prefiguring "the world to come." One passage quoted by Schoettgen and others may be given: "The people of Israel said: Lord of the whole world, shew us the world to come. God, blessed be He, answered: Such a pattern is the Sabbath" (*Jalk. Rub.* p. 95, 4). In this connexion the double ground which is given for the observance of the Sabbath, the rest of God (Ex. xx. 11) and the deliverance from Egypt (Deut. v. 15), finds its spiritual confirmation. The final rest of man answers to the idea of Creation realised after the Fall by Redemption.[3]

This view of the sabbath is not only the teaching of the church fathers like Augustine, and of rabbis, but also of modern Protestant commentators. Lenski who pointed out that "God rested 'from his works' (not 'from his labors')," noted that it was the ordained eternal rest from before creation.[4] Schneider noted further that "this 'rest' is not a forlorn bliss blotting out activity. It is rather the 'active rest' (Luther) in which the perfected Church adores and praises God."[5]

Hebrews 3 and 4 are the foundation for this interpretation of the sabbath. Canaan, the Promised Land, was a foreshadowing of the true sabbath, but the true sabbath could not be identified with it. Beyond all the types, "There remaineth therefore a rest to the people of God" (Heb. 4:9), or, it can be translated, that there remains a sabbath, or a sabbath-rest, to the people of God. As Moulton noted of Hebrews 4:10, "Man's sabbath-rest begins when he enters into God's rest (Gen. ii. 2); as that was the goal of the creative work, so to the people of God this rest is the goal of their life of 'works.' "[6]

Certain general observations can now be made concerning the sabbath. *First*, the foregoing makes clear that the sabbath has always had reference to the *future*. The *pattern* of the sabbath is in the past, from the sabbath of creation. The *entrance* into the sabbath is also in the past; for Israel, it was the redemption from Egypt; for the church, it is in the resurrection. The *fulfilment* of the sabbath is in the new creation. The sabbath is a *present* rest, based on *past* events, with a *future* reference and fulfilment.

Second, and closely related to the future reference of the sabbath, the law of the sabbath required *providence*, i.e., a provident people. Because of the short-term nature of debt, only emergency debts could be contracted. In each century, sixteen years were sabbaths, including

---

3. B. F. Westcott, *The Epistle to the Hebrews* (Grand Rapids: Eerdmans, 1952), p. 98 f.
4. R. C. H. Lenski, *The Interpretation of the Epistle to the Hebrews and the Epistle of James* (Columbus, Ohio: Wartburg Press, 1937, 1946), p. 132 f.
5. Johannes Schneider, *The Letter to the Hebrews* (Grand Rapids: Eerdmans, 1957), p. 30.
6. W. F. Moulton, "Hebrews," in Ellicott, VIII, 297.

two jubilee years. While God promised an abundant harvest for faithfulness to His law, it was still necessary for man to use that abundance providently, or else he would be unable to live. Providence in management means an obviously future-oriented perspective. Instead of a past-oriented and consumption-centered economy, the sabbath produced a production-centered, future-oriented, and rest-conscious society. A provident society can rest with peace and security, and a productive society is best able to enjoy rest.

Third, a sabbath-oriented society best gives *rest*. A generation ago, railroaders in the United States worked seven days a week, ten hours a day, every day of the year. Clearly, such working conditions were anti-Biblical and, in terms of Biblical law, criminal. Not surprisingly, the railroad tycoons were on the whole a group of thoroughly reprobate men. When the fourth commandment rules it unlawful to deny even the earth and domesticated animals their sabbath, how much more so the denial of rest to man? And yet, clearly, the shorter working hours, the paid vacations, five eight-hour-day working weeks have failed to give men true rest. The increase of heart attacks, ulcers, and other stress-induced ailments and diseases makes clear that the change in working conditions has not been any help to man. Because the older order, ungodly as it was, still was closer to a Christian faith and order, man had, in the face of lawless working conditions, a greater ability to rest than does the man of the late twentieth century. In a sabbath-oriented society, the provident man, having lived debt-free, finding rest in Christ, and able both to work and to relax, has a peace and joy in life lacking in a phrenetic generation.

But, *fourth*, since all law has reference to the future, and is in essence a plan for the future, the sabbath law is a plan for the world's tomorrow. The Biblical law works to eliminate evil and to abolish poverty and debt. The sabbath law has as its *work* the recreation of man, animals, and the earth, the whole of creation. The sabbath thus reveals the design and direction of the whole law: it is a declaration of the future the law is establishing.

Thus, while Colossians 2:16, 17 makes clear that the *formalisms* of the Old Testament observances are ended, the essence of the law is in force and is basic to all Biblical law.

Non-Christian thought, when oriented to the future, faces a double penalty. *First*, it is past-bound. The "civil rights" revolution, for example, has only the vaguest sense of the burdens of responsibility, which any person thinking in terms of reality and the future needs to have. Instead, the "civil rights" revolutionists speak endlessly of past evils, not merely real or imagined evils of their own experiencing, but all evils which they believe their ancestors suffered. Similarly, some labor union men, and American Indians, dwell endlessly on past history rather than present reality. This inability to live in the present means a radical incapacity for coping with the future.

Second, the non-Christian, as he faces the future, is at best utopian and unrealistic. As Mumford noted, "each utopia was a closed society for the prevention of human growth."[7] Man is reduced to economic man and viewed in terms of an externalism which destroys man.[8] Utopianism not only presents an illusory or dangerous picture of the future, but it also distorts and destroys the present. Utopianism thus affords man no help as he works towards the future: it gives man illusions which beget only needless sacrifice and work and produce nothing but social chaos.

7. Lewis Mumford, *The Story of Utopias* (New York: The Viking Press, 1922, 1963), p. 4.
8. *Ibid.*, pp. 239, 247.

V

THE FIFTH COMMANDMENT

1. The Authority of the Family

Before analyzing the Biblical law with respect to the honoring of parents, and their authority, it is necessary to take note of the extensive undermining of the Biblical doctrine of the family. In the Ten Commandments, four laws deal with the family, three of them directly: "Honor thy father and mother," "Thou shalt not commit adultery," "Thou shalt not steal," and "Thou shalt not covet thy neighbor's house, thou shalt not covet thy neighbor's wife, nor his man-servant, nor his maid-servant, nor his ox, nor his ass, nor anything that is thy neighbor's" (Ex. 20:12, 14, 15, 17). The fact that property (and hence theft) were family-oriented appears not only in all the law, but in the tenth commandment: to covet, whether property, wife, or servants of another was a sin against the neighbor's family. The family is clearly central to the Biblical way of life, and it is the family *under God* which has this centrality.

But it must be added that this Biblical perspective is alien to the Darwinian world-view. Evolutionary thought concedes the centrality of the family, but only as a historical fact. The family is seen as the great primitive institution, now rapidly being superseded, but important for studies of man's evolutionary past. The family is seen as the old collectivity or collectivism which must give way to "the new collectivity."[1] As the old collectivism which is resisting change, the family is steadily attacked by evolutionary social scientists, educators, and clergymen.

The evolutionary anthropology which undergirds this attack owes much, after Darwin, to William Robertson Smith (1846-1894), *The Religion of the Semites*. Darwin and Smith in turn gave Sigmund Freud (1856-1939) his basic premises. In terms of this perspective, as presented by Freud (but also made popular by Sir James G. Frazer's *The Golden Bough*), the origins of the family are in man's primitive past rather than God's creative purpose. The "primal horde," or primitive society, was dominated by the "violent primal father," who drove

---

1. Ch. Letourneau, *The Evolution of Marriage*. The Contemporary Science Series (London: The Walter Scott Publ. Co., 1911, 3rd edition), p. 356.

159

out the sons and claimed exclusive sexual possession of the mother and
the daughters. "The origin of morality in each of us" comes from the
Oedipus complex.[2] The rebellious sons, who envied and feared the
father, banded together, killed and ate the father, and then possessed
the mother and the sisters sexually. Their remorse and guilt over their
acts created three basic taboos for man, parricide, cannibalism, and
incest. For Freud, in Christianity, the son makes atonement on the
cross for killing the father, and cannibalism is transformed into a
sacrament, the communion.[3]

With this in mind, we can understand why anthropologists can say,
"The family is the most fundamental of all social groups, and it is
universal in its distribution." The next sentence informs us, however,
that the family is a "culturally determined" social form,[4] i.e., it is
entirely an evolutionary product of man's culture. Accordingly, the
subject of "Religion and Ritual" is introduced in the course of an analysis of the "Extension of Kinship."[5] The *power* of the parent and the
security of the family are in religion projected against the hostile environment to give it a participating kinship and favor to man.

Accordingly, we are told, there are two kinds of religions, the religion of the mother, and the religion of the father.

Thus, Van der Leeuw wrote,

> "There is nothing more sacred on earth than the religion of the
> mother, for it leads us back to the deepest personal secret in our
> souls, to the relationship between the child and its mother"; in these
> terms Otto Kern has crystallized the essence of our theme. Be-
> lieving that behind Power he decries the outlines of a Form, man
> recognizes therein the features of his own mother; his loneliness
> when confronted with Power thus transforms itself into the intimate
> relationship to the mother.[6]

The origin of fertility cults is seen in the worship of the mother, an
invoking of fertility as well as a return to the security of the womb. The
mother cult leads eventually to the father cult. According to Van der
Leeuw, "To every man his mother is a goddess, just as his father is a
god."[7] Moreover, "The mother creates life: the father history";[8] i.e.,
the fertility cult religions are matters of pre-history, and of primitive

2. Sigmund Freud, "The Economic Problem in Masochism"(1924), in *Collected Papers* (New York: Basic Books, 1959), II, 265.
3. Sigmund Freud, "Totem and Taboo," in *The Basic Writings of Sigmund
Freud*, A. A. Brell, translator (New York: Modern Library, 1938).
4. E. Adamson Hoebel, *Man in the Primitive World*, 2nd edition (New York:
McGraw-Hill, 1958), p. 318.
5. *Ibid.*, p. 351.
6. Gerardus Van der Leeuw, *Religion in Essence & Manifestation, A Study in
Phenomenology.* Trans. by J. E. Turner (New York: Macmillan, 1938), p. 91.
7. *Ibid.*, p. 99.
8. *Ibid.*, p. 100.

cultures, whereas the father as god is a stage of man's development in history. Van der Leeuw admitted, in commenting on Isaiah 63:16 and 64:8, that the Biblical God "is not the figure of the generator but of a creator, whose relations to man are the precise opposite of kinship, and before whose will man bows in deep but trustful dependence,"[9] but, having noted this, he returned to his evolutionary thesis.

Religion, thus, is seen as a projection of the family, and the family must therefore be destroyed in order that religion may also be destroyed. But this is not all. Private property is similarly seen as an outgrowth of the family, and the abolition of private property requires the destruction of the family as a prerequisite. Van der Leeuw spoke of the relationship between the family and property:

> Among many peoples, still further, *property* also plays a part as the common element of the family. For property is not just the object which the owner possesses. It is a power, and indeed a common power. . . . Thus we find the common element of the family bound up with blood and with property; but it is not confined to these, for it is sacred, and therefore cannot be derived without any remainder from the given.[10]

According to Hoebel,

> The essential nature of property is to be found in social relations rather than in any inherent attribute of the thing or object that we call *property*. Property, in other words, is not a thing, but a network of social relations that governs the conduct of people with respect to the use and disposition of things.[11]

This is a typical little trick of the modern humanistic intellectual: dispose of a problem by defining it away! For Hoebel, property is not "a thing but a network of social relations." And what do these social relations govern? Hoebel's last word makes it clear: they govern *things*! What are these *things* if not *property*?

But it was Frederick Engels who most plainly stated the humanistic case (and the "Marxist" thesis) concerning the relationship between property and the family. The monogamous family, he held, "is based on the supremacy of the man, the express purpose being to produce children of undisputed paternity; such paternity is demanded because these children are later to come into their father's property as his natural heirs."[12] Monogamy has reduced the importance of women and has led to "the brutality towards women that has spread since the

9. *Ibid.*, p. 179.
10. *Ibid.*, p. 249.
11. Hoebel, *Man in the Primitive World*, p. 448.
12. Frederick Engels, *The Origin of the Family, Private Property and the State, In the light of the researches of Lewis H. Morgan* (New York: International Publishers, 1964), p. 55.

introduction of monogamy."[13]   Monogamy, and the modern individual family, rests or is "founded on the open or concealed domestic slavery of the wife."[14] The original group marriage has given way to pairing marriage, and, finally, to monogamy, whose concommitants are "adultery and prostitution."[15] Communism will abolish both traditional monogamy and private property:

> We are now approaching a social revolution in which the economic foundations of monogamy as they have existed hitherto will disappear just as surely as those of its complement—prostitution. Monogamy arose from the concentration of considerable wealth in the hands of a single individual—a man—and from the need to bequeath this wealth to the children of that man and of no other. . . . Having arisen from economic causes, will monogamy then disappear when these causes disappear?

> One might answer, not without reason: far from disappearing, it will on the contrary, be realized completely. For with the transformation of the means of production into social property there will disappear also wage-labor, the proletariat, and therefore the necessity for a certain—statistically calculable—number of women to surrender themselves for money. Prostitution disappears; monogamy, instead of collapsing, at last becomes a reality—also for men.

> . . . With the transfer of the means of production into common ownership, the single family ceases to be the economic unit of society. Private housekeeping is transformed into a social industry. The care and education of the children becomes a public affair; society looks after all children alike, whether they are legitimate or not. This removes all the anxiety about the "consequences" which today is the most essential social—moral as well as economic—factor that prevents a girl from giving herself completely to the man she loves. Will not that suffice to bring about the gradual growth of unconstrained sexual intercourse and with it a more tolerant public opinion in regard to a maiden's honor and a woman's shame? And, finally, have we not seen that in the modern world monogamy and prostitution are indeed contradictions, but inseparable contradictions, poles of the same state of society? Can prostitution disappear without dragging monogamy with it into the abyss?[16]

Engels' view of marriage was that of an easily dissolved tie based only on love, with freedom for any association without penalty.[17] Very clearly, Biblical marriage was to be abolished with the abolition of private property.

It become apparent then why modern humanistic education, and especially Marxist education, is so hostile to the family, and so clearly

13. *Ibid.*, p. 64.
14. *Ibid.*, p. 65.   16. *Ibid.*, p. 67.
15. *Ibid.*, p. 66.   17. *Ibid.*, p. 73.

dedicated to replacing the "old collectivity" of the family with "the new collectivity," the state. To destroy the monogamous Biblical family means, from their perspective, the destruction, *first*, of religion, and *second*, of private property. The Marxist wants to "emancipate" woman by making her an industrial worker.[18] This is "emancipation" by definition, because it frees woman from the Biblical religion-marriage-property complex.

In order to counteract these humanistic conceptions of the family and of the parental role, the Biblical doctrine of the family which is plainly *God-centered* must be understood and stressed. The humanistic doctrine of the family is man-centered and society-centered. The family is seen as a social institution, which, in the course of evolution, provided the original and "old collectivity" and must now give way to "the new collectivity" as mankind becomes the true family of man. As already noted, the *first* characteristic of the Biblical doctrine is that the family is viewed in terms of a God-centered *function* and *origin*. The family is a part of God's purpose for man, and it functions to the glory of God in its true form, as well as giving man his own self-realization under God.

Second, Genesis 1:27-30 makes clear that God created man to subdue the earth and to exercise dominion over it under God. Although originally only Adam was created (Gen. 2:7), the creation mandate is plainly spoken to man in the married estate, and with the creation of woman in mind. Thus, essential to the function of the family under God, and to the role of the man as the head of the household, is *the call to subdue the earth and exercise dominion over it*. This gives to the family a *possessive* function: to subdue the earth and exercise dominion over it clearly involves in the Biblical perspective private property. Man must bring to all creation God's law-order, exercising power over creation in the name of God. The earth was created "very good" but it was as yet undeveloped in terms of subjugation and possession by man, God's appointed governor. This *government* is particularly the calling of the man as husband and father, and of the family as an institution. The *fall of man* has not altered this calling, although it has made its fulfilment impossible apart from Christ's regenerating work.

Third, this exercise of dominion and possession clearly involves *responsibility and authority*. Man is responsible to God for his use of the earth, and must, as a faithful governor, discharge his calling only in terms of his Sovereign's royal decree or word. His calling confers also on him an authority by delegation. To man is given authority by God

---

18. *Ibid.*, p. 148.

over his household and over the earth. In the Marxist scheme, the transfer of authority from the family to the state makes any talk of the family as an institution ridiculous. The family is to all practical intent abolished whenever the state determines the education, vocation, religion, and the discipline of the child. The only function remaining then to the parents is procreation, and, by means of birth control regulations, this too is subject now to a diminishing role. The family in such a society is simply a relic of the old order, maintaining itself only surreptitiously and illegally, and subject at all times to the intervening authority of the state. In all modern societies, the transfer of authority from the family to the state has been accomplished in varying degrees.

In the Biblical perspective, the authority of the family is basic to society, and it is a God-centered authority. Hence the common division of the commandment into two tables, or two sides, of five each, with the fifth commandment placed alongside those relating to man's duty to God.

The meaning of the family is thus not to be sought in procreation but in a God-centered authority and responsibility in terms of man's calling to subdue the earth and to exercise dominion over it.

Fourth, the function of the woman in this aspect of God's law-order is to be a help-meet to man in the exercise of his dominion and authority. She provides companionship in his calling (Gen. 2:18), so that there is a community in authority, with the clear preëminence being the man's. Man's sin is to attempt to usurp God's authority, and woman's sin is to attempt to usurp man's authority, and both attempts are a deadly futility. Eve exercised leadership in submitting to the temptation; she led Adam rather than being led; Adam succumbed to the desire to be as God (Gen. 3:5), while acting as less than a man in submitting to Eve's leadership.

But the authority of the woman as help-meet is no less real than that of a prime minister to a king; the prime minister is not a slave because he is not king, nor is the woman a slave because she is not a man. The description of a virtuous woman, or a godly wife, in Proverbs 31:10-31 is not of a helpless slave nor of a pretty parasite, but rather of a very competent wife, manager, business-woman, and mother—a person of real authority.

The key therefore to the Biblical doctrine of the family is to be found in the fact of its central authority, and the meaning thereof.

2. The Promise of Life

The fifth commandment carries a significant pledge to the obedient, the promise of life:

Honour thy father and thy mother: that thy days may be long upon the land which the LORD thy God giveth thee (Ex. 20:12).

Honour thy father and thy mother, as the LORD thy God hath commanded thee: that thy days may be prolonged, and that it may go well with thee, in the land which the LORD thy God giveth thee (Deut. 5:16).

Exodus states, and Deuteronomy, in expanded form, repeats this promise of life. Before analyzing the meaning of this promise, it is necessary to understand the condition, the honoring of parents.

Rylaarsdam's comment is an amusing example of modernist interpretation. His interpretation of Exodus 20:12 reads:

> The Fifth (Fourth) Commandment stands at the point of transition from social to civil law. The honoring of parents is a form of piety, though not a cultic observance. In Deut. 5:16 prosperity is added to the promise of length of days *in the land* offered here. Minor children were bound to strict obedience (21:15, 17; Lev. 20:9; Prov. 30:17). This commandment most especially refers to the treatment of helpless aged dependents. They are not to be sent abroad to be eaten of beasts or to die of exposure, as was the case in some societies. The possession of *the land* which *your God gives* ("is giving," "will give"—as in Deuteronomy the locus is Sinai) depends upon the maintenance of family standards.[1]

In other words, parents are "honored" if they are not exposed to die! Certainly, the custom of Eskimos was not the custom of the ancient Near East, and this interpretation is in every respect wilfully wrong. The requirement here is, *first*, a religious honoring of parents, and, *second*, it involved a general respect for one's elders. This is plainly required in Leviticus 19:32: "Thou shalt rise up before the hoary head, and honour the face of the old man, and fear thy God: I am the LORD." The respect for the aged was marked; according to Proverbs 16:31, "The hoary head is a crown of glory, if it be found in the way of righteousness." But, as Leviticus 19:32 made clear, irrespective of the moral character of the older generation, a basic respect and honor is due. Righteousness adds a "crown of glory" to the older generation.

Age commanded respect. Paul could thus appeal to his age as a factor in trying to sway Philemon: "Yet for love's sake I rather beseech thee, being such an one as Paul the aged, and now also a prisoner of Jesus Christ" (Philemon 9). Love, age, and his imprisonment for Christ all gave Paul moral authority. Because of this required respect for age, it is all the more imperative that with age we grow in wisdom. Thus, Paul counselled "That the aged men be sober, grave, temperate, sound in faith, in charity, in patience. The aged women likewise, that they

---

1. J. C. Rylaarsdam, "Exodus," in *Interpreter's Bible*, I, 985.

be in behaviour as becometh holiness, not false accusers, nor given to much wine, teachers of good things (Titus 2:2, 3).

This brings us to the *first* general principle inherent in this law: honor to parents, and to all older than ourselves, is a necessary aspect of the basic law of *inheritance*. What we inherit from our parents is life itself, and also the wisdom of their faith and experience as they transmit it to us. The continuity of history rests in this honor and inheritance. A revolutionary age breaks with the past and turns on parents with animosity and venom: it disinherits itself. To respect our elders other than our parents is to respect all that is good in our cultural inheritance. The world certainly is not perfect, nor even law-abiding, but, although we come into the world *naked*, we do not enter an empty world. The houses, orchards, fields, and flocks are all the handiwork of the past, and we are richer for this past and must honor it. Our parents especially, who provide for us and nurture us, are to be honored above all others, for, if we do not do so, we both sin against God and we disinherit ourselves. As we shall see later, there is a close connection between disinheritance in a family estate and the dishonoring of parents, the rejecting of their honor and their cultural heritage. The basic and central inheritance of culture and all that it includes, faith, training, wisdom, wealth, love, common ties, and traditions are severed and denied where parents and elders are not honored. The tragic fact is that many parents refuse to recognize that their children have disinherited themselves.

A *second* general principle inherent in this law is that of *progress rooted in the past*, of inheritance as the foundation for progress. The commandment, speaking to adults, calls for *honor*, not *obedience*. For children, the requirement is obedience: "Children obey your parents in the Lord: for this is right (Eph. 6:1). "Children, obey your parents in all things: for this is well pleasing unto the Lord" (Col. 3:20). Hodge's interpretation of Ephesians 6:1 is excellent:

> The nature or character of this obedience is expressed by the words, *in the Lord*. It should be religious; arising out of the conviction that such obedience is the will of the Lord. This makes it a higher service than if rendered from fear or from mere natural affection. It secures its being prompt, cordial and universal. That *Kurios* here refers to Christ is plain from the whole context. In the preceding chapter, v. 21, we have the general exhortation under which this special direction to children is included, and the obedience there required is to be rendered *in the fear of Christ*. In the following verses also *Kurios* constantly has this reference, and therefore must have it here. The ground of the obligation to filial obedience is expressed in the words, *for this is right*. It is not because of the personal character of the parent, nor because of his kindness, nor on the ground of expediency, but because it is *right*; an obligation aris-

ing out of the nature of the relation between parents and children, and which must exist wherever the relation exists.[2]

Many cultures have had a religious honoring of parents, but this has usually been connected with ancestor worship and has been a stifling, deadening factor in society. China's long failure to advance was due on the one hand to its relativism, and, on the other, to the social paralysis produced by its family system.

In Biblical faith, the family inherits from the past in order to grow firmly into the future. Man and wife become *one flesh*; they have in their marriage a common physical, sexual tie that makes them *one flesh*. Hence, Scripture declares, "Therefore shall a man leave his father and his mother, and shall cleave unto his wife: and they shall be one flesh" (Gen. 2:24). Marriage calls for a move forward by the man and his wife; they break with the old families to create a new one. They remain tied to the old families in that both represent a cultural inheritance from two specific families. They remain tied further by a religious duty to honor their parents. The growth is real, and the dependence is real: the new clearly and plainly grows out of and realizes the potentiality of the old.

For this reason, the church is readily spoken of as a family in Scripture. St. Paul spoke of himself as the father of the Corinthian believers, "For though ye have ten thousand instructors in Christ, yet have ye not many fathers: for in Christ Jesus I have begotten you through the gospel" (I Cor. 4:15). Again, he wrote in Philemon 10, "I beseech thee for my son Onesimus, whom I have begotten in my bonds." The church is the family of the faithful, and the ties of faith are very close ones. The ties of the family are all the stronger if the bond is of both blood and faith.

Still another aspect of *honor* will be discussed separately under the title of "The Economics of the Family."

Our concern now is with the latter part of this law-word, the promise of long life and prosperity. Solomon repeated this promise of the law, summarizing it thus, "Hear, O my son, and receive my sayings; and the years of thy life shall be many" (Prov. 4:10). Indeed, Proverbs 1-5 in their entirety deal with this promise of life.

Hodge, in analyzing this promise, observed:

> The promise itself has a theocratical form in the Old Testament. That is, it has specific reference to prosperity and length of days in the land which God had given his people as their inheritance. The apostle generalizes it by leaving out the concluding words, and makes it a promise not confined to one land or people, but to obedi-

---

2. Charles Hodge, *Commentary on the Epistle to the Ephesians* (Grand Rapids: Eerdmans [1856], 1950), p. 356 f.

ent children every where. If it is asked whether obedient children are in fact thus distinguished by long life and prosperity? The answer is, that this, like all other such promises, is a revelation of a general purpose of God, and makes known what will be the usual course of providence. That some obedient children are unfortunate and short lived, is no more inconsistent with this promise, than that some diligent men are poor, is inconsistent with the declaration, "The hand of the diligent maketh rich." Diligence, as a general rule, does secure riches; and obedient children, as a general rule, are prosperous and happy. The general promise is fulfilled to individuals, just so far "as it shall serve for God's glory, and their own good."[3]

The question has been raised as to the application of the promise: is it for the nation, or is the promise for individuals? As Rawlinson noted:

The promise may be understood in two quite different senses. (1) It may be taken as guaranteeing national permanence to the people among whom filial respect and obedience is generally practised; or (2) it may be understood in the simpler and more literal sense of a pledge that obedient children shall, as a general rule, receive for their reward the blessing of a long life. In favour of the former view have been urged the facts of Roman and Chinese permanence, together with the probability that Israel forfeited its possession of Canaan in consequence of persisting in the breach of this commandment. In favour of the latter may be adduced the application of the text by St. Paul (Eph. vi. 3), which is purely personal and not ethnic; and the exegesis of the Son of Sirach (Wisd. iii. 6), which is similar. It is also worthy of note that an Egyptian sage, who wrote long before Moses, declared it as the result of his experience that obedient sons did attain to a good old age in Egypt, and laid down the principle broadly, that "the son who attends to the words of his father will grow old in consequence."[4]

The reference to Ben Sirach is to his declaration, "He that honoureth his father shall have a long life; and he that is obedient unto the Lord shall be a comfort to his mother" (Wisd. 3:6). This is not only a repetition of the law, but an observation of fact. The reality of life is that he who loves life, and honors the God who created life, by reverencing His law and his parents under God, lives most truly, happily, and longest as a rule. To despise one's parents, or to hate them and dishonor them is to despise the immediate source of one's life; it is a form of self-hate, and it is a wilful contempt for the basic inheritance of life. From pastoral experience, it can be added that those who when rebuked for their hatred of and dishonoring activity towards parents, arrogantly say, "I didn't ask to be born," have a limited life-span, or at best, a miserable one. Their course of action is suicidal. They are saying in effect, "I'm not asking to live."

---

3. *Ibid.*, p. 358 f.
4. George Rawlinson, "Exodus," in Ellicott, *op. cit.*, I, 262 f.

This same promise of life for honoring the immediate sources of life appears in Deuteronomy 22:6, 7, and Leviticus 22:28:

> And whether it be a cow or ewe, ye shall not kill it and her young both in one day (Lev. 22:28).
> If a bird's nest chance to be before thee in the way in any tree, or on the ground, whether they be young ones, or eggs, and the dam sitting upon the young, or upon the eggs, thou shalt not take the dam with the young: But thou shalt in any wise let the dam go, and take the young to thee; that it may be well with thee, and that thou mayest prolong thy days (Deut. 22:6, 7).

A similar law appears in Exodus 23:19: "Thou shalt not boil a kid in its mother's milk" (RV). The language of the promise plainly connects these with the fifth commandment. Of Deuteronomy 22:6, 7, it is noted: "The commandment is placed upon a par with the commandment relating to parents, by the fact that obedience is urged upon the people by the same premise in both instances."[5] But it is more than a case of being "placed upon a par"; the fact is clearly indicated that one basic law is involved. Again, it will not do to say, as W. L. Alexander did, that "These precepts are designed to foster humane feelings towards the lower animals."[6] A basic premise is asserted in the fifth commandment; in these laws dealing with the birds, cows, ewes, and kids, this principle is asserted and illustrated in minimal cases to illustrate the maximal reach of the law. The earth is the Lord's and all life is the handiwork of the Lord. Man cannot on any level treat life except under law, God's law. The cry of some oppressed Persians of another generation, "We are men, and would have laws!,"[7] was a notable one. Man needs *God's* law, and the law of the Lord requires us to honor our inheritance at every level. To lay waste our inheritance, whether in the animal world or on the level of our family, is to deny life. It is playing god; it is assuming that we made ourselves and can remake our world. Paul could command obedience by children to their parents, saying, "It is right," it is by nature obligatory and proper.

Honoring parents is placed on the same level as sabbath-keeping in Leviticus 19:1-3:

> And the LORD spake unto Moses, saying,
> Speak unto all the congregation of the children of Israel, and say unto them, Ye shall be holy: for I the LORD your God am holy.
> Ye shall fear every man his mother, and his father, and keep my sabbaths: I am the LORD your God.

---

5. Keil and Delitzsch, *The Pentateuch*, III, 410.
6. W. L. Alexander in Canon H. D. M. Spence and Rev. Joseph. S. Exell, eds., *The Pulpit Commentary: Deuteronomy* (New York: Funk and Wagnalls, n.d.), p. 355.
7. Andrew Harper, *Deuteronomy* (New York: George H. Doran, n.d.), p. 304.

As Ginsburg pointed out, only twice in the entire law is the expression used, "Speak unto all the congregation of the children of Israel," in Exodus 12:3, at the institution of the Passover, and here. Of verse 3, "Ye shall fear every man his mother, and his father," Ginsburg wrote:

> The first means to attain to the holiness which is to make the Israelite reflect the holiness of God, is uniformly to reverence his parents. Thus the group of precepts contained in this chapter opens with the fifth commandment in the Decalogue (Exod. xx. 12), or, as the Apostle calls it, the first commandment with promise (Eph. vi. 2). During the second Temple, already the spiritual authorities called attention to the singular fact that this is one of the three instances in the Scriptures where, contrary to the usual practice, the mother is mentioned before the father; the other two being Gen. xliv. 20 and Lev. xxi. 2. As children ordinarily fear the father and love the mother, hence they say precedence is here given to the mother in order to inculcate the duty of fearing them both alike. The expression "fear," however, they take to include the following:—(1) Not to stand or sit in the place set apart for the parents; (2) not to carp at or oppose their statements; and (3) not to call them by their proper names, but either call them father or mother, or my master, my lady. Whilst the expression "honour" which is used in the parallel passage in Exodus xx. 12, they understand to include (1) to provide them with food and raiment, and (2) to escort them. The parents, they urge, are God's representatives upon earth; hence as God is both to be "honoured" with our substance (Prov. iii. 9), and as He is to be "feared" (Deut. vi. 13), so our parents are both to be "honoured" (Exod. xx. 12) and "feared" (chap. xix. 3); and as he who blasphemed the name of God is stoned (chap. xxix. 16), so he who curses his father or mother is stoned (chap. xx. 9).[8]

As Ginsburg pointed out, the blasphemy of God and the cursing of parents are plainly equated in the law. To reflect the holiness of God a man must begin by reverencing his parents.

Ginsburg then noted, of the second clause of Leviticus 19:3, "and keep my sabbaths,"

> Joined with this fifth commandment is the fourth of the Decalogue. The education of the children, which at the early stages of the Hebrew commonwealth devolved upon the parents, was more especially carried on by them on Sabbath days.[9]

At this point, Ginsburg missed the theological sense of the text and resorted to a historical accident. Plainly, God and the parents are associated by the text; both are to be revered, God absolutely, the parents under God. Blasphemy against God and cursing one's parents alike merit death. Both are assaults against fundamental authority and order.

---

8. Ginsburg, "Leviticus," in Ellicott, I, 421 f.
9. *Ibid.*, p. 422.

Moreover, the sabbath as rest and security in God is related to the fifth commandment in that parents provide, however faulty, some kind of rest and security for the child. The child is given life and nurture. The home represents a rest, and the godly home is truly a rest from the world, a security and pledge of victory in the face of it. Both sabbath and parents represent an inheritance from God of rest, peace, and victory. They are therefore closely associated in this law.

In this light, let us return to Deuteronomy 22:6, 7, the mother bird and her eggs or young. Very clearly, the same basic principle is applied even to animal life. Man cannot exploit the resources of the earth radically or totally. The very life that is given to him for food must be used under law. But, even if the bird in question is not a bird fit for eating, the same principle applies. The issue at stake is not the preservation of man's food supply but the reverential use of our inheritance in the Lord. There can be *no progress* without a respect for the past and our inheritance therein.

A *third* general principle appears in *the promise of life for obedience.* Some interpretations of this promise have been already noted. That of the Talmud is of interest also:

> MISHNAH. A Man may not take the dam with the young even for the sake of cleansing the leper. (For whose purification rites two birds were required, one to be slaughtered and the other to be set free into the open field, cf. Lev. XIV, 4 ff.). If in respect of so light a precept, which deals with that which is but worth an issar, the Torah said, That it may be well with thee, and that thou mayest prolong thy days, how much more (must be the reward) for the observance of the more difficult precepts of the Torah!

> *Gemara.* It was taught: R. Jacob says, There is no precept in the Torah, where reward is stated by its side, from which you cannot infer the doctrine of the resurrection of the dead. Thus, in connection with honouring parents it is written, *That thy days may be prolonged, and that it may go well with thee.* Again in connection with the law of letting (the dam) go from the nest it is written, *"That it may be well with thee, and that thou mayest prolong thy days."* Now, in the case where a man's father said to him, "Go up to the top of the building and bring down some young birds," and he went to the top of the building, let the dam go and took the young ones, and on his return he fell and was killed—where is this man's length of days, and where is this man's happiness? But *"that thy days may be prolonged"* refers to the world that is wholly long, and *"that it may go well with thee"* refers to the world that is wholly good.[10]

The editor's footnote to this reads, "The promise of bliss is to be ful-

---

10. Rabbi Dr. Epstein, ed., *The Babylonian Talmud, Seder Kodashim,* II, 823; Hullin 142a (London: Sonicino Press, 1948).

filled in the world to come, and one must not expect to receive the reward of a good deed in this world."[11] This gives a radically other-

worldly interpretation which does injustice to the law.

An examination of other promises of life in the law makes clear how plainly earthly this promise is:

> If thou wilt diligently hearken to the voice of the LORD thy God, and wilt do that which is right in his sight, and wilt give ear to his commandments, and keep all his statutes, I will put none of these diseases upon thee, which I have brought upon the Egyptians: for I am the LORD that healeth thee (Ex. 15:26).

> Thou shalt not bow down to their gods, nor serve them, nor do after their works: but thou shalt utterly overthrow them, and quite break down their images.
> And ye shall serve the LORD your God, and he shall bless thy bread, and thy water; and I will take sickness away from the midst of thee.
> There shall nothing cast their young, nor be barren, in thy land: the number of thy days I will fulfil (Ex. 23:24-26).

> Thou shalt keep therefore his statutes, and his commandments, which I command thee this day, that it may go well with thee, and with thy children after thee, and that thou mayest prolong thy days upon the earth, which the LORD thy God giveth thee, for ever (Deut. 4:40).

> O that there were such an heart in them, that they would fear me, and keep all my commandments always, that it might be well with them, and with their children for ever! (Deut. 5:29).

> Ye shall walk in all the ways which the LORD your God hath commanded you, that ye may live, and that it may be well with you, and that ye may prolong your days in the land which ye shall possess (Deut. 5:33).

> Wherefore it shall come to pass, if ye hearken to these judgments, and keep, and do them, that the LORD thy God shall keep unto thee the covenant and the mercy which he sware unto thy fathers:
> And he will love thee, and bless thee, and multiply thee: he will also bless the fruit of thy womb, and the fruit of thy land, thy corn, and thy wine, and thine oil, the increase of thy kine, and the flocks of thy sheep, in the land which he sware unto thy fathers to give thee.
> Thou shalt be blessed above all people; there shall not be male or female barren among you, or among your cattle (Deut. 7:12-16).

> If thou wilt not observe to do all the words of this law that are written in this book, that thou mayest fear this glorious and fearful name, THE LORD THY GOD:
> Then the Lord will make thy plagues wonderful, and the plagues of thy seed, even great plagues, and sore sicknesses, and of long

11. *Ibid.*, p. 823n.

continuance. Moreover he will bring upon thee all the diseases of Egypt, which thou wast afraid of; and they shall cleave unto thee.
Also every sickness, and every plague, which is not written in the book of this law, them will the LORD bring upon thee, until thou be destroyed.
And ye shall be left few in number, whereas ye were as the stars of heaven for multitude; because thou wouldest not obey the voice of the LORD thy God.
And it shall come to pass, that as the LORD rejoiced over you to do you good, and to multiply you; so the LORD will rejoice over you to destroy you, and to bring you to nought; and ye shall be plucked from off the land whither thou goest to possesss it (Deut. 28:58-63).

And he said unto them, Set your hearts unto all the words which I testify among you this day, which ye shall command your children to observe to do, all the words of this law.
For it is not a vain thing for you; because it is your life: and through this thing ye shall prolong your days in the land whither ye go over Jordan to possess it (Deut. 32:46, 47).

Even a casual reading of these passages (and more could be cited) makes clear a number of points. *First,* the promise of life is given for the whole of the law. The fifth commandment has a primacy in this promise, but all the law offers life. *Second,* the promise of life is plainly material and of this world. The promise of eternal life is clear-cut elsewhere in Scripture, but it cannot be read into these passages. *Third,* the promise is not only to covenant man if he obeys, but it is to his cattle, fields, and trees. It means freedom from plagues and diseases. It means fertility and a safe delivery of the young. It means long life for covenant man and his household. The law is thus clearly *a promise of life* to covenant man when he walks in faith and obedience. *Fourth,* the law is also *a promise of death,* of disease, sterility, and plague, to the disobedient. To reduce the law, as some antinomians do, to merely a promise of death is to deny its meaning, and finally its judgment. The law is not a mere negation: its purpose is to outlaw sin and to protect and nurture righteousness. In this respect alone, the law is a promise of life. A law against murder is a promise of death to the murderer, and a promise of life and protection in life to the godly. To remove the promise of life to the godly means to remove at one and the same time the promise of death to the murderer. When thieves and murderers are removed from society, life and property are thereby protected and furthered. When the antinomians reduce the law to a merely negative function, death to sin, they implicitly remove that death penalty also and prepare the way for *love* to become the redeemer and life-giver rather than God. They remove it by making a new principle the life-giver, *love,* God's love for man and man's love for God; death then becomes the deprivation of love, and love is the cure-all for deprivation. But the Biblical doctrine of atonement declares plainly that man's salvation is by Christ's works of law, His perfect obedience as our representative and federal head, and His substitutionary acceptance of our sentence of death. We are sentenced to death by law, and we are made righteous before God by law, but we receive this fact by faith. Faith does not eliminate the legal transaction involved, nor the requirement that we now show forth the fruits of salvation, godly works. Faith rests on a foundation of law. *Fifth*, the promise of life which the law offers is not merely a removal of the conditions of death, i.e., the elimination as it were of murderers, although this is important. It is also the fact that God, as the life-giver, prospers our life and causes us to flourish therein. As Jesus Christ declared, "I am come that they might have life, and that they might have it more abundantly" (John 10:10).

The promise of life for obedience is thus a basic premise of the law, because the law is inseparable from life. Law is a basic condition of life.

A *fourth* general principle implicit in the fifth commandment is that to dishonor one's parents is to dishonor one's self, and to invite death; similarly, to dishonor one's self is to dishonor parents. According to Leviticus 21:9, "And the daughter of any priest, if she profane herself by playing the whore, she profaneth her father: she shall be burnt with fire." Ginsburg commented:

> Whilst the married daughter of a layman who had gone astray was punished with death by strangling (see chap. xx. 10; Deut. xxii. 23, 24), the daughter of a priest who had disgraced herself was to be punished with the severer death by burning. Though the doom of the guilty partner in the crime is not mentioned here, his sentence was death by strangulation.[12]

Her sin constitutes thus a triple offense, a sin against God, against her father, and against herself. The law is thus in a sense a promise of life to the living; the dead will turn from it, for their motive is not life but profanity.

3. The Economics of Family

The word *property,* once one of the most highly regarded words in the English language, has come in recent years to have a bad connotation because of the deliberate assault on the concept by socialists. The word, however, was important enough to be a basic aspect of freedom to men during the War of Independence, when a rallying cry was "Liberty and Property." Now, however, even those who most defend

---

12. Ginsburg, "Leviticus," in Ellicott, I, 434 f.

property wince at its broader usage, the inclusion of people. Thus, most women would bridle at being described as *property*. But the word *property* should be regarded instead as a very highly possessive and affectionate term rather than a cold one. It comes from the Latin adjective *proprius,* meaning "not common with others, own, special, several, individual, peculiar, particular, proper." It also has the sense of "lasting, constant, enduring, permanent." St. Paul makes it clear that husband and wife, with respect to sex, have a property right in one another (I Cor. 7:4, 5). Even more, it can be said that a man holds his wife as his property, and his children also. But because his wife and children have certain individual, particular, special, and continuing claims on him, they have a property right in him. Laws have at various times underlined these property rights in persons; thus, some states do not permit a father to disinherit any child; the children are given a degree of permanent property rights in the father. Similarly, most states do not permit a wife to be disinherited; her property right in her husband is safeguarded. The state now claims a property right over every man by laws of inheritance. At one time, the laws of Rome permitted the father to sell his children in terms of his property right, a power very common throughout history. The rationale of this power has been the protection of the family: to maintain the continuing life of the family in a time of economic crisis, a younger member, often a girl, was sold, on the principle that it was better for the family to survive a crisis by losing one member than for all to go under in starvation. In Japan, the sale of daughters to houses of prostitution to survive economic crises is still practiced.

Such practices were routine and normal in Biblical times. They were barred to Hebrews by Biblical law:

> There shall be no whore of the daughters of Israel, nor a sodomite of the sons of Israel (Deut. 23:17).

> Do not prostitute thy daughter, to cause her to be a whore; lest the land fall to whoredom, and the land become full of wickedness.
> Ye shall keep my sabbaths, and reverence my sanctuary: I am the LORD (Lev. 19:29, 30).

This way out of economic crisis is thus strongly forbidden by the law. Even more significant is the fact that in Leviticus 19:29, 30, this bar on prostitution is clearly associated with sabbath keeping and reverence for the sanctuary; the two verses are in effect one law, and they are separated from the other verses by the declaration: "I am the LORD." Man's rest in the Lord requires a godly care and oversight with respect to his children, and a reverence for the sanctuary is incompatible with a sale of children into prostitution. Only in one sense could a father "sell" a daughter under Biblical law, into marriage. This appears in Exodus 21:7-11:

> And if a man sell his daughter to be a maidservant, she shall not go out as the menservants do.
> If she please not her master, who hath betrothed her to himself, then shall he let her be redeemed: to sell her unto a strange nation he shall have no power, seeing he hath dealt deceitfully with her.
> And if he have betrothed her unto his son, he shall deal with her after the manner of daughters.
> If he take him another wife: her food, her raiment, and her duty of marriage, shall he not diminish.
> And if he do not these three things unto her, then shall she go out free without money.

Marriage normally was by dowry: the groom gave a dowry to the bride which constituted her protection and children's inheritance. If there were no dowry, then there was no marriage, only concubinage. But here, it is clearly marriage that is in view, and the word used is marriage. The girl is taken as a wife for either the man or for one of his sons. She is legally protected from being either a concubine or a slave; she cannot even be sent out into the fields like a slave. The girl clearly has the privileges of a dowered wife, because there was a dowry. The dowry in this case went to the girl's family, not to her and her children. If the husband-to-be decided against marrying her, then the dowry is restored to him; the girl is "redeemed." If he or a son married her, and then denied her any wifely right, she then had a legitimate ground for divorce, and left without any restoration of the dowry. The reference to "duty of marriage" is to her right of cohabitation.

If the girl in question did not please the new family after the betrothal, and before consummation, she resided with that family until the dowry was restored by her family, or by another prospective husband. This is apparent in Leviticus 19:20, where "not at all redeemed" is more accurately to be translated as "not fully or entirely redeemed."[1] If, during that time, the girl is either seduced, or is guilty of fornication, "She shall be scourged," or, more accurately, "there shall be visitation *or* inquisition" to determine the truth of the matter. "This punishment (scourging) . . . she only received when it was proved that she was a consenting party to the sin" (Lev. 19:20-22).[2]

The dowry was an important part of marriage. We meet it first in Jacob, who worked seven years for Laban to earn a dowry for Rachel (Gen. 29:18). The pay for this service belonged to the bride as her dowry, and Rachel and Leah could indignantly speak of themselves

---

1. Ginsburg, "Leviticus," in Ellicott, I, 426.
2. *Ibid.*

as having been "sold" by their father, because he had withheld from them their dowry (Gen. 31:14, 15). It was the family capital; it represented the wife's security, in case of divorce where the husband was at fault. If she were at fault, she forfeited it. She could not alienate it from her children. There are indications that the normal dowry was about three years' wages. The dowry thus represented funds provided by the father of the groom, or by the groom through work, used to further the economic life of the new family. If the father of the bride added to this, it was his privilege, and customary, but the basic dowry was from the groom or his family. The dowry was thus the father's blessing on his son's marriage, or a test of the young man's character in working for it. An unusual dowry appears in Saul's demand of David, a hundred foreskins of the Philistines (I Sam. 18:25-27). Saul offered a test he felt would be too difficult for David to meet, but which David met.

The European dowry is a reversal of the Biblical principle: the girl's father provides it as a gift to the groom. This has led to an unhealthy situation with respect to marriage and the family. Girls become, in such a system, a liability. In 14th and 15th century Italy, "Fathers came to dread the birth of a girl-child, in view of the large dowry they would have to provide for her, and every year the prices in the marriage-market rose." This led to a virtual destruction of the family, whereas the Biblical dowry strengthened the family. The groom wanted the highest price before accepting a girl, and the father shopped for someone who would not bankrupt him by his demands. The protests of the clergy were to no avail.[3]

In its Biblical form, the dowry had as its purpose an economic foundation for the new family. This aspect long lingered in America. "According to an old American custom, the father of the bride gave her a cow, which was intended to be the mother of a new herd to supply milk and meat for the new family."[4]

In cases of seduction and rape, the guilty party had to endower the girl with the dowry of a virgin. If marriage followed, he lost permanently any right of divorce as well (Ex. 22:16,17; Deut. 22:28, 29). If not, the girl in such a case went into her marriage to another man with a double dowry, one of 50 shekels of silver from her seducer, and another from her husband.

The bride's dowry was not only whatever her father gave her, and what her husband endowered her with, but also the wisdom, skill, and character she brought into the marriage. As Ben Sirach wrote, "A

---

3. Iris Origo, *The World of San Bernardino* (New York: Harcourt, Brace and World, 1962), p. 52 f.
4. Clark: *Biblical Law*, 130n.

wise daughter shall bring an inheritance to her husband: but she that liveth dishonestly is her father's heaviness" (Wis. 22:4).

The importance to the family of a good wife and a godly daughter-in-law is readily apparent in any culture, but in a family-centered society, her value is all the greater. Ben Sirach commented on these things very plainly:

> A wicked woman is a chafing ox-yoke; Taking hold of her is like grasping a scorpion. A drunken woman gets very angry, And does not even cover up her own shame. A woman's immorality is revealed by her roving looks, and by her eye-lids.
> Keep a close watch over a headstrong daughter, For if she is allowed her liberty, she may take advantage of it. Keep watch over a roving eye, And do not be surprised if it offends against you. Like a thirsty traveler who opens his mouth And drinks of any water that is near, She will sit down before every tent peg, And open her quiver to the arrow.
> The grace of a wife delights her husband, And her knowledge fattens his bones. A silent wife is a gift from the Lord, And a well-trained spirit is beyond estimation. A modest wife is blessing after blessing, And a self-controlled spirit no scale can weigh. Like the sun rising on the Lord's loftiest heights, Is the beauty of a good woman as she keeps her house in order. Like a lamp shining on the holy lampstand, Is a beautiful face on a good figure. Like gold pillars on silver bases Are beautiful feet with shapely heels (Wis. 26:7-18).

This, clearly, reflected a popular Hebraic standard; the Biblical position is better stated in Proverbs 31:10-31. A conspicuous difference is that Ben Sirach reflected a common taste for a *silent* wife; this is not the Biblical requirement, which reads, "She openeth her mouth with wisdom: and in her tongue is the law of kindness" (Prov. 31:26). Ben Sirach called for a silent wife; God speaks instead of a *talking* wife, but one who speaks with wisdom and in kindness. Men as sinners prefer Ben Sirach's standard, and women as sinners want the privilege and right of speech without the requirement of wisdom and kindness.

It should be added, before leaving the subject of the dowry, that, since this often involved the family, the family exercised considerable authority and often chose the wife. In the case of Isaac, his wife Rebekah was chosen by his parent, who provided the dowry; Isaac delighted in his chosen bride. In Jacob's case, Jacob chose Rachel and provided his own dowry. The element of parental choice was not absent in Jacob's case, in that both Rebekah and Isaac sent Jacob to Padan-aram to marry (Gen. 27:46–28:9). Neither was the groom's concurrence in the parental choice absent from the arranged marriage. The whole point of the law of Exodus 21:7-11, the "sale" of a daughter, has reference to this: the girl in the household of the new family may or may not meet the approval of the prospective groom; and, if not, in that case she is to be "redeemed."

Another basic aspect of the economics of the family is the fact of *support.* This has a double aspect. *First,* the parents have a duty to provide for the children, to support them materially and spiritually. Christian education is a basic aspect of this support. The parents have an obligation to feed and clothe the child, both body and soul, and they are accountable to God for the discharge of this duty. *Second,* the children when adults have a duty also in this respect, to provide for their parents materially and spiritually as needed. Ben Sirach referred to this duty in Wisdom 3:12, 16. This duty was emphatically underscored by Jesus Christ, who, from the cross, committed His mother Mary to St. John for care and support, "Woman, behold thy son! Then said he to the disciple, Behold thy mother!" (John 19:26, 27). The oral statements of a dying criminal were a legal testament, as Buckler pointed out:

> Dalman has shown that among the rights and responsibilities of a dying criminal was the testamentary disposition of his estate and rights. For instance:
>
>> Jewish marital legislation insisted that everything should be definitely settled before it was too late. It happened, for instance, that one who was crucified gave his wife, shortly before expiring, freedom to marry again, and so a bill of divorcement could be written out, which entitled her to marry another man before the actual death of her present husband.
>>
>> The case of our Lord was parallel to that of a married man, in that a principle of *dominium* was at stake. As the firstborn of Mary, He had both the authority and responsibility, which would have devolved on her second son James. The automatic devolution was apparently undesirable, so Our Lord used the authority He possessed as a dying criminal to commit her to the care of one whom He could trust—the Beloved Disciple.[5]

The implication of this is also that, up to that moment, Jesus had maintained the responsibility for the care of His widowed mother. The other children may have assisted, but the government of the matter was in Jesus' hands.

Jesus also condemned those who gave to God, but did not fulfil their responsibility of supporting their parents:

> Well did Isaiah prophesy of you hypocrites, as it is written,
>> This people honoreth me with their lips,
>> But their heart is far from me.
>> But in vain do they worship me,
>> Teaching as their doctrines the precepts of men.

5. F. W. Buckler, "Eli, Eli, Lama Sabachtani?" in *The American Journal of Semitic Languages and Literatures,* vol. LV, no. 4 (October, 1938), p. 387.

Ye leave the commandment of God, and hold fast the tradition of men. And he said unto them, Full well do ye reject the commandment of God, that ye may keep your tradition. For Moses said, Honor thy father and thy mother; and, He that speaketh evil of father or mother, let him die the death; but ye say, If a man shall say to his father or his mother, That wherewith thou mightest have been profited by me is Corban, that is to say, Given to God; ye no longer suffer him to do aught for his father or his mother; making void the wcrd of God by your tradition, which ye have delivered: and many such like things ye do (Mark 7:6-13).

Jesus as the eldest son and main heir made John, although only a cousin and not a brother, the eldest son and main heir in His stead and gave him the responsibility for Mary's support.

This illustrates clearly a central aspect of Biblical family law and of Biblical inheritance: the main heir supported and cared for the parents, as need required it. Abraham lived with Isaac and Jacob, not with Ishmael, or with his sons by Keturah. Isaac lived with Jacob, not Esau, and Jacob lived under the care and supervision of Joseph and therefore gave to Joseph a double portion by adopting Joseph's two sons as his heirs on equal terms with all his other sons (Gen. 48:5, 6).

The converse holds equally true: *the child which supports and cares for the aged parents is the main or true heir.* For parents or the civil law to rule otherwise is to work against godly order. Inheritance is not a question of pity or feeling but of godly order, and to set aside this principle is sinful.

The question of inheritance and wills can best be understood if we examine the Biblical word for a will or testament: *blessing.* An inheritance is precisely that, a blessing, and for a parent to confer a blessing or the central blessing on an unbelieving child, or a rebellious and contemptuous child, is *to bless evil.* Although some portions of Biblical wills have the element of divine prophecy as well as testamentary disposition, it is important to note that they combine both blessings and curses, as witness Jacob's words to Reuben, Simeon, and Levi (Gen. 48:2-7). To cut off a child is a total curse.

The general rule of inheritance was limited primogeniture, i.e., the oldest son, who had the duty of providing for the entire family in case of need, or of governing the clan, receiving a double portion. If there were two sons, the estate was divided into three portions, the younger son receiving one third. The parents had a duty to provide an inheritance, as far as their means afforded (II Cor. 12:14). The father could not alienate a godly first-born son because of personal feelings, such as a dislike for the son's mother and a preference for a second wife (Deut. 21:15-17). Neither could he favor an ungodly son, an incorrigible delinquent, who deserved to die (Deut. 21:18-21). Where there was no son, the inheritance went to the daughter or daughters (Num. 27:1-11). If by reason of disobedience or unbelief, a man in effect had no son, then the daughter became the heir and son as it were. If there were neither sons nor daughters, the next of kin inherited (Num. 27:9-11). The son of a concubine could inherit, unless sent away or given a settlement (Gen. 21:10; 25:1-6). A maid could be her mistress' heir (Prov. 30:23), and a slave could also inherit (Gen. 15:1-4), since he was in a real sense a family member. Foreign bondmen could also be inherited (Lev. 25:46). The inheritance of one tribe could not be transferred to another, i.e., the land of one area could not be alienated (Num. 36:1-12). A prince could give property to his sons as their inheritance, but not to a servant, lest this become a means of rewarding them to the detriment of his family (Ezek. 46:16, 17). If some land were given by a prince to a servant, it reverted at the year of liberty to the prince's sons. The prince could not confiscate the people's inheritance or land, i.e., the state could not seize property or confiscate it (Ezek. 46:18).

This latter is an important point in view of the contemporary situation. The Biblical laws of inheritance are God's law; the modern laws of inheritance are the state's law. The state, moreover, is making itself progressively the main, and sometimes, in some countries, the only heir. The state in effect is saying that it will receive the blessing above all others. There is, however, a perverse justice and logic in the state's position, in that it is assuming the dual roles of parent and child. It offers to educate all children and to support all needy families as the great father of all. It offers support to the aged as the true son and heir who is entitled to collect all of the inheritance as his own. In both roles, however, it is the great corrupter and is at war with God's established order, the family.

A final aspect of the economics of the family: throughout history the basic welfare agency has been the family. The family, in providing for its sick and needy members, in educating children, caring for parents, and in coping with emergencies and disasters, has done and is doing more than the state has ever done or can do. The state's intrusion into the realm of welfare and education leads to the bankrupting of people and state and to the progressive deterioration of character. The family is strengthened by its discharge of those duties which always lead to the decline of welfare states. The family is the basic economic unit of society, and the strongest one. No society can prosper which weakens the family, either by removing the family's responsibilities for education and welfare, or by limiting the family's control of its property and inheritance by usurpation.

A final point, the Biblical law of primogeniture was governed by the prior standard of moral and religious requirements. Whereas in Western European history primogeniture governed almost without exception, in Biblical history, the exceptions are almost the rule. In the Biblical record, inheritance by primogeniture without moral qualification is rare. Again and again, the firstborn is set aside because of moral failure. Thus, very obviously, the spiritual and moral considerations governed inheritance, from the days of the patriarchs to Christ's testamental provision for Mary from the cross.

4. Education and the Family

A fundamental aspect of the support due a child from his parents is education in the broadest sense of the word. This involves, *first* of all, *chastisement.* According to Proverbs 13:24, "He that spareth his rod hateth his son: but he that loveth him chasteneth him betimes." Again, "Chasten thy son while there is hope, and let not thy soul spare for his crying" (Prov. 19:18); parents then were as inclined to be tender-hearted as now, but the necessity for chastening cannot be set aside by a foolish pity. Chastisement can be a lifesaver to the child: "Withhold not correction from the child: for if thou beatest him with the rod, he shall not die. Thou shalt beat him with the rod, and shalt deliver his soul from hell" (Prov. 23:13, 14). Chastening is necessary, as Kidner points out, because, Proverbs holds,

> First, "foolishness is bound up in the heart of a child"; it will take more than words to dislodge it (22:15). Secondly, character (in which wisdom embodies itself) is a plant that grows more sturdily for some cutting back (cf. 15:32, 33; 5:11, 12; Heb. 12:11)—and this from early days (13:24b: "betimes"; cf. 22:6: "Train up a child in the way he should go, and even when he is old he will not depart from it"). In "a child left to himself" the only predictable product is shame (29:15).[1]

But chastening is no substitute for sound instruction, for proper teaching. Thus, *second,* the parents have a duty to provide the child with a godly education. "The fear of the LORD is the beginning of knowledge" (Prov. 1:7); "The fear of the LORD is the beginning of wisdom" (Prov. 9:10). Wisdom rests on faith, and true knowledge has as its presupposition the sovereign God. There can be no neutrality in education. Education by the state will have statist ends. Education by the church will be geared to promoting the church. The school cannot be subordinate to either church or state.[2] The church of Christ's

---

1. Derek Kidner, *Proverbs, An Introduction and Commentary* (Chicago: Intervarsity Press, 1964), p. 51.
2. See R. J. Rushdoony, *Intellectual Schizophrenia,* 1961, and *The Messianic Character of American Education,* 1963 (Philadelphia: Presbyterian and Reformed Publishing Co.).

day taught men to give to the church, ostensibly to God, rather than providing for their parents (Mark 7:7-13). Sin was thus taught as a virtue.

Children are required to obey their parents. The counterpart to this is the parents' duty to teach the fundamentals of obedience to their children, the law of God. The law itself requires this:

> For what nation is there so great, who hath God so nigh unto them, as the LORD our God is in all things that we call upon him for?
> And what nation is there so great, that hath statutes and judgments so righteous as all this law, which I set before you this day?
> Only take heed to thyself, and keep thy soul diligently, lest thou forget the things which thine eyes have seen, and lest they depart from thy heart all the days of thy life; but teach them thy sons, and thy sons' sons (Deut. 4:7-9).

> And these words, which I command thee this day, shall be in thine heart:
> And thou shalt teach them diligently unto thy children, and shalt talk of them when thou sittest in thine house, and when thou walkest by the way, and when thou liest down, and when thou risest up (Deut. 6:6, 7).

Once every seven years, in the sabbath year, children with adults had to hear the reading of the entire law (Deut. 31:10-13).

Very early, religious leaders in Israel undertook the task of education. The prophet Nathan became the instructor of the young Jedidiah (Beloved of Jehovah) or Solomon (II Sam. 12:25).[3]

Third, because the law is intensely practical, Hebrew education was intensely practical. The common opinion held that a man who did not teach his son the law and a trade, the ability to work, reared him to be a fool and a thief. It is said that Simeon, the son of the famed Gamaliel, observed: "Not learning but doing is the chief thing."[4] Josephus, in his work *Against Apion* compared the education of the Hebrews with that of the Greeks. Greek education veered from the severely practical to the abstract and theoretical, he pointed out, whereas Biblical law has a healthy relationship between principle and practice.

Fourth, Biblical education, being family-centered and emphasizing the responsibility of parents and children, was productive of *responsible* people. A person reared and schooled in the doctrine that he has a responsibility to care for his parents as need arises, provide for his children, and, to the best of his ability, leave an inheritance of moral

---

3. A. R. S. Kennedy, "Education," in James Hastings, *A Dictionary of the Bible,* I, 647.
4. *Ibid.,* I, 646.

discipline and example as well as material wealth, is a person highly attuned to responsibility. In such an educational system, the state is not the responsible party but the family is, and the man has a duty to be a competent and provident head of his household, and the wife a skilled helpmeet to her husband. The abandonment of a family-oriented education leads to the destruction of masculinity, and it renders women either fluffy luxuries for men or aggressive competitors to men. Men and women having lost their function gyrate unstably and without a legitimate sense of function. Modern education abstracts knowledge; the specialist prides himself on knowing nothing outside his field and wears his refusal to relate his knowledge to other areas as a badge of honor. If the scholar seeks social relativity, again it is without a transcendental principle, and the result is an immersion in the social process without a value structure; all else is charged off as meaningless save the process which at the moment becomes the incarnate structure.

In modern education, the state is the educator, and the state is held to be the responsible agency rather than man. Such a perspective works to destroy the pupil, whose basic lesson becomes a dependence on the state. The state, rather than the individual and the family, is looked to for moral decision and action, and the moral role of the individual is to assent to and bow down before the state. Statist education is at the very least implicitly anti-Biblical, even when and where it gives the Bible a place in the curriculum.

Fifth, basic to the calling of every child is to be a member of a family. Virtually all children will some day become husbands and wives, and fathers or mothers. The statist school is destructive of this calling. Its attempts to meet the need are essentially external and mechanical, i.e., home economics courses, sex education, and the like. But the essential training for family life is family life and a family-oriented school and society. It means Biblical education. It means discipline, and training in godly responsibility.

The statist school, moreover, basically trains women to be men; it is not surprising that so many are unhappy at being women.[5] Nor are men any the happier, in that dominion in modern education is transferred from man to the state, and man is progressively emasculated. The major casuality of modern education is the male student. Since dominion is by God's creative purpose a basic aspect of man, any education which diminishes man's calling to exercise dominion also diminishes man to the same degree.

---

5. Carle C. Zimmerman, Lucius F. Cervantes, *Marriage and the Family,* (Chicago: Regnery, 1956), p. 310 f.

6. Julius B. Maller, "The Role of Education in Jewish History," in Louis Finkelstein, *The Jews, Their History, Culture, and Religion,* Third edition (New York: Harper and Brothers, 1960), II, 1240 f.

Sixth, Biblical education emphasized learning, godly learning. Jewish proverbs emphasized this. We have already referred to one, "Just as a man is required to teach his son Torah, so is he required to teach him a trade." Moreover, "He who teaches his neighbor's son Torah, it is as if he had begotten him." But, supremely, "An ignorant man cannot be saintly."[6] Since holiness is not a self-generating act but requires a conformity to God's law and righteousness, an ignorant man cannot be saintly. Moreover, since knowledge is not self-generating, and the meaning of factuality comes not from facts but from the Creator, knowledge requires as its presupposition in every area the knowledge of God, whose fear is the beginning of wisdom and knowledge.

It needs more than ever to be stressed that the best and truest educators are parents under God. The greatest school is the family. In learning, no act of teaching in any school or university compares to the routine task of mothers in teaching a babe who speaks no language the mother tongue in so short a time. No other task in education is equal to this. The moral training of the child, the discipline of good habits, is an inheritance from the parents to the child which surpasses all other. The family is the first and basic school of man.

5. The Family and Delinquency

The problem of juvenile delinquency appears in a law of central importance, but one unfortunately neglected by commentators, as far as any relevance to our society is concerned. The law reads:

> If a man have a stubborn and rebellious son, which will not obey the voice of his father, or the voice of his mother, and that, when they have chastened him, will not hearken unto them:
> Then shall his father and his mother lay hold on him, and bring him out unto the elders of his city, and unto the gate of his place;
> And they shall say unto the elders of his city, This our son is stubborn and rebellious, he will not obey our voice; he is a glutton, and a drunkard.
> And all the men of his city shall stone him with stones, that he die: so shalt thou put evil away from among you; and all Israel shall hear, and fear (Deut. 21:18-21).

The law is clear enough; if only the interpreters were as clear!

At this point, we see Talmudic interpretation at its worst. There is long quibbling as to what constitutes a son; it is defined in terms of a beard and pubic hair. For example, "R. Hisda said: If a minor begot a son, the latter does not come within the category of a stubborn and rebellious son, for it is written, *If a man have a son,* but not if a son (i.e., one who has not reached manhood) have a son." A discussion is also reported as to the age when a boy's sexual activity ceases to be "innocent" and becomes sinful. The pornographic discussion which follows throws no light on the text but reflects the legalistic attempts to twist the meaning of words into an alien sense.[1] Like jurists of our day, and like the U.S. Supreme Court, every attempt is made to make the law null and void by limiting the scope of its application, i.e., the son was not guilty if he drank expensive wines, because then he obviously could not get too much, so it must refer to cheap Italian wine! Again, if the delinquent has been sexually incapacitated by an accident of birth, then he is obviously not a son, we are told.[2]

In analyzing this law, certain things need to be recognized. *First,* it indicates a limitation in the power of the family. A Roman father had the power of life and death over his children. He could expose them as infants, and kill them as youths, and this power appears in many cultures. The parent as a god gave life, and as a god he took it. But, as Kline noted, "Chastening was the limit of the parents' own enforcement of their authority (vs. 18)."[3] In fact,

> The laws upon this point aim not only at the defense, but also at the limitation, of parental authority. If any one's son was unmanageable and refractory, not hearkening to the voice of his parents, even when they chastised him, his father and mother were to take him and lead him out to the elders of the town into the gate of the place. The elders are not regarded here as judges in the strict sense of the word, but as magistrates, who had to uphold the parental authority, and administer the local police.[4]

In Biblical law, all life is under God and His law. Under Roman law, the parent was the source and lord of life. The father could abort the child, or kill it after birth. The power to abort, and the power to kill, go hand in hand, whether in parental or in state hands. When one is claimed, the other is soon claimed also. To restore abortion as a legal right is to restore judicial or parental murder. It is significant that, as innocent victims are killed, and capital punishment is withheld from their murderers, the same men who plead for the murderer's life also demand the "right" to abortion. Gary North noticed, at a major university campus, the same picketeer carrying a sign one day, "Abolish Capital Punishment," and "Legalize Abortion" another day. When this was called to a liberal professor's attention, his answer was, "There is no contradiction involved." He was right: the thesis is, condemn the innocent and free the guilty.

Second, the law requires that the family align itself with law and order rather than with a criminal member. Wright held that "It is

1. *Babylonian Talmud, Seder Nezikin,* vol. III, Sanhedrin VIII; pp. 465-488.
2. *Seder Nezikin,* vol. II, Baba Bathra 126b; p. 527.
3. Kline, *Treaty of the Great King,* p. 109.
4. Keil and Delitzsch, *Pentateuch,* III, 407.

highly improbable that parents often appealed to such a law."[5] The parents are not complaining witnesses in the normal sense, and as a result they are not required to be executioners as witnesses normally were (Deut. 17:7). It is "the men of the city" who are here executioners, and hence it is a complaint in a very real sense by the community against a criminal member. It will not do to plead humanitarianism here. In those days, in neighboring cultures, the father had the power to kill his children and often did. While the Hebrews had a different standard, neither their law nor their lives moved in terms of modern humanitarianism.

If the parents refused to complain against their son, they were then guilty of condonation and/or participation in his crimes. Their role was thus a formal but necessary one: would the family align itself with justice or stand in terms of blood ties? In view of the strong nature of family loyalties, the parental participation was necessary in order to ensure freedom from feud and also to place the family firmly against its criminal members. A parent refusing to file a complaint in such a case would become a party to the offense and a defender of crime. The principle required was clear-cut: not blood but law must govern.

Third, Biblical law is case law, and this law does not deal simply with sons. It means that if a son, who is beloved of parents and an heir, must be denounced in his crime, how much more so other relatives? A family turning over its son to the law will turn over anyone. Thus, daughters were clearly included. The law said, "There shall be no whore of the daughters of Israel, nor a sodomite of the sons of Israel" (Deut. 23:17). "Do not prostitute thy daughter, to cause her to be a whore" (Lev. 19:29). The evidence would indicate that no Hebrew girl could become an incorrigible delinquent, and, in periods of law and order, remain alive. It is significant that the term used in Proverbs for a prostitute is the strange or alien woman, a foreigner. This has two possible interpretations. Possibly, the daughter who became a prostitute was read out of the family and the nation and was no longer a member of the covenant people but a foreigner. More likely, as the literal reading plainly indicates, the prostitute was a foreign girl.

Clearly then, the intent of this law is that all incorrigible and habitual criminals be executed. If a criminal son is to be executed, how much more so a neighbor or fellow Hebrew who has become an incorrigible criminal? If the family must align itself with the execution of an incorrigibly delinquent son, will it not demand the death of an habitual criminal in the community?

---

5. G. Ernest Wright, "Deuteronomy," *Interpreter's Bible,* II, 462.

That such is the intent of the law appears from its stated purpose, "so shalt thou put evil away from among you; and *all* Israel shall hear, and fear." The purpose of the law is to eliminate entirely a criminal element from the nation, a professional criminal class. The family is not permitted the evil privilege of saying, "We will stand behind our boy, come what may"; the family itself must join the war on crime. Since the law is a plan for the future, that plan clearly means the elimination of crime as any significant factor in godly society.

This law has had its effect on American law, in that habitual criminals are still technically liable to life imprisonment after so many convictions, but these laws are a weakened and declining reflection of the Biblical law. Originally, in the U.S., habitual criminals could be executed, and some states still have such legislation on the books.

Since the Biblical law has no sentence of imprisonment but only restitution, its view of crime is that the act of crime is committed, not by a professional criminal, but a weaker citizen, who must restore the stolen goods plus at least an equal amount, in order to be restored himself to his citizenship in the community. Biblical law does not recognize a professional criminal element: the potentially habitual criminal is to be executed as soon as he gives plain evidence of this fact.

Fourth, at this point the factor of pity comes into view. The common humanistic view is that such a law is pitiless. The Biblical perspective is that it is not, that, in fact, the modern perspective reflects not pity, but misplaced pity. Shall the criminal or the community be pitied? The Biblical law demands pity for the offended, not the offender.

Pity, in fact, is specifically forbidden as evil in certain cases. Obviously, in the law concerning the delinquent son, pity for the son is forbidden. But in other laws pity is specifically cited as forbidden:

> And thou shalt consume all the people which the LORD thy God shall deliver thee; thine eye shall have no pity upon them: neither shalt thou serve their gods; for that will be a snare unto thee (Deut. 7:16).

> If thy brother, the son of thy mother, or thy son, or thy daughter, or the wife of thy bosom, or thy friend, which is as thine own soul, entice thee secretly, saying, Let us go and serve other gods, which thou has not known, thou, or thy fathers;
> Namely, of the gods of the people which are round about you, nigh unto thee, or far off from thee, from the one end of the earth even unto the other end of the earth:
> Thou shalt not consent unto him, nor hearken unto him; neither shall thine eye pity him, neither shalt thou spare, neither shalt thou conceal him:
> But thou shalt surely kill him; thine hand shall be first upon him to put him to death, and afterwards the hand of all the people (Deut. 13:6-9).

But if any man hate his neighbor, and lie in wait for him, and rise up against him, and smite him mortally that he die, and fleeth into one of these cities:
Then the elders of his city shall send and fetch him thence, and deliver him into the hand of the avenger of blood, that he may die. Thine eye shall not pity him, but thou shalt put away the guilt of innocent blood from Israel, that it may go well with thee (Deut. 19:11-13).

And thine eye shall not pity; but life shall go for life, eye for eye, tooth for tooth, hand for hand, foot for foot (Deut. 19:21).

When men strive together one with another, and the wife of the one draweth near for to deliver her husband out of the hand of him that smiteth him, and putteth forth her hand, and taketh him by the secrets:
Then thou shalt cut off her hand, thine eye shall not pity her (Deut. 25:11-12).

In Deuteronomy 7:16, pity for the evil inhabitants of Canaan was forbidden; God's pity for them, and His patience, had lasted for centuries. Now the time for pity was gone: it was a time for judgment and death.

In Deuteronomy 13:6-9, pity for the subverter of the faith is forbidden, even when that person is a near and dear relative. The foundations of godly order are at stake, and pity here is an evil.

In Deuteronomy 19:11-13, pity for a murderer in a case of premeditated murder is forbidden. No extenuating circumstances can be pleaded against the fact of murder by premeditation.

In Deuteronomy 19:21, the general law of justice is stated: the punishment must fit the crime; there must be a comparable restitution or death. Pity cannot be used to set aside justice.

In Deuteronomy 25:11-12, no woman, in defending her husband who is fighting with another man, can attempt to aid her husband by mutilating the other man's sexuality. Such an offense was a particularly fearful one. It is the *only* instance in Biblical law where mutilation is the punishment, and its significance is of central importance. A wife is under God to be a help-meet to her husband, but only and always under God's law. In a quarrel between two men, she could not take unfair advantage of her husband's assailant. *Faith requires staying within the law of God, and a woman can never help her husband lawlessly.* If such were permitted, then a man could step aside and let his wife break the law for him with impunity. A lawless love is under the sentence of the law. Joab loved David as none other save Jonathan did, and Joab was often right where David was wrong, but Joab's love was often a lawless love, and he only earned the hatred of his kinsman David, and final judgment. In the case of the lawless wife, the fact of mutilation was a grim public warning: a lawless hand or help-meet was no hand or help at all. Her mutilated arm was a grim reminder to all of the prohibition of lawless love. She was not to be pitied, for pity must also move in terms of law, or it becomes the condonation of evil. Whether a wife, husband, or son be involved, pity must never become lawless.

Fifth, the crime of the delinquent son involves an assault or war on fundamental authority. Of Deuteronomy 21:18, Schroeder wrote, "He disputes the parental, i.e., divine authority in disposition and life, and indeed although it has been held before him, thus with full knowledge and purpose." Of vs. 19, he added, "With the parental, the civil authority is also endangered, and hence the case passes from that, to this."[6] Moreover, as Manley noted, "Seeing that parents stand towards their children as God's representatives, obstinate rebellion is regarded as akin to blasphemy, and is condemned to the same punishment."[7]

Sixth, the principle of capital punishment (of which more later) is involved here. Life is created by God, governed by His law, and to be lived only in terms of His law-word. All transgression faces ultimate judgment; capital offenses require the death penalty here and now, by civil authorities. *Neither the parents nor the state are the creators of life, and therefore they cannot fix the terms of life.* In this fact is man's greatest safeguard for freedom; the godly state does indeed deal severely with offenders, but it strictly limits the power of the state at any and all points in terms of the word of God. The power of parents is similarly limited under godly order: the Biblical family never has the despotic powers of the Roman or Chinese family. The parents are at all times limited by the law-word of God. Biblical law clearly favors the godly and deals severely with the lawless. As Waller wrote of the law concerning a delinquent son, "Manifestly this enactment, if carried out, would be a great protection to the country against lawless and abandoned characters, and would rid it of one very large element in the dangerous classes."[8]

Seventh, the formal charges against the son are of especial interest. We have noted the fundamental assault on authority, covered by the words "stubborn and rebellious." According to Waller, "The Hebrew words became proverbial as the worst form of reproach."[9] "A glutton and a drunkard" (cf. Prov. 23:20-22, where the same two words

6. F. W. J. Schroeder, "Deuteronomy," in John Peter Lange, *Commentary on the Holy Scriptures, Numbers–Deuteronomy* (Grand Rapids: Zondervan, n.d.), p. 161.
7. G. T. Manley, "Deuteronomy," in Davidson, Stibbs, and Kevan, *The New Bible Commentary,* p. 215.
8. C. H. Waller, "Deuteronomy," in Ellicott, II, 59 f.
9. Waller, in *Ibid.,* II, 60.

are found) adds to the picture of a rebellious, anti-social and incorrigible delinquent. The Talmud, by its re-interpretation of each term, made the law virtually inapplicable to anyone. The law, by its generalization, portrays an incorrigible delinquent whose general conduct confirms his lawless nature. The confirmed character of the son establishes, among other things, this: the delinquent and rebellious son has denied his inheritance of faith and law; in its ultimate meaning, this rebellion against his spiritual inheritance is a rebellion against life itself. Hence, the sentence of death. He is not a weak character, he is a strong one, but his character is dedicated to evil. The family is the earthly cradle of life, and the godly family gives an inheritance of life. To renounce this inheritance is finally to renounce life. Not every rebelling son goes this far in his rebellion, but the principle of his rebellion is still a rejection of his inheritance in the full sense of that word.

Eighth, as we have seen, law is a form of warfare. By law, certain acts are abolished, and the persons committing those acts either executed or brought into conformity to law. The law thus *protects* a certain class, the law-abiding, and every law-order is in effect a subsidy to the people of the law. If the law fails to enforce that protection, it destroys itself in time. The failure of the law to execute the incorrigible and professional criminal is creating a major social crisis and leading increasingly to anarchy. In Los Angeles, California, in 1968, for example, the use of city park slides by little children became difficult. Young hoodlums were burying broken bottles, jagged edge up, in the sand beneath the slides. Young hoodlums were involved in so many other activities, that the resulting conditions were beyond the effective control of the police. Again,

> Use of marijuana is so vast in the Bay Area that it is simply not in the realm of possibility for law enforcement agencies to stop it.
>
> In Berkeley on a Saturday night there may be 2000 pot parties going on—can you have an informer or a policeman at each one?[10]

In virtually every area of criminal activity, the incorrigible delinquent and the professional criminal are fast gaining a greater striking power. They outnumber the police, are a vast army of dedicated law-breakers. The courts, by making their conviction difficult, are in effect subsidizing crime and making war on the law-abiding.

6. The Principle of Authority

Statist education and statist intervention in the life of the family leads progressively to the break-down of the family. This is not

---

10. Robert McLaughlin, "A Policeman's Nightmare: Mountains of Marijuana," (quoting David Kershaw), in Los Angeles *Herald-Examiner,* Friday, December 6, 1968, p. A-13.

surprising since the principle of authority is at stake in the family.

The family is not only the first environment of the child, it is also his first school, where he receives his basic education; his first church, where he is taught his first and foundational lessons concerning God and life; his first state, where he learns the elements of law and order and obeys them; and his first vocation, where the child is given work to do, and responsibilities in terms of it. The essential world for a small child is the family, his father and mother in particular. Meredith has summarized the matter aptly: "In the eyes of a small child, a parent stands in the place of *God Himself!* For the parent is the child's provider, protector, lover, teacher and lawgiver."[1]

Hence it is that theologians through the centuries have taught obedience to civil magistrates, and to all duly constituted authorities, under the heading of the fifth commandment. It has been rightly seen how deeply involved all authority is in the authority of parents. The destruction of the family's position and authority is the destruction of all society and the introduction of anarchy.

But the introduction of radical anarchy is also precisely that which follows systematically the attack on the family. The student revolution of the 1960's had basic to it anarchism. Thus Jorge Immendorff, age 23, of Germany, called for revolution rather than reformation, because "you can't improve junk—so revolution is the only answer." The need is to "Start from scratch" with only one standard, "life itself." Anthony Duckworth, 21, of England, states that "At Oxford and Cambridge, the young teachers want to run administration policy, decide on books and courses, rooms and meals. They want to take charge." Moreover, according to John D. Rockefeller III, aged 62, "Instead of worrying about how to suppress the youth revolution; we of the older generation should be worrying about how to sustain it." This youthful "idealism" must be sustained, according to Rockefeller, and furthered.[2] But what is it that Rockefeller asks us to sustain and accept? *First,* the student and youth revolution has an immoral premise, i.e., the assertion that youth has a "right" to control and govern other people's properties. If a university belongs to the state, to a church, or to a private corporation, the student can receive an education there on the school's terms. He is free to create his own institutions, but, as a student or an instructor, he is in a school on terms set by those whose property rights govern the school. The students bewail "coercion," but their movements are among the most coercive of their century. The child has no right to govern his parents, the students

---

1. Roderick C. Meredith, *The Ten Commandments*, p. 35.
2. "The Student Rebels," in *This Week Magazine* (December 1, 1968), pp. 1, 10.

their school, nor employees their employer. *Second,* the goal of the student revolution is simply amoral power, not "idealistic" hopes. To make "life itself" the standard is to say there is no standard save anarchy. To ask for a "start from scratch" is to call for the destruction of all law and order so that the anarchist can seize what the present possessor possesses. *Third,* this anarchism is inevitable in a generation of students who have been taught neither obedience to parents and all due authority, nor honor towards them to whom honor is due. To cite Meredith again,

> The original command to "honor" father and mother applies to all of us throughout our lives, But in this place *children* (Eph. 6:1, 2), specifically, are told to *obey* their parents "in the Lord."
>
> Because of his total lack of experience and judgment, it is absolutely necessary that a child *be taught* to OBEY his parents *instantly* and *without question.* Explanations and reasons for this may and should be given to the child from time to time. But, at the moment a parental command is given, *there may not be time or opportunity to give the reason why!*
>
> Therefore, it is imperative that a child be taught the HABIT of unquestioning *obedience* to his parents. For, until the young child develops, his parents stand to him *in the place of God.* And God holds them RESPONSIBLE for teaching and directing the child properly.
>
> By direct implication, a parent is bound by the fifth command to *make himself* honorable. For to be honored, one must *be honorable.*
>
> Every parent needs to realize that he *represents God* to his child![3]

The parent represents God, because he represents God's law-order. Judges, in the law, are referred to as "gods," as are prophets (Ex. 21:6; 22:8; I. Sam. 28:13; Ps. 82:1, 6; John 10:35). Since parents represent God's law-order, they must, on the one hand, be obedient to that law-order, and on the other hand be obeyed as representatives of that kingdom.

In Exodus 21:6, the King James Version reads *judges* where the Hebrew reads *Elohim,* gods; the same is true of Exodus 22:8: The American Revised Version, and the Masoretic Text Version, read "God" and footnote "judges." In I Samuel 28:13, the witch of Endor, on seeing Samuel, cries out, "I saw gods ascending out of the earth," or, in the ARV, "I see a god coming up out of the earth." The prophet is clearly meant. In Psalm 82:1, 6, civil authorities are referred to as "gods," a usage confirmed by Jesus Christ (John 10:35). For this reason, because all due authorities represent God's law-order, the fifth

---

3. Meredith, *op. cit.,* p. 35.

commandment has often been associated with the first table of the law, i.e., with those having reference to our duties to God, as contrasted to the second table, those having reference to our duties to our neighbor. There is a validity to this division into two tables, although it cannot be pressed too far and is somewhat artificial, in that all the commandments have reference to our duty to God.

Calvin regarded the division of this commandment into the first table as foolish.[4] Curiously, he tried to use Romans 13:9 in favor of his position, as well as Matthew 19:19, but these passages are not conclusive on this matter. More pertinent are the various laws, previously treated, which relate obedience to parents to sabbath-keeping and the avoidance of idolatry (cf. Lev. 19:1-4).

But to return to the more important point, the matter of obedience: it is commonly held, by the humanistic mind, that the unquestioning and faithful obedience required by the law of children is destructive of the mind. The free person, it is held, is a product of rebellion, of the constant challenge of authority, and true education must stimulate children and youth to break with authority and deny its claims. The "culture" of youth today is this demand for instant realization combined with a defiance of authority. Ross Snyder, in *Young People and their Culture,* writes that "young people of our time are quite convinced that they are meant to *be right now.* And in all the fullness possible for them at their period of development."[5] This demand for instant realization is a characteristic of infantilism. The baby cries when hungry and voids its bladder and bowels at will. It cries with frustration and rage when gratification is not instantaneous. It is not surprising that a generation reared permissively has a high aptitude for destructive and revolutionary rage, often accompanied by gleeful public urination and defecation, and a low aptitude for disciplined work and study. The essence of the revolutionary mind is the demand for instant utopia, for instantaneous gratification, and a destructive, infantile rage against any order which fails to provide it. Freud coined the terms oral and anal personalities; the terms are irrelevant to any age of maturity or to men of maturity; they are apt in describing the ambivalent personality of an infantile and permissive age and its peoples.

But the roots go deeper. John Locke formulated the rootless psychology of the humanistic faith with his clean tablet concept. True education, he held, required that the mind be swept clean of all preconceived notions, implicitly of the teachings of parents, religion, and society. In terms of Locke's concept and psychology, education must

---

4. Calvin, *Commentaries on the Four Last Books of Moses,* III, 7.
5. Cited in a review in the *Religious Book Club Bulletin,* vol. 41, no. 15 (December, 1968), p. 2.

be revolutionary. Add to this Rousseau's natural man, and all pre-conceived notions, all forms of inheritance from the past, become chains which must be broken. Marx and Freud drew the logical conclusions from the philosophies of Locke, Rousseau, and Darwin. Darwin, by his evolutionary faith, reduced everything in the past to a lower and more primitive level, and thus added justification to the demand for a clean sweep, for revolution. This hostility to discipline and obedience has invaded almost every area of endeavor in the twentieth century. In art, the ability to master and use skills in use of paints and in draughts-manship is neglected in favor of "spontaneous" and "unconscious" expression lacking in reason and form. In religion, experience is given priority over or replaces doctrine. In politics, authority comes from below, from the lowest level, and the "charismatic" leader is the demagogue who can best satisfy the masses. In music, undisciplined emotionalism is most highly prized, and so on. The animosity towards obedience and discipline is general and deep.

But the best functioning mind is the obedient and disciplined mind. The child who is disciplined into obedience is not the servile youth but the free man. He is, by virtue of the discipline of obedience, most in command of himself and best able to command in his field of endeavor.

The older humanism, because it grew up in the context of a Christian discipline, could produce a disciplined mind. Montaigne (b. 1533), in giving counsel on educating the child, spoke without any sense of novelty as he described good training in his day:

> A few years of life are reserved for education, not more than the first fifteen or sixteen; make good use of these years, adult, if you wish to educate the child to the right maturity. Leave out super-fluous matters. If you want to do something constructive, confront the child with philosophical discourses, those that are not too complicated, of course, yet those that are worth explaining. Treat these discourses in detail; the child is capable of digesting this matter from the moment that it can more or less manage for itself (Montaigne actually wrote: "from the moment it is weaned," but probably he did not mean that too literally); the child will, in any case, be able to stand philosophical discourses much better than an attempt to teach it to write and to read; this had better wait a little.[6]

Since in Montaigne's day the child was not weaned as hastily as in our own, there is no reason to doubt Montaigne's statement. In Puritan America, children were usually taught to read by their mothers between the ages of two and four.

---

6. J. H. van den Berg, *The Changing Nature of Man* (New York: Dell [1961], 1964), p. 21.

Van den Berg cites two examples of mature children from Montaigne's era and later. They deserve citation in some detail:

We do have some data on the child's nature in Montaigne's time—the life of Theodore Agrippa d'Aubigne, Huguenot, friend of Henri IV, born in 1550. Montaigne was born in 1533, so he had reached the age of discretion when d'Aubigne was still a child. Observing young contemporaries of this d'Aubigne, Montaigne did not notice anything about maturation. Of d'Aubigne it is told that he read Greek, Latin, and Hebrew when he was six years old, and that he translated Plato into French when he was not yet eight.

Plato. Montaigne recommended the reading and explaining of philosophical discourses to children—well, if an eight-year-old child can translate Plato, what objections can there be to reading a translated version to him when he is four?

When d'Aubigne was still eight years old, he went through the town of Amboise, accompanied by his father, just after a group of Huguenots had been executed. He saw the decapitated bodies; and at the request of his father he swore an oath to avenge them. Two years later he was captured by *Inquisiteurs;* the ten-year-old boy's reaction to the threat of death at the stake was a dance of joy before the fire. The horror of the Mass took away his fear of the fire, was his own later comment—as if a ten-year-old child could know what he meant by that. And yet a child who has translated Plato and who has been used to reading classics for four years, could not such a child know what he wants, and know what he is doing? But he can hardly be called a child. A person who observes the effects of an execution intelligently, who swears an oath to which he remains true through life, who realizes for himself the interpretation of the Holy Communion, and who fathoms the horror of death at the stake—he is not a child, he is a man.

At the time Montaigne died another child was standing on the threshold of great discoveries: Blaise Pascal, born in 1623, wrote, when he was twelve years old, without assistance, a treatise on sound which was taken seriously by expert contemporaries. At about the same time he happened to hear the word *mathematics;* he asked his father what it meant, and he was given the following incomplete answer (incomplete, because his father was afraid that an interest in the mathematics might diminish his interest in other sciences): "Mathematics, about which I shall tell you more later on, is the science which occupies itself with the construction of perfect figures and with the discovery of the properties they contain." Young Pascal brooded over this answer during his hours of leisure, and unassisted, he constructed circles and triangles which led him to the discovery of the sort of properties his father must have meant—for instance, that the sum of the angles of a triangle equals two right angles.[7]

We must grant that d'Aubigne and Pascal were remarkable men and

---

7. *Ibid.,* pp. 26-28. The author, Jan Hendrick van den Berg, is professor of psychology at the University of Leyden.

child prodigies. But it must be added that in music, the sciences, and in many other fields, child prodigies were far more common then than now. We must also recognize that the intellectual level then was quite high even among the common people. The level of preaching is ample evidence of this. The ability of church members to listen to lengthy sermons of sometimes two hours, to reproduce all thirty or forty points faithfully later in the week, and to debate them or discuss them, is well documented. There was no lack of lawlessness in that era, but there was also a high order of discipline, and this discipline furthered the uses of intelligence. The men who, both in the early centuries of the Christian era, and in the Reformation and later eras, established the foundations of Western civilization and liberty were men of faith and discipline, men schooled in the academy of obedience.

A godly respect for power and authority as duly constituted and ordained by God is required by Scripture. Thus Exodus 22:28 declares, "Thou shalt not revile the gods, nor curse the ruler of thy people." Again, the ARV translates "gods" as "God" and footnotes it as "the judges." Calvin noted, of this passage, Leviticus 19:32, Deuteronomy 16:18 and 20:9, "in the Fifth Commandment are comprised by *synecdoche* all superiors, in authority."[8]

> First of all, He commands that we should think and speak reverently of judges, and others, who exercise the office of magistrate: nor is it to be questioned that, in the ordinary idiom of the Hebrew language, He repeats the same thing twice over; and consequently that the same persons are called "gods," and "rulers of the people." The name of God is, figuratively indeed, but most reasonably applied to magistrates, upon whom, as the ministers of His authority, He has inscribed a mark of His glory. For, as we have seen the honour is due to fathers, because God has associated them with Himself in the possession of the name, so also here His own dignity is claimed for judges, in order that the people may reverence them, because they are God's representatives, as His lieutenants, and vicars. And so Christ, the surest expositor, explains it, when He quotes the passage from Psalm lxxxii. 6, "I have said, Ye are gods, and all of you are children of the Most High," (John x. 34), viz., "that they are called gods unto whom the word of God came," which is to be understood not of the general instruction addressed to all God's children, but of the special command to rule.
>
> It is a signal exaltation of magistrates, that God should not only count them in the place of parents, but present them to us dignified by His own name; whence also it clearly appears that they are to be obeyed not only from fear of punishment, "but also for conscience sake," (Rom. xiii. 5) and to be reverently honoured, lest God should be despised in them. If any should object, that it would be wrong to praise the vices of those whom we perceive to abuse

8. Calvin, *op. cit.*, p. 17.

their power; the answer is easy, that although judges are to be borne with even if they be not the best, still that the honour with which they are invested, is not a covering for vice. Nor does God command us to applaud their faults, but that the people should rather deplore them in silent sorrow, than raise disturbances in a licentious and seditious spirit, and so subvert political government.[9]

That such godly obedience does not constitute an endorsement of or a submission to evil is abundantly apparent from the history of the Old Testament prophets, and from the history of the church. Rather, godly obedience is the best ground for resistance to evil, in that it stands primarily in terms of a higher obedience to God and therefore is in obedience independent, and in resistance to tyrants, obedient to the higher authority of God.

But at one point, Calvin's comment reflects (in the first sentence of the second paragraph above), not Biblical but Roman thought, when he compares rulers to parents and ascribes to them a *parental* authority. What is in common among parents, rulers, teachers, and masters is not *parenthood* but *authority*. It is a serious error to ascribe a parental power to the ruler and the state. The parents represent the authority of God to the child; the civil magistrate or ruler represents the authority of God in terms of a civil law-order to the citizens; they have, parents and rulers, *authority* in common, not *parenthood,* and even with respect to authority, it is of differing kinds. Roman law, because it divinized the state, made the state and its ruler in effect the god of the people, and the people the children of that god. The emperor was father of his country, and this was a serious aspect of the civil theology.

The heavily classical learning of medieval and Reformation scholars often led them astray. A verse sometimes cited as evidence of the parental role of the state is Isaiah 49:23. But this verse refers to the remnant of Israel, who shall be restored to Jerusalem and re-established as a state under the protection of other states, who shall be as "nursing fathers." The reference is to the re-establishment of the Hebrew commonwealth under Nehemiah, with the protection of the Medo-Persian Empire. The imagery has nothing to do with a parental role for the state and everything to do with the superior protecting role of a great empire for a small civil order which is re-constituting.

The primary and basic authority in God's law-order is the family. All other due authorities similarly represent God's law-order, but in differing realms. If parents are not obeyed by children, no other authority will be honored or obeyed. Hence, the law speaks of the key authority in terms of whose authority social order stands or falls.

9. *Ibid.,* III, 17 f.

Basic to the authority of every realm is the representation of God's law-order.

The state thus is established in order to extend God's justice. According to Deuteronomy 16:18-20,

> Judges and officers shalt thou make thee in all thy gates, which the LORD thy God giveth thee, throughout thy tribes: and they shall judge the people with just judgment.
> Thou shalt not wrest judgment; thou shalt not respect persons, neither take a gift: for a gift doth blind the eyes of the wise, and pervert the words of the righteous.
> That which is altogether just shalt thou follow, that thou mayest live, and inherit the land which the LORD thy God giveth thee.

It would be ridiculous to posit fatherhood as the purpose of this law: its goal is civil justice. Basic to the establishment of that justice is authority.

And the fifth commandment, as it speaks of parents, and by implication, all God-ordained authorities, is establishing first of all *God's authority*. God knows, after all, that parents and rulers, churchmen, teachers, and masters are sinners. God is not interested in establishing sinners: the expulsion from Eden, and the constant judgment in history, is eloquent evidence of that. But God's way of disestablishing sinners and establishing His law-order is to require that authorities be obeyed. This obedience is first of all rendered to God and is a part of the establishment of God's order. Sin leads to revolutionary anarchy; godly obedience leads to godly order.

7. The Family and Authority

The Romans conquered Judea, but, later, when Christianity conquered Rome, the Romans said of this Biblical faith of Hebrew origins, "Victi victoribus leges dederunt," "The conquered gave their laws to the conquerors."[1] The law of the later Roman Empire and of the Christian West has been largely altered by Biblical law, and fundamental to this change is the alteration of family law.

The basic Christian legal reform was instituted by Justinian and his empress, Theodora, in the sixth century. Zimmerman has summarized the basic Christian reforms with respect to sex and the family. *First,* "only heterosex relations in marriage were made publicly allowable." All sexual relations other than normal marital relations were now illegal and sinful. *Second,* this classification of all other forms of sexuality as "objectionable" was "applied to every social class" without distinction. The family became the normal and legal way of life for all. The preface to this part of the Novellae code stated:

---

1. A. Reifenberg, *Israel's History in Coins, From the Maccabees to the Roman Conquest* (London: East and West Library, 1953), p. 7.

Previous legislation has dealt with aspects of these matters piece-meal. Now we seek to put them all together and give the people certain clear rules of conduct so as to make the family (de nuptiis) the standard form of life for all human beings for all time, and everywhere. The purpose of this is to guarantee artificial immortality to the human species. This is the Christian way of life.

Third, prohibited sex activities were made punishable by law, especially forms of commercialized sex. *Fourth,* and Zimmerman notes, "fundamental," "contracts involving non-family sex activities as repayment for support or gifts were made illegal." All parties in such a contract became accessories to an illegal act. Among other things, concubinage lost its legal status. *Fifth,* these legal steps were "part of a wider movement to make the family the defined public way of life and status." The result of this legislation was the redirection of civilization. It was the creation of a "family system which would fit best into planned greatness. The authors never considered a perfect man. They sought to enroll the average man in a social system which could reach some great civilized world unity."[2]

The effects of this legislation were extensive. Two important areas of change were *inheritance* and *property.* Inheritance laws were now governed by family considerations, with the legitimate wife and her children having a status not given to a concubine or mistress and her children. The limitation of inheritance to the legitimate family made the family the significant agent and power with respect to property. The family was now far more than the basic social unit: it was in essence *the social system.* It was the social system, however, without the stultifying and immoral powers of the family system of ancestor worship. In ancestor worship, the family is geared to the past and hostile to the future. In the Christian family system, the Mosaic law as interpreted in terms of the New Testament rulings concerning the family, the perspective is on the Christian future, on the Kingdom of God and its requirements for today and tomorrow.

Without the authority of the family, a society quickly moves into social anarchy. The source of the family's authority is God; the immediate locale of the authority is the father or husband (I Cor. 11:1-15). The abdication by the father of his authority, or the denial of his authority, leads to the social anarchy described by Isaiah 3:12. Women rule over men; children then gain undue freedom and power and become oppressors of their parents; the emasculated rulers in such a social order lead the people astray and destroy the fabric of society. The end result is social collapse and captivity (Isa. 3:16-26), and

2. Carle C. Zimmerman in C. C. Zimmerman and Lucius F. Cervantes, *Marriage and the Family* (Chicago: Henry Regnery, 1956), pp. 61-63.

a situation of danger and ruin for women, a time of "reproach" or "disgrace," in which the once independent and feministic women are humbled in their pride and seek the protection and safety of a man. Indeed, seven women, Isaiah said, seek amidst the ruins after one man, each begging for marriage and ready to support themselves if only the disgrace and shame which overwhelm the lone and defenseless woman be taken from them (Isa. 4:1).[3]

Isaiah clearly saw the absence of the man's authority as productive of social chaos. The man as the head of the family is the necessary principle of order, and also the principal in order. *Dominion* is God's principle for man over nature (Gen. 1:28), and for the male in the person of the husband and father in the family (I Cor. 11:1-15). Dominion as the male's nature and prerogative is to be found throughout the animal world as a part of God's creation ordinance. In animals, as Ardrey has pointed out, there is a primacy of dominion over sexual and other drives. "The time will come when the male will lose all interest in sex; but he will still fight for his status." In fact, "dominance in social animals is a universal instinct independent of sex."[4] This male instinct for dominion reveals itself in animals in three ways: *first*, in territoriality, i.e., a property instinct and drive, and, *second*, in status, a drive to establish dominion in terms of rank in a rigidly hierarchical order, and *third*, survival, and order as a means of survival. This is true of animals in natural setting; zoo animals, being in a welfare society, are more absorbed with sex.[5] In the male, dominion leads to increased sexual potency and longevity.[6] Moreover, "It is a curious characteristic of the instincts of order that most are masculine."[7] The female's sexual and maternal instincts are personal and thus in a sense anarchistic.

These characteristics are true of human life also. The woman becomes absorbed with problems of law and order in a personal way, i.e., when her family and her family's safety is endangered by its decay. The man will be concerned with problems of society apart from a condition of crisis; the woman becomes concerned when social decay has personal implications, and her concern then is a major one.

Male and female need each other, and godly order means marriage,

---

3. It is indicative of the blindness of commentators to the context of Scripture that "reproach" is consistently taken to mean "childessness." It often does mean this *in a married woman;* but here *unmarried women* in a situation of anarchy and captivity see their position as a "reproach" or "disgrace" because they are totally defenseless and without protection against seizure, assault, robbery, and unmarried pregnancy.
4. Robert Ardrey, *African Genesis* (New York: Atheneum, 1961), p. 11.
5. *Ibid.*, p. 118.
6. *Ibid.*, p. 109.
7. *Ibid.*, p. 133.

the union of man and woman under God and to His glory and service. Apart from one another, or in contempt or at odds with one another, the emphasis of man and woman tends to become one-sided. Perhaps as telling an example of this as any, extreme almost to the point of caricature, is that of Henry VIII of England and Queen Catherine.

Catherine, more than Sir Thomas More, deserved to become the Catholic saint of her day. More was first and last a humanist; Catherine was a godly woman of intense faith and courage. The daughter of the great Queen Isabella of Spain, she shared with her sister, wrongly called Juana the Mad, an almost incredible absorption with the purely personal aspect of issues. As a result, her depraved father, Ferdinand, whom Catherine loved blindly, was able to use Catherine as a pawn for Spanish power, almost to the destruction of England. (Ferdinand had killed Juana's husband and usurped Juana's throne, and he had no scruples about taking advantage of any relative.) Catherine was equally blind in dealing with her husband Henry where more than personal issues were involved.[8]

Henry VIII, on the other hand, cannot be viewed in purely personal (and feminine) terms, as one concerned basically with his lusts. Certainly Henry was a sinner here, but his basic motive was the desire to preserve the kingdom from anarchy by gaining a male heir. Prior to his father's ascension to the throne, England had been long rent and wasted by a bloody and intermittent war of succession.[9] Henry's basic concern was to preserve order by means of an assured and strong dynastic succession, which meant to him a male heir. This was to Henry the fundamental moral consideration, even as the personal relationship was the fundamental moral consideration to Catherine.

Henry read all events in terms of his principle and justified every step in terms of it. A talented and intelligent man, he was also immature and self-righteous.[10] But he was not alone in considering England's situation and his own in terms of the impersonal issues of order and succession. Both Luther and Melancthon were ready to see the answer to Henry's plight in a legal bigamy, and Pope Clement VII made a like suggestion. Attempts are made to excuse both, with little merit to the attempts; whatever their reasons, these religious leaders made the suggestion. All, as men, were concerned with the political scene and the problem of England's order as against the purely personal problem of law and order between Catherine and Henry.

---

8. For a sympathetic study of Catherine, see Mary M. Luke, *Catherine, The Queen.* (New York: Coward-McCann, 1967).
9. A. L. Rowse, *Bosworth Field, From Medieval to Tudor England* (Garden City, New York: Doubleday, 1966).
10. See J. J. Scarisbrick, *Henry VIII* (Berkeley: University of California Press), 1968.

This episode, in sharpness and extreme form, reveals the varying natures of man and woman. But the men involved in this sorry event were at least concerned with some kind of order, even if immorally so at times. Today, men, having abdicated extensively their masculinity, are less concerned with order and more with gratification. As a result, women, because their security, and that of their children, is at stake, become involved with the problem of social decay and law and order. Social and political action thus becomes a pressing feminine concern. Their concern underscores the decay of society and the failure of men. Where women are concerned about their defense, it means normally that either a fearful outside invader is threatening the society, or else within the social order men are ceasing to function as men. Matriarchal power then develops as a substitute for a normal law-order.

The matriarchal society is thus the decadent or broken society. The strongly matriarchal character of Negro life is due to the moral failure of Negro men, their failure to be responsible, to support the family, or to provide authority. The same is true of American Indian tribes, which are also matriarchal today. In such societies, women provide a considerable portion of the family income because the moral dereliction of the men makes it necessary. A strongly permissive element predominates in child training, and the moral failure of the male is transmitted to the next generation.

The same trend towards a matriarchal society is in evidence in Western culture today. It should be stressed that, contrary to popular opinion, a matriarchal society is not a society in which women rule, but, rather, a society in which men fail to exercise their dominion, so that women are faced with a double responsibility. They must do their own work, and then work to stave off the anarchy created by man's moral failure. In a matriarchal society, women are burdened, not promoted; they are penalized, not rewarded.

The principles of Christian family order were outlined in 1840 by Matthew Sorin:

The duties arising out of (the marriage) relation. . . .

> 1. *Mutual affection.* According to the order and constitution of the divine government, man is appointed to rule in the affairs of this life. It is his prerogative to hold the reins of domestic government, and to direct the family interest, so as to bring them to a happy and honorable termination. This appointment of God is initiated in the order of the creation; and its propriety is manifested in the order of the fall. But still, as it is the right of the husband to rule, so it is his duty to rule with moderation and love—to love his wife "even as Christ loved the Church." Eph. v. 25. And so, also, the obedience of the wife is not to be the reluctant offering of an ungracious spirit, but the cheerful service of a delighted mind;

"that if any obey not the word, they also may, without the word, be won by the conversation of the wives." I Peter iii. 1-5.

2. *Mutual confidence.* Nothing is, or can be of more importance than this, in maintaining, in active and energetic exercise, conjugal affection. To destroy confidence, is to remove the foundations of all that is excellent or valuable in the family circle. . . .

3. *Mutual attention and respect.* Not the empty round of ceremonious attentions, that are ostentatiously crowded into the family circle, on certain occasions, seemingly more to please beholders, than to express the genuine sentiments of the soul. We speak of that simple, artless, and unpremeditated respect and attention, which genuine love inspires.

4. *Mutual assistance.* The first woman was given to man, not to live upon his labor, nor yet to labor for his living; she was designed to be one with himself, an equal sharer in his sorrows and joys, she was to be a help-meet for him. . . . There is a threefold assistance that married persons owe to each other, in giving interest and enjoyment to the family circle.

1. There is an assistance in promoting the temporal interests of the family.

2. Again, *there is a mutual assistance in the maintenance of order—* in the education and government of children. . . .

The rights of parents in their children are equal. If those children are honorable and prosperous in the world, it is the happiness of both. If they are prodigal and vicious, it is not more the misfortune of the one than of the other.

It is, therefore, a self-evident duty, and one most solemnly binding on parents, to contribute their united skill, influence, and authority, to "train up their children in the way they should go."

3. *There is also a mutual assistance in promoting each other's spiritual welfare.* . . .

In addition to these general views, we may here, with propriety, notice some other special duties, which are mutually due between man and wife. Thus it is required of woman to show a spirit of subordination, and to obey her husband. Eph. v. 22. But it is also required of the husband that he love and protect his wife— that he cultivate for her the most tender affection—that he protect her according to his power, in person—health—property—and reputation. Everything pertaining to her comfort, should be granted, as far as in his power, with a ready and cheerful mind. "He is to love his wife as Christ loved the Church." Eph. v. 25. "As it is required of the wife, that she reverence her husband, not as a superior being, but as her superior in the domestic economy; and that, therefore, she should not usurp authority over the man, because Adam was first formed, then Eve." I Tim. ii. 11, 14. So it is also binding on the husband not to render himself ridiculous and contemptible in the eyes of his wife, by any indecencies of speech, or vile and trifling associations. He is to maintain his place, not so much by physical power or brute force, as by the excellency of his example, and those developments of mental and moral superiority, and greater tact in the management of affairs, which it is reasonable to expect from his relation, and which will, in most cases, insure a ready and cheerful submission to rule. I Peter iii. 3, 7. Again, as it is the duty of the woman to be keeper at home, and not to be wandering from her place, like an unhappy spirit seeking rest and finding none Titus ii. 5, so most unquestionably, it is the duty of the husband to render that home as interesting and cheerful as possible. . . .[11]

Sorin's statements are cited, not because they are remarkable or unusually good in interpreting Scripture, but because they reflect the faith and practice of Christian America in the 1840's. As Bode noted:

The book is valuable not only because it gives characteristic advice but also because it describes American home life at the middle-class level. Sorin was foreign-born and so he observes us more closely, takes us less for granted, than would a native of our country. He apologizes for the inadequacies of the book, saying that it might better have been written "by one specially adapted to the principles and habits of society in this country" but he is too modest. His objectivity is buttressed by considerable insight.[12]

It is precisely the family order described by Sorin against which much revolutionary activity is directed. *Permissiveness* strikes directly at parental authority, and, in both home and school is a revolutionary concept. The prevalence of permissiveness prevents the growth of *self-discipline*. *Lack of self-discipline* is seen by many as the reason for present juvenile delinquency. This delinquency stems from "a lack of self-discipline, and a degree of selfishness which is unbelievable to adults who themselves respect the rights of others and think of them before acting." Blaine adds,

Self-discipline does not grow like Topsy, but is the result of a two-stage building process in which parents are the prime movers. Church, school, peers, and heroes play a part, too, but it is at home that the cornerstone is laid.[13]

The lack of self-discipline leads to *self-importance*. Having no authoritative criterion of judgment other than the self, permissively reared youth have no valid criterion of self-assessment. In other eras, teen-agers have been adults, and men of twenty and thirty have been men of affairs. The youthfulness of the men in the U.S. Constitutional

---

11. Cited from Matthew Sorin, *The Domestic Circle: or, Moral and Social Duties Explained and Enforced* (Philadelphia, 1840), pp. 38-61; by Carl Bode, editor, *American Life in the 1840's* (New York: New York University Press, 1967), pp. 59-70.

12. Bode, p. 58.

13. Graham B. Blaine, Jr., *Youth and the Hazards of Affluence* (New York: Harper and Row, 1966), p. 3.

Convention is evidence of the early maturity and the early capacity for disciplined action and progress of men in that era. But this maturity went hand in hand with responsibility and independence, self-support, and self-discipline: It was a natural and unified whole. Permissive youth demands, "Listen to us," and claims maturity in terms of physical growth without any attendant maturity of mind and action.[14] The result is a self-importance based on the humanistic standard of being a human, a person. This radical inner immaturity leads to juvenile delinquency, adult criminality, a higher rate of divorce, and illegitimacy.[15]

As already indicated, this self-importance of man as man *destroys all standards save that of humanity.* Thus, when youthful students visited the Soviet Union, they failed to see the essential nature of that order, because they had no criterion of judgment save humanism. They concluded,

> People are people, no matter which side of the Iron Curtain they call home. That, at least, seems to be the discovery made by a group of 16 Valley students and their teacher-leaders after returning from a six-week study-tour of the Soviet Union.[16]

This "discovery" could have been made without a journey to the Soviet Union! But, when the only standard is man, then when others are found to be men also, fellow-members of humanity, co-existence is a moral necessity. There is no thought of the moral character of men, because no law beyond man is recognized. Thus, an important issue of *Liberation* strikes out against all "illegitimate authority," i.e., any concept of transcendental law. Quite rightly, the writers see as the enemy any concept of law which has God lurking behind it. The immoral for them is the "dehumanizing," any and everything which limits man. Since every man is his own sovereign and law under this humanistic concept, Paul Goodman raises the question, "Perhaps 'sovereignty' and 'law' in any American sense, are outmoded concepts."[17] This anarchism has gone so far that "a U.S. military court has ruled that conscientious objection is a valid defense to a charge of being absent without leave." The case involved a fueler of jet planes who was "absent without leave for 41 days from his post."[18] This anarchism is a trait of old and

---

14. Peggy King, "'Listen to us' students plead," in Oakland, California, *Tribune* (Saturday, October 26, 1968), p. 5-B.
15. "An Even Bigger Crime Explosion?," *U.S. News & World Report*, vol. LXV, no. 15 (October 7, 1968), p. 16.
16. Laure Mitchell, "Students Visit Russia: People Are People Behind Soviet Iron Curtain, Too," in Van Nuys, California, *The Valley News and Valley Green Sheet*, vol. 58, no. 27 (Thursday, August 29, 1968), p. 1.
17. Paul Goodman, "Reflections on Civil Disobedience," in *Liberation*, vol. XIII, no. 3 (July-August, 1968), p. 15.
18. "Conscientious Objection 'Valid' in AWOL Defense," in Santa Ana, California, *The Register* (August 18, 1968, Thursday [m]), p. A-7.

young alike: the young are simply carrying the anarchism of their day a step further. A ludicrous example of the anarchism of the parents is the case of a woman, separated from her husband for six years, who still wanted to celebrate the 25th wedding anniversary with a large party.[19]

This anarchism erodes the family and its authority in every age. It reduces the father to a non-entity, and it gives to the mother an impossible burden, that of being the family to the children. The extent to which this legal disappearance and personal abdication of the father has gone is readily illustrated. Whereas the father as the source of authority once normally gained custody of the children in a divorce, today only six states, Alaska, Georgia, Louisiana, North Carolina, Oklahoma, and Texas, "continue to declare the father 'the preferred natural guardian.'"[20] Even more revealing is the Israeli law which denies Jewish nationality to any Jew whose mother was not Jewish, because children are in this law classified in terms of their mother, not their father.[21]

All this is *erosion,* and it is very real. But also present is a legal *assault.* From within the church comes a demand for "a genuine pluralism of sexual behavior," which we are told "will certainly occur in two main areas." *First,* there will be "the dissolving of the concept that sex and marriage are inextricably and exclusively linked to each other."[22] *Second,* there will be

> the gradual social acceptance, if not legalization, of bigamy (or polygamy) and polyandry. In the next decade or two such bigamy is most likely to resemble the older pattern of single aunts living with a family. Social acceptance of such "common law bigamy" may well be the only way to initiate the required changes. Psychologists concerned with the mental health of older persons have recommended legalization of bigamy for persons over sixty. The Church, of course, is silent so far. It has no real plans for the aged, nor for the involuntarily single. Let us hope that it will not wait too long before it even considers the merits of polygamy (and polyandry) in meeting the needs of millions of persons for whom it has no other hope to offer.[23]

But this is mild compared to the opinions of a Swedish doctor, who wants not only equal legal rights but special legal subsidies for those

19. Abigail Van Buren, "Dear Abby" column, Santa Ana, California, *The Register,* (Wednesday [m], September 20, 1967), p. B-4.
20. Mildred Adams, *The Right to Be People* (Philadelphia: J. B. Lippincott, 1967), p. 232.
21. " 'Who's a Jew?' Controversy, Supreme Court wants 'nationality' dropped from identity cards," in *The Jerusalem Post Weekly,* (Monday, November 25, 1968), p. 4.
22. Rustum and Della Roy, *Honest Sex* (New York: The American Library, 1968), p. 138.
23. *Ibid.,* p. 140.

who practice incest, exhibitionism, pedophilia, saliromania, algolagnia, homosexuality, scopophilia, and other sexual deviations.[24] Ullerstam's system is hostile to Christian law-order and would savagely penalize the Christian marital law-order.

Apart from these theoretical proposals, the legal steps are serious enough. In country after country, there are moves to legalize homosexual unions; the laws against homosexuality have been extensively dropped, so that a tacit legality exists. Other perversions are similarly allowed to go unprosecuted. The legal safeguards of the family are increasingly removed, so that again society is threatened with the anarchy of an anti-familistic state and its legalized lawlessness. In the name of equal rights, women are being stripped of the protections of the family and given no place except the perverse competition of a sexual market in which increasingly shock, perversion, deviation, and aggressiveness command a premium. The women who gain by equal rights are those clearly who are hostile to Christian law.

The law, it must be remembered, is warfare against that which is defined as evil and a protection of that which is held to be good. In the developing law-structure of humanism, warfare is implicitly waged against the parents and the family as evil, and protection is extended to perverts and law-breakers on the assumption that their "rights" need protecting.[25]

8. The Holy Family

It is not accidental that Jesus Christ, the second person of the Trinity, was also a member of a human family. The incarnation was a reality, and basic to its reality was the nativity of Jesus in a Hebrew family and as the heir of a royal line. Christ was born in fulfillment of prophecy, and in terms of laws basic to the family.

Several aspects of this fact are immediately apparent. *First,* Jesus Christ was born as heir to the throne of David, and in fulfillment of promises concerning the future meaning of that throne. In II Samuel 7:12, God declares to David, "When thy days shall be fulfilled, and thou shalt sleep with thy fathers, I will set up thy seed after thee, which shall proceed out of thy bowels, and I will establish his kingdom." This promise is celebrated in Psalm 89 and Psalm 132. This kingdom of the Messiah or Christ is "his kingdom" (II Sam. 7:12), and is defined in terms of Him.

Second, Christ's kingdom is the restoration of authority, law, and

24. Lars Ullerstam, M.D., *The Erotic Minorities* (New York: Grove Press, 1966).
25. For an analysis of the subversion of the Christian law-order, see George S. Schuyler, "The Fall From Decency to Degradation," in *American Opinion,* vol. XII, no. 1 (January, 1969), pp. 21-30.

order. As promised in Isaiah to the faithful, "I will restore thy judges as at the first, and thy counsellors as at the beginning; afterward thou shalt be called the city of righteousness, the faithful city" (Isa. 1:26). Since the judges or authorities were established at Sinai, or as a result of Sinai, so the law of God will be re-established as a result of the new Sinai, Golgotha, by the greater Moses, Jesus Christ. Accordingly, the Messiah is spoken of as the one in whom and under whom law and order are brought to fulfillment. He is the "Wonderful Counsellor, The Mighty God, The Everlasting Father, The Prince of Peace. Of the increase of his government and peace there shall be no end, upon the throne of David, and upon his kingdom, to order it and to establish it with judgment and with justice from henceforth even for ever" (Isa. 9:6, 7). We are also told of this Shoot of the stock of Jesse that "with righteousness shall he judge the poor, and reprove with equity the meek of the earth" (Isa. 11:4). He comes to bring justice and "to slay the wicked" (Isa. 11:4), to restore paradise, so that, figuratively speaking, the wolf and the lamb dwell together (Isa. 11:6, 9), and the earth is restored to greater fertility and blessedness: "The wilderness and the parched land shall be glad, and the desert shall rejoice, and blossom as the rose" (Isa. 35:1).[1]

Third, Christ's kingdom is not limited, like David's, to Canaan: it covers the earth. Christ said to His disciples, "Blessed are the meek for they shall inherit the earth" (Matt. 5:5). St. Paul said, "For the promise, that he should be the heir of the world, was not to Abraham, or to his seed, through the law, but through the righteousness of faith" (Rom. 4:13). This important declaration means, according to Hodge:

> The word heir, in Scripture, frequently means *secure possessor.* Heb. i. 2, vi. 17, xi. 7 &c. This use of the terms probably arose from the fact, that among the Jews possession by inheritance was much more secure and permanent than that obtained by purchase. The promise was not to Abraham, nor to his seed. . . . i.e., neither to the one nor to the other. Both were included in the promise. And by *his seed,* is not here, as in Gal. iii. 16, meant Christ, but his spiritual children.[2]

The second half of the verse, as Murray points out, discussing Romans 4:13 in relation to 4:16, 17, makes clear the meaning of law and faith with respect to the heirs. The real heirs are by faith:

> And these verses also establish the denotation as being not the natural descendants of Abraham, but all, both of the circumcision

1. See A. G. Hebert, *The Throne of David, A Study of the Fulfilment of the Old Testament in Jesus Christ and His Church* (New York: Morehouse-Gorham, 1941), pp. 39-49.
2. Charles Hodge, *Commentary on the Epistle to the Romans* (New York: Armstrong, 1893) p. 185.

and the uncircumcision, who are "of the faith of Abraham" (vs. 16). The "promise" is therefore that given to all who believe and all who believe are Abraham's seed.[3]

Abraham's true heirs are not by blood or law, but those who share Abraham's faith. These receive their inheritance from the King, Jesus Christ. "And if ye be Christ's, then are ye Abraham's seed, and heirs according to the promise" (Gal. 3:29).[4]

Some seek to deny Christ's kingship over the earth by citing John 18:36: "My kingdom is not of this world. . . ." Few verses are more misinterpreted. As Westcott noted, "yet He did claim a sovereignty, a sovereignty of which the spring and the source was not of earth but of heaven."[5] "My kingdom is not of this world" means it "does not derive its origin or its support from earthly sources."[6] In other words, Christ's kingdom is not derived from this world, because it is *of* God and is *over* the world.

Fourth, Christ by His virgin birth was a new creation, a new Adam: like Adam a miracle, a creation directly from God, but, unlike Adam, who had no link to any earlier humanity, Christ was linked to the old humanity by His birth from Mary. St. Luke cited both Adam and Jesus as "the son of God" (Luke 1:34, 35; 3:38). Christ is thus "the second man" or "the last Adam," (I Cor. 15:45-47), the fountainhead of a new humanity. By His birth of God, and of the Virgin Mary, Jesus Christ is head of the new race, as the new Adam, to provide earth with a new seed to supplant the old Adamic race.[7] The first Adam was tempted in paradise and fell. The new Adam was tempted in the Adamic wilderness and began there the restoration of paradise: He "was with the wild beasts, and the angels ministered unto him" (Mark 1:13). Communion was restored by "the second man" with the angels of heaven and the animals of the earth. As the true Adam, He exercised dominion (Gen. 1:28), and as the Lord of the earth, he issued His law on the mount, confirming the law He had earlier given through Moses (Matt. 5:1-7:29). In the ancient world, the king was the law-giver, and a law-giver was thus either the king or an agent of the king, as in the case of Moses. Jesus, by declaring in the Sermon on the Mount, "*I* say unto you," declared Himself to be the

---

3. John Murray, *The Epistle to the Romans* (Grand Rapids: Eerdmans, 1959), I, 142.

4. For an analysis of the heirs of Abraham as the covenant people, see Martin J. Wyngaarden, *The Future of the Kingdom in Prophecy and Fulfillment* (Grand Rapids: Baker Book House, 1955), pp. 97-107.

5. B. F. Westcott, *The Gospel According to St. John* (Grand Rapids: Eerdmans, [1881], 1954), p. 260.

6. *Ibid.*

7. See Douglas Edwards, *The Virgin Birth in History and Faith* (London: Faber and Faber, 1943).

King, and, by His Great Commission, made clear that His kingship
is over all the earth (Matt. 28:18-19).[8]

Fifth, Jesus Christ, as King of the earth, has *the right of dominion.*
This means that He attacks and overthrows all those who deny His
dominion. As God declared, "I will overturn, overturn, overturn, it:
and it shall be no more, until he come whose right it is; and I will
give it him" (Ezek. 21:27). This overturning of His enemies continues
today (Heb. 12:25-29).

Sixth, Jesus Christ was *born under the law and into law, to fulfill the
law.* This fulfillment He began from His birth, by His membership
in the holy family, where, as a dutiful son, He kept the fifth commandment all His days. As the legal heir of a royal throne, He laid claim
to the God-given promises, and, as legal king of the earth, He is in
process of dispossessing all false heirs and all enemies from His possession.

Seventh, Jesus Christ obeyed the family law. As a dutiful son, He
made provision for His mother from the cross. John was given to
Mary as her new son; to care for her. But the new "son" Christ gave
to Mary was in terms of the family of faith (John 19:25-27), so that
Christ indicated that true heirship (for the heir inherits responsibilities)
is *by faith* more than by blood. This principle He had earlier declared
with reference to His mother and brothers. When their doubts led
them to a position of fearfulness with respect to His calling, He declared
His true family to be "whosoever shall do the will of my Father"
(Matt. 12:49). He did not thereby separate Himself from His responsibility to His mother, whose care was His dying concern. In the holy
family, therefore, the Biblical law of the family is clearly exemplified.
Particularly in His *heirship,* Jesus Christ demonstrated the responsibility
of an heir. As heir of a family, He fulfilled His family responsibilities;
as heir to a throne, He met His royal obligations; as heir to the racial
mantle as the second Adam, He met His duties to the race. He thus
demonstrated that *heirship is responsibility.*

9. The Limitation of Man's Authority

The problem of authority is basic to the nature of any and every
society. If its doctrine of authority is shattered, a society collapses, or
else it is held together only by total terror. It has become commonplace on the part of scholars to avoid the fact that authority is a
religious matter; the god or ultimate power of any system is also the
authority and the law-giver of that system.

Iverach, in line with the humanistic evasion of the nature of authority,

---

8. For an analysis of Christ's kingship, see Roderick Campbell, *Israel and the
New Covenant* (Philadelphia: Presbyterian and Reformed Publishing Co., 1954).

began his analysis by stating that "The word 'authority,' as used in ordinary language, always implies a certain amount of coerciveness. The most common meaning is that of a power to enforce obedience."[1] This is certainly true as far as it goes, but it is false by its misdirection of emphasis. It is like defining a man as a creature who is largely hairless, has a thumb, and walks erect; technically, this definition is correct; practically, it has told us nothing, and has evaded the central facts concerning man. Iverach recognized this limitation, and he therefore led the argument, step by step, to the conclusion that "All authority is thus ultimately Divine authority. This is true whether we regard the world from the theistic or from the pantheistic point of view."[2] Since the starting-point of all authority is religious, then the startingpoint of all discussions of authority must be religious. God is not the final link in authority but the alpha and the omega of all authority.

All authority is in essence religious authority; the nature of the authority depends on the nature of the religion. If the religion is Biblical, then the authority at every point is the immediate or mediated authority of the triune God. If the religion is humanistic, then the authority is everywhere implicitly or explicitly the autonomous consciousness of man. Men either obey authority on religious grounds, or they disobey on religious grounds. Adam and Eve were no less religious in their disobedience than in their obedience. When they assumed that man is autonomous and has a freedom of choice with respect to God's law, and the freedom to determine what shall be law, they made a moral and a religious decision, and they acted in obedience to their new religious presuppositions. Disobedience to existing authority means that a new authority is in view. The disrespect of disobedience is a religious defiance of an authority; it is the denial of that authority in the name of another. When a child defies his parent, saying, "*I* don't want to, and *I* won't do it," he replaces parental, and religious, authority with his own will; he opposes his own demand for autonomy and moral independence against the claims of God in His word and his parents in their person. If the child obeys only through fear, it is still a religious obedience, in that power, or punishment, is the religious motive force in his life. The religions vary, but the fact that authority is religious remains constant.

Authority is rightful power; it is dominion and jurisdiction. Men respond to acknowledged authority; they resent obeying authorities they do not recognize as such. The chief priests and elders of the people asked the right question of Jesus, for the wrong reasons, being unwilling to admit what their own doctrine of authority was. But the

1. James Iverach, "Authority," in *HERE*, II, 249.
2. *Ibid.*, II, 253.

question remains: "By what authority doest thou these things? and who gave thee this authority?" (Matt. 21:23). They had already seen what His declared authority was, and had observed, "thou, being a man, makest thyself god" (John 10:23). Jesus grounded His authority on His Father, and on Himself as God incarnate.

Without a valid doctrine of authority, no order stands. To appeal to sentiment or gratitude is futile: either a religious doctrine of authority binds man, or he is not bound, save at his pleasure or convenience, which is no bond at all. Let us turn again to Egyptian moral instruction for examples of this, as witness the "Instructions" of a father to his son:

> Double the food which thou givest thy mother, carry her as she carried thee. She had a heavy load in thee, but she did not leave it to me. After thou wert borne she was still burdened with thee; her breast was in thy mouth for three years, and though thy filth was disgusting, her heart was not disgusted. When thou takest a wife, remember how thy mother gave birth to thee, and her raising thee as well; do not let thy wife blame thee, nor cause that she raise her hands to the god.

Consider also the words of Ptahhotep of the Fourth Dynasty:

> If thou art a man of standing, thou shouldest found a household and love thy wife at home, as is fitting. Fill her belly, and clothe her back; ointment is the prescription for her body. Make her heart glad, for she is a profitable field for her lord.[3]

These words are beautiful and moving, and the moral sentiment is commendable but futile. The appeal is to sentiment, not to an absolute moral law. There is here no absolute religious and moral authority undergirding the family and protecting mother and wife, nor is there a civil authority to enforce that religious law: the welfare of the mother and the wife are left to the pleasure of the individual, and so the appeal is a futile attempt to tug at the heart-strings: it is an appeal without authority.

If a doctrine of authority embodies contradictions within itself, then it is eventually bound to fall apart as the diverse strains war against one another. This has been a continuing part of the various crises of Western civilization. Because the Biblical doctrine of authority has been compromised by Greco-Roman humanism, the tensions of authority have been sharp and bitter. As Clark wrote, with reference to authority in the United States,

> It is a doctrine of both Mosaic and Christian law that governments are divinely ordained and derive their powers from God. In the Old Testament it is asserted that "power belongeth unto God," (Ps. 62:11) that God "removeth kings and setteth up kings,"

---

3. Barbara Mertz, *Temples, Tombs and Hieroglyphs, The Story of Egyptology* (New York: Coward-McCann, 1964), p. 333 f.

(Dan. 2:21) and that "the Most High ruleth in the kingdom of men, and giveth it to whomsoever he will" (Dan. 4:32). Similarly in the New Testament it is stated that ". . . there is no power but of God, the powers that be are ordained of God" (Rom. 13:1).

In Roman law it was originally considered that the emperor's power had been bestowed upon him by the people, but when Rome became a Christian state his power was regarded as coming from God. In America also God has been recognized as the source of government, though it is commonly thought that in a republican or democratic government "all power is inherent in the people."[4]

In early America, there was no question, whatever the *form* of the civil government, that all legitimate authority is derived from God. The influence of the classical tradition revived the authority of the people, which historically is equally compatible with monarchy, oligarchy, dictatorship, or democracy, but it is not compatible with the doctrine of God's authority. As a result, the authority of God has been progressively displaced in America by the authority of the new god, the people. When God is invoked, He is seen as someone who bows to the people, as a God who longs for democracy.

This is no less true elsewhere. Thus in England, Queen Elizabeth II, in her 1968 Christmas Message, declared, "The essential message of Christmas is still that we all belong to the great brotherhood of man. . . . If we truly believe that the brotherhood of man has a value for the world's future, then we should seek to support those international organizations which foster understanding between people and nations."[5] Christ, who came to divide men in terms of Himself, is seen by the queen as one who came to unite men in terms of humanity. The Marxists, because they lack this schizophrenic and/or hypocritical position, are able to function more vigorously and systematically. The Marxist authority is rigorously humanistic and is enforced by an unabashed total terror.

Under a Biblical doctrine of authority, because "the powers that be are ordained of God" (Rom. 13:1), all authority, whether in the home, school, state, church, or any other sphere, is subordinate authority and is under God and subject to His word. This means, *first,* that all obedience is subject to the prior obedience to God and His word, for "We ought to obey God rather than men" (Acts 5:29; cf. 4:19). Although civil obedience is specifically commanded (Matt. 23:2, 3; Rom. 13:1-5; Titus 3:1; Heb. 13:7, 17; I Peter 2:13-16; Matt. 22:21; Mark 12:17; Luke 20:25, etc.), it is equally apparent that the prior requirement of obedience to God must prevail. Thus, the

---

4. H. B. Clark: *Biblical Law*, p. 51 f.
5. "Queen in TV Appeal For Brotherhood," Los Angeles *Herald-Examiner* (Wednesday, December 25, 1968), p. A-13.

apostles had orders from their King to proclaim the gospel, and they therefore refused to be bound to silence by the legal authorities (Acts 4:18; 5:29; cf. I Macc. 2:22).

Second, all authority on earth, being under God and not itself God, is by nature and necessity limited authority. This limited nature of all subordinate authority is sharply set forth in a number of laws, of which an interesting one is Deuteronomy 25:1-3:

> If there be a controversy between men, and they come unto judgment, that the judges may judge them they shall justify the righteous, and condemn the wicked.
> And it shall be, if the wicked man be worthy to be beaten, that the judges shall cause him to lie down, and to be beaten before his face, according to his fault, by a certain number.
> Forty stripes he may give him, and not exceed: lest, if he should exceed, and beat him above these with many stripes, then thy brother should seem vile unto thee.

Wright observed, of the last phrase,

> *Seem vile* (KJV) is incorrect; see the RSV. The Hebrew literally has "be made light." To give a man the punishment due him for his crime was not to dishonor him as a fellow Israelite, but to beat him indiscriminately in public was to treat him like an animal rather than with the respect due a fellow human being.[6]

This point is important. Since Biblical law did not permit the growth, in times of obedience, of a class of professional criminals and incorrigible delinquents, "the wicked man" is thus not a depraved criminal but a sinful citizen and neighbor. He submits to the judgment and is reinstated in the community; he is not vile, or is not degraded, made light, in the eyes of the community or the authorities by the punishment. In fact, at a later date, according to Waller, the punishment "was inflicted in the synagogue, and the law was read meanwhile from Deuteronomy xxviii, 58, 59, with one or two other passages."[7] The reading of Deuteronomy 28:58, 59, is important: the purpose of man's judgment was declared thereby to fulfill God's requirement and avoid God's judgment, for "If thou wilt not observe to do all the words of this law. . . . Then the LORD will make thy plagues wonderful" (or extraordinary).

This brings into focus a significant aspect of *the intention of the law*. By requiring capital punishment for incorrigible criminals, the law *eliminated* the enemies of godly society, it *purged* them from society. This is the *killing* side of the law. On the other hand, by requiring *restitution* of other significant offenders, and *corporal punishment* (the

---

6. G. Ernest Wright, "Deuteronomy" in *Interpreter's Bible*, II, 479.
7. C. H. Waller, "Deuteronomy," in Ellicott, II, 67.

stripes) of minor offenders, the law worked to restore man to society, to *cleanse* and to *heal*. The man who made restitution, or who received his stripes, had paid his debt to the offended person and to society and was restored to citizenship. The reading of Deuteronomy 28:58, 59 had in mind the avoidance of God's destroying judgment by the application of God's healing judgment.

Where the law seeks to heal without killing, it kills. The surgeon must remove a hopelessly diseased organ to save the body, to heal it of its infection. But a mildly infected finger is not cut off; it is purged of infection in order to be maintained as a functioning part of the body. Whether in killing or healing, the authority of civil government is strictly governed and limited by the word of God.

The authority of the judges is thus limited authority: a maximum of forty stripes, lest it put a distance between judge and people, lest the sinning citizen become a subject of the judge rather than both together subjects of God the King. Punishment is always subject to the law of God; the normal sentence is restitution; in *minor* causes of personal controversy, it was corporal punishment, a beating. The kind of offense which was covered by corporal punishment is, among others, that of Leviticus 19:14, "Thou shalt not curse the deaf, nor put a stumbling block before the blind, but shall fear thy God: I am the LORD." According to Ginsburg, "The term deaf also includes the absent, and hence out of hearing." Moreover,

> According to the administration of the law during the second Temple, this prohibition was directed against all cursing whatsoever. For, said they, if to curse one who cannot hear, and whom, therefore, it cannot grieve, is prohibited, how much more it is forbidden to curse one who hears it, and who is both enraged and grieved by it.
>
> *Nor put a stumbling block before the blind.* In Deut. xxvii. 18, a curse is pronounced upon those who lead the blind astray. To help those who are thus afflicted was always regarded as a meritorious act. Hence among the benevolent services which Job rendered to his neighbours, he says "I was eyes to the blind" (Job xxii. 15). According to the interpretation which obtained in the time of Christ, this is to be understood figuratively. It forbids imposition upon the ignorant, and misdirecting those who seek advice, thus causing them to fall. Similar tenderness to the weak is enjoined by the Apostle: "That no man put a stumblingblock or an occasion to fall in his brother's way" (Rom. xiv. 13).[8]

Third, the law asserts *the supremacy of the written law-word of God.* Man's authority is under God and limited; God's authority is unlimited. Men have no right to interpret the will of God in terms of their wants and wishes; the will of God for man is declared in His law-word. The

---

8. C. D. Ginsburg, "Leviticus," in Ellicott, I, 423 f.

form of the civil order may vary: it may be the commonwealth governed by judges or governors (Deut. 17:8-13), or a monarchy (Deut. 17: 14-20), but the supremacy of God's law and authority remains. The only authority in any sphere of government, home, church, state, school, or other, is the written word of God (Deut. 17:9-11). This law-word must be applied to the varying conditions of man and to the diverse social contexts. *"The written word is the chain that binds.* Nor does the varying relation between the executive and legislative authority alter the principle."[9] The man who refused to recognize the authority of God's law-word as binding on himself when the verdict was given was executed, "to put away the evil from Israel," or to *purge* it from the land (Deut. 17:12, 13).

If a king ruled, he was to be (a) one of the covenant people, i.e., a man of faith because the covenant requires faith; (b) he was not to "multiply horses," i.e., instruments of aggressive rather than defensive warfare, nor "multiply wives" (polygamy), and "neither shall he greatly multiply to himself silver and gold," for his purpose must be the prosperity of the people under God rather than his own wealth; a rich state means a poor people; (c) the king must have, read, and study the law-word of God "all the days of his life, that he may learn to fear the LORD his God, to keep all the words of this law and these statutes, to do them;" and (d) the purpose of his study is not only to further God's law-order but also "That his heart be not lifted up above his brethren," since he is a fellow-subject of God, and that he may rule in obedience to God all his days (Deut. 17:14-20). Jesus Christ, as the true King, came to fulfill God's law-word and to establish God's dominion: "Lo, I come, in the volume of the book it is written of me, I delight to do thy will, O my God: yea, thy law is within my heart" (Ps. 40:7; Heb. 10:7, 9). According to Wright, writing of Deuteronomy 17:14-20, "It is impossible to imagine such writing in another nation of the ancient Near East. Kingship was as subject to the divine law as were all the other offices of the nation."[10] But in Biblical law, king, judge, priest, father, and people are all under the written law-word of God, and *the higher the position the more important is obedience.*

Thus, *fourth,* as is already apparent, personal whims cannot take precedence over God's law even where our property is concerned. A legitimate and godly heir cannot be set aside in favor of another son, simply because the father loves the second son. This is specified in the case of a polygamous marriage, where the firstborn may be the

---

9. C. H. Waller, "Deuteronomy," in Ellicott, II, 51.
10. G. Ernest Wright, "Deuteronomy," in *Interpreter's Bible,* II, 441.

son of a hated wife (Deut. 21:15-17). In *any* case, the father is not at liberty to use personal and non-religious reasons as the criterion of heirship. God's law must prevail. The only legitimate grounds of heirship are religious.

We must therefore conclude that *authority is not only a religious concept but also a total one.* It involves the recognition at every point of our lives of God's absolute law-order. The starting-point of this recognition is in the family: "Honor thy father and thy mother." Out of this commandment, with its requirement that children submit to and obey the authority of their parents under God, comes the basic and fundamental training in religious authority. If the authority of the home is denied, it means that man is in revolution against the fabric and structure of life, and against life itself. Obedience thus carries the promise of life.

VI

THE SIXTH COMMANDMENT

1. "Thou Shalt Not Kill"

The sixth commandment is, together with the eighth, the shortest statement in the table of ten (Ex. 20:13; Deut. 5:17). It appears in both Exodus and Deuteronomy without variation.

Its most elementary meaning is clearly stated by Calvin:

> The sum of this Commandment is, that we should not unjustly do violence to any one. In order, however, that God may the better restrain us from all injury of others, He propounds one particular form of it, from which men's natural sense is abhorrent; for we all detest murder, so as to recoil from those whose hands are polluted with blood, as if they carried contagion with them.[1]

It should be noted that Calvin cited *unjust* violence as forbidden by the law; capital punishment, legitimate warfare, self-defense, and similar acts are not forbidden. Calvin added, as he began his study of the details of the subordinate legislation, "It will, however, more clearly appear hereafter, that under the word kill is included by *synecdoche* all violence, smiting, and aggression."[2]

Calvin pointed out further, in a passage more than ever relevant today,

> Besides, another principle is also to be remembered, that in negative precepts, as they are called, the opposite affirmation is also to be understood; else it would not be by any means consistent, that a person would satisfy God's Law by merely abstaining from doing injury to others. Suppose, for example, that one of a cowardly disposition, and not daring to assail even a child, should not move a finger to injure his neighbours, would he therefore have discharged the duties of humanity as regards the Sixth Commandment? Nay, natural common sense demands more than that we should abstain from wrong-doing. And, not to say more on this point, it will plainly appear from the summary of the Second Table, that God not only forbids us to be murderers, but also prescribes that every one should study faithfully to defend the life of his neighbour, and practically to declare that it is dear to him; for in that summary no mere negative phrase is used, but the words expressly set forth that our neighbours are to be loved. It is un-

1. John Calvin, *Commentaries on the Four Last Books of Moses*, III, 20.
2. *Ibid.*

219

questionable, then, that of those whom God there commands to be loved, He here commends the lives to our care. There are, consequently, two parts in the Commandment,—*first,* that we should not vex, or oppress, or be at enmity with any; and, *secondly,* that we should not only live at peace with men, without exciting quarrels, but also should aid, as far as we can, the miserable who are unjustly oppressed, and should endeavour to resist the wicked, lest they should injure men as they list.[3]

Jesus in his summary of the law, declared the "two tables" of the law to be summed up in the love of God and the love of neighbors (Matt. 22:36-40). "On these two commandments hang (depend, BV) all the law and the prophets" (Matt. 22:40). The proper meaning of the law involves both the negative precept and the positive affirmation. To limit obedience, and to test character, merely by the negative factor is dangerous. It leads too often to the belief that a good man is the one Calvin singled out for his ugly example: the coward who would not dare "assail even a child" but who is incapable of any discharge of his duties. Too often the church has equated these cowards with righteous men and advanced cowardly snivellers, whose weapons are those of back-biting and tale-bearing, to positions of authority.

But all men have, as Calvin noted, "the duties of humanity as regards the Sixth Commandment." If they do not seek to prevent injury, assault, or murder, they are themselves in part guilty of the offense committed. The unwillingness in many instances of witnesses to act in cases of assault or murder may mean no entanglement on earth, but it incurs fearful entanglement and guilt before God.

Thus, a fundamental principle here appears, one which functioned in Israel, in later Christian law-orders, and which became a part of the American legal tradition, namely, *the police power of every citizen.* The law asks two things of every man, *obedience and enforcement.* To obey a law means in effect to enforce it in one's own life and in one's community. God's law is not a private matter; it is not for us to obey personally simply because we like it, meanwhile leaving other men to follow whatever law they choose. The law is valid for us because it is valid for all; to obey it means to accept a universal order as binding on us and upon all men. Obedience therefore requires that we seek a total enforcement of the law. This then is the *first* important principle which appears in this law.

But, *second*, as appears in Calvin's statement, and in our Lord's summary of the law, this commandment, "Thou shalt not kill," is more than purely political in its reference. It refers to vastly more than cases of assault and murder which are criminal offenses and subject

---

3. *Ibid.,* III, 20 f.

to trial by civil authorities. The police power and duty of the person involves a common defense of godly order. Law and order are the responsibilities of all good men without exception. Injuries to our fellow men, or to our enemies, which are not subject to civil or criminal action, are still our responsibilities. Our police power involves action against back-biting and tale-bearing. It also requires that we, in love of our neighbor, have a regard for his property as well as his reputation, to avoid injury to it. This is certainly no less true of his family, marriage, and his wife. But our police power and the prohibition against killing requires that we use the earth and its natural resources entirely subject to the word of God and under His law. Thus, only a fraction of the exercise of man's police power is political.

Third, the law makes abundantly clear that capital punishment, the death penalty, is a part of this law, so that it involves no murder to take life on God's terms and under His law. Life is created by God, and can be assailed or taken only on God's terms. The terms of life are established by God. God as the giver of all life establishes the laws for all of life, and for all things else. Hence, every aspect of this law is a religious duty. Both the giving and the taking of life are aspects of man's religious duty. This means that a man must not only avoid committing murder, and seek the apprehension of a murderer, but he must also seek the death penalty for murder.

Fourth, since the protection and nurture of man's life under God is the positive affirmation of the sixth commandment, it becomes apparent why, in Biblical tradition, both in Israel and in Western civilization, medicine has been closely linked to religion. Tournier has stated that "In the very essence of his vocation the doctor is the defender of the weak."[4] This is a strange and perverse interpretation, modern in its reading of the sick as the weak and in its orientation to the weak. The doctor is not concerned with the weak as against the strong and treats both as need or care requires it. The doctor's function is to further healing and to protect and further man's life under God. This conserving function has given medicine a conservative orientation, and one of the functions of socialized medicine has been the assault on medicine because of its conservative heritage, now rapidly being lost. The attempts at a mechanistic and materialistic medical approach function to sever the link between medicine and Biblical faith. On the other hand, psychosomatic medicine, despite its many materialistic emphases, has worked to give room again for a return to a Biblical emphasis, as has the renewed interest in the godly use of the soil and the proper growing of foods.

---

4. Paul Tournier, *The Strong and the Weak* (Philadelphia: The Westminster Press, 1963), p. 161.

Fifth, while respect for life is required by this commandment, it cannot be confused with Albert Schweitzer's anti-Biblical principle, reverence for life. Not reverence for life but reverence for God and His law-word is basic to this and every other commandment. As Ingram noted, "All rightness toward God is grounded upon strict, uncompromising observance of the First Commandment, 'Thou shalt have no other gods before me.' It is thereby against the law to put anybody or anything before God."[5] Life cannot be placed before God, neither our life nor any other man's. To view death as the ultimate evil is thus morally wrong. Rather, death is a consequence of the real evil, sin; it was sin which brought death into the world, and it is sin rather than death that man must reckon with.

Sixth, we have seen that this commandment has a political, social, and religious reference; indeed, its every reference is religious. But it should be added that the purely personal aspect is also included. Adam Clarke cited this. Establishing it on a general principle, Clarke wrote:

> God is the Fountain and Author of *life*—no creature can give life to another: an archangel cannot give life to an angel—an angel cannot give life to man—man cannot give life even to the meanest of the brute creation. As God alone gives life, so He alone has a right to take it away: and he who, without the authority of God, takes away life, is properly a *murderer*. This commandment, which is general, prohibits murder of every kind.[6]

Clarke then cited ten forms of murder, of which four concern us here:

> 6. All who by immoderate and superstitious fastings, macerations of the body, and wilful neglect of health, destroy or abridge life, are *murderers*;—whatever a false religion and ignorant superstitious priests may say of them. God will not have *murder* for *sacrifice*.
>
> 8. All who put an end to their own lives by *hemp, steel, pistol, poison, drowning*, &c. are *murderers*—whatever coroners' inquests may say of them; unless it be clearly proved that the deceased was *radically insane*.
>
> 9. All who are addicted to *riot* and *excess*; to *drunkenness* and *gluttony*; to *extravagant pleasures*, to *inactivity* and *slothfulness*; in short, and in *sum*, all who are influenced by *indolence, intemperance*, and *disorderly passions*, by which life is prostrated and abridged, are *murderers*; for our blessed Lord, who has given us a new edition of this commandment, Matt. xix. 18, proposes it thus: *Thou shalt do NO murder*,—no *kind* or *species* of murder; and all the above are either *direct* or *consequent murders*; and His

5. Ingram, *World Under God's Law*, p. 73.
6. Adam Clarke, *Discourses on Various Subjects Relative to the Being and Attribute of God and His Works* (New York: McElrath & Bangs, 1830), II, 31.

beloved disciple has assured us, that *no murderer hath eternal life abiding in him*. I John iii. 15.

10. A man who is full of *fierce* and *furious passions;* who has no command of his own temper, may, in a moment, destroy the life even of his *friend*, his *wife*, or his *child*. All such fell and ferocious men are *murderers*; they ever carry about with them the murderous propensity, and are not praying to God to subdue and destroy it.[7]

The purely personal violations of this law involve any and every abuse of our body which is destructive of our health and in violation of God's will for us. It also means that tempers of mind which are destructive and suicidal are contrary to this law.

The personal application includes markings, cuttings, and tattoos of the body, for the body must be used under God's law, and all such acts are forbidden in the law, whether for mourning, as religious marks, or for ornamental or other uses (Lev. 19:28; 21:5). Tattooing was practiced religiously to indicate that one adhered to or belonged to a god; it also indicated that a man was a slave, that he belonged to a lord or owner.[8] The believer, as a free man in Christ, indicates Christ's lordship by obedience, not by servile markings: the body is kept holy and clean unto the Lord. The persistence of a mark of slavery among men is indicative of man's perversity.

Seventh, the sixth commandment, like the first, has a reference to all ten commandments. When the law declares, "Thou shalt have no other gods before me" (Ex. 20:3), it means in part that every violation of any law involves placing ourselves and our will above God's word and is therefore a violation of the first commandment. Similarly, when the law declares, "Thou shalt not kill," it means that any violation of the first and second "tables" of the law involves a destruction of our life in relationship to God. We pass under the death penalty, and into the processes of death by disobedience. But, when we violate the fifth commandment, we also bring death to the family, as we do with violations of the seventh, "Thou shalt not commit adultery" (Ex. 20:14). Not only the family but society is assaulted or killed by violations of these and other commandments. The eighth commandment, "Thou shalt not steal" (Ex. 20:15), protects property and thereby protects the life of the family and also the social order. This is no less true of the prohibitions of the ninth and tenth commandments against false witness and covetousness: men and nations are injured and destroyed by these things.

Thus, to worship God alone is the essence of the law; to live is to worship God by using life on God's terms only. The law is total, be-

---

7. *Ibid.*, II, 32, 33.
8. "Cuttings," in *Unger's Bible Dictionary* (Chicago: Moody Press, 1957), p. 233.

cause God is totally God, absolute and omnipotent. Health for man is wholeness in terms of God's law.

Moreover, the bent and direction of every man is towards wholeness and totality in terms of a fundamental presupposition. The logic of men and nations is that they live and act out their faith; however great the social inertia, the direction of a society is governed by and moves clearly towards its fulfilment of a basic presupposition.

Man is born into a world of total meaning, so total that the very hairs of his head are all numbered; not a sparrow falls apart from God's sovereign purpose, and the wild flowers whose life-span is brief and fleeting are still a part of God's total government and have a meaning in terms of it (Matt. 6:26, 30; 10:29-31; Luke 12:6-7). All life thus has direction in terms of God's creative purpose. Even when man sins, he cannot escape meaning; in his sin, he substitutes another direction and purpose for God's purpose in imitation of God's creation mandate.

A man acts out of faith, and a man will act on his faith; "by their fruits ye shall know them" (Matt. 7:16, 20). Every fibre of man's life is geared to meaning, and he will therefore act progressively with more and more consistency in terms of his faith. The problem of a transition period in history is that men still have a hangover of the old faith, whereas they are progressively acting in terms of their new faith. Modern man, being humanistic, progressively drops his relics of Christian law and order in favor of his humanistic heart and faith. A man will act on his faith, not on his waning sentiments for a past order, and today even "conservatives" reveal their basic humanism.

Thus, some libertarian economists, whose classical economics rests on a world of law and order which presupposes God, are now increasingly espousing total relativism. They ask for a free-market for all faiths and practices, because none are true, since there is no truth. The one great enemy of the "new" libertarians is Biblical faith, since it holds to an absolute truth, and many who have had experience with these relativistic libertarians can testify that they will join forces with anyone, including Marxists, to make war on the Christians. Men will act on their faith, and there is an inescapable consistency in man, because he was created into a unified and total world of meaning and cannot live, even in sin, in any other kind of world. "Ye shall know them by their fruits. Do men gather grapes of thorns, or figs of thistles? Even so every good tree bringeth forth good fruit; but a corrupt tree bringeth forth evil fruit. A good tree cannot bring forth evil fruit, neither can a corrupt tree bring forth good fruit" (Matt. 7:16-18). There is a process of maturation, and there are diseases which from time to time infect good trees, but a tree is true to its nature, and a man acts in terms of his basic faith.

Thus, if a man's orientation is to God by His sovereign grace, then that man will be oriented to life and to obedience to the law-word of life. But if a man's presuppositions are not Biblical, if his basic faith is humanistic, then his orientation will be towards sin and death. Fearful of death, he will speak with intensity about reverence for life, but his nature begets death. The commandment, "Thou shalt not kill," prohibits suicide, for we are not our own, nor can we use or take our lives in terms of our word, but those outside God and His law-realm are suicidal. In words eminently true of himself, and applicable to the reprobate only, Oscar Wilde, in "The Ballad of Reading Gaol," wrote that "all men kill the thing they love." Certainly all reprobates do, and just as certainly all men, acting on their faith, either kill themselves by degrees, and kill their society as well, or, by God's grace and law-word, they and their societies move towards life, and that more abundantly.

2. The Death Penalty

A man will act on his faith, and, if his faith be humanistic, inevitably his basic standard will be man, not God's law. He will view the world, not as God's handiwork but as his own. A theologian of the Death of God School, William Hamilton, has called attention to the fact that man now rarely looks at the starry sky with a sense of reverence for God. Instead, he cites his experience with his son as illustrative of a new attitude:

> The other night I was out in the back-yard with one of my children who had to identify some constellations for his science homework. . . . My son is a full citizen of the modern world, and said to me, after he had located the required constellations, "Which are the ones we put up there, Dad?" He had become a technological man, and this means something religiously.[1]

The boy's reaction was clearly logical. If the God of Scripture does not exist, then man is his own god and the world's lord and maker.

Moreover, if man is his own god, then man and man's life are the highest value. The greatest sin then becomes the taking of life. Accordingly, Arthur Miller, the dramatist, declares that "life is God's most precious gift; no principle, however glorious, may justify the taking of it."[2] It follows from such a faith that the worst kind of sin is capital punishment, the deliberate taking of life by the state. This was precisely the point made by an editorial in the New York *Herald Tribune*, May

---

1. Cited from William Hamilton, "The Death of God," *Playboy*, vol. 13, no. 8 (August, 1966), p. 138; by John Charles Cooper, *The Roots of the Radical Theology* (Philadelphia: Westminster Press, 1967), p. 137.
2. Cited from *The Collected Plays of Arthur Miller* (Viking Press, 1957), p. 320, "The Crucible," by J. C. Cooper, *Roots of the Radical Theology*, p. 143. Miller cites God only to eliminate Him.

3, 1960, "A Barbarous Form of Punishment," protesting the execution
of Caryl Chessman:

> Chessman succeeded in making himself a world-wide symbol of the
> fight against the death penalty. . . .
>
> He may or may not have been guilty, twelve years ago, of robbery
> and sexual assault (called kidnapping by a strange quirk of Cali-
> fornia law). The courts found him guilty; to the end he maintained
> his innocence, and the germ of doubt thus left will continue to
> cloud the case. But certainly the man killed yesterday by the sov-
> ereign state of California was not the same man whom that state's
> courts originally sentenced.
>
> . . . California sentenced a young thug; it killed a man who had
> learned the law, and probably citizenship, the hard way. . . .
>
> The law should inculcate respect for life by itself respecting the
> sanctity of life. The state should not, as California did yesterday,
> put itself in the position of the errant father telling his wayward son,
> "Do as I say, not as I do."
>
> Death is final. It leaves no room for second thoughts, or for cor-
> rection of the errors that are a mathematical certainty in a system
> of justice based on fallible human judgment. And the quintessential
> premeditation which judicial killing represents makes it more coldly
> vicious than a crime of passion.
>
> *The very concept of a death chamber is antithetical to the ideals of
> Western civilization.*[3]

In terms of such a faith, the most vicious people of all are those who
favor the death penalty. By their offense against man, they commit the
unpardonable sin for humanism. In order to give man the pre-eminence,
the humanist logically must destroy any concept of justice as a real and
objective standard. Man must be above law and therefore above justice. Justice is therefore reduced to rationalization and organized
hatred. Thus, a University of Leicester sociologist has written of
justice,

> But could all this instead, perhaps be some kind of historical confi-
> dence trick? It has already been suggested that our idea of justice
> may be a rationalization of what is at bottom punitive behaviour.
> This would not be to argue that the idea of justice is a fake, but
> rather, that instead of taking it at face value, we might try to under-
> stand what needs it is intended to satisfy. It may appear then as
> a kind of collective psychological defence. As proof of the validity
> of our ideals, we are often inclined to refer to the sense of conviction
> that we and other people possess about them. Most of us certainly
> have strong convictions about the rightness of the ideal of justice.
> But all that a sense of conviction does is to prove its appropriateness

---

3. Cited in John Laurence, *A History of Capital Punishment* (New York: The
Citadel Press, 1960), p. xxv f.

for us: that in the present state of our emotional economy, such a belief has for us a very special and much needed part to play. But justice seen in this light is not merely the solvent of unrest within us; it is a positive outlet through which these tensions can be discharged in (as it seems to us) a constructive fashion. Through the idea of justice the bad things within us are transformed into something new and worthwhile. All this, so long as we do not look too closely at the outcome. For to stand the famous phrase upon its head and thus perhaps give it more validity: justice may more often "manifestly appear to be done" than to be done in fact.[4]

Justice William O. Douglas has pointed out the obvious fact that law once had a divine sanction and rested on "God's will." Now, however, the sovereignty of God has been replaced by "the sovereignty of the individual." In terms of this, for Douglas the civil liberties struggle is of necessity hostile to the old order. Indeed, "Law and order is the guiding star of the totalitarians, not of free men."[5] For Douglas, "Revolution is therefore basic in the rights of man,"[6] and naturally so, since man is above the law, and submission to the law is tyranny. In a "decent society" there is respect for and effort to preserve "the sovereignty and honor" as well as "the dignity of each and every individual."[7] In the anarchistic world of Douglas, what law can bind man, who is above the law? And what state can survive if free men are those who are hostile to law and order?

Clearly, a religious war is in process, between humanism and Christianity, and in that war, church, state, and school are almost wholly on the side of humanism as against Christianity. But history has never been determined by majorities but rather always and only by God.

The struggle is between God's absolute justice and His law-order and man's lawless self-assertion and autonomy. God's law-order requires the death penalty for capital offenses against that realm. Man's law claims to value life too highly to take it, but humanistic societies do exact death for those whom they deem to be their enemies.

The death penalty appears at the onset of God's covenant with Noah: "And surely your blood of your lives will I require; at the hand of every beast I will require it, and at the hand of man; at the hand of every man's brother will I require the life of man. Whoso sheddeth man's blood, by man shall his blood be shed: for in the image of God made he him" (Gen. 9:5, 6). Not only every murderer but every

---

4. Howard Jones, *Crime in a Changing Society* (Baltimore: Penguin, 1965), p. 91 f.
5. Justice William O. Douglas, "Civil Liberties: The Crucial Issue" in *Playboy*, vol. 16, no. 1 (January, 1969), p. 93 f.
6. *Ibid.*, p. 120.
7. *Ibid.*, p. 223. It is significant that Douglas' article appeared in *Playboy*, which has become the major voice perhaps of the Death of God school.

animal which kills a man must pay with its life: God requires this of a country, and brings judgment finally for non-compliance. As Rand noted, "Contrary to popular belief the Bible does not hold life cheaply. It is a serious thing to take life, and for the taking of life the murderer forfeits his life."[8] For this reason, there can be no ransoming or pardoning of murder (as distinguished from accidental killing) nor a ransom taken, for to do so is to defile the land where God dwells in the midst of His people (Num. 35:29-34).

In terms of Biblical law, the required modes of punishment, as summarized by Rand, were as follows:

1) The death penalty for capital offenses.
2) Whipping from one to forty stripes for minor offenses.
3) In cases of stealing and destruction of another man's property, restitution: to which must be added from one hundred to four hundred per cent as punishment.
4) Those who were financially unable to make restitution, or pay the fine, were compelled to contribute their work and labor until the debt had been fully paid.
5) Confinement in a city of refuge for accidental killing.[9]

The replacement of this system by imprisonment is relatively recent; "as late as 1771, a French criminologist wrote that imprisonment was permissible only in the case of people awaiting trial."[10] But "Today prison is all there is: the death penalty is out of fashion (only one man was executed for crime in the United States after legal process in 1966)."[11]

The prison system, a humanistic device, is now under attack by the humanists, who want to replace it with the mental institution and psychiatric retraining. However, since their theory holds that it is a sick society which breeds sick men or criminals, the major attempt is to have psychological reconditioning (or brainwashing) of all people by means of the schools, pulpit, press, and television. Humanistic environmentalism requires such an approach. Marxism, as a more rigorous form of environmentalism, is dedicated to a total re-making of the social environment.

This humanistic environmentalism is a form of the same basic evolutionary faith which was formulated by Lamarck. Man can be and is determined by his environment and by acquired characteristics rather than by his own inner being. Not man's sin but the world around him determines man's will. Thus, the Marxist, Lincoln Steffens, in

---

8. H. B. Rand, *Digest of the Divine Law*, p. 67.
9. *Ibid.,* p. 141.
10. Martin Mayer, *The Lawyers* (New York: Dell Publishing Co. [1966], 1968), p. 208.
11. *Ibid.,* p. 209.

referring to man's fall, blamed neither Adam, nor Eve, nor the serpent: "it was, it is, the apple," i.e., the environment, the world man lives in.[12] From such a perspective, it is wrong to blame man. It is the world which must be remade by man to be fit for man. To punish man is thus seen as evil: it is God, who made the world, and the men who under God established God's law-order, who must be punished. Thus, between Biblical law and humanistic law there is an unbridgeable gap and an unceasing warfare.

The principle involved in the Biblical law of punishment is stated in Exodus 21:23-25: "Thou shalt give life for life, eye for eye, tooth for tooth, hand for hand, foot for foot, Burning for burning, wound for wound, stripe for stripe." Some choose to interpret this literally, but the very context (Ex. 21:1-36), a delineation of offenses and penalties, makes clear that it means that the punishment must fit the crime; it must be proportionate to the offense, neither lesser nor greater. This principle is restated in Leviticus 24:17-21 and Deuteronomy 19:21. The comment of Oehler is of interest:

> The Mosaic *principle of punishment* is the *jus talionis*, as it is repeatedly expressed in the sentence, "Life for life, eye for eye, tooth for tooth" etc., Ex. xxi. 23-25; Lev. xxiv. 18ff.; Deut. xix. 21: it shall be done to him who has offended as he has done; in other words, the punishment is a retribution corresponding in quantity and quality to the wicked deed. But that the *talio* is not meant to be understood in a merely external sense is not only shown by various provisions of punishment, but by the fact that not simply the deed itself, but the guilt lying at the root of the deed, is often taken into account in determining the punishment. The *punishment of death* is attached apparently to a large number of crimes. It is prescribed not only for the crime of murder, maltreatment of parents, manstealing (Ex. xxi. 12 ff.), adultery, incest and other unnatural crimes, idolatry, and the practice of heathen divination and witchcraft (Lev. xx., Deut. xiii. 6ff.), but for overstepping certain fundamental ordinances of the theocracy,—the law of circumcision, Gen. xvii. 14; the law of the Passover, Ex. xii. 15, 19; the Sabbath law, xxxi. 14f.; the pollution of sacrifices, Lev. vii. 20ff.; sacrificing at other places than the sanctuary, xvii. 8f.; certain laws of purification, xxii. 2, Num. xix. 13, 20. Yet the peculiar expression, "to be cut off from the people," . . . is chosen for the punishment of transgressions of the latter class in distinction from the former, —an expression which, indeed, cannot refer to simple banishment (as some have interpreted it), but still, in some cases, seems to point to a punishment to be executed not by human judgment, but by the divine power, what is said in Lev. xvii. 10 with reference to the person who eats blood: "I will blot out that person." . . . When the punishment was really to be executed by human judgment,

---

12. *The Autobiography of Lincoln Steffens* (New York: Harcourt, Brace, 1931), p. 574.

the term . . . he shall be put to death, is used—as of the violation of
the Sabbath law, Ex. xxxi. 14, and in the passages of the former
kind, Ex. xxi. 12ff., Lev. xx., etc. In general, in all cases where the
people did not execute judgment on the transgressor, Jehovah
Himself reserves the exercise of justice to Himself; see, as main
passage, Lev. xx. 4-6.[13]

There are thus two kinds of capital punishment. *First,* God directly
executes judgment and death upon men and nations for certain offenses.
This He does at His time and will and none can say Him nay. *Second,*
God delegates to man the duty of inflicting death for certain offenses
and that without undue delay and without hesitation.

In examining the obligation of man to inflict the death penalty, we
see, *first,* that, normally, no ransom or fine could be paid for murder
to release the guilty. As Numbers 35:31 declared, "Moreover ye shall
take no satisfaction for the life of a murderer, which is guilty of death:
but he shall be surely put to death." The one exception to this is in
cases where an ox, with a record of goring, kills a man; the owner
then "shall be put to death," unless "there be laid on him a sum of
money, then he shall give for the ransom of his life whatsoever is laid
upon him" (Ex. 21:29, 30). In such cases, because the ox is the
primary murderer, there is a possibility of escape for the owner.

Second, as appears in the case of the goring ox, Biblical law holds
animals as well as men liable for murder charges. This clearly appears
in Genesis 9:5 as well as in the law. If a man owns an animal, and the
animal kills a man, the animal dies. The owner is not guilty if the
animal has no previous record of unprovoked violence (Ex. 21:28).
But if the animal had a record of violence in the past, then the owner
is liable for murder charges and capital punishment. For a free man,
ransom was possible; with slaves, the ransom is specified by law, thirty
shekels of silver, to prevent undue ransom being required for a slave
as the alternative to death (Ex. 21:29-32). An offense by an ox
against another man's ox is also guilty before the law and liable. If
the criminal animal had no previous record, then it must be sold, and
the proceeds divided between the two owners, and the killed ox is also
sold and the proceeds divided. But if the criminal ox had a record of
misconduct, then it is sold and the proceeds given entirely to the owner of
the dead ox, who retains possession of the proceeds of the dead ox (Ex.
21:35, 36). This principle of animal liability, and the liability of their
owners, is still a part of our law. If the executed ox was killed by
stoning, its flesh could not be eaten, having not been bled (Ex. 21:28).
A strange modern application or misapplication of this law appears in
a modernist commentary: "The animals that kill men today are not

---

13. G. E. Oehler, *Theology of the O.T.,* p. 222.

oxen but tiny organisms, germs of disease. If the possessors of these are careless in spreading them around, they too should be put to death, or charged a very high ransom."[14]

Third, we have seen that the principle is life for life, i.e., a punishment proportionate to the crime. This crime has no reference to the criminal or his mentality but only to the nature of the act. If death is the penalty for animals on the principle of life for life, then this is certainly true for men. Thus, on this principle, Biblical law has no plea of not guilty by reason of insanity. Neither is there any privileged status before the law for a minor. Murder requires the death penalty whether the offender is an animal, an "insane" man, a child, or a feeble-minded person. The modern plea of not guilty by reason of insanity arose in 1843 in the trial of Daniel M'Naughton for the murder of Edward Drummond, secretary to Sir Robert Peel. As a result of M'Naughton's trial, the M'Naughton Rules were developed. It was (a) presumed that every man is sane until the contrary is proved, but (b) a man who was insane or laboring under a defect of reason while committing the act, so that he did not realize the nature of the act or its wrongness, was not guilty by reason of insanity. M'Naughton was committed to an asylum instead of being executed. The M'Naughton Rules led to the decision in 1954 by David T. Bazelon of the Court of Appeals for the District of Columbia that no one could be held "criminally responsible if his unlawful act was the product of mental disease or mental defect."[15] This was the Durham case, the trial of Monty Durham, a housebreaker and check-passer who had been in and out of jails and mental hospitals for seven of his twenty-four years.

Such pleas as the M'Naughton and Durham Rules permit the courts to set aside the life for life principle, the principle of justice and justice itself, in favor of a humanistic concern for the life of the criminal. Supposedly, prisons are "punitive" and heartless as compared to mental treatment. But, as Mayer has noted,

> The most cursory look at our institutions reveals that some prisons, in Wisconsin, in California and in the federal system, are in fact much *less* punitive than the ordinary state mental hospital. And a man is not likely to be much better off in the job market later if his record shows a civil commitment to an institution for the criminally insane rather than a conviction for a crime.[16]

The prison system is a humanistic device, an ostensibly more humane way of treatment than the older Biblical law required. Now the mental health approach is supposedly even more humane, when in actuality, as

---

14. J. Edgar Park, "Exodus," in *The Interpreter's Bible,* I, p. 1001.
15. M. Mayer, *The Lawyers,* p. 210.
16. *Ibid.,* p. 211.

Solomon long ago noted, that here as elsewhere, "the tender mercies of the wicked are cruel" (Prov. 12:10).

But we are told by psychiatrists like Menninger that society can be made healthy only by replacing "the punitive attitude with a therapeutic attitude." To demand punishment of criminals is to reveal our own mental sickness; he speaks of it in fact as "the crime of punishment," so that in his eyes the good people of society are all criminals when they demand punishment.[17] Menninger holds that the crime of society against the criminal is greater than that of the criminal against society: "I suspect that all the crimes committed by all the jailed criminals do not equal in total social damage that of the crimes committed against them."[18] Of the criminal, Menninger says,

> We need criminals to identify ourselves with, to envy secretly, and to punish stoutly. They do for us the forbidden, illegal things we *wish* to do and, like scapegoats of old, they bear the burdens of our displaced guilt and punishment—"the iniquities of us all."[19]

As a humanist, Menninger regards man's life as the greatest good and any injury to life as the greatest evil: "the great sin by which we are all tempted is the wish to hurt others, and this sin must be avoided if we are to live and let live."[20]

Similar opinions are to be found in the legal profession and in fact dominate it. This was apparent in the 1968 convention of the American Bar Association. The kind of thinking which appealed to many was definitely to the left, and was all humanistic. Thus,

> A Negro lawyer, William Coleman of Philadelphia, argued that society should be prepared to sanction a certain amount of unrest and inconvenience as the price of progress. He contended that persons engaged in civil disobedience should be paid for their trouble in fighting unjust laws.
>
> When a cause is worthy, agreed Louis H. Pollak, dean of Yale Law School, prosecutors should refuse to press charges against persons engaged in civil disobedience. He did not set forth specific guidelines for determining whether a cause is worthy.[21]

Of course, rioters were already being extensively subsidized in their civil disobedience and rioting, as numerous studies and reports have

---

17. Karl Menninger, "The Crime of Punishment," in *Saturday Review* (September 7, 1968) pp. 21-25, 55. Menninger's book on the subject (Viking Press, New York, 1968) bears the same title, *The Crime of Punishment*.

18. Cited by Robert Kirsch, "The Book Report, Psychiatrist Analyzes Crime and Punishment in U.S.," in *Los Angeles Times*, Part IV (Thursday, December 12, 1968), p. 6.

19. Menninger, in *Saturday Review*, p. 22.

20. *Ibid.*

21. "Lawyers Look to Social Reform, Not Law, to Cure Crime Problem," in *The National Observer* (Monday, August 12, 1968), p. 4.

demonstrated, federal grants being generously given.[22] There was a dissenting voice at the ABA convention, a guest, Lord Justice Widgery of the Court of Appeals in England:

> After listening to conferences on crime and civil disorder for five days, the British jurist said it had "struck me very forcibly that I have heard not one word of commendation or criticism of the police, . . . the shock troops in the fight against crime." How do lawyers and judges expect to keep the peace, he said, "unless they have an efficient police force?"

> The lord justice also questioned the dictum expressed moments earlier by Attorney General Clark that "poverty is the mother of crime." Lord Justice Widgery dryly advised his audience not to "attach too much importance" to this theory. "Anyone who thinks relief of poverty will bring a decrease in crime is in for some kind of disappointment," he said.

> The greatest part of England's slums, he said, were razed by World War II bombing, so poor housing is no excuse for crime. And Britain has had "very great success . . . with its Robin Hood fiscal policy of taking from the rich and giving to the poor, and you would think there would be a drop in the crime figures. But nothing like this has happened. There's been an increase in every department," among the poor, the middle class, and the well-to-do.

> Crime and civil disorder continue to increase, he suggests, because societies throughout the Western world have "lost discipline," acceptance by its members of a code of discipline.[23]

In 1968, the Attorney General of the United States, Ramsey Clark, quoting the Fabian socialist, George Bernard Shaw, that "murder and capital punishment are not opposites that cancel one another but similars that breed their kind," urged Congress to abolish capital punishment for federal crimes. According to Clark's testimony before a Senate subcommittee,

> In the midst of anxiety and fear, complexity and doubt, perhaps our greatest need is reverence for life, mere life: Our lives, the lives of others, all life. . . .

> A humane and generous concern for every individual, for his safety, his health and his fulfilment will do more to soothe the savage heart than the fear of state-inflicted death which chiefly serves to remind us how close we remain to the jungle.[24]

The courts today, moving in terms of humanistic law, are already hostile to law and order. As Gardner has pointed out, "The rights of

---

22. See Patty Newman, Joyce Wenger, *Pass the Poverty Please!* (Whittier, Calif.: Constructive Action, 1966); and Shirley Scheibla, *Poverty Is Where the Money Is* (New Rochelle, New York: Arlington House, 1968).
23. *National Observer, op. cit.*
24. "Revere Life, End Capital Punishment, Says Clark," Oakland, Calif., *Tribune* (Tuesday, July 2, 1968), pp. 1, 7.

the individual are being protected, *provided the individual has committed a crime.*[25] The concern for the criminal has reached the point where prison chaplains in Germany have formed a labor union for convicts, and West Germany has given the union a charter.[26]

To return to the insanity plea, some cities already have a separate Psychiatric Court, as witness Los Angeles, to which many cases are referred. "The court handles all cases involving mental illnesses, including court commitments of persons to mental hospitals; civil and criminal narcotics cases; and determinations for the municipal courts on questions of criminal insanity."[27] The move to abolish the death penalty substitutes "medicine for morals," and it denies "the legal doctrine of individual responsibility," one of the fundamentals of godly law.[28] The door to pagan savagery is opened by this psychiatric approach. Instead of *individual* responsibility, guilt, and punishment, *group* responsibility, guilt, and punishment is stressed. The society at large and the family get the blame, not the criminal. The time is drawing closer when it will be dangerous to be innocent of crime, because innocence will constitute the greatest guilt. This is already the belief of the civil rights revolutionists.

Already, the defense in one court case indicates the direction of the law. A convicted rapist who entered a belated plea of innocent by reason of insanity has been defended in court on two grounds: (a) he has an abnormal chromosome make-up, and (b) he felt rejected by women.[29] In fact, Menninger has declared, "The unconscious fear of women goads some men with a compulsive urge to conquer, humiliate, hurt, or render powerless some available sample of womanhood."[30] The rapist is not guilty; his fears, and perhaps his chromosomes also, drive him to rape; Menninger has made clear his belief in the guilt of the innocent. The criminal is not responsible; he is "driven" by society to crime. Thus, as a Mrs. John Connolly of St. Paul, Minnesota, said of Sirhan Bishara Sirhan, when his trial for the murder of Senator Robert F. Kennedy began, "I think this poor fellow Sirhan is a very sad creature. It's hard to imagine anyone who would be driven to something like

---

25. Erle Stanley Gardner, "Crime in the Streets," in *This Week Magazine,* (August 18, 1968), p. 4.

26. "A Labor Union for Convicts," *Oakland* (Calif.) *Tribune* (Thursday, August 15, 1968), p. 3.

27. Myrna Oliver, "Insanity Plea: . . . ." in Los Angeles *Herald-Examiner* (Thursday, November 28, 1968), p. d-8.

28. E. L. Hebdon Taylor, "The Death Penalty," in T. Robert Ingram, editor: *Essays on The Death Penalty* (Houston: St. Thomas Press, 1963), p. 13 f.

29. "Rapist Felt Rejected by Women, Court Told," in *Los Angeles Times* (Friday, January 10, 1969) Part II, p. 4; and Harry Nelson, "Masculinity Doubts of XYY Defendant Told by Psychiatrist," *Los Angeles Times* (Wednesday, January 8, 1969), Part I, pp. 2, 29.

30. K. Menninger, "The Crime of Punishment," in *Saturday Review* (Sept. 7, 1968), p. 23.

this."[31] If Sirhan and other criminals are "driven" men, then someone did the driving and is therefore guilty. And if the criminal is predetermined to crime by his environment, the humanists, by asserting this, have substituted determinism by the environment for predestination by God.

Fourth, the death penalty is required by Scripture for a number of offenses. These are for

1. murder, but not for accidental killings (Ex. 21:12-14);
2. striking or cursing a parent (Ex. 21:15; Lev. 20:9; Prov. 20: 20; Matt. 15:4; Mark 7:10). It should be noted that Christ condemned the scribes and Pharisees for setting aside this law;
3. kidnaping (Ex. 21:16; Deut. 24:7);
4. adultery (Lev. 20:10-21), to be discussed later;
5. incest (Lev. 20:11-12, 14);
6. bestiality (Ex. 22:19; Lev. 20:15-16);
7. sodomy or homosexuality (Lev. 20:13);
8. unchastity (Deut. 22:20-21), to be discussed later;
9. rape of a betrothed virgin (Deut. 22:23-27);
10. witchcraft (Ex. 22:18);
11. offering human sacrifice (Lev. 20:2);
12. incorrigible delinquency or habitual criminality (Deut. 21: 18-21);
13. blasphemy (Lev. 24:11-14, 16, 23), already discussed earlier;
14. sabbath desecration (Ex. 35:2; Num. 15:32-36), already discussed earlier; now superseded;
15. propagation of false doctrines (Deut. 13:1-10), also discussed earlier;
16. sacrificing to false gods (Ex. 22:20);
17. refusing to abide by the court decision and thus denying the law (Deut. 17:8-13);
18. failing to restore the pledge or bailment (Ezek. 18:12, 13), because such an act destroyed the possibility of community trust and association.

The methods of capital punishment were by burning (Lev. 20:14; 21:9); stoning (Lev. 20:2, 27; 24:14; Deut. 21:21); hanging (Deut. 21:22-23; Josh. 8:29); and the sword (Ex. 32:27-28). The use of the sword was in an exceptional circumstance; and the basic requirement in every case was the death penalty itself rather than the form of the penalty.

Moreover, as Carey has pointed out,

Capital punishment was never to be inflicted on the testimony of less than two witnesses (Numbers 35:30; Deuteronomy 17:6, 19: 15). In specified instances capital punishment was to be executed by the witnesses themselves as in Deuteronomy 13:6-10, 17:7. In some instances execution was by the congregation (Numbers 15:

---

31. Myrna Oliver, "Sirhan Intrigues the Curious," in Los Angeles *Herald-Examiner* (Friday, January 10, 1969), p. A-3.

32-36; Deuteronomy 13:6-10), or by nearest of kin, the avenger of blood (Deuteronomy 19:11-12).[32]

To the humanistic mind these penalties seem severe and unnecessary. In actuality, the penalties, together with the Biblical faith which motivated them, worked to reduce crime. Thus, when New England passed laws requiring the death penalty for incorrigible delinquents and for children who struck their parents, no executions were necessary: the law kept children in line. Some laws secure their desired effect without any necessity for prosecution. Thus, to cite one instance, from the 1920's, as described by Llewellyn,

> The books of the New York Public Library persisted in disappearing. This was a field peculiarly of juvenile delinquency; the opportunity was open to all, but the rewards of theft so petty as to make juveniles the likely prospects. A statute was passed making exhibition for sale of a book bearing a library stamp an offense. The library officials saw to it that every second-hand book dealer in the city received notice of this statute. Promptly the thefts decreased almost into nothingness. The market had become unprofitable. There has never been a prosecution under the law. There is no need.[33]

This is not always the case, for when the religious and moral character of a people disintegrate, the law-breakers begin to outnumber the police and the law-keepers. Biblical law eliminates the incorrigible and habitual criminals; Biblical faith gives to the people a godly character and a law-abiding disposition. The breakdown of humanistic law orders is due to the radical criminal disposition of its lawless peoples. In spite of all the extensive pity for criminals, the fact remains that 80 percent of all accused persons plead guilty. Some of the remaining 20 percent are guilty, but the complaining party has dropped the charges (Mayer notes of these that many are "like our young man whose girl decided she wanted him even though he had beaten her to a pulp"). To speed up the legal log-jam, many guilty parties are allowed to plead guilty to a lesser charge to avoid delay and expense. Other studies show of every 100 picked up by the police (as against those formally accused), fifty are convicted on a guilty plea; five are convicted after trial; 30 are released without charges being brought; 13 are released "by administrative process after arraignment but before trial," and 2 are acquitted after trial. Thus, while in any fallible, human system, mistakes are made, they are obviously not very common. Justice has rough edges, but there is no alternative to justice.[34] Moreover, as Mayer noted of

---

32. Gervas A. Carey, "Thou Shalt Not Kill," in T. R. Ingram, *Death Penalty*, p. 105.
33. Cited from Karl Llewellyn, *Jurisprudence*, p. 408, by M. Mayer, *The Lawyers*, p. 167.
34. Mayer, *op. cit.,* pp. 90, 155f., 158 f., 180 f.

New York's criminal courts, lawyers never wear hats, "because if you put a hat down anywhere in a criminal court building, somebody steals it."[35] Moreover, "criminal practice is the one branch of the law where lawyers collect their fee in advance."[36] The reason, of course, is the radical dishonesty of their clients.

But more important is the situation with respect to juveniles:

> According to the FBI Uniform Crime Reports, 48 percent of all arrests for serious offenses in 1964 were arrests of children under the age of eighteen, and 43.3 percent of all those formally charged with serious crimes by the police were referred to the juvenile court for disposition. The peak comes at age fifteen. (Generally speaking, incidentally, the larger the city, the smaller the proportion of those under eighteen in the total number of arrests.) It has been estimated that one-ninth of the nation's children—one-sixth of the boys—make some contact with a juvenile court (Usually for a quite minor offense) between the ages of ten and seventeen.[37]

The figures after 1964 grew markedly worse. Too many of the children not involved in the juvenile courts are also schooled in lawlessness by humanistic education and religion. The result is the policemen's impossible task: "In Berkeley on a Saturday night there may be 2000 pot parties going on—can you have an informer or a policeman at each one?"[38]

The law breaks down when the faith behind the law is gone. The hostility to the death penalty is humanism's hostility to God's law. But God's government prevails, and His alternatives are clear-cut: either men and nations obey His laws, or God invokes the death penalty against them.

We have cited above the high ratio of guilt in all indicted persons. This does not mean that innocent men are not sometimes condemned. The Dudley Boyle case appears to have been such a case. Dudley Boyle, a mining engineer and a high-spirited young man, was arrested during the Depression for robbing the Bank of Sparks. He was defended by McCarran, later U. S. Senator for Nevada, who was convinced of Boyle's innocence. The trial revealed amazing irregularities as McCarran's daughter summarizes some of its aspects,

> One of the most unique devices used by the prosecution was that the State called to the witness stand the one man who could prove Dudley Boyle's alibi—that he had left Reno early on the morning of the robbery and journeyed by automobile to Goldfield. Summer-

35. *Ibid.*, p. 154.
36. *Ibid.*, p. 160.
37. *Ibid.*, p. 212.
38. Robert McLaughlin, "A Policeman's Nightmare: Mountains of Marijuana," Los Angeles *Herald-Examiner* (Friday, December 6, 1968), p. A-11.

field elicited the man's name and address and then dismissed him from the stand. Thereafter, McCarran, continually overruled by Judge George Bartlett, was unable to cross-examine the man, or elicit from him the confirmation of Boyle's alibi. This would be unbelievable if it were mere news reporting. The transcript is available. Even on appeal, Judge Edward A. Ducker, who had succeeded McCarran on the Supreme Court, handed down a terribly facile decision against Boyle, who had been sentenced from five to twenty years in the State Prison. He was released after six years and subsequently, committed suicide. When he had been working for parole, Boyle had written to McCarran: "You know and I know that I am innocent." This was, unfortunately in the depth of the Depression when everyone was desperately distracted. There was much to suggest that when the owner of the Bank of Sparks desired a conviction, it could be obtained.[39]

This is not an isolated case.[40] But it is not the common case. The fact is still true that virtually all indicted men are guilty, and they, in most cases, plead guilty. To avoid enforcing the law, or to break down the law, because of such cases of injustice, is to compound the injustice. The enforcement of civil and criminal law is in the hands of sinful and fallible men; it cannot be made infallible. To improve the quality of law enforcement, and to bring about greater obedience, it is necessary that we have more godly men. There is no answer, but only further decay in any weakening of the law. To use cases of injustice to destroy the law is itself a very great and deadly act of injustice.

3. Origins of the State: Its Prophetic Offices

Historically, theologians have quite regularly found the origins of the state, or civil government, in the sixth commandment, or, more accurately, in the fall of man. Before the fall, it is held, there was no need for a state, since man was sinless. After the fall, death entered the world because of sin as God's judgment on sin, and the state was created in order to keep man's sin in check and to invoke penalties up to death in judgment on sin. The state is thus God's hangman, an institution which exists between the fall and the second coming to keep man in order.

This view is extensively echoed in Cullmann, who sees the state "as something 'provisional.' "[1] According to Cullmann, Christ and Christianity reject "the Jewish theocratic ideal . . . as satanic."[2] Moreover,

---

39. Sister Margaret Patricia McCarran, "Patrick Anthony McCarran," in *Nevada Historical Society Quarterly,* Fall-Winter, 1968, vol. XI, no. 3-4, p. 28 f.

40. For a particularly shocking case, whereby a man was apparently robbed of due scientific honors, and sent to prison falsely, see Andrew A. Freeman, *The Case for Doctor Cook* (New York: Coward-McCann, 1961).

1. Oscar Cullmann, *The State in the New Testament* (London: SCM Press, 1955), p. 12.

2. *Ibid.,* p. 14.

"Jesus does not regard the State as a final institution to be equated somehow with the Kingdom of God. The State belongs to the age which still exists even now, but which will definitely vanish as soon as the Kingdom of God comes."[3] It is not necessary for the state to be Christian, but it is necessary that the state "know its *limits*."[4] Closely related to this is the Scholastic and Lutheran view which grounds the state in natural reason and thus absolves it of any direct connection with and responsibility to God.

In a sense, this position is accurate, if we hold that the provisional character of the state has reference to the *form* of the state. But the same can be said of the church: it too is provisional in its form. There will be no offices of bishops, pastors, elders, or deacons in heaven or in the final new creation. This does not mean that the church is merely provisional, any more than it means that the state is merely provisional.

Moreover, Cullmann is viciously wrong in holding that the theocratic ideal of Israel was in Christ's eyes satanic, for He had come to restore that true kingdom. It was the perversion of that ideal which was satanic, the perversion and imitation. At this point, Cullmann is right in observing that "It belongs to the Devil's inmost nature that he imitates God."[5] That which is imitated is the divine government, the Kingdom of God. This kingdom existed in Eden; its laws governed Adam and Eve and were finally broken by Adam and Eve. Civil authorities, as well as the church, school, and family, were ordained by God as varying aspects of the abiding Kingdom of God; each bears the marks of the fall, but all are ordained by God. The direct government by God has since been mediated through various institutions, of which one is the state. It is precisely because even these sin-ridden institutions still reflect God's government of the world that obedience is commanded, and resistance is declared to be resistance to God (Rom. 13:1-7). Moreover, as Calvin clearly pointed out,

> . . . to despise the providence of him who is founder of civil power, is to carry on war with him. Understand further, that powers are from God, not as pestilence, and famine, and wars, and other visitations for sin, are said to be from him; but because he has appointed them for the legitimate and just government of the world.[6]

Plague, famine, and war are results of and judgments on man for his sin, but the state is not such a visitation (although evil rulers may be) but rather an aspect of God's righteous government. There will be

---

3. *Ibid.*, p. 43.
4. *Ibid.*, p. 69.
5. *Ibid.*, p. 59.
6. John Calvin, *Commentaries on the Epistle to the Romans* (Grand Rapids: Eerdmans, 1948), ch. 13:1, p. 478 f.

government in the new creation as there is in heaven and must be on earth. The necessity to be righteous and just does not disappear in the new creation; rather, perfect obedience becomes the response to perfect government.

Now government is a vastly broader term than the state. Government means, first, self-government, then the family, church, state, school, calling, and private associations as well as much else. But the state as a "higher" but *not highest* power represents God's ministry of justice, the fulness of which is seen in heaven and hell. For the state to culminate, together with church, family, school, and calling, in the Kingdom of God in the new creation is no more its finish than the time of birth is the death of the foetus. Rather, it is truest life.

The *first* and basic duty of the state is to further the Kingdom of God by recognizing the sovereignty of God and His word and conforming itself to the law-word of God. The state thus has a duty to be Christian. It must be Christian even as man, the family, the church, the school, and all things else must be Christian. To hold otherwise is to assert the death of God in the sphere of the state. Because of its failure to require that the state be Christian, because of its implicit death-of-God theology, the church has surrendered the state to apostate reason and the devil. The church has done this because it has denied the law of God. It has, in fact, implied that God is dead outside the walls of the church, and it then must logically proclaim His death within the church.

The reason why the concept of the state as founded in the fall and in sin has failed is because the state has been separated from God except as a kind of slap from God, like a plague or a famine. Then, when a positive doctrine of the state is sought, it must be located, not in the Kingdom of God, but in natural reason, the autonomous reason of the natural man. If the state is separated from the Kingdom of God, how long will the idea of sin remain? After all, sin is an offense against God in His kingship, against the laws of His kingdom. The result is that if the state is not a part of the kingdom, then there is *no sin* in the world of justice and human relations.

This, of course, is the essence of humanism. The humanist is easily disillusioned with God, man, and society when all is not well, but he is not disillusioned with himself. Thus, the Lebanese poet Kahlil Gibran in his youth "conceived the universe as perfect and devoid of evil."[7] In reaction to his disillusionment with the world and with God, he became a disciple of Nietzsche, whose philosophy governed Gibran's writings.[8]

---

7. Anthony R. Ferris, "Introduction," to Kahlil Gibran, *Thoughts and Meditations*) New York: Bantam [1960], 1968), p. 7.
8. Annie Salem Otto, *The Parables of Kahlil Gibran* (New York: Citadel Press, 1963), p. 25.

In terms of this he saw the age of superman dawning: "We live in an era whose humblest men are becoming greater than the greatest men of preceding ages."[9] His own attitude, as the arrived superman, was one of total self-righteousness. As his own superman and god, he was beyond criticism and beyond law.

Clearly, if the state is not an aspect of the Kingdom of God, it will inevitably drop the concept of sin because it has no true God. And, because man becomes under humanism his own god, no law can then govern gods, who are their own law. As Calvin noted, without laws the state or civil magistracy "cannot subsist, as, on the other hand, without magistrates laws are of no force. No observation, therefore, can be more correct than this, that the law is a silent magistrate, and a magistrate a speaking law."[10]

A state therefore witnesses against itself when it maintains to any degree God's law-order, and, if a state does not maintain that law-order to some degree, it collapses into anarchy. The state is recognized as an order to which men under God must render obedience, and Scripture repeatedly requires this obedience where obedience is due even when the authority is a Nero. We cannot despise gold and silver simply because they are in the hands of ungodly men. On the contrary, we must seek to possess them ourselves by godly means. We must confess that gold is gold, whoever possesses it and however they use it. Similarly, the state is the state, created and destined to be a part of God's Kingdom, called to magnify God by enforcing His law-order, and it therefore cannot be despised, however ungodly the rulers of it may be. If we despise and abandon gold, we cannot complain if its new possessors are not to our taste; if we renounce the state as God's ordination and an important aspect of His Kingdom, can we complain if evil men make use of it?

The sixth commandment, "Thou shalt not kill," has both a negative aspect, the punishment of those who unjustly commit acts of violence, and a positive side, the protection of life in terms of God's law. The state is usually grounded in the negative aspect and made at best God's hangman. The state is indeed to be "a terror to . . . the evil," the protector of the good, "and the praise of the same" (Rom. 13:3). By protecting life and furthering the safety of the family and of religion, the state is clearly positive in its ministry. Protection is not a mere negation: it is a present and continual climate of peace and safety. The charge of King Jehoshaphat to the judges of Judah is revealing: "Take heed what ye do: for ye judge not for man, but for the LORD, who is with you in the judgment. Wherefore now let the fear of the

---

9. Gibran, *Thoughts and Meditations*, p. 87.
10. Calvin, *Institutes*, Bk. IV, ch. XX, xiv; II, p. 787.

LORD be upon you: take heed and do it: for there is no iniquity with the LORD our God, nor respect of persons, nor taking of gifts" (II Chron. 19:6, 7).

The law is given as principles (the ten commandments) and as cases (the detailed commandments), and its meaning is to be hammered out in experience and in trial. This does not mean that the law is a developing thing but that man's awareness of its implications develops as new situations bring fresh light on the possible applications of the law. The psalmist in Psalm 119 clearly saw the law as a positive force in his growth and in his ability to stand up to the adversities of history.

The sanctuary, as we have seen, was God's throne room. When the civil government of Israel was established, it was done before the sanctuary. God there talked with the seventy elders of the people and poured out His Spirit upon them, so that the first Pentecost was the civil Pentecost at the ordination of the civil authorities (Num. 11:16-17, 24-30). The meaning of this event is generally neglected, because the law as a whole is neglected. Moses here, as the representative of Christ the King, mediated the gift of the Spirit. That this was not an exceptional event is made clear by the anointing of Saul, who also prophesied (I Sam. 10:1-7). The fact of prophecy was not their office or calling, either with the seventy elders or with Saul: they were civil rulers. The Spirit-filled witness of the prophecy attested to their office, that it was of God's ordination. These two civil Pentecosts came at the start of the two forms of civil government in Israel, the commonwealth and the monarchy. The ordination of others was by anointing. The early church saw its continuity with the church Pentecost, by its rites of coronation. The form of the rite still remains, although the faith is gone. The oath required of Queen Elizabeth II stated:

> Will you to the utmost of your power maintain the Laws of God and the true profession of the Gospel? Will you to the utmost of your power maintain in the United Kingdom the Protestant Reformed Religion established by law? Will you maintain and preserve inviolably the settlement of the Church of England, and the doctrine, worship, discipline, and government thereof, as by law established in England? And will you preserve unto the Bishops, and Clergy of England, and to the Churches there committed to their charge, all such rights and privileges, as by law do and shall appertain to them or any of them?[11]

After this oath, the moderator of the General Assembly of the Church of Scotland brought to the queen the Bible, saying:

---

11. *The Music with the Form and Order of the Service to be Performed at the Coronation of Her Most Excellent Majesty Queen Elizabeth II in the Abbey Church of Westminster on Tuesday the 2nd Day of June, 1953* (London: Novello and Company, 1953), p. 14.

Our gracious Queen: to keep your Majesty ever mindful of the Law and the Gospel of God as the Rule for the whole life and government of Christian Princes, we present you with this Book, the most valuable thing that this world affords.

Here is Wisdom; This is the royal Law; These are the lively Oracles of God.[12]

After the anointing, which cited the anointing of Solomon, the Presentation of the Sword of State followed, with the archbishop of York, receiving it from the lord great chamberlain, presenting it to the queen with these words:

Receive this kingly sword, brought from the Altar of God, and delivered to you by the hands of us the Bishops and servants of God, though unworthy. With this sword do justice, stop the growth of iniquity, protect the holy Church of God, help and defend widows and orphans, restore the things that are gone to decay, maintain the things that are restored, punish and reform what is amiss, and confirm what is in good order: that doing these things you may be glorious in all virtue; and so faithfully serve our Lord Jesus Christ in this life, that you may reign for ever with him in the life which is to come. R. Amen.[13]

When the Orb with the Cross was given to the queen, the archbishop declared:

Receive this Orb set under the Cross, and remember that the whole world is subject to the Power and Empire of Christ our Redeemer.[14]

This service is an echo of the age-old coronation services, and of the Biblical faith, however often abused in coronation rites, that the civil order is directly under God and is established by His order as a part of His kingdom. When the people replace God as lord and sovereign, then the civil Pentecost gives away to Babel and to the confusion of tongues.

Attempts have been made by scholars to turn these seventy men of Numbers 11:16, 17 to ecclesiastical figures, but there is no warrant for this, and the parallel civil Pentecost at Saul's anointing, in echo of Numbers 11:24-30, makes clear that civil order is in view. The gift of prophecy was involved in both cases, not because they became prophets as preachers, but because the office of civil magistrates, offices of state, are *prophetic* offices, in that the civil officer must speak for God, and the primary meaning of prophet is one who speaks for God. The state thus can speak for God, and officers of state are prophets, insofar as they observe, obey, study, and enforce the law of God. For the state to seek an independent prophetic office is to renounce its office and become a false prophet.

---

12. *Ibid.*, p. 15.
13. *Ibid.*, p. 66.
14. *Ibid.*, p. 67.

Whether by laying on of hands, or by anointing, or by an oath of office and prayer, officers of church and state are inducted into the office of prophet and are men who speak for God in their respective spheres. This is a neglected fact, but a fact of Scripture all the same. The ecclesiastical point of view was expressed very bluntly by the Anglican, the Rev. R. Winterbotham, in his commentary on Numbers 11:17, 24-30: "the gifts of the Spirit are not independent of ecclesiastical order." While he added that "It is the purpose of God which is operative, not the ceremonial, however authoritative. The Spirit of God is a free Spirit, even when he elects to act through certain channels (cf. Acts i. 26; xiii. 2; 1 Cor. xii. 11; 2 Cor. iii. 17),"[15] he nonetheless restricted the Spirit to the church, a totally false point of view. Rather, the gifts of the Spirit are not independent of God's order, and both church and state can be a part of that order. They can also be hostile to and alien to God's order.

4. "To Make Alive"

As we have seen, the state is more than God's hangman; it is God's instrument for the protection of godly life by furthering justice. Although there are many remarks in Luther's writings which seem to give substance to the Lutheran reduction of the state to a hangman, Luther's actual effect was long in the other direction. As Rosenstock-Huessy noted,

> The civil servant is the result of the mutual permeation of Luther's prophecy of the universal Reformation of the prince's carrying out of their special reformation.

> The civil servant is the man who first hears the prophetic voice of universal truth, and who later enters the service of a secular authority to carry out his part in the Reform.[1]

The two important institutions in the German Reformation were *the university* and *the state*, both moving in terms of principles deeply rooted in Christendom. "Luther's prince, therefore, was not protecting Luther as a personal friend; he was standing for the right of a High Magistrate to harbour a sovereign university in his territory."[2] But Luther, in the name of God, in turn offered Frederick his protection as God's servant: "he who believes most will protect most; and because I feel that Your Grace is still weak in the faith, I cannot by any means think of Your Grace as the man who could protect or save me."[3] In

---

15. H. D. M. Spence and Joheph S. Exell, editors, *The Pulpit Commentary, Numbers,* Rev. R. Winterbotham, "Exposition and Homiletics" (New York: Funk and Wagnalls), p. 117.

1. Eugen Rosenstock-Huessy, *Out of Revolution, Autobiography of Western Man* (New York: William Morrow, 1938), p. 368.
2. *Ibid.,* p. 381.
3. *Ibid.,* p. 389.

Germany, "the universities became the heirs of the bishops' chair, the cathedra. The professor's chair was called 'Katheder.' "[4] According to Rosenstock-Huessy,

> But the prince had no grip on the universities, no more than the cobbler. The universities represented the life of the Holy Ghost in the German Nation, whereas the prince and his State were blind and deaf in matters of religion without the help of the preachers and teachers of the faith. State and government were not at all glorified by Luther. "Princes are God's hangmen and jailers," he said.[5]

This element was clearly present in Luther, but it was not the entire picture. Christian prince and Christian scholar, Christian state and the Christian ministry of the word in its broader sense to stress the scholar of the word, were the two central institutions in the German Reformation and for Luther.

But, far more than Luther, we must stress the work of the state as a ministry under God (not under the church), and with a negative task in punishing evil and injustice, which means, positively, establishing a law-order in which the godly can thrive and prosper.

Not without reason, as we have previously seen, civil and other authorities are called "gods," in that they share by God's calling and grace in His sovereign work of government. God declared through Moses, "See now that I, even I, am he, and there is no god with me: I kill, and I make alive; I wound, and I heal: neither is there any that can deliver out of my hand" (Deut. 32:39). This same declaration appears in part in I Samuel 2:6, and in Isaiah 43:13. In the Song of Moses, it is clearly related to the law: the Lord is the great law-giver and judge, and hence His power to kill and to make alive, to wound and to heal. This power is delegated to human authorities to be used in terms of God's law-word, and all authorities thus have in varying degrees the power to restrict, kill, or injure life on the one hand, and to heal or make alive by furthering God's law-order and word on the other.

This function clearly belongs to the state and to the church. The power of the keys given to the church, to forgive sins or to bind them in terms of God's word, is an aspect of this delegated authority to kill and to make alive (Matt. 18:18; 16:19; John 20:23). The church can forgive sins where God's word declares forgiveness and know that this forgiveness stands before heaven; it can refuse forgiveness where God's law-conditions are not met, confident that the forgiveness is denied in heaven. The church "makes alive" by the ministry of the word and the sacraments, not because any power to communicate life

---

4. *Ibid.*, p. 390.   5. *Ibid.*, p. 395.

resides in the church, but because God is faithful to His word where it is truly ministered.

The school too has the duty, as does the home, to kill and to make alive, to wound life in judgment where God's word requires it, and to further life by its teaching and discipline.

An important aspect of the duty to "make alive" as it appears in the Scriptures is art, in particular music. An entire book of hymns, the book of Psalms, is a part of the inspired word and repeatedly commands that God's praise be sung and played on musical instruments.[6]

Another important area of legislation to "make alive" concerns duties towards persons:

1. To widows and orphans

> Ye shall not afflict any widow, or fatherless child. If thou afflict them in any wise, and they cry at all unto me, I will surely hear their cry; And my wrath shall wax hot, and I will kill you with the sword; and your wives shall be widows, and your children fatherless (Ex. 22:22-24).

> Thou shalt not pervert the judgment of the stranger, nor of the fatherless; nor take a widow's raiment to pledge: But thou shalt remember that thou wast a bondman in Egypt, and the LORD thy God redeemed thee thence: therefore I command thee to do this thing (Deut. 24:17).

> Cursed be he that perverteth the judgment of the stranger, fatherless, and widow. And all the people shall say, Amen (Deut. 27:19).

Oppression is repeatedly cited as a particularly hateful sin in the sight of God, and rulers and judges are warned against it, and commanded to be watchful to prevent it. But, apart from the legal penalties for the particular instances of oppression, another penalty is cited: God's judgment. When the helpless cry to the Lord, then He will be their defender. The phrase "cry at all unto me" can be rendered "cry earnestly unto me." The *lex talionis* principle, life for life, tooth for tooth, is here cited by God: if men oppress the widows and orphans, their own wives and children will be widowed and orphaned by God's judgment.

2. To neighbors, i.e., fellow members of the covenant:

> Thou shalt not see thy brother's ass or his ox fall down by the way, and hide thyself from them: thou shalt surely help him to lift them up again (Deut. 22:4).

> Thou shalt not defraud thy neighbour, neither rob him (Lev. 19:13a).

> Thou shalt not avenge, nor bear any grudge against the children of

---

6. Alfred Sendrey and Mildred Norton, *David's Harp, The Story of Music in Biblical Times* (New York: New American Library, 1964). The authors rightly suggest that the Levitical musicians were of substantial assistance in the stand of the priests, prophets, and faithful kings in preserving the faith, p. 142.

thy people, but thou shalt love thy neighbour as thyself: I am the LORD (Lev. 19:18).

While animals are a part of this law, the primary concern is love of one's neighbor. This is very clearly apparent in Exodus 23:4, 5. "If thou meet thine enemy's ox, or his ass going astray, thou shalt surely bring it back to him again. If thou see the ass of him that hateth thee lying under his burden . . . thou shalt surely help with him." Neither enmity nor indifference can allow us to refuse that righteous care for our neighbor's (or enemy's) problems which God requires of us. The only basis for our relationship with other men is God's law, not our feelings.

3. To the poor:

> Thou shalt not wrest the judgment of thy poor in his cause. Keep thee far from a false matter; and the innocent and righteous slay thou not: for I will not justify the wicked (Ex. 23:6, 7).

> And when ye reap the harvest of your land, thou shalt not wholly reap the corners of thy field, neither shalt thou gather the gleanings of thy harvest. And thou shalt not glean thy vineyard, neither shalt thou gather every grape of thy vineyard: thou shalt leave them for the poor and stranger: I am the LORD your God (Lev. 19:9, 10).

> And if thy brother be waxen poor, and fallen in decay with thee; then thou shalt relieve him: yea, though he be a stranger, or a sojourner; that he may live with thee. Take thou no usury of him, or increase: but fear thy God; that thy brother may live with thee. Thou shalt not give him thy money upon usury, nor lend him thy victuals for increase. I am the LORD your God, which brought you forth out of the land of Egypt, to give you the land of Canaan, and to be your God.

> And if thy brother that dwelleth by thee be waxen poor, and be sold unto thee; thou shalt not compel him to serve as a bondservant: But as an hired servant, and as a sojourner, he shall be with thee, and shall serve thee unto the year of jubile: And then shall he depart from thee, both he and his children with him, and shall return unto his own family, and unto the possession of his fathers shall he return. For they are my servants, which I brought forth out of the land of Egypt: they shall not be sold as bondmen. Thou shalt not rule over him with rigour; but shalt fear thy God (Lev. 25:35-43).

In the courts, the poor are not to be favored ("neither shalt thou countenance a poor man in his cause" (Ex. 23:3), nor disfavored (Ex. 23: 6, 7); false matters or accusations are to be avoided, lest it lead to the injury or death of innocent men; God will in no wise justify the wicked. *In everyday living*, the deserving poor, both natives and aliens, had a legal right to glean. No farmer could harvest his fields totally; the fruit hard to reach, the grain along the fences and banks, and the lone bunches here and there on branches had to be left for the gleaners. The farmer then granted gleaning rights to certain of the poor and sometimes favored an especially deserving person, as Boaz did Ruth. In American gleaning, until World War II, some farmers carried certain families as their permanent gleaners and thus gave to these poor ones a real measure of security. The gleanings could be used either for the table or be sold for extra income. Gleaning was hard work, since it involved more effort than the regular harvest, when the fruit or grain was plentiful. In some cases, however, sometimes improvident Israelites, burdened by debt, and sometimes men beset by adversity, sold themselves as *bondsmen*. As members of the covenant, they were still brothers. Before he becomes a bondsman, when he is "fallen in decay" (or "his hand faileth"), "thou shalt relieve him," or "thou shalt lay hold of him" and give him the same consideration and care which strangers and sojourners had to receive. As the ARV reads it, "as a stranger and a sojourner shall he live with thee" (Lev. 25:35). If he is in need of funds, loans to him should be without interest or increase.

> The authorities during the second Temple defined the words which are translated "usury" (neshech) and "increase" (tarbith, or marbith) as follows: If a person lends to another a shekel worth four denarii, and gets in return five denarii, or if he lends him two sacks of wheat, and receives back three, this is usury. If one buys wheat for delivery at the market price of 25 denarii a measure, and when it rises to 30 denarii he says to the vendor, "Deliver me the wheat, for I want to sell it and buy wine," and the vendor replies, "I will take the wheat at 30 denarii and give thee wine for it," though he has no wine, this is increase. The "increase" lies in the fact that the vendor has no wine at the time, and that he may possibly lose again by the rise in wine. Accordingly, the former is a charge upon money, whilst the latter is on products.[7]

If the loan fails, then the poor man becomes a bondservant, except that, although technically such, he is a bondsman with the jubilee in prospect; he is a brother destined for liberty. Meanwhile, he cannot be treated as a slave, like an unbeliever, but rather as a hired servant who is in some sense still a free man. The reason for this is plainly stated by God: "For they are my servants" (Lev. 25:42). Both master and servant are servants of God, who governs absolutely the lives and relationships of both. In view of this, St. Paul declared, "For ye are bought with a price: therefore glorify God in your body, and in your spirit, which are God's" (I Cor. 6:20). It should be noted that the law here is mindful of the temptation to treat a weaker member of the covenant with disrespect; hence, it is stated that, while held as a

---

7. C. D. Ginsburg, "Leviticus," in *Ellicott*, I, 459.

brother, he is to be given the respect and courtesy normally accorded a stranger and a sojourner. The true believer is a free man in the Lord; thus, even in debt and in servitude he is entitled to a liberty not granted to others, who are slaves by nature.

A point of importance with respect to gleaning is that, in the older form, it was agricultural; modern life is more urban. A significant attempt at urban gleaning began some years ago, the Goodwill Industries. By collecting discarded goods and items, and then repairing and selling them by using unemployed or handicapped persons, an income for many has been provided. The rise of welfarism has limited the growth of urban gleaning, but its potentialities are very real and deserving of greater development.

4. To sojourners, aliens, or strangers:

> Thou shalt neither vex a stranger, nor oppress him: for ye were strangers in the land of Egypt (Ex. 22:21).

> Also thou shalt not oppress a stranger: for ye know the heart of a stranger, seeing ye were strangers in the land of Egypt (Ex. 23:9).

> And if a stranger sojourn with thee in your land, ye shall not vex him. But the stranger that dwelleth with you shall be unto you as one born among you, and thou shalt love him as thyself: for ye were strangers in the land of Egypt: I am the LORD your God (Lev. 19:33, 34).

> For the LORD your God is a God of gods, and LORD of lords, a great God, a mighty and terrible, which regardeth not persons, nor taketh reward: He doth execute the judgment of the fatherless and widow, and loveth the stranger, in giving him food and raiment. Love ye therefore the stranger: for ye were strangers in the land of Egypt (Deut. 10:17-19).

> Thou shalt not oppress an hired servant that is poor and needy, whether he be of thy brethren, or of thy strangers that are in thy land within thy gates: At his day thou shalt give him his hire, neither shall the sun go down upon it; for he is poor, and setteth his heart upon it: lest he cry against thee unto the LORD, and it be sin unto thee (Deut. 24:14, 15).

> Thou shalt not pervert the judgment of the stranger, or of the fatherless; nor take a widow's raiment to pledge (Deut. 24:17).

> Cursed be he that perverteth the judgment of the stranger, fatherless, and widow. And all the people shall say, Amen (Deut. 27:19).

From these verses, as well as the foregoing, an important fact comes clearly into view. Thus, while Biblical law is severe in its condemnation of crime, and of laziness (as much of Proverbs testifies), it is equally severe in its condemnation of all who oppress the weak or the stranger. To use the modern terms, society as Biblical law envisions it is competitive and free but not atomistic. The essence of both modern capitalism and of communism is that they are atomistic; because the necessary presupposition of true society, Biblical faith, has been dissolved, society has been atomistic and unable to establish true community. In order to have true community, *first*, faith is necessary, a common bond of religious doctrine and practice. *Second*, a religious humility is necessary: "ye were strangers in the land of Egypt," an awareness of our own origins and of God's grace. *Third*, the stranger and our neighbor are alike to be loved as we love ourselves, i.e., to be granted the same regard for their life, family, property, and reputation, in word, thought, and deed, as we ourselves desire. *Fourth*, not only are aliens and the weak not to be oppressed, but in their need they are to receive our help and attention. *Fifth*, the alien and the weak, widows and orphans, are to receive the same conscientious justice in courts of law as we accord to the great of our day, i.e., without favor and with due regard for the law and for their rights before the law. *Sixth*, there is to be a measure of favoritism to the needy fellow believer in loans; they are without interest, and their necessities ("a widow's raiment") cannot be taken as security. Moreover, day laborers are to be paid on the evening of their labor, "for he is poor, and setteth his heart upon it."

5. To the needy and defenseless: These appear in the foregoing classifications, but they are still singled out specifically by the law, and thus Galer rightly gives this as a distinct category of legislation.[8] Deuteronomy 24:14 and 27:19 have already been cited. Leviticus 19:14, "Thou shalt not curse the deaf, nor put a stumblingblock before the blind, but shall fear thy God: I am your LORD," was also cited previously, in another context.

6. To slaves and servants:

> If thou buy an Hebrew servant, six years he shall serve: and in the seventh he shall go out free for nothing. If he came in by himself, he shall go out by himself: if he were married, then his wife shall go out with him. If his master have given him a wife, and she have born him sons or daughters; the wife and her children shall be her master's, and he shall go out by himself. And if the servant shall plainly say, I love my master, my wife, and my children; I will not go out free: Then his master shall bring him to the judges; he shall also bring him to the door, or unto the door post; and his master shall bore his ear through with an aul; and he shall serve him for ever (Ex. 21:2-6).

Deuteronomy 24:14, 15 (cited above).

> And if thy brother, an Hebrew man, or an Hebrew woman, be sold unto thee, and serve thee six years; then in the seventh year thou shalt let him go free from thee. And when thou sendest him out free

---

8. R. S. Galer, *O.T. Law for Bible Students*, p. 142.

from thee, thou shalt not let him go away empty: Thou shalt furnish him liberally out of thy flock, and out of thy floor, and out of thy winepress: of that wherewith the LORD thy God hath blessed thee thou shalt give unto him. And thou shalt remember that thou wast a bondman in the land of Egypt, and the LORD thy God redeemed thee: therefore I command thee this thing today (Deut. 15:12-15).

The poor were to be aided in their needs, but aid could not be a subsidy. Some became, because of their inability to meet their debts, bondservants for a period of not more than six years, to the next sabbath year or little jubilee. The bondservant was not only to be well treated, but he was to be discharged with a liberal pay for his services. (This system of bondservants was a part of English law, and many Americans came from ancestors who reached America only by selling themselves as bondservants for a sabbath of years.) The bondservant, however, could not have the best of both worlds, the world of freedom and the world of servitude. A wife meant responsibility: to marry, a man had to have a dowry as evidence of his ability to head a household. A man could not gain the benefit of freedom, a wife, and at the same time gain the benefit of security under a master. If he married while a bondservant another bondservant, or a slave, he knew that in so doing he was abandoning either freedom or his family. He either remained permanently a slave with his family and had his ear pierced as a sign of subordination (like a woman), or he left his family. If he walked out and left his family, he could, if he earned enough, redeem his family from bondage. The law here is humane and also unsentimental. It recognizes that some people are by nature slaves and will always be so. It both requires that they be dealt with in a godly manner and also that the slave recognize his position and accept it with grace. Socialism, on the contrary, tries to give the slave all the advantages of his security together with the benefits of freedom, and, in the process, destroys both the free and the enslaved. The old principle of law, derived from this law, that the welfare recipient cannot exercise the suffrage and related rights of a free citizen, is still valid.

7. Reverence for the aged: "Thou shalt rise up before the hoary head, and honour the face of the old man, and fear thy God: I am the LORD" (Lev. 19:32). Again, the weak are protected by law: the protection extends thus from the young (orphans) to the aged.

8. To construct battlements:

When thou buildest a new house, then thou shalt make a battlement for thy roof, that thou bring not blood upon thine house, if any man fall from thence (Deut. 22:8).

Scholars who love to find parallels to Biblical law in other ancient legal codes are unable here (as elsewhere) to find a parallel. A principle of safety in building construction as well as a general liability principle is stated. The flat roofs of the day were commonly used for summer living; the roof had to have a wall or railing to prevent falls. A property owner had thus a general responsibility to remove occasions of hurt to legitimate persons on his land or in his home. The obligation to "make alive" is the duty to remove the potential sources of damage.

9. Gleanings and shared offerings: This has already been cited. Texts requiring gleaning are Exodus 23:10, 11; Leviticus 17:2-9; 19:9, 10; 23:22; Deuteronomy 16:10-14; 24:19-21; cf. Ruth 2. Two of these passages are not strictly with reference to gleaning (Lev. 17:2-9; Deut. 16:10-14) but have reference to shared offerings, a form of charity to the poor, to aliens, and to Levites. There is a reference to gleaning in Gideon's proverb, "Is not the gleaning of the grapes of Ephraim better than the vintage of Abiezer?" (Judges 8:2). The Chaldee interpretation of it, or paraphrase, reads, "Are not the weak of the house of Ephraim better than the strong of the house of Abiezer?"[9] The gleanings required work on the part of the recipient. The shared offerings placed the poor, the alien, and the Levites within the family of the giver as they rejoiced together before the Lord. It was not entirely nor essentially charity, in that the sojourner might be prosperous, and the Levite well off, although the fatherless and the widow (Deut. 16: 10-14) were often needy. In essence, the shared offering set forth their common life under God's gracious government. The shared offerings and the gleanings alike served also to unite men and to further community. As St. Paul declared, "Bear ye one another's burdens, and so fulfil the law of Christ" (Gal. 6:2). But, with respect to responsibility and work, as St. Paul added, "every man shall bear his own burden" (Gal. 6:5). Men are made "alive" by godly help; they are not made "alive" by being relieved of their godly responsibilities. Herman N. Ridderbos' comment on Galatians 6:5 is of interest:

> Every man is responsible for his own conduct to God. Hence, one should conduct himself as verse 4 recommends. *Burden* does not refer so much this time to the oppressive weight (as in verse 2), as to the normal duty which falls upon every man. The words *shall bear* connote the certainty of this statement, as well as the coming judgment, where it will be made manifest.[10]

Men and society are destroyed by false charity for "the tender mercies of the wicked are cruel" (Prov. 12:10), but a faithful adherence to the law of the Lord makes alive.

---

9. F. W. Farrar, "Judges," in Ellicott, II, 215.
10. Herman N. Ridderbos, *The Epistle of Paul to the Churches of Galatia* (Grand Rapids: Eerdmans, 1953), p. 215.

Since man lives in a fallen world, he has a task of *restoration*. To him is delegated by God, in every area of authority, to kill and to make alive in order to re-establish the intended dominion God ordained for man at the creation of all things. Man can never establish dominion without enforcing both aspects of this duty under God and according to His law. To kill alone accomplishes nothing; the tyrants of history are only destroyers. With all his lawless killing, Stalin gained nothing; he left Russia and the world poorer and more wretched for all his efforts to establish paradise by means of death. But, similarly, those who seek to avoid all injury, all killing, as a means of creating a new world only succeed in giving the victory to evil. Their tender mercies are cruelty, and by giving life to evil they bring death to society. Only by faithfully observing God's mandate to kill and to make alive according to His law-word can man establish dominion over the earth and accomplish the required task of restoration.

5. Hybridization and Law

The student newspaper at a fundamentalistic college carried a student attack on certain common attitudes. One of the condemned positions was summarized thus: "I can't imagine ever having a homosexual for a friend." The answer to this was, "Can you honestly imagine any of your friends not living with some awfully serious hang-ups?" The article continued,

> "Westmont students should know the Christian answer to marijuana." (Just what is the "Christian" answer? Or is there more than one possible position? Is the use of marijuana inherently evil? Is it wrong because it's illegal? What happens if the law is changed?)
> "I am repulsed by the thought of homosexuality, drug addiction, and prostitution." (Some people are repulsed by ignorance of social conditions, hypocrisy, false piety, and willing detachment from reality.)
> "I can't afford the time to become socially involved in the community problems of Santa Barbara. After all, my first responsibility is to be a student." (How can I afford not to become involved? What does being a student mean? Can it ever exclude being a person and all that that means?)[1]

Such attitudes of permissiveness and antinomianism come as a shock to many, especially when they come from ostensibly evangelical circles. But the reality is that in fundamentalistic circles, and in Lutheran, Calvinist, Anglican, Baptist, Roman Catholic, and other circles such opinions are becoming the rule rather than the exception. Those who oppose them are in the minority, and they lack the theological grounds, usually,

---

1. Kathi Robinson, "Questionable Quotes," in *Horizon* (student paper, Westmont College). (January 30, 1969), p. 3.

to be effective in their opposition, because, where the law is set aside, then *the ethics of love* takes over. Where antinomianism prevails, love becomes the new "law" and the new savior: it is then the answer to every problem, to perversion, criminality, heresy, and all things else. Where love is the answer, all law and order must give way to the imperative of love. How widely people believe in love as the cure-all appeared in the trial of a Bel-Air, California, physician who was involved in the Friars Club card cheating conspiracy, although not taken to trial after being indicted, and who also pleaded guilty to making false statements in his 1964 income tax returns.

> Dr. Lands pleaded with Judge Gray to "remand me to my family and my dog—at least I know he loves me."
> The physician declared, "I feel like a motherless child—both unloved and unwanted."[2]

Love without law is total permissiveness: it is ultimately a denial of good and evil in favor of a supposedly higher way. The ethics of love leads to situation ethics, in that, instead of God's absolute law, the morality of a situation is determined by the situation itself and the loving action it calls for. Wherever the law is denied, the logic of that position leads inevitably to situation ethics unless the rule of law is restored in life and thought. Those evangelical circles which, denying the law, are still not in situation ethics, represent merely cases of arrested development: an administrative fiat, like a papal encyclical, blocks the logical progress into situation ethics.

The law is thus necessary and basic to Christian faith. Love, in Biblical thought, is not antinomian: it is the fulfilling of the law (Rom. 13:8-10). Old-fashioned fathers are thus scripturally sound in declaring that they administer their discipline as an act of love.

Antinomianism is destructive of discrimination and of the intelligent use of things, and is forbidden. Some of the legislation in this area is extremely interesting:

> Ye shall keep my statutes. Thou shalt not let thy cattle gender with a diverse kind: thou shalt not sow thy field with mingled seed: neither shall a garment mingled of linen and woollen come upon thee (Lev. 19:19).
> Thou shalt not sow thy vineyard with divers seeds: Lest the fruit of thy seed which thou hast sown, and the fruit of thy vineyard, be defiled.
> Thou shalt not plow with an ox and an ass together.
> Thou shalt not wear a garment of diverse sorts, as of woollen and linen together (Deut. 22:9-11).

---

2. "Doctor Gets 10 Days, Fine for False Tax Statements," Van Nuys, California *The News* (Friday, February 7, 1969).

Ginsburg's comment on Leviticus 19:19 is, despite some details, to the point,

> The Holy God has made everything "after its kind" (Gen. 1:11, 12, 21, 24, 25 &c.) and has thus established a physical distinction in the order of His creation. For man to bring about a union of dissimilar things is to bring about a dissolution of the Divine laws and to act contrary to the ordinances of Him who is holy, and to whose holiness we are to attain. . . .
>
> *Not to sow thy field with mingled seed.*—According to the administrators of the law during the second Temple, the prohibition is only applicable to diverse seeds for human food, mixed together for the purpose of sowing them in the same field, as, for instance, wheat and barley, beans and lentils. These an Israelite must neither sow himself nor allow a non-Israelite to do it for him. Seeds of grain and seeds of trees, as well as seeds of different kinds of trees, may be sown together. The opening words of the parable, "A certain man had a fig-tree planted in his vineyard" (Luke xiii. 6), do not contravene this law. Seeds which were not intended for human food, such as of bitter herbs, or of vegetables intended for drugs, were exempted from this law, and like the hybrids of mixed parents, the seeds sown with diverse kinds were allowed to be used. . . . Though trees are not mentioned here, the law was applied to grafting. Hence it was forbidden to graft an apple-tree on a citron-tree, or herbs into trees. . . . According to the administrators of the law during the second Temple, an Israelite must not mend a woolen garment with a flaxen thread, and *vice versa.*[3]

Certain legal conclusions clearly appear from these laws: *First*, the commandment, "Thou shalt not kill," is a law which clearly favors fertility. To harm or destroy the fertility of men, plants, and animals is to violate this law. Hybrids are clearly a violation of this law, as these case laws of Leviticus 19:19 and Deuteronomy 22:9-11 make plain. Hybrid plants and animals are sterile and frustrate the purpose of creation, for God made all plants with their seed "in itself" (Gen. 1:12). Hybridization seeks to improve on God's work by attempting to gain the best qualities of two diverse things; there is no question that some hybrids do show certain advantageous qualities, but there is also no question that it comes at a price, bringing some serious disadvantages. Above all, it leads to sterility and thereby violates God's creation ordinance.

Second, the commandments clearly require a respect for God's creation. If God is the creator of all things, then all things have a purpose and are in their created function good. If all things have evolved, then everything, including man, has at most a demonstrated ability at survival but at worst is an evolutionary mistake and therefore destined to

---

3. Ginsburg, "Leviticus," in Ellicott, I, 425.

disappear. There is no assured *good* to anything in any evolutionary world. The law, however, requires us to respect the integrity of every living thing by refraining from hybridization. A man can kill and eat plants and animals under the law: this is within God's law. But to attempt by hybridization to alter or transcend one of God's created "kinds" is against His law.

Third, a general moral principle of total avoidance of and abhorrence for any and all violations of "kinds" is also asserted by the law. Thus, the law declares

> Thou shalt not lie with mankind, as with womankind: it is an abomination. Neither shalt thou lie with any beast to defile thyself therewith: neither shall any woman stand before a beast to lie down thereto: it is confusion (Lev. 18:22, 23).

Homosexuality and bestiality were religious practices of the cults of chaos, and their persistence and spread in the modern world is closely associated with anti-Christian and revolutionary impulses. The penalty for such offenses was death for all involved, including the animals (Lev. 20:13, 15, 16; Ex. 22:19). It is revealing of the antinomian nature of fundamentalism that Merrill F. Unger fails to cite the death penalty for homosexuality in his dictionary.[4] The New Testament makes clear that homosexuality is the *burning out* of man, the culmination of apostasy (Rom. 1:27; cf. Gal. 5:19; I Tim. 1:10), and that those who practice it are outside the Kingdom of God (I Cor. 6:9, 10; Rev. 22:15).

The laws of Puritan New England required the death penalty in terms of Scripture. Thus, John Winthrop recorded, "One Hackett, a servant in Salem . . . was found in buggery with a cow, upon the Lord's day"; in accordance with Biblical law, both man and cow were executed.[5]

Fourth, St. Paul referred to the broader meaning of these laws against hybridization, and against yoking an ox and an ass to a plow (Deut. 22:10), in II Corinthians 6:14: "Be ye not unequally yoked together with unbelievers: for what fellowship hath righteousness with unrighteousness? and what communion hath light with darkness?" Unequal yoking plainly means mixed marriages between believers and unbelievers and is clearly forbidden. But Deuteronomy 22:10 not only forbids unequal religious yoking by inference, and as a case law, but also unequal yoking generally. This means that an unequal marriage between believers or between unbelievers is wrong. Man was created in

---

4. Merrill F. Unger, *Unger's Bible Dictionary* (Chicago: Moody Press, 1957), p. 1035.
5. Gerald Carson, *The Polite Americans, A Wide-Angle View of Our More or Less Good Manners Over 300 Years* (New York: William Morrow, 1966), p. 7.

the image of God (Gen. 1:26), and woman in the reflected image of God in man, and from man (I Cor. 11:1-12; Gen. 2:18, 21-23). "Help-meet" means a reflection or mirror, an image of man, indicating that a woman must have something religiously and culturally in common with her husband. The burden of the law is thus against inter-religious, inter-racial, and inter-cultural marriages, in that they normally go against the very community which marriage is designed to establish.

Unequal yoking means more than marriage. In society at large it means the enforced integration of various elements which are not congenial. Unequal yoking is in no realm productive of harmony; rather, it aggravates the differences and delays the growth of the different elements toward a Christian harmony and association.

To return now to our second point, the respect for God's creation required by the law: Scripture makes clear that God, in creating all things, pronounced them "good" (Gen. 1:4, 10, 12, 18, 21, 25, 31). Man therefore cannot treat his fellow-men or any part of creation with contempt.

Animals are specifically referred to in the law. These references are as follows, i.e., references calling for kindness to animals:

1. Exodus 20:8-11; 23:10-12 and Leviticus 25:5-7 refer to the need for rest or a sabbath for animals. The wild animals eat of the fruit of the sabbatical year's harvest, and the domestic animals are included in the weekly sabbath rest. The sabbath year is also a rest for the land.

2. The threshing ox is included in the rewards of the harvest (Deut. 25:4). This law establishes the principle that the laborer is worthy of his hire or reward (I Cor. 9:9; I Tim. 5:18).

3. The law against killing both mother and young is directed against the destruction of a species (Lev. 22:28; Ex. 34:26b; Deut. 22:6, 7).

4. The return of stray domestic animals is required (Ex. 23:4, 5; Deut. 22:1-4); this means a kindness to one's neighbor, and also the animal, which is to be relieved if under too heavy a load.

But respect for creation means far more than kindness to animals. It means recognizing that, because God is the creator, all things have a purpose in terms of Him. In recent years, a fundamental disrespect for the world has been basic to much of science. Some of us can recall being taught in schools and colleges that some day, thanks to science, man would live in a totally germ-free and sterile world. This degenerate perspective has already wrought much havoc, as Carson's study revealed.[6] Lewis Mumford called attention to the new science and its contempt for life:

"What will be left of the plant world," Dr. Mumford states, "if we

---

6. Rachel Carson, *Silent Spring* (Boston: Houghton Mifflin, 1962).

allow the basically village culture, founded on a close symbiotic partnership between man and plants, to disappear. . . . There are plenty of people working in scientific laboratories today who, though they may still call themselves biologists, have no knowledge of this culture except by vague hearsay and no respect for its achievements.

"They dream of a world composed of synthetics and plastics, in which no creatures above the rank of algae or yeasts would be encouraged to grow."

A biological factor of safety existed when 70 to 90 per cent of the world's population was engaged in cultivating plants. "In the past century this biological factor of safety has shrunk. If our leaders were sufficiently awake to these dangers they would plan not for urbanization but for ruralization."

. . . As insects are eliminated, Dr. Mumford points out, the plants that depend on them for fertilization are doomed.[7]

Man's rash interference with the balance of nature is creating serious problems. Francois Mergen, dean of the School of Forestry at Yale University, has written:

A fuller understanding of natural processes is an absolute must if we are to avoid major environmental calamities. Some past environmental disasters are attributable to our abuse of natural systems. . . .

The World Health Organization carried on extensive programs of pest control for the people of Borneo. In order to eradicate mosquitoes, considered a pest of serious dimension, the Organization sprayed villages extensively with DDT. Shortly after the applications, palm-thatched roofs of the village houses began to collapse. It turned out that a certain caterpillar which feeds on the palm fronds had suddenly increased. Because of its habitat the caterpillar was not exposed to the DDT, but a predatory wasp which ordinarily keeps the caterpillar population at non-destructively low levels was vulnerable to the poison and consequently was annihilated.

Harrison goes on to relate further ecological reactions to spraying. To eradicate flies inside the village houses, World Health workers sprayed DDT indoors. Up to that time the flies were controlled by a little lizard that inhabits many homes in Borneo. The lizard kept on eating the flies which were now heavily contaminated with DDT, and then the lizards began to die. The lizards in turn were eaten by house-cats and the house-cats in turn died from DDT poisoning. As a result of cats being wiped out, the rats began to invade the dwellings. As we all know, rats not only consume human food but they also pose a serious threat of spreading diseases, such as the plague.

The rats appeared in such large numbers that the World Health Organization had to parachute a fresh supply of cats into Borneo

7. "Plant Dominion Key to Man's Survival," Oakland, California *Tribune* (Sunday, August 18, 1968), p. 13-CM.

in an attempt to restore a balance that had been successfully operative but unrecognized by the technicians who had come to help. I recount this true and recent story because it shows the interrelationship between living beings and their environment. To live in harmony with his environment man must modify many of his actions, and know nature. In reality we can consider ourselves lucky that none of the "scientific discoveries" has apparently interrupted the food chain processes to the extent where they have caused major catastrophes.

So far I have talked about very elementary facts that are well known to ecologists. If, however, these things are known to the administrators and engineers who plan manipulations of the environment, they seldom make it apparent. The myth that technology is the solution to all of our problems, however, is being questioned more and more by planners, as well as by the public at large. We no longer feel that the fountains of science and technology are bottomless and we are beginning to recognize that there are biological limitations imposed on our cultures. There is a greater appreciation of the fact that man is an integral part of these very complex systems and that a lack of understanding can bring about serious losses.[8]

Mergen is much too optimistic. As long as man sees himself as god in an evolving world, he will seek the technological manipulation of that world. In many areas today, problems are created by means of planned interference: squirrels increase enormously when coyotes are killed off; mosquitoes multiply when the birds, toads, and other natural checks against them are destroyed, and so on.

In eastern Pennsylvania, spraying has worked considerable damage, killing off bees and wiping out the businesses of bee-keepers. The loss of bees has its penalties: it can lead to pollination problems.[9]

On the other hand, a respect for God's creation can lead to very happy answers. In Griggsville, Illinois, a movement began in 1962 to restore a natural solution to the problem of pests:

The Griggsville campaign started modestly in 1962. The Jaycees of Griggsville installed 28 purple martin houses along its main street. The purple martins moved in, and the town had some astonishing results. Citizens found that their mosquito problem was solved! At last towns-people were able to enjoy lawns, gardens and patios without annoyance. That was only the beginning. For the town's annual Fair, it had been customary to spray with chemical pesticide to control biting insects. But that year, by some fortuitous circumstance, the usual shipment was side-tracked to another town, and failed to arrive in Griggsville in time. But the purple martins *had* arrived and were hungry. Since these birds live solely on live insects they thrived at the Fair. When the chemical firm's trouble-

8. Francois Mergen, "When It Rained Cats in Borneo," in *American Forests*, vol. 75, no. 1 (January, 1969), p. 29.
9. Robert Rodale, "Things Here and There," in *Prevention* (December, 1968), p. 12.

shooter arrived in town and apologized for the shipping delay, the Fair committee told him they no longer needed the pesticides. In their words: "We told him if he could find a fly or mosquito on the premises we'd order ten times as much spray. He couldn't and took the order back."

The Griggsville experience broadened out, to neighboring farmers, who recognized the economic values of attracting purple martins. Cattlemen, for example, learned that nesting boxes for these birds, set in stockyards, were an asset by having fewer insects bother live-stock. This yielded better cattle gains.

The initial purple martin project in Griggsville was so successful that it soon involved the local Boy Scouts, school children, com-munity park board, Western Illinois Fair Board, businessmen, farmers, orchardists, state and municipal officials, conservationists, civil workers throughout the nation, and the snowballing continues. The promotion of the purple martin spread to many other communi-ties. For example, in La Verne, Iowa, $200 worth of insecticide had already been purchased, but after attracting purple martins, they did not have to resort to even 25c worth of spray! Again, in Danville, Kentucky, a purple martin project was initiated as a direct result of the municipality's concern about the hazards of chemical pest control. Their action caused a newspaperman to editorialize: "Using natural checks on pest populations strikes us as far superior to mosquito abatement district practices of indis-criminating spraying insecticide over large residential areas. . . . We think most people would prefer the sight of martins dipping through the skies and the song of birds to the hiss of the sprayer. Such a program would also save the taxpayer money now spent on expensive chemicals and probably provide better controls. At least it should be given a try."

In publicizing this bird, the fact has often been quoted that a single purple martin can devour about 2,000 flying insects daily. Mr. Wade feels that this is a gross *underestimation.* Based on research, the actual average seems to be between 10,000 and 12,000 mosquitoes daily when these insects are plentiful! The purple martin will also eat flies, beetles, moths, locusts, weevils, and other insects which we consider damaging or as nuisance. Contrary to popular belief among some, the purple martin does *not* eat bees. The kingbird, for which the martin is sometimes mistaken, is the real culprit in bee-eating, nor does the purple martin eat any berries or seeds. Its diet is 100% live insect fare.[10]

All insects and animals have their God-given place in the life-cycle; destruction of that cycle makes pests of otherwise useful animals and insects. The work of earthworms, squirrels, moles, and gophers in pre-venting soil erosion and making possible the necessary absorption of

10. Beatrice Trum Hunter, "The Book Hunter," in *Natural Food and Farming,* November, 1968, a review of J. L. Wade, *What You Should Know About the Purple Martin, America's Most Wanted Bird* (Griggsville, Illinois: Griggsville Wild Bird Society).

water into the earth is very great. But snakes and coyotes, among others, keep these from getting out of hand, and are themselves kept in check by other creatures.

Similarly, weeds have their place in God's plan, in that they penetrate deep into the subsoil and bring necessary minerals to the top-soil. To treat weeds simply as an enemy rather than as a God-given ally is to despise creation. Weeds have rightly been called "guardians of the soil" for their restorative work.[11]

Pasteur remarked once that, in the contagion of diseases, the soil is everything, i.e., the physical health of the recipient is the determining factor. Sir Albert Howard, in his experiments in India, demonstrated the resistance which cattle, fed properly on feed grown on a healthy and well-balanced soil, had for diseases:

> My work animals were most carefully selected and everything was done to provide them with suitable housing and with fresh green fodder, silage, and grain, all produced from fertile land. I was naturally intensely interested in watching the reaction of these well-chosen and well-fed oxen to diseases like rinderpest, septicaemia, and foot-and-mouth disease which frequently devastated the countryside. None of my animals were segregated; none were inoculated; they frequently came in contact with diseased stock. As my small farm-yard at Pusa was only separated by a low hedge from one of the large cattle-sheds on the Pusa estate, in which outbreaks of foot-and-mouth disease often occurred, I have several times seen my oxen rubbing noses with foot-and-mouth cases. Nothing happened. The healthy well-fed animals reacted to this disease exactly as suitable varieties of crops, when properly grown, did to insect and fungous pests—no infection took place.[12]

The earth itself must be treated with respect. The foolish destruction of the micro-organisms which are basic to the fertility of the soil is working extensive damage in many areas. The same is true of careless tampering with natural drainage areas.[13] The introduction of new animals into an area works considerable damage, as witness the rabbit in Australia, where the rabbit's natural enemies are lacking, and perhaps now the Asian walking catfish (*Clarias batrachus*) in Florida.[14]

The Christian, as he faces the world around him, must realize three

---

11. Joseph A. Cocannouer, *Weeds, Guardians of the Soil* (New York: Devin-Adair, 1964). See also Cocannouer's *Water and the Cycle of Life* (New York: Devin-Adair, 1962); and *Farming with Nature* (Norman: University of Oklahoma Press, 1954). See also William A. Albrecht, *Soil Fertility and Animal Health* (Webster City, Iowa: Fred Hahne Printing Co., 1958); Friend Sykes, *Modern Humus Farming* (Emmaus, Pennsylvania: Rodale Books, 1959); Sir Albert Howard, *An Agricultural Testament* (London: Oxford University Press, 1940, 1956).
12. Sir Albert Howard, *An Agricultural Testament*, p. 162.
13. See Ron Taylor, "The Lake that comes and goes," in *Westways*, vol. 59, no. 10 (October, 1967), pp. 6-9.
14. "Fish Bites Dog," in *Time*, vol. 92, no. 8 (August 23, 1968), p. 56 f.

things: *First,* the world is not an enemy, nor a hostile element, but is God's handiwork and man's destined area of dominion under God. Man therefore must work in harmony with creation, not attack it as an alien and hostile force. *Second,* although the world is by nature essentially good, it is all the same a fallen world. To ascribe perfection to it, and to assume that the "natural" way is the perfect way is not Christian but humanistic. Because the world is fallen, and the ground itself under a curse (Gen. 3:17, 18), what is natural is not therefore of necessity good. Man has a restorational and healing work to do. He cannot seek hybridization, but he can work to improve a stock. He must respect the basic pattern of creation and work within its framework, but what *is,* is not for him the normative or the standard. He can never say, with the humanists, "Whatever is, is right." Even in Eden, before the fall, Adam's work was to subdue, utilize, and develop the earth under God.

"To make alive" is thus not a return to Eden, nor a return to a past standard, but a move forward in terms of the Kingdom of God and man's dominion over the earth.

The logic of the perfectionist view of nature is not only raw foods and vegetarianism, but also nudism and the avoidance of all inventions and constructions, including houses. If nature is perfect, then a return to a natural way of life requires the abandonment of all man's artifices and constructions. Cooking, clothing, and housing all become unnatural refinements and hence logically taboo. Few of those who advocate a return to nature are as logical as this, however.

In any case, the belief that nature is normative is anti-Christian and clearly unbiblical. It is God who is normative, and His law that governs man and nature alike, so that the world around is fully God's handiwork, and, although fallen, as fully to be governed by the law of God as is man.

Third, hybridization and unequal yoking involve a fundamental disrespect for God's handiwork which leads to futile experimentation, such as organ transplants, which represent sterile and limited gains in some areas, and a basic loss of moral perspective in every area. For the evolutionist, the world is fertile with potentiality because it is not fixed and set into a pattern. For the creationist, the fertility and the potentiality of the world rest precisely in its vital patterns, in its fixity, whereby man can work productively and with a full assurance of success. Knowledge and science require a basis of law, fixity, and pattern. Without this, there can be neither science nor progress. Hybridization is an attempt to deny the validity of law. Its penalty is an enforced sterility. In every area, where man seeks potentiality by a denial of God's law, the penalty remains the same, limited gains and long-range sterility.

6. Abortion

Abortion, the destruction of the human embryo or foetus, has long been regarded by Biblical standards as murder. The grounds for this judgment are the sixth commandment, and Exodus 21:22-25. Cassuto's "explanatory rendering" of this latter passage brings out its meaning:

> When men strive together and they hurt unintentionally a woman with child, and her children come forth but no mischief happens— that is, the woman and the children do not die—the one who hurt her shall surely be punished by a fine. But if any mischief happens, that is, if the woman dies or the children die, then you shall give life for life.[1]

The comment of Keil and Delitzsch is important:

> If men strove and thrust against a woman with child, who had come near or between them for the purpose of making peace, so that her children come out (come into the world), and no injury was done either to the woman or the child that was born, a pecuniary compensation was to be paid, such as the husband of the woman laid upon him, and he was to give it . . . by (by an appeal to) arbitrators. A fine is imposed, because even if no injury had been done to the woman and the fruit of her womb, such a blow might have endangered life. . . . The plural . . . is employed for the purpose of speaking indefinitely, because there might possibly be more than one child in the womb. *"But if injury occur* (to the mother or the child), *thou shalt give soul for soul, eye for eye . . . wound for wound"*: thus perfect retribution was to be made.[2]

It is interesting to note that antinomian dispensationalism sees no law here or elsewhere. Waltke of Dallas Theological Seminary sees no law against abortion here and, in fact, feels that "abortion was permissible in Old Testament law."[3]

The importance of Exodus 21:22-25 becomes all the more clear as we realize that this is case law, i.e., that it sets forth by a minimal case certain larger implications. Let us examine some of the implications of this passage: *First,* very obviously, the text cites, not a case of deliberate abortion but a case of accidental abortion. If the penalty for even an accidental case is so severe, it is obvious that a deliberately induced abortion is very strongly forbidden. It is not necessary to ban deliberate abortion, since it is already eliminated by this law. *Second,* the penalty for even an accidental abortion is death. If a man who, in the course of a fight, unintentionally bumps a pregnant woman and

---

1. Cited by John Warwick Montgomery in a letter to *Christianity Today,* vol. XIII, no. 5 (December 6, 1968), p. 28, from Cassuto, *Commentary on the Book of Exodus* (Jerusalem: Magnes Press, The Hebrew University, 1967).
2. Keil and Delitzsch, *Pentateuch,* II, 134 f.
3. Bruce K. Waltke, "The Old Testament and Birth Control," in *Christianity Today,* vol. XIII, no. 3 (November 8, 1968), p. 3(99).

causes her to abort, must suffer the death penalty, how much more so
any person who intentionally induces an abortion? *Third*, even if no
injury results to either the mother or the foetus, the man in the case
is liable to a fine and, in fact, must be fined. Clearly, the law strongly
protects the pregnant woman and her foetus, so that every pregnant
mother has a strong hedge of law around her. *Fourth*, since even a
mother bird with eggs or young is covered by law (Deut. 22:6, 7),
clearly any tampering with the fact of birth is a serious matter: to destroy life is forbidden except where required or permitted by God's law.

Christianity very early was confronted with the fact of abortion, in
that the Greco-Roman world regarded the matter as valid if the state
deemed it advisable. Plato's *Republic* is very plain-spoken on this
matter:

> I should make it a rule for a woman to bear children to the state
> from her twentieth year to her fortieth year: and a man, after getting
> over the sharpest burst in the race of life, thenceforward to beget
> children to the state until he is fifty-five years old. . . .
>
> If then a man who is either above or under this age shall meddle
> with the business of begetting children for the commonwealth, we
> shall declare his act to be an offense against religion and justice;
> inasmuch as he is raising up a child for the state, who, should de-
> tection be avoided, instead of having been begotten under the sanc-
> tion of those sacrifices and prayers, which are to be offered up at
> every marriage ceremonial, by priests and priestesses, and the
> whole city, to the effect that the children to be born may ever be
> more virtuous and more useful than their virtuous and useful par-
> ents, will have been conceived under cover of darkness by the aid
> of dire incontinence. . . .
>
> The same law will hold should a man, who is still of an age to be
> a father, meddle with a woman, who is also of the proper age,
> without the introduction of the magistrate: for we shall accuse him
> of raising up to the state an illegitimate, unsponsored, and un-
> hallowed child. . . .
>
> But as soon as the women and the men are past the prescribed age,
> we shall allow the latter, I imagine, to associate freely with whom-
> soever they please, so that it be not a daughter, or mother, or
> daughter's child, or grandmother: and in like manner we shall
> permit the women to associate with any man, except a son or a father,
> or one of their relations in the direct line, ascending or descending;
> but only after giving them strict orders to do their best, if possible,
> to prevent any child, haply so conceived, from seeing the light, but
> if that cannot sometimes be helped, to dispose of the infant on the
> understanding that the fruit of such a union is not to be reared.
>
> That too is a reasonable plan; but how are they to distinguish
> fathers, and daughters, and the relations you described just now?
>
> Not at all, I replied; only, all the children that are born between

the seventh and tenth month from the day on which one of their number was married, are to be called by him, if male, his sons, if female, his daughters; and they shall call him father, and their children he shall call his grandchildren; these again shall call him and his fellow-bridegrooms and brides, grandfathers and grandmothers; likewise all shall regard as brothers and sisters those that were born in the same period during which their own fathers and mothers were bringing them into the world; and as we said just now, all these shall refrain from touching one another. But the law will allow intercourse between brothers and sisters, if the lot chances to fall that way, and if the Delphian priestess also gives it her sanction.[4]

In this perspective, the state is the ultimate order and the working god of the system, so that the state can order abortion, infanticide, and incest. Aristotle's position was similar, in that he required abortion where state-allowed births were exceeded.[5] In Rome, when abortion was made illegal for women, it was done not on the grounds of ultimate moral law, but that it defrauded the husband of legitimate offspring.

Very early, the church condemned abortion (Didache, ii, 2). The Apostolic Constitutions (VII, iii) stated, "Thou shalt not slay the child by causing abortion, nor kill that which is begotten; for everything that is shaped, and has received a soul from God, if it be slain, shall be avenged as being unjustly destroyed, Ex. 21:23." Tertullian (Apol. 9) stated the Christian stand clearly: "To hinder a birth is merely a speedier man-killing; nor does it matter whether you take away a life that is born, or destroy one that is coming to birth. That is a man which is going to be one; you have the fruit already in its seed."[6]

The modern attitude toward abortion has been increasingly permissive. Thus, A. E. Crawley saw its main reason to be poverty, stating, indeed, that "as often as not . . . the sole reason is poverty."[7] Havelock Ellis saw civilization as leading to a decrease in abortion as life became more rational and scientific. In other words, abortion is not a sin but a primitive remedy for economic distress and for reckless sexual behavior.

However, abortions have not decreased; the decline of the authority of Biblical law has led to an increase in abortions. In 1946, the Inez Burns abortion case in San Francisco led to the realization that, whereas the annual births were 16,000, the annual abortions in that city numbered 18,000. In 1958, estimates of U. S. abortions ranged from 200,000

---

4. John Llewelyn Davies and David James Vaughan, translators, *The Republic of Plato* (New York: Macmillan, 1935), V, 461; p. 170 f.
5. *Politics,* VII, 16.
6. See also Minucius Felix, *Oct.,* XXX; Basil, *epist.* c/xxxviii, 2 and 8; Jerome, *epist.* XXII, 13; John Chrysostom, *ip epist. ad. Rom.* XXIV, 4; Augustine, *de nupt. et concup.* 1, 15; Concilium *Ancyronum* XXI.
7. A. E. Crawley, "Foeticide," in Hastings, *Encyclopedia of Religion and Ethics,* VI, 54-57.

to 1,200,000.[8] Evidence indicates that the majority of abortions are procured by married women.

An extensive program of the 1960's asserted women's "right" to abortion, a position taken by the U. S. Public Health Association.[9] In the Soviet Union, abortions are free and legal.[10] The legalization in California of therapeutic abortions, with a broad definition which permitted abortion if the mother's mental or physical health might be impaired, did not stop illegal abortions; the answer of the author of the measure was a pledge to expand the law even further.[11] Under the impact of humanism, the legal situation became badly clouded. In Boston, an unborn baby, aborted by an accident, recovered damages for wrongful injury against the owners of a truck which struck an automobile occupied by Mrs. Zaven Torigian so that her child was born prematurely.[12] This ruling was in line with Biblical law. But in New York Mrs. Robert Stewart, who gave birth to a retarded child after contracting measles and being denied an abortion, won a suit against the hospital for denying her an abortion.[13]

An important study of abortion in "primitive" societies revealed that its main functions are a revenge against the father, a hatred of responsibility (the Papuans of Geelvink Bay declare, "Children are a burden and we get tired of them. They destroy us."), a desire to avoid shame, an analogue to suicide, a hatred of life, a hatred of men, and a castration of the father. As a flight from parenthood, the motivation of abortion is (1) the preservation of beauty, (2) the continued enjoyment of freedom and irresponsibility, and (3) the avoidance of the sexual abstinence common to many cultures during pregnancy and lactation. The essence of these motives is, according to Devereaux, "a neurotic flight from maturity."[14] That even these "primitive" societies are aware that abortion is murder appears in Deveraux' section, "The Eschatology of the Fetus."[15]

A telling argument against abortion appeared in the American Bar

---

8. *Time,* (June 2, 1958), p. 70.
9. "U.S. Health Assn. Declares Women's Right to Abortion," Santa Ana, California, *The Register* (Friday [m], November 15, 1968), p. A-3.
10. "Abortions, Free, Legal in Russia," in the Los Angeles *Herald-Examiner* (Sunday, August 18, 1968), p. E-2.
11. "Illegal Abortions Still Persist Despite New Law," Los Angeles *Herald-Examiner* (Saturday, February 1, 1969), p. A-3.
12. "Unborn Baby Ruled 'Person,'" Santa Ana, California, *The Register* (Saturday [m] April 29, 1967), p. A-7.
13. "Retarded Baby Wins in NY Abortion Suit," in Santa Ana, California, *The Register* (Sunday, October 6, 1968).
14. George Devereaux: *A Study of Abortion in Primitive Societies* (New York: Julian Press, 1955), p. 126.
15. See R. J. Rushdoony, "Abortion," in *The Encyclopedia of Christianity* (Wilmington, Delaware: National Foundation for Christian Education, 1964), I, 20-23.

Association Journal, written by Dr. A. C. Mietus, professor of obstetrics and gynecology at UCLA, and his brother, Norbert J. Mietus, chairman of the division of business administration at Sacramento State College. According to them,

> They said those who deplore the loss of 5,000 to 10,000 mothers annually in illegal abortions ignore the 1 million or more unborn children "sacrificed in the process of this massive assault on human life."
>
> The Mietus brothers said some persons would justify abortion in the case of unborn infants that would be born crippled or defective.
>
> "Would any reputable doctor propose to try LIVING cripples, or mental or physical defectives, in comparable ex parte proceedings? Start by eliminating senile parents; then the millions of blind persons?
>
> "Move on to all who are bed-ridden—then those confined to wheel chairs—and finally those who use crutches? Proceed gradually with the disposition of the millions who wear spectacles, use hearing aids, are equipped with false teeth, are too stout or too thin.
>
> "Where draw the line between acceptable and the unacceptable level of fitness?" the Mietus brothers asked. "No human being is perfect. Would the world, moreover, really be a better place after the destruction of the millions of defective individuals? Has the world gained or lost from the services of the epileptic Michaelangelo, of the deaf Edison, of the hunchbacked Steinmetz, of the Roosevelts—both the asthmatic Theodore and the polioparalyzed Franklin?
>
> "It must be recognized that liberalized abortion laws would logically be followed by pressures for legalized euthanasia. The attack on life is essentially the same," they said.[16]

The essence of the demand for abortion is to return to pagan statism, to place life again under the state rather than under God. The implications of abortion concern more than the fetus; they involve every living man.

The demand for abortion is antinomian to the core. Significantly, when a group of young women invaded a New York state legislative hearing to break it up with their demand for total repeal of the anti-abortion law, they declared that "they were tired of listening to men debate something that was of primary concern to women. 'What right do you men have to tell us whether we can or cannot have a child?' shouted one of the women."[17] The logic of this position is revealing: the women held that men cannot legislate with respect to childbirth,

---

16. "First Abortion, Then Euthanasia," in the Oakland, California, *Tribune* (Monday, October 11, 1965), p. 7.
17. "Women Abort Abortion Hearing," Los Angeles *Herald-Examiner* (Friday, Februray 14, 1969 [m]), p. A-10.

because they do not experience it. The test of legislative validity in both the law and the law-makers is thus experience. By this logic, it can be held that good citizens cannot legislate with respect to murder, since the act of murder is outside their experience. Humanism (and experiential religious philosophies) reduces all things to the test of man's experience and thus under-cut all law and order. Men who cannot, like women, bear children *can* legislate with respect to abortion because the principle of law is not experience but the law-word of God.

One final note: a common rhetorical test case asks whether a doctor should attempt to save the life of the mother or of the child in a critical case. Whose life should be sacrificed? The foetus or the mother? The question is an artificial one, according to competent doctors. A doctor works in a crisis to save life and does all that he can for mother and child. No doctor questioned has had such a "choice," only the responsibility always to do all, moment by moment, to save the life of mother and child. Morality is not furthered by posing artificial questions whose purpose is to place a person in the place of God.

In California, the liberalized abortion law led rapidly to a very serious crisis, one which most people chose to ignore. Governor Reagan observed, on April 22, 1970, that the law was creating an ugly situation:

> Reagan said, "It took a lot of soul searching" for him to sign Bellenson's 1967 liberalization bill.
>
> Under that act, abortions are allowed when the prospective mother's physical or mental health is in danger, or when the pregnancy was caused by rape or incest. Previously, abortions were permitted only when the woman's life was endangered.
>
> "Let me tell you what's happened even with the liberalization that we have," Reagan told the women. Pointing to the mental health section, the governor said:
>
> "Our Public Health Department has told us its projections that if the present rate of increase continues in California, a year from now there will be more abortions than there will be live births in this state. And a great proportion of them will be financed by Medi-Cal."
>
> He said "under a technicality" a "young, unmarried girl" can become pregnant, go on welfare "and she is automatically eligible for the abortion if she wants it, under Medi-Cal. And all she has to do is get a psychiatrist—and they're finding that easy to do—who will walk by the bed and say she has suicidal tendencies."
>
> Reagan said that in Sacramento "a 15-year-old girl has just had her third abortion, with the same psychiatrist each time saying she has suicidal tendencies. I don't think the state should be in that business."[18]

---

18. "Reagan Sees Abortions Topping Births," Santa Ana, California, *The Register*, Friday (m), April 24, 1970.

As the governor spoke, Senator Anthony C. Bellenson had submitted a bill to remove all restrictions on abortion except a requirement that a physician must perform it. The Democratic gubernatorial candidate, Jess Unruh, supported Bellenson's proposal.

7. Responsibility and Law

A central aspect of Biblical law is summed up in a single sentence: "The fathers shall not be put to death for the children, neither shall the children be put to death for the fathers: every man shall be put to death for his own sin" (Deut. 24:16). This law is cited in II Kings 14:6 and II Chronicles 24:4 as the authority for King Amaziah's action in sparing the children of his father's murderers. Jeremiah emphasized the same doctrine (Jer. 31:29, 30), as did Ezekiel (18:20). Wright's comment on this law is of interest:

> Such a law as this seems superfluous in modern society when the individual is the primary unit and the sense of community solidarity is weak or entirely lacking. In patriarchal and seminomadic life, however, the sense of community responsibility was very strong, particularly that of the family. A nomadic blood feud could annihilate a whole family for a crime of one of its members (for exceptional cases of this in Israel see Josh. 7:24, 25; II Sam. 21:1-9).[1]

Wright is correct in stating that nomadic blood feuds denied the principle inherent to this law, but the same menace to this law exists in another form today. He is wrong, moreover, with respect to Achan (Josh. 7:24, 25); in Achan's case, the gold and silver hidden in the earth in the midst of the tent required the complicity of every member of the family; his interpretation of II Samuel 21:1-9 is also faulty. The common practice of antiquity was to punish, penalize, or execute the entire families of some offenders.

To analyze the law, it is important to recognize certain central aspects of it. *First*, responsibility is an aspect of every law system. Someone must be held responsible for offenses; if there is no responsibility somewhere, then no law enforcement is possible. *Who* is responsible is the important question, and the answer is a religious answer. Responsibility can be attached to the family, the community, the environment, the gods, or to the person. *Where* the responsibility is placed makes for a fundamental difference in the social order.

Second, the Biblical doctrine is, as Deuteronomy 24:16 makes clear, one of individual responsibility. It is the essence of sin, according to Genesis 3:9-13, to attempt to evade individual responsibility. Adam and Eve refused to acknowledge their guilt: they shifted the responsibility to another, Adam blaming Eve and God, Eve blaming the serpent.

---

1. G. Ernest Wright, "Deuteronomy," in *Interpreter's Bible*, II 476 f.

The godly man acts responsibly and assumes the responsibility for his actions.

Third, related to the question of responsibility is the basic one, responsibility to whom? If man is responsible, to whom is he responsible? To the family, to the community, or to the state? The Biblical doctrine of responsibility holds that man's primary responsibility is to God, secondarily to his fellow men. It is God who confronts Adam, and who at every turn confronts man, with His sovereign claims and His total law.

Fourth, in terms of this law, guilt cannot be shifted to others or passed on to the people around a man. Guilt is non-transferable; a disposition or nature can be inherited, but not guilt. Man inherits from Adam the total depravity of his nature, but his guilt before God is entirely his own, even as Adam had to bear his own guilt. This distinction between guilt and nature is fundamental to Biblical doctrine and law. It is absent in such legal systems as that of Islam. Since the law deals with guilt and punishes the guilty, the non-transferable nature of guilt in Biblical law is of central importance. Where guilt is transferable, punishment is also transferable. This is the essence of the principle of the blood-feud: if a Hatfield commits an offense, then all Hatfields share in the guilt, and all are punished. Similarly, if all Americans were guilty of President Kennedy's assassination, then all Americans must, according to this pagan theory, be punished. *Responsibility, guilt, and punishment* are inseparable in law: where there is responsibility for an offense, there is guilt, and there also punishment or penalties must be applied.

Today this doctrine of individual responsibility has been undercut by the theory of evolution. Basic to evolutionary theory is environmentalism; man is a product of his environment and has evolved in relationship to a changing environment and its actions upon him. As a result, not only is man a product of his environment, but he is also a creature of his environment rather than of God. Man is what an evolving world has made of him, and man's actions are a product of that environment and its molding of man. This means that the guilt for man's actions rests with his environment, his social and personal world, and it is this world which is punished when man sins. Thus, society is blamed for the conduct of delinquents and criminals, and parents for the sins of their children. Punishment then falls on society and on parents. In such a scheme of things, the lawless are absolved of guilt, and the guilty are made innocent.

Does the Bible teach nothing of community responsibility? As a matter of fact, Biblical law does assert community responsibility, a responsibility to see that justice is done. There is community guilt, if justice is not done.

First, to discuss community responsibility for justice. Immediately after the law concerning individual responsibility comes one of the many laws concerning justice: "Thou shalt not pervert the judgment of the stranger, nor of the fatherless; nor take the widow's raiment to pledge" (Deut. 24:17). Where there is a family, the family cannot be held guilty for the criminal's offense. Where there is no family, the community must not take advantage of the person's helplessness. If a foreigner ("the stranger") is on trial, alone and without friends, his right to justice remains unchanged. His helplessness can no more be exploited than the wealth of a criminal's relatives can be confiscated or their persons attacked. Justice is not social: it is individual. The doctrine of social justice goes hand in hand with the doctrine of social guilt. Social justice is not only an attack on individual responsibility but also on the immunity of the innocent.

Second, since the community responsibility means that justice must be enforced, it follows that community guilt ensues where justice is not done. This is dealt with in Deuteronomy 21:1-9. If a murder cannot be solved, the whole community bears the responsibility as well as the unknown murderer. The murderer bears the responsibility before God for the murder, and the community for failing to avenge the murder, for failing to bring the murderer to justice. Since the offense is against God, the leaders of the community make atonement to God for the offense, so that no guilt be incurred by them. In brief, a community could not be indifferent to any offense in their midst, and crimes going unpunished had to have ritual atonement.

The form of this law is that of the Old Testament sacrificial system; it is no longer binding on us. The substance of the law is, however, still valid. The community has a responsibility to God to see that justice is done, and it also has a responsibility to the victims of the crime.

A comment by Waller is of interest here: "It is remarkable that to our time the most effectual remedy against outrages of which the perpetrators cannot be discovered is a fine upon the district in which they occur."[2] This is in keeping with the purpose of this law; similarly, restitution to victims of the crime is an essential part of the community's atonement, as is the prayerful petitition for God's mercy by the officers of state. The latter is essential and basic, because the primary offense is always against God in any violation of law. As Ehrlich has noted, the Bible does not use the word "crime." Every offense is called a "transgression." "The absence of the term 'crime' indicates that the will of God is the sole source of all the law, and thus all punishable acts constitute sins which are in violation of God's law."[3] The concept of

---

2. C. H. Waller, "Deuteronomy," in Ellicott, II, 58.
3. J. W. Ehrlich, *The Holy Bible and the Law* (New York: Oceana Publications, 1962), p. 49.

transgression is being replaced by the doctrine of social conditioning and compulsive behavior; the life-span of such an environmental concept is relatively brief, because its impact is suicidal for any society. Moreover, basic to this pagan concept is a thorough impersonalism; man being an evolutionary product of an impersonal universe is basically governed by an impersonal world and impersonal forces. In Biblical law, man, as the creature of the personal and triune God, transgresses personally against that God in his every sin. Every offense is thus responsible because personal and is a *transgression*. Law that is geared to personal responsibility is respectful of persons: they are the central and essential figures of society. Things are not in charge; people are responsible. Law that is humanistic and evolutionary is disrespectful of persons: people are not in charge; things govern the world. Men therefore are treated callously by the social scientists who seek to play the role of gods by governing things and manipulating people. After all, why should people who have always been ruled by things object to the rule of elite men? The dechristianization of society is also the depersonalization of man.

8. Restitution or Restoration

God's purpose in redemption is the "restitution" or "restoration" of all things in, through, and under Jesus Christ as King (Acts 3:21). The goal of history is the great "regeneration," or new genesis, of all things in Christ (Matt. 19:28). "The times spoken of by the prophets are here described as times of restoration, when Christ shall reign over a kingdom in which none of the consequences of sin will any longer appear."[1]

Wright observed of the word "restoration," that "Round this word gather some of the most fascinating problems of our thought in regard to the possibilities of human destiny." It involves the declaration that humanity is to be restored to blessedness, and the earth blessed together with man.[2] This restoration or restitution does not mean universalism.[3]

The principle of restitution is basic to Biblical law; it appears with especial prominence in laws under the sixth and eighth commandments, but it is basic to the purpose of the whole law. The "eye for an eye, tooth for tooth" concept is not retaliation but restitution. Not only liberal but evangelical scholars often err at this point, as witness the premillennial, dispensationalist scholar, Unger, who reads Exodus 21:

---

1. J. Macpherson, "Restoration," in James Hastings, editor, *A Dictionary of the Bible* (New York: Charles Scribner's Sons, 1919), IV, 230.
2. T. H. Wright, "Restoration," in James Hastings, editor, *A Dictionary of Christ and the Gospels* (New York: Charles Scribner's Sons, 1908), II, 503.
3. J. C. Lambert, "Restitution," James Hastings, editor, *A Dictionary of the Apostolic Church* (New York: Charles Scribner's Sons, 1922), II, 321.

24, 25 as literal, and as vengeful retaliation.[4] But the very context of the passage cited militates against this: a pregnant woman who is struck by a man, although unintentionally, is compensated by a fine; if harm follows to either mother or child, the man pays with his life. Is this retaliation, or is it restitution? (Ex. 21:22-25). The passage which immediately follows (Ex. 21:26-35) again sets forth the principle of restitution, usually by compensation, unless death ensues. To read the eye for an eye principle as the literal blinding of a man who has put out another man's sight is to do violence to the plain statement of Scripture. The same applies to Leviticus 24:17-21; the restitution for some offenses is capital punishment, for others, compensation.

Some of the laws of restitution have reference to damages. Clark's summary of the Biblical law of damages is excellent:

> The law of damages is that one who injures or wrongs another shall make reparation or restitution. Rules concerning the duty of restitution, and the amount or measure of damages, are stated in the Scriptures. Thus restitution is required of a thief (Ex. 22:3), of one who causes a field or vineyard of another to be "eaten" (Ex. 22:5), of one who kindles a fire which escapes and burns "stacks of corn, or the standing corn, or the field" of another (Ex. 22:6); of a bailee from whom an animal delivered to be kept is stolen (Ex. 22:10, 12); and of one who kills an animal belonging to another (Lev. 24:21). One who commits an assault upon another with a stone or with his fist is required to pay for the loss of his victim's time and to cause him to be thoroughly healed (Ex. 21:19). The owner of an ox that gores another's manservant or maidservant is required to pay thirty shekels of silver to the master (Ex. 21:32). And the seducer of a damsel is required to pay fifty shekels of silver to her father (Deut. 22:29). Similarly, a husband who slanders a newly married wife is required to pay a hundred shekels of silver to the wife's father (Deut. 22:19).[5]

Some of the categories of damages are as follows:

1. for maiming persons, Lev. 24:19; Ex. 21:18-20;
2. for killing animals, or an animal killing another animal, Lev. 24:18, 21; Ex. 21:35, 36;
3. for various wrongs committed, restitution to God, Num. 5:6-8.

Many other laws of restitution deal with property. Our concern here is with injuries to persons primarily. Certain principles of liability appear: *first*, the guilty party is liable for the medical expenses of the injured: he "shall cause him to be thoroughly healed" (Ex. 21:19). *Second*, the guilty party is liable for the time lost from work (Ex. 21: 19). If the guilty party were an owner, and the injured party was his slave, then there was liability for death or for injury, but not for time lost,

---

4. *Unger's Bible Dictionary*, p. 903.
5. Clark, *Biblical Law*, p. 296 f.

since the loss was the loss of the owner; he had at this point damaged himself (Ex. 21:20, 21; Lev. 24:17-20). *Third*, the penalty applied if an animal owned by a man were guilty of the injury; if the animal had no previous record of violence to man, then the animal died (and of course the injured person was cared for and compensated). But, if the animal had a previous record of violence, the owner now became liable to the death penalty for murder (Ex. 21:28, 29). *Fourth*, the guilty party is liable to the damages laid upon him by the court for the injury, in addition to compensation for time lost and for medical expenses.

The principle of restitution is not entirely gone from law today, but there are significant differences. A study of the subject by Stephen Schafer is important in this context. According to Schafer,

> "The guilty man lodged, fed, clothed, warmed, lighted, entertained, at the expense of the State in a model cell, issued from it with a sum of money lawfully earned, has paid his debt to society; he can set his victims at defiance; but the victim has his consolation; he can think that by taxes he pays to the Treasury, he has contributed towards the paternal care, which has guarded the criminal during his stay in prison." These were the bitter and sarcastic words of Prins, the Belgian, at the Paris Prison Congress in 1895, when during a discussion of the problem of restitution to victims of crime, he could no longer contain his indignation at various practical and theoretical difficulties raised against his proposals on behalf of the victim.[6]

Restitution has long been in the background of virtually all legal systems and at times been very prominent. Thus, under early American law, "A thief, in addition to his punishment, was ordered to return to the injured party three times the value of his stolen goods, or in the case of insolvency, his person was placed at the disposal of the victim for a certain time."[7]

In modern law, the term restitution is usually replaced by "compensation" or "damages."[8] But the significant difference is this: in Biblical law, the offender is guilty before God (and hence restitution to God, Num. 5:6-8), and before the offended man, to whom he makes direct restitution, whereas in modern law the offense is primarily and essentially against the state. God and man are left out of the picture in the main. According to Schafer,

> "It was chiefly owing to the violent greed of feudal barons and mediaeval ecclesiastical powers that the rights of the injured party were gradually infringed upon, and finally, to a large extent, ap-

6. Stephen Schafer, *Restitution to Victims of Crime* (Chicago: Quadrangle Books, 1960), p. vii.
7. *Ibid.*, p. 5.
8. *Ibid.*, p. 101.

propriated by these authorities, who exacted a double vengeance, indeed, upon the offender, by forfeiting his property to themselves instead of to his victim, and then punishing him by the dungeon, the torture, the stake or the gibbet. But the original victim of wrong was practically ignored." After the Middle Ages, restitution, kept apart from punishment, seems to have been degraded. The victim became the Cinderella of the criminal law.[9]

The idea of restitution was severed from the concept of punishment. "The theory developed at the end of the Middle Ages that crime is an offense exclusively against the state had severed that connection. The concept of punishment remained untouched by the civil concept of restitution."[10] In fact, Schafer noted,

> If one looks at the legal systems of different countries, one seeks in vain a country where a victim of crime enjoys a certain expectation of full restitution for his injury. In rare cases where there is state compensation the system is either not fully effective, or does not work at all; where there is no system of state compensation, the victim is, in general, faced with the insufficient remedies offered by civil procedure and civil execution. While the punishment of crime is regarded as the concern of the state, the injurious result of the crime, that is to say, the damage to the victim, is regarded almost as a private matter. It recalls man in the early days of social development, when, left alone in his struggle for existence, he had himself to meet attacks from outside and fight alone against his fellow-creatures who caused him harm. The victim of today cannot even himself seek satisfaction, since the law of the state forbids him to take the law into his own hands. In the days of his forefathers, restitution was a living practice, and "it is perhaps worth noting, that our barbarian ancestors were wiser and more just than we are today, for they adopted the theory of restitution to the injured, whereas we have abandoned this practice, to the detriment of all concerned." "And this was wiser in principle, more reformatory in its influence, more deterrent in its tendency, and more economic to the community, than the modern practice."[11]

Certain things appear from the foregoing. *First,* the shift from restitution to imprisonment has its roots in the seizure of power by church and state, and was in its origin designed to shake down the guilty for ransom or confiscatory purposes. *Second,* the state made its doctrine of punishment the criminal law, and relegated restitution to civil law. Thus, if an injured party seeks restitution today, it involves the expense of a civil suit through the medium of an essentially uncooperative court, so

---

9. *Ibid.,* p. 8; the quotation is from William Tallack, *Reparation to the Injured; and the Rights of the Victims of Crime to Compensation* (London, 1900), pp. 11-12.
10. *Ibid.,* p. 11.
11. *Ibid.,* p. 117; the first citation is from Harry Elmer Barnes and Negley K. Teeters, *New Horizons in Criminology* (New York, 1944), p. 401; the second is from Tallack, *op. cit.,* pp. 6-7.

that, even if the injured party wins, collection is very difficult. As a result, because of this division, the criminal faces prison, a mental institution, or a correctional facility and care by an increasingly indulgent state rather than restitution. *Third*, since one form of Biblical restitution was the right of self-defense, the right under certain circumstances to kill the aggressor or thief, the increasing limitation on the right of the injured to protect himself means that we are returning to barbarism without the protection barbarism involved, i.e., freedom to defend oneself. *Fourth*, the systems of imprisonment or "rehabilitation" of criminals" involves in fact, as Prins noted, a subsidy to criminals and a tax on the innocent and the injured. It is thus a further injury to the godly which requires restitution from the hands of God and man. A society which subsidizes the criminal and penalizes the godly will end up by encouraging increasing violence and lawlessness and is thus destined for anarchy. *Fifth*, Wines noted, while giving us the false source as the preferred one, "That there are but two possible sources of civil power, viz., God and the people."[12] If power is from God, then God's law must prevail; if power be from the people, then the people's will shall prevail, and there is no principle of law above and over the people. Restitution as a principle is thus alien to a democratic society, because it is a theocratic principle which requires that man conform to an absolute and unchanging justice.

Restitution as a theocratic principle involves three things: *first,* it involves restitution to the injured person. *Second*, since the law-order broken was God's law-order, where no person existed, in the event of death, to whom restitution could be made, it was made to God (Num. 5:6-8). In cases of sin where God was directly involved, a fifth part was added in the restoration; this fifth part represented one-fourth of the original amount, another fourth, in other words (Lev. 5:14-16). In every case, restitution had to be made to God by offerings of atonement (Lev. 5:17-19). *Third*, it is apparent from these case laws that restitution is *always* mandatory for a society to be healthy before God. This carries the implication that the state must make restitution to the injured persons whenever and wherever the state, as the ministry of justice, fails to discover the offending party. The goal of godly society is *restoration*; at every point, it must be effected, with evil penalized, and the godly defended by restitution.

The goal is central to the faith, and to prayer. The Lord's Prayer declares, "Thy kingdom come. Thy will be done in earth, as it is in heaven" (Matt. 6:10). This is plainly a plea for restoration, and all true prayer must incorporate it.

---

12. E. C. Wines, *Commentaries on the Laws of the Ancient Hebrews* (Philadelphia: William S. and Alfred Martien, 1859), p. 40.

The failure of a society to ground itself on restitution, or its departure from this principle, means a growing necessity for costly protection by means of *insurance*. Much insurance is, all too often, a form of self-restitution, in that the buyer pays for protection against irresponsible people who will not make restitution. The large insurance premiums paid by responsible persons and corporations are their self-protection against the failure of the law to require restitution.

Such a society cannot in good conscience pray "Thy kingdom come," because it denies that petition by neglecting God's law. The premillennial dispensationalists who deny the law and therefore refuse to pray the Lord's Prayer are thus more consistent than the millions who use it regularly without making any effort to restore God's law order.

9. Military Laws and Production

The military laws of Scripture are of especial relevance to man, in that they involve not only laws of warfare but an important general principle.

In surveying military laws, we find that, *first*, when wars are fought in terms of a defense of justice and the suppression of evil, and in defense of the homeland against an enemy, they are a part of the necessary work of restitution or restoration, and they are therefore spoken of in Scripture as the wars of the Lord (Num. 21:14). The preparation of the soldiers involved a religious dedication to their task (Josh. 3:5).

Second, the law specified the age of the soldiers. All able-bodied men twenty years old and up were eligible for military service (Num. 1:2, 3, 18, 20, 45; 26:2, 3). This standard long prevailed and was, for example, the basis of operation in the American War of Independence. It was, however, still a selective service (Num. 31:3-6), so that, for example, out of 46,500 eligible from Reuben, 74,600 from Judah, and 35,400 from Benjamin (Num. 1), in the war against Midian, only a thousand from each tribe were taken (Num. 31:4). The eligibility of each able-bodied man was thus in principle to assert their availability in an extreme crisis.

Third, since warfare against evil is godly and serves God's task of restoration, God promised to protect His men if they moved in terms of faith and obedience. According to Exodus 30:11-16, "At the *census,* which is a military act, *each shall give a ransom* (i.e., provide a "covering") for himself."[1] As Ewing noted, "Its purpose was to make an atonement for the lives of those who went into battle." The word "plague" in Exodus 20:12 is the Hebrew *negeph*, which "comes from a primitive root meaning to push, gore, defeat, slay, smite, put to the

---

1. J. C. Rylersdaam, "Exodus," in *Interpreter's Bible*, I, 1055.

worse. This ransom was for the life of the soldier, that he might not be slain in battle." In the battle against Midian, cited above, 12,000 Israelite soldiers burned all the cities of Midian and slew their men, brought back 675,500 sheep, 72,000 head of cattle, 61,000 asses, and 32,000 unmarried women, without any loss of life. Out of this, a tithe or portion was given to the Lord.[2] Thus, where a war is waged in terms of God's law and in faith and obedience to His law-word, there men can count on His protecting and prospering care even as Israel experienced it.

Fourth, exemption from military service was provided by law. The purpose of an army should be to fight God's battles without fear (Deut. 20:1-4). Exemptions were given to several classes of men: (a) those who had built a new house and had not dedicated nor enjoyed it; (b) those who had planted a vineyard and had not yet enjoyed its fruit; (c) and those who have "betrothed a wife, and hath not taken her"; such men would have a divided mind in battle; finally, (d) all who were "fearful and faint-hearted" were excused as dangerous to army morale, "lest his brethren's heart melt as his heart" (Deut. 20:5-9). The exemption of the newlywed men was mandatory according to Deuteronomy 24:5, "When a man taketh a new wife, he shall not go out in the host, neither shall he be charged with any business; he shall be free at home one year, and shall cheer up his wife, whom he hath taken." Also exempt from military service (e) were the Levites (Num. 1:48, 49). The Levites very often fought, but they were exempt from a draft.

From these exemptions, a general principle appears: *the family has a priority over warfare.* The young bridegroom cannot serve; the new home must come first. The new farmer similarly gains exemption. *Important as defense is, the continuity of life and godly reconstruction are more important.*

A *fifth* aspect of military law requires cleanliness in the camp (Deut. 23:9-14). A latrine outside the camp is required, and a spade "to cover up your filth" (Deut. 23:13, Moffatt). "For the Eternal your God moves within your camp, to rescue you and to put your enemies into your power; hence your camp must be sacred—that he may not see anything indecent among you and turn away from you" (Deut. 23:14, Moffatt).

Another general principle appears from this law as well as the first and third laws (above), namely, that *it is not enough for the cause to be holy: not only the cause, but the people of the cause, must be holy, both spiritually and physically.*

A *sixth* military law requires that, prior to an attack, or rather, a

---

2. Charles Wesley Ewing, "The Soldier's Ransom," Faith and Freedom Bible Institute, Royal Oak, Michigan, in *Faith and Freedom Issue,* p. 4.

declaration of war, an offer of peace be extended to the enemy. The offer of peace cannot be an offer to compromise. The cause, if it be just, must be maintained; the enemy must yield to gain peace (Deut. 23:9-14). A "sneak attack" after a declaration, in Gideon's manner, is legitimate: hostilities are in progress. But, prior to a declaration of war, an attempt to negotiate with honor to the cause is required. The formal blowing of trumpets, both before war and in rejoicing at the time of victory, placed the cause before God in expectancy of victory and in gratitude for it (Num. 10:9, 10).

Seventh, warfare is not child's play. It is a grim and ugly if necessary matter. The Canaanites against whom Israel waged war were under judicial sentence of death by God. They were spiritually and morally degenerate. Virtually every kind of perversion was a religious act: and large classes of sacred male and female prostitutes were a routine part of the holy places. Thus, God ordered all the Canaanites to be killed (Deut. 2:34; 3:6; 20:16-18; Josh. 11:14), both because they were under God's death sentence, and to avoid the contamination of Israel. Among related and adjacent peoples whose depravity was similar but not as total, men (Num. 31:7; Deut. 1:1, 2, 16; 20:16, 17) and sometimes married women as well were killed (Num. 31:17, 18), but the young virgins were spared (Num. 31:18). With other foreign countries, of better calibre, any woman taken prisoner could be married, but could not be treated as a slave or as a captive (Deut. 21:10-14), clearly indicating the difference in national character between Canaanites and other peoples. These provisions are quite generally condemned by the modern age, which has hypocritically resorted to the most savage and total warfare in history. These laws were not applicable to all peoples but only to the most depraved. They assert a still valid general principle: *if warfare is to punish and/or to destroy evil, the work of restoration requires that this be done, that an evil order be overthrown, and, in some cases, some or many people be executed.* The war crimes trials after World War II represented ex post facto law (and were thus justly opposed by Senator Robert Taft); they were also based on weak legal and humanistic principles as well as unduly a product of the demands of the Soviet Union. They are thus not proper examples of this principle. But the general principle of *guilt* is a valid one; if there be no guilt in a war, then there is no justice either. This has been the case in most warfare: no justice, and hence no real concept of guilt.

Eighth, the normal purpose of warfare is defensive; hence, Israel was forbidden the use of more than a limited number of horses (Deut. 17:16), since horses were the offensive weapon of ancient warfare.[3]

---

3. See Yigael Yadin, *The Art of Warfare in Biblical Lands* (New York: McGraw-Hill Book Company, 1963), I, 86-90.

Thus, still another general principle appears: *since war is to be waged in a just cause only, and, normally, in defense of the homeland and of justice, the right of conscientious objection means that one has a moral right to refuse support to an ungodly war.*

Ninth, a very important military law appears in Deuteronomy 20:19, 20, one which also embodies a basic principle of very far-reaching implications. According to this law,

> When thou shalt besiege a city a long time, in making war against it to take it, thou shalt not destroy the trees thereof by forcing an axe against them: for thou mayest eat of them, and thou shalt not cut them down (for the tree of the field is man's life) to employ them in the siege:
>
> Only the trees which thou knowest that they be not trees for meat, thou shalt destroy and cut them down; and thou shalt build bulwarks against the city that maketh war with thee, until it be subdued.

The last portion of Deuteronomy 20:19 is rendered by various translators to read, "for is the tree of the field man, that it should be besieged of thee?" (MJV). In other words, war is not to be waged against the earth, but against men. But, even more centrally, life must go on, and the fruit tree and the vineyard represent at all times an inheritance from the past and a heritage for the future: they are not to be destroyed. Other trees can be cut down, but only as needed to "build bulwarks against the city." Wanton destruction is not permitted.

Related to this is a word of Solomon: "Moreover the profit of the earth is for all: the king himself is served by the field" (Eccles. 5:9). This is rendered by the Masoretic text, Jewish translation, as "But the profit of a land every way is a king that maketh himself servant to the field" (MJV). This word, and the law concerning fruit trees and other trees, adds up to an important general principle: *production is prior to politics.* Warfare is an aspect of the life of the political order, and its role is important, but production is more basic. Without production, without the fruit trees and the farmer, the worker and the manufacturer, there is no country to defend. *The priority of politics* is a modern heresy which is steadily destroying the world; only the great vitality of free enterprise is maintaining the productive level in the face of great political handicaps and interferences. In any godly order, therefore, production, freedom of enterprise, must always be prior to politics, in wartime as well as in peace.

Tenth, and finally, the laws of booty provided a reward to the soldiers (Num. 31:21-31, 29, 30, 42; Deut. 20:14), so that there is legal ground not only for soldiers' pay but also a pension, a reward for their services. War indemnity was an aspect of the penalty imposed on an enemy

(II Kings 3:4) as penalty for their offense, and to defray the costs of the war.

In terms of Scripture, in a sinful world, war is ugly, but it is a necessity if evil is to be overcome. Clark's summary is to the point:

> According to the Scriptures, "there is no peace unto the wicked" (Isa. 48:22; 57:41), and it is futile to cry "peace, peace, when there is no peace" (Jer. 6:14). If men would have peace, they must "seek first the kingdom of God, and his righteousness" (Matt. 6: 33), for peace is the "work of righteousness" (Isa. 32:17), and there can be no lasting and universal peace until "righteousness and peace have kissed each other" (Ps. 85:10). There shall be peace when "the inhabitants of the world . . . learn righteousness." It is "in the last days" (Isa. 2:2) and when "the Lord alone shall be exalted" (Isa. 2:11) that—
>
> ". . . the nations . . . shall beat their swords into ploughshares, and their spears into pruning-hooks: nation shall not lift up sword against nation, neither shall they learn war any more" (Isa. 2:4).[4]

10. Taxation

Commentaries and Bible dictionaries on the whole cite no law governing taxation. One would assume, from reading them, that no system of taxation existed in ancient Israel, and that the Mosaic law did not speak on the subject. Galer, for example, can cite no passage from the law concerning taxation, although he lists various passages from the historical and prophetic writings which refer to confiscatory and tyrannical taxation. He does note, however, that the census was taken under the law "for tax purposes."[1]

This failure to discern any tax law is due to the failure to recognize the nature of Israel's civil order. God as King of Israel ruled from His throne room in the tabernacle, and to Him the taxes were brought. Because of the common error of viewing the tabernacle as an exclusively or essentially "religious," i.e., *ecclesiastical* center, there is a failure to recognize that it was indeed a *religious, civil* center. In terms of Biblical law, the state, home, school, and every other agency must be no less religious than the church. The sanctuary was thus the civil center of Israel and no less religious for that fact. Once this fact is grasped, much of Biblical law falls into clearer focus. There were, then, clearly defined taxes in the Mosaic law, and these taxes were ordered by God, the omnipotent King of Israel.

There were, essentially, two kinds of taxes. *First*, there was the poll tax (Ex. 30:11-16). The fact that atonement is cited as one of the aspects of this tax misleads many. The meaning of atonement here is

---

4. Clark, *Biblical Law*, p. 81.
1. Galer, *O.T. Law for Bible Students*, p. 52.

a covering or protection; by means of this tax, the people of Israel placed themselves under God as their King, paying tribute to Him, and gained in return God's protecting care. The civil reference of this tax is recognized in part by Rylaarsdam, who cites its relation to the census, "which is a military act."[2] The amount of this tax was the same for all men, half a shekel of silver, and it had to be paid by all men twenty years of age and over. The shekel at that time was not a coin but a weight of silver. Later on, the shekels were coined and were 220 grains troy (like a U.S. trade dollar), and a half shekel was thus about 110 grains.[3] This tax was the basic and annual tax in Israel. As Fairbairn noted,

> . . . there is the clearest proof of its having been collected both before and after the captivity; allusion is made to it in 2 Ki. xii. 4; 2 Ch. xxiv. 9; and both Josephus and Philo testify to its being regularly contributed by all Jews, wherever they were sojourning, and to a regular organization of persons and places for its proper collection and safe transmission to Jerusalem (Jos. Ant. xviii. 9, sec. 1; Philo, De. Monarch. ii. t, 2, p. 234). This, then, is what the collectors came to ask of Peter; and which, as having reference to a general and indisputed custom, he at once pledged his Master's readiness to give.[4]

The fact that it was called the temple tax in the New Testament era misleads many; the temple was the civil as well as the ecclesiastical center. At the temple, priests officiated who had nothing to do with civil law. But at the temple, the Sanhedrin met as the civil power in Israel, directly under the Roman overlordship.

This head tax is specified as equal for all. "The rich shall not give more, and the poor shall not give less" (Ex. 30:15). By means of this stipulation of an equality of taxation, the law was kept from being unjust. It had to be small, since a large amount would be oppressive for the poor, and it had to be the same for all, to avoid the oppression of the rich. Thus, discriminatory taxation was specifically forbidden. This tax was collected by the civil authority and was mandatory for all males, twenty years old and older, except for priests and Levites, who were not subject to military draft. The just and basic tax, the head tax, was paid to the civil authorities as the required tax for the maintenance of a covering or atonement by the civil order.

The *second* tax was the tithe, which was not paid in a central place but was "holy unto the LORD" (Lev. 27:32). It went to the priests and Levites as they met the necessary ecclesiastical and social functions of

---

2. Rylaarsdam, "Exodus," *Interpreter's Bible,* I, 1055.
3. George Rawlinson, "Exodus," in Ellicott, I, 303.
4. Patrick Fairbairn, *Fairbairn's Imperial Standard Bible Encyclopedia,* VI, 299.

society. Sometimes the Levites served in civil offices as well, as social conditions required it (I Chron. 23:3-5). Their work in music is well known to us from the Psalms as well as all Scripture, and their teaching duties are cited often, as witness II Chronicles 17:7-9 and 19:8-11. The Levites and priests were scattered throughout all Israel to meet the needs of every community, and they received these tithes as the people gave them.

Both forms of taxation, the head tax and the tithe, are mandatory, but a major difference exists between them. The state has a right to collect a minimal head tax from its citizens, but, while *perhaps* the state can require a tithe of all men, as has often been done, it *cannot* stipulate where that tithe shall go. The state thus controls the use of the head tax; the tither controls the use of the tithe tax. This is a point of inestimable importance. Since the major social functions are, in terms of Biblical law, to be maintained by the tithe, the control of these social functions is thus reserved to the tither, not the state. The head tax supports the state and its military power plus its courts. Education, welfare, the church, and all other godly social functions are maintained by the two tithes, the first tithe and the poor tithe. A society so ordered will of necessity have a small bureaucracy and a strong people.

The head tax is thus the support of the *civil* order, and the tithe is the support of the *social* order. In Biblical law, there is no land tax or property tax. Such a tax destroys the independence of every sphere of life and government—the family, school, church, vocation, and all else—and makes every sphere dependent on and subordinate to the state, or civil government.

Since Scripture declares repeatedly that "the earth is the LORD'S, and the fullness thereof" (Ex. 9:29; Deut. 10:14; Ps. 24:1; I Cor. 10:26, etc.), a land tax is not lawful. *A tax on the land is a tax against God and against His law-order.* God Himself does not tax the land which He gives to men as a stewardship under Him; He taxes their increase, or their production, so that the only legitimate tax is an income tax, and this is precisely what the tithe is—an income tax. But it is an income tax which is set at ten percent and no more. Beyond that, what a man gives is a freewill offering; the tithe is a tax, not an offering.

The subject of taxation belongs properly to both the sixth and eighth commandments. Ungodly taxation is theft. But the modern power to tax is the power to injure and to destroy, and it is thus basically connected with the sixth commandment· A Biblically grounded tax structure will protect and prosper a social order and its citizenry, whereas a lawless tax structure spells death to men and society.

Increasingly, the function of taxation is to re-order society. By means of property, inheritance, income, and other taxes, wealth is confiscated and re-distributed. Thus, the Organization for Economic Co-operation and Development (OECD) has declared, through its Secretary-General, that the number of people working in farming must be decreased, and, at the same time, "The average size of farm enterprises has to be increased."[5] How can this be done?

Two methods are open to the various states as disguised means of confiscating land and reshaping farmers and farming. *First*, price supports favor, as Kristensen pointed out, the big farmers rather than the small farmer. *Second*, taxation can be used to wipe out the small farmer and make room for large farm operations alone. Both methods are being extensively used, and both are forms of theft and means of murder, means of destroying men and societies.

The power to tax is in the modern world the power to destroy. It is no longer the support of law and order. The more taxes increase in the twentieth century, the less law and order men have, because taxation serves the purpose of promoting social revolution. As such, modern taxation is eminently successful.

11. Love and the Law

One of the most important of all humanists was Jean Jacques Rousseau, the father of democracy. Rousseau was a tramp, a "kept" man for Madame de Warens, and a thoroughly irresponsible man. He lived for many years out of wedlock with Therese Levasseur, a hotel employee. Five children were born to them, and all were immediately carted off by Rousseau to a foundling home. This great expert on child training could not be bothered with children. Rousseau was for virtue, and he tells us that he wept when he thought about it, but in action he was a totally irresponsible and vicious man. He believed his heart, and the heart of all men, to be good; organized society, the environment, makes men bad. A very typical act of this great humanistic reformer took place in Venice. Rousseau took a prostitute to his room. After she undressed, and they both lay down in bed, Rousseau began to beg her to take the path of virtue. He was, of course, in the wrong position for such a plea, but it mattered little to him. For Rousseau, the heart, the feelings of man, were everything.

Under the influence of such humanistic beliefs, law has been extensively eroded. It is no longer the *act* of the murderer which is judged, but his *feelings* or mental state in the commission of the act. Like Rousseau, a murderer may be not guilty by virtue of his mental state. Love, thus, as the great humanistic virtue, has become all-important. Those who belong to the party of love are the holy ones of the

5. Thorkil Kristensen, "Agricultural Policies Reconsidered," in *The OECD Observer* (December, 1938), no. 37, p. 6.

humanistic world even in the commission of crimes, whereas the orthodox Christian, as a hate-monger by definition, is guilty even in the non-commission of a crime.

Love does appear in the law, but in the context of law, not humanistic feelings. Love of neighbor is required by the Mosaic law in Leviticus 19:17, 18:

> Thou shalt not hate thy brother in thine heart; thou shalt in any wise rebuke thy neighbour, and not suffer sin upon him.
> Thou shalt not avenge, nor bear any grudge against the children of thy people, but thou shalt love thy neighbour as thyself: I am the LORD.

The Berkeley Version renders the latter half of verse 17, "lest you incur sin on his account," and the Torah Version reads it as "but incur no guilt because of him." The religious authorities during the second temple era read it as "but thou shalt bear no sin by reason of it," i.e., "execute the duty of reproof in such a manner that thou dost not incur sin by it."[1] St. Paul's explanation sums up the matter: "Love worketh no ill to his neighbour: therefore love is the fulfilling of the law" (Rom. 13:10). To love one's neighbor means to keep the law in relation to him, working him no ill, in word, thought, or deed. If a neighbor's course of action leads to evil, or to problems, a word of warning is to be given as a means of preventing him ill. The meaning of neighbor in this passage (Lev. 19:17, 18) is a fellow believer. In Leviticus 19:33, 34, it includes foreigners and unbelievers. The law of love here gives no grounds for trying to govern our neighbor, nor does it reduce love to a frame of mind: it is a principle which is manifested as a totality in word, thought, and deed. The Bible is not dualistic in its view of man: it does not recognize a good heart with evil deeds. Man is a unit. As a sinner, he is clearly evil. As a redeemed man, he is in process of sanctification, and thus manifests both good and evil, but an evil thought begets an evil deed as clearly as a godly thought begets a godly act. Rousseau mistook his fantasies and illusions concerning his heart and mind as the reality concerning himself, whereas he was evil in heart and mind, and therefore in his fantasies. "Every imagination of the thoughts" of man's heart is "only evil continually" (Gen. 6:5), and it is a part of that evil imagination for man to think well of his evil.

Because man is a sinner, he cannot take the law into his own hands: "Thou shalt not avenge" (Lev. 19:18). Because man is not God, man cannot therefore assume the judgment seat of God to judge men in terms of himself. We cannot condemn men for their likes or dislikes in terms of ourselves. We can judge them in relationship to God, whose

---

1. C. D. Ginsburg, "Leviticus," in Ellicott, I, 424 f.

law alone governs and judges all men. Personal judgment is forbidden: "Judge not . . ." (Matt. 7:1), but we are required to "Judge righteous judgment" (John 7:24).

The Pauline principle states the issue clearly with respect to love: *first*, it works no ill to his neighbor; *second*, love is the fulfilling of the law.

To work *ill* to one's neighbor is thus clearly forbidden. It is a form of *killing* our neighbor's life and liberty. The fact that both life and liberty are in view in this law appears from the case laws of Scripture. Thus, the only kind of slavery permitted is voluntary slavery, as Deuteronomy 23:15, 16 makes very clear. Biblical law permits voluntary slavery because it recognizes that some people are not able to maintain a position of independence. To attach themselves voluntarily to a capable man and to serve him, protected by law, is thus a legitimate way of life, although a lesser one. The master then assumes the role of the benefactor, the bestower of welfare, rather than the state, and the slave is protected by the law of the state. A runaway slave thus cannot be restored to his master: he is free to go. The exception is the thief or criminal who is working out his restitution. The Code of Hammurabi decreed death for men who harbored a runaway slave; the Biblical law provided for the freedom of the slave. The slave in the master's house shall dwell "in that place which he shall choose in one of thy gates, where it liketh him best (where he is most suited): thou shalt not oppress him" (Deut. 23:16).

Kidnapping a fellow believer to sell him as a slave (i.e., to a foreigner or foreign country, since he could not legally be sold at home) is a capital offense, punished without exception by death (Deut. 24:7). The death penalty applied not only to the kidnapper but to his associates who received or sold the person (Ex. 21:16). The force of this law is all the clearer when we realize that Biblical law had no prison sentences. Men either died as criminals or made restitution. Biblical law requires a society of free men whose freedom rests in responsibility.

Biblical law protected a man who accidentally killed a man, as in the case of two men chopping wood, and the axe-head of one flying off and killing the other. Cities of refuge protected the man from a blood feud (Deut. 19:1-10; cf. Ex. 21:13; Num. 35:9-22, 29-34).

Murder, however, was punishable by death (Deut. 19:11-13; Num. 35:23-28, 30-33; Lev. 24:17-22; Ex. 21:12-14, 18-32), and no exception to this sentence was permitted by law.

The test of love was thus the act of love. Love works no ill to the neighbor, and love means the keeping or fulfilling of the law in relationship to other men. Love is thus the law-abiding thought, word, and act. *Where* there is no law, there is also no love. Adulterous persons do not love their spouses, although they may claim to do so; they may enjoy their wives or husbands, as well as their lovers, but love is the keeping of the law.

Humanistic man, having forsaken law, must then logically forsake love also. There are already evidences of this. Lionel Rubinoff, himself a humanist, has described the modern problem of evil in *The Pornography of Power*. As a reviewer summarizes Rubinoff's thesis,

> It is, however, in his analysis of Robert Louis Stevenson's *Dr. Jekyll and Mr. Hyde* that the assumption underlying *The Pornography of Power* is most readily grasped. Of Stevenson's portrayal of the ambivalence of human nature, Rubinoff writes: "Dr. Jekyll, the humanist, originally creates Mr. Hyde (in itself a thoroughly evil act) so that the forces of evil incarnated in a Hyde can be scientifically studied and eventually banished from the human psyche. So confident is Jekyll in the iron strength of his own virtue that he sincerely believes he can give birth to evil without being corrupted by it. Alas, the virtuous Jekyll is no match for the satanic Hyde: once the demon has been released, the angel seeks every excuse to descend himself into the depths of depravity."

> Few men can comfortably contemplate the concept of the natural supremacy of evil over good in humanity. The Judaeo-Christian tradition eases the anguish by holding out the hope of salvation through the exercise of a semblence of free will in the worldly fight with the Devil's forces. What is an increasingly secular age to do with the knowledge that evil is an inextricable part of man's nature? Face it, says Rubinoff. Bring it out into the open.[2]

Thus, as some humanistic thinkers are beginning to recognize, man faces the world, not with love and goodness, but with *evil*. The more humanistic man becomes, the more justice, authority, and legitimacy fade from the world. Lawlessness increasingly governs national and international affairs. The expression of man's heart and imagination is only evil continually. Rubinoff admits that man's evil urge leads to a demonic use of power, to what he calls the pornography of power. Rubinoff's answer is not love but evil:

> The greatest evil in becoming addicted to such pornography, says Rubinoff, is that it stunts the growth of the imagination, the only instrument by which man can truly understand—and so live with— the despairing truth of his dual nature. As examples of how to use the creative imagination in facing up to evil, Rubinoff singles out Jean Genet and Norman Mailer. Much of their writing, he says is essentially an effort to create positive values by confronting the negative and the irrational within themselves, living with it and turning it into art.

Like most programs for self-improvement, Rubinoff's ideas are

---

2. "Facing It," a review of *The Pornography of Power* by Lionel Rubinoff, in *Time*, vol. 92, no. 26 (December 27, 1968), p. 66.

The Institutes of Biblical Law

easier to talk about than to apply. On one level, his book could encourage low-grade scatology as a form of salvation. On another, *The Pornography of Power* offers an esthetic substitute for religion, by which men less creative than Genet and Mailer must try to grope their way to self-knowledge with the aid of the artist's images of evil.[3]

Rubinoff's answer is that we become artistic rather than scientific Jekylls, creating a legion of Hydes. He proposes that we enter a world of love and law by embracing evil, by expressing it boldly and freely as an artistic and creative venture. It is a program of sinning to make grace abound. What Rubinoff has expressed, his humanistic generation is practicing. Students, slum dwellers, diplomats, politicians, clergymen, teachers, and others all now practice a lawless doctrine of evil as the higher law and the higher love. Since the humanistic doctrine of love is antinomian through and through, it is inescapably therefore *the love of evil*. It is thus a logical development of humanistic love that it should become evil incarnate. Love without law is in essence the affirmation of evil and its manifestation.

12. Coercion

A society without coercion is often dreamed of by humanistic revolutionists. Anarchism is of course that philosophy which maintains that man can find fulfilment only in a non-statist, voluntaristic, and non-coercive society. Libertarianism is increasingly an openly anarchistic and relativistic philosophy. Since the libertarian definition of anarchism is the best, let us examine this position as defined by Karl Hess, who, in the 1964 presidential campaign, was Senator Goldwater's writer:

> Libertarianism is the view that each man is the absolute owner of his life, to use and dispose of as he sees fit, that all men's social actions should be voluntary and that respect for every other man's similar and equal ownership of life and, by extension, the property and fruits of that life, is the ethical basis of a humane and open society.[1]

Moreover, Hess states, "each man is a sovereign land of liberty, with his primary allegiance to himself."[2] For Hess, man is not a sinner but rather his own god. The sinner, the great evil, is the state. As he analyzes liberals and conservatives on the issue of the state, Hess states:

> Just as power is the god of the modern liberal, God remains the authority of the modern conservative. Liberalism practices regimentation by, simply, regimentation. Conservatism practices regi-

---

3. *Ibid.*
1. Karl Hess, "The Death of Politics," in *Playboy*, vol. 16, no. 3 (March, 1969), p. 102.
2. *Ibid.*

mentation by, not quite so simply, revelation. But regimented or revealed, the name of the game is still politics.

The great flaw in conservatism is a deep fissure down which talk of freedom falls, to be dashed to death on the rocks of authoritarianism. Conservatives worry that the state has too much power over people. But it was conservatives who gave the state that power. . . . Murray Rothbard, writing in *Ramparts*, has summed up this flawed conservatism in describing a "new, younger generation of rightists, of 'conservatives' . . . who thought that the real problem of the modern world was nothing so ideological as the state *vs.* individual liberty, or government intervention *vs.* the free market; the real problem, they declared, was the preservation of tradition, order, Christianity, and good manners against the modern sins of reason, license, atheism and boorishness. . . ."

For many conservatives, the bad dream that haunts their lives and their political position (which many sum up as "law and order" these days) is one of riot. To my knowledge, there is no limit that conservatives would place upon the power of the state to suppress riots.[3]

Hess is right in stating that the conservative rests on "revelation," i.e., on "the preservation of . . . Christianity," and it is the failure of conservatism that it fails to see this, that it attempts to defend on humanistic premises a Christian product. But what does Hess's position rest on? The belief in man's goodness, man's ability to live without coercion or violence, and in the sovereignty of man does not rest on either experience, history, or reason. Hess here provides his own revelation out of himself. He calls for "communities of voluntarism" and summons man "to go it alone metaphysically in a world more of reason than religion."[4] While calling his position "not quite anarchy," Hess does not distinguish it from anarchism.[5]

Modern libertarianism rests on a radical relativism: no law or standard exists apart from man himself. Some libertarian professors state in classes and in conversation that *any* position is valid as long as it does not claim to be the truth, and that therefore Biblical religion is the essence of evil to them. There must be, according to these libertarians, *a total free market of ideas and practices.*

If all men are angels, then a total free market of ideas and practices will produce only an angelic community. But if all men are sinners in need of Christ's redemption, then a free market of ideas and practices will produce only a chaos of evil and anarchy. Both the libertarian and the Biblical positions rest on faith, the one on faith in the natural goodness of man, the other on God's revelation concerning man's sinful

---

3. *Ibid.*, p. 104.
4. *Ibid.*, p. 178.
5. *Ibid.*

state and glorious potential in Christ. Clearly the so-called rational faith of such irrationalism as Hess and Rothbard represent has no support in the history of man nor in any formulation of reason. It is a faith, and a particularly blind faith in man, which they represent.

A cardinal reason for the growing lawlessness of the twentieth century is precisely relativism and moral anarchism. An inquiring reporter in Fremont, California, asking "Should Unrestricted Abortions Be Legalized in California?" received among others this answer from A. W. S., a retired salesman:

> Yes. A woman should be able to have one if that's what she wants. It's up to the individual. In a way, it is taking a human life. But if it's a medical necessity, regardless of the person's wishes, it should be done.[6]

Let us examine this statement. *First,* it is admitted that abortion "is taking a human life," i.e., is *murder.* But, *second,* it is further asserted that a woman has this power over her foetus: "It's up to the individual." What is hers, is also hers to dispose of or to murder. By logic, this position, which holds to the individual's anarchic freedom, means also that a foetus, as a subordinate life, has no such freedom. Does this mean that a mother, as a superior person, can dispose of an unwanted child by murder, or a couple rid themselves of aged parents by murder? This is an implicit position, because, *third,* the woman's desire to retain the foetus can be over-ruled: "But if it's a medical necessity, *regardless of the person's wishes,* it should be done." In other words, more powerful and knowing persons in S's anarchistic society can decree death in terms of superior scientific wisdom. In an anarchistic world, where man is his only law, the consequences of anarchism are violence to the weak by the stronger, and the destruction of intelligence by brute force.

When the humanist deals with evil, he resorts to evasion to efface man's guilt. Thus, Steve Allen has observed, "I'm not completely convinced of it, but I think there is almost no evil *intent* in the world."[7] This distinction between *intent* and *act,* now so basic to humanistic law, goes back to Greek philosophy, and to Aristotle. It is ironic that modern humanists, who rail against dualism, should themselves resort to it so heavily. In terms of this distinction, a murderer can escape from the death penalty. The courts now are ready to regard the death penalty as possibly cruel and unusual punishment and hence illegal. One of the California cases involved is of a man guilty of three murders in much

---

6. "Inquiring Reporter," San Jose (Calif.), *Mercury,* Wednesday, March 19, 1969, p. 51.
7. Bob Shane, "TV Comedy Is up Steve Allen's Alley," in Los Angeles *Times* "Calendar," Sunday, March 23, 1969, p. 34.

less than a decade. In this kind of consideration for the murderer, the victim's rights are lost and denied.[8]

In Biblical law, the act is the intent. A murder involves a murderous intent. If an axe handle obviously breaks accidentally and suddenly flies and kills a man, the act is an accident and the intent and act are thus not murder, so the penalty is not for murder.

Because history so clearly manifests evil, it is only by resorting to the dualistic distinction between intent (spirit) and act (matter) that humanism is able to claim a natural goodness (or at least a neutral nature) for man.

How then does humanism account for the obviously evil intent of men who flagrantly broke the law during the Boston police strike? Or how shall they explain the 1969 violences in Pakistan, such as cited in this report:

> Dacca, East Pakistan (UPI)—Political turmoil in East Pakistan has spawned numerous "people's courts" in the interior that are summarily issuing sentences of death by clubbing or knifing, government sources and travelers reported Tuesday.
>
> "Madness is sweeping the rural areas," said one traveler on arriving here. He said he has spent the past week in villages and towns north of Dacca.
>
> "No one is safe," he said, "servants can turn against masters." He said the people's courts have no juries and always issue the death sentence, which is carried out immediately by peasants wielding clubs or knives.[9]

It is to be noted that the flagrant evil of the Nazis is omitted here, and the most flagrant evil of the Soviet Communists. How are all these things explained? The title of the Pakistan report reveals the answer: " 'Madness' Sweeps Pakistan." Similarly, a book review of Stalin's reign of terror is titled "Mad Efficiency for Extermination."[10] This is the answer: it is not that man is a sinner but that social conditions have incited man to this reflex action which is at worst madness and at best

8. Editorial, "Victims' Rights Are Lost." Santa Ana, California, *The Register* (Thursday [m], March 13, 1969), p. D-14.
9. " 'Madness' Sweeps Pakistan," Los Angeles *Herald-Examiner*, Wednesday, March 19, 1969, p. A-14.
10. Harrison Salisbury, "Mad Efficiency for Extermination," review of Robert Conquest: *The Great Terror: Stalin's Purge of the Thirties*, in *Saturday Review* (November 9, 1968), p. 52 f. A grim commentary on the humanist mind is the next review by O. Edmund Clubb, of Alberto Moravia: *The Red Book and the Great Wall*, entitled "The Good in Red Guard"; Moravia's book is a praise of the Chinese Red Guard. Moravia, a well-to-do writer, argues that the desirable state of man is to have nothing except what is necessary, and, in terms of this, Red China by its poverty is thus a utopia, something approaching perfection. Such words from a wealthy man concerning the poor Chinese are offered as wisdom, not sin. *Ibid.*, pp. 53, 74.

revolutionary heroism. Such reasoning rests on a blind faith in man
which is immune to facts.

Moreover, because humanistic thinking cannot account for evil
except as a temporary madness (and its answer, after Rubinoff, is to
give expression to this madness in order to exorcise it), humanism cannot deal with evil or coercion honestly. It denies evil in man as the basic
fact concerning fallen man's nature, and then it denies the legitimacy
of coercion. The two facts are related. If man, as in humanism, is his
own god, then how can that god be coerced? Coercion becomes then the
great evil for a logical humanism.

Is coercion ever legitimate? The Bible, clearly, has laws against
coercion in some forms, such as murder, kidnapping, and the like. Thus
in Leviticus 24:17-22, it is declared:

> And he that killeth any man shall surely be put to death.
> And he that killeth a beast shall make it good; beast for beast.
> And if a man cause a blemish in his neighbour; as he hath done, so
> shall it be done to him.
> Breach for breach, eye for eye, tooth for tooth: as he hath caused a
> blemish to a man, so shall it be done to him again.
> And he that killeth a beast, he shall restore it: and he that killeth
> a man, he shall be put to death.
> Ye shall have one manner of law, as well for the stranger, as for
> one of your own country: for I am the LORD your God.

The laws here stated appear also in Exodus 21:12 ff., 24, 25, 33, 34.
It is the principle of restitution, and the death penalty. *Unlawful coercion* faces a severe penalty in Biblical law. The murderer, as the man
guilty of the most extreme form of physical coercion, must *without
exception* be put to death. But, it must be noted, *coercion against evil-
doers is the required and inescapable duty of the civil authority.* God
requires coercion in the suppression of lawlessness. Without godly
coercion, the world is surrendered into the hands of ungodly coercion.
No man wants a hose of water turned against his living room, but, in
case of fire, that water is a necessity and a welcome help. Similarly,
coercion is a God-ordained necessity to enable man to cope with out-
breaks of lawlessness.

The humanistic perspective is schizophrenic. Because of its basic
dualism, it denies responsibility: intent and act are divorced. Works
of evil then become, not an expression of man's sinful heart, but a form
of strange madness. Man himself is basically good, or, at worst, after
Rubinoff, neutral, part angel and part devil. Instead of restraint, humanism demands self-expression. This, of course, is the death of law
and order and the rise of massive anarchy and coercion. In the name
of abolishing coercion, humanism ensures its triumph in the form of
lawless violence.

13. Quarantine Laws

The commandment, "Thou shalt not kill," has, as its positive requirement, the mandate to preserve and further life within the framework of God's law. Basic to this framework of preservation are the laws of quarantine.

In Leviticus 13–15, detailed laws of quarantine or separation are given. The *details* of these laws are not applicable to our times, in that they have an earlier era in mind, but the *principles* of these laws are still valid. It should be noted that these laws, in particular those dealing with leprosy, were enforced in the "medieval" era and were instrumental in eliminating that disease from Europe as a serious problem. The laws in these chapters are of two varieties: *first*, those dealing with diseases, Leviticus 13:1–15:15; and, *second*, those dealing with sex, 15:16-33; since sexual rites were commonly used as a means of communion with the gods, sex was emphatically separated from worship (Ex. 19:15). Ritual prostitution at temples was an accepted part of worship in the Mosaic era among pagans. Once again, sexual acts are being restored to a ritual role by the new pagans both within and without the church. Thus, Bonthius has written, "the act of intercourse is itself to serve as an outward and visible symbol of communion, not merely between man and wife but with God."[1]

To return to the quarantine laws with respect to diseases, those cited in Leviticus 13 and 14 are generally described as *leprosy* and *plague*. The term *leprosy* has changed its meaning extensively from its Biblical and "medieval" meaning.[2] The meaning then covered a variety of infectious diseases. In terms of this, the meaning of this legislation is that contagious diseases must be treated with all necessary precautions to prevent contagion. Legislation is thus necessary wherever society requires protection from serious and contagious diseases. The state has therefore a legislative power in dealing with plagues, epidemics, venereal diseases, and other contagious and dangerous diseases. Such legislation is plainly required in the Mosaic law (Num. 5:1-4). Not only is it declared to be a matter of civil legislation but an essential aspect of religious education (Deut. 24:8).

It is clear, however, that this legislation, requiring some kind of quarantine or separation for those who are diseased, or who handle the dead (Num. 5:2), has implications beyond the realm of physical

---

1. Robert H. Bonthius, *Christian Paths to Self-Acceptance* (New York: King's Crown Press, 1948, 1952), p. 213 f. See also Derek Sherwin Bailey, *The Mystery of Love and Marriage, A Study in the Theology of Sexual Relations* (New York: Harper), p. 24, as reviewed by Otto A. Piper in *Monday Morning* (September 15, 1952).

2. See A. Rendle Short, *The Bible and Modern Medicine* (London: Paternoster Press, 1953), pp. 74-83.

294   *The Institutes of Biblical Law*

diseases. Even as the risk of physical contagion must be avoided, so likewise the risk of moral contagion must be avoided. This is plainly stated:

> And the LORD spake unto Moses, saying,
> Speak unto the children of Israel, and say unto them, I am the LORD your God.
> After the doings of the land of Egypt, wherein ye dwelt, shall ye not do: and after the doings of the land of Canaan, whither I bring you, shall ye not do: neither shall ye walk in their ordinances.
> Ye shall do my judgments, and keep mine ordinances, to walk therein: I am the LORD your God.
> Ye shall therefore keep my statutes, and my judgments: which if a man do, he shall live in them: I am the LORD (Lev. 18:1-5).

> Defile not ye yourselves in any of these things: for in all these the nations are defiled which I cast out before you (Lev. 18:24).

> Therefore shall ye keep mine ordinance, that ye commit not any one of these abominable customs, which were committed before you, and that ye defile not yourselves therein: I am the LORD your God (Lev. 18:30).

> Ye shall therefore keep all my statutes, and all my judgments, and do them: that the land, whither I bring you to dwell therein, spue you not out.
> And ye shall not walk in the manners of the nation, which I cast out before you: for they committed all these things, and therefore I abhorred them.
> But I have said unto you, Ye shall inherit their land, and I will give it unto you to possess it, a land that floweth with milk and honey: I am the LORD your God, which have separated you from other people (Lev. 20:22-24).

As the last statement declares, God identifies Himself as the God who separates His people from other peoples: this is a basic part of salvation. The religious and moral separation of the believer is thus a basic aspect of Biblical law. Even as segregation from disease is necessary to avoid contagion, so separation from religious and moral evil is necessary to the preservation of true order.

Segregation or separation is thus a basic principle of Biblical law with respect to religion and morality. Every attempt to destroy this principle is an effort to reduce society to its lowest common denominator. *Toleration* is the excuse under which this levelling is undertaken, but the concept of toleration conceals a radical intolerance. In the name of toleration, the believer is asked to associate on a common level of total acceptance with the atheist, the pervert, the criminal, and the adherents of other religions as though no differences existed. The believer has a duty of lawful behavior toward all, an obligation to manifest grace and charity where it is due, but not to deny the validity of the differences which separate believer and unbeliever. In the name of toleration, the believer is asked to tolerate all things because the unbeliever will tolerate nothing; it means life on the unbeliever's terms. It means that Biblical order is denied existence, because all things must be levelled downward.

An example, albeit a mild one, of this intolerance appeared in the Ann Landers column:

> Dear Ann Landers: Why do you pin orchids on the virgins without knowing the facts? If you could see some of those white flower girls you'd know they couldn't give it away. Why not use your valuable newspaper space to praise the sought-after, sexy girl who is constantly chased by men and is sometimes caught?
>
> I'm a woman in my middle forties who has worked ten years with young girls in a steno pool. I see the goody-goody types in their little white shirt-waist blouses and oxfords, so smug and proud of their chastity, as if they had a choice. They make me sick.
>
> Only last Friday a darling little readhead, just 21, sobbed out her story in the ladies' room. Lucy had been jilted by an executive after six months of steady courtship. They had been intimate and she was counting on marriage. It was the fourth time she'd had this terrible thing happen to her. Girls like Lucy need Ann Landers to tell them they aren't all bad. Give them encouragement, not a put-down. I've been reading your silly column for 12 years and I think you are a perfect fool.—Mama Leone.
>
> Dear Mama: Thanks for the compliment, but nobody's perfect.
>
> I don't happen to have any good conduct medals lying around for girls who think the bedroom is a shortcut to the altar. Moreover, a girl who makes the same mistake four times is what I call (in polite language) a non-learner.[3]

This letter by "Mama Leone" reveals a bitter hatred of virtue together with a strong sympathy for the promiscuous girl, who is seen as the finer person. There is no tolerance here, but only a savage intolerance.

The basic premise of the modern doctrine of toleration is that all religious and moral positions are equally true and equally false. In brief, this toleration rests on a radical relativism and humanism. There is no particular truth or moral value in any religion; the true value is man himself, and man as such must be given total acceptance, irrespective of his moral or religious position. Thus, Walt Whitman, in his poem, "To a Common Prostitute," declared, "Not till the sun excludes you, do I exclude you." *Total acceptance and total integration* are demanded by this relativistic humanism. Thus, this position, by reducing all non-humanistic positions to equality, and then setting man

---

3. Ann Landers, "Four Falls a Bad Decision," in Los Angeles *Herald-Examiner* (Tuesday, March 25, 1969), p. B-3.

above them as lord, is radically antichristian. It places man in God's place and, in the name of toleration and equality, relegates Christianity to the junk-heap.

But integration and equality are myths; they disguise a new segregation and a new inequality. "Mama Leone's" letter makes clear that, in her view, promiscuity is superior to virginity. This means a new segregation: virtue is subjected to hostility, scorn, and is separated for destruction.

Every social order institutes its own program of separation or segregation. A particular faith and morality is given privileged status and all else is separated for progressive elimination. The claim of equality and integration is thus a pretext to subvert an older or existing form of social order.

State control of education has been a central means of destroying Christian order. It excludes from the curriculum everything which points to the truth of Biblical faith and establishes a new doctrine of truth. In the name of objective reason, it insists that its highly selective hostility to Biblical faith be regarded as a law of being.

Education is a form of segregation, and, in fact, a basic instrument thereof as well. By means of education, certain aspects of life and experience are given the priority of truth and others are relegated to unimportance or are classed as wrong. Education inescapably segregates and classifies all reality in terms of certain premises or presuppositions. These premises are religious premises and are always pre-theoretical and are determinative of all thinking.

Not only education but law also segregates. Every law-order, by legislating against certain types of conduct, requires a segregation in terms of its premises. The segregation demanded by the democratic and the Marxist states is as radical and thorough as any history has seen, if not more so.

All religions segregate also, and humanism is certainly no exception. Every religion asserts an order of truth, and every other order is regarded as a lie. Humanism is relativistic with respect to all other religions, but it is absolutistic with respect to man. Man is the absolute of humanism, and all else is treated as error.

Segregation, separation, or quarantine, whichever name is used, is inescapable in any society. The radical libertarian claims that he will permit total liberty for all positions, i.e., a free market for all ideas and religions. But he outlaws all positions which deny his own. In the academic world these libertarians have proven to be ruthless enemies of Biblical faith, denying its right to a hearing. The state cannot exist, in such a libertarian order, nor can the church except on the enemy's terms. The new libertarians are congenial to Marxists, but not to Christians. While ostensibly against coercion, they are not above a common front with Marxists, as the libertarian journal *Left and Right* indicated. For the truth of Scripture, they have no toleration, nor any "common front" except a surrender on their terms. Every faith is an exclusive way of life; none is more dangerous than that which maintains the illusion of tolerance. An openly heartless faith is surely dangerous, but a heartless faith which believes in itself as a loving agent is even more to be feared.

Because no agreement is possible between truth and a lie, between heaven and hell, St. Paul declared, "Wherefore come out from among them, and be ye separate, saith the Lord, and touch not the unclean thing: and I will receive you" (II Cor. 6:17).

14. Dietary Rules

Eating and drinking are clearly regulated by Biblical law. The laws of diet, or *kosher* laws, are generally well known, but, unfortunately, here as elsewhere man in his perversity sees law, which was ordained as a principle of life, instead as a restraint on life. Moreover, the Biblical principle of eating and drinking is not ascetic: the purpose of food and drink is not merely to maintain life, important as that is, but is a part of the *enjoyment* of life. The usual picture of a robust, jolly medieval monk or priest as somehow reprobate as against the emaciated ascetic as a saint is probably in need of revision. According to Scripture, "every man should eat and drink, and enjoy the good of all his labour, it is the gift of God" (Eccles. 3:13). Note that it reads "*every* man." Again, "Behold, that which I have seen: that it is good and comely for one to eat and to drink, and to enjoy the good of all his labour that he taketh under the sun all the days of his life, which God giveth him: for it is his portion" (Eccles. 5:18). However, it should be noted that "every man that striveth for the mastery is temperate in all things" (I Cor. 9:25).

In Genesis 1:29, 30, it would appear that, prior to the flood, only permission to eat non-carnivorous foods is given, whereas in Genesis 9:3, the permission to eat meats is obviously given.[1] There is no reason to assume that any return to this original diet is possible. Again, there is reason to believe that, after the fall, permission to eat meats may have been granted. God clothed the fallen Adam and Eve in coats of skin (Gen. 3:21), and the use of cattle appeared very early. Very early, with Jabal, of the line of Cain, specialization in cattle work appeared (Gen. 4:20), indicating a demand for the meat. God's instructions to Noah before the flood referred to the distinction between clean

---

1. H. C. Leupold, *Exposition of Genesis* (Columbus, Ohio: Wartburg Press, 1942), pp. 97 f., 329 f.

and unclean beasts as an established one, indicating the legitimacy of
the distinction at least for sacrifice and probably for food. Moreover,
the warrant for meat-eating is a divine one and remains unchanged.
As a matter of fact, one of the marks of "seducing spirits, and doctrines
of devils" in "the latter times" is "Forbidding to marry, and commanding to abstain from meats, which God hath created to be received with
thanksgiving of them which believe and know the truth" (I Tim. 4:
1, 3). Religious vegetarianism thus is very sharply condemned.

The laws of diet appear in a number of passages, centrally in Leviticus 11. The reaction of most people to this legislation is that it is
strange, difficult, and oppressible to follow. In reality, the Mosaic laws
of diet are basic to the patterns of virtually every Christian country.
Certain notable breaches of these laws are apparent, but in the main the
laws are obeyed. In examining these laws, one problem is the translation
of some of the animal names. Thus, the "coney" of Leviticus 11:5 is
said to be "hyrax syriacus, a form of rock rabbit,"[2] also called a "rock
badger,"[3] but there is no certainty.

Our purpose is not to examine each particular animal but to understand the general classifications involved. According to Leviticus 11:3,
"Whatsoever parteth the hoof, and is cloven-footed, and cheweth the
cud, among the beasts, that shall ye eat." Exceptions to this rule are
also cited. With respect to sea foods, fins and scales are required, or
else the food is banned (Lev. 11:9-10). Again, a list of banned birds
is given (Lev. 11:12-19). Insects that crawl are banned, and, except
for a few exceptions, all winged insects also (Lev. 11:20-23). A variety
of animals is cited in Leviticus 11:29, 30 as forbidden. The eating of
blood is banned (Lev. 17:10-14; 19:26), as is animal fat (Lev. 7:
26, 27). Dead animals are also ruled out (Deut. 14:21). These rules
appear in Deuteronomy (14:3-20) as well as in Leviticus. In both
cases, it is given as a law of holiness (Deut. 14:1-3; Lev. 11:44-47).

Certain general rules appear in this list: *First*, the eating of blood
is forbidden on principle; the animal cannot be strangled; it must be
bled. This rule is restated in Acts 15:20. *Second*, dead, i.e., un-
butchered, animals are ruled out also. In both these cases, most Christian countries are in agreement. Pagan cultures have had no objections
normally to either dead animals or to blood. For some, the discovery
of a dead animal has been the discovery of a delicacy.

Third, animal fats are forbidden. This rule has not been observed, but it
is significant that modern medical advice tends to rule against animal fats.

---

2. Nathaniel Micklem, "Leviticus," *Interpreter's Bible*, II, 56.
3. Burton L. Goddard, *Animals of the Bible* (Lancaster, Pennsylvania: National Foundation for Christian Education, 1963), p. 27.

The Biblical ban does not extend to vegetable fats, nor, apparently, to poultry fats.

Fourth, with respect to animals and birds, and in most cases, fish also, the scavenger animals are forbidden foods. Here again the tastes of the Western world have been radically altered by Biblical law. Many of the ancient delicacies included scavengers. Among sea foods, shell fish are banned for this reason. Among fish, the partial exception is the carp, which is permitted, and is not placed in the banned class, since it has both fins and scales. The catfish, however, is forbidden. In eating kosher meats, the "scavenger" organs are banned, i.e., those organs which work to clear the body of impurities. Some recent medical testimony tends to support this ban.

The kidneys are clearly forbidden (Ex. 29:13, 22; Lev. 3:4, 10, 15; 4:9; 8:16, 25); these same verses refer also to the liver. These organs were dedicated, i.e., to be burned on the altar and not eaten. Liver is nowadays regarded as *kosher* meat by Jews. The King James Version limits the ban to "the caul that is above the liver" (Ex. 29:13); other versions render this as "the membrane." The Berkeley Version gives it as the "lobe" of the liver. Bush made it clear that "lobe" is the correct reading, i.e., "the greater lobe of the liver," and probably the gall-bladder, which is "attached to this part of the liver," is also forbidden food.[4]

Fifth, carnivorous animals are forbidden food, as witness the lion, dog, and the like. And without exception, these animals are avoided in countries influenced by Christian law. In pagan societies, as among some American Indian tribes, the dog was regarded as a choice food.

Thus far, the modern divergences are slight. The marked exceptions are the horse in France, and pork and shell fish in most countries. Pigs as scavengers are banned, and the fact that some authorities cite them as carriers of over 200 diseases is of note, as well as the fact that it is almost impossible to eliminate all of these by cooking.

Sixth, as is apparent, herbivorous animals are clearly allowed, unless they neither chew the cud nor divide the hoof. The horse thus is banned. Grain-feeding birds are also among the permitted foods, but not birds of prey.

Seventh, almost all insects except those of the locust family are forbidden. These were permitted but not prized food, usually survival fare (Lev. 11:22). When John the Baptist lived in the wilderness to typify the coming destruction and flight of the people, he lived on locusts and wild honey (Matt. 3:4), i.e., he lived off the land to typify the

---

4. George Bush, *Notes, Critical and Practical, on the Book of Exodus* (Boston: Young, 1870 [1841],) I, 180.

survival fare which would become national fare for the survivors of the coming destruction.

Eighth, no legislation is given with respect to fruits, grains, eggs, and vegetables. All these are clearly legitimate and require no lines of division as among meats. Taste, value, and practicality are the governing rules here.

Ninth, although very obvious rules of health appear in the legal prohibitions, the primary principle of division is religious, of which the medical and hygienic is a subordinate aspect. The terms used are *clean* and *unclean*, and the forbidden foods are an *abomination*; religious and moral purity is clearly in mind, of which hygienic purity is a part.

Tenth, not only was the flesh of animals which had dropped dead forbidden, but also of animals torn by wild beasts (Ex. 22:31); such an animal, if it died, had to be fed to the dogs. Since foreigners had no scruples about eating the meat of animals which died, and often were partial to them, such animals could honestly be sold for what they were to foreigners (Deut. 14:31). There was no attempt to regulate the diet of unbelievers.

Eleventh, also forbidden were all foods and liquids remaining in uncovered vessels in the tent or room of a dying or dead man (Num. 19: 14, 15). The purpose here was to preserve *cleanness* in its total sense.

Twelfth, as noted with respect to other laws, it was forbidden to seethe a kid in its mother's milk (Ex. 23:19; 34:26; Deut. 14:21). The Ras Shamra tablets indicate that such seething was a Canaanite sacred ritual. It would appear that the fertility cults believed that they could either stimulate or destroy fertility at will, since it was under their control.

Thirteenth, out of reverence for Jacob's wrestling with the Angel of the Lord, the Israelites denied themselves the sinew of the hip (Gen. 32: 32). This was not a law, however.

Fourteenth, with temperance as the rule, wines were an acceptable part of the diet. Distilled liquors are a modern invention. Wines were a part of the legitimate offerings to God (Num. 15:5, 7, 10). The use of wines, being governed by God, and governed by His law of temperance, was on the whole temperate. To this day, alcoholism is rare among Jews. The New Testament warnings against intemperance are many (Eph. 5:18; I Tim. 3:3, 8; Titus 1:7; 2:3; I Peter 4:3, etc.). On the other hand, St. Paul urged Timothy to drink a little wine for his health's sake (I Tim. 5:23). Wine was commonly used with water as a mixer (II Macc. 15:39).

In the patriarchal era, the diet included not only meats but leguminous foods (beans, peas, lentils) as a favorite food (Gen. 25:34).

Honey, spices, and nuts are also mentioned (Gen. 43:11). Milk was an important item in the diet of Israel, but more than cows' milk was used. Goats' milk and sheep's milk are both mentioned (Deut. 32:14; Prov. 27:27). Butter is often mentioned (Deut. 32:14; Prov. 30:33), as is cheese (I Sam. 17:18; II Sam. 17:29). Raisins and dried figs were common (I Sam. 25:18), date cakes (II Sam. 16:1), and the like. Game meats were favored (I Kings 4:23; Neh. 5:18), in addition to domestic meats.

To what extent are the Mosaic dietary laws still valid for us? Acts 10 is commonly cited as abolishing the old dietary restrictions. There is no reason for this opinion. Peter's vision did not instruct him to eat pork, dogs, cats, or the like: it prepared him for the coming of Cornelius' servants. The Gentiles were to be received into the kingdom: "What God hath cleansed, that call not thou common" (Acts 10:15). Peter did not see the meaning of the vision as a permission to eat forbidden foods. Rather, he said, "Ye know how that it is an unlawful thing for a man that is a Jew to keep company, or come unto one of another nation; but God hath shewed me that I should not call any man common or unclean" (Acts 10:28). There is no evidence in the chapter that the vision had anything to do with diet; it did have everything to do with the Great Commission and the admission of Gentiles into the kingdom.

However, in Colossians 2:16, 17, there is a clear reference to the dietary laws:

> Let no man therefore judge you in meat, or in drink, or in respect of an holyday, or of the new moon, or of the sabbath days;
> Which are a shadow of things to come: but the body is of Christ.

The significance of this has been noted with respect to the sabbath law. The sabbath law is no longer law for us, in that it no longer is a civil and religious offense to fail in one's observance, but it is a principle of life and a moral rule. Similarly, the dietary laws are not legally binding on us, but they do provide us with a principle of operation. The apostles, as they moved into a Gentile world, did not allow diet to be a barrier between them and the Gentiles. If they were served pork or shrimp, they ate it. On their own, they maintained the kosher rules as God's rules of health and life. St. Paul rebuked St. Peter to his face when he withdrew from the Gentiles, with whom he had been eating, because of fear of criticism on the part of some Judaizers (Gal. 2:9-15). With reference to our salvation, the laws of diet have no significance, although Phariseeism gave it such a significance (Gal. 2:16). With reference to our health, the rules of diet are still valid rules. We do not observe the sabbath of Israel, but we do observe the Lord's day. We do not regard the kosher legislation as law today, but we do observe it as a sound rule for health.

It is ironic that those churchmen who deny that Colossians 2:16 has any reference to the sabbath have still used it to deny totally any validity to the laws of diet. If the dietary laws are totally abrogated, so is the sabbath. But both remain, not as laws but as principles for the health of man, the sabbath for man's spirit, and the rules of diet for man's body. Our observance of these dietary rules should never be to place a barrier between ourselves and other men but for our health and prosperity in Christ.

15. Christ and the Law

The cross of Christ is often cited as being the death of the law, and it is commonly stated that in Christ the believer is dead to the law. Romans 7:4-6 is cited as evidence for this opinion, although nothing is said about Romans 8:4. St. Paul's point is that we are free from the law, or dead to the law, as a sentence of death against us, but we are alive to it as the righteousness of God. Christ, as our substitute, died for us, and we are dead unto the law in Him, and also alive unto the law in Him. The very death of Christ *confirmed* the law: it revealed that God regards the death penalty as binding for violation of His law, so that only the atoning death of Christ could remove the curse of the law against sinners.

In Ephesians 2:1-10, St. Paul makes clear again the meaning of the law in relationship to the cross. In commenting on St. Paul's description of sinners as "dead in trespasses and sins" (vs. 1), Calvin stated:

> He does not mean that they were in danger of death; but he declares that it was a real and present death under which they laboured. As spiritual death is nothing else than the alienation of the soul from God, we are all born as dead men, and we live as dead men, until we are made partakers of the life of Christ,—agreeably to the words of our Lord, "The hour is coming, and now is, when the dead shall hear the voice of the Son of God, and they that hear shall live" (John v. 25).[1]

In this condition of spiritual death, men are governed by demonic forces and impulses in fulfilment of their own sinful nature (vss. 2, 3) as "children of disobedience"; Calvin commented on this latter phrase, "Unbelief is always accompanied by disobedience; so that it is the source—the *mother* of all stubbornness."[2] Very bluntly, Calvin affirmed after St. Paul "that we are born with sin, as serpents bring their venom from the womb."[3]

---

1. John Calvin, *Commentaries on the Epistles of Paul to the Galatians and Ephesians,* William Pringle Translation (Grand Rapids: Eerdmans, 1948), p. 219.
2. *Ibid.,* p. 221 f.
3. *Ibid.,* p. 223.

What then is the remedy for man? Clearly, the remedy is *not* the law. Man has broken the law, is dead in sin and *cannot* keep the law. Calvin pointed out, of Ephesians 2:4, that "there is no other life than that which is breathed into us by Christ: so that we begin to live only when we are ingrafted into him, and begin to enjoy the same life with himself."[4] Our salvation is *entirely* of God's grace, *totally* His work (vs. 8). In Calvin's words, "God declares that he owes us nothing; so that salvation is not a reward or recompense, but unmixed grace. . . . If, on the part of God, it is grace alone, and if we bring nothing but faith, which strips us of all commendation, it follows that salvation does not come from us." The faith itself is the gift of God (vs. 8). *All* Scripture is emphatic: God is man's only redeemer; the law is not given as man's way of salvation but as God's way of righteousness, His law for His chosen people, His kingdom. The law therefore came "through Moses" (John 1:17)—from God through Moses—because it is the law for God's kingdom. Where converted into a way of salvation, the law is perverted. Where the law represents the government and obedience of faith, there the law fulfils its God-given purpose. In Calvin's words again, "man is nothing but by divine grace."[5]

In Ephesians 2:10, St. Paul declares, "For we are his workmanship, created in Christ Jesus unto good works, which God hath before or-dained that we should walk in them." Calvin noted,

> He says, that, before we were born, the good works were prepared by God; meaning, that in our own strength we were not able to lead a holy life, but only as far as we are formed and adapted by the hand of God. Now, if the grace of God came before our per-formances, all ground of boasting has been taken away.[6]

Plainly, therefore, we are regenerated "unto good works," that is, unto obedience to God's law-word, and the purpose of our salvation, or-dained beforehand by God, is this obedience.

But, some object, the law is called "carnal" in Scripture, as witness Hebrews 7:16. Calvin stated, "It was called *carnal*, because it refers to things corporeal, that is, to external rites."[7] When St. Paul summons believers to "temperance," he is asking for obedience in a "carnal," that is, corporeal matter as well as with respect to an attitude of mind (Gal. 5:23).

The calling of believers is unto liberty, which means, St. Paul said, to love one another, i.e., to fulfil the law in relationship to one another

---

4. *Ibid.*, p. 224.
5. *Ibid.*, p. 229 f.
6. *Ibid.*, p. 231.
7. John Calvin, *Commentaries on the Epistle to the Hebrews*, John Owen translation (Grand Rapids: Eerdmans, 1949), p. 169.

(Gal. 5:13-14). In relationship to our fellow men and to God, the works of our fallen human nature are these:

> Adultery, fornication, uncleanness, lasciviousness, Idolatry, witch-craft, hatred, variance, emulations, wrath, strife, seditions, heresies, Envyings, murders, drunkenness, revellings, and such like: of the which I tell you before, as I have told you in time past, that they which do such things shall not inherit the kingdom of God.

> But the fruit of the Spirit is love, joy, peace, longsuffering, gentle-ness, goodness, faith, Meekness, temperance: against such there is no law (Gal. 5:19-23).

St. Paul attacked the law as a saving ordinance, as man's way of sal-vation; he upheld the law as man's way of *sanctification* rather than justification. After citing lawless behavior, beginning with adultery, he cites godly behavior and says of it, "against such there is no law." Obviously, against the other catalogue of actions, beginning with adul-tery, *there is a law*, the law as given by God through Moses.

Thus, clearly, the law still stands. The implication of St. Paul's words is that there is a law against the catalogue of sins of Galatians 5:19-21; moreover, in terms of Ephesians 2:10, we are God's new creation for the purpose of keeping His law and performing good works.

In what sense, then, is the law dead, or even wrong, and in what sense does it still stand?

First, as we have seen, the law as a sentence of death is finished when the guilty party dies or is executed. For believers, the death of Christ means that they are dead in Him to the death sentence of the law, since Christ is their substitute (Rom. 7:1-6). This does not permit us to call the law "sin," for the law itself made us aware of our sinfulness before God, and our need of His Savior (Rom. 7:7-12).

Second, our salvation in Jesus Christ sets forth the salvation by God's gracious act which is the *only* doctrine of salvation all Scripture sets forth. The sacrificial and ceremonial law set forth the fact of sal-vation through the atoning act of a God-given substitute, an animal whose innocence typified the innocence of the one to come. The Mes-siah, the Lamb of God, having come, the old, typical laws of sacrifice and their priesthood and ceremonies were succeeded by the atoning work of Christ, the great High Priest (Heb. 7). It is a serious error to say that the *civil law* was also abolished, but the *moral law* retained. What is the distinction between them? At most points, they cannot be distinguished. Murder, theft, and false witness are clearly civil offenses as well as moral offenses. In almost every civil order, adultery and dishonoring parents have also been civil crimes. Do these people mean, by declaring the end of civil law, that the Old Testament theocracy is no more? But the kingship of God and of His Christ is emphatically asserted by the New Testament and especially by the book of Revelation. The state is no less called to be under Christ than is the church. It is clearly *only* the sacrificial and ceremonial law which is ended because it is replaced by Christ and His work.

Third, the law is condemned by the New Testament as a means of justification, which it was never intended to be. The law is not our means of justification or salvation, but of sanctification. Phariseeism had perverted the meaning of the law and made it "of none effect," according to Christ's declaration (Matt. 15:1-9). What the Pharisees called the law was "the commandments of men" (Matt. 15:9), and against this Christ and St. Paul levelled their attack. The law in this sense *never* had any legitimate status and must in every age be condemned. The alternative to antinomianism is not Phariseeism or legalism. The answer to those who want to save man by law is not to say that man needs no law.

Phariseeism or legalism leads to statism. If law can save man, then the answer is that society must work to institute a total law order, to govern man totally by laws and thus remake man and society. This is the answer given by statism, which invariably draws its strength from Pharisaic religion. Socialism and communism are saving law orders, and the call by preachers of the social gospel for a "saving society" is an expression of faith in *man's law* as savior. This latter point is important: God's law does not permit itself to be assigned a saving role, and as a result man devises a humanistic law-order for the total regeneration of man and society by means of total government. Biblical law has a limited role; a saving law must have an unlimited power, and as a result, Biblical law is replaced by Phariseeism with a total law. The modesty of God's law was an offense to the Pharisees. Thus, whereas the law required only one fast a year, on the Day of Atonement, and then only until sundown, the Pharisees fasted twice a week (Luke (18:12). A yearly fast which ended in a banquet involved no government over man; a twice-weekly fast both governs man and becomes a means of self-commendation before God and man.

The law is thus to be condemned when it is made into more than law, when it is made into a savior, or a favor done to God rather than man's necessary obedience and response to God's mandate and calling. Law is law, not salvation, and the law as savior leads to statism and totalitarianism.

Antinomianism, on the other hand, leads to anarchism. Religious antinomians are usually practical rather than theoretical anarchists. Their disinterest in law leads them to surrender the civil order to the enemy and to further the decline of law and order. Although antinomians would be shocked if called anarchists, they must be so desig-

nated. The logical implication of their position is anarchism. If Christ
has abolished the law, why should society maintain it? If the Christian is dead to the law, why should not the Christian church, state,
school, family, and calling be also dead to the law? A consistent faith
on the part of antinomians would require them to be anarchists, but
perhaps consistency is itself too much of a virtue, too much of a law,
and too intelligent a position to ask from such stupidity.

The law in every age sets forth the *holiness* of God. The holiness of
God is His absolute distinction from all His creature and creation, and
His transcendent exaltation above them in His sovereign and infinite
majesty. This separation of God is also His moral separation from
sin and evil and His absolute moral perfection. As Berkhof noted,

> The holiness of God is revealed in the moral law, implanted in man's
> heart, and speaking through the conscience, and more particularly in
> God's special revelation. It stood out prominently in the law given
> to Israel.[8]

There can be no holiness, no separation unto God, without the law of
God. The law is indispensable to holiness.

The law is also basic to the righteousness of God. Again, Berkhof's
phrasing is to the point:

> The fundamental idea of righteousness is that of strict adherence to
> the law. Among men it presupposes that there is a law to which
> they must conform. It is sometimes said that we cannot speak of
> righteousness in God, because there is no law to which He is sub-
> ject. But though there is no law above God, there is certainly a law
> in the very nature of God, and this is the highest possible standard,
> by which all other laws are judged. A distinction is generally
> made between the absolute and the relative justice of God. The
> former is *that rectitude of the divine nature, in virtue of which God
> is infinitely righteous in Himself*, while the latter is *that perfection
> of God by which He maintains Himself over against every violation
> of His holiness, and shows in every respect that He is the Holy One.*
> It is to this righteousness that the term "justice" more particularly
> applies.[9]

The righteousness of God is revealed in the law of God, and the norm
by which men are declared to be sinners is their violation of God's law.
The sin of Adam and Eve was their violation of God's law, and the
criterion of a man's faith is the fruit he bears, his works, in brief his conformity to the law of God, so that the law is his new life and nature
(Matt. 7:16-20; James 2:17-26; Jer. 31:33). In the neglect or defiance of God's law, there can be neither righteousness nor justice. To
forsake God's law is to forsake God.

8. Louis Berkhof: *Systematic Theology* (Grand Rapids: Eerdmans, 1941,
1946), p. 74.
9. *Ibid.,* p. 74 f.

The law is also basic to *sanctification*. Sanctification cannot be confused, as Berkhof pointed out, with mere moral rectitude or moral improvement.

> A man may boast of great moral improvement, and yet be an utter stranger to sanctification. The Bible does not urge moral improvement pure and simple, but moral improvement in relation to God for God's sake, and with a view to the service of God. It insists on sanctification. At this very point much ethical preaching of the present day is utterly misleading: and the corrective for it lies in the presentation of the true doctrine of sanctification. Sanctification may be defined as *that gracious and continuous operation of the Holy Spirit, by which He delivers the justified sinner from the pollution of sin, renews his whole nature in the image of God, and enables him to perform good works.*[10]

According to St. Paul, "faith cometh by hearing, and hearing by the word of God" (Rom. 10:17); the law is written into every fiber of that word. If this law-word is basic to faith and to hearing, it is clearly basic to the believer's growth in sanctification. Sanctification depends on our law-keeping in mind, word, and deed. The perfection of the incarnate Word was manifested in His law-keeping; can the people of His kingdom pursue their calling to be perfect in any way other than by His law-word?

If the law is denied as the means of sanctification, then, logically, the only alternative is Pentecostalism, with its antinomian and unbiblical doctrine of the Spirit. Pentecostalism does, however, represent a very logical outgrowth of antinomian theology. If the law is denied, how is man then to be sanctified? The answer of the Pentecostal movement was an attempt to fill this lack. Protestant theology left man justified but without a way to be sanctified. The holiness movement, with its belief in the instant perfection of all believers, ran so clearly counter to common sense: any observer could see that the holiness people were and are extremely far from perfection! The answer of Protestant Pentecostals and Roman Catholic ascetics and ecstatics has been this doctrine of the Spirit. Ostensibly super-normal and antinomian manifestations of the Spirit place the believer on a higher plane. Many parallel movements, like Keswick, cultivate this higher way as the alternative to law for sanctification. These movements at least represent a logical concern for sanctification, although an illicit one. Deny the law, and your alternatives are either indifference to sanctification, or Pentecostalism and similar doctrines.

The disinterest in or contempt for canon law is a part of this antinomianism.

To separate the law from the gospel is to separate oneself from the law

---

10. *Ibid.*, p. 532.

and the gospel, and from Christ. When God the Father regarded the law as so binding on man that the death of God's incarnate Son was necessary to redeem man, He could not regard that law as something now trifling, or null and void, for man. Man is saved "that the righteousness of the law might be fulfilled" in him (Rom. 8:4). To say that man is no longer under the law, and yet obliged to avoid murder, adultery, theft, false witness, and other sins, is to play with words. Either a law is a law and is binding, or it is no law, and man is not bound but is free to commit those acts.

The commandment, "Thou shalt not kill," means that man's life cannot be taken. Is not the perversion of the word of life a means of taking or injuring life? Must not false preachers be termed murderers? In an age when the foundations of law are under attack, the faithful servant of God will most zealously and clearly proclaim that law. In Martin Luther's words,

> If I profess with the loudest voice and clearest exposition every portion of the truth of God except precisely that little point which the world and the devil are at the moment attacking, I am not confessing Christ, however boldly I may be professing Christ. Where the battle rages, there the loyalty of the soldier is proven, and to be steady on all the battlefield besides, is merely flight and disgrace if he flinches at that point.

With Adam's fall, man fell, and God's law-order was broken. With Christ's victory, man in Christ triumphed, and God's law-order was restored, with its mandate to exercise dominion under God and to subdue the earth. Can any man of God proclaim less?

16. Work

Normally, *work* is considered as properly an aspect of the fourth commandment: "Six days thou shalt labour . . ." (Ex. 20:9), and this is most obviously a valid classification. Some compelling reason is necessary, therefore, to justify placing *work* elsewhere. This purpose is to be found in the original mandate, to subdue or work the earth, and to exercise dominion over it (Gen. 1:28). Work continued obviously after the fall, now with a curse on it, and with frustration (Gen. 3:17, 18), but with an obviously restorational function. By work man was originally called to subdue the earth; after the fall, man knew the frustration of sin in this calling. With the fall came a curse on man's work, but work is not a curse. With redemption, the effects of sin are steadily overcome as man works to restore the earth and to establish his dominion under God. Man, life, and the earth have been injured and killed by the effects of sin. To undo the fall, to protect and prosper life under God, means that, under the sixth commandment, man has a mandate to restore the earth by work and to inhibit and limit the injuring and killing effect of sin. The importance of *restitution* to the law is the ground whereby *work*, an aspect of the fourth commandment, is also properly an aspect of the sixth. It is also an aspect of the eighth, for "Thou shalt not steal" means "Thou shalt work" to gain whatever is needed and desired. The goal of restitution is the restored Kingdom of God as described by Isaiah 11:9: "They shall not hurt nor destroy in all my holy mountain: for the earth shall be full of the knowledge of the LORD as the waters cover the sea."

Work thus has a position of importance in Biblical thought. Proverbs repeatedly stresses its necessity, dignity, and importance; "he that gathereth by labour shall increase" (Prov. 13:11). "The hand of the diligent shall bear rule: but the slothful shall be under tribute" (Prov. 12:24). "The soul of the sluggard desireth, and hath nothing: but the soul of the diligent shall be made fat" (Prov. 13:4). "Seest thou a man diligent in his business? he shall stand before kings" (Prov. 22:29).

Work thus has as its goal the restored Kingdom of God; work therefore is a religious and moral necessity.

The effect of work as a factor in the rehabilitation of the mentally retarded is a major one. Where morons have been taken from institutions to work in factories, the results have been very good on the whole. The morons have enjoyed the work, performed it successfully, and sometimes have been regarded as the superior workmen by employers. The employers have often responded by stating that these employees appear to be as intelligent as any others.[1]

Among Hutterites, subnormal and neurotic people are treated with Christian patience but without relativism. Authority and differences are recognized.[2] The Hutterites have a religious distrust of psychologists and psychiatrists.[3] By accepting subnormals and neurotics and giving them a disciplined and accepted place in society, they make them useful and happy members of their culture. The Hutterites as a whole, with their strong belief in work from a Christian perspective, are mentally healthy and show an absence of psychosomatic and stress-induced diseases. The list of significantly lower problems includes chronic insomnia, drug addiction, asthma, food allergies, hay fever, suicides, urinary tract infections, male impotence, fear of death, coronary heart diseases, obesity, cancer, constipation, spastic colitis, menstrual disorders, female frigidity, and the like.[4]

---

1. Niall Brennan: *The Making of a Moron* (New York: Shield and Ward, 1953), pp. 13-18.
2. Joseph W. Eaton and Robert J. Weil: *Culture and Mental Disorders, A Comparative Study of the Hutterites and other Populations* (Glencoe, Illinois: The Free Press, 1955), p. 121.
3. *Ibid.*, p. 166.
4. *Ibid.*, p. 234 f.

The Hutterite "psychiatry" insists on fitting the "patient" into the "strait-jacket" of cultural conformity; it requires that the faith and life of the group be respected and maintained. "Hutterite 'psychiatry' is future-oriented." It looks ahead in Christ and demands that the individual think less of himself and more of God's requirements.[5] Because Hutterite society is a *working* society, it requires purposive work of all its members.

Moreover, no impossible burden is placed on the individual: "Taking their cue from the dogma that man is born to sin, they do not expect perfection from anyone."[6] This realism concerning man is productive of mental health. The Hutterites thus heal their neurotic members and make useful and happy their mentally retarded members by means of work.

The restorative function of work is well established. Its usefulness in dealing with neurotic and retarded persons is clearly recognized. But this function of work simply reflects a part of the basic nature of work for all society, for all men. It is the God-given means whereby man establishes dominion over the earth and realizes his calling under God.

Man should therefore enjoy work and delight in it. On the contrary, however, escape from work is a common desire among men. The lure of Marxism and similar faiths is their declaration that man is fettered to work and must be freed from it. More recently, the claim is made that automation can abolish work and that a free society is one *freed from work*. Two things which are in clear contradiction seem nonetheless all too prevalent among men, *first*, a recognition of the curative nature of work, and, *second*, a flight from work as slavery.

Why this contradiction? The contradiction exists first of all in man's being and then in man's society. Man knows in the depths of his being that work is his destiny under God, that it is his self-realization as well as his calling, that a man's manhood is essentially tied to his ability to work and his development in terms of work. But, at the same time, man comes face to face with the fact of the fall, with God's curse on his work (Gen. 3:17-19), and man flees from this reality. The curse is there, and he knows it, but, rather than recognize that he is the sinner, in rebellion against God, man frets and revolts against work, because work reveals to him the fact of the fall and the curse. Work is his calling, but his calling lays bare the ruinous work of sin in history. The moron may find contentment in work, but most men who are in rebellion against God progressively find in work their frustration, and they will not face up to the reason for it. They then either try to drown that frus-

---

5. *Ibid.*, pp. 175-178.
6. *Ibid.*, p. 192.

tration in more work, or they turn to play as a substitute for work. Socialist dreamers capitalize on man's frustration. With this frustration as their capital, they offer man a utopia in which the curse has supposedly been abolished by the abolition of a certain class of men who are called the exploiters. Somehow then paradise will be restored. According to Marx, man will be freed from the curse on man and work by the socialist paradise, in which the division of labor will disappear:

> For as soon as labour is distributed, each man has a particular, exclusive sphere of activity, which is forced upon him and from which he cannot escape. He is a hunter, a fisherman, a shepherd, or a critical critic, and must remain so if he does not want to lose his means of livelihood; while in communist society, where nobody has one exclusive sphere of activity but each can become accomplished in any branch he wishes, society regulates the general production and thus makes it possible for me to do one thing to-day and another to-morrow, to hunt in the morning, fish in the afternoon, rear cattle in the evening, criticize after dinner, just as I have a mind, without ever becoming hunter, fisherman, shepherd or critic.[7]

As Gary North points out, *"Marx's concept of human alienation was used by him as a substitute for the Christian doctrine of the fall of man."*[8] In all such thinking, man is in flight from reality and therefore from work. The worker today, whether a union member, an office worker, or an executive, all too often lives to escape work. But the escape from work to play is no escape from the basic problem, and, as a result, man's flight continues, back to work, into play, liquor, anywhere but into responsibility. The result is that man shows a chronic discontent combined with self-righteousness. But, as Brennan noted, "Anger, impatience, self-righteousness, are all the symptoms of a human being out of touch with reality. And being out of touch with reality is only a broad definition of insanity."[9] When man is in flight from reality, he is less concerned with *being* someone than with *seeming* to to be someone, with appearances rather than reality.[10] The culture then becomes radically dislocated, as this radical spiritual poverty makes hypocrisy and appearances more important than life itself. "The poor may suffer from reality, but that is better than suffering from make-believe."[11] Since the world is maintained in its social and cultural order and progress by work, not make-believe, a world in which make-believe gains the ascendency is a world moving toward collapse.

7. Karl Marx and Friedrich Engels: *The German Ideology, Parts I & II* (New York: International Publishers, 1947), p. 22.
8. Gary North: *Marx's Religion of Revolution* (Nutley, New Jersey: The Craig Press, 1968), p. 53.
9. Brennan, *op. cit.,* p. 35.
10. *Ibid.,* p. 183.
11. *Ibid.,* p. 140.

An age in which actors and actresses are public idols and heroes is a world of make-believe. Between World Wars I and II, the Hollywood actors and actresses very extensively dominated the minds of youth and adults. They have since given way to prominent socialites and jet-setters, but with these new pace-setters, the ideal remains the same, appearance and make-believe. Their new religion being appearance, the language of religion is applied to the techniques of appearance. As a prominent count and member of these "international nomads" (the jet set or cafe society) has reported:

> "Between the hair stylist and the woman," Alexandre stated to me, in a most articulate manner, caressing ever so softly his beard, "a complete communion is necessary like in a church [sic]. In order to reach this relationship there must be full confession of the client to the man she trusts with one of her most precious possessions: her locks."[12]

An actor-dominated society (and the actors need not be professionals; they may be a populace in love with appearances) is a consumption-centered society: it progressively loses its capacity to produce. In its insane self-absorption and enchantment with appearances, it commits a narcissistic suicide.

The socialist finds it easy to oppose the actor: it is ostensibly reality versus dreams. But the socialist too is in a flight from reality, equally enamored of appearances. The actor is often readily both an actor and a socialist because the two worlds are basically one. Marx's dream of man "freed" from work to be fisherman, hunter, cattleman, or critic at will is a social dream as well as a personal one. Instead of dealing with man's fallen nature, Marx dreamed of a new world to remove the curse from work. The actor and socialist are very much at peace with one another; they are united in their hostility to covenant man.

The decline of productivity and the rise of make-believe are thus signs of a society in decline. Continued very long, they point to the death of a society. "Thou shalt not kill" has as its affirmative formulation the protection and furthering of life under God and in terms of His law-word. Work is an important aspect of this free and restored life.

17. Amalek

For centuries, Assyria was scarcely known to many historians, who discounted the Biblical narrative and questioned whether so great an empire existed. The same neglect has even longer prevailed with respect to Amalek, in very ancient times "the first of the nations" (Num. 24: 20). Its origin is misunderstood even by Biblical scholars, who derive it

---

12. Lanfranco Rasponi: *The International Nomads* (New York: G. P. Putman's Sons, 1966), p. 153.

from Esau's grandson, Amalek (Gen. 36:12, 16). But, long before this Amalek's birth, the nation Amalek existed (Gen. 14:7).

Amalek is identified, with some interesting evidence, with the Hyksos by Velikovsky.[1] This identification certainly dove-tails with the narrative of Exodus 17:8-16.

The importance of Amalek to Biblical law has reference to a judgment pronounced by God against it, with God's covenant people being entrusted with its execution. Since a decree of judgment is an aspect of law, it must be considered in any discussion of law, especially when it is included in the legal code.

After Israel left Egypt, Amalek met and attacked them (Ex. 17:8-16). Two passages describe the encounter in terms of God's sentence:

> And the LORD said unto Moses, Write this for a memorial in a book and rehearse it in the ears of Joshua: for I will utterly put out the remembrance of Amalek from under heaven.
> And Moses built an altar, and called the name of it Jehovah-nissi:
> For he said, because the LORD hath sworn that the LORD will have war with Amalek from generation to generation (Ex. 17:14-16).
>
> Remember what Amalek did unto thee by the way, when ye were come forth out of Egypt.
> How he met thee by the way, and smote the hindmost of thee, even all that were feeble behind thee, when thou wast faint and weary; and he feared not God.
> Therefore it shall be, when the LORD thy God hath given thee rest from all thine enemies round about, in the land which the LORD thy God giveth thee, for an inheritance to possess it, that thou shalt blot out the remembrance of Amalek from under heaven: thou shalt not forget it (Deut. 25:17-19).

This passage states several things. *First,* in some sense Amalek was at war against God. The psalmist later cited Amalek as one of the conspiring nations: "For they have consulted together with one consent: they are confederate against thee" (Ps. 83:5, 7). Samuel declared to Saul, "Thus saith the LORD of hosts, I remember that which Amalek did to Israel, how he laid wait for him in the way, when he came up from Egypt. Now go and smite Amalek, and utterly destroy all that they have and spare them not: but slay both man and woman, infant and suckling, ox and sheep, camel and ass" (I Sam. 15:2-3). In I Samuel 28:18 reference is made to God's "fierce wrath upon Amalek." As the foregoing verses make clear, *second,* God was also at war against Amalek. *Third,* Israel had been attacked by Amalek and been savagely treated. *Fourth,* Israel was required to wage war unto death against

---

1. Immanual Velikovsky, *Ages in Chaos* (Garden City, N. Y.: Doubleday, 1952), pp. 55-101.

Amalek. This war, *fifth*, was to continue from generation to generation, and the remembrance of Amalek was to be blotted out.

To examine these points more carefully, *first*, what was the offense of Amalek against God? The Hebrew of Exodus 17:16 can be read "Because the hand of Amalek is upon (or against) the throne of heaven, therefore the Lord will have war. . . ."[2] Certainly God's enmity towards Amalek indicates that in some sense Amalek's hand was raised *against* God; hence, Moses' arms had to be raised *to* God to indicate Israel's dependence on God.

The seriousness of Amalek's offense is reflected in the Talmud. Thus, R. Jose taught, "Three commandments were given to Israel when they entered the land; (i) to appoint a king; (ii) to cut off the seed of Amalek; (iii) and to build themselves the chosen house (i.e., the Temple) and I do not know which of them had priority."[3] The Talmud showed awareness of the humanistic horror concerning God's judgment on Amalek and ascribed this horror to Saul in one of its legends:

> When the Holy One, blessed be He, said to Saul: *Now go and smite Amalek*, he said: If on account of one person the Torah said: Perform the ceremony of the red heifer whose neck is to be broken, how much more (ought consideration to be given) to all these persons! And if human beings sinned, what has the cattle committed; and if the adults have sinned, what have the little ones done? A divine voice came forth and said: *Be not righteous overmuch.*[4]

Rawlinson pointed out, with reference to Exodus 17:16, "Amalek, by attacking Israel, had lifted up his hand against the throne of God, therefore would God war against him from generation to generation."[5]

And old tradition specifies the nature of Amalek's warfare against God and Israel:

> Midrashic lore reveals how the Amalekites made themselves particularly hateful by cutting off "the circumcised members of the Israelites" (both prisoners and corpses), tossing them into the air and shouting with obscene curses to Yahweh: "This is what you like, so take what you have chosen!" This tradition is deduced from Deuteronomy 25:18, "and cut off the tails of all your stragglers," . . . alluding to Amalek's harassment of the Hebrews at Rephidim during the Exodus.[6]

The verb form "cut off the tail" can mean "to castrate," or, used as a military image, as in Joshua 10:19, its one usage other than Deuter-

---

2. Bush, *Exodus*, I, 222. Bush regarded this as "by no means an improbable interpretation," although not adopting it.
3. Sanhedren 20 b, Seder Nezikin, III, 109.
4. *Yoma* 22b, in *Seder Mo'ed*, III, 101.
5. George Rawlinson, "Exodus," in Ellicott, I, 252.
6. Allen Edwardes, *Erotica Judaica, A Sexual History of the Jews* (New York: Julian Press, 1967), p. 56.

onomy 25:18, it can mean, as rendered in the King James, "smote the hindmost," the stragglers. It may have this military usage in both cases, but the ancient tradition which cites castration as Amalek's act has perhaps truth behind it. It accounts for both the divine wrath against and the prophetic horror for, Amalek: blasphemy and perversity met in Amalek's cruel act. Amalek hated Israel because Amalek above all else hated God: hence its radical perversity with respect to Israel. This perversity continued into Esther's day in the attempt of Haman to destroy all the Jews (Esther 3).

Second, God was at war with Amalek, and this warfare is to be continued "from generation to generation" (Ex. 17:16). Note the distinction: Israel's war against Amalek is to continue until Amalek and its "remembrance" is blotted out, and Amalek as an empire is today indeed forgotten, but God's war is "from generation to generation." It is not presuming upon the text but in conformity with Biblical typology to recognize here a declaration of God's continuing warfare, from generation to generation, with the Amalekites of every age, race, and nation.

Perverse violence, contempt for God and for man, has commonly marked fallen man. Consider, for example, the report of Maurice R. Davies:

> "In Africa, war captives are often tortured, killed, or allowed to starve to death. Among the Tshi-speaking peoples 'prisoners of war are treated with shocking barbarity.' Men, women and children—mothers with infants on their backs and little children scarcely able to walk—are stripped and secured together with cords round the neck in gangs of ten or fifteen; each prisoner being additionally secured by having the hands fixed to a heavy block of wood, which has to be carried on the head. Thus hampered, and so insufficiently fed that they are reduced to mere skeletons, they are driven after the victorious army for month after month, their brutal guards treating them with the greatest cruelty; while, should their captors suffer a reverse, they are at once indiscriminately slaughtered to prevent recapture. Ramseyer and Kuhne mention the case of a prisoner, a native of Accra, who was 'kept in log,' that is, secured to the felled trunk of a tree by an iron staple driven over the wrist, with insufficient food for four months, and who died under this ill-treatment. Another time they saw amongst some prisoners a poor, weak child, who, when angrily ordered to stand upright, 'painfully drew himself upright showing the sunken frame in which every bone was visible.' Most of the prisoners seen on this occasion were mere living skeletons. One boy was so reduced by starvation, that his neck was unable to support the weight of his head, which, if he sat, drooped almost to his knees. Another equally emaciated, coughed as if at the last gasp; while a young child was so weak from want of food as to be unable to stand. The Ashantis were much surprised that the missionaries should exhibit any emotion at such spectacles; and, on one occasion when they went to give food

to some starving children, the guards angrily drove them back."
Both the regular army and the levies in Dahomey show an equal
callousness to human suffering. "Wounded prisoners are denied
all assistance, and all prisoners who are not destined to slavery are
kept in a condition of semi-starvation that speedily reduces them
to mere skeletons. . . . The lower jaw bone is much prized as a
trophy . . . and it is very frequently torn from the wounded and
living foe. . . ." The scenes that followed the sack of a fortress in
Fiji "are too horrible to be described in detail." That neither age
nor sex were spared was the least atrocious feature. Nameless
mutilations inflicted sometimes on living victims, deeds of mingled
cruelty and lust, made self-destruction preferable to capture. With
the fatalism that under lies the Melanesian character many would
not attempt to run away, but would bow their heads passively to the
club stroke. If any were miserable enough to be taken alive their
fate was awful indeed. Carried back bound to the main village, they
were given up to young boys of rank to practice their ingenuity in
torture, or stunned by a blow they were laid in heated ovens; and
when the heat brought them back to consciousness of pain, their
frantic struggles would convulse the spectators with laughter.[7]

Usually such matters are treated as evidences of primitivism, as evolutionary survivals in man rather than as evidence of his fallen nature.
Civilized man, no less than the tribes of Africa and Melanesia, is given
to perverse violence, to cruelty, and a delight in cruelty. The communist terror far surpasses the tribal terror in perversity, violence, and
scope. The evidence is here all too extensive.[8]

The use of terror is a routine political fact in the modern world of
humanism. Men are killed ostensibly to save man and society, and the
universal love of mankind is proclaimed with total hatred. Man exercises perverse violence as a means of asserting omnipotence. "To be
as God," this is man's sin (Gen. 3:5), and yet man cannot exercise
omnipotence or power to create a new world or a new man. Man turns
therefore to destruction as a means of asserting his claim to omnipotence.
As O'Brien, in *1984*, declared, "We shall squeeze you empty, and then
we shall fill you ourselves."[9] As Orwell had O'Brien say, in a famous
passage:

> Power is in inflicting pain and humiliation. Power is in tearing
> human minds to pieces and putting them together again in new
> shapes of your own choosing. Do you begin to see, then, what kind
> of world we are creating? It is the exact opposite of the stupid

7. M. R. Davies, *The Evolution of War* (Yale University Press, 1929),
p. 298 f., cited in Georges Bataille, *Death and Sensuality* (New York: Ballantine,
1969 [1962]), p. 72 f.
8. See, for example, Harold M. Martinson, *Red Dragon over China* (Minneapolis: Augsburg, 1956); Albert Kalme, *Total Terror* (New York: Appleton-
Century-Crofts, 1951); Richard Wurmbrand and Charles Foley, *Christ in the
Communist Prisons* (New York: Coward-McCann, 1968).
9. George Orwell, *1984* (New York: Signet, 1950 [1949]), p. 195.

hedonistic Utopias that the old reformers imagined. A world of
fear and treachery and torment, a world of trampling and being
trampled upon, a world which will grow not less but *more* merciless
as it refines itself. Progress in our world will be progress toward
more pain. The old civilizations claimed that they were founded on
love and justice. Ours is founded upon hatred. In our world there
will be no emotions except fear, rage, triumph, and self-abasement.
Everything else we shall destroy—everything. Already we are
breaking down the habits of thought which have survived from
before the Revolution. We have cut the links between child and
parent, and between man and man, and between man and woman.
No one dares trust a wife or a child or a friend any longer. But in
the future there will be no wives and no friends. Children will be
taken from their mothers at birth, as one takes eggs from a hen.
The sex instinct will be eradicated. Procreation will be an annual
formality like the renewal of a ration card. We shall abolish the
orgasm. Our neurologists are at work upon it now. There will be
no loyalty, except loyalty toward the Party. There will be no love,
except the love of Big Brother. There will be no laughter, except the
laugh of triumph over a defeated enemy. There will be no art, no
literature, no science. When we are omnipotent we shall have no
more need of science. There will be no distinction between beauty
and ugliness. There will be no curiosity, no employment of the
process of life. All competing pleasures will be destroyed. But always—do not forget this, Winston—always there will be the intoxi-
cation of power, constantly increasing and constantly growing
subtler. Always, at every moment, there will be the thrill of victory,
the sensation of trampling on the enemy who is helpless. If you
want a picture of the future, imagine a boot stamping on a human
face—forever.[10]

Here, plainly stated, the sin of man comes to self-realization. In order
to play at god, to gain the sensation of omnipotence, total terror
and total destruction, effected with full perversity, are man's way of
godhood.

But this perverse violence, a *pseudo-omnipotence*, brings forth God's
wrath, so that, "from generation to generation," God's enmity to every
Amalekite remains. As surely as the first Amalek was blotted out,
and in Haman, the last of the known Amalekites, so the Amaleks and
Amalekites of today are under judgment, and to be obliterated. Note
the destiny of Haman:

And Harbonah, one of the chamberlains, said before the king,
Behold also the gallows fifty cubits high, which Haman had made
for Mordecai, who had spoken good for the king, standeth in the
house of Haman. Then the king said, Hang him thereon.

So they hanged Haman on the gallows that he had prepared for
Mordecai. Then was the king's wrath pacified (Esther 7:9, 10).

10. *Ibid.*, p. 203.

Third, Israel was attacked by Amalek. According to Deuteronomy 25:17, Amalek "feared not God." Amalek's attack on Israel, according to the "Midrashic lore," was an obscene defiance of God and a contempt for God. Where men attack God's people, there we often have a covert or overt attack on God. Unable to strike directly at God, they strike at God's people. There is thus continual warfare between Amalek and Israel, between God's people and God's enemies. The outcome must be the blotting out of God's enemies.

Thus, *fourth*, the covenant people must wage war against the enemies of God, because this war is unto death. The deliberate, refined, and obscene violence of the anti-God forces permits no quarter.

Fifth, this warfare must continue until the Amalekites of the world are blotted out, until God's law-order prevails and His justice reigns.

Because God's omnipotence is total, the pseudo-omnipotence of man, the would-be god, is also total in its vain imaginations. This pseudo-omnipotence becomes progressively more and more violent, more and more perverse. It does not mellow. Its goal is the manifestation of sheer power, and, because it cannot manifest power to regenerate, it manifests power to destroy.

The typology of Moses' upraised hands (Ex. 17:11, 12) tells us of the means whereby Amalek is to be destroyed: with a full-scale offensive on all fronts, but always with a full reliance on the Lord, who is the only ground of victory.

18. Amalek and Violence

It is not surprising that a lawgiver, Solomon, spoke of the feverish desire for violence on the part of wicked men. They cannot sleep, he observed, unless they do evil: it is their life and joy to do harm, "and their sleep is taken away, unless they cause some to fall" (Prov. 4:16). Their nourishment, the food that is the life of their being, Solomon described as "the bread of wickedness, and . . . the wine of violence" (Prov. 4:17). Solomon, as a law-giver and teacher, felt that the recognition of this fact was important.

For some, "evil" is simply misplaced righteousness. The basically sound impulses of sound humanity can be misdirected into destruction or socially sterile channels; in this view, man's need is not judgment but redirection. Solomon's premise was man's depravity: the wicked enjoy their evil; it is their life and their way of life. The statement is made by Wertham, who begins with false premises, "If we do not start from sound premises, we leave the door open to false ones."[1] His basic tenet

---

1. Fredric Wertham, M.D., *A Sign for Cain, An Exploration of Human Violence* (New York: Paperback Library, 1969 [1966]), p. 23.

is environmentalism, although he tries, inconsistently, to retain responsibility.[2]

Wertham reports a number of interesting examples of violence, as, for example, the following:

> Recently two middle-aged women in Brooklyn on a summer evening were walking on a side street toward one of the larger avenues, after visiting a friend nearby. They intended to take a taxi home. About 250 feet from the avenue, a group of boys came up, crowding the sidewalk. The women drew back to let them pass. The last boy grabbed the right arm of one woman, to take her purse, then knocked her down on the sidewalk and jumped on her again and again. When she was taken to the hospital, it was found that she had a broken shoulder, broken elbow, broken arm, and a compound fracture of her right thighbone, for which an elaborate operation was necessary. She needed three nurses around the clock. And when she recovers, she will have to wear a brace from her hip to her heel and will be permanently crippled, with one leg shorter than the other. In my professional contact with this case, I learned what terrible pain and shock were caused—and that the expenses involved wiped out a family's savings. There was no sexual connotation to this attack. Since the boy had the pocketbook, there was no reason for pure gain to explain his stomping the woman so mercilessly.
>
> Twenty-five years ago this would have been an exceptional case and would have caused a sensation. Now it did not raise a ripple and was not even reported as news. It happens too often. The boys were never caught; if they had been caught, the authorities would not have known what to do with them. This is today's violence in pure culture. I have known a number of similar cases. They are as a rule not fully reported, far less solved or resolved. Those who use the fashionable explanation for violence, that it is due to domineering mothers or inadequate ones, to pent-up aggressive instincts or a revolt against early toilet training, do not know the current facts of life in big American cities. They try to reduce ugly social facts to the level of intriguing individual psychological events. In this way they become part of the very decadence in which present-day violence flourishes.[3]

To cite one more example from Wertham:

> A boy of thirteen was walking home from school in a suburban area. A short distance from the house, a car roared up and several boys jumped out. They attacked and beat him unmercifully. Then they jumped back into the car and roared away. Their victim was taken to the hospital with severe facial lacerations and concussion of the brain. He did not know his attackers and had never seen them before.[4]

---

2. *Ibid.,* pp. 3, 48, 49-74, etc.
3. *Ibid.,* p. 10 f.
4. *Ibid.,* p. 258.

320 *The Institutes of Biblical Law*

These are not extreme cases, and they are printable ones. Some of the most depraved instances of perverse violence involve sexual assaults. In cases known to this writer, no excuse of a repressive environment could be offered: the guilty persons came from loving, congenial, and permissive backgrounds where no religious inhibitions concerning sex prevailed. Instead of free, loving personalities, these persons manifested startling imaginations in their perversity and depravity.

Not only do we have this unorganized, spontaneous violence, but planned violence in the form of rioting, looting, demonstrating, and warring against the police is increasingly in evidence.[5]

As we have seen, the essence of this obscene violence is its pseudo-omnipotence. Since man cannot become the Creator God, he seeks to be a devil-god. Milton's Satan declared,

> To reign is worth ambition, though in Hell
> Better to reign in Hell than serve in Heaven
> (*Paradise Lost*, I, 262-263).

To reign as the devil-god, man must also deny and wage war against the God of Scripture. The Soviet Union in 1923 declared, "We have declared war on the Denizens of Heaven," and, again, in 1924, "The Party cannot tolerate interference by God at critical moments."[6] To abolish God and prove evolution, the Soviet scientists actually sent an expedition to Africa in the mid-twenties to create a new race by trying to fertilize apes artificially with human semen.[7] Right and wrong as objective values were abolished. Krylenko, the state prosecutor, "urged the judges to remember that in the Soviet State their decisions must not be based on whether the prisoner be innocent or guilty, but on the prevailing policy of the Government and the safety of the State." This view was stated also in Krylenko's book, *Court and Justice*.[8] When men seek to supplant God, they supplant God's justice with their perversity and violence.

When men begin to free themselves from God's law-order, and to manifest their violence, certain developments appear. *First*, violent men, because their violence is a religious act, a manifestation of pseudo-omnipotence, try to provoke a religious awe by means of *shock*. By fresh and new acts of violence, new reactions of shock are provoked. The violent feed on this fresh awe. The degenerate hoodlum who indulges in unprovoked acts of violence delights in the shocked response

5. See *Rights in Conflict*, a report submitted by Daniel Walker (New York: Boston Books, 1968).
6. R. O. J. Urch, *The Rabbit King of Russia* (London: The Right Book Club, 1939), p. 115.
7. *Ibid.*, p. 82 f.
8. *Ibid.*, p. 208.

of his victim, and of those who hear or read of his acts. The readiness sometimes of such people to confess, whether to law authorities, clergymen, friends, or even strangers, is due to this religious pleasure in the shock of violence. It feeds their lust for power.

Second, this need for a fresh shock means a continual stepping up in the *intensity* and *perversity* of violence. Violence leads to greater violence. Nothing is more absurd than the idea of some that violent acts purge the degenerate of his lust for violence: there is no "catharsis," but rather only a greater addiction. Violence does not cure itself. To wait for violence to pass away or to dissipate itself is like waiting for the sun to turn cold. Violence does not abdicate: it is either destroyed, or it destroys.

Third, the liberals and socialists believe that the answer to violence is a change of environment, by legislation, statist action, or social planning. Some hold that *love* is the cure for the violent. Pietistic Christians believe that *conversion* is the answer: the violent must be reached with the gospel offer and become born again. Some men may need love; however questionable this idea may be, let us grant it for the moment. All men do need regeneration, clearly, but again evangelism is not the answer to all problems, although it must be always operative. The restraint of the law and its punishment must at all times be operative for a society to exist in which love and evangelism can function. Violent men need conversion, or execution if they continue in violence to the point of incurring the death penalty. On the other hand, if not enough regenerate men exist in a society, no law-order can be maintained successfully. Thus, a healthy society needs an operative law-order and an operative evangelism in order to maintain its health. The law-order can keep the residue of violent men in check if it is at all times nourished by strict enforcement and the progressive growth of men in terms of the ministry of grace. In brief, love, conversion, and law-order can never be substitutes for one another: each has its place and function in social order.

Fourth, it is not surprising that we have a violent generation, in that everything has been done to flout God's law-order: education has become statist; discipline has given way to permissiveness; the church has replaced the doctrine of regeneration with social revolution, and, instead of executing incorrigible criminals in terms of God's law, society today largely subsidizes these incorrigibles. A violent generation has been fostered, and is on the increase. Not surprisingly, by 1969, the incidence of narcotics and lawlessness was greater on the high school level than on the college level. The younger the child, the more lawless his potential and his mental outlook. The very fact that violence is being fostered more intensively in the young will serve to step up the *increase in the prevalence of violence* as well as in its *intensity* and *perversity.*

Fifth, although the 1960's saw more talk about love than any previous era, no age saw less love and more hatred. Romantic love, for better or for worse, long the major theme of popular music, gave way to other themes. Winick wrote of "the virtual disappearance of idealized romantic love as a guiding principle" in popular song. Where the word "love" appears, as in the song "Careless Love," it refers to other things— in "Careless Love" to pregnancy before marriage.

> One of the most successful phonograph records ever released was "Hound Dog," a paean of hostility and a representative early rock-and-roll number with traditional chord progressions. The Marquis de Sade would have been thrilled by "boots," a more recent favorite. Nancy Sinatra is sure of a wild surge of applause when she grinds her heels into the stage as she triumphantly exults that her boots will "walk over you."[9]

A generation which thrills to this song of violence will also thrill to the Marquis de Sade. As a result, his works, long banned in every country, are now being published and promoted with high praises. The Marquis de Sade is the man of today. A generation has been reared to believe, however much it deceives itself with talk of brotherhood, that violence is the fulfilment of man, and the more perverse the violence, the more fulfilment it affords. The humanistic remedies for violence are about as effective as gasoline is in putting out a fire.

Sixth, a society which breeds violence and fosters it is characterized also by a phenomenon known as running amok (or amuck). The word comes from the Malay, among whom it is a common event. It has also been found among Fuegians, Melanesians, Siberians, and in India. It is described as "a manic and homicidal condition following a state of depression." When people from these cultures are faced with a new environment, or problems beyond themselves, their reaction is one of total violence. Grief, confusion, mental depression, brooding over circumstances all can precipitate the condition. The man works himself into a trance and then runs to do violence. It is often the case that the man running amok attacks his superiors because he cannot cope with them and fancies an insult from them.[10]

A generation brought up permissively, given to tantrums and to violence, and dedicated also to a belief in its own righteousness, is a generation virtually committed by its nature and breeding to running amok. It will do so, unless brought down, in utter conviction of its

---

9. Charles Winick, *The New People, Desexualization in American Life* (New York: Pegasus, 1968), pp. 28, 29, 33.
10. Charles Winick, *Dictionary of Anthropology* (New York: Philosophical Library, 1956), p. 21.

own righteousness and the moral necessity of its violence. Such a generation has a necessary commitment to violence.

Amalek thus is very much with us. It must be dealt with.

The education which breeds Amalekites must be replaced with Christian education. Churches which are congregations of Amalek must be replaced with Christian churches which believe, teach, and apply the whole word of God. The state must become Christian and apply Biblical law to every area of life, and must enforce the full measure of God's law. The permissive family must give way to the Christian family. Only so can Amalek be destroyed.

In 1948, George Orwell saw the future as one of horror, "a boot stamping on a human face—forever." Within twenty years, Nancy Sinatra was grinding boot heels into the stage as she sang that her boots will "walk over you," and the youth of more than one country saw her vision as one of delight. Orwell's horror had become a popular hope. Amalek was reborn.

19. Violence as Presumption

The essence of Amalek's offense was his defiance of God, a religious lawlessness whereby God was challenged and denied. This is described in the law as acting presumptuously (in the KJV), or acting with a high hand (ARV), that is, raising one's hand in defiance of the LORD, taking aggressive action against God and His law-order. Two passages in the law treat this offense as a capital crime:

> But the soul that doeth ought presumptuously, whether he be born in the land, or a stranger, the same reproacheth the LORD; and that soul shall be cut off from among his people.
> Because he hath despised the word of the LORD, and hath broken his commandment, that soul shall utterly be cut off; his iniquity shall be upon him (Num. 15:30, 31).

> And the man that will do presumptuously, and will not hearken unto the priest, that standeth to minister before the LORD thy God, or unto the judge, even that man shall die: and thou shalt put away the evil from Israel.
> And all the people shall hear, and fear, and do no more presumptuously (Deut. 17:12, 13).

The reference in Deuteronomy 17:12, 13 to the priest is to the fact that the court in Israel was often held before or at the sanctuary (God's palace and throne room), with a priest (or the high priest) included in the supreme court.

Waller observed of this passage (Deut. 17:12, 13) that "presumptuously" means "a proud self-assertion against the law. The penalty of death arises necessarily out of the theocracy. If God is the king of the nation, rebellion against His law is treason, and if it be proud and wilful rebellion, the penalty of death is only what we should expect to see inflicted."[1]

The marginal reading of Exodus 17:16 makes clear that this was basic to Amalek's position: "Because the hand of Amalek is upon (or against) the throne of heaven, therefore the Lord will have war with Amalek from generation to generation."

The essence of the Amalekite is, as we have seen, the desire to exercise omnipotence in destruction. But, because, although man is mighty, he is not almighty, his power is exercised in pseudo-omnipotence. Instead of creating a culture, the Amalekite destroys every culture he touches, both as a parasite and also as a systematic destroyer.

As an example of the strange extremes to which perversity and presumption will go is the "church" and "university" movement uncovered in April, 1969. An international movement, it made the mistake of locating a branch near a small city and thus was exposed. Leftist in orientation, using narcotics religiously, its "university" catalogue offered, among other things, a course on cannibalism, listing course number and teacher and calling the course a "co-op." Whether seriously intended or not, its framework was one of total possibility and no law:

> The participants in this co-op should be willing to help obtain some freshly killed human flesh and/or prepare it and/or eat it.
>
> We will meet weekly at a communal Sunday evening meal which we will all help prepare together, everyone cooking their own creations until we can obtain some human flesh.
>
> We will first consider the historical and legal status of cannibalism and then go on from there.
>
> The first meeting will be February 16, 1969 at 5:30 p.m. Call the Redbook at the Midpeninsula Free University, 328-4941, for information.[2]

This is not a new intellectual aberration. The Cynic philosophers of Greece espoused cannibalism as a logical use of human flesh.[3]

Behind these ideas is a religious principle. The word *libertine* comes from *liber*, "free" in the Latin, and the concept of freedom involved in libertinism is freedom from God. "One of Sade's ambitions" was "to be innocent by dint of culpability; to smash what is normal, once and for all, and smash the laws by which he could have been judged."[4] As Blanchot comments:

1. C. H. Waller, "Deuteronomy," in Ellicott, II, 51.
2. Doris Olsen, " 'Free University' Taught Cannibalism," in Santa Maria, California *Times,* Friday, April 25, 1969, p. 1. See also Gene Cowles, "Dope-'Church' Ring Vast Operation?" in Paso Robles, California, *The Daily Press,* Friday, April 25, 1969, pp. 1, 8.
3. See Philip Merlan, "Minor Socrates," in Vergilius Ferm, editor, *Encyclopedia of Morals* (New York: Philosophical Library, 1956), pp. 333-339.
4. Maurice Blanchot, "Sade," in Richard Seaver and Sustryn Wainhouse, com-

Sadean man denies man, and this negation is achieved through the intermediary of the notion of God. He temporarily makes himself God, so that before him men are reduced to nothing and discover the nothingness of being before God. "It is true, is it not, prince, that you do not love men?" Juliette asks. "I loathe them. Not a moment goes by that my mind is not busy plotting violently to do them harm. Indeed, there is not a race more horrible, more frightful. . . . How low and scurvy, how vile and disgusting a race it is!" "But," Juliette breaks in, "you do not really believe that you are to be included among men? . . . Oh, no, no, when one dominates them with such energy, it is impossible to belong to the same race." To which Saint-Fond: "Yes, she is right, we are gods."

Still, the dialectic evolves to further levels: Sade's man, who has taken unto himself the power to set himself above men—the power which men madly yield to God—never for a moment forgets that this power is completely negative. To be God can have only one meaning: to crush man, to reduce creation to nothing. "I should like to be Pandora's box," Saint-Ford says at one point, "so that all the evils which escaped from my breast might destroy all mankind individually." And Verneuil: "And if it were true that a God existed, would we not be his rivals, since we destroy thus what he has made?"[5]

The goal thus of the violent ones is total destruction; they may speak of creating a new social order, but their primary and essential work is to destroy all existing ones. They may speak, as humanists, of a love of man, but man has never before known such radical hatred as that directed against him by these violent ones.

The violent ones love perversity because it is perverse; they love a lie, because it is a lie; their pleasure and power are in deception and destruction. As a person, when caught in a lie, remarked with relish and triumph, "But I had you believing it, didn't I?"

The ultimate victory thus is to grind down man and to proclaim the death of God. In Verneuil's words, "And if it were true that a God existed, would we not be his rivals, since we destroy thus what he has made?" Men must be reduced to nothing to prove that the Amalekite, the violent one, is the new god, supplanting the supposedly dead one.

These presumptuous men, high-handed men, are, according to the law, to be executed. To deny the law and to array oneself against God is to seek to murder the whole of society and deserves the death penalty. Civil disobedience which is firmly grounded in Biblical law is one thing, but civil disobedience which places man above the law is another: it is anarchy. It is a denial of the principle of transcendental law.

---

pilers, translators, *The Marquis de Sade: The Complete Justine, Philosophy in the Bedroom, and other writings* (New York: Grove Press, 1965), p. 71.

5. *Ibid.*, p. 59.

Hence it is that God is at war with Amalek in every generation, because in every generation God's absolute law-order is the only true foundation of society, whereas Amalek, determined to be his own god, seeks to destroy every trace of God's law-order.

Because the Amalekite hates God, he also *hates life.* In the words of Christ, speaking as Wisdom, "But he that sinneth against me wrongeth his own soul: all they that hate me love death" (Prov. 8:36). This hatred of life colors the whole of life and manifests itself in every area. To cite a revealing example: in the spring of 1969, a television commercial by a prominent company manufacturing baby oils and related products used this sentence: "It isn't easy to be a baby." This repeated statement at the heart of the commercial was used because it was obviously a telling statement in this day and age. Now, logically, if it is hard being a baby, then it is a problem being alive. A generation which accepts the thesis that "It isn't easy being a baby" will certainly rebel at being youths facing oncoming responsibilities, and will rebel even more at being adults with responsibilities. If "it isn't easy being a baby," then we can expect truly violent tantrums at being an adult.

Again, violence is begotten by false teachings which, in the name of God, deny God. Thus, in 1968, in a women's Bible study group, ostensibly "fundamental" and strongly Arminian, this statement was made and accepted with almost no dissent: "Human needs come before God's law." This is an incitement to break the law, for there is not a law of God which cannot be contradicted by human need. When churchmen make such assertions, the world has no need for the Marquis de Sade or the Marxists to have violence: it is a historical inevitability that "human needs" will violently assail God's law-order.

To return to the law, as stated in Numbers 15:30, 31, in the Torah Version:

> But the person, be he citizen or stranger, who acts defiantly reviles the LORD; that person shall be cut off from among the people. Because he has spurned the word of the LORD and violated His commandment, that person shall be cut off—he bears his guilt.

That more than excommunication is meant by this is apparent from Deuteronomy 17:12, 13, where the capital penalty, death, is required for this "proud self-assertion against the law." To defy the law and treat it with contempt, to place oneself above the laws of God and man, is to be at total war with God and man, and the penalty is death.

Wherever a society refuses to exact the required death penalty, there God exacts the death penalty on that society. The basic fact of God's law-order is that, from Adam's fall on, the death penalty has been effective. Societies have fallen in great numbers for their defiance of

God, and they shall continue to fall as long as their violation of God's order continues. Every state and every society thus faces a choice: to sentence to death those who deserve to die, or to die themselves. But all they that hate God choose death. Certainly, the sin of presumption is total revolution against God and man; all who permit it have chosen death whether they recognize it or not.

All who are guilty of presumption are *hated* by God. As Solomon declared, "The fear of the LORD is to hate evil: pride, and arrogancy, and the evil way, and the froward [deceitful] mouth, do I hate" (Prov. 8:13). This is clearly a reference to *people* (not merely characteristics) of a particular kind. God hates them and expects us to hate them also if we fear Him. To fear God is to hate evil in its every form, and to love evil men is to hate God and to despise His law-word.

The humanistic mind tries to be wiser and holier than God; it claims to be able to love evil men into salvation. It views with horror those who rejoice in the downfall of evil men. God, however, makes clear His pleasure and laughter in the downfall of fools, scorners, the wilfully simple, all evil men of every kind:

> Because I have called, and ye refused; I have stretched out my hand, and no man regarded:
> But ye have set at nought all my counsel, and would none of my reproof:
> I also will laugh at your calamity; I will mock when your fear cometh;
> When your fear cometh as desolation, and your destruction cometh as a whirlwind; when distress and anguish cometh upon you.
> Then shall they call upon me, but I will not answer; they shall seek me early, but they shall not find me;
> For that they hated knowledge, and did not choose the fear of the LORD:
> They would none of my counsel: they despised all my reproof.
> Therefore shall they eat of the fruit of their own way, and be filled with their own devices.
> For the turning away of the simple shall slay them, and the prosperity of fools shall destroy them.
> But whoso hearkeneth unto me shall dwell safely, and shall be quiet from fear of evil (Prov. 1:24-33).

Not only is the *hatred* of God for evil men clearly apparent in this declaration, but also His refusal to be used as an insurance policy by them. Man is willing to grant God a place in the universe, provided that man can use God and make God serve man. Not the sovereign claims of the omnipotent God but the sovereign claims of a morally free man are asserted. This humanistic man will accept God at best as an ally and partner, although more often only as an insurance policy, a spare tire to be used in case of trouble, if used at all. But God will not be used. The presumption of those who make pious use of God is as evil as the presumption of those who, like Amalek, defy Him. There are degrees in the expression of their evil and their presumption, but presumption, explicit or implicit, governs them alike. Satan tried it first, and, after centuries of effort, is no nearer his goal.

20. Social Inheritance: Landmarks

An important law, cited in Deuteronomy 19:14, has reference basically to the eighth commandment, "Thou shalt not steal." This is apparent in the text as well as later references to the law:

> Thou shalt not remove thy neighbour's landmark, which they of old time have set in thine inheritance, which thou shalt inherit in the land that the LORD thy God giveth thee to possess it (Deut. 19:14).

> Cursed be he that removeth his neighbour's landmark. And all the people shall say, Amen (Deut. 27:17).

> Some remove the landmarks; they violently take away flocks, and feed thereof (Job 24:2).

> Remove not the ancient landmark, which thy fathers have set (Prov. 22:28).

> Remove not the old landmark: and enter not into the fields of the fatherless: For their redeemer is mighty; he shall plead their cause with thee (Prov. 23:10,11).

The reference to property is obvious, but there is also a reference to the conservation of a heritage. An inheritance is to be preserved, a heritage of land. But, quite rightly, these references in Deuteronomy and Proverbs have been seen as referring to a broader fact, a respect for the landmarks, moral, spiritual, and social, of our inheritance in God's covenant. Thus, W. F. Adeney saw in Proverbs 22:28 a reference to the landmarks of property, of history, of doctrine, and of morals.[1] There is Biblical ground for this reading, in that Hosea 5:10, in citing the religious and moral apostasy of the nation, and the corruption of its leaders, reads, in the ARV, "The princes of Judah are like them that remove the landmark: I will pour out my wrath upon them like water." Of this verse, Reynolds and Whitehouse observed, "They (the princes of Judah) break down the barrier between right and wrong, between truth and falsehood, between Jehovah and Baalim."[2] This is the significance of this law with reference to the sixth law-word, "Thou shalt not kill." To destroy the barrier between right and wrong, between truth and falsehood, and between God and false gods, is to murder society and to kill its most basic inheritance.

---

1. W. F. Adeney, in H. D. M. Spence and Joseph S. Exell, *The Pulpit Commentary: Proverbs* (New York: Anson D. F. Randolph, n.d.), p. 431.
2. H. R. Reynolds and The Rev. Prof. Whitehouse, "Hosea," in Ellicott, V, 421.

The removal of landmarks has been a major task of education and of politics in recent years. Of education, Black, in surveying the education of 19th-century America, wrote:

> As we look back on those years, we can see that the text-books and the schools themselves held the Puritan ethic as their basic moral principle. It was this ethic that shaped and unified the nation. "The value judgment," writes Ruth Miller Elson, "is their stock in trade: love of country, love of God, duty to parents, and the necessity to develop habits of thrift, honesty, and hard work in order to accumulate property, the certainty of progress, the perfection of the United States. These are not to be questioned. Nor in this whole century of great external change is there any deviation from these basic values. In pedagogical arrangements the schoolbook of the 1790's is vastly different from that of the 1890's, but the continuum of values is uninterrupted. . . . The child is to learn ethics as he learns information about his world, unquestioningly, by rote. His behavior is not to be inner-directed, nor other-directed, but dictated by authority and passively accepted."

Thus we entered the twentieth century.[3]

This description of the 19th-century textbooks is unfair in some of its terminology, but it is accurate in portraying the difference between textbooks and schools then and in the 20th century. In place of a Christian morality, a relativistic ethics is taught; instead of a respect for the landmarks of Christian society (never seen as "perfection" but as an attempt to realize godly order), a contempt of the past is taught. This has been done in the name of democracy although in contempt of popular beliefs and wishes.

The old landmarks have been denied in favor of new landmarks. Instead of affirming the sovereignty of God, the educators and intellectuals now affirm *the sovereignty of chance.* Thus Charlotte Willard declares, "Chance is the only certainty in the universe."[4] Each new faith means a new area of possibility even as it closes the door on other areas. For Willard, the sovereignty of God, an absolute morality, the movement of history in terms of God's decree to inescapable victory, and man's destiny under God, all are impossible. But new areas of possibility are opened up by a world of chance in which man assumes the role of god and creator. Willard, reviewing Jack Burnham's *Beyond Modern Sculpture: The Effect of Science and Technology on the Sculpture of This Century,* writes:

> Mr. Burnham climaxes his thesis by quoting from *Intelligence in the Universe,* by Roger MacGowan and Frederick Ordway; the

---

3. Hillel Black, *The American Schoolbook* (New York: William Morrow & Company, 1967), p. 90. The quotation by Black is from Ruth Miller Elson, *Guardians of Truth.*

4. Charlotte Willard, "Presaging the Triumph of Egghead Automata," in *Saturday Review* (February 8, 1969), p. 20.

former is chief of the Scientific Digital Branch, Army Missile Command Computation Center, Huntsville, Alabama, and the latter president of the General Astronautics Research Corporation, London. They prophesy that the intelligent life we may encounter in stellar space will probably be the product of biological evolution but will be inorganic artificially constructed intelligent life. Political leaders back on earth will soon learn that intelligent artificial automata having superhuman intellectual capabilities can be built. They believe, in fact, that these automata will take over the earth. Man, in short, will bring about his own transformation from a biological creation to an inorganic concentration of information-processing energy. Mr Burnham concludes triumphantly that "the physical boundaries which separate the sculptor from the results of his endeavors may well disappear." The final illustration in the book is a bent and upright pipe arrangement which is labeled God.[5]

Charlotte Willard's reaction to this is not a happy one, but she has no real basis for opposition. To deny God means ultimately to deny man: this is the consequence of removing the ancient landmarks. A death of God philosophy in reality spells the death of man. Man as God's creation is removed in favor of automata which are man's creation. Thus, man plays god by committing suicide, a point made by Dostoyevsky in *The Possessed*.

The old landmarks have been replaced in law with new relativistic ones. The U. S. Supreme Court has extensively replaced historic American law, with its Biblical orientation, with humanistic law. New legal landmarks have been used to modify old laws and to subvert the social order.

But a relativistic, humanistic landmark is not a landmark at all. Relativism gives only a rubber yardstick, which measures differently for every man, according to his personal measure and purpose. As a result, men can live in a crisis and fail to recognize it. Thus, although crime rose sharply between 1967 and 1969, the American public became more accustomed in those years to living in a world of crime and violence. Having no objective standard, their judgments reflected their own reactions rather than an objective fact. The Harris Survey showed that "A substantial majority of the American people, 59%, do not feel that crime is increasing in their own communities, although just over one in three still believe crime is on the rise. These results mark a sharp decrease in public apprehension over crime, compared with a similar survey taken in 1967."[6] Not surprisingly, in Los Angeles, on May 27, 1969, a large number of voters voted for Thomas Bradley, a colored candidate, because it was "the in-thing" to do.

---

5. *Ibid.*
6. Louis Harris, "Alarm Over Crime Abated Since 1967," Santa Ana, California, *The Register,* Monday (m), May 12, 1969, p. C 8.

To war against landmarks is to war against progress. When ancient China became relativistic in philosophy, the consequence was stagnation. What progress China experienced over the centuries was due to forces extraneous to its basic philosophy. Today, educational philosophers and teachers are increasingly stating in class lectures that it is impossible to set goals in education. In a world of change, how can a man know the future and educate in terms of the unknown? Since we live in a world of change, the only thing which can be validly taught is the certainty of change. Educators thus agree with Willard that "Chance is the only certainty in the universe." Thus, instead of morality, amoralism must be taught; instead of certain basic facts about man and society, there is taught instead the certainty of change. As a result, students logically demand continuous change or revolution as the one moral necessity in an amoral universe. With such an educational philosophy, education for revolution is inescapable, and only a rigorously Christian education can counteract it. Other philosophies of education, i.e., other than humanistic and Christian, are essentially nostalgic: they seek to retain a desired order but without valid cause.

In a world without landmarks, every law or landmark is a criminal offense. Thus, the moral premise of the Marquis de Sade was that, "In a criminal society one must be a criminal."[7] This means total warfare against any and every Establishment, against all social order. It also means isolation, every man being an island unto himself. As Sade said, "My neighbor is nothing to me; there is not the slightest relationship between him and myself."[8] As a result, Sade was at war with the idea of law and of courts; the only "justice" he could approve of was the vendetta, the personal act of murder. In a world of anarchism, without landmarks binding on all, every man's acts have total validity because total licence is the only law possible. As Simone de Beauvoir has summed up:

> To sympathize with Sade too readily is to betray him. For it is our misery, subjection, and death that he desires; and every time we side with a child whose throat has been slit by a sex maniac, we take a stand against him. Nor does he forbid us to defend ourselves. He allows that a father may revenge or prevent, even by murder, the rape of his child. What he demands is that, in the struggle between irreconcilable existences, each one engage himself concretely in the name of his own existence. He approves of the vendetta, but not of the courts. We may kill, but we may not judge. The pretensions of the judge are more arrogant than those of the tyrant; for the tyrant confines himself to being himself,

---

7. Simone de Beauvoir, "Must We Burn Sade?" in Austryn Wainhouse and Richard Seaver, *The Marquis de Sade: The 120 Days of Sodom and other writings* (New York: Grove Press, 1966), p. 58.
    8. Ibid.

whereas the judge tries to erect his opinions into universal laws. His effort is based upon a lie. For every person is imprisoned in his own skin and cannot become the mediator between separate persons from whom he himself is separated. And the fact that a great number of these individuals band together and alienate themselves in institutions, of which they are no longer masters, gives them no additional right. Their number has nothing to do with the matter.[9]

If a man's wishes are his only landmarks, then, in a world without meaning, man himself becomes meaningless. For Sade, the only possible *contact* with others was aggression, and the only possible *meaning* was crime. In Sade's own words, "Ah, how many times, by God, have I not longed to be able to assail the sun, snatch it out of the universe, make a general darkness, or use that sun to burn the world! Oh, that would be a crime. . . ."[10] The only reality then is *aggression*. But what if man and his aggression are only "parts" of a universal nothingness? The conclusion of Chinese relativism, and, increasingly of Western forms of the same faith, is indeed that chance is the only certainty and nothingness is the universal destiny and reality. Wang Wei (A.D. 701-761), in passing beyond the "illusions" of good and evil, wrote, "Do not count on good or evil—you will only waste your time. . . . Who knows but that we all live out our lives in the maze of a dream?"[11] The cure, according to Wang Wei, for man's loneliness and isolation in a world of relativism is "the Doctrine of Non-Being—there is the only remedy."[12] Deny all meaning as the cure for meaninglessness. In a world where landmarks are destroyed, deny the possibility of landmarks. In brief, tell the starving man that hunger is a myth. This is the conclusion of relativism.

If it is a crime to alter property landmarks to defraud a neighbor of his land, how much greater a crime to alter social landmarks, the Biblical foundations of law and society, and thereby bring about the death of that social order? If it is a crime to rob banks, then surely it is a crime to rob and murder a social order.

---

9. *Ibid.*, p. 61.
10. *Ibid.*, p. 32.
11. Chan Yin-nan and Lewis C. Walmsby, translators, *Poems by Wang Wei* (Rutland, Vermont: Charles E. Tuttle Co., 1958, 1965), p. 84.
12. *Ibid.*, p. 113.

VII

THE SEVENTH COMMANDMENT

1. Marriage

The purpose of the seventh commandment, "Thou shalt not commit adultery," is to protect marriage. It is important, therefore, to analyze the Biblical meaning of marriage in order to understand the significance of the laws governing its violation. The institution of marriage (Gen. 2:18-25) in Eden describes the meaning of marriage in relationship to man; this will be considered subsequently. At present, the meaning of marriage in relationship to God must first be understood and will be analyzed.

While marriage is of this earth, since there is no marrying nor giving in marriage in heaven (Matt. 22:29, 30), it nonetheless has reference to and is governed by the triune God, as are all things. The great statement of this fact is Ephesians 5:21-23, which begins with the general commandment, "Submitting yourselves one to another in the fear of God," rendered by the Berkeley Version, "Be submissive to one another out of reverence for Christ." Calvin commented on this:

> God has bound us so strongly to each other, that no man ought to endeavor to avoid subjection; and where love reigns, mutual services will be rendered. I do not except kings and governors, whose very authority is held for the *service* of the community. It is highly proper that all should be exhorted to be subject to each other in their turn.[1]

Thus, a general principle of subjection and service is affirmed, and marriage is then cited as illustrative of this principle. As Hodge noted, "The apostle enjoins mutual obedience as a Christian duty, v. 21. Under this head he treats of the relative duties of husbands and wives, parents and children, masters and servants."[2] Man has through the ages been in revolt against this necessity of subjection and service and dreamed rather of autonomous power. The young Louis XIV expressed his pleasure at the concept to the Duc de Gramont in 1661:

Louis: I have just been reading a book with which I am delighted.

---

1. John Calvin, *Commentaries on the Epistles of Paul to the Galatians and Ephesians*, William Pringle Translation (Grand Rapids: Eerdmans, 1948), p. 316 f.
2. Charles Hodge, *A Commentary on the Epistle to the Ephesians* (Grand Rapids: Eerdmans, 1950), p. 308.

Gramont: What is that, Sire?

Louis: *Calcandille*. It pleases me to find in it arbitrary power
            in the hands of one man, everything being done by
            him or by his orders, he rendering an account of his
            acts to no man, and obeyed blindly by all his subjects
            without exception. Such boundless power is the closest
            approach to that of God. What do you think, Gramont?

Gramont: I am pleased that Your Majesty has taken to reading,
            but I would ask if he has read the whole of *Calcandille*?

Louis: No, only the preface.

Gramont: Well then, let Your Majesty read the book through, and
            when he has finished it, see how many Turkish Em-
            perors died in their beds and how many came to a
            violent end. In *Calcandille* one finds ample proof that
            a Prince who can do whatever he pleases, should never
            be such a fool as to do so.[3]

With anarchism, this dream of autonomous power has become the hope
of a large number of people.

This general principle of subjection and service is rooted in far
more than men's interdependence; rather, it is grounded in a theocratic
faith. Men are to be in subjection to one another, and in mutual service
(Eph. 5:22-29), not because the needs of humanity require it but in
the fear of God and in obedience to His law-word. The human inter-
dependence exists because the prior dependence on God requires the
unity of His creation under His law.

Moreover, because man is not God, man is a subject, a subject
primarily and essentially to God, and to others in the Lord only. Where
man rejects his subjection to God and asserts his autonomy, man does
not thereby gain independence. The subjection of man to man continues
in pagan, Marxist, Fabian socialist, anarchist, and atheistic groups, but
this subjection is now without the restraint of God's law. The Biblical
subjection of man to man, and of a wife to her husband, is at every
point governed and limited by the prior and absolute subjection to
God, of which all other subjections are aspects. God's prior and absolute lordship thus limits and conditions every situation of man and
permits no trespass without offense. To deny the Biblical principle of
subjection is thus to open the door to totalitarianism and tyranny, since
no check then remains on man's desire to dominate and use his fellow
man. The Biblical principle of subjection conditions every relationship
by the prior requirement and totally governing jurisdiction of God's law,
so that all relationships on earth are limited and restrained by God's
law-word. Thus, wives are not placed in bondage by the Biblical

---

3. W. H. Lewis, *Assault on Olympus, The Rise of the House of Gramont
between 1604 and 1678* (New York: Harcourt, Brace and Company, 1958), p. 151.

commandment of submission (Eph. 5:22) but are rather established in the liberty and security of a God-ordained relationship.

Without Biblical faith, the only sustaining factor in marriage becomes the frail bond of *feeling*. Mary Carolyn Davies, in her poem, "A Marriage," wrote

> Took my name and took my pride
> Left me not much else beside,
> But the feeling . . . *that* insures:
> Sort of joy at being yours.
> Property! That's what it meant.
> Property! And we content!
> Now you're gone; and can I be
> Anything but property?[4]

Where *feeling* is the basis of marriage rather than a religious principle, then ultimately marriage becomes robbery, each partner using the other and then departing when there is nothing new to be gained. Again, Mary Carolyn Davies catches the materialistic impersonality of sexual relations when divorced from Biblical morality:

> "Here is a woman,"
> They'll say to all men,
> "A little soiled by living,
> A little spoiled by loving,
> A little flecked,
> A little specked—"
> Oh, they are forgiving.
> To you who did the wrong, but still of me,
> Like Cabbage in a market, critically,
> They'll say: "Not quite as fresh as she should be."[5]

Romantic feelings, mutual exploitation, and self-pity become the lot of those who reduce the man-woman relationship to one of anarchic liberty from God's law.

The Biblical principle of subjection is hierarchical in that there are classes or levels of authority, but this does not mean that all levels are not directly and absolutely liable to God in terms of His law-word. According to St. Paul, "the husband is the head of the wife, even as Christ is the head of the church: and he is the saviour of the body" (Eph. 5:23). On this foundation principle, St. Paul adds, "Therefore as the church is subject unto Christ, so let wives be to their own husbands in everything" (Eph. 5:24). The comment of the Right Rev. Alfred Barry on these verses is of interest here:

> (23, 24). . . . The words "and" and "is" are wrongly inserted, and the word "therefore" is absolutely an error, evading the difficulty of

---

4. Mary Carolyn Davies, *Marriage Songs* (Boston: Harold Vinal, 1923), p. 16.
5. *Ibid.*, "They'll Say—," p. 13.

the passage. It should be, *He Himself being the Saviour of the Body. But. . . .* This clause, in which the words "He Himself" are emphatic, notes (as if in comparison) that "Christ" (and He alone) is not only Head, but "Saviour of the Body," i.e., "of His body the Church," not only teaching and ruling it, but by His unity infusing into it the new life of justification and sanctification. Here no husband can be like Him, and therefore none can claim the absolute dependence of faith which is His of right. Accordingly St. Paul adds the word, "but." Though "this is so," yet "still let the wives," etc.

The subjection of the Church of Christ is a free subjection, arising out of faith in His absolute wisdom and goodness, and love for His unspeakable love. Hence we gather (1) that the subordination of the wife is not that of the slave, by compulsion and fear, but one which arises from and preserves freedom; next (2), that it can exist, or at any rate endure, only on condition of superior wisdom and love in the husband; thirdly (3), that while it is like the higher subordination in kind, it cannot be equally perfect in degree—while it is real "in everything," it can be absolute in nothing. The antitype is, as usual, greater than the type.[6]

This thoughtful statement misses the point of the passage in grounding the obedience on love rather than law. The obedience of the wife is not conditional upon the "superior wisdom and goodness and love in the husband"; there is nothing in the law to indicate this. Barry's interpretation denies in effect that St. Paul's statement is God's law-word: it is rather presented as a description by Barry of marital relationships. Lenski is guilty of the same error. He comments, "This is also a voluntary self subjection and not subjugation."[7] Certainly, the subjection of a wife to her husband is not slavery, nor involuntary subjugation. St. Paul is not concerned with the feelings, or the voluntarism of the wife: he is stating God's law and setting forth its meaning. To discuss law without citing the fact that it is law is certainly strange exegesis. It requires a curious blindness.

What is meant by St. Paul is that the whole universe is one of submission to authority, and that the fulfilment of each and every aspect is to discharge its duties in terms of that submission. It is the place and fulfilment of the wife to be in submission to her husband in all due authority. Even as Christ is the head of the church and the savior of His body, the church, so the authority of the husband is to be exercised toward the health and furthering of his wife and family. Even as the church must submit to Christ, so the wife must submit to her husband "in every thing" (Eph. 5:24). Hodge commented on this phrase:

6. Alfred Barry, "Ephesians," in Ellicott, VIII, 52.
7. R. C. H. Lenski, *The Interpretation of St. Paul's Epistle to the Galatians, to the Ephesians and to the Philippians* (Minneapolis: Augsburg, 1946, 1941), p. 625.

As verse 22 teaches the nature of the subjection of the wife to her husband, and verse 23 its ground, this verse (24) teaches its extent. She is to be subject . . . *in every thing.* That is, the subjection is not limited to any one sphere or department of the social life, but extends to all. The wife is not subject as to some things, and independent as to others, but she is subject as to all. This of course does not mean that the authority of the husband is unlimited. It teaches its extent, not its degree. It extends over all departments, but is limited in all; first, by the nature of the relation; and secondly, by the higher authority of God. No superior, whether master, parent, husband or magistrate, can make it obligatory on us to do what God forbids, or not to do what God commands. So long as our allegiance to God is preserved, and obedience to man is made part of our obedience to him, we retain our liberty and our integrity.[8]

In a world without submission to law and to authorities under law, very quickly only lawless force would prevail, and nothing could be more destructive of a woman's welfare, or a man's, for that matter. The world of God's law and God-ordained authorities is man's true liberty. It is *only* when we first establish the primacy of that law and authority that we can, with Barry and Lenski, speak of that voluntary submission to law and authority as man's happiness and fulfilment. Here the matter is best stated by Ingram, who begins with the law and sees the assent as assent to law:

Public witness to mutual consent and pledges of troth: these are the things that make a marriage.

The integrity of the whole moral argument of the Ten Commandments begins to stand out even more clearly in this. The mystery of making and keeping a pledge of loyalty, a promise, to God, to a spouse; the taking of the name of God in a solemn oath: these are the things upon which the moral law is built. These are the foundations of society. These are the things that are kept alive and in force by the inflicting of penalties for breaking them. Promises, vows, pledges, loyalties all vanish if they are broken with impunity. Society turns on keeping pledges and punishing violations. Credit is an extension of the principle into the business world. The contract is established by a spoken word, and is no better than that word. The bond of loyalty or the effect of a pledge lies in what we might call the spirit world: it has no shape or weight or size; it cannot be touched, seen, or heard. But it controls human life.

What an adulterer really does is to break a particular solemn vow. By his act he tramples upon marriage itself, mocks God and society, and figuratively tosses that particular promise into the trash can, making it of no value.[9]

God makes certain promises and threats to man and society con-

---

8. Hodge, *Ephesians*, p. 314 f.
9. T. R. Ingram, *The World Under God's Law*, p. 84.

ditional upon the fulfilment or violation of His law-word. Man's studied disregard of that law-word is an implicit or explicit declaration that man replaces God's authority with his own, that moral submission is denied in favor of autonomy.

The alternative to submission is exploitation, not freedom, because there is no true freedom in anarchy. The purpose of submission is not to degrade women in marriage, nor to degrade men in society, but to bring to them their best prosperity and peace under God's order. In a world of authority, the submission of the wife is not in isolation nor in a vacuum. It is set in a context of submission by men to authority; in such a world, men teach the principles of authority to their sons and to their daughters and work to instill in them the responsibilities of authority and obedience. In such a world, inter-dependence and service prevail.

In a world of moral anarchism, there is neither submission to authority nor service, which is a form of submission. A husband and father who uses his authority and his income wisely to further the welfare of the entire family is serving the welfare of all thereby. But in a world which denies submission and authority, every man serves himself only and seeks to exploit all others. Men exploit women, and women exploit men. If the woman ages, she is abandoned. If the man's income wanes, he is deserted if a better opportunity presents itself. The "jet set" world, and the arena of the theatre, provide us with abundant examples of the fact that the world of anarchism and lawlessness, i.e., the world outside God's law insofar as submission is concerned, is a world of exploitation, in particular, of sexual exploitation.

Another significant fact appears in St. Paul's Ephesian declaration: although Scripture repeatedly assumes and cites love as an aspect of a woman's relationship to her husband, love is not cited here by St. Paul with reference to the wife and her reaction to her husband. The *primacy* is given to *submission* by the wife, and *love* by the husband. The husband's love, however, is defined as *service*, and it is compared to the redemptive work of Christ for His Church (Eph. 5:22-29). Thus, the husband's evidence of love is his wise and loving government of his household, whereas the wife demonstrates her love in submission. In both cases, submission and authority are governed, not by the wishes of the parties involved, but by the law-word of God. Where the submission and authority are premised on God's law, that submission and authority interpenetrate. The husband submits to Christ and to all due authority, and the wife submits to her husband and thereby furthers his exercise of authority in every realm and becomes her husband's help-meet in his authority and dominion. The wife normally derives her status from her husband, and to undercut him is to undercut herself.

Similarly, "men ought to love their wives as their own bodies. He that loveth his wife loveth himself. For no man ever yet hated his own flesh; but nourisheth and cherisheth it, even as the Lord the church" (Eph. 5:28, 29). The basis of such a relationship is faith, and obedience by faith to God's law-word. Authority and law are not essentially physical things but primarily of the spirit; where men recognize the religion and faith which establishes authority, there the physical manifestations of authority are respected. If the religious foundations of authority are broken, then that authority rapidly crumbles and disappears. Thus, very little policing is necessary in India to keep Hindus on a vegetarian diet, since that diet is undergirded by the strictest religious faith, but it would be virtually impossible to impose such a diet on Americans today.

When the Biblical faith which undergirds Western family life is denied, then the nature of the marital relationship is also altered. The humanistic relativism of modern man dissolves the ties between man and woman as far as any objective law and value are concerned and reduces them to purely relative and personal ties. Now a purely *personal* tie is *impersonal* in its view of other people. A man whose judgment is governed by his personal considerations only, does not consider the personal considerations of other people, except insofar as they can be used to further his own ends. As a result, an *externalism* prevails. Thus, the coarse humanist, Thomas More, advocated in *Utopia* that young people view each other in the nude before deciding to marry. When Sir William Roper praised this aspect of *Utopia* and asked that it be applied to More's two daughters, whom he was courting, More took Roper to the bedroom where the two girls were asleep together, "on their backs, their smocks up as high as their armpits. More yanked off the cover, and the girls modestly rolled over. Roper slapped one on her behind, stating, "I have seen both sides; thou art mine."[10] The fact that Roper had a happy marriage does not alter the fact of the basic coarseness of both father and husband. Had not Roper and his wife both had a background of strict Catholic faith, the results would not have been as happy.

The externalism of the anarchist is alien to the hierarchy of authority which is basic to God's law-order. That authority rests on a doctrine of God, and, with respect to marriage, a central aspect of the meaning of marriage is that it is a type of Christ and His church (Eph. 5:25-32). In Ephesians 3:14, 15, St. Paul speaks of God as the Father of all families in heaven and earth, or, more literally, the "Father of all fatherhoods" according to Simpson:

God Himself is the archetype of parentage, faintly adumbrated by

10. *Aubrey's Brief Lives* (Ann Arbor: University of Michigan Press, 1957), pp. 212-214.

human fatherhood. From His creative hand have proceeded all rational beings in all their multiplicity of aspects and manners and usages, divergent or interrelated. To the "Father of Spirits" they owe their existence and the conditions that have stamped it with both an individual and collective impress, an actual or potential scope and orbit.[11]

James Moffatt's translation renders this passage thus, "For this reason, then, I kneel before the Father from whom every family in heaven and on earth derives its name and nature." The *name and nature* of all earthly relationships is derived from the triune God, so that there is no law, no society, no relationship, no justice, no structure, no design, no meaning apart from God, and all these aspects and relationships of society are types of that which exists in the Godhead. Hell has none of these things, but bare existence, which is itself God's creation. For man to deny God is to deny ultimately everything, since all things are from God and testify to Him.

According to Simpson, the typology of marriage and its relationship to Christ and the church has four implications. *First*, it sets forth the fact of *dominion*, which is basic to God's purpose and His kingdom. *Second*, it has reference to *devotion* or self-sacrifice. *Third*, it is in terms of a *design*, a sovereign purpose and destiny. *Fourth*, it declares the derivation.[12]

The "one flesh" described by St. Paul does not mean, as Hodge pointed out, an "identity of substance, but community of life."[13] Just as hell is the final and total loss of all community, so true marriage, like every aspect of the godly life, is a realization of a phase of life in community under God. St. Paul, in citing Genesis 2:24 in Ephesians 5:31, makes clear that he has simply made clear to the Church of Ephesus that which was declared from the beginning. The "great mystery" spoken of by St. Paul in Ephesians 5:32 is, according to Calvin, "that Christ breathes into the church his own life and power."[14] Where this life and power are received faithfully, and each authority, receiving God's grace directly and also as mediated through all due authorities, discharges its duties of submission and authority faithfully, there God's kingdom flourishes and abounds. With respect to salvation and God's providence, Christ is *the only mediator between God and man*. But God's grace moves, not only directly from God to man through Christ, but also *through man to man* as they discharge their duties under God. What covenant member with godly parents

11. E. K. Simpson in E. K. Simpson and F. F. Bruce, *Commentary on the Epistles to the Ephesians and the Colossians* (Grand Rapids: Eerdmans, 1957), p. 79.
12. *Ibid.*, pp. 130-134.
13. Hodge, *Ephesians*, p. 346.
14. Calvin, *Galatians and Ephesians*, p. 326.

can deny that his parents, by their prayers and their discipline, their love and their teaching, did not reveal God's grace and law-order to them? The fact that their salvation is entirely the work of God does not alter the reality of the covenantal instruments. That covenantal instruments are *instruments* in God's hands must clearly be recognized, but to deny them even that status is to deny God's order. Pastors, parents, teachers, civil authorities, and all others, as they discharge their duties under God faithfully, mediate from man to man God's order, justice, law, grace, word, and purpose. Clearly and without any doubt, "there is one God, and one mediator between God and men, the man Christ Jesus" (I Tim. 2:5). Protestantism has rightly upheld the exclusiveness of that mediation, but, it must be added, it has done harm by denying often that there is a mediation between men. A godly state, which applies God's law-order faithfully and carefully, clearly mediates God's justice to evil-doers and His care to His own. It is for this reason that Scripture refers to authorities to whom the word of God is given, i.e., who are established as authorities by God's word, as "gods," because they set forth or mediate an aspect of God's order (John 10: 34, 35). The alternative to mediation is anarchism, nor will it do to quibble at the word "mediation" until the dictionaries are altered.

Every legitimate area of administration is an area of mediation, whereby Christ's law-order is mediated through church, state, school, family, vocation, and society. To administer is to mediate, because an administrator applies not his own but a higher rule to the situation under his authority. This clearly means a hierarchy of authorities, and the higher rule or standard of all hierarchies as of all men is the Bible, God's enscriptured word.

What the Biblical doctrine of marriage makes clear is that, in life's most intimate relationships, the law-order of God not only governs every relation but is the ground of the happiness and prosperity thereof.

That Christ Himself in His incarnation confirmed the necessity of submission and the validity of authority by His own example, the New Testament abundantly testifies. To this fact also a Collect of the Mass for the Feast of the Holy Family gives beautiful witness:

> O Lord Jesus Christ, Who, being subject to Mary and Joseph, didst sanctify home life with unspeakable virtues: grant, that, by the aid of both, we may be taught by the example of Thy Holy Family, and attain to eternal fellowship with it: Who livest and reignest with God the Father in the unity of the Holy Ghost, God, World without end. Amen.

2. Marriage and Man

Man can be understood only in terms of God and His sovereign purpose in man's creation. According to Genesis 1:26-28, man was created to exercise dominion over the earth and to subdue it, and the command to "be fruitful, and multiply" was an aspect of the call to exercise dominion over the earth. Man therefore is to be understood in terms of God's kingdom and man's calling therein to manifest God's law-order in a developed and subdued earth.

Man is thus primarily and essentially a *religious creature* who is truly understood only by reference to his Creator and his ordained destiny under God. Man's destiny, to bring all things under the dominion of God's law-word, confronted man from the beginning of his creation. To subdue the earth and exercise dominion over it, as the task was assigned to Adam in Eden, had two aspects. *First, the practical aspect*: man was required to take care of the Garden of Eden (Gen. 2:15). Urban man tends to forget that fruit trees, vegetables, and plants require work and care, even in the perfect world of Eden. Adam was given the responsibility of dressing or tilling the garden and keeping or taking charge of it. *Second, the cognitive aspect*: man was required to name the creatures. Names in the Old Testament are descriptions and classifications, so that to name anything meant to understand and classify it. By work and knowledge man was called to subdue the earth, develop its potentialities, increase and multiply in order to extend his dominion geographically as well as in knowledge.

This then was man's holy calling under God, *work and knowledge* toward the purpose of subduing the earth and exercising dominion over it. Thus, *any vocation* whereby man extends his dominion, under God, to God's purpose, and without abuse of or contempt for the earth God has ordained to be man's domain under Him, is *a holy calling*. The common opinion in every branch of Christendom that a Christian calling means entrance into the ranks of the clergy could not be more wrong. Such an attitude leads to the supplanting of the Kingdom of God by the church, to ecclesiasticism as God's purpose in creation.

Thus, man was created, not as a child, so that he cannot be understood with reference either to a primitive past or to his childhood, but in terms of *mature responsibility and work*. Man realizes himself in terms of work under God, and hence the radical destructiveness to man of meaningless or frustrating work, or of a social order which penalizes the working man in the realization of the fruits of his labors. Similarly, man realizes himself as he extends the frontiers of his knowledge and learns more of the nature of things and their utility as well. Men find an exaltation in a task well done, and in knowledge gained, because in and through work and knowledge their dominion under God is extended.

The earth thus was created to be God's kingdom, and man was created in God's image to be God's vicegerent over that realm under God. The image of God involves knowledge (Col. 3:10), righteousness, and holiness (Eph. 4:24), and dominion over the earth and its creatures (Gen. 1:28). Thus, while Adam was shaped out of dust, or the topsoil, the red earth, he was still ordained to a glorious nature and destiny under God.

Man was required to know himself first of all in terms of his calling before he was given a help-meet, Eve. Thus, not until Adam, for an undefined but apparently extensive length of time, had worked at his calling, cared for the garden and come to know the creatures thereof, was he given a wife. We are specifically told that Adam named or classified all the animals, a considerable task, prior to the creation of Eve. However general and limited this classification was, it was still an accurate and over-all understanding of animal life. The Adam of Eden was thus a hard-working man in a world where the curse of sin had not yet infected man and his work.

Thus it must be noted that Adam was given Eve, *first*, not in fulfilment of a *natural* or merely *sexual* need, although this was recognized (Gen. 2:20), but, after delay, in fulfilment of his need for a "helpmeet," which is what Eve is called. She is thus very clearly a *helper* to Adam in his life and work as God's covenant man, called to exercise dominion and subdue the earth.

This means, *second*, that the role of the woman is to be a helper in *a governmental function*. Man's calling is in terms of the Kingdom of God, and woman's creation and calling is no less in terms of it. She is a helper to man in the subduing of the earth and in exercising dominion over it in whatever terms necessary to make her husband's life and work more successful. The implications of this will be discussed later in relationship to woman in marriage.

Third, God created Eve only after Adam had proven himself *responsible* by discharging his duties faithfully and well. Responsibility is thus clearly a prerequisite to marriage for the man. Hence, later, the dowry system required the bridegroom to demonstrate his responsibility by turning over a dowry to the bride as her security, and the children's security, for the future.

Fourth, since man is called to exercise dominion, and marriage and his government of the family is a central aspect of that dominion, the exercise of dominion in work and knowledge precedes the exercise of dominion as husband and father. *The covenant family* is central to the Kingdom of God and hence marriage was at its inception hedged about with safeguards in order to establish the precedent of responsibility.

Fifth, marriage is clearly a divine ordinance, instituted, together with the calling *to work* and *to know*, in paradise.

Sixth, marriage is the normal state of man, for, according to God, "It is not good that the man should be alone" (Gen. 2:18). Unless men are physically incapacitated, or else called by God to the single estate (Matt. 19:10-12), marriage is their normal state of life. Only in an age of studied immaturity do men mock at marriage as though it were bondage. What they are saying, in effect, is that responsibility, or more simply, manhood, is bondage and permanent childhood freedom. Such persons are not worth answering.

Seventh, while the family and dominion therein are a part of man's calling and a very important part thereof, it is far from being the totality of his calling. Whereas the woman's calling is in terms of her husband and the family, the man's calling is in terms of the vocation he assumes under God.

Eighth, man, before marriage, is called, as we have seen, to demonstrate two things, *the pattern of obedience* and *the pattern of responsibility,* and he is then ready to establish a new home. Genesis 2:24 makes clear that a man shall *leave* his parental home and *cleave* unto his wife. Basic to the development of man's dominion over the earth are *change and growth.* Family systems which do not permit the independence of the young couple seek to perpetuate an unchanging order, whereas change and growth are ensured by the Biblical pattern which requires a break with parents at marriage. The break does not end responsibility to parents, but it ensures independent growth.

Ninth, the Hebrew word for bridegroom means "the circumcised," the Hebrew word for father-in-law means *he who performed the operation of circumcision,* and the Hebrew word for mother-in-law is similar. This obviously had no reference to the actual physical rite, since Hebrew males were circumcised on the eighth day. What it meant was that the father-in-law ensured the fact of *spiritual circumcision,* as did the mother-in-law, by making sure of the covenantal status of the groom. It was their duty to prevent a mixed marriage. A man could marry their daughter, and become a bridegroom, only when clearly a man under God.

Thus, the parents of the bridegroom had an obligation to prepare their son for a life of work and growing knowledge and wisdom, and the parents of the bride had a duty, under Biblical standards, to examine the faith and character of the prospective bridegroom.

Maturity thus is not only basic to manhood but also to marriage. The maturity required is more than physical maturity. In other eras, marriages have often been contracted in the early teens, as in some frontier situations, but in many such cases the males were experienced and working men, the girls trained and capable women, whereas in other eras immaturity is the chronic and chosen condition of men and women. Certainly, physical maturity is wisest, but without a maturity of faith and character the marital relationship is plagued with conflicts and tensions.

Since marriage is so closely linked from creation with God's covenant with man, it is especially fitting that the Roman Catholic service, in the Blessing which concludes the Marriage Mass, should invoke the Old Testament covenant phrase. In the wording of the New Saint Andrew Bible Missal,

> May the God of Abraham, the God of Isaac, the God of Jacob be with you, and may he fulfill in you his blessing, so that you may see your children's children to the third and fourth generation and afterward possess everlasting and boundless life. Through the help of our Lord Jesus Christ, who with the Father and the Holy Spirit lives and reigns, God, forever and ever. Amen.

Finally, it must be noted that, while marriage is the ordained *sexual relationship* between man and woman, it cannot be understood simply in terms of sex. When marriage is reduced to sex, then marriage disintegrates as an institution and amoral sex replaces it. Marriage has reference first of all to God's ordination and then to man and to woman in their respective callings. Because man is to be understood in terms of his calling under God, all of man's life is to be interpreted in terms of this calling also. Dislocation in a man's calling is a dislocation in his total life. When work is futile, men cannot rest from their labors, because their satisfaction therein is gone. Men then very often seek to make work purposeful by working harder. Frustration in terms of his calling means poor health for man in terms of his physical and mental health, his sexual energy, and his ability to rest, whereas success in work means vigor and vitality to a man. Every attempt to understand marriage only in terms of sex will aggravate man's basic problem.

If marriage cannot be reduced to sex, neither can it be reduced to *love*. The Scripture gives no ground whatsoever to the idea that a marriage can be terminated when love ends. While love is important to a marriage, it cannot replace God's law as the essential bond of marriage. Moreover, a woman can make no greater mistake than to assume that she can take priority in her husband's life over his work. He will love her with a personal warmth and tenderness as no other person, but a man's life is his work, not his wife, and the failure of women to understand this can do serious harm to a marriage. The tragedy of an apostate age is that women see clearly the futility or emptiness of much of man's work, but they fail to see that a godly man's answer to a sick world is more work. Because work is man's calling, men often make the serious mistake of trying to solve all problems by working harder, whereas, in the same situation, the woman is all the more convinced of the futility of work. But to tell a man that work is futile is to tell him that he is futile. A basic and unrecognized cause of tensions in marriage is the growing futility of work in an age where apostate and statist trends rob work of its constructive goals. The area of man's dominion becomes the area of man's frustration. There are those who can recall when men, not too many years ago, worked ten hours or more daily, six and seven days a week, often under ugly and unsafe circumstances. In the face of this, they could rest and also enjoy life with a robust appetite. The basic optimism of that era and the certainty of progress, the stability of a hard money economy, and the sense of mastery in these assurances, gave men a satisfaction in their labors which made rest possible. An age which negates the meaning and satisfaction of work also negates man at the same time. Not all the more desirable conditions and hours of work can replace the *purpose* of work. Dostoyevsky pointed out that men could be broken in Siberia, not by hard labor but by meaningless labor, such as moving a pile of boulders back and forth endlessly. Such work, however slowly or lazily done, destroys a man, whereas meaningful work strengthens and even exalts him.

Because of the centrality of work to a man, one of the chronic problems of men is their tendency to make work a *substitute religion*. Instead of deriving the meaning of life from God and His law-order, men often derive their private world of meaning from their work. The consequence is a disorientation of life, family, and order.

Whether retired or actively working, a man's thinking is still in terms of the world of work, and he continues to assess reality in the same terms. Man, having been called to exercise dominion through work, is tied to work in thought and action alike. But there is no true dominion for man in and through work apart from God and His law-order.

A final note: men have through the centuries felt so closely linked to their work, that for them there has been a particular satisfaction in being near their tools. To this day, in some parts of the world, men take pleasure in having their tools close at hand. Some resistance to the Industrial Revolution came from men who enjoyed having their workshop in their home and felt a loss at moving into other premises. Not uncommonly, doctors carry their little black bags with them on a vacation, and a high point of a European tour for one doctor was the opportunity to use his medicine. Many men rest better if their tools are close at hand.

3. Marriage and Woman

The definition of woman given by God in creating Eve and establishing the first marriage is "help meet" (Gen. 2:18). This is literally "as agreeing to him," or "his counterpart."[1] Robert Young's *Literal Translation of the Holy Bible* renders it "an helper—as his counterpart." R. Payne Smith pointed out that the Hebrew is literally, "a help as his front, his reflected image."[2] The implication is of a mirrored image, a point made by St. Paul in I Corinthians 11:1-16; man was created in God's image, and woman in the reflected image of God in man. In this passage, as Hodge noted, the principle is affirmed "that order and subordination pervade the whole universe, and is essential to its being."[3] The covered head is a sign of being under authority to another person; hence, the man, who is directly under Christ, worships with uncovered head, the woman with a covered head. A man therefore who worships with covered head dishonors himself (I Cor. 11:1-4). The uncovered woman might as well be shorn or shaven, because it is as shameful for her to be uncovered as to be shaven (I Cor. 11:5-7). As Leon Morris notes with reference to vss. 8, 9, "Neither in her origin, nor in the purpose for which she was created can the woman claim priority, or even equality."[4]

Accordingly, St. Paul continued, "For this cause ought the woman to have power on her head because of the angels" (I Cor. 11:10). James Moffatt rendered "power on her head" as "a symbol of subjection," following thereby popular opinion rather than the Greek text. "Power on her head" means rather, as Morris and others have pointed out, "a sign of her authority."[5] Because angels are witnesses, a godly witness must be rendered. To many, a serious contradiction seems to be involved here: *first*, St. Paul insists on subordination, and then, *second*, speaks of what seems to to be a sign of subordination as a sign of authority. This seeming contradiction arises from the anarchic concept of authority which is so deeply imbedded in man's sinful nature. All true authority is under authority, since God alone transcends all things and is the source of all power and authority. A colonel has authority because he is under a general, and his own authority grows as the power, prestige, and authority of those above him grow, and his unity with them in mind and purpose is assured. So too with the woman: Her subordination is also her symbol of authority. Very frequently, in various societies, prostitutes have been forbidden to dress themselves in the same manner as wives and daughters, for to do so

---

1. H. C. Leupold, *Exposition of Genesis* (Columbus, Ohio: Wartburg Press, 1942), p. 129 f.
2. R. Payne Smith, "Genesis," in Ellicott, I, 21.
3. Charles Hodge, *An Exposition of the First Epistle to the Corinthians* (Grand Rapids: Eerdmans, 1950), p. 206.
4. Leon Morris, *The First Epistle of Paul to the Corinthians* (Grand Rapids: (Eerdmans, 1958), p. 153.
5. *Ibid.*, p. 153 f.

would be to claim an authority, protection, and power they had forfeited. Thus, in Assyria an unmarried prostitute who covered her head was severely punished for her presumption.[6] Similar laws existed in Rome. On the American frontier, the woman who was a wife or daughter carried an obvious authority and normally commanded the respect and protection of all men.

Men and women, St. Paul declared (I Cor. 11:11), are "mutually dependent. The one cannot exist without the other."[7] "The one is not without the other, *for* as the woman was originally formed out of the man, so the man is born of the woman."[8] Church councils very early censured long hair in men as a mark of effeminacy, as had the Romans before them. There is no evidence to support the usual portrayal of Christ and the apostles as long-haired men; the evidence of the age indicates very short hair.

> To a woman, however, in all ages and countries, long hair has been considered an ornament. It is given to her, Paul says, as a *covering*, or as a natural veil; and it is a glory to her *because* it is a veil. The veil itself, therefore, must be becoming and decorous in a woman.[9]

It is thus with Biblical grounds that a woman's hair is spoken of as her "crowning glory," and her delight in wearing it as an attractive crown is *God-given* when done within bounds, although the time some give to it is certainly not so.

The Biblical doctrine of woman thus reveals her as one crowned with authority in her "subjection" or subordination, and clearly a helper of the closest possible rank to God's appointed vicegerent over creation. This is no small responsibility, nor is it a picture of a patient Griselda. Theologians have all too often pointed to Eve as the one who led Adam into sin while forgetting to note that her God-given position was such that counsel was her normal duty, although in this case it was clearly evil counsel. Men as sinners often dream of a patient Griselda who never speaks unless spoken to, but no other wife would please them less or bore them more. Martin Luther, who dearly loved his Katie, on one occasion vowed, "If I were to marry again, I would hew a meek wife out of stone: for I doubt whether any other kind be meek." His biographer, Edith Simon, properly asks, "How would he have fared with a meek wife?"[10] The answer clearly is, not too well.

It is a common illusion that in man's primitive, evolutionary past,

---

6. J. M. Powis Smith, *The Origin and History of Hebrew Law* (Chicago: The University of Chicago Press, 1931, 1960), p. 231 f.
7. Charles Hodge, *I Corinthians*, p. 211.
8. *Ibid.*, p. 212.
9. *Ibid.*, p. 213.
10. Edith Simon, *Luther Alive* (Garden City, N. Y.: Doubleday, 1968), p. 336.

women were the merest slaves, used at will by primitive brutes. Not only is this evolutionary myth without foundation, but in every known society, the position of women, as measured in terms of the men and the society, has been a notable one. The idea that women have ever submitted to being mere slaves is itself an absurd notion. Women have been women in every age. In a study of an exceedingly backward society, the natives of Australia, Phyllis Kaberry has shown the importance and status of women to be a considerable one.[11]

Few things have depressed women more than did the Enlightenment, which turned woman into an ornament and a helpless creature. Unless of the lower class, where work was mandatory, the "privileged" woman was a useless ornamental person, with almost no rights. This had not been previously true. In 17th-century England, women were often in business, were highly competent managers, and were involved in the shipping trade, as insurance brokers, manufactures, and the like.

> Up to the eighteenth century women usually figured in business as partners with their husbands, and not in inferior capacities. They often took full charge during prolonged absences of their mates. In some instances, where they were the brighter of the pair, they ran the show.[12]

A legal "revolution" brought about the diminished status of women; "the all too familiar view of women suddenly emerging in the nineteenth century from a long historical night or to a sunlit plain is completely wrong."[13] A knowledge of early American history makes clear the high responsibilities of the woman; New England sailing men could travel on two and three year voyages knowing that all business at home could be ably discharged by their wives.

The Age of Reason saw man as reason incarnate, and woman as emotion and will, and therefore inferior. The thesis of the Age of Reason has been that the government of all things should be committed to reason. The Age of Reason opposed the Age of Faith self-consciously. Religion was deemed to be woman's business, and, the more the Enlightenment spread, the more church life came to be the domain of women and children. The more pronounced therefore the triumph of the Age of Reason in any culture, the more reduced the role of women became. Just as religion came to be regarded as a useless but sometimes charming ornament, so too women were similarly regarded.

These ideas moved into the United States through the influence of Sir William Blackstone on law, who in turn was influenced by England's

---

11. Phyllis M. Kaberry, *Aboriginal Woman, Sacred and Profane* (London: Routledge and Kegan Paul, 1939).

12. Ferdinand Lundberg and Marynia F. Farnham, M.D., *Modern Woman, The Lost Sex* (New York: Harper, 1947), p. 130.

13. *Ibid.*, p. 421.

Chief Justice Edward Coke, a calculating opportunist. As a result, the law books of the first half of the 19th-century showed woman in a diminished role. Three examples of this are revealing:

> Walker's *Introduction to American Law*: The legal theory is, marriage makes the husband and wife one person, and that person is the husband. There is scarcely a legal act of any description that she is competent to perform. . . . In Ohio, but hardly anywhere else, is she allowed to make a will, if happily she has anything to dispose of.

> Roper's *Law of Husband and Wife*: It is not generally known, that whenever a woman has accepted an offer of marriage, all she has, or expects to have, becomes virtually the property of the man thus accepted as a husband; and no gift or deed executed by her between the period of acceptance and the marriage is held to be valid; for were she permitted to give away or otherwise settle her property, he might be disappointed in the wealth he looked to in making the offer.

> *Wharton's Laws:* The wife is only the servant of her husband.[14]

There is an extremely significant clause in Roper's statement: "*It is not generally known. . . .*" The full implications of the legal revolution were not generally known. Unfortunately, they did come to be generally supported, *by men.* Even more unfortunately, the churches very commonly supported this legal revolution by a one-sided and twisted reading of Scripture. The attitude of men generally was that women were better off being left on a pedestal of uselessness. At a women's rights conference, one speaker answered these statements, Sojourner Truth, a tall, colored woman, prominent in anti-slavery circles and herself a former slave in New York state. She was 82 years of age, had a back scarred from whippings, could neither read nor write, but had "intelligence and common sense." She answered the pedestal advocates powerfully and directly, speaking to the male hecklers in the audience:

> Wall, chilern, whan dar is so much racket dar must be somethin' out of kilter. I tink dat 'twixt de niggers of de Souf and de womin at de Norf, all talkin' 'bout rights, de white men will be in a fix pretty soon. But what's all dis here talkin' 'bout?

> Dat man ober dar say dat womin needs to be helped into carriages, and lifted ober ditches, and to hab de best place everywhar. Nobody eber helps me into carriages, or ober mud-puddles, or gibs me any best place! And a'n't I a woman? Look at me! Look at my arm! . . .

> I have ploughed and planted, and gathered into barns, and no man could head me! And a'n't I a woman? I could work as much and eat as much as a man—when I could get it—and bear de lash as

---

14. Charles Neilson Gattey, *The Bloomer Girls* (New York: Coward-McCann, 1968), p. 21.

well! And a'n't I a woman? I have borne thirteen children, and seen 'em mos' all sold off to slavery, and when I cried out with my mother's grief, none but Jesus heard me! And a'n't I a woman?

Den dat little man in black dar, he say womin can't have as much rights as men, 'cause Christ wan't a woman! Where did your Christ come from? . . .

Whar did your Christ come from? From God and a woman! Man had nothin' to do wid Him.

'Bleeged to ye for hearin' me, and now ole Sojourner han't got nothin' more to say.[15]

The tragedy of the women's rights movement was that, although it had serious wrongs to correct, it added to the problem, and here the resistance of man was in as large a measure responsible. Instead of restoring women to their rightful place of authority beside man, women's rights became feminism: it put women in competition with men. It led to the masculinization of women and feminization of men, to the unhappiness of both. Not surprisingly, in March, 1969, Paris courturier Pierre Cardin took a logical step in his menswear collection show: "the first garment displayed was a sleeveless jumper designed to be worn over high vinyl boots. In other words, a dress."[16]

Thus, the age of Reason brought in an irrational supremacy for men and has led to a war of the sexes. As a result, the laws today work, not to establish godly order, but to favor one sex or another. The laws of Texas reflect the older discrimination against women; the laws of some states (such as California) show a discrimination in favor of women.

To return to the Biblical doctrine, a wife is her husband's *help-meet*. Since Eve was created from Adam and is Adam's reflected image of God, she was of Adam and an image of Adam as well, his "counterpart." The meaning of this is that a true help-meet is man's counterpart, that a cultural, racial, and especially religious similarity is needed so that the woman can truly mirror the man and be his image. A man who is a Christian and a businessman cannot find a helper in a Buddhist woman who believes that nothingness is ultimate and that her husband's way of life is a lower way. Cross-cultural marriages are thus normally a failure. Where we do find such marriages, they prove often on examination to be the union of two humanists whose backgrounds vary but whose faith unites them. Even then, such marriages have a high mortality. A man can identify character *within* his culture, but he cannot do more than identify the general character of another culture. Thus, a German reared in a Lutheran atmosphere can discern the subtle differences among women in his society, but if he marries a Moslem

---

15. *Ibid.*, p. 105 f.
16. *Time*, April 18, 1969, p. 96.

girl, he sees in her the general forms of Moslem feminine conduct rather than the fine shades of character, until too late to withdraw easily.

The Biblical doctrine shows us the wife as the competent manager who is able to take over all business affairs if needed, so that her husband can assume public office as a civil magistrate; in the words of Proverbs 31:23, he can sit "in the gates," that is, preside as a ruler or judge. Let us examine the women of Proverbs 31:10-31, whose "price is far above rubies." Several things are clearly in evidence:

1. Her husband can trust her moral, commercial, and religious integrity and competence, (vss. 11, 12, 29-31).

2. She not only manages her household competently, but she can also manage a business with ability (vss.13-19, 24-25). She can buy and sell like a good merchant and manage a vineyard like an experienced farmer.

3. She is good to her family, and good to the poor and the needy (vss. 20-22).

4. Very important, "She openeth her mouth with wisdom: and in her tongue is the law of kindness" (vs. 26). The useless woman of the Age of Reason, and the useless socialite or jet set woman of today who is a show-piece and a luxury, can and does speak lightly, and as a trifler, because she is a trifle. The godly woman, however, has "in her tongue the law of kindness." People, men and women, who are not triflers avoid trifling and cheap, malicious talk. Loose talk is the luxury of irresponsibility.

5. She does not eat "the bread of idleness" (vs. 27); i.e., the godly woman is not a mere luxury and a pretty decoration. She more than earns her keep.

6. "Her children arise up, and call her blessed; her husband also, and he praiseth her" (vs. 28).

Obviously, such a woman is very different from the pretty doll of the Age of Reason, and the highly competitive masculinized woman of the 20th century who is out to prove that she is as good as any man, if not better.

A Biblical faith will not regard woman as any the less rational or intelligent than man; her reason is normally more practically and personally oriented in terms of her calling as a woman, but she is not less intelligent for that.

Another note is added by King Lemuel in his description of the virtuous woman:

7. "Charm is deceitful and beauty is passing, but a woman who reveres the LORD will be praised" (vs. 30, Berkeley Version).

Nothing derogatory towards physical beauty is here intended, and, elsewhere in Scripture, especially in the Song of Solomon, it is highly appreciated. The point here is that, in relation to the basic qualities of a true and capable help-meet, beauty is a transient virtue, and clever, charming ways are deceitful and have no value in the working relationships of marriage.

Important thus as the role of a woman is as *mother*, Scripture presents her essentially as a *wife*, i.e., a *help-meet*. The reference is therefore not primarily to children but to the Kingdom of God and man's calling therein. Man and wife together are in the covenant called to subdue the earth and to exercise dominion over it.

There are those who hold that *procreation* is the central purpose of marrriage. Certainly the command to "increase and multiply" is very important, but a marriage does not cease to exist if it be childless. St. Augustine wrongly held that I Timothy 5:14 required procreation and defined children as the basic purpose of marriage, and many hold to this opinion.[17] But St. Paul actually said that he was requiring that the younger women, or widows, specifically marry and have children rather than seeking a religious vocation (I Tim. 5:11-15); this is very different from a definition of marriage as procreation. Luther for some time held to the belief that marriage served to provide for procreation and to relieve concupiscence. (Augustine had limited sexual relations to "the necessities of production.")[18] Edith Simon calls attention to the change in Luther's thinking on the subject:

> Before Luther had himself cast off celibacy, he had condemned it merely as a source of continual temptation and distraction to those who were not equal to perpetual chastity—in other words, his attitude then was still basically orthodox, accounting chastity as the higher state. Upon his own experience of marriage, however, that attitude was changed dramatically to one more positive. Perpetual chastity was *bad*. Only in marriage were human beings able to acquire the spiritual health which they had used to seek in the cloister. So the strange thing was that before he had ever experienced sexual release himself, Luther saw marriage as a primarily physical affair, and afterwards saw its benefits as primarily spiritual —evidently not for want of physical communion.[19]

God Himself defined Eve's basic function as a *help-meet*; important as motherhood is, it cannot take priority over God's own declaration.

4. Nakedness

There is no legislation in Scripture concerning nakedness, but a

---

17. See Jean-Marie Vaissiere, *The Family*, Part I, translated and adapted by Canon Scantlebury (no publisher or date), pp. 73-101.
18. *Ibid.*, p. 135n.
19. Edith Simon, *Luther Alive*, p. 337. Simon obviously means "celibacy" where she speaks of "chastity."

consideration of the subject is pertinent to a study of Biblical law, as we shall see.

When the word "nakedness" or "naked" is used in Scripture figuratively, as in Jeremiah 49:10 and Genesis 42:9, it has reference to being "stripped of resources, disarmed." It sometimes also means "discovered, made manifest" (Job 26:6; Heb. 4:13). The primary reference to nakedness is, however, Genesis 2:25, with respect to Adam and Eve in Eden: "And they were both naked, the man and his wife, and were not ashamed."

It is important to understand the meaning of this passage, and then its implications for history. Absurd interpretations abound. Thus, according to Simpson, it means "that they were without consciousness of sex."[1] It is a popular liberal illusion that sex is somehow connected with the fall. The Scripture gives no evidence of this; moreover, since we are informed that Adam observed sex in animals (Gen. 2:20), it is absurd to assume that he received Eve as his wife and remained celibate. Innocence does not mean asexuality.

Smith's comment is of interest in connecting this verse to the next section, but in error concerning the meaning of nakedness:

> This is the description of perfect childlike innocence, and belongs naturally to beings who as yet know neither good nor evil. It is not, however, the conclusion of the marriage section, where it would be indelicate, but the introduction to the account of the temptation, where it prepares the way for man's easy fall. Moreover, there is a play upon words in these two verses. Man is *arom* naked; the serpent is *arum* crafty. Thus in guileless simplicity our first parents fell in with the tempting serpent, who, in obvious contrast with their untried innocence, is described as being of especially subtility.[2]

This is absurd and unbiblical. Adam had not yet sinned, but he knew that to violate God's law is to do evil. Each day that he worked to subdue the earth and to exercise dominion over it, Adam had the satisfaction of knowing and doing good. Again, Smith is absurd and very unbiblical in speaking of Adam and Eve as falling "in guileless simplicity." But the whole point of Scripture is that they sinned knowingly and willfully, trying to be their own gods. To assume simplicity in Adam, who had already made a general classification of the animal world and worked with knowledge in the plant world is ridiculous; he was created a mature man, and he was now a seasoned worker and thinker, a knowledgeable man. Eve, as his wife, had come to share in that knowledge. To assume innocence and simplicity in the fall, or no guile, is to sin against God and His word.

---

1. Cuthbert A. Simpson, "Genesis," in *The Interpreter's Bible*, I, 501.
2. R. Payne Smith, "Genesis," in Ellicott, I, 23.

Leupold's comment is more to the point:

> In this brief statement one more feature is added to the picture of the primeval state of perfection: nothing had transpired to rouse in man a sense of guilt. For to feel no shame is in a perfect state due to having no occasion to feel shame. Everything was at harmony, and man was in complete harmony with himself and with his God.[3]

The shame Adam and Eve felt at their fall had reference first of all to God, from whom they hid themselves (Gen. 3:8), and second to one another. Again Leupold's comment is Biblical:

> Genesis 3:7 . . . That the sense of shame should concentrate itself around that portion of the body which is marked by the organs of generation, no doubt has its deeper reason in this that man instinctively feels that the very fountain and source of life is contaminated by sin. The very act of generation is tainted by sin. If this scripturally portrayed origin of the sense of shame be accepted as true, then all contentions of anthropologists that shame is rather the outgrowth of inhibitions and custom fall away as secondary and incidental. The scriptural account goes to the root of the matter. The only gleam of light in the verse is the fact that where shame is felt, the evildoer's case is not hopeless. He is at least not past feeling in the matter of doing wrong. God's prevenient grace allows this feeling to arise.[4]

Having dealt with the meaning of Genesis 2:25, it is necessary now to turn to its implications for history. The dream of Eden has long dominated men's minds, the hope of a return to Paradise. Very often, a part of this dream has been a return to a state of nakedness and innocence, and some groups, from the Adamites of medieval history to the nudists of today, believe that the road to innocence lies through nakedness. In other words, it is held that clothing is a provocative factor and that men will return to innocence only when they return to nakedness or nudity. The fall of man is thus ascribed to clothing. Get rid of clothing, and you thereby get rid of sin and all man's problems. Health, peace of mind, fraternity, and equality will return with nudism, it is held.

This thesis has gained support from psychologists and sociologists. It is in essence a religious faith. The editor of *Psychology Today* called it "a gentle humanism"; humanism, at any rate, it clearly is.[5] The literature on the subject so clearly underscores the return to Paradise theme that nudists as a rule claim that nudism provokes no sexual response in them.

Psychologist Leonard Blank of Rutgers did note that "nudists present

---

3. Leupold, *Genesis*, p. 137 f.
4. *Ibid.*, p. 154 f.
5. T. George Harris, "Editorial," *Psychology Today*, vol. 3, no. 1 (June, 1969), p. 17.

greater personality deviations, sexual conflicts and inhibitions, and distortions of body images, than non-nudists." His study also showed that membership or participation in a nudist camp was always a man's decision: "never did the wife want to go more than the husband."[6] Blank's title reveals more about nudism, in fact, than his entire article: "Nudity as a Quest for Life the Way it Was Before the Apple." The appeal of nudism is the desire to return to Eden. We must not overlook the voyeuristic tendencies of the men involved, but the return to Paradise is clearly an important and basic factor. Voyeurism is too fully satisfied in other ways in modern society! Blank's summary statement is both telling and amusing:

> Clothes help identify our position in society and nudity removes an important piece of sign equipment. Nudists claim they can associate with others without being categorized by clothing. Although nudists may idealize this claim somewhat, the nudist camp does effectively break down patterns found on the outside. Sex, class and power are less relevant in a nude society, and suspension of these artificial barriers increases togetherness. Even in the nudist camp there are personality clashes, cliques and intergroup disagreements. Not everyone finds Utopia there: 30 per cent of the respondents would be little if at all affected if the camp closed, 26 per cent would be somewhat affected and only 43 per cent would be very affected. Asked to list their three best friends, 49 per cent did not list a single nudist.

> Several blue-collar workers said that nudism allowed their families to associate with a better class of people without being classified by their uniforms or customary clothing. We lessen status-striving when we remove one of the major props of impression management. In nudist camps, status takes other forms: the pale skin of the sporadic visitor is looked down on. The cotton tail, or person with tanned body and white buttocks, commands less prestige but draws interested looks.[7]

Not surprisingly, psychologists and sociologists who share the myth that the road to health and innocence is through nudity are trying nudity as a therapy. Hollywood psychologist Paul Bindrim, with Dr. William E. Hartman, professor of sociology at California State College, Long Beach, California, has held "nude marathons" as therapy for troubled people. His title is to the point: "Nudity as a Quick Grab for Intimacy in Group Therapy." He believes that "at least temporarily" he has cured frigidity, male impotence, exhibitionism, arthritis, suicidal tendencies, psychosis, and "revitalized" marriages.[8] This is quite likely: people have reported even more amazing cures from little black boxes and a wild

6. Leonard Blank, "Nudity as a Quest of Life the Way It Was Before the Apple," in *ibid.*, pp. 20, 23.
7. *Ibid.*, p. 21.
8. Paul Bindrim, "Nudity as a Quick Grab for Intimacy in Group Therapy," in *ibid.*, p. 28.

variety of quackery.[9] The usual mental patient who consults a psychologist or psychiatrist is often a person who is regularly "helped" or "cured" by a wide variety of practitioners and things.

But to return to nudism and Paradise: *first* of all, a return to Eden is not a Biblical hope. Eden was free from sin but it was still *the* primitive society, man's beginning, not the end. The goal is the developed Kingdom of God, the New Jerusalem, a world order under God's law.

Second, there is no reason to assume that nakedness was a basic condition of Paradise, i.e., essential to it. The emphasis in the text is on the *shame,* not the nakedness. We can safely assume, in view of what Adam accomplished in Eden, that some time was spent there. In having the responsibility of dressing or tilling the garden, Adam had a need for tools, and we may assume that he began to develop some. Certainly the early evidence of crafts and arts in his descendants indicates early beginnings. Moreover, almost at once Adam felt some need for shelter; after all, the nightly heavy mist or dew which then watered the earth (Gen. 2:6) made shelter an immediate necessity. Bare feet on wet grass probably led Adam to decide, after his first morning, to devise some answer to that problem, so that some kind of sandal-wear was adopted probably fairly early. If not adopted before Eve's creation, it was, we can safely assume, developed very shortly thereafter at her prodding. Briefly stated, it is safe to assume that, without the fall, clothing would have been very soon invented.

Third, in some form, the ability to make garments or coverings, perhaps for sleeping purposes, had already been attained. When the shame of their fall struck them, they immediately "sewed fig leaves together, and made themselves aprons" (Gen. 3:7) or skirts. The ability was already there. Clothes may have been made before by Eve experimentally, as adornment, or as a cover against the morning dew. The *new* element was a desire to be covered because of the shame of sin.

Fourth, Adam and Eve were alone in Eden; as yet no other men existed.

Thus, it is apparent that the faith of nudism and of humanism in a cure-all in nudity is absurd. A return to primitivism is not the solution to man's problems. The desire to abolish inequalities and differences by divesting people of clothes fails to reckon with the fact that clothes do not make for the differences in society: people do, and, even in nudist camps leaders and followers, popular and unpopular people, as well as class lines do clearly appear in spite of hopes to the contrary.

The law is not oriented to the past and to nudity but rather to the future and to progress away from primitivism. It is not without reason

9. See Beverly Nichols, *Powers That Be* (New York: St. Martin's Press, 1966).

that the distinction between civilized and uncivilized peoples appears in the matter of clothing as well as in other matters. Nudism is primitivism, and it is both pathetic and suicidal as a philosophy.

5. Family Law

A strange passage of Scripture points to a fact of law commonly overlooked. Cain, on hearing his sentence for murder from God, complained, saying,

> My punishment is greater than I can bear. Behold, thou hast driven me out this day from the face of the earth; and from thy face shall I be hid; and I shall be a fugitive and a vagabond in the earth; and it shall come to pass, that every one that findeth me shall slay me.

> And the LORD said unto him, Therefore whosoever slayeth Cain, vengeance shall be taken on him sevenfold. And the LORD set a mark upon Cain, lest any finding him should kill him.

> And Cain went out from the presense of the LORD, and dwelt in the land of Nod, on the east of Eden (Gen. 4:13-16).

Because God does not change, His ultimate purposes are always implicit in His earlier acts, and therefore part of the framework of His declaration to Cain is His law-order. Certain questions thus immediately come to mind: of whom was Cain afraid? Who did he fear would kill him? That the fear was more than psychological is apparent in the fact that God "set a mark upon Cain, lest any finding him should kill him." Cain obviously needed this protection. Again, why did God, who very early made clear His requirement of the death penalty for murder (Gen. 9:6) here act to protect a murderer?

Before dealing with these questions, a brief examination of the text is of interest. Leupold rendered Genesis 4:14 thus: "Behold, thou hast this day driven me forth off the ground and I must stay hidden from Thee, and I must be shifting and straying about in the earth, and it will happen that whoever finds me will slay me." Cain's words clearly presuppose the death penalty for murder: God's law had been earlier declared, and Cain sees the need to escape from both God and man, and he complains against the odds. The fact that his was a vicious murder makes no difference to him; he feels the punishment is hopelessly unfair to him.

Furthermore, Leupold translated vs. 16b, "And Yahweh gave Cain a sign that whoever found him would not murder him." Leupold noted,

> . . . that the text does not say that God set a mark *in* or *on* Cain (Hebrew, *be*) but *for* Cain (Hebrew *le*), marking a dative of interest or advantage. Consequently, we are rather to think of some sign that God allowed to appear for Cain's reassurance, "a sign of guaranty" or a "pledge or token." As parallels might be

cited the signs vouchsafed to certain men to whom God promised unusual things: Gideon (Judges 6:36-40); Elisha (II Kings 2:9-12). God let this sign appear, therefore, for Cain, and he felt reassured. There is, therefore, no ground for supposing that Cain went about as a marked man all the rest of his life. Anyhow, *'oth* does not mean "mark."[1]

To return to the earlier questions, of whom was Cain afraid, and who did he fear would kill him, the answer is already apparent. Cain very obviously feared that God, having declared His law to mankind orally from the beginning, would Himself perhaps execute the death penalty against Cain. Moreover, he feared that other men would also kill him because God's law placed them under obligation to do so. Cain's words clearly indicate that a law-order had been instituted. Cain was a mature and married man (Gen. 4:17). Adam had a number of sons and daughters, whose names are never given to us, during his 930 years of life (Gen. 5:3-5). As a result, by the time of Abel's murder a number of persons already existed who were ready and capable of enforcing the law. Adam, as the head of his household and of the young humanity, was in a position to require enforcement of his family members.

The family thus was clearly a law-order, geared to a discipline and ready to enforce its law on its members. Cain's reaction is obvious evidence of this. God clearly had established the family as a law-order.

This brings us to our major question: why then, in apparent contradiction to the rest of Scripture, does God move here to protect Cain from being killed? Protection for crime was clearly not God's purpose. At every point, Scripture reveals God as the enemy of sin, and His demand for judgment is so strict and unwavering, that only the death of Jesus Christ could make atonement for sin by fulfiling the law to the full. Obviously, then, God's purpose here was not the protection of Cain; rather, the protection of Cain was a by-product of His central purpose. God Himself is revealed as Cain's accuser, and the very earth, because God created it, witnesses to God's law against Cain (Gen. 4:9-12). The question we must ask then is this: what kind of law-order was God maintaining which incidently led to Cain's protection? This is the key question, and, unfortunately, commentators do not ask it.

The family very clearly has a serious role in law enforcement. The family is a law-order and disciplines its members. The nature and extent of the family's punishing power can be seen by looking again at a text previously considered, Deuteronomy 21:18-21, the death penalty for juvenile delinquents. There are certain very important aspects to this

---

1. Leupold, *Exposition of Genesis*, p. 211.

law. *First,* the parents are to be complaining witnesses against their criminal son. The loyalty of the parents must thus be to God's law-order, not to ties of blood. If the parents do not assist in the prosecution of a criminal child, they are then accessories to the crime. *Second,* contrary to the usual custom, whereby witnesses led in the execution, in this case, "the men of the city" did. Thus, where the death penalty was involved, the family was excluded from the execution of the law.

Now to return to Cain: Cain was obviously reared in a family which was a disciplined law-order. Both he and Abel, as other children, were disciplined and productive workers. Cain knew of the death penalty for murder and feared it. The remarkable protection of Cain from the death penalty was due to the fact that the family was barred from an area of law enforcement, the death penalty, which properly belongs to the state. In Cain's day, mankind was made up of Adam and Eve and a number of sons and daughters. "A sign of guaranty" was given to Cain that he would not be executed by his parents or by his brothers and sisters. Very obviously, the family was informed of this, because this part of Genesis (1:1–5:1) is Adam's record. Later Cain built the first city, i.e., a *walled* community, to protect himself. Cain did not require protection from Adam's household; he did require it from his own progeny. We have Lamech's declaration of his readiness to kill if his honor were wounded (Gen.4:23-24); significantly, Lamech simply stepped up the lawlessness Cain had practiced: "If Cain shall be avenged sevenfold, truly Lamech seventy and sevenfold" (Gen. 4:24).

The family thus was created as the central law-order, but at the same time was strictly limited, in that the death penalty was withheld from it. The family can discipline, punish, and cast out a member, but it cannot kill him; at that point, it must turn to the state simply as a witness to the offense. It cannot be the executioner.

The family has real powers; a godless child can be disinherited; he can be punished in a variety of ways. But the basic fact of Biblical law is that the power to kill is not a family power, because coercion is not the strongest aspect of family law. The family is tied together by bonds of love; the husband *cleaves* to the wife, and the children obey their parents in love and duty.

Basic to family law thus is the inner bond of blood and faith. The Bible does not speak of gratitude (a word not used in the Bible); its term is thankfulness, and this is assumed, not required. We have seen previously how closely associated parental authority and God's authority are (Lev. 19:3). This is further demonstrated by Isaiah 45:9,10:

> Woe unto him that striveth with his Maker! Let the potsherd strive with the potsherds of the earth. Shall the clay say to him that fashioned it, What makest thou? or thy work, He hath no hands?

Woe unto him that saith unto his father, What begetteth thou? or to the woman, What hast thou brought forth?

The same thought appears in Isaiah 10:15. The idea of anyone being ungrateful to God or to one's parents is presented as the epitome of what is revolting and disgusting. Parents may or may not be lovable; in any case, the duty of gratitude remains. Nowadays, the lack of gratitude by children who receive not only life, but very generous and even wealthy provisions from their parents, and yet manifest ingratitude to either one or both of their parents, is especially repulsive. Such children may be free of other moral blemishes, but, if the passage from Isaiah 45:9, 10 has any meaning, they are moral monsters.

This passage from Isaiah throws light on Cain's deliverence from the death penalty. Family discipline can mean disinheritance; it can mean denouncing a child to the civil authorities. But the death penalty is reserved to God and the state. To give that power to the family is to destroy the inner tie that binds the family. The protection of Cain was thus not with reference to Cain as a person but the life of the family and its law sphere.

The one exception to this principle of the non-participation of the family in the death penalty of its members appears in Deuteronomy 13:6-9. If a member of the family tried to lead members into idolatry, their execution *required* the participation of the family. Such a person was no longer a relative: he was an alien and an enemy. Later custom saw the service of the dead read over apostates in the family circle: the apostate was no longer a member of the family but an enemy alien.

Dooyeweerd has described the psychic structure of the family as "the feeling of authority on the part of the parents, on the other hand the feeling of respect on the part of the children."[2] The absence of either authority or respect results in a serious breakdown of the family as a law-order. The family is not only a biological entity but a religious one. As such, it has inner ties which are God-ordained and religiously governed; love may be absent, but the religious authority and religious respect must remain. Their absence indicates a radical evil. No child can plead that his parents do not merit respect; love is his personal response, but respect and honor are his God-ordained duties, and failure to give respect is thus a sin against God rather than the parent.

As a result, while parents and children can and must seperate themselves from an incorrigible member and report him to the authorities, they cannot execute him. God forbids this act to any but the state. Similarly, a son or daughter can dislike a parent, and, with maturity,

---

2. Herman Dooyeweerd, *A New Critique of Theoretical Thought* (Philadelphia: The Presbyterian and Reformed Publishing Company, 1957), III, 294.

separate himself to a degree while maintaining his God-ordained duties, but he cannot deny that parent respect and honor without incurring God's judgment. Thus, not only is there a limit beyond which a parent cannot go in judging his child, i.e., the death penalty being barred, but there is also a limit beyond which the child cannot go: honor and respect must be given because of the God-ordained nature of the relationship, not because of the person of the parent necessarily. Where this respect is lacking, the child should be written off, at least for the time being, as unworthy of attention. Whatever their qualities, these children are at war at this point with God, since honor, respect, and reverence are God's requirements long before their parents ever expected them.

If God had not barred the family from killing guilty members, even at the price of allowing Cain to go free, the price would have been a fearful one. On the one hand, the development of the state as God's ministry of justice would have been impossible. The realm of the state would then have been pre-empted by the family. On the other hand, the family itself would have been destroyed by this new burden. The world would have been an anarchistic order, family arrayed against family, and the family arrayed against itself. It was thus not Cain whom God protected but, in reality, God's own law-order.

6.   Marriage and Monogamy

One of the facts which disturbs many persons with respect to Biblical laws concerning marriage is the seeming tolerance of polygamy, of more than one wife, and the total intolerance of adultery, which in the Old Testament called for the death penalty. The moralist today will tolerate adultery but not polygamy. The answer to this conflict of viewpoints lies in an analysis of the Biblical law.

First of all, very clearly the purpose of God in creation was that monogamy be the standard for man. The original, perfect standard saw the creation of Eve, one woman, for Adam, one man (Gen. 2:18-24). The normative marriage is clearly monogamous.

Second, polygamy clearly appears as a product of the fall, in a world of sin. The first recorded bigamous marriage is that of Cain's descendant, Lamech, who had Adah and Zillah as wives (Gen. 4:23).

Third, the prohibition of polygamy is implied in Genesis 2:23, 24, and is stated in one reading of Leviticus 18:18, "Thou shalt not take a wife to another, to vex her, to uncover her nakedness, beside her in her lifetime." The Berekley Version, while reading it in terms of the King James Version, still separates it from the laws of incest, Leviticus 18: 6-17, and reads the first clause as "While your wife is still living," which points to the prohibition of bigamy.

Fourth, I Timothy 3:2 makes clear that polygamy was forbidden to church officers: "The bishop then must be blameless, the husband of one wife. . . ." The Montanists read this as a ban on *all* second marriages, which they termed bigamous; a widower or a widow was thus still bound by the original marriage. There is no Biblical warrant for such an interpretation.

Fifth, there is at least an implied condemnation of polygamy in Deuteronomy 17:17, which forbad the king to "multiply wives to himself." Similarly, the high priest could only marry one wife, and that a virgin (Lev. 21:13, 14).

Sixth, it is clearly stated by Jesus Christ that marriage is the union of one man and one woman, and that this is the meaning of Genesis 2: 24; it is the *two* or *twain* who are "one flesh," i.e., a true marriage (Matt. 19:5).

Seventh, St. Paul spoke of marriage in monogamous terms: "let every man have his own wife, and . . . every woman . . . her own husband" (I Cor. 7:2).

In passage after passage, monogamy, is *assumed* to be the God-ordained standard. On the other hand, in many passages, polygamy is a recognized and accepted fact, not only among the reprobate, like Lamech (Gen. 4:19) and Esau (Gen. 26:34; 28:9; 36:2), but also among the patriarchs and saints. Jacob had two wives and two concubines (Gen. 29:15 *et seq.*); Elkanah, two wives (I Sam. 1:1, 2); Gideon, David, and Solomon, many wives, and concubines as well. Adam, Noah, Lot, Isaac, Moses, and many others, were monogamous. The instances of polygamy in the Bible are not too many, but they are conspicuous to us because of their variation from our standards and practices.

The law did recognize and regulate concubinage and polygamy. *First,* a man could not simply use a concubine. She was entitled to her food, clothing, and to sexual relations without dimunition; failure to do these three things was ground for divorce, without any recompense of the dowry or of the bridal money (Ex. 21:10, 11). Not even a war-captive woman could be denied her rights (Deut. 21:10-14).

Second, a "bondmaid betrothed to a husband" (Lev. 19:20), i.e., a girl who has been secured as a concubine, could not be put to death for adultery; both she and the guilty man could only be punished by scourging. The reason is given: "they shall not be put to death, because she was not free" (Lev. 19:20). A principle is clearly in evidence here: to whom much is given, from him much can be expected. But, since a concubine receives a limited status and receives less dignity in the marriage, only a limited loyalty can be expected. She was expected to be faithful, but in case of adultery her punishment was less, because her status was lower than that of the endowered wife. The wife had the security of her dowry and a status of authority; her punishment for adultery, as was the punishment for her husband for adultery, was death.

Third, it is thus apparent that the law tolerated polygamy while establishing monogamy as the standard. The reason for this toleration was the fact that the polygamous family was still a family, a lower form of family life, but a tolerable one (whereas polyandry is not, since it violates the basic centrality of the man and his calling). Biblical law thus protects the *family* and does not tolerate *adultery*, which threatens and destroys the family. Humanistic law protects the *anarchistic individual* by denying that adultery is a crime, and it sacrifices the family progressively to the individual.

Polygamy, thus, is tolerated in Biblical law, but the standard established by the creation ordinance and laid down by St. Paul for members (I Cor. 7:2) and for officers (I Tim. 3:2) of Christ's kingdom is monogamy.

Having said this, it is necessary to add that ancient polygamy had often other than sexual aspects. An important aspect of ancient polygamy was its governmental function. A man of wealth needed trustworthy associates to assume the government of an estate, or a ruler needed persons to act as his agents in a province or city. A wife was usually the most reliable associate under such circumstances. Very commonly the woman was the widow of an experienced officer or ruler, often elderly, so that sexual relations frequently did not occur. She was visited from time to time by her husband, whose authority re-inforced hers by his visits. If she dwelt within his home, such a wife was entrusted with the supervision of certain aspects of his business.

In Solomon's case, most of his wives and concubines represented foreign alliances and were a means of establishing both peace with Israel and favorable trade relations with it. If they were sexually attractive, this furthered their usefulness. A princess sent to Solomon's court would be accompanied by several nobly born ladies in waiting and some concubines or slave-girls; all would be sent with the advantage of the mother country in mind. Their marriage to Solomon and their pride in his power and glory made them loyal to Solomon; their national origin led them obviously to seek diplomatic and commercial advantages for their mother country. Polygamous wives have thus been a common answer to the need for a civil service.

Forms of this governmental polygamy still survive in various parts of the world, although on the wane.

Another form of polygamy is *economic*; this is especially prevalent in "primitive" cultures. In African tribes, for example, since much of the farm work depends on the wife, a second wife means another field worker. It is not at all surprising that, in economic polygamy, the over-worked wife welcomes help in the form of additional wives.

A rarer form of polygamy has been as a remedy for disaster. Such instances have been very rare, and the pretext of necessity often used. Mormon polygamy was *religious and soteriological;* women were in short supply, but polygamy was held to be a religious requirement or ordinance. The Thirty Years War saw so fearful a devastation, so many men killed, and so many women left unprotected, that the Diet legalized polygamy briefly in order to bring about a restoration of family life.

Most polygamy, especially in modern times, has been essentially sexual in purpose, and it is this kind of polygamy which most people associate with the word. The dream concept of foolish men is of a lordly male ability to use a number of women at will. This idea is very much an illusion. Several things militate against this dream. *First,* polygamous marriages are still marriages; they involve the union of two families. The wife or concubine cannot be dealt with at will without offending the in-laws. In a polygamous marriage, the woman tends to be closer to her family than to her husband. Mistreatment of the wife can mean serious trouble with in-laws who are now enemies. Very few men have been powerful enough to disregard this factor. Apart from a few monarchs, the men who have been able in any generation to disregard the woman's family have been scarce. In a polygamous family, the ties to the family of origin are usually intense and jealous.

Second, if a sultan need not fear his in-laws because he is too powerful, he still must fear his wives and concubines, who can do him much harm. The Turkish sultans drowned wives and concubines in great numbers. We know that as many as 300 women were drowned on some occasions, sometimes for intrigue, once for pleasure during the reign of Ibrahim, who, after one of his debauches, decided to get rid of his old harem and have the fun of replacing it.[1] But, it must be added, even the Turkish sultans, when not murdering their wives, moved with some fear of them. The Sultan's favorite for the night was smuggled secretly into his room, to avoid the jealous eyes of other members of the harem and of the favorite or queen. Moreover, custom as well as a satisfactory relationship required the Sultan to pay her money, jewels, and clothes to the degree of pleasure received.[2] Where the relationship between lord and harem members was so slight a one, these gifts were necessary to add incentives to the relationship. Thus, even with the power to *kill* his wives at will, the sultan still had to sneak into an appointed room like an adulterer in order to *live* with his wives.

Third, in every society, whether polygamous, or monogamous, certain

---

1. N. M. Penzer, *The Harem* (London: Spring Books, 1965), p. 185 f.
2. *Ibid.*, p. 181 f.

obligations exist between man and wife. These duties are not as strict in a monogamous marriage, because then husband and wife are normally working together for a common goal. In polygamous marriages, the obligations of the husband are spelled out more precisely to prevent the abuse of any wife. The following example is typical:

> Among several tribes of the Syrian-Arabian desert a man has to divide his marital attentions equally between his two wives. He must alternately spend one night with one and one with the other. Each of the wives cook for him a day in turn, and on that day it is the woman's right to have the husband spend the night with her, whether he cohabits with her or not. If the husband spends the night with one wife out of turn, he must compensate the other with a sheep or a goat as the price for her night. Sometimes the two wives strike a bargain and one of them buys a night from the other whose turn it is.[3]

Certain things are implicit in this which are rarely written about but are common knowledge in polygamous countries. The husband's sexual rights in a polygamous marriage are technically broad but actually severely limited; he pays for any liberty he exercises. Moreover, he faces quarrelling wives who are rivals for his favor but unite as women against him. If he has two or more wives, he must enjoy the cooking of all; if he eats lightly of one woman's cooking, she is furious and jealous. At the same time, she will brag to the other wives of how he gorged himself on the desserts she fed him at bed-time. In a like manner, each wife will boast of his sexual prowess with her. Thus, the tired man is told by a furious wife that he was passionate enough last night with another; let him prove it tonight with her, instead of resting. The next morning she will declare to the other women that she hardly slept all night, so furious and continuous was her husband's passion. As a result, the poor man is in trouble with the next wife and sure of another harried night. The distrust and hatred of women is deeply imbedded in all polygamous societies, and polygamous men are not known as home-bodies. The life of the polygamous husband is one of ostensible power but of actual bondage. It can be added that, because the harem women have their set bed rights in rotation, there is often less concern about being pleasing in person, manners, and appearance. The marital rights, the threat of in-law trouble, the prestige which comes from bearing sons, all give the woman a position of power. The man's power can be brutal, as the Turkish sultan's power to kill evidences in extreme form. The woman's power in polygamous countries comes from exploiting her strategic weapons. It is not surprising that in polygamous societies women are

---

3. Raphael Patai, *Golden River to Golden Road, Society, Culture and Change in the Middle East* (Philadelphia: University of Pennsylvania Press, 1962), p. 94.

feared as the epitome of evil. Buddha said that "Woman is the person-ification of evil." The modern Arab opinion is similar.[4]

We can thus conclude, *fourth*, that only in monogamy does the man have real rights, because only in the monogamous marriage is there a true union of man and wife. Instead of competition for a man's favor, the Christian monogamous marriage sees the woman united to her husband in godly faith and love. There is trust instead of rivalry. In such a marriage, the man commands a love, service, and loyalty which is not common to polygamous unions. He exercises rights unknown in other cultures. It is not an accident of history that in Christian countries women are more responsible, more capable of productive work, and far more attractive than in other cultures. Christian monogamous marriage is marriage in its truest form because it is faithful to the laws of creation.

The social significance of the Biblical standard is apparent in the research of J. D. Unwin. Biblical law restricts sexual intercourse to marriage and holds the monogamous marriage to be the norm. Thus, premarital chastity is required, and marital fidelity also. Unwin began his research determined to dispel the idea that any necessary connection exists between the level of civilization and its sexual morality. He found instead that, if we know the sexual regulations and conduct of a society, we can accurately "prophesy" (and the word is his) "the pattern of its cultural behavior." Mental development and cultural advance go hand in hand with the development of strict monogamy and pre-marital and post-marital chastity. A society with pre-marital and post-marital license is at a dead level culturally and mentally. It progresses to the degree that its sexual regulations move towards a strict monogamy. In three gener-ations the impact of a new morality is fully felt. As a result, Unwin felt, the strict rules of chastity and continence cannot be unnatural, since they are productive of the best in nature.[5] It is significant that Unwin's attempt to establish artificially or rationally a moral standard for a new society was an intellectual failure; nothing can replace religious motivation for moral standards.[6]

It is significant also that those who idealize promiscuity and license as an ideal for man can only find their standards in very "primitive" or degraded cultures. Two works which have greatly influenced the mod-

---

4. See Youssef El Masey, *Daughters of Sin: The Sexual Tragedy of Arab Women* (New York: Macfadden, 1963), p. 87.

5. See Joseph Daniel Unwin, *Sex and Culture* (Oxford University Press, 1934); *Sexual Regulations and Cultural Behaviour, An Address delivered before the Medical Section of the British Psychological Society, 27 March 1935* (Oxford, 1935); "Monogamy as a Condition of Social Energy," in *The Hibbert Journal*, vol. XXV, no. 4 (July, 1927), pp. 662-677.

6. See J. D. Unwin, *Hopousia, or The Sexual and Economic Foundations of a New Society* (New York: Oskar Priest, 1940).

ern anti-Christian sexual license are Bronislaw Malinowski's *The Sexual Life of Savages* (1929) and Boris de Rachewiltz' *Black Eros, The Sexual Customs of Africa from Prehistoric Times to the Present Day* (1956, in English, 1964). Malinowski's study of the Trobiand islanders has been called "virtually the Bible of all those supporting Free-Love group living.[7] Blake's comment on the supposedly ideal society of Malinowski's Trobianders is to the point:

> . . . the noted anthropologist stated unequivocally that the "Trobianders know, in their third decade of our century (1920-1930), no sexual perversions, no functional psychosis, no sex murder: they have no word for theft; homosexuality, and masturbation, to them, mean nothing but an unnatural and imperfect means of sexual gratification, a sign of disturbed capacity to reach normal satisfaction. The socially accepted form of sexual life is spontaneous monogamy without compulsion, a relationship which can be dissolved without difficulties; thus there is no promiscuity."
>
> Of course, there is no promiscuity, technically speaking, where there are no laws or social taboos. If there were no laws against murder, there would be no murder either. Where there is no obligation, no responsibility on anyone's part, it is simple enough to say that the problems of rape, adultery, child-love, non-support, etc. do not exist.[8]

Similar justifications prevail today. We are assured that Denmark has seen a drop in sexual crimes with the abandonment of laws against pornography, but we are not told that most perversions are no longer regarded as criminal offenses, so that the decline in crime is in reality a decline in law enforcement. In such a context, statistics are more than worthless: they are dishonest.

7. Incest

Biblical law prohibits incest (Lev. 18:7-17; 20:11, 12, 14, 17, 20, 21; Deut. 22:30; 27:20, 22, 23) and requires the death penalty for this offense in most cases.

The laws on incest can be summarized briefly. Sexual relations and/or marriage is forbidden with a mother, father, step-mother, sister or brother, half-sister or half-brother, a grand-daughter, with a daughter-in-law (or son-in-law), with an aunt (or uncle), with a brother's wife, or with both mother and daughter. The punishment is death except for marriage with the wife of an uncle, with a blood aunt, or with a brother's wife, where the punishment was to bear their iniquity and die childless (Lev. 20:19-21).

It is important to understand the meaning of "childless" here. It

---

7. Roger Blake, *The Free-Love Groups* (Cleveland: Century Books, 1966), p. 89.
   8. *Ibid.*, p. 94 f.

clearly did not mean that no children were born, because then and now incestuous intercourse and/or marriages have resulted in children. The Talmud reveals that a child born of incest or adultery was barred from regular marriage within the community.[1] Such a couple were childless in that they had no legal heir in their progeny.

The question which comes to the modern mind on reading the Biblical law at this point is very simply this: why was it necessary to forbid such unappealing unions? One university professor ridiculed regularly the law that he stated he saw inscribed on an English cathedral: "Thou shalt not marry thy grandmother." Who he demanded, wanted to marry his grandmother? His ignorance of history was notable. More marriages have been contracted in history, probably, with property in mind than sex. The seizure of estates by forced marriages, and the prevention of the alienation or dispersal of family funds and properties by means of inter-marriage within a family, is an old story. The decline of European royal and noble families, as well as a weakening of strength in America's Jewish aristocracy, is a development which has run parallel with extensive inbreeding.

The purpose of polyandry in Tibet was to maintain intact the inheritance in land. Instead of fractional heirship in the land, all the brothers shared a common wife and retained the land intact by conforming marriage to an ideal of a stabilized society and unbroken transmission of land.

The laws of incest were given through Moses. Prior to that time, incest was clearly not considered wrong. Moses' own father, Amram, married a young aunt, his father's sister, Jochabed (Ex. 6:20). The practice of incest continued in many areas at a much later date. Thus, in Assyria, a problem existed because of the continued practice. A son, "after the death of the father rests in the arms of his mother or step-mother," whereas the father "had to do with daughters and stepdaughters."[2] The Assyrian practice represented perverse sexuality; that of Amram and others was a pre-legislative innocence of wrong-doing.

In Egypt, full brother-sister marriages were the rule among the pharaohs, and even into the second century A.D., such marriages were the majority of unions in some districts of Egypt. The prevalence and acceptance of such marriages in Egypt made the Mosaic law all the more radical a break with the Egyptian past.

Obviously, Adam's children married one another; clearly, also, marriage with relatives did occur in subsequent history. The Bible speaks of Abraham marrying Sarah, possibly a half-sister (Gen. 20:12); the

---

1. Mekkoth, 90n, in Seder Nezikim IV.
2. Jurgen Thorwald, *Science and Secrets of Early Medicine* (New York: Harcourt, Brace & World, 1963), p. 165 f.

two supposedly had a common father. The other instance, Amram, has already been cited.

The records indicate close inbreeding in ancient times without serious or any genetic damage, whereas today the genetic damage is great. The genetic inheritance of man was at that time sufficiently broad to make the possibility of too close a genetic strain in near relatives improbable. The genetic potentialities of Adam and Eve in Eden were wholly good. After the fall, which affected the total man, defects were no doubt present but recessive, coming to the fore only with progressive inbreeding. Arthur C. Custance has called attention to the present situation with respect to inbreeding:

> From a mathematical point of view, the situation may be put in this way: that matings among first cousins (as in Darwin's case, for example, or his sister Caroline's case) result in the offspring having identical genes in a ratio of 1 to 7. Many of these genes will be recessive mutants and therefore detrimental to the possessor when inherited homozygously. Mating of uncle to niece or nephew to aunt raises this ratio to 1 to 3. Matings among brothers and sisters raises this ratio, often disastrously, to 1 to 1.[3]

This danger did not exist in early times. Genesis is written with an awareness, for example, that murder is a sin, and adultery, theft and false witness also, but with no awareness of any wrong-doing or danger existing in marriage within the prohibited degrees. At that time, no danger existed. Incest is a biological offense, but no less a fearful one, and the death penalty is God's ordinance. A study on "Risks to Offspring of Incest," in *The Lancet* (London), February 25, 1967 (p. 436), is telling concerning the danger genetically:

> Medical practitioners are sometimes asked about the advisability of the adoption of a child born as the result of incest. Such children will have an increased risk of being affected by recessive conditions. In order to get an estimate of the extent of this risk, in 1958 I invited Children's Officers to let me know prospectively of pregnancies or of new births in which it was known that the pregnancy or birth was the result of incest between first degree relatives.

> These children were followed prospectively and anonymously through the Children's Officers. The children were known to me by number only and all correspondence referred only to the child's number. Thirteen cases of incest (6 father-daughter and 7 brother-sister) were reported to me in 1958 and 59, and the latest information on them was in mid year 1965 when the children were all 4 to 6 years old. I summarize there the information on these 13 children.

> Three children are dead: one at 15 months of cystic fibrosis of the pancreas, confirmed at necropsy; one at 2½ months of progressive

3. Arthur C. Custance, *Doorway Papers, no. 51: Cain's Wife* (Ottawa, Canada: 1967), p. 8.

cerebral degeneration with blindness; and one at 7 years, 11 months of Fallot's Tetrology (this child had an IQ of 70). One child is severely sub-normal, with much delayed-milestones, and was considered non-testable at age 4 years, 9 months, when she had a vocabulary of only a few words. Four children are educatively subnormal: the known IQ of 3 are 59, 65, and 76. The remaining children are normal.

The risk of parents sharing a recessive gene will be four times greater in cases of incest between first degree relatives than it would be between first cousins.[4]

Custance draws some very important inferences from this and other data. Incest today is very clearly detrimental genetically in a very large percentage of cases. With each generation, the number of damaged genes increases rather than decreases. This means that the long history of man posited by evolutionists is impossible, in that the genetic deterioration would then be very far gone.

The Biblical record actually shows only 77 generations from Adam to Christ, and if we add to this the 2000 years since, we have something like 100 to 120 generations covering the whole of human history. Since the accumulation of defective genes is only meaningful in terms of their effect on the basis of successive generations, it is not altogether unlikely that the first human beings (namely, Adam and Eve) were indeed perfect, and that the damage started to be done following the Fall has accumulated until we reach the present situation in which there are still *some* possibilities of successful brother-sister matings, though the odds are against it. At the rate at which these mutations occur in each generation, according to the current genetical theory, one would not expect to find any undamaged segments of the individual's inherited stock of genes if the human race had been multiplying for thousands upon thousands of generations. We would all be so badly damaged by now that no brother-sister marriage could possibly succeed any longer.

On the other hand, taking the Biblical story as it stands, Adam's sons and daughters (Gen. 5:4), of whom Cain was one and his wife another, need not have been carriers of any more than a mere token of the damaged genetic stock and such a marriage need not have endangered the offspring.

There is, surprisingly enough, direct evidence in Scripture that this interpretation of the events is strictly true, for we are first of all presented with a list of immediate descendants for some ten generations from Adam to Noah who enjoyed what must be described as magnificent viability. Consider for a moment what was happening during this period of time. Previous to the Flood, man may well have been shielded against at least one source of danger to the genes, cosmic radiation, by the existence of some kind of barrier in

---

4. *Ibid.*, p. 10 f.

the upper atmosphere. There are many who believe that this barrier disappeared at the time of the Flood and could indeed have been related to that event. The pre-Flood population (both *men* and *animals,* be it noted) may therefore have suffered little damage to their genes throughout each succeeding generation while these environmental conditions existed.[5]

Clearly history has witnessed genetic deterioration. Selective breeding in Christian countries has led to a degree to the progressive elimination of many defective persons, however. Among Armenians, arranged marriages prevailed in Armenia to World War I, and a routine demand of parents, before continuing with any further negotiations, was a clear family record genetically for seven generations. As a result, many genetic defects were eliminated and unknown among Armenians. In every Christian country, some form of standard has prevailed.

We can assume, moreover, that, even as God introduced genetic problems with the fall of man, so with the progressive redemption of mankind new conditions of life will be established. The evolutionist, however, can expect only progressive deterioration, and, in fear of this, seeks to impose rigid totalitarian controls on man.

These controls are needed by and yet are impossible for humanistic man. He wants man's improvement, but he is by nature a lawbreaker. Thus, he deliberately seeks to break the very laws on which his survival depends.

Attention has been called to the perverse sensuality of the Assyrians. Incest has existed among the perverted in every generation, but in some ages it has become a matter of principle to break the law. With the Renaissance and its revived humanism, it became a common goal to be immoral in an elegant fashion. The Seigneur Pierre de Bourdeilles Brantome (*c.* 1530-1614) is an able and vivid reporter of France in that era. As Georg Harsdorfer noted, "The courtier Brantome sees all of history from the perspective of boudoir-wit."[6] Brantome's casual treatment and easy justification of incest is noteworthy:

> I have likewise heard speak of a great Lord of a foreign land, which had a daughter who was one of the fairest women in the world; and she being sought in marriage by another great Lord who was well worthy of her was bestowed on him by her father. But before ever he could let her go forth the house, he was fain to try her himself, declaring he would not easily let go so fine a mount and one which he has so carefully trained, without himself having first ridden thereon, and found out how she could go for the future. I know not

---

5. *Ibid.,* p. 11 f.
6. Georg Harsdorfer, in "Introduction" to A. R. Allinson, translator, The Seigneur De Brantome, *Lives of Fair and Gallant Ladies* (New York: Liveright, 1933), p. xxv.

whether it be true, but I have heard say it is, and that not only he did make the essay, but another comely and gallant gentleman to boot. And yet did not the husband thereafter find anything bitter, but all as sweet as sugar. He had been very hard to please if he had otherwise, for she was one of the fairest dames in all the world.

I have heard the like tales told of many other fathers, and in special of one very great nobleman, with regard to their daughters. For herein they said to have shown no more conscience than the Cock in Aesop's Fable. . . .

I leave you to imagine what some maids may do with their lovers,— for never yet was there a maid but had or was fain to have a lover,—and that some there be that brothers, cousins and kinsfolk have done the like with.

In our own days Ferdinand, King of Naples, knew thus in wedlock his own aunt, daughter of the King of Castile, at the age of 13 or 14 years, but this was by dispensation of the Pope. Difficulties were raised at the time as to whether this ought to be or could be so given. Herein he but followed the example of Caligula, the Roman Emperor, who did debauch and have intercourse with each of his sisters, one after the other. And above and beyond all the rest, he did love exceedingly the youngest, named Drusilla, whom when only a lad he had deflowered. And later, being then married to one Lucius Cassius Longinus, a man of consular rank, he did take her from her husband, and lived with her openly, as if she had been his wife,—so much so indeed that having fallen sick on one occasion, he made her heiress of all his property, including the Empire itself. But it fell out she died, which he did grieve for so exceedingly sore that he made proclamation to close the Courts and stay all other business, in order to constrain the people to make public mourning along with him. And for a length of time he wore his hair long and beard untrimmed for her sake; and when he was haranguing the Senate, the People or his soldiers, never swore but by the name of Drusilla.

As for his other sisters, when he had had his fill of them, he did prostitute them and gave them up to his chief pages which he had reared up and known in very foul fashion. Still even so he had done them no outrageous ill, seeing they were accustomed thereto, and that it was a pleasant injury, as I have heard it called by some maids on being deflowered and some women who have been ravished. But over and above this, he put a thousand indignities upon them; he sent them into exile, he took from them all their rings and jewels to turn into money, having wasted and ill guided all the vast sums Tiberius had left him. Natheless did the poor girls, having after his death come back from banishment, and seeing the body of their brother ill and very meanly buried under a few clods of earth, have it disinterred and burned and duly buried as honourably as they could. Surely a good and noble deed on the part of sisters to a brother so graceless and unnatural!

The Italian, by way of excusing the illicit love of his countryman, says that . . . "When messer Barnardo, the young ox, stand up in anger and in his passion, he will receive no laws and spare no lady."[7]

With the rise of Romanticism, an interest in incest was also revived. The poet Shelley turned to Renaissance history for the story of a degenerate family, the very wealthy Roman family of Francesco Cenci. Cenci committed incest with his daughter Beatrice (1577-1599), who, with her step-mother and her brother Giacomo, had him murdered by hired assasins, who drove a nail into Cenci's brain, September 9, 1598. Beatrice was far from beautiful and by no means moral; she gave birth before her trial to an illegitimate son. Shelley, however, made her both pure and beautiful, and turned the story in part into an attack on the papacy. His purpose in *The Cenci* he stated in the Preface: "The highest moral purpose aimed at in the highest species of the drama, is the teaching the human heart, through its sympathies and antipathies, the knowledge of itself; in proportion to the possession of which knowledge, every human being is wise, just, sincere, tolerant and kind."[8]

Mario Praz has called attention to the Romantic interest in the perverse. What for the Romantics was a subject of literary interest has become for the existentialistic and relativistic humanists of the 20th century a matter for exploration and practice, an aspect of sexual liberty.[9] It is now defended by a British sociologist.[10] A medical doctor has written on the "normalcy of incest" and of the supposed problems resulting from "suppressing incestuous desires." Such works are bringing fortunes to publishers of pornography.

To return to Blake's observations, his comments on abortion are revealing:

> Legalized abortion laws are being seriously sought by many respected physicians because of completely legitimate problems facing some of their patients. But the Free-Lovers are also the champions of new legislation in this regard simply because unwanted pregnancies are the inevitable result of their irresponsible conduct. Daughters are sometimes impregnated by their own brothers or fathers. Children from 9 to 15 often find themselves with child in these environments, and the "intellectual" advocates of this way of life offer no practical solution save the quick abortion, cheaply and competently performed.[11]

7. Brantome, *Lives of Fair and Gallant Ladies*, pp. 58-60.
8. *Complete Poetical Works, John Keats and Percy Bysshe Shelley* (New York: Modern Library), p. 300.
9. Roger Blake, *The Free-Love Groups*, pp. 69 ff., 112-124.
10. *Ibid.*, p. 171.
11. *Ibid.*, p. 188.

The free-love advocates begin by offering "life" to their followers and end by demanding death, legalized murder, in the form of abortion, as the release and escape from the consequences of their actions. This is not surprising. Death in any life and law system is an inescapable fact. The question is, death for whom? The humanist demands death for God's law-order, death for unborn babies, and death for virtue and godliness, whereas God's law requires death ultimately for evil and for rebellion against God's law-order. In Biblical law, the guilty, not the innocent, die. The penalty for incest is thus death.

A final note: the subject of inbreeding has attracted, in recent years, more than a little attention. The evidences of its dangers are many. The decline of European monarchies was in part due to the decline of the royal families due to excessive inbreeding. The serious mental and physical defects which appeared in royal families which in origin were notable for physical vigor and mental abilities is well known. Marriages were contracted by various monarchies, not in terms of inherent qualities, but in terms of "royal blood" and advantageous political alliances, so that genetic considerations were sacrificed to political ends.

The awareness of the necessity for improving the human stock has led some to advocate massive out-breeding as a means of genetic progress. As a result, racial inter-breeding has been suggested, more often orally than in writing. But new strains can add nothing to a blood-line except what they already have. Out-breeding with inferior stock can only add more problems to the already existing ones.

8. The Levirate

Mace observed, concerning "the true cause of Hebrew polygamy," that "There can be no doubt that this was the desire for an heir."[1] This is true if we realize that the desire for an heir was more than simply a love of a son. The family was basic to Biblical society and culture; the godly family had to be perpetuated, and the ungodly family cut off. The bastard was cut off from church and state, insofar as any legal status was concerned, to the tenth generation (Deut. 23:2). He might be a godly man, but he was not a citizen. In canon law, the church barred bastards from church orders, although exceptions were made by papal dispensations. The purpose of Hebrew polygamy, which was usually bigamy, to be accurate, was thus the perpetuation of the family. Moreover, in terms of the facts, as Mace pointed out, "we are bound to envisage the community as being in general almost entirely monogamous."[2]

---

1. David R. Mace, *Hebrew Marriage, A Sociological Study* (New York: Philosophical Library, 1953), p. 123.
2. *Ibid.*, p. 129.

The family as the basic social and religious unit was forbidden by the law of incest from becoming ingrown and withdrawn from its society, because the law not only forbad consanguinity but consanguinity plus affinity, that is, a father's wife, a son's wife, a brother's wife, or the like. These were classified as incest religiously although not incest genetically, although some scientific evidence for the woman's physical change by marriage may exist. The Bible clearly affirms that sexual relations do establish a profound physical relationship between two persons, so that even a casual sexual union with a prostitute establishes a union, according to St. Paul (I Cor. 6:16). As a result, union with in-laws is incest. Sexual union makes two people "one flesh" (Gen. 1:24). They may not be "one mind," but they are "one flesh." (Older versions of the Book of Common Prayer carried Ussher's "A Table of Kindred and Affinity," listing forbidden marital relationships.)

The recognition that sexual union does in some profound and as yet not understood sense establish a relationship or communicate something physically between the two parties is common to most cultures. Superstitious applications of this belief abound, as witness Tantra Yoga, and the *donnoi* relationships of the Troubadours, Cathars, and other such groups of the Middle Ages. Very commonly, old men slept with virgins, without sexual consummation, in the belief that this served as a rejuvenator. The practice was widely used in 18th century Paris, and was practiced regularly by Mahatma Gandhi.[3] The doctors who ministered to King David may have been influenced by similar ideas in making use of Abishag (I Kings 1:1-4); however, in this case, consummation seems to have been the goal of the doctors.

In more recent years, a notable example of such thinking has been the artist Pablo Picasso, who has been given not only to young women but also to robbing his young son of articles of clothing in the hopes "that some of Claude's youth would enter into his own body."[4]

These are manifest absurdities, but they do witness to the widely recognized fact that physical union does communicate something. The Biblical ban on marriage and/or sexual relations with relatives by marriage is based on this fact.

The ability of the skin to absorb and to be affected by touch and contact is not sufficiently appreciated, except where poisons are concerned. The vagina in particular is most absorbant as sexual insufflation reveals. Where a lover blows violently into the vagina, the air passes into the blood vessels and brings death to the woman from an embolism.

---

3. Omar Garrison, *Tantra, The Yoga of Sex* (New York: Julian Press, 1964), p. 126 ff.
4. Francoise Gilot and Carlton Lake, *Life with Picasso* (New York: McGraw-Hill Book Company, 1964), p. 232.

Cases of rectal insufflation have been reported among homosexuals, with death usually resulting.[5]

Because sexual union makes, according to Scripture, the two "one flesh," marriage by a widow or a widower to in-laws is barred as incest, with a single exception.

The one exception permitted is the law of the levirate (Deut. 25:5-10). According to this law, if a man died childless, his next of kin had the duty to take the widow as wife and rear up a family bearing the name of the dead man. This law was older than Moses, and was applied in Judah's household (Gen. 38:8). In *Ruth* we have a later example of the law of the levirate. The levirate was common also to other peoples of antiquity. A book of the Talmud, *Yebamoth*, is devoted to the subject.

Josephus gives us his reaction to the meaning of the law of the levirate:

> . . . for this procedure will be for the benefit of the public, because thereby families will not fail, and the estate will continue among the kindred; and this will be for the solace of wives under their affliction, that they are to be married to the next relation of their former husbands.[6]

The protection and perpetuation of the family is thus the basic purpose of the levirate for Josephus. This is, of course, the clear intent of the law: "that his name be not put out of Israel" (Deut. 25:6). According to Luther,

> The law that a man should take the wife left behind by his brother and raise up a seed for the deceased brother was established for a very good reason. First, as the text sets forth, households should not die out but should be multiplied; this concerns the fostering and enlarging of the commonwealth. Secondly, in this way God provides for widows and the pitiable sex, to sustain and support them; for the woman, by herself a weak and pitiable vessel, is even more so when she is a widow, since she is at the same time forsaken and despised. He enforces this charity, however, by means of an outstanding disgrace. Such a man is to be called shoeless, and people are to spit out before him: "Fie upon you!" He deserves the contempt of all. They are to spit on the ground and say, "You have a 'Fie on you!' coming!" because he does not cultivate or increase the commonwealth in which he sojourns and whose laws he enjoys. His bared foot is to be a sign of shame and a cause of unending denunciation. He deserves to be naked of foot, that is, without household and dependents, which are denoted by foot covering; for through this one deed he makes himself naked of foot

---

5. Dr. Georges Valensin, *Sex From A to Z* (New York: Berkeley Medallion Books, 1967), p. 129.
6. Josephus, *Antiquities of the Jews,* Bk. IV, Chap. VIII, 23.

in his obligation to sustain the household of his brother. Thus the sign is similar to the deed in which he sins.[7]

Calvin's comments are also of interest, especially since he sees the denial of the levirate as a robbery of the dead man:

> This law has some similarity with that which permits a betrothed person to return to the wife, whom he has not yet taken; since the object of both is to preserve to every man what he possesses, so that he may not be obliged to leave it to strangers, but that he may have heirs begotten of his own body: for, when a son succeeds to the father, whom he represents, there seems to be hardly any change made. Hence, too, it is manifest how greatly pleasing to God it is that no one should be deprived of his property, since He makes a provision even for the dying, that what they could not resign to others without regret and annoyance, should be preserved to their offspring. Unless, therefore, his kinsman should obviate the dead man's childlessness, this unhumanity is accounted a kind of theft. For, since to be childless was a curse of God, it was a consolation in this condition to hope for a borrowed offspring, that the name might not be altogether extinct.[8]

Calvin doubted that the term "brother" here meant literally that, since it contradicted, seemingly, the laws against incest. However, the law obviously meant "brother" and any next of kin if no brother existed; the case of Judah's sons confirms this (Gen. 38:8), as does the text case cited by the Sadducees concerning the seven childless brothers (Matt. 22:23-33), in which the lawfulness of their levirate marriages with the one woman is accepted by all.

The levirate, at any rate, was not treated as an obsolete legal relic by Luther and Calvin. It has existed through the centuries. The levirate was practiced in Scotland very commonly to the eleventh century.[9] It still exists among Christian Abyssinians, with the additional factor that, if a man is emasculated in war, and is therefore incapable of begetting children, the levirate applies.[10] There are evidences of its practice in Europe, and wealthy Jewish families in New York maintained its practice until very recently at least. Birmingham reports that "The Seligmans also followed the Jewish practice of offering widows in the family to the next unmarried son."[11]

To understand the meaning of the levirate, it is important to examine the Biblical doctrine of marriage afresh, and set it in a perspective which will throw light on the levirate.

7. Martin Luther, *Lectures on Deuteronomy*, p. 248 f.
8. John Calvin, *Commentaries on the Four Last Books of Moses*, III, 177 f.
9. George Ryley Scott, *Curious Customs of Sex and Marriage* (London: Torchstream Books, 1953), p. 102.
10. George A. A. Barton, "Marriage (Semitic)" in *ERE*, VIII, 471.
11. Stephen Birmingham, *"Our Crowd," The Great Jewish Families of New York* (New York: Dell, 1967, 1968), p. 21.

First of all, marriage is basic to the Kingdom of God, to God's creative purpose for man and the earth. The earth is to be brought under the dominion of God by man, who is to subdue the earth and rule over it under God. The Jewish marriage service, dating at least to the first century B.C., has seven blessings which cover Israel's history, recalling God's creation and His mandate, Israel's messianic hope, and the goal of godly order. The fourth and seventh of these blessings read:

> Blessed art thou, O Lord our God, King of the Universe, who hast made man in thine image, after thy likeness, and has prepared unto him, out of his very self, a perpetual fabric. Blessed art thou, O Lord, Creator of man.

> Blessed art thou, O Lord our God, King of the Universe, who hast created joy and gladness, bridegroom and bride, mirth and exultation, pleasure and delight, love, brotherhood, peace and fellowship. Soon may there be heard in the cities of Judah, and in the streets of Jerusalem, the voice of joy and gladness, the voice of the bridegroom and the voice of the bride, the jubilant voice of the bridegrooms from their canopies, and of youths from their feasts of song. Blessed art thou, O Lord, who makest the bridegroom to rejoice with the bride.[12]

Both before and after the fall, marriage remains basic to God's kingdom.

Second, because the family is God's basic institution, property is closely tied to the family. The *Kethubah,* dating back to the first century B.C., refers very specifically to the marriage settlement in the marriage vows, which were recorded: "Be thou my wife according to the Law of Moses and of Israel. I will work for thee; I will honour thee; I will support and maintain thee, in accordance with the custom of Jewish husbands who work for their wives, and honour, support and maintain them in truth." After specifying the amount of the dowry as her prior claim on his estate, the bridegroom then vowed, "All my property, even to the mantle on my shoulders, shall be mortgaged for the security of this contract and that sum."[13] This document was necessary before a marriage could be consummated:

> The Sages accordingly forbade marital relations as long as the *kethubah* had not been completed. Furthermore, they declared that it was forbidden for husband and wife to live together for a single moment without a *kethubah;* and where the *kethubah* was lost, they had to abstain from intercourse until another *kethubah* had been made out.[14]

These regulations were fully in conformity with the Biblical law. Man is a sinner, and at all points, he needs the restraint of the law. If a man

---

12. J. H. Hertz, "Foreword," *Yebamoth, The Babylonian Talmud, Seder Nashim* (London: Soncino Press, 1936), I, xvi-xvii.
13. *Ibid.,* p. xvi.
14. *Ibid.,* p. xxxiii.

is ready to be under law in relationship to other men, he should be especially ready to place his relationship to his wife under law. Such a legal relationship already exists in the marriage contract. Love is not enough to establish a marriage: a contract is required by all concerned as proof of the love. Since man, as a sinner, is often apt to take advantage of those who trust him most, to place such relationships under law is evidence of love and good faith, not of distrust. It is a recognition of reality.

Modern bankruptcy laws, despite their abuses, reflect not only the Biblical sabbatical release on debts, but the preservation to the wife and family of the home from the claim of creditors. In Biblical law, the wife is the first creditor.

Third, as we have seen, incorrigible juvenile delinquents were to be executed (Deut. 21:18-21), and also all habitual criminals. Such persons were thus blotted out of the commonwealth. When and if this law is observed, ungodly families who are given to lawlessness are denied a place in the nation. The law thus clearly works to eliminate all but the godly families.

Fourth, as we have noted, bastards could not be recognized as legitimate, nor could the offspring of a marriage within the degrees of affinity be recognized as an heir. Because *the law at no time rewards sin,* the Jewish law of divorce applied this consistently and logically:

> Perhaps the most characteristic feature of the Jewish Law of Divorce is its absolute prohibition of the adulterer to marry the adulteress. Even in cases where such a marriage had, through suppression of the true facts, been entered into, it must be dissolved.[15]

Citizenship was restricted to the godly family, and thus society was to be governed by men of godly families.

The Bible provides an exception to the Jewish law prohibiting marriage between adulterous couples, but in that exception, God Himself punished the couple even as He permitted and blessed the union. This case was that of David and Bathsheba (II Sam. 11, 12), of whom Solomon was born (Matt. 1:6) as well as Nathan (Luke 3:3), both ancestors of Jesus Christ.

Fifth, this throws light, therefore, on the levirate. The purpose of the law is to suppress, control, and/or eliminate the ungodly, and, at the same time, to establish, maintain, and further the godly families. It envisions a society in which inheritance is to the godly, and each godly generation transmits to the next a worthy inheritance of property. The creation and perpetuation of godly families is thus basic to the law. Josephus cited three purposes for the levirate: 1) the continuation of a godly family, 2) the preservation of the property, and 3) the welfare

---

15. *Ibid.,* p. xx.

of the widows. All three are clearly in view. The widow is given additional assurance of a possible child as her heir and support in old age. The levirate is still a better answer to the problems it addresses itself to than any man has been able to devise. It's general disuse today is because the laws of humanism are essentialy hostile to the family and its welfare. When the family is again restored to its Biblical place, the levirate will quietly take its place in that framework of law.

Sixth, adoption is a related fact, and its place in law is in terms of the levirate, as an alternative. The Biblical usage of the word *adoption* is theological, having reference to our adoption in Christ as sons of God. The Biblical usage reflected a fact of family life. Adoption in antiquity normally differed from the modern practice, in that usually mature men were formally adopted as heirs, men whose faith and character commended them. Abraham had adopted the mature and trusted Eliezer of Damascus as his heir and steward (Gen. 15:2, 3), Thus, because faith and character were basic to heirship, maturity was required in order to provide evidence of these facts.

9. Sex and Crime

A very common opinion not only associates sex and original sin but very logically connects sex and crime. If sex is the source of the fall, then logically, sex is the cause of crime. This opinion is read by atheists into the Bible, although without any legitimate grounds whatsoever. Actually, the origin of this belief is pagan, not Biblical. Many pagan myths indicate a belief in the sexual origin of sin. Plato's myth of the original androgynous man is a familiar example.

The sexual origin of criminality is extensively seen in neo-Freudians and in many others as well. Former San Quentin Warden Clinton Duffy wrote an exposition of this idea titled *Sex and Crime,* maintaining that

> Sex is the cause of nearly all crime, the dominant force that drives nearly all criminals. After thirty-five years of correctional experience as warden of San Quentin prison, a member of the California Adult Authority and executive director of the San Francisco Council on Alcoholism, I'm convinced that it is a rare crime that can't be traced to a sexual inadequacy of some sort. . . .

> Criminals are plagued and puzzled and upset by sexual tensions, doubts, fantasies, anxieties and hungers. In my opinion 90 per cent of the men in our nation's prisons are there because they couldn't come to grips with the problem.[1]

> We shall have sex as long as we have life, and crime as long as we have civilization. We can't wipe out sex so we can't wipe out crime. Not until we accept the relationship between the two can

---

1. Clinton T. Duffy with Al Hirshberg, *Sex and Crime* (New York: Doubleday; Pocket Books, 1965, 1967), p. 1.

we begin to make real progress in our everlasting battle against the forces of evil. We must understand that most crime is the result of sex and has to be treated as a sex problem.[2]

If this belief is true, logic requires a radical alteration in sexual standards and behavior in order to remove the causes of crime. Accordingly, the free love advocates demand an abolition of sexual regulations as the necessary step towards a free and humane society. Sexual anarchists are social utopians. A trace of this opinion is apparent in Duffy, who argued for providing sexual partners for prisoners. Mississippi permits a prisoner to have "conjugal visits" with his wife; Mexico does not limit the visit to the wife.[3]

Duffy's own report gives evidence of the non-sexual nature of crime. Ethnic groups show clear-cut patterns: thus, Orientals, with their strong family culture, "seldom get into trouble," least of all the Japanese. The Scandinavians in prison are few. Jews are normally law-abiding; their trouble with the law usually involves money, according to Duffy: "Most Jewish prison inmates are swindlers or con men or check artists or forgers." Earlier, Irish were sometimes in trouble because of drinking and fighting, Germans are rarely in trouble and then because of aggression; Italians have been in trouble where gang activities are strong; when the French are in prison, it is for "sex offenses mostly"; Mexicans are often involved in crimes of violence and narcotics, but "Few Mexicans over forty seem to get into trouble." Negroes rank proportionately very high in the prison population. In the South, "over half the inmates of state prisons are Negroes, and this is true of some prisons in the North."[4] Duffy believed that prejudice against the Negroes accounted for some of this, although he recognized that these Negro prisoners were guilty men. It is quite likely that sometimes a guilty Negro faces greater severity because of his race, but it is also true that much is tolerated and excused in him because of his race also. The Southern pattern for decades was severity in some things (such as rape) and indulgence in many things (such as petty theft, violence between Negroes, drunkenness, and the like).

The racial link with crime is very true, but it is far from the answer. No more than sex is the cause of crime can race be said to lead to crime. Since Duffy's years as prison warden, the amount of criminal activity by white youth has increased very rapidly. Their race has obviously given them no immunity against criminality. The cause must be sought elsewhere.

St. Paul states the cause plainly. The unregenerate man, the man in warfare against God, is hostile to God and hates Him; such a man

---

2. *Ibid.,* p. 176.   3. *Ibid.,* pp. 154-176.   4. *Ibid.,* pp. 67-74.

"is not submissive to God's law; in fact, cannot be so" (Rom. 8:7, BV). Such people pursue a course of religious lawlessness (Rom. 1:18-32). They suppress the truth because of their unrighteousness and worship the creature rather than the Creator.

It is this aspect of man which humanism refuses to recognize. Supposedly, man's criminality will be healed by eliminating the state, property, religion, and laws. But, since the ungodly are by nature lawbreakers, they may lower the standards as much as they will, but they will still break the law. They live to break the law. As a result, the more a revolutionary generation breaks the law, the more violent it becomes, because violations of a progressively lax standard requires progressively more flagrant actions.

Nietzsche believed rightly that disbelief in God and in immortality would create a world of violent men. Some humanists have held that if men have only this life and this world, they will treasure life and live in peace. But, since God and immortality gives this present life significance and purpose, belief curbs men, whereas unbelief cheapens life and leads to greater violence and murder. When man becomes his own god, it becomes an article of faith and an urgency of life to assert his claim by the violation of all laws not of his own choosing. The essence of life then is to be unbound, unfettered by law or by responsibility. This leads to a radical perversity, which a friend once chided the Count du Gramount for: "Is it not a fact that as soon as a woman pleases you, your first care is to find out whether she has any other lover, and your second how to plague her; for the gaining of her affection is the last thing in your thoughts. You seldom engage in intrigues but to disturb the happiness of others; a mistress who has no lovers would have no charms for you."[5] In the 18th century, the basic purpose of love affairs has been described as "a desire to seduce, and desert, for malicious sport." The "crown of his victory" was for the seducer to do his work "without the slightest emotional involvement, so that when the woman, conquered and submissive, begged at last; 'At least, tell me that you love me!' he could affect a disdainful smile and refuse." As a result, La Rochefoucauld commented, "If love is judged by most of its effects, it resembles hate more than friendship."[6] Such "love" was indeed hatred, and it began with the hatred of God. Since the goal of man, when he claims to be god, is self-sufficiency, the dependency of love is denied. It was the Age of Reason which also reduced woman's legal status to that of a slave as part of its "love." Having reduced woman to a helpless role, these men could then be romantic about this

---

5. Morton M. Hunt, *The Natural History of Love* (New York: Alfred A. Knopf, 1959), p. 263.
6. *Ibid.*, p. 279.

puppet whom they could so easily destroy. Keats burbled about this "new woman,"

> God! she is like a milk-white lamb that bleats
> For man's protection.[7]

It is not surprising that "hostility" is a basic aspect, not only of child molesters, but of those "Lolitas," small children, who welcome such advances.[8]

But every hostility has as its counterpart a new area of sympathy. Those who are hostile to God and His law will be sympathetic and friendly towards criminals. They feel a common bond uniting them in hatred for law. A European lawyer, whose perspective is definitely not Christian has observed,

> Determinism in criminal law represents an apologia in a grand manner. We must ask the further question: apologia for what? He who excuses the criminal pleads for himself. "Madame Bovary, c'est moi," Flaubert said. At a time when strong influences are breaking new ground, excusing the criminal must result in severe feelings of guilt. An effort is made by society to lessen this feeling of guilt by excusing both itself and the criminal with whom it is identified. Nietzsche referred to the wave of pity which, in the second half of the nineteenth century, swept over Europe from Paris to St. Petersburg.[9]

Sympathy for the criminal means hostility to God and His people. As Reiwald observed further, in another context, "Wherever there is some form of social life, there must be punishment."[10] The punishment in humanistic society is progressively directed against the innocent and the law-abiding. Whether with respect to taxation, discriminatory legislation, or open violence, the people of God become the objects of growing violence. In the words of Juvenal, "The depths of depravity are not reached in one step." Bronowski noted, with respect to pagan festivals, "This revolt against authority is the heart of the saturnalia everywhere."[11]

The Renaissance unleashed a great flood of violence by its hostility to godly law. According to Lo Duca,

> The liberty sought by the arts (the notion of beauty is in itself disturbing, the arts have always been the shock troops of true revolution), the liberty sought out by science (this is already more dangerous, for established power as well as for those who idolize

---

7. Cited in *ibid.*, p. 313.
8. Russell Trainer, *The Lolita Complex* (New York: The Citadel Press, 1966), pp. 36 f., 98 f.
9. Paul Reiwald, *Society and Its Criminals* (London: William Heinmann Medical Books, 1949), p. 59.
10. *Ibid.*, p. 238.
11. J. Bronowski, *The Face of Violence* (New York: George Braziller, 1955), p. 19.

the past), the liberty sought out in language and mores were all part of one capital dynamic factor: individualism.

Through individualism, liberty seeks to attain the absolute, that which leads it beyond the concepts of good and evil, to authentic anarchy. The genius of the Renaissance often masks a profound and functional anarchy, which was not destructive, being dominated and held in check by pride. Pride alone permitted this luxurious anarchy which found its morality in art.

The perfect example of Renaissance man is the condottiere. Such a condottiere as Sigismondo Malestesta is the Renaissance summed up in one man. His individualism is equal to that of Bartolomeo Colleonia or Galeazzo Maria Sforza. The "anarchy" of these warlords is based on the rejection of every law, human or divine.

Another famous condottiere, Werner von Usslingen, wore, engraved on his breastplate: *Enemy of God, Compassion and Mercy.* Men of this calibre, capable of such fierce hate, strongly marked the world arising from the ashes of the Middle Ages.

The violence of the Middle Ages was never free from obsession and cruelty, and above all the need to find a justification in invoking religious pretexts. The violence of the Renaissance did not for an instant seek to justify itself. The sentiment of guilt had disappeared, absorbed by that desperate "will to power" which will be given a name four centuries later.

Nevertheless these condottieres introduced in their society an exterior element which ravaged the continent: the soldier of fortune— mercenary or *Landsknecht*—lords of pillage and rape. Their example, as well as their crimes' impunity (war has always been a useful pretext to unleach the most infamous instincts under the cover of heroes' natural "weaknesses") strongly influenced their contemporaries.[12]

The author who gives us this summary finds also attractive to himself ancient and Greek vices, and speaks of the "fact" that "the ancients charm us with a very knowing philology on the first series of anal penetrations, either of a man or of a woman."[13] Men and societies in revolt against God's authority find a common ground in their hostility to law and moral order. Modern man thus feels a continuity with the Greeks and with the Renaissance which he definitely does not feel with the Middle Ages or with the Reformation.

Lo Duca compares the condottiere of the Renaissance with the modern man as revealed by Sade:

What the condottiere brought to the spirit of the Renaissance, Sade brought to the modern era. . . . Not only does Sade lay down the axiom that life is nothing but the quest for pleasures, and even for

---

12. Lo Duca, *A History of Eroticism* (Covina, Calif.: Collectors Publications, 1966), pp. 139-142. Adapted from the French by Kenneth Anger.
13. *Ibid.*, p. 48.

the pleasure, but he introduces the principle that pleasure is bound
to suffering, that is to say at the attempt to destroy life: ". . . the
body . . . nothing more than an instrument for inflicting pain."[14]

Where there is no submission to the law of God, there is progressive
resistance, defiance, and violation thereof. The cause of crime is not
sex: it is sin, man's defiance of God's sovereign authority and man's
attempt to be his own god. The attempt of men to find the cause of
crime in sex is a part of their attempt to overthrow God's law-order by
re-ordering sexual relations. Predictably not only with Sade but with
all those who deny God's law, the conclusion is the same: "But he that
sinneth against me wrongeth his own soul: all they that hate me love
death" (Prov. 8:36).

10. Sex and Religion

The association of sex and religion is a common one, and more than
a few writers have attempted to trace all religions to phallic worship.
The frequently close connection of sex and religion can be granted;
fertility cults are found in every part of the world, past and present.
This relationship is in fact declared in Scripture to be an attribute of
false religions. St. Paul declared, of unregenerate men,

> They claimed to be wise, but they have become fools; they have
> *exchanged the glory* of the immortal *God for the semblance* and
> likeness of mortal man, of birds, of quadrupeds, and of reptiles.
> So God has given them up, in their hearts' lust, to sexual vice, to
> the dishonouring of their own bodies—since they have exchanged
> the truth of God for an untruth, worshipping and serving the
> creature rather than the Creator, who is blessed for ever: Amen
> (Rom. 1:22-25, Moffatt).

As Murray noted, of this text, "religious degeneration is penalized by
abandonment to immorality; sin in the religious realm is punished by
sin in the moral sphere." This is not only "a natural law of consequences operative in sin," it is moreover the act of God:

> There is the positive infliction of handing over to that which is
> wholly alien to and subversive of the revealed good pleasure of
> God. God's displeasure is expressed in his abandonment of the
> persons concerned to more intensified and aggravated cultivation
> of the lusts of their own hearts with the result that they reap for
> themselves a correspondingly greater toll of retributive vengeance.[1]

The relationship of sex and religion is thus a real one: it is an aspect
of man's revolt from God. When man turns to self-worship, he ends
by worshipping his own sexual vice. Refusing to acknowledge the

---

14. *Ibid.*, p. 117.
1. John Murray, *The Epistle to the Romans* (Grand Rapids: Eerdmans, 1959),
I, 44 f.

power of God as Lord and Creator, he worships his own genital powers as creator.

An interesting example of this was cited by Herbert Asbury, in his account of *The Barbary Coast*. After the San Francisco peninsula earthquake of April 18, 1906, the reaction of countless men was to seek comfort in sex. In nearby Oakland, also badly shaken, the Police chief, Walter J. Peterson, stated, of the houses of prostitution, "All day long and at night men were lined up for blocks waiting in front of the houses, like at a box office at a theatre on a popular night."[2] As an age approaches death, man's sexual activity becomes all the more intensely perverse, because his religious hunger has increased, and sex is his substitute god.

But this is not all: man at the same time begins to justify his religious and moral depravity.

> The modern view of the orgy must at all costs be rejected. It assumes that those who took part had no sense of modesty at all, or very little. This superficial view implies that the men of ancient civilization had something of the animal in their nature. In some respects it is true that these men do often seem nearer than ourselves to the animals, and it is maintained that some of them shared this feeling of kinship. But our judgments are linked to the idea that our peculiar modes of life best show up the difference between man and animals. Early men did not contrast themselves with animals in the same way, but even if they saw animals as brothers the reactions on which their humanity was based were far from being less rigorous than ours. . . . This is why when we discuss the orgy in a very general way we have no grounds for seeing it as an abandoned practice but on the contrary we should regard it as a moment of heightened tension, disorderly no doubt, but at the same time a moment of religious fever. In the upside down world of feast-days the orgy occurs at the instant when the truth of that world reveals its overwhelming force. Bacchic violence is the measure of incipient eroticism whose domain is originally that of religion.
>
> But the truth of the orgy has come down to us through the Christian world in which standards have been overthrown once more. Primitive religious feeling drew from taboos the spirit of transgression. Christian religious feeling has by and large opposed the spirit of transgression. The tendency which enables a religious development to proceed within Christianity is connected with these relatively contradictory points of view.
>
> It is essential to decide what the effects of this contradiction have been. If Christianity had turned its back on the fundamental movement which gave rise to the spirit of transgression it would have lost its religious character entirely, in my opinion.[3]

---

2. Herbert Asbury, *The Barbary Coast* (New York: Garden City Publishing Company, 1935 [1933]), p. 263.
3. Georges Bataille, *Death and Sensuality*, p. 112 f.

By *orgy* Bataille of course means the religious festivals of antiquity which called for the religious practice of acts of chaos: adultery, homosexuality, incest, bestiality, looting, burning, killing, and general depradation. This religious spirit of transgression is described by Bataille:

> But the most constant characteristic of the impulse I have called transgression is to make order out of what is essentially chaos. By introducing transcendence into an organised world, transgression becomes a principle of an organised disorder.[4]

For these cults of chaos, every act of man was holy and sacred, since man was in continuity with the divinity of being. But Christianity, according to Bataille, desacralizes man and the world: "It reduced the sacred and the divine to a discontinuous and personal God, the Creator."[5]

As a result, there is a movement to restore "love" to its "proper" place in man's life, i.e., a place of "free" expression. It is held that "Love opens up unlimited potentialities."[6] According to Dr. Charles Francis Potter, "life is the only marvel: only life is divine."[7] This means that life, and the sexuality of life, is beyond law, because it is itself divine. Sex is then worshipped: Goldberg calls it "the sacred fire." Of the worship of sex, he writes,

> Still, sex worship did for man even more than that. It was the redeemer of his imprisoned soul. It provided an outlet for those sexual passions which the race had known in its infancy, but which later had apparently been driven out of heart and mind. Memories of them may have lingered on, as they had not been entirely effaced from the earth. At all events, the desire was there, smouldering beneath the heap of suppressions.

> Once, man was a free agent sexually. He could mate with any female that came his way. Now, he was in chains. Sex worship came to break the fetters and, if only for a brief space of time, to bring back to man the freedom that had been his. What was forbidden at large in the bush not only was permitted, but, in fact, became a duty in the temple of the gods.

> When, in the temple, man was free to do as he pleased sexually, he pleased to do it with all the freedom possible.[8]

As a result, we have studied religious assault on Biblical moral law. *First,* moral relativism is demanded; we are told that everyone must be judged in terms of his own standards. According to Danielsson,

---

4. *Ibid.*, p. 114.
5. *Ibid.*, p. 115.
6. Edward Podolsky in Preface to T. Clifton Longworth, *The Gods of Love, The Process in Early Religion* (Westport, Conn.: Associated Booksellers, 1960), p. 23.
7. Charles Francis Potter, Introduction to B. Z. Goldberg, *The Sacred Fire, The Story of Sex in Religion* (New York: University Books, 1958), p. 11.
8. B. Z. Goldberg, *The Sacred Fire,* p. 60 f.

To accuse the Polynesians of being immoral according to our Christian Western standard is of course as unreasonable as it would be for them to condemn us because we do not observe Polynesian taboo rules. Elementary justice demands that we shall employ every people's *own* moral code as a standard in trying to judge their conduct, and if we make this our starting point and compare the Polynesians' manner of observing the existing canons of behavior with our own moral standard, it is we who must be ashamed.[9]

Danielsson appeals to "elementary justice," but it is not a justice any Christian can recognize, because he has redefined justice and morality in humanistic, relativistic terms. Danielsson not only proposes moral anarchism, but he denies to those who differ from him any right to disagree. His plea for tolerance is thus grounded in a radical intolerance.

Second, these relativists then demand, to quote the wife of a former Belgian Minister of Justice, Mme. Lilar, a radical humanism, "a resacralization of human love."[10] Not surprisingly, Mme. Lilar grounds her thinking in the ancient chaos cults and the myth of the androgyne.[11] She is not an advocate of license, but she is even less an advocate of law and duty, for "Duty is as surely desacralizing as is licence." Her hope is in a "free," spontaneous, "sacred" love which will not need the law:

> Must one conclude that freedom and fidelity are irreconcilable? No. On the contrary, though a forced and conventional fidelity may have its moral and social advantages, only a spontaneous and loving fidelity, constantly renewed by being chosen in complete freedom, can strengthen the couple in its supernatural vocation. A couple must at least speculate on, bet on its ability to last. It must have faith in its love, faith in its resistance to time. If by ill fortune the love is extinguished, no duty or forced fidelity can give it back its sacral quality. What can happen then is a series of mutual adjustments in an atmosphere of association, of companionship; but it will do no good to deceive oneself—these adjustments will merely sanction the couple's passage from sacral love to profane love, and this must be held to be a falling off.[12]

The absurdity of this position is that it wants the lawlessness of the humanist while retaining the faithfulness of the Christian, an impossible combination.

But to return to the point made by Goldberg, namely, that sex is a "redeemer": this is increasingly an aspect of the modern scene. It is a serious error to see an era like the present, or the late Roman Empire,

---

9. Bengt Danielsson, *Love in the South Seas* (New York: Dell Publishing Company [1956], 1957), p. 70.
10. Suzanne Lilar, *Aspects of Love in Western Society* (London: Thames and Hudson [1963], 1965), p. 92. Translated with a preface by Jonathan Griffin.
11. *Ibid.,* pp. 119-154.
12. *Ibid.,* p. 174 f.

as a time of "over-sexed" people. As a matter of fact, the times of intense sexuality are also commonly times of low sexual vitality. When Mme. de Maintenon was over seventy, she complained because her husband, Louis XIV, "insisted on his conjugal rights every day and sometimes twice."[13] This is less likely to be a complaint in an age of decline. The end of an era sees a decline in every kind of energy, including sexual energy, and, as a result, normal sexual energy is replaced by a phrenetic one. Extremes of provocation are resorted to, because it takes more to stimulate a low and jaded appetite. It takes vastly more to excite a man in a declining era. Flagrant sexuality is thus a mark of low vitality. Perversion and violence are also required to stir the sick appetite. It becomes especially important to reject all that is normal, lawful, and a part of the ordered, godly "past." To be influenced by anything other than *the moment* is held to be wrong. Thus, when Andrei Voznesensky, a Soviet writer, was asked, "Which Russian poets of the last forty years have influenced you most?," he replied, "What a question. Being influenced by old poets is like being in love with your grandmother."[14] In such a perspective, the rootless man is the redeemed man, and Hollo speaks of Henry Miller as on "the mountaintop" of the world, "at the foot of the ladder to man's heaven."[15]

Righteousness has roots; it is grounded in God's law and moves in terms of redemptive history, past, present, and future. As a result, righteousness is the enemy for religious sexuality, whereas evil, being rootless and heedless is pure and holy. A character of O'Donoghue declares: "be not so naive as to believe that cruelty and violence must necessarily be motivated! The malicious act, set apart from the commonplace, lackluster treadmill of goal-oriented drives, attains a certain purity of its own being."[16]

Thus, it is evil, and especially *evil and perverted sexuality,* which in this perspective becomes redemptive. The 1968-1969 film *Teorema* is, we are told, "a strange, enigmatic parable dealing with corrupt contemporary society through the devastating effects a mysterious, sensual stranger has on an industrialist's family." The film was labeled obscene by the Italian government (it is an Italian production), but "the Catholic Church honored it with a prize (which was later withdrawn)." A mysterious stranger visits the household and "gives every

---

13. Nancy Mitford, *The Sun King* (New York: Harper and Row, 1966), p. 151.
14. Elizabeth Sutherland, "Interview with Andrei Voznesensky," Barney Rosset, editor, *Evergreen Review Reader*, 1957-1967 (New York: Grove Press, inc., 1968), p. 540.
15. Anselm Hollo, "A Warrant Is Out for the Arrest of Henry Miller," poem in *Evergreen Review Reader*, p. 538.
16. Michael O'Donoghue, "The Adventures of Phoebe Leit-Geist, Episode X," in *ibid.*, opposite p. 473.

member of the household the kind of sexual solace for which each yearns. The stranger reads their innermost thoughts and comforts them." Involved are a father, mother, son, daughter, and maid. When the stranger leaves "a great void—an intellectual and spiritual abyss from which no help can come—exists." The father becomes a naked homosexual roaming the streets, the mother a moral tramp; the son seeks escape in impressionistic art; the daughter becomes demented, and the maid becomes a religious hermit who performs miracles.

> What meaning can be found in all this? Is the stranger supposed to be God, the devil, or neither one. Are these people so depraved that when their artificial bourgeois existence is stripped away they have nothing left but madness?[17]

The fact that the mysterious stranger can be either "God, or the devil, or neither one," is especially telling. The point is that there is no discernible difference between God and the devil, so that such a mysterious stranger can be equally termed either, or neither. Ultimacy and morality are held to be incompatible, and therefore "God, or the devil," must rob men of their "artificial bourgeois existence" in a world of good and evil. Thus, sex in *Teorema* is a double-edged religious instrument: it can bring redemption, or it can bring damnation to those who refuse its message.

Similarly, the film "I am Curious (Yellow)," a Swedish film, is characterized by a radical defiance of authority, expressed sexually, according to sociologist-psychologist Dr. Charles Winick, a witness in favor of the film at its American trial.[18] This states it clearly: the purpose of this religious sexuality is the defiance of authority, God's authority, by the new god, man. This defiance requires the religious enactment of evil as a matter of principle.[19] The test of excellence and leadership in some groups today is depravity, the performance of various perverted acts.[20] Their thesis is "the righteousness of Lucifer," i.e., of evil.[21] A love of filth,[22] a belief in their divinity,[23] and a total warfare against every law of God is their principle.

---

17. Dale Monroe, "Movie Review: Enigmatic 'Teorema,'" in *Los Angeles Herald Examiner*, Friday, May 23, 1969, p. C-1.
18. *I am Curious (Yellow)*, film by Vilgot Sjoman (New York: Grove Press, 1968), p. 209.
19. See R. E. L. Masters, *Eros and Evil, The Sexual Psychopathology of Witchcraft* (New York: The Julian Press, 1962). For accounts of this in an earlier era, presented from a humanistic perspective, see also R. E. L. Masters and Edward Lee, *Perverse Crimes in History* (New York: The Julian Press, 1963), and Allen Edwardes and R. E. L. Masters, *The Cradle of Erotica* (New York: The Julian Press, 1963).
20. See *Freewheelin Frank*, Secretary of the Angels, as told to Michael McClure by Frank Reynolds (New York: Grove Press, 1967).
21. *Ibid.*, p. 150.
22. *Ibid.*, pp. 105, 126.
23. *Ibid.*, pp. 8, 72, 75, 107.

All this should not surprise us. It is a law of being that religious apostasy has moral consequences. As St. Paul made clear in Romans 1, the idolatry of man inescapably results in immorality, and immorality in perversity and perversions. Because such men forsake God, He forsakes them. Such men exchange the truth of God for a lie (Rom. 1:25); "By 'a lie' is meant here 'false gods,' who are the supreme embodiment of falsehood."[24] Knox's comment on Romans 1:24-27 states in part,

> The apostle's primary purpose at the moment is to point not to sins, but to judgment. He sees in the moral corruption, especially in the unnatural sexual vices, a sign that "the wrath" has already begun to work. *God gave them up . . . to impurity.* We have already seen that Paul conceived of sin and its consequences as being in the closest possible connection; decay and death followed upon sin as inevitably as life and peace upon the righteousness of faith, and indeed partook of the same character. So here he sees the prevalence of homosexuality, *the dishonoring of their bodies among themselves,* as a manifestation not only of sin, but also of its issue and punishment, i.e., corruption and death.[25]

The humanist rebels against God in order to exalt himself. The grim irony of judgment is that his act leads to dishonoring himself. The humanist seeks to glorify and honor his body, but he instead dishonors it openly and makes his disgrace a public fact.[26]

Sex and religion are thus closely and inescapably linked in every non-Biblical faith. It is the religious result of apostasy: man worships his own sexual evil and exalts his disgrace into a way of life. Humanistic man worships "the moment" and converts "the spirit of transgression" into a religious principle. Such a faith cannot create or perpetuate a culture; it can only destroy it. Men must either rebuild in terms of the triune God or be plowed under by His judgment.

11. Adultery

The approach of the humanist to Scripture is a perverse one in principle. The Bible is systematically misread. Thus, Hays writes, concerning the fall of man:

> To return to the snake, when Adam is beguiled by Eve, who has previously been told the truth by the serpent, the eyes of the primal pair are opened and they "are as gods, knowing good and evil." They also learn that they are naked and become for the first time sexually guilty—in other terms, sexual intercourse is invented.[1]

---

24. W. Sanday, "Romans," in Ellicott, VII, 208.
25. John Knox, "Romans," in *The Interpreter's Bible,* vol. 9, p. 400 f.
26. R. C. H. Lenski, *The Interpretation of St. Paul's Epistle to the Romans* (Columbus, Ohio: Wartburg Press, 1945), p. 109 f.
1. H. R. Hays, *The Dangerous Sex, The Myth of Feminine Evil* (New York: G. P. Putnam's Sons, 1964), p. 91.

The Bible, it is held, has a bad view of sex, whereas modern man has a healthy view. Even a noted psychoanalyst, however, has found the modern view rather unhealthy.

> The expression "to have fun" becomes in America more and more synonymous with having sexual intercourse. This new connotation is symptomatical of the emotional degradation of the sexual process. Sexual experience is in reality very serious, and sometimes even tragic. If it's only fun, it is not even funny any longer.[2]

It should be noted, moreover, that, not only has the Biblical view of sex and marriage been attacked, but the Christian for his profession of that view. Very early, "The moral teaching of the Christian missionaries sounded like a criticism of the private life of the Imperial family, an attack on Roman law and on the morals of Roman society."[3] We hear a great deal about the corruption and immorality of the medieval clergy and too little of the many faithful priests and monks, nor are we often told of the attempts of the immoral persons of that era to subvert the clergy. Thus, Berthold observed, "Young daughters and the young maids think of nothing but how they can seduce monks and priests."[4]

The reason for this hostility is the Biblical law, with its insistence that only marital sexual relations are legitimate and moral. The Biblical standard of marriage is seen as oppressive and unnatural:

> The merger of personalities, even when it avoids the danger of mutual devouring, runs into still another conflict with the basic mammalian sexual pattern. By and large, faithful monogamy does not seem to be a natural pattern, but a socially fabricated one; even so, it is rare to the point of seeming almost abnormal. Of one hundred and eighty-five societies analyzed in the Human Relations Area Files at Yale University, only about five percent were monogamies in which all outside sexual activity for men was disallowed or disapproved. Fidelity thus seems to some scholars difficult, unnatural, and greatly overpriced, and the insistence on it the cause of hypocrisy, guilt, unhappiness, and broken marriage. All this is the product of the identification of the selves, for infidelity is a sharing of a very intense experience with someone other than one's principal love partner, and therefore it breaches the merger. Even if the infidelity is perfectly concealed, it sets up in one person hostile barriers and dark places into which the other cannot penetrate. Dr. Abraham Stone has reported that in nearly three decades of marriage counseling he has found infidelity almost never innocuous, but practically always a cause of concealment, guilt, and impairment of personality interaction and total love.

---

2. Theodor Reik: *Sex in Man and Woman: Its Emotional Variations* (New York: The Noonday Press, 1960), p. 206.

3. Richard Lewinsohn, *A History of Sexual Customs* (New York: Harper and Brothers [1956], 1958), p. 83.

4. Herman Heinrich Ploss and Max Paul Bartels, *Woman in the Sexual Relation* (New York: Medical Press of New York), p. 34. Revised and enlarged by Ferd. F. von Reitzenstein.

Nevertheless, the discomforts of fidelity may be the price at which one buys considerable happiness and stability in marriage.[5]

In such a view, there is at best an unhappy pragmatic acceptance of monogamy, and such a perspective cannot inspire faithfulness. There is no reference here to the meaning of marriage—only to what the individual can get, at the cheapest price. Thus, even the seeming assents to Biblical law underscore the radically diverse principles of Biblical faith and humanism. Thus, Cole writes, "Christianity and psychoanalysis can agree that Rado's standard coital pattern, the insertion of the penis into the vagina prior to orgasm represents the measure of 'normal' sexuality."[6] Here is a *"measure* of normal sexuality" without any reference to the divine decree and word, only to the relation of the penis to the vagina. Normal sexuality for Christianity is marital sexuality; adultery is a violation of that relationship and an abnormal, criminal act, *an assault on fundamental order.*

In dealing with marriage, the seventh commandment singles out as the critical law word, "Thou shalt not commit adultery" (Ex. 20:14; Deut. 5:18). This same law is stated in a number of forms: it is forbidden in Leviticus 18:20 and is described as defilement. The penalty for adultery is specified as death (Lev. 20:10; Deut. 22:22).

In order to see the matter in perspective, let us examine the premarital regulations. In many cultures, adultery was forbidden to the female, but pre-marital and post-marital license was granted to the male. The Greek and Roman practice here is well known. In Chinese culture adultery was regarded, prior to communism at least, as only a female offense. The male was free to do as he pleased. Children born to a man from extra-marital relationships were brought into the man's home, and the wife had to accept them.[7] It is sometimes said that Biblical standards were similar; there is no evidence for this claim. While no law deals directly with it, the general tenor of the law, the evidence of Proverbs, and the New Testament make clear the Biblical position.

First, as we have previously noted, the law required the extermination of the Canaanites, their fertility cults, and their religious prostitution. The purpose of the law is a land purged of all these evils. The law thus addressed itself to a situation wherein these particular evils had no existence; hence, they had no legitimate existence.

Second, not only were the Canaanite prostitutes to be eliminated, but

5. Morton M. Hunt, *The Natural History of Love* (New York: Knopf, 1959), p. 394.

6. William Graham Cole, *Sex in Christianity and Psychoanalysis* (New York: Oxford University Press, 1955), p. 302.

7. David and Vera Mace, *Marriage East and West* (Garden City, N.Y.: Doubleday, 1959, 1960), p. 238.

none of Hebrew origin were to exist. Punishment was left up to the authorities, but the law clearly forbad the existence of Hebrew prostitutes or sodomites (homosexual male prostitutes):

> Do not prostitute thy daughter, to cause her to be a whore; lest the land fall to whoredom, and the land become full of wickedness (Lev. 19:29).

> There shall be no whore of the daughters of Israel, nor a sodomite of the sons of Israel (Deut. 23:17).

The punishment for a priest's daughter who turned prostitute was death (Lev. 21:9).

Third, in Proverbs, all extra-marital sexuality is condemned, and the counsels concerning the evils of prostitution, adultery, and premarital sexuality are all given as age-old wisdom and as implicit in God's law. Marital chastity is declared to be the standard (Prov. 5:1-23). It is presented, not as an impoverishing life, but as a well-spring of joy and health to man's being (Prov. 5:15-23). Adultery is especially condemned; the harlot is a moral degenerate, but the adulteress adds perversity to her evil: "For a harlot seeks only for a loaf of bread, but another man's wife stalks a priceless soul" (Prov. 6:26, BV). Adultery is a devouring fire (Prov. 6:20-35). It leads to death and ruin (Prov. 7:1-27). Sexual intercourse with prostitutes is bad, but adultery is the culminating evil and folly. All this is stated by Solomon as the wisdom of the law.

Fourth, the New Testament forbad all non-marital sexual intercourse, and pre-marital relations therefore as well, without any concern other than to restate the Biblical law for Greek and Roman converts (Acts 15:20, 29; 21:25; Rom. 1:29; I Cor. 5:1; 6:13, 18; 7:2, etc.). Christ forbad the thoughts leading to it (Matt. 5:28).

Clearly then, Biblical law is designed to create a familistic society, and the central social offense is to strike at the life of the family. Adultery is thus placed on the same level as murder, in that it is a murderous act against the central social institution of any healthy culture. Unpunished adultery is destructive of the life of the family and of social order. On the part of the wife, it is treason to the family and introduces an alien loyalty to the home, as well as alien seed. On the part of the husband, it is also treason and disloyalty, and in addition undermines his own moral authority. A morally clean husband is confident of his authority and exercises it in God-given confidence. A guilty man is less able to exercise authority and veers between arbitrariness and a surrender of authority. The law-order of the family is of a piece, and the person who breaches it at one point inevitably surrenders it at all other points. Arrests for fornication and for adultery were low in

1948;[8] by 1969, they had virtually disappeared, as had much internal family discipline. Zimmerman's comments about the strong familistic eras of history, i.e., the trustee family eras, is of interest:

> Thus in the trustee period, adultery, along with one or two other crimes, is the most infamous act against the whole society (kinship group which connects the person with life). The husband is not necessarily punished by his own family but they have to settle with the other family for his sins; so rather than put up with him, they make him subject to abandon noxal and if the other family does not kill him he must flee for life to perpetual banishment or until the crime is forgotten. In case the husband commits adultery with a woman who has no immediate family, there is no one to punish him except the woman's relatives (providing his own family do not hold him in line), but in many cases these are just the persons who will do it. Gregory of Tours reports such cases in the trustee period among the French after the Roman decline.[9]

The family is the central custodian of *property* and of *children,* two basic aspects of any society. A healthy society is one which protects the family because it recognizes that its survival is at stake.

One area of protection is against violence, or rape. The texts citing the laws on rape and seduction are the following; rape, Deuteronomy 22:23-29; seduction, Exodus 22:16, 17.

The penalty for the rape of a married woman, or of a betrothed woman, was death. The law specified that consent on the part of the woman was presumed if it occurred "in the city" and "she cried not," and she then was assumed to be a participant in adultery rather than an act of rape. As Luther observed, "The city is mentioned here for the sake of an example, because in it there would be people available to help her. Therefore she who does not cry out reveals that she is being ravished by her own will."[10] In other words, "the city" represents here available help: was it appealed to?

The cases classified as seduction are technically and realistically cases of rape also; the difference is that the girl in question is neither married nor betrothed. Why, in such cases, was not the death penalty invoked? In the former cases, marriage was already contracted; the offense was against both man and woman, therefore, and required death. In the case of a single girl, unbetrothed, the decision rested in the hands of the girl's father, and, in part, the girl. If the offender, cited simply as a seducer in Exodus 22:16, 17, and as a rapist in Deuteronomy 22:28, 29, is an acceptable husband, then he shall pay 50 shekels of silver as a

---

8. Morris Ploscowe, *Sex and the Law* (New York: Prentice-Hall, 1951), p. 157.

9. Carle C. Zimmerman, *Family and Civilization* (New York: Harper and Brothers, 1947), p. 153.

10. Luther, *Lectures on Deuteronomy*, p. 223.

dowry and marry her, without right of divorce "because he hath humbled her" (Deut. 22:29); but "If her father utterly refuse to give her unto him, he shall pay money according to the dowry of virgins" (Ex. 22: 17). If a man thus is rejected as a husband, the girl is compensated for the offense to make her an attractive wife to another man, coming as she will with a double dowry, his own and her compensation money.

To understand the background of this law, let us remember, *first,* that the Biblical law-order requires the death of incorrigible delinquents and criminals. The seducer and/or rapist of an unbetrothed girl was thus presumably not an incorrigible youth, although at this point clearly in guilt. No gain was possible from his offense. If he were allowed to marry the girl, he did so without right of divorce, and at the cost of a full dowry. If he were refused, he still had to pay a full dowry to the girl, a considerable loss to his own future.

In marriage, the woman was protected from abuse and slander by her husband. If he impugned her sexual morality, a ritual which clearly required supernatural verification revealed her innocence or guilt. If guilty of adultery, she died a lingering death. If innocent, then God blessed supernaturally (Num. 5:11-21). She "shall be sown with seed," (Num. 5:28 literal trans.), meaning moreover that her husband is required to fulfil his every duty to her.

If the husband slandered his wife's character, claiming that she was not a virgin when he married her, he was taken to court, together with his wife. If his charge was true, she died; if the charge was false, he was fined 100 shekels of silver, payable to his father-in-law, and he lost the right of divorce (Deut. 22:13-21). The wife thus was protected in marriage. She was legally guaranteed at all times her food, clothing, and "her duty of marriage," i.e., sexual intercourse, within her husband's home (Ex. 21:10). She was also guaranteed that her husband could neither be drafted nor "charged with any business" which would take him away from home during their first year of marriage (Deut. 24:5).

To return now to the question of adultery, Cole's interpretation of the New Testament view is of particular interest:

> Adultery was not merely the violation of another man's household, the trespass upon the rights of a fellow male, threatening the security of his bloodline, but a violation of his unity with his wife, a breaking of his state of "one flesh" (henosis). And adultery was not of the body only but also of the heart, "for out of the heart come evil thoughts, murder, adultery, fornication" (Matthew 15:19). Since this was true, adultery had already been committed by a lustful look or a libidinous desire (Matthew 5:27-28).[11]

11. William Graham Cole, *Sex and Love in the Bible* (New York: Association Press, 1959), p. 191.

True enough, but adultery is first and last an offense, as every sin is, against God and His law-order. As David rightly confessed, "Against thee, thee only, have I sinned, and done this evil in thy sight" (Ps. 51:4). All sin is against God essentially, and hence the God-centered emphasis cannot be overlooked in sexual offenses.

The penalty for adultery in the Old Testament was clearly death. What is the New Testament penalty? The incident of the woman taken in adultery (John 8:1-11) has often been discussed in this context, but without relevance. *First,* Jesus refused to be made a judge of legal affairs, in this case and in the matter of a contested estate (Luke 12: 13, 14). As Lord of glory, He refused to be reduced to a justice of the peace. *Second,* Jesus made clear that a judge must have clean hands, or else he is disqualified from judging: "He that is without sin among you, let him first cast a stone at her" (John 8:7). Plainly, by *sin,* He here meant adultery; His challenge was, dare you convict without convicting yourselves? Fearful of His knowledge and judgment, they left. *Third,* when the guilty woman acknowledged Him to be the "lord," then He forgave her and sent her away (John 8:10,11). This forgiveness was a *religious* forgiveness, not a *civil* judgment. He did not interfere thereby in any act the husband might take to dissolve the marriage. A murderer can be religiously assured of forgiveness and yet still executed; to confuse religious and civil forgiveness is a serious error. Achan confessed his guilt on Joshua's religious appeal, but he was still executed (Joshua 7:19-26). Thus, the incident of the woman taken in adultery, while important with respect to grace, is not pertinent to the legal issue. It can be added that the death penalty had ceased to be enforced for adultery, and the attempt to force a judgment from Jesus with respect to the woman taken in adultery was an attempt to embarrass Him. If he denied the death penalty, His declaration that He came to fulfill the law (Matt. 5:17, 18) would be challenged; if He affirmed the death penalty, He would affirm a highly unpopular position. Jesus in return judged them; the lawless cannot enforce the law, and they were lawless. The lack of any civil order in this respect appears in Hebrews 13:4: "Marriage is honourable in all, and the bed undefiled: but whoremongers and adulterers God will judge." God must judge them, because society then did not. The judgment of God is inescapable, however absent the judgment of man. But what was the judgment of God with respect to adultery?

The critical text is I Corinthians 5, a very difficult one as to some details. *First,* the case in question is a member who "is living with his father's wife" (I Cor. 5:9, RSV). In terms of Leviticus 18:8, this was incest and carried the death penalty. Paul makes clear that this sin is an offense even to Gentiles. *Second,* although it is clearly incest in terms of the Biblical law, St. Paul does not deal with it legally as a case of incest. He makes clear, in vs. 1, that it is incest, however. Instead, the man is given the general title of "fornicator," which covers a variety of offenses (I Cor. 5:9, 11). Since the father was apparently still living, since she is spoken of as "his father's wife," not widow, the offense of the man with his step-mother is adultery as well as incest. The term "fornicator" covers both factors but is less specific. *Third,* St. Paul orders them "To deliver such an one unto Satan for the destruction of the flesh, that the spirit may be saved in the day of the Lord Jesus" (I Cor. 5:5). Craig is correct in interpreting this as the death penalty.[12] Thus, the death penalty is clearly God's law for incest and/or adultery. The church, however, cannot execute a man; the death penalty does not belong to the church. The church, however, must in effect pronounce the death penalty by delivering the man to Satan; i.e., the providential protection of God is withdrawn, so that the man might be humbled and redeemed. *Fourth,* the church, however, has a duty to act, meanwhile. They must "purge out therefore the old leaven"; they must not associate with fornicators within the church, "with such an one do not to eat. . . . Therefore put away from among yourselves that wicked person" (I Cor. 5:6-13). Since the woman is not included in the judgment, it can be assumed that she was not a Christian and hence not subject to church discipline. The repentance of the offender could after a season possibly restore him to church fellowship, but always as someone with a recognized death sentence over him.

Thus, the church was given realistic legal aid for coping with the problem of capital offenses in a society which does not recognize them as such, because it was realistically recognized that this is a major problem for the church. A godly law-order will restore the death penalty, but the church must live realistically with its absence and protect itself. The proper judgment of the church both recognizes the death penalty and acts in terms of present reality.

The early church acted in terms of this. Adultery was severely judged and adulterers were received back into church fellowship only on the severest terms. In some areas, total exclusion prevailed, but this was not general.

The world into which the church moved had a variety of attitudes towards adultery, from toleration to savage mutilation. In pre-Christian Poland, "the criminal was carried to the market-place, and there fastened by the testicles with a nail; a razor was laid within his reach, and he had the option to execute justice on himself or remain where he was

---

12. Clarence Tucker Craig, "I Corinthians," in *Interpreter's Bible,* X, 62.

and die." In Rome, "Theodosius instituted the shocking practice of public construpration, which, however, he soon abolished."[13]

At present, adultery is held by many to be a cure-all for a variety of psychological problems. A Temple University professor of psychiatry has recommended love affairs as a solution to some problems.[14] As early as 1929, one researcher found that a common cause of adultery among women is the belief that they will miss something in life if they do not engage in adultery. Dr. G. V. Hamilton, who made the study, reported, according to Sherrill,

> that a large portion of these women who were adventuring outside of marriage were not doing so because of any tempermental factors. It was not more difficult for them than for others to be chaste, neither did they derive any unusual psychic satisfaction from their ventures. Rather, they appeared to be following this course of action because they felt they should carry out ideas they had formed of "spousal freedom."[15]

Because the state is steadily encroaching on the two basic social responsibilities of the family, the custody of property and of children, the state is relegating adultery to the realm of things peripheral and relatively unimportant. Not until the authority of the family in this area is re-established will adultery again become a menace to society rather than a form of entertainment. At present, adultery is seen as a personal matter and as an aspect of personal experience and pleasure, nothing more.[16]

In all cultures where the family's authority over property and children has existed, or has been re-established, adultery inescapably becomes one of the most fearful crimes, and there is a long history of brutal tortures and reprisals against offenders. The relationship is inescapable: where an offense is treason against society, there particularly severe penalties are imposed.

The Biblical answer thus is to re-establish the family in its functions, protect it in its integrity, and then penalize its offenders. In a healthy society, treason is a rare crime. In a truly Biblical law-order, adultery will also be rare. Present opinion to the contrary, it has often been rare in the past, and it is uncommon in present-day Ireland, according to Gray.[17]

---

13. "Adultery," in John M'Clintock and James Strong, *Cyclopaedia of Biblical, Theological, and Ecclesiastical Literature* (New York: Harper and Brothers, 1895), I, 86 f.

14. O. Spurgeon English, "Some Married People Should Have Love Affairs," *Pageant*, March, 1969, 108-117.

15. Lewis Joseph Sherrill, *Family and Church* (New York: Abingdon Press, 1937), p. 116 f.

16. See John T. Warren, *Wife Swappers* (New York: Lancer Books, 1966).

17. Tony Gray, *The Irish Question* (Boston: Little, Brown & Co., 1966).

A final note: the early church had a serious problem, its duty to uphold the law in a lawless age. Men whose offenses required the death penalty, as with the case in the Corinthian church, remained alive, and their return to the church on repentance posed problems. Where the Biblical law required restitution, the matter was relatively simple, but what of those offenses requiring death? Acceptance on a simple declaration of repentance was obviously to make these crimes lighter in their consequences than many lesser offenses. As a result, the penitential system evolved. Protestants, who are accustomed only to see its later flagrant abuses, almost always fail to see its earlier health, and its force as an instrument of law. Acts of penance were required of adulterers, for example, *not* as a work of atonement, but as practical acts of sanctification. The penance served a double purpose. First, it demonstrated the sincerity of the profession of repentance. Second, it constituted a form of restitution. Penance was thus a firm step towards re-establishing a law-order which the state had denied.

12. Divorce

Marriage in Scripture is the voluntary union of two persons, a man and a woman, in wedlock; although marriages were commonly arranged, consent was also secured. Without consent, the union is always in effect rape. Calvin and Luther both stressed the fact of mutual consent as necessary to a valid marriage in their discussion of the Jacob-Leah episode.[1] The question can be raised then as to why Jacob accepted Leah. The answer is clearly that he was in a coercive situation. He had been shamed and taken advantage of by Laban, who knew that Jacob had no legal recourse as a stranger. In a sense, it was a rape of Jacob, who could do nothing except protest or run away, but could not exert his legal rights successfully.

Union involves mutual consent; the *dissolution* of a marriage does not. The most common form of divorce is *by death*. This could be not only a natural death, which is not strictly a divorce, but a legal execution, which divorced the culprit from life, society, and spouse. Those who were missionaries for idolatrous cults were subject to death and therefore divorce (Deut. 13:1-11). The pre-Mosaic law required death for adultery, as the Tamar incident shows (Gen. 38:24), David expected it for his own sin (II Sam. 12:5), and it required a word from the Lord, Nathan's message, "thou shalt not die" (II Sam. 12:13) to avoid that sentence.

In some cultures, there is no divorce by death, as witness Mormonism,

---

1. See H. C. Leupold, *Genesis*, p. 798; see also Calvin, *Commentaries on the First Book of Moses Called Genesis* (Grand Rapids: Eerdmans, 1948), II, 133, translated by the Rev. John King.

in sealed marriages. In other societies, the wife was slain (as in Hinduism until recently) to prevent remarriage or continued life apart from her spouse. The Mosaic law and our Lord (Matt. 22:23-33) refused to recognize such customs by giving permission to remarry and by limiting marriage to this mortal state.

To return to divorce by death, Biblical law divorced the guilty party from the innocent by means of death for many offenses. Some of the laws whereby a woman could be divorced by death and remarry are the following, all of which require the death penalty for the man:

1. Adultery: Deut. 22:20-25; Lev. 20:10.
2. Rape: Deut. 22:25, 26.
3. Incest: Lev. 20:11, 12, 14, 17.
4. Homosexuality or sodomy: Lev. 20:13 (18:22).
5. Bestiality: Ex. 22:19; Lev. 18:23; 20:15; Num. 35:16-21.
6. Premeditated murder: Ex. 21: 12, 14; Num. 35:16-21.
7. Smiting father or mother: Ex. 21:15.
8. Death of a woman from miscarriage due to assault and battery: Ex. 21:22, 23.
9. Sacrificing children to Molech: Lev. 20:2-5.
10. Cursing father and mother: Ex. 21:17; Lev. 20:9.
11. Kidnapping: Ex. 21:16.
12. Being a wizard: Lev. 20:27 (cf. Deut. 13:1-11).
13. Being a false prophet or dreamer: Deut. 13:1-5; 18:20.
14. Apostasy: Deut. 13:6-16; 17:2-5.
15. Sacrificing to other gods: Ex. 22:20.
16. Refusing to follow the decision of judges: Deut. 17:12.
17. Blasphemy: Lev. 24:16.
18. Sabbath desecration: Num. 15:32-36 (This appears, not as a part of the legislation, but from a special instance in the wilderness).
19. Transgressing the covenant: Deut. 17:2-5.

Divorce by death was obtainable by men because of the following death penalties cited for women, and denunciation was obligatory on the believer (Deut. 13: 1-11; Luke 14:26):

1. Unchastity before marriage: Deut. 22:21.
2. Adultery after marriage: Deut. 22:22-23; Lev. 20:10.
3. Prostitution by a priest's daughter: Lev. 21:9.
4. Bestiality: Lev. 20:16; 18:23; Ex. 22:19; Deut. 27:21.
5. Being a wizard or a witch (sorceress): Ex. 22:18; Lev. 20:27.
6. Transgressing the covenant: Deut. 17: 2-5.
7. Incest: Lev. 20:11, 12, 14, 17.

It is readily apparent that the list for men is far longer. Clearly, some of the items in the list for men included women as well. Thus, a woman guilty of murder obviously suffered the death penalty. Various other offenses must have applied to women also. But, equally clear, many of these offenses were obviously masculine, because they implied greater force and strength, masculine ascendency. Thus, rape and kidnapping are almost entirely masculine offenses. Men therefore had a greater liability to the death penalty because of their position of authority. This is in terms of the Biblical principle that, the greater the privilege and authority, the greater the responsibility and the culpability, as in Leviticus 4, where the sacrifices for sin are made proportionate to the sinner's status and responsibility. Jesus referred also to this principle: "But he that knew not, and did commit things worthy of stripes, shall be beaten with few stripes. For unto whom much is given, of him shall be much required: and to whom men have committed much, of him they will ask the more" (Luke 12:48). It should be noted that ignorance does not excuse the sin or eliminate the punishment, but only lessens it; and responsibility likewise increases culpability. The sin of the one member of the family could not condemn the other members. "The father shall not be put to death for the children, neither shall the children be put to death for the fathers: every man shall be put to death for his own sin" (Deut. 24:16).

Divorce by death made remarriage possible, and freed the innocent partner from bondage to a guilty and unclean person. A second form of divorce appears in the Mosaic legislation, divorce for breach of the marital law, i.e., failure to provide food, raiment, and the due sexual relations:

1. Captive women: Deut. 21:10-14.
2. Hebrew "slave" or better, bonded girls: Ex. 21:1-10.
3. The implication is that, if breach of contract to provide is applicable for bonded girls, it is applicable as grounds for divorce for endowered wives. St. Paul referred to this law in I Corinthians 7:3-5, where the requirement of sexual relations and all "due benevolence" (or "obligations" BV) is specified. St. Paul spoke of the failure to meet the sexual responsibilities of marriages as defrauding the marital partner. (It can also be described, and has been, as a form of desertion.) The reference to Exodus 21:1-10 is clear; St. Paul spoke in the context of Biblical law.

A third type of divorce is implied, enforced by authorities, as with Nehemiah, in cases of consanguinity and mixed marriages:

1. Mixed marriages banned: Deut. 7:1-3; cf. Ex. 34:12-16; Num. 25:6-8. Divorce required: Neh. 9:2; 13:23-27; cf. Mal. 2:14.
2. Consanguinity forbidden: Deut. 22:30; 27:20-23; Lev. 18:6, 18; 20:11, 12, 14, 17, 20, 21.

A fourth type of divorce is also specified, by means of a writing or bill of divorce, given by the husband to the wife:

1. Bill of divorce: Deut. 24:1-4.
2. Bills of divorce are cited in Jer. 3:8 and Isa. 50:1, and divorced

women referred to in Lev. 21:14; 22:13; Num. 30:9 in the Old Testament.

In Jeremiah 3:8 and Isaiah 50:1 we have an insight into the meaning of a bill of divorce in God's own announced divorce from His chosen people, and divorce is here certainly *not* seen as a barely tolerated evil, as some would have it. The bill of divorce, or writing of excision or repudiation was *not* the evil *but dealt with the evil.* In Isaiah 50:1 (where mother and children are one, as J. A. Alexander has pointed out), the cause is iniquities and transgressions. "The general idea of rejection is twice clothed in figurative dress, first by emblems borrowed from the law and custom of imprisonment for debt."[2] In Jeremiah 3:8, the treachery of Judah is called adultery and ground for divorce by God as it had been for Israel. But more specifically, Judah, the wife, had defiled, desecrated, paganized the marital home, God's land (Jer. 3:9), while pretending reform from time to time in hypocrisy (vs. 10). The divorce of Israel had been due to open apostasy, open unfaithfulness (vss. 6-8), but the cause for Judah's divorce was not open apostasy but secret treachery under the guise of sincere and faithful obedience (vss. 9, 10). The adulterous nation sought her own will and gave only hypocritical lip-service to her covenant Husband, Jehovah.

In Deuteronomy 24:1-14, the ground for divorce is closely related to this. When the law speaks, it speaks relative to the situation, but in the holiness of God; it speaks moreover, to men who love the law and seek to obey it, not to give the hypocrites or ungodly an excuse. If the woman find no grace in her husband's eyes, it is with reference, not to the husband's caprice, but to the husband's holy standards as a covenant-keeper and image-bearer. The law is a part of the covenant: the husband is either a covenant-keeper and image-bearer mindful of the Lord of the covenant, or he has no interest in the law. (The pharisaic mis-use of the law, of course, came later.) Therefore, the ground for divorce here is some "nakedness of anything" found in the wife. In passing, it may be remarked that much has been made of the fact that the purpose of this particular law is not to establish divorce, but to prevent the remarriage of a divorced woman after she has become the widowed or divorced wife of another man. But, true as this is in a limited sense, the fact remains that divorce is so readily assumed, and is morally legitimated by inclusion in the law. It is moreover assumed by God to be His holy prerogative also in casting off Israel and Judah. Certainly, divorce is part of a sinful order, but no less a right for that matter in dealing with that sinful order. Warfare is a part also of a sinful order, but no less right under godly circumstances, and the right

---

2. J. A. Alexander, *Commentary on the Prophecies of Isaiah* (Grand Rapids: Zondervan, 1947, 1953), p. 248.

of the sword is by no means withheld merely because war belongs to the state of sin. Hardly an aspect of our lives can be separated from this sinful order in any full sense, but the law speaks to covenant-keepers in a sinful world, not to men in heaven.

Attempts to associate the uncleanness or nakedness of Deuteronomy 24:1 with adultery or unchastity have naturally failed. In such instances, divorce by death ensued. The word uncleanness of a thing definitely implies a serious offense; it is used elsewhere of the shameful exposure of the body (Gen. 9:22; Ex. 20:26; Lam. 1:8; Ezek. 16:36, 37), in Leviticus 18 of illicit and abnormal sexual practices, and in Deuteronomy 23:14 for human excrement. Obviously, it referred to no trifling matter but to something ungodly, abhorrent and repellant to the covenant-keeper husband who sought guidance in the law.

The answer to its meaning is a re-examination of the divorce by death lists. The women's list is shorter. Does this mean that certain sins went unpunished in women? The specification of homosexuality is definitely masculine (Lev. 20:13), and the homosexual prostitutes called "dogs" (Deut. 23:18; cf. Phil. 3:2; Rev. 22:15). Are we to conclude that this sin, cited by Paul as the culminating evidence of apostasy and unbelief (Rom. 1:26, 27), was condoned in women? Are we not rather to conclude that this constituted a nakedness or uncleanness in the woman? Her punishment was lesser than man's in most instances because her responsibility was also lesser. Again, a man, for disobeying higher authorities and refusing to follow their decision, was sentenced to die. What of a woman who disobeyed her higher authority, her husband? Was it not an uncleanness in her? When Hagar became insubordinate to Sarah, God supported Sarah's decision that she be cast out. Thus, we see already that two very important categories appear. In the man, homosexuality gave the woman a divorce by death; in the woman, it was an uncleanness. In the man, insubordination again meant death; in the woman it was an uncleanness. The testimony of Jeremiah 3:8 and Isaiah 50:1 concerning bills of divorce bears out this correlation to insubordination and rebellion, Jeremiah 3:8-10 in particular. A careful analysis of all relevant texts indicates that the nakedness or uncleanness in the woman was not to be determined in terms of the man's caprice, but in relationship to his role as the covenant man and the image bearer.

The widespread Protestant interpretation of the NT doctrine of divorce limits the recognized ground to adultery, on the basis of Matt. 19:9, and to desertion, I Corinthians 7:8-24. Many would limit it to adultery alone. The curious fact about this interpretation is that *it rests on one word alone*, and that word is *not* adultery! Let us examine the relevant texts:

1. And I say unto you, Whosoever shall put away his wife, except it be for fornication and shall marry another, committeth adultery: and whoso marrieth her which is put away doth commit adultery (Matt. 19:9).
2. But I say unto you, That whosoever shall put away his wife, saving for the cause of fornication, causeth her to commit adultery; and whosoever shall marry her that is divorced committeth adultery (Matt. 5:32).

The word rendered fornication is given as "unchastity" by Moffatt and "adultery" by Hugh J. Schonfield. Most commentators *in effect* render it *adultery*. But the two words are different: *porneia* (fornication) and *moicheia* (adultery, Matt. 15:19; to commit adultery, *moichaomai*, Matt. 19:9). Had Jesus intended *to equate* fornication with adultery, it would have not then been necessary to use a word which might lead to misunderstanding. It is *not* said that *fornication is adultery, but that marrying a woman divorced for grounds other than fornication is adultery*. The two words are different, seperate and distinct. It will not do therefore to insist that the matter is not to be "perplexed" thereby and that what Jesus meant was that fornication "on the part of a married woman is not only fornication but also adultery in the specific sense, for the simple reason that it constitutes sexual infidelity to her spouse."[3] Every act of sexual intercourse by a woman with a man other than her husband, while it may, for example, be incest as well, is always adultery: if such actions only are intended, and constitute the limits of the meaning of this statement, then the *only* word that could be legitimately used is *adultery*, not *fornication*. If, however, more than adultery is intended, homosexuality, for instance, then a word other than and broader in meaning than adultery had to be used, and was. *Scripture is never given to the idle use of words, or to their careless use.* Paul placed the weight of doctrine on the singular form of "seed" (Gal. 3:16). Jesus Himself established the doctrine of the resurrection on the very tense of a verb in His answer to the Sadducees (Matt. 22: 23-33). Certainly no one so precise in His reading of Scripture would have used words carelessly, and, had He meant adultery only, would have used the word adultery and *none other. Since, for a married person, every act of extra-marital intercourse with a person of the opposite sex can be described as adultery, to use a word other than adultery means, that besides adultery, certain acts described as and inclusive in the term fornication constitute the valid grounds for divorce. To reduce the meaning of fornication to adultery is to do violence to the text and render a distinction of no small importance null and void.* What then is the meaning of fornication?

---

3. John Murray, *Divorce* (Philadelphia: Committee on Christian Education, Orthodox Presbyterian Church, 1953), p. 21.

Let us examine its NT usage as a means of ascertaining its meaning:

1. We can see immediately that it is distinct from adultery, and a more inclusive term, in Matthew 15:19, where we have both listed as proceeding from the heart: "adulteries, fornications." See also Mark 7:21.

2. It appears frequently in a sense meaning illicit sexual intercourse generally and lewdness, and is by some rendered as whoredom at times.

   Romans 1:29 refers to sexual sins in general.

   I Corinthians 6:13, 18 refers in part to relations with prostitutes (vss. 15, 16) but has a broader reference to sexual sins.

   In I Corinthians 7:2 it means adultery and sexual disorders, mental or physical, through forced continence, and bad relations between husband and wife from forced continence.

   II Corinthians 12:21 associates it with but as distinct from uncleanness and lasciviousness.

   Galatians 5:19, 21 associates it with but distinct from a long list of the works of the flesh, including adultery, uncleanness, and licentiousness.

   Ephesians 5:3 lists it with uncleanness and covetousness as things not to be named, much less found existing, among saints.

   Colossians 4:5 lists it as one of the things to be put to death, again distinguishing it from uncleanness.

   I Thessalonians 4:3; to abstain from fornication has as its positive side to know one's own vessel in sanctification and honor.

   Revelation 9:21, here listed as one of the unrepented sins of the unregenerate, inclusive of all sexual sins.

   John 8:41, used to refer to either adultery or illicit intercourse by unmarried persons, eventuating in an illegitimate birth.

   The word thus, while inclusive of adultery, uncleanness, lasciviousness, and prosititution, is in these instances broader in significance and distinct from these words and can be and frequently is used together with them without repetition of meaning.

3. It is used specifically to refer to incest, as cited in Leviticus 18:8 and 20:11, in I Corinthians 5:1. By implication therefore the term includes the marriages prohibited in the Mosaic law, and all such intercourse as that law indicated, Leviticus 18; 20:10ff., etc. The ban on consanguinity is thus supported.

4. In Acts 15:20, 29, and 21:25, it refers to illicit sexual intercourse, although a few have seen a broader reference. The sexual laxity later referred to in I Corinthians was the type of behavior in mind at the Council of Jerusalem.

5. Even as infidelity in the OT typified the forsaking of the true God in order to worship idols, so fornication is used in Revelation 2:21, 14:8; 17:2, 4; 18:3 and 19:2 to describe rebellion against and insubordination to God and the religion and life of such rebellion.

In 2:21 actual illicit sexual practices may have been referred to. But Lenski refers to 2:21, the fornication of Jezebel at Thyatira, thus: "We take the phrase 'from her fornication' in a comprehensive sense as including all her teaching and all the corresponding deeds." In 14:8 Lenski sees it as meaning "the worship of the blasphemous beast" in imagery such as used in Isaiah 57:3-12.[4]

6. These varying usages are reflected in the LXX in such passages as the following: Genesis 38:24; Hosea 1:2; 2:2, 4, 12; I Chronicles 5:25; Ezekiel 23:19. In Judges 19:2, we have a very interesting reading, which, whether accurate or not with regard to the original, is not our present concern. It does, however, reflect the Greek usage and understanding of fornication. The LXX omits any reference to unfaithfulness, and the Chaldee softens "played the whore against him" to "she despised him." Lange suggested *"And the concubine lusted after others besides himself. The concubine was unchastely disposed. This is only a stronger expression for what the moderns mean when with palliative extenuation they say: 'she did not love her husband.' Her sensuality was not satisfied with the Levite. In this way the narrator explains the ground of her leaving him."*[5] In either case, as Lange pointed out, the Levite acted in violation of Leviticus 21:7. This passage is of particular interest because of the use made of it by Grotius, and, after him, John Milton, who wrote:

> Grotius . . . shews . . . that fornication is taken in Scripture, as tends to plain contempt of the husband, and proves it out of Judges XIX.2 where the Levite's wife is said to have played the whore against him; which Josephus and the Septuagint, with the Chaldean, interpret only of stubbornness and rebellion against her husband: and this I add, that Kimchi, and the two other rabbies who gloss the text, are of the same opinion. Gerson reasons that had it been whoredom, a Jew and a Levite would have disdained to fetch her again: And this I shall contribute, that had it been a whoredom, she would have chosen any other place to run to than her father's house, it being so infamous for a Hebrew woman to play the harlot, and so approbrious to the parents. Fornication then in this place of the Judges is understood for stubborn disobedience against the husband, and not for adultery.[6]

The account of this incident in Josephus sets it in a context of national effeminacy, luxury and pleasure. The correctness of this version is not our concern, but the reflection of the prevailing usage of the word fornication certainly is. It may be added that the Berkeley version translates Judges 19:2, "His concubine played him false and moved back to her father's house in Bethlehem of Judah for four months," and

---

4. R. C. H. Lenski, *The Interpretation of St. John's Revelation* (Columbus, Ohio: Wartburg Press, 1943), p. 434.

5. John Peter Lange, editor, F. R. Fay, *Commentary on the Holy Scriptures, Joshua, Judges, Ruth* (Grand Rapids: Zondervan [1870]), p. 242.

6. Lenski, *The Interpretation of St. John's Revelation*, p. 434.

footnotes this verse thus: "Deserting her bed and board was sometimes reason for the designation 'harlot,' as the Hebrew here intimates."

It may be objected that the word adultery is used in a similar sense in the NT. There are three such possible uses: first, in Matthew 12:39; 16:4 and Mark 8:38, we find the use of "adulterous generation." Second, in James 4:4, we read "adulterers and adulteresses," possibly literal in reference, but probably not. Third, in Revelation 2:22, the adultery of Jezebel is referred to, again questionable in meaning. Adultery on the whole is more specifically limited to the sexual violation of the marriage covenant whereas fornication commonly had a broader meaning. Had Jesus meant an exclusively physical, sexual sin by married persons, the word *adultery* would have described it. Fornication in the physical sense would have been then inappropriate usage for married persons but, in its broader sense, it ties in closely with the Mosaic law.

Let us then examine Matthew 19:2-9 in terms of its total or comprehensive meaning:

1. The Pharisees approached Him with a test question on marriage and divorce designed to embroil Him in a dangerous argument on a controversial issue. He had earlier accused them of self-justification, hearts full of abomination and trying to set aside the law by their concept of divorce, declaring, "But it is easier for heaven and earth to pass away, than for one tittle of the law to fail" (Luke 16: 14-18). Jesus had earlier also made clear his stand on the integrity of the law (Matt. 5:17-20). He came, not as a destroyer or innovater, "but to fulfil."

2. Their test question revealed their presupposition: "Is it lawful for a man to put away his wife for every cause?" (Matt. 19:3). To all practical intent, their basic conception of marriage and divorce was derived, not from the creation ordinance, but from Deuteronomy 24:1. That passage, in reading "if she doth not find grace in his eyes (for he hath found in her nakedness of anything" [Robert Young]), addresses itself to covenant man, whose doctrine of marriage is held in faithfulness to the creation ordinance. This fact the rabbis recognized and misused, declaring divorce in the proper sense to be a privilege accorded only to Israel and not to the Gentiles. The schools of Shammai and Hillel were both agreed on this point and thus completely at odds with the teaching of Christ. Although the loss of dowry by the wife was reserved for certain offenses, divorce was a right and privilege for the men of Israel for both schools. As Edersheim observed, "And the Jewish Law unquestionably allowed divorce on almost any ground; the difference being, not as to what was lawful, but on what grounds a man should set the Law in motion, and make use of the absolute liberty which it accorded him. Hence, it is a serious mistake on the part of the commentators to set the teaching of Christ on this subject by the side of Shammai."[7]

7. A. Edersheim, *The Life and Times of Jesus the Messiah* (New York: Longmans, Green, 1897), II, 333.

The School of Hillel granted the right of divorce for over-salting food or serving it too hot, or if a more attractive woman were found. In two instances cited by Edersheim, rabbis proclaimed their wish to be married for a day and divorced in exercise of their right, and he sees as basic to this "a comparatively lower estimate of woman, and . . . an unspiritual view of their marriage relation."[8]

3. Jesus, in His answer, made clear that the Mosaic ordinance was not the basic text and is not to be interpreted without the foundation of the creation ordinance of Genesis 2:18-24. The Mosaic regulation, while subordinate to that ordinance and addressed to the covenant man, is not limited in its application to him alone. The limitation of address is not the limitation of application. The creation ordinance was restored to the primacy it had been previously denied.

4. Moreover, Jesus made clear, *the creation ordinance did not contemplate any divorce at all.* This point the Pharisees immediately grasped. Jesus, in terms of the creation ordinance, saw *no ground* for divorce therein. Then why, they demanded, did Moses "command" that she be given a bill of divorce and be put away? Too much has sometimes been read into the word "command." What certainly was meant was this: if divorce was forbidden by the creation ordinance, then why does it appear in the commandments or law as an accepted and regulated fact?

5. Jesus then proceeded *to re-affirm Deuteronomy 24:1-4.* The Mosaic law came into being "for the hardness of your hearts." The fall of man followed Genesis 2 and is the great dividing line between that and subsequent history. The fact of original sin and a fallen heart made necessary the Mosaic legislation. *We can eliminate this Mosaic legislation only if we can eliminate the fall in its entirety, only if we can posit an Eden-like society. Basic to all disregarding of this fact of man's fallen world and hard heart is a heretical perfectionism.* It creates a harsh legalism which rends the church and bars sinners from the Gospel. Divorce legislation is necessary to the state of sin, and to Christians who are not yet perfectly sanctified by any means in this life, and often in ungodly marriages, living in a sinful world. Matthew 19:9 is thus Jesus' restatement of Deuteronomy 24:1 with fornication or the nakedness of anything as the ground for divorce, with this significant correction. Because the clause "if she doth not find grace in his eyes" had been interpreted, not in terms of covenant man's desire to fulfil the will of God in his home, but in terms of personal and *legislative privilege,* Jesus dropped it to focus attention on the divine legislation as such. This was upsetting even to his disciples (vs. 10), used as they were to man's *legislative* rather than *ministerial* authority in terms of the law.

6. Jesus, by making the inclusive term *fornication* the valid grounds for divorce, thereby made adultery, incest, and other offenses that once led to divorce by death now grounds for divorce by bills of

<hr>

8. *Ibid.,* II, 332.

divorce. That this was recognized to be the case in the church appears in I Corinthians 5:1-5, where in the case of incest, the death penalty was mandatory (Lev. 20:11), but Paul instead required excommunication, a spiritual surrender to death and Satan. In II Corinthians 7:7-12, it seems that, on godly sorrow and with separation, re-admittance to the church followed. Had the death penalty still been mandatory, Paul would have referred to it, but, while seeing the sin as a spiritual death, he does not see any legal ground for anything other than separation or excommunication. Paul spoke with authority, and a clearly accepted one, in Jesus Christ.

7. Finally, Jesus made it clear that any divorce for grounds other than fornication in its ratified Mosaic sense, constituted adultery, whether secured by the man or the woman (Mark 10:10), and marriage to such a divorced person was an act of adultery.

It will be seen that the New Testament's insistence on its unity with the Old Testament is taken very seriously. The Mosaic law is nowhere regarded as a lower or inferior legislation. At one point, however, there does seem to be some differences, and also Paul's approach to the problem:

1. In Exodus 34:12-16, we have a prohibition of religious covenants with the Canaanites. Alliances in antiquity were not only political and military, but religious and familist. Royal families inter-married. The gods of the superior partner were recognized by the lesser. Political alliances were thus the object of prophetic denunciation: they were inevitably idolatrous. All this Exodus 34:12-16 makes explicit.

2. In Numbers 25:1-8, it is made clear that even sexual relations with a foreign woman, a Midianitess, involved a joining to Baal-Peor and required death.

3. Deuteronomy 7:1-3 is a restatement of this same principle, and a warning.

4. Where a person clearly gave evidence of accepting Jehovah and His covenant, acceptance into the covenant could be followed by marriage within the covenant, as with Rahab (Joshua 6:24, 25; Matt. 1:5; Heb. 11:31; James 2:25) and Ruth (Ruth 1:16; 4: 5-18).

5. Where, as with the returning exiles, marriages were clearly political and religious (and not free from a sensual contempt of the covenant, Mal. 2:14), divorce was required by Nehemiah as the condition of continuation in the congregation of Israel, as the condition of participation in the covenant (Neh. 9:2; 13:23-27). The marriages had been contracted in order to maintain covenantal alliances with ungodly people of syncretistic faith.

This, then, was the background of legislation that Paul had to go on. In terms of Old Testament law, such marriages were clearly *fornication*

The Institutes of Biblical Law

and an offense to Jehovah, a violation of His covenant, and clearly banned. Paul clearly and unquestioningly reaffirmed this law, speaking to believers contemplating marriage, not to those regenerated after marriage:

> Be ye not unequally yoked together with unbelievers: for what fellowship hath righteousness with unrighteousness? and what communion hath light with darkness? And what concord hath Christ with Belial? or what part hath he that believeth with an infidel? And what agreement hath the temple of God with idols? for ye are the temple of the living God; as God hath said, I will dwell in them, and walk in them: and I will be their God, and they shall be my people.

> Wherefore come out from among them and be ye separate, saith the Lord, and touch not the unclean thing; and I receive you. And will be a Father unto you, and ye shall be my sons and daughters, saith the Lord Almighty (II Cor. 6:14-18).

In I Corinthians 7:11-24, Paul faced a different situation, not one clearly covered by the law. In vs. 12, Paul, careful never to speak *legislatively,* makes clear that he speaks *ministerially:* "But to the rest speak I, not the Lord." He does *not* therefore make his statement any the less authoritative: "so ordain I in all the churches" (vs. 17). He does, however, in terms of the doctrine of the covenant, make clear the ministerial authority whereby his statement is authoritative. What was the situation, and what was Paul's ministerial judgment?

1. Mixed marriages existed at Corinth, and Paul had been written about the matter, the Corinthians asking, quite apparently, if divorce should follow where only one member of the marriage was converted? The question was a thoughtful one. The case of incest arose among some who boasted of an antinomian liberty in Christ (I Cor. 5:2); that several parties existed in Corinth, Paul tells us (I Cor. 3:3-6). The question concerning mixed marriages did credit to those who raised it. Its implication was this: Jesus maintained the integrity of the Mosaic law, and the Mosaic law banned mixed marriages. What shall we new converts, with unbelieving mates, do therefore?

2. Paul faced a different society in Corinth than existed in the Old Testament, and to which in particular the law was delivered. Despite the attempts of the empire to create a unified culture through the emperor cult, it was basically pluralistic and atomistic. A variety of religions flourished, which, while ready to render lip service to the official cult, went their divisive way, to the consternation of many. Corinth was an industrial and commercial center. Its life was not *familist,* but *atomistic* and individualistic. Marriage in the non-Jewish sectors of society was based primarily on personal considerations, desires and advantages. In terms of this, *marriage was no longer a covenant both with a person, a people, and a faith as it had been in the Old Testament. It had become almost entirely*

a personal affair, very much as it is today. The law was still valid, and II Corinthians 6:14-18 affirms it, but it cannot be particularly applied to every mixed marriage, as will appear.

3. For a Christian to marry an unbeliever (II Cor. 6:14-18) meant a desertion of the fellowship of Christ, and a stepping now outside of the covenant into a purely individualistic and atomistic relation which was "darkness."

4. For a married unbeliever to become a believer meant that a covenant relationship had been introduced into an atomistic situation where no other covenant existed. The covenant, according to the law, extended to every member of the household, but not to visitors and hired servants (Ex. 12:43-45; Deut. 12:17, 18; Lev. 22:10; the sabbath of the land, Lev. 25:6, and the feast of weeks, Deut. 16:10, 11, included the stranger and hired servant for typical and prophetic purposes). Because no other covenant existed, God honored His covenant by the inclusion of the unbelieving partner and the children, so that God's covenant blessed the unbelieving man for his wife's sake. For the Greeks, marriage was an individual affair; in its earlier strength, it had been *familist* and *societal;* for Scripture, from beginning to end, it is *covenantal* and is in terms of the *image mandates.*

5. Another fundamental principle was involved: "Let every man abide in the same calling wherein he was called" (I Cor. 7:20). Freedom indeed was desirable for a slave, and more godly; having been bought with a price, and being Christ's servants, they were not to become servants of men (vss. 21-23). But the gospel had not come to change the *forms* of man and his society but the *heart* of man and thereby to create the culture of the Kingdom of God. Rome saw the radical implications of the gospel, as did many believers. Hence the necessity for the warning of Romans 13:1-7 to render to governments and "to all their dues" as required by God, who did not summon men to a gospel of revolution but of regeneration. Hence also the frequent counsel to slaves, men, women and children to be faithful and obedient in terms of their calling, not as pleasers of men but of God. The important note is this: "therein abide with God" (I Cor. 7:24). Hence God did not call Israel to destroy the current forms of their culture when He gave His law, but rather to make it subservient to Him in terms of His commandments and "therein abide with God."

6. If the unbelieving husband or wife departed, then the believer was no longer under bondage and free to remarry; they were then under the Mosaic sanction. In stating this, Paul did not act legislatively but ministerially. Had he introduced herein some new law, he would have been at once attacked. *No man can put asunder,* and, even if Paul had counselled *separation only,* if Christ had limited divorce to the ground of adultery, he would have been guilty of putting asunder what God had joined. But Paul answered Corinthian believers who apparently recognized the Old Testament law as still valid in terms of Christ's declaration. And Paul, by inspired collation, saw that more than one principle was here applicable, and that

a different type of cultural and religious situation prevailed, and that *only one covenant,* one with the Lord, was involved in this situation. Accordingly, his answer was strictly ministerial and as a result drew no fire from Judaizing critics who felt that he represented a break with the law.

7. Finally, because of the atomistic rather than covenantal nature of these mixed marriages in their origin, and because, whatever faith the unbelieving spouse continued to hold after the other's regeneration was by nature a *private religion* and not covenantal, the family was not involved in his unbelief and his salvation was possible (vs. 16). The religious cults of the day were essentially private religions, making their appeal primarily to men or to women, and lacking catholicity or covenant.

Thus, the law concerning marriage and divorce remains one throughout Scripture. The cultural particulars as reflected in the law can and do change, but the law itself does not. Here, as elsewhere, in a very profound sense "the scripture cannot be broken" (John 10:35).

According to Deuteronomy 4:2, Scripture consists of one revelation, one fundamental "word." Although "words" were to be added to that "word" before Old and New Testament canons were closed, another "word" could not be added. "Ye shall not add unto the word which I command you, neither shall ye diminish ought from it." Revelation is one word and cannot be broken.

Thus, the Scripture, in both Old and New Testaments, has one law with respect to marriage. The purpose of marriage is not humanistic; it is covenantal, and therefore the reasons for divorce cannot be humanistic and must be covenantal.

Unfortunately, divorce laws have been radically altered by humanism. The answer, however, is not a return to Montanism.[9] The practice of Calvin in Geneva illustrates that a strict, covenantal view of marriage and divorce is Biblical rather than having only adultery the grounds for divorce.[10]

The Biblical standards were clearly in force in the American states for many years. It is interesting to note that many states amplified the divorce by death aspect to include criminals sentenced to life imprisonment.[11]

A final word: Deuteronomy 24:1-4 forbids the remarriage by a husband of his divorced wife after her remarriage and second divorce.

---

9. For a modern example, see Otto A. Piper, *The Christian Interpretation of Sex* (New York: Charles Scribner's Sons, 1941), p. 162, where even the remarriage of widowed persons is criticized.

10. See Philip E. Hughes, editor, *The Register of the Company of Pastors of Geneva in the Time of Calvin* (Grand Rapids: Eerdmans, 1966); see also James G. Emerson, Jr., *Divorce, the Church, and Remarriage* (Philadelphia: The Westminster Press, 1961), pp. 84-108.

11. Carroll D. Wright, *A Report on Marriage and Divorce in the United States, 1867-1886* (Washington: Government Printing Office, 1891), p. 78, revised edition.

It is called an "abomination before the LORD." If the grounds for divorce are valid, and the woman is doubly divorced, the man compounds the evil by taking her back; if his grounds were dishonest and invalid, it is still evil and a contempt of law. The same applies to a woman remarrying a previous husband. Either the evil which led to the divorce is a real evil or else the evil contempt of law which led to an invalid divorce represents an equal evil, but in either case the relationship resumed after an intervening marriage represents an abomination because the intervening marriage was thus a defilement: it was a legalized adultery which the remarriage condones.

13. The Family as Trustee

Two interesting items with respect to divorce indicate an aspect of marriage too seldom considered. First, the overwhelming percentage of divorces are secured by women, not by men. Immediately after World War II, when it was assumed that many men would be divorcing unfaithful wives, the percentage was still highly on the side of feminine initiative. Earlier, 86 percent of all divorces had been gotten by wives; in 1945, it dropped to 75 percent.[1] It can be granted that many of these cases do involve masculine initiative, with the husband allowing the wife to secure the divorce for face-saving reasons, but, in spite of this, feminine initiative is surprisingly high.

Second, the better the income, the less likely a divorce. It is often assumed that divorce is most common among the wealthy; in reality, it is most common among the poor. A study by William J. Goode, from 1956, indicated this clearly:

> For although the divorce rate is often thought to be highest among the neurotic, success-driven middle class, actually it is highest among the lower economic classes: national census data show that men earning less than $3,000 a year are two to four times as likely to be divorced as men earning over $4,000 a year.[2]

Clearly, a major restraint on divorce is the possession of property. On the one hand, men are restrained from breaking up a marriage too readily because of the severe penalties of a division of community property, as well as the possibility of alimony. On the other hand, women are less likely to leave a marriage if the inducement of property and income is strong enough. It should be added that the large number of deserting fathers are to be found on the lower income levels. Property is thus an important restraint on the conduct of men and women. Private property is a stabilizing force for the family and society.

---

1. John R. Rice, *The Home, Courtship, Marriage and Children* (Wheaton, Ill.: Sword of the Lord Publishers, 1946), p. 356.
2. Morton M. Hunt, *Natural History of Love*, p. 394.

When the state dispossesses the family of property and replaces the family as the custodian of property, the marriage tie is harmed thereby. The communist thesis that marriage and monogamy are products of private property is clearly wrong, but the family is the major custodian of property in all history. To rob the family of property is to weaken its power over its children. Children and property, these are the two major areas of social function for the family, apart from the prior educational and religious functions. Socialism attacks parental control over both children and property in order to ensure the priority of the state in society.

The functions of the family are thus major and difficult ones. Its *religious* and *educational* tasks are central to life in their respective areas. They are aspects also of the family's custody of children. The care of property as an inheritance, a social force, and a religious responsibility is again important to society. Not surprisingly, marriage is seen in Scripture with tenderness but without romance. It is very clearly described as a "yoke" (II Cor. 6:14). A yoke is a tie binding two creatures together in pulling burdens. Marriage is also described in Scripture as "trouble in the flesh" (I Cor. 7:28), rendered "outward trouble" by Moffatt. Marriage is clearly a *working* partnership of man and wife in the service of God, exercising dominion in their appointed spheres.

Proverbs is revealing in its indications of marital life and standards. There is no reference in Proverbs to anything but monogamy. Together, husband and wife have a duty to instruct their children in God's law and in family discipline (Prov. 1:8, 9; 6:20, etc.). The working relationship of husband and wife can be a great joy, or a major disaster. "Every wise woman buildeth her house: but the foolish plucketh it down with her hands" (Prov. 14:1); in brief, "On her constructive womanly wisdom chiefly depends the family's stability."[3] "Whoso findeth a wife findeth a good thing, and obtaineth favour of the LORD" (Prov. 18: 22); indeed, "House and riches are the inheritance of fathers: and a prudent wife is from the LORD" (Prov. 19:14). God gives a greater inheritance than material wealth in a prudent wife. "A virtuous woman is a crown to her husband: but she that maketh ashamed is as rottenness in his bones" (Prov. 12:4). Precisely because marriage is so important an institution, personally and socially, a bad marriage is a disaster comparable only to "rottenness in his bones" which makes it difficult or impossible for a man to stand.

This partnership of man and wife acted as custodians of property, custodians because "the earth is the Lord's," and "The land shall not

---

3. Derek Kidner, *The Proverbs* (Chicago: Inter-Varsity Press, 1964), p. 50.

be sold for ever: for the land is mine; for ye are strangers and sojourners with me" (Lev. 25:23). The family is the God-given, God-ordained custodian of property. The dowry (Gen. 34:12; 30:20; Ex. 22:17) was not a bride-purchase fee but the bridal gift by the bridegroom to the bride to seal the marriage in terms of godly responsibility.

A marriage was truly and legally a marriage only when a contract specifying the property arrangements existed. Such a requirement was common to antiquity and appears, for example, in the Code of Hammurabi, 128: "If a man take a wife and do not draw up a contract with her, that woman is not a wife."[4] Clark's comments on the dowry in American law are of interest:

> Dower had likewise been an institution of the English law since early Anglo-Saxon times, and of American as well. Indeed it has been said of this right that it is as "widespread as the Christian religion and enters into the contract of marriage among all Christians." But in recent years the right has been modified or abolished in many jurisdictions by statutes conferring greater benefits upon widows than these which dower gives.[5]

> In modern law, dowry is ordinarily understood as being the right of a widow in respect of the property of her deceased husband.[6]

There is a difference, however, between the modern widow's dowry and that of Biblical law. In the modern dower, the widow is provided for only if there is an estate which will be of sufficient size to care for her. In Biblical law, the dowry preceded marriage, and the children had an obligation of support to their parents as needed.

The Biblical family can be compared to a corporation. A corporation differs, in that it is an artificial legal person and is created by the state. A corporation does not die when its founders die, or when its officers die; it continues to exist legally apart from its stockholders, who continue, as long as they are alive to draw dividends from it. Similarly, the family is a corporation, consisting of parents and children. It pays out dividends to the children in care, support, and inheritance, and it returns dividends to the parents in care and support as needed. As a corporation, it administers its properties and income in terms of its ordained and God-given purpose. For this reason, no arbitrary or purely personal decisions can govern the decisions of members of the corporation; they are both individual persons and a corporate entity, and their truest function is in terms of a full consideration of both offices under God.

---

4. J. M. Powis Smith, *The Origin and History of Hebrew Law* (University of Chicago Press, 1931, 1960), p. 199.
5. Clark, *Biblical Law*, p. 96.
6. *Ibid.*, p. 130

For the state to enter into the control of either children or property is to transgress on the sphere of the family and to claim to be that corporation whose life is the care of the family. Such a claim is a major transgression against God's law-order. If to this transgression is added *a loss of faith,* the family then becomes an institution whose main function is to provide a shelter and a sexual outlet for two atomistic and sometimes anarchistic individuals. An example of this appeared in the Ann Landers column of August 16, 1969, a man writing to declare that "all wives should be shot when they reach 40," because who wants an "old tomato?" Marriage in this perspective is a physical convenience for the satisfaction of man, or, conversely, for the satisfaction of a woman. It is in essence a lawless union, even though contracted under law. Not surprisingly, it produces lawless children with no respect for authority or for property. Instead of relying on God's law, the atomistic, antinomian person, like the decadent Romans of old, relies on the power of sex as a cure-all for man and society. The woman then must out-Venus Venus to maintain her position.[7]

The atomistic family can only create an anarchistic world. As Zimmerman has observed,

> . . . the family system plays a key role in the problem of social change. It brings the past into the present. The events of the present impinge upon it and try to alter it. Out of this past with its alterations we get the pattern generator for the culture of the future.
>
> Thus we cannot understand the family without combining three sets of ideas, the past and present natures of the family system and the tendencies for current *events* and *philosophies* to alter its nature. Neither the study of the development of the family system nor the impingement of present events upon it is sufficient unto itself alone. The family is a living growing institution, capable, as the poised bee for flight, of moving in any number of directions.[8]

Before the family can reverse its course, and that of society, it must have a Biblical law-faith rather than a humanistic and atomistic one. The family must again become the trustee of God's covenantal requirements, and a trustee under God of children and property. Not the trustee family of paganism, strong but humanistic in orientation, but the trustee family of God, this is the need.

The Biblical view of property will be discussed later, but, for the present, the case of Naboth can be cited (I Kings 21:1-14). For Naboth, the land was not his to sell. Everything he had, land and vineyard, was an inheritance from the past as a trust for the future. Naboth as a good steward had no doubt increased the value of that

7. Carle C. Zimmerman, *The Family of Tomorrow* (New York: Harper & Brothers, 1949), p. 156.
8. Zimmerman-Cervantes, *Marriage and the Family,* p. 128.

inheritance, but this did not make any of it his own. As head of a family, he had an inheritance as a trust, not as a means to self-indulgence, and therefore his basic obligation was to the future. In China, by means of ancestor worship, the trustee family was bound to the past. In Biblical faith, because of the creation mandate, the trustee family was geared to the future. The modern family, because of its atomistic humanism, is geared to the present and is thus destructive of both the past and the future. The man who proposed to Ann Landers that all wives be shot at the age of 40 was a logical humanist: the past has no meaning. Only the existential moment matters.[9]

14. Homosexuality

For some years, an extensive campaign has been underway to remove existing laws against homosexuality from the statute books and to permit homosexual relations between consenting adults.[1] A part of this campaign has been the insistence on reading the facts of homosexuality in terms of an evolutionary framework. Thus, it has been extensively described as a form of immaturity and an aspect of human development, and also as a product of certain kinds of family experience.[2] We are told that homosexuality "is a stage in the development of every human being."[3] It is "environmentally determined."[4] We are told that it is a flight from masculinity in a difficult world.[5] While theories vary from one scholar to another, they share in common an evolutionary and environmental approach.[6] Dr. Bergler, while radically critical of the homosexual's character, did not abandon this basic environmental approach for a moral and theological one.[7] The anti-Biblical presuppositions of all these writers are very apparent. One anthropologist goes so far as to hold that, behind chastity, there lurks a "passively homosexual potential,"[8] Another scholar insists that,

9. Ann Landers, "He Urges Firing Squad for Wives Over 40," *Los Angeles Herald-Examiner*, Saturday, August 16, 1969, p. A-11.
1. For an early example, see Morris Ploscowe, *Sex and the Law* (New York: Prentice-Hall, 1951), pp. 212-215.
2. See Nathan Blackman, M.D., "Homosexuality, Genesis of," in Edward Podolsky, M.D., editor, *Encyclopedia of Aberrations* (New York: Philosophical Library, 1953), pp. 271-274; Richard C. Robertiello, M.D., *Voyage from Lesbos* (New York: Avon Books, 1959).
3. Frank S. Caprio, M.D., *Female Homosexuality, A Psychodynamic Study of Lesbianism* (New York: Grove Press, 1954), p. 302.
4. *Ibid.*, p. 303.
5. Abraham Kardiner, *Sex and Morality* (London: Routledge and Kegan Paul, 1955), pp. 160-192.
6. See Irving Bilber, editor, *Homosexuality, A Psychoanalytic Study* (New York: Basic Books, 1962).
7. Edmund Bergler, M.D., *Homosexuality: Disease or Way of Life?* (New York: Hill and Wong, 1957); and *Counterfeit Sex, Homosexuality, Impotence, Frigidity* (New York: Grove Press, 1951, 1961).
8. H. R. Hays, *The Dangerous Sex*, p. 169.

Now, just as the boy's love for his father is in the strict sense homosexual, so his love for his mother is in the strict sense incestuous.[9]

Somehow, all the enemies of perversion must themselves be made
perverts!

Ullerstam, a Swedish doctor, is more open in his hostility to Christian
morality. All perversions are earnestly defended. He declares that
" 'Perversion' is a word that should be discarded," because "It has been
made to order for obscurantists and demagogues. It is saturated with
superstition, and it is an insult, to boot."[10] Perversions are good, he
holds, because they give happiness to some people.[11] He is happy to
report that incest is on the increase among his friends.[12] He defends
incest, exhibitionism, pedophilia, saliromania, algolagnia, homosexuality,
scapophilia, necrophilia, and other sexual deviations as good but does
cite an especially dangerous form of sexual intercourse:

> Of all forms of sexual intercourse the heterosexual kind certainly
> is the most dangerous, having the greatest potential risks in so-
> cial consequences. Yet this act is hedged about with fewer restric-
> tions than several other sexual expressions of a far tamer kind.
> Nevertheless we consider it a happy and healthy state of things
> that people satisfy their sexual urge in this risky manner. Would
> it not be better if we encouraged people to "perversions" instead,
> and taught them to condition their sexual secretions to other rites
> and stimuli besides heterosexual coition? Would it not be in the
> interest of the whole world to provide such education, which might,
> in the long run, prove a solution to the problem of overpopulation?[13]

The introduction to Ullerstam by Yves de Saint-Agnes is accurate in
stating that

> Present-day Sweden is living through a sexual revolution. The first
> victim to be hunted down is morality. In religious wars, absolution
> is always given for deeds of violence committed "for the cause."
> Similarly, the crusade against classical morality lends its participants
> a kind of immunity.[14]

This is an honest statement and a true one. We are in the midst of a
homosexual revolution aimed against Biblical faith and morality. The
homosexual is presented to us as the mistreated, misunderstood, sensitive
soul.[15]

For a long time, for ages, in fact, homosexuals, even where accepted,

9. G. Rattray Taylor, *Sex in History* (New York: Vanguard Press, 1954), p. 81.
10. Lars Ullerstam, M.D., *The Erotic Minorities* (New York: Grove Press, 1966), p. 351.
11. *Ibid.*, pp. 43, 82 f.   13. *Ibid.*, p. 163.
12. *Ibid.*, p. 46.   14. *Ibid.*, p. vi.
15. See R. E. L. Masters, *The Homosexual Revolution* (New York: The Julian Press, 1962); Floyd Dell, *Love in the Machine Age* (New York: Farrar & Rinehard, 1930); Diana Frederics, *Diana: A Strange Autobiography* (New York: Citadel, 1939, 1944).

have been a secret, hostile fraternity within society, very often closely linked with every kind of secret society. Louis XIV had to deal with an order of sodomites in his own court, and similar organizations have been repeatedly noted.[16]

In turning to the scholars of the church, one would hope for some resistance to this revolution, but, instead, the church is becoming a major part of the revolution.[17] Thus, one church publication demands that we treat lesbians as "individual human beings," not as homosexuals. We are asked to by-pass God's view of the matter in favor of autonomous, apostate man's view. In short, a radical sympathy for the homosexual is demanded.[18] Fantastic reasons are given for the Biblical condemnation of homosexuality.[19] The "problem" is viewed in psychological and evolutionary rather than Biblical and theological terms and standards.[20] The cause of homosexuality is said to be environment, not sin.[21] One writer, Thielicke is aware that Scripture declares that homosexuality is to be understood theologically only, but he still calls for a humanistic solution.[22]

Before analyzing the theological perspective, it is well to note some of the central characteristics of the homosexual as reported by people who are by no means hostile to them. *First,* the homosexual has an abnormal fear of aging and of death. As a result, homosexuals insist on dressing and acting on the assumption of perpetual youth, in particular, immature youth. At all times, the facade of youth must be maintained. This "worship" of youth and immaturity leads to the adoption of styles which stress these aspects and recall the innocent child to mind. An amoral world of perpetual childhood is invoked. Since maturity means responsibility, law, and standards, a *second* aspect of homosexual culture is the exaltation of studied vulgarity into high style. Martin Bender cites Susan Sontag's analysis of "camp" tastes:

> In fact, camp had been a synonym for homosexual for 40 years in England, for about a decade in New York.
>
> Miss Sontag offered more than 50 definitions of camp. A love of the exaggerated, a spirit of extravagance, "style at the expense of

---

16. Richard Lewinsohn, *A History of Sexual Customs*, pp. 222 ff., 340 ff.
17. A major document in the new morality has been *Toward a Quaker View of Sex* (London: Friends Home Service Committee, 1964).
18. Del Martin and Phyllis Lyon, "The Realities of Lesbianism," in *Motive*, vol. XXIX, nos. 6 & 7 (March-April, 1969), pp. 61-67. See on this issue, "When Are Church Magazines Obscene?" in *The National Observer*, vol. 8, no. 32 (August 11, 1969), pp. 1, 15.
19. Derrick Sherwin Bailey, *Sexual Relations in Christian Thought* (New York: Harper & Brothers, 1959), p. 242.
20. William Graham Cole, *Sex in Christianity and Psychoanalysis* (New York: Oxford University Press, 1955), p. 359.
21. William Graham Cole, *Sex and Love in the Bible*, p. 359.
22. Helmut Thielicke, *The Ethics of Sex* (New York: Harper & Row, 1964), pp. 269-292.

content," and the declaration that there is a good taste in bad taste. Camp is antiserious, appreciative of the vulgar and the banal. The examples she gave of camp taste—Aubrey Beardsley drawings, Tiffany lamps, Twenties women's clothes including feather boas and beaded dresses, Busby Berkeley musicals like *The Gold Diggers of 1933*—have become canons of faith for fashion display artists, boutique owners and department store merchandisers.[23]

This is an aspect of *homosexual antinomianism:* by replacing sound standards with arbitrary and vulgar styles, the homosexual derives a deep satisfaction: he is subverting, he believes, ultimate law and asserting man's autonomy.

Third, homosexual culture is bitterly hostile to the family, and, in its intellectual fashions, works to undercut the family and small-town culture as well. Because of the extensive control by homosexuals over fashions and publications, the mind and appearance of Western countries have been radically infected by the parasitic homosexual culture. The canons of homosexual culture are now the standards of the youth-worshipping jet set,[24] of the world of art and fashions, and of the modern intellectuals. Modern humanistic culture is to a great degree colored and imbued with homosexual culture. Many of the free-love and wife-swapping cults are strongly tinged with homosexual overtones and activities.[25]

Fourth, because the homosexual lives against reality and in a world of make-believe, he has therefore found the theater to be a happy element for his self-realization. Henriques noted "the connection of the Roman stage with homosexuality—a tradition which has persisted in the European theatre to the present day."[26] He also cited the fact that "The relationship of the stage and whoredom which had flourished since the Middle Ages was continued and enhanced in the eighteenth century."[27]

To turn now to the law, the Bible is without reservation in its condemnation of homosexuality:

> Thou shalt not lie with mankind, as with womankind: it is abomination (Lev. 18:22).

> If a man also lie with mankind, as he lieth with a woman, both of them have committed an abomination: they shall surely be put to death; their blood shall be upon them (Lev. 20:13).

---

23. Marilyn Bender, *The Beautiful People* (New York: Dell, 1968), p. 29. On the fear of death and aging see p. 27 f; on homosexuals and fashions, see pp. 231, 282.
24. Lanfranco Rasponi, *The International Nomads*, p. 78 ff.
25. Roger Blake, *The Free-Love Groups*, pp. 60, 140.
26. Fernando Henriques, *Prostitution and Society, Primitive, Classical and Oriental* (New York: Grove Press, 1962, 1966), p. 105.
27. Fernando Henriques, *Prostitution in Europe and the Americas* (New York: The Citadel Press, 1965), p. 167.

> There shall be no whore of the daughters of Israel, nor a sodomite of the sons of Israel (Deut. 23:17).

This certainly is clear enough, and there is not a single text in all the New Testament to indicate that this penalty has been altered or removed (in Romans 1:32 St. Paul in fact confirms it), yet virtually all theologians by-pass this law and disregard its requirement. In fact, St. Paul cited homosexuality as the culmination of man's apostasy (Rom. 1:18-32). St. Paul's description of the act is revealing:

> And likewise also the men, leaving the natural use of the woman, burned in their lust one toward another; men with men working that which is unseemly, and receiving in themselves that recompense of their error which was meet (Rom. 1:27).

The verb "burned" is *ekkaio*, "to burn out."[28] Homosexuality is thus the burning out of man; hence, to cite Wuest's translation of the latter half of this verse, they receive "in themselves that retribution which was a necessity in the nature of the case because of their deviation from the norm."[29]

Homosexuality is thus the culminating sexual practice of a culminating apostasy and hostility towards God. The homosexual is at war with God, and, in his every practice, is denying God's natural order and law. The theological aspect of homosexuality is thus emphasized in Scripture. In history, homosexuality becomes prominent in every area of apostasy and time of decline. It is an end of an age phenomenon.

Earlier, we made reference to the opinions of Thielicke. To return to his analysis, we find Thielicke cites the law but finds it now irrelevant:

> . . . there can be no doubt that the Old Testament regarded homosexuality and pederasty as crimes punishable by death (Lev. 18:22, 20:13). Whether direct injunctions are to be derived from this for Christians must remain a matter of discussion, at least insofar as behind this prohibition there lies the concept of cultic defilement and thus the question is raised whether and to what extent the Old Testament cultic law can be binding upon those who are under the Gospel Law. Here the problems of theological principle which are referred to in technological terminology under the subject of "Law and Gospel" become acute.[30]

If there is no Law, then there is no Gospel, because in Scripture the two are inseparable. With the law set aside, then the humanistic and amoral ethics of love can take over, in which the one real consideration is not God and His law but the *human being,* the ultimate moral norm for the ethics of love. Not surprisingly, Thielicke declares:

---

28. Kenneth S. Wuest, *Romans in the Greek New Testament* (Grand Rapids: Eerdmans, 1955), p. 36.
29. *Ibid.*
30. Helmut Thielicke, *Ethics of Sex,* p. 277 f.

It is true that the homosexual relationship is not a *Christian* form of encounter with our fellow man; it is nevertheless very certainly a search for the totality of the other *human being*. He who says otherwise has not yet observed the possible human depth of homoerotic-colored friendship. Moreover, the perversion inherent in the reduction of sexuality to mere "physical excitation" is also to be found in heterosexual relationships. To make this charge refer especially to homosexuals shows ignorance or prejudice.[31]

From the Biblical perspective, any and every "search for the totality of the other human being" apart from God is vicious, depraved, and under condemnation. This search is honored only where God is not honored in His law-word.

Thielicke is aware of the theological meaning, and he comments on Romans 1:26 f. as follows:

The wrath of God over this hubris expresses itself in God's giving man over, abandoning him (paredoken) to the consequences of this his fundamental attitude, leaving him, as it were, to the autonomy of the existence which he himself has entered upon. In consequence of this autonomy of judgment, then, *religious* confusion also lead to *ethical* chaos. It consists in confusion of the eternal with the temporal. That is to say, finite entities are vested with the sovereignty of God and men worship idols (Rom. 1:23). Because the lower and the higher, the creature and the Creator, are exchanged ("perverted"), the result is a perverse supremacy of the inferior desires over the spirit. And in this context, the *sexual* perversions are mentioned as further marks of this fundamental perversion (Rom. 1:26 f.).

What is theologically noteworthy and kerygmatically "binding" in this exposition of Paul's is the statement that disorder in the vertical dimension (in the God-man relationship) is matched by a perversion on the horizontal level, not only within man himself (spirit-flesh relationship) but also in his interhuman contacts.[32]

Without taking time to differ with details of this exposition, it can be granted that it shows awareness of the *theological* issue. But Thielicke gives priority to the *human* issue by setting aside the law in favor of understanding. The failure of the Reformaticn to come to grips with the issue of law has led ultimately to this triumph of humanism; man is not judged by God's law but as a "human being" and in terms of the purely human consequences of his actions.[33] This is not theology but rather humanistic anthropology.

It is because of the theological aspect of homosexuality, its war against God, that it is, as Thielicke is aware, also a war against man and against oneself.

It is customary now among humanists to regard homosexuality as a

---

31. *Ibid.*, p. 271 f.   32. *Ibid.*, p. 279 f.   33. *Ibid.*, pp. 287-292.

natural act which is a phase in the erotic development of man. The Biblical view is that it is an act against God and therefore against nature. It is an unnatural act, that is, an act contrary to the order of nature and a product of the fall in its ultimate implications. The hostility basic to homosexuality (both male and female) has been extensively documented by Dr. Bergler. The Marquis de Sade is a classical example of this hatred of God and law. According to Sade, "The rule of law is inferior to that of anarchy."[34] Sade's hostility to all men and to himself manifested itself in sadistic and masochistic activities. His hatred of godly order probably led him to avoid all normal sexual relations, and there is doubt as to whether his wife's children were really his.[35] Not arrested development or immaturity but deliberate and mature warfare against God marks the homosexual.

God's penalty is death, and a godly order will enforce it. Not surprisingly, a culture deeply infected by homosexuality will remove the penalties against it.

One final point: female homosexuality, or lesbianism, is a manifestation of the same evil as the masculine form, but the death penalty is reserved for the men. In the women, it is an "uncleanness" and grounds for divorce (Deut. 24:1). Why not the death penalty for women? There are two reasons for this. *First,* as seen with respect to divorce, the man's greater authority means greater moral responsibility and greater guilt in sinning. *Second,* because homosexuality is an expression of apostasy, men cannot in good conscience punish that which their own abdication of moral authority encourages. As Hosea declared, with respect to whoredom and adultery,

> I will not punish your daughters when they commit whoredom, nor your spouses when they commit adultery: for themselves are separated with whores, and they sacrifice with harlots; therefore the people that doth not understand shall fall (Hosea 4:12).

When a people reaches a certain level of moral depravity, punishment ceases to be particular and becomes national. The civil order has lost its ability to act for God, and God then acts against that order. In other words there is punishment, but the punishment is from God and the people or nation shall fall. Homosexual cultures are at war with God; in this war, there are no negotiations possible. That the modernist and the open unbeliever should be in the enemy camp comes as no surprise, but what shall we say of ostensible evangelicals who hold that "the individual homosexual would appear to be more sinned against than sinning," because his condition is either genetic or environmental in nature and thus not his fault! To agree with the Wolfenden Report, and

---

34. Cited by Simone de Beauvoir, in Sade, *The 120 Days of Sodom*, etc., p. 49.
35. *Ibid.*, p. 24.

Thielicke, is to disagree with the Scriptures. This, however, is the choice made by an article in a major "evangelical" magazine.[36] It is well to remember the words of St. Peter, that "judgment must begin at the house of God" (I Peter 4:17).

When the church has so ungodly a position, we must not be surprised at the position taken by other institutions. An "equal rights" organization for homosexuals "has been recognized as a student group at Columbia University, New York City, and has announced plans to set up similar groups at Stanford University and the University of California, Berkeley."[37] Again, Ann Landers' advice column has stated:

> The experts on homosexuality with whom I consult tell me that while the chances for a complete cure are extremely slim, the tortured homosexuals who hate themselves often profit from therapy. While it does not convert them into normal males, it helps them to accept themselves without guilt and shame and all self-destructive emotions that accompany these twin horrors.[38]

This is the goal of psycho-therapy, to sin without guilt and shame. The ungodly have at least their openly anti-God attitude to justify their position. This certainly cannot be the defense of churchmen whose vows require them to proclaim the word of God.

What faces man today in this perversion is, to use Schaeffer's apt term, "philosophical homosexuality":

> Some forms of homosexuality today . . . are not just homosexuality but a philosophical expression. One must have understanding for the real homophile's problem. But much modern homosexuality is an expression of the current denial of antithesis. It has led in this case to an obliteration of the distinction between man and woman. So the male and the female as complementary partners are finished. This is a form of homosexuality which is a part of the movement below the line of despair. But this is not an isolated problem; it is a part of the world-spirit of the generation which surrounds us. It is imperative that Christians realise the conclusions which are being drawn as a result of the death of absolutes.[39]

------

36. B. L. Smith, "Homosexuality in the Bible and the Law," in *Christianity Today*, vol. XIII, no. 21 (July 18, 1969), p. 936.

37. "Homosexual Group OK'd at Columbia," Palo Alto *Times* (California), Thursday, May 4, 1967, p. 2.

38. Ann Landers, Los Angeles *Herald-Examiner*, Sunday, October 6, 1968, p. G-4. The extent to which Ann Landers holds this opinion was apparent in another bit of advice: "Confidential to Heartbroken Mother of a Boy With a Twisted Mind: Yes, I recommend psychiatric help—not for him, but for you. Your son has learned to live with his homosexuality. In fact, he seems to have adjusted very well. Now you must learn to accept him as he is and stop torturing yourself," Ann Landers, Los Angeles *Herald-Examiner*, Monday, September 1, 1969, p. A-14.

39. Francis A. Schaeffer, *The God Who Is There* (Chicago: Inter-Varsity Press, 1968), p. 39.

All homosexuality, we would add, is a philosophical expression; this is the real nature of the "homophile's problem."

When we are confronted with a homosexual person who claims to be a Christian and demands to be recognized as such, we have a choice: we either accept the homosexual person's word, or we accept God's word as declared in Roman 1.

15. Uncovering the Springs

An unholy prudery prevents the church today from reckoning with many laws. An important example of this is the law concerning sexual relations with a menstruous woman, or with a woman not fully recovered from child-birth.

If the sexual relations with a menstruating woman are unknowingly performed, it is merely a ritual uncleanness, requiring purification but carrying no moral penalty (Lev. 15:24). On the other hand, the deliberate act is a serious offense:

> Also thou shalt not approach unto a woman to uncover her nakedness, as long as she is put apart for her uncleanness (Lev. 18:19).

> And if a man shall lie with a woman having her sickness, and shall uncover her nakedness, he hath discovered the fountain of her blood: and both of them shall be cut off from among the people (Lev. 20:18).

The cutting off "from among the people" is read by some as the death penalty, by most as excommunication. Clearly, we are dealing with a serious and significant offense. It is one of the offenses which leads to a "sickened land" and a "revolted nature."[1] This is not only an offense against God, but one of the offenses which leads the earth itself to spue out a people (Lev. 20:22). The offense of having "uncovered the fountain of her blood" means that the man has "exposed her life-spring."[2] Both the man and the woman are alike guilty.

Ezekiel's reference to the same sin throws a further light on this matter:

> But if a men be just, and do that which is lawful and right, And hath not eaten upon the mountains, neither hath lifted up his eyes to the idols of the house of Israel, neither hath defiled his neighbour's wife, neither hath come to a menstruous woman, And hath not oppressed any, but hath restored to the debtor his pledge, hath spoiled none by violence, hath given his bread to the hungry, and hath covered the naked with a garment; He that hath not given forth upon usury, neither hath taken any increase, that hath withdrawn his hand from iniquity, hath executed true judgment between man and man, Hath walked in my statutes, and hath kept my judgments, to deal truly; he is just, he shall surely live, saith the Lord GOD (Ezek. 18:5-9).

1. John Peter Lange, *Commentary on the Holy Scriptures: Leviticus* (Grand Rapids: Zondervan), p. 155.
2. *Ibid.*, p. 156.

Two things appear from these passages. *First,* sexual intercourse with a menstruous woman (or a woman before her recovery from child-birth) is classified by both Leviticus and Ezekiel with serious, *aggressive* acts. *Second,* this act is listed prominently among those which *pollute a land.* Ellison's comment here is very much to the point:

> The fact is that the popular modern conception of the individual is derived from Greek thought rather than from the Bible, and may even be regarded as anti-Biblical. We tend to think of our bodies giving us our individuality and separating us, one from the other. In the Old Testament it is our flesh—a word for body hardly exists in Hebrew—that binds us to our fellow-men; it is our personal responsibility to God that gives us our individuality. Since man ('adam) is bound to the ground ('adamah) from which he has been taken, and through it to all who live on the same ground, he cannot help influencing them by his actions. Abominable conduct causes "the land to sin" (Deut. 24:4; cf. Jer. 3:1, 9). That is why drought, pestilence, earthquake, etc., are for the Old Testament the entirely natural punishment of wickedness (cf. Psa. 107:33 f.). If a man dwelt in a polluted land, he could not help sharing in its pollution. The chief terror of exile was not that the land of exile was outside the control of Jehovah—a view that was probably held by very few—but rather that it was an unclean land (Amos 7:17).[3]

To return to the details of the law, *first,* seven days of abstinence from sexual intercourse is required during the time of menstruation (Lev. 15:19), or, if there is an ailment associated with menstruation, as long as the discharge lasts (Lev. 15:25). *Second,* the period of abstinence after the birth of a man-child is forty days (Lev. 12:2-4), and eighty days after the birth of a girl (Lev. 12:5).

We have cited two characteristics of this sin, i.e., that it is an *aggressive* act, and that it *pollutes the land.* A *third* aspect is cited by Ezekiel 22:10, its *perversity.* Ezekiel associated it with sexual intercourse with a stepmother, and he spoke of it as a *humbling* of women. This writer's pastoral experience abundantly confirmed the element of perversity in this act. It is a delight to perverse men if the act is morally and/or esthetically offensive to their wife, and, similarly, some women are interested in it if it is morally and/or esthetically offensive to their husbands. It is an attractive act only to those who want to sin against the other person, and against God.

To return to Leviticus 20:19, the sin of the man is described thus: "he has exposed her fountain." The sin of the woman is similarly described: "she has exposed the fountain of her blood" (BV). The term *fountain* is an important one here. In the natural, literal sense, it is a natural source of living water, and it is the same word as "eye" in

---

3. H. L. Ellison, *Ezekiel: The Man and His Message* (Grand Rapids: Eerdmans, 1956), p. 72.

Hebrew. The word is also used symbolically in Scripture of God (Ps. 36:9; Jer. 17:13) as the source of grace (Ps. 87:7). There are a number of such references to God and Christ. But *fountain* is also used of Israel as the father of a great people (Deut. 33:28); it is used of a good wife (Prov. 5:18) and of spiritual wisdom (Prov. 16:22; 18:4). Its usage in Leviticus 20:19 obviously combines graphically a literal and a symbolic meaning. To understand this meaning we must remember that a fountain is a source, a place on earth where living water comes forth. There is an obvious analogy to the woman's ovulation. Equally obvious is the fact that there is a symbolic sense to the term here that is basic to the severity of the punishment.

This meaning can be fathomed by stating the matter legally: it is forbidden to a man to uncover the fountain of a woman, and it is forbidden to a woman to uncover her fountain. This law thus placed the woman beyond the man's use for regular intervals of time; similarly, the woman had no right to commit herself to a man without limits or without reservation.

Man is God's creature, and God is the ultimate fountain of life. Man cannot transgress on any area, because every area of life is bound and covered by God's law and is to be discovered or uncovered in Him. Man's lordship is under God, and man cannot therefore exercise an unreserved lordship over anyone or anything. There is thus in all things a private domain which man cannot transgress; the public domain of things and of people is that covered by God's law.

No man can thus make a woman his creature, nor can any woman make herself a man's creature. Every man and every woman has those obligations of love and service to husband or wife, to parents and children, employers, employees, and neighbors, that God's law requires, but no transgression of the privacy of another person. Our fountains are in God; He alone therefore has the total right and power to unrestricted knowledge of us, and jurisdiction over us. No man can claim that right without striking at God. Even though we may love deeply a wife, husband, child, parent, or friend, we cannot have a total relationship with them, or transgress on their privacy or throw open ours without reserve.

Similarly, the state has no right to total knowledge over its citizens, or to attempt to transgress the privacy of its citizens. It must claim their obedience to law, but no more. No man and no state can claim the power to do with people as it wills.

But it is a characteristic of ungodly man to use man in terms of his own will rather than God's law. The Thirty Years War saw the ruthless and total destruction of cities, villages, and farms by both sides. Engravings of the period show us the horrors of the war: soldiers castrating

The Institutes of Biblical Law

farmers, hanging them head downward over the fire, and lining up to rape the farmer's wife. There was no restraint on the evil imaginations and actions of men. The great iniquity of the reign of Louis XIV was his treatment of the Huguenots. To have killed them for their faith would at least have been to honor it, but the policy instead was to quarter troops of the lowest kind of soldiers on the Huguenot families, to rape their womenfolk.

Napoleon showed better sense, and a contemporary account, that of the Marquis de Bonneval, reported it:

> Surgeon-major Mouton of the Guard was billeted on the Princess of Lichtenstein.
>
> Mouton, whose soldierly language was often far from choice, wrote the princess a letter complaining of the sleeping arrangements, and that in terms which were really insolent, all but indecent.
>
> This letter fell into the hands of the Prince of Neuchatel, who took it to the Emperor. Napoleon's wrath knew no bounds! He ordered the Prince of Neuchatel to produce the culprit at the following day's review, between four gendarmes.
>
> The courtyard of Schonbrunn, much larger than that of Fontaine-bleau has likewise a double flight of steps in front of the palace.
>
> The Guards having massed in this courtyard, the culprit was led in by his four gendarmes.
>
> Then Napoleon showed himself on the perron, with a paper in his hand. But instead of coming down four steps at a time, as he usually did, he advanced deliberately, followed by the whole of his brilliant staff, and still with the terrible paper in his hand.
>
> Still with measured step, he approached the culprit, and flung at him:
>
> "Was it you that signed such filth?"
>
> The wretched man hung his head by way of assent.
>
> Then Napoleon, in ringing tones:
>
> "Understand this, gentlemen, one kills men, but one never puts them to shame. Let him be shot!"
>
> The exhibition had been given, and General Dorsenne did not have the unlucky doctor shot.[4]

If Scripture does not give the power to use a person apart from the law to a husband or wife, whose relationship is one of love, how much less does it permit any other to transgress on what is God's private domain in the life of man. If a husband cannot "use" his wife apart from the law, or a wife give herself apart from the law, no other man or agency can transgress on the fountains of life without polluting the very earth and incurring judgment.

---

4. Jean Savant, *Napoleon in His Time* (New York: Thomas Nelson & Sons, 1958), p. 223.

16   The Mediatorial Work of the Law

To speak of the mediatorial work of the law is to arouse immediately the hostility of Protestant evangelicals, with their deeply rooted antinomianism. To clarify the matter as quickly as possible, Jesus Christ is the only mediator between God and man. There is no salvation except through Jesus Christ, the God-given mediator and redeemer. The mediation of Jesus Christ is *between God and man;* the law is the God-given mediator *between man and man.* The Scriptures speak of Christ as the mediator of a new and better covenant, "which was established upon better promises" (Heb. 8:6). These promises are the promises of the law as summed up in Deuteronomy 28, the blessings to obedient faith. According to Lenski,

> The promises are not better in substance compared with the promises that were made to Abraham but in the fact that we no longer need to wait for the Mediator as Abraham had to wait for him. They are, of course, better than the promises that were attached to the law-testament which was brought in 430 years after Abraham.[1]

Lenski's first sentence is correct; in his second sentence, by downgrading the Mosaic covenant, Lenski lapses into that dispensationalism which is the logical consequence of all antinomianism. Throughout Scripture, God makes one covenant for successive peoples. What is *new* in Christ's covenant was His coming and His atonement as the true sacrifice and the blood of the covenant; Christ emphasized the sameness of God's covenant by replacing Jacob's twelve sons, and Israel's twelve tribes, with twelve apostles. By this act He made clear the continuity of His covenant with that of Abraham and Adam. By celebrating His covenant at the time of the celebration of the old, the passover, Christ at the last supper again emphasized that the continuity of the covenant rested with His people. The covenant being renewed by Christ, the law of the covenant was also renewed.

Because the people of God are called to righteousness, "the righteousness of the law" (Rom. 8:4), the law is therefore a basic condition of their lives. *No direct relationship is possible between persons except through the law of God.* Attempts to by-pass the law for a person to person confrontation without God means the judgment of God, for the law is operative against its violators, and against the destruction of the true relationship of man to man under God's law.

The law of the Lord concerning sexual relations during menstruation is a clear illustration of this principle. It is impossible for man to claim that within marriage a non-theological person to person confrontation

---

1. R. C. H. Lenski, *The Interpretation of the Epistle to the Hebrews and of the Epistle of James* (Columbus, Ohio: Wartburg Press, 1937), p. 259.

is possible. The relationship is one which is entirely circumscribed by law. It is ordained by God and therefore governed by His law. We are told plainly, "Marriage is honourable in all, and the bed undefiled: but whoremongers and adulterers God will judge" (Heb. 13:4). The law extends to that bed by forbidding relations with a menstruous wife or with a wife not fully recovered from child-birth.

In every area of life, whether with respect to our enemies, neighbors, fellow-believers, husbands, wives, or children, "love is the fulfilling of the law" (Rom. 13: 8-10). Love without law is a contradiction; while love and law are not identical, the one cannot exist without the other.

If a man claims to love a woman, and then asks, in the name of a more personal and existential relationship, that they live together without marriage, the woman is justified in questioning his love. Love cannot be separated from law without denying love, nor can law be separated from love without denying law.

This means, for example, that a marriage is a valid one, and cannot be broken, where the husband and wife are faithfully discharging their duties as required by God's law in good faith towards God and their spouse, and with grace.

On the other hand, the romantic mood of the modern world seeks a person to person relationship deliberately outside the law and as a result pursues a course suicidal to the life of man. If a person to person relationship outside of God is forbidden between man and woman, it is also forbidden between man and man and woman and woman in every other area.

This means that children are not loved if they are loved outside the law; to disregard the law and attempt to exempt children from it in or out of the family is to show them anything but love.

Similarly, an employer-employee relationship is not strictly person to person. Non-Christian free-market economics has insisted that such a master-worker relationship cannot be governed by anything but the operations of the market. Modern statism has instead insisted on its right to intervene with its own statist law. The tragedy of both positions is their essential lawlessness. The one exalts the personal will into law, the other the political will; the one a market principle, the other a socialist principle. In a godless society, neither the individual nor the state can be expected to act under law; both will operate in terms of sin. As a result, their concept of law will be the exercise of power in order to increase power. But, in terms of Scripture, neither the state nor the employer can have a direct relationship with anyone apart from God.

The law of God is thus the mediator between man and man. Instead of a person to person confrontation, there is always the mediation of

God's law between persons. If the persons meet in terms of law, their relationship is blessed and is prospered; if they meet outside the law, the curse of the law works against them. The supposed purpose of person to person confrontation is a genuine existential, and truly *personal* relationship; in reality, it leads to a *radical impersonalism*. A truly personal relationship is only that which is mediated by law.

The matter can be best illustrated by turning to medicine. As Dr. Hans Selye, M.D., has pointed out, "Life just isn't the sum of its parts. . . . The more you take these living things apart, the further you get from biology. . . ."[2] Selye's work has been that of "the simple observer and correlator of the old school in biology,"[3] observing the person and working with the naked eye. Dr. Selye's respect for molecular biology is real, as is his criticism of it. His book is dedicated to a molecular biologist, Professor Humberto Fernandez-Moran, electron-microscopist of the University of Chicago. According to Selye,

> He is both a physician and a physicist who not only uses but actually builds high-power electron microscopes. I have read many of his remarkable publications, but since I had never met him, I could not resist the temptation to phone him last time I was in Chicago and he kindly invited me to his home for dinner to be followed by a visit to his famous laboratories.
>
> My interest in his research and his colorful personality was further increased by our dinner conversation and it reached a climax at about midnight in his lab when I began to realize the grandeur of his scientific contribution. There was the latest model of his famous diamond knife with which he could physically cut glycogen molecules into smaller sugars. There, I could actually see individual molecules of hemo-cyanin under his most powerful electron microscope. He explained to me that this was merely the beginning because now he was working on a still more powerful electron microscope which will show objects clearly at a magnification of two million times. I was deeply moved by what I saw and speechless with admiration. But then suddenly my iconoclastic subconscious broke out to the surface and flashed the terrifying thought through my obsolete mind: "Imagine this great genius using all his enormous intellect and knowledge to build an instrument with which to restrict his visual field two million times!"[4]

Selye's work and his great contributions to medicine have all depended on his observations of the living creature and of the laws of life, all with the naked eye. Molecular biology has made major contributions to abstract knowledge, but Selye's work has been of great practical value because of its concern with the whole, and his belief that life is more than the sum of its parts.

---

2. Hans Selye, M.D., *In Vivo, The Case for Supramolecular Biology* (New York: Liveright, 1967), p. 18 f.

3. *Ibid.*, p. 150.   4. *Ibid.*, p. 150 f.

The life of man *is* more than the sum of its parts; a basic part of the whole is the law of God. Man having been created by God, was created by and into God's law. To consider man apart from that fact is to depersonalize him.

A man can never be considered in abstraction from what he is. To hold that we can discount a man's race, heritage, intelligence, religion, and moral character, and then somehow deal with the real man is a common liberal fallacy; the result is only an abstract idea of a man, not a living man. Similarly, no man can be abstracted from the law context of his being. To attempt an approach to any man, woman, or child apart from God's law context is to attempt to approach a creature of our own making, a non-existent person. Hence the radical impersonalism of all person-to-person confrontations. Romantic love, for example, by-passes the law-context of God to get at the "real person." In such a relationship, both parties see only the uncreated person of their imagination. As both parties in such a relationship once confessed, after their grand passion cooled off, and their imagination grounded on the rocks of reality, they found themselves unable either to speak intelligently to one another or to live together.

Person to person confrontations are thus characterized by a basic impersonalism. Their attempt to reach the person outside the law, or to deal with a worker outside the law, has them using other persons, not as they truly exist, in a context of law, but as they are converted into items of use by man's imagination.

Man cannot live in the physical world without recognizing the laws thereof; to deny those laws, or to assume they can be by-passed, is to court disaster. Man did not learn to fly by leaping off a cliff in defiance of law, but by utilizing law to make possible aerial flight. Similarly, man cannot neglect the reality of God's law in any other sphere of creation. Law is as fully operative in the world of men as in any other sphere. The continuing crises of history and its chronic state of disaster are due to man's sinful failure to abide by and in the law.

The law thus does not separate people nor does it make for impersonalism. Lawlessness divides men; true law helps bring them together. Just as Christ, as mediator, is the only one who can bring man to God, so man can only be brought together with his fellow man by law, God's law. The mediation of Jesus Christ restores man into righteousness, that is, into law, and therefore communion is opened up not only with God but also with man.

17. The Transvestite

A significant law appears in Deuteronomy 22:5 which has long influenced law codes of Christian nations:

The woman shall not wear that which pertaineth unto a man, neither shall a man put on a woman's garment: for all that do so are abomination unto the LORD thy God.

The word *abomination* is of particular interest here. One Greek and four Hebrew words are translated as abomination; in this case the Hebrew word is *toebah,* which means "something loathed, especially on religious grounds."[1] "The word is used to denote that which is particularly offensive to the moral sense, the religious feeling, or the natural inclination of the soul."[2]

The law here however designates *the person* as an "abomination" to the Lord; thus, not the act or thing but the individual is singled out for this abhorrence.

No penalty is specified for the crime; it is a misdemeanor, and the punishment is left to the discretion of the lawmakers.

The comments of Biblical scholars are of interest. Wright saw it as part of the requirement of physical perfection, the duty to respect and maintain the body as God gave it, without mutilation or confusion.[3] He stated that it is

A law appearing only here and usually interpreted as directed against the simulated changes of sex in Canaanite religion. Evidence of the latter is derived, however, from sources which are much later than Israelite times. It may be that the motivation comes from the Israelite abhorrence of all that is unnatural (cf. vv. 9-11; Exeg. on 14:1-2), though in point of fact we have no certainty as to what lay behind it.[4]

Keil and Delitzsch are especially helpful:

As the property of a neighbour was to be sacred in the estimation of an Israelite, so also the divine distinction of the sexes, which was kept sacred in civil life by the clothing peculiar to each sex, was to be not less but even more sacredly observed. *"There shall not be man's things upon a woman, and a man shall not put on a woman's clothes."* (Things) does not signify clothing merely, nor arms only, but includes every kind of domestic and other utensil. The immediate design of this prohibition was not to prevent licentiousness, or to oppose idolatrous practices. . . .; but to maintain the sanctity of that distinction of the sexes which was established by the creation of man and woman, and in relation to which Israel was not to sin. Every violation or wiping out of this distinction— such even, for example, as the emancipation of a woman—was unnatural, and therefore an abomination in the sight of God.[5]

The law therefore forbids imposing a man's duties and tools on a

1. S. R. Driver, "Abomination," in James Hastings, editor, *A Dictionary of the Bible,* I, 11 f.
2. *Unger's Bible Dictionary,* p. 9.
3 G. Ernest Wright, "Deuteronomy," on 14:1, 2, *Interpreter's Bible,* II, 421.
4. *Ibid.,* I, 464.
5. Keil and Delitzsch, *The Pentateuch,* III, 409 f.

woman, and a woman's on a man. Its purpose is thus to maintain God's fundamental order. A man who allows his wife to support him when he is able-bodied has violated this law.

Alexander's comment supported the same meaning:

> The divinely instituted distinction between the sexes was to be sacredly observed, and, in order to this, the dress and other things appropriate to the one were not to be used by the other. *That which pertaineth to a man;* literally, *the apparatus of a man,* (including, not dress merely, but implements, tools, weapons, and utensils). This is an ethical regulation in the interests of morality. There is no reference, as some have supposed, to the wearing of masks for the purpose of disguise, or to the practice of the priests at heathen festivals of wearing masks of their gods. Whatever tends to obliterate the distinction between the sexes tends to licentiousness; and that the one sex should assume the dress of the other has always been regarded as unnatural and indecent.[6]

According to Baumgarten, this law

> forbids the manifestation of the primitive unnaturalness and anti-godliness that man (the husband) as the original man (human being) should obey the voice of his wife, the derived man . . . In the measure in which man persists in his estrangement from God, this fundamental error will ever make itself felt Rom. i. 26, 27 . . . But still the wrath of God reveals itself from heaven against every perversion of the sexes, in the perplexing and disturbing results of that wide-spread and ever-spreading female domination, and male servitude.[7]

We have today what Winick has called the progressive desexualization of people. The goal is increasingly "the bland man," among both the older and younger generations. Man is increasingly made into a neutral creature; the distinction between male and female is blurred. As a result, and not surprisingly, in 1964 the American Civil Liberties Union defended a man against transvestite charges, challenging the law for the first time in 119 years.[8] Moreover, "Transvestism on the part of men figures increasingly in plays and movies."[9] Unisexual clothes have become popular in London, and among some Scandinavian teen-agers.[10] Increasingly, the world and America become "the country of the bland."[11] Simultaneously, the stage has "created a number of men who were programmed for defeat" while at the same time portraying aggressive women. In fact, "Actresses are not only bigger than men at the box office; some are actually taller." Moreover, "Although women

---

6. W. L. Alexander, *Deuteronomy,* in Spence and Exell, *The Pulpit Commentary,* p. 355.
7. Quoted by F. W. J. Schroeder, in John Peter Lange, editor, *Commentary on the Holy Scriptures, Deuteronomy,* p. 165.
8. Charles Winick, *The New People,* p. 236 f.
9. *Ibid.,* p. 242.   10. *Ibid.,* p. 267.   11. *Ibid.,* p. 145 ff.

characters once represented the goal of a hero's romantic quest, today we are getting the woman as Brute."[12]

Behind this chaos lie certain ideas. *First*, the rebellion against God's ordained order is very obvious. The very principle of order is denied. Man seeks studiously to re-arrange creation in terms of his own creative mandate.

Second, equality as a philosophical and religious faith is at work. All people are equals; woman is equal to man, and man is equal to God. As a result, there must be in principle a war against differences. Not only unisex but uniman is the goal, the bland, neutral person. Henry Miller sees the return to Paradise only through the destruction of history, meaning, law, and morality. There must be a time of total destruction, the "time of the assassins," and the new world can only come when the old world is forgotten. This means a period of anarchy, racial amalgamation, and universal human hermaphroditism ("the birth of male-and-female in every individual") and then the new world may appear.[13]

To return now to the law for a fresh evaluation of its meaning, clearly it refers to garments, but its meaning is far broader. The law strikes at the general neutralization of the sexes and the confusion of their roles. The law insists on a strict line of division between male and female as the best and the God-ordained means of communication and love between them. The strength and character of male and female is best maintained by obedience to this law.

It was was once a strict principle of military conduct to enforce this law in every area. Thus, men in uniform were not permitted to push a baby carriage; it was unbecoming to the authority and strength the uniform represented to do a mother's work. If this seems now a trifling or amusing illustration, the fact is that it is still sound in principle. Its purpose was the preservation of the dignity and the masculinity of a fighting force. At the same time, under pre-World War I standards, an officer was expected to have, as were his men, versatile abilities. Their quarters had to be clean and properly cared for, and the ability to cook was not limited to the cook. The purpose was self-reliance and ability to survive. In the home, the man did no woman's work; in the barracks and in the field, the man had to be resourceful, able, and orderly in his life.

The purpose of the law is to increase the strength and the authority of men and women in their respective domains. The strength of men is in being men under God, and the strength of women is in being women under God.

---

12. *Ibid.*, p. 73.
13. Lawrence Durrell, editor, *The Henry Miller Reader* (New York: New Directions, 1959), pp. 231-239.

The definition of transvestite thus must be made broader than a mere reference to clothing.

It can be added that modern culture has a strongly transvestite character. Here as elsewhere it prefers the character of perversion to the law of God.

18. Bestiality

The law against bestiality appears in four different passages, thrice in the body of the law, once in the curses of the law:

> Whosoever lieth with a beast shall surely be put to death (Ex. 22:19.
>
> Neither shalt thou lie with any beast to defile thyself therewith: neither shall any woman stand before a beast to lie down thereto: it is confusion.
>
> Defile not ye yourselves in any of these things: for in all these the nations are defiled which I cast out before you:
>
> And the land is defiled: therefore I do visit the iniquity thereof upon it, and the land itself vomiteth out her inhabitants.
>
> Ye shall therefore keep my statutes and my judgments, and shall not commit any of these abominations; neither any of your own nation, nor any stranger that sojourneth among you:
>
> (For all these abominations have the men of the land done, which were before you, and the land is defiled);
>
> That the land spue you out also, when ye defile it, as it spued out the nations that were before you;
>
> For whosoever shall commit any of these abominations, even the souls that commit them shall be cut off from among their people.
>
> Therefore shall ye keep mine ordinance, that ye commit not any one of these abominable customs, which were committed before you, and that ye defile not yourselves therein: I am the LORD your God (Lev. 18:23-30).
>
> And if a man lie with a beast, he shall surely be put to death; and ye shall slay the beast.
>
> And if a woman approach unto any beast, and lie down thereto, thou shalt kill the woman, and the beast: they shall surely be put to death; their blood shall be upon them (Lev. 20:15, 16).
>
> Cursed be he that lieth with any manner of beast. And all the people shall say, Amen (Deut. 27:21).

The crime thus incurs the death penalty for man and beast; if the death penalty is not inflicted, the land is polluted, and the earth vomits out the degenerate people. Ginsburg's comment on Leviticus 18:25, "The land itself vomiteth out her inhabitants," restates ably this fundamental aspect of Biblical law:

> From the creation the earth shared in the punishment of man's guilt (Gen. iii. 17), and at the restitution of all things she is to

participate in his restoration (Rom. viii. 19-22). The physical condition of the land, therefore, depends upon the moral conduct of man. When he disobeys God's commandments she is parched up and does not yield her fruit (Deut. xi. 17). "The land is defiled" when he defiles himself. When he walks in the way of the Divine commands she is blessed (Levit. xxv. 19; xxvi. 4); "God is merciful unto his land and to his people" (Deut. xxxii. 43). Hence, "the earth mourneth" when her inhabitants sin (Isa. xxiv. 4, 5), and "the earth is glad" when God avenges the cause of His people (Ps. xcvi. 11-13). It is owing to this intimate connection between them that the land, which is here personified, is represented as loathing the wicked conduct of her children and being unable to restrain them. She nauseated them. The same figure is used in verse 28; chap. xx. 22; and in Rev. iii. 16.[1]

Bestiality was a common practice in antiquity; it was, moreover, a *religious* practice. Pagan religions, with their belief in an evolution out of chaos, looked downward to chaos for religious vigor, power, and vitality, not upward. Strength was believed to lie downward, in contact with the "earth," with man's primitive past. As a result, religious renewal required acts of bestiality, and in Egypt, Canaan, and many other countries, such acts were national requirements for the social welfare of the people, and personal acts by persons seeking to revitalize their lives. If God is God, then man looks upward to God for regeneration, guidance, and strength, and man conforms his life to the law-word of God. If chaos is ultimate and is the source of all things rather than God, then man must look downward to acts of chaos for his regeneration. This is exactly what man has done. Bestiality has been an important aspect of *developed* paganism. It appears thus more often in highly developed pagan cultures than in simple, backward ones; it is a prominent aspect of sexual life in the "advanced" pagan cultures.[2]

Bestiality has a history of association also with revolutionary movements and persons. The thesis of revolution is paradise through chaos, precisely the thesis of bestiality. Two members of the U.S. National Security Agency who in 1960 fled to the Soviet Union were on investigation reported to be homosexuals who also "had a penchant for indulging in peculiar sexual acts with animals."[3]

The present sexual revolution is experimenting extensively with bestiality.[4] Dr. Ullerstam has pleaded for abolition of "this moral yoke," the prohibition against bestiality, and vindicates the act.[5]

---

1. C. D. Ginsburg, "Leviticus," in Ellicott, I, 420.
2. Allen Edwardes and R. E. L. Masters, *The Cradle of Erotica* (New York: Julian Press, 1963), pp. 16, 210, 242.
3. John Carpenter, *Washington Babylon* (Phoenix, Arizona, Ron-San Corp., 1965), p. 135.
4. Michael Leigh, *The Velvet Underground Revisited* (New York: Macfadden-Bartell, 1968), pp. 53 f., 64.
5. Lars Ullerstam, *The Erotic Minorities*, p. 118.

The Bible calls the act "confusion" or "perversion" (BV). This element of perversity has always been basic to the act, and to the religious aspect of the act. The radical perversity of the Marquis de Sade is well known; his insane catalogue of acts of bestiality, coupled with sadism, with a long variety of animals is recorded in a major work.[6] In justifying the eating of feces as an erotic pleasure, Sade declared it is "the very uncleanness" of any act which pleases him.[7]

Kenneth Burke some years ago analyzed "secular conversions." While specifically discussing Freud, his concern was with all similar thinking, which he described as "conversion downwards."[8] Without accepting the framework of Burke's term, we can use this apt description as ably describing the modern concept of regeneration. Whether in literature, art, politics, or religion, vitality is sought in primitivism, in a downward quest, and vitality is assumed to abound to the degree that law is violated. A very popular cure-all for male impotence is precisely this downward quest, beginning with homosexuality, as a means of reviving a dying sexual potency.

"Conversion downward" explains also Sade's pleasure in "the very uncleanness" of any act; any perversion is a defilement, and the more violent its departure from the norm, and the more deliberate its assault on God's law-order, then the greater the "confusion," and the delight therein. Because Sade, as a classical example of a conversion downward, was in such bitter hostility to God, the more pronounced the violation of law in any act, the greater the pleasure to him. Thornton stated that

> There are still other known cases of masochism—cases, for instance, in which the individuals affected might be led by the desire for the utmost degradation of themselves to such practices as *urolagnia* and *coprolagnia*. By these terms we understand, respectively, the drinking of urine and the tasting or eating of faeces. The more he can debase himself, the lower the level to which he can reduce his humanity, the happier the true masochist is.[9]

The point of such activity is to degrade the image of God in man, to prove that man is no more than an animal.

The desire to reduce man to an animal is a part of the evolutionary faith. Popular books have been written to that end, one of the most popular being the best-selling work by Desmond Morris, *The Naked Ape,* the February, 1968, Book-of-the-Month Club selection. Shortly after the Soviet Union was established by the Bolshevik Revolution, a

---

6. Sade, *The 120 Days of Sodom,* p. 603 f.
7. *Ibid.,* p. 462 ff.
8. Kenneth Burke, *Permanence and Change, An Anatomy of Purpose* (New York: New Republic, 1935), p. 166.
9. Nathaniel Thornton, *Problems in Abnormal Behaviour* (Philadelphia: Blakiston, 1946), p. 109.

scientific expedition was sent to Africa, subsidized by millions of roubles, to attempt the crossing of men and apes. Professor Ilya Ivanovich Ivanoff and his expedition hoped to breed a new race, of ape men, in order to confirm the faith of the Anti-God Society of Soviet Russia. This expedition of 1925 failed, of course, and the Soviet press a year later reported the supposed loss in the Black Sea of the steamer bringing back Ivanoff and his female apes; and ship was said to be "lost with all hands" and apes; so, whatever happened, no survivors remained to report on the fiasco.[10] More sophisticated means are now sought to reduce man to an animal level.

Pornographic movies are now made and extensively sold; these include now many acts of bestiality. Books are advertised which give instructions on how to perform bestial acts. There is a systematic propagation of this perversion, and the training of animals to perform the act for various groups.

In one way or another, either philosophically or by means of acts of perversion, humanistic man looks downward towards chaos for his renewal.

A final note: in 1969, a motion picture was made on the subject of bestiality, the story of the "love affair" of a farmer with his pig. Film viewers were spared any of the usual sexual film fare. The Society for the Prevention of Cruelty to Animals was on hand during the filming, it was reported, to protect the pig.

19. The Architecture of Life

Once we recognize that all of God's creation has a law-structure, we can then begin to understand the fabric of law behind many declarations of Scripture which do not directly deal with law. An example of this is St. Peter's commandments concerning the relationship of husbands and wives to one another (I Peter 3:17). These words presuppose at every point the Biblical laws concerning marriage; they declare also the nature of authority in the home; they speak also of life as a "grace" from God, which, when men and women live in faith and obedience to God, they inherit, "as being heirs together of the grace of life." St. Peter also gives perspective to the meaning of marriage: contrary to popular opinion, there is no condemnation of lovely styles of hair plaiting, nor of gold jewelry, nor of beautiful apparel. What is made clear is that these are secondary at best, that the best "adornment" is a "meek and quiet spirit, which is in the sight of God of great price." Even more, the faithfulness of husband and wife to the commandments of God are required "that your prayers be not hindered" (I Peter 3:7).

---

10. R. O. G. Urch, *The Rabbit King of Russia* (London: The Right Book Club, 1939), p. 82 f. See p. 83n.

Marriage, in brief, is like all things else, to be a God-centered matter. To be God-centered does not mean that husband and wife spend their time in prayer meetings or in church activities; it means rather that they fulfil their duties to one another as God specifies them in His word.

Every area of life must be similarly God-centered, for to order life on any terms other than God's law-word is to deny Him.

The great offense of the modern era has been its humanistic re-ordering of life. Certainly humanism was prevalent in earlier eras, but never so radically and extensively at the same time. Wolf's description of Louis XIV and his construction of Versailles brings the matter into sharp focus:

> We cannot leave Versailles without reiterating that it had a purpose beyond being the residence for the king and his government. This great palace was a keystone in the new cult of royalty. In the preceding eras the great constructions were usually to the glory of God; even Philip II, when he built his great palace, made it a monastery with the chapel as the center of interest. At Versailles the bedroom of the king is the center, identifying the king as the highest power on earth, while the chapel is to one side. The impos-ing grandeur of the chateau was evidence of the wealth of the kingdom, and its construction without walls and moats was proof of the power of the king's government. Versailles was a challenge, a defiance flung out at all Europe; as impressive a display of the wealth, power, and authority of the French king as were his armies and his warships. Europe did not miss this. The century after the construction of Versailles, chateaus at Vienna, at Potsdam, at Dresden, at Munich, at St. Petersburg, and the very plans for the city of Washington, D.C., reflected the influence of the grandeur of Versailles.[1]

Louis XIV was a devout man, and his belief that God was judging him for his pride and sins darkened his later years.[2] All the same, the essential humanism of his regime persisted throughout. The bedroom rather than the chapel, romantic and sensual love rather than God, progressively dominated men's minds and hearts. Life now had a new architecture, the architecture of humanism. Much earlier, Boccaccio had stated a basic premise of the new structure, "We have nothing in this world but what we enjoy."[3]

With Hegel and Darwin, the architecture of humanism took on a firmer dimension. It now had an ostensible foundation in science, in evolution. This meant a new doctrine of man, society, and the state, a conversion downward of every aspect of life. A Princeton professor,

---

1. John B. Wolf, *Louis XIV* (New York: W. W. Norton, 1968), p. 362.
2. *Ibid.*, pp. 470, 539, 589 ff., 612, 617 f.
3. Giovanni Boccaccio, *Chamber of Love* (New York: Philosophical Library, 1958), p. 28.

far more conservative than most, laid down some logical conclusions concerning politics from the doctrine of evolution:

PROPOSITION: man is the product of Social Evolution.

Corollaries of this proposition affect the whole group of sciences pertaining to anthropology in the large sense of the word. They may be exhibited in several aspect as follows:

BIOLOGICAL

The State is the permanent and universal frame of human existence. Man can no more get out of the State than a bird can fly out of the air. . . .

The Undivided Commune is the primordial form of the State, and it antedates the differentiation of Man from the antecedent animal stock. . . .

The Individual is a distinct entity in the unit life of the State. The Individual is not an original but is a derivative.

POLITICAL

Man did not make the State; the State made Man. Man is born a political being. His nature was formed by government, requires government and seeks government. . . .

The State is absolute and unconditioned in its relation to its unit life. Government is conditioned by dependence of its functions upon structure and hence it is subject to inherent limitations. There is no absolute norm of Government but every species of the State tends to produce a type proper to its characteristics in its particular environment. Profound changes of environment produce profound changes of Government. State species unable to effect readjustments of structure to meet new conditions tend to disappear, so that from age to age there is a succession in State species analogous to that which takes place in biological species. . . .

Sovereignty is the supremacy of the State over all its parts. . . .

ETHICAL

Rights are not innate but are derivative. They exist in the State but not apart from the State. Hence rights are correlated with duties. . . .

The object of the State is the perfecting of Man, but the attainment of that object depends upon the perfecting of the State. The test of value in any institution is primarily not the advantage of the individual but the advantage of Society. Individual life enlarges by participation in a larger life; ascends by incorporation in a higher life.[4]

Ford's thesis is a sound one; if evolution is true, his deductions are logical. Revolutionists as well as the student rebels have drawn the

---

4. Henry Jones Ford, *The Natural History of the State, An Introduction to Political Science* (Princeton: Princeton University Press, 1915; London: Humphrey Milford: Oxford University Press), pp. 174-177.

logical conclusion from the doctrine, even as Ford did. Evolution logically requires perpetual revolution because of a continually changing environment. If evolution is true, then continual revolution is inescapable. The architecture of life is radically altered; man must then conform himself to a force emerging from below, to the renewing power of chaos. If we accept Scripture, then the architecture of life is structured with the enduring steel of God's law and must grow in terms of that law-word.

It is not surprising that a philosophy which begins with evolution continues by proclaiming a death of God theology, and now, finally, a death of man philosophy. Such a faith is proclaimed by Michel Foucault.[5]

To return to St. Peter's statement, if the architecture of life becomes humanistic, if a man and woman move in terms of essentially humanistic considerations, their prayers are *hindered*. They may be as devout as Louis XIV, and they may pray intensely and earnestly, but the essence of their life's structure is out of balance. It is not that a concern about every-day material things is wrong, since it emphatically is not. The question is one of structure: is the basic architecture, design, or pattern of our life in conformity to God's law-word? If we seek "first the kingdom of God, and his righteousness," then "all these things shall be added" unto us (Matt. 6:33).

But if we deny God and His law-word, then *our* word becomes law to us, and we drift into madness and death. Not surprisingly, Foucault, who has proclaimed the death of man, began an earlier work with these words: "we must renounce the convenience of terminal truths."[6] There is then nothing to *bind* man to man, nor anything to *bind* man to life. Foucault is logical: without the structure of God's truth, man cannot live, and the only conclusion which remains for man is suicide.

St. Peter presented a picture of life: obedience to God, and obedience to all due authorities under God, means that life flourishes and abounds; our prayers are not hindered, and we enjoy life as truly God's grace to us. As against humanism, this is a God-centered orientation. To be God-centered means to seek *first* God's kingdom, and His righteousness (Matt. 6:33). Today, however, humanism disguised as Christianity is all too prevalent. It occurs wherever an institution or area of life becomes an end in itself. By identifying the church with the Kingdom of God, all too many theologians have reduced the dimensions of life and the kingdom to a single aspect thereof. Protestant premillennialists and amillennialists, by their despair of this world and their surrender of

---

5. Roy McMullen, "Michel Foucault," in *Horizon*, vol. XI, no. 4 (Autumn, 1969), pp. 36-39.
6. Michel Foucault, *Madness and Civilization, A History of Insanity in the Age of Reason* (New York: Mentor [1961], 1967), p. ix.

it to the devil, not only are implicitly Manichaean, but they are also virtually reducing the kingdom to the church, in that the only legitimate area of activity becomes the church. The architecture of life then ceases to be whole: it is reduced to the size of the church. Neither church, state, school, vocation, nor any other sphere of life can be identified with the kingdom, or denied its place in the kingdom. Humanism masquerading as Christianity is humanism still.

St. Peter did *not,* as we noted, condemn gold and silver ornaments, the plaiting of hair, or lovely clothing. He simply required that these things be placed in their proper place, not as the ends of life but simply as lovely but minor aspects thereof. Similarly, neither the obedience of the wife nor the authority of the husband is the end of marriage. These things are means to the true and chief end, to serve God, and to magnify and enjoy Him forever. Man cannot provide the structure of life; God's law alone suffices as the structure and architecture of life.

20. Faithfulness

Faithfulness is a virtue stressed throughout the law and in all the Scriptures as a religious and moral necessity. The requirement of faithfulness to God, to law, to marriage, to every godly obligation, is emphatically stressed. Moses summoned Israel to observe God's law-word without turning "to the right hand or to the left," and, if they did *walk* in obedience, it would be well with them, and their days would be prolonged (Deut. 5:32, 33). Believers are called "the faithful" in the church's terminology, and the term "faithful" is in Scripture the highest praise (Prov. 20:6; Rev. 17:14; Matt. 25:21, etc.). The *walk* of the faithful is in "the paths of righteousness" (Ps. 23:3); *paths* means *ruts,* wheel-tracks, and the reference is to established habits of godliness. God establishes His faithful ones in the engrained ruts or habits of righteousness.

Sanity, character, and stability rest on faithfulness, on dependability. Irresponsibility is the consequence of faithlessness, and, ultimately, insanity so-called, which is the rejection of responsibility; it is the unwillingness to be faithful, to establish the habits of righteousness. Not surprisingly, modern philosophy, which has proclaimed so emphatically man's freedom from law and from God, has been frequently marked by the fact of mad or at best unstable men in its ranks.

The non-Christian mentality is commonly characterized by this war on faithfulness. A study of Indian sculpture speaks of "the cult of desire" as the "road to release" from the burden of life.[1] In this cult, "the other world and this were made one," and "Life and Liberation

---

1. Kanwar Lal, *The Cult of Desire* (New Hyde Park, N. Y.: University Books, 1967), p. 48.

ceased to be separate entities."[2] Salvation meant the total acceptance
of all of life as holy: "the holiness of desire would . . . sanctify any
vehicle: and if the mind is pure, all else, whether woman or man or
animal, is but means."[3] This means that the individual should "indulge
in desire irrespective of the mate, divine, human or bestial."[4]

To accept every act as holy is to deny emphatically the principle of
discrimination in terms of good and evil. *Faithfulness* is adherence to
an absolute law, and to persons and causes in terms of that absolute
law and the sovereign God of that law. As against faithfulness, *the way*
or walk is made a systematic unfaithfulness as man's life, joy, and
pleasure. Thus, in Africa, the Nandi have a saying, "A new vagina
is comforting."[5]

Because there is no principle of discrimination between good and
evil, man and animals, *persons* do not count. Danielsson's account of
Polynesian love holds that, because of the lack of standards and of
discriminations, "There was therefore no reason to prefer any particular
woman or man."[6] His description is, of course, of a degenerated culture,
as is that of Suggs, whose description is of depersonalized and degenerate
sexuality.[7]

The need for unfaithfulness as a principle came to focus in an
organized movement, romanticism. Scott's description of "the romantic
fallacy" is excellent: "it identifies beauty with strangeness."[8] The logic
of this position is that, the stranger the object, person, or act, the better
it is to the romantic. In Newton's words, "The romantic . . . can never
rejoice in the normal. What interests him must be the exceptional."[9]
This means interest in "mystery, abnormality, and conflict,"[10] a dislike
of "whatever is law-abiding, whatever conforms to a pattern." The
romantic "refuses to acknowledge the existence of law as applied to
self-expression. . . . 'Thou shalt be exceptional and follow that which
is exceptional' is his only commandment. . . . Abnormality is the negative
of law. Its very existence depends on its refusal to conform to law-
abiding behaviour."[11] This means that *freedom is identified with evil,*
sexual expression with unfaithfulness and perversion, artistic ability
with violations of standards and perversity, and character with instability.

2. *Ibid.*, p. 78.   3. *Ibid.*, p. 90.   4. *Ibid.*
5. Boris de Rachewiltz, *Black Eros, Sexual Customs of Africa from Prehistory
to the Present Day* (New York: Lyle Stuart, 1964), p. 267.
6. Bengt Danielsson, *Love in the South Seas* (New York: Dell, 1957), p. 79 f.
7. Robert C. Suggs, *The Hidden Worlds of Polynesia* (New York: Mentor,
1965), pp. 107-119.
8. Geoffrey Scott, *The Architecture of Humanism, A Study in the History of
Taste* (Garden City, N. Y.: Doubleday, 1954), p. 41.
9. Eric Newton, *The Romantic Rebellion* (New York: St. Martin's Press,
1963), p. 59.
10. *Ibid.*, p. 57.
11. *Ibid.*, p. 64.

The growth of perversion and perversity in every area of life is proportionate to the decline of faith and faithfulness.

Not only has there been a greater prevalence of perversity and perversion, but also a developing pride and boastfulness therein, as though these acts represent the wave of the future.[12] Health, vitality, and character are associated by these "new" people with sexual license, and faithfulness with Puritanism and crime.[13] In reality, the character of those given to this so-called sexual freedom is one of tormented conflicts and childish tantrums.[14]

To return to *faithfulness* itself, the Scriptures repeatedly declare it to be an attribute of God (Ps. 36:5; 89:2; Isa. 11:15, etc.). God is faithful because He is the absolute sovereign, totally self-conscious and without any dark corners in His being, without undeveloped and unconscious potentialities. Man was created in God's image, and, as redeemed in Christ, is re-established in that image. As he grows in terms of God's image, man grows in faithfulness and in his self-conscious awareness of his calling under God and his responsibilities therein. Faithfulness is stability, strength, and character. It is closely related to dominion. The term, "The faithful," used as the favorite name for baptized persons in the early church, signified their trustworthiness and strength.

Faithfulness in marriage in its truest sense means therefore sexual fidelity and much more. It means the faithful discharge of duties by husband and wife. It means dependability, trustworthiness of character, strength in adversity, and loyalty. It means initiative and ability, as appears in our Lord's words, "Well done, thou good and faithful servant" (Matt. 25:21). Faithfulness is a communicable attribute of God. It is a mark of strength and character in a man, whereas unfaithfulness in any realm is a mark of weakness and sin.

---

12. See Vincent Sheean, *Dorothy and Red* (Boston: Houghton Mifflin, 1963).

13. Arsene Eglis, *Sex Songs of the Ancient Letts* (New York: University Books, 1969), pp. 1-5. Eglis blames a variety of murders, including that of Senator Robert F. Kennedy, on the supposedly devout Christian background of the murderers!

14. See Mark Schorer, *Sinclair Lewis, An American Life* (New York: McGraw-Hill, 1961); and A. E. Hotchner, *Papa Hemingway, A Personal Memoir* (New York: Random House, 1966).

VIII

THE EIGHTH COMMANDMENT

1. Dominion

Man was created in the image of God and commanded to subdue the earth and to have dominion over it (Gen. 1:26-27). Not only is it man's *calling* to exercise dominion, but it is also his *nature* to do so. Since God is the absolute and sovereign Lord and Creator, whose dominion is total and whose power is without limits, man, created in His image, shares in this communicable attribute of God. Man was created to exercise dominion under God and as God's appointed vice-gerent over the earth. *Dominion* is thus a basic urge of man's nature.

As a result of the fall, however, man's urge to dominion is now a perverted one, no longer an exercise of power under God and to His glory, but a desire to be God. This was precisely the temptation of Satan, that every man should be his own god, deciding for himself what constitutes right and wrong (Gen. 3:5). The ultimacy of man in both law and power was asserted.

History therefore has seen the long and bitter consequence of man's perverted urge to dominion. Man has made vicious and perverted use of man individually, in gang activities, and as an army or a nation. History is a long tale of horror in which man has sought power and dominion as an end in itself. George Orwell in *1984* saw the meaning of this fallen urge to dominion: "If you want a picture of the future, imagine a boot stamping on a human face—forever." This sinful, fallen urge to dominion is prominent in every sphere of modern life, as well as in all history. It certainly governs the political world, where the state daily gains power for power's sake.

As a result of all this, many have become frightened of all power and hostile to the concept of dominion. Liberals, neo-orthodox, existentialists and others have renounced the idea of power as an illusion or a temptation, and the possession of power as an evil. The result has been to accentuate the drift to totalitarian power.

Dominion does not disappear when a man renounces it; it is simply transferred to another person, perhaps to his wife, children, employer, or the state. Where the individual surrenders his due dominion, where the family abdicates it, and the worker and employer reduce it, there another party, usually the state, concentrates dominion. Where organized society surrenders power, the mob gains it proportionate to the surrender.

This fact poses the problem, which for an Orwell, who saw the issue clearly, is impossible to answer. Fallen man's exercise of dominion is demonic; it is power for the sake of power, and its goal is "a boot stamping on a human face—forever." Its alternative is the dominion of anarchy, the bloody and tumultuous reign of the momentarily strong.

Clearly, there is no hope for man except in regeneration. The Shorter Catechism of the Westminster Divines, in dealing with the image of God declared:

> Q. 10. How did God create man?
> A. God created man male and female, after his own image, in knowledge, righteousness, and holiness, with dominion over the creatures (Gen. 1:26-28; Col. 3:10; Eph. 4:24).

The salvation of man includes his restoration into the image of God and the calling implicit in that image, to subdue the earth and to exercise dominion. Hence, the proclamation of the gospel was also the proclamation of the Kingdom of God, according to all the New Testament.

A radical deformation of the gospel and of the redeemed man's calling crept into the church as a result of neoplatonism. Dominion was renounced, the earth regarded as the devil's realm, the body despised, and a false humility and meekness cultivated. Dominion was regarded as a burden of the flesh rather than a godly responsibility. Especially with Pietism, Jesus was pictured as meek and helpless, pacifistic and mild of manner.

The word meek is a Biblical term. It is used in Numbers 12:3 to describe Moses, who is termed "very meek"; Moses hardly jibes with modern ideas of meekness. In fact, Moses is described as meek "above all the men which were upon the face of the earth." Marsh indicates the meaning of meek: "Moses does not fight for his own status before men, but is concerned to be Yahweh's servant. Therefore Yahweh cares for him and his position among the people."[1] The word meek thus refers primarily to a spiritual state in relationship to God. Elliott noted, "It may be observed, further, that the word *anav,* meek, is frequently interchanged with the cognate word *ani,* and that the meaning may be *bowed down,* or *oppressed.*"[2] The meaning is further clarified by the Beatitude: "Blessed are the meek: for they shall inherit the earth" (Matt. 5:5). Dominion over the earth is given to the meek, and meekness clearly has reference to God. The meek are the redeemed

---

1. John Marsh, "Numbers," in *Interpreter's Bible,* II, 201.
2. C. J. Elliott, "Numbers," in Ellicott, I, 516.

whom God has burdened, oppressed, and broken to harness, so that they are tamed and workable. God subjected Moses to a more rigorous discipline than any other believer of his day, and Moses accepted that oppression, grew in terms of it, and became disciplined and strong. Hence, Moses was the meekest man of his age. Meekness is thus not mousiness, but disciplined strength in and under God.

Jesus Christ described Himself as "meek and lowly in heart" (Matt. 11:29; rendered "gentle and humble" by both Moffatt and BV). He described Himself as such in relationship to those who sought Him. In His relationship to the Pharisees and Sadducees, Christ's conduct was firm and resolute. As Christ used the term meekness, it meant, *not* the surrender of dominion, but rather the wise, merciful, and gracious use of dominion. We *cannot* understand the meaning of meekness in Scripture unless we realize that it is not the surrender of dominion but rather the humble and godly use of dominion that it has reference to. The blessed meek are the tamed of God, those harnessed to His law-word and calling, who shall inherit the earth (Matt. 5:5). The blessed meek are those who submit to God's dominion, have therefore dominion over themselves, and are capable of exercising dominion over the earth. They therefore inherit the earth.

This point is of very great importance. Apart from it, the gospel is perverted. Man has a God-given urge to dominion, to power. The purpose of regeneration is to re-establish man in his creation mandate, to exercise dominion and to subdue the earth. The purpose of the law is to give man the God-appointed way to dominion. The purpose of the call to obedience is to exercise dominion.

What happens then when a caricature of Jesus is presented, when obedience is constantly demanded without the God-ordained goal of obedience being mentioned, and when man is continually summoned to prepare himself in the Lord, but for no purpose? The ministry of the church then becomes trifling, and the life of the believer, frustrating.

But the urge to dominion does not disappear simply because the church does not speak of it. Instead, it reappears as an ugly and sinful struggle for power in the church; rightful dominion being neglected or denied, sinful dominion begins then to emerge. The life of the church becomes then an ugly struggle over meaningless trifles in which the sole purpose is sinful power and dominion. All too often this sinful urge to dominion is masked with hypocritical meekness.

It is very necessary therefore to recognize that the urge to dominion is God-given and is basic to the nature of man. An aspect of this dominion is property.

It is the custom among ecclesiastical socialists to deny that there is Biblical warrant for private property. Their ground for this is the often repeated Biblical declaration, "The earth is the LORD'S" (Ex. 9:29, etc.). They choose to neglect the total witness of Scripture to private property. The so-called communism of Acts 2:41-47, also cited by ecclesiastical socialists, was simply a voluntary sharing on the part of some (Acts 5). It was limited to Jerusalem. Because the believers took literally the words of Christ concerning the fall of Jerusalem (Matt. 24:1-28), they liquidated their properties there. The wealthier members placed some or all of these funds at the church's disposal, so that a witness could be made to their friends and relatives before Jerusalem fell. Very early, persecution drove all but a nucleus out of Jerusalem (Acts 8:1).

The earth is indeed the Lord's, as is all dominion, but God has chosen to give dominion over the earth to man, subject to His law-word, and property is a central aspect of that dominion. The absolute and transcendental title to property is the Lord's; the present and historical title to property is man's. The ownership of property does not leave this world when it is denied to man; it is simply transferred to the state. If the contention of the liberals that the earth is the Lord's, not man's, is to be applied as they require it, then it must be applied equally to the state; the state then must be denied all right to own or control property.

The Scripture, however, places property in the hands of the family, not the state. It gives property to man as an aspect of his dominion, as a part of his godly subduing of the earth.

If the doctrine of dominion in and under God is weakened, then all the law is weakened also.

God grants *dominion* to man under His law, but He does not grant His *sovereignty*. God alone is absolute Lord and Sovereign. To deny God's sovereignty is to transfer sovereignty from God to man, or to man's state. Thus, Thomas Paine, in the *Rights of Man,* affirmed as a fundamental principle the sovereignty of the nation-state, declaring, *"The nation is essentially the source of all sovereignty; nor can any* INDIVIDUAL, *or* ANY BODY OF MEN, *be entitled to any authority which is not expressly derived from it."*[3] Paine and the French Revolution clearly affirmed their totalitarianism by this statement. The state as god became the source of authority, morality, and dominion. Quite logically, the Revolution became a boot, grinding down the face of man, but, by the grace of God, not forever.

God's purpose is not the dominion of sin but the dominion of redeemed man over the earth under God. According to St. Paul, the

---

3. "Declaration of the Rights of Man and of Citizens, By the National Assembly of France, in *The Complete Political Works of Thomas Paine* (New York: The Freethought Press Association, 1954), II, 95.

very creation around us groans and travails, waiting for the godly
dominion of the children of God (Rom. 8:19-23). Because of the fall,
creation is now under the dominion of sinful man and is being laid waste
by his perverted use of power. Even as the plant turns to the light,
so creation turns with longing to the restored dominion of godly man.
Even as dust and stones move in terms of gravity, so they move also
in terms of God's purposed dominion of man over them. The people
of God must therefore be schooled into the nature and requirements
of godly dominion. Anything short of this is a contempt of the supreme
authority of God, who declares in His word that He will make a
covenant with the very beasts of the field to ensure man's prosperity in
the day of his obedience:

> And in that day will I make a covenant for them with the beasts
> of the field, and with the fowls of heaven, and with the creeping
> things of the ground: and I will break the bow and the sword and
> the battle out of the earth, and will make them to lie down safely
> (Hosea 2:18).

2. Theft

The eighth commandment, one of the two shortest, declares simply,
"Thou shalt not steal" (Ex. 20:15; Deut. 5:19). Theft or stealing is
taking another man's property by coercion, fraud, or without his unco-
erced consent. Cheating, harming property, or destroying its value is
also theft. It is not necessary for the robbed to know of the theft for
it to be a sin. Thus, to ride a train or bus without paying one's fare is
theft, even though the transportation company is unaware of the act.

Theft can be accomplished in a number of ways. *First,* in simple
theft the thief robs the victim directly. *Second,* in complex but still
direct theft, the thief robs the victim as part of a group of thieves. In
such a case, a man may not be directly involved in the act of theft, but
he is a party to it all the same as a knowing party in the corporate
group of thieves. *Third,* theft can be accomplished by indirect and
legal means, i.e., by passing a law which steals from the rich, the poor,
or the middle-classes, for the benefit of a particular group. The state
then becomes the agency whereby theft is accomplished, and a pseudo-
moral cover is given by legal enactment.

Theft is not only the expropriation, legally or illegally, of another
man's property against his will or by fraud, but also the destruction of
property, or the value of property, by any wilful act or by accident.
Thus, to destroy a man's house by arson is theft, but it is also theft if
the house is burned down by carelessness. To damage a man's automobile is to rob him of its value; in this area, restitution has been made
more or less mandatory by the insurance laws of various states. Because

inflation weakens or destroys the values of paper currencies, inflation too is very definitely a form of theft.

Fraud too is clearly theft. A man may willingly purchase an item under the impression that it is what it is represented to be, but fraud on the part of the seller makes it clearly theft. To sell a man watered milk is theft; pure food and drug laws, however much abused today, are still valid laws in terms of Scripture. However, *a corrupt people begets a corrupt state, which then cannot enforce even the best of laws without corruption.*

Necessity does not justify theft; necessity cannot give man any priority over God's law. However, some Roman Catholic thinkers, following the Greek natural law tradition, have given moral countenance to theft in times of necessity:

> Thus one in danger of death from want of food, or suffering any form of extreme necessity, may lawfully take from another as much as is required to meet his present distress even though the possessor's opposition be entirely clear. Neither, therefore, would he be bound to restitution if his fortunes subsequently were notably bettered, supposing that what he had converted to his own use was perishable. The reason is that individual ownership of the goods of this world, though according to the natural law, yields to the stronger and more sacred right conferred by natural law upon every man to avail himself of such things as are necessary for his own preservation.[1]

Such a perspective gives man's life priority over God's law.

It is said that, under the influence of Phariseeism and the interpretations of lawyers, "it was not considered a crime to steal from a Samaritan or another thief."[2] In this concept of the law, the "rights" of "covenant" man were deemed to be greater than those of lesser man. In either case, whether with respect to Delany or the Pharisees, the error is in giving man priority over God's law. Such a position in effect nullifies the law.

Thus far, our definition of theft is incomplete. It must be added that theft is one form of violation of God's fundamental order. Theft is therefore more than an offense against another person; it is an offense against God. God requires us to respect the life, marriage, and property of our neighbor and enemy, not because our neighbor or enemy is not possibly evil, and not because our own needs are not great, but because His law-order takes priority over the conditions of man. Neither the nature of our neighbor's character, which may be evil, nor our own need,

---

1. Joseph F. Delany, "Theft," in *The Catholic Encyclopedia*, XIV, 564 f., 1913 edition.
2. J. Poucher, "Crimes and Punishments," in James Hastings, editor, *A Dictionary of the Bible*, I, 522.

which may be great, can justify theft. The sovereignty of God requires the priority of His law-word.

Park recognizes that this commandment "is the protection which the diligent and prudent have against the idle and careless." All the same, he adds, "Thinking men strive toward an application of this commandment which will ensure that the products of industry will be fairly divided, that the rules may ensure that each man shall have his fair share of the good things of this life."³ Park, as one of these "thinking men" does not define every man's "fair share." It is that which each man earns? Or is it a "fair share" in terms of the non-Biblical principle of equality? A new principle of justice has replaced God: it is "thinking men"!

The humanism of Delany's position is sometimes justified from Scripture by citing Proverbs 6:30, 31. It is thus important to analyze this passage. Delitzsch has, in his commentary, clarified both the text and its meaning by setting it in its context, the condemnation of adultery:

> The thief and the adulterer are now placed in comparison with one another, in such a way that adultery is supposed to be a yet greater crime.
>
> 30 One does not treat the thief scornfully if he steals
>   To satisfy his craving when he is hungry;
> 31 Being seized, he may restore sevenfold,
>   Give up the whole wealth of his house.
>
> . . . A sevenfold compensation of the thing stolen is unheard of in the Israelitish law; it knows only of a twofold, fourfold, fivefold restoration, Ex. xxi. 37, xxii, 1-3, 8. . . . This excess over that which the law rendered necessary leads into the region of the free-will: He (the thief, by which we are now only to think of him when bitter necessity has made such) may make compensation sevenfold, *i.e.,* superabundantly; he may give up the whole possessions of his house, so as not merely to satisfy the law, but to appease him against whom he has done wrong, and again to gain for himself an honoured name. What is said in verses 30 and 31 is perfectly just. One does not condemn a man who is a thief through poverty, he is pitied; while the adulterer goes to ruin under all circumstances of contempt and scorn. And: theft may be made good, and that abundantly; but adultery and its consequences are irreparable.⁴

Thus, Scripture gives no ground for violating God's law-order: men are required to work within it for their own welfare and prosperity. To defy or despise God's order is to incur God's judgment; it also brings a sorry return on man's act. An old Spanish proverb declares, "He that spits up to the sky, will get it on his face."⁵

---

3. J. Edgar Park, "Exodus," in *Interperter's Bible*, I, 987.
4. Franz Delitzsch, *Biblical Commentary on the Proverbs of Solomon* (Grand Rapids: Eerdmans, 1950), I, 153 f.
5. Dr. Mario A. Nunez, compiler, trans., *Old Spanish Sayings* (1959), p. 18.

God's order clearly includes private property. It also clearly approves of godly wealth. The Hebrew words translated as *wealth* have also the meanings of *strength, resources, goods,* and *prosperity.* According to Proverbs 13:11, "Wealth gotten by vanity shall be diminished: but he that gathereth by labour shall increase." The warning of Scripture is against the proud who forget God in their wealth, not against the fact of wealth (Deut. 8:17, 18). God blesses His saints with prosperity and wealth, as witness Job, Abraham, David, Solomon, and others. One of the possible blessings on obedience to the law is wealth (Ps. 112:3). It is arrogant and ungodly wealth which is condemned (James 5:1-6). The declaration concerning the rich and the needle's eye is commonly misused: its point is that no man can save himself; salvation is impossible with men, because it is wholly the work of God (Mark 10:23-27). Wealth is an aspect of God's blessing of His faithful ones: "The blessing of the LORD, it maketh rich, and he addeth no sorrow with it" (Prov. 10:22). The godly pursuit of property and wealth is thus fully legitimate.

As we have seen in Proverbs 13:11, the means for gaining wealth is *labor.* This is again emphasized in the New Testament, St. Paul declaring, "Let him that stole, steal no more: but rather let him labour, working with his hands the thing which is good, that he may have to give to him that needeth" (Eph. 4:28). The Berkeley Version renders this as follows: "The thief must steal no more, but rather toil to earn a living with his own hands, so he may have something to give the person in need." Very clearly, *work* and *stealing* are opposed to one another as differing approaches to property. Equally clearly, an obligation of all who work is not only *self-support* but also *charity* to those in need.

Theft as a short-cut to the possession of property seeks not only to by-pass *work* as the means to wealth but also to deny the validity of God's law-order. In terms of Scripture, wealth can be acquired by labor, inheritance, or gift. A thieving order will oppose all three means of acquisition. A thieving order will concern itself with *charity* at the price of God's law.

It is easy for those who advocate changes damaging to private property to document the evils and the sins of great corporations, wealthy men, and of social orders in which these predominate, but it is at least equally easy to document the sins of the poor as of the wealthy, to cite the evils of a worker as of a capitalist, and to call attention to the depravity of the reformers. Because a man is evil, rich or poor makes no difference to God's law: he must still be dealt with under the law. When our neighbor is a thief, we acquire no right to rob him of anything he may have. The corrective to theft is not theft. Yet we are told that "The direction of justice, then, emerges wherever adjustments and changes take place in favor of the relatively powerless by a change in the distribution or dispersion of the social power of property, a change in the distribution of the control of property."[6] This is humanism again: it is the exaltation of man's need above God's law. And man as a sinner is hardly to be trusted when it comes to defining his "needs": too often, man defines his covetousness as his need. How often has sinful man admitted to his need for judgment? There is no law where every man is his own law-maker and court.

The relationship of work to charity has been cited. True charity and love towards one's neighbor is the fulfilling of the law (Rom. 13:8-10). In terms of this Calvin wrote of the eighth commandment,

> Since charity is the end of the Law, we must seek the definition of theft from thence. This, then, is the rule of charity, that every one's rights should be safely preserved, and that none should do to another what he would not have done to himself. It follows, therefore, that not only are those thieves who secretly steal the property of others, but those also who seek for gain from the loss of others, accumulate wealth by unlawful practices, and are more devoted to their private advantage than to equity. Thus, rapine is comprehended under the head of theft, since there is no difference between a man's robbing his neighbour by fraud or force.[7]

The basic charity is thus to live in faithfulness to the law with respect to our neighbors and enemies, respecting their God-given immunities under the law. To minister to their distress by gifts is also an important aspect of the law, but in neither case can man separate or oppose charity and law.

Calvin further defined charity as against theft in these words:

> Moreover, let us communicate to the necessities, and according to our ability alleviate the poverty, of those whom we perceive to be pressed by any embarrassment of their circumstances. Lastly, let every man examine what obligations his duty lays him under to others, and let him faithfully discharge the duties which he owes them. For this reason the people should honour their governors, patiently submit to their authority, obey their laws and mandates, and resist nothing, to which they can submit themselves consistently with the Divine will. On the other hand, let governors take care of their people, preserve the public peace, protect the good, punish the wicked, and administer all things in such a manner, as becomes those who must render an account of their office to God the supreme Judge. Let the ministers of churches faithfully devote themselves to the ministry of the word, and let them never adulterate the

6. Bruce Morgan: *Christians, the Church, and Property* (Philadelphia: The Westminster Press, 1963) p. 59 f.
7. Calvin, *Commentary on the Four Last Books of Moses in the Form of a Harmony,* III, 110 f.

doctrine of salvation, but deliver it pure and uncontaminated to the people of God. Let them teach, not only by their doctrine, but by the example of their lives; in a word, let them preside as good shepherds over the sheep. Let the people, on their part, receive them as the messengers and apostles of God, render to them that honour to which the supreme Master has exalted them, and furnish them with the necessaries of life. Let parents undertake the support, government, and instruction of their children, as committed by God to their care; nor let them exasperate their minds and alienate their affections from them by cruelty, but cherish and embrace them with lenity and indulgence becoming their character. And that obedience is due to them from their children has been before observed. Let juniors revere old age, since the Lord has designed that age to be honourable. Let old men, by their prudence and superior experience, guide the imbecility of youth; not teasing them with sharp and clamorous invectives, but tempering severity with mildness and affability.[8]

Calvin further listed duties of workers and masters, and every class of men. For men to withhold work, duty, honor, or due service is to steal. "In this manner, I say, let every man consider what duties he owes to his neighbours, according to the relations he sustains; and those duties let him discharge." The law speaks with reference to all men:

Moreover, our attention should always be directed to the Legislator; to remind us that this law is ordained for our hearts as much as for our hands, in order that men may study both to protect the property and to promote the interests of others.[9]

The laws against theft thus protect not only God's order but all men who are honest and law-abiding, and they protect even the dishonest from lawless punishment.

Why then do men attack this law and the doctrine of property which the law affirms? A century ago, in his general survey of the law, Wines noted, "There are two principal sources of political, as of personal, power—knowledge and property."[10] This is the heart of the matter: property is a form of power, and wherever power is claimed for the state, there private property will be under attack.

The attack on private property can take two basic forms. *First,* by denying God's law, powerful individuals can despise the property rights of weaker individuals. The Social Darwinism which prevailed in the United States and elsewhere after 1860 led to "robber barons" who used their power to trample law underfoot. These men justified their lawlessness by appealing to evolution and "the struggle for survival."

8. Calvin: *Institutes,* II, chapt. VIII, xlvi: 1936 edition, p. 443.
9. *Ibid.,* p. 444.
10. E. C. Wines: *Commentaries on the Laws of the Ancient Hebrews* (Philadelphia: William S. and Alfred Martien, 1859), p. 452.

The Social Darwinists held that "the cultural and the biological progress
of advanced peoples is assured so long as 'the law of competition' is
allowed to operate freely and, in respect to the human species, to
assume the form of a 'struggle for existence' which only 'the strongest'
survive."[11] The Social Darwinists had no real interest in private
property; their concern was to use the theory of evolution as a guide
for society. It became a tool for justifying massive theft.

Second, other evolutionists began to emphasize "the plasticity and
creativity of man, of the dynamic character of an environment and of
the reciprocal relation between it and man."[12] For them, the state
became this "dynamic" environment whereby man could remake himself. Property for these evolutionists is simply a tool whereby the
state shapes man and the world. As a result, property is again under
lawless attack, first from individuals and corporations, now from the
state. Since property is a form of power, the totalitarian state seeks to
control or to seize private property in order to prevent the people from
having any power independently of the state.

But private property is a power which God entrusts to *man* as a
stewardship, because it is God's intention that man should have and
exercise power unto the end that the earth be subdued and man's
dominion over the earth under God be established. God gives to the
state its due power in its domain. Private property is a power given to
man to be used under God and to His glory.

3. Restitution and Forgiveness

A serious and major error which has infected Christian and non-
Christian thought alike is that *sin* can be forgiven. By *sin* is here meant
the principle of sin (Gen. 3:5), man's defiance of God and his insistence
on being his own god. Sin as this principle of independence and
autonomy *cannot* be forgiven. Custance has stated this clearly:

> Because it is hereditary, like a disease infecting the whole man, sin is
> not dealt with by forgiveness. It needs eradication somehow, or at
> least to be bypassed in the constitution of the new man. The
> fruits which are expression of it need forgiveness, but the basic
> root must be dealt with by some other method. This root is the
> locus of infection.[1]

A particular sin or sins can be forgiven; sin as a principle, original sin,
cannot be forgiven: it must be eradicated. The saving work of Jesus

---

11. Joseph J. Spengler, "Evolution in American Economics, 1800-1946," in
Stow Persons, editor: *Evolutionary Thought in America* (New York: George
Braziller, 1956), p. 216.
12. *Ibid.,* p. 222 f.
1. Arthur C. Custance: *The Development of Personality: The Old and the
New* (Ottawa: Doorway Papers, 1958), p. 23.

Christ involved a new creation, ("if any one is in Christ, he is a new creation," II Cor. 5:17 BV), restitution, the perfect keeping of the law as our federal head, and forgiveness of the particular sins of His people.

Forgiveness and restitution are inseparable. We are to forgive our brother, i.e., a fellow believer, sevenfold times (Luke 17:4), but this forgiveness always requires repentance and restitution. There are two aspects to forgiveness, the religious or God-ward aspect, and then the social and criminal aspect. Sin *always* is an offense against God, and therefore there must always be a theological aspect to every sin, i.e., some kind of settlement or judgment of man for his violation of God's order. But sin also involves other men, or the earth, and particular sins have particular requirements of restitution.

To return to the fact that, where sin is forgiven, the reference is not to sin in principle but to a particular act. The references to forgiveness in the law (Lev. cc. 4, 5; Num. 15:28, etc.) have reference to particular acts of sin. Jesus Christ pronounced the *forgiveness of sins* to those in the covenant of faith, i.e., of particular sins by the redeemed (Matt. 9:2, 5; Mark 2:5, 9; 3:28; 4:12; Luke 5:20, 23; 7:47, 48; Rom. 4:7; Col. 2:13; James 5:15; I John 2:12, etc.). For sin in itself, man must *die,* rather than be forgiven; we die in Christ as sinners who live in terms of the principle of sin, and we arise in Him as a new creation. Against *sin* as a principle, the penalty is death; for sin as a particular act, forgiveness is possible with repentance and restitution.

With this in mind, we can understand why, with respect to criminal law, the death penalty was mandatory for incorrigible criminals. By their repeated crimes, such persons make apparent that crime is their way of life, their principle, as it were. Similarly, restitution requires in other cases the death of the guilty party as the necessary counterpart to the death of the innocent person, the victim.

In Exodus 22:1-17, we have a series of laws concerning restitution. *First,* the ratio of restitution is established:

> If a man shall steal an ox, or a sheep, and kill it, or sell it; he shall restore five oxen for an ox, and four sheep for a sheep (Ex. 22:1).

Multiple restitution rests on a principle of justice. Sheep are capable of a high rate of reproduction and have use, not only as meat, but also by means of their wool, for clothing, as well as other uses. To steal a sheep is to steal the present and future value of a man's property. The ox requires a higher rate of restitution, five-fold, because the ox was trained to pull carts, and to plow, and was used for a variety of farm tasks. The ox therefore had not only the value of its meat and its usefulness, but also the value of its training, in that training an ox for work was a task requiring time and skill. It thus commanded a higher rate of restitution. Clearly, a principle of restitution is in evidence here. Restitution must calculate not only the present and future value of a thing stolen, but also the specialized skills involved in its replacement.

Second, theft could involve problems with respect to defense against the thief:

> If a thief be found breaking up, and be smitten that he die, there shall no blood be shed for him.
> If the sun be risen upon him, there shall be blood shed for him; for he should make full restitution; if he have nothing, then he shall be sold for his theft (Ex. 22:2, 3).

A housebreaker at night can be legitimately killed by householders to defend their property; it is part of their legitimate defense of themselves and their properties. There is no reason to assume that this breaking does not cover the barn or, today, a garage. In daylight, however, the killing of a thief except in self-defense is manslaughter. The thief can then be identified and apprehended, so that this in itself is a protection. If the thief cannot make restitution, he is to be sold into slavery in order to satisfy the requirement of restitution. This means today some kind of custody whereby the full income of the convicted thief is so ordered that full restitution is provided for.

Third, the law specified the restitution required of a thief caught in the act, or caught before disposing of the stolen goods:

> If the theft be certainly found in his hand alive, whether it be ox, or ass, or sheep; he shall restore double (Ex. 22:4).

In such cases, the thief was to restore the thing stolen, and its equivalent, i.e., the exact amount he expected to profit by in his theft. This is the minimum restitution. A man who steals $100 must restore not only the $100 but another $100 as well.

Fourth, certain acts, whether deliberate or accidental, incur a liability which requires restitution, for to damage another man's property is to rob him of a measure of its value:

> If a man shall cause a field or vineyard to be eaten, and shall put in his beast, and shall feed in another man's field; of the best of his own field, and of the best of his own vineyard, shall he make restitution.
> If fire break out, and catch in thorns, so that the stacks of corn, or the standing corn, or the field, be consumed therewith; he that kindled the fire shall surely make restitution (Ex. 22:5, 6).

The restitution in all such cases depends on the nature of the act; if fruit trees or vines are damaged, then future production is damaged, and the liability is in proportion thereto. Criminal law no longer has more than survivals of the principle of restitution; civil suit must now be filed by an offended party to recover damages, and then without regard to the Biblical principle.

Fifth, in Exodus 22:7-13, responsibility is determined for goods held in custody. Rawlinson summarized this law ably:

> Property deposited in the hands of another for safe keeping might be so easily embezzled by the trustee, or lost through his negligence, that some special laws were needed for its protection. ·Conversely the trustee required to be safe-guarded against incurring loss if the property intrusted to his care suffered damage or disappeared without fault of his. The Mosaic legislation provided for both cases. On the one hand, it required the trustee to exercise proper care, and made him answerable for the loss if a thing intrusted to him was stolen and the thief not found. Embezzlement it punished by requiring the trustee guilty of it to "pay double." On the other hand, in doubtful cases it allowed the trustee to clear himself by an oath (verse 10), and in clear cases to give proof that the loss had happened through unavoidable accident (verse 12).[2]

Sixth, in case of rental, or of loan, certain principles of liability are at work:

> And if a man borrow ought of his neighbour, and it be hurt, or die, the owner thereof being not with it, he shall surely make it good. But if the owner thereof be with it, he shall not make it good: if it be an hired thing, it came for his hire. (Ex.22:14, 15).

If a man borrows and damages the property of another, he is liable for the damages; he has destroyed or harmed the property of another man and is thereby guilty of theft; restitution is mandatory. If the owner came to assist him voluntarily, as a good neighbor, the damage is the owner's, because his property was damaged while under his own supervision. This is all the more true if he was working for hire, because his rental of his services, with ox, ass, tractor, or any other equipment, includes the wear and tear, the maintenance and damages, to his working equipment.

Seventh, seduction is not only an offense against the seventh commandment, but also against the eighth, in that it involves robbing a girl of her virginity (Ex. 22:16, 17). Compensation or restitution meant that "he shall pay money according to the dowry of virgins." Significantly, the word translated *pay* is in Hebrew *weigh;* money was then by weight, a weight of a shekel of silver or gold.

Restitution is cited in Scripture as an aspect of atonement. The law of the Passover, the great atonement of the Old Testament era, involved also the requirement of restitution. The sinful Egyptians, because they had defrauded Israel and had sought to kill Israel, were required to

---

2. George Rawlinson, "Exodus," in Ellicott, I, 279.

make restitution. As the Berkeley Version renders Exodus 12:35, "And in agreement with the instructions of Moses they asked the Egyptians for silver and golden articles, also for clothing." It was not enough for God to right the order by destroying Egypt with ten plagues; Israel had to be enriched by means of restitution (Ex. 12:36). A similar incident occurred earlier in Egypt to Abraham. Pharaoh's order was such that a man had no protection against seizure of his wife together with his own murder except deception (Gen. 12:11-13). There is no condemnation of Abraham for trying to stay alive: rather, God judged Pharaoh strongly (Gen. 12:17) and brought Abraham out greatly enriched by way of restitution (Gen. 12:16; 13:2). God similarly intervened to judge Abimelech (Gen. 20:3-6), even though Abimelech could plead his own integrity; nonetheless, because he headed a lawless order, God held Abimelech responsible, and restitution ensued (Gen. 20:14-18). In both instances, there is not the slightest hint of any condemnation of Abraham, every indication of God's judgment on monarchs for maintaining lawless orders in which Abraham dared not move honestly and openly.

In all these cases, there is not only judgment by God against the offender but also restitution to the offended. Restitution thus is closely linked to atonement, to justice, and to salvation. Only heresies which limit salvation to a new relationship with eternity fail to see the practical consequences of God's salvation. Calvin called attention to the social consequences of redemption. Commenting on Isaiah 2:4, he noted,

> Since, therefore, men are naturally led away by their evil passions, to disturb society, Isaiah here promises the correction of this evil; for, as the gospel is the doctrine of reconciliation (2 Cor. v. 18), which removes the enmity between us and God, so it brings men into peace and harmony with each other. The meaning amounts to this, that Christ's people will be meek, and, laying aside fierceness, will be devoted to the pursuit of peace.
>
> This has been improperly limited by some commentators to the time when Christ was born; because at that time, after the battle of Actium, the temple of Janus was closed, as appears from the histories. I readily admit that the universal peace which existed throughout the Roman empire, at the birth of Christ, was a token of that eternal peace which we enjoy in Christ. But the Prophet's meaning was different. He meant that Christ makes such a reconciliation between God and men, that a comfortable state of peace exists among themselves, by putting an end to destructive wars. For if Christ be taken away, not only are we estranged from God, but we incessantly carry on open war with him, which is justly thrown back on our own heads; and the consequence is, that everything in the world is in disorder.[3]

3. John Calvin: *Commentary on the Book of the Prophet Isaiah* (Grand Rapids: Eerdmans, 1958), I, 100 f.

There will be thus a reign of peace on earth, to the measure that God's word reigns among men, although the perfect fulfilment of this prophecy, Calvin held, "in its full extent, must not be looked for on earth."[4]

Salvation is inseparable from restitution, because God's redemption of man and of the world is its restoration to its original position under Him and to His glory. Man's work of restitution for the sin of Adam, for his own original sin as it has worked to mar the earth, is to recognize that, as a new creation in Christ, he must make the earth a new creation under Christ. The work of Christ in man is this work of restitution.

The forgiven man is the man who makes restitution. *Forgiveness* is in Scripture a juridical term. It has reference to a court of law. Since restitution is in Biblical law at all times basic to forgiveness, to re-establishment into citizenship, the word forgiveness always implies restitution in Scripture. When forgiveness is separated from law and made a matter of feeling, the end result is sentimentalism. Many modern theologians and Christians insist on an unconditional forgiveness for all men, irrespective of repentance and restitution. Such a position is simply a subsidy to and an acceptance of evil as evil. It is antinomianism.

4. Liability of the Bystander

Failure to render aid was once a serious offense, and to a limited degree, still makes the man who fails to render aid liable to serious penalties. The direction of humanistic law is progressively absolving men of any legal obligation to be a Good Samaritan. Thus, according to one decision,

> A bystander may watch a blind man or a child walk over a precipice, and yet he is not required to give warning. He may stand on the bank of a stream and see a man drowning, and although he holds in his hand a rope that could be used to rescue the man, yet he is not required to give assistance. He may owe a moral duty to warn the blind man or to assist the drowning man, but being a mere bystander, and in nowise responsible for the dangerous situation, he owes no legal duty to render assistance.[1]

In certain cases, however, the bystander must render aid or face legal action. A bystander can watch a farmer's house or barn burn and do nothing, but in the case of a forest fire (federal "property"), the bystander must render action as demanded or face penalties from a court.

Formerly, all bystanders had a legal duty to render aid to a *hue and cry.* The expression, *hue and cry,* is a legal term; formerly, when a

---

4. *Ibid.,* I, 102.
1. Bushanan v. Rose (1942) 128 Tex. 390, 159 Sw2d 109, 110 (Alexander, C.J.) cited in Clark: *Biblical Law,* p. 121.

criminal escaped, or was discovered, or an act of crime was being committed, the summons to assist was legally binding on all. Later, *hue and cry* was the name of a written proclamation asking for the apprehension of a criminal, or of stolen goods. In England, *Hue and Cry* was also the title of an official gazette publishing information on crimes and criminals.

Biblical law, however, asserts the liability of the bystander. Thus, Deuteronomy 22:1-4, declares,

> Thou shalt not see thy brother's ox nor his sheep go astray, and hide thyself from them; thou shalt in any case bring them again unto thy brother.
> And if thy brother be not nigh unto thee, or if thou know him not, then thou shalt bring it unto thine own house, and it shall be with thee, until thy brother seek after it, and thou shalt restore it to him again.
> In like manner shalt thou do with his ass; and so shalt thou do with his raiment; and with all lost things of thy brother's, which he hath lost, and thou hast found, shalt thou do likewise: thou mayest not hide thyself.
> Thou shalt not see thy brother's ass or his ox fall down by the way, and hide thyself from them: thou shalt surely help him to lift them up again.

Here again we have case law, giving a minimal case in order to illustrate a general principle. We cannot rob a man of his property by our neglect; we must act as good neighbors even to our enemies and to strangers. Lost or strayed animals, property, or clothing must be protected and held in ward with every public effort at immediate restoration.

If the bystander has an obligation to render aid "with all lost things" of another man, he has an even more pressing obligation to help rescue the man. Thus, this principle of responsibility appears in Deuteronomy 22:24. A woman assaulted in a city is presumed to have given consent if she does not raise a cry, the origin of the *hue and cry* common law. At her cry, every man within sound of her voice has a duty to render immediate aid; failue to do so was regarded as a fearful abomination which polluted the land and, figuratively, darkened the sun. The horror felt at such an offense is reflected in the rabbinic tradition:

> Our Rabbis taught, on account of four things is the sun in eclipse: On Account of an Ab Beth din (the vice-president of the Sanhedrin) who died and was not mourned fittingly; on account of a betrothed maiden who cried out aloud in the city and there was none to save her; on account of sodomy, and on account of two brothers whose blood was shed at the same time. And on account of four things are the luminaries (the moon and the stars) in eclipse: On account of those who perpetrate forgeries, on account of those who give false witness; on account of those who rear

small cattle in the land of Israel (Animals that cannot be prevented from ravaging the fields of others); and on account of those who cut down good trees.[2]

It is significant that this offense is rated as worse than giving false witness; the false witness misrepresents the truth; the non-interfering bystander becomes an accomplice to the crime by his refusal to render aid. Asaph said of those who were indifferent to the need to render aid,

When thou sawest a thief, then thou consentedst with him; and has been partaker with adulterers (Ps. 50:18).

Quite properly, the marginal references cite Romans 1:32 and I Timothy 5:22. In the latter passage, those who consent to the hasty ordination of novices in the faith, or by their silence give consent, are "partakers of other men's sins." It is not unreasonable to assume that the penalty for the inactive bystander was like that of the false witness. The penalty of the crime applied to the false witness (Deut. 19:18, 19); the inactive bystander is also a kind of witness, and one who consents to the crime by his failure to act. The inactive bystander is thus an accomplice, an accessory to the crime, and liable to the penalty for the crime.

Solomon also called attention to the same crime in sharp and pointed words declaring,

If thou forbear to deliver them that are drawn unto death, and those that are ready to be slain;
If thou sayest, Behold, we know it not; doth not he that pondereth the heart consider it? and he that keepeth thy soul, doth not he know it? and shall not he render to every man according to his works? (Proverbs 24:11, 12).

Kidner's comment on Proverbs 24:10-12 is worth noting in this connection:

Exceptional strain (10) and avoidable responsibility (11, 12) are fair tests, not unfair, of a man's mettle. It is the hireling, not the true shepherd who will plead bad conditions (10), hopeless tasks (11) and pardonable ignorance (12); love is not so lightly quieted —nor is the God of love.[3]

Delitzsch's comment on Proverbs 28:17 is very fitting here also:

Grace cannot come into the place of justice till justice has been fully recognized. Human sympathy, human forbearance, under the false title of grace, do not stand in contrast to this justice.[4]

---

2. Sukkah 29a; in Seder Mo'ed, *The Babylonian Talmud*, III, 130 f.
3. Derek Kidner: *The Proverbs, An Introduction and Commentary*, (Chicago: Inter-Varsity Press, 1964), p. 154.
4. Franz Delitzsch: *Biblical Commentary on the Proverbs of Solomon* (Grand Rapids: Eerdmans), II, 234.

The Biblical law thus makes clear the liability of the bystander; it states, in fact, that he cannot be a bystander. An older decision of an American court stated the matter briefly: the law "requires the doing of good at all times."[5] The *police power* of the citizenry rests in Deuteronomy 22:1-4, 24. When a neighbor's property went astray or was lost, or when a man or woman raised a cry of distress, every man had a duty to answer that cry and enforce the law. All citizens have the right of arrest to this day in the United States as a result of this Biblical heritage.

Under common law, a sheriff still has the right to muster every male citizen of a community of 15 years or older to assist him in the enforcement of law.[6]

With respect to citizen's arrest,

> William B. Saxbe, Attorney General of Ohio, spelled out some of the ground rules of citizen's arrest. With some state-by-state variations, United States law holds that a private person may arrest someone for committing or attempting to commit a felony or a misdemeanor in his presence. He may also arrest someone whom he has *reasonable cause* to believe has previously committed a felony, but *not* for a misdemeanor, in the past. Some states allow citizen's arrest *only* for felonies, while others provide broad arrest powers for citizens for all crimes.
>
> Saxbe noted that felonies are almost always crimes that are basically wrong or evil, while misdemeanors are lesser crimes.[7]

Usually, however, the police power of the citizen is best exercised in rendering aid to the police and to victims of crimes. Police prefer that witnesses summon them, take sharp note of the events, and assist as they are required by the police. In Germany, persons failing to assume police powers to defend others can be fined from $1.25 to $2,500, or receive a year in prison. France and Italy have similar laws.[8]

American law has become contradictory since the old common law has been superseded by statute law. A man's car can be commandeered to apprehend a criminal, but he has no legal grounds for claims against the city if his car is destroyed in the process.[9] Warnick's comments are to the point:

> It is not a crime in any state—as it is under common law and quite generally in Europe—for a citizen to fail to disclose commission of a felony to police on his own initiative. But by act of Congress such "misprision of a felony" is a crime in the United States if it is

---

5. Moore v. Strickling (1899) 46 W.Va. 515, 33 SE 274, 50 LRA 279, 282; in Clark, *op. cit.,* p. 120.
6. Dorothy Brant Warnick, "The Police Powers of Private Citizens," in *The American Legion Magazine,* June, 1967, p. 17.
7. *Ibid.*
8. *Ibid.,* p. 20.   9. *Ibid.,* p. 21.

a *federal* felony that goes unreported. A layman's view of this is that if you saw a store robbery and went your quiet way you'd be on the right side of the law if not your conscience. But if you saw a mail robbery and didn't call the cops you would have committed a federal felony.

What has brought all of this to the fore again is, of course, the resurgence of crime and mob violence in America; the downgrading of the police to the point where fewer people even want to be police; and the shocking apathy of many people toward "becoming involved" in crimes. . . .

If the law does not require you to call the cops when the store is robbed or someone is brutally beaten; if you are liable to false arrest charges even when acting most reasonably on your own; if you may not be protected against injury or liability when obeying an officer, then you are privileged to take a position—even against your own feelings—that society itself isn't really serious about controlling crime. Society in this case is the legislatures and the courts.

Why isn't "misprision of a felony" a state offense as it is a federal offense? Legislatures can restore the common law principle that made it so.[10]

The civil legal situation may be an equivocal one; the Biblical legal requirement is not. Misprision, i.e., the concealment of a crime, is a serious offense. The inactive bystander is a party to the crime. The parable of the Good Samaritan (Luke 10:29-37) was firmly based on Biblical law.

In the parable of the Good Samaritan, the priest and the Levite avoided the victim and "passed by on the other side." The religious leaders claimed to obey the law; they tithed "mint and rue and all manner of herbs, and pass over the judgment and the love of God" (Luke 11:42). It was an easy matter to tithe mint; it sometimes required moral courage to help a victim; in the case of the victim Jesus described, not even courage was required, only assistance in terms of the law to a victim abandoned by the criminals. The religious leaders kept the law only when it cost them little or nothing to do so. Jesus confounded them from the law.

It is thus a serious error to reduce the parable of the Good Samaritan to the level of feeling alone, or to a matter of charity; these things are subordinate to the law in this case. Those who despise the law are also without charity. They profess to love the law, but they choose simple matters for obedience and despise the things which are difficult. Too many churchmen today reduce the law to simple rules about the Sabbath and adultery and by-pass or violate the rest of the law with impunity. This is Phariseeism.

---

10. *Ibid.,* p. 53.

5. Money and Measures

A greatly misunderstood law is Leviticus 19:35-37 concerning honesty in measurements:

> Ye shall do no unrighteousness in judgment, in mete-yard, in
> weights, or in measure.
> Just balances, just weights, a just ephah, and a just hin shall ye
> have; I am the LORD your God, which brought you out of the land
> of Egypt.
> Therefore shall ye observe all my statutes, and all my judgments,
> and do them: I am the LORD.

The word judgment here refers to all that follows; *mete-yard* was a
measure of length or surface, i.e., yard, cubit, foot, and the like; *weight*
had reference to the talent, shekel, and other weights of money;
measure refers to measures of capacity, the homer, ephah, hin, etc.;
balances means scales and *weights, ephah,* and *hin* cites again the
forms of measurement already listed.[1]

That *weights* means money has long been known. *Fairbairn's Bible
Encyclopedia,* like others, discusses the shekel under the classification
of "Weights." The Bible speaks of money as a *weight.* For example,
we are told that "David gave to Ornan for the place six hundred shekels
of gold by weight" (I Chron. 21:25). Opinions differ as to the exact
nature of the talent, menah, shekel, bekah, zuza (Reba), and gerah,
but Bonar's table of weights is perhaps as good as any.[2] The shekel
was probably half an ounce, avoirdupois weight.

Bonar has been referred to deliberately, because he is also the author
of a commentary on Leviticus. In commenting on Leviticus 19:35-37,
he devotes three pages to a basically evangelistic homily. In two sentences, he refers to the specific point of the text to say:

> In markets, in trade, in their shops—in meting out land with the
> yard and cubit, or weighting articles in the balance, or trying the
> capacity of solids. The balances and its weights, the *ephah,* and
> its subdivision the *hin,* must be strictly exact.[3]

It is possible to speak of *the studied irrelevance* of much preaching and
comment on Scripture. A law of central importance to the monetary
and economic morality of a nation is treated casually or not at all. The
Biblical materialism of the Jews prevented them from being so irrelevant. The Talmud thus noted,

> Raba said: Why did the Divine Law mention the exodus from
> Egypt in connection with interest, fringes and weights? The Holy
> One, blessed be He, declared, "It is I who distinguished in Egypt

---

1. George Bush: *Notes, Critical and Practical on the Book of Leviticus* (New
York: Ivison & Phinney, 1857), p. 214.
2. Horatius Bonar, "Weights," in *Fairbairn's Bible Encyclopedia,* VI, 330.
3. Bonar: *Leviticus,* p. 356.

between the first-born and one who is not a first-born; even so, it
is I who will exact vengeance from him who ascribes his money
to a Gentile and lends it to an Israelite on interest, or who steeps
his weights in salt, or who (attaches to his garment threads dyed
with) vegetable blue and maintains that it is (real) blue."[4]

The point here is that the first-born or elect of God are those who abide
by His law. Those who have outwardly enjoyed the privileges of the
covenant and a covenant culture but who deny its laws are the subject
of especial vengeance from the Covenant God.

C. D. Ginsburg also referred to this aspect of the law and cited its
enforcement during the time of the second Temple:

> It will be seen that the Lawgiver uses here exactly the same phrase
> with regard to meting out right measure which he used in connection
> with the administration of justice in verse 15. He, therefore, who
> declares that a false measure is a legal measure is, according to
> this law, as much a corrupt judge, and defrauds the people by false
> judgment, as he who in the court of justice wilfully passes a wrong
> sentence. Owing to the fact that men who would otherwise disdain
> the idea of imposition often discard their scruples in the matter of
> weights and measures, the Bible frequently brands these dealings
> as wicked, and an abomination to the Lord, whilst it designates
> the right measure as coming from God himself (Deut. xxv. 13, 15;
> Ezek. xlv. 10, 12; Hosea xii. 8; Amos viii. 5; Micah vi. 10, 11;
> Prov. xi. 1, xvi. 11, xx. 10, 23). According to the authorities
> during the second Temple, he who gives false weight or measure,
> like the corrupt judge, is guilty of the following five things. He (1)
> defiles the land; (2) profanes the name of God; (3) causes the
> Shekinah to depart; (4) makes Israel perish by the sword, and
> (5) to go into captivity. Hence they declared that "the sin of
> illegal weights and measures is greater than that of incest, and is
> equivalent to the sin of denying that God redeemed Israel out of
> Egypt." They appointed public overseers to inspect the weights
> and measures all over the country; they prohibited weights to be
> made of iron, lead, or other metal liable to become lighter by
> wear or rust, and ordered them to be made of polished rock, of
> glass, &c., and enacted the severest punishment for fraud.[5]

This law has therefore a number of very important implications.
First, the old Latin and modern laissez-faire principle, *caveat emptor,*
let the buyer beware, is not Biblical. Dishonest merchandising is as
serious a matter as dishonest judges and courts. At this point, the
modern liberals have been closer to Biblical requirements than conservatives have been. The supposed evolutionary law of the jungle is not
Biblical morality. On the other hand, the liberal principle, "let the
seller beware," is not Biblical either. The law cannot encourage irresponsibility on the part of either buyer or seller. Laissez-faire counte-

4. *Baba Mezi's* 61b: in *Seder Nezekin,* I, 366 f.
5. C. D. Ginsburg, "Leviticus," in Ellicott, I, 429.

nanced irresponsibility by the seller; liberalism and socialism encourage irresponsibility by the buyer. Honest goods are necessary, but also honest payments. The state, as the ministry of justice, does have a duty to maintain justice in the market-place, but it cannot confuse justice with charity. True, the state as the policeman can be corrupt; in fact, if the society as a whole is corrupt, the state will also be corrupt. In a healthy and godly society, the state will function successfully to restrain the minority of evil-doers. The key to the situation is not the state but the religious health of the society. The law specifically states that false weights and measures are "unrighteousness in judgment," or injustices in matters calling for justice. Since justice is the ministry of the state, these are matters for the state to adjudge.

Second, mete-yards are measures of length or surface, of yards, feet, inches, cubits, meters, and the like, including acres, as we have noted. Justice requires the maintaining of strict standards in these matters, and the penalizing of those who defraud by means of false measures. Frauds in this area involve frauds in land transactions, in goods and materials, and in a variety of ways basic to commerce.

Third, fraud in weights is essentially fraudulent money. Very obviously, Biblical money was by weight, a weight of silver or of gold, and every form of coinage in later times was by weight. Earlier, money was not by minting or coining, but was a piece of silver or gold of a specific weight. The gold coinage of the United States followed the Biblical pattern by establishing itself with reference to weight, the ounce, .900 fineness, or fractions of an ounce.

Fractional reserve banking, unbacked or partially backed paper money, and inflation of money by debt and credit, is thus a violation of this law. Isaiah, in listing the charges in God's bill of indictment against Jerusalem, declared that "Thy silver is become dross, thy wine mixed with water" (Isa. 1:22). The reference is to false weights, silver replaced with baser metals, or heavily alloyed with them, and to false measures, a quart of wine made into a gallon by mixture with water.

Thus the law clearly requires the condemnation of all fraudulent money. The law of the guilty bystander thus clearly condemns *all* ministers, priests, and teachers who do not declare the sentence of the law against fraudulent money. Their silence means a guilt comparable to that of corrupt judges or of counterfeiters, in that they counterfeit God's word by their silence or by false interpretations.

As surely as a false yardstick or a false cup measure defrauds a man, just as surely a false money defrauds a man. Even worse, dishonest money introduces a false weight into every monetary transaction in a society, so that radical corruption and injustice prevail. If in every business transaction in any society a basic fraud prevails in the form of dishonest and counterfeit money, then the entire society is polluted, honest men are robbed, and thieves prevail. This is precisely what monetary fraud and inflation perpetrate, the triumph of thieves over godly men. Silence in the face of such radical corruption is an inexcusable ignorance and an evil. Ginsburg (supra) cited the texts condemning false weights. They are declared to be an "abomination" to the Lord, as witness Solomon's declaration:

> Divers weights, and divers measures, both of them are alike abomination to the LORD (Prov. 20:10).
> Divers weights are an abomination unto the LORD; and a false balance is not good (Prov. 20:23).

In Ezekiel 45:9-12, God specified the exact ratio of the shekel to its lesser and greater weights as well as dealing with balances and measures of capacity. The lack of justice here God through Ezekiel termed "violence and spoil" as well as "exactions."

Fourth, measures here in this law refers to measures of capacity, and the law required strict honesty here as elsewhere. Liquid and dry measures alike are covered by this law. We have noted Isaiah's condemnation of watered wine; a gallon of wine which has been watered may provide an accurate gallon, but it is still dishonest because its contents have been mixed with water. Fruit watered shortly prior to marketing gives a dishonest weight and lesser flavor. Cows given salted feed in order to make them drink heavily and increase their weight represent fraud, as do forms of trucking cows to the sales yard which will dehydrate them and reduce their weight. Fraud thus extends beyond the scales or the bushel basket.

Fifth, just balances refers to what is today called weights. Honest scales are basic to just commerce, and the regulation of scales is thus basic to the ministry of justice. The poor in particular are victimized by dishonest balances (Amos 8:4-8). They are least able to protect themselves and suffer the most from the consequences.

Sixth, the consequences of violations of this law are apparent in the land itself, which will cast out the people. Even as the Nile floods Egypt, so judgment shall sweep over the people (Amos 8:8). The law is emphatic on the relationship of this law to life:

> Thou shalt not have in thy bag, divers weights, a great and a small. Thou shalt not have in thine house divers measures, a great and a small.
> But thou shalt have a perfect and just weight, a perfect and just measure shalt thou have; that thy days may be lengthened in the land which the LORD thy God giveth thee (Deut. 25:13-15).

This statement has been well noted by Luther, who observed that

a just weight and just measure should be preserved in the community, so that a poor person and one's neighbor are not cheated. This also has general validity for all exchanges of all contracts, that the seller give just and equable wares for the money of the buyer. Here greed knows unbelievable injustices and tricks in changing, cheapening, imitating, and adulterating merchandise; therefore it is no small part of the concern of government to have an eye here to the common good.[6]

Luther is clearly right. The commandment, "Thou shalt not steal," plainly forbids "changing, cheapening, imitating, and adulterating merchandise," and such fraud or theft is "no small part of the concern of government." But the culminating point is too often neglected, the promise of life for obedience to this law, as well as the fifth commandment. Conversely, life is denied to those who violate this law; a land given to theft faces judgment and death. In other words, God shortens the life of the nation that condones short-changing and defrauding, by fraudulent money, scales, and other measures.

Calvin said, of Leviticus 19:35,

Now, if the laws of buying and selling are corrupted, human society is in a manner dissolved; so that he who cheats by false weights and measures, differs little from him who utters false coin; and consequently one, who, whether as a buyer or seller, has falsified the standard measures of wine, or corn, or anything else, is accounted criminal.[7]

The reformers, like the earlier church fathers, were not silent with respect to this law.

In evaluating this law, it is important to set it in the context of the legal tradition of the modern era, in order to understand the basic conflict of principles. The legal tradition can be divided into three basic positions. *First* a principle of the older liberalism and more recent conservatism joins the concepts of laissez-faire and self interest. Noninterference by the state in economic affairs is required, and it is held that the self-interest of all individuals adds up to the public good. *Caveat emptor* reigns, and no attempt is made to enforce this Levitical law. This position clearly posits *the rule of the individual* as well as his ultimacy in the social order. The self-interest of the individual leads to the greatest good of the greatest number of people.

Second, the new liberalism as well as socialism affirms *the rule of the state.* The self-interest of the state leads to the greatest good, because the state has the welfare of all the people at heart. Legislation is therefore necessary to enforce honest weights and measures.

In the first, there is no protection for men and society from the sin

---

6. Luther: *Deuteronomy,* p. 249.
7. Calvin: *Commentaries on the Four Last Books of Moses,* III, 120.

and rapacity of men; in the second social order, there is no defense for men against the power and depravity of the state.

Third, Biblical law declares the rule of God and His law. God's self-interest is alone the true foundation of law and order. God as all-holy, righteous, and just, does most wisely decree and govern all things. Only as men are redeemed and submit, by grace and/or by compulsion to God's law-order can there be justice. If God's law is not respected, then neither men's self-interest nor the state's self-interest can preserve the social order. "Except the LORD build the house, they labour in vain that build it" (Ps. 127:1).

6. Usury

Few laws are more misunderstood than the usury laws of the Bible. The word *usury* itself confuses the issue. It does not refer to exorbitant interest in Biblical usage, but to any interest at all. To avoid misunderstanding at this point, the American Revised Version of 1901 will be used. The laws read as follows:

> If thou lend money to any of my people with thee that is poor, thou shalt not be to him as a creditor; neither shall ye lay upon him interest.
> If thou at all take thy neighbor's garment to pledge, thou shalt restore it unto him before the sun goeth down:
> for that it is his only covering, it is his garment for his skin; wherein shall he sleep? and it shall come to pass, when he crieth unto me, that I will hear; for I am gracious (Ex. 22:25-27).

> And if thy brother be waxed poor, and his hand fail with thee; then thou shalt uphold him: as a stranger and a sojourner shall he live with thee.
> Take thou no interest of him or increase, but fear thy God; that thy brother may live with thee.
> Thou shalt not give him thy money upon interest, nor give him thy victuals for increase.
> I am Jehovah your God, who brought you forth out of the land of Egypt, to give you the land of Canaan, and to be your God (Lev. 25:35-38).

> Thou shalt not lend upon interest to thy brother; interest of money, interest of victuals, interest of anything that is lent upon interest.
> Unto a foreigner thou mayest lend upon interest; but unto thy brother thou shalt not lend upon interest, that Jehovah thy God may bless thee in all that thou puttest thy hand unto, in the land whither thou goest in to possess it (Deut. 23:19, 20).

First of all, in two of the three statements of this law, it is specifically stated that the law has reference to the poor, and, moreover, to poor fellow believers or covenant members. Deuteronomy is in part a summary of the law and apparently assumes the same fact. This point is very important, in that much of the misunderstanding of this law stems from misconstructions of the word "brother." For centuries, the church assumed that "brother" referred to every believer, and it accordingly banned all interest among Christians. The Talmud followed a similar interpretation: all interest payments between Israelites were forbidden. However, a variety of evasions arose, and it became the practice for an Israelite to ascribe "his money to a Gentile and (he) lends it to an Israelite on interest."[1] A number of technicalities were also developed, whereby interest could be exacted without being regarded as interest. The same was true of medieval theory and practice.

Calvin altered this brotherhood thesis. In Nelson's curious terminology, he "charted the path to the world of Universal Otherhood, where all became 'brothers' in being equally 'others.' "[2] Nelson's conclusion is highly questionable. Calvin clearly recognized that the law did not abolish interest but rather called for help to the deserving poor brother. In commenting on Exodus 22:25, Calvin stated:

> The question here is not as to usury, as some have falsely thought, as if He commanded us to lend gratuitously, and without any hope of gain; but, since in lending, private advantage is most generally sought, and therefore we neglect the poor, and only lend our money to the rich, from whom we expect some compensation, Christ reminds us that, if we seek to acquire the favour of the rich, we afford in this way no proof of our charity or mercy; and hence He proposes another sort of liberality, which is plainly gratuitous, in giving assistance to the poor, not only because our loan is a perilous one, but because they cannot make a return in kind.[3]

The point Calvin then made boldly, breaking with the entire tradition stemming from Aristotle which held all interest to be an evil, was that interest is not in itself evil. Calvin had no liking for interest, or for money-lending. He was conscious of the weight of prejudice against it, and he stated that he would prefer a world without it, "but I do not dare to pronounce upon so important a point more than God's words convey."[4]

> I have, then, admonished men that the fact itself is simply to be considered, that all unjust gains are ever displeasing to God, whatever colour we endeavor to give it. But if we would form an equitable judgment, reason does not suffer us to admit that all usury is to be condemned without exception. If the debtor have protracted the time by false pretenses to the loss and inconvenience of his creditor, will it be consistent that he should reap advantage

---

1. *Baba Mezi'a,* 61b; p. 367. See S. Stein, "Interest Taken By Jews From Gentiles," in *Journal of Semitic Studies* (1956), I, 141-164.
2. Benjamin N. Nelson: *The Idea of Usury, From Tribal Brotherhood to Universal Otherhood* (Princeton: Princeton University Press, 1949), p. 73.
3. Calvin: *Commentary on the Four Last Books of Moses,* III, 126 f.
4. *Ibid.,* III, 132.

from his bad faith and broken promises? Certainly no one, I think, will deny that usury ought to be paid to the creditor in addition to the principal, to compensate his loss. If any rich and monied man, wishing to buy a piece of land, should borrow some part of the sum required of another, may not he who lends the money receive some part of the revenues of the farm until the principal shall be repaid? Many such cases daily occur in which, as far as equity is concerned, usury is no worse than purchase. Nor will that subtle argument of Aristotle avail, that usury is unnatural, because money is barren and does not beget money; for such a cheat as I have spoken of, might make much profit by trading with another man's money, and the purchaser of the farm might in the meantime reap and gather his vintage. But those who think differently, may object, that we must abide by God's judgment, when He generally prohibits all usury to His people. I reply, that the question is only as to the poor, and consequently, if we have to do with the rich, that usury is freely permitted; because the Lawgiver, in alluding to one thing, seems not to condemn another, concerning which he is silent.[5]

The total condemnation of interest has led to very ugly moral consequences. Money-lenders and bankers have as a class been regarded with distrust because of the lingering condemnation of usury. From the medieval period, such persons were seen as a kind of evil conspiracy against mankind, and this opinion has grown instead of subsiding. We are continually told by both conservatives and socialists that international bankers and the "money trust" are in conspiracy against mankind. Although no evidence for this is ever presented, the fable has been so often repeated, that it is assumed to be true because so many people believe it. The 16th century Dean of Durham, the Rev. Dr. Thomas Wilson, a vigorous enemy of all interest, clearly revealed the moral confusion this position leads to. In describing the wickedness of money-lenders, Wilson cited an example:

I knowe a gentelman borne to five hundred pounde lande, and entring into usurie uppon pawne of his lande did never receyve above a thousand pound of nete money, and within certeyne yeres ronnyage stil upon usurie, and double usurie, the merchantes termyng it usance and double usance by a more clenly name, he did owe to master usurer five thousand pounde at the last, borowyng but one thousand pounde at first; so that his land was clean gone, beynge five hundreth poundes inherytance, for one thousande pound in money, and the usurie of the same money for so few yeres, and the man nowe beggeth. I will not saye but this gentleman was an unthrift dyvers waies in good cheere, maye in evill cheere I may call it, in wearing gaye and costly apparell, in roysterynge with many servauntes mo then needed, and wyth mustrrynge in monstrous great hose, cardes and dyce, as tyme served. And yet I

---

5. *Ibid.,* III, 130 f.

do saye, he loste more by the usurer than hee did by all those unthriftye meanes: for his vayne expences was not much more than a thousand pound, because hee had no more: whereas the usurer had not only his thousand pounde agayne, but fower tymes more, whiche is five Thousand pounds in the whole, and for want of this payment the five hundred pounde lande was wholly his. And this gayne onlye for tyme.[6]

The heir in question spent all the income from his estate, plus his thousand pound loan, in riotous living, and ended a beggar. He spent more than the loan sum, therefore, and Wilson was thus in error here. The interest seems high, but here we cannot judge, because we do not know the years of this wayward heir's life. The sixteenth century saw much inflation in England; interest rates during inflation climb proportionately, and interest figures are thus relative. The loan was probably a legitimate loan; very clearly, the morality of the heir was bad. The evil in this case was, very plainly, mainly that of the heir, and possibly entirely his. Wilson gives us no evidence of clear-cut wrong-doing on the part of the money-lender; instead, his position is that money lending is in itself evil. As a result, he passes lightly over the obvious moral dereliction of the young gentleman, who deserved to be a beggar.

This habit of condemning others for our own sins has become deeply ingrained in Western man as a result of this hostility to money-lending. It has also been a fertile ground for anti-semitism.

Second, the nature of the loan to the poor deserves careful attention. According to Rylaarsdam, commenting on Exodus 22: 25-27,

The real point is that in his regulations with a poor man, possibly his own employee, an Israelite must be generous. If he gives him an advance payment on his wage, he must not insist on payment by the end of the day at the risk of the man's doing without the *garment* he has given as pledge for the loan (vs. 26). The original admonition was not so much a prohibition of interest as a demand that one be ready to "risk an advance" without material security. Amos 2:6 condemns Israelites for having treated such advances in a strictly legal manner, even at the cost of making the poor destitute. As a barter economy developed into a money economy the problem of interest became increasingly acute (Deut. 23:19-20; Lev. 25:26); between Israelites interest on commercial loans was prohibited. (In Hebrew the word "interest" means "bite"!) To take a *neighbor's garment in pledge* for any time longer than the working hours of the day, when he does not wear it, is equivalent to making him pledge his life (cf. Deut. 24:6, 17). This prohibition ultimately makes enslavement for debt impossible.[7]

6. Thomas Wilson: *A Discourse Upon Usury* (1572), (New York: Augustus M. Kelley, 1963), p. 228. With a historical introduction by R. H. Tawney.
7. Rylaarsdam, "Exodus," *Interpreter's Bible*, I, 1008.

Rylaarsdam's evolutionary faith leads him to assume a later date for the laws in Leviticus and Deuteronomy, and hence a different meaning. For this there is no evidence. He is right, however, in citing this law as evidence of advance payment of wages. The pledge taken was of the outer garment or cloak in which the poor worker slept. The reference is to the poor people with the lender, to "my people *with thee* that is poor," to people working on his land with him. The same meaning appears in Leviticus 25:35-38, and it is expanded. If a poor fellow believer who is employed by the well-to-do believer is in financial distress because of some crisis, he is to receive the same hospitality which a foreigner or a traveller would receive, the hospitality due to a visitor. The charity is thus to be gracious, and the loan without interest. Wright's comment on Deuteronomy 23:19, 20 bears this out:

> No interest is to be charged on loans to a fellow Israelite, though it is permissible in the case of a foreigner. Since most loans in Israel were for the purpose of relieving distress, the principle behind the law was that another's need should not be the occasion for profit. The use of loans in international commerce was for another purpose. Hence the foreigner is excluded from the requirement.[8]

It is commendable when a rich man lends to poor fellow believers, but this is an act of voluntary charity, whereas the law, as the wording of Leviticus makes clear, requires this charity as mandatory towards employees. No rich believer has the ability to lend to every needy fellow believer. He does have the ability to help those whom he employs. His responsibility here is to advance them loans without interest, against their wages, and to give emergency loans in times of crisis. The prohibition against interest is thus limited to a specific type of case, and it involves more than a mere prohibition, in that an active duty towards those under our authority is required.

Third, while charity is clearly the purpose of this law, charity is not confused here with a gift, a loss, or foolishness. A pledge or security can be, although it need not be, required. As Gary North points out, this forbids fractional reserve banking, in that the security cannot be used to negotiate a second loan, in that it is held by the lender during the day. The pledge requirement was a protection against irresponsibility on the part of the poor worker. If the poor worker were a trustworthy man, the employer would not require the pledge. The pledge or security was thus insurance against failure to repay, or to work out the loan. The charity in this case is thus a gift of the interest, not of the loan.

The indictments of usury in the prophets are indictments of loans to workmen at interest, to seize their small holdings of land. In Psalm

---

8. G. Ernest Wright, "Deuteronomy," *Interpreter's Bible,* II, 472.

15:5, such usury is coupled with taking "reward against the innocent," i.e., bribe-taking. In Proverbs 28:8, we are told that "He that augmenteth his substance by interest and increase, gathereth it for him that hath pity on the poor," i.e., the man who charges interest to his poor employees who are believers will be judged finally by God, and his wealth given to those who take pity on their poor brethren. Jeremiah faced the hostility of men who enslaved their fellow believers rather than helping them (Jer. 15:10). Ezekial referred to the same kind of oppression (Ezek. 22:12; 18:13). Nehemiah required a return to the Biblical law (Neh. 5:1-13).

Jesus referred to the same kind of loan without interest in passing, in Luke 6:34, 35. His approval of interest on commercial loans is clearly apparent in Luke 19:23, and Matthew 25:27.

Unger's summary statement is thus clearly in the main correct:

> The Israelites not being commercial people, money was not often loaned for the purpose of business, but rather to aid the struggling poor. This last is the only kind of interest forbidden in the law, and the avoiding of this is sometimes given among the characteristics of the godly man (Ps. 15:5; Jer. 15:10; comp. Prov. 28:8).
>
> The practice of mortgaging lands, sometimes at exorbitant interest, grew up among the Jews during the captivity, in direct violation of the law (Lev. 25:36; Ezek. 18:8, 13, 17); and Nehemiah exacted an oath to insure its discontinuance (Neh. 5:3-13). Jesus denounced all extortion, and promulgated a new law of love and forbearance (Luke 6:30, 35). The taking of usury in the sense of a reasonable rate of interest for the use of money employed in trade is different, and is nowhere forbidden; and is referred to in the New Testament as a perfectly understood and allowable practice (Matt. 25:27; Luke 19:23).[9]

There is no ground for calling our Lord's statements "a new law of love and forbearance," when it is no more than a summation of the law of the Old Testament.

Fourth, while interest is permitted on commercial loans, all such loans are under the restriction of the sabbath law, i.e., their life is limited to six years. According to Deuteronomy 15:1-6,

> At the end of every seven years thou shalt make a release. And this is the manner of the release: every creditor shall release that which he hath lent unto his neighbor: he shall not exact it of his neighbor and his brother: because Jehovah's release hath been proclaimed. Of a foreigner thou mayest exact it: but whatsoever of thine is with thy brother thy hand shall release. Howbeit there shall be no poor with thee (for Jehovah will surely bless thee in the land which Jehovah thy God giveth thee for an inheritance to possess it), if only thou diligently hearken unto the voice of Jehovah

9. *Unger's Bible Dictionary,* p. 1129.

thy God, to observe to do all this commandment which I command thee this day. For Jehovah thy God will bless thee, as he promised thee; and thou shalt rule over many nations, but they shall not rule over thee.

Short term loans are alone permitted. No godly man has the right to mortgage his future indefinitely; his life belongs to God and cannot be forfeited to men. Thus, every kind of debt by believers, whether as charity or for business reasons, must be a short term debt. The sabbath is basically and essentially *rest* rather than *worship,* and basic to the sabbath rest is debt-free living. Long-term debts are clearly a violation of the sabbath, and many churches that profess to be devout sabbath-keepers are flagrant sabbath-breakers here. The normal life of the covenant man is to be debt free, to owe no man anything save the obligation of rendering tribute, honor, fear, and custom wherever due, and of rendering that love which is the fulfilling of the law (Rom. 13:7-8). If this and all other laws of God be kept, there will be "no poor" among the people of God. This is a firm and unqualified statement; it presupposes that the godly man can keep the law to that degree necessary to receive this blessing.

Fifth, the unbelieving are excluded from the charity required by this law, both the interest-free loans and the termination of the debt in the sabbatical year. The ungodly are already slaves to sin by nature; the true slave cannot be weaned from slavery, and it is foolishness to treat him as a free man. The godly are free men by nature; in times of distress, they need relief to regain their freedom. Freedom cannot be given to a man who loves slavery, and it is foolishness to attempt it by means of money. Regeneration is his only solution.

Sixth, on citing their deliverance from Egypt, God reminds His people that the purpose of His law is to deliver man into freedom, even as He delivered them from slavery to freedom. The purpose of the laws governing interest, and the purpose of the whole law, is man's freedom under God. To speak of deliverance from the law is to speak of deliverance from freedom. The law cannot be freedom to the sinner, but rather a sentence of death for his failure to keep it. The law-breaker is a man in slavery to his sin, a man unable to live in terms of freedom. The law therefore is a continual indictment and a death sentence to him, in that it underscores his impotence and his inability to rule himself: "what I hate, that I do" (Rom. 7:15). To the redeemed, however, the law is the way of freedom.

Seventh, the pledge was, as we have seen, a pawn or deposit as security for a debt. Certain kinds of pledges were forbidden:

No man shall take the mill or the upper millstone to pledge; for he taketh a man's life to pledge (Deut. 24:6).

Thou shalt not wrest the justice due to the sojourner, or to the fatherless, nor take the widow's raiment to pledge; but thou shalt remember that thou wast a bondman in Egypt, and Jehovah thy God redeemed thee thence; therefore I command thee to do this thing (Deut. 24:17, 18).

When thou dost lend thy neighbor any manner of loan, thou shalt not go into his house to fetch his pledge. Thou shalt stand without, and the man to whom thou dost lend shall bring forth the pledge without unto thee. And if he be a poor man, thou shalt not sleep with his pledge; thou shalt surely restore to him the pledge when the sun goeth down, that he may sleep in his garment and bless thee: and it shall be righteousness unto thee before Jehovah thy God (Deut. 24:10-13).

That the reference in Deuteronomy 24:10-13 is essentially to workers serving a wealthy fellow believer appears in the passage immediately following, Deuteronomy 24:14-16. A pawn or pledge cannot involve anything necessary to a man's work or living, for to do so would be to endanger the man's "life," i.e., his freedom. Moreover, the dignity of the borrower cannot be broken or harmed; the "widow's raiment" cannot be taken from her, nor can a creditor enter a man's home to choose the pawn or pledge. Even a poor man's home has a sanctity which a creditor cannot challenge. "A man's house is his castle." The source of this principle is Deuteronomy 24:10-13. The dignity of the borrower cannot be infringed by the man making the loan, whether with or without interest. The horror for degrading pawns is expressed in Job 24:9, 10.

There is, however, an analogous obligation on the part of the borrower. No man has the right to risk those things which are basic to his life and liberty, nor to borrow on those things, even if someone is ready to make the loan. The cloak of the poor workman, his sleeping garment, is as much as a man can pledge, and even then only for the day-time hours. The widow's cloak cannot be pledged.

Eighth, failure to restore a pledge or pawn when repayment is made is robbery, and it is linked to pagan worship, adultery, theft, and murder, as is also exacting usury of a poor fellow believer. This appears clearly in Ezekiel 18:10-13:

If he beget a son that is a robber, a shedder of blood, and that doeth any one of these things, and that doeth not any of these duties, but even hath eaten upon the mountains, and defiled his neighbor's wife, hath wronged the poor and needy, hath taken by robbery, hath not restored the pledge, and hath lifted up his eyes to the idols, hath committed abomination, hath given forth upon interest, and hath taken increase: shall he then live? He shall not live: he hath done all these abominations; he shall surely die; his blood shall be upon him.

Ezekiel had in mind here the coming fall of Jerusalem, but he still cited God's basic judgment on all who fail to restore a pawn.

The law here has been subjected to extensive attack by socialism and every form of totalitarianism. Statism assumes that its law rather than God's regenerating power is the principle of freedom. As a result, it legislates against Biblical law. Modern "civil liberty" and "civil rights" legislation requires an equalizing of all men, so that an employer cannot hire or favor his fellow believers in distinction from unbelievers. The end result is the enslavement to the state of all men; the need for charity remains, but the state now makes itself the source of charity and the judge as to who shall receive it. An impersonal and political test replaces the test of faith.

7. Responsibility

An important aspect of Biblical law is its doctrine of responsibility. In a law previously considered, Exodus 21:28-32, it was established that animals are responsible for their actions, and an ox goring a person was sentenced to death. Animals are clearly held to be accountable. But responsibility also rests with the owner of the ox: if the ox's previous behavior indicated that it was a dangerous animal, and the owner "hath not kept him in," then the owner is also responsible. *Responsibility is thus not a one-way street.* Both owner and animal have a responsibility. This being case law, the reference is to the ox, and to more than an ox, as St. Paul made clear with respect to the law concerning the muzzling of an ox treading out grain (Deut. 25:4; I Cor. 9:9; I Tim. 5:18).

In terms of this, certain observations can be made. *First,* a parent is responsible for a child if nothing is done to curb, punish, or bring to judgment an irresponsible or delinquent child. If a man is responsible for the actions of an ox, he is certainly responsible for the actions of a delinquent son, if he "hath not kept him," if no attempt has been made to prevent the son from giving vent to his delinquency.

Second, the responsibility of the parent does not absolve the child of his responsibility. The goring ox is always guilty; the owner is only guilty if his negligence can be proven. The prior responsibility is always that of the acting party. The owner or parent can be an accessory to the crime only if he has been delinquent in his responsibility.

Third, transgression beyond a certain point ends responsibility. Thus, in the law of the delinquent son (Deut. 21:18-21), the parents' responsibility to provide for and protect their son ended with the son's delinquency; their duty and their moral responsibility then became denunciation of and separation from their son.

As previously noted, responsibility is not a one-way street. The responsibility of parents for a child ends when that child refuses to submit to the godly authority and discipline of the parents.

The same is true of the responsibility of children for their parents. Again, it is not a one-way street. To cite illustrations which will throw some light on this problem: A daughter assumed responsibility for her sick father when the brothers rejected their responsibility. As a devout Christian, she felt duty-bound to care for her father, who remained in her home as an invalid until death. During the more than ten years in her home, the father was a bed patient much of the time. Because he was only interested in the sons and grandsons who would carry on his name, he treated his daughter and her family as non-entities or at best as servants, with never a word of gratitude. He made out his will in favor of his sons and their sons, although his sons were both prosperous. He gave lavish gifts at holidays to his sons and their sons, and never a gift nor a thanks to his daughter and her family. Clearly, the daughter's interpretation of the law was faulty. As surely as an ungodly son must be cast out and turned over for judgment, so an ungodly father (for his *conduct* revealed him to be such) had no place in her home, having denied plainly any responsibility to it.

Another illustration: a mother, a militant liberal or modernist in religion, made her home with her daughter and son-in-law, both devout, orthodox believers. The mother regarded the family's faith, church, and family worship with contempt, belittled it to her grandchildren and daily ridiculed her daughter for her "ignorant, reactionary" faith. Having denied openly the authority of her son-in-law, and having denied the faith of the family, she had forfeited any right to its care and protection. The family's patient suffering was not godly. Because responsibility is a two-way street, the mother had the duty to respect the family's faith, her son-in-law's authority, and her daughter's devotion.

Other illustrations can be added: a daughter was expected by her parents to remain unmarried and to care for them. Lacking friends because of their bad character, they demanded that she include them in all her social activities. The result was that the girl lost all her friends because of her parents. From start to finish, the relationship was lawless, and the daughter's sense of responsibility was misguided.

Another instance: a mother felt duty-bound to use her meager funds to help her only child, an ungrateful man whose income was good and whose sense of responsibility was very bad. The mother limited herself severely to provide him the luxuries he demanded as necessary to maintain a pretended social position. Again, the relationship was lawless on both sides and required breaking.

An Ann Landers column gives the letter of a girl reporting on a family problem. A 20-year-old paralyzed brother in a wheel-chair, angry at life for his condition, treats his parents and sisters with hateful contempt and rage. The family, sick at heart, dances to his whims.[1] No one, sick or healthy, has any right to behave so without judgment. Many paralyzed people have trained themselves into useful work. This youth has no right to eat food he does not deserve and is ungrateful for.

Thus, we may say that, not only does transgression beyond a certain point end responsibility, but *fourth,* if responsibility is maintained beyond that point it becomes a *robbery.* Where a juvenile delinquent is tolerated or protected, or a lawless parent allowed to be an affront to the family's faith and authority, the other members of the family are robbed of their due. Unconditional honor and service are due to God alone, not to man. St. Paul's admonition is "Render therefore to all their dues: tribute to whom tribute is due, custom to whom custom; fear to whom fear; honour to whom honour" (Rom. 13:7). *No relationship between man and man can be absolutized. We have no absolute bond which ties us unconditionally to any man, either to obey or to love him.* Marriage is dissolved by certain transgressions. The parent's duty to the child is nullified by his incorrigible conduct. The child's duty to the parent is limited by his prior obedience to God and the maintainence of God's law-order. In every human relationship, the only absolute is God's law, not man's relationship.

Fifth, not only does the absolutizing of a human relationship involve theft, in that the indulgence of a delinquent family or society member is the robbing of another, but it also involves theft God-ward as well as man-ward. *It is an infraction of God's order to indulge evil.* It involves robbing one person of his due in order to reward or indulge another, and this means also the violation of God's order to continue man's disorder.

To repeat again, responsibility is not a one-way street. If the ox, an animal of limited intelligence, is accountable for his acts, then every man in his station is also responsible. In every relationship, there is responsibility on every side by every person.

Modern man is hostile to responsibility; he replaces responsibility with sensitivity, sensitivity being defined as awareness of humanity. Thus, a rebellious nun of the Immaculate Heart of Mary Sisters defies authority and declares, "These men (church officials) have no right to make a judgment when they don't know us."[2] This nun had entered an order requiring authority but had refused to submit to it. Her freedom to leave and establish her own way of life was not in question.

---

1. Los Angeles *Herald-Examiner,* Tuesday, November 25, 1969, p. A-15, Ann Landers Column.
2. Terrence Shea "A Community Divided. Dissident Nuns Now Face A Bigger Split—With Rome Itself," *The National Observer,* Monday, November 17, 1969, p. 14.

She denied the principle of any responsibility beyond that which she owed to herself. Similarly, an actor, Steve McQueen, complained about the views of Midwestern farmers, adding, "When they understand that black people make love, and they make it good, then we'll be on our way. We've got to learn to live together."[3] For McQueen, the fact of being human, of belonging to a species, is the only criterion for judgment; responsibility, morality, have nothing to do with man. It is the Midwestern farmer's moral perspective and insistence on responsibility which McQueen condemns. For such a man, there is no meaning to life; hence, no moral criterion can be applied to it. Asked about his future, McQueen said, "with a shrug," that "I'll make mistakes—The main thing—(Then he stopped, sharp, and shook his head). No, there is no main thing."[4] In a world of brute factuality, all facts are equally important, and equally meaningless, and there can be "no main thing." It is a world, therefore, without responsibility. But a world without responsibility is a world of the dead.

8. Stealing Freedom

Thus far our analysis of the eighth law-word has dealt essentially with matters pertaining to property and restitution. Certain modern German scholars, by no means orthodox, have pointed out that the eighth commandment has primary reference to something other than property. Thus, Noth, commenting on Exodus 20:15, wrote:

> In the commandment against stealing the unnamed object is not so clear as in the two preceding commandments. The position of this commandment among a group of commandments which are concerned with the person of the "neighbour," and the difference in content which is to be assumed between this commandment and the last in the Decalogue suggests that, as elsewhere when this particular verb occurs, a human object is imagined (cf. e.g. Gen. 40:15). It probably therefore has in mind the loss of freedom, particularly of free Israelites; it is forbidden to enslave free Israelites by force whether it be for one's own use or to sell to another.[1]

Von Rad's observation on Deuteronomy 5:19 is even more explicit:

> It is today regarded as certain that the prohibition of stealing referred originally to the kidnapping of a free person (Ex. 21:16; Deut. 24:7).[2]

There is more than a little merit to this conclusion. Commandments six through ten are concerned with man's relationship to man; they are personal. The eighth commandment can thus be expanded to read,

---

3. John Hallowell, "McQueen," Los Angeles *Times,* November 23, 1969, p. 36.
4. *Ibid.*
1. Martin Noth: *Exodus, A Commentary* (Philadelphia: Westminster Press [1959], 1962), p. 165 f.
2. Gerhard von Rad: *Deuteronomy, A Commentary* (Philadelphia: Westminster Press [1964], 1966), p. 59.

"Thou shalt not steal another man's freedom by forcibly enslaving his person or his property." The purpose of man's existence is that man should exercise dominion over the earth in terms of God's calling. This duty involves the restoration of a broken order by means of restitution. To kidnap a man and enslave him is to rob him of his freedom. A believer is not to be a slave (I Cor. 7:23; Gal. 5:1). Some men are slaves by nature; slavery was voluntary, and a dissatisfied slave could leave, and he could not be compelled to return, and other men were forbidden to deliver him to his master (Deut. 23:15, 16). This implied some liberty on the part of slaves, and a duty of just treatment by their masters. Ben Sirach confirms this, speaking of both the duty of the master to correct and discipline his slaves, and also to be just towards them, and to avoid defrauding them of their liberty (Ecclesiasticus 42:1, 5; 7:21; 33:24-28). This is also confirmed by St. Paul: "Masters, give unto your servants that which is just and equal; knowing that ye also have a Master in heaven" (Col. 4:1).

The purpose of freedom is that man exercise dominion and subdue the earth under God. A man who abuses his freedom to steal can be sold into slavery in order to work out his restitution (Ex. 22:3); if he cannot use his freedom for its true purpose, godly dominion, reconstruction, and restoration, he must then work towards restitution in his bondage.

Kidnapping was punished by death. Its purpose was usually to sell a person as a slave in another country, where forcible slavery was the rule. In any case, whatever the purpose of kidnapping, this theft of a man's freedom was punished by death. The law specifically calls the kidnapper a *thief:*

> And he that stealeth a man, and selleth him, or if he be found in his hand, he shall surely be put to death (Ex. 21:16).

> If a man be found stealing any of his brethren of the children of Israel, and maketh merchandise of him, or selleth him; then that thief shall die; and thou shalt put evil away from among you (Deut. 24:7).

Certain things clearly appear in these two laws. *First,* Exodus 21:16 forbad the kidnapping of any man, whether Israelite or foreigner, whereas Deuteronomy 24:7 forbad the kidnapping of Israelites. The kidnapped Israelite would almost surely be sold abroad, and this second crime would be more difficult to detect, since care would be taken to put some distance between the enforced slave's new home and his homeland, lest the slave as a runaway expose the kidnappers.

Second, the selling of slaves was forbidden. Since Israelites were voluntary slaves, and since not even a foreign slave could be compelled to return to his master (Deut. 23:15, 16), slavery was on a different basis under the law than in non-Biblical cultures. The slave was a member of the household, with rights therein. A slave-market could not exist in Israel. The slave who was working out a restitution for theft had no incentive to escape, for to do so would make him an incorrigible criminal and liable to death.

Third, the death penalty is mandatory for kidnapping. No discretion is allowed the court. To rob a man of his freedom requires death. The law does not have reference to wartime captives, however.

Fourth, Deuteronomy 24:7 forbids stealing a man by anyone who "maketh merchandise of him, or selleth him." The ARV mg reading is "chattel" for "merchandise," and *Young's Literal Translation* reads "hath tyrannized over him." The meaning is cruelty, or cruel dealing; it refers to a depersonalized, brutal treatment of a man. Man must be treated as a man at all times; the penalties he suffers must be deserved penalties as a man, not penalties intended to degrade or destroy him as a man. The woman war captive had very specific rights under the law (Deut. 21:10-14); this relationship is strictly circumscribed by law as are all other relationships.

Rylaarsdam states that the Code of Hammurabi had a similar protection against kidnapping.[3] This is not entirely correct. The exact reading of the law, in the Code of Hammurabi 14, is "If a man has stolen the minor child of another man, he shall be killed." This is radically different from the Biblical law, in that only a child is protected. Moreover, compulsory slavery was legal in the Code of Hammurabi, and "Helping another's slave to escape or harboring a fugitive slave was punishable by death (15-16)."[4] Moreover, as Gordon pointed out, in Hammurabi's law "the entire population is theoretically in slavery to the king."[5]

To return to the interpretation of theft as, essentially, the robbing of a man's freedom: false weights and measures, fraudulent money, and the destruction, impairment or theft of property all diminish or destroy a man's freedom. Property is basic to man's freedom. A tyrannical state always limits a man's use of his property, taxes it, or confiscates that property as an effective means of enslaving a man without necessarily touching his person. The interpretation of Noth and von Rad, instead of altering the traditional interpretations of the eighth commandment rather reinforce them, in that theft is seen as more than the lawless seizure or destruction of property: it is at the same time an assault on a man's freedom.

---

3. Rylaarsdam, "Exodus," *Interpreter's Bible,* I, 998.
4. Cyrus H. Gordon: *Hammurabi's Code, Quaint or Forward-Looking?* (New York: Holt, Rinehart and Winston, 1960), p. 5.
5. *Ibid.,* p. 11.

Neither the state nor any individual has any right to transgress this law.

The state does transgress this law not only by acts of confiscation, manipulation of money, and by taxation, but also by any and every undercutting of Biblical faith and education. State supported and controlled education is theft, not only in its taxation plan, but also by virtue of its destruction of public character, so that a godly society is turned into a thieves' market. The 1860's in the United States saw a decline of Christian faith, a rise of statist education, and the birth of social Darwinism. On Wall Street, Drew, Fiske, Gould and other men manipulated the market and corporations with radical contempt for morality. All the same, there was then still enough Biblical morality in the people at large to make possible some surprising evidences of public character. It should be remembered too that, at this time, New York City represented a radically lower moral standard than other settled areas of the United States and was widely regarded as another Sodom. All the same, Sobel reports, on the public morality of the day on Wall Street, in the 1860's.

> This type of integrity might be illustrated by noting that the rob-beries of gold which had led to the formation of the Exchange Bank came to an end, and the honor of the Street returned. By the late 1860s gold was transported openly, carried by messengers in heavy canvas bags. From time to time one of the bags would burst, and its contents—usually $5,000 in coin—would scatter in the street. The custom on these occasions was for a crowd to form a circle around the area, not moving until the messenger had picked up all the coins. Anyone who stooped to take a gold piece would receive a boot in the rear.[6]

The problems of law and order in 19th-century New York were serious, unusual, and critical. But, because of a national basis of char-acter, a measure of public integrity could be established, as this incident witnesses. The same would not be true today. It would be impossible to carry sacks of gold openly and regularly on Wall Street or elsewhere, and a broken bag would be usually beyond recovery.

This loss of public character robs every godly man of considerable peace and security. This theft is chargeable against the state and its anti-Christian schools.

During the law-abiding time of Israel's history, houses lacked doors. A curtain was hung in place of a door. Pagan dwellings in surrounding areas had heavy doors, sometimes of stone, carefully fitted into the stone wall, as a necessary protection against other men. This difference, discovered by archeological work, is a striking one. When morality

---

6. Robert Sobel: *Panic on Wall Street, A History of America's Financial Dissenters* (New York: Macmillan, 1968), p. 116.

was prevalent, men at peace with their neighbors, and the law obeyed and enforced, the purpose of a door was merely to insure privacy, and a curtain, in a moderate climate, was sufficient. In lawless neighboring countries, stone doors were required, and men lived as prisoners within their own homes, in effect besieged by a lawless world.

The same lawless siege-living condition again prevails. By their destruction of godly education and of Biblical law, the nations have robbed their people of freedom, and the people, by their apostasy, have denied themselves freedom. The psalmist long ago observed, of those who attempt to build up a city and to safeguard it without God, that,

> Except the LORD build the house, they labour in vain that build it: except the LORD keep the city, the watchman waketh but in vain (Ps. 127:1).

To return again to the definition of theft as the stealing of freedom, the implication is clearly that property is freedom. A man is free if his person and his possessions are under his control. To the degree that his person is free, and to the degree that he has property free of hindrances, to that degree a man is free. The old word *freeman* has as one of its older meanings the member of a corporation, a property owner. The same is true of the word *freeholder*. The restriction of suffrage to property owners had as its basis in part the restriction of the vote to freemen.

9. Landmark and Land

The law with respect to landmarks has already been considered with respect to its meaning in matters of social inheritance. This meaning has long been a familiar one, common among the church fathers and schoolmen. Luther remarked, "That landmarks are not to be moved from where they have been placed by the former dwellers means that we are to add nothing to the doctrine transmitted by the apostles, as though one could give better advice in matters of conscience."[1] The primary meaning of the law, however, has reference to land:

> Thou shalt not remove thy neighbour's land mark, which they of old time have set in thine inheritance, which thou shalt inherit in the land that the Lord thy God giveth thee to possess it (Deut. 19:14).

The law is cited also in Deuteronomy 27:17, Proverbs 22:28; 23:10; Job 24:2.

This law appears also in other ancient law codes. In Rome, removal of the landmarks was punishable by death. According to Calvin,

> . . . for that every one's property may be secure, it is necessary that

---

1.　Luther: *Deuteronomy,* p. 198.

the land-marks set up for the division of fields should remain untouched, as if they were sacred. He who fraudulently removes a landmark is already convicted by this very act, because he disturbs the lawful owner in his quiet possession of the land; whilst he who advances further the boundaries of his own land to his neighbour's loss, doubles the crime by the deceptive concealment of his theft. Whence also we gather that not only are those thieves, who actually carry away their neighbour's property, who take his money out of his chest, or who pillage his cellars and granaries, but also those who unjustly possess themselves of his land.[2]

Calvin's point is a valid one: the deceit of the act makes it *a double crime.* It is both theft and false witness. Because the law is a unit, the violation of one law is a violation of the whole law. As St. James summarized it, "For whosoever shall keep the whole law, and yet offend in one point, he is guilty of all" (James 2:10). Thus, this crime involves violation of the eighth and ninth commandments, and also the tenth, coveting our neighbor's land. Crimes against the land can also involve the fourth commandment, the sabbath law, and the sixth, "Thou shalt not kill."

Land laws are an important aspect of the Biblical legislation. The Talmud comments on these laws at length. The land, the rabbis noted, remained holy unto the Lord ("For mine is the land," Lev. 25:23) even in the hands of the heathen; hence, the heathen are accountable to God for the care of the land and for the tithe.[3] The reason for the sabbatical year, according to R. Abbahu, is that "The Holy One, blessed be He, said to Israel, sow your seed six years but omit the seventh, that ye may know that the earth is mine."[4] Of particular interest is the comment of R. Eleazar:

> R. Eleazar said: Any man who has no wife is no proper man; for it is said, *Male and female created He them and called their name Adam.*
>
> R. Eleazar further stated: Any man who owns no land is not a proper man, for it is said, *The heavens are the heavens of the Lord; but the earth hath he given to the children of men.*[5]

Since man's calling is to exercise dominion, the rabbis recognized that the two basic areas for the exercise of dominion are in the family and in relation to the earth; man's duty here is binding on all men.

The land laws required a sabbath rest for the land (Ex. 23:10-11; Lev. 25:1-11). The true meaning of the sabbath is rest, rather than worship, and a rest due to the land itself for the revitalizing of the

---

2. Calvin *Commentaries on the Four Last Books of Moses,* III, 121.
3. *Gittin,* 47a; p. 208; *Kiddushin,* 38b; p. 188.
4. *Sanhedrin,* 39a; p. 250.
5. *Yebamoth,* 62b-63a; p. 419.

earth. To deny a sabbath to the land is to defraud the land and to rob it of its due. Bonar commented on this law that "It has been well said that by the weekly Sabbath they owned that they themselves belonged to Jehovah, and by this seventh-year Sabbath they professed that the land was His, and they His tenants."[6]

At the heart of the land law is the declaration, "The land shall not be sold for ever: for the land is mine; for ye are strangers and sojourners with me" (Lev. 25:23). This law sounds especially strange in modern ears, for farm land has become, especially in North America, an area for speculative buying and selling, and the changes of ownership in some areas are very many. In most of the world, land has been and is still regarded as an inalienable family possession. Perhaps the most important resistance to communism and the communist empire has come, not from foreign countries, but from the long-suffering and stubbornly resisting peasants. The sale of land, and the confiscation of land, these are things the peasant refuses to accept: land is an inheritance which cannot be alienated. The peasant parties of the various European countries have been responsible groups and their leaders superior politicians and statesmen. Significantly, the International Peasant Union, with its stubborn resistance to the Soviet Empire, has as its emblem a green flag, the color of budding crops and of hope.[7]

It is important therefore to analyze carefully the meaning, of Leviticus 25:23-28, and then its significance for our times. *First,* the general rule is that "the land shall not be sold forever," or literally, "to annihilation, i.e., so as to vanish away from, or be for ever lost to, the seller."[8] Sales were in effect leases, because no man had the right to alienate the Lord's land.

Second, if a man became poor and "sold" his farm, his kinsman could redeem the land and restore it at once to him (Lev. 25:25, 48, 49).

Third, if the owner had no relatives able to redeem the land for him, and he earned enough to do it himself, he could calculate the years remaining until the jubilee year and pay off the buyer for the years of his lease which still remained (Lev. 25:26, 27).

Fourth, if the owner had no money to buy back the land, it would still revert to him after the seven sabbath years, in the jubilee (Lev. 25:28).

Fifth, God made it clear that the Israelites were "strangers and sojourners" in their own land; God being the owner, their status was

6. Bonar: *Leviticus,* p. 446.
7. Henry C. Wolfe, "Peasants vs. Communism," *Christian Economics,* vol. XXI, no. 21, (November 11, 1969), pp. 1, 3.
8. Keil and Delitzsch: *The Pentateuch,* II, 461.

similar to that of their stay in Egypt; they were there at the suffrance of the Lord and on His terms.

Sixth, town houses could be permanently alienated or sold, once the purchase was completed. Being built by men, these properties could be freely transferred (Lev. 25:29-34).

Seventh, it was apparently possible to sell the land permanently if the sale were to a family member, if Jeremiah 32:7, 8 is any indication.

Ginsburg gives an important insight into the meaning of this law in his comment on Leviticus 25:23:

> God has not only helped the Israelites to conquer the land of Canaan, but has selected it as His own dwelling-place, and erected His sanctuary in the midst of it (Ex. xv. 13; Num. xxxv. 34). He therefore is enthroned in it as Lord of the soil, and the Israelites are simply His tenants at will (chaps. xiv. 34, xx. 24, xxiii. 10; Num. xiii, 2; xv. 2), and as such will have to quit it if they disobey His commandments (chapts. xviii. 28, xx. 22, xxvi. 33; Deut. xxviii. 63). For this reason they are accounted as strangers and sojourners, and hence have no right absolutely to sell that which is not theirs.[9]

Because the tabernacle and then the temple had the Holy of Holies, God's throne, the seat of His visible government of Israel, the land of Israel had a particular fixity required by law. God as its landlord alloted it to the various tribes, and he required that a stable character be given to the land by an unchanging family ownership of rural land. This act alone gave to Israel a rural conservatism comparable to that of peasant Europe.

The important question for us is the present status of this law. Does it still have the same binding force? If so, how shall it be applied, and, if not, does any significance remain to the law?

It would appear that the binding force of this law had reference to the rural lands of the original allotment to the twelve tribes. The Tribe of Dan later acquired a northern territory by conquest (Judges 18), and we are not given any indication that the same law of the land applied to the new territory, which began almost as a territory outside the law. There is no evidence later that the Jews in dispersion felt that this law was mandatory outside of Israel, although the same loyalty to the land remained. The inalienability of the land was thus a characteristic of the Throne area. A comparable concept on a lesser scale is the modern Vatican State, owned by the Vatican entirely and hence not on the market for sale. The Holy Land was God's Throne area, and hence not for sale.

On the other hand, God's ownership of the whole earth is basic to

---

9. C. D. Ginsburg, "Leviticus," in Ellicott, I, 456.

Biblical law, so that the Throne rights extend very clearly to every part of the earth. The Throne, however, is now in heaven, which has in full the *unchanging status* once required of Canaan. Obviously, therefore, land can now be sold.

Just as obviously, God does intend that land laws give a stability to society. The absence of any land and property tax in Biblical law very definitely protects enduring ownership, whereas modern tax laws destroy ownership. To cite an example, in one city, a lovely area of very superior homes, from ten to twenty rooms, some of stone construction, became, in about 25 years, so heavily taxed, that the homes either had to be torn down to make way for apartments, or sold for use as dormitories. The ownership of these homes was made prohibitive to impossible by means of taxes.

In another area, taxes led to the deterioriation of the area, as people moved out and homes were made into multiple dwellings. Taxes then went down, and others moved in, so that a 90 percent change in population occurred in less than ten years. People who had built there, expecting to remain for life, lost heavily. Taxation of property is a means of destroying property and is a form of robbery.

Taxation makes for the speculative use of land, and it destroys the stability of communities. There is a marked hostility today to the development and preservation of communities by religious and ethnic groups, and such hostility leads to the destruction of property. The destruction of the Boston West End Italian community by urban redevelopment and "slum clearance" has been ably described by H. J. Gans. A family centered society, extensively policing and disciplining itself, was broken up by a "slum clearance" project, because the area was coveted by planners. Both the taxing power, and the eminent domain exercised, are anti-Biblical.[10]

Eminent domain is a divine right. It belongs to God alone. The "right" of the state to eminent domain has no place in Biblical law.[11] The state has a duty to protect man and his property, but not to tax or to confiscate it.

To summarize the Biblical tax laws in relationship to the ownership of land, the basic tax was the poll or head tax (Ex. 30:11-16), which had to be the same for all men. It was paid by men only, all men of age twenty and over. This tax was collected by the civil authority for the maintainance of the civil order, to provide all men with a covering or atonement of civil justice.

---

10. For an account of the Boston West End, see Herbert J. Gans: *The Urban Villagers* (New York: The Free Press of Glencoe, 1962).
11. See R. J. Rushdoony: *The Politics of Guilt and Pity*, chap. on "Eminent Domain" (The Craig Press, Nutley, N.J., 1970).

The tithe met the general religious and social needs of the community, education, welfare, and the like.

There was thus no land tax or property tax. Since "the earth is the LORD'S and the fullness thereof" (Ex. 9:29, etc.), a land tax usurps God's rights and is unlawful. The purpose of Biblical law with reference to land is to ensure the security of man in his property; a property tax of any kind is a denial of this God-ordained security.

10. The Virgin Birth and Property

The strong vein of Manichaeanism in the church has led it to disregard the material world for the world of the spirit, or, in the case of the modernists, to choose the material order as against the spiritual. Those who disregard the material world become antinomians; the gospel for them has no law for the material world, because that world must perish and must be renounced. The mandate to subdue the earth, the promises concerning a restored creation, and, at the end, of a resurrection body, are not taken seriously. The world and the flesh are linked with the devil as an unholy trinity.

The modernists affirm the world of matter and renounce the law for a like reason. The two alien worlds of spirit and matter cannot, according to Manichaean theology, be linked. The material world is therefore its own source of law, and the consequence is a social gospel, a gospel derived from society rather than God, and a situation ethics, a morality governed by the existential, material moment.

The modernist turns the birth narratives of Jesus Christ into a myth; the evangelicals convert the history into a sweet, other-worldly tale. The reality of that history is totally anti-Manichaean and totally relevant to time and eternity. The Manichaean mind has so extensively infected the Western world that to write or speak of "The Virgin Birth and Property" comes as a shock: the twain should never meet.

The annunciation (Luke 1:26-38) declared that Jesus would be given "the throne of his father David: And he shall reign over the house of Jacob for ever; and of his kingdom there shall be no end" (Luke 1:32, 33). At this point, churchmen hasten to tell us that this throne and kingdom are spiritual and have no reference to this world, except insofar as men are saved and enter the ark of the church. That the meaning includes a spiritual and an eternal frame of reference can be fully granted, and must be. But there is no ground for the exclusion of a reference to time and history. Plainly, Jesus Christ shall be lord and sovereign of the nations in terms of messianic prophecy. He comes to reclaim His realm, His property, as sovereign lord.

Mary clearly so understood it, as the Magnificat makes clear (Luke 1:45-56). The Magnificat is simply a joyful recital of Old Testament

prophecies on the subject. It is, in fact, "almost wholly made up of
Old Testament quotations."[1]

The Virgin Mary celebrated "the mighty reversal of things which in
principle has already been accomplished by the entrance of God upon
the course of history and in the life of mankind, through the coming
Messiah, her promised Son."[2] This "mighty reversal of things" is the
over-turning of the dominion of sin over man and history. It is the
mighty re-ordering of all things under the dominion of the King, Jesus
the Messiah, because God's "mercy is on them that fear him from
generation to generation" (Luke 1:50):

> He hath shewed strength with his arm; he hath scattered the proud
> in the imagination of their hearts.
> He hath put down the mighty from their seats, and exalted them of
> low degree.
> He hath filled the hungry with good things; and the rich he hath
> sent empty away.
> He hath holpen his servant Israel, in remembrance of his mercy;
> As he spake to our fathers, to Abraham, and to his seed for ever
> (Luke 1:51-55).

Very obviously, Mary meant that history would see a mighty reversal
of things because of her Son's birth. By His strength, the vain imaginations of men would be confounded. The mighty would be dethroned,
and the blessed meek of the Lord exalted. The hungry people of God
would be filled, and the rich sinners would be cast out to beg. All this
would be in fulfilment of the prophecies to patriarchs and prophets that,
through the seed of Abraham and of David, the Israel of God would
possess the whole material earth.

To say that Mary believed this, but that a "spiritual" fulfilment was
instead intended by God, is to trifle with Scripture. The plain meaning
of Mary is unmistakable. If her words can be spiritualized into a
non-material fulfilment, then the creation narrative and the reports of
the virgin birth can also be spiritualized into a non-material fulfilment.
Either Scripture means what it says, or it means nothing.

Obviously then, a very real and material fulfilment is the only valid
meaning here. Very generally, then, this meaning is as follows: *First,*
the earth is the property of Jesus Christ, because He is the messianic
King, the very Son of God as well as the royal Son of David.

Second, this King has the right of eminent domain and can do as He
pleases with His property. He can turn out the ungodly and give the
kingdom to those who obey Him. As Jesus declared, "Therefore I say
unto you, The kingdom of God shall be taken from you, and given to

---

1. Norval Geldenhuys: *Commentary on the Gospel of Luke* (Grand Rapids:
Eerdmans, 1951), p. 84.
2. *Ibid.,* p. 86.

a nation bringing forth the fruit thereof" (Matt. 21:43). The purpose of His coming is to dispossess the present world leadership and to give His domain to His people.

Third, this means that the people of God must expect His kingdom, enforce its laws, and be faithful to the creation mandate to subdue the earth and to exercise dominion over it (Gen. 1:26-28).

Fourth, "Through the Messiah, God will dethrone all enemies."[3] This plainly means total victory. The Magnificat clearly prophesies the total victory of Jesus Christ and the uprooting of the kingdom of man. The ungodly will be openly confounded and turned out, and the people of God equally openly brought to power and victory. Israel, the covenant people of God, shall be established in full power. It will not do to say, as did Lenski,

> "And Mary said" hints at no divine inspiration; neither this nor revelation were needed for the contents of this hymn. Unlike that of Elisabeth, it contains no prophecy and no proof of knowledge that is supernaturally communicated. Elisabeth's hymn is directed to Mary, and properly so; Mary's to God, and again most properly. Elisabeth's is a continuation of Gabriel's address to Mary, Mary's a continuation and an expression of her brief reply to Gabriel. While Mary's is most beautiful in phrase and form it is on a lower level than Elisabeth's.[4]

As against Lenski, the Magnificat very clearly does contain and is prophecy. Moreover, it restates Old Testament prophecy. If only that which is labelled inspired in the Bible is actually inspired, then many a prophecy must be demoted. Mary prophesied; either she was not inspired and was merely extravagant and emotional, or else she clearly prophesied in the Spirit of God. The annunciation (Luke 1:26-35) clearly indicates that more than the womb of Mary was set apart by God for His holy purpose, and it does violence to Scripture, to limit the workings of God to Mary's womb. The fact that Lenski added, after the above statement, that "Mary herself furnishes no cause for Mariolatry" makes clear his purpose, to under-rate Mary. It is not Mariolatry to do justice to Scripture.

Fifth, the law, "Thou shalt not steal," means also that man cannot rob God of His prerogatives, nor of His property. God casts the thieves out of His vineyard (Matt. 21:33-44) and grinds to powder His enemies.

The virgin birth therefore is the confirmation of God's law and an emphatic assertion of God's property rights *over man* and the earth. This miracle sounds the note of victory and restoration.

---

3. William F. Arndt: *The Gospel According to St. Luke* (Saint Louis: Concordia, 1956), p. 60.
4. R. C. H. Lenski: *The Interpretation of St. Luke's Gospel* (Columbus, Ohio: Wartburg Press, 1948), p. 84.

11. Fraud

According to Leviticus 19:13, "Thou shalt not defraud thy neighbour, neither rob him: the wages of him that is hired shall not abide with thee all night until morning." Ginsburg noted,

> Here oppression by fraud and oppression by violence are forbidden. It is probably in allusion to this passage that John the Baptist warned the soldiers who came to him: "And he said to them, Do violence to no man, neither accuse any falsely: and be content with your wage" (Luke iii. 14).

> From the declaration in the next clause, which forbids the retention of the wages over night, it is evident that the day labourer is here spoken of, as he is dependent upon his wages for the support of himself and his family; the Law protects him by enjoining that the earnings of the hireling should be promptly paid. This benign care for the labourer, and the denunciation against any attempt to defraud him, are again and again repeated in the Scriptures (Deut. xxiv. 14, 15; Jer. xxii. 13; Mal. iii. 5; James v. 4). Hence the humane interpretation which obtained of this law during the second Temple: "He who treats a hireling with harshness sins as grievously as if he hath taken away life, and transgresses five precepts."[1]

According to Clarkson, the law requires "integrity in daily transactions" and honesty:

> "Ye shall not steal, neither deal falsely" (v. 11). "Thou shalt not defraud thy neighbour, neither rob him" (ver. 13; see vers. 35, 36). Nothing could be more explicit than this, nothing more comprehensive in suggestion. No member of the Hebrew commonwealth could (1) deliberately appropriate what he knew was not his own, or (2) rob his neighbour in the act of trading, or (3) deal falsely or unrighteously in any transaction or in any relation, without consciously breaking the Law and coming under the displeasure of Jehovah. The words of the Law are clear and strong, going straight to the understanding and to the conscience. Every man amongst them must have known, as every one amongst us knows well, that dishonesty is sin in the sight of God.[2]

Calvin stated that the force of this law is to prohibit "all unjust oppression," any seizure of the goods of another.[3] Frederic Gardiner stated that Leviticus 19:13 "deals with faults of power, 'the conversion of might into right.' The particulars mentioned are oppression (comp. xxv. 17-43), robbing, and undue retention of wages. The last is spoken of more at length (Deut. xxiv. 14, 15. Comp. James v. 4)."[4]

---

1. C. D. Ginsburg, "Leviticus," in Ellicott, I, 423.
2. W. Clarkson, in Spence and Exell: *The Pulpit Commentary, Leviticus* (R. Collins, A. Cave, F. Mayrick), (New York: Funk & Wagnalls), p. 300.
3. Calvin: *Commentary on the Four Last Books of Moses*, III, 112.
4. Frederic Gardiner, "Leviticus," in John Peter Lange: *Exodus-Leviticus*, p. 150.

Gardiner brings us to the heart of this law. We have here a variation of the law against theft which is particularly directed against abuses of power, against oppression. Wages are to be paid promptly, at the specified and contracted time. In antiquity, payment was by the day; this meant that payment had to be made at the end of the working day, not the next morning. Failure to pay at the required time was thus a criminal act: it was theft.

This point is an important one. Many of the goals sought by modern liberals are a part of the Mosaic law, but with a significant difference. Biblical law required the just treatment of the laborer; it forbad fraud in foods, measures, money, and drugs. It required soil conservation, and much else, but *not* by administrative agencies. The criminal law forbad murder and theft, and all harmful drugs and foods were forbidden as destructive of life; fraudulent foods and goods were theft, and so on. In modern society, these offenses are too often the jurisdiction of arbitrary administrative agencies, as are labor problems, with the result that the criminal law is subverted and the very purpose of this law, the prevention of oppression, nullified. Moreover, because civil statute law has replaced Biblical law, men can be harmed and their lives shortened by dangerous drugs and sprays, and no crime exists unless a statute covers the specific offense. The combination of statute law and administrative law has created oppression, whereas the common law of Scripture gives man a principle of justice and a basis for a public understanding of law.

It is possible to defraud our neighbor by a variety of ways. His property can be alienated by expropriation, injury, restrictive legislation, and a variety of other means. A man's *property,* moreover, includes more than his land, home, material possessions, and money. A man has a property also in his ideas and inventions. *Patents* thus have a long history in Western culture as an outgrowth of the law against theft. The fact that patent laws have sometimes been very poor during that long history does not nullify their necessity. One of the reasons for the progress of Western civilization has been patent laws, whereby men could develop an invention and prevent the theft of their ingenuity. The Plant Patent Act of 1930 brought great progress to plant breeding and to nurserymen, in that it protected their investments of time and money.[5] The present erosion of patent laws by judicial and administrative interpretations is a major threat to future progress.

Copyright laws have a complicated history, which is not our concern here, but they too rest on the premise that a man has a property right in his written works.

---

5. Ken and Pat Kraft: *Fruits for the Home Garden* (New York: William Morrow, 1968), p. 22.

The Berkeley Version translates the first clause of this law, "Neither use extortion toward your neighbor," and the Torah translation reads it as "You shall not coerce your neighbor." The reference is to any kind of oppression, *legal or illegal,* whereby another man is deprived of his property and possessions. Legal and illegal extortion tend to go hand in hand. When men are given to lawlessness, their society will also be lawless, as will be their laws and courts. In legal extortion or fraud, men use the agency of the state or its courts to conduct their robberies. Laws which discriminate against the poor because they are poor, or against the rich because they are rich, are laws of extortion. Laws which seek to equalize men's incomes are laws of extortion.

The basic intention of this law, since it deals with "the faults of power," is to legislate against the various forms of legalized robbery which so often accompany the control of the state by one class or another. The references to this law in Scripture are many. To cite a few, Proverbs 22:22, 23 declares,

> Rob not the poor, because he is poor: neither oppress the afflicted in the gate;
> For the LORD will plead their cause, and spoil the soul of those that spoiled them.

Again, in Proverbs 28:24, reference is made to the oppression of parents by children who twist the law or the courts to their advantage: "Whoso robbeth his father or his mother, and saith, It is no transgression; the same is the companion of a destroyer." The guilt is compounded by the technical legitimacy which enables the thief to say, "It is no transgression." The judgment of God upon the pious extortioners is death: "This is the portion of them that spoil us, and the lot of them that rob us" (Isa. 17:14). The extortioners and oppressors create a social order which will ultimately destroy them also; ". . . he that getteth riches, and not by right, shall leave them in the midst of his days, and at his end shall be a fool" (Jer. 17:11).

These latter statements give us an insight into the dimensions of Biblical law. Modern civil law foresees only civil enforcement. Biblical law requires civil enforcement and declares the certainty of ultimate divine judgment in history for failure to enforce His laws. Biblical criminal law is thus essentially religious law, and it has in mind two courts, the God-ordained courts of the social order, and the Supreme Court of Almighty God.

Ehrlich's comment is to the point:

> It is difficult to compare Biblical sins with statutory crimes since in the former all are based on moral and spiritual values whereas in

the latter only that is a crime which fits into the structure of the statute sought to be enforced.[6]

Precisely. Biblical law is the word of God; it therefore represents an ultimate order which is written into the texture of all creation and into the heart of man. Hence, a jury system is valid in terms of Biblical law, since the decision is in terms of a fundamental law which all men know, whether they acknowledge it or not. Civil statutes represent only the will of the state, not an objective and absolute moral order. Statutory law creates lawlessness, because society is then no longer governed by an absolute standard of justice but rather by the fiat will of the state. Like fiat money, fiat law lacks substance, and it quickly destroys itself, and all who rely on it. It is a form of fraud, and a major form.

12. Eminent Domain

Eminent domain is the claim to sovereignty by the state over all the property within the state, and it is the assertion of the right to appropriate all or any part thereof to any public or state use deemed necessary by the state. Compensation for the appropriated property is normally given, but it is not regarded as a binding limitation on the state.[1]

Eminent domain is an assertion of sovereignty, and in Scripture is ascribed to God alone. Because of His right of eminent domain, God brought judgment upon Egypt (Ex. 9:29). Because of His right of eminent domain, God moreover gave the law of the domain to Israel and declared it to be for all the earth and to all people, "for all the earth is mine" (Ex. 19:5). This affirmation is again stated in Deuteronomy 10:12-14:

> And now, Israel, what doth the LORD thy God require of thee, but to fear the LORD, thy God, to walk in all his ways, and to love him, and to serve the LORD thy God with all thy heart and with all thy soul,
>
> To keep the commandments of the LORD, and his statutes, which I command thee this day for thy good?
>
> Behold, the heaven and the heaven of heavens is the LORD'S thy God, the earth also, with all that therein is.

This fact of God's eminent domain is celebrated in Scripture as the ground for the confidence of His people (Ps. 24:1; 50:12; I Cor. 10:26, 28, etc.). The eminent domain of the state was not recognized in Israel, as the incident of Naboth's vineyard makes clear (I Kings 20),

---

6. J. W. Ehrlich: *The Holy Bible and The Law,* p. 92.
1. For an analysis of the concept of eminent domain, see R. J. Rushdoony: *The Politics of Guilt and Pity,* Section IV, Chapter 5. The discussion in that chapter is not repeated in this chapter.

although it is prophesied as one of the consequences of apostasy from God the King (I Sam. 8:14). It is specifically forbidden in Ezekiel 46:18.

The origins of eminent domain are in pagan kingship. The *term,* eminent domain, may originate in Grotius in 1625. Since then, it has had a significant development. More important, the *concept* did not originate with Grotius, and it became significant in Christendom only as *natural law* thinking was developed. Because the philosophy of natural law locates the ultimate law within nature, it therefore locates the sovereign power within nature also, with the result that sovereignty is ascribed to a temporal power. "Sovereignty ('majesty,' 'supremacy,' etc.), in the theory of Natural Law, not only means a particular form or quality of political authority; it also means political authority itself, in its own essential substance."[2]

According to Cochran and Andrews, "The power of eminent domain is a sovereign, inherent power which cannot be contracted away or separated from the state"[3] This power was not claimed by the original colonies and states but did grow as a consequence of the natural law philosophy and the influences of English law. With respect to the theory of eminent domain in American law, a paragraph in William M. McKinney and Burdett A. Rich, *Ruling Case Law* (1915), gives an excellent summary of the concept as it developed in the 19th century in the United States:

> 10. Eminent Domain as Exercise of Sovereignty.—It was the theory of Grotius that the power of eminent domain was based on the principle that the state had an original and absolute ownership of the whole property possessed by the individual members of it, antecedent to their possession, and that their possession and enjoyment of it being subsequently derived from a grant by the sovereign, it was held subject to a tacit agreement or implied reservation that it might be resumed and all individual rights to it extinguished by a rightful exertion of this ultimate ownership by the state. This explanation of the basis of the power of eminent domain was adopted by several of the state courts in their earlier decisions. Grotius' theory however, was not adopted by all of the other political philosophers, Heineccius quoting Seneca to the effect that to kings belongs the control of things, to individuals the ownership of them. It was objected by some of the judges of this country, imbued with the spirit of individual liberty, that such a doctrine is bringing the principles of the social system back to the slavish theory of Hobbes, which, however plausible it may be in regard to land once held in absolute ownership by the sovereignty, and directly granted by it

---

2. Otto Gierke: *Natural Law and the Theory of Society 1500 to 1800* (Boston: Beacon Press, 1957), p. 40 f.
3. Thomas C. Cochran and Wayne Andrews: *Concise Dictionary of American History* (New York: Charles Scribner's Sons, 1962), p. 328.

to individuals, is inconsistent with the fact that the securing of pre-existing rights to their own property is the great motive and object of individuals for associating into governments. Besides, it will not apply at all to personal property, which in many cases is entirely the creation of individual owners; and yet the principle of appropriating private property to public use is fully as extensive in regard to personal as to real property. Accordingly it is now generally considered that the power of eminent domain is not a property right or an exercise by the state of an ultimate ownership in the soil, but that it is based on the sovereignty of the state. As that sovereignty includes the right to enact and enforce as law anything not physically impossible and not forbidden by some clause of the constitution, and the taking of property within the jurisdiction of the state for public use on payment of compensation is neither impossible nor prohibited by the constitution, a statute authorizing the exercise of eminent domain needs no further justification. The question is largely academic, but is of some practical importance in deciding whether the United States may exercise the right of eminent domain within the District of Columbia, notwithstanding a provision in the act of cession that the property rights of the inhabitants should remain unaffected. It was held that as eminent domain was a right of sovereignty and not of property, the provision had no application.[4]

There are a number of interesting presuppositions in this paragraph, but we shall confine ourselves to two. *First,* the natural right of the state to eminent domain has been presupposed and the Tenth Amendment to the U. S. Constitution has been over-ruled in terms of it. There is no express delegation of eminent domain to the federal government in the Constitution, which means that it was prohibited to it, if the Tenth Amendment has any meaning. But a prior right, a law of nature, is assumed, after Grotius, which grants to every state a supposed right which no law or constitution can alter. Thus, although the U. S. Constitution does not grant eminent domain to the federal government, and although the act of cession of the District of Columbia to the federal government specifically required "that the property rights of the inhabitants should remain unaffected," this provision was held to have no application because of an absolute right on the part of the state. *Second,* this absolute right to eminent domain is derived from "the right of sovereignty." Again, this is an amazing assumption, in that the U. S. Constitution at no time uses the word "sovereignty," and, in fact, avoids it. The Puritan tradition reserved the word properly to God, and the separation of the United States from King George III made them especially hostile to any political revival of the concept of sovereignty. There is thus no "right of sovereignty" envisioned in the U. S. Constitution of 1787-1791.

---

4. 10 R.C.L., 10.

In terms of this claim to sovereignty and to eminent domain, no constitution and no law has validity, in that all legislation can be set aside by means of an assertion of a prior sovereign power in the state. No legislation can give citizens any immunity against a state wherein the courts maintain a doctrine of eminent domain, whereby every law is subject to rejection wherever the sovereign power of the state so decrees.

Quite logically, the federal income tax legislation calls what the taxpayer is allowed to keep an "exemption" by the state, i.e., an act of grace. *All* a man's property and income, his artistic and commercial products, are, in terms of this claim to sovereignty and eminent domain, the property of the state, or at the least under the control and use of the state.

Only as the sovereign power and saving grace of the triune God are asserted and accepted can the claims of the state to be the source of sovereignty and grace be undercut and nullified.

In the United States, George Mason, author of the Virginia Declaration of Rights, specifically excluded eminent domain in that document. The Virginia Declaration states "That no part of a man's property can be taken from him, or applied to public uses, without his own consent, or that of his legal representatives." This principle, ostensibly restated in the Fifth Amendment to the U. S. Constitution, was poorly worded and left grounds for the re-introduction of eminent domain.

Not surprisingly, the assertion of the sovereignty of the state, a humanistic concept, led in the 18th and 19th centuries to a counter-assertion, the sovereignty of the individual, again a humanistic principle.

For Bakunin, the state was a sham god to be destroyed. Bakunin's trust was in natural law, and he held that natural law knows no state or any theory of state, but only man. "Man can never be altogether free in relation to natural and social laws." Freedom does not consist in revolting against all laws; "in so far as laws are natural, economic, and social laws, not authoritatively imposed but inherent in things," they are to be obeyed, said Bakunin. "If they are political and juridical laws, imposed by men upon men," whether by force, deceit, or universal suffrage, they are not to be obeyed.

> Man Cannot Revolt Against Nor Escape from Nature. Against the laws of Nature no revolt is possible on the part of man, the simple reason being that he himself is a product of Nature and that he exists only by virtue of those laws. A rebellion on his part would be . . . a ridiculous attempt, it would be a revolt against himself, a veritable suicide. And when man has a determination to destroy himself, or even when he carries out such a design, he acts in accordance with those same natural laws, from which nothing can

exempt him: neither thought, nor will, nor despair, nor any other passion, nor life, nor death.

Man himself is nothing but Nature. His most sublime or most monstrous sentiments, the most perverted, the most egoistic, or the most heroic resolves or manifestations of his will, his most abstract, most theological or most insane thoughts—all that is nothing else but Nature. Nature envelopes, permeates, constitutes his whole existence. How can he ever escape this Nature?[5]

If man is "nothing but Nature," then man's every impulse has the status of sovereign will. As against the sovereignty of the state and its right of eminent domain, anarchism holds to the sovereignty of the individual and the individual's right of eminent domain.

Accordingly, Bakunin called for "The negation of God and the principle of authority, divine, and human, and also of any tutelage by a man over men," and for "The negation of free will and the right of society to punish,—since every human individual, with no exception whatever, is but an involuntary product of natural and social environment."[6] Because "man is a social animal," man is truly man only in society; therefore, "Social solidarity is the first human law; freedom is the second law."[7] How can man live in society, when every man is his own law? For Bakunin, nature being absolute, the natural order is of necessity the good and the true order. It follows, then, that

> VIII. The primitive, natural man becomes a free man, becomes humanized, a free and moral agent; in other words, he becomes aware of his humanity and realizes within himself and for himself his own human aspect and the rights of his fellow-beings. Consequently man should wish the freedom, morality, and humanity of all men in the interest of his own humanity, his own morality, and his personal freedom.

> IX. Thus respect for the freedom of others is the highest duty of man. To love this freedom and to serve it—such is the only virtue. That is the basis of all morality; and there can be no other.[8]

If nature is the ultimate order, then Nature must also be the source of true order. Bakunin's logic is sound, however false his premises. If the state is the true manifestation of natural law, then the state is that area where man will realize true life and true morality. If the individual is this true expression of Nature and of natural law, then the anarchism of the individual, and a society of anarchism, represents true order. Anarchism and statism thus have been two rival humanistic claimants to the right to represent natural law and to claim eminent domain.

---

5. G. P. Maximoff, editor: *The Political Philosophy of Bakunin: Scientific Anarchism* (New York: The Free Press of Glencoe, 1964), p. 263.
6. *Ibid.,* p. 338.
7. *Ibid.,* p. 339.   8. *Ibid.,* p. 341.

It should be added that anarchism does not give land to the individual but to "society," to natural man as a social group, so that eminent domain in anarchism is usually exercised by the social group, not the individual.

As against the natural law philosophies, Biblical law declares the sovereignty of the triune God and His sole right to eminent domain. All property is held in trust under and in stewardship to God the King. No institution can exercise any prerogative of God unless specifically delegated to do so, within the specified area of God's law. The state thus is the ministry of justice, not the original property owner or the sovereign lord over the land. Accordingly, the state has no right of eminent domain.

The chronic humanistic quarrel between statism and anarchism cannot be resolved except by the rejection of both alternatives in favor of the triune God and His supernatural law.

One final point: many who grant the menace of statist and anarchistic eminent domain still balk at rejecting the statist doctrine for technological reasons. How else, we are told, can roads then be built and the air waves controlled? The answer to a technological problem must be technological, not a theological surrender. Technology can, if freed from statist controls, make possible the simultaneous use of various wave lengths and channels by radio and television. A different kind of society will develop without eminent domain. That development is a technological matter.

13. Labor Laws

The several laws on labor are as follows:

> Thou shalt not defraud thy neighbour, neither rob him: the wages of him that is hired shall not abide with thee all night until the morning (Lev. 19:13).

> Thou shalt not oppress an hired servant that is poor and needy, whether he be of thy brethren, or of thy strangers that are in thy land within thy gates:
> At his day thou shalt give him his hire, neither shall the sun go down upon it; for he is poor, and setteth his heart upon it: lest he cry against thee unto the LORD, and it be sin unto thee (Deut. 24:14, 15).

The first two of these laws forbids fraud and oppression with respect to workmen. Prompt payment of wages is required. The rabbinic interpretation of this law during the second Temple era stated: "He who treats a hireling with harshness sins as grievously as if he hath taken away life, and transgresses five precepts."[1] This law thus clearly re-

---

1. C. D. Ginsburg, in Ellicott, I, 423.

quires, *first,* that all who are employers, all who are in a superior position, use that power with kindliness, thoughtfulness, and mercy. Offenses against labor are made criminal offenses. Instead of administrative law, criminal law governs labor relations. Failure to pay due wages is fraud or theft, and to be prosecuted as such.

Second, God declares that His own supreme court is the proper court of appeals for labor. This is clearly a promise of judgment against thieves among employers and a thieving state which does not prosecute theft.

The strong sense of horror against the abuse of power by employers is apparent in Biblical declarations, and in Ben Sirach, who wrote, "he that defraudeth the labourer of his hire is a bloodshedder" (Ecclus. 34:22). The word of the Lord through Jeremiah was one of judgment concerning such men: "Woe unto him that buildeth his house by unrighteousness, and his chambers by wrong; that useth his neighbour's services without wages, and giveth him not for his work" (Jer. 22:13). The word through Malachi is similar:

> And I will come near to you to judgment; and I will be a swift witness against the sorcerers, and against the adulterers, and against false swearers, and against those that oppress the hireling in his wages, the widow, and the fatherless, and that turn aside the stranger from his right, and fear not me, saith the LORD of hosts (Mal. 3:5).

The same note reappears in the New Testament:

> Behold, the hire of the labourers who have reaped down your fields, which is of you kept back by fraud, crieth: and the cries of them which have reaped are entered into the ears of the Lord of sabaoth (James 5:4).

The reference in these texts is to failure to pay, short-changing on wages, or delay in payment of wages. Delay in payment then and now was and is a means of fraud. Thus, one small company which rendered material and services to a major corporation, rejoicing in its biggest single contract, over a million dollars, was not paid for almost a year. The interest on borrowed money to pay due obligations almost wiped out the small company; the larger company had used this strategy of failure to pay with several companies all at one time in order to accumulate capital without interest; they had rightly reckoned that, long before charges entered against them ever came to trial, they would repay and end the case against them without further ado.

Third, while the intent of the law is to promote the godly use of power, the honest treatment of workmen is not a favor to them but an obligation. St. Paul summarized the principle of the law succinctly: "Now to him that worketh is the reward not reckoned of grace, but of debt" (Rom. 4:4), rendered by the Berkeley Version as "Now, to a workman wages are not credited as a favor, but as an obligation." Work done for us or by us is a debt which must be promptly paid as per contract, or it is theft and to be prosecuted as such.

Fourth, the property owner is the sole governor of his property, and, provided he deals honestly with his workmen, can do as he pleases with his own. Thus, in the parable of the householder who hired men at different hours of the day, some in the morning, others at the third, sixth, and ninth hours, yet paid them all the same wages, the Lord declared, "Is it not lawful for me to do what I will with mine own? Is thine eye evil, because I am good?" (Matt. 20:15). The master had said to each, "Whatsoever is right, that shall ye receive" (Matt. 20:7), and if some worked only one hour but received a full day's wages, no injustice was done to those who worked all day and received a full day's wages. The owner is in debt to the extent of the labor performed; control of his money and property, however, does not thereby pass to the workman.

Fifth, a principle with respect to pay is established in Deuteronomy 25:4, "Thou shalt not muzzle the ox when he treadeth out the corn" or grain. This, of course, is the classic example of case law, a general principle of law illustrated by a minimal case. If the ox deserves his pay, his food, how much more so man? Therefore, "the workman is worthy of his meat" (Matt. 10:10) or "the labourer is worthy of his hire" (Luke 10:7). As St. Paul summarized it, in speaking of the pay of pastors,

> Let the elders that rule well be counted worthy of double honour, especially they who labour in the word and doctrine.
> For the scripture saith, Thou shalt not muzzle the ox that treadeth out the corn. And, The labourer is worthy of his reward (I Tim. 5:17, 18).

This is an extremely important law, and its understanding is of central importance. On its economic side, a correlation is asserted between the work done and the pay received. Because work is a debt contracted by an employer, the extent of that debt depends on the nature and extent of the services. An ox gets his feed and his care; a laborer is worthy of his hire; the nature of the services determines the extent of the debt. Thus, a ditch-digger does not command the pay of an engineer; the debt contracted for his services is an obviously lower one in virtually any market-place or society. There can be no equality of pay because there is no equality of debt. There can be no "fair price" for a particular kind of service, because the value of the service varies in the nature of the debt it contracts in terms of the need for the service.

On the non-economic side, it is clear that, while economics are not by-passed, the relationship of master and workman is not reduced to economics alone. The ox is not "muzzled"; but the ox is also trained by the master and cared for by him. The apostles and ministers have more than an economic relationship to those whom they serve; the relationship is definitely not one of charity, but it is not merely economic. The law calls the workman "thy neighbor," indicating a social relationship as well as an economic one. The relationship of worker and employer cannot be reduced to the bare bones of economics, neither can it defy economics. Between the two, there is a vast world of personal relationships. The relationship of Japanese capital and labor has been called paternalistic and feudal, but it is an economically sound relationship and yet personal. Western humanism has depersonalized and atomized relationships with unhappy results. A variety of institutions and organizations now intrude into the relationship: statist administrative agencies, labor guilds and unions, and manufacturer's organizations. On top of that business has systematically depersonalized itself and widened the gap.

The correlation between the nature of work and pay for that work is again asserted by St. Paul in I Corinthians 3:8, "and every man shall receive his own reward according to his own labour"; or, in the Berkeley Version, "each will receive his own pay in agreement with his particular labor." It is asserted with respect to the ministers who served the Corinthian church, a non-economic ministry and yet with an economic principle appealed to by St. Paul. At no point is this economic principle abandoned, therefore, nor at any point is the fact of a personal relationship by-passed.

The pressing question with respect to labor relations is the "right to strike." Does a moral right to strike exist? Hazlitt has raised questions with respect to it.[2] Read has denied that such a moral right exists: "No person, nor any combination of persons, has a moral right to force themselves—at their price—on any employer, or to forcibly preclude his hiring others."[3] As Read further states,

> To say that one believes in the right to strike is comparable to saying that one endorses monopoly power to exclude business competitors; it is saying, in effect, that government-like control is preferable to voluntary exchange between buyers and sellers, each of whom is free to accept or reject the other's best offer. In other words, to sanction a right to strike is to declare that might makes right—which is to reject the only foundation upon which civilization can stand.

Lying deep at the root of the strike is the persistent notion that an

2. Henry Hazlitt: *Economics in One Lesson* (New York: Pocket Books, 1948), p. 125 f.
3. Leonard E. Read: *The Coming Aristocracy* (Irvington-on-Hudson, New York: The Foundation for Economic Education, 1969), p. 169

employee has a right to continue an engagement once he has begun it, as if the engagement were his own piece of property. A job is but an exchange affair, having existence only during the life of the exchange. It ceases to exist the moment either party quits or the contract ends. The right to a job that has been quit is no more valid than the right to a job that has never been held.[4]

Interference by the state into economics has led to the rise of monopolies, monopolies in business and in labor. The areas of monopoly are exclusively the areas of statist interference.

Many will object that, without this statist interference, the employer will be free to rob the worker. This is to assume that the world is not under God's law; but, because it is under God's law, theft ultimately brings on judgment.

To cite one example: after World War II, a garment manufacturer built a plant in a community of retired people living on pensions. Inflation was forcing many wives and widows to look for work in a community with little employment opportunities. The manufacturer used political associations to make himself immune to various codes and inspections; he paid the minimum wage, had women lining up for jobs, and had ensured against union interference, so that no attempt was made to unionize his plant. Union members cited this as a classic case of a sweat-shop, geared to out-compete other manufacturers; for them, it "proved" the necessity for unionism. The manufacturer, however, was bankrupt and out of business in a very few years. Paying very poor wages, he could only employ those who could not get jobs elsewhere. Morale was low, and workmanship very poor. Although using quality materials, his products were sub-standard and were soon turned down by all good retailers. If he trained a good employee, that employee moved on to a better job. Thus, an attempt to use politics and misfortune to take advantage of workers ended in a major financial disaster.

But let us examine the same problem morally. The attempt to use violence to force an employer to pay a desired non-economic wage is clearly robbery. It is a demand that either the employer rob himself or his customers, which can mean pricing himself out of the market. True, many employers are evil men, and many workmen are evil men also. Neither has the right to rob the other. If neither is violating a criminal law, there is no right on the part of either to call in the state. No individual has the right to attempt by force to convert or regenerate another man.

The false premise of contemporary policies is that by means of statist action utopia can be made a reality in a short time. Most people

4. *Ibid.*, p. 170 f.

define utopia, moreover, in terms of what they want. Thus, the major U.S. business corporations, around 1900, were unable to withstand the competition of smaller rivals, and a marked decentralization was under way. Legislation on a national scale against "monopolies" actually make monopolies possible, and it saved the day for "big business."[5] This concentration of economic power has been furthered by union monopolies. Supposedly, by these moves towards stabilization of the economic scene, utopia and prosperity are assured. In reality, stagnation and decay are guaranteed as the stabilization increases. Economic progress is not stabilization but a process of growth and destruction, competition and advance. Morally, no man can be converted by force, and "conversion by violence" leads only to deeper divisions in a society, and to more unresolved conflicts. No more than frosting on a cake of mud will make it a pastry, will force resolve the problems of man and convert men into saints.

The law, as its instrument, requires force, and force can be used legitimately where men violate the criminal law, where they steal, kill, and the like. The law can govern men's behavior where justice is violated, but it cannot change the heart of man. Even more, the law cannot be used to deprive a property owner of his property rights. We may agree that a man is evil, or that he is unpleasant to deal with, but unless that man violates the law, we cannot touch him. The law must allow us to recover property from a thief, but it cannot legitimately allow us to steal from that thief. When business and labor use the law to steal from the consumer, or from one another, they are denying the rule of law in favor of the rule of might, of violence, for might apart from right is violence. Theft is theft, whether it be stealing from the rich, the poor, or the middle classes. The premise of pro-business legislation is this: It is right to steal for the sake of business, since business is good for the country. The premise of pro-labor legislation is: It is right to steal for the sake of labor, since the workingman is poor, and also because he has many votes. The word of God is very clear: Thou shalt not steal.

A labor association may call itself Christian, but if it accepts the basic premises of unionism, it becomes morally compromised. Thus, the "Principles and Practices of the Christian Labor Association of Canada" equates equalitarian principles with Scripture. Its second principle reads,

> Discrimination in employment because of color, creed, race or national origin conflicts with the Biblical principle of equality of all human beings before God and the law of love toward all men.

All men are *not* equal before God; the facts of heaven and hell, election

---

5. Gabriel Kolko: *The Triumph of Conservatism, A Reinterpretation of American History,* 1900-1916 (New York: The Free Press of Glencoe, 1963).

and reprobation, make clear that they are not equal. Moreover, an employer has a property right to prefer whom he will in terms of "color, creed, race or national origin." A Japanese Christian church in Los Angeles has the right to call a Christian Japanese pastor. A Swedish or a Negro employer has a right to hire whom he will, in terms of what is most congenial to his purposes.

The fifth principle reads,

> Creational resources may not be exploited for personal gain or the enrichment of a group or a community, but must be developed for use in the service of all mankind.

This is simply socialism, theft made into a principle of operation. Not a word in all Scripture gives any ground for such a statement.

The fact that a worker is poor gives him no more right to steal than an employer's power gives him a right to defraud. Theft is not a privilege or right pertaining to any class of men.

14. Robbing God

Every crime is an offense against God's law order, but certain acts are in particular singled out as especially offensive. One of these is the failure to tithe, which is described as robbing God (Mal. 3:8-12).

Before analyzing the implications of that fact, let us review the basic laws in this area. *First,* the basic civil tax in Scripture, the only tax, is the poll or head tax, paid by every man twenty years of age and older (Ex. 30:11-16). The same tax was assessed on all men: "The rich shall not give more, and the poor shall not give less" (Ex. 30:15). All have the same stake in justice and therefore pay the same tax.

Second, no man is allowed to tax his own future by means of debt. The length of a debt is limited to six years (Deut. 15:1-4). No man has a right to mortgage his future, since his life belongs to God.

Third, the tithe is required of all men (Lev. 27:30-32; I Cor. 9:12-14; Num. 18:21-28; Mal. 3:8-12; Prov. 3:9-10; 11:24 f.; Matt. 23:23; Heb. 7:1-8. The regular tithe, ten percent of one's income (Deut. 14:22), was then tithed to the priests, who received ten percent of the tithe (Num. 18:21-28). Thus, the church tithe was a fraction of the total tithe. The poor tithe, paid every other year (Deut. 14:28; Amos 4:4), alternated with the rejoicing tithe (Deut. 14:22-26) on each six-year cycle out of seven. Thus, the combined poor tithe and religious tithe, averaged out to about 15 percent per year; some say 18 percent. Some of the regular tithe went for levitical services to worship, and to music; much of it went to general social financing, i.e., to godly education and a number of other related services.

If this be true, when then is the failure to tithe held to be robbing God? The answer is very clear: without the tithe, a totalitarian state progressively develops to play god over society. With the tithe, the rule of society is restored to God through His ordained tax. A variety of agencies are created by the tithe to minister to the needs of godly society and to provide the needed social financing. The tithe belongs to neither church nor state: it belongs to God and is to be given by God's people to those who will administer it under God. Its social consequences have been ably described by Ewing:

> If we were living in a theocracy, with the Divine constitution, the tithe would cover everything, but at present we are living under man-made governments and man-made governments collect their own taxes. But the tithe still belongs to God. "Render therefore unto Caesar the things which are Caesar's, and unto God the things that are God's" (Matt. 22:21; Mark 12:17; Luke 20:25; Rom. 13:1-8). The extra tax exacted by governments of our day is the penalty we pay for not accepting God's rule over us nationally. Israel was told of this very thing when she demanded a king, to become like other nations, that he would misappropriate the tithe (I Sam. 8:11-18).[1]

In view of the radical implications of the tithe for society, the failure of the church to teach its importance and meaning constitutes a form of robbing God as surely as does the failure to pay the tithe.

Another form of robbery against God is the failure to provide for gleaning. According to Leviticus 19:9-11, total harvesting is prohibited; "the poor and stranger" are to gain some harvest from "the corners" of the field or trees. Here again God has provided a means of social welfare whereby the state is by-passed.

Modern urban gleaning includes the work of Goodwill Industries. Even more, it once included all garbage and trash collections by private parties. Paper was bought and re-processed for use; rags were important for a variety of uses, garbage for hog feed, or for compost, metals for scrap, old bottles for re-use, and so on. Private enterprise made profitable use of trash, whereas today most cities, having made trash collections a socialist monopoly, have mountains of expensively collected trash accumulating and creating major problems. Not too many years ago, trash collection was a business many immigrants entered as poor men and sometimes left as prosperous citizens.

Failure to observe the sabbath years with respect to the land means not only robbing the earth of its rest, but robbing God. Noth rightly observed, "The Sabbatical year and the Year of Jubilee have each in a special way the same theme—the *restitutio in integrum* or restoration to an original state."[2] Restoration is God's purpose and man is sum-

---

1. Curtis Clair Ewing: *The Law of Tithing in Scripture* (Sierre Madre, California, 1969), p. 9.
2. Martin Noth: *Leviticus,* p. 183; see Noth's *Exodus,* p. 189 f.

The Institutes of Biblical Law

moned to fulfil, not to impede it. All restoration looks ahead to the times of jubilee. The times of jubilee were once basic to Western man's hope and resounded in his song. However misguided, many Civil War soldiers sang songs looking to jubilee, in the belief that their struggle brought it closer. The jubilee is referred to in "Marching Through Georgia," "Kingdom Coming," and other songs of the period.[3]

Turning again to the tithe, how the early church understood the tithe is important, in that it is clear that they saw it as a binding law the purpose of which was broader than the church. Thus, *The Apostolic Constitution* says of the clergy,

> Let him use those tenths and first-fruits, which are given according to the command of God, as a man of God; as also let him dispense in a right manner the free-will offerings which are brought in on account of the poor, to the orphans, the widows, the afflicted, and strangers in distress, as having that God for the examiner of his accounts who has committed the disposition to him. Distribute to all those in want with righteousness, and yourselves use the things which belong to the Lord, but do not abuse them. . . .[4]

The Apostolic Constitutions made the bishop and clergy the dispensers of the tithes.[5] With this, we cannot entirely agree. However, the important fact is the functions covered by the tithe and gifts in a time of oppression and persecution, and the fact that the tithe was seen as a basic, continuing law.[6]

A pseudo-Augustinian sermon stated that refusing to tithe is simply theft:

> Whoever will not give the tithe appropriates property that does not belong to him. If the poor die of hunger, he is guilty of their murder and will have to answer before God's judgment seat as a murderer; he has taken that which God has set aside for the poor and kept it for himself.[7]

Another such sermon stated:

> Our ancestors had more than they needed because they gave God tithes and paid their taxes to the Emperor. However, since we do not wish to share the tithes with God, everything will soon be taken from us. The tax collector takes everything which Christ does not receive.[8]

With Charlemagne the tithes were made mandatory for all citizens. The Council of Seville, A.D. 590, had passed a canon ruling that, "If

---

3. Irwin Silber, editor: *Soldier Songs and Home-Front Ballads of the Civil War* (New York: Oak Publications, 1964), pp. 78, 92.
4. *The Apostolic Constitutions*, II, sec. iv; *Ante-Nicene Christian Library*, vol. XVII, p. 55.
5. *Ibid.*, Bk. VIII, sec. iv; p. 243.
6. Irenaeus: *Against Heresies*, IV, xviii; *Ante-Nicene Library*, V, pp. 431-436.
7. Lukas Vischer: *Tithing in the Early Church* (Philadelphia: Fortress Press, 1966), p. 20.
8. *Ibid.*, p. 21.

anyone does not tithe everything, let the curse which God inflicted upon Cain for not rightly tithing be heaped upon him."[9] The state, however, had not yet recognized the social centrality of the tithe. The existence of the tithe made possible the development of religious orders and foundations which undertook to provide hospitals and medical care, education, welfare, patronage to religious art and music, and a variety of other services.

The tithe has functioned where both church and state recognize the principle of the tithe.[10] Since it is a tithe to the Lord, it cannot be restricted to the church or controlled by the state, although both have a right to make it mandatory. The tithe is to the Lord. Thus, in the days of Elisha, a man from Baal-shalisha brought his tithe to Elisha and his school rather than to the priests (II Kings 4:42). In so doing, he was exercising his right to give to that which served the Lord best, rather than to an official but apostate priesthood.

The decline of tithing in the 19th and 20th centuries led to a variety of devices for raising funds for churches, Protestant and Catholic, and to a decline in Christian social financing. The result was a shift of power to the state, and also the growth of taxation to remedy the lack of social financing. Without the restoration of the tithe, there can be no restoration of Christian social order, nor can power be restored to the Christian man under God.

In "reviving" tithing, the modern church has personalized the framework. It has referred the promises of Malachi 3:8-12 to the individual: they clearly refer to a national blessing. The tithe creates a radically different social order, and hence a blessing to the nation is spoken of, both as a consequence of tithing, and as a result of God's favor. Moreover, the modern church calls for tithing to the church, an erroneous view which cuts off education, health, welfare, and much else from the tithe. "Medieval" culture saw all these things as a function of the tithe, and when existing orders failed to minister God's gifts properly, new orders arose to receive and administer them. The result was resentment on the part of parish priests, of course, but a healthier social order as well.[11] Tierney's comment on the care of the poor then is striking: "when parishioners who were prepared to bring all kinds of charges against their priests very seldom did raise the issue of the neglect of the poor, the most obvious inference is that it was not a common failing among resident parsons and vicars."[12]

9. Ewing, *op. cit.*, p. 6.
10. Joseph Bingham: *The Antiquities of the Christian Church*, Bk. V, Chapt. v, I, 190.
11. Giles Constable: *Monastic Tithes, From Their Origins to the Twelfth Century* (Cambridge: At the University Press, 1964).
12. Brian Tierney: *Medieval Poor Law, A Sketch of Canonical Theory and Its Application in England* (Berkeley: University of California Press, 1959), p. 106.

The modern social order robs God by stripping virtually every area from His jurisdiction, from His ordained government and care. Within a generation after the abolition of the legally required tithe in the United States, the state supported and controlled schools came into existence. Because revivalism and antinomianism led to the decline of the tithe (denounced as "legalism" and bondage to law), by the beginning of the 20th century welfare came to be a statist function. A new social order came with the abandonment of the tithe, and the rapid increase of taxes ensued, or statist double and triple tithes and more, to further that new order. Foundations, once an instrument of the Christian tithe, became humanistic social agencies with statist ideals. The City of God was progressively replaced with the City of Man. The effective lord of an order is always the essential taxing and tax-collecting power. If the church collects the tax, the church rules society; if the state collects the tax, the state rules society. If, however, the people of God administer the tithe to godly agencies, then God's rule prevails in that social order. In the modern world, the operative god is the state.

A final note: even during the Maccabean period, in spite of the social turmoil, the poor tithe provided for widows and orphans on a regular basis. "Then the high priest told him that there was . . . money laid up for the relief of widows and fatherless children" (II Maccabees 3: 10); the total amount available was 400 talents of silver, and 200 talents of gold.

An age which today both rejects God's order, and God's son as well, is surely cursed with a curse and destined for judgment.

15. Prison

A concordance will quickly reveal that many references to prisons appear in the Bible, but none in the law itself. Prisons were a part of Egyptian life and law (Gen. 39:20-23; 40:3, 5; 42:16, 19), but not of Israel under the law. During the wilderness journey, there are two references to confinement, "in ward" (Lev. 24:12; Num. 15:34), pending a hearing, but there is no reference to imprisonment as a punishment. According to Unger, "imprisonment was not directed by the law," and "we hear of none till the time of the kings, when the prison appears as an appendage to the palace, or a special part of it (I Kings 22:27)."[1] According to Kennedy and Barclay, "Imprisonment, in the modern sense of strict confinement under guard, had no recognized place as a punishment for criminals under the older Hebrew legislation. The first mention of such, with apparently legal sanction, is in the post-exilic passage

---

1. *Unger's Bible Dictionary*, "Prison," p. 889.

Ezra 7:26."[2] The reference in Ezra 7:26 is part of a proclamation of Artaxerxes and thus has reference to Persian rather than Biblical law.

The prison appears in Biblical law only as a place of custody, pending trial. There is no direct reference to prisons. The methods of dealing with criminals was basically threefold: *First,* capital punishment was required for capital offenses, and for incorrigible criminals. *Second,* for all other offenses, restitution was the law; where an order of law had been violated, restoration was the basic function of the courts. Emphatically, in Biblical law the goal is *not punishment but restoration,* not the infliction of certain penalties on criminals but the restoration of godly order. The center of attention is thus not the criminal but the righteous man and the total godly order. *Third,* where criminals were unable to make restitution, bond-service was mandatory in order to work out the required restitution.

In Leviticus 18:24-30, there is a strong summons to righteousness coupled with a warning. Sin is a defilement of man and of the land: it destroys or upsets God's order, and its consequences is God's judgment. Man must therefore "keep" the law lest the land "spue" him out for his "abominations" and "iniquities." Justice builds up and exalts a land; it is a restoration and a construction, whereas iniquity destroys a land and creates a moral vacuum that cries for judgment.

Western civilization began as an unhappy compromise between the Biblical standard of *restitution* and a Greco-Roman and pagan criminology which, while having elements of restitution, leaned heavily towards *punishment.* The prison thus had a place in Christendom, as an ugly, bastard compromise. It was not only a place of custody, but also a place for torture and punishment, a place to hold men for ransom or for elimination from a threatening position in the state. The prison was an accepted and illegitimate part of the social order. Thus, it could be stated that, into the 18th century,

> It must be borne in mind that all this time the prisons were primarily places of detention, not of punishment. The bulk of those committed to their safe keeping were accused persons awaiting trial in due process of law, or debtors; and of these again by far the most numerous class were the impecunious and the unfortunate, whom a mistaken system locked up and deprived of all means of paying their liabilities. Now and again an offender was sentenced to be imprisoned in default of payment of fine, or to pass the intervals between certain periods of disgraceful exposure on the pillory. Imprisonment has as yet no regular place in the code of penalties, and the jail was only the temporary lodging of culprits duly tried

2. A. R. S. Kennedy and R. A. Barclay, "Prison," in James Hastings, editor; revised edition by Frederick C. Grant and H. H. Rowley: *Dictionary of the Bible* (New York: Charles Scribner's Sons, 1963), p. 789.

and sentenced according to law. The punishment most in favour in these ruthless times was death.[3]

The rise of humanism led to a number of radical changes. Humanism was an intellectual movement among a self-appointed elite, and this elite was notoriously contemptuous of the poorer members of society. As a result, an already severe law-structure, dominated by an aristocracy, gave way to a more severe one in which the answer to almost every offense was the death penalty.

Colonial needs later led, in England, to another solution, deportation. Criminals were deported in great numbers, especially to Australia, both as a means of colonization and also as a punishment.

The next alternative was the prison system, and a major movement resulted in a demand for both more humane treatment in prisons, and the punishment of imprisonment as the solution to the problem of crime. It came to be believed that imprisonment could have a saving effect on man, that punishment in the form of a loss of liberty would lead to reformation.

Punishment next gave way, in the humanist ideology, to rehabilitation, and prisons began to be converted into rehabilitation centers. Thus, in California, one class of prisons is known as a "correctional facility." The "old doctrine . . . that the purpose of the criminal law is to exact from the criminal a retributive suffering proportionate to the heinousness of the offense" has given way to "the effort . . . to combine deterrence and public protection with restoration of the offender to a more self-sustaining role in the community."[4] This opinion reveals certain basic errors. *First,* criminal law is invested with a religious and messianic role, a duty to save criminals. This is asking of the law more than law can deliver. *Second,* it misinterprets history. Retribution is seen as exacting suffering; this was true of humanistic law, but not of Biblical law, wherein retribution or vengeance is the prerogative of God and His instruments and involves giving justice where justice is due (Luke 18:1-8). *Third,* this opinion is individualistic, not social, and it concentrates on the person of the criminal, not the victim. Thus, Bennett notes, "The current trend in the disposition of offenders is unmistakably toward individualized penal treatment administered within the frame-

---

3. Major Arthur Griffiths, "Prison Discipline," in *The Encyclopaedia Britannica,* Ninth Edition, The R. S. Peale Reprint (Chicago: R. S. Peale, 1892), XIX, 747. For a history of the early developments towards penal punishment, see Ralph B. Pugh, *Imprisonment in Medieval England* (Cambridge: University Press, 1968).

4. James V. Bennett, "The Sentence and Treatment of Offenders," in *The Annals of the American Academy of Political and Social Science,* vol. 339 (January, 1962), p. 142. *Crime and the American Penal System.*

work of a flexible criminal code."[5] Salvation is personal, and the law now concerns itself with saving the person of the criminal.

This personal frame of reference has led to the newer emphasis on mental health, on psychiatric treatment as the answer to criminality.

Humanism thus has come full circle. It began by replacing restitution with the prison system. It concludes now by restoring restitution, by requiring that society make restitution to the criminal for its supposed neglect. Because of its environmentalism, humanism blames a lack in the environment for a man's crimes. This means that society must atone for that lack by restitution. Both criminology and welfarism rest on this humanistic doctrine of restitution. Restitution must thus be made to all who are criminals, perverts, or lazy, to all who will not work, or who are failures, to all who give birth to illegitimate children, and to all who in any way are sub-standard. Restitution has once again become the social standard, but it is a humanistic restitution which works in total opposition to God's order.

Humanistic restitution is anti-law in that it is fundamentally hostile to any concept of absolute law. Absolute law is replaced with the absolute person. The result is the end of any law-order, and its replacement with a lawyer-order. The difference between the two is a great one.

The Puritans of the Massachusetts Bay Colony were fearful of the tendencies of English society towards a lawyer-order, and they began by banning a professional, paid lawyer-class. Every man had an obligation to know the law by means of the Bible. The jury system was developed in America to a far-reaching power on the premise of a Biblical law order in which every citizen knows the law. The requirement that jury members be believers was not a church requirement but a state requirement: the law order required men knowledgeable in Biblical law. The jury system was strong as long as the law was the common law of Scripture, not an esoteric doctrine open only to a professional class. There was room, after the distrust of the early years, for lawyers in America. In fact, America saw the rise of several generations of great lawyers who dominated national life and politics and gave powerful expression to national aspirations. These lawyers were nurtured in the same Biblical law-word as the people; however much both lawyers and people drifted from that faith, they continued to share certain basic premises. The lawyers thus could find a well-nigh universal response to their formulations of issues because they evoked a common faith in a common law. When lawyers turned instead to positive law (statist law) and statute law (in place of Biblical law), they cut themselves off from the people and became steadily a by-word for deceit because they were beyond the comprehension of the people

5. *Ibid.*

with their esoteric, humanistic law. A lawyer-society had replaced a law-society.

A comparison with Japan is instructive. Japan's immediate background is a Shinto law-order; Japan is in process of being transformed into a modern, humanistic lawyer order. Much of Japanese society is still governed by ancient traditions, loyalties, duties, and relationships which provide a wide cover of law without lawyers. In Japan, "10,000 members of the Japanese Bar Association suffice for a nation with half the population of the U.S. The U.S. has 340,000 lawyers."[6]

In a lawyer order, the social cement has eroded, and the commonly accepted ties which bind men and facilitate communication are gone. An artificial body of statutes, lacking in social roots and having been rationally conceived, replace the old order, and the lawyer becomes the interpreter of these esoteric laws. In a Christian law order, "ignorance of the law is no excuse," because the law is an open book to all, since it is Biblical in nature and represents a common faith and order. In humanistic lawyer orders, ignorance of the law is unavoidable, because thousands of statute laws, having no basis in any ultimate moral order, are regularly passed. Not only is ignorance of these laws unavoidable for the laymen, but also for the lawyer, who must become a specialist in a particular area of law and then engage in continuing research in order to keep up with its esoteric intricacies.

The lawyer order, being alien to law, becomes a social order managed by social scientists. Since environment rather than sin is blamed for crime, treatment of the offenders and restitution to them becomes the order of the day. In 1966, a presidential commission blamed poverty for criminality and urged treatment instead of imprisonment for all except a hard core of incorrigibles.[7] The humanists, who gave us the prison system, are now condemning it and are damning it as a "conservative" instrument.[8] The idleness of prisoners in county and city jails leads to a variety of serious problems. Homosexuality and homosexual rape is a major problem. Of homosexual rape in prisons, a report stated:

> Philadelphia—Robert, a 20-year-old accused car thief and check forger, should be in a county jail here. But even though Robert couldn't raise his $800 bail, Judge Alexander F. Barbieri Jr. set him free to await trial.
>
> Why? "This boy simply wouldn't be safe in a Philadelphia prison," the judge explained. "Even if he's guilty, it would be a greater crime to keep him in prison, than to allow him to repeat his offenses."

6. "Bernie, Go Back!" in *Forbes* vol. 104, no. 11 (December 1, 1969), p. 21.
7. Monroe W. Karmen, "Combating Crime," in *The Wall Street Journal*, Pacific Coast Edition, vol. LXXV, no. 125 (Wednesday, December 28, 1966) p. 1.
8. "Prison System Breaking Down? Search For a Better Way," in *U.S. News & World Report* (August 11, 1969), pp. 60-63.

Judge Barbieri so ruled because Robert, a slightly built youth, was the victim of homosexual rape several times, perhaps as many as 10 times, while held in pretrial custody here.

Triggered by the disclosure of similar incidents—one involving a 17-year-old victim whose only "crime" was running away from home —a recent two-month investigation found that "sexual assaults are epidemic in the Philadelphia prison system." Investigators conservatively estimate that in two years there were about 2,000 sexual assaults in jails here.

These assaults aren't unique to Philadelphia. They are common in many metropolitan jails, authorities say. Homosexual rapes recently have been revealed in county and city prisons in Washington, D.C., and its suburbs and in Chicago, among other places. "It's a result of warehousing a hodgepodge of prisoners in antiquated prisons where they have little or nothing to do," says E. Preston Sharp, secretary of the American Correctional Association.[9]

These facts are not surprising. A prison holds in enforced community a large number of incorrigible criminals who deserve death, and a number of offenders who should be required to work out restitution. To keep such a collection of people from evil would require more guards than most prisons can afford. Instead of dealing with the root problem, the departure from the Biblical principle of restitution, humanistic reformers compound the evil. As radical legal positivists, they deny any absolute concept of justice and concern themselves instead with the individual, the person of the criminal. Humanistic restitution then functions to give every possible advantage to the criminal. Note, for example, the case of one convicted slayer:

> The convicted slayer of a Long Beach police officer has been granted an unprecedented $500 expense account, a valet and other extraordinary privileges while he prepares to defend himself at his fifth penalty trial.
>
> Superior Judge John F. McCarthy did so, according to a formal court order of Oct. 29, because he feels that the funds and other privileges are needed by Doyle A. Terry, 40, to adequately prepare his defense.
>
> The county will provide Terry with a licensed private investigator, two legal runners (one of whom will serve as Terry's valet), an additional cell in which to store his files, all the unsupervised personal telephone calls he wants to make and use of the jail law library practically at will.
>
> Terry, who has spent nearly nine years on San Quentin's Death Row, was convicted in 1960 for the slaying of officer Vernon J. Owings.

---

9. Charles Alverson, "The Jail Jungle," in *The Wall Street Journal*, vol. LXXX, no. 39, Pacific Coast Edition (Tuesday, February 25, 1969), p. 1. Note the environmentalism of Sharp's statement.

Terry previously was sentenced to death in 1960, 1962 and 1965. Another penalty trial in 1965 ended when the jury was unable to agree unanimously on whether he should be sentenced to death or life in prison.

Each of his death penalty sentences was reversed by the State Supreme Court, which retroactively applied decisions of the U.S. Supreme Court.

Terry won his second trial because in the first the prosecution commented (as permitted at the time) on the deterrent effects of the death penalty. He got his third trial because in the second the prosecution (as it then was allowed to do) told the jury he would be eligible for parole if given a life sentence.

His latest reversal came because prospective jurors opposed to the death penalty automatically (as then was permitted) were excluded.

All the privileges granted by Judge McCarthy to Terry appear to exceed those allowed other prisoners acting as their own lawyers after refusing the services of a public defender. . . .

. . . Judge McCarthy said . . . "The Supreme Court might just tell us, 'Here, you deprived this man of a fair trial because you didn't let him have telephones.' And I don't think they would pay too much attention to us if we told them the money hadn't been budgeted."

Officer Owings, 31 at the time, was shot in the head June 24, 1960, when he and his partner stopped to aid what they thought were two men, one of them Terry, having car trouble on Terminal Island.

Terry was captured by pursuing officers a mile from the scene of the shooting.

At his first trial he also was convicted of five counts of robbery and one of conspiracy to commit robbery . . .[10]

It must be stressed again that this is environmentalistic restitution. For environmentalism, evil is in the environment, not in the sinner; therefore, the environment must be penalized and restitution made to the sinning individual. For the environmentalist, proof of the innocence of a criminal is to find evidence of some unhappy interaction with the environment. Thus, because a murderess had been a fat girl who later became very attractive, it was held that this transformation made her into a murderess. A probation report on this murderess, Kristina Cromwell, quoted her mother as saying that "When she lost weight and found that she was attractive to men, she couldn't handle it."[11] The probation report "At the very least . . . implied that the crime for which she was sentenced to life imprisonment Tuesday was rooted in her physical

---

10. Ron Einstoss, "Killer Gets Expense Account and Valet to Defend Self Again," in the Los Angeles *Times*, Sunday, Nov. 16, 1969, Section C, pp. 1, 4.
11. "Life For Kristina," in the Los Angeles *Herald-Examiner*, Wednesday, April 2, 1969, p. A-3.

turnabout and the personality change it provoked."[12] This kind of opinion is to be found very widely today among the clergy, educators, and sociologists, among others.

The result of such opinions is a growing inability of society to cope with crime. The bail system, legitimate in a godly social order, has become a source of major abuse in modern society, so that President Nixon in 1969 proposed denial of bail to accused persons whose release is likely to menace the community.[13] In one California case, it was reported that "A Van Nuy's man free on $15,000 bail pending court action involving attacks on nine women and girls in the Van Nuys area has been arrested on charges of attacking a 13-year-old girl." This offense led to his arrest on April 10, 1969; in February of 1969, this man, Anthony J. Iannalflo, was arrested and "later arraigned on 12 counts, including four forced rapes, for child molestation, three kidnap and one robbery. The charges allegedly were the results of attacks on women and girls in the Van Nuys area since last June (1968)."[14]

Without God's moral absolutes, man becomes eventually unable to cope with evil. Instead of fighting it, he seeks a compromise with it. According to one sociologist, compromise is society's best hope.

> Should state and federal authorities attempt to negotiate with the Cosa Nostra, just as our State Department negotiates with hostile foreign powers? Such diplomacy might well serve the interest of noncriminals, suggests Dr. Donald R. Cressey, professor of sociology at UC Santa Barbara.
>
> "A little cold-blooded appeasement is not necessarily a bad thing, especially when our side is losing," he writes. He states that some form of negotiation (or accommodation or communication) by state and federal officials—such as is carried on by local officials, often in a haphazard and corrupt fashion—might lessen the danger that organized criminals will achieve a monopoly on democratic processes in the United States.[15]

Such appeasement already existed illegally, even as the professor wrote. Thus, according to reliable federal and other sources, it was held that "La Cosa Nostra spends $2 billion annually to corrupt public officials all the way up from the county sheriffs and courthouse right on into the Supreme Court."[16]

---

12. Jerry Cohen, "Diet That Made Women Slender May Have Made Her a Killer," Los Angeles *Times*, Wednesday, April 2, 1969, Part I, p. 32.
13. "Crimes While on Bail—The Hunt For a Remedy," in *U.S. News & World Report*, vol. LXVI, no. 7 (Feb. 17, 1969), p. 42.
14. "Rapist Suspect, Out on Bail, Arrested in New Attack Case," in Van Nuys, California, *The Valley News and Green Sheet*, vol. 58, no. 156, (Friday, April 11, 1969), p. 1.
15. "News From The Academy," in the Kingsburg (Calif.) *Recorder*, Thursday, Dec. 18, 1969, p. 8.
16. Victor Riesel, "Web of Mafia Control," Los Angeles *Herald-Examiner*, Sunday, Dec. 21, 1969, p. B-7.

The direction of any godless system of justice is only downward; it is, to use Van Til's phrase, integration into the void.

According to Leviticus 18:24-30, every departure from God's law is a defilement of men and a defilement of the land: it is the basic pollution of all things. The modern prison system is an important aspect of the defilement of our times.

16. Lawful Wealth

According to the Westminster Shorter Catechism, the question of acquiring wealth is directly related to the eighth commandment:

> Q. 73. Which is the eighth commandment?
> A.   The eighth commandment is, Thou shalt not steal.
> Q. 74. What is required in the eighth commandment?
> A.   The eighth commandment requireth the lawful procuring and furthering the wealth and outward estate of ourselves and others.
> Q. 75. What is forbidden in the eighth commandment?
> A.   The eighth commandment forbiddeth whatsoever doth or may unjustly hinder our own or our neighbour's wealth or outward estate.

Answer 75 had in mind the love of pleasure, drunkenness, gluttony, laziness, and theft and cited Proverbs 21:17; 22:20; 28:19, and Ephesians 4:28. Alexander Whyte saw this commandment as covering "all matters connected with the earning, saving, spending, inheriting and bequeathing of money and property."[1] Whyte added,

> All a man's possessions, go back to the beginning of them, go down to the bottom of them, will always be found to represent so much self-denial, labour, industry. Obscure as may be the origin, history, and growth of this or that particular estate, yet it must in its beginning have been due to some man's obedience to the Creator's law of labour and reward. "Be fruitful, and multiply, and replenish the earth, and subdue it." This is the original charter of the right of property.[2]

Whyte further added, "Akin to the habit of industry is the sister habit of frugality and forethought."[3]

Capitalization is the accumulation of wealth, the conversion of work, savings, and forethought into tangible working assets. No progress is possible without some measure of capitalization. It is a serious error to assume that socialism and communism are opposed to capitalization or to capitalism; their opposition is simply to *private capitalism,* but their dedicated policy is to *state capitalism.* For the state to plan any

---

1. Alexander Whyte: *A Commentary on the Shorter Catechism* (Edinburgh: T. & T. Clark, 1961; reprint), p. 145.
2. *Ibid.,* p. 145 f.   3. *Ibid.,* p. 146.

program of progress, public works, or conquest, work, frugality, and forethought are necessary. The work is exacted from the people by force; the frugality or savings is again forced out of the people by means of wage controls, compulsory savings and bond-buying programs, and slave labor, the forethought is provided by the state planners.

State capitalism is seriously defective for a number of reasons. Most notably, *first* of all, it represents *theft*. The private capital of the people is expropriated, as well as their work and savings. It is thus a radically dishonest capitalization.

Second, forethought is divorced from work and frugality, that is, the planners are not the ones who provide the work and the sacrifice. As a result, the planners have no brake of immediate consequences imposed upon them. They can be prodigal in their waste of manpower and capital without bankruptcy, in that the state compels the continuance of their non-economic and wasteful planning. The consequence is that, wherever planning is separated from work and savings, instead of capitalization, the result is decapitalization. Socialism is thus by nature imperialistic, in that it must periodically seize or annex a fresh territory in order to have fresh capital to gut by expropriation. State capitalism is thus an agency of decapitalization.

Private capital is acquired basically in three ways, excluding private theft as an illegal and immoral means. These three ways are by work, inheritance, and gift. Private capital must then be utilized by planning, and the loss is the planner's loss, so that there is an incentive to efficiency in private capital, even where received by gift or by inheritance, which is lacking in state capitalism. The immediacy of consequences, the direct liability of the private capitalist to loss, makes private capital more responsible even where the private capitalist is a thief. Where criminal syndicates like the Mafia enter into business, they do so with a ruthless eye towards profits and efficiency which is lacking in state capitalism.

Lawful wealth is that wealth which comes to man as he abides by God's law and applies work, thrift, and forethought to his activities. Lawful wealth is a covenant promise; hence the warning by Moses in Deuteronomy 8:11-20, culminating in vs. 18 with the statement, "But thou shalt remember the LORD thy God: for it is he that giveth thee power to get wealth, that he may establish his covenant which he sware unto thy fathers, as it is to this day." Man must not say in his heart, "My power and the might of mine hand hath gotten me this wealth" vs. 17). Wright's comment on this is good:

> The pride is most terrible and insidious because it flouts the plainest of facts, by asserting the virtual deity of self: "My power and the might of my hand have gotten me this wealth" (vs. 17). Yet Israel must remember that the wealth is by God's power, not her own, and

it is given in accord with his covenanted promises, not in payment for what the nation deserves (vs. 18). This is one of the strongest and most powerful passages in the Bible on this characteristic and distressing problem of human life. Wealth here is not by natural right; it is God's gift. Yet man must beware of the terrible and self-destructive temptation to deify himself which comes with it.[4]

True wealth, godly wealth is a product of covenant blessings on work, thrift, and foresight; it is inseparably connected with the law. The commandments are given "that ye may live, and multiply, and go in and possess the land" (Deut. 8:1).

Scripture distinguishes throughout between godly wealth and ungodly wealth. Wealth in itself therefore is not a sign of God's favor; it can be a witness to theft and fraud. Wealth can be, however, a sign of God's favor and an evidence of covenantal blessings where accompanied by lawful means and godly faith.

To return to the matter of capitalization, capitalization in a society requires a background of faith and character. In every era of history, capitalization is a product of the Puritan disposition, of the willingness to forego present pleasures to accumulate some wealth for future purposes. Where there is no character, there is no capitalization but rather decapitalization, the steady depletion of wealth. Society becomes consumption centered rather than productive, and it begins to decapitalize the centuries-rich inheritance which surrounds it.

Thus, decapitalization is preceded always by a breakdown of faith and character. Where men feel that private happiness is man's purpose and goal rather than serving and glorifying God, and finding joy in Him, where men feel that life owes them something rather than seeing themselves as debtors to God, and where men feel called to fulfil themselves apart from God rather than in Him, there society is in rapid process of decapitalization.

To return now to Deuteronomy 8:1, 18, the purpose of wealth is the establishment of God's covenant; its *goal* is that man prosper in his task of possessing the earth, subduing it and exercising dominion over it. The *means* to lawful wealth is the *covenant* law, the law of God. Capitalization is thus a radical and total task. Man must seek to subdue the earth and gain wealth as a means of restitution and restoration, as means of establishing God's dominion in every realm. Wherever godly men establish their superior productivity and gain wealth, they thereby glorify God. Wealth in itself is good, and a blessing of the Lord. It is *trust* in wealth rather than God which Scripture condemns (Ps. 49:6, 7). We are told that, "When Rehoboam had established the kingdom, and had strengthened himself, he forsook the law of the LORD, and all

---

4. G. Ernest Wright, "Deuteronomy," *Interpreter's Bible,* II, 389.

Israel with him" (II Chron. 12:1). "The rich man's wealth is his strong city, and as a high wall in his own conceit" (Prov. 18:11; cf. 10:15; BV, "The rich man's wealth is his strong city and as a high wall—so he thinks").

Godly wealth is basic to God's purposes for the earth. It is a vital link in the task of restoration.

> Benjamin Franklin, in his Memoirs, mentions a merchant named Denham, who failed in his business at Bristol, compounded with his creditors, and went to America. In a few years he accumulated a plentiful fortune, returned to England in the same ship with Franklin, called his creditors together to an entertainment, and paid the full remainder of his debts, with interest up to the time of settlement.[5]

Personal restitution is godly, but much more is required. Man must restore the earth, must make it truly and fully God's kingdom, the domain in which His law-word is taught, obeyed, and honored. Man must gain wealth and use it to the glory of God, but, to gain lawful wealth, man must know and obey the law. Godly wealth is to be acquired, held, and used in good conscience; it is a happy result of the covenant of God.

17. Restitution to God

Another aspect of the law of restitution appears in two interesting laws:

> And the LORD spake unto Moses, saying,
> If a soul commit a trespass, and sin through ignorance, in the holy things of the LORD; then he shall bring for his trespass unto the LORD a ram without blemish out of the flocks, with thy estimation by shekels of silver, after the shekel of the sanctuary, for a trespass offering:
> And he shall make amends for the harm that he hath done in the holy thing, and shall add the fifth part thereto, and give it unto the priest: and the priest shall make an atonement for him with the ram of the trespass offering, and it shall be forgiven him (Lev. 5:14-16).

> And the LORD spake unto Moses, saying,
> Speak unto the children of Israel, When a man or woman shall commit any sin that men commit, to do a trespass against the LORD, and that person be guilty;
> Then they shall confess their sin which they have done; and he shall recompense his trespass with the principal thereof, and add unto it the fifth part thereof, and give it unto him against whom he hath trespassed.
> But if the man have no kinsman to recompense the trespass unto,

---

5. John Whitecross: *The Shorter Catechism Illustrated from Christian Biography and History* (London: Banner of Truth Trust, [1828] 1968), p. 114.

let the trespass be recompensed unto the LORD, even to the priest: beside the ram of the atonement, whereby an atonement shall be made for him.
And every offering of all the holy things of the children of Israel, which they bring unto the priest, shall be his.
And every man's hallowed things shall be his: whatsoever any man giveth the priest, shall be his (Num. 5:5-10).

In the Leviticus passage, the reference, according to Ginsburg, is to "inadvertently keeping back the things which belong to the sanctuary, and to the service of the Lord, as, for instance, the tithes, the firstfruits, or not consecrating or redeeming his firstborn (Exod. xxviii. 38; Num. v. 6-8)."[1] The reference is to "the holy gifts, sacrifices, first-fruits, tithes, etc., which were to be offered to Jehovah, and were assigned by Him to the priests for their revenue"; it means "to sin in anything by taking away from Jehovah that which belonged to Him." It does not refer to deliberate sin but to a trespass committed "in a forgetful or negligent way."[2] A trespass offering, compensation for the amount of the tithe or offering due, plus a fifth of the amount more as penalty was the required restitution.

In the Numbers passage, the reference is to a similar offense, but in this case against a neighbor. The Talmud stressed the reference in 5:6 to woman ("When a man or woman shall commit any sin"), declaring that "Women are also subject to the law of torts."[3] At any rate, the natural inference, by virtue of its echo of Leviticus 5:14-16 is that here again minor, inadvertent offenses are referred to. Serious guilt, such as a runaway fire, is dealt with elsewhere in the law. Here, the offenses are real but neither capital nor major. The noun *maal,* trespass, here used, together with its cognate verb, "implies stealth, or secrecy in action."[4] Through carelessness or neglect, a man or woman, sinning against a neighbor, then guiltily conceals the offense. Restitution, however, must be made, and, when found guilty, the person must make an offering of atonement, make restitution, and add a fifth of its value to his restitution. It is possible, in times of turmoil, or of sudden death, for an offender to find no one left to make restitution to: the family is dead or has moved out of the country, and no relatives survive. In such cases, restitution is made to the priest or pastor. The guilty party, in coming forward to confess his guilt voluntarily, is protected in his confession. "These gifts could be personal, so that they needed not to flow into the Temple treasury. By this it was made possible for these cases of guilt to be treated more confidentially, which

1. C. D. Ginsburg, "Leviticus," in Ellicott, I, 355.
2. Keil and Delitzsch: *The Pentateuch*, II, 313.
3. *Baba Kamma*, 15a; p. 63.
4. C. J. Elliott, "Numbers," Ellicott, I, 497.

also gave the greater encouragement to the confession of guilt and to restitution."[5]

Many commentators refer the sins of this law to Leviticus 6:2, 3, but this is clearly a separate law, although closely related. It would appear that Numbers 5:5-10 refers to sins of negligence and inadvertence, as does Leviticus 5:14-16, whereas Leviticus 6:1-7 refers to minor offenses of a deliberate nature involving property:

> And the LORD spake unto Moses, saying,
> If a soul sin, and commit a trespass against the LORD, and lie unto his neighbour in that which was delivered him to keep, or in fellowship, or in a thing taken away by violence, or hath deceived his neighbour;
> Or have found that which was lost, and lieth concerning it, and sweareth falsely; in any of all these that a man doeth, sinning therein:
> Then it shall be, because he hath sinned, and is guilty, that he shall restore that which he took violently away, or the thing which he hath deceitfully gotten, or that which was delivered him to keep, or the lost thing which he found,
> Or all that about which he hath sworn falsely; he shall even restore it in the principal, and shall add the fifth part more thereto, and give it unto him to whom it appertaineth, in the day of his trespass offering.
> And he shall bring his trespass offering unto the LORD, a ram without blemish out of the flock, with thy estimating, for a trespass offering, unto the priest:
> And the priest shall make an atonement for him before the LORD: and it shall be forgiven him for any thing of all that he hath done in trespassing therein (Lev. 6:1-7).

Although such offenses are called "violence," Noth points out that in the Hebrew "the context scarcely suggests a forcible robbery or a regular theft, but rather some deceptive way of appropriating someone else's property."[6]

In all three of these laws, certain common legal principles appear. The *first* is clearly the fact that restitution must be made to God. In Exodus 22:1-14 the basic laws of restitution are given, but these laws have no reference to a trespass offering to the Lord, as we find in Leviticus 5:14-16; 6:1-7, and Numbers 5:5-10, nor to a sin offering. The general laws of sacrifice assumed such offerings. Why then is it specifically cited in the case of these laws? The very fact of the minor character of these offenses, inadvertence in two cases and petty offenses in the other, gives us the clue. Marsh has observed of Numbers 5:5-10, that, "While there could be a sin against God alone, any sin against

---

5. John Peter Lange: *Numbers,* p. 35.
6. Martin Noth: *Leviticus, A Commentary* (Philadelphia: The Westminster Press, 1965), p. 49.

man was also reckoned a sin against God, so that a guilt offering had to be made."[7] Ginsburg stated it even more plainly, with reference to Leviticus 6:1-7:

> It will be seen that the trespass against God is, strictly speaking, a violation of the rights of a neighbour's property. As fraud and plunder are most subversive of social life, a crime of this sort is described as an insult to God, who is the founder and sovereign ruler of his people.[8]

The law permits no one to forget that the slightest offense is also an offense against God; by requiring in these cases a restitution to God, as well as a restoration of the damaged or misappropriated property, the total jurisdiction of God is asserted as well as the fact that the slightest breach of order is a breach of God's order. At every point, God's order must be restored.

Second, in greater offenses, restitution involves double or fivefold return, here, only 20 percent. In every case, the same principle is at work, which in part certainly involves also the removal of all profit from sin. "The law of the Lord removes all profit from stealing and imposes severe penalties upon those who steal."[9] Apart from the law of restitution, crime does very commonly pay. An English professional criminal, asked about the risks involved in his thefts, his prison sentences, and the likelihood of an eight-year prison term when next caught, replied:

> I don't want to do eight years, no—but if I have to I have to, and that's all there is to it. If you're a criminal, what's the alternative to the risk of going to prison? Coal-miners don't spend their time worrying about the risk they might get killed by a fall at the coal-face either. Prison's an occupational risk, that's all—and one I'm quite prepared to take. I'll willingly gamble away a third of my life in prison, so long as I can live the way I want for the other two-thirds. After all, it's my life, and that's how I feel about it. The alternative —the prospect of vegetating the rest of my life away in a steady job, catching the 8:13 to work in the morning, and the 5:50 back again at night, all for ten or fifteen quid a week—now that really does terrify me, far more than the thought of a few years in the nick.[10]

This criminal's position was a logical amoral conclusion. The profit in theft far outweighed the penalty for him. Modern humanistic law does tend to make crime profitable while at the same time lessening

---

7. John Marsh, "Numbers," *Interpreter's Bible,* II, 166.
8. C. D. Ginsburg, "Leviticus," in Ellicott, I, 356.
9. H. B. Rand: *Digest of the Divine Law,* p. 73.
10. Tony Parker and Robert Allerton: *The Courage of His Convictions* (New York: W. W. Norton, 1962), p. 88.

its significance in terms of the moral law. Saxon law dealt brutally with criminals. According to Sir William Blackstone,

> Our ancient Saxon laws nominally punished theft with death, if above the value of twelve pence; but the criminal was permitted to redeem his life by a pecuniary ransom; as, among their ancestors the Germans, by a stated number of cattle: But in the ninth year of Henry the First, this power of redemption was taken away, and all persons guilty of larceny above the value of twelve pence were directed to be hanged; which law continues in force to this day.[11]

Capital punishment for larceny continued in English law into the reign of George IV, at which time the law was altered. In such a perspective, the law seeks to repress crime by imposing heavy and disproportionate penalties. This is contrary to the Biblical law where restoration is primary, not repression. Both capital punishment and restitution in Biblical law are in terms of justice, not repression; the professional criminal or murderer is executed in order to eliminate iniquity and restore order, and restitution is made for other crimes to reestablish that godly and working social order which is necessary to God's creation mandate. Neither hanging a thief, nor imposing a disproportionate ransom or fine on him, constitutes justice.

A *third* factor is very important also. The requirement of restitution in little things is a God-given law which makes for better relations with neighbors. The modern tendency is to "overlook" little things, as though it constitutes nobility to do so. Thus, if a woman drops and breaks a platter belonging to her neighbor, the modern tendency is to "forgive and forget." The Biblical principle is to restore a sum equivalent to the platter, or the same kind if available, plus a fifth of its value as compensation. Such restitution replaces annoyance with neighborly love, for "love is the fulfilling of the law" (Rom. 13:10). Much of the petty annoyances between friends and neighbors would be eliminated by observance of this law. By means of this law, God is clearly aware of the necessity for governing the minor problem which are so often the main factors in our lives.

A *fourth* aspect of this law is confession. Making restitution to a neighbor is a form of confession, of course. When the neighbor is dead or has migrated, and no kinsman is left to whom restitution can be made, confession is made to God through the priest. Numbers 5:5-10, "emphatically insists on confession, and finally enacts also, that if the individual against whom the trespass was committed has no Goel (kinsman), the compensation money shall, together with the ram to be offered, devolve to the Lord, i.e., be paid to the priest."[12] There is thus

11. Cited in J. W. Ehrlich: *The Holy Bible and The Law,* p. 224.
12. G. F. Oehler: *Theology of the O.T.,* p. 302.

a place for confession in the law. True confession does not create a mediating institution: it simply upholds the sovereignty of God's law and the necessary fact of restitution.

True confession is restitution. Forgiveness is a juridical term in the Bible and means that charges are dropped because satisfaction has been rendered. Forgiveness thus means "satisfaction" or restitution. Confession is worthless, and forgiveness invalid, where restitution has not been made.

18. The Rights of Strangers, Widows, and Orphans

The law repeatedly speaks of various groups of peoples whose rights are more readily or easily endangered. Two important such laws are the following:

> Thou shalt neither vex a stranger, nor oppress him: for ye were strangers in the land of Egypt.
> Ye shall not afflict any widow, or fatherless child.
> If thou afflict them in any wise, and they cry at all unto me, I will surely hear their cry;
> And my wrath shall wax hot and I will kill you with the sword; and your wives shall be widows, and your children fatherless (Ex. 22:21-24).
> And if a stranger sojourn with thee in your land, ye shall not vex him.
> But the stranger that dwelleth with you shall be unto you as one born among you, and thou shalt love him as thyself; for ye were strangers in the land of Egypt: I am the LORD your God (Lev. 19:33, 34).

These laws speak, *first* of all, about foreigners. The aliens referred to are permanent residents of the community. There is no reference here to a traveller passing through the country: such people are governed by the laws of hospitality. Again, this law does not refer to foreign businessmen, temporarily in the land to transact business: such transactions are governed by all the requirements of honesty and the prohibitions of theft. The term "stranger" as used in Exodus 22:24 can refer to an alien resident of the country, or to a fellow Israelite who is in the territory of another tribe, such as Beerothites in Gittaim (II Sam. 4:3). "The classification was tribal and social, not primarily religious."[1] Thus, it would apply to a Frenchman in California, or a Southerner or a Negro in California. The law is repeated in Exodus 23:9, with some variation: "Also thou shalt not oppress a stranger: for ye know the heart of a stranger, seeing ye were strangers in the land of Egypt." Israel was reminded of the discrimination and persecution it experi-

---

1. J. Coert Rylaarsdam, "Exodus," in *Interpreter's Bible*, I, 1007.

enced in Egypt and asked therefore to beware of placing other men under similiar sufferings.

In Leviticus 19:33, 34, the reference is somewhat more restricted, in that it apparently refers to the alien who has become a believer. According to Ginsburg, this "stranger" is one who has become circumcised, fasted on the Day of Atonement (Lev. 16:29), obeyed the laws of sacrifice (Lev. 17:8, 9; 22:18; 22:10, 15), and has practiced the laws of chastity (Lev. 18: 26), as well as obeyed other moral laws (24: 16-22). "Having once been admitted into the community, the Israelites were forbidden to upbraid him with his nationality or throw at him the fact that he was originally an idolater."[2] In Solomon's day, there were 153,000 "strangers" in Israel.[3]

The very closeness which life as a fellow-believer placed the alien in relationship to an Israelite made possible more tension than with a non-believing alien. The closer a relationship, the more likely are tensions and problems. It is easier to have problems with one's own husband or wife than with someone a mile away. As a result, the law speaks more attentively and precisely where relationships are the closest.

Second, such people are not to be *vexed,* oppressed, or wronged. The word has reference to specific aggressive and discriminatory acts. The discrimination is an act not permitted by God's word; thus, eunuchs could not become members of the congregation, although they could be believers; bastards and certain Canaanites were excluded for some generations from membership (but not faith) because of their nature or their low moral background (Deut. 23:1-6). The discrimination forbidden is one of our own making.

Israel was reminded of its own experience in Egypt. The evil in that experience was not their segregation into Goshen: that was a favor and an advantage. The evil was in the oppression and enslavement, in the legal discriminations against them.

Precisely because this is a law, it is limited in scope. It requires justice for the "stranger." Life in that day was family and clan life. Alliances and relationships were established by blood and by marriage. Hospitality was readily extended, to a remarkable degree, to passing strangers, but normally friendships were in a restricted circle governed by faith and family. To call for the modern, humanistic society with an open relationship to all men would have appeared to the Israelites as the ultimate in tyranny. This law did not require any such a re-ordering of any man's private life: It simply required justice in dealing with all men.

The closed inner circle of Biblical life made possible the open outward

2. C. D. Ginsburg, "Leviticus," in Ellicott, I, 429.
3. *Ibid.*

circle. Abraham was ready, in Biblical manner, to greet and receive
passing strangers with every possible kindness (Gen. 18:1-8). Again,
he was ready to go to the rescue of the Canaanite kings, as well as to
rescue his nephew Lot (Gen. 14); had Abraham's concern been only
Lot, he could have ransomed him easily and at no risk to himself. A
man's home was open in its hospitality to passing strangers in need,
and his responsibility to his neighbors in a common defense was great.
On the other hand, the inner circle of the home was severely restricted.
Abraham did not become a close friend of the Canaanites, and he sent
to Mesopotamia for a bride for Isaac, in order to assure a godly marriage (Gen. 24). It must be noted, therefore, that personal friendship
and contacts were very severely limited in Biblical life and law, to a
degree which would be regarded as unlawful by humanism, whereas
hospitality, assistance to neighbors, and a common lawful defense were
required to a degree rarely recognized today.

Third, it must be noted that violations of this law are serious in
God's sight. This law against oppression is placed in Exodus immediately after laws against seduction, idolatry, and witchcraft (Ex. 22:
16-20). As Rawlinson noted,

> The juxtaposition of laws against oppression with three crimes of
> the deepest dye seems intended to indicate that oppression is among
> the sins which are most hateful in God's sight. The lawgiver, how-
> ever, does not say that it is to be punished capitally, nor, indeed,
> does he affix to it any legal penalty. Instead of so doing, he declares
> that God Himself will punish it "with the sword" (verse 24). Three
> classes of persons particularly liable to be oppressed are selected for
> mention—(1) strangers, *i.e.,* foreigners; (2) widows; and (3)
> orphans.[4]

Such oppression is serious, because it indicates that, to all practical
intent *no law exists.* True law gives a common protection to all those
who are law-abiding; where the weak are unable to get such protection,
no law exists. If the law discriminates against the weak because they
are weak, and the strong because they are strong, then it ceases to be
law and is an instrument of oppression. True law discriminates against
those who are wrong-doers by seeking to enforce restitution and/or
death against them, and is in favor of the law-abiding, in that it protects
them in their lives and properties, and compels restitution for offenses
against them. If the lives and properties of foreigners, widows, and
orphans are not protected by the civil order, then that order has become
lawless.

No penalties are affixed to these laws, Rawlinson to the contrary,
not because there are none, but because the law already provides them:

---

4. George Rawlinson, "Exodus," in Ellicott, I, 271.

restitution for theft, death for rape, and so on. The particular form of oppression calls for its particular penalty.

Fourth, widows and orphans are included in this law together with strangers as helpless classes of peoples. In a very real sense, none of these, nor anyone else in society has any rights as such: what they do have is a common law which protects all men who are law-abiding and exacts penalties of all who are criminals.[5] Thus, we use the title "The Rights of Strangers, Widows, and Orphans" in order to point to the fact that the only true right of any person is the law of God. The point of the legislation at hand is to declare the inclusiveness of that law: it is the refuge of foreigners and of helpless peoples. Where there is no right, there are no rights; without God's law, no rights exist. Volumes of legislation can confer no justice where no sense of right exists.

Fifth, an order without justice is subject then to the judgment of God. Rylaarsdam has observed, in comparing this law with the code of Hammurabi, "What is uniquely stressed here is the immediate and dynamic role the God of Israel plays in this concern for and accomplishment of justice. He is directly related to the historical process and has not, like an absentee, entrusted his work to an agent, such as Hammurabi, who can play an independent role."[6] This point is emphatically made in Biblical law, and, on many occasions. Thus, according to Deuteronomy 10:17-19,

> For the LORD your God is God of gods, and LORD of lords, a great God, a mighty, and a terrible, which regardeth not persons, nor taketh reward:
>
> He doth execute the judgment of the fatherless and widow, and loveth the stranger, in giving him food and raiment.
>
> Love ye therefore the stranger: for ye were strangers in the land of Egypt.

Of this last sentence, Rashi's comment was appropriate: "The blemish which is upon thyself thou shalt not notice in thy neighbour."[7]

Where the courts are lawless, the Supreme Court of God must be appealed to: "I will surely hear their cry" (Ex. 22:23). We must not confuse the suffering of the afflicted with their concern for justice; the afflicted may be as disinterested in justice as their oppressors, and as ready to persecute and oppress if given the opportunity. There must therefore be an appeal, not only for deliverance, but for justice. Where there is no appeal for justice, there is no interest in justice.

---

5. T. Robert Ingram, " 'Right' and 'Rights,' " in *The Presbyterian Journal,* Jan. 26, 1970, p. 9 f.

6. Rylaarsdam, *op cit.,* I, 1007.

7. Cited by C. H. Waller, in "Deuteronomy," Elliott, II, 36.

19. Injustice as Robbery

Injustice by courts and judges is a major form of robbery in much of history. The thieves that men must deal with are all too often on both sides of the bench. The law declares,

> And thou shalt take no gift: for the gift blindeth the wise, and perverteth the words of the righteous (Ex. 23:8).

> Ye shall do no unrighteousness in judgment; thou shalt not respect the person of the poor, nor honour the person of the mighty: but in righteousness shalt thou judge thy neighbour (Lev. 19:15).

> Thou shalt not wrest judgment: thou shalt not respect persons, neither take a gift: for a gift doth blind the eyes of the wise, and pervert the words of the righteous.
> That which is altogether just shalt thou follow, that thou mayest live, and inherit the land which the LORD thy God giveth thee (Deut. 16:19, 20).

Calvin's comment on these laws is very much to the point:

> This kind of theft is the worst of all, when judges are corrupted either by bribes, or by affection, and thus ruin the fortunes which they ought to protect: for, since their tribunal is as it were a sacred asylum, to which those who are unjustly oppressed may fly, nothing can be more unseemly than that they should there fall amongst robbers. Judges are appointed to repress all wrongs and offenses; if therefore they shew favour to the wicked, they are harbourers of thieves; than which there is no more deadly pest. And besides, since their authority excludes every other remedy, they are themselves like robbers with arms in their hands. The greater, therefore, their power of injury is, and the greater the damage committed by their unjust sentences, the more diligently are they to be beware of iniquity; and thus it was necessary to keep them in the path of duty by special instructions, lest they should conceal and encourage thievery by their patronage. Now, as avarice is the root of all evils, when it thus lays hold of the mind of judges, no integrity can continue to exist.[1]

The judge must not favor either the rich or the poor. In Exodus 23: 3, 6, the judge is forbidden to "countenance a poor man in his cause," or to "wrest the judgment of the poor in his cause." Luther, in his comment on Deuteronomy 16:18-20, observed:

> Moreover, He lays down this rule to these judges and officers: they are to judge justly, that is, according to the Law of God and not according to their own understanding. Then He forbids corrupt feelings; they are not to leave the Law behind and be led and motivated by the consideration of persons and bribes. These two things tend to distort and misdirect all justice, and therefore he here adds this aphorism: "Bribes blind the eyes of the wise and subvert the cause of the righteous" (v. 19). Partiality towards

---

1. Calvin, *Commentaries on the Four Last Books of Moses,* III, 136 f.

persons includes such things as these: fear of persons great, mighty, or wealthy; love of relatives; regard for friends; contempt for the lowly; sympathy toward those stricken by calamity; and fear of peril to one's own life, reputation, and property. "Bribes," however, include gain, advantage, ambition, and the insatiable and boundless gulf of greed. Therefore in Ex. 18:21 Jethro advises Moses to choose men who are without greed, that is, birds that are as rare as a black swan.[2]

There is a point of especial importance in these laws; where bribery is involved, the offense is the judge's, not the briber's. The word for bribe or bribery is in Hebrew *kopher*, redemption. The reference thus is to a payment for redemption. The judge who accepts a bribe is granting a false or undeserved redemption or salvation to a man who should be judged.

As we have seen, a 1969 report indicated that bribery by the Cosa Nostra of public officials in the United States is $2 billion a year. The crimes of this criminal syndicade are real and many and require judgment, but, with respect to bribery, the offense in terms of Biblical law is not theirs but the judges'. In every social order, there will be some lawbreakers; no perfect society is possible this side of heaven. In no social order, therefore, will judges be free from temptation, if not to bribery, then at least to favoritism. The sin of bribery is thus cited in Scripture as the offense, not of the giver, but of the taker.

By taking a bribe, the public official or judge thereby makes a thief of himself, and a thieves' domain of his office. The most deadly and dangerous thieves are those who operate within the law and especially as the officers of the law. As Calvin rightly saw, "This kind of theft is the worst of all." The whole social order is then converted into an instrument of evil.

According to Exodus 23:8, a bribe blinds the wise judge, but it is a onesided blinding, i.e., it blinds him to justice. The requirement of Deuteronomy 16:19, "thou shalt not respect persons," is in Hebrew literally, "Thou shalt not recognize faces." The judge thus must be blind to the *persons* in the case, and must see the *issues* involved. The bribe exactly reverses this: the judge is then *blind* to the *issues* and *sees* only the *persons*.

Since the judge or civil officer must continually deal with evil, and commonly faces some lawbreaker in matters brought before him, the reality of attempts to blind justice is always before him: it is a condition of his office. The offense therefore is his offense; it is a demonstration of the fact that he is on the wrong side of the bench, sitting as a judge rather than facing arraignment as a lawbreaker.

---

2. Luther: *Deuteronomy*, p. 163.

The golden rule is often cited, and properly so, as a summation of the law: "Therefore all things whatsoever ye would that men should do to you, do ye even so to them: for this is the law and the prophets" (Matt. 7:12). To observe the law in relationship to our neighbor, recognizing his right to life, home, property, and reputation, is to love him, and to do to him as we would have others do unto us. Not only is this a fundamental principle of Scripture, but its reverse is equally fundamental. As Obadiah stated it, "as thou has done, it shall be done unto thee: thy reward shall return upon thine own head" (Obad. 15; cf. Judges 1:17; Ps. 137:8; Ezek. 35:15; Joel 3:7, 8).

What have corrupt judges done, and what is their penalty? Josephus reported on the penalty: "If any judge takes bribes, his punishment is death: he that overlooks one that offers him a petition, and this when he is able to relieve him, he is a guilty person."[3] Why this penalty? If a judge accepts a $50 bribe, why should he die for it, and the bribe-giver suffer no penalty? The point at issue is more than $50: it is the life of the society. Is the society dedicated to furthering justice in terms of God's law order, or is it a thieves' order and court? Every corrupt official of state, and especially the judge, is guilty of using his office to destroy the foundations of social order, to kill godly society, and to replace it with a society of polite and legal thieves and murderers. Hence, the principle inherent in the golden rule, "as thou has done, it shall be done unto thee," requires his death. First and last, the major form of treason to any civil order is to destroy it as a representative of justice. Injustice therefore is not only robbery but murder. It robs individuals and murders the social order.

In the King James Version we read that the bribe "perverteth the words of the righteous" (Ex. 23:8; Deut. 16:19); the Torah renders this, that bribes "upset the pleas of the just." The Berkeley Version of Exodus 23:8 reads that a bribe or present "thwarts a just man's testimony" or "subverts the cause of the innocent" (Deut. 16:19). The bribe blinds the judge's eyes to the issues of justice and closes his ears to its pleas. The essence of a just order in court is that the cry for justice be heard. All the procedural care of a court of law has as its function to sift out truth from error and perjury and to listen with sensitivity and care for the truth. The bribe thus destroys the basic communication required to maintain a law order. To receive a bribe is as serious therefore as to cut off a man's air. Just as the man strangles without air, so the social order dies without justice. Calvin was right: "This kind of theft is the worst of all." It is also perhaps the most prevalent.

---

3. Flavius Josephus: *Against Apion*, II, 27; in William Whiston: *The Works of Flavius Josephus* (Philadelphia: David McKay), p. 919.

An important point with respect to this law is that it is *civil* law. The impersonality required of the civil courts is markedly different from the personalism of decisions in other realms. In the family, judgments can be more lenient and more severe, depending upon the situation. The family must live with the offending member; it may be more severe if it feels he is hopeless, or more lenient if it feels the offender has learned his lesson. In the church, because believers are members of one another, the same is true. They are not to resort to the impersonality of the civil courts unless the member refuses to accept the church's discipline. In that case, he is a heathen and a publican and is dealt with impersonally (Matt. 18:7). Family and church justice is personal, and, in a sense, partial, respecting persons, although still just. In the state, where persons of varying backgrounds confront one another, impersonality and impartiality must be the rule of justice. Family and ecclesiastical justice, being personal, can be concerned with rehabilitation; civil justice must be tied to restitution only, the principle of justice. Where the state assumes a parental role, or a pastoral role, it not only usurps the jurisdictions of family and church, but also forsakes the impersonal justice it must administer. The state then becomes a class agency, or an instrument of a race or some dominant group. If it substitutes rehabilitation or punishment for restitution, it penalizes the injured party in favor of the criminal.

Within the family, an impersonal justice is fatal. For husband and wife to deal with one another impersonally is to destroy their relationship, which must be one of justice surely, but also of mutual forbearance. Every area of personal relationships is similar. But traffic laws cannot be personal, and marital laws cannot be impersonal. When ecclesiastical discipline becomes impersonal, it means, practically, excommunication. The counsel to Christians to avoid the courts against one another (I Cor. 6:1-10) in part presupposes this requirement of justice tempered with forbearance in personal relationships.

20. Theft and Law

The eighth commandment reads very simply, "Thou shalt not steal" (Ex. 20:15); of this, there is little question: theft is forbidden, and clearly so. It is necessary to ask, to whom does this law apply? The usual answer by churchmen is, "Why, to all men, of course," and this answer is faulty. The commandment applies to all men *and* to their institutions, corporations, and forms of government. Failure to extend the law to its full jurisdiction has been productive of more than a little evil.

At the root of this error is the unhappy fact that most churchmen treat the commandments as simple matters of morality, not as law.

The Mosaic law is indeed a moral code, but it is inescapably law as well. To deny to the Mosaic legislation its force as law is to surrender the world to the devil.

In one of the most incisive studies of the law, Frederick Nymeyer, who titled his study "Essays Against Organized Sanctimony and Legalized Coercion," wrote in criticism of the ideas of Dr. Bruins Slot, stating:

> Everything stands or falls on this simple question: does a government have more authority than its citizens? If so, it must have got that authority from some greater source than the citizens. The only greater sources are God or Satan. Satan is never considered by Calvinists to be the source of governments; (governments are manifestations of the "common grace" of God!). Therefore Hitler had a "peculiar inherent authority" directly *from God*! Now we can realize how *De Standaard* came to follow the course it did during World War II.
>
> Grant the foregoing to Abraham Kuyper, to *De Standaard*, to the Anti-Revolutionary Party and to Bruins Slot and where do you end up? Here are four propositions that follow naturally from Bruins Slot's major idea:
> 1. God has restricted individual men by and to the Ten Commandments.
> 2. But God has given to government more authority or rights than individual men have.
> 3. Therefore, governments have direct authority to go beyond the Ten Commandments, that is, they may violate the Ten Commandments.
> 4. It is exactly that right to violate the Ten Commandments which constitutes the purpose of claiming a "peculiar inherent authority" for government.
>
> Hitler, you see, was operating quite within his "rights" derived directly from God. Concentration camps, firing squads, lies, violence, wars, oppression—all these are products of the "peculiar, inherent authority" of government. Men are bound by the Decalogue; governments are not![1]

Nymeyer, who with Ingram stands almost alone in doing justice to the Biblical law, has stated the case clearly. All authority is either from God or Satan. If authority is from God, then it is either under God's law, and an agency of God's law, or else it has some special pipeline to God which enables it to sidestep God's law, and for this Scripture gives no evidence.

In a delightful footnote, Nymeyer added:

> A person reading this manuscript with some amusement worked out the obvious syllogisms:

---

1. Frederick Nymeyer: *Progressive Calvinism* (South Holland, Ill.: Libertarian Press, 1955), I, 331 f.

1. The powers that be are ordained of God;
2. Satan is one of the powers that be;
3. Therefore, Satan is ordained of God!

Then he outlined the succeeding syllogism:

1. All the powers ordained of God must be obeyed;
2. Satan is a power ordained of God;
3. Therefore, Satan must be obeyed![2]

Such absurd thinking is far from absent in evangelical circles. In July, 1967, this writer became the target of a demand for investigation as one teaching false doctrines because of a filmstrip text entitled *The Moral Foundations of Money*. In that text, unbacked paper money was called a form of counterfeiting, and inflation a form of larceny. One of the accusations made by the Rev. Albert G. Edwards of the Orthodox Presbyterian Church, was as follows:

> This is accusing the state of robbery, which seems to go quite contrary to what Paul says in the 13th chapter of Romans, where we are told to give what is asked of us in regard to taxation and to recognize the right of the state in this. (Edwards spoke of paper money inflation as a "hidden tax," rather than larceny.) To call taxation larceny seems to be an act of open rebellion against the state and contrary to Scripture which admonishes us to be subject to the ordinances of men, for God's sake.[3]

On August 7, 1967, this writer answered in part as follows:

> You speak of paper money as a form of hidden tax, which is true. But your point with regard to Romans 13 I do not regard as valid. You yourself I have heard criticize certain actions of civil government as morally wrong, or in various ways wrong. Did you impugn thereby Scripture? Elijah called the seizure of Naboth's vineyard theft and murder; was he impugning God's law? The state has a legitimate authority, but not everything it does is thereby legitimate. As Hodge, in another context than Romans 13, says of all authority, "It extends over all departments (of its domain), but is limited in all; first, by the nature of the relation; and secondly, by the higher authority of God." The work of the ministry must be prophetic, i.e., it must speak for God, and it must therefore deny to the state what belongs to God. The state thus has no right, for example, to usurp the education of children. This is a responsibility of the covenant, of parents, not the state. The state has no right to violate God's law. "Thou shalt not steal," and paper money is theft, and what you call a "hidden tax" is actually hidden theft. I cannot hold to the immunity of the state from moral judgment.

In too many churchmen, we find the exemption of the state from

---

2. *Ibid.*, p. 331.
3. Letter of July 17, 1967, to R. J. Rushdoony, from Rev. Albert G. Edwards.

the law, and from judgment in terms of the law. The roots of this position go back to pagan divinization of the state. Practically, where men exempt the state from the law of God, they make it an instrument of Satan.

The law is the law for everyone. If the citizen has no moral right to steal, neither does the state. If the citizen cannot expropriate his neighbor's property, neither can the state. "Thou shalt not steal" applies to corporations, governments, and men equally. It forbids socialism, communism, inflation, bad checks, and every other form of theft. It forbids false advertising, and dishonest processing and adulteration of foods. It forbids featherbedding by workers' associations, and it forbids the cheating of workers. All men, their institutions, corporations, and forms of government are equally under the law of God. The reduction of the Ten Commandments to the status of a moral code only is the destruction of the law.

If all authority is not under God, then, instead of a universe, we have a multiverse; instead of one Creator and Law-giver, we have many gods acting as creators and law-givers in their realms. If all authority comes from God, then all authority is plainly under God's law-word and entirely subject to it. "Thou shalt not steal" cannot then be restricted to the individual man but must be applied to every area of life.

The concept of a multiverse has become prominent in the 20th century, and, with it, the consequences of polytheism. Pre-Christian paganism, being evolutionary, was also polytheistic: the world has seen multiple origins and hence had multiple gods.

In the 20th century, educators have spoken of the university at times as a *multiversity*, having room for a variety of ideas and faiths. The teaching of witchcraft, astrology, and related concepts by some schools is related to this concept of the multiversity. High schools in a major city have introduced yoga and palmistry. If the world is a multiverse, then all things are permissible except a sovereign God and a universal law-order. Hence our polytheistic world is tolerant of almost every kind of belief except orthodox Christianity. A universal law-order and a sovereign God rule out the possibility of a polytheistic multiverse. But, because the sovereign and triune God of Scripture rules, there is no multiverse but rather a universe and a unified law-order.

The law, "Thou shalt not steal," applies therefore not only to the state but to the church as well. Where the church does not faithfully teach the whole counsel of God, His entire law-word, it is then plainly guilty of theft. It is robbing the people and the social order of its vital nerve; it is undercutting all authority when it limits the law on which all authority rests.

As Nymeyer has observed, "What gold is to money, the law of God is to liberty."[4] Without the law of God, men, unions, corporations, and states feel free to be a law unto themselves, to play god. Failure to teach the law of God is thus to pave the way for tyranny.

James Madison said of God's law:

> We have staked the whole future of American civilization, not upon the power of government, far from it. We have staked the future of all of our political institutions upon the capacity of mankind for self-government; upon the capacity of each of us to govern ourselves, to control ourselves, to sustain ourselves according to the Ten Commandments of God.[5]

4. Frederick Nymeyer, *Progressive Calvinism* (South Holland, Ill.: Libertarian Press, 1957), III, 209.

5. Cited by F. Nymeyer, in *Progressive Calvinism* (South Holland, Ill.: Libertarian Press, 1958), IV, 31.

IX

THE NINTH COMMANDMENT

1. Tempting God

The ninth commandment, "Thou shalt not bear false witness against thy neighbour" (Ex. 20:16), has been widely misinterpreted to mean that "Thou shalt at all times and under all circumstances tell the truth to all men who may ask anything of you."

On October 15 and 16, 1959, this writer lectured to a Christian school teachers' conference at Lynden, Washington. The substance of the lectures, with additional material, was later published as a book, *Intellectual Schizophrenia*. Both at the time of the lectures, and after publication, various "Reformed" clergymen sharply attacked this writer for his remarks concerning Rahab and her lie about the Israelite spies whom she hid, and whose lives she saved. It was pointed out that

> Rahab had a choice to make: 1) she could tell the truth and surrender the spies, two godly men, to death. 2) she could lie and save their lives. This is the kind of situation the moralist hates and refuses to accept. Either course involves some evil, however the moralist seeks to deny it. The question is, which is the lesser of two evils? Our choices are rarely black and white ones; we rarely have the luxury of an absolute choice. But we do have the continual opportunity to make decisions in terms of an absolute faith, however gray the immediate situation. This faith Rahab had. Whether she lied or not was relatively unimportant as compared to the lives of two godly men. She lied and saved their lives. For this James singled her out, together with Abraham, as an instance of vital faith, of faith which was not a mere opinion but a matter of life and action (James 2:25). Again, Hebrews 11:31 singled this same act as an instance of true faith. It is useless evasion to try to abstract something from the act as praiseworthy while condemning her for the lie, and a violation of the unity of life. Rahab clearly lied, but her lie represented a moral choice as against sending two godly men to death, and for this she became an ancestress of Jesus Christ (Matt. 1:5). For the moralist, it is important that he stand in his own self-righteousness, and Rahab's alternative is intolerable, because it makes some kind of sin inescapable at times. For the godly man, who stands, not in his own righteousness but the righteousness of Christ, his own purity is not the essence of the matter but that God's will be done. And God, in this situation, certainly willed that the lives of the spies be saved, not that the individual come forth able to say, I never tell a lie.

But, we are told by the moralist, if Rahab had told the truth, God would have been bound to honor her integrity and to deliver her and the spies, and Rahab had an obligation to tell the truth irrespective of the consequences. Several fallacies, characteristic of moralism, are involved here:

1. Moral choice, it is held, involves a simple, uncomplicated, rational issue.
2. It is always a choice between absolute right and wrong.
3. The central issue is always the preservation of the individual's moral purity rather than a transcendent factor.
4. Poetic justice is always operative; virtue is always rescued and rewarded, and truth always triumphant.

But this is not biblical Christianity, but 18th century Deism with a strong dash of Spenser's *Faerie Queene!* Paul could say, echoing the Psalmist (Ps. 44:22) "For thy sake we are killed all the day long; we are accounted as sheep for the slaughter" (Rom. 8:26). That Scripture affirms an ultimate triumph of the *godly* (as differentiated from the *moral*) is beyond question, but it does not affirm the concept of poetic justice. We cannot allow so radical a falsification of the faith to be projected onto Scripture.

The doctrine of poetic justice in effect requires a rewriting of Scripture, history and literature. . . .[1]

It has been insisted by these critics that God will bless and deliver the person who tells the truth at all times. It must be added that these champions of truth-telling at all times have been notorious liars. They feel that they have a right to deny that they have made a statement unless the exact wording, to the last syllable, is exactly reproduced. Such pharisaic reasoning is characteristic of their thinking.

But does God require us to tell the truth at all times? Such a proposition is highly questionable. The commandment is very clear: we are not to bear false witness against our neighbor, but this does not mean that our neighbor or our enemy is ever entitled to the truth from us, or any word from us, about matters of no concern to them, or of private nature to us. No enemy or criminal has any right to knowledge from us which can be used to do us evil. Scripture does not condemn Abraham and Isaac for lying in order to avoid murder and rape (Gen. 12:11-13; 20:2; 26:6, 7); on the contrary, both are richly blessed by God, and the men who placed them in such an unhappy position are condemned or judged (Gen. 12:15-20; 20:3-18; 26:10-16). Like examples abound in Scripture. No one who is seeking to do us evil, to violate the law in reference to us or to another, is entitled to the truth. More than that, it can with scriptural grounds be called an evil to

---

1. R. J. Rushdoony: *Intellectual Schizophrenia, Culture, Crisis and Education* (Philadelphia: Presbyterian and Reformed Publishing Company, 1961, 1966, 1971), p. 79 f.

tell the truth to evil men and enable them thereby to expedite their evil. Asaph declared, "When thou sawest a thief, then thou consentedst with him, and hast been partaker with adulterers" (Ps. 50:18). To see theft and to be silent is to be party to the theft. To see men planning theft or murder, and then to answer truthfully concerning the whereabouts of the man, woman, or property they mean to kill, rape, or steal, is to be party to their offense. Such truth-telling is then participation in the crime. In terms of this, Rahab, had she told the truth, would have been an accessory to the death of two men.

The fact that the ninth commandment does not require or command a surrender of privacy has long been recognized and has passed into law. The Fifth Amendment to the U. S. Constitution of 1787 declared that no man "shall be compelled, in any criminal case, to be a witness against himself." A man may confess; he may choose to testify in his own behalf, in which case he must not perjure himself, but he cannot be forced to be witness against himself. If testifying in his own behalf, he cannot be asked questions extraneous to the case at hand. For this reason, the Christian must oppose the use of the lie detector with any man, voluntarily or otherwise, because the subject can then be made to testify to extraneous matters and his privacy is thereby invaded.

To return to the matter of truth-telling, the Christian is under obligation to God to tell the truth at all times where normal communicaion exists. This truth-telling means, not the exposure of our privacy, but bearing a true witness in relation to our neighbor. It does not apply to acts of war. Spying is legitimate, as are deceptive tactics in warfare. Protection from thieves requires concealment and walls.

To believe that we can tell the truth in a situation comparable to Rahab's, and that God will miraculously deliver us and the men whose lives are at stake, is not only foolish but also demonic theology. To hold that God must deliver us in such circumstances is to be guilty of the satanic temptation, testing God. Satan's second temptation to Jesus Christ, the last, or second, Adam, was to cast himself down from a pinnacle of the temple and summon God to rescue Him. Jesus said to Satan, "It is written again, Thou shalt not tempt the Lord thy God" (Matt. 4:7). Jesus Christ made it clear that no man could put God on trial, or impose a requirement on Him. No man can heedlessly expose two men to death on the pretext that his duty is to tell the truth irrespective of the circumstances, expecting God to deliver the men whom he himself refuses to deliver. It was Satan who held that man has a duty to test God: "Yea, hath God said?" (Gen. 3:1).

In this connection, the position of John Murray, an outstanding theologian, deserves examination. In answer to the question, "What is truth?" Murray stated:

Our Lord's answer to Thomas, "I am the way, the truth, and the life" (John 14:6) points the direction in which we are to find the answer. We should bear in mind that "the true" in the usage of John is not so much the true in contrast with the false, or the real in contrast with the fictitious. It is the absolute as contrasted with the relative, the ultimate as contrasted with the derived, the eternal as contrasted with the temporal, the permanent as contrasted with the temporary, the complete in contrast with the partial, the substantial in contrast with the shadowy.[2]

Jesus, in declaring that He is the truth, "is enunciating the astounding fact that He belongs to the ultimate, the eternal, the absolute, the underived, the complete."[3] Truth refers to "the sanctity of the being of God as the living and true God. He is the God of truth and all truth derives its sanctity from him."[4] Murray recognized the validity of a concealment of truth:

It is quite true that the Scripture warrants concealment of truth from those who have no claim upon it. We immediately recognize the justice of this. How intolerable life would be if we were under obligation to disclose all the truth. And concealment is often an obligation which truth itself requires. "He that goeth about as a talebearer revealeth secrets; but he that is of a faithful spirit concealeth a matter" (Proverbs 11:13). It is also true that men often forfeit their right to know the truth and we are under no obligation to convey it to them.[5]

However, in dealing with the case of Rahab, and like ones in Scripture, Murray equivocates:

It should not go unnoticed that the New Testament Scriptures which commend Rahab for her faith and works make allusion solely to the fact that she received the spies and sent them out another way. No question can be raised as to the propriety of these actions or of hiding the spies from the emissaries of the king of Jericho. And the approval of the actions does not logically, or in terms of the analogy provided by Scripture, carry with it the approval of the specific untruth spoken to the king of Jericho. It is strange theology that will insist that the approval of her faith and works in receiving the spies and helping them to escape must embrace the approval of *all* the actions associated with her praiseworthy conduct.[6]

Murray to the contrary, we must insist that it is a very strange theology which will admit that God approved of the faith and the act of Rahab, but that the lie on which the whole rescue rests is somehow bad. Murray's position has no scriptural evidence: it involves wrongly dividing the word, trying to divide and act from itself, and denying that God's praise of the act was indeed praise.

---

2. John Murray: *Principles of Conduct* (Grand Rapids: Eerdmans, 1957), p. 123.
3. *Ibid.*, p. 124.
4. *Ibid.*, p. 125.　　　5. *Ibid.*, p. 146 f.　　　6. *Ibid.*, p. 138.

The same pharisaic nonsense is indulged in with respect to the midwives who saved the lives of Israelite babies who were to be killed at
birth. According to Murray,

> The apparent prevarication of the midwives in Egypt has been
> appealed to as warrant for untruth under proper conditions. "And
> the midwives said unto Pharaoh, Because the Hebrew women are
> not as the Egyptian women; for they are lively, and are delivered
> ere the midwives come in unto them. And God dealt well with the
> midwives" (Exodus 1:19, 20). The juxtaposition here might seem
> to carry the endorsement of the reply to Pharaoh. . . .
>
> Let us grant, however, that the midwives did speak an untruth and
> that their reply was really false. There is still no warrant to con-
> clude that the untruth is endorsed, far less that it is the untruth that
> is in view when we read, "And God dealt well with the midwives"
> (Exodus 1:20). The midwives feared God in disobeying the king
> and it is because they feared God that the Lord blessed them (cf.
> verses 17, 21). It is not at all strange that their fear of God should
> have coexisted with moral infirmity. The case is simply that no
> warrant for untruth can be elicited from this instance any more than
> in the cases of Jacob and Rahab.[7]

This is amazing reasoning. Murray calls the midwives' report, "pre-
varication" and "untruth"; let us call it, more honestly, a lie. Even
more, what shall we call Murray's separation of the midwives' lie which
saved the lives of babies sentenced to death from God's blessing of the
midwives? It is clearly presented as cause and effect. The midwives
lied *because* they feared God more than Pharaoh. Their fear of God
was manifested precisely in the lie, at the risk of their own lives possibly, to save the lives of God's covenant children. Their lie was not,
Murray to the contrary, "moral infirmity" but moral courage, even as
Rahab's lie was. The moral infirmity in the matter is entirely Murray's,
and his pupils'. Pharaoh was at war with God and with Israel; Israel
had been enslaved, its people abused, and its newborn babies sentenced
to death. This was clearly war; even more, it was legalized, wholesale
murder. The midwives lied to Pharaoh to save the lives of the babes.
It was clearly lying; it was clearly justified. And it was clearly blessed
by God.

There is a long tradition here of straining at gnats and swallowing
camels. St. Augustine indulged in peculiar reasoning to accept the
Scripture's statement concerning the midwives, declaring, "For if a
person who is used to tell lies for harm's sake come to tell them for the
sake of doing good, that person has made great progress."[8] In other
words, the midwives had been nasty liars, and now they had improved:

---

7. *Ibid.,* p. 141 f.
8. St. Augustine: *De Mendacio* (On Lying), 7, in *Nicene and Post-Nicene
Fathers,* First Series, III, 460.

they lied for a good cause! For Augustine, "these testimonies of Scripture have none other meaning than that we must never at all tell a lie."[9] If we always tell the truth, Augustine held, misusing a text, God will always make a way of escape (I Cor. 10:13).[10]

The midwives suffered at Calvin's hands also, in spite of God's blessing. According to Calvin,

> In the answer of the midwives two vices are to be observed, since they neither confessed their piety with proper ingenuity, and what is worse, escaped by falsehood. . . . Wherefore both points must be admitted, that the two women lied, and, since lying is displeasing to God, that they sinned. . . . Nor is there any contradiction to this in the fact that they are twice praised for their fear of God, and that God is said to have rewarded them; because in his paternal indulgence of his children he still values their good works, as if they were pure, notwithstanding they may be defiled by some mixture of impurity. In fact, there is no action so perfect as to be absolutely free from stain; though it may appear more evidently in some than in others. . . . Thus, though these women were too pusillanimous and timid in their answers, yet because they had acted in reality with heartiness and courage, God endured in them the sin which he would have deservedly condemned.[11]

Calvin would have had the midwives not only tell the truth to Pharaoh but also make a witness to him, converting the audience into a kind of testimonial meeting. Not only would such a witness by two women have been impossible at a royal audience, but it would have been immoral in terms of Christ's words: "Give not that which is holy unto the dogs, neither cast ye your pearls before swine, lest they trample them under their feet, and turn again and rend you" (Matt. 7:6).

Much else in Scripture militates against Calvin's belief that the women should have witnessed to Pharaoh. According to Solomon,

> He that reproveth a scorner getteth himself shame: and he that rebuketh a wicked man getteth himself a blot.
> Reprove not a scorner, lest he hate thee: rebuke a wise man, and he will love thee (Prov. 9:7, 8).

In one respect Calvin was right: the women lied, but, Calvin to the contrary, God in no way disapproved of their action.

Hodge, however, cited the case of the midwives as "an intention to deceive" which was not "culpable."[12] He did not develop the point, however, and unfortunately, his position has had too few followers. Park commends the midwives, but he grounds their action in "humane-

---

9. *Ibid.*, 42; p. 476.
10. *Ibid.*, 43; p. 477.
11. Calvin: *Commentaries on the Four Last Books of Moses*, I, 34 f.
12. Charles Hodge: *Systematic Theology* (New York: Charles Scribner's Sons, 1891), III, 440.

ness" and calls it "true religion," which gives a humanistic twist to the text which is not there.[13]

The Southern Presbyterian theologian Dabney, in analyzing the significance of the ninth commandment, declared that "Man may kill, when the guilty life is forfeited to God, and He authorizes man to destroy it, as His agent. So, I conceive, extreme purposes of aggression, unjust and malignant, and aiming at our very existence, constitute a forfeiture of rights for the guilty assailant."[14] Thus, lawless aggression results in "a forfeiture of rights for the guilty assailant," and Rahab, the midwives, and the other saints of old were innocent of wrongdoing.

Scripture does speak at length of the fact that lying is hateful to God (Prov. 6:16-19; 12:22; Lev. 19:11; Col. 3:9, etc.). Satan is spoken of as the father of lies (John 8:44; Acts 5:3). The critics of Rahab and of the midwives (as well as of Abraham, Isaac and others) fail to cite verses like I Kings 22:22, 23, where God is declared to have put a lying spirit in the mouths of the false prophets in order to deceive a false king. The reason is that it militates against their absolutism. And this is the heart of the matter. Shall we, in platonic fashion, absolutize truth-telling as a word, idea, or universal above God, or is God alone absolute? To absolutize truth-telling is to make Scripture an absurdity, because God in His sovereign power is alone absolute. Truth-telling is always in relation to and in terms of the absolute God and His law. Man has an obligation to speak truthfully in all normal circumstances, but he cannot permit evil men to steal, murder, or rape by his truth-telling, which must at all times have reference to an absolute God rather than an absolute idea.

The Westminster Shorter Catechism, in questions 77 and 78, brings us to the heart of the matter with its answers:

> Q. 77. What is required in the ninth commandment?
> A. The ninth commandment requireth the maintaining and promoting of truth between man and man, and of our own and our neighbour's good name, especially in witness-bearing.
> Q. 78. What is forbidden in the ninth commandment?
> A. The ninth commandment forbiddeth whatsoever is prejudicial to truth, or injurious to our own or our neighbour's good name.

If we are not permitted by this law to injure "our neighbour's good name," how much less are we permitted to aid evil men to steal his property, rape his women-folk, and kill him as well? Truth-telling under such circumstances is not a virtue but moral cowardice.

The concept of truth-telling implicit in the critics of Rahab, the mid-

---

13. J. Edgar Park, "Exodus," *Interpreter's Bible*, I, 856.
14. Robert L. Dabney: *Syllabus and Notes of the Course of Systematic and Polemic Theology* (Richmond, Virginia: Presbyterian Committee on Publication, 1871, 1890), p. 425 f.

wives, Abraham, Isaac, and others is related to a pagan doctrine of sanctification. In paganism, the self-perfection of the individual is the religious ideal and the purpose of sanctification. The perfect individual is his own ultimate. The goal pursued, whether by the Sufis or by Buddha, has no reference to God and His law-order, and, very often, little reference to other men as well. The self is the world of pagan holiness, and the perfection of the self, the goal. The result is a concept of holiness and of truth-telling which is *abstract*, i.e., it is abstracted from the reality of God and His law, and the reality of a world at war. An abstract, non-Christian moralism can thus declare that it is holy to tell the truth to enemies and thereby lead to the killing of friends, neighbors, or loved ones, because the only issue is the abstract purity of the soul. Such a doctrine is clearly not Christian.

2. Sanctification and the Law

Since the ninth commandment, like the third, deals with the spoken word, it is important in this connection to restate and examine carefully a particular word in God's law, "holy." The law is repeatedly given as the way of holiness or sanctification, and the demand, "Ye shall be holy: for I the LORD your God am holy" (Lev. 19:2), is a prefix in the law to every law. In this Leviticus 19:2 citation, it is a prefix to the ban on gossip and on false witness in court (Lev. 19:16).

The law is the way of holiness, the way of sanctification. One portion of the Pentateuch is in fact called "The Holiness Code" (Lev. 17–26) because of its especial insistence on the law as the means of sanctification. From beginning to end, the Scripture makes clear that salvation, justification is by the grace of God through faith, and that sanctification is by law, God's law.

The sin of Phariseeism was that it converted the law, and works of law, into the way of salvation. In the process, it also adulterated the law and gave primacy to its reinterpretation of the law. The law was thus clouded in its meaning and given a function which was not proper for it to bear. Much has been written on the sins of Phariseeism which needs no repeating here. Too little has been said of the comparable sins and often apostasies of the church with respect to the law.

The infiltration of Hellenic thought into the Christian community meant, among other things, the introduction of a new doctrine of sanctification. The Biblical doctrine is thoroughly practical: it calls for the progressive submission of man and the world to the law of God. It is a program for conquest and victory. Even its partial observance has served to give eminence to a people or culture. The greatness of medieval culture was built on the bedrock of an obedience to the law, and the same was true of Puritanism. The staying power of the Jew in the face of adversities has been the measure of his loyalty to the law.

But Hellenic thought, like all pagan philosophies of its day, was dualistic. The world was basically two seperate substances or beings held together in dialectical tension. On the one hand, there was spirit, light, or goodness, or the good god, and, on the other, matter, darkness, or evil, or the bad god. If the division were pushed too far, the result was a collapse of the dialectic and some form of radical dualism, a form in which the dialectical relationship was shattered and two alien, warring worlds left.

Salvation, in both the dialectical and dualistic perspectives, was deliverance from the bad order to the good order, from matter to spirit, from will to reason, from material preoccupations to spiritual pre-occupations, or, possibly, vice versa. Instead of the whole man, mind and will, matter and spirit, being fallen, only one segment of him was fallen, the other remaining by nature pure.

In such a perspective both salvation and sanctification involved a desertion of the one realm for the other. Sanctification thus meant forsaking the world; it meant "spirituality," and spiritual exercises. Before the church became infected by such thinking, Jewish believers who were Hellenic in their thinking had already chosen the path of asceticism and the renunciation of earthly things. The Hellenic world was pro-ducing a great variety of ascetics who were forsaking the world and the flesh in order to gain holiness. Simeon Stylites (390-459) showed more clearly the influence of pagan Syrian Atargatis cult than any Biblical faith. Simeon lived on a 66-foot pillar, topped with a flat summit three feet wide; on this he spent 37 years in all kinds of wild austerities. For 40 years of his life, he passed the whole of Lent without taking any food. The practices of Simeon Stylites had nothing to do with Biblical holiness. They were a neoplatonic and pagan contempt of the flesh and an attempt to transcend it.

A long and dreary chronical of horrors could be cited to illustrate the ways in which men have sought sanctification apart from the law. Self-torture, flagellations, fastings, hairshirts, and a great variety of devices have been used in order to give the seeker sanctification. The result has been neither peace nor holiness. Men have rolled themselves in thorn bushes, treated their bodies as a satanic enemy, and still found evil resting in the essence of their thoughts. Weak bodies have not made for strong souls.

The Reformation restated clearly the doctrine of justification, but it failed to clarify the doctrine of sanctification. The confusion is apparent in the Westminster Confession of Faith; chapter XIII, "Of Sanctification," is excellent as far as it goes, but it fails to specify precisely what the *way* of sanctification is. In chapter XIX, "Of the

Law of God," one of the errors of the Confession appears, in that Adam is placed under "a covenant of works," the law. However, in paragraph II, it is stated that "This law, after his fall, continued to be a perfect rule of righteousness; and, as such, was delivered by God upon Mount Sinai, in ten commandments, and written in two tables." The law is thus seen as the rule of righteousness, i.e., the way of sanctification. However, in paragraph IV, without any confirmation from Scripture, it is held that the "judicial laws" of the Bible "expired" with the Old Testament. We have previously seen how impossible it is to separate any law of Scripture as the Westminster divines suggested. In what respect is "Thou shalt not steal" valid as moral law, and not valid as civil or judicial law? If we insist on this distinction, we are saying that the state is free to steal, and is beyond the law, whereas the individual is under the law. At this point, the Confession is guilty of nonsense. In paragraph VI, it is stated that the law is "a rule of life informing" believers "of the will of God, and their duty; it directs and binds them to walk accordingly." That which is a rule of life for man is also a rule of life for his courts, civil governments, and institutions, or else God is then only a God of individuals and not of institutions.

Somewhat earlier, the Formula of Concord (1576) had declared, in Article V, II, "We believe, teach, and confess that the Law is properly a doctrine divinely revealed, which teaches what is just and acceptable to God, and which also denounces whatever is sinful and opposite to the divine will." In Article VI, the law was declared to be, in its third purpose, "that regenerate men, to all of whom, nevertheless, much of the flesh still cleaves, for that very reason may have certain rules after which they may and ought to shape their lives." The law gives us the way of sanctification as against the "impulse of self-devised devotion" (Article VI, Affirmative III).[1]

In spite of this early and excellent statement, Protestantism has by and large by-passed the law as the way of sanctification in favor of the "impulse of self-devised devotion." Moreover, the more it has followed in this course, the more self-righteous and pharisaic has it become, a natural course where men make the word of God of none effect through their traditions (Matt. 15:6-9). The sanctified person in Protestantism is too often a sanctimonious law-breaker who goes to Sunday School, attends church twice each Sunday, prayer-meeting in the week, gives testimonies when asked, and is amazed if he is told that the law of God, rather than man-made spiritual exercises, constitutes the way of sanctification. Many preachers stress long hours of prayer as a mark of holiness, in plain defiance of Christ's condemnation

---

1. See Philip Schaff: *The Creeds of Christendom* (New York: Harper, 1877) III.

of those who thought, with their long prayers, they would "be heard for their much speaking" (Matt. 6:7).

In Arminian churches, and especially the so-called "holiness" churches (Pentecostal and others), sanctification is associated with various emotional binges which are far closer to the methods of ancient Baal worship, which, in its extreme, went into cutting and even castrating oneself (I Kings 18:28). St. Paul said of the Judaizers who were substituting law for grace, and then man's traditions for the law of God, that he wished these men who challenged him and troubled the churches would prove their greater holiness by means of their own logic: "I wish those who are unsettling you would also become eunuchs" (Gal. 5:12, Berkeley Version). Lenski's comment here is to the point:

> With their circumcision these Judaizers want to outdo Paul and take the Galatians away from him. But if they have no more to offer than Paul offers, if, as they claim, he, too, still preaches circumcision, how will they be able to outdo him? Well, there is a way—would that they might try it! Let them have themselves castrated! Then they would, indeed, leave Paul behind who, as they say, still preaches only circumcision.[2]

Since these men had no law, only man's traditions, the logical way to prove their superiority to the flesh was to cut it off at the critical point! More than once, in the history of the church, this temptation has been succumbed to, as a means of holiness, and Origen is the best-known instance.

Where sanctification is a matter of spiritual exercises under the "impulse of self-devised devotion," there all kinds of errors abound. Caldwell cites the statement of a "holiness" church member who felt superior to others who testified because he had been the bigger sinner and could give a greater testimony and be more sanctifying to the congregation. He had earlier committed adultery with "a sister-preacher" and with two married women at the same time, all of which made him more "holy" because he had ostensibly forsaken more.[3]

During the 1950's and well into the 1960's, the Orthodox Presbyterian Church was deeply troubled and divided over the issue of Peniel teachings, which had infected many of its most earnest ministers. These men, deeply troubled by the lack of spiritual growth among their members, began to seek the answer in the guidance of the Holy Spirit. Because sanctification was sought through the Holy Spirit but without

2. R. C. H. Lenski: *The Interpretation of St. Paul's Epistle to the Galatians, to the Ephesians, and to the Philippians* (Columbus, Ohio: Wartburg Press, 1937, 1946), p. 271.
3. Erskine Caldwell: *Deep South, Memory and Observation* (New York: Weybright and Talley, 1966, 1968), pp. 58-62.

reference to the law, the result was irrationalism and spiritual pride, a basic lawlessness. Tragically, these were precisely the men who sensed the need for growth, the inadequacy of current preaching and living, and who felt that sanctification was somehow the key. Their quest of a way of sanctification apart from the law was a radical failure. On the other hand, those who condemned them simply continued in their own spiritually immature, or, more commonly, sterile condition, spiritual eunuchs by choice.

The modernists have denied both Biblical doctrines, justification and sanctification. They have returned to a modified phariseeism and seek to save man by man's works and traditions. Love then becomes the means of sanctification, a non-discriminating love of all men. Because of its radical antinomianism, modernism is often congenial to various aspects of Pentecostalism, speaking in tongues in particular. In all these manifestations, man's way is paramount.

In our analysis of truth-telling, attention was called to the abstract concept of holiness implicit in many churchmen, a doctrine which is in essence paganism. The perfect individual is seen as his own ultimate. His actions are abstracted from the reality of God and His world, and an abstract standard of reality and holiness is insisted on. The personal perfection of the midwives in Egypt (Ex. 1:17-21) is more important than anything else. Champions of this position within the church are quick to claim that this perfection is Biblical perfection and God's desire, but they clearly contradict the Scripture and disapprove that which God clearly approves of. It is more important to them that Rahab, the midwives, and they themselves preserve their abstract purity than that godly lives be saved in the warfare of the world against God.

Let us examine, with this in mind, the definition of sanctification as given by a very able Calvinistic scholar. According to Berkhof, "Sanctification may be defined as *that gracious and continuous operation of the Holy Spirit, by which He delivers the justified sinner from the pollution of sin, renews his whole nature in the image of God, and enables him to perform good works.*"[3] As far as it goes, this definition is good, but how are the good works to be defined? How do we know specifically and precisely what good works are? According to Berkhof, "good works" are those "works that are essentially different in moral quality from the actions of the unregenerate, that are the expressions of a new and holy nature, as the principle from which they spring."[4] This is still very vague. Then Berkhof adds, "They are not only in external conformity with the law of God, but

---

3. Louis Berkhof: *Systematic Theology.* Third revised and enlarged edition. (Grand Rapids: Eerdmans, 1946), p. 532.

are also done in conscious obedience to the revealed will of God, that is, because they are required by God."[5] Here, finally, the truth is out: sanctification does require obedience to the law of God because God commands it. Since the law is basic to sanctification, why then mention it only in a left-handed way in a chapter of 17 pages, and then only in passing? Is it any wonder that most people miss this point and seek sanctification, not in the law, but in spiritual exercises?

Earlier, both in teaching and in practice, the law was the rule of sanctification. The law was basic to sanctification in the medieval church, although commands of the church came to be added to it, and it was the rule also in many Protestant circles. Thus Heyns, in writing on sanctification, described "The Law of God as Rule," declaring in part:

> We, however, confess: "according to the law," which means that the Law only is the rule of sanctification, for so the Word of God teaches. Isa. 8:20; Ps. 119:105. And our fathers were so zealous in adhering to God's ordinances and to them alone, that they even objected to the observance of the Christian feastdays and weekday prayer services. They feared that desiring to do more than that which the Lord had commanded in His Word would result in relaxing with respect to that which he had instituted.
>
> Isa. 8:20, To the law and to the testimony! if they speak not according to this word, surely there is no morning for them.
>
> Ps. 119:105, Thy word is a lamp unto my feet, and light unto my path.[6]

Now, in many quarters of Protestant evangelicalism, sanctification is equated with attending church twice each Sunday, and the weekday prayer service as well. But such practices fail to satisfy man's spiritual hunger, and other spiritual exercises are added. Thus, one Los Angeles doctor began, while still in Berkeley in 1942, to set his alarm for 5:30 A.M. in order to spend an hour in prayer. He reported his experience the first morning:

> I felt my way out into the dark living room. I switched on a light, knelt down in front of the sofa and started to pray.
>
> I prayed for my family, friends, patients, the other doctors at the hospital, doctors at other hospitals, doctors who didn't have hospitals, our country, our soldiers, the enemy, all the missionaries I knew. At last I looked at my watch. Only 20 minutes had gone by.
>
> I went back over the whole list in more detail, and at last 60 minutes crawled past. I was exhausted. . . .

---

4. *Ibid.,* p. 540 f.
5. *Ibid.,* p. 541.
6. W. Heyns, *Manual of Reformed Doctrine* (Grand Rapids: Eerdmans, 1926), p. 296.

Week by week, God was not only becoming more real to me, He was becoming the meaning in all reality, and the hour that had started out seeming so long now became more and more precious. My whole life, in fact, was different, and I knew the investment of time was paying off.[7]

After the war, this doctor established a prayer-group in Berkeley. I do not know the doctor personally, but many of the members of his group were familiar to me, as were a few of their sessions. All glowed with a strong self-righteousness, had grown adept at long prayers, and were concerned that their method was the key to true spiritual growth and sanctification. The only visible result of this "impulse of self-devised devotion" was a growth in phariseeism, and a growing dis-interest in any real knowledge of Scripture. Prayer without law-keeping can induce self-satisfaction, but only prayer with law-keeping is honoring to God. I received, in fact, some valuable theological and Biblical studies from one member of the group who was now interested in this "deeper" life. The condemnation by our Lord of those who "think they shall be heard for their much speaking" (Matt. 6:7) still stands.

The call to sanctification, "Ye shall be holy, for I the LORD your God am holy" (Lev. 19:2) is *a summons to obey the law: it is the rule of sanctification.* This is no new word: it is as old as Scripture. It was taught by many saints through the Middle Ages, and it was basic to Luther's perspective. In his comment on Romans 3:31, "We establish the law," Luther declared:

> On the other hand, the Law is established and confirmed when its demands or injunctions are heeded. In this sense the Apostle says: "We establish the Law"; that is: We say that it is obeyed and fulfilled through faith. But you who teach that the works of the Law justify without faith, make the law void; for you do not obey it; indeed, you teach that its fulfillment is not necessary; the Law is established *in us* when we fulfill it willingly and truly. But this no one can do without faith. They destroy God's covenant (of the Law) who are without the divine grace that is granted to those who believe in Christ.[8]

Moreover, in his Small Catechism, Luther taught, "the Law teaches us Christians which works we must do to lead a God-pleasing life. (A rule)."[9] Unfortunately, in other places Luther replaced law with love,[10] and Calvin, also self-contradictory here, at times required the

---

7. Dr. Ralph L. Byron, Jr.: "Lenten Guideposts: Prayer Hour Changed Doctor's Life," Los Angeles *Herald-Examiner* (Monday, February 16, 1970), p. A-6.
8. Martin Luther: *Commentary on the Epistle to the Romans.* Translated by J. Theodore Mueller (Grand Rapids: Zondervan, 1954), p. 64.
9. *Luther's Small Catechism* (St. Louis: Concordia, 1943), p. 86.
10. Luther: *Deuteronomy,* p. 70.

law as the rule of life, surpassing Luther in his insistence that the state enforce both tables of the law.[11] Calvin, in fact, cited the law as "the rule of life."[12] The failure of men in every age to be clear-cut in this matter does not absolve the people of God: they have the law.

3. The False Prophet

The false witness which is banned by the ninth commandment includes a false witness concerning God. In Deuteronomy 18:9-22, we have, not only a prophecy of Christ's coming but also a test of false prophets.

The law begins by banning certain forms of idolatry which are "unlawful means of communication with the unseen world."[1] No trick of magic, nor any kind of ritual, can coerce God. God does not reveal Himself in answer to ritual or rite, nor does He prosper men in response to gifts and bribes. Instead of turning to these "abominations" which only brought judgment on the Canaanites (Deut. 18:12, 14), "Thou shalt be perfect (or upright) with the LORD thy God" (Deut. 18:13). Rashi's comment is worth quoting: "Thou shalt walk with Him in sincerity, and wait for Him. And thou shalt not pry into the future. But whatsoever cometh upon thee, take it with simplicity, and then thou shalt *be with Him*, and be his portion."[2]

More important, however, is the fact that the purpose of these unlawful rites is prediction, the desire to know the future and to predict it. In a very central sense, the believer must walk by faith, not by sight. Precise and personal prediction and preview of the future is closed to him.

In another sense, however, the law itself is given as the God-ordained means of prediction for a nation. The central purpose of Deuteronomy 27–31 is to provide the people of God with a true means of prediction, and that means of prediction is the law. If men disobey the law, certain curses ensue; if they obey the law, blessings result. Because the law is concerned with prediction, the people of God will avoid all lawless claims to prediction. The one principle of prediction is the sovereign power and decree of God; the other principle of prediction is the demonic power which seeks to establish an independent and revolutionary concept of power and control.

The law was given through Moses, but the means whereby the law was given was terrifying to Israel and brought them close to the

---

11. William A. Müeller: *Church and State in Luther and Calvin* (Garden City, New York: Doubleday Anchor Books, [1954], 1965), p. 128.

12. Calvin, "Catechism of The Church of Geneva," in *Tracts and Treatises.* T. F. Torrance translation (Grand Rapids: Eerdmans, 1958), II, 56.

1. C. H. Waller, "Deuternomy," in Ellicott, II, 54.

2. *Ibid.*

presence of judgment. God will therefore raise up another Prophet, another Moses or law-giver, "and will put my words in his mouth; and he shall speak unto them all that I shall command him" (Deut. 18:18). The Great Prophet is thus given in terms of the original law, and as the law-giver. The key to the relationship of the Prophet to Moses is the law.

False prophets shall arise representing another god or power, and therefore another law. Their falsity will be revealed by their false predictions. Because the principle of true prediction is the law-word of God, all the prophets, culminating in Jesus Christ, spoke, inspired of God, in terms of that law. Jeremiah, in prophesying the captivity, echoed the law-prediction of Deuteronomy 27–31; because he also spoke by God's inspiration, he could also declare that the captivity would last seventy years (Jer. 25:11).

The key to the matter is the law. Where there is no law, there is no true prophecy, neither a true speaking for God nor true prediction. Whenever and wherever Christians have become neglectful of the law, they have been easily and readily misled by charlatans.

A classic example of this was Peregrinus Proteus, a Cynic philosopher who died in A.D. 165, but who has had his defenders among some modern philosophers, as well as among those of his era like Aulus Gellius. The career of Peregrinus saw him in many areas—in Rome (from whence he was banned for an insult to Emperor Antoninus Pius), in Athens as a teacher, in Syria, where he was imprisoned, and so on. In his youth, he wandered into Armenia, with unhappy results, according to Lucian:

> This creation and masterpiece of nature, this Polyclitan canon, as soon as he came of age, was taken in adultery in Armenia and got a sound thrashing, but finally jumped down from the roof and made his escape, with a radish stopping his vent. Then he corrupted a handsome boy, and by paying three thousand drachmas to the boy's parents, who were poor, bought himself off from being brought before the governor of the province of Asia.

> All this and the like of it I propose to pass over; for he was still unshapen clay, and our "holy image" had not yet been consummated for us. What he did to his father, however, is very well worth hearing; but you all know it—you have heard how he strangled the aged man, unable to tolerate his living beyond sixty years. Then, when the affair had been noised abroad, he condemned himself to exile and roamed about, going to one country after another.[3]

Peregrinis headed for Palestine and quickly associated himself with various antinomian Christians, and became their "prophet, cult-leader,

---

3. Lucian, "The Passing of Peregrinus," in *Works of Lucian* (Cambridge: Harvard, 1936, 1962), V, 11.

head of the synagogue, and everything, all by himself." He became to
these people their new lord: "they revered him as a god, made use of
him as a lawgiver, and set him down as a protector, next after that
other, to be sure, whom they still worship, the man who was crucified
in Palestine, because he introduced this new cult into the world." He
came to be called "the new Socrates."[4]

Peregrinus also picked up Hindu ideas and generally made himself
into a kind of universal prophet.

Imprisoned in Syria, he was liberally helped by these pseudo-
Christians, and the Roman governor of the province freed Peregrinus
as an unjustly persecuted philosopher.

Peregrinus now had a professional garb: he wore his hair long,
dressed in a dirty mantel, "had a wallet slung at his side, the staff was
in his hand, and in general he was very histrionic in his get-up."[5] Returning to his home, a small Greek town, he found hostility there because of his murder of his father for the estate. Peregrinus gave the
sizable estate to the town, and the murder charges were dropped. The
people hailed him as " 'The one and only philosopher! The one and
only patriot! The one and only rival of Diogenes and Crates!' His
enemies were muzzled, and anyone who tried to mention the murder
was at once pelted with stones."[6]

Later, he became objectionable to his pseudo-Christian following,
and he sought new worlds to conquer by studying under a famous
pagan ascetic.

> Thereafter he went away a third time, to Egypt, to visit Agathobu-
> lus, where he took that wonderful course of training in asceticism,
> shaving one half of his head, daubing his face with mud, and dem-
> onstrating what they call "indifference" by erecting his yard amid a
> thronging mob of bystanders, besides giving and taking blows on
> the back-sides with a stalk of fennel, and playing the mountebank
> even more audaciously in many other ways.[7]

He then went to Rome, was banished, went to Athens, and again
stirred up trouble. Finally, with his reputation falling, he devised a
publicity-provoking plan: at the next Olympic games, a year away, he
would burn himself up. Peregrinus was immediately in the limelight
again. Some held that he hoped that his plans would be forbidden,
because the site chosen was a holy place, or near one. Peregrinus himself announced that he would "become a guardian spirit of the night;
it is plain, too, that he already covets altars and expects to be imaged
in gold."[8] On the appointed day, for the pre-pyre funeral service,
Peregrinus came out, and, in a long speech, declared, "I wish to benefit

---

4. *Ibid.,* p. 13.
5. *Ibid.,* p. 17.
6. *Ibid.,* p. 19.

7. *Ibid.,* p. 19 f.
8. *Ibid.,* p. 31.

mankind by showing them the way in which one should despise death."
Some cried out, "Preserve your life for the Greeks!," but most shouted,
"carry out your purpose!"[9] When the games ended some days later,
Peregrinus jumped into the flames; Lucian described him as "a man
who (to put it briefly) never fixed his gaze on the verities, but always
did and said everything with a view of glory and the praise of the
multitude, even to the extent of leaping into fire, when he was sure
not to enjoy the praise because he could not hear it."[10]

The case of Peregrinus has been cited in some detail precisely because it is now, in average circles, non-controversial and therefore
illustrates readily the problem of antinomian religious leaders. They
are, like Peregrinus, *first* of all, lawless, antinomian men. There may
be degrees of difference in their morality, but their basic character is
the same. *Second*, instead of a zeal for the law-word of God, there is
a zeal for self-promotion and self-glory.

There are many claimants to special revelations and a fresh word of
prophecy. Thus, a 1970 advertisement spoke of the continuing "campaign" of one "evangelist" whose Sunday night subject was "Jesus
Walked into my Room and Talked With Me in Jerusalem."[11] Can anyone imagine St. Paul conducting such a "campaign"?

However, those who fail to teach the whole word of God are no
less guilty of being false prophets. They who neglect the law have
no gospel, for they have denied the righteousness of God which is
basic to the gospel.

The death penalty is required for those who "presume to speak a
word in my name, which I have not commanded him to speak, or that
shall speak in the name of other gods, even that prophet shall die"
(Deut. 18:20). This law is in part responsible for the executions of
heretics in the medieval and Reformation eras, and these executions
are now strongly condemned. Clearly, in most cases, these executions
involved other presuppositions. Moreover, the point of this law was
misconstrued. The heresies were often serious, and the executions
were sometimes unjustified, but the law here does not deal with heresies,
or matters of doctrine, important as they are, but with predictive
prophecy in terms of an alien or false god and law. Such predictive
prophecy rested, like the child sacrifice, witchcraft, magic, and related
practices described at the beginning of this law (Deut. 18:9-14), on
an anti-God faith, constituted treason to the society, and represented
an alien and revolutionary law-order. Their toleration is suicidal.

Those who deliberately teach a revolutionary law-order are traitors

---

9. *Ibid.*, p. 37 f.
10. *Ibid.*, p. 47 f.
11. Los Angeles *Herald-Examiner*, Saturday, Feb. 21, 1970, p. A-9.

3

to the existing law-order. Those who preach by cupidity, greed, or antinomian tendencies a defective view of Scripture are also traitors, although not in the same sense or to the same degree.

No society can escape penalizing those who vary from its fundamental faith. Marxist societies execute those who vary from or challenge its fundamental dogma. Socialist and democratic states are less severe, but they still execute traitors who give aid and comfort to the enemy. The fundamental religious presupposition of every society is either defended, or the society perishes. In a Christian social order, it is not the ecclesiastical deviations which must be the civil concern, but rather the challenges to its law-structure. To permit revolution is to perish. Toleration is due to differences within a law-system, but not to those dedicated to overthrowing the law-system. Rome, in persecuting the early church, was trying to preserve its law-order; the emperors clearly saw the issue: Christ or Caesar. Their moral and religious premise was false, but their civil intelligence was sound: either the pagan empire or the church had to die. They failed to see that the empire was already dying, and that the death of Christians would not save Rome's failing life. It was Constantine's grasp of this fact that led to the recognition of Christianity.

The relationship of the various kinds of false prediction (witchcraft, magic, spiritualism, etc.) to subversion deserves extensive study. It is no coincidence that May Day, the ancient fertility cult festival of witches, has repeatedly been a day of central importance to revolutionaries, as witness the Marxists. The anti-Christian lawyers who celebrate it as "law-day" have an anti-Christian law in mind.

4. The Witness of the False Prophet

In analyzing the work of the false prophet (Deut. 18:9-22), we saw that the purpose of the magic, sacrifice, divination, and related rites of false prophecy is *prediction*. The prediction involved in the rites described (Deut. 18:9-14) has as its basic premise the belief that real and ultimate power resides elsewhere than in God. The practice of false prophecy could involve child sacrifice, divination, astrology, enchantment, witchcraft, charms, spiritualism, wizardry, necromancery, and the like. It could also involve simply the belief that Satan is the ultimate power.

Satan tempted Jesus to become a false prophet. In the culminating temptation, we are told,

> Again, the devil taketh him up into an exceeding high mountain, and sheweth him all the kingdoms of the world, and the glory of them; And saith unto him, All these things will I give thee, if thou wilt fall down and worship me.

> Then saith Jesus unto him, Get thee hence, Satan: for it is written,
> Thou shalt worship the Lord thy God, and him only shalt thou
> serve (Matt. 4:8-10).

The meaning of this temptation is of central importance. Satan, in
approaching Jesus in this final attempt to make Him a false prophet,
had, among other things, two basic ideas in mind. *First*, Satan asked
Jesus to admit the rightness of his rebellion, to affirm that the creature
had a legitimate right to independence from the Creator. Had Jesus
in the slightest degree offered any excuse for man's sin, conceded to
the environmental excuse, or felt that some independence from God
on man's part is justifiable, He would have conceded to Satan a moral
justification. This Jesus refused to do: "Thou shalt worship the Lord
thy God, and him only shalt thou serve."

Second, Satan claimed a world power that was not his to claim or
to give. A fundamental premise of the law-word is that "The earth is
the LORD'S" (Ex. 9:29; Deut. 10:14; Ps. 24:1; I Cor. 10:26).
Satan neither rules it nor holds title to it, nor can he give it to
anyone.

At this point, many people are seriously in error. Genesis 3 gives
us the Biblical answer: Adam and Eve were guilty before God of rebellion, of apostasy. They compounded their sin by each placing the
blame on someone else: the serpent, and the woman. The guilt of Satan
made no difference to the fact that Adam and Eve were primarily and
essentially guilty for their own sin.

Others disagree with God's word. The Marxist answer was clearly
stated in terms of Genesis 3 by Lincoln Steffens some years ago at a
Jonathan Club dinner meeting in Los Angeles. At a second meeting,
with about a hundred prominent citizens present, Steffens summed it up
to his listeners, who included John R. Haynes, William Mulholland, the
Episcopal bishop, and others:

> You want to fix the fault at the very start of things. Maybe we can,
> Bishop. Most people, you know, say it was Adam. But Adam, you
> remember, he said that it was Eve, the woman; she did it. And
> Eve said no, no, it wasn't she; it was the serpent. And that's where
> you clergy have stuck ever since. You blame that serpent, Satan.
> Now I come and I am trying to show you that it was, it is, the
> apple.[1]

Steffens' answer is good Marxism; it affirms the economic determinism:
"it was, it is, the apple." This doctrine is a denial of the personal responsibility affirmed by Scripture.

Equally deadly, however, is the very common doctrine of satanic

---

1. *The Autobiography of Lincoln Steffens* (New York: Harcourt, Brace, and
Company, 1931), p. 574.

determinism. At this point, Steffens was right, when he told the clergy present: "You blame that serpent, Satan." Too many churchmen have laid the foundation, over the centuries, for a doctrine of satanic determinism. We can call it also the conspiracy theory.

Now very clearly Scripture affirms the fact of conspiracies; Psalm 2 is a classic statement of their reality. This same psalm, however, strongly underscores their futility; God laughs at the conspiracies of the ungodly nations and summons His people to share in His laughter.

Conspiracies prosper only when moral order declines. In every society, there are criminals, thieves, and murderers. Only as a society goes into a moral decline and collapse do these elements gain any ascendancy. The declining Roman Empire saw a proliferation of cults espousing revolution, communism, free love, homosexuality, and much more. When Christendom went into moral decline after the 13th century, again these criminal secret societies began to abound. Some affirmed communism, others staged nude protests and marches, and still others plotted revolution. As Schmidt observed of the Reformation era, "The whole of Europe around Calvin was polluted by fraternities, some spreading 'enlightenment' and some scepticism."[2] The Reformation and the Counter-Reformation led to the temporary decline of these groups, which rose again as Christian faith, law, and order declined.

But those who bear false witness, who ascribe to Satan powers which belong only to God, are not content to recognize that conspiracies exist. They go much further. *First*, they ascribe to conspiracies a moral order and a discipline which is an impossibility. Satan cannot construct or create; he is merely a destroyer, a murderer, and he has power *only* to the extent that we forsake the true power of God. The Soviet Union, to cite an international conspiratorial government, is a corrupt, bumbling, and radically incompetent agency. It has required the repeated aid of other countries plus imperialistic looting in order to survive. The Hoover relief of the 1920's, the Roosevelt recognition of the 1930's, and continuing proppings have kept it alive. The communist problem is not their evil power and ability but rather the steady moral collapse of Christian churches and nations, and their radical apostasy.

Second, the power of evil is weak and limited; it is under God's control and is His scourge of the nations. The weakness of evil conspiracies means that they can normally only occupy a vacuum. The roots of Soviet power are in the moral decay of Russia and its Kenotic Christianity; the Soviet victories in the Baltic countries are due to the morally compromised position of the Western Allies, who sold these countries out.

2. Albert-Marie Schmidt: *Calvin and the Calvinistic Tradition* (New York: Harper, 1960), p. 58.

Third, the key to overcoming evil conspiracies is not a concentration on evil but godly reconstruction. One of the sins Jesus Christ condemned in some members of the church at Thyatira was their concern with studying "the depths of Satan," which can be translated as "exploring the deep or hidden things of Satan" (Rev. 2:24). The non-Christian conservative movements are radically given to studying or exploring the deep things of Satan, as though this were the key to the future.

Fourth, implicit in all this is the belief, as noted, in satanic determination, which makes of these conservatives staunch Satanists. To deny the sovereign power of conspiracies is one of the surest ways of antagonizing many of the people, who will then argue with religious passion for the sovereign, predestinating power of Satan. They will insist that every national and international act is a carefully planned and manipulated conspiracy, all governed by a master plan or plot, and a secret master council. That the plotters and plans exist, and are many, can be granted, but the Christian must hold to their futility. They rage in vain; they "imagine a vain thing" when they plot together against the Lord and His anointed (Ps. 2:1, 2).

To blame the world's evils, and to ascribe the world's government, to hidden satanic conspiracies is to be guilty of false witness against God. It is comparable to resorting to magic, witchcraft, or human sacrifice. It denies that God only is the source of prediction and ascribes power and prediction to Satan instead.

Far better than most theologians, Berle has described the laws of power:

> Five natural laws of power are discernible. They are applicable wherever, and at whatever level, power appears, whether it be that of the mother in her nursery or that of the executive head of a business, the mayor of a city, the dictator of an empire.
>
> They are:
>
> *One*: Power invariably fills any vacuum in human organization. As between chaos and power, the latter always prevails.
>
> *Two*: Power is invariably personal. There is no such thing as "class power," "elite power," or "group power," though classes, elites, and groups may assist processes of organization by which power is lodged in individuals.
>
> *Three*: Power is invariably based on a system of ideas or philosophy. Absent such a system or philosophy, the institutions essential to power cease to be reliable, power ceases to be effective, and the power holder is eventually displaced.
>
> *Four*: Power is exercised through, and depends on, institutions. By their existence, they limit, come to control, and eventually confer or withdraw power.

Five: Power is invariably confronted with, and acts in the presence of, a field of responsibility. The two constantly interact, in hostility or co-operation, in conflict or through some form of dialogue, organized or unorganized, made part of, or perhaps intruding into, the institutions on which power depends.[3]

Berle is right. Power is based on a faith, a philosophy. When the faith or philosophy behind a culture begins to die, there is a shift of power. Today, because Christian faith has waned and has become anti-nomian, it cannot maintain or create a law-order. As a result, ancient criminal impulses and movements grasp at power. The key to displacing these grasping evil powers is not a study of the deep things of Satan, nor a belief in their power, but godly reconstruction in terms of Biblical faith, morality, and law. For many non-Christian conservatives, the test of a true conservative is simply this: Does he believe in the existence, plan, and power of the conspirators, call them what you will? This test is a satanic one: it holds almost as much danger to society, if not more, as does the belief that the apple is to blame, i.e., as economic determinism. It is a form of Moloch worship. God confronted Adam and Eve in Eden with *their* responsibility; Nathan declares to David, "Thou art the man" (II Sam. 12:7).

The Biblical position involves not only an affirmation of man's essential responsibility, but it also declares that God alone is the almighty one, and He alone predestines and governs all things. To ascribe to conspiracies a power, discipline, and government of the past, present, and future which is not theirs is another form of affirming witchcraft and like "abominations." It is to become a false prophet, and to make a false witness.

It means also incurring God's judgment. To affirm another power is to deny God and His law. Not surprisingly, an antinomian age has readily subscribed to such beliefs. But God will no more respect the antinomianism of the church members than He will the lawlessness of the ungodly. At this point, men face the only effective "conspiracy": God's "conspiracy" against all who deny or forsake Him.

The commandment, "Thou shalt not bear false witness," means that we must bear true witness concerning all things. We must not bear false witness concerning God or man, and we are not to bear false witness concerning Satan by ascribing to him power that belongs only to God. The true witness of the apostles was not a testimony about the powers of Satan but of the triumphant Christ. The world they faced, as a very small handful, was far more entrenched in its evil than our own, but the apostles did not spend their time documenting the depravity, perversity,

---

3. Adolf Augustus Berle: *Power* (New York: Harcourt, Brace & World, 1969), p. 37.

and power of Nero. Instead, St. Paul, who was aware of the approach of persecution, still wrote confidently to the Christians in Rome: "And the God of peace shall bruise Satan under your feet shortly" (Rom. 16:20). The confidence of St. John is similar: "this is the victory that overcometh the world, even our faith" (I John 5:4).

Today, however, many so-called Christian conservatives not only spend their time studying the work of Satan but become angry if you question the omnipotence of Satan. They insist that every step of our world history is now in the hands of satanic manipulators who use men as puppets. To deny this is to be classed as some kind of heretic; the practical meaning of this position is Satan worship. But St. John tells us that, at the supreme moment of Satan's conspiracy, when Christ's death was decreed, the secret purpose of God was being most fulfilled (John 11:47-53). It is always God who reigns, never Satan. Any other faith is a false witness and an especially evil one.

5. Corroboration

A fundamental aspect of Biblical law appears in the commandment, "Thou shalt not bear false witness." Basic to this law is its reference to the courts and to perjury. The courts represent God's vengeance as ordered and channelled through human but God-ordained agencies. Within the courts, for justice to prevail, honest and faithful testimony is a necessity. However, because man is a sinner, and the agencies of human society reflect man's sin, checks and balances are necessary. The testimony of a witness must be subject to cross-examination and to corroboration. The law is clear at this point:

> One witness shall not rise up against a man for any iniquity, or for any sin that he sinneth: at the mouth of two witnesses, or at the mouth of three witnesses, shall the matter be established (Deut. 19:5).

> At the mouth of two witnesses, or three witnesses, shall he that is worthy of death be put to death; but at the mouth of one witness he shall not be put to death (Deut. 17:6).

> Whoso killeth any person, the murderer shall be put to death by the mouth of witnesses: but one witness shall not testify against any person to cause him to die (Num. 35:30).

This law is echoed in the New Testament:

> Moreover, if thy brother shall trespass against thee, go and tell him his fault between thee and him alone: if he shall hear thee, thou hast gained thy brother.
> But if he will not hear thee, then take with thee one or two more, that in the mouth of two or three witnesses every word may be established (Matt. 18:15, 16).

In the mouth of two or three witnesses shall every word be established (II Cor. 13:1).

Against an elder receive not an accusation, but before two or three
witnesses (I Tim. 5:19).

He that despised Moses' law died without mercy under two or three
witnesses (Heb. 10:28).

As noted previously, we are not under any moral obligation to tell
the truth to an enemy seeking to harm or destroy us. The duty to tell
the truth is reserved for normal relationships which are within the framework of law, and to the proceedings of courts of law in church, state,
and other institutions.

Even here, however, there are limitations on the power of the court
or the demands of other persons. The Biblical law of testimony does not
permit torture or coerced confessions. Voluntary confession is possible,
but two or more witnesses are required for conviction. More strictly,
confession is never cited in the law; its place in a court was apparently
only in connection with corroborating evidence. Thus Achan's confession required confirming evidence before he was sentenced and executed (Josh. 7:19-26). The voluntary aspect of Achan's confession
must be noted. Biblical law preserves the integrity of the individual
against forced confession; the right of citizens to be protected from the
power of the state to compel their self-incrimination does not appear
outside of the Biblical legal tradition. The Fifth Amendment to the
U. S. Constitution of 1787 embodied this protection: no person can be
placed in double jeopardy, "nor shall be compelled, in any criminal
case, to be a witness against himself."

The objection of self-incrimination means that a Christian must oppose the use of lie detectors as a matter of principle. The lie detector
reverses a basic principle of justice. It is the duty of the law enforcement officials to prove guilt when a man is accused: the defendant is
innocent until proven guilty. By demanding that a suspect submit to a
lie detector test, this legal principle is denied: the suspect is assumed to
be guilty and is challenged to prove himself innocent by submitting to
that test.

Another point of interest with respect to lie detector tests has been
cited by a Christian police officer. An innocent man may submit to the
test in the hopes of clearing himself, but, once under test, his total
privacy is subject to invasion. He can be asked about religious beliefs
(in an anti-Christian society), political opinions, does he own any
guns, and almost anything the examiners choose to ask him. The
result is a forced confession.

Like lie detectors, wire-tapping is a form of illegal invasion of privacy; it involves a form of coerced confession, a destruction of the integrity of communication, which makes it clearly immoral and wrong.

There are other limitations on testimony. The right to silence on the grounds of privileged communication is to a degree granted to pastors and doctors. The presupposition in both cases is the same. The statements or confessions made by a person to his pastor or doctor in the course of a formal or professional relationship are privileged communications, because the person in question is in effect confessing to God in the form of a ministering agent. Both doctor and pastor are concerned with health, the one with physical and the other with spiritual health. Salvation literally means health. The religious nature of a doctor's calling is a deeply rooted one. Doctors were formerly monks, and hospitals until fairly recently were entirely and exclusively Christian institutions. The modern divorce of both pastor and doctor from Biblical faith does not alter the essential nature of their calling. Privileged communication rests on the presupposition of the religious function of pastor and doctor as God's servants in the ministry of health. A person's relationship to them is thus not the property of the human agent but of God. This does not deny the duty of pastor and doctor to urge a person to make restitution where restitution is due, or to urge confession where confession is due. It is their duty to uphold the law of God by urging compliance with it of all who come to them, but they cannot go beyond that fact of counsel.

At the present time, there are wide variations in the legal status of privileged communications with a pastor.[1] These differences reflect in part the theological uncertainties and instabilities of the various churches.

There are other limitations on the extent of testimony. Thus, conferences with one's attorney are privileged communications, since the attorney serves as the defendant's agent and representative in court. To compel an attorney's testimony is to deny the defendant his liberty and privacy. Similarly, the spouse of a defendant is barred from testimony on similar grounds, since it would involve self-incrimination. There are exceptions to these rules under certain circumstances, but the basic principle remains true. One such exception is in cases where a husband or wife assaults the other. The normal purpose of the restriction on testimony by a spouse concerning the marital partner is not only to protect against self-incrimination but to prevent the destruction of the marital relationship. In communist countries, the requirement that children and marital partners spy on one another is destructive of family life.

There are areas of conflict over the matter of privileged communi-

---

1. See William Harold Tiemann: *The Right to Silence, Privileged Communication and the Pastor* (Richmond, Va.: John Knox Press, 1964).

cation. Corporations have largely been held to have no immunity, and their books and records can be opened. Internal Revenue has regularly compelled individuals to open their records. The immunity of privileged communications has been held to apply to both civil and criminal cases, and both federal and state courts, despite some conflicts in the past.

If privileged communication and immunity from self-incrimination did not exist, then corroboration, the basic premise of the Biblical law of testimony, would not exist, because the routine method of "evidences" would be to force testimony out of the defendant. The law requires corroboration because it forbids coerced self-incrimination.

Thus, not only are we under no obligation to tell the truth to a lawless enemy who is bent on doing us harm, or destroying us, but the requirement to tell the truth in a court of law is strictly governed by law.

On the other hand, witnesses to a crime are under strict requirement to testify. As a general rule, men have a duty to give their testimony to courts of law in all inquiries where their testimony may be material, and the court is the judge of whether their witness is material. Inconvenience is no excuse. The judge and jury have the duty of assessing the value of the witness' testimony, not he himself. The court can also assess the credibility of the witness. Thus, for a long time U. S. courts did not regard as admissible the testimony of an unbeliever, since he could not subscribe to an oath; in his own behalf only could such a person testify, and then his testimony was subject to being discounted since the fear of God was not an essential aspect of his character.

The duty to testify is a part of the citizen's police power, his part in the administration of law. "It is a general rule of law and necessity of public justice that every person is compellable to bear testimony in the administration of the laws by the duly constituted courts of the country."[2] The duty to enforce the law is not merely a police and court responsibility but a public duty. The citizen is not himself the court or the prosecutor but as a witness must serve as an agent of justice by providing such material evidences as are necessary to determine the nature of the case. The court determines their validity. Until recently, the court could also examine the witness' religious beliefs, to determine his competency, because, "Clearly, a witness must be sensible to the obligation of an oath before he can be permitted to testify."[3] Until recently also, the criminal character of a man was a factor in assessing the man's testimony, although full pardon could restore competency. The details and variations are many, but the

---

2. William M. McKinney and Burdett A. Rich, editors: *Ruling Case Law,* vol. 28, Witnesses, 3; p. 419. 1921.
3. *Ibid.,* vol. 28, para. 41; p. 453.

central fact is the responsibility of all non-privileged witnesses to testify.

Failure to testify in Biblical law means being an accessory to the crime: "When thou sawest a thief, then thou consentedst with him, and has been partaker with adulterers" (Ps. 50:18).

Corroboration cannot exist as an instrument of justice if the citizenry is not mindful of its responsibilities in the enforcement of a law-order.

6. Perjury

Perjury is regarded as a very serious offense in Biblical law. Precisely because the procedures of Biblical law rest, not on coerced self-incrimination but on honest testimony, any perjury constitutes a destruction of the processes of justice. The law is thus explicit and severe in its attitude towards perjury:

> And ye shall not swear by my name falsely, neither shalt thou profane the name of thy God: I am the LORD (Lev. 19:12).

> At the mouth of two witnesses, or three witnesses, shall he that is worthy of death be put to death: but at the mouth of one witness he shall not be put to death.
> The hands of the witnesses shall be first upon him to put him to death, and afterwards the hands of all the people. So thou shalt put the evil away from among you (Deut. 17:6, 7).

> If a false witness rise up against any man to testify against him that which is wrong:
> Then both the men, between whom the controversy is, shall stand before the LORD, before the priests, and the judges, which shall be in those days;
> And the judges shall make diligent inquisition: and, behold, if the witness be a false witness, and hath testified falsely against his brother;
> Then ye shall do unto him, as he had thought to have done unto his brother: so shalt thou put the evil away from among you.
> And those which remain shall hear, and fear, and shall henceforth commit no more any such evil among you.
> And thine eye shall not pity; but life shall go for life, eye for eye, tooth for tooth, hand for hand, foot for foot (Deut. 19:16-21).

> A false witness shall not be unpunished, and he that speaketh lies shall not escape (Prov. 19:5).

> A false witness shall not be unpunished, and he that speaketh lies shall perish (Prov. 19:9).

> A man that beareth false witness against his neighbour is a maul, and a sword, and a sharp arrow (Prov. 25:18).

The law against false witness is repeatedly affirmed in the New Testament (Matt. 19:18; Mark 10:19; Luke 18:20; Rom. 13:9, etc.).

The law equates perjury with blasphemy, since it is God's justice which is offended (Lev. 19:12). The priests have a part in the procedures of the court, in that the witness' oath is made to the Lord, "before the priests, and the judges" (Deut. 19:17). *The courts are inescapably religious establishments.* The law they administer represents a religion and a morality, and the procedures of a court rest on the integrity of the oath under which testimony is given. Humanistic courts of law are thus doomed to decline in integrity and to collapse into radical injustice, because every man becomes his own law, and the court a law unto itself. Both oath and law are religious; alter the religion behind them, and the society is in revolution. Thus, it is apparent, *first* of all, that perjury is a religious as well as civil and criminal offense. While the Bible places severe limits on the ability of a court or of any man to invade the mind of an individual, it does clearly declare that all legally required testimony must be an honest and faithful witness, or else a criminal offense against God and man has been committed. Pagan cultures basically expected false testimony and relied on torture to extract the desired statements, whether true or false. Because Biblical law does not permit torture, nor does it permit testimony beyond certain limits, it requires the strictest honesty within those limits or else justice is thwarted. Because the Bible respects the person, it requires much of the person and therefore punishes that person who fails to maintain the God-ordained standard.

Second, the presupposition of Biblical law is individual responsibility and guilt. The Bible is not environmentalist in its explanation of sin. Deuteronomy 17:7 concludes, "So thou shalt put the evil away from you." Waller's comment on this sentence is especially telling:

> *The evil.*—The Greek version renders this "the wicked man," and the sentence is taken up in this form in I Cor. v. 13, "and ye shall put away from among you *that wicked person.*" The phrase is of frequent occurrence in Deuteronomy, and if we are to understand that in all places where it occurs "the evil" is to be understood of an individual, and to be taken in the masculine gender, the fact seems to deserve notice in considering the phrase "deliver us from evil" in the Lord's Prayer. There is really no such thing as wickedness in the world apart from some wicked being or person.[1]

Evil does not exist in the abstract. When we are confronted with sin, we are confronted with a person or persons, and we must deal with that person. The environmentalist approach detaches sin from the person and places it in the environment, which was precisely the thesis of Satan in Eden. Since God is ultimately our environment, this means that *every environmentalist is essentially at war with God.*

This point is of especial importance. Environmentalists disguise the basic issue by their sentimental appeals. A common saying has it that

---

1. C. H. Waller in Ellicott, II, 50.

we should "love the sinner and hate the sin." In terms of Scripture, this is an impossibility. Sin does not exist apart from man; it does not exist as an abstraction. There is no murder except where there are murderers, no adultery where there are no adulterers. Murder and adultery exist as possible violations of the law *by persons.* By separating the sin from the sinner, judgment is withheld from the actuality, the person, and placed upon the possibility, the sin. Because the sin is possible because God so created man, the judgment and guilt for this possibility are thus transferred to God. As Adam said to God, "The woman whom thou gavest to be with me, she gave me of the tree, and I did eat" (Gen. 3:12). God, having created the possibility, was thus blamed by Adam. The environmentalist is always at war with God.

Third, the penalty for perjury is in terms of the principle of an eye for an eye. Here Wright is surprisingly to the point:

> The principle of an eye for an eye is that on which Israelite law is based. It is one of the most misunderstood and misinterpreted principles in the O.T., owing to the fact that it is popularly thought to be a general command to take vengeance. Such an understanding is completely wrong. In neither the O.T. nor the N.T. is a man entitled to take vengeance. That is a matter which must be left to God. The principle of an eye for an eye is a legal one which limits vengeance. It is for the guidance of the judge in fixing a penalty which shall befit the crime committed. Hence it is the basic principle of all justice which is legally administered.[2]

This principle means that, in cases where the defendant's life is at stake, the false witness must be executed. If restitution of $1,000 is involved, the false witness must make a payment of $1,000. The penalty of the case falls on the perjurer.

It is important to realize that this Biblical law was once a part of American law. It is still on the books in some cases. Clark noted that "In Texas law, where perjury is committed on a trial of a capital felony, the punishment of the perjury shall be death. (See 32 Tex Jur 825, para 40;)"[3] In a California court, it was stated,

> It is time that the citizens of this state (California) fully realized that the Biblical injunction: "Thou shalt not bear false witness against thy neighbour," has been incorporated into the law of this state, and that every person before any competent tribunal, officer, or person, in any of the cases in which such an oath may by law be administered, wilfully and contrary to such oath, states as true any material matter which he knows to be false, is guilty of perjury, and is punishable by imprisonment in the state prison for not less than one nor more than fourteen years. People v Rosen (1937) 20 Cal. App. 2nd 445, 66, P2d 1208, 1210 (McComb J)[4]

2. G. Ernest Wright, "Deuteronomy," *Interpreter's Bible,* II, 454 f.
3. Clark, *Biblical Law,* p. 235, n 15.
4. *Ibid.,* p. 234, n. 13a.

In some states at least, if a prosecutor knowingly introduces false testimony, the verdict is nullified in that a fair trial has been denied the defendant.

The Apocrypha gives us a famous story of the death penalty being applied against two false witnesses who testified against Susanna. It is stated that "according to the law of Moses they did unto them in such sort as they maliciously intended to do to their neighbour: and they put them to death."

Fourth, the law forbids pity towards a perjurer, and, in general, towards malefactors: "thine eye shall not pity" (Deut. 19:21). In particular, pity towards one who bears false witness is a radically revolutionary emotion, in that it aligns us with those who are destroying social order. A Christian law-order cannot survive the breakdown of its courts, and every toleration of perjury, as of false witness in general, dissolves justice and communication and atomizes society. The fact that perjury is relatively unpunished today, and that false witness generally is tolerated, is no small aspect of our social decay.

Fifth, the significance of the sentence, "So thou shalt put the evil away from you," has already been cited, and also its relationship to the Lord's Prayer. The petition, "Deliver us from evil" (Matt. 6:13), is better translated, "deliver us from the evil one." Evil, again, is not abstract. It is Satan, and it is every evil person in the world. Immediately after this petition is the doxology, "For thine is the kingdom, and the power, and the glory, for ever. Amen" (Matt. 6:13). The kingdom, the power, and the glory belong to the triune God, not to the evil one. Those who ascribe to hidden conspiracies a radical step by step control over men and events are ascribing the kingdom to Satan and are Satanists. This is the greatest of false witnesses and is perjury.

Evil is serious, vicious, and deadly, because sinners are so. We need to pray for deliverance from the evil one. We are given the law in order to cope with every evil one. Punish the perjurer without pity. Do unto him as he sought to do unto others. Move in every case against those who bear false witness, steal, murder, or in any way trample on God's law presumptuously. Pity the righteous, the victims, the offended, the poor and the needy, widows and orphans, but move against the lawless. "So thou shalt put the evil away from among you."

7. Jesus Christ as The Witness

In Biblical law, the witness not only must give true and accurate testimony but must participate in the execution of the offender if it is a capital offense. According to Deuteronomy 17:6, 7,

At the mouth of two witnesses, or three witnesses, shall he that is worthy of death be put to death; but at the mouth of one witness he shall not be put to death.

The hands of the witnesses shall be first upon him to put him to death, and afterwards the hands of all the people. So thou shalt put the evil away from among you.

The same principle is affirmed in Leviticus 24:14 and Deuteronomy 13:9. The police power of all the people is implicit in this law. All have a duty to enforce the law, and, in an execution, the witnesses have a leading part. The enforcement of law requires the participation of all law-abiding citizens, and the law requires their involvement.

The meaning of "witness" has been confused, however, because of a post-Biblical development of the Greek word for *witness*. The Hebrew word for witness, *ed, edah*, is given in the Greek New Testament as *martus, marturion*. The Greek word is the proper translation for the Old Testament word, as Matthew 18:16, Mark 14:63, and many other passages make clear. But the Greek word *martus* is the origin of the English word "martyr," and the result is an amazing confusion. The witnesses to Christ were executed by the Roman Empire, and the result was a strange reversal of meaning. In the Bible, the witness is one who works to enforce the law and assist in its execution, even to the enforcement of the death penalty. "Martyr" now has come to mean the exact reverse, i.e., one who is executed rather than an executioner, one who is persecuted rather than one who is central to prosecution. The result is a serious misreading of Scripture.

The point is all the more important because Jesus Christ is identified as supremely *the* Witness:

And from Jesus Christ, who is the faithful witness, and the first begotten of the dead, and the prince of the kings of the earth. Unto him that loved us, and washed us from our sins in his own blood.
And hath made us kings and priests unto God and his Father; to him be glory and dominion for ever and ever. Amen (Rev. 1:5, 6).

And unto the angel of the church of the Laodiceans write; These things saith the Amen, the faithful and true witness, the beginning of the creation of God (Rev. 3:14).

The witness of Jesus Christ has reference to His earthly mission; then His death and resurrection are cited in Revelation 1:5, His triumph over the false witness against Him, and then in vss. 5 and 6, His enthronement over time and eternity and His enthronement of His people together with Him.[1] In the letter to the Laodiceans, Christ identifies Himself again as "the faithful and true witness." The meaning is obvious thereby: Jesus Christ testifies against that church and promises

---

1. R. C. H. Lenski: *The Interpretation of St. John's Revelation* (Columbus, Ohio: The Wartburg Press, 1943), p. 44.

to execute sentence against them if they do not repent (Rev. 3:15 ff.). As the greater Moses, as Himself the great Prophet (Deut. 18:15-19), Jesus Christ is both the giver and enforcer of the law. Israel rejected Him, and called His witness false; therefore, He sentenced Israel to death (Matt. 21:43 f.; 23:23-24; 28). The law was applied to Israel. It had borne false witness against Jesus Christ (Matt. 26:65 f.; 27:22) and had sentenced Him to death. The Biblical penalty for such perjury is death (Deut. 19:16-19). The significance of Jesus Christ as "the faithful and true witness" is that He not only witnesses against those who are at war against God, but He also executes them.

Associated with this title of "witness" is another, "the Amen" (Rev. 3:14). God's Amen means that He is faithful, i.e., "Thus it is and shall be so," whereas man's "amen" is an assent to God's and means "so let it be."[2] The Amen was frequently an assent to the law (Deut. 27:15; cp. Neh. 5:13). Jesus Christ is the Amen of God, because through Him "the purposes of God are established, II Cor. 1:20."[3] In Revelation 3:14, Jesus is the Amen because He is "the faithful and true witness," He who declares the law, gives testimony concerning all offenses against it, and, where men will not accept their death penalty in Christ's atonement, He executes sentence against the offender.

Jesus Christ as the witness is therefore the Lord and Judge over history. He gives witness concerning men and nations, passes sentence against them, and then proceeds to their judgement or execution. He is Shiloh, who bears the sceptre, who is the law-giver, and to whom the gathering of the people shall be (Gen. 49:10). As Lord of history and "the faithful and true witness," Jesus Christ therefore witnesses against every man and nation that establishes its life on any other premise than the sovereign and triune God and His infallible and absolute law-word. The cross of Christ witnesses against man; it declares that man has not only broken God's law and then compounded his guilt with self-righteous excuses, but he has further borne false witness against the Lord of glory and demanded His death (Matt. 21:38). Man has sought to seize the inheritance, the Kingdom of God (Matt. 21:38), on his own terms. The cross therefore requires judgment. The false witness concerning Jesus Christ, to which all unbelievers, all apostate churchmen, and all nations and institutions which deny His sovereignty and His law-word, with one accord assent, that law requires their death (Deut. 19:16-21). So Christ puts evil away from His realm, both in time and in eternity.

To speak of Christ as a *martyr* in the modern sense is thus a per-

2. W. E. Vine: *An Expository Dictionary of New Testament Words* (Westwood, N. J.: Fleming H. Revel, 1940, 1966), I, 53.
3. *Ibid.*

version of Scripture. As the witness in the continuing judgment, as well as the last judgment, and as King and judge over men and nations, He is not a martyr but the executioner, not a victim but the great victor over evil.

The ninth commandment, therefore, has eschatological significance. It is unusual among the commandments in that its key word, "witness," becomes a messianic title. This particular law-word is thus in itself a witness to the Witness, an affirmation of the inescapable triumph of Christ and His kingdom. The failure of the church to recognize the eschatological significance of this law concerning witness and the title, "the faithful and true witness," does not alter its importance or the inevitability of Christ's judgment and triumph. The failure of the churches serves only to make them at best castaways (I Cor. 9:27), fit only to be laid on a shelf, or to be tossed aside as useless.

On His way to the cross, Jesus turned to the women who wept for Him, saying, "Daughters of Jerusalem, weep not for me, but weep for yourselves, and for your children. For, behold, the days are coming, in the which they shall say, Blessed are the barren, and the wombs that never bare, and the paps which never gave suck. Then shall they begin to say to the mountains, Fall on us; and to the hills, Cover us" (Luke 23:28-30). Thus spoke Christ the Witness, who had already passed sentence of execution on the world and church of His day.

8. False Witness

In discussing "false witness" we are dealing with a variation of perjury, and, in a sense, could declare that the subject is closed simply by stating that false witness in its every form is prohibited. The subtle but important varieties of false witness are cited in the law, however, and we need to recognize them. By examining the specific context of the law, sometimes much is indicated as to its meaning. Thus, the meaning of Exodus 23:1, 2, 7 becomes clearer if verses 1-9 are examined:

> Thou shalt not raise a false report: put not thine hand with the wicked to be an unrighteous witness.
> Thou shalt not follow a multitude to do evil; neither shalt thou speak in a cause to decline after many to wrest judgment:
> Neither shalt thou countenance a poor man in his cause.
> If thou meet thine enemy's ox or his ass going astray, thou shalt surely bring it back to him again.
> If thou see the ass of him that hateth thee lying under his burden, and wouldest forbear to help him, thou shalt surely help with him.
> Thou shalt not wrest the judgment of thy poor in his cause.
> Keep thee far from a false matter; and the innocent and righteous slay thou not; for I will not justify the wicked.
> And thou shalt take no gift: for the gift blindeth the wise, and perverteth the words of the righteous.

Also thou shalt not oppress a stranger: for ye know the heart of a stranger, seeing ye were strangers in the land of Egypt.

Before examining this passage, let us note what Isaac Barrow long ago said of the ninth commandment:

> It is in the Hebrew, Thou shalt *not answer* (to wit, being examined or adjured in judgment) *against thy neighbor as a false witness;* so that primarily, it seems, bearing false testimony against our neighbour (especially in matters of capital or of high concernment to him) is prohibited; yet that not only this great crime, but that all injurious (even extra-judicial) prejudicing our neighbour's reputation, and consequently his safety or his welfare in any sort, is forbidden, we may collect from that explication of this law, or that parallel law, which we have in Leviticus: *Thou shalt not,* it is said there, *go up and down as a talebearer among thy people; neither shalt thou stand against the blood of thy neighbour*: as talebearer, that is, a merchant, or trader in ill reports and stories concerning our neighbour, to his prejudice; defaming him, or detracting from him, or breeding in the minds of men an ill opinion of him; which vile and mischievous practise is otherwise under several names condemned and reproved. . . .[1]

The law against false witness is thus primarily with reference to a court of law, and secondarily with reference to life in a community. Exodus 23:1-9 sets the law of false witness, in both its meanings, in the context of a broader requirement of justice. Rylaarsdam has called vss. 1-9 a "group of principles and admonitions" designed to give "the spirit of justice" and to "permeate all legal decisions."[2] Several principles appear in these laws. *First,* a godly man must move in terms of God's law, not the mob or "multitude," because the spirit of the mob, however powerful in governing man, is rarely if ever the law of God (vs. 2). A man must have courage and faith; not the power of man but the power of God must govern him. *Second,* just as he cannot be moved by the mob, neither can he be governed by personal considerations, i.e., pity for the poor (vs. 3), nor friendliness to the rich (vs. 6). Bribes are even greater instances of distortion of law, in that they blind man to the real issues, so that he deliberately gives a false witness, whether as witness or judge (vss. 7, 8). A stranger or alien must receive the same justice as a friend (vs. 9), and an enemy is due the same justice and assistance in real need as a friend (vss. 4, 5). *Third,* malicious witness is condemned, as are false reports, in the first verse, and we can infer that all the following verses give instances of such false reports or malicious witness. In brief, there is a close and necessary correlation between words and deeds. Malice in words means malice in deeds also. A man who issues a false and malicious report

---

1. *The Works of Isaac Barrow* (New York: John C. Riker, 1845), III, 38.
2. J. Coert Rylaarsdam, "Exodus," in *Interpreter's Bible*, I, 1009 f.

or witness concerning his neighbor, in or out of court, is likely also to be unwilling to assist that man if his ox is astray, and his ass overburdened. A dishonest witness is also essentially a corrupt neighbor.

In the modern perspective, words are often theoretically treated as though they are nothing. Freedom of speech is interpreted to mean the total right of expression without consequence, an ideal never fully established in practice.

The dream of absolute free speech is a myth and a delusion. No society has ever granted it. We do not recognize the right of a man to shout "fire!" in a crowded theatre, nor to call for the execution of the President, nor to publish totally false and malicious statements with respect to a man. Speech must be responsible to be free, and there is a social necessity for freedom of responsible speech. The advocates of free speech are logical in also demanding free action, freedom from all responsibility in speech and act. No society can exist if such total freedom from responsibility is permitted. Not surprisingly, the most vocal champions of free speech today are those who champion a revolution which will deny free speech to all others tomorrow. They suppress free speech in a very real fear of the responsible word as well as the irresponsible one. The foundations of their fear of contrary words is in part political safety, and in part religious fear.

In ancient pagan belief, the word had magical power. Word and act were *creatively* related. Because man is the god of all humanism, and paganism was humanistic, therefore man's word is held to have creative power. Hence the ancient search for the magic word which governed especially potent acts, "open sesame," "abracadabra," and the like. By possession of the word, man possessed special powers. This belief is echoed in occultism today, and in secret lodges with their special passwords and hidden terms.

It is not lacking from secular and public humanism, however, where the magical identification of word and act is often implicit. The partiality to the phrase-maker is perhaps evidence of this: American liberals preferred the impotent John F. Kennedy, who mouthed the language of the intellectuals, to the very substantial socialist gains of Lyndon B. Johnson, who lacked the verbalizing powers the liberals rejoice in.

A clearer example is the faith of the humanists in the power of rationally conceived plans and ideas. Because man's creative word is assumed to have divine power, so that the word is the act, *as with God*, so the humanistic intellectuals assume that once their rational or scientific plans are conceived they need only to be declared by the state in order to become a reality. The result is a very great humanistic faith in the power of legislation.

Van der Leeuw has summed it up ably:

> It is the word that decides the possibility. For it is an act, an atti-
> tude, a taking one's stand and an exercise of power, and in every
> word there is something creative. It is expressive, and exists prior
> to so-called actuality.[3]

For the humanist, the words of the non-humanist, of the uninformed,
the unenlightened, are empty words; the words of the elite are creative,
divine words.

The Biblical position is that man, created in the image of God,
speaks, not a creative word, but an analogical word, that is, he can
think and speak God's thoughts after Him, and therein is man's
power. Man exercises power and dominion under God to the extent
that he speaks and acts in terms of God's creative word.

It was the temptation of Satan that man could speak his own divine
and creative word: "Ye shall be as gods, knowing good and evil" (Gen.
3:5). Man, according to Satan, will then establish his own divine word,
speak and declare for himself what is good and evil; reality will be
re-ordered and re-created by man's own word. In the world of Satan,
man's word is the act, and the new world is born when man separates
himself by word from God.

Because man is created in the image of God, speech is important to
man. *Words* are the subject of two commandments, the third and the
ninth. When man gives false witness, when he takes the name of the
Lord in vain or acts in violation of it, man then denies the image in
favor of Satan's claim that man makes himself. When Sartre insists
that man makes his own essence, i.e., that man defines himself and
brings himself into being out of nothingness, he is affirming Satan's
position. But wherever man gives true witness in the full sense of
the word, there he grows in terms of the restored image of God.

The context of Exodus 23:1-9 makes clear thus that a faithful
witness is a part of a way of life, a spirit of justice. A faithful witness
transcends personal issues such as friendship or enmity towards a
man. Where men have no right to the truth, it is not because we dislike
them, but because they are at war with God's law, trying to extract
the truth from us for evil and unlawful ends.

The point is that the law of God must govern us. As Van Til has
observed with respect to philosophical thought, "God is the original
and . . . man is derivative."[4] Moreover, "If one does not make human
knowledge wholly dependent upon the original self-knowledge and

3. G. Van der Leeuw: *Religion in Essence and Manifestation* (New York:
Macmillan, 1938), p. 403.
4. Cornelius Van Til: *A Christian Theory of Knowledge* (Presbyterian and
Reformed Publishing Co., 1969), p. 16.

consequent revelation of God to man, then man will have to seek knowledge within himself as the final reference point."[5]

Translated into the world of law, this means that the point of reference in speech is not man. The law of God does not permit us to use words with reference to our love and hatred, likes and dislikes, or our profit and loss. The analogical word means the obedient word. The words of Rahab and the midwives were obedient words, and David cites also as the man of God, "He that sweareth to his own hurt, and changeth not" (Ps. 15:4), i.e., the man who gives honest testimony in a court of law to his own detriment. The entire psalm, in fact, stresses the significance of a total true witness:

> LORD, who shall abide in thy tabernacle? who shall dwell in thy holy hill?
> He that walketh uprightly, and worketh righteousness, and speaketh the truth in his heart.
> He that backbiteth not with his tongue, nor doeth evil to his neighbour, nor taketh up a reproach against his neighbour.
> In whose eyes a vile person is contemned; but he honoureth them that fear the LORD. He that sweareth to his own hurt, and changeth not.
> He that putteth not out his money to usury, nor taketh reward against the innocent. He that doeth these things shall never be moved (Ps. 15).

This psalm is a commentary on Exodus 23:1-9. The analogical word is the word of a faithful witness in the act of obedience. True witness has reference, first and last, to God and His justice, not to man and his wishes.

Where God's absolute law-word is gone, truth and true witness quickly vanish. A book by Sam Keen, *To a Dancing God*, begins:

> I, Sam Keen, wrote this book. The voice that speaks to you in these essays is mine. It is not the voice of Philosophy, or Theology, or Modern Man. What I offer is a series of personal reflections upon issues, problems, and crises with which I have had to wrestle. The conclusions I have reached are not inescapable. Both my doubts and my certainties may be too intimately connected to unique elements in my autobiography to be typical of that nebulous creature called "modern man." When I speak with assurance it is because I have discovered some elements of a style of life that are satisfying for me. However, the affirmations I make have no authority unless you choose to add your voice to mine. This is how it is with me. I cannot say how it is with you. Nevertheless I would invite you to replace the "I" of these essays with "we" when you find yourselves in agreement.[6]

---

5. *Ibid.*, p. 17.
6. Quoted in the April, 1970, Religious Book Club Bulletin. Mr. Keen's book was the club choice. Keen is a Fellow of the Western Behavioral Sciences Institute and Center for the Study of Persons.

Without God's absolute word, man can only offer a "life-style," not the truth; authority is also gone when truth is gone. The ability to distinguish between good and evil, right and wrong, is also gone, because, in an existential world, all things are relative, and man is beyond good and evil. Billy Graham, having moved progressively into an experiential concept of truth, could thus say, as cited in 1970 by Robert Davis in his "News Briefs," that "he refused to discuss Communism although he had once been known as a great foe of that system. 'For years I have not spoken about that,' he said. 'I cannot go around the world and say who is right and who is not right.' Graham's comments came in an interview with *Der Spiegel*, a German news magazine."

When truth and truth-telling are both divorced from God and His absolute law-word, they both disappear.

9. False Freedom

In Proverbs 19:5 we have a summation of the ninth commandment and its necessary enforcement: "A false witness shall not be unpunished, and he that speaketh lies shall not escape." The word "speaketh" can perhaps be translated "breathes out." In brief, the law requires, *first*, the prosecution of a false witness, and, *second*, the prosecution of liars and slanderers.

The Biblical law with respect to speech is therefore not a declaration of freedom of speech but a prohibition of false witness in court, and of malicious and false statements with respect to men and events in everyday affairs. The distinction is a very important one. The Biblical law gives freedom to the truth, not to false witness in its broadest sense. True freedom of speech rests on the prohibition of false witness.

At this point, a serious mis-reading of the U. S. Constitution of 1787 is very prevalent. Amendment I reads in part: "Congress shall make no law respecting an establishment of religion, or prohibiting the free exercise thereof; or abridging the freedom of speech, or of the press. . . ." This has now come to mean the prevalence of federal interpretation in every area of the United States; originally, it meant that the federal government was barred from any power to legislate with respect to religion, speech, or the press, because these areas were reserved to the citizens and/or the states. The various states had religious establishments and had no desire for a federal religious establishment to govern them. To understand the thinking of Americans on the subject seventy years after the writing of the Constitution, the comments of John Henry Hopkins, Episcopal bishop of the Diocese of Vermont, are most revealing:

The religious rights of the citizens of the United States consist in the enjoyment of his own conscientious choice, amongst all the forms of our common Christianity which were in existence at the time when the Constitution was established. This must be taken as the full limit of fair and legal presumption, as the two first chapters have sufficiently proved. Therefore I hold it preposterous to suppose that a band of Hindoos could settle in any part of our territories, and claim a *right*, under the Constitution, to set up the public worship of Brahma, Vishnu, or Juggernaut. Equally unconstitutional would it be for the Chinese to introduce the worship of Fo or Buddha, in California. Neither could a company of Turks assert a right to establish a Mosque for the religion of Mahomet. But there is one case, namely, that of the Jews, which forms an apparent exception, although it is in fact supported by the same principle. For, the meaning of the Constitution can only be derived from the *reasonable intention of the people of the United States*. Their language, religion, customs, laws, and modes of thought were all transported from the mother country; and we are bound to believe that whatever was tolerated publicly in England, was doubtless meant to be protected here. On this ground, there is no question about the constitutional right of our Jewish fellow-citizens, whose synagogues had long before been established in London. But with this single exception, I can find *no right* for the public exercise of any religious faith, under our great Federal Charter, which does not acknowledge the divine authority of the Christian Bible.[1]

Most present-day Americans would not agree with Hopkins, but in 1857 most were in agreement, and there was an extensive legal history supporting their position. The Bill of Rights was then a bill of immunities against federal legislation in certain areas, not a prohibition of state or local legislation.

By the twentieth century, in America as in Europe, the ideal social order and civil government was believed to be one which was dedicated to *liberty*, one which made basic to its purpose freedom of religion, speech, and press. But a society which makes freedom its primary goal will lose it, because it has made, not responsibility, but freedom from responsibility, its purpose. When *freedom* is the basic emphasis, it is not responsible speech which is fostered but irresponsible speech. If freedom of press is absolutized, libel will be defended finally as a privilege of freedom, and if free speech is absolutized, slander finally becomes a right. Religious liberty becomes the triumph of irreligion. Tyranny and anarchy take over. Freedom of speech, press, and religion all give way to controls, totalitarian controls.

The goal *must* be God's law-order, in which alone is true liberty.

---

1. John Henry Hopkins: *The American Citizen: His Rights and Duties, According to the Spirit of the Constitution of the United States* (New York: Pudney & Russell, 1857), p. 77 f.

The law against false witness is basic to true freedom. Today, in the name of free speech and free press, false witness is tolerated, and the laws against slander and libel are progressively eroded. If false religion has rights, why not false witness? To exalt freedom over all else, to absolutize liberty, is to deny the distinction between true and false witness.

Where freedom is absolutized and made the prior and ultimate consideration as against good and evil, truth and falsity, then Gresham's Law becomes operative in that area also. Just as bad money drives out good money, so a lie drives out the truth, pornography drives out good literature and clean entertainment, and so on.

Because of the emphasis on free speech and free press, the United States and other countries have seen the rapid triumph of dishonest advertising and merchandising.[2] The most flagrant kind of evil prevails in these areas, and every attempt to cover them by statute law leads to new avenues of evasion. Neither statute laws nor administrative agencies of civil government have been able to cope at all effectively with this problem. However, if the criminal law were grounded on Biblical law, then every form of false witness would be a criminal offense. Every instance of false merchandising, advertising, and misrepresentation would be a criminal offense.

Where false witness is given protection by law in the name of freedom, there a progressive deterioration of quality appears in every area. If free enterprise can be interpreted to mean freedom for dishonest enterprise, for fraudulent goods and merchandising, then the freedom of honest enterprise is diminished. Shoddy goods marketed as quality items tend to drive out, in terms of Gresham's principle, better merchandise which is sold of necessity at a higher price.

Because almost all laws against false witness have been gone for some generations, there has been a progressive replacement of honest enterprise with a radically dishonest enterprise. Even the remnants of slander and libel laws require civil action by the offended party, in that the criminal law is mainly unconcerned with false witness.

The press, for almost two centuries, has been a major threat to freedom rather than an asset to it. The newly gained immunity from statist interference was rapidly interpreted to mean anarchy, and the press has an ugly history of abuse of power. It has consistently borne false witness and defended its right to do so as "freedom of the press." A 1970 news report gave a measure of indication of the nature of the problem:

There is a growing concern, reported the *Sunday Telegraph* of Lon-

---

2. See Sidney Margolis: *The Innocent Consumer vs. The Exploiters* (New York: The Trident Press, 1967).

don recently, following seven months of secret investigations by a Subcommittee of the U. S. House of Representatives Inter-State and Foreign Commerce Committee, which uncovered evidence of "deceptive reporting by American news organizations, national magazines, and their 'slanted,' 'doctored,' and 'arrogant' treatment of the news."

The report found that a television team, assigned to a student demonstration in California, had arrived at the spot with its own picket signs, which it distributed to the demonstrators they were to film; that news organizations have participated in court cases, a fact which Washington terms "inexcusable interference with the administration of justice"; that the news department of C.B.S. had attempted to finance a "commando invasion of Haiti"—a definite plan to "intrude on the conduct of foreign affairs."

The investigative team also uncovered evidence that C.B.S. reportedly staged a pot (marijuana) party among college students in suburban Chicago. The film of the party appeared later as a legitimate news report to document the widespread use of drugs "among upper-class college students," and to push for a radical change in the narcotic laws.

The Congressional committee recommended finally, according to the *Sunday Telegraph*, that "a section of the Federal Communication Act, prohibiting 'deceptive practice' in television entertainment, be extended to make 'falsification' of news a Federal offense."[3]

The systematic distortion of the news has been reported by newsmen themselves.[4]

Whenever freedom is made into the absolute, the result is not freedom but anarchism. Freedom must be under law, or it is not freedom. The removal of all law does not produce freedom but rather anarchy and a murderer's paradise. The Marquis de Sade demanded such a world; the liberty he required made a potential victim of all godly men and assured only the freedom for murder, robbery, and sexual violence. Only a law-order which holds to the primacy of God's law can bring forth true freedom, freedom for justice, truth, and godly life.

Freedom as an absolute is simply an assertion of man's "right" to be his own god; this means a radical denial of God's law-order. "Freedom" thus is another name for the claim by man to divinity and autonomy. It means that man becomes his own absolute. The word "freedom" is thus a pretext used by humanists of every variety—Marxist, Fabian, existentialist, pragmatist, and all others—to disguise man's claim to be his own absolute.

---

3. *The Review of the News*, vol. VI, no. 12 (March 25, 1970), p. 14.
4. Herman H. Dinsmore, *All the News that Fits, A Critical Analysis of the News and Editorial Content of the New York Times* (New Rochelle, N.Y.: Arlington House, 1969).

Freedom in itself means freedom for something in particular. If all men are "free" to murder, then there is no freedom for godly living; no peace or order is then possible. Men are then no longer free to walk the streets in safety. If men are "free" to steal without penalty, then there is no freedom for private ownership of property. If men have unrestricted free speech and free press, then there is no freedom for truth, in that no standard is permitted whereby the promulgation or publication of a lie can be judged and punished. False witness is then favored and the importance of truth is denied. The commandment of James was this: "So speak ye, and so do, as they that shall be judged by the law of liberty" (James 2:12). There is a law of liberty; without law, there is no liberty.

The "free speech" movement at the University of California at Berkeley in the early 1960's was a logical application of the idea of lawless liberty. The students used the public address system to shout obscenities in the name of free speech, and to demand the "right" to copulate openly on the campus like dogs. The students were more logical than their teachers; they insisted on carrying free speech to its logical conclusion, and they recognized the hypocrisy of the liberals who advocated free speech but flinched at practicing it. They were logical too in their sexual demands: if free speech is a valid standard, why not free actions? Their choice of irresponsible freedom was an honest if wrong one: they pushed the liberal ideal to its logical conclusion.

The liberal intellectual objects to any restraint on his absolute standard of freedom on two grounds usually. *First*, he holds that freedom of speech is more important than any other consideration, and similarly freedom of press is more important than responsibility. *Second*, he may agree that pornography is bad, but "how can you define it?" A student reported that a university professor and class concluded that pornography does not exist, because they found themselves unable to define it. This is the rationalistic fallacy that only the rational is real, and the rational includes that which can be precisely and scientifically defined. Instead of life being prior to definition, definition is prior to life. A thing does not exist for the intellectual until he has defined it, until his supposedly creative and defining word calls it into being. It is easy to recognize pornography; it is not as easy to define it. It is easy to recognize a friend, but it is less easy to define what a friend is. Much of reality escapes a definition. Hence the weakness of statute law: because it insists on defining each particular variety of a crime precisely, it creates a problem for law enforcement. It is not enough for statute law that a murder or a theft has been committed; a definition by statute must be found and "fitted" to the crime, and the definition must fit the crime, or the law will not recognize the crime. Biblical law simply states, "Thou shalt not kill," and "Thou shalt not steal," easily recognizable and not in need of definition. Since reality always escapes full definition, the precise definition of crimes by statute means that much criminal activity is not included in the catalog of crimes.

10. The Lying Tongue

Scripture has much to say about the lying tongue. Solomon's comment on the matter is especially revealing:

> These six things doth the LORD hate: yea, seven are an abomination unto him:
> A proud look, a lying tongue, and hands that shed innocent blood;
> An heart that deviseth wicked imaginations, feet that be swift in running to mischief.
> A false witness that speaketh lies, and he that soweth discord among brethren (Prov. 6:16-19).

Of the seven sins here cited, three are directly matters of speech, i.e., the "lying tongue," the "false witness," and "he that soweth discord among brethren." As Delitzsch commented, the point made by Solomon is "that no vice is a greater abomination to God than the (in fact satanical) striving to set men at variance who love one another."[1] These seven sins are closely related. "The first three characteristics are related to each other as mental, verbal, actual."[2] The fourth deals with the heart; the fifth, with feet running with haste to evil; the sixth is again verbal, as is the seventh. "The chief of all that God hates is he who takes a fiendish delight in setting at variance men who stand nearly related."[3]

How the Hebrews understood this matter appears in Ben Sirach's comments on the law. Ben Sirach condemned all who relied on dreams and divinations, on false prophecy of any kind. Echoing Scripture, he asked, "From an unclean thing what can be clean? And from something false what can be true?"[4] He added that "The law must be observed without any such falsehoods, And wisdom finds perfection in truthful lips" (Ecclus. 34:8). Even more, Ben Sirach declared that "A thief is better than a habitual liar, But they are both doomed to destruction" (Ecclus. 20:25). This point is of especial importance. A thief takes a man's property, but he does not thereby harm a man's reputation, whereas a liar does damage to a man's reputation and robs him of peace, not only once but continuously, as the lie circulates and remains.

---

1. Franz Delitzsch: *Biblical Commentary on the Proverbs of Solomon* (Grand Rapids: Eerdmans, [1872] 1950), I, 146.
2. *Ibid.*, p. 147.
3. *Ibid.*, p. 148 f.
4. Ecclesiasticus 34:4. From the J. M. Powis Smith translation.

Hence the sharp condemnation of the lying tongue by Solomon and all of Scripture.

Both slander and libel are thus very serious offenses. Slander is false witness concerning a man by word of mouth; it is gossip which does injury to a man's character or property, his office or profession. Libel is false witness by means of writing, pictures, or signs. Both libel and slander are forms of false witness.

In every age, false witness has been extensive because man is a sinner, but in the modern era it has particularly been developed into a refined science. Humanistic man, from Machiavelli, through Hegel, Marx, Nietzsche to the present, having no belief in an absolute law, has revived the platonic doctrine of the right of the state to lie. Especially with the birth of the revolutionary era, lying has become a major instrument of civil polity. The vicious slanders and libels of Louis XVI, Marie Antoinette, and Napoleon persist in the textbooks to this day. With the two world wars, lying became especially prominent in international politics.

At this point, a distinction must be made. Warfare requires strategic deception, but no false witness concerning the character of the enemy is justifiable. Like Rahab, we are not under obligation to tell the truth to someone seeking to kill a godly man, but we are under obligation to bear true witness concerning our enemy. The false witness made with respect to Germany in World War I was thus clearly evil. The stories of German atrocities were manufactured and were vicious and totally false.

The false witness born during World War II with respect to Germany is especially notable and revealing. The charge is repeatedly made that six million innocent Jews were slain by the Nazis, and the figure—and even larger figures—is now entrenched in the history books. Poncins, in summarizing the studies of the French Socialist, Paul Rassinier, himself a prisoner in Buchenwald, states:

> Rassinier reached the conclusion that the number of Jews who died after deportation is approximately 1,200,000 and this figure, he tells us, has finally been accepted as valid by the Centre Mondial de Documentation Juive Contemporaine. Likewise he notes that Paul Hilberg, in his study of the same problem, reached a total of 896,292 victims.[5]

Very many of these people died of epidemics; many were executed. We will return to this matter again.

Meanwhile, let us note that not much has been said of the very extensive mass murders perpetrated by the Communists. The United

5. Vicomte Leon de Poncins: *Judaism and the Vatican* (London: Britons Publishing Company, 1967), p. 178.

States assisted in these by handing over General Wlassov and his army of anti-communist Russians to the Communists for execution. The Communists executed 12,000 Polish army officers in the Katyn Forest; 400,000 Poles died on their deportation journey. Of 100,000 German prisoners captured at Stalingrad, only 5,000 came back alive; 95,000 died in the prison camps; 4,000,000 of the Germans deported by the Communists from Silesia died, and so on.[6] The British and the Americans on February 13, 1945, attacked by air Dresden, a hospital city, and killed 130,000 people, almost twice the toll at Hiroshima, without any good military reason.[7] Thus without going into the Pacific arena of the war, it is clear that all concerned were engaged not only in warfare but murder as well, with the Communists pursuing it as a commonplace policy of state.

Let us turn now to another aspect of the same problem. A popular post-war novel described events at Auschwitz during the war and presented its material not only as fact but actually used the real names of living persons. Thus, a Polish physician who was a prisoner of war in the camp and serving in the camp medical corps was charged with having performed 17,000 "experiments" on Jewish prisoners in surgery without anaesthetics. The doctor immediately sued the novelist for libel. The trial, held in London, quickly reduced the 17,000 cases to 130 contested ones; sterilization of Jewish women and the castration of men were basic to the "experiments." Had the doctor refused, a witness stated, he himself would have been killed. The number of *established* cases was few; 17,000 was a false figure. The judge, in his summation to the jury, stated that he could give them no "guidance about morals." The doctor won the case, his award being the smallest coin of the realm, one halfpenny; his share of the legal costs was about 20,000 pounds.[8] The jury agreed that he had been the victim of libel, but it also believed his guilt to be still real enough to merit only a token victory.

This trial brings to focus the basic insensitivity to truth which too extensively characterizes this age. The fact that a doctor under any pressure would perform such operations is itself an ugly fact. If only ten were performed, or even one alone, instead of 130 or 17,000, the

---

6. *Ibid.,* p. 101 f. See also J. K. Zawodny: *Death in the Forest, The Story of the Katyn Forest Massacre* (Notre Dame, Indiana: University of Notre Dame Press, 1962); Edward J. Rozek: *Allied Wartime Diplomacy: A Pattern in Poland* (New York: John Wiley and Sons, 1958); Albert Kalme: *Total Terror, An Expose of Genocide in the Baltics* (New York: Appleton-Century-Crofts, 1951); and Harold M. Martinson: *Red Dragon Over China* (Minneapolis: Augsburg, 1956).
7. David Irving: *The Destruction of Dresden* (New York: Holt, Rinehart & Winston, 1964).
8. Mavis M. Hill and L. Norman Williams: *Auschwitz in England, A Record of a Libel Action* (New York: Stein and Day, 1965).

crime is real and very serious. Why then the gross exaggeration? Why too the malicious misrepresentation of men who were opposed to Allied policy, such men as Laval and Quisling, in their own way "patriots," no better than some of the Allied leaders, worse than some, and perhaps better than most?[9]

Let us examine again the mass murders of World War II, and the background of false witness during World War I and later. Life had become so cheap and meaningless to these heads of state and their camp followers that a murder or two meant nothing. Likewise, a generation schooled to violence in motion pictures, radio, literature, and press could not be expected to react to a murder or two. The result was a desperately twisted mentality which could only appreciate evil as evil on a massive scale. Did the Nazis actually execute many thousands, tens, or hundred thousands of Jews? Men to whom such murders were nothing had to blow up the figure to millions. Did the doctor perform a number of experiments on living men and women? A few sterilized women and a few castrated men and their horrified tears and grief are not enough to stir the sick and jaded tastes of modern man: make him guilty of performing 17,000 such operations. The evils were all too real: even greater is the evil of bearing false witness concerning them, because that false witness will produce an even more vicious reality in the next upheaval. Men are now "reconciled" to a world where millions are murdered, or are said to be murdered. What will be required in the way of action and propaganda next time?

During World War II, a brief and popular book gave a hint of the new mentality. Kaufman called in 1941 for the total sterilization of all Germans and the elimination thereby of the German nation.[10] Kaufman was not alone. The novelist Ernest Hemingway called for the mass sterilization of all members of Nazi party organizations in the preface to his book *Men at War*.[11] The Harvard anthropologist, Ernest A. Hooton, called for the "wiping out" of German leadership and "the subsequent dispersal throughout the world of the rest of the German people."[12]

In view of this massive insensitivity to murder, so that false witness is resorted to, the exaggeration of evil to make it seem evil, evil itself is growing in order to keep pace with the imagination of men, an evil imagination grounded in a false witness. In World War I, the Turks

---

9. Hubert Cole: *Laval, A Biography* (London: Heinemann, 1965); Ralph Hewins: *Quisling, Prophet Without Honor* (New York: The John Day Company, 1960).

10. Theodore N. Kaufman: *Germany Must Perish!* (Newark, New Jersey: Argyle Press, 1941).

11. *Time Magazine* (December 21, 1942), p. 108.

12. "Non Germanic Germany is One Solution," San Francisco *Chronicle* (Friday, April 17, 1942), p. 2.

sought to murder all Armenians; at that time, it horrified the world. Today, some Negroes speak freely of the mass murder of all whites, and some whites long for the death of all Negroes, and the shock of such thinking lessens daily.

Basic to all lying tongues is the unwillingness to accept responsibility. Satan is called the father of lies by our Lord (John 8:44), and Adam and Eve, after accepting Satan's principle, immediately lied about their guilt (Gen. 3:9-13). Where men are evading their responsibility, they are liars. In denying their guilt and their responsibility, they must affirm the guilt and responsibility of their environment, human and otherwise. Thus, to return to Poncins, the thesis of his study is that the Church of Rome has been victimized by the Jews. The plight of the church is not the responsibility of the church; churchmen from the pope down are all whitewashed.[13] For Poncins the guilt always lies elsewhere, with the Jews or with the Freemasons.[14] Satan did tempt Eve, and other people may tempt us, but, in the sight of God, the basic and primary responsibility is always ours. We cannot escape from guilt by blaming others; we then add a lying tongue to our offenses, and we then become progressively insensitive to the reality of evil. Just as a narcotic addict needs a progressively larger dose to maintain his habit, so the liar needs both a more monstrous lie and a more perverse reality in order to maintain his stability in terms of evil. A liar is thus more dangerous than a thief: he destroys far more, and he lets loose greater evils.

Poncins, bitterly anti-Jewish, is ready to report the errors in the accounts of Nazi murders of Jews; he is not ready to be distressed that *any* were brutally murdered. Poncins is hostile to lies about the numbers of Jews killed, but is he not repeating the lie of Adam and Eve in blaming the evils of the church on everyone except the church? With Eve, Poncins says the serpent gave me, and I did eat; it was therefore not my fault. Poncins must blame someone other than churchmen who have great powers, because to do so would be to accept the guilt of the church, and of its members, including himself.

Every false witness is dangerous, in that it sets loose a vast chain of consequences which cannot be recalled; it unleashes a taint which spreads and leads finally to action. Solomon was right in the sequence of consequences: first the thought, then the word, and finally the act.

A final note: false witness has no privileged status. For a person to confide in us a piece of gossip, asking us not to disclose his name, does not mean that we are to respect his wishes. To do so is to become

---

13. Poncins, *op. cit.*, pp. 32 ff., 80, 160 ff.
14. Vicomte Leon de Poncins, *Freemasonry and the Vatican* (London: Britons Publishing Company, 1968).

a party to his slander of another person, group, or race. Rather, we must refuse to accord to any lie the status of a privileged communication and must instead correct and/or rebuke the liar, and, if need be, expose his tactics.

11. Slander Within Marriage

Biblical law forbids slander within marriage, i.e., slander by husband or wife with respect to their spouse. As Clark has pointed out, such slander makes a husband, for example, liable not only to his wife but to her family.[1] This law is an important example of case law:

> If a man take a wife, and go in unto her, and hate her,
> And give occasions of speech against her, and bring up an evil name upon her, and say, I took this woman, and when I came to her, I found her not a maid:
> Then shall the father of the damsel, and her mother, take and bring forth the tokens of the damsel's virginity unto the elders of the city in the gate:
> And the damsel's father shall say unto the elders, I gave my daughter unto this man to wife, and he hateth her:
> And, lo he hath given occasions of speech against her, saying, I found not thy daughter a maid: and yet these are the tokens of my daughter's virginity. And they shall spread the cloth before the elders of the city.
> And the elders of that city shall take that man and chastise him;
> And they shall amerce him in an hundred shekels of silver, and give them unto the father of the damsel, because he hath brought up an evil name upon a virgin of Israel: and she shall be his wife; he may not put her away all his days.
> But if this thing be true, and the tokens of virginity be not found for the damsel:
> Then they shall bring out the damsel to the door of her father's house, and the men of her city shall stone her with stones that she die: because she wrought folly in her father's house: so shalt thou put away evil from Israel (Deut. 22:13-21).

Before analyzing the implications of this law for its bearing on false witness, it should be noted that this is a most unusual law from the legal perspective. *First*, in every trial under this law, a conviction inevitably follows. Either the wife is found guilty, or the husband is found guilty, for having brought false charges against her. When a marriage reaches this point, an inner penalty is inescapable; the public penalty is also inescapable when the matter reaches trial.

Second, this law is also unusual in that it seems to reverse all normal procedure in court cases. In all other kinds of trials, the accused is innocent until proven guilty, and it is the duty of the witnesses to prosecute the case by providing evidence of guilt. As the Talmud[2]

---

1. Clark: *Biblical Law,* pp. 184, 296 f.
2. *Kethuboth,* 251 ff.

gives evidence, witnesses to prosecute were still necessary, and a normal part of the proceedings in such cases. All the same, however, the wife must clearly prove her innocence. The reason for this unusual aspect of such a case is that the case is in reality a double prosecution. The husband has accused his wife of coming to the marriage with a background of unchastity. The father of the bride initiates the prosecution; he prosecutes the husband in order to silence the slander of his daughter, and, as prosecutor, he must produce evidence and witnesses, evidence of his daughter's virginity, and witnesses to the slander. The husband must produce evidence of unchastity or pay a very heavy penalty.

The fine and the penalty are worth noting in some detail. A fine of 100 shekels of silver (Deut. 22:19) was a very considerable sum. A quarter shekel was considered a notable gift for a great man (I Sam. 9:8). The annual poll tax of all males in Israel, 20 years of age and older, was half a shekel (Ex. 30:15). Under Nehemiah, with the Persian Empire providing many of the civil functions and also exacting a tax, the poll tax was cut to a "Third part of a shekel" (Neh. 10:32). Thus, 100 shekels of silver was an extremely heavy fine and one which would virtually wipe out most husbands and make them in effect their wife's servant or slave thereafter. The fine was paid to the bride's father, and thus kept out of the control of the husband, who could nullify the effect of the penalty if the money were in his wife's possession. Control of the wife would then lead to control of the money. The father-in-law would not be subject to such control and could administer the funds for his daughter's and grandchildren's welfare. Not only was the husband so penalized, but all recourse to divorce was then barred to him. This did not mean that the wife now had a license to sin; she could still be put to death for any future adultery. Such an offense was criminal action. The power of divorce was taken from the husband. Corporal punishment was also inflicted on the husband (Deut. 22:18). On the other hand, the bride paid for her unchastity with her life. She was stoned to death, an ancient method of execution. Its place in the Bible is due to the ability of the witnesses and the community to take part in the execution, since the police power of the people required that they recognize their duty to witness and to execute in all cases of established crime. The principle of general police power is still valid and basic.

It should be noted that this law has a lingering effect on divorce laws, in that, until recently, mutual consent did not terminate a marriage but rather actual and proven guilt. Failure to prove guilt nullified the action.

Now, to examine the law itself with respect to false witness, certain things must be noted. *First*, this is case law. If slander by a husband is forbidden, and carries such severe penalties, then slander by a wife is also forbidden. If the penalty is so severe for such a slander, then any slander between man and wife carries severe penalties in Biblical law. The fine imposed for lesser offenses of slander would still be proportionately high.

Clearly, therefore, Biblical law requires a high degree of care and thoughtfulness of speech between husband and wife. Instead of being an area of laxity, where man and wife can cut loose with carelessness of consequences, marriage is an area where words must be weighed with especial care because the relationship is so important. Scripture gives extensive evidence of this requirement. Thus, St. Paul declares that "So ought men to love their wives as their own bodies. He that loveth his wife loveth himself. For no man ever yet hated his own flesh; but nourisheth and cherisheth it, even as the Lord the church" (Eph. 5: 28-29). St. Peter calls attention to the behavior of Sarah and her respectful speech and conduct towards Abraham (I Peter 3:5-6).

An old Russian proverb states the matter pointedly: "A dog is wiser than a woman: he won't bark at his master." Too many men and women are guilty of such stupidity: they bark and snarl at those nearest to them, and the consequence is only unrest to themselves. Any man or woman who belittles his or her spouse only hurts himself in the long run. False witness and a loose tongue bring only dishonor to a person.

Second, the matter of slander within the family is a criminal and public offense, not merely a private matter. Damages are due to the bride's parents, and a penalty is imposed by the state, because the disruption of the peace of family life is a major breach of public peace and order. The centrality of the family makes slander within the family particularly dangerous to society. The charge is that the husband "hath brought up an evil name upon a virgin of Israel": the wife is in this charge identified, not in terms of her family, but the nation. The husband has lashed out at more than his wife and her family: he has attacked moral standards upheld and underscored by the nation itself.

Third, this law in particular fines and punishes the husband. A fine of the wife would be in part a penalty on the husband also, and it would also be evidence of his inability to govern his own home. It is the duty of the husband to be, among other things, the protector of his wife and children. If he instead defames them, defames his wife in particular, it is an indication of both an inability to protect and to govern, and a sick mentality which invites shame and disgrace. The man has denied to his family a standard of godly conduct, which is a basic necessity of life. Another Russian proverb points out that, "If the father is a fisherman, the children know the water." Its meaning is clear: the father's life has a major teaching function. Where the father fails to set a pattern of responsible and thoughtful life and speech, the children are deprived of a major stabilizing and educating force.

A husband can defame his wife not only by speech but by distrust. If he refuses to allow her those duties and privileges which she is competent to administer, he has defamed her. To cite an example: a husband regularly belittled his wife's financial competence and often cited as a joke a foolish checkbook error she had made. The error was real enough, but it was not a true report of her character. Her little gift shop had twice saved him from serious trouble in his own business; on one occasion, he had over-expanded too rapidly when business was very good and then faced bankruptcy; her nest egg, derived from her shop, saved him, but it was never repaid nor publicly acknowledged. On another occasion, bad investments hurt him financially, and her funds provided a needed payment on his building. This husband regularly slandered his more capable wife without ever formally telling a lie: he simply cited a few facts which gave a false picture of a very capable woman. Truth itself can be slanderous, if it is used to give a partial or distorted picture.

Fourth, the ninth commandment requires that we bear no false witness against our "neighbour," and this law makes clear that our most important neighbor is our wife or husband. F. W. J. Schroeder observed that "Man is free only as he maintains veracity; the lie destroys his true freedom."[3] Man finds his richest freedom in family life under God; this freedom is destroyed, and the home turned into a prison, where men and women bear false witness against one another.

Fifth, turning again to the fine imposed on the husband, we get a further glimpse of the seriousness of slander within marriage. In Deuteronomy 22:29, we see that the fine imposed for rape or seduction, in a case involving an unbetrothed virgin and a young man without a criminal record, was 50 shekels of silver; if marriage followed, i.e., if the guilty man were accepted as a husband, no divorce was possible. The fine for slandering a wife by a false accusation of premarital unchastity was thus twice the fine for rape and/or seduction. In either case, the fine was very heavy, but the penalty for slander is greater because it strikes at an existing marital relationship and undercuts it brutally. The ravished girl had a dowry of 50 shekels to take into another marriage, if her father rejected the offender as a possible husband; she could begin a new life with another man with the advantage of an extra dowry (Ex. 22:16, 17). The offended wife had no such opportunity; her children might well bind her to her husband. (The

---

3. Schroeder, in Lange: *Deuteronomy,* p. 167.

loss of the right of divorce was his, not hers.) The fine was thus especially severe in order to prevent the occurrence of such offenses.

In modern humanistic law, there is virtually an open season on slander
within marriage, and the results are predictably bad.

A final note: virtually every people has a background of wife-beating
(and, on occasion, husband-beating). There is no evidence of this in
Scripture. The severity of the law with respect to slander makes clear
that, by analogy, physical abuse is worse and unthinkable. A relationship is required between husband and wife which is grounded on faith,
not fear.

12. Slander

Leviticus 19:16, 17 is usually cited as that instance where *gossip*
is condemned by the law, and is often read as a denunciation of gossip
rather than court-related law. An examination of the text makes clear
that, while gossip is condemned, the courtroom is in view:

> Thou shalt not go up and down as a talebearer among thy people:
> neither shalt thou stand against the blood of thy neighbour: I am
> the LORD.
> Thou shalt not hate thy brother in thine heart: thou shalt in any
> wise rebuke thy neighbour, and not suffer sin upon him.

The first part of vs. 16 can be rendered, "Thou shalt not go about
slandering. . . ." The word is translated as *slander* in Jeremiah 6:28;
9:4; and in Ezekiel 22:9 marginal note. True witness must be given
both in and out of court: the circulation of slander anywhere is prohibited. According to Ginsburg,

> This dangerous habit, which has ruined the character and destroyed
> the life of many an innocent person (I Sam. xxii. 9; Ezek. xxii. 9,
> &c.), was denounced by the spiritual authorities in the time of Christ
> as the greatest sin. Three things they declared remove a man from
> this world, and deprive him of happiness in the world to come—
> idolatry, incest, and murder, but slander surpasses them all. It kills
> three persons with one act, the person who slanders, the person
> who is slandered, and the person who listens to the slander. Hence
> the ancient Chaldee Version of Jonathan translates this clause:
> "Thou shalt not follow the thrice accursed tongue, for it is more
> fatal than the double-edged devouring sword."[1]

Ben Sirach spoke strongly against slander, declaring,

> Curse the whisperer and double-tongues: for such have destroyed
> many that were at peace. A backbiting tongue hath disquieted
> many, and driven them from nation to nation: strong cities hath it
> pulled down, and overthrown the houses of great men. A backbiting
> tongue hath cast out virtuous women, and deprived them of their
> labours. Whoso hearkeneth unto it shall never find rest, and never

1. C. D. Ginsburg, "Leviticus," in Ellicott, I, 424.

dwell quietly. The stroke of the whip maketh marks in the flesh: but the stroke of the tongue breaketh the bones. Many have fallen by the edge of the sword: but not so many as have fallen by the tongue. Well is he that is defended from it, and hath not passed through the venom thereof; who hath not drawn the yoke thereof, nor hath been bound in her bands. For the yoke thereof is a yoke of iron, and the bands thereof are bands of brass. The death thereof is an evil death, the grave thereof were better than it. It shall not have rule over them that fear God, neither shall they be burned with the flame thereof. Such as forsake the Lord shall fall into it; and it shall burn in them, and not be quenched; it shall be sent upon them as a lion, with thorns, and devour them as a leopard. Look that thou hedge thy possession about with thorns, and bind up thy silver and gold, and weigh thy words in a balance, and make a door and bar for thy mouth. Beware thou slide not by it, lest thou fall before him that lieth in wait (Ecclus. 28:13-26).

A folk proverb once popular with children has it that, while sticks and stones may break our bones, *words* can never hurt us. This is mere bravado: words do hurt us; it is only because we are so scarred by the malice of gossip that it provokes only a sad and wry humor.

But the law of God *never* sees gossip as an *idle* matter: hence the concern of the law with all slander. Verse 16 states "neither shall thou stand against the blood of thy neighbour." According to Micklem, this means "to seek to get him put to death (cf. Exod. 23:7)."[2] Ginsburg commented on the variety of implications of this statement:

This part of the verse is evidently designed to express another line of conduct whereby our neighbour's life might be endangered. In the former clause, "the going about" with slanderous reports imperiled the life of the slandered person, here "the standing still" is prohibited when it involves fatal consquences. The administrators of the law during the second Temple translating this clause literally, *thou shalt not stand still by the blood*, &c., interpreted it to mean that if we see any one in danger of his life, *i.e.*, drowning, attacked by robbers or wild beasts, &c., we are not to stand still by it whilst his blood is being shed, but are to render him assistance at the peril of our own life. Or if we know that a man has shed the blood of his fellow creature, we are not to stand silently by whilst the cause is before the tribunal. Hence the Chaldee Version of Jonathan renders it, "Thou shalt not keep silent the blood of thy neighbour when thou knowest the truth in judgment." Others, however, take it to denote to come forward, and try to obtain a false sentence of blood against our neighbours, so that this phrase is similar in import to Exod. xxiii, 1, 7.[3]

All these meanings are certainly implied, but it is better to look at the simplest sense of the text. There is an obvious parallelism drawn be-

---

2. N. Micklem, "Leviticus," in *Interpreter's Bible,* II, 96.
3. Ginsburg, *op. cit.,* p. 424.

tween slandering someone and standing against his blood, i.e., seeking his death. Slander is a form of murder: it seeks to destroy the reputation and the integrity of a man by insinuating falsehoods. The reason why the rabbis regarded it as worse than idolatry, incest, and murder was because its moral consequences are fully as deadly if not worse, and it is a crime easily committed and not too readily detected. Moreover, slander, because it passes from mouth to mouth quickly, involves far more people in a very short time than does idolatry, incest, or murder.

Gossip is thus forbidden by law; this is not merely moral advice; it is criminal law. Because the Puritans took Biblical law seriously, they did punish the gossip by court action. Slander and libel today are matters of civil suit, not normally of criminal action, and the result is the widespread liberty for malicious gossip. Irresponsibility has been given a privileged position.

In verse 17, the proper course of action is described. If a "brother" or "neighbour" is actually guilty of wrong-doing, we must go to him and seek to dissuade him from his evil course. Otherwise, we "suffer sin upon him," or "so thou bear not sin on his account," i.e., we become an accomplice to his evil by our silence. The "brother" here clearly has reference to a man of the covenant, not a reprobate who will not respond to godly counsel. We must speak to the brother; we may, depending on the situation, speak to the ungodly, but we are not required to do so. This meaning is clearly confirmed by the use of this law in Matthew 18:15-17.

Thus, the negative formulation of this law forbids slander: we must not bear false witness. The positive formulation, however, clearly requires more than true witness. Our witness must not only be true but responsible. By our speech, we must not only avoid slander but rebuke and discipline it, and, in a godly society, bring it before the courts of church and state. The law positively requires us to promote, not an anarchistic freedom of speech which permits slander, but a responsible speech which works to preserve and further integrity, industry, and honesty. The commandment has reference to social order, not merely personal moral counsel, as Calvin read it.[4] It is moral counsel, but it is first and last God's law for His kingdom which all must obey. Calvin took for granted the Christian law structure which Geneva had inherited from earlier centuries; his Puritan followers were wiser when they stressed the importance of that law.

If God's absolute law is replaced with anarchistic freedom, then meaning is withdrawn from the world, and a responsible witness ceases, because there is no one to be responsible to, no God who can absolutely

---

4. Calvin: *Commentaries on the Four Last Books of Moses,* III, 183-185.

require man to be responsible to Himself and to His world of men. Colin Wilson has stated the implications of this anarchism: "I thought I had seen the final truth that *life does not lead to anything*; it is *an escape from something*, and the 'something' is a horror that lies on the other side of consciousness."[5]

If life becomes "an escape from something," then it is an escape from truth, because truth is related to reality, whereas a lie is related to fantasy. Reality is anathema to men interested in escape, and as a result the "necessary" lie is cultivated by such men, as Nietzsche evidenced in his own life and philosophy.

But freedom too is related to reality rather than to fantasy, and thus to seek escape from reality is also to escape from freedom. Thus, for the surrealists, living with reality is a compromise. For them, liberty means denying "the world and man's flesh and blood existence."[6] The surrealist prefers dreams to reality; he demands a totally man-made world; such a dream cannot be realized in the real world. The totally man-made world is therefore sought in dreams. Surrealism believes "in the omnipotence of dreams" because this is the area of man's supposed power.[7] It prizes a dream world where "the heart reigns supreme."[8] This is comparable to mysticism, for, "to a mystic, absolute liberty goes hand in hand with the destruction of the contingent world."[9] There must therefore be a perpetual revolution against the real world in terms of the dream world. A surrealist statement declares that "Not only must the exploitation of man by man cease, but also that of man by the so-called 'God,' of absurd and provoking memory. . . . Man, with his arms and equipment, must join the army of Man."[10]

Whenever man, institutions, and societies forsake God, they forsake reality. They cease to bear true and responsible witness and begin to live a lie because in the world of the lie, they can play god. The church which believes it can live in the world and neglect the problems of the world is living in a realm of dreams. By failing to relate the law-word of God to the whole world, they are living a lie, however formally correct their religion. They may boast of being "evangelical" or "orthodox," but they are in reality irrelevant and are liars, because there is nothing irrelevant about God. Because God is the Lord and Creator of all things, there is a total relevance of all things to God and a total subordination of all things to the law-word of God. The church which fails to speak to the whole of life in terms of the total word of God

---

5. Colin Wilson: *Religion and the Rebel* (Boston: Houghton Mifflin, 1957), p. 16, cited in Herbert S. Gershman: *The Surrealist Revolution in France* (Ann Arbor: University of Michigan Press, 1970), p. 133.
6. Gershman, p. 12.
7. *Ibid.*, p. 35.
8. *Ibid.*, p. 46.
9. *Ibid.*, p. 132.
10. *Ibid.*, p. 109.

will soon be a savage liar with respect to any man who seeks to shake it out of its world of dreams. The truth is not in such a church or such men, and we cannot expect the truth from them.

When responsible witness ceases, then man has neither the ability to face reality nor the ability to be free. He becomes chained to the false witness of his own imagination. The ultimate end of all false witness is that it lives in a world of its own imagination. Living a lie, the unregenerate man ultimately has no world but his lie. This is true of all unregenerate men, as epistemological self-consciousness takes them to their logical conclusion. The Marxists are trapped in the dream world of their lie; they live in hell and call it the gate of paradise. The believers in democracy are also prisoners of their lie; they create deep and savage class and race hostilities by law and call it peace and equality.

The rabbis were right about false witness: it is death to the man who utters it and lives by it, death to the society which tolerates it, and it breathes out murder against its neighbor. To avoid false witness, a society must first of all avoid all false gods. False gods breed false men and a false witness.

13. Slander as Theft

In Leviticus 19:11, we have another reference in the law to slander: "Ye shall not steal, neither deal falsely, neither lie to one another." Ginsburg refers this to the previous law, Leviticus 19:9, 10, on gleaning, but the connection he makes is not too valid a one. The Berkeley Version renders "deal falsely" as "cheat," which clarifies that section of this law. Lange's comment is of historical interest with respect to the history of exposition:

> This and the following precepts take the usual negative form of statutory law. The eighth commandment is there joined with the offences recounted in vi. 2-5 of falsehood and fraud towards others. St. Augustine here (Qu. 68) enters at length into the casuistical question of the justifiableness of lying under certain peculiar circumstances, citing the example of Rahab among others. He concludes that it was not her lying, as such, which received the divine approbation, but her desire to serve God, which indeed prompted her lie. However this may be, it is plain that the law here has in view not extraordinary and exceptional cases, but the ordinary dealings of man with man. Such law is of universal obligation. Comp. Col. iii. 9.[1]

Lange was right in citing Colossians 3:9, 10, "Lie not one to another, seeing that ye have put off the old man with his deeds, And have put on the new man, which is renewed in knowledge after the image of him that created him." The ninth law-word lines up truth and reality

---

1. Lange, *Leviticus,* p. 150.

under God, and separates the world of false witness, all flight from reality, and every rejection of truth into the realm of Satan.

Meyrick's comment is also of interest:

> Stealing, cheating, and lying are classed together as kindred sins (see ch. vi. 2, where an example is given of theft performed by means of lying; Eph. iv. 25; Col. iii. 9).[2]

The citation of Ephesians 4:25 is again of interest, in that it speaks of the line of division: "Wherefore putting away lying, speak every man truth with his neighbour: for we are members one of another."

A very obvious fact about this law, Leviticus 19:11, is that two forms of violation of the eighth commandment, stealing and cheating, are given together with lying, a violation of the ninth commandment. All the laws are closely interdependent in that all come from the hand of the same God, but the connection of some is more immediate than that of others. The form of the law establishes an obvious connection: stealing and cheating do involve false witness, cheating especially so. Theft is a form of false witness when the thief purports to own the goods, sells them as his own, and lives off the proceeds as though they represented his own wealth.

Another important relationship between lying and theft is that slander does in fact rob a man of his reputation, his standing in the community, and his peace of mind. Although slander has largely passed from criminal to civil law, and restitution or damages are less and less awarded, historically, because of the background of Biblical law, restitution has been a necessary part of the law with respect to slander.

Slander is extensively denounced in Scripture. To cite a few examples: "An hypocrite with his mouth destroyeth his neighbour" (Prov. 11:9). "Put them in mind . . . to speak evil of no man (B.V., not to slander anyone)" (Titus 3:1, 2). "Let no corrupt communication proceed out of your mouth" (Eph. 4:29). "Speak not evil of another" (James 4:11). "He that uttereth a slander is a fool" (Prov. 10:18). "Whoso privily slandereth his neighbour, him will I cast off" (Ps. 101:5). It is clear that slander is seen not only as theft, but also as a form of murder (Prov. 11:9). It is therefore necessary that restitution be made.

The basic law reads that we are not to bear false witness against our "neighbour" (Ex. 20:16). The word "neighbour" is in Hebrew *rea* or *rach*, meaning "to feed or nourish," and *rach* also appears in Scripture as the verb "to feed." The neighbor, whether a close relative or friend, an enemy, or a fellow creature, is one whom we are thus to nourish, even as he has a duty to nourish us. We nourish one another, are good

---

2. F. Meyrick, in Spence and Exell, *The Pulpit Commentary, Leviticus*, p. 287.

neighbors or feeders one of another, when we establish and further a law-order which feeds and strengthens our common life. When we bear true witness, we feed one another with the truth. True witness is by no means to be confused with flattery, or with concealing evil. It does involve working together to further godly law-order. Slander destroys that mutual feeding; it breaks the bonds of community life and is a murder and theft directed both against individuals and against the community.

The word *neighbor* also gives us an insight into the nature of Biblical welfare. To be neighbors one to another means to establish a society which feeds and nourishes its members by means of godly law-order, and which ministers to its members' needs in terms of that law. Here, in deference to Ginsburg, we can acknowledge a connection between this law and the preceding one, Leviticus 19:9, 10. The laws of gleaning do require us to help our neighbor to feed himself.

Biblical welfare does not mean a class of people receiving monetary grants without work and living parasitically off of other men's labors. As previously noted, the laws of gleaning do require hard work. Moreover, the word *neighbor* applies to every man, rich and poor alike; i.e., not only the poor are to be fed in a neighborly society, but rich and poor are to nourish one another by working together to establish a godly social order in which all good men can flourish.

Such a society cannot flourish where there is no faith. As Pascal observed,

> Man is nothing but insincerity, falsehood, and hypocrisy, both in regard to himself and in regard to others. He does not wish that he should be told the truth; he shuns saying it to others; and all these moods, so inconsistent with justice and reason, have their roots in his heart.[3]

Without faith, men simply tend progressively to reflect their fallen nature, which lives, believes, and prefers a lie.

This is why the two "tables" of law are inseparable one from the other. Since moral order rests on theological order, man cannot long maintain a neighborly relationship to his fellow man if his relationship to God is broken. As ever, truth is in order to goodness; truth is the foundation and mainspring of moral character.

14. "Every Idle Word"

If the existentialists are right, then we live in a world without moral absolutes or transcendental law. In a world without absolute laws, whatever god or gods may exist can, together with men, give only

---

3. Cited in Alexander Whyte: *The Shorter Catechism*, p. 149.

advice, and that advice at best can be only pragmatic. There is, then, no law to appeal to. Of slander, therefore, such advice from the gods can say only that it may perhaps get a man into trouble, in that others will resent it. It is not in and of itself wrong; it can be advantageous, but it also can be disastrous.

Too often, instead of presenting the Biblical teaching concerning slander as law, the church has taught it as pragmatic advice. Not surprisingly, an age taught by antinomian churchmen has become existentialist. Many passing condemnations of gossip and slander appear in the Bible. Some of the more interesting ones are the following, interesting in the variety of forms of slander which are condemned:

Luke 6:41-45. Slander comes from an evil heart.
Ps. 109:3. It arises from hatred.
I Tim. 5:13. Lack of faith plus idleness breed slander.
Prov. 11:9. Hypocrites are addicted to slander towards the just.
Ps. 50:19, 20. The wicked are so addicted to it that they slander even their family.
Rev. 12:10. The devil is an "accuser" or slanderer.
Ps. 52:4. The wicked love to destroy men with their slander.
Prov. 10:18. Anyone who indulges in slander is a fool.
Titus 2:3. Older women are warned against indulging in it.
I Tim. 3:11. The wives of church officers are warned against it.
Matt. 26:60. Christ was the target of perjury.
Jude 8. Rulers are exposed to slander by "filthy dreamers" or false idealists.
Rom. 3:8; II Cor. 6:8. St. Paul was the target of slander.
Ps. 38:12; 108:2; I Peter 4:4. The people of God are exposed to it.
Ps. 15:1, 3; 34:13; I Peter 2:12; 3:10; 3:16; Eph. 4:31; Titus 3: 1, 2; I Cor. 4:13; Matt. 5:11. The saints are given instructions concerning their conduct in relationship to false witness.
Some of the practical effects are cited as separating friends (Prov. 16:28); deadly wounds (Prov. 18:8; 26:22); strife (Prov. 26:20); discord among brethren (Prov. 6:19); murder (Ps. 31:13; Ezek. 22:9).
James 3:1-12. The unbridled tongue represents an evil desire to lord it over other men by debasing them, and it receives "the greater condemnation" or judgment, possibly greater accountability. The law is clearly in mind as St. James speaks.

The most telling reference is our Lord's declaration: "But I say unto you, That every idle word that men shall speak, they shall give account thereof in the day of judgment" (Matt. 12:36). The word *idle* is also rendered "useless" (B.V.), "careless" (Moffatt), and "inoperative, non-working word" (Amplified Version). Alford's comment on this word brings out an essential meaning:

Idle is perhaps best taken here in its milder and negative sense, as not yet determined on till the judgment; so that our Lord's declara-

tion is a deduction, "a minori," and if of every *idle* saying, then
how much more of every *wicked* saying?[1]

To restate this, our Lord declared, *first*, that a man's life must be a true
witness; i.e., he must bear good fruit unto God, because, as a creature,
he is created to produce results for God (Matt. 12:33-35). There is
thus a requirement of every man to exercise dominion under God to
bear witness to God. *Second*, the "idle words" are those pointless ones,
i.e., words apart from man's calling under God. They shall be judged
finally, but, for the time, man is given time to turn to God and be converted from an idle life and idle words to a productive one under God.
Third, this clearly implies that every wicked saying, every instance of
perjury and slander, must be dealt with by judgment now, whether
spoken by sinner or saint. The appointed agencies of law must deal
with the *evil* word; God in His time judges every *idle* word. *Fourth*,
"For by thy words thou shalt be justified, and by thy words thou shalt
be condemned" (Matt. 12:37). The Berkeley Version reads, "For by
your words you shall be acquitted and by your words you will be condemned," a translation which makes clear the basically legal reference
of this statement. The courts of this world must hold a man accountable
for his words, and God holds man accountable also. Words are clearly
shown thus to be a basic aspect of man's "fruit," his self-revelatory
production, and words, like actions, are entirely within the realm of
judgment.

At this point it is imperative to make clear that the law against false
witness is not a counsel of sweetness and light. We are not counselled
to be evasive in our speech, or to flatter, nor are we forbidden to tell
the truth about evil, or to condemn it. Our Lord commanded, "Judge
not according to appearance, but judge righteous judgment" (John
7:24). We are nowhere told to abdicate moral standards and judgments; we are forbidden to judge in terms of personal and humanistic
criteria (Matt. 7:1, 2). Christ spoke bluntly and sharply to and about
the Pharisees; He called Herod a "fox," and His language was blunt and
forceful. The usual counsel to say nothing unpleasant about anyone is
a call to bear false witness; it has given a generation of humanists a
bad conscience about telling the truth.

The law is thus clearly the context of all Biblical teaching with respect
to the "unbridled tongue." The framework of reference is always the
law, not merely pragmatic counsel. There is future judgment for a life
of idle words, and there must be present judgment for every evil word.

The seriousness of the law with respect to slander is apparent in
Revelation 22:15, where those denied citizenship in the New Jerusalem

---

1. Henry Alford: *The New Testament for English Readers* (Chicago: Moody
Press), p. 90.

are cited: "dogs," i.e., homosexuals; "sorcerers," or those who practice magic, those who seek to control the natural and supernatural and to play god; "whoremongers," or the sexually unchaste; "idolaters," worshipers of false gods; "and whosoever loveth and maketh a lie" (B.V., "those who fabricate and love lies"). On the other hand, "Blessed are they that do his commandments, that they may have right to the tree of life, and may enter in through the gates into the city" (Rev. 22:14).

The humanistic era has given, however, the unbridled tongue and the idle word a new eminence. Slander and libel have been common enough in every age, but a humanistic age has an amazing interest in false witness. Humanism exalts man, and in every humanistic era men have a particularly zealous desire to defame and degrade man. Man being the god of humanism, sinful men especially delight in turning on this new god, in hearing filthy and vicious gossip concerning men of eminence.

The gossip columnist plays an important role in a humanistic society. In every age, there is curiosity about the lives of great men and women and prominent persons. But in the twentieth century this interest has been geared increasingly to a new stage, the world of the theatre, the jet set, persons of notoriety, and criminals, many of whom have been lionized, whereas a delight has been taken in reporting real or invented scandal about important people. William Randolph Hearst, of newspaper publishing fame, expressed his personal dislike of Walter Winchell, and ordered that his staff "Keep him far away from me," but he used him profitably to increase reader interest.[2] Gossip made Winchell a wealthy and important man. According to McKelway, Winchell, a man of dubious calibre, had in the past amazing protection:

> His valuable life, once zealously protected by bodyguards assigned him by his friends Owney Madden and Lucky Luciano, has in recent years been watched over by agents on the payroll of the Federal Bureau of Investigation, assigned to him by his friend J. Edgar Hoover.[3]

McKelway cites an amazing case in 1934 where both FBI agents and Capone gunmen were giving Winchell a courtesy guard: Chicago detectives were also a part of the special protection Winchell received. Was he being protected from the people?[4]

Noted Americans courted Winchell, men like Herbert Bayard Swope, M. Lincoln Schuster, Burton Rascoe, Heywood Broun, Alexander

2. Lyle Stuart: *The Secret Life of Walter Winchell* (Boar's Head Books, 1953), p. 115.
3. St. Clair McKelway: *Gossip, The Life and Times of Walter Winchell* (New York: The Viking Press, 1940), p. 20.
4. *Ibid.*, pp. 122 ff.

Woollcott, Alice Duer Miller, and others.[5] Winchell was attacked, however, by Marlen Pew, the editor of *Editor & Publisher*.[6] Winchell's
importance is now ended, but not the humanistic zeal for gossip.

Humanism exalts man and therefore the *motives* of men. Thus, if
there is a conflict between truth and the desires of men, truth is sacrificed. An important instance of this is the case of Dr. Frederick A.
Cook, who, on April 21, 1908, became the first man to reach the North
Pole. A year later, a civil engineer in the U. S. Navy, Robert E. Peary,
reached the pole on April 6, 1909. Peary began a campaign to discredit
Cook, in which men in high places joined.

Later, Cook was sent to prison for a term of fourteen years nine
months, in Leavenworth, and fined $12,000 for a supposed oil swindle
of a company he served as officer and geologist. Actually, the oil field
was already producing and became "one of the most productive oil and
gas areas of Texas and Arkansas." Cook, the largest single investor,
had received no salary, commission, or profits. The judge, John M.
Killits of Toledo, Ohio, in passing sentence, said to Dr. Cook in words
which will remain as a landmark of injustice:

> This is one of the times when your peculiar and persuasive hypnotic
> personality fails you, isn't it? You have at last got to the point
> where you can't bunco anybody. You have come to the mountain
> and can't reach the latitude; it's beyond you.
>
> First we had Ananias, then we had Machiavelli; the twentieth cen-
> tury produced Frederick A. Cook. Poor Ananias, he is forgotten,
> and Machiavelli—we have Frederick A. Cook.
>
> Cook, this deal of yours and this conception of yours, and this
> execution of yours was so damnably crooked that I know the men
> who defended you, defended you with their handerchiefs to their
> noses, rank, smelling to heaven.
>
> I wish I could do with you as I might, the way I feel about you; I
> wish I were not circumscribed by some conventions that I think
> are mistakes. . . . I don't think you ought to run at large at all;
> you are dangerous.
>
> Undoubtedly you have got those ill-gotten gains of your laid away.
>
> . . . I don't see how any living man who has any appreciation of the
> standards of decency or honesty can suggest that you ought to hold
> a penny of it . . . because every penny of it was robbed from orphans
> and widows and credulous old people; people in the depth of
> poverty; people anxious to get money enough so as to ensure a
> decent burial. . . .
>
> Oh God, Cook, haven't you any sense of decency at all, or is your
> vanity so impervious that you don't respond to what must be
> calls of decency to you? Aren't you haunted at night? Can you
> sleep? . . .

5. *Ibid.*, pp. 82 f., 140 f.   6. Stuart, p. 84 ff.

What's the use of talking to you? Your effrontery, vanity, and nerve are so monumental, so cold-steel, so impervious, so adamantine to what I have to say that the only satisfaction I get in saying that is that I know I am voicing the feelings of the decent people of Texas without any question; those of them that have brains enough not to fall for what some of these foolish people call your personality. I don't know where it is. They call it "personality," whether it is poker face or false face. . . .

It is strange . . . that the prosecuting officers have suggested to me that I be not quite so stiff on you. It is my own disposition and my abhorrence for such a crook as you. . . .[7]

The amazing thing about these remarks is that they were recorded; perhaps the importance of the trial made a full record mandatory. However, anyone who has spent time in courtrooms, observing proceedings, will recognize the arrogance, contempt, and air of infallibility which characterizes all too many humanistic judges. A faithful transcript of many proceedings would leave most people incredulous.

Dr. Cook's claims have been established as valid, but the textbooks still do not mention him as the discoverer of the Pole, nor cite his many great attainments. Dr. Cook made the mistake of surpassing in achievement Peary, an employee of the federal government.

The lives of the Wright brothers were similarly embittered by the unwillingness of federal authorities to give them priority for the first successful airplane flight. The Wrights had erred by being independent and not a part of either a federal agency or the academic world. Priority was claimed for the work of S. P. Langley, a federal employee on the staff of the Smithsonian Institute, and fraud was resorted to in order to buttress that claim. Some reference works now give priority to Langley, and the Wright brothers are being pushed into a secondary position.

None of this should surprise us. When a state denies God, it denies the principle of truth. It will inevitably exalt itself into the place of God, and then lie to maintain its power and prestige.

Americans are often amused when they read that the Soviet Union claims that the automobile, telephone, and other inventions were discovered first by Russians. There is nothing illogical about these claims, however false. If the United States can distort history to favor federal employees, why should not the U.S.S.R. distort history to make claims for its citizens? The object is not truth but power and prestige.

The humanistic age is unwilling to see its faults or to recognize its radical evils. St. Alphonsus de Liguori was very fond of the music of the licentious music halls of his day in Naples. To enjoy the music with-

---

7. Andrew A. Freeman: *The Cast for Doctor Cook* (New York: Coward-McCann, 1961), p. 244 f.

out having to be responsible for viewing the stage, he hit upon the device, being nearsighted, of taking off his glasses as soon as he seated himself in a box well away from the stage.[8] Ligouri's little foible is a major obsession with humanism: it is determined not to see those errors which reveal the radical guilt and evil of humanism. It is bent on bearing false witness concerning itself. It will therefore all the more readily bear false witness concerning others. Its idle words shall soon be judged. Its hopes shall be confounded.

Humanism dreams of unity, the unity of man, but it contributes instead to man's disunity. St. Bernard of Clairvoux, in his *De considera- tione* (1152), contrasted collective unity to constitutive unity. Collective unity can be obtained by heaping stones together; constitutive unity exists when many members make one body, where things or persons are members one of another.

The unity humanism achieves is collective, and it does violence to true unity, which is possible only in Christ, who bears witness to the only true unity. Unless Christ feeds us, we cannot be fed. Every word of humanism is an "idle word."

15. Trials by Ordeal and the Law of Nature

Trial by ordeal has had a long and important history in the laws of many nations; it appeared in primitive traditions, in Arabian and Islamic cultures, among Babylonians, Celts, Chinese, Greeks, Hindus, Burmese, Iranians, the Malagasy, Romans, Slavs, and Teutons. It was used also during the Middle Ages.

The trial by ordeal subjected the accused person to a fearful physical test, such as plunging the hand in boiling water, drinking poison, carrying a hot iron, and the like; injury meant proof of guilt. In West Africa, the ordeal was the preferred method of trial.

The ordeal has had opposition. The Koran forbad it. Roman law avoided it entirely, although it lingered among Romans. It was, however, common among the Celts, Teutons, and Slavs, who were responsible for its use in the Middle Ages. The church opposed it; chapter 18 of the fourth Lateran Council in 1215 excluded the clergy from participation in ordeals. The Norman kings of England strongly opposed it, and there is no record of its use after the reign of John.[1]

The ordeal involved essentially a trust in nature as normative. The belief was that the test or trial would result in nature's vindication of the innocent and rejection of the guilty. The test or trial was at times psychologically valid. Thus, some African tribes favor the poison

---

8. Phyllis McGinley: *Saint-Watching* (New York: The Viking Press, 1969), p. 19.
1. See Hastings *ERE,* IX, pp. 507-533.

ordeal; the innocent, confident of acquittal, vomit the distasteful poison at once, whereas the guilty, tense and fearful, are unable to throw it up and die. The ordeal has thus had a record of limited success.

Its basic premise, however, is unsound, and its major results have of necessity been unsound also. The history of such injustices is a long one, but it is not our concern. The question is, rather, does the ordeal have a place in Biblical law?

The only passage in Scripture which seems to indicate some kind of trial by ordeal is the trial of jealousy, Numbers 5:11-31. Kelsen has been savage in his denunciation of this law as "highly repulsive."[2] Selbie, on the other hand, recognized that there was a difference here: "It is evident that the efficacy of the ordeal described is regarded as due entirely to divine intervention; the ingredients employed are innocuous."[3]

This is the heart of the matter. The trial by ordeal required *nature* to deliver the innocent party by a miraculous intervention; nature is normative, and the law of nature perfect, according to the trial by ordeal. As a result, the accused took poison, or plunged his hand into boiling water, on the supposition that nature would protect the innocent.

In the Biblical law of jealousy, it is not nature but God who is the judge. Holy water and dust are swallowed, ingredients which are not likely to do any harm. The water and the dust of the sanctuary both represented the holiness of God. The penalty for the woman's offense (i.e., her sexual guilt) was serious ailments in her reproductive organs; if innocent, she was blessed with fertility. This ritual was used where other evidence of adultery was entirely lacking, but suspicion remained. This law is thus related to Deuteronomy 22:13-21, and the penalty on the husband was thus the same. There may be some evidence, in the meaning of the Hebrew word for "bitterness," that there is implied "a potential fatal effect of the water."[4]

Of interest too is the uncovering of the woman's head during the ritual (Num. 5:18), i.e., "not only the removal of the head-covering, but also letting the hair become loose and dishevelled. (Comp. I Cor. xi. 5-10)."[5] During the trial, the marks of her submission to her husband and to due authority were removed from her, to symbolize the implications of the trial. If she were innocent, and her husband's jealousy had falsely denied her the authority and protection due to her,

---

2. Hans Kelsen: *What Is Justice? Justice, Law and Politics in the Mirror of Science* (Berkeley: University of California Press, 1957), p. 28 f.
3. J. A. Selbie, "Ordeal (Hebrew)," in *ERE*, IX, 521.
4. Martin Noth: *Numbers, A Commentary* (Philadelphia: The Westminster Press, 1968), p. 51.
5. C. J. Elliott, "Numbers," in Ellicott, I, 498.

then she was permanently restored to his authority and support without any right of divorce allowed to him (Deut. 22:19).

Because adultery involves more than merely a relationship between a man and a woman, the trial does not limit the issue to the husband and wife. The husband had to bring an offering, and the wife held the offering during a portion of the trial (Num. 5:25), to signify the fact that both adultery and false jealousy are offenses against God's order.

To return to the contrast between the ordeal and this Biblical law: in the ordeal, nature is normative, unfallen, innocent, and therefore the evil-doer is rejected. In Biblical law, man and nature are alike fallen and therefore are not normative but rather under judgment. Only the direct intervention of God made the trial of jealousy efficacious.

For the ordeal, nature is the source of law, because law is a product of nature and therefore inescapable in every confrontation with nature. (The doctrine of poetic justice is related to this concept of the ordeal and is a sophisticated version of it.)[6] In this perspective, judgment comes from nature, and nature will ultimately right every wrong.

The ordeal largely disappeared in Europe during the Middle Ages, but not the faith behind the ordeal. The natural law concept succeeded the ordeal as the representative of this faith in nature. In turn, the natural law concept has given way to positivism in law, which sees the state as the source of law and hence normative.

In terms of Biblical law, the ordeal has no place and is entirely alien to its declaration of the sovereignty of God. The Bible has no such terms as "Nature." Not Nature but God is the source of all natural phenomena. "Nature" is simply a collective name for an uncollectivized reality; the myth of nature is a product of Hellenic philosophy.[7]

If nature is normative, then man too, as a part of the world of nature, becomes normative to the degree that he is "natural." This is basic to Rousseau and to existentialism, and to the belief in democracy, the divinity of the common man. There is now a widespread belief on the part of many people that they are qualified to act as agencies of judgment precisely because they represent the lower levels of society. Thus, students, because they are young, believe that they bring a special and fresh wisdom to bear on issues. Negroes, because they are low on the social scale, are increasingly imbued with this mysticism of naturalness and primitivism. Common laborers are often convinced that they alone know how things should be run. On June 4, 1970, an Arizona bakery truck driver hijacked a jetliner and demanded a $100 million ransom

---

6. See R. J. Rushdoony: *The Biblical Philosophy of History* (Nutley, New Jersey: Presbyterian and Reformed Publishing Company, 1969), pp. 77-86.
7. See R. J. Rushdoony, "The Myth of Nature," in *The Mythology of Science,* (Nutley, New Jersey: The Craig Press, 1967), pp. 96-98.

before the FBI succeeded in arresting him. His attitude after arrest was described as arrogant and defiant. This unemployed truck driver, prior to his arrest, radioed this message to President Nixon and the State Department: "You don't know how to count money and you don't even know the rules of the law."[8] This lecture on "the rules of the law" came from a man threatening to kill passengers and personnel, and already in the act of theft and kidnapping. This same 49-year-old man had lost his job seven years earlier.

> B— sued the Teamsters Union when it would not support him in a dispute with his employer. Vern Case, secretary-treasurer of the Teamsters Local 274, said B—'s troubles stemmed from his feeling that "he was the only one who knew how to run the company."[9]

His wife defended him, saying, "He's a man who believes in his country. He believed in what he was fighting for in World War II, and now look at what they've done to him."[10] There is no sense of guilt expressed here, but rather a belief in the "truth" of the common man and his opinion. The background of this thinking is the acceptance of nature as normative.

The Biblical perspective and law denies that either nature or man is normative. Neither the common man, nor an aristocracy, nor intellectuals are to be trusted. All without exception have sinned, and all alike are under God's judgment unless regenerated in Christ (Rom. 3:9-18). Not man but God and the law of God are normative, and His law must be the criterion of judgment. The trial of jealousy is a law which spoke clearly against the whole principle of the ordeal.

A book of the Talmud, *Sotah*, is extensively devoted to the trial of jealousy. The trial was efficacious only when the husband himself was innocent, and the trial was abolished in the first century A.D. because adultery on the part of husbands became so common.[11] The trial was invalid if the husband cohabited with his wife after making the accusation and before the trial. Some rabbinic commentators have seen a reference to this law in Psalm 109:18. The *Sotah* makes clear that more than mere jealousy was required to start the trial. The wife had to have a record of too close an association with another man; the husband had to issue a warning against the relationship. The question then was one of reference to an actual situation: was the relationship innocent, or was it guilty? Was the husband unfairly jealous, or did his suspicions have grounds? In such cases, no witnesses of wrong-doing

---

8. "Shootout Ends 'Ransom' Skyjack," Los Angeles *Herald-Examiner* (Friday, June 5, 1970), p. 1, 2.
9. "Hijacker's Troubles Started When He Lost His Job," Los Angeles *Herald-Examiner* (Friday, June 5, 1970), p. A-2.
10. *Ibid.*
11. Selbie, *op. cit.,* p. 521.

existed, but, on the other hand, mere feelings on the husband's part were insufficient grounds; an existing relationship, whether innocent or not, was the ground of his complaint.

The rabbis related both adultery and slander to a haughty spirit. One rabbi declared,

> Every man in whom is haughtiness of spirit, the Holy One, blessed be He, declares, I and he cannot both dwell in the world; as it is said, *Whoso privily slandereth his neighbour, him will I destroy; him that hath an high look and a proud heart will I not suffer* (Ps. CI. 5)—read not "him" (I cannot suffer), but "with him" I cannot (dwell). There are some who apply this teaching to those who speak slander; as it is said, "*Whoso privily slandereth his neighbour, him will I destroy.*"[12]

The trial of jealousy was thus radically different from and in direct contrast to the ordeal. It is the worst kind of false witness for a scholar like Banks to declare, of Numbers 5:11-31, the law of jealousy, that "The subsequent practice of ordeals in the West was based on the OT institution."[13] When the background of pagan European trials by ordeal is ignored, and the ordeal charged against a Biblical law hostile to it, we are justified in seeing a radical hostility to God and His law-word in such cases.

The word *ordeal* is of Anglo-Saxon origin, and its best-known occurrences in the English-speaking world are of Anglo-Saxon derivation.

According to E. B. Tylor, the ordeal in certain cases is "closely related to oaths, so that the two shade into one another."[14] There is a measure of truth to this. Both the ordeal and the oath invoke a curse or a blessing, depending on the truthfulness of the person under oath. The oath, however, reserves ultimate judgment to God, or to His appointed courts of justice where perjury is discovered, whereas the ordeal held that nature would immediately confirm the truth or falsity of an oath on a demand for judgment concerning a charge. There is thus a very real similarity as well as a marked difference. The oath in terms of Biblical law presupposes the ultimate and infallible supreme court of God. The oath and ordeal of pagan law presuppose the immediate and infallible court of nature. The two are in this sense mutually exclusive and in radical contradiction.

A final word on the law of jealousy. An interesting comment in the *Sotah* makes clear that the trial did not work, nor the supernatural intervention of God occur, when the man was not free from iniquity.

---

12. *Sotah,* 5a; p. 19 f.
13. J. S. Banks, "Jealousy," in James Hasting, editor: *A Dictionary of the Bible,* II, 554.
14. E. B. Tylor, "Ordeal," in *The Encyclopaedia Brittanica* (Chicago: 1892), XVII, 819.

Then "the water does not prove his wife." The ground for this was in Scripture, Hosea 4:14: "I will not punish your daughters when they commit whoredom, nor your spouses when they commit adultery: for themselves are separated with whores, and they sacrifice with harlots: therefore the people that doth not understand shall fall."[15] Their destiny is then judgment.

16. Judges

In any civil order, one of the most important positions is that of the judge. The courts of law cannot represent any real justice if the judge and his office are defective by nature and authority. For a social order to prosper and to provide its people with stability and peace, it is necessary, *first* of all, for the state to require all people with serious grievances to submit them to a court of law. Men cannot be allowed to take the law into their own hands. While the citizenry is important and basic to the execution of law and justice, it cannot identify itself with law without destroying law. The law transcends the people, and the law requires an agency separated from the people and immune to their partial and personal feelings.

Second, the courts of law must have the power of the state to enforce their decrees, or else anarchy prevails. Every decision of a court will displease at least one party. While the court can never be infallible, the decision of the court must be protected, and appeal against its decision must be made within the structure of the courts, not outside them nor against them, otherwise anarchy prevails.

Third, the court must represent a transcendental concept of law and justice, a standard beyond man and above man, a law-structure derived, however faultily, from God. The whole idea of a court and a judge implies transcendence: to gain justice, something more than the victory of the most powerful litigant or party is required. If the judge and the court represent a political party or idea, or a class or a caste, instead of providing the transcendence a court requires, they simply magnify the original evil by compounding it. If a powerful and evil man, class, or group can push an innocent man out of his property, or in any way abuse him, the evil is compounded if they can command the state to help them in their theft. Justice then becomes more difficult. Similarly, if in a democracy the masses of the poor can use the courts to defraud the prosperous, justice is again made more remote in that society. The court must transcend the passions of the day. It must represent a law-order which judges the entire social order, and this is possible only if the judges represent God, not the people or the state.

This means, *fourth*, that the election or selection of the judges is not

---

15. *Sotah,* 47b; p. 251 f.

the real issue, but their character and faith, and the character and faith of the citizenry at large. In the United States, federal judges are generally appointed, and state judges normally elected. Both methods have produced their quota of superior judges and degenerate judges; the method of selection has not been at fault and has been basically immaterial. The real issue has been the religious standards of the day. If a strong faith has marked the social order, the judges have been usually superior men; if relativism and pragmatism prevail, the courts and judges have reflected it. The quality of judges and courts is not a product of methodology.

The institution of graded courts in Israel was pragmatic; it was Jethro's wise counsel, designed to relieve Moses of the pressure of cases (Ex. 18:13-16). The graded courts were to govern the tens, the hundreds, and the thousands of Israel (Ex. 18:21). The reference to this decimal structure, and the basic unit of ten, is assumed by many to refer to ten men.[1] Since the basic governmental structure of Israel was by families (and hence by tribes of families), it is safe to conclude that the tens refers to ten families. For each ten families one judge was appointed to deal with minor matters and to refer other cases to a higher jurisdiction.

Moses made clear the purpose of courts of law: "the people come unto me to enquire of God: When they have a matter, they come unto me: and I judge between one and another, and I do make them know the statutes of God, and his laws" (Ex. 18:15, 16). In this he echoed God's purpose (Deut. 16:18). We have referred previously to the civil pentecost, whereby God filled the civil officers of Israel with His Spirit, to signify that they were prophets of God, called to speak for God in the ministry of justice (Num. 11:16).

Every reformation in Israel involved in part a return to the prophetic nature of civil office. It was awareness of this fact which led the Protestant reformers, as well as the medieval reformers within the church, to address their call to reformation to both church and state. It is a modern heresy that a country can have a "revival" without a reformation of the state as well as the church. Jehoshaphat's reform involved precisely such a step. After Jehoshaphat had allied himself with Ahab, seeking by coalition to strengthen himself against Syria, a prophet rebuked him. Jehu, the son of Hanani the seer, declared, "Shouldest thou help the ungodly, and love them that hate the LORD? therefore is wrath upon thee from the LORD" (II Chron. 19:2). In recognition that the only true defense is not an ungodly alliance, but rather in faith and justice, Jehoshaphat reformed the courts, instructing the judges,

---

1. George Rawlinson, in Spence and Exell, *The Pulpit Commentary, Exodus,* II, 92.

"Take heed what ye do: for ye judge not for man, but for the LORD, who is with you in the judgment. Wherefore now let the fear of the LORD be upon you: take heed and do it: for there is no iniquity with the LORD our God, nor respect of persons, nor taking of gifts" (II Chron. 19:6, 7).

The office of judge is thus clearly a theocratic office; the minister declares the word: the judge applies it to the conflicts of life. If the judge represents a class or party rather than God and His law, a radical perversion of justice is introduced into the life of the nation. Because man is a sinner, even the most godly of judges will be fallible and erring, but, by virtue of his faith, will be guided by the law-word of God and His Holy Spirit. The ungodly judge, having no such standard, will naturally be partisan: he will represent a faction or class. For him to accept a bribe is thus logical, however evil: he is there to represent human power, not the law of God and His righteousness. Thus, in terms of Biblical law, while it is a crime for a judge to accept a bribe, it is not a crime for a man to bribe a judge. The judge sins against his office; the man who bribes him deals realistically with the situation. If a piece of meat thrown to a snarling and dangerous dog will enable a man to pass in safety, he will throw the meat and spare his person.

The godly judge is warned against bribes, perjury, and miscarriages of justice (Ex. 23:6-8; Lev. 19:15; 24:22; Deut. 1:12-18; 16:18-20; 25:1; 27:25). He is only secondarily an officer of state; he is primarily an officer of God. If the judge does not represent God's law order, he is ultimately a political hack and hatchet man whose job it is to keep the people in line, protect the establishment, and, in the process, to feather his own nest. Ungodly judges are to be feared and hated: they represent a particularly fearful and ugly form of evil, and their abuse of office is a deadly cancer to any society.

17. The Responsibility of Judges and Rulers

A basic promise of Biblical law appears in a law of central importance. According to Deuteronomy 21:1-9, it is the responsibility of judges and rulers to right every wrong, whether the culprit is located or not:

If one be found slain in the land which the LORD thy God giveth thee to possess it, lying in the field, and it be not known who hath slain him:
Then thy elders and thy judges shall come forth, and they shall measure unto the cities which are round about him that is slain:
And it shall be, that the city which is next unto the slain man, even the elders of that city shall take an heifer, which hath not been wrought with, and which hath not drawn the yoke;
And the elders of that city shall bring down the heifer unto a rough valley which is neither eared nor sown, and shall strike off the heifer's neck there in the valley:

And the priests and sons of Levi shall come near; for them the LORD thy God hath chosen to minister unto him, and to bless in the name of the LORD; and by their word shall every controversy and every stroke be tried:
And all the elders of that city, that are next unto the slain man, shall wash their hands over the heifer that is beheaded in the valley:
And they shall answer and say, Our hands have not shed this blood, neither have our eyes seen it.
Be merciful, O LORD, unto thy people Israel, whom thou hast redeemed, and lay not innocent blood unto thy people Israel's charge. And the blood shall be forgiven them.
So shalt thou put away the guilt of innocent blood from among you, when thou shalt do that which is right in the sight of the LORD.

The observations of some of the commentators is of interest with respect to details of this law:

The slaying of the animal was not an expiatory sacrifice, and consequently there was no slaughtering and sprinkling of the blood; but, as the mode of death, viz. breaking the neck (*vid.* Ex. xiii. 13), clearly shows, it was a symbolical infliction of the punishment that should have been borne by the murderer, upon the animal which was substituted for him. . . . If the murderer were discovered afterwards, of course the punishment of death which had been inflicted vicariously upon the animal, simply because the criminal himself could not be found, would still fall upon him.[1]

According to Manley,

The sixth commandment taught that human life is sacred, and now Moses rules that murder must be atoned for. . . . Rashi comments: "A yearling heifer which had borne no fruit, shall come and be beheaded in a place which yieldeth no fruit, to atone for the murder of the man whom they did not suffer to bear fruit." The ideas of atonement and cleansing are combined, and both point to Calvary (Heb. ix. 13).[2]

In analyzing the implications of this law, certain things appear and are of particular importance. *First,* the entire community has a responsibility to right the wrongs committed within its jurisdiction. This is an aspect of the police power of the citizenry. As Wright noted,

Crime is not merely a private matter between individuals. The whole community bears the responsibility as well as the unknown murderer. It is necessary therefore that the community shall acknowledge this fact and act to secure divine forgiveness.[3]

Second, if the community cannot locate the guilty party, then it must

1. Keil and Delitzsch: *The Pentateuch,* III, 404 f.
2. G. T. Manley, "Deuteronomy," in Davidson, Stibbs, and Kevin: *The New Bible Commentary,* p. 215.
3. G. Ernest Wright, "Deuteronomy," in *The Interpreter's Bible,* II, 460.

take steps to right the wrong all the same, or else it becomes guilty, along with its courts and rulers. The point of the ceremony is to "put away the guilt of innocent blood" (Deut. 21:9). In this sense only is there a collective guilt. However, those who fail to work to institute God's requirement of restitution are *individually* guilty, even though they number millions, whereas those who uphold the principle of restitution are absolved from the *individual* guilt. The collective guilt is thus essentially individual. There is, however, a collective judgment on the nation or community from the hand of God.

Third, this is case law, and it must be understood in terms of its basic principle, restitution. This law clearly affirms that crime must be atoned for, and the wrong righted. If God must be reckoned with, then man also must be reckoned with: the principle of restitution is a total one and requires restoration in every area. The symbolic death of the murderer means that the community believes that the restoration of true order is mandatory.

This brings us to the principle of restitution for murder. We have previously studied restitution from a number of perspectives; now a further implication needs to be drawn. One aspect of the law of restitution for murder is capital punishment. Another aspect is monetary compensation, which appears in Exodus 21:30-32. The personal property of the murderer is liable to seizure (but not that of his wife) for sale to compensate the relatives of the deceased. The history of Biblical law in its use in history makes clear that a crime could have a double penalty, because of its implications. Thus, in medieval courts, failure to pay a contracted debt meant not only the requirement to repay, but punishment for perjury by the court, since the contract to pay, being broken, represented false witness.[4]

Where society apprehends a criminal, it is a duty before God to require restitution; where it fails to apprehend the criminal, the duty to make restitution still remains. The state must in all such cases make restitution out of special funds for that purpose, either tax or fine funds accumulated for such a cause.

Clearly, it is God's purpose that every wrong be righted. Where the criminal cannot be apprehended, the state or the community must make atonement and restitution. The meaning of atonement is simply restitution; atonement implies restitution in a more total sense, in relationship to God and the whole of God's reality.

This principle did enter into Western law. Thus, Waller, writing with Britain in view, wrote,

It is remarkable that in our own time the most effectual remedy

---

4. F. R. H. DuBoulay: *An Age of Ambition, English Society in the Late Middle Ages* (New York: The Viking Press, 1970), p. 138.

against outrages of which the perpetrators cannot be discovered is a fine upon the district in which they occur.[5]

The absence of such a law has made many counties of the United States profitable areas of criminality. Murder, theft, and a variety of offenses flourish in these areas to the profit of corrupt officials and businessmen, and with no penalty from any law of restitution. Such a law would soon lead to a pragmatic moral outrage. The present alliance of courts, public officials, and businessmen to countenance crime because it is profitable cannot exist where restitution is required in every case.[6]

Fourth, the presence of the priests in the court is to be noted. Josephus recorded the fact that Levites were regularly assigned to all courts as a part of the implied requirements of the law of Moses:

> Let there be seven men to judge in every city, and these such as have been before most zealous in the exercise of virtue and righteousness. Let every judge have two officers allotted them out of the tribe of Levi. Let those that are chosen to judge in the several cities be had in great honour; and let none be permitted to revile any others when these are present, nor to carry themselves in an insolent manner to them; it being natural that reverence toward those in high offices among men should procure men's fear and reverence toward God. Let those that judge be permitted to determine according as they think to be right, unless any one can show that they have taken bribes, to the perversion of justice, or can allege any other accusation against them, whereby it may appear that they have passed an unjust sentence; for it is not fit that causes should be openly determined out of regard to gain, or to the dignity of the suitors, but that the judges should esteem what is right before all other things; otherwise God will by that means be despised, and esteemed inferior to those, the dread of whose power has occasioned the unjust sentence; for justice is the power of God. He, therefore, that gratifies those in great dignity, supposes them more potent than God himself. But if these judges be unable to give a just sentence about the causes that come before them, (which case is not infrequent in human affairs,) let them send the cause undetermined to the holy city, and there let the high priest, the prophet, and the sanhedrin determine as it shall seem good to them.[7]

In the determination and application of the law, these Levites were authoritative; the civil judges dealt with the guilt of the criminal and the hearing of the evidence, the Levites with the specific nature and application of the law.

> And by their word shall every controversy and every stroke be tried; literally, *And upon their mouth shall be every strife and every stroke,* i.e., by their judgment the character of the act shall be de-

---

5. C. H. Waller, "Deuteronomy," in Ellicott, II, 58.
6. See Ovid Demaris: *Captive City* (New York: Lyle Stuart, 1969).
7. Josephus: *Antiquities of the Jews,* Bk. IV, viii.

termined, and as they decide so shall the matter stand (cf. ch. x. 8; xvii. 8). In the present case the presence of the priests at the transaction gave it sanction as valid.[8]

Fifth, we saw, with respect to the trial of jealousy, that, according to Hosea 4:14, when guilt becomes prevalent, God's *specific judgment* of guilty wives *is replaced with a general judgment.* The ceremony of breaking a heifer's neck ended at about the same time as the trial of jealousy, in the first century A.D. According to the Talmud,

> Our Rabbis taught: When murderers multiplied the ceremony of breaking a heifer's neck was discontinued, because it is only performed in a case of doubt; but when murderers multiplied openly, the ceremony of breaking a heifer's neck was discontinued.[9]

In every culture, *where specific judgment fails, then general judgment follows.* Judgment is inescapable wherever there are offenses. If the offender is not brought to the court and required to make restitution, then the civil order must make restitution. The just claims to atonement by God, the great Lord and owner of all men and all the earth, and the just claims of offended men must be met. If they are not met, then God's judgment on the entire social order will ultimately follow.

Christ's atonement to God is His act of restitution for His new humanity; by His perfect obedience to God's law, and His vicarious death for the elect, Jesus made restitution for His people. Those who are the Lord's race, the new humanity, will make restitution between man and man as their response to God's grace. Men who have no atonement with God through Christ will make no atonement towards men.

Churches which are Christian in name only will not preach restitution, neither will they right wrongs. Their answer to their own problems is pragmatic. If lay officers are morally wrong but are important men, the pastor is transferred to avoid conflict. If the pastor is morally guilty or unfit for the ministry, he is transferred all too often and too seldom demitted. Not restitution but institutional security is usually the goal.

18. The Court

The law of atonement for all offenses (Deut. 21:1-9) makes clear the participation of a Levite, i.e., an expert in God's law, a theologian, in the civil courts. Josephus confirms the fact that Israel's history was marked by this fact, i.e., that *the court is a religious establishment.* The presence of the priests or Levites did not mean a confusion of

---

8. W. L. Alexander: *Deuteronomy*, p. 338; Spence and Exell: *The Pulpit Commentary.*
9. *Sotah*, 47b; p. 251.

church and state: it meant rather the total permeation of church and state, as well as every other institution, by the authority of God's word. The Levites in question were experts in God's law, *lawyers*. The frequent reference to lawyers in the New Testament was precisely to these experts who were members of the court. The law required this:

> If there arise a matter too hard for thee in judgment, between blood and blood, between plea and plea, and between stroke and stroke, being matters of controversy within thy gates: then shalt thou arise, and get thee up unto the place which the LORD thy God shall choose;
> And thou shalt come unto the priests the Levites, and unto the judges that shall be in those days, and enquire; and they shall shew thee the sentence of judgment:
> And thou shalt do according to the sentence, which they of that place which the LORD shall choose shall shew thee; and thou shalt observe to do according to all that they inform thee:
> According to the sentence of the law, and according to the judgment which they shall tell thee, thou shalt do: thou shalt not decline from the sentence which they shall shew thee, to the right hand, nor to the left (Deut. 17:8-11).

Waller's comment on this law is extremely important:

> It is not sufficiently observed that this defines the relation between the Church and the Bible from the time the Law . . . was delivered to the Church, and that the relation between the Church and the Bible is the same to this day. The only authority wherewith the Church (of Israel, or of Christ) can "bind" or "loose," is the written Law of God. The binding (or forbidding) and loosing (or permitting) of the Rabbis—the authority which our Lord committed to His Church—was only the application of His written word. The Rabbis acknowledge this from one end of the Talmud to the other by the appeal to Scripture which is made in every page, sometimes in almost every line. The application is often strained or fanciful; but this does not alter the principle. *The written word is the chain that binds.* Nor does the varying relation between the executive and legislative authority alter the principle.[1]

The reference of our Lord was thus clearly to this law when He spoke of binding and loosing:

> And I say unto thee, That thou art Peter, and upon this rock I will build my church; and the gates of hell shall not prevail against it.
> And I will give unto thee the keys of the kingdom of heaven: and whatsoever thou shalt bind on earth shall be bound in heaven: and whatsoever thou shalt loose on earth, shall be loosed in heaven (Matt. 16:17, 18).

> Verily I say unto you, Whatsoever ye shall bind on earth shall be bound in heaven: and whatsoever ye shall loose on earth shall be loosed in heaven (Matt. 18:18).

---

1. Waller, "Deuteronomy," in Ellicott, II, 51.

It is not our purpose to discuss the doctrine of the church here, but it is at least clear that *"the keys of the kingdom" are inseparable from the law, and the faithful declaration of the law.* It can be said, indeed, that *"the keys of the kingdom" which bind and loose are the law;* the church, by being constituted as the New Israel of God, the new covenant people, was thus also given the law as the means of governing the New Israel, civil and ecclesiastical. The keys are thus neither an episcopal or papal power per se nor private interpretation: they are the law as the only instrument of true power under God, of condemning and acquitting, binding, or loosing. It is the law of God, not the church, which binds or looses men, and only as the church faithfully declares the law is there any true binding or loosing. Whenever the church attempts to bind or loose men's conscience and conduct apart from the law-word of God, it is itself bound, that is, it is itself under judgment.

The state similarly cannot bind or loose men apart from the law-word of God, and the state needs the faithful exposition of that law from the church and from theologians in the service of the state. The Westminster Confession declared, in Chapter XXXI, v,

> Synods and councils are to handle, or conclude nothing, but that which is ecclesiastical: and are not to intermeddle with civil affairs which concern the commonwealth, unless by way of humble petition in cases extraordinary: or, by way of advice, for satisfaction of conscience, if they be thereunto required by the civil magistrate.

This is true of the church; it does not apply to the religious teacher, who can be a servant or administrator in church, state, or school, and has a duty to make clear the law-word of God.

Every court, because it is inescapably concerned with law, is a religious establishment. A religious establishment requires religious education. The education within a state will either teach the religion of the state or else the state will be revolutionized. The establishment of state-controlled schools in the United States, in a movement led by two Unitarians, Horace Mann and James G. Carter, was the beginning of a major religious and legal revolution in the United States.[2] The courts, precisely because of their importance in the life of a nation, must in particular be informed of the nature of God's law-word. Legal training is a form of theological training, and modern law schools are humanistic religious establishments. In terms of Biblical law, the courts and judges should be informed, both in their schooling and in their operation, of God's law.

---

2. See R. J. Rushdoony: *The Messianic Character of American Education.* (Nutley, New Jersey: Presbyterian and Reformed Publishing Company, 1963, 1968).

The expression in Deuteronomy 17:8, "between blood and blood," means a decision between murder and manslaughter. "Between plea and plea" means between one type of plea for right as against another. "Between stroke and stroke" refers to varieties of bodily injury; "matters of controversy within thy gates" means matters of controversy within the community. In these very practical questions of law and the application of the law, the ultimate authority which binds and looses is God's law-word. This law must govern the court, and the court must at the very least be fully grounded in the law.

Neither church nor state can bind or loose if it does not adhere to the law of God as the sole source of binding and loosing, of condemning and acquitting. In every culture, the true god of that system is the source of law, and if church or state, or any other agency, function as the creator of law, i.e., issuing laws without any transcendental basis, then they have made themselves into gods. Their *right* to command is then gone. For the people of God under their jurisdiction, the routes open are, first, peaceful resistance, using the instruments of the law; second, emigration to another church or another country; third, obedience, but with the full awareness that they are obeying as unto God, to preserve order, not unto man, recognizing that, while the powers have no right to command apart from God's word, sometimes the duty to obey remains as the moral course, and the pragmatic course; fourth, disobedience as a moral duty under the leadership of authority; such disobedience must be conscientious obedience to God rather than to man.

The more a power departs from God's law, the more impotent it becomes in coping with real offenses, and the more severe it becomes with trifling offenses or with meaningless infractions of empty statutes which seek to govern without moral authority and without reason.

Thus, in many major cities, especially in the eastern United States, widespread rioting and looting was tolerated in the 1960's and early 1970's, but, at the same time the police were under orders to pick up traffic violators for the most insignificant or trifling infractions. The fines were a rich source of money for nearly bankrupt cities. Witness also the implications of the following report from Washington, D. C., scene of many flagrantly lawless demonstrations:

> "A dozen footmen, mounted policemen and officers on motor-scooters charged the group and arrested three. . . . After running into a parked car and falling, Donohoe was pounced upon by four officers, one of whom blackjacked him as he was pinned to the ground by other park policemen. . . ." What does this April Washington *Post* story describe? Police overreacting to anti-war demonstrators? No, it describes federal park police arresting citizens of Washington, D. C. for violating a bizarre ordinance that prohibits

. . . kite-flying. By the 19th fifteen persons had been arrested during April for flying kites.[3]

When the law, whether in church, state, school, or family, ceases to command men morally, it breaks down, and two possibilities then exist. A *first* consequence is anarchy. We should not be surprised at the anarchy in family life, the business world, or in the state, nor at the lack of discipline in churches. Men will not obey a law which lacks moral structure. Many children are rebellious against parental authority, but too many parents, as humanists, have no moral grounds for commanding obedience and have only transmitted moral anarchy to their children. The rebellion of youth in the second half of the twentieth century has been logical; it has been based on the moral premises taught by home, church, state, and school. Christian homes which have sent their children into public schools have denied their faith and asked for moral anarchism. This moral anarchism saturates every area, including business and employment.

Second, the alternative to moral anarchism is naked coercion, the use of terror. Karl Marx saw logically no valid philosophy save anarchism; pragmatically, he recognized the need for solidarity and hence he favored communism. Marxism has, however, communicated moral anarchism. As a result, the logical course for a working Marxist, as Lenin quickly realized, is the institution of terror. The Red Terror thus became a necessary and accepted substitute for moral force.

Nowhere should moral authority be greater than in the church. Because the church is commissioned to teach the word of God, when it teaches it faithfully its authority is very great. Discipline is then written into the hearts and sinews of the people. More than a church court then demands it: the lives of the people create it. Where the discipline is lax, or it is grudgingly obeyed only under pressure, the people are either unconverted, or the church is either apostate or irrelevant, and irrelevancy is a form of apostasy.

The court is a religious establishment. For the court to function, the religion of the court must also be the religion of the people. If the moral discipline is not in the hearts of the people, no revolution can put it there, nor give it to the courts. Instead of moral discipline, the result is terror. *If men will not obey God, they will not obey men*: they will then require the gallows and the gun as the necessary instruments of order. Their protests against the new order they have created by their lawlessness are as morally unfounded as that new order, and less effective. This new order then has one destiny—to kill and to be killed.

---

3. "For Your Information," *Triumph*, vol. V, no. 6 (June, 1970), p. 6.

19. The Procedure of the Court

The procedures of the court have been discussed in part in studying the laws of witnessing and of evidence.

Other aspects of court procedure which are of particular note are, *first*, the place of the court, at the city gates (Deut. 21:19; 22:15; 25: 7; Amos 5:12, 15; Zech. 8:16), or, on cases of appeal to the highest courts, at the Porch of Judgment at the king's palace (I Kings 7:7). Symbolically, justice was thus the gate of the city; symbolically too, justice, having nothing to hide and everything to gain by being public, was totally open. The hearings of the court were available to all. The concept of a *public* trial, as against the secret trial so common to antiquity and to tyrannies, was thus basic to Biblical law. The public execution was part of this same principle. Secret or closed executions, promoted in the name of dignity, are in reality a sign of growing statism and incipient tyranny. Ultimately, in a tyrant state, the deaths are not only in secret but are not even reported. In countries where weather does not permit public outdoor trials, indoor trials became only logical, but the principle of a public hearing must be retained.

Second, we must not assume, as humanistic scholarship would lead us to, that trials in Biblical eras were primitive and unrecorded. Long before Moses, written records were mandatory. Job, whose time is the patriarchal age, mentions in passing the court procedures of his day:

> Oh that I had one to hear me!
> (Lo, here is my signature, let the Almighty answer me)
> And that I had the indictment which mine adversary hath written!
> (Job 31:35 ARV).

Written charges and records were thus an early aspect of court procedure in order to fix the fine points of evidence and testimony.

Third, contempt of court was forbidden (Ex. 22:28), and, where involving a radical rejection of the court's authority, was punishable by death (Deut. 17:12, 13).

Fourth, witnesses had to take an oath before testifying (Ex. 22:10, 11). The oath was a conditional curse, with specified penalties for violation (Lev. 6:1-7).

Fifth, cases could be appealed to the highest court of the land, to Moses, the judges of the nation, or to the king (I Kings 3:9). Indeed, the most important function of the chief magistrate or authority in a nation was, in Biblical law, the duty to function as a final court of appeals. We cannot understand the greatness of Solomon and his reign without a recognition of this fact. The whole point of I Kings 3:5-15 is that the young king Solomon pleased God by desiring, above all else, to be a wise chief justice of Israel. He asked for "understanding to discern justice" (I Kings 3:11 ARV). It is a commentary on our times that Solomon is best known to us for his harem; in his age it was ability as the supreme judge of the nation which gained him the greatest renown. His request of God was precisely this:

> Give therefore thy servant an understanding heart to judge thy people, that I may discern between good and bad: for who is able to judge this thy so great a people? (I Kings 3:9).

Trained by the prophet Nathan, a champion of the law, Solomon's major concern was the law, which was the cornerstone of the greatness of his reign. When men today think of Solomon's "wisdom," they modernize the concept into something abstract, academic, and intellectualistic. The Biblical reference to Solomon's wisdom means most centrally his wisdom as a judge, the wisdom he prayed for, and, secondarily, his wisdom in administration. The Proverbs of Solomon are essentially a practical commentary on the law, and this is their wisdom.

Solomon, by providing a godly and practical wisdom as judge in all cases appearing before him, ensured thereby that the final court of appeals in Israel would be a court of justice. The result was a great confidence amongst the peoples and a prosperity under conditions of justice. Solomon's later folly never entirely undercut the basic justice of his reign.

Sixth, although arrests could be made on the sabbath (Num. 15: 32-36), trials were held only during other days of the week. In American law, "an offender may not be tried and convicted on Sunday," although he may be arrested, committed, or discharged by the magistrate.[1]

Seventh, the right to a speedy trial, to justice without delay, was not only a feature of the public hearings of the court, but also stressed, as an instrument of sound administration, by Artaxerxes in his orders to Ezra: "And whosoever will not do the law of thy God, and the law of the king, let judgment be executed speedily upon him, whether it be unto death, or to banishment, or to confiscation of goods, or to imprisonment" (Ezra 7:26). This order brought together Persian authority and law with Hebrew law and tradition. (This Persian order, cited also in the Apocrypha, I Esdras 8:24, is of particular interest in that it cites a form of judgment alien to Biblical law, i.e., imprisonment. It remained alien, although used by the Herodians. The imprisonment of men like John the Baptist was in essence an illegal act.)

Eighth, since in Biblical law the function of the state is to be the ministry of justice, the highest office in the state was inseparable from justice and the courts. Administration, now most closely associated

---

1. Clark: *Biblical Law,* p. 280.

with the highest office in a state, was then a function reserved to officers of the king, members of the harem, eunuchs, and others. The basic functions of the chief officers of the land, whether a judge in the earlier era, or a king later, were twofold, to be the military leader, and to be the chief justice of the country. The military office was not a constant one; it could be delegated to others, as, in David's case, to Joab. The office of chief justice was a continuous one and most basic to the state. This function of the king was common to medieval monarchs, and the success or failure of an English king, for example, very commonly depended largely on his abilities as the supreme judge of the nation. The very name for the king's audiences and his associates reflects this function: court, and courtier. The king's court was originally not a showplace nor a center of social functions but a seat of justice. When kings' courts began to change into ladies' promenades, monarchy was in process of rendering itself obsolete.

In any civil government where administrative offices gain centrality, a growth of centralized power becomes inescapable, because not justice to the people but government over the people becomes basic to the nation and the state. Prior to Lincoln, American presidents were not as central to American life as they have since become, and the growth of presidential power has been a necessary result of the growth of the importance of administration over justice. Prior to Lincoln, presidents in the United States tended to regard themselves as a variety of judges, and vetoes were based on legal considerations, on questions of constitutionality, and the presidential office was seen as an agency of judicial review over the acts of Congress. Much of the early uncertainty over the role of the U.S. Supreme Court was due to the fact that the historical background saw the chief magistrate as the final court of appeal over the justices of courts. The presidential power of pardon is a survival of this fact. Questions of constitutionality were at first raised by President Washington, only much later by the court. Appeals to the president to right wrongs long continued in American history as an echo of his undefined role as supreme justice of the American system. The administrative role took precedence finally, and a different kind of America began to take shape.

In the Old Testament, Moses was the chief justice of Israel, a judge. The tribal leaders were various administrative heads of the nation; their "federal union" under Moses and Joshua was essentially military and judicial. They were under one law, and Moses was the chief justice of that federal union as well as its supreme commander. The military functions Moses delegated to Joshua; the legal responsibilities Moses himself discharged.

Samuel, as chief justice, made a circuit of the entire country annually (I Sam. 7:16, 17) to bring justice to the people, to ensure the right of appeal by making appeal immediately available.

Ninth, and finally, the judge was not to be an impartial referee but a partisan champion of the law of God, actively concerned with bringing God's justice to bear on every situation "by requiting the wicked, by recompensing his way upon his own head; and by justifying the righteous, by giving him according to his righteousness" (II Chron. 6:23).

20. The Judgment of the Court

The judgments of the court in Biblical law are of two kinds: *first,* judgments of money and property, to make restitution, and, *second,* judgments upon the person, from corporal to capital punishment. The nature of these judgments has already been discussed.

It is important to recognize that in Biblical law the judgments are the judgments of God:

> Ye shall not respect persons in judgment; but ye shall hear the small as well as the great; ye shall not be afraid of the face of man; for the judgment is God's: and the cause that is too hard for you, bring it unto me, and I will hear it (Deut. 1:17).

The thesis here is the same as that of St. Paul in Romans 13:1-4, but it is more specific: the *judgment* of the court is the judgment of God, whenever faithfully delivered. Because the court is identified so closely with the activity of God, the judges themselves are referred to as "gods" in Scripture. Psalm 82:1 reads, "God standeth in the congregation of the mighty; he judgeth among the gods." The Berkeley Version renders this "God stands in the congregation of God; in the midst of the judges He gives judgment." Judges thus are "the congregation of God," an assembly of men God has called to represent Him in justice; through them, God gives judgment or justice. Thus, a fundamental aspect of God's order, of His kingdom must be and can only be manifested in and through the courts of law. If the court fails to give the judgment of God by its apostasy from God, it will inevitably give the judgment of man in terms of the satanic principles of independence and lawlessness. When the judges fail to dispense justice to the weak and the orphan, to the wretched and the needy, to the great and the small without favor or respect of faces, then they reveal their blindness and wilful ignorance. The apostasy of the judges means, according to the Berkeley Version, that "All the foundations of the earth are shaking" (Ps. 82:5).

Judges by their office are made into gods, and sons of God (Ps. 82:6). By their failure to render the judgment of God, they shall perish (Ps. 82:7). The plea of Asaph, in the face of false judges, is this: "Arise,

O God! Judge the earth, for Thou dost possess all nations!" (Ps. 82:8 BV).

Jesus, in citing this psalm, declared that judges are those "unto whom the word of God came, and Scripture cannot be broken" (John 10:35). In other words, *the word of God was written in large measure for judges*; it is a book, among other things, for the organization of civil society in terms of the word of God. It is attempting to "break" Scripture to deny its civil application, or the role of judges under God; and to limit its application to the church and purely personal piety is surely heresy. The test of judges as the sons of God is to do the work of God, to dispense justice in terms of God's law-word. The test of Jesus Himself is similar: He does the work God ordains for Him. "If I do not the works of my Father, believe me not. But if I do, though ye believe not me, believe the works: that ye may know, and believe, that the Father is in me, and I in him" (John 10:37-38). In both cases, the test is the same. A false messiah would not do the work ordained by God in His word, the Bible; because Jesus came in perfect fulfilment of the prophetic word, He and none other is the Messiah of God. Similarly, a false judge will not function as a son of God, to render justice strictly in terms of God's law-word, whereas a godly judge will render judgment in terms of God's law-word.

Clearly then, Scripture declares that judges are true judges only if they are faithful to God's law. What then of Paul's words in Romans 13:1-4, which declares that all civil authorities are ministers of God? The difference is between legitimacy and integrity: a man may be the legitimate son of his father, and that fact cannot be honestly denied, but he may lack the integrity and respect his father commands; he may, in character, be a false son. Similarly, a judge, a minister of justice, or a clergyman, a minister of grace, may be a legitimate officer, having full title to his office in terms of all the human requirements, but he may be at the same time unfit for office morally. God requires us to recognize the human legitimacy and to honor the office if not able to honor the man; judgment beyond a certain point is in God's hands. This does not mean that lawful means of protest and change should not be used; in fact, they must be used.

Reform, however, involves more than a recognition of evil and a distaste or hatred of it. A very eloquent and well reasoned attack on corruption in government was made in October, 1931, in *Liberty* Magazine by Al Capone. He came out strongly against communism and subversion; he attacked the easy money mentality and stock market speculation, and the amalgamation of weak companies into large corporations which worked greater havoc with their collapse. Capone, who claimed that he had fed about 350,000 needy persons a day in Chicago during the previous winter, condemned graft also:

> "Graft," he continued, "is a byword in American life today. It is a law where no other law is obeyed. It is undermining this country. The honest lawmakers of any city can be counted on your fingers. I could count Chicago's on one hand!
>
> "Virtue, honor, truth, and the law have all vanished from our life, We are smart-Alecky. We like to be able to 'get away with' things. And if we can't make a living at some honest profession, we are going to make one anyway." . . .
>
> "The home is our most important ally," Capone observed. "After all the madness the world has been going through subsides, we'll realize that, as a nation, very strongly. The stronger we can keep our home lives, the stronger we can keep our nation.
>
> "When enemies approach our shores we defend them. When enemies come into our homes me beat them off. Homebreakers should be undressed and tarred and feathered, as examples to the rest of their kind."[1]

In the course of this same interview, Capone predicted that the Democrats would win the 1932 elections with "a record vote," with either Owen Young or Roosevelt.

Capone's basic position was thus for law and order, as long as he was not bothered. This is the failure of most reform movements. Evil is recognized and opposed everywhere except in ourselves. Hence, the cry of political reform movements is to throw out all the rascals, except themselves.

During the Kennedy Administration, a humorous critique of the Kennedy critics had more than a little truth to it. The typical critic went to public schools, riding there on a county bus on a public highway; he went to college on the GI bill, bought a house with an FHA loan, started a business with a loan from the Small Business Administration, made money, retired on social security, and then sat back to criticize the welfare program, demanding that the freeloaders be put to work.

In terms of God's law, true reform begins with regeneration and then the submission of the believer to the whole law-word of God. The degenerate pretenders to reform want to reform the world by beginning with their opponents, with any and everyone save themselves. True reform begins with the submission of our own lives, homes, and callings to God's law-word. The world is then recaptured step by step as men institute true reform in their realms. Any other kind of reform has as much integrity and value as Al Capone's words. We can accept the

---

1. Cornelius Vanderbilt, Jr., "How Al Capone Would Run This Country," reprinted in Richard Armour, *Give Me Liberty* (New York: World Publishing Co., 1969), p. 155.

sincerity of Al Capone's words; like all sinners, he wanted a better world to live in, but not at the price of his own surrender to God's law-order.

The judgments of God in His word must become the judgments of God's people. Only as a people are recalled to God and His order can they expect the benefits of that order. According to Solomon, "Where there is no vision, the people perish [or "run wild," B.V.], but he that keepeth the law, happy is he" (Prov. 29:18). *Vision* is here equated with keeping the law.

God's law is a total law: it is not limited to a segment of creation such as man's private life, his church life, or any other partial area. No more than reform can come by a mere changing of politicians without a change in the lives of the people, can reform come simply because man applies it to a restricted area of life. When men, in terms of God's law, deliver the judgments of God in their homes, churches, schools, vocations, and in the state, then too the courts will deliver the judgments of God's total law.

21. Perfection

A declaration in the law reads, "Thou shalt be perfect with the LORD thy God" (Deut. 18:13). This is restated in the Sermon on the Mount, Christ declaring, "Be ye therefore perfect, even as your Father which is in heaven is perfect" (Matt. 5:48).

The law does not command us to do what man cannot do. How then shall we understand this requirement, and wherein can we be perfect before the Lord without bearing false witness concerning ourselves?

We are told that Noah was "perfect" (Gen. 6:9), and Abraham was called to be perfect (Gen. 17:1). In Psalm 37:37, we have a reference to the "perfect man" as a fact of everyday life. In Psalm 101:2, David declared, "I will behave myself wisely in a perfect way. . . . I will walk within my house with a perfect heart."

The Old Testament words translated as "perfect" mean upright, having integrity, blameless, and the New Testament words have the meaning of mature, complete.[1] Clearly, this is something other than sinlessness. Lenski's comment is very much to the point with respect to the confusion of Biblical "perfection" with sinlessness:

> The English translation "perfect" is largely responsible for the idea of absolute sinlessness often given as the meaning . . . and it is unfortunate that we have no derivative from "goal" adequate to render the Greek. The fact that absolute sinlessness is not the thought expressed here we see from v. 6 (of Matt. 5), where the blessed disciples still hunger for righteousness, and from v. 7, where they still need mercy and are blessed by constantly obtaining it.

---

1. W. E. Vine, *An Expository Dictionary of New Testament Words* (New York: Revell [1940], 1966), III, 175 f.

. . . Perfectionism may imagine that it is able to attain sinlessness in this life; this goal we shall not reach until we enter glory. Equally incorrect is the idea that in these expositions of the law Jesus offers only "counsels for the perfect" which are unattainable on the part of lesser Christians. Christ has no double standard. His greatest saints are found among the common believers who by grace have become pure in heart (v. 8).[2]

Perfection means uprightness and maturity in terms of a goal or purpose, an end established by God. Our maturity in heaven will include sinlessness, but our maturity here is of a different sort.

In this life, we can be perfect in the sense of being blameless in our faithfulness to God's purpose, but to be blameless does not mean being faultless. Thus, G. Campbell Morgan once wrote of his experience with his young son. Morgan was in America, and a letter arrived from his son, who had just learned to read and write. The letter, full of errors, expressed the boy's love of his father, and his longing for him. The letter, Morgan noted, was clearly not faultless, but it was blameless. The Berkeley Version translates Deuteronomy 18:13, "You, however, must be blameless before the LORD your God."

What is blameless in a child is not blameless in an adult; maturity requires continuous growth towards God's appointed purpose. Then too, the greater the responsibility, the greater the maturity required to be blameless. What a minister, a doctor, judge, or civil officer does, and, in many cases, what their wives do, is more important than what others do. A remark blameless in others may be a serious offense from them.

To cite an example: Martha Mitchell, wife of U. S. Attorney General John Mitchell, is apparently a charming, intelligent, and witty woman; her mouth is usually open. Her remarks have repeatedly had national news coverage, and many people have agreed with her. The effect of her remarks in Washington has been to widen breaches, stir up trouble, and create a number of unhappy problems. It is possible thus to say, with all due respect to Martha Mitchell as a superior woman, that she is blameworthy, and she has sought the limelight too often at the expense of the administration's policies. Even when ordered by her husband to be silent, she managed to get into the news:

> For months now, the lady's outspoken statements have been conspicuously missing from the press—in obedience, no doubt, to an injunction from U. S. Attorney General John Mitchell. Henceforth, he has decreed, if his wife Martha must speak out in public, it must be in Swahili. But what husband has ever silenced his wife? Administering the oath of office to the new president of the American Newspaper Women's Club in Washington last week, Martha spoke in near-faultless Swahili: "*Je unaabe kwa kweli*

---

2. R. C. H. Lenski, *The Interpretation of St. Matthew's Gospel*, p. 253.

kwemba usaziunga. . . ." Ruled the Attorney General, who was present: "The oath in Swahili is perfectly legal."[3]

This kind of witty and irrepressible desire to make news is entertaining from a distance; for those near at hand, it is a problem, and it does represent thoughtlessness of consequences, and Biblical perfection or maturity is not geared to the moment but to God's ordained goals.

The influence of pietism has been an important one in modern history, and it has borne false witness concerning God's requirements. Its emphasis on sinless perfection has in fact begotten sin. Where men expect a sinless perfection of other men, they are readily led into a sinful intolerance of human frailties. This sinful perfectionism especially abounds at the end of an age, or in any era when men find their problems either temporarily or permanently unsurmountable. Where problems are insoluble, men then turn on one another. Their basic unhappiness over the insoluble problems manifests itself in trying to "dissolve" from their midst people who irk them. As the fall of Rome began to loom, men long before had fled from the cities, recognizing their hopeless future. Their reaction, however, was far from sound. Christians and pagans alike turned on men and renounced them, becoming desert hermits. But being alone solved nothing, and the inner torments of these desert refugees indicated that their flight gave them neither peace nor an answer to the world's problems. Today again, as problems appear to be insoluble, the irritation of man with man increases. There is a low level of tolerance with children, neighbors, husbands, wives, friends, and associates. Instead of solving problems, this kind of perfectionism only aggravates them. Giving an exaggerated emphasis to human frailties is to bear false witness concerning them.

The law here is plain-spoken: "Bear ye one another's burdens, and so fulfil the law of Christ" (Gal. 6:2). This has reference, very clearly, as Galatians 6:3-5 makes clear, to our faults and weaknesses. We are to recognize that each of us has a burden of weaknesses, and "every man shall bear his own burden" (Gal. 6:5). We sometimes need correcting, but, much of the time, we must live together mindful of our common frailties and work together to gain that maturity which comes from seeking first the Kingdom of God and His righteousness (Matt. 7:33).

Our greatest strength is thus in what is termed "perfection" and which means maturity, an integrity in terms of God's purpose which gains God's blessing even amidst serious troubles. Maturity is the ability to grow in terms of our experiences and to use them to draw closer to God's purpose for us.

3. "People," *Time* Magazine, vol. 96, no. 2 (July 13, 1970), p. 28.

The *problem*, from the modern perspective, is too often seen as *subversion*, when it is more commonly a *moral failure*, inability to grow and become mature. Societies which concentrate on problems of subversion are near death: they have lost their capacity to cope with their problems. This does *not* mean that subversion is to be neglected or condoned, but the only permanent answer to it is growth. The cause is reconstruction.

During the War for Independence, the subversives ostensibly on the American side were undoubtedly many. It now is maintained that Benjamin Franklin was a British agent during the entire struggle.[4] At least through the War of 1812, the number of British and French agents in America were numerous, but the basic health of the leadership, and a sufficient element of men of character, plus the grace of God, enabled the American cause to prosper in the face of radical subversion.

Without that maturity, no cause can survive. Without the ability to grow in terms of a goal, no cause can endure merely by rooting out its subversive elements. The salt that has lost its savor is "good for nothing, but to be cast out, and to be trodden under foot of men" (Matt. 5:13). There is no divine protection for men and nations who lose their calling and "savor." In fact, there is then no escaping judgment: it is "As if a man did flee from a lion, and a bear met him; and went into the house, and leaned his hand on the wall, and a serpent bit him" (Amos 5:19).

---

4. Richard Deacon and Tom McMorrow, "Famous British Historian Claims Benjamin Franklin Was a British Spy," in *Argosy*, July, 1970, p. 24 ff.

X

THE TENTH COMMANDMENT

1. Covetousness

The tenth commandment is one of the longer statements of principle in the Decalogue. In its two versions, it reads:

> Thou shalt not covet thy neighbour's house, thou shalt not covet thy neighbour's wife, nor his manservant, nor his maidservant, nor his ox, nor his ass, nor any thing that is thy neighbour's (Ex. 20:17).

> Neither shalt thou desire thy neighbour's wife, neither shalt thou covet thy neighbour's house, his field, or his manservant, nor his maidservant, his ox, or his ass, or any thing that is thy neighbour's (Deut. 5:21).

Much has been said by silly triflers about the place of the wife in each of these sentences, before and after the house, and also that she is supposedly on the same level as the ox and the ass. Fools should be left to their folly; the wise will occupy their time with other matters.

The meaning of this law depends on the meaning of *covet*. The rest of the law deals with the *actions* of men; does the law in this case deal with man's emotions instead, or have we misunderstood the meaning of *covet*? Noth has pointed out that *covet* in fact does mean much more than the emotion of coveting.

> The commandment in v. 17 is formulated with a verb which is rendered "covet." But it describes not merely the emotion of coveting but also includes the attempt to attach something to oneself illegally. The commandment therefore deals with all possible undertakings which involve gaining power over the goods and possessions of a "neighbour," whether through theft or through all kinds of dishonest machinations. The first object to be named is the neighbour's house. The term "house" can in a narrow and special sense describe the dwelling-place, primarily the built house but also in every case the tent-"house" of the nomad; it can, however, also be used in a more or less wide or transferred sense to mean, for instance, the family, or to sum up everything which is included in the house.[1]

Thus, when Exodus begins by forbidding coveting a neighbor's house, by house it means, as it then goes on to specify, the wife, the servants, animals, and all other possessions of our neighbor. First, the general

---

1. Martin Noth, *Exodus* (Philadelphia: Westminster Press, 1962), p. 166.

term *house* is used, and then specific aspects of the "house" are described. In Deuteronomy, the citations are apparently all of specifics, including the "house."

Von Rad wrote of "covet" in equally telling terms:

> If in the last commandment the translation of the verb as "covet" were correct, it would be the only case in which the decalogue deals not with an action, but with an inner impulse, hence with a sin of intention. But the corresponding Hebrew word (*hamad*) has two meanings, both to covet and to take. It includes outward malpractices, meaning seizing for oneself (Josh. 7:21; Micah 2:2, etc.).[2]

When Jesus cited the tenth commandment in Mark 10:19, He clearly cited it in terms of a sin of action, and the Greek text uses the word *aposteresis*, to defraud of a thing, and it is translated in the King James Version as "defraud."

The observations of Noth and Von Rad represent no novelty in interpretation. Clearly, our Lord gave it the same meaning, and, just as clearly, this was known by Christian scholars in earlier eras. Thus, the great Anglican scholar of the 17th century, Dr. Isaac Barrow, writing on the tenth commandment, observed:

> This law is comprehensive and recapitulatory, as it were, of the rest concerning our neighbour, prescribing universal justice toward him (whence St. Mark, it seems, meaneth to render it in one word, by . . . *deprive not*, or bereave not your neighbour of any thing; Mark x. 19) and this not only in outward deed and dealing, but in inward thought and desire, the spring whence they do issue forth. . . .[3]

Adam Clarke was also aware of the meaning of covet, and declared:

> Thou shalt not covet, ver. 17 . . . *lo tachemod*—the word . . . *chamad*, signifies an *earnest* and *strong* desire after a matter, on which all the affections are concentrated and fixed, whether the thing be *good* or *bad*. This is what we commonly term *covetousness,* which word is taken both in a *good* and *bad* sense. So when the Scripture says, that *covetousness is idolatry*: yet it also says, *covet earnestly the best things*; so we find that this disposition is sinful or holy, according to the object on which it is fixed. In this command, the *covetousness* which is placed on forbidden objects, is that which is prohibited and condemned. To covet in this sense, is intensely to long after, in order to enjoy as *property,* the *person,* or *thing,* coveted. He breaks this command, who by any means endeavours to deprive a man of his *house,* or *farm,* by some *underhand* and *clandestine* bargain with the original landlord; what is called in some countries, *taking a man's house and farm over his*

---

2. Gerhard Von Rad, *Deuteronomy, A Commentary* (Philadelphia: Westminster Press, 1966), p. 59.
3. Isaac Barrow, *Works* (New York: John C. Riker, 1845), III, 39.

head. He breaks it also, who lusts after his neighbour's wife, and endeavours to ingratiate himself into her affections, by striving to lessen her husband in her esteem:—and he breaks it, who endeavours to possess himself of the servants, cattle &c. of another, in any clandestine or unjustifiable way. This is a most excellent moral precept, the observance of which will prevent all public crimes: for he who feels the force of the law which prohibits the inordinate desire of any thing that is the property of another, can never make a breach in the peace of society by an act of *wrong* to any of even its feeblest members.[4]

The misconception of this law began with pietism, which limited God's law to moral precepts. Religion was internalized and therefore actions ceased to be as important as the "heart." On top of that, the idea that gain of any sort was somehow "unspiritual" was also propagated, so that covetousness took on an exclusive evil meaning.

Habakkuk 2:9 gives us an example of the fact that Scripture made a distinction betwen good and evil covetousness. The meaning of the passage appears as both the King James and Berkeley Versions are examined:

Woe to him that coveteth an evil covetousness to his house, that he may set his nest on high, that he may be delivered from the power of evil! (KJV).

Woe to him who acquires an evil gain for his house, in order to set his seat on high, to be out of the reach of calamity! (BV).

Covetousness is here equated with gain; it is evil covetousness or gain which is condemned. Honest gain and godly covetousness are clearly not condemned.

St. Paul, in I Corinthinans 12:31, used the word "covet" in its good sense: "But covet earnestly the best gifts"; the Berkeley Version renders "covet" as "aim hard for," work earnestly and zealously for the best gifts.

Thus, what is clearly condemned by the tenth commandment is every attempt to gain by fraud, coercion, or deceit that which belongs to our neighbor. On this principle, alienation of affection suits were once a part of the law of the land. Their abuse by a lawless age led to their abolition, but the principle is sound. A person who works systematically to alienate the affections of a husband or wife in order to gain him or her for himself, sometimes together with his monetary assets, is guilty of violating this law.

This law thus forbids the expropriation by fraud or deceit of that which belongs to our neighbor. The tenth commandment therefore does sum up commandments six through nine and gives them an additional

---

4. Adam Clarke, *Discourses on Various Subjects*, II, 36 f.

perspective. The other commandments deal with obviously illegal acts, i.e., clear-cut violations of law. The tenth commandment can be broken within these laws. To cite a Biblical example. David committed adultery with Bathsheba, a clearly illegal act. His subsequent acts were technically within the law: Uriah was put in the forefront of the battle and orders were so issued as to insure Uriah's death in battle. It was not technically murder, but it was clearly a conspiracy to kill, with David and Joab both guilty of murder.

Thus, a variety of laws in Western civilization are based on this principle of the fraudulent use of the law to defraud or to harm. Many of these laws legislate against the conspiracy aspect of fraud. They legislate against the covetous seizure of our neighbor's possessions by evil although sometimes legal means. The law against dishonest gain is thus a very important one, and the tenth commandment, instead of being a vague appendage to the law, is basic to it.

This law against dishonest gain is directed by God, not merely to the individual, but to the state and all institutions. The state can be and often is as guilty as are any individuals, and the state is often used as the legal means whereby others are defrauded of their possessions. The law against evil covetousness is thus an especially needed one in the 20th century. The pietism which earlier undercut this law has now become a pervasive social attitude.

Pietism emphasizes the *heart*, the attitudes of man, and underrates the importance of man's actions. Its roots are in the pagan, Greek, and Stoic deprecation of matter as against spirit. The goal in these philosophies was to be passionless. The true philosopher was above feeling grief for material things: his house could burn down, his wife and children die, and he sought to be unconcerned. Only those things which are of the mind or spirit supposedly concerned him.

The influence of these philosophies on the church made all coveting evil. Man was supposed to be without desire in order to be holy. To be ambitious was evil, because it represented desire with respect to material things. Shakespeare and Fletcher reflected this in their play, *Henry VIII*, in which Cardinal Wolsey says,

> Mark but my fall, and that that ruined me.
> Cromwell, I charge thee, fling away ambition:
> By that sin fell the angels; how can man, then,
> The image of his Maker, hope to win by it?
> Love thyself last: cherish those hearts that hate thee.
> (Act III, sc. II).

Such a philosophy meant that ambition had no Christian legitimacy, and that desire for better things was always a sin. As a result, the only legitimate ambition and desire was that which renounced Christianity

for humanism. Pietism led Christianity, both before and after the
Reformation, into false paths of feeling as against a wholebess of life.

Pietism, in origin pagan and humanistic, re-infected humanism in the
modern era. As a result, liberals who have no real love of Negroes,
Indians, and others, flit from cause to cause by working up a flood of
feeling as the real solution to all problems. The result of such pietistic
emotionalism is no real advance in anyone's cause but only an emotional
bath for the humanistic pietists.

2.   The Law in Force

In the Sermon on the Mount, Jesus applied some of the laws of
Scripture to the heart of man, i.e., declared that the law has not only a
requirement to make of man's actions but also of man's heart. God,
being total in His sovereignty, issues a total law.

Some of the implications of the law as stated in the Sermon on the
Mount are not within the scope of civil law (Matt. 5:21, 22, 27, 28).
To hate our brother, or to look with lust at a woman, are offenses
which God can judge, but the courts can judge only if some action ensues in terms of those feelings.

Some of the implications of the law, as they ensue in action, are
covered by the tenth commandment. We have cited alienation of
affection suits.

Even more common are those actions, technically within the law,
which violate the spirit of the law, actions whereby man expropriates
the property of others by abuse of the letter of the law. The law must
be "confirmed," i.e., put into force in all its implications, not a barren
legalism which uses the law to break the law. This is clearly required
in Deuteronomy 27:26:

> Cursed be he that confirmeth not all the words of this law, to do
> them. And all the people shall say, Amen.

Moffatt's translation:

> "A curse on the man who will not give effect to the words of this
> law!" And all the people shall answer, "So be it."

To cite an example of this, the law requires payment of debts; failure
to pay is a form of theft as well as perjury. The lender does need protection in business loans, because many people are "deadbeats" and
all too ready to defraud their creditors. However, contracts are now
usually dishonest because of the many clauses which, while designed to
protect against defrauders, become tools to defraud the unwise and the
ignorant. The "fine print" of contracts today may include such things
as waiver of defenses, contingency liability, written notification, confession of judgment, liability waivers, and pre-existing health condition

clauses, all of which penalize the individual as against the company. In a world of limited liability many of these contracts re-introduce an illegitimate form of unlimited liability. The Christian must favor unlimited liability, but not in this one-sided way. Both parties to a contract should be governed by its conditions.

In an analysis of such contracts, Jean Carper wrote:

> Reluctant to sell the house they had lived in 35 years, a couple in an Eastern state signed a contract for $2,500 to have it renovated. Unfortunately, three weeks later, their contractor died of a heart attack, and the work was never begun.
>
> Soon afterward, the couple received notice from a finance company demanding monthly payments to fulfill the contract of $2,500. The couple wrote explaining the situation, made no payments, and thought no more about it. Two months later the sheriff served papers notifying them that the finance company had foreclosed on the house and would put it up for auction—unless they produced the cash to cover the contract, plus legal fees. They sought help in every direction, but could not raise the money. Thus, incredibly— to pay for a job never done—their house was auctioned off. Worth perhaps $30,000, it was sold to an officer of the finance company for $20,000.
>
> In another state, a 56-year-old widow bought automobile insurance from a company recommended by her insurance agent. Her policy was cancelled a year later with no explanation. Then, nearly three years later, she received a letter from a lawyer ordering her to pay the state $291.49 because she was liable for claims against this now-defunct company that had once insured her car. Out of her meager earnings, she was forced to pay a little every month until the entire amount was paid off.
>
> How are such things possible? The explanation is: "fine print." It appears on installment contracts, insurance policies, credit cards— on almost any legal document you sign. And as many have discovered, its potentiality for disaster cannot be underestimated.[1]

In the first case, the couple had signed a contract with a waiver of defense, unaware of its meaning. In the second case, according to Miss Carper, the widow had signed with a company having a contingency liability, which "in effect makes the policy holder a part owner of the company and responsible for its debts."[2] Miss Carper cites many other similar examples of contracts which defraud the unwary.

These contracts have a common characteristic: the legal terminology involves liabilities of which the signer is not aware. For the average person with a credit card, loan, or debt, a lawyer would be necessary to explain the traps and pitfalls in such contracts. These people, how-

---

1. Jean Carper, "Before You Sign—Read the Fine Print," in *Family Weekly*, supplement to the Santa Ana (Calif.) *Register*, April 12, 1970, p. 13.
2. *Ibid.*

ever, are precisely the ones who cannot afford a lawyer. Thus, the very
people who need the supervision of a legal counsellor are the ones who
have no practical access to one.

Another aspect of the contracts appears from the above illustrations.
The state is clearly involved in both, as are the courts. The business
of the state courts is increasingly the business of the state, and of
powerful creditors against helpless and foolish people. When, under
pressure, the state bans one form of extortion by statute, it leaves loop-
holes for several more. The legal reforms of a couple of generations,
designed to "protect" the small American, the "little people," have only
left such persons more vulnerable. Moreover, the federal government
has paved the way for easier credit and thus more exploitation. Thus,
the federal government has boasted of making housing more readily
available by means of easy credit restrictions, but the 30- and 35-year
notes have led to shoddy construction, a multitude of frauds, and a
deeply rooted exploitation of the people. The reforms of a state which
denies God are no more to be trusted than the reforms of a man with
a gun in his hand, robbing us of our money.

This is not to deny that certain limited legal steps are to the good,
nor that some judges institute honest measures. It is the basic direction
of the law which concerns us. (One New York cab driver reported that a
thief who robbed him of his cab and his money returned subway fare
home to the man with an air of nobility and generosity.)

An example of reform by an apparently concerned judge is the work
of Judge M. Peter Katsufrakis of the small claims court of Division 4
of the Los Angeles Municipal Court.

The small claims court, designed as a resort for ordinary people with
small claims and no means for legal fees, has become largely a collection agency for finance companies, stores, and utilities. Most of
their cases were won by default, because the defendant failed to show
up. They failed to show up because the various defendants might be
living anywhere in California from the Oregon border to the Mexican
border and could not afford to journey to Los Angeles for the trial. The
company involved instituted proceedings in Los Angeles, its home office,
knowing it could win by default. Judge Katsufrakis directed that all
such cases be tried in the jurisdiction in which the defendant lived or
entered into the business dealing. Shaw reported an exchange in one
hearing:

> A contractor's representative had entered into an agreement with
> a young married couple and now the contractor was suing them.
>
> "The contractor didn't do everything his representative said he'd
> do," the husband told the court.
>
> "I can't be bound by what he told you," the contractor replied,

pointing to his representative. "He wasn't authorized to make any agreement. He isn't my agent. He . . ."

"Wait a minute, fellas," Katsufrakis cut in. "Don't try that tic tac toe routine with me. I've seen this man in here representing you before, and if you're going to tell me he isn't your authorized agent now, I'll go back through the records and void every judgment he's been involved in."[3]

Most small claims courts, however, are not conducted with much regard for justice and are regarded by judges as unhappy positions from which they hope to graduate.

The character of the courts, judges, and legal system cannot be long maintained if the character of the people is delinquent and degenerate. Courts and judges do not exist in a vacuum: they are a part of the faith, culture, and moral standards of the people at large, of the nation of which they are a part. It is the principle of the revolutionist that a deep moral cleavage does exist, that the establishment is in nature and essence evil, and the people innocent and good. This revolutionary principle undergirds almost all radicalism and conservatism, and it leads to the mentality which ascribes all ills to conspiracies and virtually none to man's fallen nature. The orthodox Christian denies that a moral cleavage exists between the establishment and the people; instead, the moral cleavage is between all unregenerate men, great and small, and the redeemed of God. This moral cleavage cannot be bridged by revolution but only by regeneration. A resort to arms is thus not the answer. When Christians have resorted to arms in the past, it has usually been in self-defense, not as an instrument of regeneration.

The tenth commandment forbids dishonest use of the law to defraud our neighbor. A society which is established on a dishonest principle, on a lawless, anti-God foundation, will inevitably make civil covetousness a way of life, and its principle of gaining wealth will increasingly become expropriation.

Deuteronomy 27:26 requires us to put the law into force. This forbids us to "obey" the law by mere negation. We cannot be "broken-field runners," evading by deft footwork all violations of the law. There is no holiness in such a course. A curse is pronounced upon all who do not put the law into force, who fail to give effect to, or "confirm" the law, by obeying it in the fullest sense of the word. The law is to be obeyed from the heart.

3. Special Privilege

In Romans 7:7 and 13:9, the word "covet" appears, a translation

---

3. David Shaw, "Fair Shake. Small Claims Court Judge Leads Revolt," in Los Angeles *Times*, LXXXIX (Wednesday morning, June 10, 1970), pp. 1, 18, 19.

of a Greek word for desire, to set one's heart upon, to long for. The word "covet" in these verses has reference to seeking things forbidden, but the sense of "covet" is good or bad in terms of its context. The law in Deuteronomy 5:21 condemns coveting, desiring or taking by force what is not rightfully ours.

If all desiring and taking by force or by law what is our neighbor's is strictly against God's law, it follows that the organization of such covetousness into a system is the creation of an anti-God society. A welfare economy—socialism, communism, or any form of social order which takes from one group to give to another—is thus lawlessness organized into a system.

In such a society, this lawless seizure can lay hold of what belongs to our neighbor by asking the state to serve as our instrument of seizure; to covet by law is no less a sin.

One of the common justifications for such a covetous society is that it is supposedly morally necessary to war against special privilege. The term *special privilege* is one of the most abused as well as most dangerous of names. It brings up visions of exploitation and abuse, and it creates a prejudiced situation wherever it is used. The term is one which has done no small damage; a common insult from the left, it has been extensively picked up and used by the right. If a thing is called "special privilege," it is sufficient in most cases to arouse hostility to it.

The truth is that no society has ever existed without special privileges, nor is it likely that any will. Special privileges can be good or bad, depending on the situation. A president has special privileges; a wife and a husband have special privileges with each other; special privileges are an inescapable part of life.

Let us examine the possible social orders and their relationship to special privilege.

The *first* possible form of social order is one of total equality. The Marxist states hold formally to the principle of, from each according to his abilities, to each according to his needs. In varying degrees, all welfare and socialist societies hold to this principle, although its strict interpretation is actually abandoned even by communist countries. However, this Marxist principle does not actually eliminate either special privilege or inequality. Even if most strictly applied, the Marxist principle only means an equality of wealth, not of work. The wealth of the successful is given to the unsuccessful. Special privileges are thereby given to the incompetent, the unsuccessful, and the lazy. The more strictly a Marxist society, or any state, seeks to be equalitarian, the more radical the inequalities and special privileges it creates. There is no "equality" in an order where men of ability are retarded or handicapped. Special privilege has not been eliminated in Russia: a mildly coercive and frequently unjust order of special privilege has been exchanged for a social order based on total coercion, radical injustice, and bitter special privileges.

A *second* possible social order is what has been called meritocracy. This to a large degree is the goal of Fabian socialist states, Great Britain in particular. The principle of the civil service is applied to the whole social order. Parkinson has cited the Chinese origin of the competitive written examination.[1] The purpose of the written examination was originally to examine the candidates in classical education; gradually, the test has become modernized and has tested aptitude, psychological factors, and general intelligence.

A meritocracy thus is insistent on examinations and is hostile to the family, because the family is the major instrument in all history in furthering special privileges for its members. Goethe expressed the matter thus:

> Really to own what you inherit
> You must first earn it by your merit.

This means that inheritance taxes must be used to destroy the family's desire to confer special privileges on its members. Michael Young, in his satire on meritocracy, has stated the issue clearly:

> Aristocratic influence would never have lasted so long, even in England, without the support of the family: feudalism and the family go together. The family is always the pillar of inheritance. The ordinary parent (not unknown today, we must sorrowfully admit) wanted to hand on his money to his children rather than to outsiders or to the state; the child was part of himself and by bequeathing property to him the father assured a kind of immortality to himself: the hereditary father never died. If parents had a family business which in a sense embodied themselves, they were even more anxious to pass it on to someone of their own blood to manage. Parents, by controlling property, also controlled their children; a threat to cut a child out of a will was almost as effective an assertion of power in industrial as it had been in agricultural Britain. . . .
>
> For hundreds of years society has been a battleground between two great principles—the principle of selection by family and the principle of selection by merit. . . .
>
> We have had to put up with the failings of the family. We have had to recognize that nearly all parents are going to try to gain unfair advantages for their offspring. The function of society, whose efficiency depends upon observing the principles of selection by merit, is to prevent such selfishness from doing any serious harm. The family is the guardian of individuals, the state the guardian of collective efficiency, and this function the state is able to perform be-

---

1. C. Northcote Parkinson, *Parkinson's Law* (Cambridge: The Riverside Press, 1957), p. 49 f.

cause citizens are themselves divided in their interests. As members of a particular family, they want their children to have every privilege. . . . We underestimate the resistance of the family. The home is still the most fertile seed-bed of reaction.[2]

In a family-oriented society, not only do people favor their own relatives and their friends, but they add to the special privilege factor by increasing the advantages of those who are advanced or are hard-working and pleasing. The most offensive statement of special privilege ever made is probably the declaration of Jesus Christ, "For unto every one that hath shall be given, and he shall have abundance: but from him that hath not shall be taken away even that which he hath" (Matt. 25:29). This flagrant rewarding of initiative and success is an outrage to many.

In a meritocracy, a rigid system of examinations determines who shall have more education and advanced training, and who shall enter the professions. The supply of superior intelligence is limited, and all the professions need superior minds. The system of tests is intended to locate and develop such minds. This means that, because a meritocracy has a supposedly scientific testing method for determining intelligence and aptitude, those who fail are in a true sense failures. In a special privilege society, Young notes, the failures can blame the system and claim they never had a chance; in a meritocracy, they are forced to conclude, on scientific grounds, that they are inferior. The so-called equality of a testing method thus creates a deeper rift.[3]

Not only does a meritocracy create a deeper sense of inequality, but it does not bring the best abilities to the top. The testing method comes, significantly, from the background of the civil service. It does identify and foster the bureaucratic mentality, not the inventor or entrepreneur. It is geared to a statist mentality, not a Christian or a free mind.

Thus, the meritocracy creates a new elite, a specially privileged class of intellectuals and bureaucrats, who thrive under the examination system. It creates a new ruling class strictly organized in terms of these new standards. Britain is replacing its old lords with a new House of Lords, made up of intellectuals and labor politicians. Special privilege has not been avoided: it has simply shifted from one group to another. Moreover, state officials, in every socialist society, give special privileges to their children; the family thus re-asserts itself, but now re-enforced with the power of a monolithic state.

The rise of meritocracy has a relationship to the student rebellions of the second half of the 20th century. The students, as products of the

---

2. Michael Young, *The Rise of Meritocracy, 1870–2033, An Essay on Education and Equality* (London: Thames and Hudson, 1958), p. 24 f.
3. *Ibid.*, pp. 83-100.

state schools, believed in the authority of science and the machine. The computer and its tests carried weight. In terms of meritocracy, many saw themselves as potential failures. Their first great slogan of rebellion was borrowed from the computer: "Do not fold, staple, or mutilate." Fearing failure in the inhuman world of meritocracy, they "dropped out." Would the computer and its tests reveal them to be "slobs"? They became dirty, unkempt slobs in protest. As against the Fabian socialist meritocracy, the primitive communist equalitarianism appealed to them.[4]

A *third* form of society, Biblical in character, is family oriented. The state is limited to a ministry of justice, and free enterprise and individual initiative are given the freedom to develop. The state is then barred from all respect of persons in processes of law. Every channel of state is then concerned with justice, not special privilege. Families, organizations, and employers are then free to give special privileges as they see fit.

In the parable of the laborers in the vineyard, Jesus told of the householder who hired men in the morning, mid-morning, noon, and afternoon, and then paid them all the same wages. There was an economic basis for his action, perhaps. Often, because of weather, grapes must be picked in a single day. As the day progressed, perhaps it became more urgent to get the still available workmen before others hired them. The price of labor would tend to rise in such a situation. The parable, however, does *not* seem to give any ground for such an interpretation. The late-comers were standing idle, unemployed. The grape-pickers protested at being paid identical wages; the wages were not below standard. Their protest was an attack on the special privilege of the late-comers, who received the same pay as they did. Jesus' answer is important both as a religious and an economic principle, a principle, in fact, for all of life: "Is it not lawful for me to do what I will with my own? Is thine eye evil because I am good?" (Matt. 20:15). The contract with those first hired had been honestly paid. It was the privilege of the householder to grant whatever he wished to any man. The right to give special privileges is a basic aspect of *freedom*, and of *private property*. If the individual's freedom to confer special privileges is denied, then freedom and private property are denied.

Even more, the world is reduced to an impersonal and mechanistic world. Special privileges exist, because people exist. The hard-working are rewarded by being granted something more than their due compensation as an act of gratitude, or to create incentive.

The hostility to the family in socialistic states is due to the fact that the family is a special-privilege-oriented group. The family will be

---

4. On merit, see F. A. Hayek, *The Constitution of Liberty* (University of Chicago Press, 1960), pp. 85-102.

both harder on its members than society will be, and more generous. In a family-oriented society, churches, organization, and communities tend to be dominated by a family-motivated morality and will be personalistic. Special privileges will then become routine. Conant has made clear his hostility to the family as an "aristocratic," i.e., special privilege, institution. For him, it is alien to democracy.[5] For Conant and others, the state school is an agency to further democracy and to limit the family's power.

The attitude of the grape-pickers in the parable was a covetous one; it involved a desire to prevent others from receiving what was lawfully theirs. It was an attack on "special privilege." Every such attack is an attempt to coerce lawlessly in order to apportion privilege in terms of our own desires.

Every law which seeks to legislate apart from God's law is a case of lawless coercion. Examples of such laws are many. Turner gives a telling illustration:

> Two people could have walked down any U. S. street in 1930—one with a bottle of whiskey under his arm and one with a bar of gold in his pocket, and the one with the whiskey would have been a criminal whereas the one with the bar of gold would have been considered a good law abiding citizen. If the same thing happened in any U. S. city in 1970, the one with the whiskey would be the law abiding citizen and the one with the gold bar would be the criminal.[6]

Such laws further lawlessness, in that they violate the fundamental principle of Biblical law, that all judgments and all legislation rest on the righteousness of God rather than the will of man and the policies of state.

4. Offenses Against Our Neighbor

The tenth commandment, like the ninth, makes mention of our neighbor, our fellow man. In the tenth commandment, the word neighbor appears three times (Ex. 20:17, Deut. 5:21). Clearly, the entire second half of the law deals with offenses against our neighbor, but the tenth commandment is especially pointed in this respect.

In Exodus 20:17, one word is used for "covet." In Deuteronomy 5:21, two words are used, the first translated "desire," meaning to delight in, want, desire; the second, rendered "covet," means to lust after, according to traditional exegesis. As we have noted, Von Rad has shown that the word *covet* "has two meanings, both to covet and

---

5. James Bryant Conant, *Education in a Divided World, The Function of the Public Schools in Our Unique Society* (Cambridge: Harvard University Press, 1948), p. 8.
6. W. W. Turner, *The Amazing Story of the British Sovereign* (Nashville, Tenn.: 1970), p. 4.

to take.""[1] Why has the meaning become limited to the one aspect, the mental attitude? The cause rests in the basic dualism of pagan thought, and of the Hellenic philosophies which have extensively influenced Western thought, including theology. Mind and body are separated into two separate realms, and the separation has led to serious consequences. Intent and act have become divorced, and the consequences of actions have been separated from the consequences of thought. At times, acts, have been irrelevant, because the mind has been basic to the definition of man. At other times, the mind has been free to indulge in every vagary, because only acts have been ascribed responsibility. Dualism has thus led to a basic irresponsibility.

This commandment, as law, is concerned with the acts of men, illegal and immoral seizures of what is properly our neighbor's. It grounds this lawless variety of action in the intent of man, his mind. The immoral act begins with a lawless thought, and the two are inseparable. Dr. Damon gives us an illustration of this:

> Boys are gossips; believe me, I know. They boast about their sexual triumphs. In secret, they may feel guilty if they have been the first one with a girl; this leads them perversely to tell another boy about how willing she was and urge him to "try her out." He wants someone to share his blame. Soon a girl who allows intimacy or intimacies, even if she is lucky enough not to get pregnant, finds herself paying a terrific penalty: she becomes cheap. Even if she leaves one school and goes away to another and tries to bury her mistakes, a rather tawdry past has a way of catching up with her.[2]

Guilty men (and guilty women) want to reduce others to their level. This is an important aspect of their philosophy and behavior. Thus, one writer, in surveying sexual mores among office-holders in Washington, D.C., finds that the sexual sin there is not enough to suit him. His answer to world and national problems is more sexual sinning, because there would then be fewer standards to divide us. Without standards, he believes we would have more peace. A common guilt is thus for him the means to a common peace. That a national magazine of ostensibly superior calibre published this article is an interesting commentary on the times. But let us hear John Corry speak for himself:

> It could be a spectacular thing for the country if the President, his Cabinet, and any number of other important men in Washington, J. Edgar Hoover coming quickly to mind, were from time to time locked up in a whorehouse, not a fine whorehouse on the Upper East Side of New York, but something sweatier and more imagina-

---

1. Von Rad, *Deuteronomy*, p. 59.
2. Virgil G. Damon, M.D., and Isabella Taves, *I Learned About Women From Them* (New York: David McKay Company, 1962), p. 243.

tive, where someone like Jean Genet was the idea man. This would not make the important men in there any smarter, but it could make them more sympathetic to the rest of us. Washington does not take for granted the weaknesses of the flesh, and sometimes it does not even recognize them. Important men in Washington are not accustomed to feeling guilty the way the rest of us do, worrying all the time that we are doing something wrong, but if they did it could turn the country around, and the important men might know more about us, too. Guilt makes you kinder and more tolerant of others, and a real case of whorehouse guilt could work wonders on, say, the Justice Department. Strom Thurmond would bleed for the black man, the liberals would lay off the labor unions, and everyone would want to get out of Vietnam tomorrow.[3]

If guilt makes men "kinder and more tolerant of others," as Corry believes, it is strange that history has not given evidence of it. From the ancient tyrants, Roman emperors, Renaissance rulers, to the modern bureaucrats, communist rulers, and dictators, guilt has produced only greater guilt and a radical brutality.

Corry's error is in part his dualism. He fails to recognize that a guilty mind will continue to produce guilty acts, and that there will be a growth both of evil and of guilt.

The ten commandments do not permit such a dualism as Corry represents. The law of God links the mind and body of man to law, and it ties man's law-keeping to his covenant-keeping with God.

In the Book of Common Prayer, the Collect which precedes the reading of the law emphasizes this unity of thought and act:

> Almighty God, unto whom all hearts are open, all desires known, and from whom no secrets are hid: Cleanse the thoughts of our hearts by the inspiration of thy Holy Spirit, that we may perfectly love thee, and worthily magnify thy Holy Name; through Christ our Lord. Amen.

The response of the people to the law is similarly grounded on this unity: "Lord, have mercy on us, and incline our hearts to keep this law." (The foregoing Collect is also a part of the Ordinary of the Mass in the Roman Catholic service.)

Because Judea had been so extensively Hellenized during the inter-testamental period, part of the Sermon on the Mount was given to a rejection of dualism in the name of the law. The tie between the mind of man and murder and adultery was cited by Jesus as illustrative of this fact (Matt. 5:21-28). On another occasion, He declared, "that which cometh out of the mouth, this defileth a man" (Matt 15:11). Explaining this to the uncomprehending disciples, He added, "those

---

3. John Corry, "Washington, Sex, and Power," in *Harper's* Magazine, vol. 241, no. 1442 (July, 1970), p. 68.

things which proceed out of the mouth come forth from the heart; and they defile the man. For out of the heart proceed evil thoughts, murders, adulteries, fornications, thefts, false witness, blasphemies: these are the things which defile a man" (Matt. 15:18-20).

The lawless thought is thus not merely an inconsequential fact: it is a first step in the unified life of man, and that first step either culminates in a lawless act or is retracted by another step into covenant-keeping. Our thoughts have an ultimate effect on our neighbor.

The tenth commandment thus presupposes and embodies an important philosophy of man and the law.

5. The System

As we have seen, *covet* means both to *desire* and to *take*. We are forbidden unlawful desire and seizure of our neighbor's wife, his house, field, servants, his livestock, or anything that is our neighbor's. In Ephesians 5:5, St. Paul calls such covetousness a form of idolatry. In evil covetousness, a man takes a lawless course and redefines it as a justifiable one. Men are ever prone to justify their every act. Justification is a necessary cover for man, and as a result men will work to justify the most flagrant offenses.

Abraham Ruef, in describing the course of action which led him to the central position of power and corruption in San Francisco's politics at the beginning of the twentieth century, justified his position by describing the foolishness of democracy. Ruef graduated from the University of California and the University of California law school with exceptional honors. "His first political convention, he tells us in his Confessions, showed him that representative government was a farce." From an organizer of a club for civic reform, he immediately turned to being an "errand boy" for powerful and corrupt political bosses.[1]

The principle involved in such actions was well stated by someone in speaking to this writer some years ago. He vindicated political corruption, declaring, "When the people are larcenous, they deserve to be taken, and somebody will." We are not, however, justified in robbing a thief because he is a thief. The cure for public corruption is not more corruption.

Ruef's career illustrated well the operation of an ancient political structure, known as far back as the days of Abraham in Nuzi documents, which Hichborn calls "the system." "The system" is the organization of corruption and graft into a form of political order.

---

1. Franklin Hichborn, *"The System," as Uncovered by the San Francisco Graft Prosecution* (San Francisco: James H. Barry Company, 1915), p. 13 f., ft.

Labor, business, and civil government unite to form a system of entrenched theft and covetousness which exploits the people. "The system," however, rests on the fact of the already existing corruption of the people. Where "the system" exists, reform is much talked about but never or rarely ever desired, because every man has a vested interest in loose law enforcement, in corruption, and in perpetuating evil.[2]

A group of wealthy men, headed by Rudolph Spreckels and James D. Phelan, instituted the investigation which led to a partial exposure of "the system." The "reform" demanded by many earlier became unpopular when its ramifications began to appear, and Spreckels and Phelan were the targets of hostility. Hostility to Phelan reached even Washington, D. C., to prevent him from receiving a cabinet appointment in the Wilson Administration.[3] Ruef's morality had been wrong, but his judgment sound in this respect: the people did not want honest government. Every honest man is a threat to a thief, and a man of integrity is an offense to a liar, because honesty and integrity are a standing indictment to evil-doers.

The liar, the thief, the adulterer, and the covetous man refuse to change, and the best of incentives are not enough to reform them. An amusing episode in the life of the painter Breugel illustrates this fact. Of Breugel we are told that,

> As long as he lived in Antwerp, he kept house with a servant girl. He would have married her but for the fact that, having a marked distaste for the truth, she was in the habit of lying, a thing he greatly disliked. He made an agreement or contract with her to the effect that he would procure a stick and cut a notch in it for every lie she told, for which purpose he deliberately chose a fairly long one. Should the stick become covered in notches in the course of time the marriage would be off and there would be no further question of it. And indeed this came to pass after a short time.[4]

The sinner, instead of changing, seeks to remake the world in his own image. The result is coercion, covetousness. The covetous man strikes out at the honesty or happiness of others. Jesus characterized this attitude in these words: "Is thine eye evil, because I am good?" (Matt. 20:15). Moffatt renders it, "Have you a grudge because I am generous?"

---

2. See Ovid Demaris, *The Captive City*; Lincoln Steffens, *The Shame of the Cities* (New York: Sagamore Press, 1904, 1957); Walter Bean, *Boss Ruef's San Francisco* (Berkeley: University of California Press, 1952, 1967); Frank Gibney, *The Operators* (New York: Harper, 1960); the important study is Hichborn's.
3. Hichborn, p. 456.
4. F. Grossmann, *Breugel, The Paintings* (London: Phaidon Press, 1955; rev. ed., 1966), p. 7 f.

It is the privilege of God the Creator to make and remake man and the world. Unto man God gives the opportunity to share in that remaking by means of work and the law, the God-ordained means of establishing dominion and bringing all things into captivity to Christ. The wickedly covetous man steps outside this lawful path and seeks by lawless means to remake his life and world; hence his assault on his neighbor's property, home, and wife.

Thus, the covetous man has his "system" too; he seeks a state of affairs where by lawless means the consequences of law are obtained. He wants a society to further his lawlessness and yet to protect him in it. Just as the political "system" is the organization of corruption and graft into a form of political order, so the personal "system" is the use of covetousness and lawlessness as the means to a new form of personal and social order. Instead of order, the result is moral anarchism and social collapse.

The names for the society whereby men can covet everything that is their neighbor's may vary: socialism, communism, a welfare economy, rugged individualism, fascism, and national socialism are a few of the names common to history. Their goal is the same: under a facade of morality, a system is created to seize what is properly our neighbor's. Not surprisingly, such a system shows a general decline in morality. Theft, murder, adultery, and false witness all increase, because man is a unity. If he can legalize and "justify" seizing his neighbor's wealth or property, he will then legalize and justify taking his neighbor's wife.

The more self-righteous his profession of morality becomes, the wider the gap between profession and performance grows. Thus, the 20th century has seen a widespread advocacy of reverence for life, the abolition of the death penalty, and a proliferation of peace movements. At the same time, it has also seen these same leaders create a world of massive pollution and destruction of life, more murders than before, savage world wars and national wars, prison camps, massive torture, enslavement, and murder, and all this while professing the noblest morality.

Add to this the movements legalizing abortion. Congressman John G. Schmitz reported,

> Here in Congress, legislation has been introduced in both House and Senate to allow the killing of unborn children throughout the United States, and to remove the Federal personal income tax for all children after the second. Testimony before the House Committee on Interstate and Foreign Commerce revealed a bill is pending in the Florida State Legislature which would legalize the killing of old people ("euthanasia"), and that a bill in the Hawaii State Legislature would compel the sterilization of all women after

they have their second child. Such legislation heralds the coming of a new Nazism to our land.[5]

In the words of St. Paul, "Professing themselves to be wise, they became fools" (Rom. 1:22). Professing themselves to be lovers of life and mankind, they revealed themselves as haters and murderers of men.

---

5. John G. Schmitz, "Government Against Life," *Weekly News Report*, Aug. 19, 1970.

XI

THE PROMISES OF LAW

1. The Use of Law

Biblical law has receded in its relevance in the modern era. The rise of pietism in the late medieval era, and the deep infection of both Protestantism and the Roman Catholic Church with pietism has led to a decline of emphasis on Biblical law. Pietism emphasizes "spiritual" religion; law stresses a very material religion in every sense of that word, relevant to the world and practically concerned with everyday affairs.

The law suffered badly at the hands of Martin Luther. Partly in reaction to the peasant uprising, and to the Anabaptists, Luther turned sharply against the law, which he denounced intemperately, in a sermon of 1525, "How Christians Should Regard Moses." Luther held that the law of Moses binds only the Jews and not the Gentiles. "We will not have Moses as ruler or lawgiver any longer." Luther found three things in Moses: "In the first place I dismiss the commandments given to the people of Israel. They neither urge nor compel me. They are dead and gone" except as an example or a precedent. "In the second place I find something in Moses that I do not have from nature: the promise and pledge of God about Christ. This is the best thing." Neither of these uses of Moses has anything to do with law, and the third even less so. "In the third place we read Moses for the beautiful examples of faith, of love, and of the cross, as shown in the fathers, Adam, Abel, Noah, Abraham, Isaac, Jacob, Moses, and all the rest." We are also given examples of godless men and their destinies. But, "where he gives commandment, we are not to follow him except so far as he agrees with the natural law."[1]

Luther thus paved the way for the full-fledged return of scholasticism and the natural law, as did Calvin by his sometimes weak views on Biblical law. The first revival of scholasticism came thus in Protestant rather than Catholic areas of Europe.

Kevan, in commenting on the origin of antinomianism, noted that

> Antinomianism was the theological contrary to Puritanism in its doctrine of the Law of God in Christian experience. Apart from its early appearance in New Testament times, and in Valentinian

---

1. *Luther's Works*, vol. 35, *Word and Sacrament* (Philadelphia: Muhlenberg Press, 1960), I, 161-173.

651

Gnosticism, the formal rise of antinomianism has usually been associated with Johannes Agricola, sometimes called Islebius, an active leader in the Lutheran Reformation. In his search for some effective principle by which to combat the doctrine of salvation by works, Agricola denied that the believer was in any way obliged to fulfil the moral Law. In the Disputation with Luther at Wittenberg (1537), Agricola is alleged to have said that a man was saved by faith alone, without regard to his moral character. These views of Agricola were denounced by Luther as a caricature of the Gospel, but in spite of this, the Antinomians made repeated appeal to Luther's writings and claimed his support for their opinions. This claim, however, is based merely on certain ambiguities in Luther's expressions, and general misunderstanding of the Reformer's teaching.[2]

Kevan to the contrary, the "ambiguities in Luther's expressions" rested in very serious ambiguities in Luther's thinking.

In 1529, Luther, in the *Small Catechism*, gave a sounder view of the law, but his brief statements therein could not undo the damage of his more extended attacks on the law. Too often Luther felt that the only way to establish the doctrine of justification by faith was to deny works and sanctification. He wrote on August 1, 1521, to Melanchthon, "Sin cannot separate us from God, even if we commit murder and fornication a thousand times a day."[3] With saints like this, the world has little need for sinners.

If man wants a spiritual or mystical religion, then the law is his enemy. If he wants a material religion, one fully relevant to the world and man, then Biblical law is inescapably necessary for him. Leviticus 26:3-45 emphasizes the material relevance of the law. This "Great Exhortation" makes clear that there can be no successful material life for man apart from the law.

This "Great Exhortation" can be divided into three parts. In vss. 3-13, the material blessings of obedience to the law are declared. There will be rain, good harvests, excellent wine yields, peace, prosperity, no evil beasts, victory against their enemies, and God's favor as well as His presence with them. This favor is a very great one, so that "ye shall chase your enemies, and they shall fall before you by the sword. And five of you shall chase an hundred, and an hundred of you shall put ten thousand to flight: and your enemies shall fall before you by the sword" (Lev. 26:7-8).

In the second section, vss. 14-33, the curse upon disobedience to the law is declared. Disobedience leads to a mounting judgment, to

---

2. Ernest F. Devan, *The Grace of Law, A Study of Puritan Theology* (Grand Rapids: Baker Book House, 1965).
3. Cited in Friedrich Heer, *The Intellectual History of Europe* (Cleveland: World Publishing Company [1953], 1966), p. 221.

disease, defeat, want, terror, drought, plagues, and conquest. The national morale will be so bad that "ye shall flee where none pursueth you" (Lev. 26:17). These judgments will culminate in conquest, cannibalism, and a scattering among the nations. The earth will itself disappoint a people under judgment, as will the heavens. The heaven will be as iron (no rain), and the earth as brass (unwatered and sterile) to the disobedient (Lev. 26:19).

The third section, vss. 34-45, declared that a judged land will be given its sabbath rest. The people will know terror in captivity. Repentance, however, will lead to restoration.

First of all, the "Great Exhortation" is clearly addressed to Israel. Just as clearly, the Sermon on the Mount is addressed to the disciples, and the Epistles to particular churches, but this does not limit their application to the particular persons or churches addressed. Either the Word of God is a unity, and is God's word to all men, or it is not. To deny any part of Scripture is ultimately to deny all.

Second, we cannot believe that God has no judgment for men and nations in the Christian era. Hebrews 12:18-29 makes clear that the same God and the same law and judgment apply to the church as to Israel, and man and nations receive a similar shaking, in order to destroy all those which can be shaken and leave only God's "kingdom that cannot be shaken." Calvin held that in the Old Testament era, "God manifested Himself more fully as a Father and Judge by temporal blessings and punishments than since the promulgation of the Gospel."[4] As evidence of this, Calvin declared,

> The earth does not now cleave asunder to swallow up the rebellious: God does not now thunder from heaven as against Sodom; He does not now send fire upon wicked cities as He did the Israelitish camp: fiery serpents are not sent forth to inflict deadly bites: in a word, such manifest instances of punishment are not daily presented before our eyes to make God terrible to us; and for this reason, because the voice of the Gospel sounds much more clearly in our ears, like the sound of a trumpet, whereby we are summoned to the heavenly tribunal of Christ.[5]

This is silly and trifling reasoning. Miraculous judgments were *not* "daily presented" in the Old Testament era; they were few and far between. The short time span of the New Testament saw as many miraculous judgments: on Judas, on Jerusalem and Judea, on Ananias and Sapphira, on Herod (Acts 12:21-23), and on many others. It also saw miraculous deliverances: an angel freed Peter (Acts 12:7-10), Paul and Silas in Philippi (Acts 16:25-31), the many persons healed by Christ and the apostles, Paul's deliverance from shipwreck, and so on.

4. Calvin, *Commentaries on the Four Last Books of Moses*, III, 217.
5. *Ibid.*, III, 215 f.

Calvin confused the miraculous with the law. Apart from these miracles, the judgments and the blessings of the law are apparent in the Old Testament world, on Israel and the nations, and they are apparent in Christian history as well.

To deny the permanence of God's law is to fall into dispensationalism and ultimately into Manichaeanism. Instead of an unchanging God, at the very least a changing God is posited, if not two dissimilar gods. Calvin was wiser in declaring,

> Inasmuch as in the Law the difference between good and evil is set forth, it is given for the regulation of the life of men, so that it may be justly called the rule of living well and righteously.[6]

Exactly so. If God created all things, then all things can be used properly and safely only in terms of His law, "the rule of living well and righteously." The law gives us a set of "manufacturer's instructions" which can be disregarded only at our peril.

Third, because man's life is a material life, he must be governed by a material law, a law relevant to his life. The materialism of the law is thus a necessary aspect of the law. The "Great Exhortation" is as a result as valid today as when delivered by Moses. As long as the earth remains, the law remains. Those who seek to "deliver" man from Biblical law violate a law stated in both Old and New Testaments, in Deuteronomy 25:4, I Corinthians 9:9, and I Timothy 5:18: the ox which treads out the corn must not be muzzled, because the laborer is worthy of his hire. The law spells out both the punishment and the hire of man. Clearly, God's rewards and punishments are far to be preferred to the promises of nations or any mythical natural law.

Reference was made earlier to John Agricola (1492-1566), the antinomian. In 1537, Agricola wrote, "Art thou steeped in sin—an adulterer or a thief? If thou believest, thou art in salvation. All who follow Moses must go to the devil; to the gallows with Moses."[7]

Antinomianism, having denied the law, runs into mysticism and pietism. As it faces a world of problems, it has no adequate answer. To supply this lack, antinomianism very early became premillennial; its answer to the problems of the world was to postpone solutions to the "any moment return" of Christ. Antinomianism thus led to an intense interest in and expectation of Christ's return as the only solution to the world's problems, Christ's law being denied the status of an answer. Not surprisingly, one of the results of John Darby and the Plymouth

---

6. *Ibid.*, III, 196.
7. Daniel Steele, *A Substitute for Holiness, or, Antinomianism Revived, or The Theology of the So-Called Plymouth Brethren Examined and Refuted* (Boston: Christian Witness Co., 1899), second edition, p. 47.

Brethren, leaders in this movement, was a sorry fact recorded in 1877 by Steele:

> A handful of Americans, fragments of families, possessed by this infantile interpretation of Scripture, are eking out an existence in Jerusalem. They have adopted and are called by the name of "The American Colony." They are determined to be at the head of the line of office-seekers when the new administration comes in.[8]

2. The Law and the Ban

A very important declaration which is a part of the declared law is Deuteronomy 7:9-15:

> Know therefore that the LORD thy God, he is God, the faithful God, which keepeth covenant and mercy with them that love him and keep his commandments to a thousand generations;
> And repayeth them that hate him to their face, to destroy them: he will not be slack to him that hateth him, he will repay him to his face.
> Thou shalt therefore keep the commandments, and the statutes, and the judgments, which I command thee this day, to do them.
> Wherefore it shall come to pass, if ye hearken to these judgments, and keep, and do them, that the LORD thy God shall keep unto thee the covenant and the mercy which he sware unto thy fathers:
> And he will love thee, and bless thee, and multiply thee: and will also bless the fruit of thy womb, and the fruit of thy land, thy corn, and thy wine, and thine oil, the increase of thy kine, and the flocks of thy sheep, in the land which he sware unto thy fathers to give thee.
> Thou shalt be blessed above all people: there shall not be male or female barren among you, or among your cattle.
> And the LORD will take away from thee all sickness, and will put none of the evil diseases of Egypt, which thou knowest, upon thee; but will lay them upon all them that hate thee.

First, while this is a part of covenant law, its application is not restricted to Israel. The covenant circumscribes all men without exception. The original covenant was with Adam; the renewed covenant was with Noah. All men are either covenant keepers or covenant breakers; all men are thus inescapably tied to the covenant and its promises of love and hate, blessings and curses. Christ, in renewing the covenant, made it clear that all men were involved in it. According to John 12:32, 33,

> And I, if I be lifted up from the earth, will draw all men unto me.
> This he said, signifying what death he should die.

By becoming the sacrifice, the priest, and the divine renewer of the covenant of God with man, Jesus would draw all men to Him, i.e.,

---

8. *Ibid.*, p. 355.

become the principle of judgment and of salvation, of curses and of blessings. The covenant and the law of the covenant, as well as the Lord of the covenant, thus judge every man.

Second, the covenant God identifies Himself as "God, the faithful God," which means, in Wright's words, that "he alone is sovereign Lord, and he is reliable, trustworthy; what he has said, he will do."[1] An aspect of God's trustworthiness is His jealousy, His wrath, hate, and judgment of those who despise His covenant and law. God promises love and hate as an aspect of His absolute justice and faithfulness.

Third, this means retribution. He promises to repay "those who hate Him, by destroying them; He does not delay with those who hate Him but repays them personally" (Deut. 7:10, BV). Thus, retribution is an aspect of God's law which men must apply, because it is first of all God's principle of operation which He applies. Those whom He loves, i.e., those who obey His covenant law, He blesses with "fertility of womb, of land, of flocks and herds, and freedom from the notorious *evil diseases of Egypt*."[2]

Fourth, God asserts His sovereign rights. In verse 12, He refers to His "judgments." As W. L. Alexander has pointed out,

> *Judgments*, i.e., rights, rightful claims. God, as the Great King, has his rights, and these are to be rendered to him by his subjects and servants.[3]

Keil and Delitzsch interpreted judgments (in Deut. 4:1) to mean "rights, all that was due to them, whether in relation to God or to their fellow-men."[4] However, God's law is an assertion of God's righteousness and rights over mankind. Secondarily, because man is God's creature, his only true rights are in God and God's law. It is interesting to note that one of the Greek New Testament words for judgment is *krisis*, which means a separating and then a decision. The law and the judgment of the law is a declaration of God's rightful claims, His rights over all men. Hence His right to love and to hate them in terms of their reaction to His rights.

Fifth, as already noted, fertility and abundance are promised to all who are obedient to God's covenant law. To the degree that even an ungodly man respects God's law, to that degree he flourishes. Nations rise and fall in terms of this fact. Disobedience, on the other hand, leads to judgment.

This brings us to a point of especial importance. It was stated earlier that the covenant circumscribes all men without exception: covenant-

---

1. G. Ernest Wright, "Deuteronomy," *Interpreter's Bible*, II, 381.
2. *Ibid.*, II, 382.
3. W. L. Alexander, *The Pulpit Commentary, Deuteronomy*, p. 136.
4. Keil and Delitzsch, *The Pentateuch*, III, 308.

keepers are blessed, and covenant-breakers are cursed. This is apparent in the "ban" which precedes and follows Deuteronomy 7:9-15—vss. 1-8 and 16-26. Israel was called upon to cast out and destroy the inhabitants of the land, because now their iniquity was "full" (Gen. 15:16). The whole point of the *ban* was that these Canaanite peoples were morally offensive to God (Deut. 20:16-18).

The *ban* could be issued only by God, not by man. By the ban, God declared a people to be outside the law and under sentence of death. The *ban* is the reverse of communion, and it declares the end of communion with God and man; the banned people are given over to death as their judgment.

Communion and community can exist where there are strong personal differences and enmity. Van der Leeuw cites a good example of this:

> To-day the finest example is still the peasant, who has no "feelings" but simply belongs to his community, as contrasted with the *citoyen* invented in the eighteenth century! Even peasants who fight, or engage in law-suits, remain neighbours and brothers; a peasant in the Eastern Netherlands who has a mortal enemy in the village nevertheless knows that on market-days he is obliged to greet his foe and walk up and down with him once, when the peasant community of the whole district is gathered in the country town, thus demonstrating to the eyes of "strangers" the fellowship of the village *ad oculos*.[5]

The point in such a custom is this: disagreement exists, law-suits are in process, but such differences are a part of life in a community and a form of community. Thus, differences are inescapable in every marriage; with godly people, the differences serve to increase the areas of communion and agreement by bringing problems to the surface for settlement. A community *requires* dissension and disagreement in order to have progress. The *ban* instead means the end of community; it indicates a situation beyond disagreement; it means that the curse has taken over.

The relationship of community and disagreement is well illustrated by an incident in a small California farm area in 1970. A woman notorious for her brawling and argumentative ways tried to start a major argument with Mrs. E. S., whom she had met only once before. Mrs. S., with a superb feminine logic and wisdom, walked out on her, observing, "don't pick a fight with me! I don't know you that well!" Her point was well taken; there was no community whatsoever between them, and thus no ground whatsoever for any communication or any disagreement.

---

5. G. Van Der Leeuw, *Religion in Essence and Manifestation*, p. 243.

The ban is more than the *absence* of community; it is rather the *end* of all community, of any possible agreement or disagreement. The Jewish custom of reading the service of the dead over a member of the family who has transgressed beyond a certain point is a very sound one: the person is then under the ban. Where the ban validly exists, there the curse takes over.

In the curse, man invokes God to judge a man or people he regards beyond communion, whose sins require total judgment. God will not hearken to an undeserved curse, as in the case of Balaam (Deut. 23:5), but turned it into a blessing. The causeless curse accomplishes nothing (Prov. 26:2). When God pronounces the curses which appear in the law and the epilogue to the law upon disobedience, He is thus placing all such persons under the *ban*.

The law forbids us from cursing certain persons. We are forbidden, in Exodus 22:28, to curse rulers or "the gods" or judges, or to curse parents (Ex. 21:17), or the deaf (Lev. 19:14). This does not mean the alternative is servile obedience, but it does forbid us to curse superior authorities, or the helpless. God Himself pronounces curses on godless authorities.

The fact of the *ban* and of curses thus makes clear that the scope of the law is beyond the realm of Israel or the church. God as the Creator of all men intends His law to govern all men. All men are thus liable to judgment and death for disobedience to the law of God.

The Talmud, in dealing with land laws, insisted on God's ownership of the earth. Because of God's total lordship and sovereignty, the land, even in the hands of heathens, is under God's jurisdiction. The heathen thus are accountable, according to the Talmud, to God for the care of the earth under law, and for the payment of the tithe.[6] It is fashionable for many "Christians" to express their contempt for the Talmud; despite its many vagaries, at this point, and elsewhere, the Talmud gave better practical recognition to the sovereignty of God than did Luther, Calvin, and many others. Luther, having denied the law of God, pushed his hostility to the point of denying everything associated with it, including the Jews and the Talmud.

Having denied the law of God, Lutheranism then had to deny the victory promised by that law. Accordingly, in the Augsburg Confession, Article XVII, in the last paragraph, it is declared of the Lutheran churches that,

> They condemn others also, who now scatter Jewish opinions, that, before the resurrection of the dead, the godly shall occupy the kingdom of the world, the wicked being every where suppressed

---

6. *Gittin*, 47a, p. 208; *Kiddushin*, 38b, p. 188.

(the saints alone, the pious, shall have a worldly kingdom, and shall exterminate all the godless).[7]

The movement of the church so charted is from victory to defeat.

Luther himself began with victory and ended in defeat, a self-tortured, guilt-ridden, and bloated man. He who had been the hope of the Christian poor had been denounced by them as Herr Luder, Mr. Liar, decoy, law scoundrel, or carrion. Luther could rightfully plead that his was not a theology of social revolution, but he had raised false hopes among the peasants. "Sola Scriptura" was his standard: the word of God alone. This to the people meant not only justification by faith but also the sovereign law of God. To that law they appealed, and Luther denounced God's law in favor of statist law.

Melanchthon did not betray Luther when "he constructed a new doctrine of natural law based on Aristotle and Biblical theology which in many respects is identical with that of St. Thomas. The similarity to Thomism was not accidental."[8] Having denounced God's law, the only alternative was Thomism and natural law. The Reformation was thus stillborn.

Lutheranism has maintained the standard, "Sola Scriptura," but it has denied the validity of God's law. It has, more than any other church, discouraged interest in the book of Revelation, since that book so emphatically declares the total relevancy of God and His law to this world. If the people were to read too much in Revelation, a crisis of faith might arise, and the people might call their church Luderan instead of Lutheran.

Calvin also made possible the revival of natural law by his loose views of the law of God. The Puritans for a time saved Calvinism from itself by their emphasis on Biblical law, only to succumb themselves to the intellectual climate of neoplatonism and also the lure of the natural law. The Reformation as a whole moved from victory to defeat, from relevance to irrelevance, from a challenge to the world to a surrender to the world or a meaningless withdrawal from it. Rome, Geneva, Wittenberg, and Canterbury retreated also into an ineffectual pietism. They were all now of the world but not in the world!

To forsake the law is to forsake the blessing and victory which the law confers upon all who are obedient. Pagan nations which reject God but still are in obedience to some of His laws, maintaining true family order, observing laws concerning murder, theft, and false witness, and also respecting the laws concerning the use of the earth, such nations prosper and flourish to the degree of their obedience. Great

7. Philip Schaff, *The Creeds of Christendom* (New York: Harper, 1877, 1919), III, 18.
8. Friedrick Heer, *The Intellectual History of Europe*, p. 240.

nations have arisen as a result of the discipline of the law and have fallen
on forsaking it.

If to forsake the law is to forsake victory and blessing, and to keep
the law is to prosper and flourish, and if this be true for pagan nations,
how much more so for the godly? If a people acknowledge Jesus
Christ as Lord and King, and obey His sovereign law, their blessing and
victory will be all the greater, even as, in lawlessness and unbelief,
their condemnation will surpass all others.

3. The Curse and the Blessing

In Deuteronomy 27 and 28, we have a further and important insight
into the implications of the law. These chapters give us the curses and
blessings associated with the law.

Curse, ban, and *anathema* are basically the same concepts. That
which is under a curse, ban, or anathema is *devoted* or *dedicated,* i.e.,
given over to destruction at the requirement of God. In the church, the
concept of the curse, ban, or anathema appears as excommunication.[1]

According to Harper, the Biblical purpose of the ban is always ethical,
and its purpose was "to preserve religion when gravely endangered."[2]

The ban, curse, or anathema does not disappear from a society when
it abandons Biblical faith. The ban is simply transferred to a new area
of life. Thus, writing early in the century, Harper noted:

> Notwithstanding that the Church of the New Testament is the
> bearer of the higher interests of humanity, we are taught that when
> it is least definite in its direction as to conduct, when it is most
> tolerant of the practices of the world, then it is most true to its
> original conception. We are told that an indulgent Church is what
> is wanted; rigour and religion are now supposed to be finally di-
> vorced in all enlightened minds. This view is not often categorically
> expressed, but it underlies all fashionable religion, and has its
> apostles in the golden youth who forward enlightenment by playing
> tennis on Sundays. Because of it too, Puritan has become a name
> of scorn, and self-gratification a mark of cultured Christianity.
> Not only asceticism, but *askesis* has been discredited, and the moral
> tone of society has perceptibly fallen in consequence. In wide
> circles both within and without the Church it seems to be held that
> pain is the only intolerable evil, and in legislation as well as in
> literature that idea has been registering itself.[3]

Harper was right. Earlier in the 20th century, *pain* was under the
ban of a humanistic society. Now, war, poverty, discrimination with
respect to race, color, or creed, and orthodox Christians are steadily
being placed under a ban and are targets of legislation.

1. J. Denney, "Curse," in Hastings, *Dictionary of the Bible,* I, 534 f.
2. Andrew Harper, *The Book of Deuteronomy* (New York: Doran, n.d.),
p. 173 f.
3. *Ibid.,* p. 185.

No society can escape having a ban; the important question is, what shall be banned?

According to Deuteronomy 27:15-26, it is violations of God's law (not the law of the state or of the church) which place men under the ban or curse. Twelve curses are pronounced, equal to the number of the tribes of Israel, to indicate a totality. These twelve curses are:

1. against secret breaches of the second commandment (Ex. 20:4), vs. 15;
2. against contempt of or lack of due respect of parents (Ex. 20:17), vs. 16;
3. against all who remove their neighbor's landmarks (Deut. 19:14), vs. 17;
4. against men who lead the blind astray (Lev. 19:14), vs. 18;
5. against all who pervert the justice due to foreigners or widows, and orphans (Deut. 24:17), vs. 19;
6. against incest with a stepmother (Deut. 23:1; Lev. 18:8), vs. 20;
7. against bestiality (Lev. 18:23), vs. 21;
8. against incest with a sister or half-sister (Lev. 18:9), vs. 22;
9. against incest with a mother-in-law (Lev. 18:8), vs. 23;
10. against murder (Ex. 20:13; Num. 35:17 ff.), vs. 24;
11. against anyone who accepts a bribe either to kill a man outright, or to bring about his death by false witness (Ex. 23:7, 8), vs. 25;
12. against any man who fails to put the law into effect, who does not make the law the model and standard of his life and conduct.

> From this last curse, which applied to every branch of the law, it evidently follows, that the different sins and transgressions already mentioned were only selected by way of example, and for the most part were such as could easily be concealed from the judicial authorities. At the same time, "the office of the law is shown in this last utterance, the summing up of all the rest, to have been preeminently to proclaim condemnation. Every conscious act of transgression subjects the sinner to the curse of God, from which none but He who has become a curse for us can possibly deliver us." (Gal. iii. 10, 13, O. v. Gerlach).[4]

The principle and the ground of blessings and of curses is very plainly *the law* (Deut. 28:1, 15). The foregoing curses specify particular sins of a depraved character, sins which are acts of viciousness. The twelfth curse, however, includes every law of God and thus allows no area of escape from the curse except in obedience.

Deuteronomy 28, especially vss. 1-26, gives us a magnificent declaration of blessings and curses. Two very obvious and important facts are in evidence. *First*, these blessings or beatitudes promise life, prosperity, and success to those who obey God's law. Kline is right in stating,

---

4. Keil and Delitzsch, *The Pentateuch*, III, 434 f.

Israel, if faithful to the covenant oath, would come out on top in every military and commercial encounter with other nations. Within the kingdom there would be abundance of the earth's goodness. Canaan would be a veritable paradise, flowing with milk and honey. Of primary import, Israel would prosper in her relationship to her covenant Lord. This is the secret of all beatitude, for his favor is life.[5]

Obedience to the law is an act of faith that God is faithful and will give to His people an abundant life and a goodly earth. David affirmed the faith of all Scripture in declaring,

> For evildoers shall be cut off: but those that wait upon the LORD, they shall inherit the earth.
> For yet a little while, and the wicked shall not be: Yea, thou shalt diligently consider his place, and it shall not be.
> But the meek shall inherit the earth; and shall delight themselves in the abundance of peace (Ps. 37:9-11).

David's words cannot be understood apart from Deuteronomy 28, nor can Christ's beatitude, "Blessed are the meek: for they shall inherit the earth" (Matt. 5:5). The meek, the tamed of God who obey Him, are literally promised the earth for their obedience. They are blessed in the city and in the field, in the fruit of their body and the fruit of the field, in basket and in store, and in everything. The promise is that "The meek shall eat and be satisfied" (Ps. 22:26). "The meek will he guide in judgment: and the meek will he teach his way" (Ps. 25:9), i.e., He will guide them in justice and teach them the way of life. The law is thus very clearly the way to a rich life on earth. There is no promise of any prosperity apart from the law. The obedience of faith is the law.

Second, with respect to curses, "Banishment from the promised inheritance was the extreme of malediction."[6] Just as the law opens up life and the land, so lawlessness opens up curses, defeat, and finally death. The major part of the chapter is given over to a precise specification of the consequences of the curse.

It was the curse on lawlessness, when Adam and Eve denied God as the principle of life and law, as their Sovereign, that led to their expulsion from paradise. It has been the same curse on lawlessness which, age after age, has doomed man to frustration, defeat, and death. To deny God is to deny His law and sovereignty, or, conversely, to deny God's law and sovereignty is to deny God. To affirm God's law is to accept His sovereignty and His lordship. Faith and law are inseparable, for "faith without works is dead" (James 2:20).

In fact, "The blessings are represented as actual powers, which follow

---

5. Meredith G. Kline, *Treaty of the Great King,* p. 125.
6. *Ibid.*

the footsteps of the nation, and overtake it."[7] Not only does Scripture teach a doctrine of *sovereign and irresistible grace*, but it also teaches a doctrine of *sovereign and irresistible blessings and curses* for obedience and disobedience to God's law. This is the inescapable meaning of Deuteronomy 28.

In Deuteronomy 28:2, we are told that "all these blessings shall come on thee, and overtake thee, if thou shalt hearken unto the voice of the LORD thy God." In vs. 15, it is stated that "all these curses shall come upon thee, and overtake thee." In both cases, an irresistible consequence is declared.

Man is not at liberty, however, to choose the consequence, i.e., he cannot declare that, because he is due to be blessed, he chooses to be blessed by means of money, a new wife, or four sons. Similarly, man cannot choose his punishment. The world of curses and blessings is not a smorgasbord affair, where man can exercise his free choice and choose to his taste. At all times, God is sovereign, and "He shall choose our inheritance for us" (Ps. 47:4).

The history of that irresistible curse began with the fall and continues to this day. The irresistible blessings began in Eden, and throughout history have been in effect wherever obedience has prevailed. By His beatitudes, Jesus Christ confirmed Deuteronomy 28 and made Himself known as the Lawgiver. This was sensed by His hearers, for "the people were astonished at his doctrine: For he taught them as one having authority, and not as the scribes" (Matt. 7:28-29). The scribes interpreted the law; Jesus Christ declared the law as its maker. As the maker of the law, His words were a revelation of the law. Therefore, the curses and the blessings of the law depended upon hearing and obeying His "sayings" (Matt. 7:24-27).

Man wants and needs a world of curses and blessings. Everything in his nature, because it is God-created, demands a world of consequence and causality. However, because man has fallen and is in rebellion against God, he wants those curses and blessings to be meted out on his terms, in relationship to his demands and his estimate of justice. Not too many years ago, this writer had more than a little experience with gamblers in Nevada. Although generally profane men, they sometimes prayed, and they held it against God that their prayers were not answered according to their heart's desire. Sometimes when gambling with desperation, they prayed for sensational success, promising God that a large portion of the winnings would go to the priest, minister, or church. One man even promised to repay his mother some

---

7. Keil and Delitzsch, *The Pentateuch*, III, 435 f.

money he had long owed her. Somehow, because of their "noble" declarations, God as their "partner" was supposed to bless them, and it was evidence of the fraud of religion that God did not bless them. In all such cases, men establish the conditions, rules, or laws of blessing and then expect God to comply. Since this kind of bargaining is blasphemous, it can only merit judgment, not a blessing. An unsound enterprise is not made good by naming God a partner. Man cannot break God's law without being broken.

Examine again the curses. A man is not exempt from the curse of the law because he has avoided the first eleven secret offenses. The curse applies to all who fail to put the whole law of God into effect. When God arraigns us for violating His law, we therefore cannot plead that we did not commit incest, nor bestiality. We are given a total law, and the declaration is, "Cursed be he that confirmeth not all the words of this law to do them" (Deut. 27:26). There are many aspects of the law of which the worst of men approve. In prison societies, murderers despise rapists, thieves despise murderers, and so on. Each criminal wants all the world of law and order except his personal area of exemption. Some criminals are proudly self-righteous of their areas of compliance. No thief is exempt from prison because he has not murdered, nor is any murderer exempt because he has not committed rape. Similarly, in the sight of God, we are accountable for the total law, and we cannot ask to be exempted from the curse if we keep ninety-nine percent of it and then treat the other one percent with total casualness or contempt. Repeatedly, God has placed moralistic churchmen under His curse for this kind of reasoning. "For whosoever shall keep the whole law, and yet offend in one point, he is guilty of all" (James 2:10).

4. The Unlimited Liability Universe

A limited liability company is one in which the liability of each shareholder is limited to the amount of his shares or stocks, or to a sum fixed by a guarantee called "limited by guarantee." The purpose of limited liability laws is to limit responsibility. Although the ostensible purpose is to protect the shareholders, the practical effect is to limit their responsibility and therefore encourage recklessness in investment. A limited liability economy is socialistic. By seeking to protect people, a limited liability economy merely transfers responsibility away from the people to the state, where "planning" supposedly obviates responsibility. Limited liability encourages people to take chances with limited risks, and to sin economically without paying the price. Limited liability laws rest on the fallacy that payment for economic sins need not be made. In actuality, payment is simply transferred to others.

Limited liability laws were unpopular in earlier, Christian eras but have flourished in the Darwinian world. They rest on important religious presuppositions.

In a statement central to his account, C. S. Lewis described his preference, prior to his conversion, for a materialistic, atheistic universe. The advantages of such a world are the very limited demands it makes on a man.

> To such a craven the materialist's universe has the enormous attraction that it offered you limited liabilities. No strictly infinite disaster could overtake you in it. Death ended all. And if ever finite disasters proved greater than one wished to bear, suicide would always be possible. The horror of the Christian universe was that it had no door marked Exit. . . . But, of course, what mattered most of all was my deap-seated hatred of authority, my monstrous individualism, my lawlessness. No word in my vocabulary expressed deeper hatred than the word Interference. But Christianity placed at the center what then seemed to me a transcendental Interferer. If its picture were true then no sort of "treaty with reality" could ever be possible. There was no region even in the innermost depth of one's soul (nay, there least of all) which one could surround with a barbed wire fence and guard with a notice of No Admittance. And that was what I wanted; some area, however small, of which I could say to all other beings, "This is my business and mine only."[1]

This is an excellent summation of the matter. The atheist wants a limited liability universe, and he seeks to create a limited liability political and economic order. The more socialistic he becomes, the more he demands a maximum advantage and a limited liability from his social order, an impossibility.

In reality, living with the fact that the universe and our world carry always unlimited liabilities is the best way to assure security and advantage. To live with reality, and to seek progress within its framework, is man's best security.

The curses and the blessings of the law stress man's unlimited liability to both curses and blessings as a result of disobedience or obedience to the law. In Deuteronomy 28:2 and 15, we are told that the curses and blessings come upon us and "overtake" us. Man cannot step outside of the world of God's consequence. At every moment and at every point man is overtaken, surrounded, and totally possessed by the unlimited liability of God's universe.

Man seeks to escape this unlimited liability either through a denial of the true God, or by a pseudo-acceptance which denies the meaning of God. In atheism, the attitude of man is well summarized by William

---

1. C. S. Lewis, *Surprised by Joy* (New York: Harcourt, Brace, 1956), p. 171 f.

Ernest Henley's poem, "Invictus." Henley boasted of his "unconquerable soul" and declared,

> I am the master of my fate:
> I am the captain of my soul.

Not surprisingly, the poem has been very popular with immature and rebellious adolescents.

Pseudo-acceptance, common to mysticism, pietism, and pseudo-evangelicals, claims to have "accepted Christ" while denying His law. One college youth, very much given to evangelizing everyone in sight, not only denied the law as an article of his faith, in speaking to this writer, but went further. Asked if he would approve of young men and women working in a house of prostitution as whores and pimps to convert the inmates, he did not deny this as a valid possibility. He went on to affirm that many of his friends were converting girls and patrons wholesale by invading the houses to evangelize one and all. He also claimed wholesale conversion of homosexuals, but he could cite no homosexuals who ceased the practice after their conversion; nor any whores or their patrons who left the houses with their "evangelizers." Such lawless "evangelism" is only blasphemy.

In the so-called "Great Awakening" in colonial New England, antinomianism, chiliasm, and false perfectionism went hand in hand. Many of these "holy ones" forsook their marriage for adulterous relations, denied the law, and claimed immediate perfection and immortality.[2]

What such revivalism and pietism espouses is a limited liability universe in God's name. It is thus atheism under the banner of Christ. It claims freedom from God's sovereignty and denies predestination. It denies the law, and it denies the validity of the curses and blessings of the law. Such a religion is interested only in what it can get out of God: hence, "grace" is affirmed, and "love," but not the law, nor God's sovereign power and decree. But smorgasbord religion is only humanism, because it affirms the right of man to pick and choose what he wants; as the ultimate arbiter of his fate, man is made captain of his soul, with an assist from God. Pietism thus offers limited liability religion, not Biblical faith.

According to Heer, the medieval mystic Eckhart gave to the soul a "sovereign majesty together with God. The next step was taken by a disciple, Johannes of Star Alley, who asked if the word of the soul was not as mighty as the word of the Heavenly Father."[3] In such a

---

2. C. C. Goen, *Revivalism and Separatism in New England, 1740–1800, Strict Congregationalists and Separate Baptists in the Great Awakening* (New Haven: Yale University Press, 1962), p. 200 f.
3. Friedrich Heer, *The Intellectual History of Europe*, p. 179.

faith, the new sovereign is man, and unlimited liability is in process of being transferred to God.

In terms of the Biblical doctrine of God, absolutely no liabilities are involved in the person and work of the Godhead. God's eternal decree and sovereign power totally govern and circumscribe all reality, which is His creation. Because man is a creature, man faces unlimited liability; his sins have temporal and eternal consequences, and he cannot at any point escape God. Van Til has summed up the matter powerfully:

> The main point is that if man could look anywhere and not be confronted with the revelation of God then he could not sin in the Biblical sense of the term. Sin is the breaking of the law of God. God confronts man everywhere. He cannot in the nature of the case confront man anywhere if he does not confront him everywhere. God is one; the law is one. If man could press one button on the radio of his experience and not hear the voice of God then he would always press that button and not the others. But man cannot even press the button of his own self-consciousness without hearing the requirement of God.[4]

But man wants to reverse this situation. Let God be liable, if He fails to deliver at man's request. Let man declare that his own experience pronounces himself to be saved, and then he can continue his homosexuality or work in a house of prostitution, all without liability. Having pronounced the magic formula, "I accept Jesus Christ as my personal lord and savior," man then transfers almost all the liability to Christ and can sin without at most more than a very limited liability. Christ cannot be accepted if His sovereignty, His law, and His word are denied. To deny the law is to accept a works religion, because it means denying God's sovereignty and assuming man's existence in independence of God's total law and government. In a world where God functions only to remove the liability of hell, and no law governs man, man works his own way through life by his own conscience. Man is saved, in such a world, by his own work of faith, of accepting Christ, not by Christ's sovereign acceptance of him. Christ said, "Ye have not chosen me, but I have chosen you" (John 15:16). The pietist insists that *he* has chosen Christ; it is *his* work, not Christ's. Christ, in such a faith, serves as an insurance agent, as a guarantee against liabilities, not as sovereign lord. This is paganism in Christ's name.

In paganism, the worshiper was not in existence. Man did not worship the pagan deities, nor did services of worship occur. The temple was open every day as a place of business. The pagan entered the temple and bought the protection of a god by a gift or offering. If the god failed him, he thereafter sought the services of another. The

---

4. Cornelius Van Til, *A Letter on Common Grace* (Philadelphia: Presbyterian and Reformed Publishing Company, 1955), p. 40 f.

pagan's quest was for an insurance, for limited liability and unlimited blessings, and, as the sovereign believer, he shopped around for the god who offered the most. Pagan religion was thus a transaction, and, as in all business transactions, no certainty was involved. The gods could not always deliver, but man's hope was that, somehow, his liabilities would be limited.

The "witness" of pietism, with its "victorious living," is to a like limited liability religion. A common "witness" is, "Praise the Lord, since I accepted Christ, all my troubles are over and ended." The witness of Job in his suffering was, "Though he slay me, yet will I trust him" (Job 13:15). St. Paul recited the long and fearful account of his sufferings *after* accepting Christ: in prison, beaten, shipwrecked, stoned, betrayed, "in hunger and thirst, . . . in cold and nakedness" (II Cor. 11:23-27). Paul's was not a religion of limited liability nor of deliverance from all troubles because of his faith.

The world is a battlefield, and there are casualties and wounds in battle, but the battle is the Lord's and its end is victory. To attempt an escape from the battle is to flee from the liabilities of warfare against sinful men for battle with an angry God. To face the battle is to suffer the penalties of man's wrath and the blessings of God's grace and law.

Apart from Jesus Christ, men are judicially dead, i.e., under a death sentence, before God, no matter how moral their works. With regeneration, the beginning of true life, man does not move out from under God's unlimited liability. Rather, with regeneration, man moves from the world of unlimited liability under the curse, to the world of unlimited liability under God's blessings. The world and man were cursed when Adam and Eve sinned, but, in Jesus Christ, man is blessed, and the world progressively reclaimed and redeemed for Him. In either case, the world is under God's law. Blessings and curses are thus inseparable from God's law and are simply different relationships to it. The world of regenerate men is the world of the law.

Men inescapably live in a world of unlimited liability, but with a difference. The covenant-breaker, at war with God and unregenerate, has an unlimited liability for the curse. Hell is the final statement of that unlimited liability. The objections to hell, and the attempts to reduce it to a place of probation or correction, are based on a rejection of unlimited liability. But the unregenerate has, according to Scripture, an unlimited liability to judgment and the curse. On the other hand, the regenerate man, who walks in obedience to Jesus Christ, his covenant head, has a limited liability to judgment and the curse. The unlimited liability of God's wrath was assumed for the elect by Jesus Christ upon the cross. The regenerate man is judged for his transgressions of the law of God, but his liability here is a limited one, whereas his liability for blessings in this life and in heaven are unlimited. The unregenerate can experience a limited measure of blessing in this life, and none in the world to come; they have at best a limited liability for blessing.

Man thus cannot escape an unlimited liability universe. The important question is this: in which area is he exposed to unlimited liability, to an unlimited liability to the curse because of his separation from God, or to an unlimited liability to blessing because of his faith in, union with, and obedience to Jesus Christ?

XII

THE LAW IN THE OLD TESTAMENT

1. God the King

The Hebrew word for "law" is *torah*, meaning "a pointing out, a direction, or authoritative direction" from the Lord.[1] From the very beginning of Israel's relationship to God, there was thus of necessity a law, or authoritative direction. Previously, authoritative direction had been given to Adam, the line of Seth, Noah and his descendants, Abraham and his heirs, as well as to other men (as witness Melchizedek and Job). It is impossible for a relationship with God to exist without law.

Since the modernist lacks a faith in the sovereign God, he cannot accept the existence of a given law from the beginning. He must posit instead an evolution in man's self-awareness and a development of law in terms of man's experience with reality. As a result, the modernist sees the law as a late codification of Israel's national experience. S. R. Driver, in his very influential work, *An Introduction to the Literature of the Old Testament* (1897), assumed an evolutionary position and made no attempt to prove his thesis; the faith of the day was with him. The same position was given an important restatement by Robert H. Pfeiffer, in his *Introduction to the Old Testament* (1941). The basic premise of such critics is an evolutionary and philosophical humanism. Not surprisingly, with Darwin such a faith came into its own. The comment of Allis on this point is telling:

> Even a cursory examination of the literature of the higher criticism makes it clear that it has been increasingly dominated by three great principles of evolutionary theory: (1) that development is the explanation of all phenomena, (2) that this development results from forces latent in man without any supernatural assistance, and (3) that the "comparative" method, which uses a naturalistic yardstick, must determine the nature and rate of this development.[2]

In Biblical history, because the law is always the assumed perspective of every book of the Old Testament, the judgments of the prophets and writers are always on the premise of the law.

---

1. S. R. Driver, "Law (in the Old Testament)," in Hastings, *A Dictionary of the Bible*, III, 64.
2. Oswald T. Allis, *The Five Books of Moses* (Philadelphia: Presbyterian and Reformed Publishing Company, 1943), p. 228 f.

The book of Joshua, for example, begins with the reminder to the people that it is their privilege and strength that they are the people of the law, that they have God's authoritative direction (Josh. 1:7-9). They are repeatedly reminded that the law is their source of strength and the sign of their covenantal bond, as a nation, with God (Josh. 22:5; 23:1-16; 24:1-27). The individual mark of the covenant, circumcision, is cited in Joshua 5, as well as the passover. The laws of the ban and of conquest appear in chaps. 6:17; 9:23; and 11:20. The division of the land in terms of the law is described in chaps. 13:14-33; 14:1-15; and 17–19; and the cities of refuge in chap. 20.

Skipping over to Ruth, we find here the practices of gleaning, redemption of the land, and the levirate.

The book of Judges is especially sharp in its presupposition of the law. It describes the apostasy of Israel from God and His law (Judges 2:1-2, 10, 15, 17; 3:7-8; 5:8; 6:1, 10, 25 f.; 10:13, 14, etc.).

The central point and theme of Judges is stated repeatedly (17:6; 18:1; 21:25): "In those days there was no king in Israel: every man did that which was right in his own eyes" (21:25). The same point prefaces an ugly account of depravity in chapters 19 and 20 (19:1).

Myers' interpretation of this statement is that "Because *there was no king* in Israel there was no restraint upon families except that of tribal authority and custom."[3] He assumes the meaning to be the lack of a human monarch and the institution of monarchy. Farrar's sorry comment is similar:

> This shows that these narratives were written, or more probably edited, in the days of the monarchy. . . .
>
> *Did that which was right in his own eyes.*—This notice is added to show why there was no authoritative interference of prince or ruler to prevent idolatrous or lawless proceedings. (Deut. 12:8: "Ye shall not do after all the things which we do here this day, *every man what is right in his own eyes.*")[4]

The surprising fact about Farrar's blindness is that he cited Deuteronomy 12:8, which is part of a statement of God's kingship and the claim of His sovereign law. The point of Judges is that Israel repeatedly forsook God the King, and abandoned His law, to go "a whoring after other gods," failing to obey "the commandments of the LORD" (Judges 2:17). God was Israel's lawmaker both as sovereign God and universal King and as Israel's covenant King. Human kingship is not the answer. In fact, the pagan oppressors of Israel had human kings, and Israel itself had, over part of its realm, a human king, Abimelech (chaps. 9

---

3. Jacob M. Myers, "Judges," in *Interpreter's Bible*, II, 801.
4. F. W. Farrar, "Judges," in Ellicott, II, 254.

and 10). The kingship of Abimelech is presented as an aspect of the denial of the kingship of God.

Another vivid contrast is drawn between the kingship of Jabin, king of Canaan, reigning in Hazor, whose captain was Sisera (Judges 4:2), and the kingship of God. The Song of Deborah gives us a poor picture of Israel, defeated, cowardly, and ill-armed. The battle was won by God, the King of Israel: "They fought from heaven; the stars in their courses fought against Sisera" (Judges 5:20). God as universal King had used the elements to defeat and destroy the Canaanite armies. As King, He then meted out curse and blessing in terms of loyalty to His cause.

> Curse ye Meroz, said the angel of the LORD; curse ye bitterly the inhabitants thereof; because they came not to the help of the LORD, to the help of the LORD against the mighty.
> Blessed above women shall Jael the wife of Heber the Kenite be; blessed shall she be above women in the tent (Judges 5:23-24).

Here we have the curse and the blessing of the law pronounced by the giver of the law, the King.

After describing Jael's execution of Sisera, Deborah declared:

> The mother of Sisera looked out at a window, and cried through the lattice, Why is his chariot so long in coming? why tarry the wheels of his chariots?
> Her wise ladies answered her, yea, she returned answer to herself, Have they not sped? have they not divided the prey; to every man a damsel or two? to Sisera a prey of divers colours, a prey of divers colours of needlework, of divers colours of needlework on both sides, meet for the neck of them that take the spoil?
> So let all thine enemies perish, O LORD: but let them that love him be as the sun when he goeth forth in his might (Judges 5:28-31).

Deborah's language is intense and graphic. The "damsels" Sisera's men dreamed of possessing is literally "uterus," "to every man a uterus or two."[5] Keil and Delitzsch translate the latter part of verse 31 thus: "But let those that love Him be like the rising of the sun in its strength," and state that this "is a striking image of the exaltation of Israel to a more and more glorious unfolding of its destiny."[6] Even more, it is an image of the blessing of God the King on those who love, serve, and obey Him.

In a psalm celebrating the law of God (Ps. 19:7-14), God's rule over the universe is also cited, and again we have the image of "the sun; Which is as a bridegroom coming out of his chamber, and rejoicing as

---

5. Keil and Delitzsch, *Joshua, Judges, Ruth* (Grand Rapids: Eerdmans, 1950), p. 324.
6. *Ibid.*, p. 325.

a strong man to run a race" (Ps. 19:4, 5). It is after he describes the law and order apparent in the heavens, the firmament, the earth, and the sun, that David joyfully declares "The law of the LORD is perfect, converting the soul" (Ps. 19:7). The glory of God is revealed in all the universe by His law order; that same glory is manifested in man and his world when the law is obeyed. This same image is in mind in Deborah's song. It was because the law and kingship of God were denied by Israel, and "every man did that which was right in his own eyes," that, instead of being comparable to the sun in its glory among the nations, Israel was instead all too often in captivity to alien powers.

Returning to *torah*, or direction, a pointing out, Jesus Christ referred to Himself as the torah when He declared, "I am the way, the truth, and the life: no man cometh unto the Father, but by me" (John 14:6). The Greek word for "way" is *'odos*, a proceeding, a course of conduct; in Acts 13:10, Romans 11:33, and Revelation 15:3, according to Joseph Henry Thayer's *Greek-English Lexicon of the New Testament*, it means "the purposes and ordinances of God, his way of dealing with men." The use of "I am" echoed the divine name (Ex. 3:14); the reference to the "way" spoke of the law. Jesus Christ, as the incarnate God, was also the declaration of God's righteousness and law. By this sentence, Christ made Himself inseparable from either the Godhead or from the law. He is the *torah* or direction of God; by His declaration, Christ made both Himself and the law more readily identifiable.

The alternative to Christ and the law is thus anarchy and lawlessness; it means a life without meaning or direction. Christ is the declaration of God's direction or law; the law points us to the right road. Sin, *hamartia*, is missing the mark; it does involve moving in the right direction, but it is a falling short, a missing of the mark. *Anomia*, sin, is lawlessness; it means moving in the wrong direction and denying direction. It is anarchy. "If we say we have no sin (*hamartia*), we deceive ourselves and the truth is not in us" (I John 1:8). It is the godless who are sinners in the sense of being anti-law, hostile to God's direction. The word used is *anomos*, lawless or without law (Acts 2: 23; II Thess. 2:8; II Peter 2:8). However, all men who commit sin (*harmartia*) habitually and carelessly are in reality not Christians and are guilty of lawlessness (*anomia*). "Whosoever committeth sin (*hamartia*, i.e., all who practice sin as their way of life) transgresseth also the law (*anomia*, such persons are actually anti-law, lawless); for sin (*hamartia*, i.e., the habitual practice of sin) is the transgression of the law (*anomia*, is the practice of lawlessness)" (I John 3:4).

The law is an indictment, a death sentence, if we are headed in the wrong direction. If we move in God's directed path, the law is a schoolmaster, guiding us all our days into God's way of righteousness and truth. Galatians 3:24, 25 states that, "after faith is come, we are no longer under a schoolmaster" (Gal. 3:25). Does this mean the end of the law? On the contrary, we now learn, not from the law as an indictment, but from Christ the way, and God our Father, how to walk in the appointed direction or in the law, "For ye are all the children of God by faith in Christ Jesus" (Gal. 3:26). The contrast is not between law and no law, but between "the immature life of slavery under a tutor (and) the life of sonship, with all its privileges and rights."[7] Luther saw both the law and sin as abolished and declared that, "To the extent that I take hold of Christ by faith, therefore to that extent the Law has been abrogated for me."[8] This is antinomianism, and alien to St. Paul. St. Paul attacked man-made laws, and man-made interpretations of the law, as the way of justification; the law can never justify; it does sanctify, and there is no sanctification by lawlessness.

2. The Law and the Prophets

The function of the prophets in Israel was to speak for God in terms of the law, and, under inspiration, also to predict specifically the curses and blessings of the law as they would occur in the nation's history. The burden of the prophetic word was summed up by Isaiah thus:

> To the law and to the testimony: if they speak not according to this word, it is because there is no light in them (Isa. 8:20).

No other recourse—to monarch, armies, wizards, foreign allies, or other gods—was of any use. The faithful could say to all enemy nations: "Take counsel together, and it shall come to nought: speak the word, and it shall not stand: for God is with us" (Isa. 8:10).

In analyzing Isaiah 8:20, it is sad to note that the very able Edward J. Young did not firmly link "law" with the Mosaic law.[1] Plumptre even denied anything but a remote connection to the law of Moses: " 'The law and the testimony' are obviously here, as in verse 16, the 'word of Jehovah,' spoken to the prophet himself, the revelation which had come to him with such an intensity of power."[2] Such an opinion destroys the unity of Scripture and denies the whole purpose of prophecy. Alexander, before their day, stated the meaning simply and clearly:

> Instead of resorting to these unprofitable and forbidden sources, the

---

7. Herman N. Ridderbos, *The Epistle of Paul to the Churches of Galatia* (Grand Rapids: Eerdmans, 1953), p. 146.
8. Jeroslav Pelikan, Walter A. Hansen, editors, *Luther's Works*, vol. 20, *Lectures on Galatians, 1535* (St. Louis: Concordia, 1963), p. 350 f.
1. Edward J. Young, *The Book of Isaiah* (Grand Rapids: Eerdmans, 1965), I, 319.
2. E. H. Plumptre, "Isaiah," in Ellicott, IV, 443.

disciples of Jehovah are instructed to resort *to the law and to the testimony* (i.e., to divine revelation, considered as a system of belief and as a rule of duty)—if they speak (i.e., if any speak) not according to this word (another name for the revealed will of God), *it is he to whom there is no dawn* or morning (*i.e., no relief from the dark night of calamity).*[3]

Alexander should have added that, while all Scripture is God's law word, the heart of that law is the law of Moses.

When Israel rejected God as King and chose a man to be king, God declared that it was a rejection of Himself: "they have rejected me, that I should not reign over them" (I Sam. 8:7). In terms of their choice, God then *prophesied* their destiny (I Sam. 8:9-18; 12:6-25). Because of their departure from God the King, and from the law of that King, certain consequences would follow. The prophecy of God in the epilogue to the law, in the body of the law, and through Samuel, gives us both the formal condition and the basic content of all subsequent prophecy.

The new monarchy, not less than the old commonwealth, had a responsibility to obey God and His law, and Saul was accordingly judged in terms of the law (I Sam. 15:22-35). David was called to be faithful, blessed for his faithfulness, and severely punished for his breach of law (II Sam. 12:9-14). The reign of Solomon similarly records blessings and penalties in terms of obedience and disobedience, and the same is true of all the subsequent rulers of both Judah and Israel. The reforms recalled men to the law; apostasy meant a contempt for and abandonment of the law, and the God of the law. The captivity to Babylon is shown to be a fulfilment of the curses of the law. Jeremiah, in terms of the law, had pronounced its curse upon Judah, and the Babylonian captivity came "To fulfil the word of the LORD by the mouth of Jeremiah, until the land had enjoyed her sabbaths: for as long as she lay desolate she kept sabbath, to fulfil threescore and ten years" (II Chron. 36:21).

To separate prophecy from the law is to render both meaningless. Both the law and the prophets have reference to one basic fact, the Kingdom of God, God's rule by law over all the earth. As Edersheim observed in the Warburton Lectures of 1880-1884,

The one pervading and impelling idea of the Old Testament is the royal reign of God on earth. . . . Almost a thousand years before Christ rises the longing cry after the future Kingdom of God—a kingdom which is to conquer and win all nations, and to plant in Israel righteousness, knowledge, peace, and blessing—that Kingdom of God in which God, or his Vicegerent, the Messiah, is to be

3. Joseph Addison Alexander, *Commentary on the Prophecies of Isaiah*, p. 193.

King over the whole earth, and all generations are to come up and worship the Lord of Hosts.[4]

The champions of premillennialism have been right in one respect: the goal of Biblical history is the Kingdom of God. They have erred in making it purely eschatological, beyond the scope of present history, and they have in effect denied the kingdom by denying the validity of its law today. By their doctrine of a parenthesis between the Old Testament kingdom and the ostensible future, millennial kingdom, they have denied the law, the prophets, and the kingship of Christ. If we deny the King's law, we deny the King. By separating the kingdom from the Christian era, the rule of God is denied, and the world is turned over to Satan. Not surprisingly, persons of the Scofieldian, dispensational school declare this present age to be ruled by Satan.

Throughout the Old Testament, when the prophets charged that the nation had forsaken the covenant, the theme of virtually all the prophets (I Kings 19:10, etc.), they were plainly charging the nation with deserting God the King and His covenant law. Without a covenant, there is no law; a covenant requires a law. To renew the covenant, as was done repeatedly in the Old Testament, and supremely by Christ at the Last Supper, was to renew the law of the covenant. Thus, every renewal of the covenant was a renewal of the law of the covenant. This was true of Josiah's reformation, and of every other reformation in Biblical history:

> And the king stood by a pillar, and made a covenant before the LORD to walk after the LORD, and to keep his commandments and his testimonies and his statutes with all their heart and all their soul, to perform the words of this covenant that were written in this book. And all the people stood to the covenant (II Kings 23:3).

The text of Chronicles also emphasizes the same fact, while making clear that the desire for reformation came from the king and was imposed on the people:

> And the king stood in his place, and made a covenant before the LORD, to walk after the LORD, and to keep his commandments, and his testimonies, and his statutes, with all his heart, and with all his soul, to perform the words of the covenant which are written in this book.
> And he caused all that were present in Jerusalem and Benjamin to stand to it. And the inhabitants of Jerusalem did according to the covenant of God, the God of their fathers (II Chron. 34:31-32).

The covenant law declares God to be the sovereign Lord, who "hath his way in the whirlwind and in the storm, and the clouds are the dust

---

4. Edersheim was quoting here from Keim. Alfred Edersheim, *Prophecy and History* (Grand Rapids: Baker Book House, 1955), p. 48.

of his feet" (Nahum 1:3). Storm and pestilence are His tools in dealing with a rebellious realm.

This appears with especial force in the challenge issued by God through Elijah to the priests of Baal. God ordained a fearful drought in Israel. Ellison's account of the struggle is excellent:

> As the excavations at Ugarit have shown us, Baal was above all the god of the winter rains. But let Jezebel, her priests and prophets howl to Baal as they would, there would be no rain in Israel, no, not even dew, until *Jehovah* gave it, and He would announce its giving beforehand through His servant Elijah, lest any should give the glory to others. There is no suggestion that the famine was punishment, though punishment it was at the same time; it was above all an undeniable proof of Jehovah's power and Baal's impotence precisely in that realm which was considered Baal's specialty.

> He allowed the lesson to sink in thoroughly. Three winters passed without rain and three summers without harvest (I Ki. 18:1). We can easily imagine how the worshippers, prophets and priests of Baal were reduced to despair. Only then did God tell him to come out of hiding and tell Ahab that Jehovah would have mercy on a land that must have been near its last gasp.

> It was not enough, however, to give rain in the name of Jehovah. The war had to be carried into the enemy's camp. This Elijah did by challenging Baal on his own ground. Not only was the seaward end of Carmel claimed by Phoenicia, but it was considered especially sacred to Baal. Here on Baal's own ground he was challenged to send his lightning flashes from heaven, for his worshippers looked on him as the controller of the thunderstorm. How successful Elijah was in his purpose may be seen by translating the cry of the people literally, "Jehovah, He is the Mighty One; Jehovah, He is the Mighty One!" (I Ki. 18:39).[5]

The prayer of Elijah was in terms of Deuteronomy 28:23, God's declaration that the heaven would be as brass (no rain), and the earth as iron (producing no crops), if God's people disobeyed His law.

Elijah thus prayed in terms of God's law, for God's curse on a lawless people. It is a requirement of true prayer that it be within the framework of the law. We can pray that sinners be converted, but not that they be blessed in their lawlessness. We can pray for God's blessing on our obedience, but not for a blessing on disobedience. Prayer cannot be antinomian.

To pray for grace to a sinner is to pray within the law, for the basic fact about grace is that it is not antinomian. The·sinner accepts God's

---

5. H. L. Ellison, *The Prophets of Israel* (Grand Rapids, 1969), p. 30 f. The extent to which the law is echoed throughout the Bible appears in Elisha's request for a double portion of Elijah's spirit (II Kings 2:9), of which Ellison accurately observes, "He was asking for the first-born's share (cf. Deut. 21:17), and not that he should be greater than his master" (p. 44); Elisha was asking to be named the heir to Elijah's office.

law-judgment on his sin when he accepts God's grace, and grace is inseparable from that judgment.

The reason why Elijah's prayer was effectual was simply because it was the prayer of a righteous man within the context of God's law.

The prayer of Elijah for a drought was a prayer to further God's kingdom; it is cited as the type of true prayer by James (5:16-18). The goal of that effectual prayer was to break the power of false authorities and to establish God's reign in the midst of His enemies.

The concern of the law and the prophets was the Kingdom of God. The judges were in a sense kings under God. As Ellison has noted, "The word which in the Old Testament we render judge (*shophet*) was among the Phoenicians their title for king. The fact of rule was never contrary to God's will."[6] It was the rejection of God's kingship which marked the establishment of Saul's monarchy that God condemned. The whole point of I Samuel 8 was that their human kings would give them a man-made law, together with all its evils and injustice. The indictments of the prophets are bills of particular offenses against God's law and judgments in terms of that law. The law can no more be separated from the prophets than wetness from water, for it is then no longer water, but something else.

But this is not all. *The law cannot be separated from God without destroying it.* Too often in our times the law is abstracted from God and seen in isolation. To cite a specific example, very commonly in our day private property is strongly advocated by conservatives without at the same time giving more than lip service to God and no attention to the law of the tithe. But Scripture makes clear that the earth is the Lord's and therefore subject to His law, and to His tax, the tithe. Private ownership apart from His law is accursed. Each man ends up a lonely island on his property, surrounded by a lawless, alien world of ravenous men. The alternative is no better: a communistic society in which men have land in common, but life in silent hostility and suspicion. Obviously, no arrangment of property can supply the loss of God and His regenerating power. On the other hand, among regenerate men, a variety of economic orders can prevail successfully. The Hutterites, a sect of communally oriented Christians who hold all things in common, are able to out-compete their neighbors in America who live on privately owned farms. The reason is that the motive force is not private property but faith. Clearly, the Bible does establish private ownership as the God-ordained form of land-holding, but just as clearly it does not identify land arrangement as the source of blessing. Moreover, since the Hutterite community is a voluntary order resting on a

---

6. *Ibid.*, p. 129.

faith, it is clearly not communistic and thus does not violate the concept of private property any more than partnership in a business, membership in a country club, or shares in a business violates private ownership simply because there are multiple owners. Multiple ownership is not state socialism.

Multiple ownership, however, is no more successful than sole ownership where God is left out. In our cities and towns, the sole owner of property is increasingly threatened by lawless forces, but so is the owner of a condominium. In fact, the condominium may include and increasingly does include lawless men; the guard at the door cannot keep out the enemy within. Similarly, the worst threat to many sole owners is their own families—lawless sons and daughters.

Clearly, the law cannot be separated from God without destroying it. The law is then rootless and soon dead. The prophets never presented a rootless law but always the living God and His sovereign will, the law.

3. Natural and Supernatural Law

The Bible does not recognize any law as valid apart from the law of God, and this law is given by revelation to the patriarchs and Moses, and expounded by prophets, Jesus Christ, and the apostles. To have two kinds of law is to have two kinds of gods; not surprisingly, the ancient world, like the modern, was polytheistic; having many laws, it had many gods.

Some will deny this. After having adopted a Greek and rationalistic concept of natural law, they attempt to graft it into Biblical religion. Witness, for example, the reason of Melanchthon in *Loci Communes*:

> Some laws are natural laws, others divine, and others human. Concerning natural laws, I have seen nothing worthily written either by theologians or lawyers. For when natural laws are being proclaimed, it is proper that their formulas be collected by the method of human reason through the natural syllogism. I have not yet seen this done by anyone, and I do not know at all whether it can be done, since human reason is so enslaved and blinded—at least it has been up until now. Moreover, Paul teaches in Rom. 2:15 in a remarkably fine and clear argument that there is in the Gentiles a conscience which either defends or accuses their acts, and therefore it is law. For what is conscience but a judgment of our deeds which is derived from some law or common rule? The law of nature, therefore, is a common judgment to which all men give the same consent. This law which God has engraved on the mind of each is suitable for the shaping of morals.[1]

By this thesis, to which the Reformation leaders virtually all gave as-

---

1. Wilhelm Pauck, editor, *The Library of Christian Classics*, vol. XIX, *Melanchthon and Bucer* (Philadelphia: Westminster Press, 1969), p. 50.

sent, they denied the Reformation. Unregenerate, fallen man, unable
to save himself and guilty of holding down or suppressing the truth of
God in unrighteousness (Rom. 1:18), is somehow able to know a law
inherent in nature and make it a ground "for the shaping of morals"!

Let us examine now these laws of nature which Melanchthon reports
to us, and see how worthy these are of replacing the law of Moses:

> I pass over those things which we have in common with the beasts,
> the instinct of self-preservation, of giving birth, and procreating
> from self. The lawyers relate these things to the law of nature,
> but I call them certain natural dispositions implanted commonly in
> living beings.
>
> Of the laws that pertain properly to man, however, the principal
> ones seem to be the following:
>
> 1. God must be worshiped.
> 2. Since we are born into a life that is social, nobody must be
>   harmed.
> 3. Human society demands that we make common use of all
>   things.[2]

With such thinking as this, the Reformers were busy castrating themselves! Melanchthon gets his first natural law from Romans 1 rather
than nature. The second he grounds feebly in Genesis 2:8, although
why he needs a single verse to support his position, having disposed of
all the books of Moses, he does not tell us. The "natural" foundation
for Melanchthon's second law of nature is majoritarianism:

> Therefore, those who disturb the public peace and harm the innocent
> must be coerced, restrained, and taken away. The majority must
> be preserved by the removal of those who have caused harm. The
> law stands: "Harm no one!" But if someone has been harmed, the
> one who is responsible must be done away with lest more be
> harmed. It is of more importance to preserve the whole group
> than one or two individuals. Therefore the man who threatens the
> whole group by some deed that makes for a bad example is done
> away with. This is why there are magistracies in the state, this is
> why there are punishments for the guilty, this is why there are wars,
> all of which the lawyers refer to the the the law of nations (*ius gen-
> tium*).[3]

With these words Melanchthon joined hands with Caiaphas, who said
concerning Christ, "that it is expedient for us, that one man should die
for the people, and that the whole nation perish not" (John 11:50).
The persecution of the early Christians, and of all disturbing minorities,
is given firm ground in this natural law.

Melanchthon's third natural law led to a dangerous Anabaptist
communism, and thus it was necessary both to affirm this majoritarian,

---

2. *Ibid.*, p. 50 f.   3. *Ibid.*, p. 51 f.

mass man concept and also to retain private property, princely domains, universities, professors, and lords in their estates. As a result, he posited "contracts" as the means of "sharing" things, so that by contract the rulers could maintain their uncommon possession of common things. Melanchthon as a result "condensed" the three basic laws into four and added a proud epilogue:

> So much for the general rules of the laws of nature, which can be condensed in the following way:
> 1. Worship God!
> 2. Since we are born into a life that is social, a shared life, harm no one but help everyone in kindness.
> 3. If it is impossible that absolutely no one be harmed, see to it that the number harmed be reduced to a minimum. Let those who disturb the public peace be removed. For this purpose let magistracies and punishments for the guilty be set up.
> 4. Property shall be divided for the sake of public peace. For the rest, some shall alleviate the wants of others through contracts.
>
> He who wants to do so may add to this particular ideas from the poets, orators, and historians that are generally related to the law of nations (*ius gentium*), such as one can read about here and there concerning marriage, adultery, the returning of a favor, ingratitude, hospitality, the exchange of property, and other matters of this kind. But I thought it adequate to mention only the most common forms. And do not rashly consider just any thoughts of the Gentile writers to be laws, for many of their popular ideas express the depraved affections of our nature and not laws. Of this sort is this thought from Hesiod: "Love him who loves you, and go to the one that comes to you. We give to the one who gives to us, and do not give to him who does not give to us" (Hesiod, *Works and Days*, 353-354). For in these lines friendship is measured by utility alone. Such also is that popular saying: "Give and take." The statement that "force must be repelled by force" is pertinent here, like that which appears in Euripides' *Ion*: "It is fine for those who are prosperous to honor piety, but whenever anyone wishes to treat his enemies badly, no law stands in the way."
>
> Also, so-called civil law contains many things which are obviously human affections rather than natural laws. For what is more foreign to nature than slavery? And in some contracts that which really matters is unjustly concealed. But more about these things later. A good man will temper civil constitutions with right and justice, that is, with both Divine and natural laws. Anything that is enacted contrary to divine or natural laws cannot be just. So much about the laws of nature. Define them with more exact and subtle reasoning if you can.[4]

The main purpose of God's law through Moses would appear to be to convict man of sin, so that man can then be saved by grace and

4. *Ibid.*, p. 52 f.

delivered from God's law to nature's law. Salvation is in effect from God to nature. "The law demands impossible things such as the love of God and our neighbor."[5] However, "That part of the law called the Decalogue or the moral commandments has been abrogated by the New Testament."[6] Some of the Anabaptists practiced what Melanchthon preached but were only damned for it. The Spirit leads Christians "to do the law" even though the law is now abrogated![7] The Holy Spirit is thus obviously more law-minded than Melanchthon.

Melanchthon was not alone in this kind of nonsense. Bucer, in *De Regno Christi*, demanded a totalitarian regime as a consequence of his natural law faith. His advice to Edward VI of England was revealing, and it should be noted that Bucer cited Plato, not the Bible:

> And in this it must be ordered, first, that nobody should be allowed to enter merchandising whom officials have not judged suitable for this sort of thing, having found him to be pious, a lover of the commonwealth rather than of private interest, eager for sobriety and temperance, vigilant and industrious. Secondly, that these should not import or export merchandise other than that what Your Majesty has decreed. And he shall decree that only those things are to be exported of which the people of the realm really have an abundance so that their export may be of no less benefit to the people of this realm, to whom these things are surplus, than to those who take them to foreign countries and make a profit on them. So also he should permit no merchandise to be imported except what he judges good for the pious, sober, and salutary use of the commonwealth. Finally, that a definite and fair price should be established of individual items of merchandise, which can easily be arranged and is very necessary (so fiery is human avarice) for conserving justice and decency among the citizens.

> The same statutes must apply to peddlars and retailers, to which task, as it is lowly and sordid, no one should be admitted unless he is lacking in ability or has a physical incapacity so as to render him unsuitable for more liberal skills, as was the opinion of Plato also (Plato, Republic, II, 371 c-d.).[8]

They uttered blasphemy and called it reformation. They set aside the law of God for man's rationalizing and declared it to be a superior law for men and nations.

Bucer, having booted out God's law for Plato, still spoke piously of God's law and transferred its moral premises to man's natural law:

> For inasmuch as we have been freed from the teaching of Moses through Christ the Lord, so that it is no longer necessary for us to observe the civil decrees of the law of Moses, namely, in terms of the way and the circumstances in which they are described, nevertheless, insofar as the substance and proper end of these command-

---

5. *Ibid.*, p. 117.
6. *Ibid.*, p. 121.

7. *Ibid*, p. 124.
8. *Ibid.*, p. 344 f.

ments are concerned, and especially those which enjoin the discipline that is necessary for the whole commonwealth, whoever does not reckon that such commandments are to be conscientiously observed is certainly not attributing to God either supreme wisdom or a righteous care for our salvation.[9]

The main function of this re-introduction of the Mosaic law is to buttress the power of the state with the death penalty, the duty of obedience, and the like.[10]

We have seen that Melanchthon was so proud of his formulation of natural law that he proudly declared, "Define them with more exact and subtle reasoning if you can." Many did just that. Every man had his own natural law in his fallen nature. The 18th century and deism, and in the 20th century Lenny Bruce and the hippies, stood with the poet Pope in affirming, "Whatever is, is right." Everything in nature, every crime and every perversion, was, according to the Marquis de Sade, a law of nature; the only violation of natural law was for him the Christian religion. Thus, wherever nature has been held to be the source of law, law has ended up by reflecting or being identical with the sin of man.

How does the Bible relate law and nature? Psalm 1 is as clear a statement as any. When it speaks of law, it means "the Law of Moses."[11] Jackman translates verse 1 thus: "Blessed is the man that walketh not in the counsel of the lawless, nor standeth in the way of the unlawful, nor sitteth in the seat of the scornful." In verses 4-6, "ungodly" is also rendered as "lawless."[12] The man whose delight is in the law of the Lord, the Biblical law, is "like a tree planted by the rivers of water, that bringeth forth his fruit in season" (vs. 3). Note the ready link between obedience to Biblical law and prospering in the natural world. It is God's supernatural, revealed law on which the godly man meditates and which he obeys, and it means a natural flourishing on earth. To have roots in the revealed law of God is to have roots in the natural world of God, because God having created it, that world is totally responsive to the same purposes as His word.

But this is not all. The psalm makes clear also that the best if not the *only* way to have one's roots in the natural world is to be firmly rooted in God's supernatural law. "His leaf also shall not wither; and whatsoever he doeth shall prosper." The ungodly, or, after Jackman, the lawless, those who deny God's law, "are not so: but are like the

---

9. *Ibid.*, p. 378.
10. For Luther's meandering views on law, see Ferdinand Edward Cranz, *Harvard Theological Studies XIX, An Essay on the Development of Luther's Thought on Justice, Law, and Society* (Cambridge: Harvard University Press, 1959).
11. J. A. Alexander, *Psalms*, p. 10.
12. T. R. Jackman, *Psalms for Today*, p. 7.

chaff which the wind driveth away" (vs. 4). To be rootless in God means to be rootless in this world, and to be no better than chaff, which is blown away by the first adverse wind.

The natural world around us is totally governed by God and His law. There are laws operative in and over the natural world, laws of biology, physics, and the like, but never as closed systems. When and where God's revealed law is denied, God's absolute decree and law in the natural world is also ultimately denied. It is impossible to create a natural law philosophy: it vanishes into nothingness. The same is true of those modern substitutes for natural law which go by the name of common grace. If the sovereign and triune God be denied, all law everywhere is in effect also denied.

Thus the Bible, while not a textbook of physics or biology, all the same is basic to physics and biology. Without the sovereign God of Scripture and His law word, no science, no fact, and no learning could exist. No fact exists in and of itself. As Van Til has made clear, all reality is revelational of God and cannot be truly understood apart from Him. "If God exists there are no brute facts; if God exists our study of facts must be the effort to know them as God wants them to be known by us. We must then seek to think God's thoughts after Him. To assume that there are brute facts is therefore to assume that God does not exist."[13]

Therefore, *because* God exists, there are no brute facts, nor any brute laws (an impossible concept), in that world of brute factuality. The natural law philosophy seeks to find brute laws in a world of brute facts, i.e., ultimately meaningless laws in an ultimately and immediately meaningless world of facts. Natural law philosophers attempt to present us God's world without the God of Scripture and Scripture's law, and they succeed only in presenting us with a specimen of themselves.

The only tenable approach to the laws operative over and within the natural world is thus through the supernatural law word of God. If they will not have Moses, neither will they have this world or any law in it. The choice thus is not between Biblical law and natural law: it is between law and no law. To reject Moses is to reject the God of Moses.

Reduced even to a choice between Moses and Plato, Bucer's choice was a very sorry one. Having God's revealed law, why should any man wish to form a moral and civil law out of the fallen and perverted elements of man's mind?

The reason why men choose to look for a foundation in man is

---

13. Cornelius Van Til, "A Calvin University," in *The Banner*, Nov. 9, 1939; reprinted in C. Van Til, *Science Articles, a syllabus* (Philadelphia: Westminster Theological Seminary), p. 26.

because of their quest for a common ground with all men and all reality outside of God. They want to avoid what they call " 'a sectarian' system of thought." They declare that the need is for "the *philosophia perennis*," a philosophy common to all men as men, apart from theological considerations. By this means these thinkers claim that they can establish all the truths of Biblical religion in a rational manner satisfying to all men. Thus, instead of an exclusive or parochial revelation, a better, common ground can be established, it is held. In such a philosophy, the state, instead of a God-ordained ministry of justice, becomes "a 'natural' institution," a product of man's " 'social' being."[14] As men live socially, conflicts arise because of varying desires.

> Obviously there arises the necessity of some compromise; individual differences must be resolved; somebody, or some group selected to deliberate and speak for the whole community, has to make the decisions. And so arises, just as naturally and just as clearly God-given in origin as man's societal nature itself, the institution of authority.[15]

Such a natural law philosophy rests authority, not on an absolute God, nor on an absolute law, but on *compromise*. The basis of authority is thus relativism; compromise, not truth.

This natural law philosophy rests itself on the ultimacy of man's mind and it appeals to a common rationality in all men. But the fallen man uses his reason as an instrument of his warfare against God, and thus the common aspect of the rationality of apostate men is the determination to exclude the sovereign God of Scripture.

But if the natural man, without saving faith, can work his way up to God and a universal law, then he in fact needs neither God nor God's law, nor does he need the Bible, theologians, nor any revelation from God; man himself is then the principle of revelation and truth, the walking source of law. Where natural law and natural theology, or its modern common grace variations, prevail, there the church has very limited options left. It can become the handmaid of the state and work for social action, or it can forsake the world by means of pietism and mysticism. In any case, it has no God left apart from man.

The source of law is also the location of the god of any system, and if law is located in the rationality of men, then man is the god of that philosophy. Not surprisingly, Western thought, having adopted a natural law basis for its social orders, first viewed law as *logic*, an aspect of man's rationality, and then as *experience*, an aspect of man's being. And what does experience mean? "The very considerations which

---

14. Harold C. Gardiner, S.J., *Catholic Viewpoint on Censorship* (Garden City, N. Y.: Hanover House, 1958), p. 14.
15. *Ibid*, p. 20.

judges most rarely mention, and always with an apology, are the secret root from which the law draws all the juices of life. I mean, of course, considerations of what is expedient for the community concerned."[16] Natural law began with *compromise*, and it ends with *expediency*, having travelled, after much effort, nowhere at all. In the process of standing still, it has accomplished something: it has lost truth and authority, and has no common ground left, because the experience and the expedience of every man is his private world of compromise. Every man becomes his own world of law, his own realm of experience, and his own criterion of expediency.

Natural law philosophy begins on "the assumption that the non-Christian mode of reasoning is the only possible mode of reasoning."[17] As Van Til observed further, in contending against the same philosophy calling itself a doctrine of common grace:

> A doctrine of common grace that is constructed so as to appeal once more to a neutral territory between believers and non-believers is, precisely like old Princeton apologetics, in line with a Romanist type of natural theology. Why should we then pretend to have anything unique? And why then should we pretend to have a sound basis for science? Nothing short of the Calvinistic doctrine of the all-controlling providence of God, and the indelibly revelational character of every fact of the created universe, can furnish a true foundation for science. And how can we pretend to be able to make good use of the results of the scientific efforts of non-Christian scientists, if, standing on an essentially Romanist basis, we cannot even make good use of our own efforts?
>
> Why live in a dream world, deceiving ourselves and making false pretense before the world? The non-Christian view of science:
> (a) presupposes the autonomy of man,
> (b) presupposes the non-created character, i.e., the chance-controlled character of facts; and,
> (c) presupposes that laws rest not in God but somewhere in the universe.
>
> Now if we develop a doctrine of common grace in line with the teachings of Hepp with respect to the general testimony of the Spirit then we are incorporating into our scientific edifice the very forces of destruction against which that testimony is bound to go forth.[18]

The only true common ground is in God, i.e., in the fact that He created and governs all things, so that all things are revelational of Him. The understanding of all things begins therefore in Him, the submission

---

16. O. W. Holmes, Jr., *The Common Law* (Boston: Little, Brown, 1881), p. 35.
17. Cornelius Van Til, *Common Grace* (Philadelphia: Presbyterian and Reformed Publishing Co., 1947), p. 48.
18. C. Van Til, *A Letter on Common Grace* (Philadelphia: Presbyterian and Reformed Publishing Co., 1955), p. 66.

by man to God's judgment, salvation, and law-word. Van Til, in arguing against the opinions of a Reformed leader, Masselink, observed:

> But I have argued at length, particularly against Barth, that the image of God in man consists of actual knowledge content. Man does not start on the course of history merely with a capacity for knowing God. On the contrary he begins his course with *actual* knowledge of God. Moreover he cannot even eradicate this knowledge of God. It is this fact that makes sin to be sin "against better knowledge."
>
> . . . Roman Catholic theology thinks of the creature beginning as it were from the borders of non-being. There is according to Roman theology in man, as in created reality generally, an inherent tendency to sink back into non-existence. Hence the need of supernatural aid from the outset of man's being. There is in Roman theology a confusion between the metaphysical and the ethical aspects of man's being. . . . The destructive tendency of sin is not to be seen in a gradual diminution of man's rationality and morality. Man is not less a creature, a rational moral creature of God when he turns his back to God and hates his maker than he was before. Therefore when God gives to man his grace, his saving grace, this does not reinstate his rationality and morality. It reinstates his *true* knowledge, righteousness and holiness (Col. 3:10; Eph. 4:29). It restores man *ethically*, not metaphysically. So too if we take common grace to be that which has to do with the restraint of sin, then it is an ethical and not a metaphysical function that it performs. It does not maintain, as Dr. Masselink seems to contend, the creational characteristics of men. It does not sustain the image of God in "the wider sense," consisting of man's rationality and morality. It keeps the man who will be rational anyway from expressing his hostility to God in the field of knowledge to such an extent as to make it impossible for himself to destroy knowledge. And in restraining him in his ethical hostility to God, God releases his creatural powers so that he can make positive contributions to the field of knowledge and art. Similarly in restraining him from expressing his ethical hostility to God there is a release within him of his moral powers so that he can perform that which is "morally" though not spiritually good. As constitutive of the rationality and morality of man these powers had not diminished through sin. Man cannot be *amoral*. But by sin man fell ethically; he became hostile to God. And common grace is the means by which God keeps man from expressing the *principle* of hostility to its full extent, thus enabling man to do the "relatively good."[19]

Van Til has suggested "creation grace" as the better term than "common grace." Certainly the term "common grace," which has come to be a sign of humanism and of warfare against God, needs to be abandoned as a bastard term, bringing as it does two alien concepts together illegitimately.

---

19. *Ibid.*, p. 36.

In brief, to begin with anything less than God's law as the only foundation for social order is to end up with no law and only the rule of man's logic and experience.

Thus, the laws of physics, economics, biology, and every other science or study are firmly grounded in God's eternal decree; because God's predestinating and sovereign power is total, there are laws in every area. These laws derive, not from "nature" but from God. When the eternal decree is denied, the laws are in effect also denied, and they gradually wither away.

It was the humanism of the Enlightenment which developed natural law philosophy as its alternative to the sovereign, predestinating God of Scripture. Later, their heirs attacked the natural law concept as one which pointed to God; better to eliminate all law and leave no signposts to God, no evidences of design in the universe to speak of its Creator. The world was ready to accept Darwin and a blind, lawless, evolving universe to escape a God whose law governed all reality.

The concept of "inherent natural law . . . came between nature and God and . . . was conceived as independent of any external law-giver for its validity and operation."[20] In accepting natural law as a substitute for God, the Enlightenment saw it progressively in mechanistic terms. "Reality was no longer primarily a question of personal will and purpose."[21] The universe was compared to clockwork.

> Yet nothing is more hopeless from the Christian point of view than the comparison of the universe to a piece of clockwork. This pottage for which the biblical birthright was traded was a substitution of design for purpose; the surrender of the concept of goal for a conglomeration of mechanical ends expressed in philosophical terms of order, beauty, harmony, and perfection. The arguments from design point backward to creation, not forward to a consummation. . . .
>
> Grotius, the archetype of humanism, developed the distinction between the law of God and the law of nature, where nature included man and his history. The result of this distinction between Providence and the processes of life and history was that there arose the possibility of moulding life and history apart from any law of God. And this was a desirable end, since the law of God permitted wars and disasters. The moulding of history according to natural law pointed toward the idea of progress and thus bore directly upon the question of an eschatology. Man would now work out his own salvation, but in a radically different sense than in the meaning of the biblical word, and of course without fear and trembling (Phil. 2:12).[22]

---

20. James P. Martin, *The Last Judgment in Protestant Theology from Orthodoxy to Ritschl* (Grand Rapids: Eerdmans, 1963), p. 102.
21. *Ibid.*, p. 103.
22. *Ibid.*, p. 107.

As a result of this development, the law of nature, which in its pagan antiquity was the law of nations, again became the law of nations, man's law. Since neither God nor nature had eliminated wars, man, the new god and law-giver, would mold the nations and all men to eliminate wars.

The general and the particular government of God would be replaced by man's general and particular government. God's general government establishes man in a framework of total law; God's particular government is mindful of our every need, and not a hair falls apart from His sovereign care and oversight. The new sovereign state works to enfold us in a progressively total framework of law, and to watch us in its network of particular oversight. The senior editor of a major American periodical gave its approval to this radical invasion of privacy by the modern state's total government in a major editorial:

> As technology increasingly depersonalizes and dehumanizes our lives, it is spawning in us a need to reassert that which is most basic and vital in us, our instincts. Moreover, technology is sweeping us into an epoch when privacy is becoming literally impossible. It will become impossible on one hand, because of sheer population density, and, on the other, because of rapidly advancing technical means of surveillance in a civilization whose societies obviously intend to keep all individuals under constant watch.

> One paramount need thus is dawning: the need to dwell, more or less as human beings, in a society in which privacy is out of the question. Our answer apparently is going to be to adopt a mode of life in which privacy is no longer considered necessary. So I suspect that public sex should be seen as the wave of the future. . . .[23]

Natural law always ends up as the law of the state, and an anti-Christian state at that.

4. The Law as Direction and Life

The basic Biblical word for "law" is *tora* (or *torah*). *Tora* means not only instruction or teaching, but, fundamentally, "direction." The law thus gives the God-ordained direction to life; a lawless life is a directionless life in the sense that no true meaning exists apart from God. Evil is not an absence or thinness of being, but is an ethical, not a metaphysical, departure from God. The greater the departure, the greater the loss of meaning. Hell has no community or meaning. It is the collapse of all community, meaning, and life into a radical negation.

The book of Proverbs is essentially a book about the law as the direction and guide of life. The *tora* in Proverbs,

> Where it occurs unqualified (28:9; 29:18) it is clearly the divine law (it is also the Jewish term for the Pentateuch); but *my law,* "thy mother's law" (1:8), *etc,* refers to the present maxims and

23. Frank Trippett, "What's Happening to Sexual Privacy?" in *Look*, vol. 34, no. 21 (Oct. 20, 1970), p. 50.

to the home teachings, based indeed on the law, but not identical with it.[1]

Thus, all *direction* rests and must rest on God's fundamental *tora*, law, or direction. A parent's law, a teacher's or employer's law, must be an application of God's law. God's law when so applied becomes the fabric of life and the direction of society. As Solomon stated it,

> Whoso despiseth the word shall be destroyed: but he that feareth the commandment shall be rewarded.
> The law of the wise is a fountain of life, to depart from the snares of death (Prov. 13:13-14).

As Kidner observes,

> The phrase *law of the wise* (man) (AV, RV) indicates that *law (tora)* is here used in its original sense of "direction" or "instruction"; it is the voice of spiritual experience rather than divine command, though it will be in harmony with *the* Torah (as its proximity to verse 13 emphasizes).[2]

God's law is given to all men; the godly society and godly men will mediate that law to each new generation and will thus ensure their health and welfare. As Delitzsch summarized it,

> the proverb is designed to state that the life which springs from the doctrine of the wise man, as from a fountain of health, for the disciple who will receive it, communicates to him knowledge and strength, to know where the snares of destruction lie, and to hasten with vigorous steps away when they threaten to entangle him.[3]

This restates the basic meaning of *tora*, direction, and the direction provided by the law is the way of health, knowledge, and life. Moreover,

> They that forsake the law praise the wicked: but they that seek the law contend with them.
>
> Evil men understand not judgment: but they that seek the LORD understand all things (Prov. 28:4, 5).

Turning again to Delitzsch:

> They who praise the godless turn away from the revealed word of God (Ps. lxxiii. 11-15); those, on the contrary, who are true to God's word (xxix. 18) are aroused against them, they are deeply moved by their conduct, they cannot remain silent and let their wickedness go unpunished. . . . He who makes wickedness his moral element, falls into the confusion of the moral conception; but he whose end is the one living God, gains from that, in every situation of life, even amid the greatest difficulties, the knowledge

---

1. Derek Kidner, *Proverbs, An Introduction and Commentary* (Chicago: Inter-Varsity Press, 1964), p. 63.
2. *Ibid.*, p. 103.
3. Franz Delitsch, *Biblical Commentary on the Proverbs of Solomon* (Grand Rapids: Eerdmans [1872], 1950), I, 279.

of that which is morally right. Similarly the Apostle John (I John ii. 20): "Ye have an unction from the Holy One, and ye know all things": i.e., ye need to seek that knowledge which ye require, and which ye long after, not without yourselves, but in the new divine foundation of your personal life; from thence all that ye need for the growth of your spiritual life, and for the turning away from you of hostile influences, will come into your consciences. It is a potential knowledge, all-comprehensive in its character, and obviously a human relative knowledge, that is here meant.[4]

Forsaking the law means forsaking direction and life; a society and men which forsake God's law lose wisdom thereby and all direction. Relativism commands the society, and, with it, a moral paralysis. Kidner's comments bring this out clearly:

> 28:4. God's law man's bastion.
> Without revelation, all is soon relative; and with moral relativity, nothing quite merits attack. So, *e.g.*, the tyrant is accepted because he gets things done; and the pervert, because his condition is interesting. The full sequence appears in Romans 1:18-32.

> 28:5. God's law man's light.
> Romans 1:21, 28 illuminates line 1, as Romans 1:18-32 the preceding proverb. On line 2, *cf.* Psalm 119:100; John 7:17, and other references given in RVmg.[5]

One of the most persistent desires of men is to walk by sight, i.e., with a knowledge of the future of what lies ahead. It was this motive which led Saul to seek out the witch of Endor. Through her, Saul wanted to know the outcome of his war with the Philistines, and what he should do (I Sam. 28:15). The 19th and 20th centuries have seen a major revival of various forms of occultism whereby man seeks to probe the future and to gain light to walk by.

Scripture forbids all such attempts to probe the future apart from God. The means provided whereby man can know the future is the law-word of God. In terms of this, the psalmist declared, in his great meditation on the law, Psalm 119,

> Thy word is a lamp unto my feet, and a light unto my path.
> I have sworn, and I will perform it, that I will keep thy righteous judgments (Ps. 119:105-106).

This concept of the law as man's guide appears again and again in Scripture. These same words were also stated, perhaps first of all, by Solomon:

> For the commandment is a lamp; and the law is light; and reproofs of instruction are the way of life (Prov. 6:23).

In this verse, as Kidner notes, parental rules based on God's law "are

---

4. *Ibid.*, II, 226.   5. Kidner, *op. cit.*, p. 169.

regarded as expressions of the absolute, divine law."[6] Even more basic is the fact that God's law, in its Biblical statement as well as when faithfully mediated through family, church, state, or school, is the God-ordained means of *light*, the valid means of prediction. Man, walking by faith in obedience to God's law, walks to a great degree by sight. To walk without law is to walk in darkness.

The mediated law cannot take the place of the basic law, God's *tora*. The mediated law must in fact be identical with the divine *tora*. Application, not innovation or addition, is the duty of a mediating person or agency. Solomon therefore connected three things: first, the fear of the Lord and His instruction, direction, or law; second, the same law or instruction as applied by father and mother to the son; third, the consequence of obedience to this direction is an ornament or crown of life to the son.

> The fear of the LORD is the beginning of knowledge: but fools despise wisdom and instruction.
> My son, hear the instruction of thy father, and forsake not the law of thy mother:
> For they shall be an ornament of grace unto thy head, and chains about thy neck (Prov. 1:7-9).

By the term "beginning of wisdom" is meant "the first and controlling principle, rather than a stage which one leaves behind."[7] Delitzsch renders verse 9 thus: "For these are a fair crown to thy head, and jewels to thy neck."[8] The controlling principle of life, which crowns a man and enriches his days with wisdom, is the fear of the Lord, and this fear is inseparable from the law, instruction, or direction of God.

The centrality of the law to life is set forth powerfully in two further proverbs:

> He that turneth away his ear from hearing the law, even his prayer shall be an abomination (Prov. 28:9).
> Where there is no vision, the people perish: but he that keepeth the law, happy is he (Prov. 29:18).

If a man denies God's law or direction, he has denied himself any relationship to God, and "even his prayer shall be an abomination" to God, a moral offense, for to pray to the God whose direction we despise is to add insult to our offenses. Moreover, "without a revelation a people become ungovernable," as Delitzsch rendered Proverbs 29:18.[9] God's revelation is also His law, which is man's only road to true happiness, and the only acceptable means of serving God.

When Jesus Christ said, "I am the way, the truth, and the life: no

---

6. *Ibid.*, p. 73.
7. *Ibid.*, p. 59.

8. Delitzsch, *op. cit.*, I, 59.
9. *Ibid.*, II, 251.

man cometh unto the Father, but by me" (John 14:6), the word He used for "way" was *hodos*, a natural path, road, way, traveller's way, or metaphorically, a course of conduct, way of thinking, or righteousness.[10] Westcott cited the use of the word "way" in the mysticism of Lao-tse by way of comparison.[11] There is nothing mystical about the use of "way" by our Lord. He is the only direction to God, and, in identifying Himself as the direction, He declared in effect, "I am the Torah." The law as the expression of God's righteousness and rights is man's only valid road or direction. Christ kept the law perfectly, because the law was the expression of His being; He was sinless and could not sin, because the law was none other than His righteousness and rights set forth. He could not set the law aside, for to do so would have been to deny Himself and to cease existing. Tyrannical politicians have declared, "I am the law," and finally perished under God's law, but Jesus could declare absolutely, I am the way or law, the truth and the life. The law cannot be separated from Christ, nor Christ from the law.

5. The Law and the Covenant

The prophet Isaiah indicted Judah in the name of God as a law-breaker, and his prophecy begins with an indictment as well as a summons to return to the Lord. "Hear the word of the LORD, ye rulers of Sodom; give ear unto the law of God, ye people of Gomorrah" (Isa. 1:10). The curses of the law, of Deuteronomy 28, shall descend upon Judah and Jerusalem, "Because they have cast away the law of the LORD of hosts, and despised the word of the Holy One of Israel" (Isa. 5:24).

But this is not all. The nations of antiquity were also indicted by God (Isa. 13:1–23:18). The world's sin will be severely judged by God the King (Isa. 24:1–27:13). Judah and Jerusalem, because of their ungodly relations to Egypt and Assyria, are also again the target of still further indictments (Isa. 28:1–33:24). Edom is also the subject of an indictment (Isa. 34).

The judgment on Judah shall be so radical that only a tithe or tenth shall return, and this tenth shall be eaten or consumed until only a holy seed shall remain (Isa. 6:13). The judgment on other nations will be even more radical: "Behold, the LORD maketh the earth empty; and maketh it waste, and turneth it upside down, and scattereth abroad the inhabitants thereof" (Isa. 24:1). The reason for this is plainly stated: "The earth also is defiled under the inhabitants thereof, because

---

10. W. E. Vine, *Expository Dictionary of New Testament Words*, IV, 203.
11. B. F. Westcott, *The Gospel according to St. John* (Grand Rapids, Eerdmans [1881], 1954), p. 202.

they have transgressed the laws, changed the ordinance, broken the everlasting covenant" (Isa. 24:5). According to Alexander, "The three terms used (laws, ordinance, covenant) are substantially synonymous, *law, statute, covenant*, being continually interchanged."[1] This point is of especial importance. It again emphasizes the position of all Scripture that all men and nations are inescapably tied to God's covenant, whether as covenant-keepers or as covenant-breakers. God's covenant is "the everlasting covenant" with all men. Man's relationship to that covenant can change from blessings to curses, but the covenant remains. As Copass noted,

> All sinning peoples come under the temporal judgment of omnipotent, Holy God, who is mighty to save, who knows that without judgment on sin there can be no salvation.

> Further, persistent sinners will know *final separation and eternal punishment.*[2]

Law and covenant are thus used synonymously, and all men are inescapably involved in that reality. Because God is God, the absolute sovereign and sole creator of all things, no independence from Him is at all possible. Man is inescapably tied to God on God's terms, His covenant or law. Although an elect people is the witness to that covenant, its witness must be on the claim of God and His covenant on all peoples without exception. For their failure to heed that covenant and its witness, all the nations of antiquity were judged and condemned.

In Jeremiah, there is a similar judgment on Judah, and also on the foreign powers (Jer. 46:1–51:64). Judgment is pronounced on Babylon "for she hath sinned against the LORD" (Jer. 50:14). Moreover, the reverse of the golden rule is the principle of God's judgment against Babylon: "take vengeance upon her: as she hath done, do unto her" (Jer. 50:15); "according to all that she hath done, do unto her" (Jer. 50:29). Against Moab, Jeremiah's word from God is that "cursed be he that keepeth back his sword from blood" (Jer. 48:10). The curses of Deuteronomy 28 are pronounced by Jeremiah on Judah and all nations for their disobedience to God, and this "is the vengeance of the LORD, the vengeance of his temple" (Jer. 51:11). Since the temple (and the tabernacle before) was God's throne room and governmental center, this means that God the King exercises vengeance on all who break His law.

Judgment upon the nations appears in Ezekiel 25:1–32:32, and elsewhere. Daniel gives us a view of the great empires and their

---

1. J. A. Alexander, *Commentary on Isaiah*, p. 406.
2. Benjamin Andrew Copass, *Isaiah, Prince of Old Testament Prophets* (Nashville: Broadman Press, 1944), p. 146.

judgment. All the prophets stress the law and the covenant, and summon men and nations to repentance, or pronounce judgment.

The conclusion of Malachi summons men thus, "Remember ye the law of Moses my servant, which I commanded unto him." If the fathers and the children are not united in faith and obedience, God declares that He shall "come and smite the earth with a curse" in the day of the Lord, the time of judgment when the Messiah is rejected (Mal. 4:4-6).

St. Paul summed up this aspect of Scripture in Hebrews 12:18-29. The superiority of the renewed covenant is strongly stressed. With "Jesus, the mediator of the new covenant," they who are of the church have come to something far greater than the fearful manifestations of Mt. Sinai. It is the same God, "a consuming fire" (Heb. 12:29; Ex. 20:18, 19), and that fact is more plainly stated by St. Paul than by Moses. The contrast between Mt. Sinai and Moses on the one hand, and Christ on the other, makes obedience to the greater all the more mandatory, and disobedience all the more damning. The ages until Christ's coming represented a great shaking of the nations, which would culminate in the fall of Jerusalem. The next great shaking would remove all those things which can be shaken, "as of things that are made, that those things which cannot be shaken may remain" (Heb. 12:27). The "things that are made" are man-made inventions which seek to supplant God's law and kingdom with the city of man. But God's elect have received "a kingdom which cannot be moved" or is unshaken (Heb. 12:28); they must therefore serve God acceptably, with reverence and awe.

Thus, even as the Old Testament era saw the radical destruction of all nations which rejected God, so the Christian era will see a great shaking of the powers that be, because of their unbelief, apostasy, and lawlessness.

The covenant which exists between God and His people has been rightly called a *covenant of grace*. It is precisely that, a covenant of grace or blessing made by the sovereign God with those whom He redeems in Christ. Opposed to the covenant of grace or blessing is *the covenant of death or curses*. The promise of God to disobedience to His law was, from the beginning in Eden, death (Gen. 2:17). The curse was operative immediately when man fell (Gen. 3:16-19; 4: 10-12). Cain was "cursed from the earth" (Gen. 4:11) for his murder of Abel, and his life thereafter manifested a covenant of death.

The people of God cannot make a covenant with those who break God's covenant (Deut. 7:2). Those who wander after other gods and covenant themselves to them shall inherit all the curses of the law (Deut. 29:18-24). The destiny of the covenant breakers is death (Rom. 1: 31-32). This is emphatically declared in Isaiah 28:14-18:

Wherefore hear the word of the LORD, ye scornful men, that rule this people which is in Jerusalem.

Because ye have said, We have made a covenant with death, and with hell are we at agreement; when the overflowing scourge shall pass through, it shall not come unto us: for we have made our lies our refuge, and under falsehood have we hid ourselves:

Therefore thus saith the LORD GOD, Behold, I lay in Zion for a foundation a stone, a tried stone, a precious corner stone, a sure foundation: He that believeth shall not make haste.

Judgment also will I lay to the line, and righteousness to the plummet: and the hail shall sweep away the refuge of lies, and the waters shall overflow the hiding place.

And your covenant with death shall be disannulled, and your agreement with hell shall not stand; when the overflowing scourge shall pass through, then ye shall be trodden down by it.

The key to the meaning of this prophetic word is well stated by Young in his comment on verse 15:

In this verse Isaiah gives a reason why the men of scorn should hear the Word of the Lord and also why it is necessary for God to lay in Zion a corner stone. What is given is not the actual language of the scorners but an evaluation of their actions. Were these actions translated into words, they would be words such as these. To state it otherwise, here is an expression of the carnally devised thoughts and purposes of the scorners; and inasmuch as thoughts such as these have motivated their actions, God Himself will intervene and erect in Zion a stone.

Isaiah addresses the rulers of "this people." *Ye have said*—Not in so many words, but this is what they purposed in their hearts. . . . If one has made a covenant with death, death will not harm him, for he and death are at peace. "You are acting," so the prophet's thought would seem to be, "as though death and the grave will not overcome you nor claim you. They come to others, but you are exempt. Round about you you have beheld others fall, and even seen the ten tribes go into captivity, but you think that death will pass you by."[3]

A covenant with death and with hell is thus the assumption that God's covenant law is not operative, that God is to all practical intent dead. It is a rejection of the world of law and causality and an insistence that man lives in a neutral, non-causal world of brute factuality. A covenant with death and hell is thus an attempt to nullify death and hell; it is a rejection of God's law-order in favor of a man-made order. Such a covenant with meaninglessness is rejected by God, and those who make it are trodden under foot by God's judgment (Isa. 28:18). This covenant with death characterizes all unbelief, and the promise of God, as rendered by the Berkeley Version, is judgment upon all.

---

3. Edward J. Young, *The Book of Isaiah* (Grand Rapids: Eerdmans, 1969) II, 282.

Isaiah's word to the scoffers of Jerusalem was this, "Now therefore, scoff no more, lest your bondage be aggravated; for of a determined annihilation upon the whole earth have I heard from the Lord God of hosts" (Isa. 28:22).

Man and nations make a covenant with death, with meaninglessness, to escape the law of God, but the response of God is to give them death, "a determined annihilation" in terms of His sovereign purpose. There is no escape from law and meaning. As Ezekiel made clear, God's purpose is to overthrow all things which oppose Christ and His kingdom: "I will overturn, overturn, overturn it; and it shall be no more, until he come whose right it is; and I will give it him" (Ezek. 21:27). God's declaration, repeated many times throughout Ezekiel, is that His judgment falls upon the lawbreakers to the end that "ye shall know that I am the Lord GOD" (Ezek. 23:49, etc.). Similarly, the law was given, and God's justice made known, the sabbath ordained "that ye may know that I am the LORD your God" (Ezek. 20:19-20, etc.). Both the law and the judgments of the law have as their purpose the revelation of God.

The law as revelation is thus a basic aspect of God's manifestation of Himself. It is, in fact, impossible to think of a revelation of God without law, for this would mean that God has no nature, no person of defined and totally self-conscious purpose. Because God is totally self-conscious and without potentialities, without undeveloped aspects, He has a full and developed law, and that law is basic to His revelation of Himself. God cannot reveal Himself without law, nor can the law be set forth without revealing God.

The implication of this is that no knowledge of God is possible if the law is rejected. To reject the law is to deny God's nature, and to deny the meaning of God the Son and His atonement. The knowledge of God is not *by* the law, but by the grace of God through faith, but this knowledge of God is inseparable from the law. The priority is with God, not with the law, but the law can no more be divorced from God than His nature can be alienated from Himself.

Barthianism, because it is antinomian, logically presupposes a god who is unknowable and beyond definition. The Barthian god gives no law because he has no law within himself, no fixed nature. By the term, "the freedom of God," Barthians mean the freedom from any law or nature. Not surprisingly, the next step theologically was to announce the death of this god.

XIII

THE LAW IN THE NEW TESTAMENT

1. Christ and the Law

One of the most important and most misunderstood of all Biblical declarations concerning the law is our Lord's declaration in the Sermon on the Mount:

> Think not that I am come to destroy the law, or the prophets: I am not come to destroy, but to fulfil.
> For verily I say unto you, Till heaven and earth pass away, one jot or tittle shall in no wise pass from the law, till all be fulfilled (Matt. 5:17, 18).

Two different words are used for the idea of fulfilment. The word translated as "fulfil" in verse 17 is *plerosai*, related *pleroma*; it means to make full, to the top, to fill, diffuse, to cause to abound, to pervade. Christians are said to be *plervusthai*, filled with the power of the Holy Spirit (Col. 2:10; Eph. 3:19). Christ "fills" the universe with His power and activity (Eph. 4:10, *pleroun*). The word means to fill and to keep full, i.e., to put into force as a continuous thing. Thus, our Lord declared that He had come to put the law into force and to keep it in force.

In verse 18, the word used is *genetai*, from *ginomai*, to become, to come to pass, happen. The law thus shall become the reality of the world's life to the end of the world. This gives us a very different perspective on the meaning of "fulfil" than those interpretations which see its meaning as ended, i.e., the fulfilment of the law as the end of the law. There is no hint of such a meaning in the text.

Rather, Christ as the Messiah or King, because He has come, declared afresh the validity of the law and His purpose to put it into force. This was powerfully stated in "A Sermon Preached Before the House of Commons in Parliament at their Public Fast, November 17, 1640," by Stephen Marshall:

> First. . . .
>
> This is the Scepter whereby Christ rules: The dwelling of his Word with a people, is the greatest proofs of their owning him for their *Prince*, and his acknowledging them for his owne *Subjects*. Is any Country esteemed a part of a Prince's Dominion, that it is not ruled by his Lawes? Neither can any Land be accounted Christ's

Kingdome, where the preaching of the Word, which is the *Rod of his power* is not established. And the Lord hath ever esteemed the hinderers of his Word, to bee the men that would not have Christ rule over them.

Secondly, if all the good Lawes in the world were made, without this, they would come to nothing; order what you can, leave this undone, you will never doe the thing you aime at. Magistrates and Ministers of Justice will not execute them, and people will not obey them. *The dark places of the Land are ever full of the habitations of wickednesse.* But if Christ *smite the earth with the rod of his mouth, the Wolfe shall dwell with the Lambe, and the Leopard shall lye down with the kid, the calfe, and the young Lion, and the fatling together, and a little Child shall leade them.* There shall nothing hurt nor destroy, where Christ's Scepter rules: Your Lawes cannot give men new hearts, nor new strength; that is the privilege of the Lawes of Christ.[1]

The fact that the King was coming to enforce His kingship and His law was very bluntly stated by John the Baptist. He spoke of "the wrath to come" (Matt. 3:7; Luke 3:7), i.e., the judgment of the King. "And now also the axe is laid unto the root of the trees: therefore every tree which bringeth not forth good fruit is hewn down, and cast into the fire" (Matt. 3:10; Luke 3:9). The King intended to judge and "thoroughly purge" His realm (Matt. 3:12). When the believing people asked John, "What shall we do then?" (Luke 3:10), John answered that they should do two things: first, obey the law, and, second, manifest charity towards those in need (Luke 3:11-14).

The temptation of Christ cannot be understood apart from the law. The temptations offered by Satan required a declaration of independence from God and His law and the choice of the creature's will as ultimate law. The answer of Christ to each temptation was a quotation from the law: Deuteronomy 6:16; 8:3, and 10:20 (cf. Josh. 24:14; I Sam. 7:3). The direction for history had to be derived not from man's will but from God's law. As King, Jesus declared God's way or "torah," and as King, He cast out demons (Luke 4:31-37). The demons acknowledged His kingship in the process (Luke 4:34; cf. Isa. 49:7). Jesus declared Himself to be "the Son of man" and "Lord" of the sabbath day (Matt. 12:8; Luke 6:5; Mark 2:28).

The Sermon on the Mount in particular identifies Christ as King and Lawgiver. He invited comparison with Moses by declaring the law from a mountain (Matt. 5:1); He made clear that He was greater than Moses, that He was God the King, by declaring, not "Thus saith

---

1. Robin Jeffs, ed., *The English Revolution, Fast Sermons to Parliament*, vol. I, Nov. 1640–Nov. 1641 (London: Cornmarket Press, 1970), p. 151 f. The texts by Marshall are Ps. 74:20 and Isa. 11:4 ff.

the Lord," but by declaring, "I say unto you" (Matt. 5:18).[2] In Deuteronomy, God pronounces the curses and blessings; in the Sermon on the Mount, Jesus Himself pronounces the blessings or beatitudes (Matt. 5:3-11). As sovereign and universal King, Jesus is also the source of all law, and Himself the law or direction of being. As thus the principle of the law and the source of all blessing, He declared Himself to be the new shibboleth whereby men are to be tested and judged. St. Peter identified Jesus as the shibboleth of God: "Neither is there salvation in any other: for there is none other name under heaven given among men, whereby we must be saved" (Acts 4:12).

As King, Jesus emphatically underscored His sovereign law:

> Whosoever therefore shall break one of these least commandments, and shall teach men so, he shall be called the least in the kingdom of heaven: but whosoever shall do and teach them, the same shall be called great in the kingdom of heaven.
> For I say unto you, That except your righteousness shall exceed the righteousness of the scribes and Pharisees, ye shall in no case enter into the kingdom of heaven (Matt. 5:19-20).

Since He is the law-giver, Jesus also determines the curses and the blessings of the law; here He spoke of the temporal and eternal consequences of the law and declared Himself the determiner of those consequences. This was an implicit identification of both God and the law with Christ.

Christ then proceeded to develop the full implications of the law, their personal as well as civil implications, their requirements of the heart as well as of the hand. To be angry "without a cause" with a covenant brother is to have murder in the heart (Matt. 5:21-24). Adultery is forbidden in thought as well as in act (Matt. 5:27-28). Against the loose practices of the day, the Biblical law of divorce is restated (Matt. 5:31-32). The third commandment is enforced and stressed as against the careless use of oaths (Matt. 5:33-37). The limitations of the law in dealing with an alien power which controls the law are cited in Matthew 5:38-42; the law cannot be enforced by enemies of the law. Our obligation even then is to observe the law, and love is the fulfilling of the law, towards our enemies (Matt. 5:43-48).

The laws of charity are also analyzed in terms of their inward obedience, as are the requirements of worship and prayer (Matt. 6:1-23).

Confidence in the rule of the king is required (Matt. 6:24-34). God

---

2. On Moses as King (Deut. 33:5), and the Messiah as the New Moses, see H. L. Ellison, *The Centrality of the Messianic Idea for the Old Testament* (London: The Tyndale Press, 1953, 1957), pp. 9, 15 ff.

the King knows our needs; we dare not doubt His government, nor to be "of little faith" (Matt. 6:30).

Personal standards cannot be made into a principle of judgment; the law of God is the only criterion (Matt. 7:1-5). Warnings are given to enable us to judge, and we are commanded to trust God, who is more faithful in our behalf than our human parents.

The test of citizenship in God's kingdom is obedience to "these sayings of mine" (Matt. 7:24). To build on Christ and His law-word is to build upon a "rock" (an ancient symbol for God), but to build on man's word is to build on sand. The one course leads to security, the other to disaster (Matt. 7:21-27).

We are told of the astonishment of His hearers, "for he taught them as one having authority, and not as the scribes" (Matt. 7:29). The word translated as "authority" is *exousia*, which means power of choice, authority, the liberty of doing as one pleases, the power of right. Jesus taught with authority; He declared Himself to be the principle of curses and blessing; men stand or fall in terms of Him. Deuteronomy 28 is reinforced in His person, for He is the law incarnate, God incarnate, the "way" (John 14:6).

The Pharisees and the rulers understood all this better than the disciples and the people. As against their loose interpretation of the law, Jesus had declared Himself to be the champion of the law in its full force, and Himself the Law-giver. They sought therefore in the case of the woman taken in adultery to embarrass Him by forcing an unpopular decision from Him (John 8:11). With respect to taxation, they again tried to crowd Him into a declaration which would harm His position as champion of the law (Matt. 21:15-22; cf. Mark 12:14; Luke 20:22). The Sadducees tried to reduce to nonsense the doctrine of resurrection as well as the law of the levirate, and again Jesus confounded them from Scripture (Matt. 22:23-33).

The repeated challenges to Jesus by the leaders of the people were in terms of the law. A determined effort was made to deny to Him the status of the champion of the law, for, as the established law order, as the rulers of their day, Christ's claims were an indictment of these men. Thus, the counterpart to the beatitudes of the Sermon on the Mount is the curse upon the leaders of the people, these perverters of the law, which Christ repeatedly pronounced, especially in Matthew 23. Upon these perverters of God's law would descend "all the righteous blood shed upon the earth" (Matt. 23:35), demanding the full vengeance of the law. No more fearful curse could be pronounced; hence their judgment was the severest of all history: "For there shall be great tribulation, such as was not since the beginning of the world to this time, no, nor ever shall be" (Matt. 24:21). This was the judgment of the King who declared that "All power is given unto me in heaven and earth" (Matt. 28:18). That power brings the total curse to those who oppose Him, His kingdom, and His law; but He Himself is the beatitude of His covenant people.

2. The Woman Taken in Adultery

During the course of our analysis of the law, repeated references were made to the confirmation of the law in the Gospels. It is not our purpose here either to repeat those confirmations or to attempt an exhaustive catalogue of every reference to the law in the Gospels. One event, however, although cited in some detail earlier, deserves further attention: the story of the woman taken in adultery in John 8:1-11. Because this particular incident has been cited as an instance of the setting aside of the law, as the prime example, in fact, it needs further attention because it in fact is a *confirmation* of the law.

Had the incident been at all antinomian, it would have provided the scribes and Pharisees with exactly the charge they wanted with which to condemn Jesus. The charge of Jesus against the scribes and Pharisees was precisely their antinomianism; He had strongly denounced them publicly for their neglect of the law for tradition (Matt. 15:1-10). No answer was possible against this charge: clearly, the leaders of the people had set aside the law by means of their humanistic legal tradition. The whole point of the attack of these leaders was to try to show that Jesus, when confronted by the hard facts of a concrete case, would be no more a strict champion of the law than they were. The culminating example of this attempt to embarrass Jesus was this incident of the woman taken in adultery. To ask for the full enforcement of the law, the death penalty, would have been to invite hostility, because the prevailing attitude was one of moral laxity. To deny the death penalty would have enabled the Pharisees to charge Jesus with hypocrisy: He would then have been in the same school of thought as the Pharisees He condemned. Quite obviously, Jesus did not take an antinomian stand, because the Pharisees left, confounded, and the incident obviously confirmed Jesus as the champion of the law.

A woman had been "taken in adultery, in the very act" (John 8:4). The woman was "brought unto him." We cannot assume that she came voluntarily. She may have been dragged there, but the text does not indicate this. Apparently "the scribes and Pharisees" involved had police powers, or had, with the assistance of the authorities, used such legal powers as were necessary to compel her compliance. Having such legal authority, they were also requiring that Jesus preside at the hearing. The man involved in the act was not brought forward; we have no knowledge of the reason for this, although it would appear that it would have aggravated the "offense" of Jesus had He either demanded the death penalty for a woman, or, on the other hand, allowed an adulterous woman to go free. More emotional reaction could be milked by the use of an adulterous woman than an adulterous man. "Now Moses in the law commanded us, that such should be stoned: but what sayest thou? This they said, tempting him, that they might have to accuse him" (John 8:5-6). The reason for the incident is plainly stated: grounds for an accusation against Jesus were sought. Would Jesus persist as the champion of the law, or would He retreat into the use of some aspect of the pharisaic tradition?

"But Jesus stooped down, and with his finger wrote on the ground, as though he heard them not" (John 8:6). At this point, the comment of Burgon is most telling and deserves full citation:

> The Scribes and Pharisees bring a woman to our SAVIOR on a charge of adultery. The sin prevailed to such an extent among the Jews that the Divine enactments concerning one so accused had long since fallen into practical oblivion. On the present occasion our LORD is observed to revive His own ancient ordinance after a hitherto unheard of fashion. The trial by bitter water, or water of conviction (See Num. v. 11-31), was a species of ordeal, intended for the vindication of innocence, the conviction of guilt. But according to the traditional belief the test proved inefficacious, unless the husband himself was innocent of the crime whereof he accused his wife.

> Let the provisions of the law, contained in Num. v. 16 to 24, be now considered. The accused Woman having been brought near, and set before the LORD, the priest took "holy water in an earthen vessel," and put "of the dust of the floor of the tabernacle into the water." Then, with the bitter water that causeth the curse in his hand, he charged the woman by oath. Next, he wrote the curses in a book and blotted them out with the bitter water; causing the woman to drink the bitter water that causeth the curse. Whereupon if she were guilty, she fell under a terrible penalty,—her body testifying visibly to her sin. If she was innocent, nothing followed.

> And now, who sees not that the Holy One dealt with His hypocritical assailants, as if they had been the accused parties? Into the presence of incarnate JEHOVAH verily they had been brought: and perhaps when He stooped down and wrote upon the ground. it was a bitter sentence against the adulterer and adulteress which He wrote. We have but to assume some connexion between the curse which He thus traced "in the dust of the floor of the tabernacle" and the words which He uttered with His lips, and He may with truth be declared to have "taken of the dust and put it on the water," and "caused them to drink of the bitter water which causeth the curse." For when, by His Holy Spirit, our great High Priest in His human flesh addressed these adulterers,—what did He but present them with living water (v. 17. So the LXX) "in an earthen vessel" (2 Cor. iv. 7; v. 1)? Did He not further charge them with

an oath of cursing, saying, "If ye have not gone aside to uncleanness, be ye free from the bitter water: but if ye be defiled"—On being presented with which alternative, did they not, self-convicted, go out one by one? And what else was this but their own acquittal of the sinful woman, for whose condemnation they had shewed themselves so impatient? Surely it was "the water of conviction" as it is six times called, which *they* had been compelled to drink; whereupon, "convicted by their own conscience," as St. John relates, they had pronounced the other's acquittal. Finally, note that by Himself declining to "condemn" the accused woman, our LORD also did in effect blot out those curses which He had already written against her in the dust,—when He made the floor of the sanctuary His "book."[1]

Because this incident took place in the temple (John 8:2), Burgon's comment is all the more to the point. The temple dust He wrote in met the requirements of the law. His action placed every accuser on trial immediately; that they were aware of this, the text makes clear, for we are told that all felt "convicted by their own conscience" (John 8:9).

Charges had been made against the woman by the "scribes and Pharisees." Their charges represented a clear-cut case against a woman taken in "the very act" of adultery. The counter-charges by Jesus, by His actions and by His declaration, "He that is without sin among you, let him first cast a stone at her" (John 8:7), broke them. As themselves guilty men, they suspected secret evidence on His part against them. They were busy trying to collect evidence against Jesus; this made it easier for them to believe that Jesus had done the same to them.

These scribes and Pharisees had preferred charges against the woman in the place of her husband; Jesus placed them in the husband's category by invoking Numbers 5 by His writing in the dust. If they were guilty, and Jesus knew of their guilt, then, if He invoked the death penalty, could He not charge them also? By invoking Numbers 5, Jesus in effect placed them on trial also: did they come to judgment with clean hands?

It will not do to plead the "high moral standards" of Pharisees. These men were planning the death of Jesus. In the face of their deliberate and calculating plans against God's Messiah, the sin of adultery was a trifling matter to such men. They had no stomach for an accusation against them which could cite God's requirement of a death penalty.

When Jesus said, "He that is without sin among you, let him first cast a stone at her" (John 8:7), He was not referring to sins in general but to the sin of adultery. A general statement would mean no court of law is possible; the specific reference meant that men

---

1. John W. Burgon, *The Woman Taken in Adultery*, p. 239 f. On the ms. evidences for the authenticity of this passage, see p. 246 ff.

guilty of a crime were not morally free to condemn that crime in another *unless* they condemned it in themselves. We are told that all these scribes and Pharisees were then "convicted by their own conscience" (vs. 9).

Moreover, Jesus had *confirmed* the death penalty; He had simply demanded honest witnesses to step forward and execute her, to "first cast a stone at her" (vs. 7). To remain as witnesses against her was to invite witnesses against themselves; to testify to a witnessed fact and confirm a death penalty against the woman was to invite a witness unto death against themselves. They left.

> When Jesus had lifted up himself, and saw none but the woman, he said unto her, Woman, where are those thine accusers? hath no man condemned thee?
> She said, No man, Lord. And Jesus said unto her, Neither do I condemn thee: Go, and sin no more (John 8:10-11).

At this point, it is necessary to distinguish between civil or juridical forgiveness. Civil forgiveness occurs when a condemned person pays the penalty for his crime, when restitution is made and the moral claims of the law are satisfied. A thief who had robbed a man of an ox and restored fivefold is thereupon forgiven. Religious forgiveness requires as a prior condition restitution, or civil forgiveness. A thief cannot be forgiven religiously if he has not made restitution.

There is a similar distinction between civil condemnation and religious condemnation. Civil condemnation is for offenses against the civil law; religious condemnation is both for offenses against the civil law and for disbelief of God and His law-word. The two kinds of forgiveness and condemnation are distinct but related.

Jesus had been asked to make a pronouncement on the civil law with respect to adultery; He affirmed the death penalty. The witnesses, however, had withdrawn their charge and had disappeared. There was thus no *legal* case against the woman. Legally, Jesus could not therefore sustain a case: "Neither do I condemn thee."

But a moral case existed. The humility of the woman, who acknowledged Him to be "Lord," indicates some evidence of change in her, and perhaps regeneration. But Jesus simply said, "Go, and sin no more," an echo of His words in John 5:14, "sin no more, lest a worse thing come unto thee."

It is more than possible that she was religiously a changed person, and forgiven by God's grace. We are simply told that no ground for legal condemnation existed at the moment. This does not rule out subsequent legal condemnation; her husband, if she had one, is not evident in this episode, but he would have had grounds for some kind of action, under existing law, if he chose. This is not the concern of the text. She was granted acquittal in terms of the evidences of the immediate "hearing." Jesus recognized the reality of her offense by His warning, "Go, and sin no more." The fact of this warning indicates some evidences of a change in her, since it was contrary to our Lord's practice to warn those who would not be warned (Matt. 7:6). For Christ to tell an unregenerate person to "sin no more" is unreasonable. The particular sin referred to was adultery. She was charged with a responsibility to chastity as an aspect of her new life in Christ.

The woman addressed Jesus as "Lord" (John 8:11); the scribes and Pharisees simply called Him "Master" (vs. 4), and the disciples themselves often spoke of Him as simply "Rabbi" (John 1:49). Her conduct here indicated a changed person.

In brief, instead of any evidence of antinomianism, this episode confirmed emphatically the position of Jesus as the champion of the law, and He confounded the attempts of the scribes and Pharisees to prove otherwise.

The sin of Phariseeism was thus exposed. Phariseeism, *first* of all, denied the necessity of conversion. Man, by his unaided free will, is able to save himself, to choose between good and evil and make himself good. Both free will and self-salvation were thus affirmed, and predestination and conversion or regeneration denied.[2] *Second*, the Pharisees had, while professing to hold to the law of God, converted it into the traditions of men. Thus, they had denied the Biblical doctrines of justification and sanctification and were accordingly the particular target of Christ's denunciation. The Pharisees, professing to be champions of God's word, were in fact its enemies and perverters.

3. Antinomianism Attacked

Several issues divided the religious leaders from Jesus. They rejected His implicit and explicit declaration of His calling as Messiah; they denied His unique status as the Son of God; they rejected His demand for a religious reformation in terms of Himself; and they resented strongly His attack on tradition. As champions of the law according to their religious and civil tradition, the leaders of the people resented Jesus' accusation that they were in fact lawless. Tradition was for them the vital and necessary development of the law; priority was thus given to tradition over the law. The Pharisees, however, saw their tradition as inseparable from the law. Jesus, on the other hand, attacked their traditions as a perversion of the law.

The issue was sharply stated at the third passover. According to Mark 7:1-23 (cf. Matt. 15:1-20), the scribes and Pharisees attacked

---

2. See Hugo Odeberg, *Phariseeism and Christianity* (St. Louis: Concordia, 1964).

Jesus for the supposed violation of the law by some of His disciples. These disciples ate their meal "with defiled, that is to say, with un-washen hands" (Mark 7:2). This does not mean that these disciples ate with dirty hands but rather with ceremonially unpurified hands. This was "the tradition of the elders" (vs. 3). It was a ritual form of separation from an "unclean" world and was seen as an aspect of the laws and a form of holiness.

The attack of Jesus on this seemingly harmless custom was very strongly worded:

> He answered and said unto them, Well hath Esaias prophesied of you hypocrites, as it is written, This people honoureth me with their lips, but their heart is far from me.
> Howbeit in vain do they worship me, teaching for doctrines commandments of men.
> For laying aside the commandment of God, ye hold the tradition of man, as the washing of pots and cups: and many other such like things ye do (Mark 7:6-8).

The disciples of Jesus had been charged with breaking the law; the answer of Jesus was to deny the validity of their man-made religious law and call their law "the commandments of men," or "the tradition of men." The scribes and Pharisees were called "hypocrites" and their worship described as "vain" or futile. Alexander's comment on verse 7 is of interest:

> The literal translation of the Hebrew words is, *and their fearing me* (i.e., their worship) *is* (or *has become*) *a precept of men, a thing taught.* . . . In our Saviour's application of the passage to the hypocrites of his day, he has reference particularly to religious teachers, as corrupting the law by their unauthorized additions.[1]

The elevation of a harmless tradition to a status equal to the law of God and equally binding on man is totally condemned by Jesus. Law means the law of God, not the commandments of men. Thus, the charge of the scribes and Pharisees against some of the disciples was turned against them: they were the lawbreakers. "Many other such like things ye do" (vs. 8).

One of these things is then specifically cited:

> And he said unto them, Full well ye reject the commandment of God that ye may keep your own tradition.
> For Moses said, Honour thy father and thy mother; and Whoso curseth father or mother, let him die the death:
> But ye say, If a man shall say to his father or mother, It is Corban, that is to say, a gift, by whatsoever thou mightest be profited by me; he shall be free.

---

1. Joseph Addison Alexander, *Commentary on the Gospel of Mark* (Grand Rapids: Zondervan, [1864]), p. 185.

> And ye suffer him no more to do aught for his father or his mother;
> Making the word of God of none effect through your tradition, which
> ye have delivered: and many such things ye do (Mark 7:9-13).

The law of Moses (vs. 10) is identified as "the commandment of God"
(vs. 9) and "the word of God" (vs. 13). The law of Moses cannot
be reduced to the dimension of a national law for Israel only, nor to
a passing thing: it is the unchanging commandment or word of the
unchanging God. The scribes and Pharisees are charged with altering,
rejecting, and nullifying the law of God.

The law of God requires honoring parents, and supporting them
economically in their need. To curse one's parents is to incur the death
penalty. Failure to support one's parents is a form of cursing them,
according to Jesus.

The scribes and Pharisees, however, exempted men from the obligation to support their parents. By pronouncing their funds "Corban,"
such men could specify the whole or part of their income as a gift to the
temple or to the priests and Levites. "That such things were permitted
and applauded may be proved by certain dicta of the Talmud, and
especially by a famous dispute between Rabbi Eliezer and his brethren,
in which the very act here described was vindicated by the latter."[2]
Religion was thus used to condone the violation of God's law (vs. 12).
Again Jesus declared, "Many such like things do ye" (vs. 13). Their
violation of God's law was not occasional: it was basic and radical. They
were making the word of God of none effect by their tradition.

The scribes and Pharisees prided themselves, St. Paul informs us,
of being leaders of the blind, "a guide of the blind" (Rom. 2:19).
Their traditions they saw as a valid and important instrument in guiding
the blind. Now, informed that the Pharisees were offended by His remarks, Jesus pressed the matter further:

> But he answered and said, Every plant, which my heavenly Father
> hath not planted, shall be rooted up.
> Let them alone: they be blind leaders of the blind. And if the
> blind lead the blind, both shall fall into the ditch (Matt. 15:13-14).

The Pharisees were "blind leaders of the blind," and their destiny was
the ditch. But even more, Jesus emphatically rejected *every law* except
those laws given by God: "Every plant, which my heavenly Father
hath not planted, shall be rooted up." Since the issue at stake is the
law, His reference in "plant" is clearly to the law, although more is
intended, because a generalization is made. The particular example
from which the generalization is made is God's law, and the primary
meaning is law. Thus, every law order not planted by God, not faith-

---

2. *Ibid.*, p. 189.

fully grounded on the law of God, "shall be rooted up." Not only is antinomianism condemned but also legalism, which is the substitution of man's law for the law of God.

The things which defile a man, which render him unclean before God, come from within. Lawlessness is the substitution of man's way for God's way, of man's law for God's law. Lawlessness declares, "Yea, hath God said . . .?" (Gen. 3:1). The outward act of lawlessness is the product of an inner defilement, which then defiles the world outside by its actions:

> And he said, That which cometh out of the man, that defileth the man.
> For from within, out of the heart of men, proceed evil thoughts, adulteries, fornications, murders,
> Thefts, covetousness, wickedness, deceit, lasciviousness, an evil eye, blasphemy, pride, foolishness:
> All these evil things come from within, and defile the man (Mark 7:20-23).

The Pharisees were environmentalists; that which came from without defiled the man. As against this, Jesus emphatically stressed the heart of man as the source of defilement. Environmentalism leads to antinomianism, because it denies responsibility in favor of environmental conditioning. The law of God stresses responsibility and allows no man to escape it. Purity for the Pharisees was progressively becoming a ceremonial matter, a question of isolating themselves from a contaminating world. According to Jesus, however, every man is his own source of contamination; "from within," He declared, as against the Pharisees, not from without, comes the defilement. Because of this antinomianism, the Pharisees were logically developing a new law, the tradition of men, to escape from the anti-environmentalist force of God's law. Their ceremonial washings were thus not harmless: by such washings they assumed that the world was the source of contamination, not their own fallen nature. It was inescapable therefore that they preferred their tradition to the law of God. In attacking the Pharisees, Jesus was therefore condemning every form of antinomianism in every age. Antinomianism can thus never legitimately call itself Christian.

If the world is the basic source of contamination, the logic of law requires environmental reconditioning; the world must be remade in order to save man. If the basic source of defilement is, as Jesus declared, "from within, out of the heart of men," then the salvation of man is conversion or regeneration. Man must be remade if the world itself is to be saved. We have thus two opposed doctrines of salvation and of law.

4. The Transfiguration

The relationship between Jesus and Moses is stressed by the Gospels. Like Moses, Jesus gives the law from the mountain. Moses mediated between God and Israel, setting forth therein the function of the greater Moses. The prophecy concerning the Messiah was that He would be like Moses (Deut. 18:18-19). Even as Moses led God's people from captivity to freedom, so the greater Moses would lead God's covenant race.

The comparison made between Moses and Christ is especially clear in the accounts of the transfiguration (Matt. 17:1-9; Mark 9:2-10; Luke 9:28-36). At several points, the comparison is marked.

First of all, the incident occurred on a mount. Most commentators are concerned with identifying the mountain rather than analyzing the significance of a mountain retreat. Privacy in other places would also have been possible. Clearly the choice of a mountain invited comparison with Moses, and Jesus self-consciously fulfilled the prophecy inplicit in the typology. Even as Moses went up into the mountain, after the first disastrous episode, to return with renewed tables of law, and himself transfigured, so Jesus ascended the mountain. He had already given the law from the mountain, i.e., His confirmation of the law in the Sermon on the Mount. Now, like Moses, He was to be transfigured. The transfigured Moses gave the directions for building the tabernacle; the transfigured Christ, as the true tabernacling presence of God, fulfilled all that the sacrifices of the old tabernacle typifyed. The fact that the disciples tended to expect the literal restoration of Israel's political power was confirmed by the transfiguration event; in the framework of their insistent expectations, the transfiguration seemed to confirm their hope.

Second, Jesus was "transfigured before them." Matthew tells us that "his face did shine as the sun, and his raiment was white as the light" (Matt. 17:2). Mark states that "his raiment became shining, exceeding white as snow; so as no fuller on earth can white them" (Mark 9:3), and Luke states that "the fashion of his countenance was altered, and his raiment was white and glistening" (Luke 9:29). The transfiguration of Moses is thus repeated and surpassed.

> And it came to pass, when Moses came down from mount Sinai with the two tables of testimony in Moses' hand, when he came down from the mount, that Moses wist not that the skin of his face shone while he talked with him.
> And when Aaron and all the children of Israel saw Moses, behold, the skin of his face shone; and they were afraid to come nigh him (Ex. 34:29-30).
> And till Moses had done speaking with them, he put a vail on his face.

But when Moses went in before the LORD to speak with him, he took the vail off, until he came out. And he came out, and spake unto the children of Israel that which he was commanded.

And the children of Israel saw the face of Moses, that the skin of Moses' face shone; and Moses put the vail upon his face again, until he went in to speak with him (Ex. 34:33-35).

The experience of Moses is repeated on the mount to point to Jesus as the greater Moses.

Third, "And there appeared unto them Elias with Moses: and they were talking with Jesus" (Mark 9:4). In their persons, the law and the prophets witnessed to the Great Lawgiver and the Supreme Prophet.

There was, it was obvious, a singular fitness in each case. One was the great representative of the Law, which was a "schoolmaster" or "servant-tutor" leading men to Christ, the other of the whole goodly fellowship of the prophets. Of one it had been said that a "Prophet like unto him" should come in the latter days (Deut xviii. 18), to whom men should hearken; of the other, that he should come again to "turn the hearts of the fathers to the children" (Mal. iv. 5). The close of the ministry of each was not after the "common death of all men." No man knew the sepulchre of Moses (Deut. xxxiv. 6), and Elijah had passed away in the chariots and horses of fire (2 Kings ii. 11). Both were associated in men's minds with the glory of the kingdom of the Christ. The Jerusalem Targum on Ex. xiii. connects the coming of Moses with that of the Messiah. Another Jewish tradition predicts his appearance with that of Elijah. Their presence now was an attestation that their work was over, and that the Christ had come.[1]

Rather than witnessing, however, that their work was over, of which the text gives no hint, the presence of Moses and Elijah with Jesus attests to their unity. Their work and ministry was one word and one ministry; no division can be made between Jesus and the law and the prophets. Moses and Elijah "appeared in glory" (Luke 9:31), and Jesus Himself was transfigured and glorified, so that the three reveal together the glory of God.

Fourth, "they spake of his decease which he should accomplish at Jerusalem" (Luke 9:31), literally, "the decease or departure of him." The word translated as "decease" is in Greek *exodon,* our English word "exodus." Luke's choice of word was not accidental. Moses led the people of God in their exodus from Egypt; Elijah witnessed to their apostasy and thus implicitly to the coming exodus from the land of promise. Now Jesus was to accomplish the true exodus at Jerusalem. By His atoning death and resurrection, Jesus would lead the people of God from the land of bondage into true freedom. Hebrews 4 de-

---

1. C. J. Gloucester and Bristol, commentary on Matthew XVII. 3, in Ellicott, VI, 104.

velops this same point by contrasting Joshua and Jesus as each led God's people into their sabbath or rest. The emphasis here is on the exodus to be accomplished at Jerusalem, not on the vision itself. Hence, when Peter sought to concentrate on the fact of the vision rather than its call to action in history, his statement was disregarded (Luke 9:33).

Nixon has called attention to the extensive use of the Exodus theme in the New Testament. A few of the many events cited are the baptism of Jesus by John, a "sacramental representation of the historical Exodus of Israel and, at the same time, an introduction to the New Exodus of salvation"; the forty days of temptation in the wilderness "are a miniature of the forty years which Israel spent in the wilderness. . . . The temptations put to Christ are basically those to which Israel had yielded":

> Where they had been dissatisfied with Yahweh's provision of manna, He is tempted to turn stones into bread. Where they put God to the test at Massah demanding proof of His presence and power, He is tempted to jump from the Temple pinnacle to force God to honour His promises. Where they forgot the Lord who had brought them out of Egypt and substituted a molten calf for Him, He is tempted to fall down and worship Satan. Christ is shown to meet the temptations not arbitrarily but deliberately from Moses' summary in Deuteronomy of the history of Israel in the wilderness. If Jesus really was the true representative of God's people, he too must be shown to have had his wilderness journey and endured the test which proved his person, only without sin.[2]

The sending of the Seventy (Luke 10:1 ff.) is also an echo of the Exodus experience (Num. 11:16 ff.). "There is then to be a new conquest of Canaan. Its cities will be destroyed in a day of judgment (Mk. 8:12; Mt. 16:4; Mt. 12:39; Lk. 7:31 f.)."[3]

Fifth, Jesus was thus attested to by the law and the prophets, and by God Himself, as the Greater Moses. The voice of God out of the cloud (a symbol of God in judgment) declared, "This is my beloved Son, in whom I am well pleased; hear ye him" (Matt. 17:5). St Peter tells us exactly what this meant:

> For Moses truly said unto the fathers, A prophet shall the Lord your God raise up unto you of your brethren, like unto me; him shall ye hear in all things whatsoever he shall say unto you.
> And it shall come to pass, that every soul which will not hear that prophet, shall be destroyed from among the people (Acts 3:22-23).

---

2. R. E. Nixon, *The Exodus in the New Testament* (London: The Tyndale Press, 1962), p. 14 f.
3. *Ibid.,* p. 17.

Moses gave the law; those who refused to hear him refused to submit to the law of God; they revealed their unregenerate nature thereby. Jesus is like unto Moses; He is the great and ultimate Lawgiver incarnate. To listen to Him is to listen to all the law and the prophets and much more. To reject Him is to deny the law and the prophets as well as His person. Every person who fails to hear Him should be "destroyed from among the people." In Deuteronomy 18:19, which Peter quoted, the text reads, "I will require it of him." The threat or promise of destruction appears in Exodus 12:15, 19; Leviticus 17:4, 9, etc. The ultimate meaning of "cutting off" is required here and is applied by Peter because to disobey the law-word of Jesus Christ is to be a radically lawless person.

God's "hear ye him" did not call for hearing Jesus as against Moses and Elijah, for they appear in glorified unity with Him. The command to hear Jesus is to hear the Christ, whose word is the totality of Scripture, as against the scribes and the Pharisees, the leaders of the people. They are to hear Jesus Christ, which means hearing Moses and Elijah, as against the powers of this world, and as against its philosophers and religious leaders. They are to hear Jesus rather than the men of a "faithless and perverse generation" (Luke 9:41).

It is blasphemy therefore to separate the law from Jesus Christ. The fact that this is being done is an evidence of religious decline and collapse. As evidence of this fact, witness a letter from a first year student at a prominent seminary which prides itself on its "orthodoxy":

> Dr. W. put the whole discussion (of abortion) in the purely academic sphere when he divorced morality from society by saying that since this is a *democracy*, the state would have to base its decision concerning abortion laws on the will of the majority of the people. If they think abortion is harmful to society, they ought to prohibit it, if not, then let 'er rip!! His antinomianism is appalling.

> I suppose that is the thing I find most troubling here (more in students than professors, but in the latter to some extent)—the antinomianism. The old "I never mix religion and politics . . ." line. . . . It is so bad among some of the folks that when I was trying to discuss God's law in politics and society with one of the students here in the first week I was here, he said that the trouble with me was that I was "tight-assed!"

> Now, I've associated a lot of things with desiring to keep God's law, but never *that!!!*

> One thing that disturbed me about that abortion thing was that it was more or less assumed by all there, even those who opposed general abortion, that "therapeutic abortion" was morally justifiable. If you are trying to save the mother, murder is justified. . . . So murder (of anyone?) for a "good cause" is OK. It is

hard to see why they can't see the fallacy of that. Murder is murder.[4]

Such a position is anti-Biblical and anti-Christian, as all antinomianism inescapably is.

Salvation is by the grace of God through faith; sanctification is by the law of God. Those outside of grace feel the law as an indictment; it is a death sentence against them. Those who are in the covenant are in a covenant of grace which is also a covenant of works. The grace enables them to perform the works which are required of them. The warfare of Jesus was not against Moses: it was against the scribes and Pharisees who perverted Moses. It is a perversion of Scripture to separate the law and the prophets from Jesus. The mount of transfiguration witnessed to their unity.

Foulkes has rightly pointed to the covenant and the law as a unity, the covenant as the principle of prediction, and also the basis of prayer.

> It is significant also that for Israel the Law is not just a statement of abstract principles, a carefully worked out code of behaviour formulated as such. The Law is the expression of the righteousness and mercy of God. It is the statement of the principles of the covenant. The Old Testament setting of the Law is the giving of the covenant at the Exodus. The Decalogue begins, "I am the Lord thy God, which brought thee out of the land of Egypt, out of the house of bondage. . . ."
>
> The Law, therefore, contains not just a code for Israel to keep, but the principles of God's actions in the past, which remain the same for the present and the future.[5]

Antinomianism has furthered the development of a humanistic law, and humanistic law has stimulated the growth of antinomianism. When men have seen humanistic law assume a messianic character and at the same time dissolve the foundations of society, it has been easy for them to develop a theological hostility to law. In Scripture, however, the law is proclaimed to the elect people, to the covenant of grace; and the opening sentence of the law, as Foulkes noted, celebrates that grace.

5. The Kingdom of God

Luke reports an interesting statement by our Lord on the relationship of the law and the prophets to the Kingdom of God:

---

4. From a letter of October 17, 1970. (With respect to cases where supposedly the doctor must choose between the life of the mother or the life of the baby, I have been unable to find doctors who can cite any such cases. I cannot believe God ever puts any man in a situation where he must play God. The whole matter of therapeutic abortions is an attempt to create situations where man must play God.—RJR)
5. Francis Foulkes, *The Acts of God, A Study of the Basis of Typology in the Old Testament* (London: The Tyndale Press, 1955), p. 17.

And the Pharisees also, who were covetous, heard all these things: and they derided him.

And he said unto them, Ye are they which justify yourselves before men; but God knoweth your hearts: for that which is highly esteemed among men is abomination in the sight of God.

The law and the prophets were until John: since that time the kingdom of God is preached, and every man presseth into it.

And it is easier for heaven and earth to pass, than one tittle of the law to fail (Luke 16:14-17).

The force of this last verse can in no wise be diminished. "The scribes and Pharisees had been tampering with the sacredness of the laws which are not of to-day or yesterday—fixed as the everlasting hills— and they are told that their casuistry cannot set aside the claims of those laws in any single instance, such, e.g., as that which immediately follows."[1] Plainly, verse 17 makes clear that the law is in no sense done away with; it is still in force. Geldenhuys comments on verses 17 and 18:

17. But although it is a fact with His advent a new order, a new dispensation is entered upon, this does not mean that the revelation of God under the Old Covenant is set aside or rejected. Although it is of a preparatory nature, it remains (naturally in a moral and spiritual sense and in the full light of the divine revelation in and through Jesus) absolutely authoritative.

18. The moral laws, e.g., may be violated—adultery continues to be adultery, even although the time of preparation is superseded by the time of fulfilment.[2]

The problem is with respect to the first part of verse 16, "The law and the prophets were until John," or, as the Berkeley Version renders it, "Till John we had the law and prophets." This cannot mean that the law and prophets are no longer valid or in force, for this would conflict with the conclusion of verse 17. If "it is easier for heaven and earth to pass away than for one iota of the law to lapse" (vs. 17, B.V.). then the law has not lapsed and something else is intended by verse 16. The next clause of verse 16 makes clear what is intended: "Since that time the kingdom of God is preached." Until John, the *preaching* was

---

1. Gloucester and Bristol, "Luke," in Ellicott, VI, 322.
2. Norval Geldenhuys, *Commentary on the Gospel of Luke* (Grand Rapids, Eerdmans, 1951), p. 421. With respect to Luke 16:18, many hold that this bars divorce or at least the remarriage of divorced people. Thus, it is held by one scholar that "The remarriage of divorced persons is prohibited in Scripture" (H. C. Hoeksema, "About Marriage Regulations for Priests in Leviticus," *The Standard Bearer*, vol. XLVII, no. 5 [Dec. 1, 1970], p. 115). The Mosaic law permitting divorce is nowhere set aside; I Cor. 7:15 confirms it. The point of Luke 16:18 is that the lawless divorces of the day, such as those condoned by the Pharisees' perversion of the law, have no standing before God. Matt. 19:9 makes clear that the permission for remarriage is denied only to those who lack Biblical grounds for divorce; divorce and remarriage are not barred to those who have godly grounds.

from the law and the prophets; now God the King, in Christ's person, preaches. Both clauses deal with a proclamation: the one with a fore-telling, the other with an advent. Christ the King has come: the King is the Lawgiver and the great enforcer. As the King, He comes to gather His people together and to possess their inheritance for them.

The consequence is that "every man presseth into it" (vs. 16). Lenski translates this verse thus: "The law and the prophets—till John, from then on the Kingdom of God is preached as good news, and everyone is energetically pressing into it."[3] This means, as Plummer noted, that "the Jew has no longer any exclusive rights."[4] All nations are summoned into the new covenant now. This change does not, however, invalidate the law. "There are several Jewish sayings which declare that anyone who is guilty of interchanging any of these similar letters (the iotas and the letters they distinguish) in certain passages in the O.T. will destroy the whole word."[5] These sayings are echoed by Christ in verse 17.

Those who "press" into the kingdom did not include the leaders of the people, as Jesus made clear in the "parable" of Lazarus and the rich man (Luke 16:19-31). Nowhere else is a person in a parable named. Tertullian, in *De Anima* (vii) held the name to be evidence that the narrative was not a parable but history. What the story does clearly teach is that the prominent men of Judea would not believe: "Neither will they be persuaded, though one rose from the dead" (vs. 31), as Christ soon did. On the other hand, peoples from all over the world pressed into the kingdom and submitted to its law. Thus, on the one hand, the scribes and the Pharisees rejected Jesus Christ and ex-changed the law for human tradition; on the other hand, many peoples pressed into the kingdom, accepting Christ as their Redeemer and King and submitting to His law. Edersheim noted that "The Parable itself is strictly of the Pharisees and their relation to the 'publicans and sinners' whom they despised, and to whose stewardship they opposed their own proprietorship."[6] Of verse 17, Edersheim observed,

> Yes—it was true that the Law could not fail in one tittle of it. But, notoriously and in everyday life, the Pharisees, who thus spoke of the Law and appealed to it, were the constant and open breakers of it. Witness here the teaching and practice concerning divorce, which really involved a breach of the seventh commandment.[7]

The King had come, and therefore the Kingdom of God was now

---

3. R. C. H. Lenski, *Interpretation of St. Luke's Gospel* (Columbus, Ohio: The Wartburg Press, 1946, 1951), p. 839.
4. Alfred Plummer, *A Critical and Exegetical Commentary on the Gospel According to S. Luke* (Edinburgh: T. & T. Clark, 1910), p. 389.
5. *Ibid.*, p. 389.
6. Alfred Edersheim, *The Life and Times of Jesus the Messiah* (New York: Longmans, Green, 1897), II, 277.
7. *Ibid.*

manifested in a sense not possible when God ruled from the tabernacle. The King, by declaring His universal kingship and summoning all the peoples of the earth to press in, was thereby taking away the kingdom from His false deputies (Matt. 21:43). Edersheim observed, of the kingdom passages of the New Testament,

> In fact, an analysis of 119 passages in the New Testament where the expression "Kingdom" occurs, shows that it means *the rule of God;* which was *manifested in and through Christ;* is *apparent in the Church; gradually develops amidst hindrances*; is *triumphant at the second coming of Christ* ("the end"); and finally, *perfected in the world to come.* Thus viewed, the announcement of John of the near Advent of this Kingdom has deepest meaning, although, as so often in the case of prophetism, the stages intervening between the Advent of Christ and the triumph of that Kingdom seem to have been hidden from the preacher. He came to call Israel to submit to the Reign of God, about to be manifested in Christ. Hence, on the one hand, he called them to repentance—a "change of mind"—with all that this implied; and, on the other, pointed them to Christ, in the exaltation of His Person and Office. Or rather, the two combined might be summed up in the call: "Change your mind"—repent, which implies, not only a turning from the past, but a turning to the Christ in newness of mind. And thus the symbolic action by which this preaching was accompanied might be designated "the baptism of repentance."[8]

In Matthew 11:20-24, Jesus denounced the cities of Israel for rejecting Him. Sodom and Tyre would fare better on judgment day than these cities, where Phariseeism was enthroned. As against the leaders of Israel, Jesus offered an easy "yoke" (Matt. 11:29-30). The expression refers to a common Jewish expression of the day, "to take up the yoke of the kingdom of heaven," meaning "to vow obedience to the law."[9] The law of Israel had come to be the unbearable yoke of human tradition which made the law of God of none effect. In its place, Jesus offered the easy yoke of God's law. "In his teaching the kingdom once more becomes a kingdom of grace as well as of law, and thus the balance so beautifully preserved in the Old Testament is restored."[10] The term "kingdom of heaven" is the same as "kingdom of God"; the Jewish habit of avoiding the use of the name of God led to a frequent use of the former phrase.[11]

In the Lord's Prayer, the great petition at the beginning is, "Thy kingdom come. Thy will be done, in earth as it is in heaven" (Matt. 6:10). The prayer concludes, "For thine is the kingdom, and the

---

8. *Ibid.*, I, 270.
9. Geerhardus Vos, *The Teaching of Jesus Concerning the Kingdom and the Church* (Grand Rapids: Eerdmans, 1951), p. 18.
10. *Ibid.*, p. 19.
11. *Ibid.*, p. 24.

power, and the glory, for ever. Amen" (Matt. 6:13).[12] The entrance into that kingdom is by God's electing grace; the rules of that kingdom are the commandments of God, His law. For those in grace, the yoke is easy, and the burden is light, because grace answers to the law.

6. The Tribute Money

One of the best-known stories of the New Testament is the one concerning the tribute money question: "Is it lawful to give tribute unto Caesar or not?" Christ's answer, "Render therefore unto Caesar the things which are Caesar's; and unto God the things that are Gods" (Matt. 22:15-22; Mark 12:13-17; Luke 20:20-26), is one of the most familiar sentences of Scripture. The general implications have long been recognized; in the specific application, there has been much variation.

The purpose of the Pharisees is again to "entangle him in his talk" (Matt. 22:15); Luke is more specific, "And they watched him, and sent forth spies, which should feign themselves just men, that they might take hold of his words, that so they might deliver him unto the power and authority of the governor" (Luke 20:20-26). The Roman governor was meant. Apparently the expectation was that Jesus, in faithfulness to the law, would declare that only a theocracy was valid in Israel, not Roman rule and law. Behind this strategy were the Pharisees and the Herodians (Matt. 22:16; Mark 12:13), a minor, political, non-religious party of the day. The Herodians favored the Roman tax and the Herodian dynasty, which they regarded as preferable to direct Roman rule. The Pharisees were normally hostile to the Herodians, but they joined forces in hostility to Jesus. If Jesus opposed the tax, He could be denounced and delivered to the Roman authorities for arrest and trial.

The question was prefaced with fulsome flattery; the questioners asked as if motivated by a tender conscience rather than a desire to entrap. They attempted to push Jesus into an answer heedless of consequences by asserting that "thou art true, and carest for no man; for thou regardest not the person of men, but teachest the way of God in truth" (Mark 12:14). Such an integrity, they hoped, would compel Him to deny the legitimacy of the Roman tax. "Is it lawful for us to give tribute unto Caesar, or no?" (Luke 20:22).

The Greek text makes clear that the tax was a "capitation tax," not an indirect tax.[1] "Luke uses *phoros*, the wider word for 'tribute' as it is

---

12. For the ms. evidence for this petition, see Edward F. Hills, *The King James Version Defended* (Des Moines, Iowa: Christian Research Press, 1956), pp. 97-102.

1. Plummer, *Luke*, p. 465.

paid by one nation to another; Matthew and Mark use the more specific *kenos* or poll tax that is levied upon every individual for his own person and is thus especially galling as a mark of servitude to the Roman power."[2]

Israel already had a poll tax, that required by God's law in Exodus 30:11-16. Its purpose was to provide for civil atonement, i.e., the covering or protection of civil government. Every male twenty years old or older was required to pay this tax to be protected by God the King in His theocratic government of Israel. This tax was thus a civil and religious duty (but not an ecclesiastical one).

There was thus a particular aggravation in the fact that Rome also required a poll or head tax. The Roman Empire and emperor were progressively assuming divine roles, requiring religious assent, and claiming priority over religion. The poll tax was thus a particularly offensive tax, in that it seemed to require a polytheistic faith, the worship of a god other than the true God. Moreover, the Herodian tax was so heavy that twice the imperial government compelled Herod to reduce his tax demands in order to avoid serious trouble. Judas Galilaeus had earlier presented himself as the messiah and had summoned Israel, in the name of God and Scripture, to refuse to pay the tax. The Romans were merciless in putting down the rebellion (Acts 5:37).

The matter had been aggravated as early as A.D. 29 by Pilate, who for a time issued coinage "bearing the *lituus*, the priest's staff, or the *patera*, the sacrificial bowl—two symbols of the imperial philosophy which were bound to be obnoxious to the people."[3] These coins were later withdrawn, but they did serve to underscore the fact that their bondage to Rome had religious overtones.

The right to issue coins had religious overtones for Israel as I Maccabees 15:6 implies, and it was thus important to them. " 'Coin' and 'power' were regarded as synonyms, so that the coin was the symbol of the ruler's dominance."[4] In the second century A.D., Bar Kochba, the false messiah, replaced Roman coinage with his own coins as a means of asserting his power. To give tribute to Caesar thus meant to acknowledge Caesar's power; to approve of giving tribute to Caesar was to acknowledge the legitimacy of Caesar's power. The question implicit in the Herodian's statement was whether any government other than God's has any legitimacy. Christ's assertion of His messiahship was seen by his accusers as a denial of Caesar's right to tax (Luke 23:2), since the Messiah as King had to have exclusive sovereignty, in their

---

2. Lenski, *Luke*, p. 988.
3. Ethelbert Stauffer, *Christ and the Caesars* (Philadelphia: Westminster Press, 1955), p. 119.
4. *Ibid.*, p. 125.

perspective. For Jesus to have denied Caesar's right to tax Israel was a mark of insurrection and would make Him liable to arrest. For Jesus to have affirmed Caesar's right to tax would have been, in the eyes of the people, a denial of His messiahship.

The answer of Jesus was to ask for a denarius; He asked it of His questioners. As Stauffer, whose chapter on "The Story of the Tribute Money" is very important, has written:

> Jesus asked for a penny, a *denarius*. Why? There were a great many coins in the wide Roman empire which passed as legal currency, old and new, large and small, imperial and local, gold, silver, copper, bronze and brass. In no country did so many different kinds of money circulate as in Palestine. But the prescribed coin for taxation purposes throughout the empire was the *denarius*, a little silver coin of about the worth of a shilling. (It can only be the silver *denarius* which is intended in Mark 12:16, Luke 20:24 and Matt. 22:19, not a gold coin as Titian supposed, in his representation of the tribute scene, nor a Herodian coin, as is often asserted; for the Herodian coins were not called *denarii* and were not tribute coins, but were local copper coins.) Jesus knew this, and so He asked for the silver imperial tax coin, using the Latin word, the Roman technical expression, which had become current in Palestine along with the coin itself. Bring me a *denarius*, He said. He did not produce one from His own pocket. Why not? The point now is not whether Jesus had such a coin in His pocket but whether His opponents had. With Socratic irony, he added: "That I may see it?" Why? He had the maieutic purpose with his questioners, He wanted to deliver them, in the Socratic manner, not *a priori*, but *a posteriori*. Not their logical or moral sense, but their historical situation and attitude would bring the truth to light. Something is to be seen, and deduced, from the *denarius* itself.[5]

When the coin was handed to Jesus, He did not yet answer their question, "Is it lawful to give tribute to Caesar, or not?" Instead, He asked another question: "Whose is this image and superscription?" (Matt. 22:20; Mark 12:16; Luke 20:24). The answer was, of course, "Caesar's." According to Geldenhuys,

> After their acknowledgment that it is Caesar's, the following two facts are vividly brought to light through Jesus' masterly handling of the situation:
>
> (1) Coins with Caesar's image and superscription are in use among the Jews.
>
> (2) The coins are evidently the property of Caesar, otherwise they would not have borne his image and superscription.
>
> From these two facts it thus follows that the Jews had accepted the imperial rule as a practical reality, for it was the generally current view that a ruler's power extended as far as his coins were in use.[6]

---

5. *Ibid.*, p. 122 f.   6. Geldenhuys, *Luke*, p. 504.

The practical reality was thus made clear. These men used the coins of Tiberius which carried a "bust of Tiberius in Olympian nakedness, adorned with the laurel wreath, the sign of divinity." The inscription read, "Emperor Tiberius August Son of the August God," on the one side, and "Pontifex Maximus" or "High Priest" on the other. The symbols also included the emperor's mother, Julia Augusta (Livia) sitting on the throne of the gods, holding the Olympian sceptre in her right hand, and, in her left, the olive branch to signify that "she was the earthly incarnation of the heavenly Pax."[7] The coins thus had a religious significance. Israel was in a certain sense serving other gods by being subject to Rome and to Roman currency. The point made by implication by His enemies, that tribute to Caesar had religious overtones, was *almost* confirmed by Jesus, even as He proved their own submission to Caesar.

Then came His great answer: "Render to Caesar the things that are Caesars, and to God the things that are God's (Mark 12:17). According to Stauffer, *render* here means "give back." "That is the first great surprise in this verse, and its meaning is: the payment of tribute to Caesar is not only your unquestioned obligation; it is also your moral duty."[8] St. Paul used the same term in Romans 13:7, "Render to all their dues: tribute to whom tribute is due; custom to whom custom. . . ." Judea was living within the Roman Empire, gaining military and economic benefits from that empire whether it wanted them or not. Even if the benefits of the empire were outweighed by its liabilities, the people were still to render Caesar his due.

The fact still remained that two poll taxes stood in opposition, one paid to the emperor, the other to God. The imperial tax provided "for the daily sacrifice for the welfare of the Roman emperor"; it maintained the empire as a religious entity.[9] The other tax, called then the temple tax, was God's tax for maintaining His holy order. How could both taxes be paid? According to Stauffer, "He affirmed the symbolism of power, but He rejected the symbolism of worship. But this reservation was not made as a negative statement, but rather as a positive command. 'Render to God what is God's' "[10] Stauffer is right in asserting that, according to Numbers 8:13 ff., this means that "Everything belongs to God."[11] At the time that Jesus spoke, the Biblical poll tax was being collected in the spring, in the month of Adar. More specifically, Jesus asked that Caesar's tax be rendered to Caesar, and God's tax be rendered to God. The early church was apparently aware of this fact. Jerome, commenting on Matthew 22:21, declared, "Render unto Caesar the things that are Caesar's, namely, coins, tribute, money; and to God

7. Stauffer, *op. cit.*, p. 124 f.   9. *Ibid.*, p. 131.   11. *Ibid.*
8. *Ibid.*, p. 129.   10. *Ibid.*, p. 132.

the things that are God's, namely, tithes, first-fruits, vows, sacrifices."[12]

Israel's departure from God's rule and law had placed them under Roman rule and law; they owed to Rome the tribute due to Rome. Rome did not serve God, but neither did Israel. Obedience is due to all authorities under whom we find ourselves (Rom. 13:1-7). Rome was now their master, and Rome had to be obeyed. Obedience to God requires obedience to all those whom we find ourselves in subjection to. In the temptation in the wilderness, Satan had tempted Jesus to follow a way of empire: give the people bread and miracles; enable them to walk by sight. Now, through other tempters, the temptation was offered of rejecting all empires, all earthly powers.

> Christ conquered this temptation afresh with His words about the double duty of obedience to the way and to the goal of history, to the kingdom of the world and to the kingdom of God. Mark 12:17 is spoken by Christ *in conspectu mortis*, in the sight of the messianic death. Holy Week is the existential exegesis of His words: submission to the dominion of Caesar, submission to the dominion of God—united in the acceptance of that monstrous judicial murder by which Caesar's most wretched creature fulfils *sub contrario* the work of God (Matt. 26:52 ff.; John 19:11).[13]

Let us return to St. Jerome's words. Two kinds of taxation exist, and Christ requires our obedience to both. The world of Caesar seeks to create a new world without God, and without regeneration; it exacts a heavy tax and accomplishes little or nothing. We are, as sinners, geared by our fallen nature to seeking Caesar's answer. We pay tribute to Caesar thus, in our faith and with our money. The answer to Caesar's world is not civil disobedience, the final implication of which is revolution. This is Caesar's way, the belief that man's effort by works of law can remake man and the world.

The answer rather is to obey all due authorities and to pay tribute, custom, and honor to whom these things are due. This is the minor aspect of our duty. More important, we must render, give back to God what is His due, our tithes, first-fruits, vows, and sacrifices. The regenerate man begins by acknowledging God, the author and Redeemer of his life, as his lord and savior, his King. At *every* point in his life, he renders to God His due service, thanksgiving, praise, and tithe. His salvation is God's gift; the bounty he enjoys is God's gift and providence; the regenerate man therefore renders, gives back to God, God's appointed share of all things.

The way of resistance to Rome chosen by Judea led to the world's worst war and to the death of the nation. Neither the Roman imperial answer nor the Judean revolutionary answer offered anything but

---

12. *Ibid.*   13. *Ibid.*, p. 135.

death and disaster. Self-consciously, the Christians followed their Lord. Justin Martyr wrote:

> And everywhere we, more readily than all men, endeavour to pay to those appointed by you the taxes both ordinary and extraordinary, as we have been taught by Him; for at that time some came to Him and asked Him, if one ought to pay tribute to Caesar; and He answered, "Tell me, whose image does this coin bear?" And they said, "Caesar's"; And again He answered them, "Render therefore to Caesar the things that are Caesar's, and to God the things that are God's." Whence to God alone we render worship, but in other things we gladly serve you, acknowledging you as kings and rulers of men, and praying that with your kingly power you be found to possess also sound judgment. But if you pay no regard to our prayers and frank explanations, we shall suffer no loss, since we believe (or rather, indeed, are persuaded) that every man will suffer punishment in eternal fire according to the merit of his deed, and will render account according to the power he has received from God, as Christ intimated when He said, "To whom God has given more, of him shall more be required."[14]

Christ's answer did not prevent His enemies from charging Him with "perverting the nation, and forbidding to give tribute to Caesar" (Luke 23:2). His answer in reality had demolished all grounds for any accusation against Him.

Their duty, Jesus had declared, was "to render back" "to pay what is owing"[15] to Caesar and to God. What is due to Caesar is due to Caesar only by the providence, purpose, and counsel of God. What is due to God, what all men owe Him, is everything. Jesus set forth "God's absolute and peculiar right in respect of every man individually and of all men collectively—an exclusive and paramount right possessed by God alone."[16]

Those who reduce this great sentence of Christ's to a declaration about church and state have missed the point of the incident.

7. The Cultural Mandate

In 1970, a resolution was adopted by the Thirty-fourth General Synod of the Bible Presbyterian Church, meeting on Friday, October 9, in the Christian Admiral Hotel, Cape May, New Jersey. This measure, Resolution No. 13, said to have been written by Dr. McRae and Dr. Carl McIntire, was on "The Cultural Mandate" and declared:

Resolution No 13

THE CULTURAL MANDATE

We, the members of the 34th General Synod of the Bible Presbyterian Church, meeting at Cape May, New Jersey, in October, 1970,

---

14. Justin Martyr, *First Apology*, chap. XVII.
15. Geldenhuys, *op. cit.*, p. 507. 16. *Ibid.*, p. 508.

wish to express our opposition to the false doctrine, sometimes called "*the cultural mandate*." The mandate under which Christians obey their Lord is the Great Commission of Matthew 28: 19-20, which requires that we teach and honor all things "whatsoever I have commanded you." This so-called "cultural mandate" erroneously builds its case on Genesis 1:28 before the Fall and the promise of redemption in the seed of the woman. The conditions of Genesis 1:28 will never again be available to man until after the Return of Christ and sin is removed. The cultural mandate declares that it is the Christian's duty to pursue these pre-Fall realities, just as it is their duty to preach the Gospel. This same command was renewed to Noah (Genesis 9) after the flood without any reference to the word "and subdue it." Furthermore, the verse has nothing to do with culture, in the present sense of the word. The so-called "cultural mandate" is based entirely on one word of the verse, the word that is translated "and subdue it." Like all words of Scripture, this word should be interpreted in context. Here the context is that of filling the empty earth with people. It says that the earth should be brought under cultivation, to enable these people to survive and multiply. That, and that alone, is what it means. Calvin saw in this verse neither a mandate nor anything relating to culture, and the same is true of the other great exegetes of Christian history.

We oppose the "cultural mandate" also because it gives a false idea of the place of the Christian in this age of sin, and cuts the nerve of true missionary work and of evangelism.

Christians have a right to enjoy the fruits of various cultural developments under common grace and to participate in all the good things that God has created. But the high duty of Christians between the Fall and the Return of Christ is to witness to God's righteousness in all things, to live godly lives, and to use every effort to bring individuals to the knowledge of the Saviour, that they may be redeemed through His precious blood and may grow in grace and in the knowledge of His Word.

Unanimously adopted on Friday, October 9, 1970, by the Thirty-fourth General Synod of the Bible Presbyterian Church, meeting in the Christian Admiral Hotel, Cape May, New Jersey, October 5-9, 1970.

Before analyzing this measure, let us examine the term *cultural mandate*. *Culture* means "To educate or refine; cultivate. 1. Cultivation of plants or animals, especially with a view to improvement. 2. The training, improvement, and refinement of mind, morals, or taste; enlightenment. . . ." *Mandate* means "An authoritative requirement; a command; order; charge." The cultural mandate is thus the obligation of covenant man to subdue the earth and to exercise dominion over it under God (Gen. 1:26-28). The law is the program for that purpose and provides the God-ordained means of improving and developing plants, animals, men, and institutions in terms of their duty to fulfil God's purpose. In every age, men have a duty to obey God and to train and improve themselves, i.e., to sanctify themselves, in terms of God's law. All enemies of Christ in this fallen world must be conquered. St. Paul, summoning believers to their calling, declared,

> (For the weapons of our warfare are not carnal, but mighty through God to the pulling down of strong holds;)
> Casting down imaginations, and every high thing that exalteth itself against the knowledge of God, and bringing into captivity every thought to the obedience of Christ;
> And having in a readiness to revenge all disobedience, when your obedience is fulfilled (II Cor. 10:4-6).

The Berkeley Version renders verse 6 thus: "We are prepared also to administer justice upon all disobedience, when your obedience is fully shown." Moffatt brings out the force of this verse even more clearly: "I am prepared to court-martial anyone who remains insubordinate, once your submission is complete." Moffatt renders verse 5, "I demolish theories and any rampart thrown up to resist the knowledge of God, I take every project prisoner to make it obey Christ."

St. Paul was talking about the cultural mandate. Before the fall, the task was less complicated. Now man needs regeneration. Thus, the *first* step in the mandate is to bring men the word of God and for God to regenerate them. The *second* step is to demolish every kind of theory, humanistic, evolutionary, idolatrous, or otherwise, and every kind of rampart or opposition to the dominion of God in Christ. The world and men must be brought into captivity to Christ, under the dominion of the Kingdom of God and the law of that kingdom. *Third,* this requires that, like Paul, we court-martial or "administer justice upon all disobedience" in every area of life where we encounter it. To deny the cultural mandate is to deny Christ and to surrender the world to Satan.

The cultural mandate cannot be equated with the natural man's view of culture and progress. It is not to be summed up in operas, physical comforts, or childish self-indulgences. Clement of Alexandria gives us some amusing examples of the attempts of decadent Romans to prove their culture and wealth by absurd displays:

> It is a farce, and a thing to make one laugh outright, for men to bring in silver urine-vases and chamber-pots of crystal as they usher in their counsellors, and for silly rich women to get gold receptacles for excrements made; so that being rich, they cannot even ease themselves except in a superb way.[1]

---

1. Clement of Alexandria, "The Instructor," Bk. II, ch. iii; *Ante-Nicene Christian Library*, IV, 214.

Culture in the Soviet Union, and increasingly in the Western world, is identified with the ballet, an opera house, and an art gallery, which may be slightly better than the golden chamber-pots of Roman women, but is still false.

Culture is religion externalized, and it is the development of man and his world in terms of the laws of his religion. The laws of Rome had no ultimate and absolute foundation; they were relativistic and pragmatic; they were the products of events, not the God-given *shaper* of events. In speaking of this Roman environmentalism, of the faith in Fate, Tatian, an Assyrian Christian of the middle of the second century, declared:

> But we are superior to Fate, and instead of wandering demons, we have learned to know one Lord who wanders not; and, as we do not follow the guidance of Fate, we reject its lawgivers. . . .

> And how is it that Kronos, who was put in chains and ejected from his kingdom, is constituted a manager of Fate? How, too, can he give kingdoms who no longer reigns himself?[2]

Tatian pin-pointed the Roman dilemma with his citation of Kronos: how can men or gods who are themselves the products of and governed by Fate and environment rule that environment? Are they anything more than puppets or a reflex action? The psychology of Marxism is derived from Pavlov; it is conditioning; man is governed by reflex actions and is socially conditioned. The philosophy of Marxism is dialectical materialism; men and ideas are socio-economic products. Soviet law thus is in radical contradiction to itself: it insists, in practice, on individual guilt while affirming, in theory, total conditioning. Men are in practice held responsible, whereas in theory they are entirely victims. A Soviet jurist has said:

> Only when everyone is fully conscious of what it means to be a Soviet citizen will there be no crime. . . .

> There is no such thing as human nature. Man is the product of his surroundings, of the social and economic system which molds him. Change the mold and you change the man. And that is what we are doing. You know the church used to talk loud and long about original sin; it was a good way to keep the masses in their miserable places. But we junked that idea long ago.

> We are doing something, we are doing a great deal, about removing the artificial societal arrangements that foster crime—and this is where I think that socialism shows its greatest advantage over capitalism. . . . You see, man is essentially good; only private property and everything he learned from it corrupted him. We're

---

2. Tatian, "Address to the Greeks," ch. ix; *Ante-Nicene Christian Library*, III, 14.

restoring his goodness and at the same time making him infinitely richer in every way. Don't you see the glory in that?[3]

Western humanistic law has adopted basically the same premises as Soviet law and in some cases practiced it more rigorously and systematically. By all of this their religion is revealed; the culture of modern man is one of surrender to environment, to Fate. Humanism, whether in its liberal or Marxist forms, has no cultural mandate but rather a cultural surrender; it is an aggressive philosophy of surrender.

The Bible Presbyterian statement is no better; it too calls for a surrender of the world to the devil.

The implications of surrender are, however, anarchy and social chaos. Where man is a covenant breaker, anarchy is a major problem and a terrifying one. Man's prospect then is a war by every man against all others. His answer is the state.

> *Imperium* is a necessity, otherwise man's world falls to pieces in a *bellum omnium contra omnes*. That, so to speak, was the political testament of the oriental world empires right down to the time of Alexander, a testament that was executed in a new and unique way in the world empire of Rome. Wherever the *imperium romanum* went, there also went the *pax romana*. As long as the *imperium* lasted the world was protected against chaos. That was why the *imperium* had to stand as long as the world itself remained, and also why the Roman empire was to be an everlasting one.[4]

Because man has again denied the cultural mandate, he seeks protection against chaos by means of empire—the Soviet empire, the United Nations, and various other alliances and efforts. Aggression replaces faith and law as man's defense against anarchy.

The answer of God to this crisis of man is His sovereign act of grace, the incarnation. Stauffer's comment here is to the point:

> There are two demands that the pre-Christian story of the concept of destiny has to make upon the Church's soteriology. The whole world is so involved in Adam's sin that the situation can be redeemed, if at all, only by God himself. Then the fate of this world is so radically bound up with that of man that the actual work of deliverance can only be effected in terms of a human life. Both requirements are fulfilled in the coming of Christ.[5]

> But this honour of the Christ is not self-glorifying encroachment, not demonic seizure of God's honour, but on the other hand, a service to the *gloria dei* that God himself has willed.

Matthew and Luke in their prefaces to their Gospels try another way

---

3. George Feifer, *Justice in Moscow* (New York: Simon and Schuster, 1964), pp. 330-332.

4. Ethelbert Stauffer, *New Testament Theology*, trans. by John Marsh (New York: Macmillan, 1955), p. 82.

5. *Ibid.*, p. 116 f.

of expressing the twofold concern of the NT christology. Christmas
Day is the day of the new creation, and the hour of Christ's birth
is the long expected critical hour of cosmic history. Why? The
Spirit of God mentioned in Gen 1:1 comes into action in a new
Genesis (Matt. 1. 18) and a divine miracle (Luke 1. 37) creates a
new man who realizes the promises of Gen. 3. 15 and fulfils the
frustrated hope of Gen. 4. 1. Like the first man, Adam (Luke
3. 38), the new man comes directly from God. But he is not
only, as Adam was, simply the recipient of the divine breath of
life. He was conceived by the Holy Ghost of the Virgin Mary
(Luke 1. 35; Matt. 1. 18). So Jesus is at one and the same time
both Adam's son and God's.[6]

The purpose of the new Adam is to undo the work of the fall,
restore man as covenant-keeper, make of man again a faithful citizen
of the Kingdom of God, and enable man again to fulfil his calling to
subdue the earth under God and to restore all things to God's law and
dominion. Those who submit to this calling and dominion inherit the
earth (Matt. 5:5).

The joyful news of the birth of Christ is this restoration of man to
his original calling with the assurance of victory. This has long been
celebrated in Christmas carols. Isaac Watts in 1719 wrote, in "Joy
to the World,"

> No more let sins and sorrows grow,
> Nor thorns infest the ground;
> He comes to make his blessings flow
> Far as the curse is found.

Johannes Olearius in 1671, in "Comfort, Comfort Ye My People,"
wrote

> For the herald's voice is crying
> In the desert far and near,
> Bidding all men to repentance,
> Since the kingdom now is here.
> O that warning cry obey!
> Now prepare for God a way;
> Let the valleys rise to meet him,
> And the hills bow down to greet him.
>
> Make ye straight what long was crooked,
> Make the rougher places plain;
> Let your hearts be true and humble,
> As befits his holy reign.
> For the glory of the Lord
> Now o'er earth is shed abroad;
> And all flesh shall see the token,
> That his word is never broken.

---

6. *Ibid.*, p. 117.

The cultural mandate and post-millennialism is either explicit or implicit in Christmas carols. Edmund H. Sears, in 1850, wrote "It Came Upon a Midnight Clear," which concludes thus:

> For lo, the days are hast'ning on,
> By prophet bards foretold,
> When with the ever-circling years
> Comes round the age of gold;
> When peace shall over all the earth
> Its ancient splendors fling,
> And the whole world give back the song
> Which now the angels sing.

Hymn writers, as they reflected on the Christmas glory and the prophecies concerning it, reflected at times a theology with greater content than they themselves held.

In His ascension, Jesus underscored again the creation mandate, declaring:

> All power is given unto me in heaven and in earth.
> Go ye therefore, and teach all nations, baptizing them in the name of the Father, and of the Son, and of the Holy Ghost:
> Teaching them to observe all things whatsoever I have commanded you: And, lo, I am with you alway, even unto the end of the world. Amen (Matt. 28:18-20).

Lenski rendered "teach all nations" as "disciple all nations." Two domains are cited where Christ's total royal authority prevails, heaven and earth. "The universality of the commission is made plain by . . . 'all nations' of the earth. Here we have the fulfilment of all the Messianic promises concerning the coming kingdom."[7]

In the ascension, "the exalted Christ ascended his throne." According to Stauffer,

> We read that the final subjection of God's enemies will only take place at the end of the days, though it is presupposed, in saying this, that the fundamental beginning has already been made (Mark 14:62; Rev. 3:21; 14:14). We read again that the subjection has already taken place, though here the celebration of the triumph is held back until the time of the end (Eph. 1:20 ff.; Heb. 1:13; 10:12 f.; 12:2). But wherever the emphasis falls, this much is clear: The Lord has from now on all authority in heaven and on earth, and he is "with" his Church always, even unto the end of the world (Matt. 28:18 ff.).[8]

All nations are to be *subdued* by baptism and teaching, i.e., by regeneration and the word of God. Originally, the first Adam faced a naturally good and unfallen world to subdue, the second or last Adam

---

7. R. C. H. Lenski, *The Interpretation of St. Matthew's Gospel* (Columbus, Ohio: The Wartburg Press, 1943), pp. 1170, 1172.
8. Stauffer, *op. cit.*, p. 138.

faced rebellious and fallen nations and a fallen world, a wilderness or desert to be made fertile and productive unto God. More than a garden was now to be subdued; the nations and empires of the world were to be brought under the dominion of Christ and His members.

This fallen world mobilizes itself against Christ and His people. It denies Christ and curses Him, first in the massacre at Bethlehem, later by crucifixion, and since then by its condemnations. Instead of accepting the transfiguration of Christ as the revelation of God and His law-order through His only-begotten Son, the world seeks to transfigure itself, sometimes by exalting its most wretched persons. Thus, in Rome, an underground basilica of a cultic hellenistic brotherhood presented a lesbian deified. "On its apse it carried a picture of the transfiguration of Sappho."[9]

But Christ turned the curse of the cross into victory, and the condemnations of the world into judgments against the world.

> The Church, persecuted by the ejected dragon and yet freed from a tremendous burden, sings its hymns to Christ: "Now is come the salvation, and the power, and the kingdom of our God, and the authority of his Christ; for the accuser of our brethren is cast down, which accuseth them before our God day and night. And they overcame him because of the blood of the Lamb!" (Rev. 12:10 f.). This is the new situation for the world that dates from the ascension.[10]

If men are not regenerated by Christ, and if they will not submit to His calling, to the cultural mandate, they will be crushed by His power.

8.   The Law in Acts and the Epistles

Few things better illustrate what has happened in theological circles than an examination of Richard Watson's *Biblical and Theological Dictionary*. Watson (1781-1833) was a Wesleyan theologian; his dictionary was published in 1832. For Watson, the law was not superseded; rather, the Christian era called for its more intensive and wider application. Watson showed that the New Testament not only restated the whole Decalogue but extended its force.

> Thus, then, we have the obligation of the whole decalogue as fully established in the New Testament as in the Old, as if it had been formally reenacted; and that no formal reenactment of it took place, is itself a presumptive proof that it was never regarded by the lawgiver as temporary, which the formality of republication might have supposed. It is important to remark, however, that, although the moral laws of the Mosaic dispensation pass into the Christian code, they stand there in other and higher circumstances; so that the New Testament is a more perfect dispensation of the

9. *Ibid.*, p. 139.   10. *Ibid.*

knowledge of the moral will of God than the Old. In particular, (1) They are more expressly extended to the heart, as by our Lord, in his sermon on the mount; who teaches us that the thought and inward purpose of any offense is a violation of the law prohibiting its external and visible commission. (2) The principles on which they are founded are carried out in the New Testament into a greater variety of duties, which, by embracing more perfectly the social and civil relations of life, are of a more universal character. (3) There is a much more enlarged injunction of positive and particular virtues, especially those which constitute the Christian temper. (4) By all overt acts being inseparably connected with corresponding principles in the heart, in order to constitute acceptable obedience, which principles suppose the regeneration of the soul by the Holy Ghost. This moral renovation is, therefore, held out as necessary to our salvation, and promised as a part of the grace of our redemption by Christ. (5) By being connected with promises of divine assistance, which is peculiar to a law connected with evangelical provisions. (6) By having a living illustration in the perfect and practical example of Christ. (7) By the higher sanctions derived from the clearer revelation of a future state, and threatenings of eternal punishment. It follows from this, that we have in the Gospel the most complete and perfect revelation of moral law ever given to men; and a more exact manifestation of the brightness, perfection, and glory of that law, under which angels and our progenitors in paradise were placed, and which it is at once the delight and the interest of the most perfect and happy beings to obey.[1]

Contrast this statement by Watson, one of the very greatest men in Wesleyan history, with the work of a modern British evangelical scholar, F. F. Bruce. Bruce's 1968 "Payton Lectures" at Fuller Theological Seminary, Pasadena, California, discussed *The New Testament Development of Old Testament Themes*. Bruce's antinomian work ignores the law entirely; "The Rule of God" is discussed in Chapter II without any reference to the law of God.[2] Chapter IV is on "The Victory of God" and begins with an important statement:

> The salvation of God is the victory of God: as at the Exodus, so in the redemptive act of Christ the victory of God is the salvation of His people. The Hebrew words for "salvation" are readily translated "victory" in our common English versions when the context makes this rendering preferable.[3]

Exactly. But because Bruce by-passes the law, a central aspect of God's plan and program for victory, he can only look for victory in death or martyrdom and in the end of the world. "The conqueror-in-

1. Richard Watson, "Law," in *A Biblical and Theological Dictionary*, p. 576 f. (New York: Mason and Lane, 1832, 1840).
2. F. F. Bruce, *The New Testament Development of Old Testament Themes* (Grand Rapids: Eerdmans, 1968), pp. 22-31.
3. *Ibid.*, p. 40.

chief is the Davidic Messiah, . . . who appears, however, as the sacrificial Lamb restored to life after winning his victory by submission
to death; his followers share in his victory by similar submission."[4]
This is a program for defeat.

One of the central texts used by antinomians is Acts 15:5: "But there
rose up certain of the sect of the Pharisees which believed, saying, That
it was needful to circumcise them, and to command them to keep the
law of Moses." How shall this be understood? There is no evidence
whatsoever that the Ten Commandments ceased to be law after the
Council of Jerusalem; the epistles repeatedly restate the law; thus,
St. Paul, in Ephesians 6:2, not only restates the fifth commandment
but reminds us of its promises, all still valid. The laws of God against
sin were never repealed by this council.

The issue was justification; Judaism had misused the law. *First*, it
had replaced it with the traditions of man, which it made into law, and,
second, the law, which is the way of sanctification, was made into the
way of justification. This was the problem both with Phariseeism and
with the Judaizers. Paul at Antioch declared of Jesus Christ:

> Be it known unto you therefore, men and brethren, that through
> this man is preached unto you the forgiveness of sins;
> And by him all that believe are justified from all things, from which
> ye could not be justified by the law of Moses (Acts 13:38-39).

This was the issue, *justification by law*. Moreover, the Pharisees called
their rabbinic interpretations "the law of Moses," although Christ
called them "the traditions of men." Plumptre rightly called Paul's
statement on justification, at Antioch, "the germ of all that was most
characteristic in St. Paul's later teaching."[5] Paul never attacked the
law as the way of sanctification, but only as the way of justification.
The issue in the council was the conversion of some Gentiles; up to
that time, all converts were Jews, already in the old covenant and law.
Now members were added directly by conversion. It was the protest
and phrasing of the Pharisees which we read in Acts 15:5, "saying, That
it was needful to circumcise them, and to command them to keep the
law of Moses." By law was thus meant the law as viewed by rabbinic
tradition. It was this "yoke" against which Peter protested (Acts 15:
10). He would not have dared to call obedience to God's law tempting
God. The issue, St. Peter stated, is that men are saved by "the grace
of the Lord Jesus Christ" (Acts 15:11); the issue was the doctrine of
justification. Also at issue was the ceremonial law and the laws of
separation. The Jewish converts needed no instruction; they already

observed all the necessary, i.e., Biblical, laws (Acts 15:21). According to Plumptre, on verse 21,

> The Jews, who heard the Law in their synagogues every Sabbath, did not need instruction. It might be taken for granted that they would adhere to the rules now specified. So, in verse 23, the encyclical letter is addressed exclusively to "the brethren of the Gentiles."[6]

Clearly, verse 21 emphasizes the still binding character of the law and does not disturb the Jewish converts who obeyed the law. The use of the word "synagogues" can refer to the Jewish synagogues, still attended by many, or to Christian gatherings.

The instruction to the gentile Christians is summed up in verse 20: "But that we write unto them, that they abstain from pollution of idols, and from fornication, and from things strangled, and from blood." Does this mean that the Gentiles were free to have other gods, to blaspheme, dishonor parents, murder, steal, bear false witness, or covet? Obviously not, and just as obviously the issue was not whether the law was to be retained, but *how* to be retained: as the means of justification, or of sanctification? Very clearly, the law was rejected as the way of justification and retained as the way of sanctification. The instructions of Acts 15:20 and 29 clearly presuppose the law and *emphasize how far the law was retained. First*, the gentile believers are commanded to abstain from "pollutions of idols." In verse 29 this is defined as the eating of "meats offered to idols." A serious problem existed in the cities, in that meats were sacrificed to idols and their eating represented a religious rite. "Josephus says, that some of the Jews at Rome lived on fruits exclusively, from fear of eating something unclean."[7] Later, in Romans 14, St. Paul revised this ruling; Calvin spoke of Paul's ruling as a remodelling of the law.[8] Does this change mean that no law was in force? On the contrary, both the council and St. Paul held that a law of God was at stake; the question was as to how to maintain obedience to that law. The pollution of idols, in terms of the law of separation, had to be avoided as a matter of law. If a man could regard the idols as nothing, and the meat simply as food, his conscience would not be troubled, nor would the use of the meat compromise him; he would be a "strong man," unpolluted by his use of meat. The weak, however, were right in avoiding meat, in that there was no inner separation possible for them. In either case, the law was respected.

Second, fornication must be abstained from, i.e., sexual sins in gen-

---

6. *Ibid.*, VII, 98.
7. Charles Hodge, *Commentary on the Epistle to the Romans* (New York: Armstrong, 1882, 1893), p. 656.
8. John Calvin, *Commentary Upon the Acts of the Apostles* (Grand Rapids: Eerdmans, 1949), II, 79n.

eral, and lasciviousness. For many pagans, these acts were not sin and were in fact sometimes religious acts. Because of the proneness of pagans to sexual sins, especially in that era, particular stress was laid on such offenses. Theft and murder were condemned by the pagans, but the morality of the day viewed sexual offenses with growing casualness.

Third, "things strangled" had to be avoided as food, and, *fourth,* blood. These two are closely related, in that strangled animals are not bled. For many peoples, such meats are preferred. The law, however, specifically forbad the eating of blood (Gen. 9:4; Lev. 3:17; 17:14; Deut. 12:16, 23). This law was never at any time amended or altered in the epistles. *Thus, of the four commandments to the Gentiles by the council, three concerned food.* Instead of declaring the law to be ended, the Council of Jerusalem therefore clearly established or sustained the law as the way of sanctification and *retained even the dietary aspects of the law.*

There is a significant change, however. In Acts 15:5, the demand of the Pharisees in the church was also for circumcision. This demand, the Gentiles were told in the encyclical, was "subverting your souls, saying, "Ye must be circumcised, and keep the law: to whom we gave no such commandment" (Acts 15:24). Circumcision was thus dropped, and Peter's baptism of the Gentiles sustained, as the mark of the renewed covenant; the keeping of the law in pharisaic sense of being justified by the law (Acts 13:39) was rejected. Bruce is wrong thus in assuming that the issue at stake was "the obligation to keep the Mosaic law."[9] Lenski holds that "all these Levitical regulations (concerning foods) had been abrogated." He explains the council decision as pragmatic:

> James mentions these two points because the Jewish Christians were especially sensitive regarding them. They, too, knew that these points of the law were abrogated but they still felt a horror of eating blood or any meat that had retained the blood. The Gentile Christians were asked to respect this feeling and thus from motives of brotherly love, and from these alone, to refrain from eating blood and meat that still had its blood.[10]

But the point at issue was not the feelings of the Jewish Christians as such; no such consideration enters into the text. In stating that the issue is one of "motives of brotherly love, and from these alone, to refrain from eating blood, . . ." Lenski was reading into the text what

---

9. F. F. Bruce, *Commentary on the Book of Acts* (Grand Rapids: Eerdmans, 1954), p. 301.
10. R. C. H. Lenski, *The Interpretation of the Acts of the Apostles* (Columbus, Ohio: The Wartburg Press, 1944), p. 616.

was not there. The issue was plainly raised by the Pharisees in the church with a false view of law and of justification.

In Colossians 2:16, St. Paul states that we are not to be judged with respect to meats (the eating of meats offered to idols), *or* sabbaths. There is no evidence that sabbaths were abolished by this statement. If the incident St. Paul describes in Galatians 2:11-21 is the same as that of Acts 13:39, or related to it, and thus preceded the council, clearly the issue at stake was that St. Peter, fearful of the criticism of the Pharisees in the church, conformed to their practice. St. Paul's principle was that no artificial barrier could be made by foods to approaching the Gentiles and converting them.

Turning now to Romans, we find that St. Paul, far from setting aside the law and its penalties, appeals to the death penalty against homosexuals as an established and continuing fact (Rom. 1:32). Of the expression "the judgment (or ordinance) of God," Murray comments, " 'The ordinance of God' in this case is the judicial ordinance of God" which expressly calls for death, here more than temporal death, while including it.[11]

In Romans 6:14, however, St. Paul declares, "for ye are not under the law, but under grace." Murray is again to the point:

> "Law" in this case must be understood in the general sense of the law as law. That it is not to be understood in the sense of the Mosaic law as an economy appears very plainly from the fact that many who were under the Mosaic economy were the recipients of grace and in that regard were under grace, and also from the fact that relief from the Mosaic law as an economy does not of itself place persons in the category of being under grace. Law must be understood, therefore, in much more general terms of law as commandment.[12]

The comment of Charles Hodge is also very telling at this point. Writing of this same verse, Hodge said in part:

> By *law* here, is not to be understood the Mosaic law. The sense is not, "Sin shall not have dominion over you, because the Mosaic law is abrogated." The word is not to be taken in its widest sense. It is the rule of duty, that which binds the conscience as an expression of the will of God. This is plain: 1. From the use of the word through this epistle and other parts of the New Testament. 2. From the whole doctrine of redemption, which teaches that the law from which we are delivered by the death of Christ, is not simply the Mosaic law; we are not merely delivered from Judaism, but from the obligation of fulfilling of the law of God as the condition of salvation.[13]

---

11. John Murray, *The Epistle to the Romans* (Grand Rapids: Eerdmans, 1959), I, 51.
12. *Ibid.*, I, 228 f.   13. Hodge, *Romans*, p. 322.

The law in this general sense is a way of salvation; it is man's belief that, by keeping God's general law as he knows it, man will save himself and merit heaven. Freedom from the law as a way of salvation does *not* give man the right to sin (Rom. 6:15-16); man has a duty to obey God as now a "servant of righteousness" rather than a "servant of sin" (Rom. 6:17-23).

According to Murray, "Romans 7:1-6 is to be connected with what the apostle had stated in 6:14, 'Ye are not under law, but under grace.' "[14] In Romans 7:4, Paul speaks of having become "dead to the law by the body of Christ"; as Murray noted, "that death is our death to the law in the death of Christ."[15] The illustration of marriage is used by Paul; even as a woman is "bound by the law to her husband so long as he liveth; but if the husband be dead, she is loosed from the law of her husband" (vs. 2), so we too, by the death of Christ in our stead are dead to the law. The point in this illustration is *not* that the law is dead, but that we in Christ are dead, i.e., the death sentence of the law is fulfilled against us. As Hodge noted, "It is not the law that dies."[16] To return to the illustration, if a husband dies, it is *not* the institution of marriage which dies but a particular man who is dead to marriage.

What is then the meaning of this illustration and phrase? In verse 5 we are plainly told that, while we were sinners, the effect of the law in our lives was to further our rebellion against God; the law of God made us all the more zealous in affirming our own will in rebellion. The result was "fruit unto death." The law was a death sentence to us: it declared that, for our apostasy, our covenant-breaking with God, we deserved to die. The death sentence being fulfilled against us in the person of Jesus Christ, we are now judicially dead in the eyes of the law. Therefore, those who are truly saved can never again be sentenced to death by the law. However, being raised from the dead, i.e., the death of sin, by the work of Christ, we are now "married to another, even to him who is raised from the dead, that we should bring forth fruit unto God" (vs. 4). The sinner, having made himself god in his own eyes (Gen. 3:5), is at war with God; the law of God only incites him to more warfare. The law thus drove us into more bondage to sin. By regeneration, however, our union is no longer with sin but with Christ. Being alive in Christ, we are now *alive to the law*, not as a death sentence against us, but as that which represents our new life, the "newness of spirit" (vs. 6), our life in Christ, whereby the law is now our happy way of life. The law does not die; the old man, the unregenerate man, dies; the new, regenerate man now has a new relationship to the law, no longer in "the motions of sin" but "in newness of spirit." Whereas

14. Murray, *op. cit.*, p. 239.
15. *Ibid.*, p. 242.   16. Hodge, *op. cit.*, p. 337.

for the sinner the violation of God's law is the drive and nature of his being, for the regenerate man obedience to the law in Christ is the delight of his being.

Paul makes emphatic that "the law is spiritual" (7:14); "the law is holy, and the commandment holy, and just, and good" (vs. 12); the law, moreover, "was ordained to life" (vs. 10); in his sin, because he was then in principle breaking the law because it is good, he consents "unto the law that it is good" (vs. 16). As a redeemed man, working out his salvation, growing in sanctification, he can declare, "For I delight in the law of God after the inward man" (vs. 22). "The law of sin," his fallen nature, dead judicially in Christ but not eradicated from his being, wars against his new nature, so that one aspect of his being, the new man, serves "the law of God," another, "the law of sin" (vss. 23-25). Clearly, the law is the standard for the new man. Indeed, the goal of sanctification is "that the righteousness of the law might be fulfilled in us" (8:4). Murray's comment here is again noteworthy:

> It is all the more significant in this context because he had repre-
> sented deliverance from the power of sin in 6:14 as proceeding from
> the fact that we are not "under law" but "under grace." In chap-
> ter 7 he had returned to that theme and showed that we are not
> "under law" because "we had been put to death through the body
> of Christ" and "have been discharged from the law" (7:4, 6). He
> had also demonstrated that the law was unto death because sin
> took occasion from the law to work all manner of lust (7:8-13).
> And, finally in this chapter he had just spoken of the impotence
> of the law (8:3). How then can he construe the holiness of the
> Christian state as the fulfillment of the law's requirement? The fact,
> however, cannot be disputed, and it is conclusive proof that the
> law of God has the fullest normative relevance in that state which
> is the product of grace. To construe the relations of law and grace
> otherwise is to go counter to the plain import of this text. We had
> been prepared for this, however, in earlier notifications to this
> same effect (cf. 3:31; 6:15; 7:12, 14, 16, 22, 25). And in the
> subsequent development of the subject of sanctification there is
> abundant corroboration (cf. 13:8-10).

> The term "fulfilled" expresses the plenary character of the fulfil-
> ment which the law receives and it indicates that the goal contem-
> plated in the sanctifying process is nothing short of the perfection
> which the law of God requires.[17]

Briefly, to restate the matter, it is not the law that is dead, but we who die in Christ and are therefore dead to the law as an indictment and a sentence of death. As regenerate men, in Murray's words, "the law of God has the fullest normative relevance in that state which is the product

---

17. Murray, *op. cit.*, p. 283.

738   *The Institutes of Biblical Law*

of grace. *To construe the relation of law and grace otherwise is to go counter to the plain import of this text."*

Galatians 2:19 must be read in the same sense: "For I through the law am dead to the law that I might live unto God." Again, the law is not dead, but rather the sinner. In Galatians 2:21, the contrast is between justification by law and justification by the grace of God through Jesus Christ; in the use of law as a means of justification, no righteousness can be gained. In Galatians 5:16-18, the contrast is between the way of "the flesh," fallen, unaided human nature, and the way of "the Spirit," the redeemed and aided new man. The law is associated in this context with "the flesh," so that the reference is again clearly to the misuse of the law as a way of justification. In Ephesians 2:15, the reference to the law is very clearly the law as a sentence of death to the unbeliever.

St. Paul thus is no support for those who declare that the law is dead, nor for those who hold that the redeemed man is dead to the law. Not only does St. Paul affirm the law, but in letter after letter he appeals to the law in settling church conflicts, in giving instructions, and in giving counsel concerning sanctification.

Murray is right: "The law of God has the *fullest* normative relevance in that state which is the product of grace."

XIV

THE CHURCH

1. The Meaning of Eldership

Few offices have deteriorated more radically than that of the elder.
Its original purpose has been obscured, its functions lost, and its purpose
altered.

To understand the meaning of the office of elder, it is necessary to
remember that the office was not created by the church but taken over
from the practices of Israel. As Morris has written,

> The first Christians were all Jews, and it is a reasonable inference
> that they took over the office of elder from the Judaism with which
> they were familiar. It will repay us accordingly to give some atten-
> tion to the Jewish elders.

> These men were officials responsible for the administration of
> Jewish communal life. They had responsibilities in both what we
> would call civil and ecclesiastical affairs. Probably they made no
> hard and fast distinction between the two, for their law was the
> law of Moses which deals impartially with both. Moreover, their
> unit of organization was the synagogue congregation, and the syna-
> gogue, in addition to being a place for worship, was a place of
> instruction, a school. The Rabbis dealt with all manner of subjects.
> They did not confine themselves to what we would call religious
> matters, but laid down regulations for the conduct of civil affairs
> as well.

> The elders were elected by the community and held office for life.
> They were admitted to their functions by a solemn rite, which in
> New Testament times was apparently an act of enthronement. The
> laying on of hands does not appear to have been practised at this
> time, and it probably did not make its appearance until the war of
> Bar Kochba or later. . . . The function of the elder was apparently
> centred on the law. They were to study it, expound it and deal
> with people who had offended against it.

There are obvious similarities between this office and that of the
first Christian elders. The importance of this similarity is heightened
when we reflect that the Christian Church appears to have been
regarded at first as a branch of Judaism. Her assemblies seem to
have been modelled on the synagogue pattern. Any ten male adult
Jews could form a synagogue. And it is probable that the first
assemblies of Christians were organized as synagogues. In fact
one is called by this very name in James 2:2 and there is evidence
that "The Christian congregations in Palestine long continued to

739

be designated by this name" (J. B. Lightfoot, *Saint Paul's Epistle to the Philippians*, p. 192). . . . These would supervise the affairs of the new society in the same way as Jewish elders looked after the synagogue.[1]

In order to understand the Hebrew background of the office, it is important to recognize its origin in the family and tribal structure of Israel. The elder, *first*, was what the name indicated, an older man in a position of authority. The term *elder* was comparative, so it could mean a man ruling over his household. This head of the household, or of a group of families, supervised the discipline and justice within his family, its education, worship, and economic support; he was also responsible for its defense against enemies. Thus, very clearly, *law and order* were basic functions of the elder but in far more than in a police sense, in that it was the duty of the elder to train his charges into a way of life. The concern of the elder was thus religious, civil, educational, and vocational. He also provided for the welfare of his household.

Second, elders formed the basis of civil government. Since men who governed in so extensive a way their own households were best trained to govern, Moses turned to the elders, at the command of God, to form a group of seventy to rule Israel (Num. 11:16). These men governed under Moses and aided him in instructing the people in the implications of the law (Deut. 27:1). Local government was in the hands of elders (Deut. 19:12; 21:2; 22:15; 25:7; Josh. 25:4; Judges 8:14; Ruth 4:2). These elders are also referred to in the Gospels (Matt. 16:21; 26:47; Luke 7:3). In the New Testament era, some elders ruled in the Sanhedrin and were experts in the law, and others ruled in localities.[2]

Third, elders were rulers of synagogues, as Morris has indicated. Within the synagogue, the elder was the teacher, enforcer, and expert student of the law.

The fact that the elder ruled in church, state, and family in the Old Testament era did not make this office one institution. The fact of unity came not from the absorption of one institution into another, but in their common subordination to the law and their common use of the law.

The fact that the church took over the office of elder from Israel is an aspect of its claim to be the new and true Israel of God. The church was now God's true synagogue, and its people the new Israel. The purpose of the office was to create a new society, the Kingdom of God,

---

1. Leon Morris, *Ministers of God* (London: Inter-Varsity Fellowship, 1964), p. 70 f.
2. W. E. Vine, *Expository Dictionary of N. T. Words*, p. 20 f.; J. A. Selbie, "Elder (in O. T)," in James Hastings, *Dictionary of the Bible*, I, 676 f.

to institute the new creation by means of the discipline of its law-word. The seal of God's approval on the church as the new Israel, and the elders as the new office-bearers of God's law, was the laying on of hands and the implied anointing of the Holy Ghost (I Tim. 4:14).

The office of elder has, among its qualifications, the ability to teach, and the ability to rule (I Tim. 3:2-5). Significantly, the tie to the origin of the office remains. The elder was originally and always a man who ruled a household; hence, in Israel, a ruler (and all rulers were in a real sense elders) had to be a married man, a man tested in authority and government. St. Paul restates this qualification as an inescapable fact, "For if a man know not how to rule his own house, how shall he take care of the church of God?" (I Tim. 3:5). The office of elder requires a family-centered society.

The government of the new Christian society was complicated by the fact of persecution. The offices of deacons and widows, created to function under the elders, had government as their function, the relief of the needy, ministering to the younger, education, etc. The elder as a teacher thus functioned in the early church in one sphere after another, in the church, in the family, in the area of welfare by delegation and supervision, in education, and, by their avoidance of civil courts, as a civil government.

Precisely because the Roman courts were "unjust" (I Cor. 6:1), the elders served as a court to judge controversies among Christians (I Cor. 6:1-3). If a church member refused to heed a correction (Matt. 18:15-17), then he could be treated as "an heathen man and a publican" and taken, if need be, to a civil court. Normally, the ungodly court is to be avoided even at a sacrifice (Matt. 5:40). No restriction against the use of courts exists in the Old Testament, because the courts there were either in the hands of the elders or reflected their influence. American courts, despite their corruption, have not lost their Christian character or Biblical law heritage.

Paul in I Corinthians 6:2 declares, "Do ye not know that the saints will judge the world?" Some, because of the reference to angels in verse 3, refer this judging to the world to come, but its true meaning is with reference to time and eternity. The word judge here has the Old Testament sense of *govern*. Moffatt translates it as *manage*. *Manage* does convey the meaning of a continuing government by the saints over the Kingdom of God, in time and in eternity.

One of the consequences of existing in a hostile world was that the church had to assume the function of a total society for its members. The elders or presbyters were central to this function. The office of elder began with the family. It retained not only the *office* but the concept of the *family* in the new society of Christ. All true believers

were members of the family of Christ. A congregation and a community
of believers thus cared for its own, for "whoso hath this world's good,
and seeth his brother have need, and shutteth up his bowels of compassion from him, how dwelleth the love of God in him?" (I John
3:17). The literature of the early church underscores this position. At
the same time, there was no toleration of indolence: "If any would not
work, neither should he eat" (II Thess. 3:10). Moreover, "if any
provide not for his own, and specially for those of his own house, he
hath denied the faith, and is worse than an infidel" (I Tim. 5:8). The
goal of the elders and their teaching was thus to create a community of
responsible believers, responsible for themselves and their household
and for their fellow believers.

But this is not all. Because the saints were called to *manage* or
govern the world, very quickly it became their purpose to move into
positions of authority and power. The letters of St. Paul show clearly
that prominent Romans were converted. The salutations include those
"that are of Caesar's household" (Phil. 4:22). In the Puritan era, the
pressure of the saints on every kind of office in church, state, school,
and commerce was very extensive.

Law is equivalent to rule or reign: it is the expression of a rule or
reign and the application of a sovereignty to the area of jurisdiction.
The elders, as officers of a law, God's law, are thus called to apply the
law of God to every sphere of life. It is the duty of the Christian home,
school, and church to train elders who will apply the law of God to
all the world. The elder is not governed by the church as a subordinate
officer who is sent out as an imperial agent into the world. Rather, the
elder governs in his sphere, even as the church in her area, each as
imperial agents of Christ the King. At points, the elder is under the
authority of the church, and at other points independent of it.

The church calls and ordains her elders, but there is little reason to
limit the office to the church. Christians in education, civil government,
the sciences, law, and other professions can constitute themselves as
Christian bodies and examine and ordain men who will further the law
and rule of God in their sphere. The eldership is a calling from God, and
the church is one agency in which the calling is fulfilled. This was the
form of the office in Israel, and there is no evidence of any change in the
nature of the office in the New Testament. The fact that the very name
of the office, *elder*, was retained emphasizes the continuity.

In Revelation, moreover, we meet with "four and twenty elders,"
symbolizing the fulness of the church of both the Old and New Testaments. The Jewish practice of enthronement of elders is echoed also,
in that these elders "cast their crowns before the throne" (Rev. 4:10),
indicating the supreme kingship of God. Elders were enthroned, an

echo of the original calling of Adam to be a priest, prophet, and *king* over creation under God. The restoration of that kingly rule under Christ is the function of the elder, and it is a calling in every domain of life.

The concept of eldership or ministry was strongly revived by Luther with respect to the university and the professors. The professor's chair was the heir of the synagogue elder's chair, and there was a comparable enthronement. To this day, many professors are inducted into an endowed "chair" without realizing the meaning of that term. Rosenstock-Huessy pointed out that "The universities represented the life of the Holy Ghost in the German Nation."[3] The work of the Holy Spirit through the office and ministry of the elder was seen as manifested through the professor.

However, not until every legitimate calling is seen as an area of potential eldership and is brought under the rule of God's law-word by presbyters or elders serving God will the meaning of eldership be fully realized.

2. The Office of Elder in the Church

The people of God, in church, state, family, vocation, and every other sphere, have a continuous duty to reform themselves into conformity with the word of God. There are many areas of church life today which are seriously in need of reformation. In discussing the office of elder, it is not our purpose to indicate this as more erring an area than others but simply to call attention to some problems within this area.

The office of elder has for some generations been seriously in decline in importance and function. In many churches, it became by 1900 mainly an honor accorded to prominent members. Moreover, the function of the elder became largely that of a judge sitting in monthly review on the minister, and sometimes dealing with matters concerning the building and the premises. Since the early church for perhaps two centuries had no church buildings but met in homes, the administration of a building was clearly not a part of the original function of an elder. Again, there is nothing in Scripture to indicate that a session, or a board of elders, has as its central function the judgment of a pastor, or a supervision of his work. Indeed, we can term such a function as a rare one, necessitated by an emergency, for the welfare of the church. Similarly, since the early church had no choirs, no Sunday School, no youth leagues or women's guilds, none of these tasks of supervision are basic to the office of elder, and, we can add, to the office of pastor.

It is our purpose to examine the evidences of patristic literature con-

---

3. Eugen Rosenstock-Huessy, *Out of Revolution, Autobiography of Western Man* (New York: William Morrow, 1938), p. 395.

cerning the office of elder, in order to throw light thereby on the Biblical meaning and practice. The Reformed interpretation of the office is assumed, and Calvin's summary statement that "the appellations of bishops, elders, pastors, and ministers" all "express the same meaning."[1] Put in modern terms, the offices of pastor and bishop are identical.

But the episcopal position clearly has strong support in patristic literature. Very early the office of bishop is seen as separate from the office of elder or presbyter. This is clear in Ignatius, who died possibly in A.D. 107 and thus reflected a very early practice and was a contemporary of some apostolic leaders. Thus, in the Epistle of Ignatius to the Trallians, written from Smyrna, we read, "It becomes every one of you, and especially the presbyters, to refresh the bishop, to the honour of the Father, of Jesus Christ, and of the apostles" (ch. XII). Ignatius clearly distinguished the two offices. Thus, he declared, "As therefore the Lord did nothing without the Father, being united to Him, neither by Himself nor by the apostles, so neither do ye anything without the bishops and presbyters."[2] This authority of the bishop was a spiritual authority: "It is fitting, then, not only to be called Christians, to be so in reality: as some indeed give one the title of bishop, but do all things without him."[3] The duties of a bishop were outlined by Ignatius to Polycarp.[4] Polycarp's flock is told, "Give ye heed to the bishop, that God also may give heed to you. My soul be for theirs that are submissive to the bishop, to the presbyters, and to the deacons, and may my portion be along with them in God!"[5] Clearly, the offices of bishop, presbyter, and deacon in Ignatius are our familiar offices of pastor, elder, and deacon. But there is a serious difference in function, so that both the modern episcopal and presbyterian functions would appear to be deviations. Ignatius is again revealing here:

> See that ye all follow the bishop, even as Jesus Christ does the Father, and the presbytery as ye would the apostles; and reverence the deacons, as being the institution of God. Let no man do anything connected with the church without the bishop. Let that be deemed a proper Eucharist, which is (administered) either by the bishop, or by one to whom he has entrusted it. Wherever the bishop shall appear, there let the multitude (of the people) also be; even as, wherever Jesus Christ is, there is the catholic church. It is not lawful without the bishop either to baptize or to celebrate a love-feast; but whatsoever he shall approve of, that is also pleasing to God, so that everything that is done may be secure and valid.[6]

1. Calvin, *Institutes*, bk. IV, ch. III, no. viii.
2. *Epistle of Ignatius to the Magnesians*, ch. VII.
3. *To the Magnesians*, ch. IV.
4. *To Polycarp*, chs. I-V.
5. *To Polycarp*, ch. VI.
6. *Epistle of Ignatius to the Smyrnaeans*, ch. VIII.

Certain things clearly appear from this. *First*, the church then was not an institution, or a building; it was a body of believers, meeting in a home and bound together in a hostile world by their common faith in Jesus Christ as their Redeemer. *Second*, these small churches in homes were scattered across the empire, and beyond its frontiers. The church was not able to, nor did it attempt to provide each little congregation with a pastor or bishop. Therefore, even as St. Paul continued in his journeys to keep a governing hand on the churches in Corinth, Thessalonica, and elsewhere, so the successors of the apostles continued to do the same. As perambulating pastors, missionaries, or evangelists, they found it necessary to govern these little congregations by epistles as well as visits; hence the epistles of Ignatius and others. These men were termed bishops; we could as well term them missionary pastors. *Third*, these bishops or pastors appointed and ordained presbyters or elders in the various local congregations to carry on the worship of God and the study of Scripture in that church during the absence of the travelling pastor. Since a pastor or bishop might cover a larger or smaller area, with a home base, very often the local presbyter or presbyters had to maintain the church by their own leadership. If the pastor were in the nearest large city, and the congregations met in scattered homes within the city and the surrounding villages, the contact could be a close one. In other cases, extensive correspondence became a necessity. Thus, both in the New Testament and patristic eras, epistles were a basic pastoral tool. *Fourth*, the bishop or pastor alone could conduct the services of baptism and communion, but he could, as Ignatius declared, delegate the administration of the sacraments to the presbyters. Thus, while the presbyters or elders could administer the sacraments, this was true only when they were so instructed by the pastor or bishop in view of his distance and his confidence in the presbyter. The presbyter or elder thus not only taught but also had a subordinate responsibility with respect to the sacraments. *Fifth*, the office of bishop here appears very different from the sacerdotal conception of episcopalians. We might add that Joseph Bingham, in his *Antiquities of the Christian Church*, declared that the bishops inherited the apostolic office, and that the title of *apostle* "is thought by many to have been the original name for bishops, before the name bishop was appropriated to their order."[7] As a matter of fact, Ignatius rather compares the presbyters or elders to the apostles: "See that ye all follow the bishop, even as Jesus Christ does the Father, and the presbytery as ye would the apostles."[8] Are we to conclude that bishops are like unto God, and presbyters the successors of the

7. Bk. II, ch. II.
8. *Ibid.*

apostles? Is the meaning not rather that a principle of obedience to authority, when that authority is faithful to ultimate authority, is taught?

As a matter of fact, Irenaeus did assert the apostolic succession of elders or presbyters: "Wherefore it is incumbent to obey the presbyters who are in the church—those who, as I have shown, possess the apostolic succession from the apostles; those, who, together with the succession of the episcopate, have received the certain gift of truth, according to the good pleasure of the Father."[9] This succession Irenaeus defined as those who taught the apostolic faith, not some hidden esoteric doctrine imparted to "the perfect." Irenaeus was warring against those who were "wiser . . . even than the apostles" and opposing to them the presbyters and bishops who were in apostolic succession, that is, who subordinated themselves to the Biblical authority.[10] The authority of the faith is paramount, not the physical succession; apostolic succession meant a succession in the faith of the apostles, and it set forth a loyalty and subordination to that faith.[11]

Sixth, the purpose of this supervision of the elders by the bishop or pastor was "that everything that is done may be secure and valid."[12] To protect the church from heresy and disorders, the missionary pastors or bishops had, from New Testament times on, a responsibility for every flock under their jurisdiction.

Seventh, this means that the episcopal tradition has wrongly exalted one pastor or bishop above others, while the presbyterian tradition has tended to degrade the office of presbyter or elder to a largely inactive and ineffectual board. Instead of being governed in action by the pastor, it sits to govern the pastor. Instead of being an effective office for the growth of the church beyond the abilities of the pastor's reach, or to follow his work by effective development, it has become a *voting* rather than a *functioning* office. The main task of most elders today is to vote in session, consistory, or vestry, and in presbytery, classis, synod, or general conference.

Can the office of presbyter be resurrected in its original function? There are many who hold that it cannot be done, that the modern man is too sophisticated to tolerate anything but the most trained seminary leadership and the most attractive services of worship, with choir, beautiful sanctuary, and organ. Is this true?

In recent years, numerous organizations have demonstrated the superior vitality of lay outreach. Two illustrations will suffice, *first*, the John Birch Society. This illustration is deliberately chosen. It is

---

9. *Against Heresies*, bk. IV, ch. XXVI, 2.
10. *Ibid.*, bk. III, ch. II, 2; III, 1.
11. *Ibid.*, bk IV, ch. XXVI, 3, 4.   12. Ignatius, *op. cit.*

not our concern, nor is it relevant, to discuss here the pros and cons of that organization. It is important to our purpose that this society is both criticized, hated, and attacked as the early church was to a far greater degree, and that it is led by volunteer laymen. Groups of men, women, and youth, normally not exceeding twenty persons, meet in homes regularly to follow a course of study under a leader. These leaders are usually surprisingly busy men: doctors, dentists, businessmen, and others who have a full schedule but still take time to prepare a lesson, invite friends and neighbors, and recruit, with help from other members, new members. These chapter leaders can be called elders, directed by area coordinators, who function as bishops or pastors. The total membership of the society is unknown, although it is estimated to range from 60,000 to 100,000. However, there is a continual turnover in membership, as some, having studied a year or two, leave the society without abandoning its basic philosophy. Based on this writer's travels, the total number of those who have been influenced by the society in its brief history may number five million. Other conservative movements have arisen from time to time with greater followings but less impact. The key to the John Birch Society's effectiveness has been a plan of operation which has strong resemblance to the early church: have meetings, local "lay" leaders, area supervisors or "bishops."

The *second* illustration is personal: this writer's weekly Bible and theological studies are tape-recorded and circulate across the United States and sometimes beyond its frontiers. Some of these studies are appearing also in print, as witness *The Foundations of Social Order, Studies in the Creeds and Councils of the Early Church* (1968). This work, regarded by some pastors as too difficult or theological, is still circulating heavily among laymen. It is listened to by groups in various states in home meetings. The usual situation is that a man or woman opens his home to friends, provides refreshments, and holds weekly study sessions to a steadily increasing audience.

Clearly, the Biblical pattern does work, and it is time the churches used it again. Living as we do in a humanistic age, where the true church is a small minority, we need again an active and functioning eldership.

A second consideration, apart from that of basic function, must be noted. The church today has fallen prey to the heresy of democracy. For many laymen and women, and for many elders, the essence of their Christian duty is to speak their mind. The pastor or bishop is continually hamstrung by a democratic impulse which makes him the errand boy of the congregation. *The Apostolic Constitutions* makes an interesting statement here: "It is not equitable that thou, O bishop, who art the head, shouldst submit to the tail, that is, to some seditious person among the laity, to the destruction of another, but to God alone. For it is thy privilege to govern those under thee, but not to be governed by them.[13] In brief, *the church is a monarchy, not a democracy.* Christ is the King, and all offices derive their authority from Him, not from the people. The assent and vote of the people is a part of their assent to Christ. Unless the pastor or elder is disobedient to the Lord, he must be obeyed and respected. But we cannot be perfectionist in our demands of office-bearers. Thus, the patristic literature states, "Hear your bishop, and do not weary of giving all honour to him; knowing that, by showing it to him, it is borne to Christ, and from Christ it is borne to God; and to him who offers it, it is requited manifold. Honour, therefore, the throne of Christ."[14] Granted that an exaggeration of this attitude led to Roman Catholic authoritarianism, but is it not also a perversion when some champions of presbyterianism cite their church as the cradle of democracy? The church of Jesus Christ is a monarchy, and the purpose of its representative form of government is to strengthen the preservation of the "Crown Rights of King Jesus." Not the rights of the people but the sovereign rights of Christ the Lord are to be championed by members, deacons, elders, and pastors or bishops. The session, or consistory, or vestry is not a democratic forum but a ruling body for Christ. Pastors or bishops are examined by presbytery in terms of the canon or rule of Scripture in order to preserve the dominion of Christ. Unless the church purposes to be a democracy, a similar examination for the office of elder is a necessity.

In the Orthodox Presbyterian Church, *The Standards* require that, at the ordination or installation of ruling elders, "the minister shall state, in the following or similar language, the warrant and nature of the office":

> The office of ruling elder is based upon the kingship of our Lord Jesus Christ, who provided for his church officers who should rule in his name. . . .
>
> It is the duty and privilege of ruling elders, in the name and by the authority of our ascended King, to rule over particular churches, and, as servants of our great shepherd, to care for his flock.[15]

The monarchistic orientation of the office is plainly affirmed, and it needs to be stressed afresh in the churches. Unfortunately, too often,

---

13. *Apostolic Constitutions*, bk. II, sec. III, xiv.
14. *The Clementine Homilies*, ch. LXX.
15. *The Standards of Government Discipline and Worship of the Orthodox Presbyterian Church* (Philadelphia: Committee on Christian Education, O.P.C., 1957), p. 84, ch. VI, B.

as in the Orthodox Presbyterian service, the office is formally recognized but in reality it is sterile.

We have thus seen, *first*, that the office of elder is pastoral in nature, that the elder in the early church functioned as an arm of the pastor or bishop in maintaining and extending the gospel. *Second*, we have noted that this office is not a part of an ecclesiastical democracy but of a monarchy. *Third*, the elder or elders are a court of the church. In this area, much has been done to restore the ancient function of the elder, and church discipline has been stressed in those circles which stand on Reformed doctrines. It is thus sufficient to add simply that important and necessary as this judicial function is, it becomes a distortion if the basic pastoral function is neglected and the elder becomes primarily a judge, and the session, consistory, or vestry essentially a court. The pastoral function must at all times be primary.

It is thus important to recognize, *fourth*, that the essential task of the elder is not to sit in session but to act to the furtherance of the gospel and the lordship of Christ. Turning again to Polycarp, let us note his comment on the duties of presbyters:

> And let the presbyters be compassionate and merciful to all, bringing back those that wander, visiting all the sick, and not neglecting the widow, the orphan, or the poor, but always "providing for that which is becoming in the sight of God and men"; (Rom. xii. 17; 2 Cor. viii. 31) abstaining from all wrath, respect of persons, and unjust judgment; keeping far off from all covetousness, not quickly crediting (an evil report) against any one, not severe in judgment, as knowing that we are all under a debt of sin. If then we entreat the Lord to forgive us, we ought also ourselves to forgive (Matt. vi. 12-14); for we are before the eyes of our Lord and God, and "we must all appear at the judgment-seat of Christ, and must every one give an account of himself" (Rom. xiv. 10-12; 2 Cor. v. 10). Let us then serve Him in fear, and with all reverence, even as He Himself has commanded us, and as the apostles who preached the gospel unto us, and the prophets who proclaimed beforehand the coming of the Lord (have alike taught us). Let us be zealous in the pursuit of that which is good, keeping ourselves from causes of offense, from false brethren, and from those who in hypocrisy bear the name of the Lord, and draw away vain men into error.[16]

It is the ministry of the state to be a ministry of justice, to insure law and order and to be a court of justice. It is the calling of the church to be a ministry of grace, to proclaim Christ's redemptive work, so that its basic task is redemptive, not judicial. This too must be the basic orientation of every office of the church. Pastors and elders are not primarily a court but a ministry of grace, proclaiming that salvation is of our God by Jesus Christ, and summoning all men to submit to Christ

---

16. *The Epistle of Polycarp to the Philippians*, ch. VI.

their King. The very real judicial function of pastors and elders is to preserve the integrity of this, their basic calling, and the churches in their charge, from corruption and defection from their calling. *To rule* as a ruling elder thus means more than sitting in session as a judge; it means even more extending and maintaining the rule of Christ the King. Thus, an elder who assumes leadership in establishing Christian schools is truly fulfilling his office. The same is true of an elder who uses his home as a center for a study group, a little home-church, as a nucleus for a new congregation. The faithful elder may also be one who makes it his duty to call on the sick and needy of Christ's flock, or to preach under the supervision of a pastor to a struggling new congregation, or to begin a new work. Again, he may assume major responsibilities in his own church, in order to free his pastor for further work. In brief, a *judge* deals with offenders only; a *ruler* deals with the whole life of the people. Elders are called to be ruling, not judging elders. This distinction is vital, and its abuse is paralyzing to the church.

Clement of Alexandria, in citing the threefold division of offices as bishop, presbyter or elder, and deacon, declared that the true elder is

> a true minister (deacon) of the will of God, if he do and teach what is the Lord's; not as being ordained (or, elected) by men, nor regarded righteous because a presbyter, but enrolled in the presbyterate because righteous. And although here upon earth he be not honoured with the chief seat, he will sit down on the four-and-twenty thrones, judging the people, as John says in the Apocalypse.

> For, in truth, the covenant of salvation, reaching down to us from the foundation of the world, through different generations and times, is one, though conceived as different in respect of gifts.[17]

Clearly, this is a spiritual office, and it is a ruling office; it becomes a judging office when circumstances require it. But, even as Aaron and Hur bore up the arms of Moses unto victory over Amalek (Ex. 17:10-12), so the presbyters or elders of our day must bear up the arms of their bishops or pastors unto victory over the powers of darkness, the Amaleks of our day, unto the end that we can rejoice that "The kingdoms of this world are become the kingdoms of our Lord and of his Christ, and he shall reign for ever and ever" (Rev. 11:15).

A final note: the characteristic weakness of church and state is to over-govern. The answer of the state to all problems tends to be new laws, and the answer of the church to its problems is "discipline." Such actions cannot replace the need for Christian character and growth. The church can have no better source of discipline than sound and thorough teaching, but it finds it easier to diminish the responsibilities and the freedom of members than to provide them with the means of

---

17. Clement of Alexandria, *The Miscellanies*, bk. VI, ch. xiii.

mature growth. The best discipline is the word of God and the workings of the Holy Spirit; church "discipline" should be a last resort, a necessary instrument but a subordinate one.

3. The Christian Passover

One of the most obvious facts about the Last Supper is that it was celebrated at the passover meal. The continuity of the renewed or new covenant with the old was marked by the coincidence of the two rites. The fact that Jesus had selected twelve disciples made clear that His community was the new Israel of God. There is no possibility of understanding the New Testament if its continuity with the Old is denied or under-rated.

While they were eating the passover, Jesus called attention to the planned betrayal by Judas and then sent Judas out (Matt. 26:21; John 13:30). Then "as they were eating" (Matt. 26:26; Mark 14:22), Jesus instituted the Christian passover in His body and blood.

To understand the Christian passover, it is imperative that the Hebraic passover be analyzed. Certain aspects of the original passover require attention, therefore.

First of all, the passover celebrated the deliverance from Egypt and from the tenth plague, the death of the firstborn. It was thus the Old Testament *salvation*, and marked the beginning of sabbaths, the day of rest in the Lord, commemorating salvation (Deut. 5:15; Ex. 12: 12, 13). The first day of the festival falls on the 15th of Nisan (March-April) and lasts for eight days. The passover ritual, if it begins on a weekday, commences thus:

> Blessed art thou, O Eternal, our God, King of the Universe, Creator of the fruit of the vine.
>
> Blessed art thou, O Eternal, our God, King of the Universe, who selected us from among all people and exalted us among nations, and did sanctify us with his commandments. And thou, O Eternal, our God, hast given us (Sabbath days for rest and) festival days for joy, (this Sabbath and the days of) this feast of the unleavened bread, the time of our deliverance (in love) remembrance of the departure from Egypt. For us hast thou selected, and sanctified from amongst all nations, in that thou causedst us to inherit thy holy (Sabbath and) festival days (in love and favour). Blessed art thou, O Eternal, who hallowest (the Sabbath and) Israel and the festival days.

These words make plain the fact of election, and the fact that sanctification is by law: God "didst sanctify us with his commandments." The orthodox service thus still reflects sound doctrine—justification by electing grace and sanctification by law. Chapters 12 and 13 of Exodus witness to the fact of grace and cite the requirement of obedience to law (13:9).

Likewise, the Christian passover celebrates the Christian day of salvation, the victory of Christ over sin and death, and hence the day of resurrection marked the beginning of the Christian sabbath. In most liturgies of the sacrament, the reading of the law, of the Ten Commandments, is basic to the service. In the Book of Common Prayer, the law is read at the beginning of the service, although it can be omitted if it is read at least one Sunday each month. If omitted, the summary of the law is read. In Calvin's last communion service order, and in Knox's first communion in Scotland, the law was not read, but it appeared in their liturgies in the form of excommunications pronounced specifically against all transgressors of the law.

Second, the Hebraic passover is a *family* service, and God ordered that the son not only ask a ritual question but that the service be addressed to him (Ex. 13:14). The youngest son thus normally asks the question about the meaning of the service, and the purpose of the priest-father's words is to make the meaning of the passover known to him. The youngest present asks "The Four Questions," which inquire as to the meaning of the night's ritual. The story of the deliverance from Egypt and its meaning is then declared by the head of the household and other participants.

The Christian passover is also a celebration by the family of Christ. Accordingly, children partook of the elements. The early church met in homes, usually at night, since the first day of the week was then a work day. The sacrament was celebrated as an agape feast, a love feast, a pot-luck dinner of all the members. Children shared in the meal. Nothing is clearer than the fact that infants were baptized, confirmed, and partook of the elements for perhaps the first nine or ten centuries of the Christian era.

The Hebraic pattern of the Old Testament law was very strong in the church. (Even today, a Roman Catholic missal notes, in its order of the mass, that, at one point, "Celebration of the Word," "This has been taken from the synagogue service of Israel.")[1] As a result, it required the action of a church council to depart from the practice of baptizing on the eighth day. Fidus, an African bishop, had raised a question as to "whether infants were to be baptized, *if need required*, as soon as they were born, or not till the eighth day, according to the rule given in the case of circumcision?" The synodical answer of St. Cyprian and a council of sixty-six bishops was this:

> As to the case of infants, whereas you judge that they ought not to be baptized within two or three days after they are born; and that the rule of circumcision should be observed, so that none should

---

1. *The New Saint Andrew Bible Missal* (New York: Benziger Brothers, 1966), p. 903. Prepared by a Missal Commission of Saint Andrew's Abbey.

be baptized and sanctified before the eighth day after he is born; we were all in our council of the contrary opinion. It was our unanimous resolution and judgment, that the mercy and grace of God is to be denied to none as soon as he is born.[2]

The obvious intention of this decision was to permit the baptism of new-born babes who might die before the eighth day and thus remain unbaptized. Apparently that early fear prevailed that such children would be denied the covenant salvation because they lacked the covenant rite. In essence, the eighth day requirement of the Old Testament was recognized and was set aside only to care for emergencies. It is not our purpose here to analyze the view of baptism held by the council, but simply to call attention to the persistence of the Old Testament pattern. To return to the service of the communion, the evidence is clear "that the communion itself was given to infants, and that immediately from the time of their baptism." As Bingham noted, this fact "is frequently mentioned in Cyprian, Austin, Innocentius, and Gennadius, writers from the third to the fifth century. Maldonat confesses it was in the church for six hundred years. And some of the authorities prove it to have been continued two or three ages more, and to have been the common practice beyond the time of Charles the Great."[3] This fact represented the persistence of the Old Testament pattern, very clearly. No Biblical reason can be given for eliminating children from the sacrament. The sense of covenant life is destroyed by their exclusion and God's law violated. The reason for their exclusion is found in I Corinthians 11:28, the requirement of self-examination, just as the limitation of the meal to a token is based on verses 22 and 34. There may be grounds for the latter fact, although there cannot be a limitation of the sacrament to the token meal only. However, self-examination was a part of the Hebraic ceremony.

This brings us to our *third* point of importance, the aspect of *preparation* for the passover. In the Hebrew home, on the 13th of Nisan, in the evening, the head of the household searched the house with a lighted candle, to eliminate all leaven, including all bread made from leavened dough of wheat, barley, spelt, oats, and rye.[4] Then, in the Seder, the first two days of the Passover Festival, "the emphasis on children's participation" was pronounced.[5] How do these two facts reconcile themselves with the requirement of preparation and self-examination? How can children be included?

---

2. Joseph Bingham, *The Antiquities of the Christian Church* (London: Bohn, 1850), I, 495; bk. XI, ch. IV, 11.
3. *Ibid.*, p. 545; bk. XII, ch. I, 3.
4. W. J. Moulton, "Passover," in Hastings, *Dictionary of the Bible*, III, 691.
5. "Seder," in David Bridges, Samuel Wolk, *The New Jewish Encyclopedia* (New York: Behrman, 1962), p. 436.

The ritual of searching the house to eliminate all leaven was an enacted symbol of the need to eliminate corruption from the life of the family and from the individual. As such, it was a vivid sign to all children from their earliest days of the need for self-examination, the need to eliminate every corrupting influence and habit from their lives. The child, as a member of the covenant, was thus from his earliest memories instructed in the meaning of membership in the covenant. The early Christians pushed the implications further than did the Hebrews, in that babes in arms had the elements placed in their mouths; more than a little superstitious belief may have entered into this practice. This does not eliminate the Biblical requirement that the service include all children able to ask the question as to the meaning of the service. The service, moreover, is both a celebration and a teaching service, to instruct all present in the fact of salvation and its meaning.

Fourth, the passover commemorated a victory and looked forward to more victory. The word *salvation* can also be translated as *victory*. The orthodox Jewish service reads at one point: "May He who is most merciful, break the yoke of our captivity from off our neck, and lead us securely to our land." This is a future-oriented faith, one which expects victory, and then looks to Elijah to come as its herald.

Similarly, the Christian passover has its purpose stated by St. Paul: "For as often as ye eat this bread, and drink this cup, ye do shew the Lord's death till he come" (I Cor. 11:26). According to Hodge, the meaning of this verse is that,

> As the Passover was a perpetual commemoration of the deliverance out of Egypt, and a prediction of the coming and death of the Lamb of God, who was to bear the sins of the world; so the Lord's supper is at once the commemoration of the death of Christ and a pledge of his coming the second time without sin unto salvation.[6]

This is true enough, but is it all that this statement means? Calvin commented,

> The Supper then is (so to speak) a kind of memorial, which must always remain in the Church, until the last coming of Christ; and it has been appointed for this purpose, that Christ may put us in mind of the benefit of his death that we may recognize it before men. Hence it has the name of the Eucharist (From *having given thanks*).[7]

This is better, in that Calvin spoke "of the benefits of his (Christ's) death." The meaning of the Lord's death is the death of sin and of death: it means salvation or victory. The Christian passover must

---

6. Charles Hodge, *Commentary on the First Epistle to the Corinthians* (Grand Rapids: Eerdmans, 1950 reprint), p. 229 f.

7. John Calvin, *Commentary on the Epistles of Paul the Apostle to the Corinthians* (Grand Rapids: Eerdmans, 1948), I, 384.

declare the victory of God and of the people of God. "The meek shall inherit the earth; and shall delight in the abundance of peace" (Ps. 37:11.)

The dimension of victory is so basic to the sacrament that to observe it without a declaration of that victory is to deny the sacrament. The Old Testament passover, which is the heritage of all Christians, saw the firstborn of all Egypt slain, and the people of God delivered from bondage. The New Testament passover saw the people of God, sinners in themselves, delivered by the death of God's firstborn, in whom they have victory.

Fifth, the death of the firstborn is basic to the passover. In the Old Testament passover, the firstborn of Egypt were slain; the requirement of Israel was that "all the firstborn, whatsoever openeth the womb among the children of Israel, both of man and of beast; it is mine" (Ex. 13:2). The firstborn of God's enemies are slain; all the firstborn of the covenant, representing all within the covenant, are either given or dedicated to God, or must be slain (Ex. 13:13). The passover is life and victory to those who are faithful to the covenant: it leads to the promised land.

In the Christian passover, the death sentence upon the firstborn of the covenant, who are all sinners, is assumed by God's firstborn, Jesus Christ, the new Adam. The death sentence is ultimately enforced on all others. For the people of the covenant of Christ, the passover means deliverance to the promised land. This is victory in time and eternity. The Jews for weary ages have celebrated their passover, declaring, Next year in Jerusalem. Such a spirit echoes the victory of the original passover. The victory of the Christian passover is far greater. For an observance of the Lord's Table to be devoid of this note of victory is to deny the sacrament.

The Christian passover thus means that all men outside the covenant are under the tenth plague. Only those within are covered by the blood of the Lamb and assured of victory and deliverance to the promised land, the new creation of God. St. Paul referred both to the self-examination (purging the house of leaven), and the victory over all enemies, when he wrote: "Purge out therefore the old leaven, that ye may be a new lump, as ye are unleavened. For even Christ our passover is sacrificed for us: Therefore let us keep the feast . . ." (I Cor. 5:7, 8).

4. Circumcision and Baptism

The relationship between circumcision and baptism, the one succeeding the other as the sign of the covenant, was so close that, as we have seen, it required in Cyprian's day the action of a church council to permit baptism before the eighth day. Because the law of circumcision required that the rite be performed on the eighth day (Gen. 17:12; Lev. 12:3), it was believed that baptism should not precede the eighth day, and council action was necessary to alter this. The early church thus not only recognized that baptism was the successor to circumcision as the covenant sign, but also that the same laws governed both. Precisely because this fact was always recognized, infant baptism was inescapably a fact in the early church.[1]

Circumcision, as the mark of the covenant, made a witness concerning fallen man's nature, and the need for a new nature in God's covenant. As Vos noted,

> Circumcision has something to do with the process of propagation. Not in the sense that the act is of itself sinful, for there is no trace of this anywhere in the O.T. It is not the act but the product, that is, *human nature*, which is unclean and disqualified in its very source. Sin, consequently, is a matter of the race and not of the individual only. The need of qualification had to be specifically emphasized under the O.T. At that time the promises of God had proximate reference to temporal, natural things. Hereby the danger was created that natural descent might be understood as entitling to the grace of God. Circumcision teaches that physical descent from Abraham is not sufficient to make true Israelites. The uncleanness and disqualification of nature must be taken away. Dogmatically speaking, therefore, circumcision stands for justification and regeneration, plus sanctification (Rom. 4:9-12; Col. 2:11-13).[2]

Circumcision, by a symbolic cutting of the organ of generation, declared that in generation there is no hope, but only in regeneration; man can only reproduce his fallen nature; he cannot transcend it.

Symbolically, circumcision thus represented a form of death, a cutting off of life. It also represented the removal of an impediment; in Exodus 6:12, 30, it is used metaphorically "for the removal of disqualification of speech." Repeatedly, the unregenerate heart is spoken of as uncircumcised (Lev. 26:41; Deut. 10:16; 30:6; Jer. 4:4; 6:10 speaks of the ear; 9:25, 26; Ezek. 44:7; Rom. 2:25-29; Phil. 3:3; Col. 2:11-13).[3]

Circumcision as a sign of death pointed to the death of Christ as man's representative. Trumbull noted that "in the rite of circumcision it was Abraham and his descendants who supplied the blood of the

---

1. For a development of the Biblical evidences for infant baptism, see John Murray's able exposition, *Christian Baptism* (Philadelphia: Committee on Christian Education, The Orthodox Presbyterian Church, 1952; Presbyterian and Reformed Publishing Co., 1972).

2. Geerhardus Vos, *Biblical Theology, Old and New Testaments* (Grand Rapids: Eerdmans, 1948), p. 104 f.

3. *Ibid.*, p. 104.

covenant, while in the passover sacrifice it was the Lord who commanded the substitute blood in token of his blood-covenanting."[4]

Because Christ came as very man of very man, and very God of very God, He supplied the blood of the covenant, dying as true man for man's violation of the covenant, and, as very God, dying as our sinless substitute and perfect law-keeper, who by His death broke the dominion of sin and death. The blood of circumcision and the blood of the passover lamb typified the work of Christ. His work on the cross having been accomplished, blood ceased to be, except in a memorial sense, an aspect of the covenant rites. In the Christian passover, life-giving, refreshing wine is substituted as the sign of His shed blood. The old rites looked ahead to Christ; they looked back to Adam and Abraham, and to the passover in Egypt. The new rites of the covenant look back to Abraham and Adam, and to Christ's death and resurrection; they look forward to His victory and reconquest of the earth, and to a new creation. The old covenant was inaugurated with blood after the fall and with Abraham; it looked ahead to Christ's atoning blood, set forth typically in the blood of sacrificial animals. The renewed covenant in Christ began in His blood but looks forward to the glorious reign of the King in a realm of peace, as foretold by Isaiah. As a result, because of this fact, blood ceased to be an aspect of the covenant rites.

Baptism sets forth our death and resurrection in Christ, our regeneration, adoption, and incorporation into the covenant of grace. It is a witness to grace rather than grace itself. As St. Augustine noted, it is "the sacrament of grace, and the sacrament of absolution, rather than grace or absolution itself."[5] The early church saw illumination as an aspect of baptism, the new understanding of a redeemed heart; baptism was also called "the royal mark or character, and the character of the Lord."[6] Mindful of its relationship to the Old Testament rite, some church fathers spoke of baptism as "the great circumcision."[7] In obedience to Matthew 28:19, it was from the beginning regarded as valid only when done in the name of the Trinity.

Certain classes of people were barred from baptism unless they forsook their profession: charioteers, gladiators, racers, curators of the common games, participators in the Olympic games, musicians, vintners, and others, all of whose callings were parts of pagan religious ceremonies. Also excluded under all circumstances were astrologers, magicians, diviners, witches, and the like. The theater and circus

---

4. H. Clay Trumbull, *The Blood Covenant, A Primitive Rite and Its Bearing on Scripture* (Philadelphia: John D. Wattles, 1893), p. 351.
5. Bingham, *Antiquities*, I, bk. XI, ch. 1, sec. 2; p. 473.
6. *Ibid.*, I, bk. XI, 1, 7; p. 476.
7. *Ibid.*, I, bk. XI, 1, 10; p. 477.

being especially debauched aspects of paganism, frequenters thereof were refused baptism. Polygamists were rejected also.

Since baptism meant in part the believers' death and rebirth or resurrection in Christ, it was very early associated with the Easter season, although not exclusively so. This same aspect, rebirth, led to an interesting custom which survived for some centuries as basic to baptism, namely, baptism, usually by immersion, in the nude. Sprinkling and immersion were both used by the church, which recognized sprinkling, after Ezekiel 36:25, as the mark of the new covenant. Aspersion was also very early a common practice. The emphasis on death and rebirth led to a stress on immersion as symbolically representative of this fact. Men were born naked; hence, they were reborn naked in baptism. No works of the unregenerate man could be carried into heaven; therefore, the candidate symbolically stripped himself of all clothing to indicate that he had nothing save God's grace. There were two baptistries thus in churches for some generations, since men and women were baptized separately. Romans 6:4 and Colossians 2:12 were passages cited to confirm this practice of symbolic burial and resurrection. This practice of naked baptism indicates how seriously the Biblical symbolism was taken by the early church; nothing was avoided, and sometimes over-literal applications resulted.

An aspect of the symbolism of nakedness was the comparison to Adam:

> St. Chrysostom, speaking of baptism, says, Men were naked as Adam in paradise; but with this difference; Adam was naked because he had sinned, but in baptism, a man was naked that he might be freed from sin; the one was divested of his glory which he once had, but the other put off the old man, which he did as easily as his clothes. St. Ambrose says, Men came as naked to the font, as they came into the world; and thence he draws an argument by way of illusion, to rich men, telling them, how absurd it was, that a man was born naked of his mother, and received naked by the church, should think of going rich into heaven. Cyril of Jerusalem takes notice of the circumstance, together with the reasons of it, when he thus addresses himself to persons newly baptized: As soon as ye came into the inner part of the baptistery, ye put off your clothes, which is an emblem of putting off the old man with his deeds; and being thus divested, ye stood naked, imitating Christ, that was naked upon the cross, who by his nakedness spoiled principalities and powers, publicly triumphing over them in the cross. O wonderful thing! ye were naked in the sight of men, and were not ashamed, in this truly imitating the first man Adam, who was naked in paradise, and was not ashamed. So also Amphilochius in the Life of St. Basil, speaking of his baptism, says, He arose with fear and put off his clothes, and with them the old man. . . . Athanasius, in his invectives against the Arians, among other things, lays this to their charge, that by their persuasions the Jews

and Gentiles broke into the baptistry, and there offered such abuses to the catechumens as they stood with their naked bodies, as was shameful and abominable to relate.[8]

Baptism, as we have seen, is cited by St. Paul as typifying, among other things, our death and rebirth in Christ (Rom. 6:4; Col. 2:12). This was also an aspect of circumcision. Circumcision not only signified new life in the covenant Lord but also, for those who broke or denied the covenant, it signified death. As Kline has pointed out,

> The general and specific considerations unitedly point to the conclusion that circumcision was the sign of the oath-curse of the covenant ratification. In the cutting off of the foreskin the judgment of excision from the covenant relationship was symbolized.[9]

The covenant sacrifice of Genesis 15:9 ff. as well as the mark of circumcision testified to the cutting off, the curse on the covenant breaker.

Kline is right in calling attention to the same aspect of judgment in baptism.

> Paul described Israel's Red Sea ordeal as a being baptized (I Cor. 10:2) and Peter in effect calls the Noahic deluge ordeal, a baptism (I Pet. 3:21). . . . But of particular relevance at this point is the fact that John the Baptist himself used the verb *baptizo* for the impending ordeal in which the One mightier than he would wield his winnowing fork to separate from the covenant kingdom those whose circumcision had by want of Abrahamic faith become uncircumcision and who must therefore be cut off from the congregation of Israel and devoted to unquenchable flames. With reference to this judicially discriminating ordeal with its dual destinies of garner and Gehenna John declared: "He shall baptize you with the Holy Ghost and with fire" (Matt. 3:11 f.; Lk. 3:16 f.; *cf.* Mk. 1:8).[10]

To be faithless to the covenant meant to be cut off, to be wiped out by the flood of judgment, to be destroyed by the fire of God's wrath. Thus, the very marks of the covenant are also signs of God's unfailing judgment on covenant breakers from the beginning of history. All men are covenant breakers, but the circumcised of the Old Testament church (and it was called a church in Acts 7:38) and the baptized of the New, are doubly so. This knowledge may have contributed to the delayed baptisms in the early church, many deferring it to the point of death: such a practice was, of course, a sin against the covenant. Kline's comment on the baptism of Jesus brings out the aspect of judgment clearly:

8. *Ibid.*, I, bk. XI, 11, 1; p. 536.
9. Meredith G. Kline, *By Oath Consigned, A Reinterpretation of the Covenant Signs of Circumcision and Baptism* (Grand Rapids: Eerdmans, 1968), p. 43.
10. *Ibid.*, p. 57.

Jesus' reception of John's baptism can be more easily understood on this approach. As covenant Servant, Jesus submitted in symbol to the judgment of the God of the covenant in the waters of baptism. But for Jesus, as the Lamb of God, to submit to the symbol of judgment was to offer himself up to the curse of the covenant. By his baptism Jesus was consecrating himself unto his sacrificial death in the judicial ordeal of the cross. Such an understanding of his baptism is reflected in Jesus' own reference to his coming passion as a baptism; "I have a baptism to be baptized with" (Lk. 12:50; *cf.* Mk. 10:38). Jesus' symbolic baptism unto judgment appropriately concluded with a divine verdict, the verdict of justification expressed by the heavenly voice and sealed by the Spirit's anointing, Messiah's earnest of the kingdom inheritance (Matt. 3:16, 17; Mk. 1:10, 11; Lk. 3:22; *cf.* Jn. 1:32, 33; Ps. 2:7 f.). This verdict of sonship was contested by Satan, and that led to the ordeal by combat between Jesus and Satan, beginning with the wilderness temptation immediately after Jesus' baptism and culminating in the crucifixion and resurrection-vindication of the victorious Christ, the prelude to his reception of all the kingdoms of the world (the issue under dispute in the ordeal; *cf.* esp. Matt. 4:8 ff.; Lk. 4:5 ff.).[11]

The covenant sign thus places the recipient under God's particular blessings and curses. As an unredeemed man, he is already under the curse. In receiving the covenant sign, a man is under a double threat of judgment if he violates that covenant. It was for this reason that Moses was in peril of the curse for embarking on God's covenant calling without circumcising his son (Ex. 4:24-26). For this reason also "judgment must begin at the house of God" (I Peter 4:17), both because of the double offense and to cleanse God's covenant race. All who receive the covenant mark are required to bind those under them to the law of God, and Christ's judgment on His church is the exercise of His authority as the baptized of God, the new Adam.

The baptism of Jesus tells us more about the meaning of baptism: "And Jesus, when he was baptized, went straightway out of the waters: and, lo, the heavens were opened unto him, and he saw the Spirit of God descending like a dove, and lighting upon him" (Matt. 3:16). Vos gives major insight into this aspect of the baptism:

> The O.T. nowhere compares the Spirit to a dove. It does represent the Spirit as hovering, brooding over the waters of chaos, in order to produce life out of the primeval matter. This might be found suggestive of the thought, that the work of the Messiah constituted a second creation, bound together with the first through this function of the Spirit in connection with it.[12]

Baptism thus is entrance into the new creation, whose king is the new

---

11. *Ibid.*, p. 58 f.
12. Vos, *Biblical Theology*, p. 346.

Adam, Jesus Christ. It is the covenant sign of the new paradise of God and of the citizens thereof.

In a document of the early church, we read, "Now, regeneration is by water and spirit, as was all creation: 'For the Spirit of God moved on the abyss' (Gen. i. 2). And for this reason the Saviour was baptized, though not Himself needing to be so, in order that He might consecrate the whole water for those who were being regenerated.[13] Baptism was thus emphatically seen as the sacrament of the new creation, whereby the old is purged and remade. Both the Spirit and the water signify agencies of cleansing:

> VIII. "The water above the heaven." Since baptism is performed by water and the Spirit as a protection against the twofold fire,— that which lays hold of what is visible, and that which lays hold of what is invisible; and of necessity, there being an immaterial element of water and a material, it is a protection against the twofold fire. And the earthly water cleanses the body; but the heavenly water, by reason of its being immaterial and invisible, is an emblem of the Holy Spirit, who is the purifier of what is invisible, as the water of the Spirit, as the other of the body.[14]

Despite the rather involved and strange hints of dualism in this passage, what is clear is that baptism was seen, in its inward and outward aspects, as the recreation of the world, material and spiritual, by means of the recreation of the whole man.

The promises to the covenant people in the Old Testament are remarkable ones; these are not retracted in the New, but rather expanded. As Murray so ably observed,

> Finally, we cannot believe that the New Testament economy is less beneficent than was the Old. It is rather the case that the New Testament gives more abundant scope to the blessing of God's covenant. We are not therefore led to expect retraction; we are led to expect expansion and extension. It would not accord with the genius of the new economy to suppose that there is the abrogation of so cardinal a method of disclosing and applying the grace which lies at the heart of God's covenant administration.[15]

The waters of baptism echo the judgment of the flood and of the Red Sea crossing; they also promise a new world, a promised land in Christ. They point to the fulness of blessing as surely as they reflect God's judgment on the old humanity, the fallen Adam in all of us.

5. The Priesthood of All Believers

It is a Protestant fallacy that "the priesthood of all believers" is a "New Testament doctrine" which came to light with the Reformation.

---

13. "Selections from the Prophetic Scriptures," in *Ante-Nicene Christian Library*, vol. XXIV *Early Liturgies and Other Documents* (Edinburgh: T. & T. Clark, 1872), p. 118 f.
14. *Ibid.*, p. 119. 15. John Murray, *Christian Baptism*, p. 53.

The doctrine is in fact an Old Testament article of faith, as Exodus 19:5-6 makes clear, as do many other passages:

> Now therefore, if ye will obey my voice indeed, and keep my covenant, then ye shall be a peculiar treasure unto me above all people: for all the earth is mine:
> And ye shall be unto me a kingdom of priests, and an holy nation. These are the words which thou shalt speak unto the children of Israel.

First of all, these words preceded the giving of the law, so that God's requirement ("if ye will obey my voice indeed, and keep my covenant") has reference to the covenant law, the Ten Commandments and the subordinate laws. Without obedience to the law of God, no valid priesthood can exist. Priesthood before God is thus conditional upon obedience to the covenant law of God.

Second, the people of God shall be "a kingdom of priests." The realm is the Kingdom of God; the priesthood of believers thus has reference to that kingdom. It is not a sacerdotal nor a sacrificing priesthood. This appears clearly, not only in the Old Testament, where the work of offering tabernacle sacrifices was limited to the line of Aaron, but also in the New Testament, where the word *hierus*, priest in the sacrificing sense, is never applied to believers.[1] The basic priesthood, that of all believers, is always with reference to the Kingdom of God. Its purpose is thus the establishment of God's order, and the law is given for that purpose. The "sacrifices" of this priesthood are "spiritual," i.e., an obedient and faithful service in the Holy Spirit; they are called to be "a royal priesthood, an holy nation, a peculiar (or unique) people" (I Peter 2:5, 9). The goal of this priesthood is to "reign on earth" (Rev. 5:10; 20:6); the instrument of this reign or rule is God's law. The work of sacrifice which belonged to the priesthood of Aaron was brought to its completion and purpose by the sacrifice of Christ. The believer priests of the Old Testament always had the duty of offering sacrifices of service, praise, and thanksgiving (rather than atonement), and this duty continues in the believer priests of the church (Rom. 12:1; Heb. 13:15).

Third, the believer priest of the Old Testament served as a priest-ruler over his household and in his calling. The same responsibility remains with the Christian priest-ruler. His family and his calling are areas within which the law-word of God must be enforced and the dominion of God exercised.

It was the believer priest of the Old Testament who established the synagogue as a means of furthering the teaching of the law and the

---

1. J. Denney, "Priest in N.T.," in James Hastings, editor, *A Dictionary of the Bible*, IV, 100.

worship of God. It must be emphasized that worship cannot be restricted to the synagogue or church; it is an aspect of the daily life
of man. Grace before meals is a form of worship, as are other forms
of the family's study of Scripture and praise of God. Worship in
connection with work is and has been common. The church has the
ministry of the word (although not exclusively) and of the sacraments;
while worship is an aspect of the life of the church, worship is not the
exclusive prerogative of the church.

The Biblical mandate for the synagogue was found in Exodus 18:20:
"And thou shalt teach them ordinances and laws, and shalt shew them the
way wherein they must walk, and the work that they must do." The
origins of the synagogue were perhaps in the Babylonian exile. The
synagogue was not only a place of worship but also an elementary
school. The synagogue was also regarded as a kind of adult school;
it was a place for lectures, and also the scene of legal decisions.[2]

It has become a requirement in Judaism that ten men are necessary
to organize a synagogue. Even more important than this number is
the fact that, from of old, the believer priest organizes the synagogue,
not a religious hierarchy. The synagogue was thus created by the
believer priests as an aspect of their priestly responsibility.

In the New Testament, the *church* or "assembly" is also called in
the Greek original a *synagogue* (James 2:2). The church is the Christian synagogue, having the same officers (elders) and the same basic
function as brought to its fulness in Christ. The church in the New
Testament was created in the same way as the synagogue. The apostolic
missionaries brought the converts to Christ; the converts then organized
a church, electing elders or rulers as the apostles gave instructions concerning their qualifications (I Tim. 3). The election of the officers was
the function of the local congregation, not of the apostles, who could,
however, declare the law-word of God concerning not only officers but
also members and their discipline (I Cor. 5:4-5). This power of the
missionary overseer was subject to the word of God, so that St. Paul
found it necessary to state the Biblical legal foundations for his judgments (I Cor. 5:1-13; 7:1-40; 8:1-13, etc.).

The local church was thus "planted" by missionaries, but it was the
local believers who established and governed the church. Their local
self-government did not mean autonomy, but neither did their subordination to the church at large have any weight or binding power apart
from Scripture. All authority being grounded in Scripture was therefore limited by Scripture.

Fourth, the priesthood of all believers means what the Rev. V.

2. W. Bacher, "Synagogue," in *ibid.*, IV, 636-642.

Robert Nilson, in a sermon in Long Beach, California, in 1970, called "an every believer ministry." St. Paul, in Ephesians 4:7, declared "But unto every one of us is given grace according to the measure of the gift of Christ." Every believer is given a mature responsibility in terms of Christ's kingdom. In Ephesians 4:11, St. Paul cites some of the offices of that ministry; not all are called to these particular and higher offices, but "every one of us" is still called to serve God in a particular priestly calling. We have a duty to profit by the ministry of others and to grow, "That we henceforth be no more children, tossed to and fro, and carried about with every wind of doctrine" (vs. 14), but, as mature men (vs. 13), meeting our responsibilities and exercising dominion in our appointed realm.

The training of such mature men is the function of the church. The purpose of the church should not be to bring men into subjection to the church, but rather to train them into a royal priesthood capable of bringing the world into subjection to Christ the King. The church is the recruiting station, the training field, and the armory for Christ's army of royal priests. *It is a functional, not a terminal, institution.*

The church has by and large paid lip service to the priesthood of all believers, because its hierarchy has distrusted the implications of the doctrine, and because it has seen the church as an end in itself, not as an instrument.

Fifth, because the priesthood of all believers has a practical purpose, so does the church. To limit the church's faithfulness to a profession of faith is as wrong as limiting the believer's faithfulness to a profession of faith. Such a profession is necessary, but it is not enough. "Thou believest that there is one God; thou doest well: the devils also believe, and tremble. But wilt thou know, O vain man, that faith without works is dead?" (James 2:19, 20). Long before the disciples were fully aware of our Lord's true nature and calling, devils confessed Him to be the Christ and the Son of God (Matt. 8:29; Mark 1:24; 3:11; 5:7; Luke 4:34; cf. Acts 19:15). A good tree brings forth good fruit: thus it is by their fruits that we shall know men (Matt. 7: 16-20). True faith reveals itself in works.

It is thus very wrong for men to argue that it is wrong to secede from a church because its formal profession of faith is still orthodox. Most modernist churches still retain orthodox creeds and confessions. The statement that "To secede from a denomination that is still doctrinally sound officially is, to be sure, a most serious business,"[3] is nonsense. Every professional thief is formally an honest man; he does not advertise himself as a thief. Virtually every apostate or derelict church

---

3. John Vander Ploeg, "Secession Is a Serious Business," *Torch and Trumpet,* vol. 20, no. 11 (Nov., 1970), p. 6.

denies that it is anything but a true church, so that to be "doctrinally sound officially" is meaningless. Is it doctrinally sound in deed as in thought, in its profession as in its practice?

Sixth, the priesthood of all believers is, as we have seen, a "royal priesthood," and has reference to the Kingdom of God. As Van Til has pointed out, "the Kingdom of God is man's summum bonum."

> By the term kingdom of God we mean the *realized program of God for man*. We would think of man as (a) adopting for himself this program of God as his own ideal and as (b) setting and keeping his powers in motion in order to reach that goal that has been set for him and that he has set for himself. We propose briefly to look at this program which God has set for man and which man should have set for himself.
>
> The most important aspect of this program is surely that *man should realize himself as God's vicegerent in history*. Man was created God's vicegerent and he must realize himself as God's vicegerent. There is no contradiction between these two statements. Man was created a character and yet he had to make himself ever more of a character. So we may say that man was created a king in order that he might become more of a king than he was.[4]

The purpose of man's calling as priest is thus to realize himself as God's vicegerent and to dedicate himself, his areas of dominion, and his calling to God and to the service of God's kingdom. Man's *self-realization* is possible only when man fulfils his priestly calling.

The tendency of institutions—church, state, and school—and of callings, is to absolutize themselves and to play god in the lives of men. The answer of men to this problem has come to be "democracy." Democracy, however, only aggravates the centralization of power into institutional hands, because democracy has no solution to the problem of human depravity and often fails even to admit the problem.

The doctrine of the priesthood of all believers, when properly developed, gives a Christian answer to the problem. The centralization of institutional power cannot flourish where priesthood flourishes. The practical application of the concept of priesthood led Judaism through the centuries to the creation of a state within a state and a society within societies. The doctrine of the priesthood of all believers, where adhered to, is a program for not only survival but victory as well. The modern concept of democracy is a sorry parody of this doctrine.

6. Discipline

An important and basic aspect of church law is discipline; it is also a very much misunderstood subject in church, school, and family life.

---

4. Cornelius Van Til, *Christian Theistic Ethics* (Nutley, N. J.: Presbyterian and Reformed Publishing Co., 1971), p. 44 (vol. III of *In Defense of the Faith*).

To illustrate this misunderstanding, the case of a pious couple with an erring and seriously delinquent daughter can be cited. Complaining because of her behavior, her unmarried and pregnant condition, and her contempt of their authority, the parents insisted that they had "disciplined" her regularly. She had been deprived of various privileges, and had been frequently slapped and spanked when younger. All of this was true, but the fact remained that the child had grown up radically undisciplined. The parents had confused, as all too many people do, chastisement or punishment with discipline, and the two are markedly different. Discipline is systematic training and submission to authority, and it is the result of such training. Chastisement or punishment is the penalty or beating administered for departure from authority. Clearly, *discipline* and *chastisement* are related subjects, but just as clearly they are distinct.

What churches mean when they boast of a "strict discipline" is not discipline at all usually, but strict punishment. A church which administers no punishment is most likely also an undisciplined church. However, a church which is continually involved in matters of punishment is also most likely an undisciplined church. The same observation is true of schools and families. In the case of the delinquent daughter cited above, this was very definitely the case. The girl, almost twenty years of age, was pregnant and in bad company, given to experimenting with narcotics and much else, but she did not know how to sew or cook, study or work, or obey a simple order. Her parents had raged at her, and punished her, and she had raged back at them, but discipline had been radically lacking in the home. Where there is no discipline, chastisement is ineffective and comes closer to being abuse than correction.

Failure to understand this distinction between discipline and punishment is responsible for much of the disorder in the church. In almost every church, where *discipline* is spoken of, in reality *punishment* is meant. In the confusion of the two, it is discipline that is usually lost. Thus, "The Book of Discipline" of the Orthodox Presbyterian Church is, typically, a book about judicial procedures for ascertaining and punishing sin and misconduct. Nothing is said about true discipline. The same is true in church after church.

What is discipline in essence? We have used the dictionary definition, i.e., that discipline is systematic training and submission to authority, and the result of such training. It should be added that discipline comes from disciple, which is the Latin word *discipulus*, in turn derived from *disco*, learn. *To be a disciple and to be under discipline is to be a learner in a learning process. If there is no learning, and no growth in learning, there is no discipline.*

First and foremost in considering church discipline is the fact that learning or discipline is by the word of God, by Scripture. An undisciplined church is a church in which there is a failure in the proclamation and teaching of Scripture. A church which denies the word cannot have discipline. A church which simply preaches for conversion but not for growth cannot have discipline. A church which is antinomian has denied the premise of growth and thus cannot have discipline. St. Paul declared that "Faith cometh by hearing, and hearing by the word of God" (Rom. 10:17). Regeneration is inseparable from the word of God. A living church is a church which hears the word, grows in terms of it, and is thus disciplined by it.

Second, ecclesiastical punishments, however necessary and scriptural, cannot replace the word of God as the means of discipline. Because the word is always accompanied by the power of God, it has a capacity to discipline or teach which is wholly lacking in any acts of synods or councils apart from the word. God's word accomplishes its purposes without fail, we are assured:

> For as the rain cometh down, and the snow from heaven, and returneth not thither, but watereth the earth, and maketh it bring forth and bud, that it may give seed to the sower, and bread to the eater:
> So shall my word be that goeth forth out of my mouth: it shall not return unto me void, but it shall accomplish that which I please, and it shall prosper in the thing whereto I sent it. (Isa. 55:10, 11)

Alexander identified "word" here as "everything that God utters either in the way of prediction or command."[1] Plumptre identified "word" with "the purposes of God."[2] Calvin recognized the identity of this *word* with Scripture, and with "the power and efficacy of preaching" when it is fully faithful to Scripture. It will condemn the wicked and save and strengthen the elect in terms of God's purpose.[3]

For a church to put its confidence in the disciplinary power of its own word, and its punishing powers, and to by-pass the teaching power of God's word, is to forsake true discipline for anarchy. There is a supernatural teaching or disciplining power inherent in the word of the supernatural God which is lacking in the words and actions of men. Wherever the church forsakes, neglects, or limits the word, there also the church forsakes the divine power of God's word for a purely humanistic teaching. It is not surprising, therefore, that antinomian churches have produced impotent and humanistic Christians and the world around them has steadily collapsed into humanism.

---

1. J. A. Alexander, *Isaiah*, p. 332.
2. E. H. Plumptre, "Isaiah," in Ellicott, IV, 554.
3. John Calvin, *Commentary on the Book of the Prophet Isaiah* (Grand Rapids: Eerdmans, 1956), IV, 172.

Third, in true discipline, the learning process is guided and furthered by the Holy Spirit, which is given to the elect that they might know the things which are of God. As St. Paul stated it,

> But as it is written, Eye hath not seen, nor ear heard, neither have entered into the heart of man, the things which God hath prepared for them that love him.
> But God hath revealed them unto us by his Spirit: for the Spirit searcheth all things, yea, the deep things of God.
> For what man knoweth the things of a man, save the spirit of man which is in him? even so the things of God knoweth no man, but the Spirit of God.
> Now we have received, not the spirit of the world, but the spirit which is of God; that we might know the things that are freely given to us of God (I Cor. 2:9-12)

Turning now to church chastisement, the central passage is Matthew 18:15-20, which is usually assumed to be the basis of discipline. In reality, the procedure outlined simply determines if the wrong-doer is amenable to chastisement, i.e., if there is any discipline of the word in his or her life. The assumption is that there is an actual trespass by a member or officer of the church. The *first* step (vs. 15) is to confront the person with their trespass in terms of God's law. Do they know the law of God, and are they ready to submit to it? If they do submit to that law of God, then indeed they are a "brother" in the Lord.

Second, if they neglect the word and refuse to hear it, their refusal is to be confirmed in the mouth of at least one other witness, so that at least two witnesses can testify to their apostasy and/or unbelief (vs. 16). The reference here again is to the law of God, an offense against it, a rebuke in terms of that law, and the failure to accept that law.

The *third* step is to declare the unwillingness of the guilty party to the church, "but if he neglect to hear the church, let him be unto thee as an heathen man and a publican" (vs. 17). The only possible judicial process which can take place in this third stage is if the accused party denies that the charges are true. A hearing then can determine whether the charges are true or false, i. e., if God's law has been transgressed. Failure by any party to accept God's law must lead to a break with him, to excommunication. He is to be regarded as a heathen or a publican.

The premise and ground of the authority of the individual who confronts the guilty party, and of the church in its excommunicating power, is the law-word of God. Where men "bind" on earth the consciences of men in faithfulness to that word, their actions are valid in heaven. Where in faithfulness to that word they forgive men on repentance and restitution, whom they loose on earth is loosed in heaven (vss. 18, 19). This authority is ministerial, not legislative, i.e., man is bound to God's word, not God to man's word. Where man acts in faithfulness to God's word, there he can fully expect God's supporting faithfulness. "For where two or three are gathered together in my name, there am I in the midst of them" (vs. 20). The primary reference here is to the judicial acts of chastisement and forgiveness, but the reference is also general, so that, whatever believers and churches do in faithfulness to the law-word of God, they can then count on the presence and supporting and over-ruling power of the Lord Himself.

Matthew 18:15-20 refers to and is based on laws given in the Old Testament: Leviticus 19:17 requires the rebuke; Deuteronomy 17:6 and 19:15 require at least two witnesses. Christ restated this law, and the apostolic epistles repeatedly confirm it: Luke 17:3; James 5:20; I Peter 3:1; John 8:17; II Corinthians 13:1; Hebrews 10:28; I Timothy 5:19-20; Romans 16:17; I Corinthians 5:9; II Thessalonians 3:6, 14; II John 10; Matthew 16:19; John 20:23; I Corinthians 5:4-5; Matthew 5:24; James 5:16; I John 3:22; 5:14. All these verses clearly confirm the full validity of the Old Testament laws. In James 5:16 and I John 3:22; 5:14, the relationship between obedience to the law and efficacious prayer is strongly stressed.

Thus, there can be no true discipline in a church, or in school and home, unless there be also a full and faithful preaching of the law-word of God. Antinomianism cannot produce discipline.

It must be added, however, that, even as discipline cannot be equated with chastisement, so neither can discipline be equated with order. Order of sorts can also be an outcome of stagnation and death; the graveyard is usually an orderly place, far more orderly than the best of cities, but this is hardly a commendable order for life. False order is as alien to discipline as disorder. The common expression "law and order" sums up the matter. True order is a product of true law. The discipline of God's law-word is alone productive of true order.

It should be added that there is an alternative in some cases to chastisement. This is separation. In Acts 15:36-41, we read of a serious disagreement between Paul and Barnabas. The answer to this conflict was not Matthew 18:15-20, followed by church trials and appeals. Had Paul and Barnabas chosen this course, neither would have been able to accomplish much work. Paul could have been tied down with endless appeals and trials on charges of slandering John Mark, or he could have accused Barnabas of failing to punish Mark for neglect of duty. Instead of Mark's Gospel and Paul's epistles, we would have had endless legal documents from both, if some modern churchmen would have their way. Instead, Paul and Barnabas separated, and both accomplished much in their separate courses.

7. Rebukes and Excommunication

In I Timothy 5:1-16, St. Paul discusses the *rebuke* of church members. Elders are to be first entreated "as a father," younger men are to be rebuked as "brethren," "the elder women as mothers, the younger as sisters." Widows, men and women, the idle and busybodies, are all mentioned by St. Paul in his declaration of the rebuke. The rebuke is the first stage in chastisement and has reference to Matthew 18:15; it has reference to a known and obvious offense which is brought to the attention of the offender by pastor or member in the light of Scripture; it can also be the last step in some matters which call for a public rebuke (I Tim. 5:20).

In this epistle, St. Paul is plainly concerned with the law (I Tim. 1:3-11). The areas of concern for rebuke, chastisement, and excommunication are then cited in terms of church problems: they are essentially matters of faith and morals, of authority and law. The goal of such actions is not the church but God's kingdom, not an institution but God's reign. Some, although by no means all, of the areas cited by St. Paul are, *first*, authority. Men must assume the leadership in matters of the faith as well in the home, and women must not step outside the bounds of their position (I Tim. 2:8-15). St. Paul, from this statement of authority, goes on to deal with the authority, in terms of qualifications, of a bishop or presbyter. Authority is given only to men who can exercise authority, and whose ability at disciplining themselves and their household is a proven one (I Tim. 3:1-13).

Second, areas of doctrine and false teaching concerning doctrine and morality are discussed (I Tim. 4:1-16). Asceticism and sacerdotal celibacy are condemned. We have here no new law, but the Biblical law as a whole, and Biblical faith as a whole, affirmed. No new dispensation has rendered the Old Testament view of meats and marriage obsolete.

Third, areas of morality are cited as areas for rebuke. It is the obligation of parents to teach their children godliness. Let us examine specifically what St. Paul says. In I Timothy 5:3 he commands, "Honour widows that are widows indeed." Moffatt accurately paraphrases this as, "Widows in real need must be supported from the fund." The meaning of honoring father and mother clearly involves support. The widows excluded from church support are, as Lenski summarized it, "such as have relatives and such as plunge into a gay life."[1] Worthy widows, in return for their support, work for the church.

---

1. R. C. H. Lenski, *The Interpretation of St. Paul's Epistles to the Colossians, to the Thessalonians, to Timothy, to Titus, and to Philemon* (Columbus, Ohio: The Wartburg Press, 1937, 1946), p. 655.

Widows with families are then cited. These have a teaching function, as does the church, in relation to their children and grandchildren:

> When a widow has children or grandchildren, they (the children and grandchildren) must learn that the first duty of religion is to their own household, and that they should make some return to those who have brought them up. In God's sight this is commendable indeed (I Tim. 6:4, Moffatt).

Failure to care for members of one's family thus constitutes a violation of the fifth commandment; it is also a violation of the eighth, in that it is a form of theft. This same point, the duty of providing for one's family, is restated in vs. 8;

> Whoever does not provide for his own relatives and particularly for his own family, has repudiated the faith: he is worse than an infidel (Moffatt).

Lenski's comment on this verse is very much to the point:

> This is stated in the strongest form. . . . In v. 4 it is: "Let them learn!" Here the sense is: "If one will not learn, this is the verdict to be pronounced on him." But in v. 4 we have the case of only one widow; here it is a question of any and of all dependents. The reference of "anyone" is perfectly plain: it is the person who has a household, whose business it is to provide for the members of this household. The verb means "to think beforehand" and thus (intensified) to carry out this thinking, i.e., "to provide." Paul states it in the most comprehensive way: "provide for his own and especially his family members." The preferred reading has only one article, for Paul does not refer to two distinct groups. . . . "His own," are all who belong to the head of the house, servants and members of the family. . . . Here is a strong argument regarding the support of a widowed mother or grandmother; one ought to provide for even his servants, how much more then for one's own mother or grandmother. But all dependents are included: father and mother, if these are dependent, wife and children, also other relatives such as orphaned nephews and nieces.
>
> This is the Christian teaching. Now he who will not live up to that "the faith . . . he denies," etc. . . .
>
> In order to make plain the enormity of such an action, Paul adds in an explicative way: "and is worse than an unbeliever," one who never believed and never professed to believe. The thought is not that an unbeliever would always provide for the members of his family and his servants—many do not; but when an unbeliever does not do so, bad as he is, bad as his action is, it is not as bad as having the true teaching and then flagrantly denying it. What the congregation should do with a member of this kind does not need to be added. His verdict is written here.[2]

---

2. *Ibid.*, p. 663 f.

Those who do not support their own are first to be rebuked and then excommunicated.

Where false doctrine is involved, we are required to "avoid" such persons (Rom. 16:17), indeed, to "reject" them "after the first and second admonition." We are not to receive such persons into our house, nor to bid them God speed, to do so makes us partaker of their evil deeds (II John 10, 11).

Where immorality, such as non-support is involved, such men are also to be rejected. The same is true of unrepentant fornicators who are church members; they are to be excommunicated (I Cor. 5:9-11).

Just as "honor" means more than verbal respect and includes support, so "requite" and "provide" mean more than merely financial support. To provide for one's children includes a Christian education, for the child's mind and body must both be provided for. Placing children in a public school or in an atheistic school is a failure to provide for them adequately.

It should be noted that the apostolic church, and for centuries later the Christian church, provided for widows, orphans, and the sick, for all needy persons, as a part of its duty. In I Timothy 5:10, reference is made to lodging strangers, and elsewhere to hospitality (I Tim. 3:2). In those days, outside of Palestine inns were usually houses of prostitution as well and hence no place for Christians to stay. As a result, the duty of caring for travelling Christians was an important one. The early church was thus a very extensive government, and it continued to be so almost to the twentieth century.

It is important to restate here the meaning of *government* in its historic Biblical sense. The basic government of man is the self-government of Christian man. The family is an important area of government also, and the basic one. The church is an area of government, and the school still another. A man's calling is an area of government, and society at large governs men by its standards and opinions. The state is thus one government among many; it is civil government, and it cannot be permitted to usurp or claim areas which do not belong to it.

Because of the Biblical understanding of government, many law spheres exist, and each has its inner authority, discipline and requirements. These spheres are separate but interlocking. The state thus must require children to support their parents, but the church, whether or not the state acts, has a duty to teach and to chastise or to excommunicate its members in this same matter. Similarly, the family is required to teach such support (I Tim. 5:4) and to deal with its erring members for failure to obey.

Another area of morality cited by St. Paul is with respect to wages. The principle, previously considered in relation to Deuteronomy 25:4,

"Thou shalt not muzzle the ox when he treadeth out the corn," is that "The labourer is worthy of his reward" (I Tim. 5:18). Economic considerations are not set aside by this requirement but rather reinforced. The wise man is a good steward not only of money and materials but also of men. The man who pays his workers as little as possible is ultimately the loser before God.

It is clear thus that the punishment inflicted by the church has primary reference to man's behavior before God and man; the reduction of much church chastisement to offenses against the church is a perversion of Scripture and a limitation of the church's jurisdiction.

8. Power and Authority

St. Paul, in reminding the Corinthian Christians of their destiny, said, "Do ye not know that the saints shall judge the world?" (I Cor. 6:2). Moffatt renders this, "Do you not know that the saints are to manage the world?," a meaning we need to remind ourselves of. Church government is a prelude to world government, not by the church but by "the saints." In trying to establish the necessary church government towards this end, Paul's constant appeal was, not to the form of church government or to the members, but to the law of God and the growth of the saints in terms of it (I Cor. 6:15–9:27). Judging, governing, or managing of the world is in terms of God's law.

When St. Paul expressed indignation at the idea of Christians going to a Roman court, he was speaking as a good Jew, in the tradition of the law (I Cor. 6:1). To go to an outside court was forbidden in Israel, under normal circumstances, in problems between Jews. In such instances resort was had to Jewish courts, a tradition of law maintained to this day in many circles. Similarly, St. Paul felt that, between believers, the church authorities constituted the governing body. Between a Jew and a Gentile, or between a Christian and a non-Christian, there could be a legitimate use of the outside or civil courts. These courts not being governed by God's law were therefore not trustworthy agencies of justice.

Let us turn now to Homer's *Odyssey*. Odysseus returned home after many years of wandering. During that time, it had not occurred to him that chastity might be required of him, although he expected it of his wife and slave girls. The suitors of his wife—for Odysseus was presumed dead—raped some of these slave girls. Odysseus himself acknowledged this: "Ye dogs, ye said in your hearts that I should never more come home from the land of the Trojans, in that ye wasted my house, and lay with the maidservants by force, and traitorously wooed my wife while I was yet alive." The nurse Eurycleia said that twelve of his fifty slave-girls were involved: "Of these twelve in all have gone

the way of shame, and honour not me, nor their lady Penelope." After
killing the suitors, Odysseus and his son Telemachus, and others,
turned to the girls, to execute them. Telemachus hung all twelve on
one cable. The reason for the execution was stated by Telemachus:
"These . . . have poured dishonour on my head and on my mother, and
have lain with the wooers."¹ The offense of the girls was not against
God: it was against Odysseus and Telemachus. The involvement of
these girls with the men who had raped them, or perhaps seduced them,
was not as important as the "dishonour" felt by Odysseus and Telemachus. Law for them had no higher reach than themselves. "The
girls were property. The disposal of property was then, as now, a
matter of expediency, not of right and wrong."²

The same was true in early Rome. The father had power over his
children: they were property. Law did not transcend man, and it was
essentially limited to the family of man. Subsequently, the state took
over the family's powers and made itself the father of its people and
the source of law.

In either case, law was essentially humanistic and man-centered.
Since man as family head or man as statist leader issued the law, the
law was total. This appeared very clearly in Plato's *Laws*:

> The principal thing is that none, man or woman, should ever be
> without an officer set over him, and that none should get the mental
> habit of taking any step, whether in earnest or in jest, on his indi-
> vidual responsibility . . . in a word, we must train the mind not
> even to consider acting as an individual or know how to do it.³

If no law of God exists, man's humanistic alternatives, when pressed to
their logical conclusions, mean either anarchism or totalitarian statism.
Brophy's comment on the Leopold and Loeb case is revealing at this
point:

> What emerges from reading an account of the case is a failure—
> or, rather, a confusion—on the part of society, which, in all its deal-
> ings with Leopold and Loeb, in their education and in what
> amounted to their further education, their trial, never offered them
> any reason why they should not murder or why they should feel
> remorse.
>
> What it did offer them was God, and they saw through him. "He
> gave up the idea that there was a God," states one of the medical
> reports on Leopold, "saying that if a God exists some pre-God
> must have created him." In this line of thinking he reasons by
> analogy. . . . Having been taught that the moral law drew its
> sanction from God, the young men were simply being logical in

1. Homer, *Odyssey*, bk. XXII, S. H. Butcher and Andrew Lang translation.
2. Aldo Leopold, *A Sand County Almanac* (New York: Sierra Club/Ballan-
tine Book, [1949], 1970), p. 237.
3. *Laws*, 942 AB.

concluding that to jettison God was to jettison the moral law as well. Indeed, this, in society's eyes, was their crime—or at least the crime of Leopold, the more intelligent of the two: he reasoned. And, having worked out his position by reason, he could not be induced to change it under emotional pressure from the threat of death. As the medical report records, "he stated that consistency has always been a sort of God to him."

Society could make nothing of Leopold except to classify him as abnormal, by which it meant he was a non-conformer—in his sexual tastes, his very imagination. . . .[4]

Anarchism or totalitarianism, these are the alternatives. Either people, after Plato's hope, who do "not even . . . consider acting as an individual or know how to do it," or individuals who are an absolute law unto themselves—these are the alternatives humanism offers to man.

But the saints are to govern the world in terms of God's law, which means that they must know that law. Thus, a basic requirement of healthy church life is a constant study of God's law, its implications and its applications.

The question of *authority* is inseparable from law in any Biblical sense. A primary meaning of authority is, "The right to command and to enforce obedience; the right to act officially." The origin of authority is a Latin word, *augeo*, increase. Authority has a natural increase to it. True authority prospers and abounds. Power and authority are not identical words. Power is strength or force; power can and often does exist without authority. The power of Odysseus and Telemachus, and the powers of the Roman Empire, were real powers, but, in terms of God's law, they lacked authority, although they had a formal authority merely as legitimate governments in their societies. As Denis de Rougemont pointed out, "One does not become a father by stealing a child. One can steal the child, not paternity. One can steal power, not authority."[5]

The church must, by its faithfulness to the law-word of God, establish, strengthen, and increase its authority. Its power will increase, St. Paul indicated to the Corinthians, as Christians obey the law of God and as the church applies it to its internal affairs, and as it calls upon its member-citizens to apply it to the world around them.

The ground of this increased power is Jesus Christ, who declared, "All power is given unto me in heaven and in earth" (Matt. 28:18). As the absolute possessor of all power, He is the predestinating source of all immediate power. He is also the perfect coincidence of power

---

4. Brigid Brophy, *Black Ship to Hell* (New York: Harcourt, Brace and World, 1962), p. 30 f.

5. Denis de Rougemont, *The Devil's Share* (Washington, D. C.: Bollingen Series II, 1944), p. 31.

and authority. In the school of history, the church is held back, rebuked, and humbled whenever its power ceases to be grounded in the
authority of Christ's law-word, or wherever its authority seeks support
in other lords than Christ. The church is required to teach all men and
nations "to observe all things whatsoever I have commanded you:
and lo, I am with you alway, even unto the end of the world" (Matt.
28:20). His presence and His power undergird those who teach the
observance of all that Christ commands.

Power, when divorced from godly authority, becomes progressively
demonic. Authority can be legitimate in a human sense, resting on
succession or election, and yet be immoral and hostile to God's order.
Thus, the authority of Nero was somewhat legitimate, and Christians
were required to obey him, but his authority was ungodly and implicitly
and explicitly satanic in its development. True order requires that
both power and authority be godly in their nature and application.

Some of the aspects of this problem can be best illustrated by the report
of an able and thoughtful Christian, who suddenly realized that his
day dreams were probably satanic. He dreamed of having enough
power to eliminate by execution all traitors and communists, and to
have all Americans miraculously turned into converts. In his thinking,
he gave assent to Christ; in his imagination he was asking Christ to
submit to Satan's temptation. He wanted to compel belief by miracles
(Matt. 4:5-7), and to provide security from problems miraculously
(Matt. 4:1-4).

Then he raised a very discerning question: is the alternative merely
the way of conversion and love, without any law-order and coercion,
and without miracles, or do miracles, laws, and coercion somehow have
a place?

To answer this question, let us first look at Matthew 13:58, which
tells us that in "his own country," Nazareth (Matt. 13:54), Jesus
"did not many mighty works there because of their unbelief." It is a
serious error to say that Jesus' power to perform miracles was conditional
upon faith on the person's or the audience's part. His power was entirely from Himself, by virtue of His deity; it was not in any sense
dependent on the response of the people. There had to be, thus, another reason for the limited number of miracles performed in Nazareth.
Some were performed, although apparently not publicly, for we are told
that "he did *not many* mighty works," which implies *some* were done.
The miracles were never performed to convert people; the demand
of the scribes and Pharisees for a "sign" specifically aimed at compelling
them to belief, or, rather, at making faith unnecessary because of sight,
was rejected by Jesus (Matt. 12:38, 45; 16:1-5).

The purpose of the miracles was to glorify God, and the reaction of faith to the miracles was to glorify God also (Mark 2:12). There is thus a very important place in the life of the converted person for miraculous and providential help from God; it is an aspect of His governing care.

Similarly, there is a place for coercion. Justice and law require it. They are futile, however, without a basis in a people of faith who can maintain and develop a social order. If tomorrow all the internal and external enemies of the United States were miraculously destroyed, the major result would be the further decline and decay of American life; there would then be the freedom to sin with impunity insofar as historical consequences are concerned. If all or almost all Americans were at the same time miraculously converted, the evil would be compounded. The point of the daydream was humanistic: its purpose was national peace and freedom. Had it been international peace and freedom, the humanism would have been no less real. The chief end of such a dream is human order and man's peace. It is thus a variation of the social gospel.

The primary purpose of conversion is that man be reconciled to God; reconciliation with his fellow man and with himself is a secondary aspect of this fact, a *necessary* by-product but still a by-product. The purpose of regeneration is that man reconstruct all things in conformity to God's order, not in terms of man's desire for peace. This purpose and mission involves law and coercion.

Regeneration is God's sovereign act in terms of His sovereign purpose. It is coercive in that it is God's act, and yet, because man himself is God's act, regeneration is not coercive in that it comes as a climax to God's work within man's heart. Neither conversions nor miracles are man's work. For man to seek forced conversions or miracles in terms of his own hopes is wrong; man can require obedience to God's law, but he cannot play God.

Where power and true authority are together, there man does not play God; he serves God in terms of His law and He prays to God. Power and authority are used to further godly order, not human hopes of order. God's order required the fall of Rome, not its peace. Many Christians prayed for Rome, and rightfully so; they sinned when they limited God's work to the framework of the empire.

9. Peace

A central purpose of God's plan for man and the earth is the establishment of His peace. This peace is often described symbolically as a peace, not only with God, but between man and man, and man and nature. We are told thus that

The wolf shall dwell with the lamb, and the leopard shall lie down with the kid; and the calf and the young lion and the fatling together; and a little child shall lead them.

And the cow and the bear shall feed; and their young ones shall lie down together; and the lion shall eat straw like the ox.

And the sucking child shall play on the hole of the asp, and the weaned child shall put his hand on the cockatrice' den.

They shall not hurt nor destroy in all my holy mountain: for the earth shall be full of the knowledge of the LORD, as the waters cover the sea (Isa. 11:6-9).

Another equally familiar symbol involves the vine and the fig tree, both symbols not only of peace but of fertility and prosperity as well. We meet with it repeatedly in Scripture (II Kings 18:31; Isa. 36:16), but its best-known statements are following:

And he shall judge many people, and rebuke strong nations afar off; and they shall beat their swords into plowshares, and their spears into pruninghooks; nation shall not lift up a sword against nation, neither shall they learn war any more.

And they shall sit every man under his vine and under his fig tree; and none shall make them afraid: for the mouth of the LORD of hosts hath spoken it (Micah 4:3, 4).

And Judah and Israel dwelt safely, every man under his vine and under his fig tree, from Dan even to Beersheba, all the days of Solomon (I Kings 4:25).

In that day, saith the LORD of hosts, shall ye call every man his neighbour under the vine and under the fig tree (Zech. 3:10).

Of these, Micah 4:3, 4 and Zechariah 3:10 are messianic prophecies, describing the culmination of the Messiah's reign.

Jesus cited Himself as the source of this peace, as the true vine, declaring, "I am the true vine" (John 15:1). More directly, He said, "Peace I leave with you, my peace I give unto you: not as the world giveth, give I unto you. Let not your heart be troubled, neither let it be afraid" (John 14:27). When Jesus cursed the fig tree (Matt. 21: 19 ff.; Mark 11:13, 14), it was Israel's peace which was cursed by Him who is the true peace.

Before the fall, not only did man dwell in peace in Eden, but the earth also, and the animals. Their peace was broken by man's sin, and now, St. Paul declares, "the whole creation" waits earnestly for the deliverance and restoration to be worked through Christ and the children of God (Rom. 8:19-23).

The restoration of that peace begins with man's restoration to life by the regenerating work of Jesus Christ. Man is then a new creation (Moffatt, II Cor. 5:14, "There is a new creation whenever a man comes to be in Christ; what is old is gone, the new has come.").

The concept of the peace which is the inheritance of every man in

Christ is a part of the doctrine of the sabbath, of man's rest in his Lord. The very earth too is required to be given its rest and peace, because the earth is the Lord's.

This concept of peace had a profound influence on law. Keeton's comment on the medieval doctrine of the peace in England is very instructive:

> Another factor of importance which influenced the growth of the criminal law in the first century after the Conquest was the concept of the King's peace. In Saxon law every freeman has a peace. So also had the Church, and the peace of God governed all holy days. For breaches of a person's peace, e.g., by the commission of a crime within it, compensation must be paid, as well as compensation to the victim or his kin. Above all other peaces was that of the King, and even in Saxon times we hear of the efforts made by strong kings to preserve it, especially on "the King's highway." In the hands of the royal administrators after the Conquest this proved a dynamic concept, and, as Maitland once expressed it, eventually the King's peace swallowed up the peace of everyone else. This happened in two ways. Gradually the money payments in respect of the breach of the peace of other persons ceased to be levied, whilst the conception of the King's peace was extended to the entire realm. Any serious crime thus became a breach of King's peace, and a felony. Already by the time of Bracton, in the thirteenth century, it has become a common form to charge an accused in the following terms: "Whereas the said B was in the peace of God and of our Lord the king, there came the said N. feloniously as a felon," etc. Even today a person accused of a felony is charged that he did "feloniously and contrary to the peace of our sovereign lady, the queen," etc.

> It was the characteristic of outlaws that they had put themselves out of the King's peace, so that every man's hand was against them. Moreover, the King's peace was at first conceived as existing so long as the King was alive.[1]

Maitland's statement is well phrased: "Eventually the King's peace swallowed up the peace of everyone else." *Peace was viewed not as an aspect of God's order, but as a product of the state's life.* The difference between these two perspectives can scarcely be overstated.

The meaning of the word *peace* in Hebrew is revelatory of its Biblical significance. According to Brown,

> PEACE, the translation in OT of the Heb. . . . *shalom* (from the root . . . "to be whole"—"wholeness," "soundness," hence health, wellbeing, prosperity; more particularly, peace as opposed to war, concord as opposed to strife. . . .

> The fundamental meaning of *shalom* is prosperity, wellbeing, good of any kind, a meaning which reappears in the Gr. *eirene*. . . .

1. George W. Keeton, *The Norman Conquest and the Common Law* (London: Ernest Benn Ltd.; New York: Barnes & Noble, 1966), p. 175.

> In the primary sense of prosperity, peace is a blessing of which God alone is the author (Isa. 45:7 . . .). . . .
>
> Among the blessings to which Israel looks forward in the Messianic time none is more emphasized than peace. . . .
>
> The NT shares with OT the view of peace as a characteristic of the Messianic time (Lk. 1:79, 2:14, 19:38, Acts 10:36). In this sense is probably to be understood the greeting of the disciples on their missionary journey (Mt. 10:12, 13, Lk. 10:5, 6). The gospel of the Messiah is expressly called a gospel of peace (Eph. 6:15, Acts 10:36). . . . Jesus Himself is the great peace-maker. . . .
>
> Characteristic of NT is the view of peace as the present possession of the Christian. . . .[2]

In the Biblical sense, peace is that order and prosperity which flows out of reconcilation to God and a restoration to life under God. Life in Eden was marked by peace with God and therefore peace with man, within man, and with and within nature. Life in Christ means the progressive restoration of that peace as man grows in Christ and as the world is brought under His dominion. The source of peace is man's regeneration in Christ; it is more than the cessation of hostilities: it is the growth of communion and it is personal fulfilment in Christ as well.

Statist peace is at best the absence of hostilities and the suppression of criminal activities. Because the state cannot regenerate man, it cannot establish even this limited form of peace. The state's power is the power of the sword essentially. The state can thus order men to love one another and to live in peace, but its repressive measures only add another element of hostility to the situation.

The state, moreover, in its efforts to impose a repressive and armed peace on its citizens, destroys the peace of those citizens as it usurps God's peace and the freeman's peace. The state can only be an instrument for peace when it is an instrument of God and a ministry of Christ. Its efforts then are limited to their proper realm, to be a ministry of justice.

Clearly, *peace* as prosperity and well-being is very closely connected with *salvation*, victory, and health. The picture of peace, every man under his vine and under his fig tree, is one of prosperity, safety, contentment, and joy. Peace and salvation are thus God-centered concepts which also mean the fulfilment of man. God being the author and creator of all things, there can be no fulfilment for man apart from Him. Therefore, "the wicked are like the troubled sea, when it cannot rest, whose waters cast up mire and dirt. There is no peace, saith my God, to the wicked" (Isa. 57:21).

---

2. W. Adams Brown, "Peace," in Hastings, *Dictionary of the Bible*, III, 733.

This peace, however, is more than the absence of hostilities: it is peace with God. Peace with God means warfare with the enemies of God. Christ made clear that allegiance to Him meant a sword of division (Matt. 10:34-36). In a sinful world, some warfare is inescapable. A man must therefore pick his enemies: God or sinful man? If a man is at peace with sinful men, he is at war with God. Peace in one sector means warfare in another. God alone, however, can give inner peace now, and, finally, world peace through His sovereign law (Micah 4:2).

XV

NOTES ON THE LAW IN WESTERN SOCIETY

In the canons of the early church, the importance of Biblical law is readily apparent. The churches clearly felt that Biblical law was binding on believers.

Not all went as far nor were as literal as the Church of Armenia, in which in those days and for centuries thereafter, "only those are appointed to the clerical orders who are of priestly descent (following in this Jewish customs)." This practice was condemned by Canon XXIII of the Quinisext Council (or the Council in Trullo) in 692.[1] Canon XCIX of the same council referred also to the fact that "certain persons boil joints of meat within the sanctuary and offer portions to the priests, distributing it after the Jewish fashion." Strabo gives an account of a similar custom in the West in the ninth century.[2] But this is not all. The Armenian Church had animal sacrifices after the Old Testament law, continuing them long after the Jews abandoned them, well into the twentieth century. These took place at the church door and were a freewill offering to the Lord, commemorating the Old Testament sacrifices, and given as a result of vows made to the Lord as a part of prayer. The animal had to be levitically acceptable—a yearling, and free from all blemish—according to the law. The prayer read in part as follows:

> For through thy blessed prophet Moses thou enjoined on thy people Israel to offer up to thee sacrifices, of their flocks and sheep and of other pure animals, bringing them to the door of the tent of witness, to the Levite priests, who should lay their hands on them and pour out their blood on thy holy altar, O Lord; and thereby sins were expiated and petitions fulfilled.
>
> Yet in all this thou prefiguredst, as in a shadow, the things to come, that true salvation which thou hast graciously given us through thy coming into the world. For thou thyself, all-merciful and beneficent Lord, through thy foreseeing Spirit declaredst by the prophet, saying: I accept not of your steers the fat, but offer a sacrifice of praise to God, and with willing mind tender unto God a bloodless

---

1. Henry R. Percival, *The Seven Ecumenical Councils*, Second Series of Philip Schaff and Henry Wace, *Nicene and Post-Nicene Fathers* (Grand Rapids: Eerdmans, 1956), XIV, 381. This writer comes from an ancient line of such hereditary Armenian priests; his father, the son of a priest, was a Presbyterian clergyman, as he is also.
2. *Ibid.*, p. 407.

victim. For is there not the saying: The sacrifice of God is an afflicted spirit, and a humble spirit doth God not despise?

So now that we have sinned and are unworthy, humbled in our hearts fall down before thine infinite pity: and supplicate for thy abundant love of mankind and mercy, and for thy unfailing promise which thou madest to thy beloved ones, to our fathers.

Condescend, O Lord, to this our offering, and accept it from our hands; even as thou didst the whole burnt-offerings of rams and steers, and as thou didst the innumerable offerings of fat lambs.

Graciously grant our petitions, that we may not become the sport of our enemies, but rather rejoice in thy salvation. For if thou weighest all the mountains and the plains in thy glance, and holdest heaven and earth in the hollow of thy hand, and sittest in the height of heights on the throne of the cheribim, and the abysses are not hidden from thee, and all four-footed animals and all that have the breath of life suffice thee not for the whole burnt offering—how dare we to presume before thee and to offer sacrifice?[3]

The Greek church also had prayers for animal sacrifices.[4]

The levitical regulations concerning the priesthood were also applied to the clergy of the church, and Leviticus 21:17-23 was carefully obeyed. Since eunuchs were thus barred from the ministry, a problem was created when Rome or the barbarians deliberately castrated the clergy to destroy their validity of orders or ordination. The Council of Nicea in 318 declared that "those castrated by barbarians" could "remain among the clergy," in view of the circumstances of their blemish.[5] The Council of Ancyra, Canon XI, in 314 had to consider the cases of betrothed virgins who had been raped; in such cases, no blemish was ascribed to the girl. The canonical epistle of St. Gregory Thaumaturgus made a similar point in Canon I.[6]

Ancyra, in Canon XXI, dealt severely with abortion (ten years of penance); transvestites were excommunicated; various sexual offenses were repeatedly cited as cause of life-long excommunication (since the church had no power to enforce a death penalty); murder, divination, the worship of angels, heresy, and other matters were dealt with in terms of the Biblical law, as far as the church could go.[7]

Restitution was basic to canon law and to penance. The Apostolic Constitutions cite it in Canon LXXII, as did St. Gregory Thaumaturgus in his canonical epistle, Canon VIII.[8]

The canons and regulations concerning the sabbath are of especial

3. F. C. Conybeare, editor, *Rituale Armenorum* (Oxford: Clarendon Press, 1905), p. 56.
4. *Ibid.*, p. 403 f.
5. Canon I in Percival, *op. cit.*, p. 8.
6. *Ibid.*, pp. 68, 602.
7. *Ibid.*, pp. 70 f., 73 f., 82 f., 150, 606-609, etc.
8. *Ibid.*, pp. 598, 603.

interest. Timothy, bishop of Alexandria, required that man and wife forbear from "the conjugal act . . . On Saturday, and the Lord's day; for on those days the spiritual sacrifice is offered."[9] This was in terms of Exodus 19:15 and was designed to separate any fertility cult element from worship. Christians were not always free to rest on the Lord's Day, the Christian sabbath, and necessity was thus a legitimate excuse; respect for the Jewish sabbath, however, was forbidden:

> Christians must not judaize by resting on the Sabbath, but must work on that day, rather honouring the Lord's Day; and, if they can, resting then as Christians. But if any shall be found to be judaizers, let them be anathema from Christ.[10]

Because the Lord's Day was a time of rest and joy, fasting on Sunday was condemned and required excommunication.[11] The same council, Gangra, condemned those who condemned marriage (Canon I); it condemned vegetarianism (Canon II); it condemned those who separated themselves from a married clergy (Canon IV); and so on.

The early church thus clearly obeyed Biblical law. This is not to say that its obedience was by any means perfect. Custom at times overruled the law. The first canonical epistle of Basil, archbishop of Caesarea in Cappadocia, to Amphilochius, bishop of Iconium, made note of this in Canon IX:

> Our Lord is equal, to the man and woman forbidding divorce, save in case of fornication; but custom requires women to retain their husbands, though they be guilty of fornication. . . .[12]

There was, however, no lack of intelligent application of the law. Thus Canons XXXIII and LII of Basil declared that child neglect which led to death was murder.[13]

The church thus was mindful of the centrality of Biblical law to Christian faith, and its canon law was the application of the rule of that law to the problems of life. The church, however, was within the framework of the Roman Empire and Roman law. It is necessary to cite briefly some aspects of the interpretations of Roman law within the context of Christian faith.

Rome had reached a centralization and over-simplification of the control of men which had begun to hamper and destroy social order. C. Dickerman Williams has said, of the period of the Theodosian Code (313-468),

> The Theodosian Code and Novels concern a period in history

---

9. *Ibid.*, p. 613.
10. *Ibid.*, p. 148; Canon XXIX of the Synod of Laodicea, A.D. 343-381.
11. *Ibid.*, p. 99; Canon VXIII, Council of Gangra or Paphlagonia, 325 or 380.
12. *Ibid.*, p. 605.
13. *Ibid.*, pp. 606, 608.

much like ours in many of its problems. But in that day it was no longer possible to attempt to solve problems by greater centralization and officialdom. At the time of the earliest edict included in the Code the centralization of society could go no further because it was already complete. An area which was for its inhabitants the entire world had been welded into a single organization. Social, economic and religious activities were administered or rigidly controlled by the state. The authority of the Emperor was unchallenged. The edicts compiled in the Theodosian Code and Novels represent the often desperate efforts to make the system work. But during these years it was the tendency to disintegration that was irresistible. The enactments designed to keep the organization together failed. Within only a few years after the last of the edicts the Empire had been shattered into a thousand fragments. Thus that era, unlike ours, was one of disintegration, albeit a disintegration that was most involuntary.[14]

Exhaustion, spiritual and physical, was destroying the empire. The centralization of power only aggravated the basic irresponsibility which had led to the destruction of resources. Williams is again to the point in his comment:

> Now the Empire's problem was shortages: shortages of grain, of materials, and of men. . . . Throughout the Mediterranean basin agriculture had been operated to supply the distant mistress of the world. The rewards of the consumer had been too attractive; those for the producer not enough. Lands, especially in Italy, had gone out of cultivation. Areas in Africa from which Rome had drawn grain and meat for centuries were becoming desert. Spain and other countries had been deforested to provide fuel for the public baths of Rome. "The decline of the Roman Empire is a story of deforestation, soil exhaustion and erosion. . . . From Spain to Palestine there are no forests left in the Mediterranean littoral, the region is pronouncedly arid instead of having the mild, humid character of forest-clad lands, and most of its former bounteously rich topsoil is lying at the bottom of the sea" (White and Jacks, *Vanishing Lands*, p̃. 8).

> Today it is fashionable in some quarters to scoff at occasional warnings of the exhaustion of natural resources. Such levity would have found no echo at the courts of the later Emperors.[15]

The emperors were helpless to reverse the trend. Power had been centralized, and the empire was now in the hands of the emperor and his bureaucracy, who could not begin to cope with the problems on the grass-roots level, where most of the problems were. "The management of the gigantic administrative machine was simply beyond their ca-

---

14. C. Dickerman Williams, "Introduction," in Clyde Pharr with T. S. Davidson and M. B. Pharr, translators, editors, *The Theodosian Code and Novels and the Sirmondian Constitutions*, p. xvii.

15. *Ibid.*, p. xix f.

pacity."[16] After a certain point of centralization, a bureaucracy becomes unrelated to reality; it is busy managing management and governing the machinery of power. "The wonder is that the Empire's territorial integrity was preserved so long." After a certain point a bureaucracy also becomes cannibalistic.

> The Emperors relied for their political support upon the urban proletariat, especially that of the city of Rome, and upon the civil and military bureaucracy. To maintain that support, it was necessary to favor those consumer elements in the population, especially vis-a-vis the rural producers. The effect of that policy was to discourage production and to tempt the farmers to move to the cities. The Code and the Novels show that in order to get supplies for the city dwellers and government personnel, it was then necessary to adopt harsh measures such as rural serfdom and taxes payable in kind. The enforcement of such measures required an increased state apparatus of administration and repression, which in turn withdrew more and more men from production. The harassed farm managers, continually under pressure to meet their quotas of supplies, could pay little attention to the conservation of soil and forests. Their consequent deterioration accentuated the difficulties of production. The state machine finally became so complex as to be unmanageable.[17]

As a result, it was then possible for wandering tribes of barbarians to bring about the fall of Rome. The empire had disintegrated because of its inner decay.

The disintegration of Roman law was equally real. The Theodosian Code shows the influences of Christianity, but it is still Roman law. In analyzing the laws of marriage we have noted the radical Christianization of Roman law under Justinian I (*c.* 482-565), in the *Corpus Juris Civilis*. Roman law now continued in its development, but it became progressively an expression of Biblical law. Justinian's *Institutes* (with the Digest, Code, and Novels, a part of the *Corpus Juris Civilis*) clearly reflects what is called "natural law," but that concept was now becoming something other than Roman law had known it.[18] Natural law, whether in the hands of jurists, scholastics, or Deists, was in essence an anti-trinitarian doctrine, but it was still more Christian than Roman. Natural law became a form of Christian heresy and ascribed to nature legislative powers and absolute laws which were clearly borrowed from the God of Scripture. Thus, both Roman law and natural law became so thoroughly Christianized with the centuries that no Roman would have recognized them. Even where the wording of

16. *Ibid.*, p. xxii.
17. *Ibid.*
18. Thomas Collett Sanders, translator, editor, *The Institutes of Justinian*, 12th revised edition, 1898 (London: Longmans, Green, 1905).

ancient Roman laws was retained, a new content and interpretation rendered the ancient meaning remote and barren.

The same is true of pagan laws. Clearly, many pagan laws survived and colored Western law codes, but again they were subjected to radical alteration in most cases. Moreover, it must be noted that a very real defect of scholars has been their ignorance of Biblical law. As a result, much has been called pagan which was in reality Biblical. Thus, in a Harvard scholar's source book on medieval history, we are told, concerning Alfred the Great in ninth-century England:

> Here are a few characteristic laws included by Alfred in the code which he drew up on the basis of old customs and the laws of some of the earlier Saxon kings. . . .
>
> If any one smite his neighbor with a stone, or with his fist, and he nevertheless can go out with a staff, let him get him a physician and do his work as long as he himself cannot.
>
> If an ox gore a man or a woman, so that they die, let it be stoned, and let not its flesh be eaten. The owner shall not be liable if the ox were wont to push with its horns for two or three days before, and he knew it not; but if he knew it, and would not shut it in, and it then shall have slain a man or a woman, let it be stoned; and let the master be slain, or the person killed be paid for, as the "witan" shall decree to be right.
>
> Injure ye not the widows and the stepchildren, nor hurt them anywhere; for if ye do otherwise they will cry unto me and I will hear them, and I will slay you by my sword; and I will cause that your own wives shall be widows, and your children shall be stepchildren.
>
> If a man strike out another's eye, let him pay sixty shillings, and six shillings, and six pennies, and a third part of a penny, as "bot." (Compensation rendered to an injured person.) If it remain in the head, and he cannot see anything with it, let one-third of the "bot" be remitted.
>
> If a man strike out another's tooth in the front of his head, let him make "bot" for it with eight shillings; if it be the canine tooth, let four shillings be paid as "bot." A man's grinder is worth fifteen shillings. If the shooting finger be struck off, the "bot" is fifteen shillings; for its nail it is four shillings.
>
> If a man maim another's hand outwardly, let twenty shillings be paid as "bot," if he can be healed; if it half fly off, then shall forty shillings be paid as "bot."[19]

These are, of course, clearly Biblical laws adapted to the English coinage and scene.

Biblical law played a central role in the shaping of Western civilization as it entered society from still another source, the Jews of Europe.

---

19. Frederick Austin Ogg, *A Source Book of Mediaeval History* (New York: American Book Company, 1908), p. 104 f.

Unfortunately, the history of the Jews, as normally reported, tends to stress their sufferings rather than their accomplishments. This is an unhappy preoccupation which characterizes many other able peoples, but it is not good history, whether done by Jews, Armenians, Poles, Frenchmen, U. S. Southerners, or anyone else.

Western civilization owes a large debt to the culture of its towns and cities. Towns and cities were products of merchantmen and their communities, and these were largely Jewish. Commercial law and urban law thus had their origins in the Jewish communities and their intense devotion to Biblical law. While some Syrians or Phoenicians continued into the Christian era as the merchants of Europe, as Christian merchantmen, increasingly the major role was played by Jews. The influence of the Jews on their Christian imitators in the commercial realm was extensive. Their power also was very great. In a work of very great importance, Irving A. Agus has written,

> Moreover, it was in the centuries preceding the crusades that this remarkable group played a most heroic role in northwestern Europe. The few thousand Jews that constituted this group in the pre-Crusade period were so powerful that they bent the rulers of Europe to their will. They forced these rulers to bring about a radical change in basic Church policy toward the Jews. The latter were allowed to practice their religion undisturbed, to employ Christian servants and sometimes even Christian slaves, to hold positions of authority over Christians and to manage the financial activities of large estates, even of bishoprics. These few Jews forced the prelates of the Church to become their benefactors. In the midst of almost universal personal subjugation, the Jews alone were politically free; in the midst of turbulence and war, they alone could travel in comparative safety and could carry valuable merchandise over long distances. When practically every man owed to his superior services and dues that constituted a sacrifice of from fifteen to fifty percent of his income-producing time, the Jews paid as taxes but a tiny fraction of their income. They organized self-governing communities, developed supra communal institutions, enacted ordinances on a national scale, and employed a most efficient and most remarkable form of group organization and group government, one that afforded every individual effective help and protection even when he was hundreds of miles away from home. They instituted practices and procedures that gave them great power and resilience, enabled them to deal with the princes of Church and state from a position of strength, and created for them opportunities for powerful economic growth and great physical expansion.[20]

This power was grounded in a systematic and faithful obedience to Biblical law, to a system of justice which maintained the community

---

20. Irving A. Agus, *Urban-Civilization in Pre-Crusade Europe* (New York: Yeshiva University Press, 1968), I, 16 f.

in times of difficulty and gave it an instrument for coping with internal and external affairs. Life in a community meant life in the law of God. In terms of this, the modern city, a product of Jewish merchantmen and their communities, is a unit brought together by law, not by blood, and maintained by justice essentially, rather than by brute force. These Jewish courts were moreover *stateless courts,* forerunners of the medieval Fair Courts, and of modern arbitration.

The influence of Maimonides (Rabbi Moses ben Maimon, 1135-1204) on European thought rests on this urban orientation of Jewish life and thought. As medieval Europe became urban Europe, it looked to the fathers of urban life. Maimonides had codified the Jewish applications of Biblical law to urban and commercial life, and, as a result, his influence was inescapable.

Maimonides is best remembered for his influence on European philosophy, for helping introduce Aristotelianism into European thought as well as into Judaism. His philosophical works were denounced by the Jews of Provence to the Inquisition, which burned these writings. His compendium of Biblical law, much neglected by scholars today, was far more influential in his day than even his philosophical writings. In a Europe intensely concerned with law, with the development of cities and of national states, Maimonides' legal studies were important. Because of their common allegiance, with differences, to Biblical law, Christians and Jews were very close in their relations then, as well as very much at odds at times. The Biblical nature of Maimonides' legal studies made them influential.[21]

Another source by means of which Biblical law has exercised a major influence on Western civilization has been through the common law. Whatever local customs, or elements of "Roman" law, there may be in it, common law is essentially Biblical law. "Common law was Christian law."[22] As Keeton noted, "The judges of earlier times spoke with a certainty which was derived from their conviction that the Common law was an expression of Christian doctrine, which none challenged."[23] In trying to eliminate Biblical law from Western civilization, scholars have studiously strained out whole herds of camels in search of gnats.

The importance of the tithe in the development of Western civilization deserves study, but at present an assessment of its part is not possible.

---

21. See the Yale Judaica Series: vol. II, *The Code of Maimonides, Book Thirteen, The Book of Civil Laws*; vol. III, *Book Fourteen, The Book of Judges*; vol. V, *Book Twelve, The Book of Acquisition*; vol. IX, *Book Eleven, The Book of Torts*; etc. (New Haven, Conn.: Yale University Press, 1949).

22. Eugen Rosenstock-Huessy, *Out of Revolution, Autobiography of Western Man,* p. 270. See also David Little, *Religion, Law, and Order, A Study in Pre-Revolutionary England* (New York: Harper, 1969), p. 103n.

23. George W. Keeton, *The Norman Conquest and the Common Law* (London: Ernest Benn, 1966), p. 221.

There are indications, however, that the tithe was basic to social reforms and ecclesiastical reforms, to education and to welfare, and that the tithe was a major factor in social change and progress. Some of the English Puritans were not entirely happy with the established form of the tithe as a part of a stagnant establishment, but their own voluntarily given tithes and offerings were responsible for the extensive reshaping of English society.[24]

In America, especially in New England, as a part of the Christian conservatism, a harking to the past, and radicalism, a return to the root of matters, of the Pilgrims and Puritans, as well as other colonists, there was a self-conscious adoption of Biblical law. The attitude was best summed up by John Cotton in *Moses His Judicials*, when he observed, "The more any Law smells of man the more unprofitable."[25]

Significantly, when Massachusetts in 1641 framed its laws in terms of the English and Puritan understanding of Biblical law, that document was called the *Body of Liberties*. God having called man to serve Him through the law had made that law man's charter of liberty. The Puritans took very literally the words of Isaiah 33:22, which, as they cited it, reads, "Jehovah is our Judge, Jehovah is our Lawgiver, Jehovah is our King; he will save us." Cotton's earlier summary of law had been theoretical; the *Body of Liberties* was Biblical in perspective but directly applied to the problems of the colony and hence a practical code concerned with immediate matters.[26] The fidelity of the laws of Massachusetts to Scripture tends to be under-rated at times by scholars, and Powers, who gives occasional evidence of this, still provides abundant evidence of the Biblical character of the law. A Committee of the General Court repudiated the "Jewish Code" in 1851, but it clearly had been in force earlier.[27]

---

24. See W. K. Jordan, *Philanthropy in England, 1480–1660* (New York: Russell Sage Foundation, 1959, 1964). In Scotland, well into the 19th century, monthly "Kirk-plate allowances" were distributed to the poor by the church elders, according to H. C. Preston MacGoun, *The Elder and His Wife* (London: T. N. Foulis, n.d.), p. 11. Meanwhile, the civil poor laws had, from 1536 to 1834, created a permanent crisis in England. A chronic problem of unemployment was created by means of poor relief, and, because sub-standard wages were supplemented with civil relief, employers felt free to underpay and thereby aggravate the social problem (Henry Hazlitt, "The Poor Laws of England," in *The Freeman*, vol. 21, no. 3 [March, 1971], pp. 137-146). The solution to the problem in 1834 borrowed some of its ideas from the old Puritan pattern and was a part of the reforms introduced by the evangelical movement.

25. W. C. Ford, "Cotton's Moses His Judicials," in *Massachusetts Historical Society, Proceedings* (Series 2), vol. XVI (1902), p. 184.

26. For the text of the *Body of Liberties*, see Richard L. Perry and John C. Cooper, *Sources of Our Liberties* (New York: American Bar Foundation, 1959), pp. 148-161.

27. Edwin A. Powers, *Crime and Punishment in Early Massachusetts 1620–1692, A Documentary History* (Boston: Beacon Press, 1966), p. 315. See also George Lee Haskins, *Law and Authority in Early Massachusetts* (New York: Macmillan, 1960).

Where the legislators moved into areas not covered by Biblical law, they did so "according to the more Generall Rules of Righteousness," as the New Haven Colony Laws made clear:

This Court thus frames, shall first with all care and diligence from time to time provide for the main-tenance of the purity of Religion, and suppresse the contrary, according to their best Light, and direc-tions from the word of God.	1. Psal. 2:10 11, 12 I Tim. 2:2
Secondly, though they humbly acknowledge, that the Supreme power of making Lawes, and of repeal-ing them, belongs to God onely, and that by him this power is given to Jesus Christ as Mediator, Math. 28:19. Joh. 5:22., And that the Lawes for holiness, and Righteousnesse, are already made, and given us in the Scriptures, which in matters morall, or of morall equity, may not be altered by humane power, or authority, *Moses* onely shewed *Israel* the Lawes, and Statutes of God, and the *Sanedrim* the highest Court, among the Jewes, must attend those lawes. Yet Civill Rulers, and Courts, and this Generall Court in particular (being intrusted by the freeman as before) are the Ministers of God, for the good of the people; And have power to declare, publish, and establish, for the plantations within their Juris-dictions, the Lawes he hath made, and to make, and repeale Orders for smaller matters, not particularly determined in Scripture, according to the more Gen-erall Rules of Righteousnesse, and while they stand in force, to require due execution of them.[28]	2. Isa. 33:22 Deut. 5:8 Deut. 17:11 Rom. 13:4

Precisely because lawyers, courts, and scholars today are usually radical humanists and antichristian, there is commonly a hostility towards any full acknowledgment of the Biblical nature of the legal heritage of Western civilization. On the contrary, the effort is to dis-mantle that legal structure and to replace it with humanistic law.

Such a challenge is not new. It has been repeatedly attempted over the centuries, and one such attempt culminated in Renaissance tyranny. The force of Biblical law has thus ebbed and flowed. Some aspects of that law have retained greater force than others. Criminal law has been very much a product of the Biblical requirements. Dietary ob-servances very steadily lost their force in most areas as far as pork and shell-fish are concerned, and horse meat in France, although re-taining their force with some peoples. Diet is less readily affected by conversion than are other aspects of a people's life, because diet is

---

28. *New-Haven's Settling in New-England, And some Lawes for Government* (London, 1656), in Charles Hoadly, editor, *Records of the Jurisdiction of New Haven, From May, 1653, to the Union* (Hartford: Case, Lockwood, & Co., 1858), p. 569.

usually closely linked to the economic limitations of a society. Moreover, with the passing of the centuries, the stricter faithfulness of the
Jews tended to condemn dietary laws as anti-Jewish feelings arose.
As against the barbarian converts to Christianity, the Jewish communities represented a higher moral and cultural level.

It should be remembered that the Saxons, for example, practiced
human sacrifice until, after twenty years of war, Charlemagne both
defeated them and compelled their baptism in 782 in order to break
the tie to offensive pagan practices. Only by means of placing the
Saxons under the sign of the God of Scripture, whose wrath would be
manifested against those who practiced such rites as human sacrifice,
was a break made with the past. Their forcible conversion made the
Saxons and other peoples open to civilization, but their level of accomplishment was clearly below that of the Jews for some centuries.
People hate few things in others more than superiority. The hostilities
were thus real. They were not helped by the fact that Jews, as merchantmen, often dealt in Christian slaves. (As slave owners, the Jews were
vulnerable, in that by law a slave, owned by a Jew, gained his freedom
if he became a Christian.)

Hostility to Jews thus became hostility in many cases to Kosher laws,
and many people at times took a delight in trying to render Jewish
wines ritually impure. The lack of a knowledge of Scripture because of
an inability to read furthered the division and aggravated the ignorance
of many Biblical ordinances.

Moreover, as time passed, the interpretation of some laws became
ecclesiastical rather than social. Thus, the sabbath, very clearly ordained for rest, came steadily to mean worship and the church; a
secondary application came to be the primary emphasis and meaning.
The requirement to rest, and to rest in the Lord, is still basic to
Scripture. It means a rest for man, his working animals, and for the
earth; in this respect, the strictest sabbatarian churches are clearly
derelict in their sabbath-keeping. The sabbath law is still necessary for
man, as is the whole law, and its observance is mandatory for the
health of society. The church, having in one area after another abandoned the law of God, or, having reduced it to a purely ecclesiastical
or moral concern, has led society in its dereliction. John Cotton was
right: "The more any Law smells of man the more unprofitable."
Humanistic law has led to social chaos and crisis. It is time to turn
again with the Puritans to the words of Isaiah 33:22: "For the LORD
is our judge, the LORD is our lawgiver, the LORD is our king; he
will save us."

Humanistic man seeks salvation from man, sometimes through politics
and the state, at other times by means of anarchism. But anarchism

leads to social collapse and warfare, and the state, reflecting man's sin, can only compound it. Father Francis Edward Nugent has cited, after Fulton Lewis III, the corruption of members of Congress, and has added:

> The state legislatures are no less open to the low and corrupt: consider unhappy New Hampshire where the House of Representatives now sitting includes one man who was convicted of using the mails to defraud, another who was arrested for stealing an ambulance while under the influence of drink and a third who was convicted of the statutory rape of a mentally retarded 15 year old girl.[29]

Clearly, with the growing decline of public and private morality, no arrangement of men or political institutions can provide relief. The evil is primarily in man, and in his institutions and environment insofar as they reflect his nature. Rabshakeh was right with reference to Egypt: "Now, behold, thou trustest upon the staff of this bruised reed, even upon Egypt, on which if a man lean, it will go into his hand and pierce it: so is Pharaoh king of Egypt unto all that trust on him" (II Kings 18:21). The future does not rest with pierced hand politics but with the sovereign and triune God and His absolute law.

---

29. Father Francis Edward Nugent, in *Christendom*, February, 1971, p. 3n.

APPENDICES

1. The New Testament as Law

According to H. L. Hoeh, the church for some time celebrated, not the modern Easter, but the Hebrew passover as its annual Christian passover (or communion), and the resurrection festival was in terms of the passover day, irrespective of what day it fell on.[1] There is more than a little evidence that the early church continued to celebrate the passover and to find in the Old Testament rite the New Testament requirement. Bingham gives evidence that the early church did observe "Easter, or the Paschal festival," at the same time as the Jewish passover.[2] The Venerable Bede cited seventh-century papal rebukes to the Scots for continuing to observe the Hebrew passover as the only valid occasion for "keeping Easter."[3] Hostility between Christians and Jews helped push the two observances apart, and the apostasy of some Christians to Judaism[4] furthered the break with the law. An anonymous "Epistle to Diognetus" gives an excellent example of this hostility, and of the seriousness of the problem to some churchmen of the day:

> Chapt. IV. But as to their scrupulosity concerning meats, and their superstition as respect the Sabbaths, and their boasting about circumcision, and their fancies about fasting and the new moons, which are utterly ridiculous and unworthy of notice—I do not think that you require to learn anything from me. For, to accept some of these things which have been formed by God for the use of men as properly formed, and to reject others as useless and redundant;— How can this be lawful? And to speak falsely of God, as if He forbade us to do what is good on the Sabbath-days,—how is this impious? And to glory in the circumcision of the flesh as a proof of election, and as if, on account of it, they were specially beloved by God,—how is it not a subject of ridicule? And as to their observing months and days, as if waiting upon the stars and the moon; and their distributing, according to their own tendencies, the appointments of God, and the vicissitudes of the seasons, some for festivities, and others for mourning,—who would deem this a part of

---

1. Herman L. Hoeh, "Four Thousand Years of Easter," in *Tomorrow's World* vol. III, no. 3 (March, 1971), pp. 42-46.
2. Joseph Bingham, *The Antiquities of the Christian Church*, vol. II, bk. XX, chap. V, sec. 1-4.
3. The Venerable Bede, *The Ecclesiastical History of the English Nation* (London: J. M. Dent, 1913, 1939), II, 19; p. 100.
4. Bingham, *op. cit.*, II; bk. XVI, chap. VI, sec. 1-3.

794

divine worship, and not much rather a manifestation of folly? I suppose, then, you are sufficiently convinced that the Christians, properly abstain from the vanity and error common (to both Jews and Gentiles), and from the busy-body spirit and vain boasting of the Jews; but you must not hope to learn the mystery of their peculiar mode of worshipping God from any mortal.[5]

There was much more in this vein—attempts to discourage by ridicule Christian obedience to Old Testament practices, and to discourage the attendance of Christians to *both* church and synagogue, a custom Bingham noted. Quite obviously, Christians were not only keeping the laws concerning diet but also observing the laws of sabbath observance and circumcision. Clearly, while the church had some problem with antinomianism, it also had many members eager to keep the whole law of God without any departures from Hebraic practices.

The reason is easily seen. The law was readily stressed by the apostolic literature.[6] Thus, in *Barnabas* we read,

Loose every bond of injustice, untie the knots of forcibly extracted agreements. Release the downtrodden with forgiveness, and tear up every unjust contract. Distribute your food to the hungry, and if you see someone naked, clothe him. Bring the homeless into your home, and if you see someone of lowly estate, do not despise him nor (despise) anyone of your own household. . . . Give your food to the hungry without hypocrisy, and have mercy on the person of lowly estate.[7]

Moreover, *Barnabas* stressed the fact that "Christians have received *the* covenant (not a *new* covenant) through Jesus," to cite Kraft's words.[8] The covenant remained the same, but a "new people" was substituted for the old.[9] In discussing the typology of circumcision, *Barnabas* did not reject circumcision as such; he simply argued "that circumcision is a matter of understanding and obedience" (Kraft).[10] In discussing the Old Testament food restrictions, *Barnabas* is similarly concerned with typology. He does condemn Israel for believing that the essential meaning of the dietary laws is "actual food" rather than spiritual meaning, but he cannot call good what typologically signifies evil, or vice versa.[11] The *Didache* says of the matter, "Now concerning food, observe the traditions as best you can."[12] This is not an abandonment; it follows the Pauline requirement that the dietary

---

5. "The Epistle to Diognetus," in *Ante-Nicene Christian Library*, vol. I, *The Apostolic Fathers* (Edinburgh: T. & T. Clark, 1867), p. 306 f.
6. "The First Epistle of Clement," in *ibid.*, chap. I, II, XXI, pp. 8 f., 22 f.
7. "Barnabas," III:3, 5; in Robert A. Kraft, *The Apostolic Fathers, A New Translation and Commentary*, vol. 3, *Barnabas and the Didache* (New York: Thomas Nelson & Sons, 1965), p. 86 f.
8. *Ibid.*, p. 90 f.
9. *Ibid.*, V, 7, p. 94.   11. *Ibid.*, 10:1-12; pp. 109-114.
10. *Ibid.*, IX:I–X:12, pp. 106-109.   12. *Ibid.*, "Didache," 6:3; p. 163.

laws be not used to create a barrier with the unbelieving who are being evangelized, but rather observed as godly counsel.

The typology, moreover, stressed the importance of the original law and thus, despite disapproval, the original law never quite disappeared. Circumcision clearly was replaced by baptism, but circumcision has been extensively practiced "for medical reasons" which have a semi-Biblical authority. Attempts to revive the Hebrew sabbath have been commonplace through the centuries, as well as efforts to transfer to the Christian sabbath the Hebrew severities.

Two impulses thus have been a continuing factor. *First*, hostility to Judaism has led to hostility to the law, and a rejection of some or all of the law, i.e., to antinomianism in varying degrees; *second*, a respect for Scripture as the word of God has led to an unwillingness to see any aspect of the law as superseded by Christ's coming or altered by His re-interpretation. As a result, an Old Testament emphasis has at times occurred, and a retention of practices in their pre-New Testament form.

To deny that the Hebrew sabbath still governs us is not to abandon the sabbath. To deny circumcision as a covenant rite need not obscure its medical values. To recognize the centrality and authority of the law does require that the law be understood in terms of the whole of Scripture. The Gospels themselves were seen in the early centuries as books of law, since they were the words of a King. As Derrett has pointed out, the *Milindapanha*, a Buddhist work of about A.D. 150, cited the Gospels and Christ's words on taxation (Matt. 17:24-27) as legal precedent in the Far East.[13] The royal word is always a law-word, and as such is an inescapable part of the body of law. By the miraculous attestations given to the apostles, that royal word and power was declared to be in them also. Thus, the whole of the New Testament speaks as a unity with that law given in the Old Testament.

It is this aspect of kingship which has been neglected in recent years, because kingship in the modern state is largely decorative rather than operative. The ancient power of the king, however, was inseparable from his law-making power. His word was literally law. For Jesus to claim to be Messiah-King over all the world meant that He Himself regarded His own every word as inescapable law. For converts in the world of antiquity, Christ's word was law, and to despise the law of a king was a serious offense. Even the thief on the cross had confidence in the law-word of that King (Luke 23:39-43), and his confidence was recorded by Christ and man. The fact that this King placed His authority behind the law of Moses (Matt. 5:17-19; Luke 16:17) made it difficult for the church to set aside that law. As a result, the per-

---

13. John Duncan Martin Derrett, *Law in the New Testament* (London: Darton, Longman & Todd, 1970), p. 255.

sistence of the strictest kind of observance remained in many sectors of the church for centuries.

Reference has been made to the practice, by many Christians, of attending both synagogue and church, and of observing both the Jewish sabbath and the Christian sabbath. The Synod of Laodicea, A.D. 348-381, in Canon XXIX, referred to this practice:

> Christians must not judaize by resting on the Sabbath, but must work on that day, rather honouring the Lord's Day; and, if they can, resting then as Christians. But if any shall be found to be judaizers, let them be anathema from Christ.[14]

This canon not only reveals the continuing practice but also reflects the change in sabbath observance noted by St. Paul. "If they can," the Christians are to rest, but their life under an alien state and economy made such observance at times, or usually, impossible. The force of the law, however, was sufficiently strong among Christians that many erred on the side of obedience by observing both Jewish and Christian sabbaths.

Of interest too is the answer of Timothy, bishop of Alexandria, at the First Council of Constantinople, A.D. 381, to Question XIII of a series of questions proposed to him:

> When are man and wife to forbear the conjugal act?
> *Answer*: On Saturday, and the Lord's day; for on those days the spiritual sacrifice is offered.[15]

The source of this ruling is Exodus 19:5, a commandment which was designed to prevent Biblical religion from any confusion with fertility cult practices when the law was given. Again, we have an illustration of the belief, however misapplied at times, that the law was still binding upon believers.

2. The Implications of I Samuel 8

I Samuel 8 has been a popular chapter since Western civilization rejected monarchy as a form of government, and it has been used as evidence of an anti-monarchistic perspective in the Bible. Dissenters from this opinion search the Scriptures for a pro-monarchistic viewpoint, or see evidence of both opinions.

But is the main point of this chapter the monarchy? Is it not rather the rejection of God's government for man's government? The Lord said to Samuel, "They have not rejected thee, but they have rejected me, that I should not reign over them" (I Sam. 8:7). Thus, very clearly, God saw Israel's decision as primarily and essentially a rejection of

---

14. H. R. Percival, *The Seven Ecumenical Councils*, p. 148.
15. *Ibid.*, p. 613.

His government. Moreover, the rejection was essentially religious, and it was a rejection whatever the form of the civil government Israel might choose. "According to all the works which they have done since the day that I brought them up out of Egypt even unto this day, wherewith they have forsaken me, and have served other gods, so do they also unto thee" (I Sam. 8:8). Clearly, whether Israel chose a monarchy, a republic, democracy, dictatorship, or any other form of civil government, it was an abandonment of God. In choosing a king, they were doing openly what they had repeatedly done in the period of the Judges. A godly king could restore God's government, as David and others did, but the essential purpose of the nation's demand for a king was to be ruled like other nations (I Sam. 8:5, 20). The complaint against Samuel's sons was not a demand for reform (vss. 1-5); the corruption of Samuel's sons was an excuse for their demand for a centralized government and a professional warrior-ruler and his armed men (vs. 20). It was a surrender of God's law-order for a humanistic law-order.

At God's command, Samuel reviewed the implications of the new order (vss. 11-17). The key to this review is *first* the new form of taxation, which will be a taxation taking sons and daughters by conscription, fields, produce, livestock, and servants. *Second*, the tithe is cited and they are told that the taxation of their new order will be a ruthless tithe of capital as well as income.

Here we have the heart of the difference between the two orders. God's government exacted only the head or poll tax for civil government (Ex. 30:11-16), and fines perhaps; the rest of the government functions were provided for by the tithe, thereby insuring a decentralized society, as well as one governed both by godly principles and by God's tax.

Unless we see this chapter as the formal rejection of God's law-order for another law-order, we miss the meaning of this central and revolutionary event. The people clearly rejected God's government (vss. 19-20), in the face of God's clear warning that He would reject them (vs. 18). While they attempted to maintain a formal allegiance to God, in reality they had rejected Him. It was possible for them to have a king and retain God's law, as Samuel made clear (I Sam. 12:14-15); the key was to rebel not "against the commandment of the LORD," i.e., to retain the law of God as the law of the social order.

The captivity came, Jeremiah declared, because the nation had abandoned God's law, and seventy years of captivity were decreed to give the land the sabbaths denied it (Jer. 25:9, 10; 29:10). Ball wrote of the like declaration of II Chronicles 36:21,

> We have no right whatever to press the words of the sacred writer, in the sense of assuming that he means to say that when Jerusalem

was taken by the Chaldeans exactly seventy sabbatical years had been neglected—that is, that the law in this respect had not been observed for 490 years (70 × 7), or ever since the institution of monarchy in Israel (490 + 588 = 1,078).[1]

Ball to the contrary, we have no right to deny that this is exactly what Jeremiah and the Chronicler are telling us, when they plainly say so. Thus, we are told that, with the monarchy, the sabbaths of the land were abandoned. The implication of I Samuel 8 is that the tithe was also being abandoned, because they were warned that the state tax would constitute another tithe, and a far more extensive one.

Clearly then, while Israel intended to be "moral," i.e., to decry adultery, murder, and theft, it intended also to abandon God's law as the absolute and governing rule for man and society. The Chronicler tells us of the price they paid for it.

3. Stewardship, Investment, and Usury: Financing the Kingdom of God

by Gary North

But, I hope, it will never be complained, That the Ministers of the Gospel, are by any Sinful Silence, accessory to the Transgressions, which *Deny* the *Doctrine of God our Saviour*, among a People, that are under peculiar Obligations to *Adorn* it. It shall not be complained, That the Ministers do so confine themselves to Preach *Faith* and *Repentance*, that the People forget *Moral Honesty*, thro' any Default of ours.
Cotton Mather
Fair Dealing between Debtor and Creditor (1716)

The question of usury is one which has challenged the exegetical skills of Christian commentators for two thousand years. A considerable proportion of the works devoted to the practical application of Christian principles—casuistry—was devoted to this very issue, from the 12th century through the 17th. Before the Christian era, Hebrew leaders and prophets struggled against the constant pressure of usury. Pre-exilic and post-exilic prophets warned their contemporaries against their continual violations of the Mosaic ordinances regarding lending. Jeremiah, in condemning his brethren for their persecution of him, pointed to his innocence of the crime of usury: "I have neither lent on usury, nor men have lent to me on usury; yet every one of them doth curse me" (Jer. 15:10b). Nehemiah warned the rulers of his day not to

---

1. C. J. Ball, "II Chronicles," in Ellicott, III, 453.

extort any usurious returns from God's people, for they were oppressed by the ravages of famine and the costs of redeeming their brethren out of bondage (Neh. 5:1-13). The rulers were wise enough to heed his warning, going so far as to return both principal and interest to the debtors (5:11-12). It is unlikely that this example will be followed in our modern, enlightened Christian circles.

Usury, Interest, and Charity

The prohibition against usury as it appears in the Mosaic law refers specifically to the brother who is poor: "If thou lend money to any of my people that is poor . . ." (Ex. 22:25); "And if thy brother be waxen poor . . ." (Lev. 25:35). It was legitimate to take a return above the sum lent from the religious stranger (Deut. 23:20). A tenth of this increase would therefore be tithed to God, thereby extracting from the unregenerate at least a portion of the tithe that all men owe to God. As a slave to sin, the stranger was not protected from the bondage imposed on a poor man by every usurious contract. But to the poor Hebrew brother his lending brother was to show mercy; no increase of any kind beyond the original money or goods could be legitimately claimed by the creditor (Lev. 25:37).

Historically, these restrictions were not acknowledged as binding by the Hebrew commonwealth. The continual violations of all aspects of the Mosaic law brought condemnation on the nation. God had not left them without warning:

> He that hath not given forth upon usury, neither hath taken any increase, that hath withdrawn his hand from iniquity, hath executed true judgment between man and man, Hath walked in my statutes and hath kept my judgments, to deal truly; he is just, he shall surely live, saith the Lord God. . . . [He that] Hath given forth upon usury, and hath taken increase: shall he then live? he shall not live: he hath done all these abominations; he shall surely die; his blood shall be upon him (Ezek. 18:8-9, 13).

The definition of usury is precise Biblically: *any increase taken from the poor in return for having made a loan.* There is no Biblical evidence, nor have Christian casuists generally argued, that the prohibition restricted interest received on business loans, so long as the lender shared the risks of failure along with the borrower. This interpretation of the usury prohibition was basic to the expositions of medieval and early Protestant casuists.[1] By sharing in the risk of a profit-making business,

---

1. J. Gilchrist, *The Church and Economic Activity in the Middle Ages* (New York: St. Martin's, 1969), pp. 65 ff. Cf. John T. Noonan, *The Scholastic Analysis of Usury* (Cambridge, Mass.: Harvard University Press, 1957), pp. 40, 41, 46, 59, 136. As Noonan shows, the acceptance in the late 15th century by Roman Catholic theologians of the validity of the *contractus Trinus*—a partnership in which one partner bore all risks of failure and paid the other a fixed return

a lender has the right to participate in a portion of the returns. The problem for the casuists came only when the lender was guaranteed a return on his investment irrespective of the success or failure of the enterprise.[2]

The prohibition of usury, as it appears in the Bible, is simultaneously coupled with a requirement that godly men lend to all brethren in truly dire circumstances (Deut. 15:7 ff.). This requirement, if it were universally respected, would have a definite impact on the illicit, immoral usury market. People in emergencies would have access to more money and goods than they would have been able to gain access to had the requirement to lend never been given by God. Christians with extra funds are brought into the emergency loan market apart from an economic incentive. With more funds available, the demands of desperate borrowers can be met more readily. Thus, the prevailing rate of return on the usury market is forced lower: those receiving the charitable loans have no need to enter the usury market, and their presence does not therefore raise rates in that illicit market. They are not bidding up the usury rate because their needs are being met outside of that market.

It must be stressed, however, that the kind of emergency described by the relevant passages is a true emergency. It arises when a poor man has nothing left but his cloak, and even that may be legitimately

on a loan, irrespective of failure or success of the enterprise—destroyed the medieval objections to usury. One of the defenders of this lattitudinarian contract was John Eck, a hireling of the German banking firm of Fuggers, and the most notable theological opponent of Martin Luther. It was against this liberalization of the usury prohibition that Luther reacted so vehemently. See Martin Luther, "Trade and Usury" (1524), in *Luther's Works* (Philadelphia: Muhlenberg Press, 1962), vol. 45, pp. 249-305. Noonan traces the liberalization of usury legislation in a concise essay, "The Amendment of Papal Teaching by Theologians," in (improbably) Charles E. Curran ed., *Contraception: Authority and Dissent* (New York: Herder & Herder, 1969), pp. 41-75. On the traditional, conservative, semi-medieval attitude of Calvinist thinkers, see Charles H. George, "English Calvinist Opinion on Usury, 1600-1640," *Journal of the History of Ideas*, XVIII (1957), 455-474. Richard Baxter, in his massive study, *A Christian Directory* (1673), began a loosening of the earlier prohibitions. He held to the Biblical position: the poor brother need not pay interest, but interest could be taken from someone who makes a profit on the borrowed funds. Baxter, *Chapters from A Christian Directory*, edited by Jeanette Tawney (London: Bell, 1925), pp. 119 ff., 130-131. As Richard Schlatter writes, "The divines of the Restoration had no revolutionary contribution to make to the discussion of borrowing and lending." Schlatter, *The Social Ideas of Religious Leaders, 1660–1688* (London: Oxford University Press, 1940), p. 217. Baxter's subtlety was lost on his contemporaries.

2. This, of course, was the kind of arrangement established by the *contractus trinus*. It is the essence of the modern banking contract: a fixed, guaranteed, compound rate of interest. It is impossible to guarantee such returns over long periods of time, since profits are not guaranteed in this world, and therefore such an insured rate of return is fraudulent. The bank will eventually go bankrupt, or else it will pay off in depreciated fiat currency. Cf. Gary North, "The Theology of the Exponential Curve," *The Freeman*, May, 1970, pp. 305-306. This journal is published monthly, at no subscription charge, by the Foundation for Economic Education, Irvington-on-Hudson, New York, 10533.

demanded as collateral in the daytime (thus keeping the debtor from using the collateral to secure multiple loans). The emergency is a situation of desperation; godly men and women are not to indebt themselves for anything less than this. "Owe no man anything, but to love one another" is the binding rule for all non-emergency circumstances (Rom. 13:8a). *Charity* loans were required of affluent believers; *consumer* loans at no interest were not contemplated. No one was supposed to ask for them, so there was no requirement to provide them at zero return. It was assumed that consumer loans were products of a slave mentality. From the ethical slave—the stranger—it was legitimate to take interest. Those who did not regard themselves as slaves were (and are) expected to heed the words of Solomon: "The rich ruleth over the poor, and the borrower is servant to the lender" (Prov. 22:7).

Operationally, the rate of interest, like all prices, is a product of supply and demand. In a non-monetary economy, it would reflect the supply and demand for goods and services; the presence of money confuses the picture somewhat by adding another factor to the equation: the supply of and demand for money. The fact that these two aspects are present in the single rate of interest can lead to highly concrete practical problems, namely, the boom-bust cycle of inflation-depression.[3] For the purposes of this essay, it is not necessary to pursue this dualistic aspect of the interest rate. The problem here is simpler: Why is it that people expect to gain a return above the capital loaned, and why are others willing to pay it?

This highly theoretical problem baffled economists for centuries. Professional economists are not yet completely agreed on the subject, but in the last hundred years a general solution has appeared. A man can claim a rate of return on his money or goods loaned out for three reasons. *First,* because he forfeits the use of the money for a given period of time. This is the so-called *time-preference* factor, also called the originary rate of interest. The use of a good right now is more valuable to a person than the promise of the use of that good at a later time (assuming that tastes do not change, of course). Every rational person *discounts* the value of future economic goods. Men are mortal; they are subject to the burden of time. Each man places a premium on the use of his wealth over time; he will not voluntarily forfeit that use without compensation. His personal time-preference sets his discount rate for the enjoyment of future goods and services that his money

---

3. Ludwig von Mises, *Human Action* (New Haven, Conn.: Yale University Press, 1949), chap. 20. The revised edition of this work is presently published by Henry Regnery Co., Chicago. For an introduction to the literature supporting Mises' theory of the business cycle, see Gary North, "Repressed Depression," *The Freeman*, April, 1969.

might buy immediately. That rate of discount sets the rate of interest that he will demand from someone who wants to borrow his money. Because money is more highly valued now than the same amount of future money is valued now (assuming a stable purchasing power for money), some men are willing to pay to get access to money now.

A future-oriented society will display a lower rate of interest. Such men do not value the present that much in terms of the future; as a result, the price spread between present money and future money is narrowed. Here is one possible avenue of investigation open for anyone interested in explaining the rapid rates of growth experienced in the past century by the West, and especially the Protestant West. A future-oriented culture produces lower rates of interest, making it easier for capitalist entrepreneurs to gain access to funds for economic development.[4]

The *second* component of the rate of interest is the *risk premium*. The lender knows that he may not get his money back. The borrower may go bankrupt, or he may run away with the loan. To compensate the lender for his risk—a factor which can be estimated with some accuracy by modern statistical techniques—he demands a payment above and beyond his time-preference return. Naturally, in a culture which honors the creditor's claim, the risk premium will be lower. Morality does influence the rate of interest. A society that takes seriously the Psalmist's warning with respect to both borrowing and lending will find a godly "easy money policy," and not a Keynesian, inflationary one: "The wicked borroweth, and payeth not again: but the righteous showeth mercy, and giveth" (37:21). The merciful lender, as we have already seen, helps to keep the illicit usury rate down, and the honest borrower in a business helps to keep the risk premium lower. Christian nations that are not seduced by antinomianism should produce a smaller black market for loans (emergency, usurious loans) and a lower interest rate for commercial loans.

The *third* factor is the *inflation premium*. A lender wants to be paid back in money that will purchase as many goods as the money he lent. In an inflationary society, the lender will add a new demand: enough money to compensate him for the expected fall in the value of the nation's circulating media. Again, if a society honors Isaiah's condemnation of debased precious metals (used by ancient kingdoms as money), and if it also honors the Mosaic law against multiple indebtedness (thus stifling the inflation produced by modern fractional reserve

4. On the distinction of "upper class" cultures from "lower class" cultures in terms of "future orientation" vs. "present-mindedness," see Edward C. Banfield, *The Unheavenly City* (Boston: Little, Brown, 1970).

banking), it will not experience much price inflation.[5] In fact, an expanding economy, given a relatively fixed money supply, will produce a gradually falling price level.[6] It could fall enough to lower the *money* rate of interest (though not the actual rate of interest in terms of purchasing power). A society could conceivably produce a negative money rate of interest if the value of the purchasing power of money were rising at a faster rate than the market's registered rate of time-preference plus the risk premium. If you could buy *more* with the money received in the future, you might need to ask only for an *equal* amount of paper money or coins as a return.[7]

With this as background to the theory of the interest rate, it should be easier to grasp the implications of the *charitable loan* that comes under the usury prohibition. The lender faces a sure loss on his loan. First, he bears the risks associated with loans to the impoverished, for he can ask no extra payment as a risk premium attached to the rate of interest. Second, he receives back goods in the future, but future goods are less valuable to a man than the same goods in the present. He therefore forfeits the use of his goods over time without any compensation. He receives back less-valuable goods, for he has lost the one thing that creatures cannot restore: *time*. Third, during inflationary times, he also forfeits the lost purchasing power if his loan is one in terms of paper money, as it would normally be. He therefore bears two, and possibly three, costs of the loan. That is the extent of his charity. He suffers a loss for the sake of his needy brother. This loss is required of him by God.

Stewardship, Investment, and Charity

The concept of Christian stewardship is a fundamental tenet of the Christian social order. The Bible declares that God is the sovereign owner of all His creation.[8] He delegated the responsibility for the

---

5. Currency debasement is prohibited by Isaiah 1:22; cf. Gary North, "The Sin of Debased Currency," *Christian Economics*, Oct. 31, 1967, p. 4. Fractional reserve banking is prohibited, since it is a special manifestation of multiple indebtedness—more debts outstanding than resources to meet those obligations on demand if all are presented simultaneously. Multiple indebtedness is prohibited by Ex. 22:25 ff.: the cloak taken as collateral by a lender cannot therefore be used by the borrower to obtain loans from other people.

6. Gary North, "Downward Price Flexibility and Economic Growth," *The Freeman*, May, 1971. Cf. Mises, *The Theory of Money and Credit* (New Haven, Conn.: Yales University Press, [1912] 1953), p. 417; F. A. Hayek, *Prices and Production* (London: Routledge & Kegan Paul, [1931] 1960), p. 105.

7. Governments are always inflating the money supply, so this is not a statement subject to historical verification in modern times. However, the rate of interest on almost risk-free federal bonds during the 1930's fell as low as one-half of one percent in the United States. With falling prices, increasing unemployment, failing businesses, money increased in purchasing power. Thus, the money rate of interest fell to almost zero. It was considered safer to buy a government bond than to hold cash by many investors.

8. Lev. 25:23; Ps. 24:1; 50:10-12; Hag. 2:8. Cf. Gustave Oehler, *Theology of the Old Testament* (Grand Rapids, Mich.: Zondervan, 1883), p. 235; Milton

care of the earth to Adam, the representative head of mankind (Gen. 1:28). Throughout the Bible man is cautioned to exercise dominion over the earth in terms of God's requirements; God's law-order is the means by which man is to bring the earth into subjection. Any deviation from this law-order involves man in rebellion against God and the destruction of God's property. The great enemy of God, Satan, is pictured in the parable of the tares as the one who violates the rules of planting in order to defy God and to thwart God's plan (Matt. 13:24 ff.). The parable of the husbandman who prepared his vineyard and then turned it over to servants who proved to be unfaithful thieves indicates the hostility of God against those who would violate His rights of ownership (Matt. 21:33 ff.). The faithful steward is he who treats God's universe with respect, causing it to flower and grow in productivity. He is the one who invests his Lord's money wisely, turning an honest profit, expanding the value of the goods entrusted to him (Matt. 25:14 ff.).[9] Yet he is also a man who should be merciful in his dealings with others, as God has been merciful to him. (Matt. 18:23 ff.).

Faithful stewardship therefore involves, at the minimum, the following: (1) a recognition of the sovereignty of God over His creation; (2) obedience to the law-order God has established for the governing of His creation; (3) the productive, fruitful administration of one's vocation or calling; (4) the recognition of the lawfulness of the tithe, in theory and practice; (5) the voluntary giving of alms on a selective, godly basis.[10] Stewardship can be summarized into two overarching principles: *calling* and *charity*. The first of the five aspects of stewardship—the recognition of the sovereignty of God—is the foundation of both the calling and charity.

Charity and calling are linked, and yet they are separate. The principle enunciated by Jesus, "unto whomsoever much is given, of him shall be much required," indicates the link (Luke 12:48b). God grants plenty to men, His vicegerents on earth, but He expects honesty and charity from them. Men are warned specifically against the great danger

---

G. Evans, "Biblical Teaching on the Righteous Acquisition of Property," *Biblical World*, XVII (1906), p. 277; Vernon Bartlet, "The Biblical and Early Christian Idea of Property," in Charles Gore, ed., *Property: Its Duties and Rights* (New York: Macmillan, 1915), p. 86 ff.

9. The word translated as "usury" by the early 17th-century translators ought to be rendered "interest" in Matt. 25:27, since it refers to a lawful business transaction rather than an emergency charity loan to paupers. The bias of the translators against all forms of interest is indicated by their selection of the prejudicial term "usury."

10. On the selective nature of Puritan almsgiving, see W. K. Jordan's crucially important study, *Philanthropy in England, 1480–1660* (London: George Allen & Unwin, 1959). Jordan writes: "The children of the poor were to be taught a trade and set to work; alms were to be raised by voluntary means in each parish for the support of the helpless poor; while casual alms, so typical of medieval piety, were now declared to be harmful and were carefully restricted" (p. 85).

of benefiting from the open hand of God only to forget the sovereign demands of the giver; destruction will be the result (Deut. 8:11 ff.). But the distinction between investment and usury stands as a reminder against the fusing of charity into the realm of the calling. One may not make a living through loans to needy brothers; such a living is an abomination in the sight of God. It is not the case, as one advocate of a totally laissez-faire free market has attempted to argue, that the best form of charity is a profit-making investment in capital which will create jobs.[11] To accept that premise the Christian would have to blur the God-given distinctions between business and voluntary charity. Business involves an economic return (or at least a potential for making a profit) to the investor; charity involves the transfer of scarce economic resources to another, with no thought of return (Matt. 10:8; Luke 6:35).

A man can hardly call himself a faithful steward if he seals off charity from business in an absolute manner. Businesses are supposed to earn profits if they are to be successful, as several parables of Jesus indicate. However, ruthless competition that is utterly devoid of mercy is also condemned in the parables. But the fact that a particular young ruler was told to sell all of his goods and give everything to the poor does not stand as the requirement for every steward. Nor does the example of the church at Jerusalem in Acts 4:32 prevail as the model for all churches. A man must be careful not to drown out the revelation of God in His word, listening only to the parables of profit or only to the examples of total poverty. He is responsible before God to respond to the leading of God's Spirit at different times and along each turn in life's path. We are warned to grow spiritually by means of earthly parables of economic stewardship. The fact that God may demand a man to give up all that he has does not imply that God is sanctioning the moral validity of continual economic losses. What God is saying is that one must not be morally ruthless in business, nor morally wasteful in charity. "Share the wealth" is a Biblical principle, and the normal means of this sharing is the tithe. The general principle is not "destroy all wealth" through universal, indiscriminate giving. In short, business is not charity, though it may be and should be merciful. Charity should be carefully administered in a "business-like" fashion—with honest accounting, budgeting, etc.—but it is not a business, i.e., not a profit-making economic endeavor. They are separate, sovereign realms. Their differences must be respected.

One important difference is in the very bureaucratic structure produced by each form of stewardship. Professor Mises has distinguished

---

11. F. A. Harper, "The Greatest Economic Charity," in Mary Sennholz, ed., *On Freedom and Free Enterprise* (Princeton: Van Nostrand, 1956), pp. 94-107.

two basic models of management. The first is the *business* form, the one geared to *profit and loss* statements. It will be characterized by a central entrepreneurial hierarchy that makes the basic decisions as to general goals of the corporation. These goals are transmitted to the lower ranks by professional managers who earn a salary, but who do not participate in the true economic profits. (Profits are the residuals left after all costs are met: taxes, salaries, interest, raw materials. It is a residual based on the accurate forecasting of formerly unknown events; superior forecasters of the future reap profits, while the less-efficient take losses.[12]) The lower ranks of the bureaucracy are left relatively free to do whatever turns a profit in each subdivision, within the general goals of the company. There is far more flexibility at the lower levels precisely because the magnitude of profit and loss is not rigidly fixed in advance. In contrast to this flexible, risk-oriented, free market management is the *government bureaucracy,* or the non-profit charity's bureaucratic structure. They are on *fixed allocations* determined by taxpayers or givers. These bureaucracies have far less flexible budgets, for they are financed from above. They do not make profits and they do not sustain losses, at least not in the sense of the profits and losses sustained by a firm in a competitive market. The only way to increase revenues is to get more money from the taxpayers or the donors. This kind of bureaucracy allows far less freedom to lower echelon bureaucrats to spend as they please; they must follow *carefully delineated budgets* that are fixed in advance. These men are less flexible than their free market counterparts because their budgets are centrally directed, far less flexible, and as a result, the men involved are not subject to the direct competition of the market.[13]

To a limited extent, the tax law structure of the United States acknowledges the validity of both Mises' analysis and the Biblical separation of business and charity. Non-profit corporations are supposed to be essentially charitable—educational, eleemosynary, service oriented, cultural, etc.—and employees are just that—salaried employees. They are paid in terms of services rendered to the functioning of the corporation. They are not allowed to receive all residuals after all costs are

---

12. The nature of profit under capitalism was first analyzed in a systematic manner in Frank H. Knight's classic study, *Risk, Uncertainty and Profit* (New York: Harper Torchbook, [1921], 1965). Cf. Mises, *Human Action,* pp. 286-297. Joseph Schumpeter, who studied economics with Mises under Böhm-Bawerk, emphasized the role of the entrepreneur as innovator: *The Theory of Economic Development* (New York: Oxford University Press, [1934] 1961), chap. 4. It should be clear that both accurate forecasting and meeting expected demand through efficient, innovative techniques are both a part of entrepreneurial profit-making activity.

13. Mises, *Bureaucracy* (New Rochelle, N. Y.: Arlington House, [1944] 1969). Cf. Gary North, "Statist Bureaucracy in the Modern Economy," *The Freeman,* Jan., 1970.

The Institutes of Biblical Law

met, and, for that reason, the civil government grants to these corporations the right to escape a very important operating cost: taxes. The taxable business, however, is allowed to keep profits for the owners, distributing these profits in any way the owners decide.[14] Charitable organizations pay for services rendered; profit and loss corporations try to gain for the owners as much profit as possible. Gains from the first are limited, ultimately, by civil law; gains from the second, except in the case of regulated monopolies or semi-monopolies, are not. The tax laws recognize a distinction between a *return for service* and a *return on an investment*. Charity is not business.

God's Institutional Monopoly

At this point it is mandatory to recognize another distinction. Just as stewardship encompasses both the calling and charity, so the concept of the Kingdom of God includes the work of the institutional church and the godly activity of Christian men in all other legitimate human institutions. This point was made clear by the great Dutch thinker, Abraham Kuyper, when he developed his concept of sphere sovereignty. The Roman Catholic Church is erroneous in equating the Kingdom of God with the institutional church; the kingdom is something far wider than the mere dispensing of the sacraments. It involves the work of Christians in all their various activities.[15]

A crucial question now appears. Is the institutional church primarily under the rules governing those aspects of the kingdom concerned with profit-making business, or is it more properly under the rules governing the charitable organization? The official answer of the churches has to be that the second alternative is the valid one. The business of the church is not the profit-and-loss statement; the business of the church is the spreading of the gospel, collective worship under godly discipline, and the administration of the sacraments. The concern of the institutional church is with spiritual income and economic giv-

---

14. Were it not for the enforcement of the state-imposed limited liability laws, corporation owners would be far more responsible for the affairs of corporations. The "separation of ownership and control" which has bothered many scholars— James Burnham, A. A. Berle, Gardiner Means—would be far less likely. Cf. Rushdoony, *Politics of Guilt and Pity* (Nutley, N. J.: Craig Press, 1970), p. 254 ff. Schumpeter has argued that such separation of ownership and control in giant corporations has destroyed the older meaning of property and responsibility, thus helping to break the path into socialism: *Capitalism, Socialism and Democracy* (3rd ed.; New York: Harper Torchbook, [1950] 1962), p. 139 ff. He might better have argued that the weakening of personal responsibility implied and created by limited liability laws has led to the creation of giant companies with their huge stock issues. The partnership of the closely held corporation would be the outcome of truly responsible ownership. People would not risk all their assets in huge, impersonal, and vaguely responsible corporations.
15. Kuyper, *Lectures on Calvinism* (Grand Rapids: Eerdmans, [1898] 1961); Henry R. Van Til, *The Calvinistic Concept of Culture* (Philadelphia: Presbyterian and Reformed, 1959).

ing; its concern, unlike the Christian business, is not with spiritual income through economic residuals.

Unlike the American fundamentalists' claim that "full-time Christian service" is limited to the affairs of the institutional church or its missionary appendages, the Calvinist recognizes the validity of all godly callings as full-time Christian service. But the principle of sphere sovereignty requires that we distinguish the nature of each calling in contrast to all others. That which is valid for the Christian businessman is not always valid for the church elder or seminary administrator. Simply because all godly callings are valid, we are not allowed to conclude that all of them are identical. They are governed by different rules, and their successes and failures are estimated by different standards.

If any example in the Bible stands out as the premier example, it is the account of Christ and the temple moneychangers. The moneychangers, as the name indicates, were in the business of foreign currency exchange. Part of the annual sacrifice requirements of the Mosaic law was the offering of a census payment of half a shekel of silver (Ex. 30:12-15). Jerusalem was flooded with visiting Hebrews from all over the Mediterranean during the passover, adding to an already diverse population (cf. Acts 2:5 ff.). Various coins from many lands would have to be converted to the proper offering, the shekel. The moneychangers performed this service, and as the hostility of Jesus indicates, they did so at a profit.

What was their crime? The gaining of profit from foreign exchange transactions is an old and respected profession. The most rigorous of the medieval commentators allowed banks to make profits from this service; this was considered banking's foremost legitimate function.[16] Why the overwhelming hostility of Jesus against them? The reason almost certainly lies in the location of their tables. They were set up in the outer court of the temple.[17] The presence of the temple added an obvious, unmistakable aura of holy sanctity to the men whose services were being offered there. The visiting Hebrews would not have to deal with gentile moneychangers on the outside. They could trust the men of the temple, or so they thought. An implicit, and in all likelihood an explicit, demand was being made by the rulers of the temple: the sacrifices required by God should be obtained from the moneychangers (and dove salesmen) inside the jurisdiction of the Lord's house. The moneychangers were reaping a monopoly return because of their close

---

16. Raymond de Roover, *The Rise and Decline of the Medici Bank, 1397–1494* (New York: Norton, 1963), p. 10 ff.
17. Matthew Poole, *A Commentary on the Holy Bible* (London: Banner of Truth Trust, [1685] 1969), III, 98.

connection to the institutional church. They were not subject to the competitive pressures of a free market in money exchange. They were shielded by the name of God. By so using God's name they dishonored Him. Monopoly profits are not to be earned in this way.

We can only surmise that the rates of exchange were unfavorable in comparison to rates available outside the temple court. We can only acknowledge the fact that the power to reap monopoly economic returns is one which is unlikely to be ignored over long periods of time. Again, we can only surmise that the moneychangers turned a portion of their profits over to the temple authorities. It would seem reasonable that temple authorities would demand a cut of monopoly returns that had their origin in the very aura of the temple. It is possible that the moneychangers were even salaried employees of the temple. But whatever the concrete economic arrangements, Christ's words made their position in God's eyes quite clear: "It is written, My house shall be called the house of prayer; but ye have made it a den of thieves" (Matt. 21:13). The dove salesmen, the moneychangers, those who bought, those who sold: Jesus cast them all out of the court. Such economic transactions were an abomination. The house of God had its support in the tithes and offerings of His people; He did not sanction huckstering in His name as a means of increasing "holy" revenues.

The institutional church is the means of preaching the gospel, disciplining the saints, and administering the sacraments. It is quite openly a spiritual monopoly. It is *the* monopoly in men's affairs. Christ made it clear that this position of monopoly is not to be exploited by men for their own profit. Payment to God's ordained servants in the service of the institutional church is for services rendered. Economic returns to the church are not to be in terms of the principle made famous in Frank Norris' book, *The Octopus*: "All the traffic will bear." The institutional church is not a business—not a money-changing business, not a bingo business, and not an insurance business. It is the house of prayer.

Men who come in the name of the Lord and who claim the prerogatives granted to His ordained must be scrupulously careful to distinguish their profit-making callings from their service callings. Paul was a tentmaker. He did not use his position as an apostle to reap monopoly returns from the brethren. He did not market his wares under the auspices of the local church, charging a price higher than the market price because he was ordained. He kept his trade because he desired to relieve the institutional church of the economic burden of supporting him, not because he intended to set up Apostolic Tents, Inc. (available only at your local church).

The institutional church and its related institutions possess legitimate, but limited, sovereignty. When this sovereignty—a monopoly grant from God—is transgressed, a violation of God's law-order occurs. The institutional church then becomes a destroyer, a thief. The institutional church is not a business. It is the house of prayer.

Christian Usury

With this as background, it is time to turn to that practice which is euphemistically known as the "Christian stewardship program." It has many facets, and many, many practitioners. It involves virtually every Protestant denomination. It involves mission societies, institutions of Christian learning, medical aid societies, and Christian charities. Almost any denominational magazine will contain, in any given issue, several appeals for loans of various kinds. There is one contemporary magazine, the official publication of a supposedly Reformed denomination of 250,000 members, that runs almost a dozen such advertisements every issue.

When I began to gather data on these "stewardship" programs, I sent out requests to various Protestant organizations for booklets, charts, or other information. The data poured in, and always by first class mail. Personal letters were sent, and every letter offered to supply further information on request. Then came the telephone calls and the personal visits by "stewardship" expediters. I had two such visits within a month, and I live in an isolated part of a town that is many miles from the offices of the men who came by to talk to me. In my first ten years as a Christian, I had one visit from a local church's elders. That was initiated by the request of the denomination's multi-millionaire, who insisted that they visit me. I was not home at the time, and they never returned or phoned. But the interest that was shown to me when I inquired about "stewardship"! I was a man whose Christian soul needed the uplifting experience of true Christian fellowship! An 80-mile round trip was not too far to drive. One would almost be led to conclude that God was wrong—that we *can* serve God and mammon. It is almost as if God had said that He came that men might have profits, and that they might have them more abundantly. Indeed, here were men who were *really* involved in "full-time Christian service"!

What surprised me initially was the remarkable similarity of these programs. The tax laws apparently create this uniformity. Some of these programs use the very same pamphlet, but with their own names stamped or printed on the folder. They offer the prospective "steward" many ways of "giving." Here are a few of the titles of the brochures: *Faithful Stewardship Through Christian Investment* (World Vision); *Christian Living—Stewardship Giving, Inseparably Linked* (Christian and Missionary Alliance); *Effective Giving Through Gift Annuities* (Bible Study Hour). The grotesque link among "investment," "steward-ship," and "giving" is so open, so incredibly blatant, that it should shock the sensibilities of all Christians. Obviously, it doesn't. A con-fusion of Biblical categories so thorough, so willful, and so profitable financially (in the short run), would be difficult to match. The sup-posedly conservative, orthodox denominations and ministries are right back in the Roaring Twenties world of Bruce Barton, where Jesus could be considered seriously as "The Founder of Modern Business."[18]

Usury, in its Biblical definition, involves the loaning of money to the needy brother and then demanding a repayment of principal plus interest. The question then arises as to the status of the institutional church; I assume that it has already been established that this institu-tion is not to be regarded as a profit-making business. Therefore, to demand the payment of interest by a church for any kind of loan offered to it is a usurious demand. The hierarchy of the church is equally guilty, for the Bible makes it plain that it is immoral to enter into such a transaction, either as lender or borrower (Jer. 15:10b). The *institutional church* must be regarded as a *charitable ministry*, something to be supported by the tithes and offerings of its members. It is not comparable to a corporation. It is not to be financed through the sales pitches of hucksters who offer misleading hopes to elderly couples (as I intend to demonstrate), and who offer them usurious contracts, "guaranteed" annual returns for life, or any other of a mul-titude of schemes dreamed up by insurance companies and congressional tax committees.

Interest may be taken from businessmen who need to raise money to launch some hopefully profitable enterprise. Interest becomes (Bib-lically) usury when it is taken from charitable, legally non-profit firms that are not operating in a competitive market in´ order to *increase*

---

18. Bruce Barton, *The Man Nobody Knows* (New York: Grosset & Dunlap, 1924). This has been republished in *The Book and the Man Nobody Knows* (Indianapolis: Bobbs-Merrill, 1959). Condensed versions of the volume appeared in *Reader's Digest* in March and June of 1965! Barton's words are almost un-believable today: "Surely no one will consider us lacking in reverence if we say that every one of the 'principles of modern salesmanship' on which business men pride themselves, are brilliantly exemplified in Jesus' walk and work" (Grosset & Dunlap edition, p. 104). Or again: "He would be a national advertiser today, I am sure, as he was the great advertiser of his own day" (p. 140). Barton's book was only one of a number of such studies. The most complete—perhaps three times as large—was *The Business Man of Syria*, by Charles Francis Stocking and William Wesley Totheroh (Chicago: Maestro Co., 1923), which went through at least five editions in the year of its publication, the year prior to the publica-tion of *The Man Nobody Knows*. Forgotten today, it boggles the imagination. The chapter on John the Baptist is titled, "The Advance Agent Appears." The Sermon on the Mount: "The Business Charter Given"; and " 'Method & Secret' Revealed." But the perspective of the book, like Barton's, is liberal, reformist Protestantism.

revenues, but which are in fact *distributing* revenues in the name of God. Stewardship is undoubtedly involved in the support of the church and its appendages, but it is the *stewardship of charity* rather than the stewardship of a profitable calling. To transfer the concept of the *stewardship of business* to that of charity, thereby justifying usurious loan contracts, is nothing short of blasphemy. He who accepts such a loan is as guilty as he who offers it.

The request for loans to support the work of the church is legitimate in times of emergency, just as the appeal is valid for an impoverished individual. It is not legitimate otherwise. But an appeal for a loan at interest is always usurious, always immoral, and always under the curse of God, if it is made in terms of the need for charity. Men can shut their eyes and stop up their ears, but that is what the Bible affirms. There is no escape from the truth; God only delays the judgment.

The issue of the so-called "life-income contracts" is more difficult to assess, at least for the person who has not had some training in economic theory. Consider the booklet published by "Charitable Giving Publications" and distributed by a leading conservative seminary and the Bible Study Hour. It is written by Robert Sharpe; the seminary version is dated 1967, and the Bible Study Hour version is dated 1968. It presents the case for "gift annuities." These contracts involve the payment of a lump sum in cash; the institution uses these funds, and it pays the investor a stated annual return in dollars until he dies. On his death, the remaining money in the fund (if any) goes to the surviving husband or wife or else it goes to the institution, depending upon the type of contract signed. We are informed by the booklet:

> You accomplish two main purposes with a gift annuity.
> FIRST . . . You make a gift to a charity, an educational or other charitable organization. Such organizations must meet certain qualifications for your gift to offer you the tax advantages discussed later.
> Second . . . You are providing yourself with a regular and assured income.

Both statements are misleading. A gift is a present sacrifice made to a charity or a person without any thought of return. It is not the same, morally or legally, as a legacy after death (as any tax collector will be careful to explain). A gift involves the sacrifice of the living donor, not the sacrifice of his surviving relatives. That, at least, is the Biblical idea of a gift. An investment is not a gift, either. For example, an annuity may be taken out with a commercial insurance company, a fact admitted in the brochure. Is this to be regarded as a "gift" to Prudential or John Hancock? Is it not rather a form of

risk-taking, with the insurance company betting that you will not outlive
the actuarial average life expectancy for someone of your age group
and sex? Is the company not betting that the accumulated interest on
your money plus the principal will be greater, at your death, than the
payments made to you during your lifetime?

If the contracts are the same, why does a person go to a church or a
missionary organization to make provisions for his "lifetime income"?
Because the church comes to him in the name of the Lord. The church
calls his investment a gift, calls his risk-taking charitable stewardship,
calls his usury commendable. A commercial insurance organization
does not bear the name of Christ, and it must pay taxes on its profits.
It is not really so competitive among the faithful as the church's insurance scheme is. Like the moneychangers, the church's insurance
salesmen (and loan brokers) are "inside the temple court." The church
possesses that crucial spiritual monopoly, and its administrators have
learned that such a spiritual monopoly can be easily converted into a
very successful (in the short run) economic monopoly.

Is this an exaggeration? Listen to the words of Mr. Stanley L.
Bjornson, of the Christian and Missionary Alliance, in that organization's official pamphlet promoting the "Treasures Tomorrow" program:

> We call it "Treasures Tomorrow," adapted from Christ's injunction
> to "lay up for yourselves treasures in heaven." Of course, many
> financial plans offered by the Alliance provide income opportuni-
> ties for the near future, others in years to come. *All, however, are
> investments in behalf of God's work* which he has promised to bless
> (italics in original).

Naturally, these organizations prefer an outright gift to an investment which requires them to repay something to the investor. But
donors are not always able to meet the needs of the various organizations, so potential usurers in the audience must be encouraged to embark on a new, more immediately profitable path to "charitable giving." Ezekiel was no doubt right in his day to condemn such practices,
but then he was "under law, not grace." We supposedly live in a new
dispensation, as Mr. Bjornson indicates:

> The best gift possible, of course, is the outright gift which becomes
> immediately available for use; however, many Christians "yearn to
> give but need earnings to live." For them, income-giving gifts,
> annuities or trusts are preferable and beneficial. It is our sincere
> desire to serve all who wish to "lay up treasures in heaven" by
> giving and investing in the Lord's work today.[19]

Christians who play such games with language are laying up something
in heaven, no doubt, and perhaps they will be skillful enough to convince

---

19. *Christian Living—Stewardship Giving, Inseparably Linked* (n.d.).

themselves (on earth) that the thing being stored up for them is a "treasure," but there will come a day of accounting. Whether their stores are treasures or not will be examined by fire (I Cor. 3:12 ff.).

So the pastors of the flock make usurers of the sheep. In order to gain funds for their "kingdom projects," the pastors have turned the house of prayer into a den of thieves—all for a good purpose, of course. The truth or falsity of the Bible's stand against usury is not even a topic for consideration. Men skilled in the most tortuous kind of detailed Biblical exegesis, men trained in the original Biblical languages, men who can spot a flaw in a creedal formulation in an instant, find themselves unconcerned with the practical issue of usury. That is the blight of antinomian pietism: precision in things narrowly theological, utter blindness in anything beyond the scholar's footnote. Its product is cultural impotence. The years of studied irrelevance catch up to a church; the pastors are no longer capable of applying Biblical norms even in the narrow realm of the institutional church. The standards of the world of high finance are assumed, *a priori*, to be eminently transferable to the world of the institutional church. If the tax authorities (once called *publicans*) grant to non-profit corporations certain tax advantages on annuity programs, that is assumed to sanction the practice in God's eyes. And indebtedness, like a narcotic, is very difficult to abandon once the practice is begun. Those lifetime annuities must be paid off in part by the financing of more lifetime annuities. That is the modern way. "Owe no man any thing, but to love one another" is disregarded; that was for first century Rome, not for modern times. We live in a new dispensation.

Inflation and Annuities

Risk is basic to all life. Nothing on earth is a "sure thing." Society has devised many institutions to predict the future and to spread risk, and the insurance company is the most notable of these institutions. A "no-risk contract" is a contradiction in terms: companies go bankrupt, disasters strike, people steal money and disappear, governments devalue currencies or freeze accounts in banks. There are low-risk investments, but never no-risk ones.

Consider the implications of the statement by Mr. Bjornson, in answer to the question, "What is a charitable gift annuity?":

> This is the transfer of money, securities or property to a charity in return for a *guaranteed income for life*. The amount of fixed income depends upon the donor's age at the time of the gift. In addition to certain tax benefits *the donor has the assurance of regular income, free from investment concern and economic fluctuations* (emphasis in original).

The World Vision organization is almost as blatant in its promises concerning safety of the "donor's" so-called "gift":

> An annuity provides a fixed income for life and makes it unnecessary to concern yourself with personal management of the transferred funds. Annuities offer financial security, and because of a saving on taxes, give you additional funds for the Lord's work.[20]

Ah, the wonders of risk-free living, giving, and investment! The mass-produced *Effective Giving Through [So and So's] Gift Annuities pamphlet* spells out the nature of the contract in glowing terms:

> 1. You have an income which you cannot outlive—it is for your lifetime, plus you are giving support to this organization.
>
> 2. You have an income which will never be reduced—it is set at the time you make the gift, and it cannot be changed.

Here is the financial world's answer to the perpetual motion machine. "An income which will never be reduced!" What a marvelous promise to some elderly couple. They lived through the depression, and like so many of their generation, that experience left permanent scars on them. They think of economic catastrophe in terms of collapsing prices and low pay. Europeans of their same generation know better. The more normal form of economic catastrophe is inflation, where pensions and savings accounts are wiped out by the depreciation of a nation's currency. But in America, the appeal is made to the terror that is available, and that terror is the absence of monetary income. So the *Effective Giving* pamphlet presents the reader with a totally meaningless economic statement: "Increasingly, the American economy is based on income rather than wealth." The sales pitch is then made for the safety of guaranteed income. The unsophisticated are encouraged to sign the irrevocable contract; their savings are permanently transferred, by law, to the organization, in return for a fixed money payment (annual, semi-annual, or quarterly).

One unstated premise underlies the promise of permanent income: *income in dollars is the economic equivalent to income in goods and services*. The assumption is made by the buyer of the contract—the so-called "donor"—that the purchasing power of money income will remain stable over the remainder of his lifetime. He is involved in a form of gambling, although the unsophisticated person may not be aware of this gamble. He is betting his savings on the huge gamble that there will be no more monetary inflation by the civil government, and therefore prices will remain stable or even fall. That gamble, since at least 1965, has been a very poor one. It is worse than poor; it is suicidal. From 1958 through 1968, the increase in the American

---

20. *Faithful Stewardship Through Christian Investments*, p. 4.

money supply exceeded 90 percent. Prices are rising at an annual rate of over six percent; this rate will climb much higher in the 1970's and 1980's. Only price and wage controls will call a halt to this *visible* increase in prices, and the controls will destroy many segments of our free market economy.[21] Inflation has become a way of life for Americans, both politically and economically.

Usury is a crime against God. Today Christians have become usurers in response to the appeals of their leaders. They are no doubt sinning in ignorance. The fact remains, however, that they are involved in rebellion against God's law-order, and there is judgment coming. The miracle of God's universe is its marvelous regularity; its lawfulness is beyond human comprehension.[22] Those who have purchased such usurious contracts have made an economically irrevocable decision. Their hopes are being eaten away by inflation. Their real income is steadily dropping, as value of money tumbles. The usurers are being destroyed by inflators. God will not be mocked.

The American Institute for Economic Research, a respected investment service, is noted for its conservative attitude towards highly speculative investments. The Institute has published a study of the various forms of annuities, evaluating each separately. The *retirement annuities*, whereby a man sets aside a large sum of money, transfers it to the corporation in question, and waits for, say, 25 years for it to mature, at which time he receives a fixed payment for life, is evaluated as follows:

> From an investment point of view, the interest earned on the annual premiums is not especially favorable, because the guaranteed return over a long period of years is less than that paid by most savings banks. . . . if there is any substantial improvement in the average length of life in the future, the option on an annuity may be valuable. On the other hand, probable inflation and the threat of another devaluation of the dollar indicate that deferred contracts of this nature may not be favorable.[23]

Recent reports made available to the news media by the federal government have announced that a marked drop in the average life expectancy for males over five years old has appeared. The pressures of industrial life, coupled (one suspects) with the physically degenera-

---

21. Gary North, "Price-Wage Controls: Effects and Counter-Effects," *The Commercial and Financial Chronicle*, Aug. 21, 1969, p. 13; North, "Inflation and the Return of the Craftsman," *The Whole Earth Catalog*, Jan., 1971, p. 8.

22. Cf. Eugene P. Wigner, "The Unreasonable Effectiveness of Mathematics in the Natural Sciences," *Communications on Pure and Applied Mathematics* XIII (1960), pp. 1-13. Wigner is a Nobel Prize winner in physics.

23. AIER, *Life Insurance and Annuities from the Buyer's Point of View*, Aug., 1969, p. 25. The Institute does not argue that annuities are totally unwise economic investments, but only that a person should invest but a part of his assets in them. The greater the rate of inflation, the less should be invested.

tive effects of processed foods, have combined to reduce the average life expectancy for males by as much as five years. So the purchaser of a deferred annuity loses both ways: he lives a shorter life and is paid off in depreciated currency.

"Strictly as an investment," the Institute goes on to say, "most retirement annuities are not especially desirable. The interest yield to the maturity of the policy is lower than probably can be obtained from a wise selection of other investments." The study adds this warning: "During an inflationary period, funds should be invested principally in the types of securities that will tend to preserve purchasing power." Publications sent by the Institute since the issuing of this one indicate that in the opinion of the Institute's staff, runaway inflation is now a distinct possibility. The higher the rate of inflation, the poorer the investment in annuities of any kind. The AIER staff recommends that elderly people purchase Swiss annuities only (April 19, 1971).

Since the economic effect of inflation on annuities and other kinds of insurance contracts, as well as on long-term loans, is to destroy the investor's capital, should the churches continue to promote such contracts (even if they were not usurious, which they are)? Can the church's leaders afford not to analyze the causes and effects of inflation, and then bring the warning to their flocks? Does not this aspect of preaching fall under the general requirement of preaching the whole counsel of God? The answer of most of our pastors today is simple: *no*.

When R. J. Rushdoony spoke in a church on the nature of inflation at a special midweek conference, he received a letter from a pastor who was critical of such a message even being presented inside the church's building.[24] On another such occasion, one minister was threatening to have him publicly disciplined by his denomination for having narrated a filmstrip critical of the inflationary policies of the Federal Reserve System. Any number of arguments can be used by the antinomian clergy against this kind of preaching: "Separation of church and state (and never mind about our tax law break)!" "The Bible doesn't talk about inflation!" "The Bible isn't a textbook of economics." "We're under grace, not law." So they continue to lead their unsophisticated, trusting congregations into usury and economic self-destruction. No warnings are offered, no attempt is made to abandon the loan contracts. There is every evidence in our churches today of judicial blindness, a curse imposed by God comparable to the one promised by Isaiah and administered by Christ: "By hearing ye shall hear, and shall not understand; and seeing ye shall see, and shall not perceive" (Matt. 13:14).

24. R. J. Rushdoony, *The Biblical Philosophy of History* (Nutley, N. J.: The Craig Press, 1969), p. 141.

Irrevocable lifetime annuities, in the context of mass inflation, is irrevocable economic suicide. A pastor who fails to warn his flock of this fact, thus exposing the lies printed in his own denomination's huckstering pamphlets, is nothing but a destroyer—a wolf in sheep's clothing who seeks to impoverish the weakest members of his congregation. The pastors have become proponents of pauperization, encouragers of usury. They are the middlemen of economic whoredom. By validating a wholly illegitimate transfer of moral business practices to the realm of the institutional church, they have become financial pimps.

Hierarchical Autonomy

Hayek, in his masterful book, *The Road to Serfdom*, includes a chapter entitled, "Why the Worst Get on Top." His argument is that centralized power, especially economic power, is a lure for the most unscrupulous men in society. He believes that by the very fact of the concentration of economic power in the sphere of civil government, a strong impulse toward totalitarian rule is established. What he says about the civil government could be easily applied to any non-market, essentially non-competitive religious institution. The more economic power that is lodged at the higher levels of the bureaucratic hierarchy, the less responsive will the leaders be to the demands of the membership. Grant any such organization a large degree of financial autonomy, and it becomes a likely target for take-over by the unscrupulous.

The twentieth century has witnessed the liberalization of virtually every Christian church, both Protestant and Catholic. Theological liberalism and political liberalism have been cooperating partners.[25] A major factor in the success of the conversion of the churches to unorthodox creeds and actions is clearly the hearts of the congregational members. They have listened to the false prophets in the pulpits, complaining only when their leaders' radicalism has infringed on some cultural or economic preserve dear to the hearts of particular members. But a crucial institutional factor leading to the take-over has been the

---

25. The most forthright statement of the link between political liberalism and theological liberalism is found in R. J. Rushdoony, *Politics of Guilt and Pity,* sec. IV, esp. pp. 313-317. Cf. J. Gresham Machen, *Christianity and Liberalism* (Grand Rapids: Eerdmans, [1923]), Introduction. For historical accounts of the parallel developments of the two liberalisms in America, see Rushdoony, *The Nature of the American System* (Nutley, N. J.: The Craig Press, 1965), chap. 6; C. Gregg Singer, *A Theological Interpretation of American History* (Nutley, N. J.: The Craig Press, 1964). The chief flaw in Singer's book is his overemphasis on the role of Deism in the coming of the American Revolution. That movement was essentially a Christian counter-revolution: Rushdoony, *This Independent Republic* (Nutley, N. J.: The Craig Press, 1964); Carl Bridenbaugh, *Mitre and Sceptre* (New York: Oxford University Press, 1962); Alice M. Baldwin, *The New England Clergy and the American Revolution* (New York: Ungar, [1928] 1958); Edmund S. Morgan, "The Puritan Ethic and the American Revolution," *William and Mary Quarterly,* XXIV (1967), pp. 3-43.

existence of endowed agencies within the churches: mission boards, educational institutions, denominational publishing houses, and so forth. The financial autonomy from the weekly contributions of the members has been a basic means of subversion.[26] Part of this autonomy is provided by the irrevocable annuity schemes and long-term loan contracts. These favor the perpetuation of the institution in question apart from the theological commitment of the institution. Its future supposedly rests more on income from "prudent investments" than on the preservation of its original theological standards. This, of course, is inevitable, given the nature of the trust agreements, as indicated by the following sales pitch:

> Long after you have gone home to heaven your influence can live on . . . here on earth. A gift to missions—to the ongoing work of the worldwide Church—can mean that your Christian influence will live on through the years in dedicated hearts, hands and feet of the servants of Christ in the far corners of the earth.[27]

What an irresistible appeal for some elderly, unsophisticated widow who has a few thousand dollars saved! And what a curse to the organization which offers her the appeal; it is sealing its own doom, theologically. The structure may survive, but the goals will change. Perpetual annuities and trusts reverse the promise of Solomon: "The wealth of the sinner is laid up for the just" (Prov. 13:22b). Instead, we find that the wealth of the just is laid up for the sinner.

The hypocrisy of the appeal to the elderly Christian to part with his money like this should be manifest. The donor (or in this case, the usurer), is led to believe that the institution, in and of itself, can and will maintain its commitment to the establishment of God's kingdom. What the institution needs, the donor-usurer is told, is a permanent fund. The fund is crucial, and not a commitment to theology. Theology will take care of itself; what is needed is *money!* The fund must expand, even if this means that Christians are turned into usurers, and economically imprudent usurers at that (given the fact of inflation). If the

---

26. Another important factor in the take-over of the Protestant churches is an attitude best described as "Protestant sacerdotalism." It regards the minister as standing above and distinct from the ordained elders, and it regards the laity as not merely functionally subordinate but also intellectually inferior. Cf. Paul Ramsey, *Who Speaks for the Churches?* (Nashville: Abington, 1968). For a classic example of the arrogance of the pastors whose votes place denominations in support of radical positions, in direct opposition to the stated opinion of the majority of the members, see John C. Bennett, "Christian Responsibility in a Time that Calls for Revolutionary Change," in John C. Raines and Thomas Dean, eds., *Marxism and Radical Religion* (Philadelphia: Temple University Press, 1970), pp. 75-76. An excellent critique of Protestant sacerdotalism is provided in E. L. Hebden Taylor, *Reformation or Revolution* (Nutley, N. J.: The Craig Press, 1970), p. 413 ff.

27. Bob Pierce, founder of World Vision, in his introductory statement to *Faithful Stewardship Through Christian Investment*, p. 1.

fund can just be built up, the leaders will be able to operate, irrespective of the hostility of the membership; the threat of funds cut off cannot exercise the same force. God save the fund!

Financial autonomy of the hierarchy of an institution is the death knell of its original goals. There were many reasons why all debts were cancelled in the Old Testament every seventh year. Surely this was one of them: the civil government, the banks (in whatever form they took), the lenders, the debtors, and all other institutions were prohibited from living in terms of perpetual debt and "irrevocable annuities," whether secular or usurious. The prohibition must have helped to preserve the responsibility of the bureaucrats of all kinds to the wishes of the people, just as the requirement of the tithe kept the people from becoming tyrants. Plural sovereignties were protected by the various provisions of the law; each had its own rights, and each had its own limitations. None was to become permanent apart from the continuous renewal of God and continual acknowledgment of His sovereignty as absolute.

The essence of *Christian stewardship* is simply this: *full-time, irrevocable, personal responsibility before God.* By their very nature, irrevocable trusts and annuities involve both "giver" (usurer) and debtor in *revocable theological responsibility.* The rate of interest may be irrevocable and utterly impersonal, but that is the only part of the arrangement that is. Christians are not allowed the luxury of such "stewardship," for this kind of irrevocable finance is the *abolition* of Christian stewardship.

There is justice in all of this. The churches that have been too mild and "tolerant" to demand that their members *tithe* (though, of course, not to the church alone, which *would* be illegitimate Biblically) find themselves making usurers of their members because funds are so scarce. Too soft-hearted to enforce the law of the tithe, they have been utterly ruthless in devising a whole complex of usury schemes. But in doing so, they have linked their impersonal economic futures—their irrevocable external "protection"—to the survival of an inflationary economy. When price and wage controls are imposed, the endowments full of "blue chips" will fast turn into "buffalo chips": these controls destroy both stocks and bonds.[28] To the extent that our Christian institutions have participated in the "economic genius" of the modern world, they will perish in terms of such genius. They will learn to their dismay that guaranteed prosperity, like guaranteed income for the widows, is never so simple as it seems. Debts incurred in faith of perpetual economic expansion cannot but fail in the long run; there is no such thing as linear, irreversible, irrevocable growth—of population,

---

28. Gary North, "Price-Wage Controls: Effects and Counter-Effects," *Commercial & Financial Chronicle*, Aug. 21, 1969, p. 13.

of money in the bank, of new members, or the rate of interest. At some point, mathematical law informs us, the exponential curve flattens out or falls.[29] Judgment is coming.

The Pitfalls of Huckstering

Where will it all end? An indication of where we are going came to me in the mails, unsolicited, under the "Postage Paid" stamp of a non-profit organization. The organization is Pallotine Missionaries of Baltimore, Maryland. I shall quote from the envelope itself: "Postmaster, Contents: Sweepstakes notification numbers enclosed. $14,000 SWEEPSTAKES. You have 5 chances to win 112 PRIZES." On the back: "TWO 1970 OLDSMOBILES OR $3500 CASH . . . 100 KODAK MOVIE CAMERAS OR $35 . . . TEN COLOR T.V.'s OR $350 CASH." Inside was the promotional:

> *Today May Be Your Lucky Day. . .Why Such a Fantastic Giveaway???* Because a group of supporters of the Pallotine Missions got together and came up with the bright idea of donating all the prizes [tax-deductible, of course—G.N.]. . .God bless them. . .and just think you may be a winner. *Why a Sweepstakes???* Simply to call attention in a dramatic way to the needs of the poor, hungry and sick children in the Pallotine Missions. . . . Mail me your contribution today. . . . A person with a heart full of love has always something to give, especially to help children. . .Just as loving never empties the heart—giving never empties the purse.

When Bruce Barton wrote *The Man Nobody Knows* half a century ago, he was trying to bring a degree of sanctity into the world of business. He was trying to prove, however ludicrously, that Jesus was a successful organizer, and He was worth imitating, even if a man were in business. Barton's liberal theology at least let him try to bring ethics into business, although it involved a rewriting of church history. Today, all good pastors, liberal or conservative, officially ridicule Barton's book (if they have ever heard of it). Yet they have become far more perverse than Barton. They are not telling the businessman to imitate Jesus; they are trying to convince the followers of Jesus to imitate the businessman, and not the ethical businessman, but the huckster. Tell the half-truth (unchanging income, permanent, for life), but get that contract signed! Promise those color television sets, but make sure the sheep empty those wallets that never empty! "Tell ya what I'm gonna do . . . This week, and this week only . . . All your money down, but a whole lifetime to get it back. . . ."

---

29. Gary North, "The Theology of the Exponential Curve," *The Freeman,* May, 1970. Cf. Garrett Hardin, "The Cybernetics of Competition: A Biologist's View of Society," in Helmut Schoeck and James W. Wiggins, eds., *Central Planning and Neomercantilism* (Princeton: Van Nostrand, 1964), pp. 60-90.

The institutional church is not an insurance company. It is not a raffle service. It is not a place for bingo, even Protestant bingo. It is a house of prayer.

The Riverside, Calif., *Press-Enterprise* (August 29, 1970) printed a column under "Religion Today" by Rev. Lester Kinsolving. The article was run under this headline: "Shearing of the Sheep." Mr. Kinsolving provided a whole rogues' gallery of ordained fundamentalist ministers who promoted the sale of bonds, in this case, Baptist bonds. The church bond market today is a $500,000,000 market. Kinsolving writes:

> Potential investors were promised an opportunity to "do your Christian duty" (at 7 per cent) by investing in bonds issued by BBU [Bethel Baptist University], "a high calibre, accredited university that doesn't mock God, teach 'Apeism' . . . or wreck the student's faith."

> Pious investors poured more than $1 million into this Oklahoma enterprise only to learn, after its operators had vanished, that it had never been accredited and that its final enrollment had been four students.

> Such shearing of the sheep is no rarity:

> One promoter arranged a $20,000 bond issue for a small Arkansas church—but sold $40,000 worth, skipping town with the difference.

> The Golden Circle Gospel Federation sold $44,000 worth of what it claimed were church bonds—and then tried to invest the money in a Santa Barbara oil exploration firm when the Securities and Exchange Commission caught up with them.

> Claude M. Bond, of Gideon Church Builders, was permanently enjoined from selling bonds issued by 30 churches in the Dallas-Ft. Worth area. The SEC charged that Bond had misled investors by telling them "there has never been a known defaulted church bond."

> Not only investors but many state and municipal governments have proven exceptionally naive about such practices. For church sponsorship of such bond issues often means there is no requirement [that] the stock be registered or backed up with evidence of the institution's ability to repay.

Horrifying? Exceptional? What else should Christians expect when churches encourage the violation of God's imposed limitations on the members, the hierarchy, and the type of financing legitimate for each aspect of God's kingdom? Protestants may complain that such examples of defaulting or huckstering are not typical. That is not the point, however. What is crucial is not the fact that these fundamentalist "entrepreneurs" may be in control of only a small percentage of church trust funds; what is crucial is that the churches establish the funds in

the first place. It is not simply that the churches are not so efficient as
General Motors is in the handling of their internal and external debt;
what is intolerable is that they should imitate the kind of debt contracts
that General Motors, as a profit-making business, finds it profitable to
agree to. General Motors is not the institutional church, and it is not
under the same restrictions regarding the giving and taking of interest.
General Motors, unlike the institutional church, is not a house of
prayer.

4. The Economics of Sabbath-Keeping

by Gary North

> Six days shall work be done, but on the seventh day there shall
> be to you an holy day, a sabbath of rest to the Lord: whoso-
> ever doeth work therein shall be put to death. Ye shall kindle
> no fire throughout your habitations upon the sabbath day (Ex.
> 35:2, 3).

One of the very few Old Testament ceremonial ordinances that contemporary Christians still claim to respect is the sabbath. Usually, the
defense of a required rest on the sabbath is made in terms of the "creation ordinance" argument, and not simply in terms of the fourth
commandment (Ex. 20:8-11). It is argued that God rested on the
seventh day of the creation, and this serves as an example to be followed
by all people in all cultures. God's covenant people are especially
required to abstain from all secular employment on Sunday. No profits
are legitimate that are made on Sunday. Only those people who work
in occupations that offer aid to those in some emergency, or the people
who enforce public law, are allowed to labor on the sabbath. This
would include doctors, policemen, firemen, soldiers who are on duty,
and emergency telephone operators. (Why these people should accept
payment for these services is seldom explained. Christ defended the
right of a man to pull a beast of burden out of a ditch, but He did not
say men should operate "beast-retrieval" companies for profit on the
sabbath. Puritan preachers sometimes saw this more clearly. Thomas
Gouge, a contemporary of Owen and Baxter in 17th-century England,
praised as shining examples several Christian physicians who refused
payment for Sunday labor.[1])

Despite their official appeal to the "creation ordinance" argument,
modern sabbatarians invariably appeal also to specific Old Testament

---

1. On Gouge, see Richard Schlatter, *The Social Ideas of Religious Leaders,
1660–1688* (London: Oxford University Press, 1940), pp. 129, 137.

passages to support their interpretation of the requirements for sabbath observance. The same verses as cited by the Westminster Confession of Faith and the Larger Catechism in the annotations are used today, over three centuries later.[2] Isaiah 58:13 is a common reference, as is Jeremiah 17:21-27. It never seems to disturb them that these "Hebrew" applications of the sabbath came comparatively late in the English Reformation. Sabbatarianism had been a minor part of medieval Catholicism, and what rigor was asserted in theory by Catholic commentators was opposed vehemently by the Lollards and Luther. They were not willing to countenance anything which magnified the authority of the Roman Church.[3] Calvin followed the tradition laid by Irenaeus and Augustine, interpreting the sabbath as an allegory of the believer's rest in Christ from the bondage of sin, a rest to be made perfect in eternity.[4] This, of course, was simply the teaching of Hebrews 4, and Calvin was unwilling to break from its perspective. He went lawn bowling after church on Sunday, a fact which later sabbatarians have chosen to ignore. The Church of England took a position midway between the Lutheran and the Catholic positions: it denounced superstitious celebrations but reserved Sunday as a day of rest, although recreations of many sorts were considered legitimate, to the horror of later Puritans. It was only in the 1590's that the Anglicans, reacting against rigorous Puritan sabbatarians, drifted back in the direction of the Roman Church, with its holiday rests on certain saints' days.[5] Professor Knappen, the foremost authority on Puritanism in England during the 16th century, has therefore come to this conclusion:

> Modern English Sabbatarianism is therefore not Reformed or Calvinistic in its origins. So far as it had any theoretical background, it is to be found in the medieval doctrine which survived in Anglican teaching and legislation, that the day was to be devoted wholly to religious ends. This remained the official doctrine of the church under Elizabeth, as set forth in homily, catechism, and injunction. But the Queen's conduct did not conform to such standards. . . . By permitting her churchmen to perpetuate a high doctrine on the subject and then flouting it, Elizabeth invited a reaction which eventually took the form of an even higher doctrine.[6]

The reaction, according to Knappen, began when the Paris Garden

---

2. *The Confession of Faith* (Publications Committee of the Free Church of Scotland, 1967); WCF, chap. xxi; Larger Cat., QQ. 115-121.
3. M. M. Knappen, *Tudor Puritanism* (Chicago: University of Chicago Press, [1939] 1965), pp. 444-445.
4. On Augustine and Irenaeus, see Knappen, *ibid.*, p. 443. Calvin's viewpoint can be seen in his *Commentary on Hebrews*, chap. 4; cf. *Tracts and Treatises* (Grand Rapids: Eerdmans, 3 vols., 1958), II, 61-62. His ambivalence in the *Tracts* stands in contrast to his more rigid exegesis of Exodus 20:8 ff.
5. Christopher Hill, *Society and Puritanism in Pre-Revolutionary England* (New York: Schocken, 1967), p. 155 ff.
6. Knappen, *Tudor Puritanism*, p. 447.

bearbaiting pit collapsed on Sunday, January 13, 1583, and killed eight
people. Rev. John Field took up the gauntlet and blamed this event on
the violation of the sabbath, equating the Christian sabbath with the
Hebrew sabbath, an altogether new idea.[7] Others then followed his
lead. The hostility to any form of recreation on the sabbath is manifested in many Puritan works of the last decade of the 16th century,
notably Nicholas Bownde's *Doctrine of the Sabbath* (1595) and Richard
Greenham's *Treatise of the Sabbath* (1592).[8] The Puritan position
absolutely commanded labor on the last six days of the week, and absolutely forbade any sort of amusement on the first day. The extent
of their hostility to anything resembling a "five day work week" is
reflected in a statute that appears in the May 11, 1659, minutes of the
General Court of Massachusetts, one of the few political jurisdictions
that Puritans ever controlled:

> For preventing disorders arising in several places within this juris-
> diction, by reason of some still observing such festivals as were
> superstitiously kept in other countries, to the great dishonor of God
> and offence of others, it is therefore ordered by this Court and the
> authority thereof, that whosoever shall be found observing any such
> day as Christmas or the like, either by forbearing of labor, feasting,
> or any other way, upon such accounts as aforesaid, every such
> person offending shall pay for every such offence five shillings, as
> a fine to the county.[9]

The Larger Catechism, hammered out between 1643 and 1647 by
the Westminster Assembly, is straightforward enough. It prohibits
"all prophaning the day by idleness, and doing that which is in itself
sinful; and by all needless works, words, and thoughts, about our
worldly employments and recreations" (A. 119). The defense of
such Sunday rigor is made with numerous Old Testament citations. In
his chapter on "The Uses of Sabbatarianism," the English historian
Christopher Hill comments: "Some of the extremes to which later Sabbatarianism resorted arose from belief in the literal inspiration of the
Bible and the equation of Sunday with the Jewish Sabbath. But these
extreme views came later, *after* the hierarchy had broken with the
virtual unanimity of early Elizabethan times on the subject of Sunday
observance. . . ."[10] The coming of strict sabbatarianism cannot be
separated from the political and ecclesiastical conflicts in England from
1590 to 1660. The modern sabbatarian who is ignorant of the origins

---

7. *Ibid.*, p. 448.
8. Hill, *Society and Puritanism*, pp. 168, 170.
9. Nathaniel B. Shurtleff, ed., *Records of the Governor and Company of the Massachusetts Bay in New England* (Boston: Commonwealth of Massachusetts, 1854), vol. IV, pt. I, p. 366. I have modernized the spelling.
10. Hill, *Society and Puritanism*, p. 159.

of his peculiar heritage has failed to see the extent of his deviation from the Augustinian-Calvinistic tradition.[11]

What modern sabbatarians generally argue is that the so-called "purely ceremonial" aspects of the sabbath were temporary. This includes the very foundation of Hebrew sabbath worship, namely, the penalty for all violations, the death sentence. The fact that enforcement was absolutely and invariably connected to the observance of the sabbath disturbs our contemporary rigorists not in the slightest. More rigorous than the New Testament would permit, the modern sabbatarian is nevertheless too humanistic to let anything like fixed Old Testament law interfere with his lax view of sabbath *enforcement*. No exegetical argumentation is offered to explain why the unity of Old Testament sabbath observance and enforcement can be broken; it is simply taken for granted. Sabbatarians merely assume that God is somehow honored by their own inconvenience on Sundays, while a violation of His specific sabbath enforcement provisions simultaneously brings Him much glory.

Equally "ceremonial" are the debt provisions of the sabbath years, in which all slaves were to be freed and all debts canceled in the seventh year. The land was to go uncultivated as well. So we find self-proclaimed strict sabbatarians who are in debt for seven times seven years, or who mine the soil unmercifully; nevertheless, they pride themselves on their rigor. Their claim rests on the fact that they are not employed for profit on Sundays, and they do not watch the Green Bay Packers play the Cleveland Browns on television. Some of them will not listen to a news broadcast or read the Sunday newspaper. And the truly holy among them do not read the Monday morning issue either, knowing that it was printed on Sunday.

Naturally, the Monday morning sabbatarian quarterbacks who at least enjoy *reading* about the Packers-Browns game, even though it is immoral to watch it or play it, resent the rigor of their fellow sabbatarians who refuse to read the Monday afternoon account of it (the

---

11. Hill erroneously attributes the later Puritan sabbatarian position to Calvin, although he is forced to admit that Calvin's willingness to bowl on Sunday worried more zealous sabbatarians. Unlike Knappen, Hill shows little sign of having read Calvin's own writings on the sabbath. He writes in a footnote on the same page that "[Richard] Baxter was also a little uneasy in his attempts to explain away Calvin's and Beza's laxness." Hill, *ibid.*, p. 170. It is perhaps understandable that Hill, as a Marxist scholar specializing in 17th-century English history, would not be familiar with the details of Calvin's writings. There is no excuse for the statement by Professor John Murray of Westminster Seminary, in a desperate attempt to avoid the thrust of Calvin's view of the sabbath, that Calvin's views have simply been misinterpreted. Murray's Scottish heritage just will not conform to Calvin's "lax" teachings, so he has chosen to rewrite Calvin. See Murray's letter to the editor, *The Presbyterian Guardian*, June, 1969. On the fantastic, ludicrous rigor of the 17th-century Scottish sabbatarians, see Hill, p. 183.

morning edition, as I have already mentioned, goes unread). They think of the others as "legalists," while extremists who follow the implications of their position naturally view their weaker brethren as "latent antinomians." Such is the way of men: he who resents getting his toes stepped on calls his brother a legalist; he who delights in stepping resents all others' obvious inconsistency. It is too often a question of whose ox is getting gored (or, to fulfil the analogy, whose ox has fallen into what ditch).

What are the implications of sabbath-keeping? It no doubt meant much more to the ancient Hebrew culture than any one of us can realize. In the modern world we would find the full enforcement of sabbath rest, as practiced in ancient Israel, enormously disruptive of our familiar patterns of living. Thus, I have chosen to limit my enquiry to only the most obvious implications for the single sphere of economics. This narrow focus in no way covers the sweeping impact of the Old Testament sabbath provisions for other spheres of human society—family, government, military, and so forth. In any case, the implications of sabbath observance for the narrow realm of economic affairs should be disconcerting enough for those who like to think of themselves as strict sabbatarians. Hopefully, they will be forced to reconsider either their *actions* or their *definition* of the sabbath as it applies to our age.

The passage which introduced this essay, Exodus 35:2, 3, sets forth the general provisions for the enforcement of the Hebrew sabbath. It was a capital crime to kindle sticks on the sabbath. Orthodox commentators have taken two basic views of this passage. First, that "kindle" must have referred to the starting of a fire, literally and figuratively, from scratch. It was a difficult task to light up a fire once it had gone out, and this constituted extra labor which could have been avoided merely by paying attention to the home fire which should have been started a day before. The second view holds that "kindle" refers to a fire used in business, such as in the case of a blacksmith. The latter view is singularly unconvincing. (A third possibility, that no fires were going in Israel, even in the cold of winter, is unlikely, especially in the light of Jesus' liberal interpretation of sabbath observance [Matt. 12:1 ff.].) Thus, it seems reasonable to assume that it was illegal to start a fire on the sabbath, but legitimate to keep yesterday's fire burning.

The case presented in Numbers 15 should be interpreted in this light. A prohibition against starting a fire had to apply equally to the gathering of materials that might be used in kindling such a blaze. God made it plain to the Hebrews that such an extension of the general principle was required.

And while the children of Israel were in the wilderness, they found a man that gathered sticks on the sabbath day. And they that found him gathering sticks brought him unto Moses and Aaron, and unto all the congregation. And they put him in ward, because it was not declared what should be done to him. And the Lord said unto Moses, The man shall surely be put to death: all the congregation shall stone him with stones without the camp. And all the congregation brought him without the camp, and stoned him with stones, and he died; as the Lord had commanded Moses (Num. 15:32-36).

This passage is crucial to the understanding of what the sabbath ordinances demanded of God's covenant people. The violation of the sabbath in so "small" a matter as the gathering of sticks involved the offender in a capital crime. Judicially, there was no distinction between this crime and murder. Both required the death penalty. The modern sabbatarian, by citing Old Testament references to the sabbath in support of his position, inevitably involves his position with this passage. He is required to regard the tiniest violation of the sabbath with the same horror as he would regard the murder of a member of his family. All offenses, from stick-gathering through playing professional football, have to be seen as capital crimes. There is no escape from this situation: if the standards of Hebrew practice are worth proclaiming, then the requirements of Hebrew jurisprudence are worth enforcing. While our contemporary civil codes do not presently impose the death penalty on sabbath violators, consistent sabbatarians should not rest on the other six days of the week until the civil government is persuaded to impose such a sanction against the violators. *If covenant law is binding, then covenant law's enforcement is equally binding.* The man who deviates from this principle is, Biblically, an antinomian.[12] Any so-called "humanitarian" leniency in the enforcement of Biblical law is no less a violation of God's absolute standards of righteousness than the open denial of the validity of the legal standard in question. *At the very minimum*, based on expediency until our civil codes can be changed, any denomination or congregation that proclaims sabbath law as binding must enforce sabbath law on all its members through the process of the threat of excommunication. If Hebrew standards of sabbath observance are in any way assumed to be applicable in New Testament times, then the churches must regard sabbath breakers with the same horror as they regard (or should regard) murderers, kidnappers, and sodomites.

The churches, as everyone knows, do not now nor have they ever

---

12. This has been my basic charge against the neo-Dooyeweerdians of both the Netherlands and the English-speaking Calvinist community. For specifics, see my essay, "Social Antinomianism," *International Reformed Bulletin*, Oct. 1967.

so regarded sabbath violators. Paul went so far as to announce the doctrine that "One man esteemeth one day above another: another esteemeth every day alike. Let every man be fully persuaded in his own mind" (Rom. 14:5). He did not say, it should be pointed out, that the day or days in question were something called "Hebrew new moons or sabbath days," as desperate sabbatarian scholars have tried to argue. He simply said *day*.[13] Such an *option of the Christian's conscience* was not open to the stick-gatherers of Numbers 15. This ought to lead us to the conclusion that the application of the sabbath principle in New Testament times is radically different from what was required in Old Testament times. Similarly, Paul asks the individual Christian to decide; the ecclesiastical system that infringes on this right of conscience is in open violation of the New Testament standard. A church may enforce attendance at a Sunday service; it has no right to do more than this. The rights of the individual conscience in this particular case may not be infringed upon by any ecclesiastical authority.

If the twisted exegesis of the sabbatarians is accepted, and Paul's appeal to conscience is not regarded as applying to the weekly sabbath (with the forced exegesis also applying to Col. 2:16, 17), then a major dilemma appears: either the church's standards of sabbath-keeping are in flagrant violation of the Old Testament's far more rigorous standards, or else the hypothetically proper creedal provisions are presently unenforced, and have been unenforced for at least two centuries. More than this: it appears that they are completely unenforceable. *The creeds are less rigorous than the Old Testament; the contemporary church's enforcement is less rigorous than the creeds.* The sabbatarian who tries to escape this truth is deluding himself. Furthermore, what has happened in the case of the enforcement of these provisions—Old Testament or creedal—by the civil government is vastly worse. The sabbatarian cannot avoid this problem, either. If he finds it easy to ignore the failure of the civil government to enforce the sabbath laws, then he ought to be equally unconcerned with the state's failure to enforce the Biblical laws regarding marriage, prostitution, homosexuality, theft, and almost everything else that the Ten Commandments might be concerned with. The man who takes lightly the state's laxity in enforcing any or all of these is simply an antinomian. If he believes that the sabbath laws do apply, yet bothers himself not at all with the thought that the state has not done its job properly in this field, then he is defying the scriptural principle of law: a law worth proclaiming is worth enforcing.

---

13. There is some evidence that the King James translations of the Greek and Hebrew words for "month" were incorrectly translated "moon" in a limited number of cases, including Col. 2:16. On this point, see Curtis Clair Ewing, *Israel's Calendar and the True Sabbath* (Los Angeles: The National Message Ministry, 1958), pp. 7-8.

It should also be noted that a five-day work week is an open violation of the sabbath laws. The Lord did not offer anyone the option of taking a day off during the week. "Six days shall ye labor," He commanded, the AFL-CIO notwithstanding. Let's see the church enforce *that*! The Puritans did; they were threatened with jail for preaching it or following it.[14] They took that risk.

Sabbatarians and Fuel

The gathering of sticks is a fine example of Hebrew case law as applied in the light of a general requirement of the Decalogue. It shows, perhaps, better than any other instance, the implications of the fourth commandment for the Hebrew nation. Consider the economic implications. What was involved in the gathering of sticks? Sticks could be used for at least four purposes:

1. *Heating* the home
2. *Lighting* the home
3. *Cooking* the meals
4. *Selling* the sticks for uses 1-3

As far as actual use was concerned, the case in Numbers 15 applied more to the daily life of Hebrew women than it did to the men of the family. It is more often the man and his work which are the focus of modern sabbatarian concern, but this was not necessarily the case in a rural, pre-industrial community. The gathering of sticks was more likely to be the task of children; women were to use them for household tasks, once gathered. Men were to reap the benefits of both the gathering and actual use of the sticks, but in general they would not have much to do with the actual handling of sticks. There could be a few exceptions, of course, but one exception seems to be far more likely, namely, that of the professional stick-gatherer. His work would be most in demand on the sabbath, precisely the day on which the prohibition against work was enforced. A woman who failed to gather sticks earlier in the week could buy some from a professional.

We are not told that the man in Numbers 15 was such a professional, but the severity of the punishment clearly would have made it far more dangerous for such a class of professionals to have come into existence. There was a need for a harsh penalty, men and women being what they are. There is always a delight in violating God's commandments if one is a sinner; if that violation also brings with it certain superficial benefits above and beyond the mere pleasure of defiance, so much the better. Sabbath prohibitions involved heavy costs for the obedient; enforcement of the sabbath required stiff penalties, thus burdening violators with high costs in the form of high risk.

---

14. Hill, *Society and Puritanism*, p. 155 ff.

What were the costs of the sabbath? For the man, it was the forfeiture of all income—monetary (less likely in a rural society), psychological, or in physical property—for that day. But women also paid.
They had to gather all sticks earlier in the week. It meant more work
during the week, either in longer days or by increasing the intensity of
the working day—or both. Had the working day not been lengthened
or intensified, then other tasks which it was desirable to accomplish
would have to have been foregone, and that, as any wife knows, also
involves costs (especially if a husband or a mother-in-law notices the
failure in question). There would always be a temptation to forego
the gathering of sticks during the week, especially if a professional
would come by with a load of wood on the sabbath for a reasonably
cheap price. If his price was less than the woman's estimation of the
costs involved in gathering the wood earlier in the week, a bargain was
to be expected. By imposing a rigorous and permanent form of
punishment on the violator, the community was able to force up the
price of the sticks; risks would be so high that few professionals could
survive. How many women could or would pay the costs? It would
be cheaper to buy them or gather them earlier in the week. Stick-
gathering was made an unlikely source of profitable employment on
the sabbath. Since the market for sticks on the sabbath was restricted
because of the high prices for the sticks (due to the risks involved),
the opportunities for temptation were thereby reduced to a minimum.
It did not pay anyone to violate the sabbath, and it was too expensive to
hire someone to violate it.

To the degree that the penalties are weakened in a case like this,
to that degree it becomes *a matter of conscience* as to whether or not
one violates the sabbath or pays someone else to do it. Conscience
stands without the protection of higher economic costs to keep a man
acting in a holy fashion. In the mid-twentieth century, rest on Sunday
is based primarily on tradition and labor unions; where these restraints
are overcome, conscience is the only barrier against the violation of
the Old Testament application of the sabbath principle. Men who value
leisure less than other forms of income will tend to seek out employment
on the sabbath, especially when the market is restricted, for one reason
or another, against the entry of competing laborers. "Overtime" payments add incentive.

If we accept the principle that it is wrong for us to hire another
person to commit a crime for our benefit and his profit, then certain implications follow. Sabbath violations were capital crimes. If strict
sabbatarians regard Old Testament provisions as binding on Christians,
then it is as wrong to hire a man to violate the sabbath as it is to
hire someone from Murder, Inc. to kill a neighbor. The execution of

the crime and the guilt of the hiring party are in both cases equal. Capital crimes are major ones. *If the Hebrew sabbath is morally binding today, its implications and applications are equally binding.*

I have heard Christian people charge their fellow Christians with a violation of the sabbath because the latter have dared to go out to a restaurant to eat after church services are over. The same supposedly holds for those who purchase food in a supermarket on the sabbath. Why should this be a violation? Clearly, only on the grounds that it is a violation of the sabbath to encourage another's violation of the sabbath by paying him to remain open for business. *If* the standards of the Hebrew sabbath are binding, then entering a place of business on the sabbath *is* morally a capital crime, and an abomination in the sight of God. Therefore, pastors and elders must tell their flock to refrain from entering into trade of any sort on the sabbath.[15] If a man wishes to take the standards even of the Westminster Confession of Faith (a pre-industrial document, it should be pointed out) in all of its pre-industrial rigor, then he should encourage his elders to enforce the provisions. Of course, the provisions of the Confession do not even approach the requirements of Numbers 15, i.e., the true Biblical standards in the eyes of a consistent sabbatarian, but at least they are something. If the creeds are valid in their 1646 interpretation, then 1646 standards of enforcement ought to be applied. If such standards are not applied, then it is a clear admission that *the church no longer recognizes as valid the 1646 definition of the sabbath.*

Let us pursue the charge against the "restauranteers" with rigor. Those same people who make the charge pride themselves on their sabbath observance because *they* do not go out to restaurants on the sabbath. *They* do not shop in supermarkets. *They* have stored up provisions to eat at home. Quite properly, if one is a sabbatarian, for it is of the very essence of sabbath-keeping that one store up provisions in advance of the sabbath. But the Old Testament required more than the mere storing up of food. The passage we have referred to, Numbers 15, makes it explicit that not only food but the *fuel* was to be stored up in advance; fuel for heating the home, cooking the meals, and lighting the room had to be procured in advance. It was a capital offense in the eyes of a righteous and holy God to gather sticks—fuel— on His sabbath. The modern sabbatarian thinks that his is the way of

---

15. The utter confusion of many sabbatarian pastors is seen in their prohibition against paying for any book bought from the church's book room on a Sunday. The book(s) may be taken home but not paid for until Monday or later. An economic transaction made on credit is not regarded as an economic transaction if the church book room is concerned. However, a purchase of gasoline or any other item bought on credit on a Sunday is regarded by the same pastors as a flagrant violation of the sabbath. Anyone who can make sense out of these two positions is a rival of the medieval scholastic theologians.

the holy covenant of God simply because he buys his food early; his brother in Christ supposedly is a vile sinner because he has failed to do so. But under the provisions of Numbers 15, both are equally subject to death, for both have paid specialized fuel producers to work on the sabbath. There is this difference, however: the man who enters the restaurant is not self-righteous about his supposed keeping of the sabbath, and he has made no charges against his fellow Christians. He has undoubtedly violated the sabbath provisions of Numbers 15, but that is the extent of his guilt. The modern sabbatarians I have met too often violate both the sabbath and the commandment against gossip, or at least they indulge in the "judgment of the raised eyebrow and clicking tongue." They neglect Christ's warning: "Judge not, that ye be not judged. For with what judgment ye judge, ye shall be judged . . ." (Matt. 7:1, 2a).

The very architecture of our churches is a standing testimony to the unwillingness of contemporary Christians to accept the implications of the sabbath. We fill our buildings with all sorts of electrical appliances; we heat and cool the rooms to a comfortable 75 degrees, both winter and summer. We often pride ourselves on the efficiency of modern technology, forgetting that many men and women must go to work and operate the machines that provide the power—the fuel—for our gadgets. These workers are committing sabbatarian capital crimes each Sunday, and every Christian sabbatarian who uses these gadgets, apart from some legitimate emergency, sends people to hell every Sunday, morning and evening, as he sits in the comfort of his air-conditioned church. If the sabbatarian creeds are correct, then sabbatarians are weekly condemning others to the flames of eternal torment, just so that they can sit in 75-degree comfort.

Naturally, sabbatarians can always defend a 75-degree temperature in the name of a vital emergency. It can be seen by some to be the equivalent of an ox which has fallen into a ditch. Freezing churches would drive away unbelievers in winter; stifling churches would do so in the summer. Possibly this argument is legitimate, if this *really* is the reason we heat our churches. Or perhaps our bodies really could not stand what our Puritan forefathers went through to establish Reformed worship in America; perhaps we could not bear churches so cold that communion bread would freeze solid. Possibly we would die if our present technological comforts were to be taken away from us (as apocalyptic pessimists have asserted may be a prospect in the near future). But if mere comfort is our defense of our power-consuming central heating systems, then we are not giving much thought to our sabbatarian creeds. It has become altogether too fashionable to adapt the interpretation of the sabbath to each new technological breakthrough; sabbatarians cling religiously to standards written centuries ago, while violating the terms of those creeds regularly. It is schizophrenic. The wording of the creeds should be altered, or else sabbatarians should alter their easy acceptance of a radically non-sabbatarian technology.

This plea should not be regarded as something new. It was made by one of the strictest and most consistent sabbatarians in the history of the post-Reformation Protestant church, Robert Murray McCheyne. He minced no words in his condemnation of his fellow Christians:

> Do you not know, and all the sophistry of hell cannot disprove it, that the same God who said, "Thou shalt not kill," said also, "Remember the Sabbath day to keep it holy"? The murderer who is dragged to the gibbet, and the polished Sabbath-breaker are one in the sight of God.

Andrew Bonar has preserved McCheyne's teachings on the sabbath question in his *Memoirs of McCheyne,* and the self-proclaimed strict sabbatarian would do well to ponder what McCheyne wrote. If the standards of Numbers 15 are still in effect, how can a man who proclaims the sabbath escape the thrust of McCheyne's words? McCheyne saw clearly what the industrial revolution would mean. He challenged the right of the railways to run on Sunday, but he was not followed by his sabbatarian colleagues in Scotland. They chose, as sabbatarians ever since have chosen, to turn their backs on the implications of their creed, while vainly proclaiming the validity of that creed. McCheyne has a word for those who today enjoy having others work on the sabbath to provide them with fuel at reasonable prices:

> Guilty men who, under Satan, are leading on the deep, dark phalanx of Sabbath-breakers, yours is a solemn position. You are *robbers.* You rob God of His holy day. You are *murderers.* You murder the souls of your servants. God said, "Thou shalt not do any work, thou, nor thy servant"; but you compel your servants to break God's law, and to sell their souls for gain.

Sabbatarians should heed McCheyne's warning. Those who stand in pride because of their sabbatarian position ought to consider the implications of that position. God will not be mocked!

When the provisions of the Westminster Confession of Faith are rigorously enforced, then the sabbath debate can take on some meaning other than the playing of theological games. Then, and only then, will the issues be drawn clearly and honestly. When the elders of the church *begin at home* to follow the sabbatarian standards of the Old Testament, and when they impose such standards on their recalcitrant wives who love their stoves, their hot running water, and their air-conditioning systems, then the non-sabbatarian will be impressed. Let them turn off their electrical appliances, or purchase a generator to provide the power. Let them turn off the natural gas, or else purchase butane in advance. Let them cease phoning their friends for "Christian fellowship," so that the lines might be kept open for truly emergency calls. Let them stop using the public mails on Friday, Saturday, and Sunday, so that mail carriers and sorters will not have to miss their observance of the sabbath. Let them, in short, shut their eyes to the offenses of others until the church, as a disciplinary force, begins to enforce more rigorous requirements on all the membership, *starting at the top of the hierarchy* and working down from there. Let all the self-righteousness be abandoned until the full implications of the economics of sabbath-keeping are faced squarely. Until that time comes, non-sabbatarians will continue to be simultaneously amused and appalled at the shoddy thinking and self-righteous confidence of those who hypocritically call themselves strict sabbatarians, but who are unfaithful to the very standards that they seek to impose on others. They are too much like the double-minded Judaizers of Galatians 6:12, 13. The non-sabbatarian will not be able to take the strict sabbatarians seriously until the latter impose upon themselves the considerable economic costs of sabbath-keeping. Until then, the debate over the sabbath will remain a farce at best, and an embarrassment to Christ's church at worst.

Rethinking the sabbath question will involve a rethinking of the whole of Western industrial civilization. It will certainly involve the questioning of the last two centuries of rapid economic growth. Strict sabbatarians should at least be aware of the possible effects of their proposals. If the world should be conformed to Christian standards of Biblical law, and if the standards of Hebrew sabbath practice are, in fact, still the rule for the Christian dispensation, how would these standards be imposed on the population at large? Would it not make impossible our modern version of industrial, specialized society? In other words, if such standards had been enforced for the past two centuries, could this civilization, which most modern Christians accept as far as its technological conveniences are concerned, have come into existence? How much of our economically profitable, efficient Sunday technology would we be forced to destroy?[16] The costs, I suspect, would be considerable. It is time for strict sabbatarians to count those costs.

---

16. An obvious example is the steel industry. The cost involved in shutting down a steel plant and then restarting it are prohibitive. Steel could not be manufactured under such condititions. The power needed to heat up a steel foundry, to say nothing of the lost man-hours, would force steel producers to cease production. Once again, strict sabbatarians will have to regard steel production as a case of emergency. Everything, in fact, that would involve more discomfort than sabbatarians of any generation are accustomed to bear is thrown into that ever-increasing catch-all classification, "emergency service."

5. In Defense of Biblical Bribery

by Gary North

The three heresies of humanism, moralism, and legalism often manifest themselves simultaneously, even in supposedly Christian circles. All three center their focus on man. The primary assumption of *humanism* is that man—his goals, needs, desires, standards—is the central focus of life. It argues that man is not merely God's vicegerent over the creation, laboring in order to achieve dominion over the earth for the glory of God, but rather that the earth is to be subdued "by the people, for the people," as if creation were "of the people." *Moralism* is grounded on the doctrine that man is capable of demonstrating his own worth before God by acts of charity and self-denial. Moralists strive toward "being good" through acts of inherent goodness. *Legalism* is usually a parallel creed of moralism. God is viewed as being bound by the same laws that bind mankind; God, like His creation, is under law and must therefore conform Himself to the desires and demands of men who act in terms of His law. Legalism is a blood relative of magic, since the magician also seeks to manipulate reality by means of rigid incantations and self-abnegation, compelling the secret powers to perform in accord with the prescribed formulas. Legalism must assume the validity of moralism, and both are essentially humanistic: the salvation of man is accomplished by the deeds of man.

Orthodox Christianity, by definition, denies all three positions. Against humanism, Christianity asserts the sovereignty of God. The whole creation must give God all the glory, for that is its function (Isa. 45:22, 23; Rom. 14:11; Phil. 2:10, 11). Against moralism, Christianity says that there is nothing in man that can ever merit favor in God's eyes; man is totally depraved. All our righteousness is as filthy rags (Isa. 64:6). Sanctification is therefore equally as much a gift from God as is justification. "A man's heart deviseth his way: but the Lord directeth his steps" (Prov. 16:9). In short, moralism, by asserting man's intrinsic worthiness, is fallacious. Finally, Christianity rejects legalism, even as it rejects magic. God is above His creation; law is under God, not over Him. God covenants with man, of course, but the perversion and rebellion of man invariably leads to a situation where God's covenant blessings are delivered only because of Christ's ultimate righteousness; man receives a blessing only because of his participation in the covenant through faith, or, lacking saving faith, only because he lives in a universe temporarily shielded from God's wrath out of God's respect for Christ, Christ's people, and Christ's work in time (Calvin, *Inst.* II, 7, 4). God is in no way compelled by the feeble attempts at righteousness by the legalist or the manipulations by the magician to respect the cry of man. *God can resist the legalistic manipulations of men.* A failure of recognition of this basic fact led Job, as well as his three comforters, into a sinful misinterpretation of God's sovereign plan (Job 32–41). Orthodox Christianity declares that God is totally sovereign over His creation; He may do with it as He pleases, bestowing wrath or grace as He sees fit. He can make light and darkness, peace or evil (Isa. 45:9), and none may charge Him with sin or error (Rom. 9:19 ff.). The purposes of the laws of God are invariably theocentric, not humanistic.

Any Christian who gives tacit approval in principle to what has been said so far can test himself in terms of several Biblical particulars. Is law truly theocentric? Should our obedience be in terms of a covenantal law structure that aims *solely* at the glory of God? If so, then in what way should we regard the activities of Rahab?

It must be pointed out that the Bible is unhesitating in its praise of Rahab. Both the author of Hebrews (11:31) and James (2:25) testify to her wisdom in deciding to shield the Hebrew spies, and no criticism is given of her method of doing so. We are specifically told that for her actions she received a reward (Josh. 6:25). She made a covenant with the two representatives of the Hebrew nation (Josh. 2:12 ff.) and, by way of implication, with the God of the Hebrews. By faith she was justified, showing her faith by her works: here is the message of Rahab through the ages. The harlot who was grafted into the covenant line of Christ (Matt. 1:5), the only survivor, along with her family, of the fall of Jericho, was clearly favored by God. There is not the slightest hint anywhere in the Bible that *any* aspect of her defense of the Hebrew spies is in some way suspect. Calvinists, including Calvin, have rushed in where angels fear to tread; legalism runs deep in the rebellious hearts of men.

Rahab, we find, had to resort to lying in order to protect her visitors (Josh. 2:3 ff.). In his explanation of verse 4, Calvin writes of her *treason* in abandoning her people that "there was no criminality in abandoning them." However, her *lie* is not so easily dismissed:

> As to the falsehood, we must admit that though it was done for a good purpose, it was not free from fault. For those who hold what is called a dutiful lie to be altogether excusable, do not sufficiently consider how precious truth is in the sight of God. . . . And yet the particular fault does not wholly deprive the deed of the merit of holy zeal; for by the kindness of God the fault is suppressed and not taken into account. Rahab was wrong when she falsely declares that the messengers were gone, and yet the principal action was agreeable to God, because the bad mixed up with the good was not imputed.[1]

---

1. John Calvin, *Commentaries on the Book of Joshua* (Grand Rapids: Eerdmans, 1949), pp. 47-48.

Calvin set the precedent, and Calvinistic commentators have tended to follow his example. Very little space is devoted to Rahab's crime of treason, but the lie which she used in order to commit treason has come under close scrutiny. Matthew Poole, the 17th-century Puritan commentator, minced no words: "*I wist not whence they were*: her answer, contained in these and the following words, was palpably false, and therefore unquestionably sinful; howsoever, her intention was good therein: see Rom. iii. 8."[2] Nevertheless, it is a modern commentator who brings Calvinistic legalism to its highest point in the treatment of Rahab, although he would deny being a legalist as previously defined. So desperate is he to avoid the obvious implications of Rahab's example—that lying is legitimate in some cases and that God can be glorified in a lie—that he resorts to the most embarrassing kind of exegetical squirming:

> The vindication of deliberate untruth under certain circumstances receives more plausible support from the case of Rahab the harlot. That Rahab uttered an explicit falsehood is apparent. . . . How could her conduct in reference to the spies be so commended, we might say, if the untruth by which she shielded them were itself wrong?
>
> It should not go unnoticed that the New Testament Scriptures which commend Rahab for her faith and works make allusion solely to the fact that she received the spies and sent them out another way. No question can be raised as to the propriety of these actions or of hiding the spies from the emissaries of the king of Jericho. And the approval of these actions does not logically, or in terms of the analogy provided by Scripture, carry with it the approval of the specific untruth spoken to the king of Jericho. It is a strange theology which will insist that the approval of her faith and works in receiving the spies and helping them to escape must embrace the approval of *all* the actions associated with her praiseworthy conduct. And if it is objected that the preservation of the spies and the sequel of sending them out another way could not have been accomplished apart from the untruth uttered and that the untruth is integral to the successful outcome of her action, there are three things to be borne in mind. (1) We are presuming too much in reference to the providence of God when we say that the untruth was indispensable to the successful outcome of her believing action. (2) Granting that, in the *de facto* providence of God, the untruth

---

2. Matthew Poole, *A Commentary on the Whole Bible* (London: Banner of Truth Trust, [1685] 1962), I, 411. This exegesis was by no means representative of most Puritan thought on the matter of legitimate lying. The leading Puritan casuists, William Perkins and William Ames, both accepted the validity of the *dolus bonus* (good deceit), and they were followed in this by the chief Anglican casuist, Jeremy Taylor. On the various Puritan opinions concerning the acceptability of lying, especially by the magistrate, see George L. Mosse's study, *The Holy Pretence* (Oxford: Basil Blackwell, 1957). The key New Testament passage regarding God's use of the delusion in His plan is II Thes. 2:10-12. Those who are unrighteous are compelled by God to believe a lie.

was one of the means through which the spies escaped, it does not follow that Rahab was morally justified in using this method. God fulfils his holy, decretive will through our unholy acts. . . . [Point three compares Jacob's lie to Isaac and the resulting blessing: the blessing was justified, the lie was wrong.] We see, therefore, that neither Scripture itself nor the theological references derived from Scripture provide us with any warrant for the vindication of Rahab's untruth and this instance, consequently, does not support the position that under certain circumstances we may justifiably utter an untruth.[3]

What we see, on the contrary, is the difficulty of imposing onto the account of Rahab the legalistic limitations of a strained exegesis. Rahab's great faith and works burst such legalistic limits as thoroughly as Samson burst his ropes. This hypercautious exegesis simply refuses to come to grips with the plain teaching of Scripture: Rahab was justified in God's eyes, and not a single word in the whole of Scripture's references to her hints at any wrongdoing on her part. And consider the author's statement that "No question can be raised as to the propriety of these actions or of hiding the spies from the emissaries of the king of Jericho." In short, treason, under the circumstances, was perfectly normal, utterly reasonable. But the sin of lying—how awful! Legalism strains at the ethical gnat and swallows the ethical camel. To return the author's own barb, this is indeed "a strange theology." The author does not seem to comprehend the extent to which he is committed to the very legalism which his own theology of grace in principle denies.

"If only she hadn't lied!" our commentators seem to be saying. Then she would have been truly holy! Holy indeed; she would have been holier than God Himself required of her, which is the ultimate goal of all consistently applied legalism. Her lie, by all the standards of the ancient world, involved her in treason against the gods of her city. To covenant with Israel's God inevitably meant blasphemy and treason against the gods of the established culture, a fact made inescapably clear to Christians in the Roman Empire.[4] Even the most committed legalist cannot escape this fact, so legalists do not criticize Rahab for treason (for that was necessary by definition), but only for her lie (which "somehow" was not necessary). The capital crime of treason is sometimes legitimate, the legalist admits; the sin of telling a lie is *always* unrighteous. The world of legalism is an upside-down universe. We

---

3. John Murray, *Principles of Conduct* (Grand Rapids: Eerdmans, 1957), pp. 138-139.

4. On this point, see Ethelbert Stauffer, *Christ and the Caesars* (Philadelphia: Westminster Press, 1955). On the close connection between the state and the gods of the ancient city-state, see Fustel de Coulanges, *The Ancient City* (Garden City, N. Y.: Doubleday, [1864] 1936). For a survey of the theological warfare between early Christianity and the humanism of the ancient city-state, see R. J. Rushdoony, *The Foundations of Social Order* (Nutley, N. J.: The Craig Press, 1968).

should expect this, for all forms of humanism reverse the order of creation.

It may be objected that such an exegesis of Rahab as the quoted example represents is not legalistic, given the definition offered at the beginning of this essay. There is no explicit statement that God is bound by certain laws and that man can manipulate God in some way. True enough; there is no *explicit* statement of this kind. But it is clearly stated that "We are presuming too much in reference to the providence of God when we say that the untruth was indispensable to the successful outcome of her believing action." The critics of Rahab's lie apparently think her case is analogous to David's adultery with Bathsheba, a union which ultimately produced Solomon. We are not, of course, bound to praise David's actions simply because Solomon's rule produced many desirable results (such as the construction of God's temple). We are *specifically told* that David's adultery was abhorrent in the eyes of God; we are *not* so informed about Rahab's actions. It is dangerous exegetically to read into the story of Rahab sin which is not explicitly shown to be present, especially in the face of such overwhelming Biblical praise of her actions. Thus, we find Rahab's critics arguing that in some unstated way she could have responded truthfully or remained silent, while simultaneously preserving the lives of the spies. God just *had* to have some alternative plan to put into operation! If she had not lied to the king's men, she still would have survived, somehow, and the spies would have escaped, and Jericho would have fallen. In other words, *because man does good, God must see to it that His plan produces good.* God is therefore bound to honor man's good response, irrespective of what the obvious consequences of that good action may be (e.g., execution of all those involved by the king). This implies a kind of manipulation of God and His plan by man. It is never said what she should have done, but treason with lies, unlike treason without lies, is evil. Legalists will see it in no other light.

If the imposed exegesis of legalism were valid, then we should expect to find the greatest Biblical praise heaped on the closed-mouth traitors of Scripture: the traitor of Judges 1:24-26 or the regicide of Judges 3:12 ff. Who can quarrel, from the legalist's perspective, with the fact that in the latter example, "the children of Israel sent a present unto Eglon the king of Moab" (3:15b)? The "present" may have been a knife in the belly, but no one complains that Ehud gained access to the king's chambers by promising to deliver this present. "It's all in what we call a thing. Rahab told a lie, which was wrong; Ehud delivered a sharp present, which was perfectly honest." But the Bible does not reserve the greatest praise for these men; Rahab is the recurring example of godly obedience. This fact should warn us against the consequences of exegetical tampering with the plain truth of Scripture. What Rahab was, by the standards of Jericho, was a treasonous whore. The Bible regards her as an obedient saint. The legalists see her as a naughty girl: she told a white lie. Legalism misses the issues involved, whether from the point of view of the Jericho authorities or from the point of view of the covenantal history of God's people. Legalism dilly-dallies with the periphera of life while men live and die in terms of crises. Where legalism flourishes, Christians grow ethically over-cautious and culturally impotent.

With this as background, we come to the heart of this essay. Bribery is a sin, *if* it is a sin, of far less impact than treason, though admittedly it seems to be far more dangerous than telling "white lies." Would a pastor in an American pulpit ever preach on the legitimacy of a Christian's offering a bribe to a state official under certain circumstances? Would he counsel such a thing in private? Probably no pastor would ever think of offering such counsel, at least not until some crisis comes—and then he would no doubt feel guilty. Therefore, the principles of exegetical legalism must be focused on the enormous task of explaining the following verses out of existence: "A gift is as a precious stone in the eyes of him that hath it: whithersoever it turneth, it prospereth" (Prov. 17:8), and "A gift in secret pacifieth anger: and a reward in the bosom strong wrath" (Prov. 21:14). The author of these proverbs offered us his advice, but few pastors will be willing to follow his lead. That is how deeply legalism is imbedded in contemporary Christianity. It is better not to prosper, apparently, than to pay a bribe; better not to pacify the anger of some corrupt official than to pay him off: this is the inescapable set of conclusions that a consistent legalistic exegesis must produce. It makes a person wonder why Solomon bothered to insert such lines; it is as if he did so only to give nightmares to legalistic commentators. The congregation that listens to the preaching of legalism may someday find itself threatened by an apostate state bent on the persecution of Christians, and that congregation will be helpless. It will die as surely as the two spies would have died if, given the circumstances in which God had placed them, Rahab had not been so "naughty." Scratch a legalist, and underneath you will find a sanctimonious ostrich. Legalism hardens the heart and softens the brain. It results in cultural impotence.

What the Bible condemns is the *taking* of bribes, since it is assumed that godly men will enforce God's laws without payoffs. A bribe may not be accepted for one's own personal profit, either for perverting justice or for administering justly. But the Bible nowhere condemns the *giving* of bribes in order to impede the progress of *apostate* governments. "Bribery" as such is no more condemned than "treason" as such; it all depends on whose laws or whose nation is being defied. There can be no neutral, universal application of a word like "bribery," for, to make such a universal definition, we would have to assume the existence of some universal, neutral, and completely accepted legal code. That is the basic presupposition of humanism, but Christianity denies such neutrality. Neutrality does not exist. Everything must be interpreted in terms of what God has revealed. The humanistic goal of neutral language (and therefore neutral law) was overturned at the Tower of Babel. Our *definitions* must be in terms of *biblical revelation*. Resistance to unjust laws is not anarchy; resistance to just laws is anarchy. Rahab was right, though her apostate state would have regarded her as treasonous; Judas Iscariot was wrong, though an apostate state regarded his actions as exemplary, and rewarded him handsomely. There is no universal definition of a concept like treason. God's law and His specific guidance determine what is or is not treasonous or anarchistic. Rahab was the saint and Judas was the traitor. The exegesis of legalism inevitably forces its followers to conclude that the officially disobedient underground church in Hitler's days or in Red China today is really in the same position as the officially disobedient Black Panther Party or the contemporary satanistic cults; no doubt Romans 13 would be cited and Acts 5:29 utterly ignored. "What's sauce to the goose is sauce to the gander," legalism and other forms of humanism assert. Christianity denies it, for Christianity denies its premise: there can be no universal, neutral principles of law, language, or culture.

God's requirement for men is that they subdue the earth in terms of His revealed law structure, and that they do it to His glory. This means that whenever Christian men are in positions of authority in any government—family, civil, educational, financial, ecclesiastical—they are to render judgment in terms of God's standards. (This may help to explain why the early Christian churches often prohibited their members from serving in positions of high responsibility in the civil government; only after the accession of Constantine to the emperor's dominion was it to become proper to serve as a high civil official.) God therefore made it plain to the Hebrew rulers that any taking of bribes was illegal in terms of His law. Men were to govern in God's civil kingdom in a righteous manner and for His glory. Personal gain through bribes was illegitimate. It was assumed in the holy commonwealth that all cases of bribe-taking were motivated by the desire to pervert God's judgment for the sake of personal profit. When we examine the various passages dealing with bribery that are found in the law, we discover that bribes are linked with unrighteous judgment. The basic formula dealing with bribe-taking is found in Ex. 23:8: "And thou shall take no gift: for the gift blindeth the wise, and perverteth the words of the righteous." A parallel and even more explicit passage is Deuteronomy 16:18, 19. Rulers are to be "able men, such as fear God, men of truth, hating covetousness . . ." (Ex. 18:21). Perverting God's judgment for personal gain is what is condemned, and it should come as no surprise that only a few sentences away from Solomon's advocacy of giving a bribe (Prov. 17:8) we find this warning: "A wicked man taketh a gift at his bosom to pervert the ways of judgment" (17:23). This same perversion of judgment was the sin of Samuel's sons (I Sam. 8:3). It was the sin catalogued in Isaiah 1:23, Amos 5:12, Psalms 26:10, and I Samuel 12:3.

God's criticism is straightforward: men are wicked if they take bribes to pervert *righteous* judgment. God's laws are our only standard; we are to follow His lead in the appropriate way, the way creatures must follow, analogously: "Wherefore now let the fear of the Lord be upon you; take heed and do it: for there is no iniquity with the Lord our God, nor respect of persons, nor taking of gifts" (II Chron. 19:7). Yet we are told that God *does* take gifts in this very book, 32:23. Thus, we must see the evil of gift-taking as the evil associated with unrighteous judgment and taking respect of persons; it is not gift-taking as such that is evil. Taking a *bribe* is synonymous with perverting judgment in the Scriptures; it is prohibited in the affairs of *civil* justice. The example of the father who accepts a gift from his child is analogous to God's acceptance of the gifts in II Chronicles 32:23: he must not favor the child with judgments contrary to God's law due to his respect for the gift.

The setting in which God laid down His law was one in which an earthly civil kingdom was being established. In the New Testament times, civil power had been transferred to a pagan ruler. The change of setting involves a different emphasis on the responsibilities of those who are ruled. Jesus' parable of the unjust judge is typical. The judge, first of all, "feared not God, neither regarded men" (Luke 18:2). The widow comes to him in order to be avenged of her adversary, and she harasses the judge continually. Finally, he can stand it no longer. He announces, in desperation: "Though I fear not God, nor regard man; yet because this widow troubleth me, I will avenge her, lest by her continual coming she weary me" (vss. 4, 5). It is ethically proper for a widow with a righteous cause to harass an unrighteous judge if she believes that by doing so she will receive righteous judgment. This in no way sanctions the right of a corrupt woman to disturb the peace of a righteous judge who is truly too busy to give immediate attention to her case. In a very real sense, the woman of the parable offers the judge a bribe: if he renders judgment, she offers him peace.

The legalist is usually stunned by the implications of certain portions of the Sermon on the Mount. Jesus offers some remarkable suggestions—remarkable from the legalist's point of view—for the conduct of day-to-day life. What Jesus was giving to His disciples was a series of recommendations for the ethical conduct of a *captive* people. For example, "Agree with thine adversary quickly, whiles thou art in the way with him; lest at any time the adversary deliver thee to the judge, and the judge deliver thee to the officer and thou be cast into prison" (Matt. 5:25). That rule was a wise one in Judean lands during the time of the Roman Empire. It should not lead us to believe that the Christian attitude toward an enemy of God ought to be one of perpetual forgiveness and unending toleration when Christians have the power and authority legally to prosecute and convict him. If Christians, as God's people, should be given the power of the sword, then the adversaries of God should take seriously the warning of Matthew 5:25: let *them* agree with the Christian, lest for their outward lawlessness in disagreeing, the Christian should see to it that righteous judgment be applied in a civil suit, and the adversaries be severely punished.

On the other hand, to the extent that any Christian's position in any period of time should resemble the plight of the Christians under Roman rule, then he should take heed. Under the rule of a Hitler or a Stalin, the Christian's proper response is outward subservience. He should bribe the dictator's lieutenants, lie if necessary, join a Christian underground, and gain freedom of action through the lies and bribes to continue preaching and publishing. And if, as in the case of Ehud, the Christians are faced with an evil, triumphant, invading army (such as Christians in the Netherlands and other countries faced in World War II), a successful execution of the invading tyrant might be the proper course of action. Give him his "present"; he deserves it.

Christ warns His people explicitly: "And if any man will sue thee at law, and take away thy coat, let him have thy cloak also. And whosoever shall compel thee to go a mile, go with him twain" (Matt. 5:40, 41). Christ therefore informs His followers that they should give to those in power over them (i.e., if any *compel* thee) *an extra quantity of goods and services* over and above the original request. If such a gift were voluntary, we would call such an action a tip or charity. What, then, should we call such an action under conditions involving external coercion? There is a word for it, of course, but legalists may shrink from it. What Jesus advocates is for Christians to *bribe* the offending official. A bribe is a gift over and above what is legally required or asked for—a gift which will encourage the offending party to leave the Christian and the church in peace. It enables the Christian to escape the full force of the wrath that, in principle, a consistent pagan would impose on Christians if he realized how utterly at war Christ and His kingdom are against Satan and his kingdom. In other words, the bribe pacifies the receiver, just as Solomon said it does. The ethic of the Sermon on the Mount is grounded on the principle that a godly bribe (of goods or services) is sometimes the best way for Christians to buy temporary peace and freedom for themselves and the church, assuming the enemies of God have overwhelming temporal power. Such a bribe must be given in good conscience in order to achieve a righteous end. Christian citizens or servants are not thereby granted a license to offer the rulers bribes in order to achieve unrighteous ends. Nevertheless, this one fact should be apparent: turning the other cheek is a bribe. It is a valid form of action for only so long as the Christian is impotent politically or militarily. By turning the other cheek, the Christian provides the evil coercer with more peace and less temporal danger than he deserves. By any economic definition, such an act involves a gift: it is an extra bonus to the coercing individual that is given only in respect of his power. Remove his power, and he deserves punishment: an eye for an eye, and a tooth for a tooth. Remove his power, and the battered Christian should either bust him in the chops or haul him before the magistrate, and possibly both.

It is only in a period of civil impotence that Christians are under the rule to "resist not evil" (Matt. 5:39). When Christians are given power in civil affairs, the situation is different, and another rule is imposed: "Submit yourselves therefore to God. Resist the devil, and he will flee from you" (James 4:7). The same holds true for the devil's disciples. Martin Luther once saw the devil, or something he thought was the devil, and he hurled an inkwell at him. He had other suggestions, even more earthy, as to how we should handle the devil. That should be the attitude of all Christians who possess authority. We pay the bribe until the day that God's adversaries lose power, but not one day longer.

6. Subversion and the Tithe

During the 11th century, Manichaean ideas spread rapidly in northern Italy and southern France, having come there from North Africa, Byzantium, and Bulgaria. The headquarters in Europe of this movement was in Bosnia, whence a leader or "pope" is said to have ruled his followers. Most of these followers came to be known as Catharists. The Catharists attacked the Christian church as the church of Satan, mocked at infant baptism, communion, and orthodox doctrine. They held that the material world was created by Satan, the apostate son of God, while men's souls belonged to the true kingdom of heaven.

In particular, the Catharists struck at the foundations of Christendom by speaking against the tithe and urging people not to pay tithes. This fact alone "drew adherents in many localities."[1]

This fact, moreover, contributed to the changed attitude of the church towards these groups, and the suppression of all such movements began. Runeberg sees a connection between the Catharist movement, which went underground, and the rise of witchcraft.[2] The Catharists apparently allied themselves with the ancient religious practices and superstitions of rural peoples and gave them a Manichaean development. Thus, an ancient and dying paganism was converted into an aggressive heresy which was striking at the foundations of Christendom by attacking the tithe.

There was thus a dual movement underway, first, an attack on Christendom by means of an attack on its material mainstay, the tithe, and, second, an attempt to tie the tithe too closely to the church, which also undercut the vitality of Christian renewal. As long as the tithe flows freely to reforming agencies, renewal is constant. When it is tied to the church, the church's power is enhanced, not the vitality of Christendom.

In England, however, the monastic foundations impropriated the tithes from the parochial clergy, who had long given the poor tithe careful attention. By the early 12th century, this was creating problems. As the monastic foundations lost interest in the poor, there were complaints in parliament against these impropriations. In spite of this, the parish churches still did much to minister to the poor.[3] The ruthless impropriations of monastic properties by Henry VIII were in part made possible by this background. The monetary inflation of the Tudor regimes then worked to destroy the ability of the parish church to minister to the poor with its existing funds, and the clergy itself became needy.[4]

The tithe thus can be subverted in more than one way. It can be subverted by an attack on the law of tithing. It can be undercut by appropriating the tithe to the church (or state) rather than to the Lord's work directly from the people of God. It can be nullified by monetary inflation, whereby endowed funds are reduced to a pittance, and long-range provisioning made of none effect.

Without the tithe, the need for social financing remains, and thus the state tax takes over, as well as statist corruption and misappropriation. A limited state without a tithe is an impossibility, and political conserva-

---

1. *Societas Scientiarum Fennica, Commentationes Humanarum Litterarum XIV*, 4, Arne Runeberg, *Witches, Demons and Fertility Cults* (Helsingfors, 1947), p. 21.
2. *Ibid.*, p. 22 ff.
3. W. K. Jordan, *Philanthropy in England, 1480–1660* (New York: Russell Sage Foundation, [1959] 1964), pp. 80-83.
4. *Ibid.*, pp. 308-310.

tives who dream of such an order are fools and dreamers, as are anarchists who dream of existing with no state at all. A strong familistic
society *and* a tithing society can create a wide variety of institutions,
schools, and agencies which can take over the basic functions of church,
school, health, and welfare and thereby shrink the state to its proper dimensions. Social financing is necessary: either the people of God undertake it, or the state will.

7. Notes

1. An important question with respect to homosexuality is raised
by I Corinthians 6:9-11. Romans 1:24-32 cites homosexuality as the
culmination of apostasy and a burning-out of man, whereas I Corinthians
6:9-11 seems to open the door of salvation to "abusers of themselves
with mankind." In this passage Paul lists ten representative forms of
unrighteousness which bar men from God's kingdom, unless God's grace
intervenes in some cases. One of these, the "effeminate," has reference
to voluptuaries.[1] The catalogue of sins covers "false religion and irreligion, . . . sexual vices, sins against property, and sins of the tongue."[2]
St. Paul was telling the Corinthians of the kind of offense which separated men from God. He was not charging the Corinthians with commission of all these offenses. All were redeemed sinners, but "some of
you," St. Paul reminds them, were guilty of grosser sins prior to their
conversion. According to Hodge, on vs. 11, "and such were some of
you." "The natural explanation is, that the apostle designedly avoided
charging the gross immoralities just referred to upon all the Corinthian
Christians in their previous condition."[3] This verse thus does not tell
us that former homosexuals were among the redeemed in the Corinthian
Church. It can be noted, however, that, in Greek education, youth were
commonly seduced into homosexual practices by their tutors and
teachers, a charge much earlier made with justice against Socrates. The
burning-out of man described in Romans is not to be confused with
the sins of some of these Corinthians as young boys in the hands of
degenerate teachers. Perhaps I Corinthians 6:9-11 covers persons
seduced into this vicious type of practice and experience and thus makes
their redemption an open question, whereas Romans 1:26-32 presents
the homosexual as the burned-out and reprobate mind in action, and as
a culmination of apostasy and reprobation.

---

1. R. C. H. Lenski, *The Interpretation of St. Paul's First and Second Epistle
to the Corinthians* (Columbus, Ohio,: Wartburg Press, [1937] 1946), p. 248.
2. *Ibid.*, p. 249.
3. Charles Hodge, *An Exposition of the First Epistle to the Corinthians* (Grand
Rapids: Eerdmans, 1950), p. 99.

2. In July, 1562, the Council of Trent considered the matter of children and communion and issued a statement, one of four points on the sacrament, with four anathemas. This fourth point, and all four anathemas, read as follows:

> IV. Children below the age of reason are not obliged to receive the sacrament of Communion, because at that age they cannot lose grace. However, the opposite custom, which is ancient and preserved in some places, is not to be condemned, because it is doubtless to be believed that it was not done as necessary for salvation but for some other reason.

In conformity with this doctrine four anathemas were read:

> I. Against whoever says that all the faithful are obliged to receive the Eucharist under both kinds, either by divine command or as necessary for their salvation.

> II. Against whoever says that the Catholic Church has no good reason or that it has erred in giving the laity and those not celebrating Mass Communion under the form of bread alone.

> III. Against whoever denies that Christ, fount and author of all grace, is received under the form of bread alone.

> IV. Against whoever says that the sacrament of the Eucharist is necessary for children below the age of reason.[4]

It is significant that Trent recognized that communion by children was a practice "ancient and preserved in some places" and "not to be condemned." Calvin, who at one point opposed the practice, left room for it in his last communion service, with an exhortation fencing the table, however, from "all who are rebellious against fathers and mothers."[5]

3. The rising civil demand for restitution to victims of crime has gained legal attention and minor enactment. The May/June 1972 issue of *Trial* (vol. 8, no. 3), the legal magazine published by the American Trial Lawyers Association, was extensively devoted to compensation. The basic idea, however, is compensation by the state to the victim, rather than restitution by the criminal to his victim.

4. Samuel Willard, Puritan divine in New England, is an example of the Puritan view of the law. He held that the norm of sanctification is the law of God and opposed the antinomian view of the law. See Seymour Van Dyken, *Samuel Willard, 1640–1707: Preacher of Orthodoxy in an Era of Change* (Grand Rapids: Eerdmans, 1972), p. 131.

---

4. Sarpi, *History of Benefices, and Selections from History of the Council of Trent*, Peter Burke, trans., ed. (New York: Washington Square Press, 1967), p. 220.
5. Charles W. Baird, *The Presbyterian Liturgies* (Grand Rapids: Baker, 1957), p. 53.

SCRIPTURE TEXTS

OLD TESTMENT

Genesis			*Genesis*	
1:1	728		4:14	358
1:1–5:1	360		4:16b	358
1:2	761		4:17	359
1:4	257		4:19	363
1:10	257		4:20	297
1:11	255		4:23	362
1:12	255, 257		4:23–24	360
1:18	257		4:24	360
1:21	255, 257		4:26	117
1:24	255, 376		5:3–5	359
1:25	255, 257		5:4	371
1:26	257, 448		5:29	146
1:26ff	8, 449, 495, 342, 724		6:5	13, 285
1:27	448		6:9	628
1:27–30	163		7:11	13
1:28	3, 147, 201, 210, 308, 343, 724, 805		9:1ff	724
			9:1–17	8
1:29	297		9:3	36
1:30	297		9:4	36, 734
1:31	257		9:5	47, 77, 227, 230
2:1ff	410		9:6	36, 47, 77, 227, 358
2:6	357		9:22	405
2:7	163		12:1	16
2:8	680		12:11–13	462, 543
2:15	342		12:15–20	543
2:15–17	8		12:16	452
2:17	695		12:17	462
2:18	164, 257, 344, 347		13:2	462
2:18–24	362, 410		14:1ff	532
2:18–25	333		14:7	313
2:20	354, 343		14:15	21
2:21	257		14:20	52, 170
2:23	257, 362		15:1–4	181
2:24	167, 340, 344, 362, 363		15:2	381
2:25	354, 355		15:3	381
3:1	544, 709		15:7–21	44
3:5	3, 117, 149, 164, 316, 448, 458, 578, 736		15:9ff	759
			15:16	93
3:7	355, 357		16:10	29
3:8	355		16:13	29
3:9–13	269, 589		17:1	41, 58, 628
3:12	571		17:9–14	41
3:15	728		17:12	137, 756
3:16–19	695		17:35	58
3:17	262, 308, 438		18:1–8	532
3:17–19	310		18:2–4	29
3:18	262, 308		18:13	29
3:21	297		18:14	29
4:9–12	359		18:17–19	41
4:10	36		18:33	29
4:10–12	695		20:2	543
4:11	695		20:3–6	462
4:13–16	358		20:3–18	543

APOCRYPHA

NEW TESTAMENT

INDEX

Abomination, 435
Abortion, 186, 263-269, 290, 649, 714n
Abraham, 3, 8, 24, 41, 44, 49, 180, 210
462, 532, 543
Absolute, 17, 66, 119
Abstaining from meats, 37, 298
Abyssinian, 378
Achan, 269, 566
Act, 291
Acton, Lord, 59
Actors, actresses, 312
Adamites, 355
Adams, M., 207n
Adeney, W. F., 328
Administration, 341, 623
Adoption, 381
Adultery, 286, 304, 364, 392-401, 405ff,
454, 610, 646, 700, 702-706
Advertising, 582
A.F.L.-C.I.O., 831
Africa, 315f, 446, 606f
Agathobulus, 558
Age, 165
Age of Reason, 349, 351f, 383f
Aged, 251
Agnosticism, 112
Agricola, John, 652, 654
Agus, I. A., 788
Albrecht, W. A., 141, 261n
Albro, John A., 2n
Alcoholism, 300
Alexander, J. Addison, 116, 404, 674f,
683n, 694, 707, 767
Alexander, W. L., 169, 436, 617n, 656
Alford, Henry, 602n
Alfred the Great, 787
Algolagnia, 208
Alienation of affection suits, 634, 636
Aliens, 249f
Allen, Steve, 290
Allenson, A. R., 372n
Allerton, R., 528n
Allis, Oswald T., 29n, 52n, 670
Alphonsius de Liguori, St., 605f
Altar, 73-78
Alverson, C., 519n
Amalek, 312-323, 750
Ambition, 635
Amen, 574
American Bar Association, 232f
American Civil Liberties Union, 436
American Inst. for Econ. Research, 817
Ames, Wm., 839n
Amok, 322
Amphiloschius, 758, 784
Anabaptist, 651, 682

Anarchism, 40, 118, 192, 206, 207, 289,
305, 306, 502ff, 775, 848
moral, 290, 338
Anarchy, 3, 17, 61, 66, 95, 100, 115, 121,
192, 200, 206f, 241, 288, 290, 305,
325, 334, 338, 449, 581, 583, 611,
621, 673
Ancestor worship, 419
Andrews, W., 500
Angel of the Lord, 28, 29
Animals, 246f, 257ff
Anne, Queen, 51
Annunciation, 493f, 495
Anthropology, 159, 443
Anti-Christ, 14n, 15n, 119
Anti-God Society, 441
Anti-semitism, 476, 589
Antinomianism, 2, 3, 4, 18, 19, 21, 171,
173, 253, 263, 267, 288, 305, 307,
422, 463, 514, 559, 564, 651, 654,
677, 697, 702, 706-709, 713f, 732ff,
767, 769, 803n, 825, 830
meaning of "dead to the law," 3, 302,
306
not warranted by Scripture, 3, 6
Antoninus Pius, 557
Apeman, 441
Apostasy, 10, 21, 34, 621
Apostles, 23, 301
Apostolic Constitutions, 265, 512, 747f,
783
Apple, 561
Aquinas, 659
Ardrey, Robert, 201
Arians, 758
Aristocracy, 97
Aristotle, 265, 290, 474, 789
Arizona, 609f
Ark, 73
Armenia, 372, 557, 589, 782f, 788
Arminianism, 326, 552
Arndt, W. F., 495n
Asbury, Herbert, 387
Asceticism, 297, 770
Assyria, 24, 312, 348, 369, 372
Astrology, 35
Atargatis, 550
Atheism, 112
Atonement, 3, 4, 6, 17, 18, 45, 174, 271,
461f, 526, 617
Attack, sneak, 278f
Augsburg Confession, 658f
Augustine, St., (Austin), 155, 156, 353,
546f, 598, 753, 757, 825
Aulus Gallius, 557
Auschwitz, 587

872

Tallack, W., 275n
Tallant, R., 61n
Talmud, 20, 85, 171, 185f, 191, 314, 369, 377, 379f, 464f, 468f, 474, 489, 526, 590, 609, 617, 658, 708
Tantra Yoga, 376
Tatian, 726
Taton, R., 104n
Tatooing, 84, 223
Taves, Isabella, 645n
Tawney, J., 801n
Taxation, 34f, 50, 56f, 90, 97, 98f, 281-284, 492f, 510
  equality in, 97f
  poll tax, 281-284, 719, 721f
  unjust, 13, 283
Taylor, E. L. H., 820n
Taylor, G. R., 152n, 420n
Taylor, J., 839n
Taylor, Ron, 261n
Technology, 504, 834-856, 847
Teeters, N. K., 275n
Telemachus, 774f
Temple, 809f
Temple U., 400
Temptation of Jesus, 26, 699
Tempting God, 542-549
Teorema, 390f
Tephil!in, 22
Terror, 59, 62, 101, 120, 214, 621
Terry, D. A., 519f
Tertullian, 265, 716
Testimony, 566f
Thayer, J. H., 126n
Theatre, 422
Theft, 11, 13f, 223, 283, 304, 452-458, 483, 484-488, 509, 510-514, 534-541, 598-600
Theodosian Code, 784ff
Theodosius, 400
Theology, 493, 645
Thielicke, H., 421, 423f, 426
Thirty Years War, 365, 429f
This Week Magazine, 91n, 192n
Thompson, J. A., 7n
Thompson, P. W., 50n, 53, 54n
Thoreau, H. D., 122
Thornton, N., 440
Thorwalk, J., 369n
Throne, 69-73, 242
Thurmond, S., 646
Tibet, 369
Tiemann, W. H., 567n
Tierney, B., 513
Time Magazine, 261n, 266n, 287, 588n, 630n
Timothy of Alexandria, 784, 797
Tithe, 12, 13, 35, 39, 50-58, 283f, 510-514, 789f, 798, 806, 821, 846-848
  failure to, 510-514
  laws of the, 52, 282f
  subversion and the, 846-848
  poor, 54f
Toledo, Ohio, 604
Tolerance, toleration, 5, 113, 294f

Torigian, Mrs. Zaven, 266
Totalitarianism, 33, 40, 58, 67, 99, 101, 451, 481, 581, 775, 819
Tournier, Paul, 221
Transfiguration, 710-714
Transgression, 271f
Transvestites, 87, 434-438
Treason, 38f 66ff, 118
Trees, 280
Trial, 849
Trials by ordeal, 606-611
Tribute money, 718-723
Trippett, F., 689n
Triumph, 621n
Trobian Islands, 368
Trotsky, 130n
Troubadors, 376
Trumbull, H. C., 756f
Truth, 295f, 580
  absolute, 17, 224, 289
  is one as God is one, 18
  no agreement with lie, 297
  telling, duty of, 602
Tse-Tung, Mao, 5
Turkey, 365f, 588f
Turner, W. W., 644
Tylor, E. B., 610
Tyranny, 101, 123, 581
Tyre, 32

Ullerstam, Lars, 208, 420, 439
Ultimacy, 4f, 33, 113
Unbelief, 39, 112, 302
Unger, M., 223n, 256, 272f, 435n, 478, 514
Union for convicts, 234
Unions, 507ff
U. S. News and World Report, 206n, 518n, 521n
United States of America, 348f, 487, 586f, 605, 616, 624
  Civil War, 97, 512
  Congress, 624
  Constitution, 68, 115, 501f
  General Welfare clause, 101
  Fifth Amendment, 502, 544, 566
  First Amendment, 580
  oaths of office, 111
  President, 624
  Supreme Court, 91, 101, 124, 186, 330, 624
  Tenth Amendment, 501
  National Security Agency, 439
  War of 1812, 631
  War of Independence, 174, 277, 631
  Washington, D. C., 620, 645f
U. S. Public Health Assn., 266
Unity, 16ff, 23, 30, 100, 200, 606
Universalism, 20, 272
University of California, Berkeley, 106, 426, 584, 647
U. of Leicester, 228
Unruh, Jesse, 269
Unwin, J. D., 367